FINANCIAL ACCOUNTING
A USER PERSPECTIVE

Second Canadian Edition

FINANCIAL ACCOUNTING

A USER PERSPECTIVE

Second Canadian Edition

Robert E. Hoskin
University of Connecticut

Maureen R. Fizzell
Simon Fraser University

Ronald A. Davidson
Arizona State University West

John Wiley & Sons Canada, Ltd
Toronto • New York • Chichester • Weinheim • Brisbane • Singapore

This textbook was created entirely by electronic means using the Macintosh platform — QuarkXpress, Illustrator, and Photoshop. Film was produced using disk-to-film technology.

Canadian Cataloguing in Publication Data

Hoskin, Robert E., 1949-
    Financial accounting : a user perspective

2nd Canadian ed.
Includes index.
ISBN 0-471-64372-6

1. Accounting. I. Fizzell, Maureen. II. Davidson, Ronald Allen. III. Title.

HF5635.H68 1999   657'.044   C99-932899-9

Production Credits
Acquisitions Editor: John Horne
Publishing Services Director: Karen Bryan
Developmental Editor: Karen Staudinger
Cover Illustration: Anson Liaw
Cover and Interior Design: Interrobang Graphic Design Inc.
Printing and Binding: Tri-Graphic Printing Limited
Printed and Bound in Canada
10 9 8 7 6 5 4 3 2

To my husband, Charles,
who spent many Sundays on his own
while I worked on this second edition,
and to my children, Carrie and Scott

ABOUT THE AUTHORS

Robert E. Hoskin

Robert E. Hoskin has been an associate professor in the School of Business Administration at the University of Connecticut since 1986. In 1990, he spent six months with Price Waterhouse in Hartford as a faculty intern. This lead to the development of a course in property and liability insurance, now published by Price Waterhouse under the name *Crash: An Introduction to Property and Liability Insurance*. Prior to the University of Connecticut, he was an assistant professor at Fuqua School of Business. In 1979-1980, he was an accounting lecturer at Cornell University and Duke University. Robert Hoskin is the author of 12 papers and publications and the co-author of two financial accounting books. Robert Hoskin received a Ph.D. and M.A. from Cornell University, an M.Sc. in Chemistry from Bowling Green State University, and a B.Sc. in Education from Ohio State University.

Maureen R. Fizzell

Maureen R. Fizzell, B.Ed., B.Comm., M.Sc., CMA has been teaching at the university level for 15 years, nine years at the University of Saskatchewan and 6 years at Simon Fraser University, where she is now a Senior Lecturer. In September 1995, she was appointed as the Director of the Undergraduate Program in the Faculty of Business Administration at Simon Fraser University. Over her university teaching career she has taught financial accounting from the introductory to the advanced level. Maureen is an active CMA member serving on the B.C. Board of Directors and the Management Accounting Institute Board from 1997 to 1999. As well, she has been a member of the Saskatchewan Provincial Council, critiqued exams and acted as liaison between university students and the Society. During her 15 years, she has received numerous teaching awards. Some of them are: Most Effective Professor in the Classroom Award at the University of Saskatchewan in 1990; Canada Trust Distinguished Teaching Award in 1996, and membership in the Teaching Honour Roll in 1997 at Simon Fraser University.

Ronald A. Davidson

Ronald Davidson, a Chartered Accountant for 30 years, is the Director of Accountancy Programs at Arizona State University West. He was previously on the faculties of Simon Fraser University and the University of Calgary. He also taught at the University of Arizona, the University of Bahrain, the University of Saskatchewan, and the University of Alberta. He has more than 30 publications in leading accounting and management journals. He has a Ph.D. in accounting and auditing from the University of Arizona, an MBA from York University, and a B.Com. from the University of Manitoba. His main research interests are the behavioural aspects of auditing and accounting education. He is a member of the Institute of Chartered Accountants of British Columbia, the Canadian Institute of Chartered Accountants, the Canadian Academic Accounting Association, and the American Accounting Association.

PREFACE

Background

In the early nineties, organizations like the Accounting Education Change Commission (AECC) recommended a change in emphasis at the introductory level of accounting. Previously, many schools had emphasized the "how to" of accounting, showing students how financial items are measured, recorded, and reported. This type of knowledge is important for students who intend to become accountants but students in introductory accounting have a broad range of career goals covering all aspects of business. What is important to all students is the accounting information that is at the backbone of many decisions made in organizations. As a result, the AECC and other organizations advocated a shift to an emphasis on accounting information and how it affects decision- making. For most students, how the information can be used is more important than how it was prepared.

The first edition of *Financial Accounting: A User's Perspective* set out to address that shift by complementing the fundamental procedural aspects of accounting with information about who uses accounting information and what decisions they make from it. The text was designed to achieve a balance between the preparation and use of accounting information. This balance not only continues in the second edition — it is enhanced.

New In This Edition

The focus on accounting in the real-world that brings accounting to life has been enriched:

• All chapters are now introduced with a Chapter Opening Vignette, Chapter Preview, Study Objectives, as well as a brief written introduction that places the material in context.

• "Accounting in the News" boxes appear throughout the chapters and relate key topics to what is happening in the real world of business.

• The number of examples from real companies has been increased by more than 50%. Many of these companies will be familiar to students.

• The emphasis on GAAP has been downplayed, with the focus now being on Canadian practice.

The number of problems has been substantially increased to provide greater selection to both students and professors:

• There are two new problem types: Management Perspective problems, and Beyond the Book. Many of the Beyond the Book questions ask students to do research on the worldwide web.

The text has been reorganized to introduce students to the subject of accounting at a better pace:

• Chapter 3 (Manufacturing Corporations) has been removed.

• Accounting Systems content has been divided into two chapters —Transaction Analysis and Accounting Entries & Double-Entry Accounting Systems.

And all chapters have been updated to reflect the latest standards and practices. Most notably, Chapters 5 (Cash Flows Statement) and 8 (tax coverage) have been updated to reflect the latest CICA Handbook changes.

Text Organization

In order to focus on the understanding and use of financial statements and to emphasize the importance of topics such as decision-making, cash flows, and ratio analysis, this text is organized in a unique manner.

Chapter 1 lays the conceptual groundwork for the mechanics of the accounting system, and guides students through the annual reports of Big Rock Brewery Limited and Future Shop Limited. Students learn basic accounting terminology and are introduced to the three major accounting statements: income statement, balance sheet, and statement of changes in financial position. This chapter also presents background material on the standard setting process and the conceptual framework underlying accounting.

Chapters 2 & 3 build on the basics from Chapter 1, presenting the traditional presentation of the accounting system using the basic accounting equation and a full description of the double entry accounting system and the accounting cycle. The early introduction of the cash flow statement enables students to appreciate the differences between the income statement and cash flow statement that are crucial to understanding accrual basis financial statements.

Chapter 4 caps the discussion of the income statement with revenue recognition criteria and methods. This topic is often not emphasized in introductory texts. However, the authors recognize that the revenue recognition policies established by a company can have a major impact on its operating results. It is, therefore, important for students to have some understanding of these policies early in the course.

Chapter 5 reflects the importance of the cash flow statement in at least two ways: it is unique in covering the interpretation as well as the construction of the statement and secondly, the coverage occurs earlier than in other introductory texts. Because this topic is a difficult one for many students, the chapter explains the linkage of the cash flow statement to the operating policies of the company (accounts receivable, inventory, and accounts payable policies) helping students to interpret the information in the operating section of the cash flow statement. By the end of Chapter 5 students will have a basic understanding of the three major financial statements. Because of the complexity of the cash flow statement, some instructors prefer to teach the topic later in the course. The chapter has been designed so that it can be taught after chapter 11 instead of after chapter 4.

Chapters 6 through 11 discuss the major asset, liability, and equity accounts that students will see in published financial statements. In each of these chapters, students are alerted to the important aspects of these items so that they can better interpret financial accounting information. The chapter material and the questions at the end provide numerous examples of disclosures from the financial statements of real companies.

Financial statement analysis issues are discussed in all chapters and are summarized and extended in Chapter 12 after students have learned about the major asset, liability and equity accounts. Financial ratios associated with the topics under discussion are introduced in each chapter. From their first exposure to accounting, students are given tools that they can use to analyze financial statements. By the time they reach Chapter 12 where all the ratios are summarized and extended, they have worked with all the ratios. Chapter 12 gives them an opportunity to pull the analysis together and work with the total corporate entity. In some cases, this takes the coverage slightly beyond what is usual in introductory texts.

Because real corporations are complex, and generally prepare consolidated financial statements, an appendix that covers long-term investments in other corporations and the consolidation process is included. Recognizing that consolidation procedures are complicated and beyond the scope of an introductory textbook, this discussion is kept very simple. In keeping with the user orientation, the financial statement impacts of the consolidation policies are considered.

Features of This Book

The text's user orientation not only supports the goals set out by the Bedford Report and the AECC, it has been successful followed at universities across Canada. In addition to the content and organization, a variety of pedagogical features support the approach.

The Use of Financial Statements

Virtually all introductory accounting students, both graduate and undergraduate, will become users of accounting information, while only a few will become preparers.

The user perspective that continues in this text focuses on the understanding and use of corporate financial statements as a primary source for accounting information. Over the last few years, instructors across the country have found this approach to be an effective way of preparing students to work with accounting information. As well, it provides a solid foundation for students who continue on in accounting.

Integral to this approach is the extensive use of real financial statement data. Throughout the text you will find excerpts from the annual reports of actual corporations, reprinted exactly as they originally appeared. The financial statements of both Big Rock Brewery Limited and Future Shop Limited are presented in their entirety, along with a variety of excerpts from over 55 Canadian and international corporations. Each chapter provides a unique set of problems in the "Reading and

Interpreting Published Financial Statements" section, which requires students to analyze and interpret corporate financial statement disclosures.

An International Perspective: Reports from Other Countries

International issues are integrated into the text in several ways. Where appropriate, international differences are discussed in the main body of the text. Additional international material is set off from the main body in boxed-in areas that often feature "NAFTA Facts". Actual foreign financial statements are included in some of the boxed-in areas and are included in some of the problems at the end of the chapters.

Ethics in Accounting

Ethical issues are raised in most chapters by special boxed-in sections. These exhibits are designed to raise the reader's consciousness on ethical issues, and to provide a source of in-class discussion topics.

Critical Thinking & Communication

While many of the problems in the "Reading and Interpreting Published Financial Statements" sections are challenging problems, special critical thinking problems and case questions have been included at the end of most chapters. These problems require students to critically analyze issues. They can be used as the basis for term papers, class discussion and debates, providing opportunities for students to polish written and oral communications skills.

In-Text Student Aids

Each chapter includes the following sections: text, summary problem, synonyms & abbreviations, glossary, and problems:

Summary Problem The summary problem at the end of each chapter is designed to illustrate the main points in the chapter. Many of these problems elaborate on topics discussed in the chapter and provide an example for students to aid them when tackling the end of chapter problems.

Synonyms & Abbreviations This section contains terms used in the chapter and their common synonyms as well as any common abbreviations that are used in the chapter.

Glossary   There is a glossary at the end of each chapter that defines the key terms introduced in the chapter. Key words are boldfaced in blue the first time they are used in a chapter.

Problems   The problem section of each chapter is divided into seven parts: Assessing Your Recall, Applying Your Knowledge, Management Perspective Problems, Reading and Interpreting Published Financial Statements, Beyond the Book, Case, and Critical Thinking Question. As mentioned earlier, the Management Perspective Problems and Beyond the Book are new to this edition.

- The *Assessing Your Recall* section is designed to assess the understanding of basic terms and concepts introduced in the chapter.

- The *Applying Your Knowledge* section asks students to apply the concepts and procedures discussed in the chapter in a hypothetical situation. These problems are most like those found in a traditional text and will often re-enforce the technical side of accounting.

- The *Management Perspective Problems* let students assume the role of a particular user and to consider and discuss chapter topics from that perspective.

- The *Reading and Interpreting Published Financial Statements* section is unique to this book and contains problems that make use of corporate financial statement disclosures. The problems typically involve some type of analysis and interpretation of financial statement data.

- The *Beyond the Book* section provides an opportunity for the instructor to have students do individual or group research. The Beyond the Book section in chapter 1 gives several library and internet sources of corporate financial statements that students can use throughout the course. Students are asked to find financial information about a company of their choice and to answer questions about topics introduced in each chapter.

- The *Case* is a hypothetical scenario in which students are asked to identify problems, evaluate situations and make recommendations. The required part of the case often asks for a written report.

- The *Critical Thinking Question* often takes students beyond the structured data in the chapter by asking them to consider controversial areas associated with one or more of the chapter's topics.

Acknowledgements

I would like to thank Robert Hoskin who developed the original concept for this book and who put so much thought and energy into its construction.

I would also like to thank Ron Davidson who worked with me on the first edition of this text. His work on the first edition made my work on the second edition easier.

I would like to acknowledge the many reviewers who provided very valuable comments on the first edition and on the revised chapters of the second edition as they were written. As a result of their comments several changes were made to the organization of material in the book and within chapters. As well, their comments helped me simplify some areas and provide clearer descriptions in others. The reviewers are:

Deborah Crane, St Mary's University
Alireza Daneshfar, University of Ottawa
Charles Draimin, Concordia University
Darrell Herauf, Carleton University
Cameron Morrill, University of Manitoba
Fred Phillips, University of Saskatchewan
Catherine Seguin, University of Toronto
Shu-Lun Wong, Memorial University

I am very grateful to everyone at John Wiley and Sons Canada, Limited: John Horne, who convinced me to write this second edition; Diane Wood, who always makes me feel part of the author team at Wiley; Carolyn Wells, who comes up with a wealth of ideas on how to effectively market the book; Karen Bryan, who handled all of the publishing details; and all of the sales representatives who did the leg work in getting the book into the hands of instructors and students. I want to convey a special thanks to Karen Staudinger, my editor, who has worked tirelessly on the book managing the whole publishing process from the initial reviewing of manuscripts to the final printing. She is a gem.

I would also like to acknowledge Michelle Czornobay, who worked with me getting permissions and type-setting problem solutions; Zahwil Dossa, who worked on problem solutions; and Victor Grigore, who worked on the appendices.

As well, I would like to thank all of the other people that Karen had working behind the scenes to provide stories, newspaper articles, editing and problem solution verification. They are: Elizabeth d'Anjou, Aleli Balagtas, Jane Broderick, Zofia Laubitz, and Enola Stoyle.

Concluding Remarks

I hope that both students and instructors will find the materials contained in this book useful as they attempt to understand the extremely complicated world of corporate financial reporting. I have tried to be careful in the editing of the book and the associated solutions manual and instructors' manual so that there area a minimum number of errors. The remaining errors are, of course, mine and I look forward to hearing from you concerning any that you find so that I can improve upon the product.

Maureen Fizzell
Simon Fraser University, December, 1999

BRIEF TABLE OF CONTENTS

TABLE OF CONTENTS

It's Like Your Scorecard

Raj Randhawa admits accounting wasn't his favourite class at the University of Saskatchewan, where he received his Bachelor of Commerce degree. But as manager and co-owner of Horizon Computer Solutions, a computer hardware, software, and service provider in Saskatoon, he uses it every hour of his business life.

Beginning in 1995 with three employees, by 2000 Horizon had 26 employees and $10 million in sales annually. This rapid growth has been made possible by sound finance decisions, all of which rely on accounting information. For example, Horizon recently began focusing more on service—programming, network support, and so on—than on hardware sales. "Profit margins in hardware are about 10 or 11% in this business," explains Mr. Randhawa, "whereas in services they can be much higher. In addition, by selling customers a whole package—the computer and the service—we provide better value and gain loyalty." The change has helped the company's sales soar in recent years.

By contrast, Mr. Randhawa regrets not thinking through all of the relevant financial accounting issues when, in 1997, Horizon renovated its stores. "We paid for the renovation with our line of credit," he says. "Bad idea." It would have been cheaper and simpler, he now realizes, to obtain a loan for the purpose. "It seemed like it was going to be a small job at first," he explains, "but it got bigger and bigger."

He learned his lesson. The company just installed a new, $15,000 telephone system (the old one wasn't Y2K compliant, and didn't have enough voice mail ports for all the new staff). Before taking the plunge, Mr. Randhawa and his partner carefully investigated two financing options: purchasing and leasing. "The lease made much more sense in the end," he explains. But

they would never have known that without a careful review of the numbers.

"Nothing in school could have prepared me for the real world of business," he sighs. But a good grasp of accounting helps him make a lot of decisions. "Say you need a loan at the bank. They're very wary of small businesses; they want to see all your financial statements. Whether you apply certain expenses in this month or next can make a big difference in how profitable your company looks to them. Or say you want to invest in a lot of new training for your staff. It's expensive—is it worth it? If it will increase your revenue and result in cost savings, then yes."

"Accounting is like your scorecard," Mr. Randhawa muses. "It lets you know what's going on at any moment. It shouldn't be at the forefront of your business; you have to be concentrating on what you do or make, like a player concentrates on the game. But it is in the background all the time so that you can check to see how you are doing and it provides you with input to your next strategy. Everything has to work together to make a business successful."

chapter 1

OVERVIEW OF CORPORATE FINANCIAL REPORTING

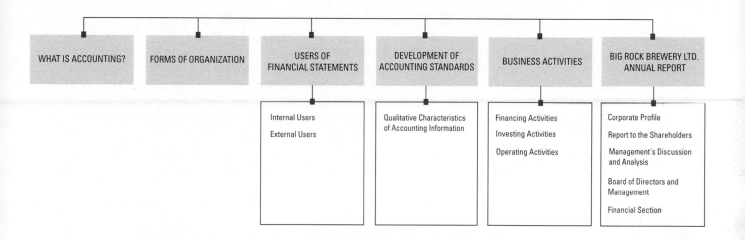

WHAT IS ACCOUNTING?	FORMS OF ORGANIZATION	USERS OF FINANCIAL STATEMENTS	DEVELOPMENT OF ACCOUNTING STANDARDS	BUSINESS ACTIVITIES	BIG ROCK BREWERY LTD. ANNUAL REPORT
		Internal Users External Users	Qualitative Characteristics of Accounting Information	Financing Activities Investing Activities Operating Activities	Corporate Profile Report to the Shareholders Management's Discussion and Analysis Board of Directors and Management Financial Section

Learning Objectives

After studying this chapter, you should be able to:

1. *Define accounting and understand its relationship to economic decision-making.*
2. *Understand what an annual report is and what it contains.*
3. *Describe the major forms of organization in which accounting is used.*
4. *Identify several users of financial statements and begin to understand how they use accounting information.*
5. *Know what Generally Accepted Accounting Principles (GAAP) are.*
6. *Identify the qualitative characteristics of accounting information.*
7. *Describe the three fundamental business activities.*
8. *Identify the major financial statements and describe their major components.*
9. *Begin to understand the role of ethics in financial accounting.*

The opening story tells how accounting and business success work hand in hand. Whether you are performing day-to-day operations, borrowing money for expansion, planning a new avenue of operations, or deciding to purchase or lease, you need to have information which will enable you to make the most advantageous decisions. One of the most important sources of that information is the accounting system.

WHAT IS ACCOUNTING?

Learning Objective

1

Define accounting and understand its relationship to economic decision-making.

Accounting is the system whereby the underlying economic conditions of organizations and, indeed, individuals are recorded, summarized, reported, and understood. Accounting can be as simple as balancing your individual cheque-book or as complex as recording and reporting on the economic condition of a multinational corporation such as Microsoft or a government such as the federal government of Canada. All of these entities need to have economic information in order to continue to operate efficiently and effectively. Accounting is the system that provides the information. It is the very framework around which people and organizations make decisions. It is therefore important that you, as future users, have at least a basic understanding of what accounting is (and is not): what it is trying to accomplish and how it goes about doing so.

Learning Objective

2

Understand what an annual report is and what it contains.

The focus of this book is going to be on the accounting information produced by profit-oriented organizations, although we will occasionally make reference to not-for-profit organizations or governments. We will concentrate mainly on the **financial statements**, which are the reports from the management of companies to their owners summarizing how the company performed during a particular period. The financial statements are the final set of documents, produced at the end of an accounting period. They are included in a larger **annual report** that is the main method management uses to report the results of the company's activities during the year. The annual report is sent to all owners, but many other parties that have an interest in the company—for example, lenders, analysts, and credit-rating agencies—use it as well. Many companies have created websites and include their most recent financial statements as part of the information users can access.

The primary goal of this book is to help you become an intelligent reader of corporate financial statements. You may become a manager, accountant, banker, or financial analyst; even if you don't, you probably will become an investor in the shares or bonds of a company at some time in your career. In your various business roles, you will make decisions about companies, such as whether to invest in their shares or to lend them money or to sell them goods or services on credit. In making these decisions, it will be important for you to understand the information that is presented in corporate financial statements. You must know not only what each piece of information tells you about the company, but also what it doesn't tell you. You should also recognize that some important information is not contained in the financial statements, yet is useful in certain decision-making contexts.

We have written this book for a broad readership, understanding that many of you will play multiple roles as owners (shareholders), creditors, and managers of companies. We have assumed that you know little or nothing about accounting. We have not assumed that you are training to be an accountant, although that may be your objective. Therefore, this book does not emphasize accounting procedures. Instead, the underlying concepts of accounting and the analysis of financial statements are emphasized. However, a complete understanding of the end result of the accounting process is probably not possible without an overall view of how the accounting system works. For this reason, the first few chapters present the mechanics of the accounting system. Subsequent chapters are devoted to accounting issues and concepts, and to analyzing financial statements.

Throughout the book, information from real companies is used to illustrate the topic at hand. In addition to numerous examples of financial statement information from a variety of companies, the complete annual report of Big Rock Brewery Ltd. for 1999 is included as Appendix A at the end of the book. A second complete annual report, that of Future Shop Ltd., has been included as Appendix B at the end of the book. The inclusion of two complete annual reports, one for a manufacturing company (Big Rock Brewery) and one for a retailer (Future Shop), will provide you with more reference material. Many references will be made to the Big Rock (BR) report and the Future Shop (FS) report throughout the text. Page numbers from these annual reports will be preceded by "BR-" or "FS-"; that is, page 10 from an annual report will be referred to as "BR-10" or "FS-10." Additional problems, labelled "Beyond the Book," require that you find a company of your own choosing or one suggested by your instructor. At most universities, annual reports of various companies may be accessed through electronic means. Reports are also currently available on the Internet through the SEDAR filings. Your instructor may provide you with information about how to access this information on your campus, or you can contact your university librarian.

Because different companies use slightly different terminology to refer to items in their financial statements, it is sometimes confusing to read their statements. To assist you in interpreting these financial statements, lists of abbreviations and synonyms are provided at the end of most chapters. A glossary that briefly defines or explains the terms used in the chapter is also provided at the end of each chapter.

An International Perspective

Reports from Other Countries

Another goal of the book is to expose you to financial statement requirements in countries other than Canada. Integrated into the discussion of most chapters are examples of how accounting standards in other countries might differ from those in Canada. These sections are set off from the main text, as is this paragraph, so that you can easily identify discussions of international standards rather than Canadian ones. Some of these international boxes are used to highlight accounting principles used in the United States and Mexico, which we have labelled "NAFTA FACTS."

FORMS OF ORGANIZATION

Learning Objective

3

Describe the major forms of organization in which accounting is used.

Financial information is used in many different types of organization: profit-seeking entities like corporations; governing organizations like federal, provincial, and municipal governments; service entities like hospitals and academic institutions; and not-for-profit entities like charities and clubs. Although these entities have different objectives, they all need to tell their users whether they are still viable, whether they are meeting their goals, and whether they have a future. Financial statements attempt to capture financial information about an **entity** and present it to users so that they can make informed decisions. Because these entities have different objectives, the underlying accounting associated with them may be different. To try to capture the variations adequately would make this book too complicated. We are, therefore, concentrating on the profit-seeking entities, although we will occasionally add information about the other types of entity.

Organizations of many different types or forms conduct business in Canada. Although the accounting issues discussed in this book apply to some degree to all these forms of organization, attention is directed primarily towards the accounting issues facing corporations. Almost every large business in Canada is a corporation. Other forms of business include *sole proprietorships*, *partnerships*, *limited partnerships*, *joint ventures*, and *crown corporations*. These forms of organization are discussed in more detail in Chapter 11.

In all business organizations the owners make some type of initial investment in the business entity in the form of cash or property. In sole proprietorships and partnerships this ownership interest is referred to as the *owner's* or *partner's capital*. In a corporation, owners make similar investments in the company but their ownership interest is referred to as **shareholders' equity** and is represented by a document known as a *share*. A share is simply a document that represents ownership in the corporation. The owners therefore are referred to as **shareholders**. One advantage of the corporate form of business is that the shares can be easily transferred to another investor, allowing one investor to sell and another to buy ownership in a given company. It is not as easy to transfer ownership in a sole proprietorship or a partnership. Corporations whose shares are held by a small number of individuals are sometimes referred to as **private corporations**. The shares in these corporations do not trade on public stock exchanges, which makes the transfer of ownership more difficult. Corporations whose shares are held by a larger number of individuals or entities and that trade on a public stock exchange (such as the Toronto Stock Exchange) are referred to as **publicly traded** corporations. Some portion of their ownership often changes hands on a daily basis.

Except for some small corporations, shareholders typically do not become involved in the day-to-day operation of the business. Because of the large number of shareholders and their lack of involvement in the day-to-day activities, the shareholders typically elect a **Board of Directors** to represent them. The Board of Directors then hires (and fires) individuals known as senior management to manage the day-to-day operations. These senior managers, along with the managers they hire, are collectively referred to as **management**. To keep shareholders informed of the performance of their investment in the company, management reports periodically to the shareholders. This periodic report typically is sent to shareholders on a quarterly basis in a quarterly report. The fourth-quarter report is combined with the prior three quarters to produce financial statements that cover the entire fiscal year. These annual financial statements are included in the company's annual report.

USERS OF FINANCIAL STATEMENTS

Accounting is primarily concerned with the communication of financial information to users. Accountants must first identify what information should be recorded, then ensure that the company's accounting system will accurately collect and record this information. Because businesses are involved in many thousands of transactions each year, accountants must summarize this information in a format understandable, and therefore useful, to users. Accountants are very concerned that the information they provide is both reliable and relevant to users.

Although annual reports and corporate financial statements are prepared by managers primarily for shareholders, other users of financial data who are both external and internal to the company also analyze them. Exhibit 1-1 lists some of these users.

■ **Learning Objective**
④
Identify several users of financial statements and begin to understand how they use accounting information.

■ **Users of Financial Statement Information**

Internal users:
    Management
    Board of Directors
External users:
    Shareholders
    Potential investors
    Creditors (for example, bankers and suppliers)
    Regulators
    Taxing authorities
    Other corporations, including competitors
    Security analysts
    Credit-rating agencies
    Labour unions

EXHIBIT 1-1

Internal Users

Management and the Board of Directors

Management and the Board of Directors, as primary internal users, use accounting data to make many types of decisions such as pricing products and deciding whether to buy or lease equipment. Because of their position in the company, managers have access to many sources of financial information beyond what is included in the financial statements. Their uses of accounting data are important, but are generally covered in courses and books devoted to **management accounting** or **cost accounting** and will not be discussed in this text. Our primary focus will therefore be on the value of accounting data to external users. **Financial accounting** courses are oriented primarily to the study of the accounting data provided to these outside users. In most academic programs, both a financial and a management accounting course are required, to expose students to both types of accounting information.

External Users

The information disclosed in financial statements is sensitive to the needs of external users, because management, which prepares the statements, wants to communicate information to shareholders, creditors, and others about the financial status of the company. Management can, therefore, disclose almost any information it considers important for an understanding of the company, subject to some limitations set by various regulatory bodies.

Shareholders and Potential Investors

Shareholders and potential investors need information that will enable them to assess how well management has been running the company. They want to make decisions about buying more shares or selling some or all of the shares they already own. They want to decide if the people currently sitting on the Board of Directors are adequately overseeing the management team they have selected. Information in the financial statements will affect those decisions. Other sources of information for these users include press releases, business newspapers and magazines, and experts like stockbrokers and financial advisors.

Creditors

Creditors usually come from three major groups. The first group includes those who sell goods or services to the company and are willing to wait a short period of time for payment. These users are very interested in the short-term cash level in the company because they want to be paid. The second group is financial institutions, such as banks, that have lent money to the company. They are also interested in the cash level of the company, but they need to assess the cash flow further into the future. They want not only the principal of the debt repaid, but also an interest charge paid. The third group is investors who have purchased long-term debt instruments, such as corporate bonds, from the company. Similar to banks, these users have both a long-term and a short-term interest in the cash level. These creditor groups use the financial statements as a source of information, enabling them to assess the future cash flows of the company. They will make their lending or investing decisions based on their assessment of the risk of non-collection.

Regulators

The regulators who are interested in the financial statements are numerous. For example, the government establishes regulations for the manner in which a business becomes incorporated and for its conduct after incorporation. It is, therefore, interested in ensuring that the company follows those regulations. Environmental groups monitor the activities of companies to ensure that environmental standards are being met.

Taxing Authorities

The federal taxing authority in Canada, Parliament, has established Revenue Canada as its collection agency. Parliament establishes the rules for how taxable income should be measured. The tax rules use accounting financial statements extensively in the assessment of the amount of tax to be paid by businesses, but there are several areas in which they deviate. Later in this text we will describe some of those deviations and explain their impact on the financial statements.

Other Users

Additional users of financial statement information include other companies, security analysts, credit-rating agencies, and labour unions. Other companies may want information about the performance of a company if they enter into cooperative agreements or contracts with that company. Security analysts and credit-rating agencies use the information in financial statements to provide information about the strengths and weaknesses of a company to people who want to invest. Labour unions need to understand the financial health of the company in order to negotiate labour issues with management.

All of these users, with their various needs, use the same set of financial statements. It is therefore important that the financial statements provide information for the widest possible group of users. As you would guess, however, there are many pieces of information particular users may want but cannot find in the financial statements. They therefore must develop alternative sources of information.

DEVELOPMENT OF ACCOUNTING STANDARDS

In Canada, the **Accounting Standards Board (AcSB)** of the Canadian Institute of Chartered Accountants (CICA) sets accounting guidelines, which are published in the *CICA Handbook*. These accounting guidelines have the force of law as they are recognized in both federal and provincial statutes that regulate business corporations. In the United States, the Financial Accounting Standards Board **(FASB)** sets accounting standards for American corporations.

Learning Objective

5

Know what Generally Accepted Accounting Principles (GAAP) are.

The set of accounting guidelines that corporations use is referred to as Generally Accepted Accounting Principles, or GAAP (usually pronounced "gap"). Many different methods of deriving these principles have been used over time. Deductive methods start with some generally accepted definitions (of assets, liabilities, and income, for instance) and concepts, and then logically derive accounting methods and other accounting principles from them. These methods are similar to the process mathematicians use in the development of mathematical theory. The problem with this approach has been the difficulty in achieving a consensus on the underlying definitions and concepts. Inductive approaches generally take into consideration the methods in current practice and attempt to develop (induce) general principles from these methods. Current standard-setting under the CICA combines a deductive approach and an inductive approach. On the deductive side, the CICA has developed a set of underlying objectives and concepts called financial statement concepts, or the **conceptual framework**. This framework is then used deductively to justify new accounting standards. On the inductive side, the conceptual framework and the new accounting standards have all been established by a political process of reaching consensus among the various users of financial information.

AN INTERNATIONAL PERSPECTIVE

Reports from Other Countries

The development of accounting standards has, in general, been a country-specific process. Each country has developed its own standards, which reflect its political, social, and economic environment. With the development of world markets for both products and financial capital, there has been an increasing need for better understanding among countries with regard to financial reporting. Over the years, numerous organizations have attempted to set international accounting standards. There are currently several groups involved in the process of trying to formulate international accounting standards; predominant among them is the **International Accounting Standards Committee (IASC)**. The IASC is an independent, private-sector body that is funded by donations from accounting organizations around the world and the **International Federation of Accountants (IFAC)**. By the end of 1998, the IASC had issued 39 **International Accounting Standards (IAS's)**. The IASC has developed relationships with the primary standard-setting bodies in numerous countries, including the CICA in Canada, in order to promote the development of international accounting standards. The IASC encourages countries to change their accounting standards so that they more closely resemble the international standards.

The purpose of the conceptual framework is to describe the concepts that underlie financial accounting. This framework is used to develop accounting guidelines from which financial statements are prepared so that external users can find information on which to base decisions about the entity. The financial statements should describe what the entity owns, to whom it has obligations, and what is left over after the obligations are satisfied. They should also show how cash flowed in and out of the entity. The final purpose of financial statements should be to describe the results of the operations of the entity.

Qualitative Characteristics of Accounting Information

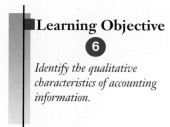

Learning Objective
6

Identify the qualitative characteristics of accounting information.

Accounting data should possess four essential characteristics. Exhibit 1-2 provides a hierarchy of these characteristics.

Characteristics of Accounting Information

EXHIBIT 1-2

Understandability
Relevance
    Predictive value and feedback value
    Timeliness
Reliability
    Representational faithfulness
    Verifiability
    Neutrality
    Conservatism
Comparability

Understandability, the first qualitative characteristic, is related to the user of accounting information. The information must be understandable to the user. For example, if you see an item called "Current portion of long-term debt" listed on a financial statement, you should understand that this means that over the next year the amount listed for this item will be paid in cash to the group that lent the money to the company. If preparers of the financial statements were not interested in understandability they would show the amount of long-term debt in total without backing out the amount that has to be paid back in the next year. Then, users would not be able to assess the probable cash outflow from the company in the coming year. The underlying assumptions behind this qualitative characteristic are that the users are reasonably well informed about accounting terminology and procedures and that the users have a reasonable understanding of the business environment. It is unlikely that you have such a background, which means that initially you will find the financial statements difficult to understand.

Relevance refers to whether the information is capable of making a difference in a decision. If you were told that you had an exam next week, that would be relevant to you. However, if you were told that it was snowing at the North Pole, you would probably not find that relevant. From an accounting perspective, the market value of a short-term investment is likely a relevant piece of information to a user. If the investment is short-term, it means that the company intends to sell it in the near future. Knowing what its market value is at a point in time enables the user to estimate the potential cash inflow from its sale.

Information may have three kinds of value: predictive value, feedback value, and timeliness. **Predictive value** means that the information is useful in predicting future results and, therefore, should be useful to users who make decisions that depend on accurate predictions of future events. Predictive value is based on an underlying assumption that the past is a good predictor of the future. The example in the previous paragraph has potential predictive value in that the market value of the investment may be a good predictor of future cash inflows. **Feedback value** is information that allows users to assess the outcomes of previous decisions, providing them with feedback on decisions made in the past. This can be helpful as users learn from their past successes and failures. Following the investment example, if the user saw financial statements following the sale of the investment, the user could determine whether the investment sold for the market value previously disclosed. If it did, the user would be confident that relying on the market value was a reasonable decision. If the investment sold for less or more, the user might decide that the market value was one piece of information but that predicting cash inflows requires other sources of information. Finally, **timeliness** is important because old information loses its relevance to users. If the information is not timely, it may lose its ability to make a difference in a decision. For example, if you were interested in investing in a company, one of the things you would want to see is its financial statements. Companies produce financial statements for the public every three months (quarterly) and annually. If you request information from a company, this is what you will receive. If it is June and the most recent financial statements you can get are dated March 31, is this timely information? With the rapid changes in the business environment that are evident around us, timeliness will in future become even more important in decision-making. It may be that, in the future, companies will publish monthly financial statements in order to satisfy the demand of users for timely information.

Reliability of information rests on four fundamental characteristics: representational faithfulness, verifiability, neutrality, and conservatism. **Representational faithfulness** means that the information faithfully represents the attribute, characteristic, or economic event that it purports to represent. For example, suppose the accounting system produces a dollar total for sales that is supposed to represent all sales made during a single year. This amount should include all sales made in that year and exclude all sales made in any other year. If it does, the information has representational faithfulness.

Verifiability means that independent measurers using the same measurement methods should agree on the appropriate value. Determining the cost of an item based on evidence such as invoices and cancelled cheques possesses a high degree of verifiability. Determining the market value of a piece of real estate possesses a much lower degree of verifiability, because it is based solely on opinions.

Neutrality means that the information is not calculated or presented in a way that would bias users towards making certain desired decisions and not making other, undesired decisions. For example, an inflated estimate of the value of inventory on hand is biased and not neutral. On the other hand, recording inventory at what you paid for it is neutral.

Conservatism means that, if estimates must be made in financial statements, they should err on the side of understating rather than overstating net assets and net income. For example, if a company bought a piece of land for $50,000, it would be on its records at the $50,000. If there was a downturn in the economy and the market value of the land dropped to $40,000, the company would be required to reduce the land on the records to $40,000 and recognize a loss in the value of the land. This writedown is necessary even though the company has no intention of selling the land in the near future. The writedown illustrates conservatism. If instead of declining to $40,000, the market value of the land increased to $100,000, no change would be made in the company's records unless the company actually sold the land for the $100,000. This also represents conservatism. Note that conservatism may conflict with neutrality. If conflict occurs, conservatism overrides neutrality.

Comparability generally refers to the ability of information produced by different companies, particularly within a given industry, to be compared. A high degree of comparability allows for better comparisons across companies and potentially better decisions. Within Canadian GAAP, however, there are no guidelines requiring all companies in an industry to use the same accounting methods. Because different methods will produce different financial statement amounts, it is important for users to understand what methods are available to companies and how the various methods will impact on the accounting numbers. Comparability is enhanced with the consistent application of accounting methods by a given company over time. Much of the predictive value of accounting information depends on the trends of the data over time. If different methods are used to produce that information over time, the predictive value of the information is diminished.

Finally, there are two overriding constraints that affect the information provided by management: the cost/benefit constraint and the materiality criterion. The **cost/benefit constraint** states simply that the value of benefits received from information should exceed the cost of producing it. The value of benefits received from information, however, is very difficult to measure. This can lead to problems, because the company bears the cost of producing the information yet the benefits are perceived mainly by outside users. For example, a company could consider publishing financial statements every week instead of every three months. To publish the financial statements every week would be very costly in terms of hours required to produce the financial statements and ensure their accuracy. It is likely that it would take at least a week to produce the statements and then it would have to start again on the week just ended. The company could measure how much it would cost to engage in this activity. It would then have to estimate the amount of benefit users would get from seeing weekly financial statements. If there was perceived to be very little benefit from weekly financial statements, the company would not do it, because the cost would exceed the benefit.

Materiality is a pervasive concept that affects many aspects of the production of information. It is generally thought of as the minimum size of a transaction that can significantly affect decisions. For example, when a company purchases a building, the amount spent is usually substantial. Because the building will be used for several years, it is appropriate to spread that cost over several years, which affects the company's profitability. The effect on profitability over a period of years may affect an investor's decision to buy shares. On the other hand, if the company purchases a pencil sharpener, the cost is so small that it will not affect an investor's decision. Materiality is used by the company's **external auditors** in their annual audit of the financial statements. Auditors are an independent third party that the shareholders hire to review the financial statements presented by management. They provide a professional opinion as to whether the financial statements fairly present the results of the operations of the company. In their tests of the financial statements, auditors will ignore discrepancies below a certain dollar level, because the explanation of the discrepancy would not significantly change their opinion about the financial statements. More is said about the work of the auditor later in the chapter. Both materiality and the cost/benefit constraint are kept in mind as the CICA adopts and implements new accounting guidelines and as accountants implement these guidelines.

These qualitative characteristics and constraints help form the underlying basis on which accounting guidelines are established. As we discuss these guidelines in the book, referring back to these characteristics and constraints should help you understand and remember the guidelines being used.

BUSINESS ACTIVITIES

Learning Objective

7

Describe the three fundamental business activities.

To understand the information in financial statements, it is useful to think about the fundamental types of activities that all businesses engage in and report on. The basic activities of businesses are **financing**, **investing**, and **operating**.

Financing Activities

Financing refers to the activity of obtaining **funds** (cash) that can be used to buy major assets such as the buildings and equipment used by virtually every business. This activity is necessary to start the business, of course, but it is also a continuing activity as the business grows and expands its operations. Funds are obtained from two primary sources outside the company: **creditors** and **investors**. Creditors expect to be repaid on a timely basis and very often charge the business in the form of interest for the use of their money, goods, or services. The amount to be repaid is generally a fixed amount. Examples of creditors are banks that offer both short-term and long-term loans and suppliers who are willing to provide goods and services today with the expectation of being paid for those products later. Investors, on the other hand, invest in the company in the hope that their investment will generate a profit. They earn profits either by receiving **dividends** (withdrawals of funds from the company) or by selling their shares to another investor. Of course, investors may experience either a gain (receive more than the initial amount paid for the shares) or a loss (receive less than the initial amount paid for the shares) on the sale of their shares.

A primary internal source of new funds to the company is the profit generated by the business that is not paid out to shareholders in the form of dividends. These profits are called **retained earnings**. If the company is not profitable, or if all profits are distributed to shareholders in the form of dividends, the only way the company can expand is either to get more funds from investors (existing shareholders or new investors) or to borrow more from creditors. How much to borrow from creditors and how much to obtain from investors are important decisions that the management of the company must make. Those decisions can determine whether a company grows, goes bankrupt or is bought by some other company. Examples of financing activities follow.

> **TYPICAL FINANCING ACTIVITIES**
>
> Borrowing money
> Repaying loans
> Issuing shares
> Repurchasing shares
> Paying dividends on shares

Investing Activities

Once the company obtains funds, it must invest those funds to accomplish its purposes. Most companies make both long-term and short-term investments. Most short-term investments are considered operating activities, such as the purchase of raw materials and inventories. Some short-term investments, such as the investment in the shares of other companies (called marketable securities), and most long-term investments are considered investing activities. Long-term investment in property, plant, and equipment to produce goods and services for sale is one such investing activity. Long-term investments in the shares of other companies would also be considered an investing activity. Examples of investing activities follow.

> **TYPICAL INVESTING ACTIVITIES**
>
> Purchase of property, plant, and equipment
> Sale of property, plant, and equipment
> Investments in the shares of other companies
> Sale of investments in the shares of other companies

Operating Activities

Operating activities are those associated with developing, producing, marketing, and selling the products and/or services of the company. While financing and investing activities are necessary in conducting operations, they tend to occur on a more sporadic basis than the activities thought of as operating activities. The day-to-day continuing activities are generally classified as operations. Examples of operating activities follow.

TYPICAL OPERATING ACTIVITIES
Sales to customers
Collection of amounts owed by customers
Purchase of inventory
Payment of amounts owed to suppliers
Payment of expenses like wages, rent, and interest
Payment of taxes owed to the government

Financial statements provide information about the operating, financing, and investing activities of a company. By the end of this book, you should be able to interpret financial statements as they relate to these activities. To start you on the journey to becoming a successful user of financial statement information, we have included for you, as Appendix A at the back of the book, the annual report of a Canadian corporation, Big Rock Brewery Ltd. A survey of the various types of information contained in the Big Rock Brewery annual report follows.

BIG ROCK BREWERY LTD. ANNUAL REPORT

The 1999 annual report for Big Rock constitutes Appendix A at the back of the book. As mentioned earlier, references to its page numbers are prefixed by "BR-." The Big Rock annual report will probably appear very complex, particularly if you have never before been exposed to accounting. The fact is, however, that Big Rock is a fairly simple company. We selected it because it is a good example of annual reporting, it illustrates almost all the reporting issues discussed in this book in spite of its simplicity, and it offers a challenge to you, the reader: to understand the workings of a modern company. The "pain" in trying to understand Big Rock will be rewarded by the "gain" in your understanding of real, complex business organizations.

A survey of the various types of information contained in the Big Rock Annual Report follows.

Corporate Profile

On the last page of the annual report, Big Rock includes a short section describing the business activities and history of the company. Most companies will put this profile near the front of the annual report. Big Rock produces and markets quality craft beers across five provinces and two territories in Canada and into 23 states in the United States. Its headquarters are in Calgary, Alberta.

When you evaluate a company for the first time, it is extremely important that you know what kinds of businesses it is in so you can assess the risk of the company. You may be deciding whether to invest in the company or whether to lend it money. The decision will be heavily influenced by the risk being taken. An investment in an oil exploration company, for instance, would have a much greater risk than an investment in a grocery store chain. When you read the financial statements, you must weigh the financial results against the level of risk of the investment. On pages

BR-4 through BR-7, Big Rock includes a section called A Marketing Glance. This section gives you more information about where they are currently selling their products. This information should help you in your risk assessment.

Report to the Shareholders

The report to the shareholders appears on pages BR-1 through BR-2. The report is written by the Chairman and Chief Executive Officer. Here, he has the opportunity to give a global view of where the company has been, what it accomplished last year, and where it is going in the future. You can see that he has highlighted his report with information about product development, distribution, and the future.

Management's Discussion and Analysis

Many companies use this report (pages BR-8 to BR-11) to make more extensive, detailed comments on the company and its operating results. This report provides an opportunity for senior management to discuss with shareholders the performance of the company. Often the information is presented from the perspective of the various divisions of the company. Also, it is one of the few places in the annual report where you will find prospective (i.e., forward-looking) information. As you will discover shortly, most of the information presented in the annual report is retrospective (i.e., based on past events). If your interest is in the future of the company, management's discussion and analysis is a good place to get management's opinion about the future directions and prospects of the company. The report should be read sceptically, however, since much of what is said reflects the opinion of top management. In such a report, there is an inherent bias towards presenting results to the shareholders in the best possible light.

Board of Directors and Management

Somewhere in every annual report there is a list of the Board of Directors of the company. Sometimes the report also includes their pictures. These directors are elected by shareholders to serve as their representatives, and as such they provide advice and counsel to the management of the company. They also have broad powers to vote on issues relevant to shareholders, and to hire and fire management. A listing of the senior management of the company is also included somewhere in the report; for Big Rock, this list can be found on page BR-21.

Financial Section

The remainder of the annual report contains all the financial information about the performance and status of the company (BR-3 and BR-12 through BR-20). In general, this section has the following major components:

COMPONENTS OF THE FINANCIAL SECTION

Summary of financial highlights for the past five to 10 years
Auditors' report
Financial statements:
  Income Statement
  Balance Sheet
  Statement of Retained Earnings
  Statement of Cash Flows
  Notes to the financial statements
Supporting schedules

Each of these components is discussed at some length in the sections that follow. Virtually all the disclosure contained in this section is in compliance either with the guidelines in the *CICA Handbook* or with the Alberta Securities Commission (ASC), although management would surely disclose most of this information voluntarily to shareholders in the absence of requirements by the CICA or the ASC.

There are three major statements that appear in all sets of financial statements. They are the **income statement**, the **balance sheet**, and the **statement of cash flows** (sometimes called the Statement of Changes in Financial Position). In addition to these, a company will often include a **statement of retained earnings**. In this chapter, only the income statement, balance sheet, and statement of cash flows will be discussed.

Learning Objective

8

Identify the major financial statements and describe their major components.

INCOME STATEMENT   The income statement (BR-14) is also known as the statement of earnings. This statement describes the results of the operating activities of the current period. The results of those activities add up to the net income amount, or bottom line. In companies, net income is defined as **revenues** (money or resources flowing into the company as a result of sales transactions) less **expenses** (money or resources flowing out of the company related to sales transactions). This is different from the concept of income used in preparing individual income tax returns. Income to individuals, for tax purposes, is generally the gross amount of money earned by the individual (salary) with very few deductions allowed. Individuals cannot, for example, deduct the cost of groceries or clothing. In a business, the rules are such that almost all expenditures qualify as expenses in the determination of earnings. There may be a delay in recognizing some expenditures as expenses. Because items such as machinery contribute to the generation of revenues over several years, we will normally recognize as an expense a portion of the original cost of the machine each period over its life. This expense is called **amortization**. Eventually, the entire expenditure will have been expensed in the determination of net income.

Refer to the Statement of Operations and Retained Earnings for Big Rock (BR-14). Note that this statement combines the income and retained earnings statements. Companies will sometimes produce a combined statement instead of two separate ones. The statement covers the period indicated at the top of the statement, where it reads "Years ended March 31." The revenues and expenses are the amounts recognized during the year ended March 31, 1999 and the year ended March 31, 1998. The activities reported in this statement are primarily the operating activities of the corporation. The statement is a report of the operating performance of the corporation during the year and measures the inflow of revenues and the outflow of expenses from the shareholders' point of view. For this reason, it is sometimes called a **flow statement**. Another way of putting it is that the earnings statement captures the net change in the shareholders' wealth, as measured in the accounting records, across a designated time period. In this case, that period is one year.

As you will note in the statement, there is one revenue category called Sales, which represents the inflow of resources from the sale of inventory—namely, beer. There is a second category called Government Taxes and Commissions. You will notice that the amount is deducted from the sales amount. In 1999 the amount of $9,821,360 is shown in parentheses, which means it is deducted from the previous amount. Items like these that are deducted from a revenue amount are often referred to as **contra-revenue amounts**. The government taxes and commissions represent the various Liquor Control Board commissions charged to the company for the beer. Governments often impose special taxes on the alcoholic beverage industry. Depending on the operating activities of a company, you might also find revenue from performing services or earning interest. The level of detail provided in a company's statement depends on the usefulness of the disclosure. Since Big Rock is involved only in the brewery business, the statement can be quite simple.

Another related reason for the breakdown into different types of revenue is that shareholders (and other users of financial statements) want to forecast the performance of the company. The amounts that are reported in the financial statements are largely historical in nature. For example, the values reported for the assets of the company are generally based on what the company historically paid for them, not on what they are currently worth on the market. These historical numbers may be useful in forecasting. Because of the differences in the nature of various aspects of a company, the growth rates of the different types of revenues and expenses may differ greatly. If the reader of the financial statements is not provided with any detail about the breakdown in revenues and expenses, it will be very difficult for the reader to forecast them accurately.

Costs and expenses are also listed under various categories, including cost of sales or cost of goods sold (the expenditures for goods sold during the period) and operating expenses. These cost and expense categories are also provided to explain to the shareholders, in more detail, the performance of the company. Big Rock's income statement has a couple of interesting expenses that likely require further explanation. The Amortization Expense represents the allocation of the original cost of a long-lived asset like a building. Big Rock owns buildings and equipment that it uses to make the beer which it sells to generate revenue. The cost of using the buildings and equipment, the amortization, is included every year as an expense. The Loss on Sale of Capital Assets represents the fact that Big Rock sold some of its long-lived assets (capital assets) for an amount that was below the recorded amount on the **books**. The value of these items had dropped below their carrying value on the records of Big Rock. The last expenses, Income Tax (Recovery) Expense and Large Corporation Tax, which represent the provision for income taxes, are listed as separate expenses because they depend on both the revenues and expenses reported. Taxes are calculated on the amount by which revenues exceed expenses.

At the bottom of the income statement is an earnings per share disclosure. Basic **earnings per share** is the net income of the company divided by the average number of **common shares** that are outstanding during the year. Shareholders find this calculation useful since it puts the performance of their investment in the company into proper perspective. In other words, a shareholder who holds 1,000 shares of Big Rock can determine his or her share of the earnings during the period. In 1999, Big Rock had a loss of $0.11 per share. Therefore, that investor's share of the earnings for 1999 would be a negative $110. Big Rock listed its earnings per share as Basic & fully diluted, which indicates that the company has either debt or share options that can be converted into common shares (Note 2, page BR-17, states that there are common share options outstanding). If they were converted, the earnings per share would remain at ($0.11) per share. In other words, when the additional shares are issued the earnings per share will not be negatively affected.

For a second example of an income statement, review Exhibit 1-3, the Consolidated Statements of Earnings of Future Shop Ltd. for 1999. Note that like Big Rock it is an uncomplicated income statement. Future Shop does not have fully diluted earnings per share, which means that it holds no potentially dilutive financial instruments. Use the Future Shop Statement of Earnings to review the components of the income statement.

EXHIBIT 1-3

CONSOLIDATED
STATEMENTS OF EARNINGS (LOSS)

	Period from April 1, 1998 to April 3, 1999	Year ended March 31, 1998
	(in thousands of dollars except per share amounts)	
Sales	$ 1,960,274	$ 1,760,160
Cost of sales	(1,546,723)	(1,370,773)
Gross profit	413,551	389,387
Selling, general and administrative expenses	(432,444)	(386,080)
Unusual items (Note 6)	(83,830)	-
Earnings (loss) before income taxes	(102,723)	3,307
Income tax recovery (Note 7)	20,478	654
Net earnings (loss)	$ (82,245)	$ 3,961
Earnings (loss) per share	$ (6.48)	$ 0.31
Weighted average number of common shares outstanding ('000)	12,692	12,670

Big Rock is a simple company with all of its operations run out of two business entities. Big Rock Brewery Ltd. is the parent, and it has one subsidiary company, Big Rock Brewery (Sask.) Ltd., which it controls. Both of these companies are separate business entities, but when Big Rock prepares its annual financial statements it prepares **consolidated financial statements**. These consolidated financial statements are a combination of all the elements of the subsidiary's financial statements and the elements of the parent's financial statements. More detail concerning consolidated financial statements is contained in Appendix C at the end of the book. When businesses expand they will often establish other companies or buy shares in other companies. This enables them to expand operations and diversify the risk.

When the subsidiary company is in a business that is fairly similar to the parent company's business, consolidated financial statements provide much useful information. However, when the business of a subsidiary is very different from that of the parent company, the combined set of financial statements may not be easy to interpret because of the complexity of the combined companies. In Canada, parent companies must prepare consolidated financial statements unless there is some impediment that prevents the earnings of the subsidiary from flowing to the parent.

Reviewing the income statement for Big Rock, you can see that the earnings (net loss) for 1999 were ($556,745). You will notice that the net loss is a drop from the $288,981 of the previous year. Companies provide the previous year's results along with the current year so that users can better evaluate the current year. They will often round amounts to the nearest $100, $1,000, or, in the case of very large companies, $1,000,000. The units in which the numbers are expressed must be stated somewhere on the statement. Usually they can be found in parentheses at the top of the statement. This brings up an issue that was discussed earlier, in the development of accounting standards section: materiality. If an auditor were to find a $2,000 mistake when trying to verify how fairly the statements presented the earnings of a company, how much difference would it make if the company rounded its amounts to the nearest $1,000? The answer is: It would not make much difference in the overall analysis of the financial status of the company. On the other hand, a $2,000 mistake in the tax reporting of an individual's earnings would certainly get the attention of Revenue Canada. The materiality of an item often depends, in part, on the size of the entity being considered.

Below is a list of some of the more common items you can expect to see on an income statement.

COMMON INCOME STATEMENT ITEMS	
Sales Revenues	The total amount of sales for the period.
Other Income	Various types of revenues or income to the company other than sales.
Cost of Goods Sold	The cost of the units of inventory that were sold during the period.
Selling, General, and Administrative Expense	The total amount of other expenses of the company during the period that do not fit into any other category.
Amortization Expense	The allocation of part of the cost of long-lived items like equipment.
Interest Expense	The amount of interest incurred on the debt of the company during the period.
Income Tax Expense (Provision for Taxes)	The taxes levied on the profits of the company during the period.

BALANCE SHEET The balance sheet (BR-13) is also known as the Statement of Financial Position. Financial position suggests that this statement represents the financial status of the company at a particular point in time. In fact, at the top of the statement "As at March 31" appears. The amounts in the statement are those that exist on March 31 in 1999 and 1998, respectively. These dates may also be thought of as the beginning and end points of the current accounting period. In the transition from one accounting period to the next, the ending balances of one accounting period become the beginning balances of the next accounting period. This statement has been described by various authors as a snapshot of the financial position of the company at a particular point in time.

So what makes up the financial position of the company? Individuals, if asked about their own financial positions, would probably start by listing what they own, such as a car, a computer, or a house, and then listing what they owe to other people, such as bank loans and credit-card balances. The net of what is owned less what is owed would be a measure of their net worth (wealth or equity) at a particular point in time. A company lists exactly the same types of thing in its balance sheet. In Big Rock's statement, there are two major categories: the first is a category for **assets**, and the second is a category for **liabilities and shareholders' equity**.

Assets When asked for a simple definition of an **asset**, many people reply that it is something of value that the company either owns or has the right to use. In fact, the accounting definition of an asset is very similar. In this book, assets will be those things that meet the following criteria: (1) the company owns or has the right to use them; (2) they have probable future value, which can be measured; and (3) the event that gave the company the ownership of or right to them has already happened. The word "future" has been added to value since the company would not want to list things that had value in the past but will not have value in the future. "Probable" has been added because businesses exist in an uncertain world and the value of an asset is subject to change. One of the risks of ownership of an asset, in fact, is that its value may change over time.

> **CHARACTERISTICS OF AN ASSET**
>
> 1. Something that has probable future value that can be measured.
> 2. The company owns or has the right to use the probable future value.
> 3. The event that gave the company the ownership or right has already occurred.

The assets that Big Rock lists in its balance sheet include cash, accounts receivable, income tax receivable, inventories, prepaid expenses and other, capital assets, and deferred charges and other. A full discussion of how each of these meets the criteria of ownership and probable future value is left to later chapters. As an example, however: Ownership of inventory by the company is evidenced either by possession or by legal documentation. It has future value because the company can later sell the inventory and receive cash in the amount of the selling price. The presence of the inventory or the documents indicates that the event that gave ownership to the company has already happened. The cash, in turn, has value because the company can use it to obtain other goods and services. The total assets of Big Rock as at March 31, 1999, are $29,165,835. Following is a list of assets normally found in a balance sheet.

COMMON BALANCE SHEET ASSETS

Cash	The amount of currency that the company has, including amounts in chequing and savings accounts.
Temporary Investments	Short-term investments in securities of other companies, such as treasury bills, shares, and bonds.
Accounts Receivable	Amounts owed to the company that result from credit sales to customers.
Inventory	Goods held for resale to customers.
Prepaid Expenses	Expenses that have been paid for but have not yet been used. An example is prepaid insurance.
Capital Assets	Investments in land, buildings, and intangibles that the company uses over the long term. Intangibles are investments in assets such as patents, trademarks, and goodwill.

Big Rock prepares a **classified balance sheet**. A classified balance sheet is one in which the assets and liabilities are classified as **current** and **noncurrent**. For assets, current means that the asset will be turned into cash or consumed (used up) in the next year or operating cycle. The **operating cycle** of a company refers to the time period between the initial investment of cash in products or services and the return of cash from the sale of the product or service. Assets such as cash, accounts receivable, and inventories are classified as current, and assets such as capital assets are classified as noncurrent.

Assets and liabilities are listed on the balance sheet in *liquidity order*. **Liquidity** refers to how quickly the company can turn the asset into cash. Noncurrent assets are the least liquid, because they will be used over a long period of time and will not quickly be turned into cash. Accounts receivable, on the other hand, are amounts owed to the company by its customers who bought goods or services on credit. The company hopes that these will be collected quickly (many companies have collection policies that give customers 30 days to pay). Therefore, accounts receivable are fairly liquid. Inventories are less liquid than receivables since they must be sold first, which normally results in an account receivable. Cash is then received when the account receivable is collected.

An **unclassified balance sheet** is, then, a balance sheet in which current assets or liabilities are not distinguished from noncurrent assets or liabilities. Even in an unclassified balance sheet, however, assets and liabilities are still listed primarily in the order of their liquidity. For instance, the cash, receivables (current receivables), inventories, and capital assets will have the same order as they do in the Big Rock report even if they are not specifically identified as current or noncurrent.

Using the information you have just been given about assets, examine the balance sheet of Future Shop Ltd. in Exhibit 1-4. You will notice that it lists assets similar to those of Big Rock. Is it a classified balance sheet? The current assets are identified but the noncurrent ones are not, although they do follow the current ones and the liquidity order has been maintained.

EXHIBIT 1-4

CONSOLIDATED
BALANCE SHEETS

		As at April 3, 1999		As at March 31, 1998
		(in thousands of dollars)		
ASSETS				
CURRENT				
Cash and short-term deposits	$	-	$	58,945
Cash held in escrow (Note 5)		20,251		-
Accounts receivable		25,099		15,121
Inventory		160,092		254,690
Prepaid expenses		1,544		1,634
Future income taxes (Note 7)		14,343		2,648
		221,329		333,038
CAPITAL AND OTHER ASSETS (Note 3)		114,217		108,269
FUTURE INCOME TAXES (Note 7)		2,970		-
	$	338,516	$	441,307
LIABILITIES				
CURRENT				
Bank indebtedness, secured by a general security agreement covering all assets	$	23,828	$	-
Accounts payable and accrued liabilities		219,550		309,838
Current portion of extended warranty plan		10,500		4,480
		253,878		314,318
EXTENDED WARRANTY PLAN		26,945		28,283
DUE TO AFFILIATED COMPANY (Note 4)		1,364		1,364
FUTURE INCOME TAXES (Note 7)		-		7,476
		282,187		351,441
SHAREHOLDERS' EQUITY				
Capital stock (Note 5)		58,051		29,851
Special warrants (Note 5)		20,508		-
Retained earnings (deficit)		(22,230)		60,015
		56,329		89,866
	$	338,516	$	441,307

Commitments (Note 8)

APPROVED BY THE BOARD

Hassan Khosrowshahi   (signed) Director

Gary Patterson, CA   (signed) Director

Liabilities A simple definition of liabilities might be "amounts that the company owes to others." The accounting definition of liabilities encompasses this concept and, consistent with the earlier definition of assets, will be used to refer to items that require a probable future sacrifice of resources. In most cases the resource is cash, but with the recognition that a company could satisfy a liability with services or goods. For example, a warranty liability could be satisfied with a new part or with the services of a repair person.

Big Rock, in its classified balance sheet, lists among its liabilities bank indebtedness, accounts payable and accrued liabilities, long-term debt, deferred income taxes, and commitments. Note that Big Rock classifies liabilities as current or noncurrent in its balance sheet. Current liabilities are those that will require the use of current assets or will be replaced by another current liability in the next year or operating cycle. The following list includes some of the more common liabilities found in financial statements.

COMMON BALANCE SHEET LIABILITIES

Bank Indebtedness	Amounts owed to the bank on short-term credit.
Accounts Payable	Amounts owed to suppliers from the purchase of goods on credit.
Notes Payable	Amounts owed to a creditor (bank or supplier) that are represented by a formal agreement called a note (sometimes called a promissory note).
Dividends Payable	Amounts owed to shareholders for dividends that are declared by the Board of Directors.
Accrued Liabilities	Amounts owed to others based on expenses that have been incurred by the company but are not yet due, such as interest expense and warranty expense.
Taxes Payable	Amounts owed to taxing authorities.
Long-term Debt	Amounts owed to creditors over periods longer than one year.
Deferred Income Taxes	Amounts representing probable future taxes the company will have to pay to Revenue Canada.

Refer back to Future Shop's balance sheet in Exhibit 1-4 and review the liability items listed there. Notice that Future Shop has two warranty liabilities—one for the current portion of warranties (those that will come into effect within the next year) and the extended warranty plan, which represents the portion of the warranties that extends beyond one year. Because many of the inventory items sold by Future Shop have warranties, you would expect to see this liability on its balance sheet.

Shareholders' Equity The last major category in the balance sheet is the equity section. It is frequently referred to as shareholders' equity. In Big Rock's section on shareholders' equity, note the listings for share capital and retained earnings. This section captures the value of the shareholders' interest in the company as measured by the accounting guidelines. Note that the total assets equal the total liabilities plus the equity. Big Rock lists both as $29,165,835 on March 31, 1999. This relationship is described by the basic accounting equation:

BASIC ACCOUNTING EQUATION

Assets = Liabilities + Shareholders' Equity

This equation gives meaning to the description of this statement as the balance sheet. If the equation is rearranged, it can be seen that shareholders' equity is equal to assets minus liabilities:

BASIC ACCOUNTING EQUATION (REARRANGED)

Shareholders' Equity = Assets − Liabilities
(Net Assets)

To state this relationship another way, shareholders' equity is the difference between what the investors own and what the company owes to others, as measured in the **accounting records**. Because of this relationship, shareholders' equity is sometimes referred to as the *net assets* of the company (net refers to the net of the assets less the liabilities) or the *net book value* of the company. It is the equivalent of an individual's personal net wealth. The shareholders' wealth as measured by the accounting statements is a residual concept. The shareholders can claim the residual of the assets that are left over after all of the liabilities are paid. You should note that the market value of the shares of a company is another measure of the shareholders' wealth in the company. By **market value** we mean the price at which the shares trade in the stock market. This value could be very different from the book value of shareholders' equity, because accounting records are not necessarily based on market values.

We can look at the proportion of liabilities and shareholders' equity on the balance sheet to gain a better understanding of the financing strategy used by the company. For Big Rock, total liabilities are $12,718,178 and total shareholders' equity is $16,447,657. The proportion of liabilities is 44% ($12,718,178/$29,165,835), which is almost 50%. This means that Big Rock uses both debt and shareholders' equity to finance activities in the company.

Shareholders' equity is generally made up of two accounts: **share capital** and **retained earnings**. The first, share capital, is used to record the amount that the investors originally paid (invested) for the shares that the company issued. The retained earnings account is used to keep track of the earnings of the company less any amounts that are paid from the company to the shareholders in the form of **dividends**. Dividends will be paid to shareholders only when approved by a vote of the Board of Directors. The change in the retained earnings of a company during a given period can be explained by the net income less the dividends declared as follows:

CHANGE IN RETAINED EARNINGS

Change in Retained Earnings = Net Income − Dividends

Other accounts can appear in this section. In the first part of this book, these other accounts will be ignored in order to concentrate on common share capital and retained earnings. The other accounts will be discussed in later sections of the book. Following is a list of some of the more common account titles that appear in the shareholders' equity section.

COMMON BALANCE SHEET SHAREHOLDERS' EQUITY ACCOUNTS	
Share Capital	Represents the shares that have been issued by the company and is usually stated at an amount equal to what was originally paid by investors for the shares. Shares can be of different types, with different rights and privileges attached to each.
Retained Earnings	The earnings of the company (as measured on the Income Statement) that have been kept (retained) and not paid out in the form of dividends.

Refer back to the balance sheet of Future Shop in Exhibit 1-4. Note that instead of the term Share Capital, Future Shop uses the term Capital Stock to refer to the share portion of shareholders' equity. Other terms that you might see are Common shares or Preferred shares, which refer to the type of shares that the company has issued.

STATEMENT OF CASH FLOWS The statement of cash flows, sometimes called the Statement of Changes in Financial Position (BR-15), is a flow statement that is, in some ways, similar to the income statement. It measures inflows and outflows during a specific period of time. Note how the words at the top of the statement indicate that the statement is "For the years ended March 31," which is the same terminology used on the income statement. The difference is that instead of measuring the increase and decrease in shareholders' wealth, this statement measures the increase and decrease in cash and highly liquid assets and liabilities called cash equivalents. Remember that a liquid item is one that can be converted very quickly to cash. Since cash is very important to the operation of the company, this statement is vital to any user's evaluation of a company.

Today the statement of cash flows has three sections that report the sources and uses of cash and cash equivalents for the three business activities described earlier: operating, financing, and investing.

SUBSECTIONS OF THE STATEMENT OF CASH FLOWS
Cash from operating activities
Cash from financing activities
Cash from investing activities

In order to evaluate the liquidity position of a company, users need to evaluate where cash is coming from and where it is being spent. Big Rock generated a positive cash flow of $2,113,702 from its operating activities in 1999.

Operating activities include all inflows and outflows of cash related to the sale of goods and services of the company. The starting point in this section is net income, which is a summary of the income from operating activities from the income statement. There are adjustments to this number, because the recognition of revenues and expenses (as will be seen in the future chapters) does not necessarily coincide with the receipt and payment of cash. For instance, sales could be either cash sales or sales on account (i.e., the customer can pay at a later date, resulting in an account receivable rather than cash). Expenses may also be paid later if the company is given credit by its suppliers (this would result in an account payable). Because the operating activities are the backbone of the company, a positive cash flow from operations is essential to the company's health.

The negative cash flow of ($2,548,712) from financing activities indicates that Big Rock used cash to pay off its short- and long-term borrowing and to repurchase some of its own common shares. **Financing activities**, as you will recall, are those transactions that either provide new funds from investors or return funds to investors. Investors can be either shareholders or lenders, and the typical activities in this category are the issuance and repurchase of shares and the issuance and repayment of debt.

Investing activities generally involve the purchase and sale of long-term assets such as property, plant, and equipment as well as investment in other companies. These typical activities can be seen from the disclosure by Big Rock. The positive cash flow of $318,616 from investing activities indicates that Big Rock made an investment in new capital assets during the year and sold off some of its surplus capital assets. The proceeds from the sale more than offset the cost of the new assets. In the future the company will use the new capital assets for operating activities. If the current year is an indicator of future results, the future operating activities will generate a positive cash flow and the company's investment in new capital assets will have been a worthwhile investment. These amounts in 1999 indicate that Big Rock is doing quite well with respect to cash flow. From operating activities, it has generated a larger cash flow than the previous year even though the company had a net loss in 1999. Big Rock is paying off its debt, which will free up more cash in the future.

Examine the cash flow statement for Future Shop in Exhibit 1-5. You can see that in 1998 it had no financing activities at all although it purchased new capital assets worth $34,301,000. This new investment was financed entirely from internally generated funds. Like Big Rock, Future Shop is using internal financing.

The preparation and interpretation of the statement of cash flows are discussed in detail in Chapter 5. Until you study the statement in more detail, confine your study of this statement to understanding what the three sections of the statement are measuring.

SUMMARY OF FINANCIAL STATEMENTS

INCOME STATEMENT
- Measures the operating performance of a company over a period of time.

BALANCE SHEET
- Measures the resources controlled by a company (assets) and the claims to those resources (liability and equity holders) at a given point.

STATEMENT OF CASH FLOWS
- Measures the change in cash flow through operating, financing, and investing activities over a period of time.

EXHIBIT 1-5

CONSOLIDATED STATEMENTS
OF CHANGES IN FINANCIAL POSITION

	Period from April 1, 1998 to April 3, 1999	Year ended March 31, 1998
	(in thousands of dollars)	
OPERATING ACTIVITIES		
Net earnings (loss)	$ (82,245)	$ 3,961
Items not involving cash		
Depreciation and amortization	31,496	28,294
Loss on disposal and write-down of capital and other assets	34,989	41
Future income taxes	(21,634)	(2,125)
Extended warranty plan	(1,338)	(831)
Cash provided by (used in) operations	(38,732)	29,340
Change in non cash operating working capital	(10,443)	20,736
Net cash provided by (used in) operations	(49,175)	50,076
FINANCING ACTIVITY		
Issue of special warrants	48,201	-
INVESTING ACTIVITIES		
Business acquisition	(12,894)	-
Proceeds on disposal of capital assets	1,056	1,607
Purchase of capital and other assets	(69,961)	(34,301)
	(81,799)	(32,694)
NET CASH (INFLOW) (OUTFLOW)	(82,773)	17,382
CASH POSITION, BEGINNING OF YEAR	58,945	41,563
CASH POSITION (INDEBTEDNESS), END OF YEAR	$ (23,828)	$ 58,945

NOTES TO THE FINANCIAL STATEMENTS   You may have noticed that various items on the financial statements direct the reader to specific notes. In such notes to the financial statements (BR-16 to BR-20), management has a chance to provide more detail about the referenced items. For example, on Big Rock's income statement the income taxes item includes a reference to Note 8. Note 8 goes into greater detail about taxes owed, deferred taxes, and tax rates. Financial statements are thus kept simple and uncluttered through the inclusion of additional explanations in notes rather than on the financial statements themselves.

A full discussion of notes will be left to succeeding chapters, but some attention should be paid to the note that discusses Significant Accounting Policies. It is usually the first or second note. It is the second note in Big Rock's financial statements. Within GAAP there are choices and judgements to be made by management. This note describes the choices that were made by management. The auditors, of course, review these choices for conformity with GAAP. As you progress through the book, you will see that the choices made by management have important implications for the interpretation of the statements. As an example, note how, on page BR-16, Big Rock's inventories are valued primarily using the first-in first-out, or FIFO, method. This method will produce a different balance in the inventory account on the balance sheet from that produced by a similar company using an alternative method, such as the last-in first-out, or LIFO, method. Comparing the two companies using these two different methods would pose difficulties. To aid users in comparing various companies, management must disclose their major accounting policies in this note.

SUMMARY OF INDUSTRY SEGMENTS   Information about various segments of the company is provided as a part of the notes to the financial statements. This is a requirement for any company that has more than one significant segment. A segment represents a business activity. Big Rock has only one business activity, the production and marketing of specialty draught and bottled beer, which means that it discloses very little in this section. It does, however, sell outside of Canada, and in Note 10 it tells you that 3.3% of its sales were outside Canada. This information is important to the reader, because it helps to explain the kinds of risks an investor takes when buying Big Rock shares. Segments can differ significantly with regard to risk and are affected in different ways by economic factors such as commodity prices, inflation, exchange rates, and interest rates. It is important to know the relative amounts invested in these segments when making an overall assessment of the risk of this company. Because companies produce consolidated financial statements, which provide aggregate information, it would be difficult to assess segment risks without this additional information.

SELECTED FINANCIAL DATA   (Five- to 10-Year Summaries) Another part of the notes to the financial statements provides key financial figures for a greater period of time than that covered by the main financial statements. For many companies, a five-year summary is provided, but it is not uncommon to see 10-year summaries. This type of information is useful to the reader for spotting trends in the data that would not be evident in the two years' worth of income data, cash flow data, or balance sheet data that are presented in the main financial statements. Big Rock provides a five-year summary near the beginning of the annual report (BR-8) rather than in the notes to the financial statements. Future Shop provides a five-year summary just before the financial statements (see FS-11 in Appendix B at the end of the book).

ethics in accounting

■ The management of a company has both a moral and a legal obligation to safeguard the investment that shareholders have entrusted to them. To ensure that management fulfils this stewardship function with regard to the resources of the company, shareholders typically provide some incentives for and controls over management. Management compensation arrangements are often tied to the financial statement performance of the company, to provide incentives for management to make decisions that are in the best interests of the shareholders. Also, auditors are hired to review the financial statements to ensure they adequately reflect the transactions of the company. There are also legal responsibilities placed on the behaviour of management.

Learning Objective

9

Begin to understand the role of ethics in financial accounting.

MANAGEMENT DISCUSSION OF FINANCIAL RESPONSIBILITY   This section, which is often included with the financial statements, contains a statement by management that it is responsible for the contents of the annual report. In addition, it discusses the steps management has taken to ensure the safekeeping of the company's assets and to assure the shareholders that management is operating in an ethical and responsible way. Big Rock includes this statement in its annual report on BR-12. Future Shop includes one also. Review Exhibit 1-6 to see what a typical statement says.

EXHIBIT 1-6

FINANCIAL REVIEW

Management's Responsibility for Financial Statements

The management of Future Shop Ltd. is responsible for the integrity of the accompanying consolidated financial statements and all other information in the annual report. The financial statements have been prepared by management in accordance with generally accepted accounting principles, which recognize the necessity of relying on some best estimates and informed judgements. All financial information in the annual report is consistent with the consolidated financial statements.

To discharge its responsibilities for financial reporting and safeguarding of assets, management depends on the Company's systems of internal accounting control. These systems are designed to provide reasonable assurance that the financial records are reliable and form a proper basis for the timely and accurate preparation of financial statements. Management meets the objectives of internal accounting control on a cost-effective basis through the prudent selection and training of personnel and the adoption and communication of appropriate policies.

The Board of Directors oversees management's responsibilities for financial statements primarily through the activities of its Audit Committee. This committee meets with management and the Company's independent auditors, Deloitte & Touche LLP, to review the financial statements and recommend approval by the Board of Directors. The financial statements have been audited by Deloitte & Touche LLP. Their report is presented below.

Hassan Khosrowshahi
*President, CEO and
Chairman of the Board*

Gary Patterson, CA
Chief Financial Officer

INDEPENDENT AUDITORS' REPORT   The financial statements are prepared by the management of the company. Independent auditors are hired by shareholders to provide an opinion about the fairness of the presentation and the conformity to accounting guidelines. **Auditors** are professionally trained accountants who add credibility to the financial statements by expressing their professional opinion as to whether the financial statements fairly present the results of the company's operations.

Companies such as Big Rock are audited not by one person alone but by a firm of auditors. Auditors apply a set of procedures to test the financial statements to determine whether they comply with generally accepted accounting principles and to assess the fairness of the presentation. Audit reports are often expressed in a standard format of three paragraphs. The first paragraph states what financial statements have been audited, that the financial statements are the responsibility of management, and that the auditors' responsibility is to express an opinion about the financial statements. The second paragraph explains how they conducted the audit using accepted auditing standards. The third paragraph is the auditors' opinion about the financial statements. The audit report of Big Rock (BR-12) follows this format. We have included the auditors' report from Future Shop in Exhibit 1-7 so that you can see the similarities between the two statements. A standard format like this is called an **unqualified opinion**. It means that the financial statements present fairly, in all material respects, the financial position, results of operations, and cash flows of the entity in conformity with generally accepted accounting principles.

EXHIBIT 1-7

AUDITORS' REPORT

To the Shareholders of Future Shop Ltd.

We have audited the consolidated balance sheets of Future Shop Ltd. as at April 3, 1999 and March 31, 1998 and the consolidated statements of earnings (loss), retained earnings (deficit) and changes in financial position for the period from April 1, 1998 to April 3, 1999 and the year ended March 31, 1998. These financial statements are the responsibility of the Company's management. Our responsibility is to express an opinion on these financial statements based on our audits.

We conducted our audits in accordance with generally accepted auditing standards. Those standards require that we plan and perform an audit to obtain reasonable assurance whether the financial statements are free of material misstatement. An audit includes examining, on a test basis, evidence supporting the amounts and disclosures in the financial statements. An audit also includes assessing the accounting principles used and significant estimates made by management, as well as evaluating the overall financial statement presentation.

In our opinion, these consolidated financial statements present fairly, in all material respects, the financial position of the Company as at April 3, 1999 and March 31, 1998 and the results of its operations and the changes in its financial position for the period from April 1, 1998 to April 3, 1999 and the year ended March 31, 1998 in accordance with generally accepted accounting principles.

Deloitte & Touche LLP
Chartered Accountants
Vancouver, British Columbia
May 14, 1999

In Canada the unqualified opinion, or **"clean" opinion**, is the most commonly seen opinion. Companies like to have a clean opinion attached to their financial statements. If the auditors are contemplating an opinion other than an unqualified one, management is informed about the reason(s) for the opinion prior to the issuance of the financial statements. Management then has an opportunity to change the financial statements to resolve the problem(s) the auditors have detected. If the issue is controversial, there may be some negotiation between management and the auditors as to how best to resolve the problem. If no resolution is reached and management decides to issue the statements as originally prepared, a **qualified or adverse opinion** will be included with the statements. This rarely happens in practice because the problems are usually resolved prior to statement issuance. As the following article indicates, sometimes the auditors withdraw from an audit if they do not think they can find enough information to allow them to verify the amounts on the financial statements.

accounting in the news

AUDITORS RESIGN BEFORE CERTIFYING STATEMENTS

In relatively rare cases, a company is not able to provide certified financial statements. In June 1998, Deloitte & Touche LLP resigned as auditors to YBM Magnex International Inc., refusing to certify the U.S.-based industrial magnet-maker's 1997 financial results. Deloitte released a letter stating that it was unlikely further audit procedures would "reduce to an acceptable level the risk of material misstatement in YBM Magnex International Inc.'s financial statements for the year ended December 31, 1997, due to error or fraud."

The troubled company had been banned from trading on the Toronto Stock Exchange for several weeks after it delayed producing financial statements for 1997. YBM had also been the subject of scrutiny on both sides of the border. U.S. federal authorities had raided its Pennsylvania headquarters as part of an organized-crime investigation, while the Ontario Securities Commission was looking into YBM's financial statements.

Source: "Deloitte Pulls Away from YBM Situation," by Bertrand Marotte, *Vancouver Sun*, June 12, 1998, page E1.

In any set of financial statements, the auditors' report should be read, because it can alert the reader to major problems the company may be experiencing. In other words, it can provide a "red flag." Readers must then investigate further to make their own assessments of the extent of the problems the company is facing. Also, recognize that there may be significant problems that the auditors did not identify with their tests or that are beyond the responsibility of the auditors.

Most large companies are audited by large accounting firms because of the size and expertise needed on the audit team. Until the late 1980s, the eight largest accounting firms were known as the Big Eight. The Big Eight audited virtually all the large companies in Canada and, as international firms themselves, many companies in other parts of the world. In the late 1980s, two mergers among the Big Eight resulted in what became known as the Big Six. In 1997, merger talks began between two of the Big Six, Price Waterhouse and Coopers & Lybrand. In 1998, that merger was finalized to form PricewaterhouseCoopers, the largest public accounting firm in Canada. The remaining four firms of the now Big Five are, in alphabetical order, Arthur Andersen & Co., Deloitte & Touche, Ernst & Young, and KPMG Peat Marwick. There are also several large and medium-sized national accounting firms performing audits in Canada.

In Canada there are three professional accounting organizations that establish the professional standards of accountants. The members of the Canadian Institute of Chartered Accountants are called Chartered Accountants (CAs). Members of CMA Canada are Certified Management Accountants (CMAs). The Certified General Accountants' Association of Canada establishes the standards for the Certified General Accountants (CGAs). These professional accountants perform audits, supervise and perform accounting functions within organizations, and fulfil decision-making functions within and outside organizations. Canada is one of the few countries in the world to have more than one professional accounting body. There have been attempts to combine the three bodies into one, but so far all attempts have been unsuccessful.

ethics in accounting

■ Auditors are hired by the shareholders to review the financial statements presented to the shareholders by the management of the company. The auditors, as they conduct their review, must maintain their independence from management. In order to ensure their independence and encourage ethical behaviour, the professional accounting organizations have developed codes of professional conduct. The codes state the responsibilities of auditors to the public, clients, and colleagues. For example, accountants normally cannot audit companies in which they own shares. In addition, the codes describe the scope and nature of the services provided by auditors. Each professional accounting organization has also developed a peer review process to monitor itself in the performance of its audit work.

SUMMARY

In this chapter we discussed what accounting is and what financial statements are. We looked at the activities in which companies engage. We discussed the various users of financial accounting information and provided an overview of the types of information that they would need. A brief introduction to the development of accounting standards that underlie accounting guidelines was included so that you can begin to understand the basic concepts governing how we collect and report financial information. The greater part of the chapter was used to provide a detailed explanation of the various components of an annual report using Big Rock Brewery Ltd. as an example. In the annual report, you discovered the information components of three major financial statements: the income statement, the balance sheet, and the statement of cash flows. Subsequent chapters will build on this framework. In Chapters 2 through 5 the mechanics of preparing these statements and more information about their decision-making capabilities are discussed. In Chapters 6 through 11 details of each individual asset, liability, and shareholders' equity account are discussed. Chapter 12 considers financial statement analysis to provide some tools for interpreting and linking the major financial statements. To provide some understanding of complex business organizations and the major accounting issues related to mergers, acquisitions, and consolidated financial statements, Appendix C has been included; it goes into these issues.

SUMMARY PROBLEM

The major financial statements of Celanese Canada Inc. from its 1998 annual report are included as Exhibit 1-8.

1. Find the following amounts in the statements:
   a. Revenues in 1998
   b. Operating costs in 1998
   c. Other income and expense in 1998
   d. Income tax expense in 1998
   e. Net income (earnings) in 1998
   f. Inventories at the end of 1998
   g. Accounts payable and accrued liabilities at the beginning of 1998
   h. Retained earnings at the end of 1998
   i. Deferred pension and post-retirement benefit cost at the beginning of 1998
   j. Cash provided from operating activities in 1998
   k. Cash payments, net of disposals, to acquire capital assets in 1998
   l. Dividends paid in 1998
   m. Cash proceeds from issuing new shares in 1998
   n. Cash provided from investing activities in 1998

2. Does Celanese Canada Inc. finance its business primarily with debt or with shareholders' equity? Support your answer with appropriate data.

3. List the two largest sources of cash and the two largest uses of cash in 1998. (Consider operations to be a single source or use of cash.)

4. Does Celanese use a classified balance sheet? Explain.

EXHIBIT 1-8
PART A

CONSOLIDATED
BALANCE SHEETS

(dollar amounts in thousands)

As at December 31	1998	1997	1996
		(restated)	(restated)
Assets			
Cash and short-term investments	$147,348	$102,055	$ 31,252
Accounts receivable	110,465	126,863	87,427
Inventories (note 4)	77,632	63,936	80,092
Prepaid expenses	1,749	759	1,754
Future income tax assets (note 3)	5,472	6,586	4,090
Total current assets	342,666	300,199	204,615
Property, plant and equipment	847,537	829,924	817,029
Accumulated depreciation	563,382	530,752	509,052
Net property, plant and equipment (note 5)	284,155	299,172	307,977
Deferred costs	14,112	18,094	17,294
Total assets	$640,933	$617,465	$529,886
Liabilities and Shareholders' Equity			
Accounts payable and accrued liabilities	$ 64,164	$ 73,948	$ 59,053
Dividends payable	8,147	8,147	8,147
Income taxes payable	11,697	19,467	4,471
Total current liabilities	84,008	101,562	71,671
Future income tax liabilities (note 3)	18,884	14,121	1,765
Deferred pension and post-retirement benefit obligations (note 6)	25,875	25,717	33,113
Minority interest	17,192	22,908	20,407
Shareholders' equity:			
Share capital (note 7)	50,122	50,114	50,106
Retained earnings	444,852	403,043	352,824
Total shareholders' equity	494,974	453,157	402,930
Total liabilities and shareholders' equity	$640,933	$617,465	$529,886

The accompanying notes and the segmented information are integral parts of these consolidated financial statements.

On behalf of the Board:

Donald S. Macdonald, Director
Paule Gauthier, Director

EXHIBIT 1-8

PART B

CONSOLIDATED *Statements of* INCOME

(amounts in thousands, except per share amounts)

For the years ended December 31	1998	1997	1996
		(restated)	(restated)
Net sales	$696,465	$796,533	$561,154
Operating costs:			
Cost of goods sold	553,052	602,551	423,725
Selling and administrative	13,624	13,929	9,806
Research and development	5,040	6,479	4,410
Total operating costs	571,716	622,959	437,941
Operating income	124,749	173,574	123,213
Other income and expense	13,123	3,013	3,371
Income before minority interest and income taxes	137,872	176,587	126,584
Minority interest (note 1)	(22,528)	(48,224)	(23,227)
Income before income taxes	115,344	128,363	103,357
Income taxes (note 3)	40,947	45,557	36,676
Net income	$ 74,397	$ 82,806	$ 66,681
Net income per share	$ 1.83	$ 2.03	$ 1.64
Weighted average shares outstanding during year	40,735	40,734	40,734

EXHIBIT 1-8

PART C

1998 ANNUAL REPORT

(CONSOLIDATED) *Statements of*

CASH FLOWS

(dollar amounts in thousands)

For the years ended December 31	1998	1997	1996
		(restated)	(restated)
Cash flows from operations:			
Cash receipts from customers	$712,863	$757,097	$538,641
Cash paid to suppliers and employees	(554,760)	(564,151)	(436,608)
Interest income received	6,480	1,399	4,848
Cash from other income and expense	6,716	1,889	(2,142)
Income taxes paid	(42,840)	(20,701)	(29,621)
Cash flows from operations	128,459	175,533	75,118
Cash flows from investing activities:			
Additions to property, plant and equipment, net of proceeds on disposal	(22,342)	(22,778)	(156,262)
Deferred costs	–	(3,650)	(15,695)
Cash flows from investing activities	(22,342)	(26,428)	(171,957)
Cash flows from financing activities:			
Dividends paid	(32,588)	(32,587)	(52,954)
Distribution to minority interest holders	(28,244)	(45,723)	(15,818)
Shares issued (note 7)	8	8	–
Cash flows from financing activities	(60,824)	(78,302)	(68,772)
Increase (decrease) in cash and short-term investments	45,293	70,803	(165,611)
Cash and short-term investments:			
at beginning of year	102,055	31,252	196,863
at end of year	$147,348	$102,055	$ 31,252

The accompanying notes and the segmented information are integral parts of these consolidated financial statements.

SUGGESTED SOLUTION TO SUMMARY PROBLEM

All answers are in thousands of dollars unless otherwise stated.

1. The following answers are found on the financial statements included in Exhibit 1-8:
   a. Revenues in 1998 = $696,465
   b. Operating costs in 1998 = $571,716
   c. Other income and expenses in 1998 = $13,123
   d. Income tax expense in 1998 = $40,947
   e. Net income in 1998 = $74,397
   f. Inventories at the end of 1998 = $77,632
   g. Accounts payable and accrued liabilities at the beginning of 1998 = $73,948 (the end of 1997 is the same as the beginning of 1998.)
   h. Retained earnings at the end of 1998 = $444,852
   i. Deferred pension and post-retirement benefit costs at the beginning of 1998 = $25,717
   j. Cash produced from operating activities in 1998 = $128,459
   k. Cash payments, net of disposals, to acquire capital assets in 1998 = $22,342 (additions to property, plant, and equipment under the investing activities)
   l. Dividends paid in 1998 = $32,588 (listed under the financing activities on the Statement of Cash Flows)
   m. Cash proceeds from the issuance of new shares in 1998 = $8
   n. Cash provided from investing activities in 1998 = ($22,342)

2. Celanese Canada Inc. uses more shareholders' equity to finance its business than debt. You can see this when you compare the total liabilities to the total shareholders' equity (balance sheet) as shown below:

   Total liabilities (12/31/98) $145,959
   Total shareholders' equity (12/31/98) $494,974
   Total liabilities and shareholders' equity $640,933
   Total liabilities are, therefore, 23% ($145,959/$640,933) of the total sources of financing for Celanese Canada Inc.

3. The two largest sources of cash are proceeds from operating activities ($128,459) and proceeds from the issuance of shares ($8). The two largest uses are dividends ($32,588) and distribution to **minority interest** holders ($28,244).

4. Celanese Canada Inc. does use a classified balance sheet but this is not obvious on the balance sheet, because it has not labelled a section for current assets or current liabilities. It has, however, totalled all of the current assets and current liabilities and given you a total for these items. With respect to the noncurrent items, it has given you a subtotal for property, plant, and equipment but not for total noncurrent assets, nor has it given you a total for noncurrent liabilities.

ABBREVIATIONS USED

AcSB	Accounting Standards Board	GAAP	Generally Accepted Accounting Principles
ASC	Alberta Securities Commission		
CA	Chartered Accountant	IAS	International Accounting Standards
CGA	Certified General Accountant		
CICA	Canadian Institute of Chartered Accountants	IASC	International Accounting Standards Committee
CMA	Certified Management Accountant	IFAC	International Federation of Accountants
FASB	Financial Accounting Standards Board		

SYNONYMS

Accounts Receivable/Current Receivables

Balance sheet equation/Accounting equation

Capital Assets/Property, Plant, and Equipment/Plant Assets/Fixed Assets

Common Shares/Share Capital/Capital Stock

Earnings Statement/Statement of Earnings/Income Statement/Net Income Statement/Consolidated Statement of Earnings/Profit and Loss Statement

Equity/Owners' Equity/Shareholders' Equity

Financial reporting books/Reporting books/Books/Accounting records

Liabilities/Debt

Managerial accounting/Cost accounting

Net income/Profit/Earnings

Retained Earnings/Earnings Retained in the Business/Earnings Reinvested in the Business

Statement of Changes in Financial Position/Cash Flow Statement/Statement of Cash Flow/Consolidated Statement of Cash Flow

Statement of Financial Position/Balance Sheet/Consolidated Balance Sheet

GLOSSARY

Accounting Standards Board (AcSB)   The CICA committee that sets accounting standards in Canada.

Assets   Elements of the balance sheet that have probable future value that can be measured, are owned or controlled by the company, and are the result of a past transaction.

Auditor   A professionally trained accountant who examines the accounting records and statements of the company to determine whether they fairly present the financial position and operating results of the company in accordance with GAAP.

Balance sheet   A financial statement showing the asset, liability, and shareholders' equity account balances of the company.

Basic accounting equation   The equation that describes the relationship between assets, liabilities, and shareholders' equity. It is as follows:

$$Assets = Liabilities + Shareholders' Equity$$

Board of Directors   The governing body of a company elected by the shareholders to represent their ownership interest.

Books   The accounting records of the company. Usually this term refers to the records reported to shareholders rather than to any other body, such as the tax authority.

Capital Stock   Synonym for Share Capital.

Cash Flow Statement   See Statement of Cash Flows.

Classified balance sheet   A balance sheet in which the assets and liabilities are listed in liquidity order and are categorized into current and noncurrent sections.

Clean opinion   Synonym for unqualified opinion.

Common Shares   The shares issued by a company to its owners. Shares represent the ownership interest in a company.

Comparability   A quality of accounting information that improves the ability of financial statement readers to compare different sets of financial statements.

Conceptual framework   The framework set out in section 1000 of the *CICA Handbook* to guide the AcSB as they set new accounting standards.

Consistency   A quality of accounting information that requires consistent application of accounting principles over time.

Consolidated financial statements   Financial statements that represent the combined financial results of a parent company and its subsidiaries.

Cost accounting   A branch of accounting that studies how cost information is used internally within the company.

Cost/benefit constraint   A constraint that states that the cost of implementing a new accounting standard should be less than the benefits that will be derived.

Creditors   Individuals or entities that are owed something by the company.

Current asset/liability   For assets, current means that the asset will be turned into cash or consumed in the next year or operating cycle of the company. For liabilities, current means that the liability will require the use of cash or the rendering of service or will be replaced by another current liability within the next year or operating cycle of the company.

Dividends   Payments made to shareholders that represent a return on their investment in the company. Dividends are paid only after they are declared by the Board of Directors.

Earnings   The profits generated by a company during a specified period. Earnings are determined by subtracting expenses from the revenues of the company.

Earnings per share   A ratio calculated by dividing the earnings for the period by the average number of shares outstanding during the period.

Entity   The business reported by the financial statements, usually a company.

Equity   A term sometimes used to describe the sum of liabilities and shareholders' equity; sometimes also used to refer simply to the shareholders' equity section, which can lead to some confusion in the use of this term.

Expenses   The resources used in the production of revenues by the company; representing decreases in the shareholders' wealth.

FASB   Financial Accounting Standards Board, the regulatory body that currently sets accounting standards in the United States.

Feedback value   A quality of accounting information that gives it relevance to decision-makers. The information provides feedback on previous decisions.

Financial accounting   The study of the accounting concepts and principles used to prepare financial statements for external users.

Financial reporting books   The accounting records that are summarized and reported to shareholders and other users via the financial statements.

Financing activities   Activities of the company in which funds are raised to support the other activities of the company. The two major ways to raise funds are to issue new shares or borrow money.

Flow statement   A statement that describes certain types of inflows and outflows of the company. The cash flow statement and the income statement are both examples of this type of statement.

GAAP   Generally Accepted Accounting Principles—the set of accounting principles that corporations use.

Investing activities   The activities of the company involved with long-term investments, primarily investments in property, plant, and equipment and in the shares of other companies.

Liability   An element of the balance sheet characterized by a probable future sacrifice of resources of the company.

Liquidity   The length of time required to turn assets into cash.

Management   The individuals responsible for running or managing the company.

Management accounting   The study of the preparation and uses of accounting information by the management of the company.

Materiality   A concept used to indicate items that will affect decision-making. In auditing it means those items that are large enough to have a significant effect in the evaluation of the presentation of the financial results of a company.

Minority interest   The shareholders, other than the parent company, of a subsidiary company who own shares of the company. Usually they own less than 50% of the shares.

Minority shareholders   Synonym for minority interest.

Net income   Synonym for earnings.

Neutrality   A quality of accounting information indicating that the methods or principles applied should not depend on the self-interest of the company being measured but should be neutral with regard to the potential outcomes of the company.

Noncurrent asset/liability   Assets or liabilities that do not fit the definition of current assets and liabilities.

Operating activities   The activities of the company that involve the sale of goods and services to customers.

Operating cycle   The time period between the initial investment of cash in products or services and the return of cash from the sale of the product or service.

Owners   Synonym for shareholders.

Predictive value   A quality of accounting information that makes the information relevant to decision-makers. Its relevance stems from its ability to predict the future.

Privately held company   A company whose shares are held by a few individuals and do not trade in an active stock market.

Publicly traded company   A company whose shares are traded in a public stock market.

Qualified opinion   An audit opinion that finds some exception to the fair presentation of the financial results.

Relevance   A quality of accounting information indicating that the information should be relevant to the decisions of the user.

Reliability   A quality of accounting information indicating that the information should be reliable to be of use to decision-makers.

Reporting books   Synonym for financial reporting books.

Representational faithfulness   A quality of accounting information indicating that the information should accurately represent the attribute or characteristic that it purports to represent.

Retained Earnings   Earnings that are retained within the company and not paid out to shareholders in the form of dividends.

Revenues   Inflows of resources to the company that result from the sale of goods and/or services.

Share capital   The investment in a company by the shareholders.

Shareholders   The individuals or entities that own shares in a company.

Shareholders' equity   The section of the balance sheet that represents the shareholders' wealth; equivalent to the assets less the liabilities.

Statement of Cash Flows   A statement that describes the inflows and outflows of cash during a specified period categorized into operating, investing, and financing activities.

Statement of Changes in Financial Position   Synonym for statement of cash flows.

Statement of Financial Position   Synonym for balance sheet.

Tax books   The accounting records the company keeps to report to the taxing authority.

Taxing authority   An agency that assesses taxes owed by the company and collects them.

Timeliness   A quality of accounting information indicating that information must be timely in order to be relevant to decision-makers.

Unclassified balance sheet   A balance sheet that does not classify assets and liabilities into current and noncurrent categories.

Unqualified opinion   An audit opinion that states that the financial statements present fairly the financial position and operating results of the company in conformity with GAAP.

Verifiability   The capability of accounting information to be verified by an independent measurer.

Working capital   The difference between the current assets and the current liabilities.

Assignment Material

Assessing Your Recall

1-1 Describe and illustrate the three major types of activities in which all companies engage.

1-2 Describe and illustrate the three major categories of items that appear in a typical balance sheet.

1-3 Describe the purpose of the three main financial statements that are contained in all annual reports.

1-4 Discuss the meaning of Generally Accepted Accounting Principles, and describe the organizations that establish these principles.

1-5 What is the purpose of an auditor's opinion, and what types of opinions can auditors render?

1-6 Identify at least three major users of corporate financial statements, and briefly state how they might use the information from the statements.

1-7 List three types of information that users should be able to obtain from financial statements.

1-8 List and briefly describe the major qualitative characteristics that accounting information should possess according to the CICA conceptual framework.

1-9 Explain the meaning of the term "books" as it is used in accounting.

Applying Your Knowledge

1-10 (What is accounting?)
In the opening story to this chapter, Raj Randhawa compared accounting to a scorecard.

Required:
Write a paragraph explaining why this comparison is appropriate.

1-11 (Identification of financing, investing, and operating transactions)
For a company like Big Rock Brewery, provide two examples of transactions that you would classify as financing, investing, and operating.

1-12 (Identification of financing, investing, and operating transactions)
For a company like the Hudson's Bay Company, provide two examples of transactions that you would classify as financing, investing, and operating.

1-13 (Application of qualitative characteristics)
The AMAX Company purchased land several years ago for $70,000 as a potential site for a new building. No building has yet been constructed. A comparable lot near the site was recently sold for $110,000.

Required:

a. At what value should AMAX carry the land on its balance sheet? Support your answer with consideration for the relevance and reliability of the information that would result.

b. If AMAX wanted to borrow money from a bank, what information about the land would the bank require? Explain your answer.

1-14 (Comparison of the income statement and the statement of cash flows)
Compare and contrast the statement of income and the statement of cash flows with regard to their purpose.

1-15 (Identifying items on financial statements)
Use the following abbreviations to respond to this question.
    CA   Current Assets
    NCA Noncurrent Assets
    CL   Current Liabilities
    NCL Noncurrent Liabilities
    SC   Share Capital
    RE   Retained Earnings
    NI   Income statement item
    SCF Statement of cash flows item

Required:
Classify the following items according to where the item would appear in the financial statements:

a. Temporary investment

b. Taxes payable

c. Interest expense

d. Inventory

e. Dividends

f. Sales to customers

g. Manufacturing equipment

h. New issuance of common shares

i. Cash

j. Bonds payable (debt due in 10 years)

1-16 (Identifying items on financial statements)
Use the following abbreviations to respond to this question.

CA   Current Assets
NCA Noncurrent Assets
CL   Current Liabilities
NCL Noncurrent Liabilities
SC   Share Capital
RE   Retained Earnings
NI   Income statement item
SCF   Statement of cash flows item

Required:
Classify the following items according to where the item would appear in the financial statements:

a. Wages payable

b. Administrative expenses

c. Purchase of equipment

d. Amounts owed to suppliers

e. Short-term bank loan acquired from the bank

f. Cost of inventory sold to customers

g. Building

h. Net income for the year

i. Prepaid expenses

j. Amounts owed by customers to the corporation

1-17 (Classifying items on the statement of cash flows)
Use the following abbreviations to respond to this question.

OA Operating Activities item
FA Financing Activities item
IA Investing Activities item

Required:
Classify each of the following transactions according to whether they are operating, financing, or investing activities:

a. Cash collected from customers

b. Repayment of debt

c. Payment of dividends

d. Purchase of a truck for use in deliveries

e. Purchase of a truck for resale (by a truck dealer)

f. Purchase of shares of another company

g. Sale of a building

h. Issuance of shares

1-18 (Identify items on the balance sheet and income statement)
Indicate whether each of the following items will be reported in the balance sheet (BS), income statement (IS), neither the balance sheet nor the income statement (N), or both the balance sheet and the income statement (B).

a. Cash

b. Loans payable

c. Building and equipment

d. Interest income

e. Sales of goods and services

f. Dividends distributed to shareholders

g. Salary expense

h. Sales anticipated next period

i. Payment made to pay off a bank loan

j. Common shares

1-19 (Identify items on the balance sheet and income statement)
Indicate whether each of the following items will be reported in the balance sheet (BS), income statement (IS), neither the balance sheet nor the income statement (N), or both the balance sheet and the income statement (B).

a. Accounts receivable

b. Selling expenses

c. Retained earnings

d. Current portion of long-term debt

e. Purchase of property, plant, and equipment

f. Cost of goods sold to customers

g. Interest expense

h. Temporary investments

i. Payment made to reduce a bank loan

j. Deferred income tax

1-20 (Determine missing balance sheet amounts)
Compute the missing balance sheet amounts in each of the following independent situations:

	A	B	C	D
Current Assets	?	$550,000	$230,000	$80,000
Noncurrent Assets	250,000	?	500,000	?
Total Assets	?	1,050,000	?	290,000
Current Liabilities	75,000	500,000	200,000	50,000
Noncurrent Liabilities	?	150,000	?	60,000
Shareholders' Equity	225,000	?	80,000	?
Total Liabilities and Shareholders' Equity	350,000	?	?	?

1-21 (Determine missing retained earnings amounts)
Compute the missing amounts in the reconciliation of retained earnings in each of the following independent situations:

	A	B	C	D
Retained Earnings Dec. 31, Year 1	$40,000	$100,000	?	$60,000
Net Income	18,000	?	400,000	32,000
Dividends Declared and Paid	6,000	35,000	250,000	?
Retained Earnings Dec. 31, Year 2	?	130,000	600,000	82,000

1-22 (Prepare a simple income statement)
Josephine Friesen operated a small pizza business called Hot Stuff Inc. During the month of July the following things occurred: she spent $125 on the telephone system and $266 on electricity and water; the rent on the premises was $1,000; she took in $18,730 from selling pizzas; the ingredients for the pizzas cost her $5,733; she paid $229 for gas and repairs to the delivery vehicle; and she paid her employees $6,240 in wages.

Required:

a. Prepare an income statement to determine how much Josephine Friesen earned in July.

b. Are there any other costs that you think Josephine Friesen might have incurred in July that were not listed?

1-23 (Prepare a simple income statement)
Pavel Bains ran an outdoor adventure company called Call of the Wild, Ltd. His busiest months were June through September although he did operate some limited excursions later in the fall. For the month of August he recorded the following items: he paid $21,120 for employee wages; he spent $5,780 on advertising; people paid him $64,200 for excursions in August; the supplies used in August cost $10,674; the telephone and electricity in the office came to $574; and it cost $1,300 for gas and repairs to the vehicles.

Required:

a. Prepare an income statement for Call of the Wild, Ltd. to determine how much it earned in August.

b. Are there any other costs that you think Pavel Bains might have incurred in August that were not listed?

1-24 (Prepare a simple balance sheet)

Problem 1-22 introduced Josephine Friesen and her pizza business. At the end of July, the following items were in her records:

Inventory	$ 4,277
Wages owed to employees	1,650
Bank loan owed to the bank	10,000
Cash held in the chequing account	10,361
Cost of the ovens used to cook the pizza	21,695
Prepaid rent for August	1,000
Common shares	15,000
Retained earnings	10,683

Required:

a. Identify each of the items in her records as an asset, liability, or shareholders' equity item.

b. Prepare a balance sheet for the end of July.

c. Josephine Friesen does not have accounts receivable in her records. Explain why it is unlikely that she will have an account called "accounts receivable."

1-25 (Prepare a simple balance sheet)

Problem 1-23 introduced Pavel Bains and his outdoor adventure company. At the end of August, the following items were in his records:

Bank loan owed	$15,000
Supplies on hand to be used in September	4,220
Cash in bank accounts	18,450
Common shares	10,000
Tents, rafts, etc.	15,590
Retained earnings	27,190
Vehicles	32,400
Amounts paid for trips to be taken in September	18,470

Required:

a. Identify each of the items in his records as an asset, liability, or shareholders' equity item.

b. Prepare a balance sheet for the end of August.

c. Does Pavel Bains have any inventory? Explain.

d. Pavel Bains does not have accounts receivable in his records. Explain why it is unlikely that he will have an account called "accounts receivable."

1-26 (Identification of assets and liabilities)

For each of the following companies, list at least two types of assets and one type of liability that you would expect to find on its balance sheet (try to include at least one item for each company that is unique to its business):

a. Petromet Resources Limited This company is involved in oil and gas exploration and production.

b. Fletcher Challenge Canada Limited This company is primarily in the forest products business, selling both paper and wood products.

c. Sask Tel (Saskatchewan Telephone Company) This telecommunications company provides phone service and equipment in Saskatchewan.

d. Sun Life This is a multiline (property/casualty, life, health, etc.) insurance company.

e. Bombardier Inc. This company manufactures transportation equipment and other industrial products.

f. Scotiabank This is a major commercial bank.

1-27 (Identification of income statement items)
For each of the companies listed in Problem 1-26, list at least two line items that you would expect to find on its income statement (try to include at least one item for each company that is unique to its business).

1-28 (Identification of statement of cash flow items)
For each of the companies listed in Problem 1-26, list at least two line items that you would expect to find on its statement of cash flows (try to include at least one item for each company that is unique to its business).

Management Perspective Problems

1-29 (Use of accounting information)
You are the accounting manager for a Canadian company that has just been acquired by a German company. Helmut Schmidt, the CEO of the German company, has just paid you a visit and is puzzled as to why Canadian companies use different information when reporting to Revenue Canada and to the shareholders. In Germany, the same set of information is sent to both parties.

Required:
Draft a memo explaining to Helmut why the two groups of users accept different information. In answering this question, consider the reporting objectives of the two groups.

1-30 (Information for decision-making)
Suppose that the CICA proposed that inventory be accounted for at its current market price (i.e., what you could sell it for) rather than its historical cost. Provide an argument that supports or opposes this change on the basis of relevance and reliability.

1-31 (Information for decision-making)
Suppose that you started your own company that assembles and sells laptop computers. You do not manufacture any of the parts yourself. The computers are sold through orders received over the Internet and through mail orders.

Required:
Make a list of the information that you would think would be relevant to running this type of business. When you are through, discuss how you would reliably measure the information that you would want to keep track of.

1-32 (Information for decision-making)
Suppose that you own and operate your own private company. You need to raise money to expand your operation and approach a bank for a loan. The bank loan officer has asked for financial statements prepared according to GAAP.

Required:

    a. Why would the loan officer make such a request?

    b. Assuming that your statements were prepared according to GAAP, how could you convince the loan officer that this was so?

1-33 (Value of auditors)

In order for a company's shares to be listed (i.e., traded) on a Canadian stock exchange, the company's financial statements must be audited by an independent auditor. Why?

1-34 (Raising new capital)

Suppose that your best friend wanted to start a new business providing website construction services to customers. Your friend has some savings to start the business but not enough to buy all of the equipment that she thinks she needs. She has asked you for some advice about how to raise additional funds.

Required:

Give her at least two alternatives and provide the pros and cons for each alternative.

1-35 (Value of future-oriented information)

From time to time there have been calls from the user community for management to disclose their own forecasts of future expectations such as net income.

Required:

As an external user of the financial statements, discuss the relevance and reliability of this type of information.

1-36 (Distribution of salary in a partnership)

Suppose that you and a friend form a partnership in which you contribute the same amount of cash and agree to share in the profits on a 50-50 basis. Further suppose that you are responsible for running the day-to-day operations of the company but your friend is a "silent partner" in the sense that he doesn't work in the business (he has another job). Since you have no other job, the partnership agrees to pay you $1,500 per month.

Required:

How should the partnership treat this payment, as a distribution of profits (like a dividend) or as an expense of doing business? What difference would it make to the distribution to you and your partner?

Reading and Interpreting Published Financial Statements

Base your answers to problems 37–42 on the financial statements for Big Rock Brewery in Appendix A at the end of the book.

1-37 (Find dividends declared)

Determine the amount of dividends that Big Rock declared in 1999. Assume that the only events that affect retained earnings are dividends and net income.

1-38 (Verify basic accounting equation)

Verify that total assets equal total liabilities and shareholders' equity for Big Rock in 1999.

1-39 (Find financial statement balances)

Find the following amounts in the statements of Big Rock:

    a. Revenues from the sale of beer in 1999.

    b. Cost of sales in 1999.

    c. Interest expense in 1999.

    d. Income tax expense in 1999. (Include the Large Corporation tax.)

    e. Net income in 1998.

    f. Inventories at the end of 1999.

    g. Accounts payable and accrued liabilities at the beginning of 1999.

    h. Retained earnings at the end of 1999.

    i. Long-term borrowings at the beginning of 1999.

    j. Cash produced from operating activities in 1999.

    k. Cash payments to acquire capital assets in 1999.

    l. Cash proceeds from new borrowings in 1998.

    m. Cash produced from or used for investing activities in 1999.

    n. Cash payments to reduce long-term debt in 1999.

1-40 (Identify sources and uses of cash)
List the two largest sources of cash and the two largest uses of cash in 1999. (Consider operations to be a single source or use of cash.)

1-41 (Net income versus cash from operations)
Suggest some reasons why, in 1998, income was $288,981 yet cash flow from operations was $1,665,863.

1-42 (Comparison of change in sales with change in net income)
During 1999, sales were approximately $1,000,000 higher than they were in 1998. However, net income in 1999 was approximately $800,000 lower than in 1998. Examine the income statement and provide some reasons why this occurred.

Base your answers to problems 43–50 on the 1998 financial statements for AT Plastics Inc. in Exhibit 1-9.

1-43 (Find dividends declared)
Determine the amount of dividends that AT Plastics Inc. declared in 1998. The only events that affected retained earnings were dividends and earnings.

1-44 (Verify basic accounting equation)
Verify that total assets equal total liabilities and shareholders' equity for AT Plastics Inc. in 1998.

1-45 Calculation of current assets–current liabilities)
AT Plastics Inc. prepared a classified balance sheet. Calculate the difference between the current assets and current liabilities at the end of 1998. This amount is referred to as **working capital**. State explicitly what assets and liabilities you have included as current for the purpose of your calculation.

1-46 (Find financial statement balances)
Find the following amounts in the statements of AT Plastics Inc.:

    a. Revenues from sale of goods in 1998

    b. Cost of sales in 1998

    c. Interest expense in 1998

    d. Income tax expense (current and deferred) in 1998

EXHIBIT 1-9

PART A

22   AT Plastics 1998 Annual Report

consolidated balance sheets

December 31, 1998 and 1997

(thousands of dollars)	1998	1997
Assets		
Current		
Cash	$ 4,292	$ 411
Accounts receivable	32,028	31,809
Inventory (Note 2)	46,877	47,426
Prepaids	1,113	906
	84,310	80,552
Fixed (Note 3)	386,271	255,419
Other (Note 4)	35,040	22,225
	$ 505,621	$ 358,196
Liabilities		
Current		
Accounts payable	$ 41,384	$ 30,362
Current portion of long-term debt (Note 5)	12,555	8,351
	53,939	38,713
Long-term debt (Note 5)	242,825	149,362
Deferred income taxes	21,149	15,628
	317,913	203,703
Shareholders' Equity		
Capital stock (Note 6)	153,937	128,404
Retained earnings	33,771	26,089
	187,708	154,493
	$ 505,621	$ 358,196

See accompanying notes to consolidated financial statements.

Approved by the Board

Gordon Pearce
Director

John Abell
Director

EXHIBIT 1-9

PART B

23   AT Plastics 1998 Annual Report

consolidated statements of operations and retained earning

Years ended December 31, 1998 and 1997

(thousands of dollars, except per share amounts)	1998	1997
Sales	$ 229,976	$ 218,644
Cost of sales and other expenses	194,170	182,582
Income before the undernoted items	35,806	36,062
Less		
Interest on long-term debt	5,858	7,785
Depreciation and amortization	9,680	9,741
Interest income	(229)	(136)
Other expense	1,361	1,642
	16,670	19,032
Income before income taxes	19,136	17,030
Income taxes (Note 7)		
Current	2,264	1,060
Deferred	6,104	5,629
	8,368	6,689
Net income for the year	10,768	10,341
Retained earnings at beginning of year	26,089	18,501
Dividends	(3,086)	(2,753)
Retained earnings at end of year	$ 33,771	$ 26,089
Net income per share (Note 8)	$ 0.62	$ 0.68

See accompanying notes to consolidated financial statements.

EXHIBIT 1-9

PART C

consolidated statements of changes in financial position

Years ended December 31, 1998 and 1997

(thousands of dollars)	1998	1997
Cash from (used in)		
Operations		
Net income for the year	$ 10,768	$ 10,341
Add items charged to income not affecting cash		
Depreciation and amortization	9,680	9,741
Deferred income taxes	6,104	5,629
Amortization of exchange on long-term debt	1,432	462
Write-off of discontinued projects	–	877
Cash flow before change in working capital and other liabilities	27,984	27,050
Change in non-cash working capital and other liabilities	11,145	(3,412)
	39,129	23,638
Financing activities		
Long-term debt issued	100,433	70,000
Long-term debt repaid	(8,641)	(6,070)
Common shares issued	24,949	–
	116,741	63,930
Dividends paid	(3,086)	(2,753)
Investing activities		
Purchase of fixed assets	(140,457)	(92,612)
Change in other assets	(8,446)	(7,018)
	(148,903)	(99,630)
Increase (decrease) in cash during the year	3,881	(14,815)
Cash at beginning of year	411	15,226
Cash at end of year	$ 4,292	$ 411

See accompanying notes to consolidated financial statements.

    e. Net income in 1998

    f. Inventories at the end of 1998

    g. Accounts payable at the beginning of 1998

    h. Retained earnings at the end of 1998

    i. Long-term borrowings at the beginning of 1998

    j. Cash produced from operating activities in 1998

    k. Cash payments to acquire capital assets (fixed assets) in 1998

    l. Cash proceeds from new borrowings in 1998

    m. Cash produced from or used for investing activities in 1998

1-47 (Determine financing strategy)
Did AT Plastics Inc. finance the company mainly from creditors (total liabilities) or from shareholders (shareholders' equity) in 1998? Support your answer with appropriate data.

1-48 (Identify sources and uses of cash)
List the two largest sources of cash and the two largest uses of cash in 1998. (Consider operations to be a single source or use of cash.)

1-49 (Net income versus cash from operations)
Suggest some reasons why, in 1998, net income was $10,768,000 yet cash flow from operations was $39,129,000.

1-50 (Firm valuation)
The prices of AT Plastics' common shares in the fourth quarter of 1998 ranged from $11.00 to $8.05 per share. There were 17,760,916 common shares outstanding at the end of 1998. Compute the average total market value of the common shares of AT Plastics Inc. in the fourth quarter of 1998. Compare this with the value of shareholders' equity at the end of 1998 as represented in the balance sheet. If these numbers are different, offer an explanation for this discrepancy.

Base your answers to Problems 51–57 on the 1998 financial statements of Mosaid Technologies Incorporated, which are in Exhibit 1-10. Mosaid Technologies, an Ontario corporation, designs memory chips and supplies engineering test systems around the world.

1-51 (Fiscal year end)
When is the business year end for Mosaid Technologies Inc.?

1-52 (Find financial statement balances)
Find the following amounts in the statements of Mosaid Technologies Inc.:

    a. Revenues from operations in 1998

    b. Research and development in 1998

    c. Interest revenue in 1998

    d. Income tax expense in 1998

    e. Net income in 1997 (net earnings)

    f. Inventories at the end of 1998

MOSAID Technologies Incorporated   f i n a n c i a l   s t a t e m e n t s   1 9 9 8

EXHIBIT 1-10

PART A

MOSAID Technologies Incorporated
Consolidated Statement of Earnings and Retained Earnings

(in thousands, except per share amounts)

	Year ended	
	May 1, 1998	May 2, 1997
Revenues		
Operations	$ 40,672	$ 38,853
Interest	707	946
	41,379	39,799
Expenses		
Labour and materials	9,434	9,051
Research and development (Note 8)	13,956	10,009
Selling and marketing	7,157	6,276
General and administration	5,627	5,270
Bad debt	542	–
Unusual item (Note 9)	–	500
	36,716	31,106
Earnings from operations	4,663	8,693
Gain on sale of assets	3,897	670
	8,560	9,363
Income tax (Note 10)	3,012	3,381
Non-controlling interest	337	2,234
Net earnings	5,211	3,748
Retained earnings, beginning of year	20,610	16,862
Retained earnings, end of year	$ 25,821	$ 20,610
Earnings per share (Note 14)		
Basic	$ 0.73	$ 0.53
Fully diluted	$ 0.67	$ 0.49
Weighted average number of shares		
Basic	7,143,500	7,071,576
Fully diluted	8,024,505	7,781,487

See accompanying Notes to the Consolidated Financial Statements.

EXHIBIT 1-10

PART B

MOSAID Technologies Incorporated (INCORPORATED UNDER THE ONTARIO BUSINESS CORPORATIONS ACT)
Consolidated Balance Sheets
(in thousands)

	As at	
	May 1, 1998	May 2, 1997
Current Assets		
Cash and short-term marketable securities	$ 19,625	$ 18,337
Accounts receivable	9,489	11,250
Revenues recognized in excess of amounts billed	4,003	3,656
Inventories (Note 2)	5,512	4,490
Prepaid expenses	476	576
	39,105	38,309
Capital Assets (Note 3)	14,593	7,440
Technology Acquisitions (Note 4)	1,239	995
Long-term Investments (Note 5)	5,814	1,712
	$ 60,751	$ 48,456
Current Liabilities		
Accounts payable and accrued liabilities	$ 5,150	$ 4,988
Mortgage payable (Note 6)	128	–
Income taxes payable	1,069	301
Deferred revenue	630	636
Deferred income taxes	430	383
	7,407	6,308
Mortgage Payable (Note 6)	5,842	–
Deferred Income Taxes	461	713
	13,710	7,021
Shareholders' Equity		
Share capital (Note 7)	21,220	20,825
Retained earnings	25,821	20,610
	47,041	41,435
	$ 60,751	$ 48,456

See accompanying Notes to the Consolidated Financial Statements.

Thomas I. Csathy
Director

Robert F. Harland
Director

MOSAID Technologies Incorporated
Consolidated Statement of Changes in Financial Position
(in thousands)

	Year ended	
	May 1, 1998	May 2, 1997
Operating		
Net earnings	$ 5,211	$ 3,748
Items not affecting cash		
Amortization	3,301	2,405
Gain on long-term investment	(4,103)	–
Loss on disposal of capital assets	206	22
Non-controlling interest	337	2,234
Deferred income taxes	(205)	49
	4,747	8,458
Change in non-cash working capital items	1,301	(3,710)
	6,048	4,748
Investing		
Acquisition of capital assets – net	(10,357)	(5,366)
Acquisition of technology	(547)	(1,169)
Long-term investments	(4,002)	(2,570)
Proceeds of disposition of long-term investment	3,781	–
	(11,125)	(9,105)
Financing		
Issue of mortgage	6,000	–
Repayment of mortgage	(30)	–
Issue of common shares	395	876
	6,365	876
Net cash inflow (outflow)	1,288	(3,481)
Cash position, beginning of year	18,337	21,818
Cash position, end of year	$ 19,625	$ 18,337
Cash comprises the following:		
Cash	$ 1,367	$ 3,028
Marketable securities	18,258	15,309
	$ 19,625	$ 18,337

See accompanying Notes to the Consolidated Financial Statements.

g. Accounts payable and accrued liabilities at the beginning of 1998

h. Retained earnings at the end of 1998

i. Mortgage payable at the end of 1998 (current and long-term)

j. Cash produced from operating activities in 1998

k. Cash payments to acquire capital assets in 1998

l. Dividends paid in 1998

m. Cash proceeds from new share issuances in 1998

n. Cash produced from or used for investing activities in 1998

1-53 (Determine financing strategy)
Did Mosaid Technologies Inc. finance its business primarily from creditors (total liabilities) or from shareholders (shareholders' equity) in 1998? Support your answer with appropriate data.

1-54 (Identify sources and uses of cash)
List the two largest sources of cash and the two largest uses of cash in 1997. (Consider operations to be a single source or use of cash.)

1-55 (Net income versus cash from operations)
Suggest some reasons why, in 1998, net income was $5,211,000 yet cash flow from operations was $6,048,000.

1-56 (Dollar changes in assets and liabilities)
List the three assets and the three liabilities that experienced the largest dollar changes from the end of 1997 to the end of 1998.

1-57 (Determine financing strategy)
Total assets of Mosaid Technologies Inc. at May 2, 1997, and May 1, 1998, were $48,456,000 and $60,751,000, respectively. Total shareholders' equity at these same two dates was $41,435,000 and $47,041,000, respectively. Compute the ratio of debt to total assets for each of 1997 and 1998. How has Mosaid Technologies Inc. been financing its business?

Base your answers to problems 58–63 on the financial statements of Métro-Richelieu Inc., which are included in Exhibit 1-11. Métro-Richelieu, a Quebec company, is involved in the food industry.

1-58 (Fiscal year end)
When is Métro-Richelieu's fiscal year end?

1-59 (Find financial statement balances)
Find the following amounts in the statements of Métro-Richelieu Inc.:

a. Sales in 1998

b. Cost of goods sold and operating expenses in 1998

c. Interest expense in 1996 (both short-term and long-term)

d. Income tax expense in 1998

e. Net earnings in 1998

f. Inventory at the beginning of 1998.

g. Prepaid expenses in 1998

h. Retained earnings at the end of 1998

Consolidated statement of earnings

MétroRichelieu

EXHIBIT 1-11
PART A

Year ended September 26, 1998
(Millions, except for earnings per share)

	1998	1997	1996
Sales	$ 3,653.0	$ 3,432.3	$ 3,266.0
Cost of goods sold and operating expenses	3,483.1	3,277.7	3,124.0
Depreciation and amortization *(note 2)*	39.7	39.2	37.0
	3,522.8	3,316.9	3,161.0
Operating income	130.2	115.4	105.0
Financing costs			
Short-term	1.1	1.2	1.2
Long-term	3.8	4.1	1.8
	4.9	5.3	3.0
Earnings before income taxes and the following items	125.3	110.1	102.0
Labour relations settlement	24.1	—	—
Gain on disposal of investment	(6.1)	—	—
Earnings before income taxes	107.3	110.1	102.0
Income taxes *(note 3)*	41.9	43.9	41.0
Net earnings	$ 65.4	$ 66.2	$ 61.0
Earnings per share			
Basic	$ 1.28	$ 1.29	$ 1.00
Fully diluted	$ 1.25	$ 1.26	$ 0.96
Weighted average number of shares outstanding	50.9	51.2	61.1

See accompanying notes

Additional information excluding labour relations settlement and gain on disposal of investment			
Net earnings	$ 75.9	$ 66.2	$ 61.0
Earnings per share			
Basic	$ 1.49	$ 1.29	$ 1.00
Fully diluted	$ 1.45	$ 1.26	$ 0.96

Consolidated statement of retained earnings

Year ended September 26, 1998
(Millions of dollars)

	1998	1997	1996
Balance, beginning of year	$ 138.5	$ 85.2	$ 115.4
Net earnings	65.4	66.2	61.0
	203.9	151.4	176.4
Dividends	10.4	7.7	6.7
Share redemption premium	8.8	5.2	84.5
Stock options settled in cash	1.1	—	—
	20.3	12.9	91.2
Balance, end of year	$ 183.6	$ 138.5	$ 85.2

See accompanying notes

23

EXHIBIT 1-11
PART B

Consolidated balance sheet   MétroRichelieu

As at September 26, 1998 *(Millions of dollars)*		1998		1997		1996
Assets						
Current						
Cash	$	—	$	—	$	3.1
Accounts receivable		160.9		147.1		144.2
Income taxes		10.7		3.5		—
Inventories		166.9		164.8		145.0
Prepaid expenses		11.3		10.3		10.0
Current portion of investments *(note 4)*		0.7		2.4		2.5
		350.5		328.1		304.8
Investments *(note 4)*		17.0		18.2		17.4
Capital assets *(note 5)*		420.0		379.2		340.9
	$	787.5	$	725.5	$	663.1
Liabilities and shareholders' equity						
Current						
Bank loans	$	0.5	$	7.5	$	—
Outstanding cheques		33.1		11.6		5.9
Accounts payable		329.3		301.7		285.4
Income taxes		—		—		6.0
Current portion of long-term debt *(note 6)*		3.5		2.7		6.5
		366.4		323.5		303.8
Long-term debt *(note 6)*		48.6		94.6		106.2
Deferred income taxes		29.9		11.2		12.6
		444.9		429.3		422.6
Shareholders' equity						
Capital stock *(note 7)*		159.0		157.7		155.3
Retained earnings		183.6		138.5		85.2
		342.6		296.2		240.5
	$	787.5	$	725.5	$	663.1

See accompanying notes

On behalf of the Board:

Jean-Pierre Boyer
Director

Gilles Lamoureux
Director

EXHIBIT 1-11

PART C

Consolidated statement of changes in financial position   MétroRichelieu

Year ended September 26, 1998
(Millions of dollars)

	1998	1997	1996
Operating activities			
Net earnings	$ 65.4	$ 66.2	$ 61.0
Items not affecting cash			
Amortization and depreciation of capital assets	39.7	39.2	37.0
Loss (gain) on disposal of assets	(6.1)	1.2	(1.1)
Deferred income taxes	18.7	(1.4)	0.3
	117.7	105.2	97.2
Net change in non-cash working capital items	3.5	(16.2)	(3.1)
	121.2	89.0	94.1
Financing activities			
Increase in long-term debt	3.6	7.5	120.4
Repayment of long-term debt	(48.8)	(22.9)	(39.5)
Issuance of capital stock	3.0	3.8	6.9
Redemption of Subordinate Shares	(10.5)	(6.6)	(123.4)
Stock options settled in cash	(1.1)	—	—
	(53.8)	(18.2)	(35.6)
Investing activities			
Acquisition of investments	(4.2)	(3.6)	(4.1)
Disposal of investments	13.2	2.9	1.8
Net acquisitions of capital assets	(80.5)	(78.7)	(56.6)
	(71.5)	(79.4)	(58.9)
Dividends	(10.4)	(7.7)	(6.7)
Decrease in cash during the year	(14.5)	(16.3)	(7.1)
Cash position, beginning of year	(19.1)	(2.8)	4.3
Cash position, end of year	$ (33.6)	$ (19.1)	$ (2.8)

Cash consists of cash less bank loans and outstanding cheques.

See accompanying notes

    i. Long-term borrowings at the beginning of 1998 (both current and long-term portions)

    j. Cash produced from operating activities in 1998

    k. Cash payments to acquire capital assets in 1998

    l. Dividends paid in 1998

    m. Cash produced or used for financing activities in 1998

1-60 (Determine financing strategy)
Did Métro-Richelieu Inc. finance its business primarily from creditors (total liabilities) or from shareholders (shareholders' equity) in 1998? Support your answer with appropriate data.

1-61 (Identify sources and uses of cash)
List the three largest sources of cash and the three largest uses of cash in 1998. (Consider operations to be a single source or use of cash.)

1-62 (Determine causes of change in retained earnings)
Explain the change in retained earnings from the end of 1997 to the end of 1998.

1-63 (Net earnings versus cash balance changes)
Net earnings has stayed about the same in 1998 as it was in 1997, yet the cash balance (i.e., bank loans and outstanding cheques—Métro-Richelieu Inc. has no cash but rather short-term bank loans) has declined over the same period. From the major categories presented on the statement of changes in financial position, can you suggest reasons why Métro-Richelieu Inc. has experienced this decrease in cash?

Base your answers to Problems 64–67 on the 1997 financial statements of Daimler-Benz and Subsidiaries presented in Exhibit 1-12.

1-64 Find the following amounts in the consolidated statements of Daimler-Benz (express your answers in Deutsche Marks [DM]):

    a. Net revenues in 1997

    b. Cost of sales in 1997

    c. Financial income in 1997

    d. Tax expense in 1997

    e. Net income (result) in 1997

    f. Inventories at the beginning of 1997

    g. Accounts payable (trade liabilities) at the beginning of 1997

    h. Retained earnings at the end of 1997

    i. Capital stock at the beginning of 1997

    j. Property, plant, and equipment in 1997

    k. Cash and cash equivalents in 1997

    l. Earnings per share in 1997

1-65 (Determine financing strategy)
Did Daimler-Benz finance its business primarily from creditors (total liabilities) or from shareholders (shareholders' equity) in 1997? Support your answer with appropriate data.

Consolidated Statements of Income

EXHIBIT 1-12

PART A

in millions of DM, except per share amounts	Note	Consolidated			Financial Services		
		1997	1996	1995	*1997*	1996	1995
Revenues	24	*124,050*	106,339	102,985	*9,499*	8,379	7,661
Cost of sales	4	*(98,943)*	(84,742)	(86,686)	*(8,650)*	(7,752)	(7,239)
Gross margin		*25,107*	21,597	16,299	*849*	627	422
Selling, administrative and other expenses	4	*(17,433)*	(15,955)	(20,834)	*(608)*	(476)	(366)
Research and development		*(5,663)*	(5,579)	(5,369)	*0*	0	0
Other income		*1,620*	1,402	1,742	*161*	113	89
Income (Loss) before financial income and income taxes		*3,631*	1,465	(8,162)	*402[1]*	264[1]	145[1]
Financial income, net	5	*618*	496	929	*7*		8
Income (Loss) before income taxes		*4,249*	1,961	(7,233)	*409*	264	153
Tax benefit relating to a special distribution		*2,908[2]*					
Income taxes		*1,074[3]*					
Total income taxes	6	*3,982*	712	1,620	*(210)*	(127)	(82)
Minority interest		*(189)*	89	(116)	*(1)*	(4)	2
Net income (loss)		*8,042[4]*	2,762	(5,729)	*198*	133	73
Earnings per share (in DM)							
Basic earnings (loss) per share	25	*15.59[4]*	5.37	(11.17)	–	–	–
Diluted earnings (loss) per share	25	*15.30[4]*	5.35	(11.17)	–	–	–

1) Equal to the operating profit of the Group's Financial Services.
2) Reflects the tax benefit relating to a special distribution of DM 20.00 per share.
3) Includes non-recurring tax benefits of DM 1,962 relating to the decrease in valuation allowance as of December 31, 1997, applied to the domestic operations that file a combined tax return.
4) Excluding the non-recurring benefits, 1997 net income would have been DM 3,172 and basic and diluted earnings per share would have been DM 6.15 and DM 6.08, respectively.

The accompanying notes are an integral part of these Consolidated Financial Statements.

Consolidated Statements of Income

Consolidated Balance Sheets

in millions of DM		Consolidated		Financial Services	
Assets	Note	December 31, 1997	December 31, 1996	December 31, 1997	December 31, 1996
Intangible assets	7	1,915	1,951	100	80
Property, plant and equipment, net	7	20,656	18,225	76	57
Investments and long-term financial assets	13	3,453	3,536	205	60
Equipment on operating leases, net	8	14,931	11,941	15,055	12,748
Fixed assets		40,955	35,653	15,436	12,945
Inventories	9	14,390	13,602	988	645
Trade receivables	10	12,006	10,864	373	382
Receivables from financial services	11	25,924	19,052	25,953	19,073
Other receivables	12	12,251[1)	8,959	897	826
Securities	13	14,687	9,783	91	92
Cash and cash equivalents	14	5,833	4,557	684	269
Current assets		85,091	66,817	28,986	21,287
Deferred taxes	6	10,462	9,603	27	162
Prepaid expenses		591	388	81	65
Total assets		137,099	112,461	44,530	34,459
Liabilities and stockholders' equity					
Capital stock		2,584	2,577		
Additional paid-in capital		5,247	5,080		
Retained earnings		26,508[1)	19,033		
Other equity		746	(297)		
Stockholders' equity	16	35,085	26,393	2,642	2,094
Minority interest		1,170	936	55	52
Accrued liabilities	17	36,618	34,886	576	523
Financial liabilities	18	39,302	28,850	38,383	29,171
Trade liabilities	19	11,079	9,027	176	132
Other liabilities	20	10,116	8,792	901	800
Liabilities		60,497	46,669	39,460	30,103
Deferred taxes	6	2,003	2,253	1,345	1,244
Deferred income		1,726	1,324	452	443
Total liabilities and stockholders' equity		137,099	112,461	44,530	34,459

1) Includes a tax receivable/tax benefit of approximately DM 2.9 billion relating to the special distribution of DM 20 per share.

The accompanying notes are an integral part of these Consolidated Financial Statements.

Consolidated Balance Sheets

69

1-66 (Fiscal year end)
When is Daimler-Benz's fiscal year end?

1-67 (Format of balance sheet)
The balance sheet of Daimler-Benz is organized differently from the Canadian balance sheets that you have seen in this chapter. Describe the areas where there are major differences.

Beyond the Book

The Beyond the Book problems are designed to give you the opportunity to find and utilize company information found outside the book.

1-68 (Using the library and other sources to find company information)
Familiarize yourself with the resources that are available at your university to access information about corporations. Most universities have some type of electronic database of financial statement information. The following is a short list of resources that may be available:

LEXIS/NEXIS Database—This is an incredibly large database that contains all sorts of news and financial information about companies. It contains information about Canadian, U.S., and international companies. The financial information is in full text form.

Carlson On-line Service—A directory site with Canadian investment information. Research any company traded on a Canadian exchange for links to other sites that have reliable and up-to-date information on that company.

Compact/Disclosure Canada—Contains descriptive and financial data for over 8,500 public, private, and Canadian government-owned (crown) corporations. Provides more than 60 financial items, including assets, liabilities, sales, profits, number of employees, and selected ratios.

CD-Disclosure—This database contains full text financial footnote information for thousands of companies but does not contain full text of the major financial statements.

EDGAR Filings—The EDGAR filings are electronic forms of the SEC filings which are included in the LEXIS/NEXIS database but are also accessible through the Internet.

ABI Inform (UMI, Inc.)—This database contains full text information from numerous business periodicals.

You can also surf the web for sites that list information about companies. The **SEDAR** website (http://www.sedar.com) contains most securities-related information required by the Canadian securities regulatory authorities. The **Wall Street Research Net** (http://www.wsrn.com) lists over 17,000 companies on the NYSE, NASDAQ, AMEX, OTC Bulletin Board, TSE, VSE, ME, and Alberta stock exchanges.

1-69 (Find information about a new company)
For a company of your choosing, answer the following questions:

   a. What are the products (or product lines) and/or services that your company sells? Please be as specific as possible.

   b. Who are the customers of your company?

   c. In what markets, domestic and global, does your company sell its products and/or services?

d. Who are the major competitors of your company?

e. What are the major inputs your company needs to produce its product? What are the suppliers of these inputs?

f. Are any of the items listed in the questions above changing substantially? Use a two-year time span as a window to address this question.

To answer these questions it will be useful to collect a series of articles concerning your company over the most recent two-year period. Try to find at least five reasonably long articles. Use these as references to write a two- to three-page background paper about your company.

1-70 (Find information about a new company)
For a company of your choosing, answer the following questions:

a. What are the major sections included in your annual report?

b. What are the three most important points made in the letter to the shareholders?

c. What are the titles to the major financial statements included in the report?

d. What are the total assets, total liabilities, and total shareholders' equity of the company? What percentage of the company's total assets are financed through liabilities?

e. Is the balance sheet classified or nonclassified? If classified, what are the major categories used?

f. What were the net sales in the most recent year? Is this up or down from the prior year (answer in both dollar and percentage amounts)?

g. What is the net income and earnings per share in the most recent year? Is this up or down from the prior year (answer in both dollar and percentage amounts)?

h. What is the net cash provided (used) by operating, financing and investing activities for the most recent year?

i. What is the last day of your company's fiscal year end?

j. Who are the independent auditors and what type of opinion did they give the company?

Critical Thinking Question

1-71 (Appropriateness of accounting guidelines for different businesses)
Donna Bovolaneas and Pankaj Puri (*CA Magazine*, October 1995) argue that the accounting guidelines for life insurance companies, banks, trust companies, and securities dealers should be similar.

1. Briefly discuss the differences in the business activities undertaken by corporations in these industries compared to the business activities of most other corporations.

2. Briefly discuss why the accounting guidelines for these industries might be different from those of other industries.

3. Briefly discuss why accounting guidelines should be identical for all industries.

4. Briefly discuss why accounting guidelines should not be identical for all industries.

"I Can Do This!"
Starting Up a Business

To hear Jennifer Crowe tell it, starting up a successful retail clothing store is easy. "I woke up one morning and said to myself, 'I can do this!'" she explains. "Then I went to the bank and asked them to give me a whole bunch of money—and they did. That was four years ago, and we've been successful pretty much ever since."

Upon reflection, she admits that she encountered complications she hadn't foreseen during the startup period for Grateful Threads, which sells clothing and jewellery ranging from classic to funky in Edmonton's hip Old Strathcona district. "There were all the costs I had expected, like leasing the store, buying inventory, and renovating (we hated the fluorescent lights that used to be in here!). And, while I've heard horror stories from other small-business owners, I had no trouble getting the licences I needed. But I hadn't thought ahead about joining the Retail Merchants' Association, which is an expense but brings your costs down in the long run, or about fire insurance. And who'd have thought I'd need to pay for an engineering certificate for our sign because it hangs over a City easement?"

Grateful Threads' balance sheet looks for the most part like that of any small retail business, with lines for cash, accounts receivable, and inventory (which Ms. Crowe, who keeps the books herself, divides into sweaters, other clothing, and jewellery/miscellaneous). But she currently has an unusual item under assets: antiques. "Those are pieces we bought for the window display," she explains. "Eventually I'll get tired of them and I guess we'll sell them and come up with something new!"

The liabilities side is notable for what isn't there—rare for a small business, the company has never had a loan. "I financed the startup from a line of credit," says Ms. Crowe. She was lucky enough to turn a profit quickly and pay down the credit, and has stayed in the black ever since, with a return on assets that averages about 8%. The secret? Well, besides a lot of great clothes and excellent customer service, Ms. Crowe stresses that she keeps her accounting—and all the store's administration—as simple as possible, so she can focus on making her customers look great.

chapter 2

TRANSACTION ANALYSIS
AND ACCOUNTING ENTRIES

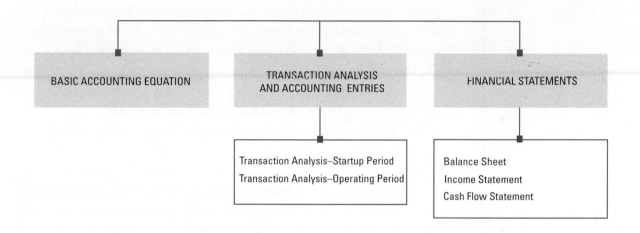

| BASIC ACCOUNTING EQUATION | TRANSACTION ANALYSIS AND ACCOUNTING ENTRIES | FINANCIAL STATEMENTS |

Transaction Analysis–Startup Period
Transaction Analysis–Operating Period

Balance Sheet
Income Statement
Cash Flow Statement

Learning Objectives:

After studying this chapter, you should be able to:

1. *Understand the basic accounting equation.*
2. *Analyze simple transactions and describe their effect on the basic accounting equation.*
3. *Identify operating activities and describe their impact on retained earnings.*
4. *Describe how inventory is accounted for when it is purchased and when it is sold.*
5. *Describe the difference between accrual basis accounting and cash basis accounting.*
6. *Describe the revenue recognition and matching criteria.*
7. *Prepare a balance sheet, income statement, and cash flow statement after a series of transactions.*
8. *Calculate three profitability ratios.*
9. *Begin to analyze the information on a cash flow statement.*

Jennifer Crowe owns and manages a successful business. What makes that business a success? She obviously has a good sense of what customers want. The clothing industry is very competitive and successful retailers must be able to accurately judge what will appeal to customers. She is able to buy inventory at competitive prices and sell it with enough markup to cover her other expenses and make a profit. How does she know what price will be high enough to cover all of her costs? How does she know that she has made a good deal when she buys new inventory? How does she know whether she is making a profit? The answer to all of these questions is that she keeps records. By keeping records she is able to compare her selling prices and costs over time, determine where prices might be increased or costs decreased, and measure how well she is doing. In this chapter and the next three, we are going to show you what some of those records look like. Similar to Jennifer Crowe, we are going to try to keep it simple. Our aim is not to make you an accountant but rather to give you enough knowledge about how the information is collected and reported for you to make sound decisions from the information that accountants provide.

The accounting system measures, records, and aggregates the effects on the company of numerous economic events. To interpret the information in the financial statements, you must be able to understand the process by which accounting information is obtained, and the guidelines by which it is classified and aggregated for financial statements. Only then can you use accounting information knowledgeably to make decisions. Chapter 1 provided an overview of the types of information that are presented in financial statements. This chapter and the next are devoted to explaining how accountants collect, classify, and aggregate that information. This chapter is necessarily technical in nature.

There are several possible approaches to understanding the accounting systems that companies use. The approach taken in this chapter is to focus on the balance sheet to discuss how a typical set of transactions would be reflected in the financial records and also how the three major financial statements would be prepared using the transaction information. We will use the basic accounting equation discussed in Chapter 1.

Learning Objective

Understand the basic accounting equation.

BASIC ACCOUNTING EQUATION

The basis of all accounting systems is the basic accounting equation. This equation was stated in Chapter 1 as:

BASIC ACCOUNTING EQUATION
Assets = Liabilities + Shareholders' Equity

When transactions are recorded in the accounting system, the equality of this equation must always be maintained. The balance sheet provides readers with information about this equality at the beginning and at the end of the current accounting period by showing amounts from the previous year in the outside column and amounts from the current year in the inside column. A statement with the amounts for two years is called a *comparative statement* (see Future Shop's balance sheet in Appendix B at the end of the book). The users of financial information typically want to know more than just the balance sheet amounts. They usually want to know something more about how the company's financial position changed from the beginning to the end of the year. An income statement and a cash flow statement are both useful for this purpose. The balance sheet equation will be used to record a set of typical transactions for a hypothetical company, and an income statement and a cash flow statement will be constructed from this information.

In Chapter 1 we showed you that retained earnings (one of the components of shareholders' equity) increased when the company earned net income (revenues minus expenses) and decreased when the company declared a dividend (a payment of earnings back to the investors). To help you understand the linkages of the financial statements and how the various items are affected by transactions, we are adding the following notations beside the amounts: R—revenue, E—expense, and D—dividend. Similarly, to help you understand the cash flows we will designate them as follows: O—operating, F—financing, and I—investing.

TRANSACTION ANALYSIS AND ACCOUNTING ENTRIES

The basic accounting equation can now be used to illustrate the functioning of the accounting system and the preparation of financial statements. We will use the typical transactions of a retail sales company to demonstrate the analysis and recording of transactions in the accounting system.

Assume that the Demo Retail Company, Ltd., is formed as a company in December of 20x0[1] with the issuance of common shares for $7,500.[2] Before the end of December, Demo uses $4,500 of the cash received from that issuance to buy equipment. It also buys $2,500 of inventory on account. ("On account" means that Demo has been extended credit by its suppliers and will be required to pay for the inventory at some later date. Typical terms for this type of credit include payment within 30 days.)

Learning Objective
2

Analyze simple transactions and describe their effect on the basic accounting equation

Transaction Analysis—Startup Period

On December 31, 20x0, just prior to commencing operations, Demo would like to prepare financial statements. Because Demo has not yet begun its normal operation

---

[1] The problems and examples in the text that do not use data from real companies are given artificial dates so as not to confuse them with real companies. Therefore, a designation of "20x0" represents year zero, "20x1" represents year one, and so on.

[2] The numbers used in this and most other made-up examples are stated in small round numbers for ease of presentation. If you want to think of them in more realistic terms, you might multiply all numbers by one thousand or one million.

of selling goods to customers, it has not yet earned any income. Therefore, it has no need for an income statement. It could, however, prepare a cash flow statement and a balance sheet. The cash flow statement for December would simply show the cash inflow from the issuance of shares ($7,500) and the outflow to buy equipment ($4,500). To prepare the balance sheet, we would use the basic accounting equation developed earlier.

Balance sheet preparation begins with an analysis of the transactions. In December 20x0, there were three transactions to record. They are as follows:[3]

A. Issuance of common shares for $7,500.

B. Purchase of equipment for $4,500.

C. Purchase of inventory for $2,500, on account.

Each of these transactions is analyzed in the following subsections and recorded in the balance sheet equation that appears in Exhibit 2-1. Note that the beginning balances in all the accounts are zero, because this is a new company.

DEMO RETAIL COMPANY, LTD.

BASIC ACCOUNTING EQUATION

(Amounts in Dollars)

	Cash	+	Inventory	+	Assets = Equipment	=	Liabilities Accounts Payable	+	Shareholders' Equity Common Shares	+	Retained Earnings
Balances	0	+	0	+	0	=	0	+	0	+	0
Transaction #											
A	+7,500 F					=			+7,500		
B	−4,500 I				+4,500	=					
C			+2,500			=	+2,500				
Ending											
Balances	+3,000	+	2,500	+	4,500	=	+2,500	+	7,500	+	0
Totals					10,000	=	10,000				

Transaction A

Demo issued common shares for $7,500.

ANALYSIS   The shareholders of the company have contributed $7,500 to the company in exchange for ownership rights. The cash received by the company increases its cash asset, and the ownership interest is represented by an increase in common shares. Look again at Exhibit 2-1. The entry can be summarized as follows:

EFFECTS OF TRANSACTION A
Assets (Cash) increase by $7,500
Shareholders' Equity (Common Shares) increases by $7,500

---

[3] We will designate these transactions with letters to distinguish them from the numbered transactions in January, which are discussed later in this chapter.

See Exhibit 2-1 for the recording of this transaction. The transaction can be summarized as follows:

EFFECTS OF TRANSACTION A ON THE BALANCE SHEET (EXHIBIT 2-1)		
Assets =	Liabilities +	Shareholders' Equity
Cash + Inventory + Equipment =	Accounts Payable +	Common Shares + Retained Earnings
+7,500 F =		+7,500

Note that the entries maintain the balance in the basic accounting equation. Also note that the cash transaction has been designated "F," indicating that this is a financing-type cash flow.

Transaction B

Demo purchased equipment for $4,500.

ANALYSIS Because the purchase of equipment requires an outflow of cash, cash decreases. The equipment purchased is generally regarded as a long-term asset because it will be used by the company over several future periods. The asset will be used up or consumed over those future periods, and the annual amount that is consumed or used will be shown as an amortization expense. The expensing of part of this amount is shown later in the transactions for January. By the end of December, however, none of the asset has been used up or consumed and the full amount should be reported as an asset. The entry can be summarized as follows:

EFFECTS OF TRANSACTION B
Assets (Cash) decrease by $4,500
Assets (Equipment) increase by $4,500

See Exhibit 2-1 for the recording of this transaction. The transaction can be summarized as follows:

EFFECTS OF TRANSACTION B ON THE BALANCE SHEET (EXHIBIT 2-1)		
Assets =	Liabilities +	Shareholders' Equity
Cash + Inventory + Equipment =	Accounts Payable +	Common Shares + Retained Earnings
−4,500 I +4,500 =		

Note that the cash outflow has been designated "I," indicating that it is an investing cash flow.

GAAP The treatment of this transaction under GAAP is based on an assumption of **accrual basis** accounting. Under accrual accounting, costs (such as the cost of the equipment) are represented as decreases in the shareholders' wealth (expenses) only when the item is consumed or the company relinquishes its ownership of the item (such as in a sale transaction). In this transaction, therefore, the view under GAAP is that one asset (cash) has been exchanged for another asset (equipment) and there has been no change in the shareholders' wealth. Accrual basis accounting is different from **cash basis** accounting, in which costs are represented as decreases in shareholders' wealth (expenses) when the cash is paid. In the cash basis system, therefore, this transaction would result in an expense that would be reported on the income statement. GAAP requires accrual basis accounting. It is discussed in more detail in the context of Transaction 1, which appears later in this chapter.

Transaction C

Demo purchased $2,500 of inventory on account.

ANALYSIS   The substance of this transaction is that Demo has received an asset (inventory) from its supplier and in exchange has given the supplier a promise to pay for the inventory at a later date. The promise to pay represents an obligation of the company and is therefore recorded as a liability. These liabilities are usually referred to as **accounts payable**. The inventory is usually recorded at the amount the company will have to pay to acquire it (its cost). The entry can be summarized as follows:

EFFECTS OF TRANSACTION C
Assets (Inventory) increase by $2,500
Liabilities (Accounts Payable) increase by $2,500

See Exhibit 2-1 for the recording of this transaction. The transaction can be summarized as follows:

EFFECTS OF TRANSACTION C ON THE BALANCE SHEET (EXHIBIT 2-1)
Assets = Liabilities + Shareholders' Equity
Cash + Inventory + Equipment = Accounts Payable + Common Shares + Retained Earnings
+2,500 = + 2,500

GAAP   As with Transaction B, this transaction involves the purchase of an asset, but this time no cash changes hands immediately. The inventory will be held until it is sold, and GAAP requires that the inventory be recorded at its cost and held as an asset until it is sold. The cost is, therefore, recorded as an asset until the company relinquishes title to it. There is no immediate income-statement impact from this transaction. It will affect the income statement only in the period in which the inventory is sold. Note that the transaction also has no impact on the cash flow statement in December, since no cash changed hands. Cash flow will be affected when the company pays the supplier.

At the bottom of Exhibit 2-1, you can see the net result of transactions A, B, and C. These figures represent the balance sheet at the end of December 20x0. The balance sheet could be formally represented as shown below. Note that the total assets of Demo equal the sum of the liabilities and shareholders' equity, as they should, to satisfy the basic accounting equation.

DEMO RETAIL COMPANY, LTD. Balance Sheet As at December 31, 20x0			
Assets		**Liabilities**	
Cash	$ 3,000	Accounts payable	$ 2,500
Inventory	2,500		
Equipment	4,500	**Shareholders' equity**	
		Common shares	7,500
		Retained earnings	0
Total assets	$10,000	Total liabilities and shareholders' equity	$10,000

Now that you have seen how a few simple transactions are analyzed and reported on the financial statements, we are going to continue with the example. Assume that during January the following events occurred that affect the account balances of Demo:

1. Demo sold units of inventory to customers, on account,[4] for $2,500.[5] The units sold were from the inventory purchased in December.

2. The cost of the units removed from inventory for sale in January totalled $1,800.

3. Purchases of new inventory to replace the units sold in January totalled $2,100. All of these purchases were made on account.

4. During the month, Demo received $2,200 from customers as payments on their accounts.

5. Demo made payments of $2,700 on its accounts payable.

6. Demo paid $360 in cash on January 1 for an insurance policy to cover its inventory from January 1, 20x1, through June 30, 20x1.

7. Demo's accountant determined that the equipment should be amortized $150 for January.

8. On the first day of January, Demo purchased land for $15,000 as a site for a future retail outlet. In order to pay for the land, Demo raised money by borrowing $10,000 from the bank and issuing new shares for $5,000.

9. The interest rate charged on the loan from the bank in Transaction 8 is 6%.

10. Dividends in the amount of $250 were declared and paid in January.

Transaction Analysis—Operating Period

For each of the events or transactions that affect the company, the accountant must analyze the economic substance of the transaction. The accountant must decide what accounts are affected and by how much. We call this **transaction analysis**. We

Learning Objective

Identify operating activities and describe their impact on retained earnings.

---

[4] The term "on account" in a sales transaction means that the company is granting the customer credit. The customer will then pay for the goods at some later date based on the agreement with the seller about the terms.

[5] The dollar amounts here are aggregate totals of all units that were sold during the month. Information about individual units would likely be recorded daily and would be of use to the sales or marketing manager, but in this example we are interested in the aggregate effects of sales.

have already done this for transactions A, B, and C, which occurred in December. It is at this stage of the accounting process that the accountant's training and knowledge are most needed. Not only must the economic substance of the transaction be analyzed, but also the accountant must know which accounting guidelines apply to the transaction.

For each of the preceding transactions the substance will be analyzed and an appropriate entry proposed. GAAP for the transaction will then be discussed. The transaction will be entered into the "accounting system" (the basic accounting equation). The recording of the transactions appears in Exhibit 2-2, but you may want to try to construct your own exhibit as you work through the transactions.

EXHIBIT   2-2

DEMO RETAIL COMPANY, LTD.

BASIC ACCOUNTING EQUATION

(Amounts in Dollars)

	Cash +	Accounts Receivable +	Inventory +	Prepaid Insurance +	Land +	Equipment =	Accounts Payable +	Interest Payable +	Bank Loan +	Common Shares +	Retained Earnings
					Assets		**=**	**Liabilities**		**+ Shareholders' Equity**	
Balances	3,000 +	0 +	2,500 +	0 +	0 +	4,500 =	2,500 +	0 +	0 +	7,500 +	0
Transaction #											
1		+2,500				=					+2,500 R
2			−1,800			=					−1,800 E
3			+2,100			= +2,100					
4	+2,200 O	−2,200				=					
5	−2,700 O					= −2,700					
6a	−360 O			+360		=					
6b				−60		=					−60 E
7						−150 =					−150 E
8a	+5,000 F					=				+5,000	
8b	+10,000 F					=			+10,000		
8c	−15,000 I				+15,000	=					
9						=		+50			−50 E
10	−250 F					=					−250 D
Ending balances	1,890 +	300 +	2,800 +	300 +	15,000 +	4,350 =	1,900 +	50 +	10,000 +	12,500 +	+190
Totals						24,640 =	24,640				

Transaction 1

Learning Objective

4

Describe how inventory is accounted for when it is purchased and when it is sold.

Demo sold units of inventory to customers, on account, for $2,500. The units sold were from the inventory purchased in December.

ANALYSIS   The substance of a sale transaction is that the company has exchanged an asset that it possesses for an asset that the customer possesses. The asset given up by the company may be an item of inventory if the company is a retailer or a manufacturer, or it may be some type of expertise or service if the company is a service provider. In this case, Demo is a retailer and the asset given up is inventory. The asset received in exchange from the customer is generally cash, but other possibilities exist. For example, when a new car is purchased, the buyer's old car is often traded in as part of the deal. Also, the customer may exchange a promise to pay later. This is typically called a **sale on account**, and it results in the company receiving a promise to pay—that is, an **account receivable**—in exchange for the inventory. The term "account receivable" means the account will be received in the future. It is "receivable" on the day the inventory is sold. This transaction is a sale on account.

Because this is an exchange, there are two parts of the transaction to consider: the inflow of the asset received in the exchange and the outflow of the asset given up. The inflow increases the wealth of the shareholders and increases assets (accounts receivable). The outflow decreases assets (inventory) owned by the company and decreases the wealth of the shareholders (retained earnings). If the inflow is worth more than the outflow in the exchange, the company has generated a **profit** from the sale transaction. If the inflow is less than the outflow, a *loss* results. The increases and decreases in shareholders' wealth in this transaction are typically called the **sales revenue** (inflow) and **cost of goods sold** (outflow), respectively. Because the analysis shown in Exhibit 2-2 focuses only on the balance sheet, the effects of both the sales revenue and the cost of goods sold will be shown as affecting the retained earnings portion of the shareholders' equity. Remember that net income (revenue minus expenses) increases retained earnings. It should, therefore, be logical that revenues will increase retained earnings and expenses will decrease retained earnings.

The remaining question in the analysis is how to value the inflow and the outflow. Based on the information in Transaction 1, the total selling price of the goods sold was $2,500. Therefore, sales revenue (retained earnings) and accounts receivable both increase by $2,500. There is no information given in Transaction 1 regarding the cost of goods sold. This is covered in Transaction 2. It may seem odd to analyze and record these two simultaneous events separately. Nonetheless, this is typical of how events are recorded in most companies. For example, in a department store, when a clerk rings up a sale, a record is made of the sales revenue amount and the increase in cash (or accounts receivable in the case of a sale on account). The sales person does not know the cost of the item sold at the time of sale. The cost is determined at the end of the period as described under Transaction 2. To summarize:

> **EFFECTS OF TRANSACTION 1**
>
> Assets (Accounts Receivable) increase by $2,500
> Shareholders' Equity (Retained Earnings) increases by $2,500

GAAP The timing of the recognition of revenues and expenses is an important decision that management must make in preparing financial statements. There is an underlying conflict between reporting income information in a timely manner and being assured that the transaction is a bona fide sale. To take two extreme positions: at one extreme it might be argued that a company should recognize a sale when a customer signs a contract for the future delivery of the product; at the other extreme it might be argued that the company should wait until cash is collected before recognizing the transaction as a sale. In the first case, the company is counting on delivering the product and ultimately collecting the cash from the sale. These

Learning Objective

Describe the difference between accrual basis accounting and cash basis acccounting.

are both uncertain events and, if they do not materialize, shareholders may be mis-led by the income statement into thinking the company is doing better than it really is. In the second case, delaying recognition of the sale until cash is collected (assum-ing that it isn't collected when the goods change hands), makes it clear that by then the transaction is a bona fide sale, but it may not be providing shareholders with a very good measure of the company's performance (on the income statement) during the period prior to collection of the cash. Sales that had been made but were in the process of collection would not appear on the income statement.

The two extremes just discussed have evolved over time into two bases on which accountants generally prepare financial statements: the *accrual basis* and the *cash basis*. The accrual basis attempts to measure performance (i.e., revenues and expenses) in the period in which the performance takes place rather than when the cash is collected. When the accrual basis is used, **revenue recognition criteria** are considered to determine if performance has been achieved. These criteria are dis-cussed in detail in Chapter 4. In brief, the criteria state that revenue can be recog-nized as earned when (1) the company has performed the majority of the things it has to do associated with the sale (i.e., completed the work, transferred the inven-tory to the buyer, etc.), (2) the amount that has been earned is known, and (3) there is reasonable assurance that the amount will collected. You can see from these cri-teria that when a customer signs a contract as described in the previous paragraph, revenue would not be recognized, because the first criterion, that of completion of the work, was not achieved. The company still must deliver the product which is a major part of the earning process. Once the product is delivered, however, revenue could be recognized even if cash was not received at that point, provided the other two criteria were met. The criteria are set to provide shareholders with assurance that the amounts stated as revenues and expenses are reasonable and that there is a high probability that the revenues and expenses recorded will ultimately result in similar cash flows. The accrual basis is used by most businesses and will be used throughout this book.

Learning Objective
6

Describe the revenue recog-nition and matching criteria.

When the cash basis is used, events are recorded only when their cash effects occur. For example, sales revenue is recorded only when cash is received from the customer, and the cost of goods sold is recorded only when the cash is paid out for inventory. You can see that on this basis you could be recording expenses for inven-tory earlier than you recorded the revenue for selling it. Or, if the company pur-chased its inventory on account (to be paid for later), you could be recording the cash from the sale before you record the expense for the inventory. In either case, if the financial statement were prepared between the cash collected for the sale and the payment of cash for the inventory, you would have revenue in one period and its associated expense in another. The mistiming of recording activities such as this would make it difficult for managers to make decisions about pricing and inventory acquisition. Because of the potentially misleading information produced by the cash basis, it is not used very often. It is, however, still used by some farmers, lawyers, and professional service companies to account for their businesses. In the past, most *not-for-profit organizations* used the cash basis, but today many of them are switching to the accrual basis.

In a business such as Demo, the revenue recognition criteria are generally met when the product is exchanged with the customer. Therefore, in the preceding analysis, the result of Transaction 1 is to recognize revenues (increase retained earnings). Demo should not wait until the cash is collected (see Transaction 4). On a cash basis, of course, Demo would not recognize revenue as a result of Transaction 1.

Another aspect of accrual basis accounting is the **matching concept**. This concept requires that all costs associated with generating sales revenue be matched with the revenue earned on the income statement; that is, the cost of goods sold related to this revenue should be recognized in the same period as the sales revenue. See the analysis of Transaction 2 for the recording of the cost of goods sold.

Refer to Exhibit 2-2 and the following summary for the proper recording of Transaction 1 in the basic accounting equation. Note that the equation is balanced after the entry is made. The effects on the basic accounting equation can be summarized as follows:

EFFECTS OF TRANSACTION 1 ON THE BALANCE SHEET (EXHIBIT 2-2)

Assets						=	Liabilities			+ Shareholders' Equity	
Cash +	Accounts Receivable +	Inventory +	Prepaid Insurance +	Land +	Equipment	=	Accounts Payable +	Interest Payable +	Bank Loan +	Common Shares +	Retained Earnings
+2,500						=					+2,500 R

Note that this transaction has no effect on cash. The cash effects of the sale of goods will be felt by the company only in the period in which the receivable is collected. This will lead to a difference between the cash received from operations and the net income for the period. Note also that the entry to the retained earnings account has been designated "R," indicating that this is a revenue that will be reported on the income statement for the accounting period.

Transaction 2

The cost of units removed from inventory for sales in January totalled $1,800.

ANALYSIS As explained in the analysis of Transaction 1, there are two parts to the sale transaction. Transaction 1 included information about the revenue side of the transaction. Here in Transaction 2, the costs that are to be matched with the revenue are given. The effect of the outflow of the inventory is to decrease the inventory asset and to decrease the shareholders' wealth, because the company no longer holds title to the inventory. The decrease in shareholders' wealth (that is, retained earnings) by the cost of goods sold is one of the many expenses that the company shows on its income statement. To summarize:

EFFECTS OF TRANSACTION 2

Assets (Inventory) decrease by $1,800
Shareholders' Equity (Retained Earnings) decreases by $1,800

GAAP As explained earlier, in the analysis of Transaction 1, when the revenues from the sale are recognized, the matching concept requires that the costs associated with that revenue be recognized as well. For a retailer such as Demo, the cost of the inventory is simply the wholesale price that Demo paid to acquire the inventory. Under accrual basis accounting the cost of the inventory is held in the inventory account until it is sold. Typically, the cost of goods sold is determined at the end of the period by physically counting the number of units still available in inventory and then attaching unit costs to those units. Knowing the cost of the inventory still unsold at the end of the period (ending inventory) and the cost of the inventory with which the period began (beginning inventory), as well as the purchases during the period, the accountant can calculate the cost of those units that were sold as follows:

COST OF GOODS SOLD CALCULATION
Beginning Inventory
+   Purchases
=   Cost of Goods Available for Sale
−   Ending Inventory
=   Cost of Goods Sold

The determination of the cost of the units of inventory that are sold is discussed in greater depth in Chapter 7.

Refer to Exhibit 2-2 for the recording of this transaction. The entry is summarized as follows:

EFFECTS OF TRANSACTION 2 ON THE BALANCE SHEET (EXHIBIT 2-2)											
Assets						=	Liabilities			+ Shareholders' Equity	
Cash +	Accounts Receivable +	Inventory +	Prepaid Insurance +	Land +	Equipment =	Accounts Payable +	Interest Payable +	Bank Loan +	Common Shares +	Retained Earnings	
		−1,800				=				−1,800 E	

Note that this transaction has no effect on cash. The cash flow effects of inventory occur at the time that payment for the inventory is made. This leads to a difference between the cash from operations and the net income for the period. Note further that the entry to the retained earnings account has been designated "E," indicating that this is an expense that will be reported in the income statement for this accounting period.

Transaction 3

Purchases of new inventory to replace the units sold in January totalled $2,100. All these purchases were made on account.

ANALYSIS   The purchase of inventory has the effect of increasing the inventory asset. Because the inventory is bought on account, Demo has given the seller a promise to pay at some time in the future. Demo should record an increase in accounts payable to indicate its liability to the seller. The term "accounts payable" means the account will be paid in the future. It is "payable" on the day the inventory is purchased. Note that on the seller's books this transaction results in a corresponding account receivable. To summarize:

EFFECTS OF TRANSACTION 3
Assets (Inventory) increase by $2,100
Liabilities (Accounts Payable) increase by $2,100

GAAP With the accrual basis of accounting, inventory is considered an asset until the revenue recognition criteria are met. The valuation principle for inventory under GAAP is that it be recorded at its acquisition cost (i.e., the price paid to obtain it). When inventory is purchased on account, the inventory is valued at the amount of the liability incurred in the transaction—that is, the value of the accounts payable. Accounts payable are liabilities that are generally settled in a short period of time (30 to 60 days) and are valued at the gross amount owed. There is generally no recognition[6] of interest on an account payable even though it is a "loan" from the seller. Occasionally, inventory is purchased on longer-term credit, which results in a formal loan document called a **note payable**. In the case of a note payable, interest is usually explicitly recognized. The interest would be recorded as an expense and as either an outflow of cash, if it is paid, or as a new liability on its own, if the interest is going to be paid in the future. The accounting for interest is explained further in Transaction 9.

See Exhibit 2-2 for the recording of this transaction in the accounting system. The entry is summarized as follows:

EFFECTS OF TRANSACTION 3 ON THE BALANCE SHEET (EXHIBIT 2-2)										
Assets						= Liabilities			+ Shareholders' Equity	
Cash +	Accounts Receivable +	Inventory +	Prepaid Insurance +	Land +	Equipment =	Accounts Payable +	Interest Payable +	Bank Loan +	Common Shares +	Retained Earnings
		+2,100				= +2,100				

Note that this transaction had no effect on cash. The cash effects of purchasing inventory will be shown when the account payable is paid. Also note that it had no effect on shareholders' wealth (retained earnings). Income will be affected when the inventory is sold.

Transaction 4

During the month, Demo received $2,200 from customers as payments on their accounts.

ANALYSIS The receipt of cash from customers means that cash increases. Because the customer no longer owes this amount to the company, the value of the customer's account receivable decreases by the amount of the payment. The entry can be summarized as follows:

EFFECTS OF TRANSACTION 4
Assets (Cash) increase by $2,200
Assets (Accounts Receivable) decrease by $2,200

[6] The term "recognition" means an item in the accounting system.

GAAP　Accounts receivable generally are short-term loans from the seller to the buyer and do not typically result in the recognition of interest. The amount of the receivable is stated at the selling price to the buyer. If this were a *note receivable* that explicitly included interest, the cash received would be larger than the selling price, and the excess amount above the selling price would represent interest revenue. See Exhibit 2-2 for the recording of this transaction. The transaction can be summarized as follows:

		EFFECTS OF TRANSACTION 4 ON THE BALANCE SHEET (EXHIBIT 2-2)								
	Assets					=	Liabilities		+ Shareholders' Equity	
	Accounts		Prepaid				Accounts Interest	Bank	Common Retained	
Cash +	Receivable +	Inventory +	Insurance +	Land +	Equipment =		Payable + Payable +	Loan +	Shares + Earnings	
+2,200 O	−2,200					=				

Note that this transaction does affect cash but does not affect shareholders' wealth (retained earnings). The income effect related to accounts receivable was recorded earlier, when the original sale occurred. Note further that the cash entry has been designated "O," indicating that this is an operating cash flow.

Transaction 5

Demo made payments of $2,700 on its accounts payable.

ANALYSIS　Cash payments result in a decrease in cash. In this case, because the payment is on an account payable, there is a corresponding decrease in the accounts payable account. To summarize:

EFFECTS OF TRANSACTION 5
Assets (Cash) decrease by $2,700
Liabilities (Accounts Payable) decrease by $2,700

GAAP　Note that no part of the payment is interest. When longer-term loans are involved, the payment would have to be divided between the amount that represents interest and the amount that represents repayment of the original amount of the loan. See Exhibit 2-2 for the recording of the transaction. The transaction can be summarized as follows:

		EFFECTS OF TRANSACTION 5 ON THE BALANCE SHEET (EXHIBIT 2-2)								
	Assets					=	Liabilities		+ Shareholders' Equity	
	Accounts		Prepaid				Accounts Interest	Bank	Common Retained	
Cash +	Receivable +	Inventory +	Insurance +	Land +	Equipment =		Payable + Payable +	Loan +	Shares + Earnings	
−2,700 O						=	−2,700			

Note that cash is affected by this transaction but shareholders' equity (retained earnings) is not. The income effects of inventory are shown in the period in which the inventory is sold. The period of sale could be either prior to or after the payment of cash. The cash flow will be reported in the operating section of the cash flow statement.

Transaction 6

Demo paid $360 in cash on January 1 for an insurance policy to cover its inventory from January 1, 20x1, to June 30, 20x1.

ANALYSIS   This transaction is an example of a *prepaid expense*. The cost of the insurance coverage is paid in advance of the coverage period. At the date of the payment (January 1 in this case), the cost of the policy should be shown as an asset since it has not been used up yet. Another way to think about this as an asset is to consider what would happen if you cancelled the policy immediately after it was paid. Except for any cancellation and/or processing fees, you should be entitled to get your money back—because the insurance company has not provided any coverage yet. Only as time passes is the coverage "consumed." In this example the amount of the coverage that is consumed in January is one month's worth, or $60, assuming that we simply spread the coverage out evenly over the six-month period. Therefore, by the end of January, $60 of the insurance should be treated as an expense, to represent the month that has been consumed, and the rest ($300) should be treated as an asset, to represent the coverage to which the company is still entitled as of the end of January.

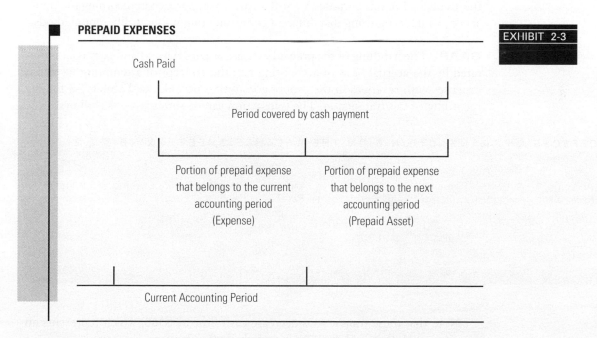

PREPAID EXPENSES

EXHIBIT 2-3

Cash Paid

Period covered by cash payment

Portion of prepaid expense that belongs to the current accounting period (Expense)

Portion of prepaid expense that belongs to the next accounting period (Prepaid Asset)

Current Accounting Period

Exhibit 2-3 displays a timeline that highlights the effects of a prepaid expense and the timing issue involved. Note that the proportions illustrated in the exhibit are not representative of the situation for Demo. Part of the cash payment results in an expense being recognized in the current period, with the remaining portion an asset for the following period.

There are several ways that a company might record this transaction. One way would be to record the initial cash outflow of $360 on January 1 as a decrease in cash and an increase in a prepaid asset account (Transaction 6a). Then on January 31 the company would have to record a decrease in the prepaid asset account and a decrease in retained earnings for the $60 that is now an expense (Transaction 6b). The net result would be to record a decrease in cash of $360, a decrease in retained earnings of $60, and an increase in a prepaid insurance account of $300. This set of effects is shown below:

EFFECTS OF TRANSACTION 6A
Assets (Prepaid Insurance) increase by $360
Assets (Cash) decrease by $360

EFFECTS OF TRANSACTION 6B
Shareholders' Equity (Retained Earnings) decreases by $60
Assets (Prepaid Insurance) decrease by $60

An alternative to this treatment would be to record the transaction as a net result of the analysis above in one entry. A third possible treatment would be to initially show all of the cash outflow as an expense and then at the end of the month adjust the expense from $360 to $60 and at the same time record an increase in a prepaid asset account of $300. All three of these treatments would result in the same net effect on the accounts. For our purposes, we will use the first approach in recording the transaction, while recognizing that different companies might follow different methods.

GAAP   The handling of the prepaid expense as part expense and part asset is dictated by the accrual basis of accounting and the concept of attempting to match expenses with revenues in the proper accounting period. See Exhibit 2-2 for the recording of this transaction. The transaction can be summarized as follows:

EFFECTS OF TRANSACTION 6 ON THE BALANCE SHEET (EXHIBIT 2-2)										
Assets						= Liabilities			+ Shareholders' Equity	
Cash +	Accounts Receivable +	Inventory +	Prepaid Insurance +	Land +	Equipment =	Accounts Payable +	Interest Payable +	Bank Loan +	Common Shares +	Retained Earnings
Transaction 6a										
−360 O			+360			=				
Transaction 6b										
			−60			=				−60 E

Note that these transactions decrease cash flow by $360, which represents an operating cash flow, and decrease income by $60 in January.

Transaction 7

Demo's accountant determined that the equipment should be amortized $150 for January.

ANALYSIS Whenever a company makes an expenditure to acquire an asset, there are three general questions to ask regarding the nature of the transaction:

1. Has an asset been created?
2. If so, what is the value of the asset?
3. How does the asset get used up over time, and when does it cease to exist?

To address the first question, one must evaluate the criteria for an asset. Does the item have probable future value, and does the company own it or have the rights to use it? If the answer to both of these questions is yes, an asset exists and should be recorded. When Demo originally purchased its equipment, the answer to both recognition criteria questions was yes. Demo owned the equipment (because it held title to the equipment), and the equipment had future value (because it was to be used to sell products and thus generate revenues). The equipment, therefore, qualified as an asset.

The answer to the second question is that, under GAAP, the equipment is valued at its acquisition cost (sometimes called *historical cost*). In the example, assume that the $4,500 value of the equipment at December 31, 20x0, represents its historical cost.

The third question is a little more difficult to answer. For an asset such as inventory, the answer is relatively simple: the asset ceases to exist when it is sold and the company gives up title it. The inventory stays on the books until it is sold, and then the cost appears as an expense (cost of goods sold) on the income statement. For equipment, the answer is more complicated. The equipment is used up as time passes, and the equipment is used to generate revenues from the sale of the company's products. Equipment has an estimated **useful life**. For example, it may last for only five years, at which time it is sold, discarded, or traded in for a new piece of equipment.

Because the asset is used up over time, some of the cost of the asset should be shown as an expense in each period in which it is used. Another reason to show some of the cost as an expense is that the expense of using the equipment should be matched (the matching concept) with the revenues generated from the use of the equipment. How much should be shown as an expense in any period is a function of how much of the asset gets used up during that period of time. The amount shown as an expense in any period is called the **amortization** of the asset. There are numerous ways to calculate how much amortization should be taken in a given period. These methods are discussed in detail in Chapter 8. The most common method used is **straight-line amortization**, which assumes that an asset is used evenly throughout its life and that the same amount of amortization should be taken in every time period. The formula for calculating straight-line amortization is:

$$\text{Straight-line Amortization} = \frac{\text{Original Cost} - \text{Estimated Residual Value}}{\text{Estimated Useful Life}}$$

Two estimates are required to perform the calculation. The **useful life** of the asset must be estimated. This could be expressed in either years or months, depending on the length of the accounting period. In the Demo example, it would be months. The second estimate is **residual value**. This is an estimate of what the asset will be worth at the end of its useful life. The quantity in the numerator of the calculation is sometimes called the **amortization value** of the asset, because it is the amount that should be amortized over the useful life of the asset.

In the case of Demo Retail Company, Ltd., if it is assumed that the equipment had an original cost of $4,500, an estimated useful life of two years (24 months), and a residual value at the end of two years of $900, the monthly amortization would be calculated as:

$$\text{Straight-line Amortization} = \frac{\$4,500 - \$900}{24 \text{ months}}$$

$$= \$150/\text{month}$$

At the end of each month, Demo should reduce the value of the equipment by $150 and show a $150 expense on the income statement (amortization expense). To summarize:

EFFECTS OF TRANSACTION 7
Assets (Equipment) decrease by $150
Shareholders' Equity (Retained Earnings) decrease by $150

GAAP   Several amortization methods are commonly used by companies and are discussed in Chapter 8. The choice of method is influenced by the pattern of use of the asset and the most appropriate method for capturing that pattern of use.

See Exhibit 2-2 for the recording of this transaction. The transaction can be summarized as follows:

EFFECTS OF TRANSACTION 7 ON THE BALANCE SHEET (EXHIBIT 2-2)										
Assets					=	Liabilities			+	Shareholders' Equity
Cash +	Accounts Receivable +	Inventory +	Prepaid Insurance +	Land +	Equipment =	Accounts Payable +	Interest Payable +	Bank Loan +	Common Shares +	Retained Earnings
					−150 =					−150 E

Note that the reduction in the equipment account is taken directly out of this account. In practice, the reduction in a capital asset due to amortization is kept in a separate account called *accumulated amortization*. Over time, this account collects all of the reductions in the asset account. It is shown with the capital asset account and is called a *contra asset account*, because when it is added to the capital asset account the net amount is reduced. By creating this special account, we can keep the original cost of the capital asset intact. Users find that the original cost of a capital asset is a piece of information that helps them in their decision-making. For now, however, to make things simple the number of accounts is being kept to a minimum and we are going to reduce the asset directly. In Chapter 3 we will start to use an accumulated amortization account. Note that this transaction has no effect on cash. The cash outflow due to equipment is shown in the period in which the asset is purchased. There might also be a cash inflow in the period in which the equipment is sold.

Transaction 8

On the first day of January, Demo purchased land for $15,000 as a site for a future retail outlet. In order to pay for the land, Demo raised money by borrowing $10,000 from the bank and issuing new shares for $5,000.

ANALYSIS It is instructive to view Transaction 8 as a combination of three transactions: the issuance of shares, the borrowing of money, and the purchase of land. These three are discussed as if each occurred separately.

Issuance of Shares One way for a company to raise money is to issue new shares. New shareholders will provide cash to the company in exchange for share certificates that signify ownership in the company. In this case, the shares are worth $5,000. The shares could be directly exchanged for the land (if the previous landowner was willing to accept them in exchange for the land), or they could be issued to a new group of investors to obtain cash and then the cash paid to the landowner. We will assume the latter. In either case, the appropriate way to value the shares is to take their **fair market value** at the date of the transaction. The effect of the transaction is that cash increases by $5,000 and shareholders' equity increases by $5,000. The new shareholders have made a contribution to the company.

In Canada, shares generally are recorded at the amount that the shareholders paid for them. To summarize (this part of the transaction is referred to as Transaction 8a):

EFFECTS OF TRANSACTION 8A

Assets (Cash) increase by $5,000
Shareholders' Equity (Common Shares) increases by $5,000

Borrowing Money A second method for raising money is to borrow it. In this case, Demo has borrowed $10,000 from the bank. The effect of this transaction is that cash increases and a new obligation is created to show the amount owed to the bank. The amount of the loan is called the *principal* of the loan. The principal does not include interest. Interest will be added to the amount owed to the bank as time passes. For example, if the interest rate on this loan is 8% per year (interest rates are generally stated on an annual basis), the interest added in the first year of the loan will be 8% of the principal of $10,000, or $800. The terminology is that *interest accrues on the loan at 8%*. The accrued interest at the end of the first year will be $800. At the point of acquiring the loan, the accountant records only the principal of the loan, because no time has passed since the loan was taken out. To summarize (Transaction 8b):

EFFECTS OF TRANSACTION 8B

Assets (Cash) increase by $10,000
Liabilities (Bank Loan) increase by $10,000

Purchase of Land The purchase of land for cash means that cash decreases by the amount of the purchase price and that land increases by the same amount. GAAP requires that land be recorded at its acquisition cost. Land is an asset because it has probable future value and the company holds title to it. The probable future value can be viewed as either its future sales price or its future use (in this case, its use as a site for a retail outlet). Land is not amortized because it is not consumed the way other capital assets, like equipment, are. Buildings and equipment will wear out from use, but land usually stays in a useable condition. To summarize (Transaction 8c):

EFFECTS OF TRANSACTION 8C

Assets (Cash) decrease by $15,000

Assets (Land) increase by $15,000

GAAP Cash transactions are usually easy to value under GAAP because there is an objective measure of the value given up. In exchange transactions, where cash is not involved, the "cost" is not as easily determined. If, for example, in this transaction the loan had been made by the original owner of the land and the shares had been issued to the original owner of the land, and no cash had changed hands, it might be difficult to assign values to the shares and the loan. These types of transactions are called **nonmonetary exchanges**. Under GAAP, the general rule is that these transactions be valued at the fair market value of the consideration given up in the transaction. In this example, that would be the fair market value of the shares and the loan. In our example, it is assumed that the share issuance and bank borrowing are separate from the purchase of the land. The transaction is, therefore, a monetary exchange, even though there is no net effect on cash. See Exhibit 2-2 for the recording of the net effects of this transaction in the basic accounting equation. Remember that the transaction has been split up into separate transactions labelled 8a, 8b, and 8c. The transaction can be summarized as follows:

EFFECTS OF TRANSACTION 8 ON THE BALANCE SHEET (EXHIBIT 2-2)

				Assets		=	Liabilities			+ Shareholders' Equity	
Cash +	Accounts Receivable +	Inventory +	Prepaid Insurance +	Land +	Equipment =		Accounts Payable +	Interest Payable +	Bank Loan +	Common Shares +	Retained Earnings
Transaction 8a											
+5000 F						=				+5000	
Transaction 8b											
+10,000 F						=			+10,000		
Transaction 8c											
−15,000 I				+15,000		=					

Note that these transactions do not affect income (retained earnings) but do affect cash, although in this case the effects on cash are offsetting. As we will point out in Chapter 5, this particular transaction would qualify as a noncash transaction and as such would not be reported directly in the cash flow statement. It would, however, be given more complete disclosure in the notes to the financial statements. For the purposes of this chapter, however, we will treat the components of this transaction as separate and report them all in the cash flow statement.

Transaction 9

The interest rate charged on the loan from the bank in Transaction 8 is 6% and is paid quarterly (at the end of every three months).

ANALYSIS Interest is the amount charged by lenders for the use of their money. From the point of view of the borrower, interest is an expense and therefore results in a decrease in the shareholders' wealth during the period in which it is incurred. By the end of January the $10,000 loan has been outstanding for one month and therefore one month's interest expense should be recognized. Since the interest has not been paid yet (and will not be paid until the end of March), Demo will have to recognize a liability for its obligation to pay the interest at the end of the quarter. This is an example of an *accrued expense*. As illustrated in Exhibit 2-4, accrued expenses are expenses that are recognized on the income statement in the period in which they are incurred, which is prior to the period in which they are paid in cash. Note that the proportions illustrated in the exhibit are not representative of the situation for Demo.

ACCRUED EXPENSES

EXHIBIT 2-4

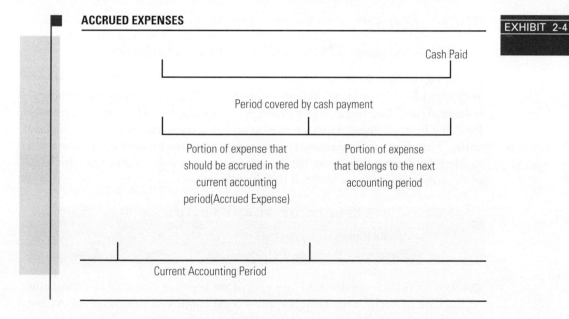

To calculate the amount of interest expense, you multiply the amount of the loan (known as the *principal*) by the interest rate and then by the fraction of the year that has passed (since the interest rate is always expressed as a yearly rate). In Demo's case, therefore, the amount of interest incurred in January is $50 [$10,000 × 6% × 1/12]. Shareholders' equity (retained earnings) should, therefore, decrease by $50 to recognize the interest expense, and liabilities (interest payable) should increase by $50 to recognize the obligation to pay the interest. To summarize:

EFFECTS OF TRANSACTION 9

Shareholders' Equity (Retained Earnings) decreases by $50
Liabilities (Interest Payable) increase by $50

GAAP Accrual basis accounting requires that expenses be recognized in the period in which they are incurred rather than the period in which they are paid. Accrued expenses, therefore, typically result in a liability that appears on the balance sheet at the end of the period representing the amount of expenses that have been accrued by that date, which will be paid in the subsequent period. See Exhibit 2-2 for the recording of this transaction. The transaction can be summarized as follows:

EFFECTS OF TRANSACTION 9 ON THE BALANCE SHEET (EXHIBIT 2-2)										
		Assets				=	Liabilities		+ Shareholders' Equity	
Cash +	Accounts Receivable +	Inventory +	Prepaid Insurance +	Land +	Equipment =	Accounts Payable +	Interest Payable +	Bank Loan +	Common Shares +	Retained Earnings
					=		+50			−50 E

Note that this transaction affects income (retained earnings) but it does not affect cash. Because the interest is paid quarterly, the effect on cash will occur at the end of the quarter.

Transaction 10

Dividends in the amount of $250 were declared and paid in January.

ANALYSIS Dividends are payments to the shareholders of the company as authorized by the company's board of directors. They are a return to the shareholders of part of the accumulated earnings of the company. They are not expenses for doing business because they are not incurred for the purpose of generating revenues. The effect of Transaction 10 is to reduce the shareholders' equity (retained earnings) and either to increase liabilities (dividends payable), if they have not been paid, or to decrease assets (cash), if they have been paid.

EFFECTS OF TRANSACTION 10
Assets (Cash) decrease by $250
Shareholders' Equity (Retained Earnings) decreases by $250

GAAP Dividends are declared by a vote of the board of directors of a company. At the date of declaration, they become a legal liability of the company. As just illustrated, the accounting records should show a decrease in retained earnings (usually through an account called the **dividends declared** account) and an increase in the dividends payable account. The dividends declared account affects retained earnings. The change in this account explains part of the change in the retained earnings account from the beginning of the period to the end of the period. It is very important, however, to note that dividends are not an expense and do not appear on the income statement. They will appear on a cash flow statement when they are paid, and many companies prepare a statement of retained earnings, which shows the dividends declared during the period. There is generally a delay between the date the dividends are declared and the date they are paid, and therefore the cash effects are not recognized until the payment date. In the case of Demo, dividends are declared and paid in the same accounting period, so that the dividends payable account is ignored.

See Exhibit 2-2 for the recording of the effects of this transaction in the balance sheet equation. The transaction can be summarized as follows:

EFFECTS OF TRANSACTION 10 ON THE BALANCE SHEET (EXHIBIT 2-2)

	Assets					=	Liabilities			+ Shareholders' Equity	
	Accounts		Prepaid				Accounts	Interest	Bank	Common	Retained
Cash +	Receivable +	Inventory +	Insurance +	Land +	Equipment =		Payable +	Payable +	Loan +	Shares +	Earnings
−250 F						=					− 250 D

Note that dividends are not part of income but do appear on the cash flow statement, because they do affect cash.

FINANCIAL STATEMENTS

Balance Sheet

This completes the analysis of the 10 transactions of the Demo Retail Company, Ltd. The balance sheet for Demo could now be constructed as follows:

Learning Objective

7

Prepare a balance sheet, income statement, and cash flow statement after a series of transactions.

DEMO RETAIL COMPANY, LTD.
Balance Sheet

	January 31, 20x1	December 31, 20x0
Current Assets		
Cash	$ 1,890	$ 3,000
Accounts receivable	300	0
Inventory	2,800	2,500
Prepaid insurance	300	0
Total current assets	5,290	5,500
Land	15,000	0
Equipment	4,350	4,500
Total assets	$24,640	$10,000
Current Liabilities		
Accounts payable	$ 1,900	$ 2,500
Interest payable	50	0
Total current liabilities	1,950	2,500
Bank loan	10,000	0
Total liabilities	11,950	2,500
Common shares	12,500	7,500
Retained earnings	190	0
Total shareholders' equity	12,690	7,500
Total liabilities and shareholders' equity	$24,640	$10,000

Note that the Demo balance sheet is a classified balance sheet in which current assets and liabilities are distinguished from noncurrent assets and liabilities. Because the accounting period involved is one month, the balances for both the beginning of the month[7] and the end of the month are shown.

---

[7] Note that the beginning balances in January are the same as the ending balances from December.

Income Statement

The income statement can be constructed from the information on the transactions recorded in the retained earnings account in Exhibit 2-2 (refer back to Chapter 1 for a description of the income statement). Note that the dividend amount does not belong on the income statement, because it is not an expense used to derive net income. Rather, it is a payment of earnings to the shareholders. The income statement would be constructed as follows:

DEMO RETAIL COMPANY, LTD.	
Income Statement	
For the month ended January 31, 20x1	
Sales revenues	$2,500
Less:	
Cost of goods sold	(1,800)
Gross profit	700
Amortization expense	(150)
Insurance expense	(60)
Interest expense	(50)
Net income	$ 440

Demo operated profitably during the month of January, earning a net income of $440.

By itself, a net income of $440 tells users nothing about a company other than that it has a positive income flow. To understand the profitability of a company more fully, users will often use ratio analysis, a technique you will see used frequently throughout this text. A ratio divides one financial statement amount by another financial statement amount. This allows users to understand how some amounts are related to other amounts. As you have seen from the financial statements illustrated so far, there are many numbers from which meaningful relationships can be derived. Ratios allow users to compare different companies that are of different sizes, or to compare the same company over time. Ratio analysis can be used to assess profitability, the effectiveness of management, and the ability of the company to meet debt obligations. As we introduce new topics to you, we will be showing you ratios that can help users understand and evaluate a set of financial statements. A complete discussion of these ratios can be found in Chapter 12.

We are going to start by using the Demo example to examine profitability ratios. Profitability ratios are usually constructed by comparing some measure of the profit (net income) of the company to the amount invested, or by comparing it to the revenues of the company. We will calculate three such measures.

Learning Objective

8

Calculate three profitability ratios.

Profitability Ratios

The **profit margin ratio** is calculated by dividing the profit generated by the company by the revenues that produced that profit. For Demo, this ratio is 17.6% (net income/revenues = $440/$2,500). This indicates that Demo earned, as profit, 17.6% of the revenue amount. Stated another way, of the $2,500 in initial revenues generated by the company, Demo retained 17.6% and increased the company's wealth by this amount.

The **return on assets** invested is another measure of profitability. It is calculated by dividing the profit of the company by the average total assets invested in the company. The average assets can be calculated using the information in the balance sheet. For Demo, the average is $17,320 [($10,000 + $24,640)/2]. In January of 20x1, the return on assets was 2.5% (net income/average total assets = $440/$17,320). Remember that a company invests in assets so that it can use them to generate profits. Demo's return of 2.5% means that for each $100.00 invested in assets Demo earned $2.50 of profit.

The third measure of performance is the **return on equity**. This measure compares the return (profit) with the amount invested by the shareholders (average total shareholders' equity). The measure is 4.4% (net income/average shareholders' equity = $440/$10,095) for Demo. The $10,095 is the average of the sum of the shareholders' equity accounts (common shares and retained earnings). The average is calculated as [($7,500 + $12,690)/2]. This measure means that the shareholders have earned a 4.4% return on their investment in one month.

The interpretation of these ratios must be made either within the context of the past performance of the company or in comparison with other companies in the same industry. More will be said about these ratios and their interpretation in Chapter 12.

Cash Flow Statement

A cash flow statement can now be constructed from the information in the cash column in Exhibit 2-2. The cash flow statement explains the changes in cash flow by detailing the changes in operating, financing, and investing activities (refer back to Chapter 1). Remember that we marked all of the cash transactions in the exhibit with an O, I, or F to make the preparation of this statement easier. The operating section of Demo's cash flow statement appears to be somewhat different from that of Future Shop's cash flow statement, shown in Chapter 1. The reason is that GAAP allows for this section to be prepared using either a direct or an indirect method. The direct method has been used here, whereas the indirect method has been used by Future Shop. The explanation for this difference is presented in Chapter 5.

DEMO RETAIL COMPANY, LTD.
Cash Flow Statement
For the Month Ended January 31, 20x1

Cash from operating activities:		
Cash receipts from customers	$2,200	
Cash disbursement to suppliers	(2,700)	
Cash disbursement for insurance	(360)	
Cash flow from operating activities		$ (860)
Cash from investing activities:		
Purchase of land		(15,000)
Cash from financing activities:		
Proceeds from issuance of common shares	5,000	
Proceeds from bank loan	10,000	
Dividends paid	(250)	
Cash flow from financing activities		14,750
Decrease in cash		($ 1,110)

EXHIBIT 2-5

Consolidated Statement of Changes in Cash Position
(in millions except per share figures)

Year ended December 31		1998		1997
Cash provided by (used for)				
Operating				
Income (loss) for the year	$	(16)	$	427
Adjustments to reconcile to net cash provided by operations				
Depreciation, amortization and obsolescence		292		258
Gain on sale of investments (notes 1a & 4)		(57)		(201)
(Gain) loss on sale of other assets		27		(35)
Deferred income taxes		(23)		17
Deferred pension expense		34		(38)
Amortization of deferred foreign exchange		32		20
Amortization of deferred gains		(16)		(20)
(Increase) decrease in accounts receivable		62		(80)
Increase in spare parts, materials and supplies		(46)		(38)
Increase in accounts payable and accrued liabilities		172		53
Increase (decrease) in advance ticket sales		(40)		130
Aircraft lease payments in excess of rent expense		(73)		(79)
Other		(52)		(48)
		296		366
Financing				
Issue of share capital		1		7
Reduction of long-term debt		(95)		(482)
Long-term borrowings		180		235
Other		(26)		(26)
		60		(266)
Investing				
Proceeds from sale and leaseback of assets		–		137
Proceeds from sale of investments and other assets		97		375
Additions to property and equipment (net of recovered progress payments)		(730)		(439)
Investments and advances		(7)		22
		(640)		95
Increase (decrease) in cash position		(284)		195
Cash position, beginning of year		650		455
Cash position, end of year	$	366	$	650
Cash flow per share from operations				
– Basic	$	1.66	$	2.34
– Fully diluted	$	1.59	$	2.04

See accompanying notes.

The important part of the cash flow analysis is interpreting what the cash flow statement shows about the health of the company. Subsequent chapters discuss many of the detailed analyses that can be done with the data in the cash flow statement. For now, there are two basic questions that can serve as a start for the analysis of this statement. The first is: Is the cash from operations sufficient to sustain, in the long run, the other activities of the company? A company can be healthy in the long run only when it produces a reasonable amount of cash from operations. Cash can be obtained from financing activities (issuance of new debt or shares) and from investment activities (the sale of investments or capital assets), but these sources cannot sustain the company forever because there are limits to the company's access to them.

Learning Objective

9

Begin to analyze the information on a cash flow statement.

The second question relates to the first: Which of the sources and uses of cash are continuing items from period to period, and which are simply sporadic or non-continuing? A large source or use of cash in one period may not have long-term implications if it does not continue in the future. To address this question, you must consider the historical trend in the cash flow statement data. The cash flow statement for Air Canada is shown in Exhibit 2-5. Note that cash from operations generated a positive amount in each of the two years presented and that the amount decreased over those two years.

To assess whether the cash from operations is adequate to meet Air Canada's needs, look at the major uses of cash. In 1998, the three largest uses of cash were as follows (in millions):

Additions to property and equipment	$730
Reduction of long-term debt	95
Other	26
	$851

The total of these uses was more than the cash produced from operations of $296 million. To make up for the shortfall from operations, Air Canada used cash on hand of $284 million, borrowed $180 million, and sold some investments and other assets for $97 million, for a total of $561 million. In trying to forecast whether operations will be sufficient to cover these major uses, the company must assess whether these uses are likely to continue at the same level. If they continue at the same level, Air Canada will have to make up for the shortfall from operations with other sources of cash. This would not be good, because it would require further borrowings or issuances of shares.

Of the three major uses, the acquisition of property, plant, and equipment seems to be greatly increased in the current year. Replacing capital assets is common practice, especially for a company in the airline industry, since there is a continuing need to replace them if the company wants to continue its current activities or to grow. Air Canada also seems to borrow and repay long-term debt. Judging by the information for 1998 and 1997, Air Canada has not used the issuance of shares very extensively as a way of generating cash. If the net cash provided by (used in) financing activities is considered, it is obvious that, over the last two years, Air Canada has been borrowing and repaying its debt. Air Canada had a loss of $16 million in 1998, compared to a profit of $427 million the previous year. If Air Canada can return to a profit from operations, it will likely be able to decrease its reliance on outside sources of cash.[8]

---

[8] One caveat should be stated here: A complete analysis of Air Canada's cash position is not possible without a review of all of the financial statements and related notes.

Returning to the analysis of Demo Retail Company, even though the company was profitable, based on the income statement ($440), the analysis of cash flow indicates a negative cash flow from operations of $860 and an overall decrease in cash of $1,100. Further, considering the starting balance in cash of $3,000, it is clear that Demo could operate for a few more months at this rate and still have some cash remaining. It cannot, however, continue to operate indefinitely with a negative cash flow (i.e., net cash outflow). The company would run out of cash in a little over three months. This should raise questions about why Demo has this cash drain, even though it appears to be profitable. When we look at the three types of activities, the biggest concern is the negative cash flow from operations. Analyzing why Demo is having difficulty generating cash from operations is beyond the scope of this chapter, but Demo's problem represents an important issue that will be addressed in various sections of this book, most thoroughly in Chapter 5. In fact, problems related to cash flows are key reasons why new businesses fail in their first year. For now, it is important to understand that, while the income statement provides important information about the changes in the shareholders' wealth, it does not reveal everything that is important for one to know about the company. The cash flow statement can provide additional useful information about the company's operations that is not adequately captured by the income statement. On the basis of only one month's worth of data for Demo, it is impossible to comment on the continuing nature of the items on Demo's cash flow statement.

SUMMARY

This chapter has introduced the accounting system using the basic accounting equation. A basic set of transactions were examined in detail and the effect of the transactions on the basic accounting equation was demonstrated. A retail company served as the example in this explanation, but the same procedures would be used in any profit organization. From the transactions, the three basic financial statements were developed. The additional explanations that accompanied the financial statements build on the information provided in Chapter 1. In the next chapter we will use the same example to expand on the operation of the accounting system in a more formal way.

SUMMARY PROBLEM

The balance sheet of Sample Retail Company Ltd. as at January 1, 20x1, is shown in Exhibit 2-6. The following transactions occurred during 20x1:

SAMPLE RETAIL COMPANY, LTD.
Balance Sheet
January 1, 20x1

Cash	$ 4,500
Accounts receivable	500
Inventory	7,500
Prepaid rent	1,200
Total current assets	13,700
Equipment	9,200
Total assets	$22,900
Accounts payable	$ 5,400
Accrued salaries payable	400
Income tax payable	360
Total current liabilities	6,160
Bank loan	800
Total liabilities	6,960
Common shares	3,600
Retained earnings	12,340
Total shareholders' equity	15,940
Total liabilities and shareholders' equity	$22,900

1. Goods with an aggregate selling price of $80,000 were sold, all on account.

2. A review of accounts receivable showed that $750 remained uncollected as at December 31, 20x1.

3. Salaries totalling $20,500 were earned by employees. Cash payments for salaries totalled $20,375.

4. Purchases of inventory, all on account, totalled $39,700. (Assume that this is the only item that affects accounts payable.)

5. Payments on accounts payable totalled $37,300.

6. A count of inventory at December 31, 20x1, revealed that $9,700 remained unsold in ending inventory.

7. Rent for each month is prepaid on the last day of the preceding month. Monthly payments during 20x1 were $1,300.

8. Interest on the bank loan accrues at 9% and is payable at the end of each month. On December 31, 20x1, $200 of the principal of the loan was repaid.

9. Amortization expense on the equipment totalled $2,000.

10. New equipment was purchased for $4,500.

11. The tax rate is 40% for 20x1. Taxes are computed at the end of each quarter and are paid one month later. Assume that the taxes on income in 20x1 were evenly spread across the four quarters of the year.

12. Dividends of $210 were declared and paid.

Required:
Analyze the effect of the transactions above using the basic accounting equation.
Prepare an income statement, balance sheet, and cash flow statement.

SUGGESTED SOLUTION TO SUMMARY PROBLEM

The basic accounting equation analysis is shown in Exhibit 2-7. The entries are numbered to correspond with the transaction number in the problem. Financial statements are shown in Exhibits 2-8, 2-9, and 2-10. One note regarding the cash flow statement: Under GAAP, companies report interest and tax payments as operating items even though you could think of interest as a part of financing activities and tax payments as being spread over all types of activities. Therefore, all interest and tax amounts are shown in the operating section of Exhibit 2-10.

EXHIBIT 2-7

SAMPLE RETAIL COMPANY, LTD.

BASIC ACCOUNTING EQUATION
(Amounts in Dollars)

	Cash	+ A/R	+ Inv	+ Prepaid Rent	+ Equip	=	A/P	+ Accrued Salaries	+ Tax Payable	+ Loan	+ CS	+ RE
Beginning Balance	4,500	+500	+7,500	+1,200	+9,200	=	5,400	+400	+360	+800	+3,600	+12,340
Trans #						=						
1		+80,000				=						+80,000 R
2	+79,750 O	−79,750				=						
3a						=		+20,500				−20,500 E
3b	−20,375 O					=		−20,375				
4			+39,700			=	+39,700					
5	−37,300 O					=	−37,300					
6			−37,500			=						−37,500 E
7a	−15,600 O		+15,600			=						
7b			−15,500			=						−15,500 E
8a	−72 O					=						−72 E
8b	−200 F					=				−200		
9					−2,000	=						−2,000 E
10	−4,500 I				+4,500	=						
11a						=			+1,771			−1,771 E
11b	−1,689 O					=			−1,689			
12	−210 D					=						−210 D
Ending Balance	4,304	+750	+9,700	+1,300	+11,700	=	7,800	+525	+442	+600	+3,600	+14,787
Totals					27,754	=	27,754					

The following detail is provided for selected transactions:

Transaction 2. The ending balance of $750 is provided in the problem. The cash receipts from customers are then determined using this and other information about the beginning balance of accounts receivable and the sales on account given in Transaction 1.

Transaction 3. Salaries earned during the period should be shown as expenses. Salaries paid during the period reflect the payment of salaries from the previous period (i.e., the beginning balance in the accrued salaries payable account) as well as the payment of salaries during the current period. The ending balance in the salaries payable account reflects the salaries that were earned during the current period but not paid at year end.

Transaction 6. The physical count of unsold inventory provides the ending balance in the inventory account. The cost of goods sold is then determined by considering the beginning balance, the purchases of inventory, and the ending balance. Refer back to the explanation given for Transaction 2 for Demo Retail if you want to review the calculation of cost of goods sold.

Transaction 7. The beginning balance ($1,200) in prepaid rent is the payment made on December 31 of the prior year that covers rent expense in January of 20x1. This, along with 11 months of payments (11 x $1,300/month = $14,300) during 20x1, constitutes the rent expense for the year of $15,500 ($1,200 + $14,300). The final payment in 20x1 of $1,300 applies to the first month in 20x2 and is, therefore, the ending balance in the prepaid rent account.

Transaction 8. Because the interest expense is paid at the end of each month, there is no accrued liability to be shown at the end of the period. The cash payments for interest, in this case, are the same as the expense. The expense is calculated by multiplying the principal ($800) times the interest rate (9%) times one year. Remember that interest rates are expressed as an annual rate.

Transaction 11. To determine the tax expense for the period, you must first determine income before taxes. The income before taxes is $4,428. The tax expense is then calculated by taking 40% of this number, resulting in $1,771 for the year (40% × $4,428 = $1,771). The beginning balance in the taxes payable account is the tax computed for the last quarter of the previous year that is paid in January of 20x1. The quarterly payments in 20x1 are $443 ($1,771/4), assuming the income is evenly distributed across the quarters. The payment for the beginning balance in the taxes payable account and three of the quarterly payments constitute the payments for taxes in 20x1 of $1,689 [$360 + (3 × $443)]. The last quarter's amount of $442 ($1 less than the other three quarterly payments due to rounding error) is still payable at December 31, 20x1, and is, therefore, the ending balance in the taxes payable account. It will be paid in January of 20x2.

EXHIBIT 2-8

SAMPLE RETAIL COMPANY, LTD. **Income Statement** **For the year ended December 31, 20x1**		
Revenues		$80,000
Expenses:		
Cost of goods sold	$37,500	
Salary expense	20,500	
Rent expense	15,500	
Amortization expense	2,000	
Interest expense	72	
Total expenses		75,572
Income before taxes		4,428
Tax expense		1,771
Net income		$ 2,657

SAMPLE RETAIL COMPANY, LTD.
Balance Sheet
As at December 31

	20x1	20x0
Assets		
Current assets		
Cash	$ 4,304	$ 4,500
Accounts receivable	750	500
Inventory	9,700	7,500
Prepaid rent	1,300	1,200
Total current assets	16,054	13,700
Equipment	11,700	9,200
Total assets	$27,754	$22,900
Liabilities		
Current liabilities		
Accounts payable	$ 7,800	$ 5,400
Accrued salaries	525	400
Taxes payable	442	360
Total current liabilities	8,767	6,160
Bank loan	600	800
Total liabilities	$9,367	$6,960
Shareholders' equity		
Common shares	3,600	3,600
Retained earnings	14,787	12,340
Total shareholders' equity	18,387	15,940
Total liabilities and shareholders' equity	$27,754	$22,900

SAMPLE RETAIL COMPANY, LTD.
Cash Flow Statement
For the year ended December 31, 20x1

Cash from operating activities:		
Cash receipts from customers	$79,750	
Cash disbursements to suppliers	(37,300)	
Cash disbursements for salaries	(20,375)	
Cash disbursements for rent	(15,600)	
Cash disbursements for interest	(72)	
Cash disbursements for taxes	(1,689)	
Cash flow from operating activities		$4,714
Cash from investing activities:		
Purchase of new equipment		(4,500)
Cash from financing activities:		
Repayment of bank loan	(200)	
Dividends paid	(210)	
Cash flow from financing activities		(410)
Decrease in cash		($196)

ABBREVIATIONS USED

A/R	Accounts receivable	Inv.	Inventory
A/P	Accounts payable	RE	Retained earnings
CS	Common shares	SE	Shareholders' equity
Equip.	Equipment		
GAAP	Generally Accepted Accounting Principles		

SYNONYMS

Amortization/Depreciation

Profit/Net Income/Return/Earnings

GLOSSARY

Accounts payable   The liabilities that result when the company buys inventory or supplies on credit. It represents a future obligation.

Accounts receivable   The assets that result when a customer buys goods or services on credit. It represents the right to receive cash from the customer.

Accrual basis   The accounting basis, used by almost all companies, that recognizes revenues and expenses in the period in which they are earned or incurred, and not necessarily in the period in which the cash inflow or outflow occurs.

Amortization   The expense taken each period based on the use of a noncurrent asset, such as plant or equipment. Amortization is a process that uses a systematic and rational method, such as the straight-line method, to allocate the cost of a noncurrent asset to each of the years of its useful life. Amortization is sometimes referred to as depreciation.

Amortization value   The portion of the cost of a noncurrent asset, such as plant or equipment, that is to be amortized over its useful life. The amortization value is equal to the original cost of the asset less its estimated residual value.

Cash basis   The accounting basis used by some entities in which revenues and expenses are recognized when the cash inflow or outflow occurs.

Cost of goods sold   The expense that is recorded for the inventory sold during the period.

Depreciable cost   A synonym for amortization value.

Depreciable value   A synonym for amortization value.

Depreciation   A synonym for amortization.

Dividends declared   A distribution of assets (usually cash) to the shareholders of a company. The Board of Directors of the company votes to formally declare the distribution, at which point it becomes a legal obligation of the company. The distribution of cash occurs at a date specified at the time of declaration.

Fair market value   The value of an asset or liability based on the price that could be obtained from, or paid to, an independent third party in an arm's-length transaction.

GAAP   Generally accepted accounting principles.

Matching concept   A concept in accounting that requires all expenses related to the production of revenues to be recorded during the same period as the revenues. The expenses are said to be matched with the revenues.

Net income   The difference between the revenues and the expenses recognized during the period.

Nonmonetary exchange   An exchange of goods or services in which the assets or liabilities exchanged are not cash.

Note payable   A formal document representing the amount owed by a company. There is usually interest on this type of debt.

Profit   A synonym for net income.

Profit margin ratio   A ratio that compares the profit (net income) during an accounting period with the related revenues.

Residual value   The estimated value of an asset at the end of its useful life. The estimate is made when the asset is purchased.

Return on assets   A ratio that compares the net income for the period with the investment in assets.

Return on equity A ratio that compares the net income for the period with the investment that shareholders make in the company.

Revenue recognition criteria Criteria established within GAAP that stipulate when revenues should be recognized in the financial statements.

Sale on account A sale in which the seller receives from the buyer a promise to pay at a later date.

Sales revenue The amount of sales recognized during the accounting period based on the revenue recognition criteria.

Straight-line amortization An amortization method that calculates the amount of amortization expense for each period by dividing the amortization value by the estimated number of years of useful life.

Transaction An exchange of resources with an outside entity or an internal event that affects the balance in individual asset, liability, or shareholders' equity accounts.

Transaction analysis The process by which the accountant decides what accounts are affected, and by how much, by an economic transaction or event.

Useful life The estimate of the expected life over which an asset will be used.

Assignment Material

Assessing Your Recall

2-1 Discuss why dividends do not appear on the income statement but do appear on the cash flow statement.

2-2 What advantages and disadvantages are there in using the cash basis of accounting rather than the accrual basis?

2-3 Identify the three major sections in the cash flow statement and briefly describe the nature of the transactions that appear in each section.

2-4 Respond to each of the following statements with a true or false answer:

   a. Revenues increase shareholders' equity.

   b. Cash receipts from customers increase accounts receivable.

   c. Dividends declared decrease cash immediately.

   d. The cash basis recognizes expenses when they are incurred.

   e. There is no such thing as a prepaid rent account on the cash basis.

   f. Dividends are an expense of doing business and should appear on the income statement.

   g. Under the accrual basis, interest should be recognized only when it is paid.

2-5 Briefly describe how a company typically calculates the cost of goods sold.

2-6 What are revenue recognition criteria, and how does the matching concept relate to these criteria?

2-7 Explain how a prepaid expense (like rent) gets handled under accrual basis accounting.

2-8 Explain how an accrued expense (like interest) gets handled under accrual basis accounting.

2-9 Suppose that a company had an accounting policy that recognized warranty expense only when warranty service was provided. Discuss whether this meets the matching concept under accrual basis accounting and suggest other ways that this transaction might be handled.

2-10 Explain what amortization is and how it is calculated using the straight-line method.

Applying Your Knowledge

2-11 (Cash basis versus accrual basis)

Given the following transactions, what income would be reported on the cash basis and on the accrual basis?

Credit sales to customers totalled $16,000.

Cash collections on account from customers totalled $14,000.

Cost of goods sold during the period was $9,000.

Payments made to suppliers of inventory totalled $8,500.

Salaries of $4,000 were paid; salaries of $400 remained unpaid at year end; there were no salaries unpaid at the beginning of the year.

Insurance premiums on a two-year policy were paid in the amount of $600. At year end, 18 months of coverage remain.

2-12 (Nature of retained earnings)

Explain why you agree or disagree with the following statement: "Retained earnings are like money in the bank; you can always use them to pay your bills if you get into trouble."

2-13 (Income statement and cash flow statement)

Compare and contrast the income statement and the cash flow statement.

2-14 (Transaction analysis)

For each of the transactions below, indicate which accounts are affected and whether they increase or decrease.

    a. Issue common shares for cash.

    b. Buy equipment from a supplier on credit (short-term).

    c. Buy inventory from a supplier partly with cash and partly on account.

    d. Sell a unit of inventory to a customer on account.

    e. Receive a payment from a customer on his or her account.

    f. Borrow money from the bank.

    g. Declare a dividend (to be paid later).

    h. Pay a dividend (that was previously declared).

    i. Recognize wages earned by employees (to be paid at the end of the next pay period).

2-15 (Transaction analysis and the basic accounting equation)

For each of the following transactions, give the effect on the basic accounting equation.

    a. Issuance of shares for cash.

    b. Payment of a liability.

    c. Purchase of land for cash.

    d. Purchase of equipment on credit.

    e. Payment of cash to shareholders reflecting a distribution of income.

    f. Receipt of a loan from the bank.

2-16 (Transaction analysis)

For each of the following transactions, indicate how income and cash flow are affected (increase, decrease, no effect) and by how much:

a. Issue common shares for $20,000.

b. Sell for $150, on account, a unit of inventory that cost $105. The unit is already in inventory.

c. Purchase equipment for $700 cash.

d. Amortize plant and equipment by $200.

e. Purchase a unit of inventory, on account, for $100.

f. Make a payment on accounts payable for $600.

g. Receive a payment from a customer for $75 on his or her account.

h. Declare (but do not pay yet) a dividend for $300.

i. Pay a dividend for $300 that was declared.

2-17 (Transaction analysis and the basic accounting equation)
Show how each of the following transactions affects the basic accounting equation:

a. Borrow $1,500 from the bank.

b. Buy land for $20,000 in cash.

c. Issue common shares for $5,000.

d. Buy inventory costing $3,000 on account.

e. Sell inventory costing $2,500 to customers, on account, for $3,500.

f. Receive a payment from a customer for $500 representing a downpayment on a unit of inventory that must be ordered.

g. Make a payment of $250 to the electric company for power used during the current period.

h. Declare a dividend of $350.

i. Amortize equipment by $500.

2-18 (Transaction analysis and the basic accounting equation)
Show how each of the following transactions affects the basic accounting equation:

a. Issue common shares for $10,000.

b. At the time of sale of a piece of inventory, recognize the warranty cost, which is estimated to be $500. Hint: This is a possible future cost to the company. If the sale is recognized in the current period, all associated expenses should be matched to that revenue in the same period.

c. Receive a payment from a customer on his or her account in the amount of $325.

d. Make a payment to the bank of $850. Of this amount, $750 represents interest and the rest is a repayment of principal.

e. Return a unit of inventory costing $200 that was damaged in shipment. You have already paid for the unit and request a refund from the supplier.

f. Dividends of $175 that were previously declared are paid.

g. Purchase equipment costing $6,800. You pay $1,200 in cash and give the supplier a note payable for the balance of the purchase price.

h. Sales on account of $15,000 are reported for the period.

i. A count of physical inventory at the end of the period indicates an ending balance of $575. The beginning balance was $485, and the purchases for the period were $11,500. Record the cost of goods sold.

2-19 (Transaction analysis and the basic accounting equation)
For each of the following transactions, indicate how it immediately affects the basic accounting equation and what other effects there will be in the future as a result of the transaction:

a. Purchase equipment.

b. Borrow money from the bank.

c. Purchase inventory on account.

d. Pay rent in advance for a warehouse.

e. Pay for an insurance policy on an office building.

f. Sell inventory for cash to customers.

g. Sign a warranty agreement with a customer that covers a product that was sold to them. See 18 (b) for more information about this type of transaction.

h. Buy a patent for a new production process.

2-20 (Transaction analysis and the basic accounting equation)
Indicate the effects of the following transactions on the basic accounting equation developed in the chapter. Assume that the fiscal year end of the company is December 31.

a. Borrow $2,500 from the bank on Jan. 1, 20x1.

b. Pay interest on the bank loan described in (a) on Dec. 31, 20x1. The interest rate is 10%.

c. Buy equipment on Jan. 1, 20x1, for $4,000. The equipment has an estimated useful life of five years and an estimated residual value at the end of five years of $500.

d. Record the amortization for the equipment as at Dec. 31, 20x1, assuming the company uses the straight-line method.

e. Sales for the period totalled $15,500, of which $3,500 was on account. The cost of the products sold was $11,600.

f. Collections from customers on account totalled $2,800.

g. Purchases of inventory on account during 20x1 totalled $12,700.

h. Payments to suppliers totalled $12,900 during 20x1.

i. Employees earned salaries of $800 during 20x1.

j. All employee salaries were paid by year end except the salaries for the last week in December, which totalled $50.

k. Dividends were declared and paid in the amount of $100.

2-21 (Transaction analysis and the basic accounting equation)
Indicate the effects of the following transactions on the basic accounting equation developed in the chapter. Assume that the fiscal year end of the company is December 31.

a. Issue common shares for $25,000.

b. Pay an insurance premium of $600 on July 1 that provides coverage for the 12-month period starting July 1.

c. Recognize the amount of insurance expense that has been used from July 1 through December 31, assuming the facts in Transaction b.

d. Sales recorded for the period totalled $60,000, of which $25,000 were cash sales.

e. Cash collections on customer accounts totalled $37,000.

f. Sign a contract to purchase a piece of equipment that costs $1,200, and put a downpayment of $100 on the purchase.

g. Dividends of $1,300 are declared.

h. Dividends of $1,150 are paid.

i. Amortization of $3,300 was taken on the property, plant, and equipment.

j. Purchase $31,350 of inventory on account.

k. Inventory costing $35,795 was sold.

2-22 (Transaction analysis and the basic accounting equation)
Sunshine Company Ltd. reported assets of $90,000, liabilities of $35,000, and shareholders' equity of $55,000 on January 1, 2000. During the year, Sunshine Company:

a. Purchased land for $21,000 cash.

b. Purchased equipment costing $30,000 by signing a three-month note payable.

c. Paid liabilities of $15,000.

d. Issued new common shares for $28,000 cash.

e. Borrowed $7,000 from a local bank on a six-month note payable.

Required:
Compute the totals reported in each of the three major categories of the basic accounting equation following the transactions.

2-23 (Basic accounting equation evaluation)
Ballentine Company Ltd. has assets of $10,000, liabilities of $3,000, and shareholders' equity of $7,000. Using the basic accounting equation, answer each of the following independent questions:

a. At what amount will liabilities be stated if total assets increase by $200 and shareholders' equity remains constant?

b. At what amount will shareholders' equity be stated if Ballentine pays off $150 of liabilities with cash?

c. At what amount will assets be stated if total liabilities increase to $525 and shareholders' equity remains constant?

d. At what amount will assets be stated if total liabilities decrease by $100 and shareholders' equity increases by $250.

e. What would be the impact on the accounting equation for Ballentine if the shareholders received $550 in cash as a dividend?

2-24 (Preparation of an income statement)
Jack's Shoe Mart Ltd. had the following account balances at the end of December 20x1:

Cost of goods sold	$30,000
Rent expense	6,000

Sales	60,000
Dividends declared	2,000
Wages expense	18,000
Advertising expense	1,800
Bank loan	5,000

Required:

a. Prepare an income statement for the year ended December 31, 20x1. Follow the format given in the chapter.

b. You did not need to use all of the items listed. For every item that you did not use, explain why you did not use it.

2-25 (Preparation of an income statement)

The Wizard's Corner, a company selling adventure games, figures, cards, and clothing, had the following account balances at the end of June, 20x1:

Wages expense	$ 35,000
Sales	160,000
Accounts receivable	14,000
Rent expense	12,000
Cost of goods sold	100,000
Common shares	30,000
Advertising expense	6,000
Dividends declared	3,000

Required:

a. Prepare an income statement for the year ended June 30, 20x1. Follow the format given in the chapter.

b. You did not need to use all of the items listed. For every item that you did not use, explain why you did not use it.

2-26 (Preparation of an income statement)

The Garment Tree Ltd. sells sports clothing. At the end of December 20x1, it had the following account balances:

Miscellaneous expense	$ 2,000
Wages expense	22,000
Wages payable	500
Cost of goods sold	62,000
Sales	100,000
Rent expense	9,000
Inventory	22,000
Advertising expense	3,000

Required:

a. Prepare an income statement for the year ended December 31, 20x1. Follow the format given in the chapter.

b. You did not need to use all of the items listed. For every item that you did not use, explain why you did not use it.

2-27 (Preparation of the balance sheet)

The Tree Top Restaurant Ltd., a restaurant chain with restaurants in several cities across Canada, had the following account balances at December 31, 20x1:

Accounts payable	$40,000
Accounts receivable	20,000
Common shares	50,000
Cash	33,000
Land	20,000
Inventory	24,000
Retained earnings	4,000
Wages payable	3,000

Required:

Prepare a classified balance sheet for Tree Top Restaurant Ltd. for December 31, 20x1. Follow the examples in the chapter.

2-28 (Preparation of the balance sheet)

At the end of its first year of operations, December 31, 20x1, Black's Books Ltd. had the following account balances:

Cash	$ 4,000
Sales	90,000
Cost of goods sold	54,000
Retained earnings	?
Salaries expense	22,000
Other expenses	9,000
Dividends declared	1,000
Inventory	15,000
Accounts receivable	8,000
Accounts payable	3,000
Common shares	20,000

Required:

a. Identify the income statement accounts and calculate net income.

b. Subtract the dividends declared from the net income you calculated in part a. to find the amount of retained earnings at December 31, 20x1.

c. Prepare a classified balance sheet for December 31, 20x1, following the format given in the chapter. Use the amount calculated in part b. for retained earnings.

2-29 (Preparation of the balance sheet)

Little Tots Ltd. sells children's clothing. At the end of December 20x1, it had the following account balances:

Cash	$ 3,000
Wages payable	500
Display counters	4,000
Wages expense	15,000
Cost of goods sold	32,000
Sales	55,000
Rent expense	3,600
Bank loan	1,800
Advertising expense	800
Telephone expense	100
Electricity expense	200

Dividends declared	1,200
Common shares	9,000
Accounts payable	2,000
Inventory	8,000
Other expenses	400
Retained earnings	?

Required:

a. Prepare a computation to determine the amount of retained earnings.

b. Use what you need to prepare a classified balance sheet following the format given in the chapter.

2-30 (Transaction analysis and financial statement preparation)
The T. George Company started business on Jan. 1, 20x2. Listed below are the transactions that occurred during 20x2.

Required:

a. Use the basic accounting equation to analyze the transactions for 20x2.

b. Prepare a balance sheet, an income statement, and a cash flow statement for 20x2.

Transactions:

1. On Jan. 1, 20x2, the company issued 10,000 common shares for $175,000.

2. On Jan. 1, 20x2, the company borrowed $125,000 from the bank.

3. On Jan. 2, 20x2, the company purchased (for cash) land and a building costing $200,000. The building was recently appraised at $140,000. Hint: Because the building will be amortized in the future and the land will not, you must record the land and building in separate accounts.

4. Inventory costing $100,000 was purchased on account.

5. An investment was made in Calhoun Company Ltd. shares in the amount of $75,000.

6. Sales to customers totalled $190,000 in 20x2. Of these, $30,000 were cash sales.

7. Collections on accounts receivable totalled $135,000.

8. Payments to suppliers totalled $92,000 in 20x2.

9. Salaries paid to employees totalled $44,000. There were no unpaid salaries at year end.

10. A physical count of unsold inventories at year end revealed that inventory costed at $10,000 was still on hand.

11. The building was estimated to have a useful life of 20 years and a residual value of $20,000. The company uses straight-line amortization.

12. The interest on the bank loan is recognized each month and is paid on the first day of the succeeding month; that is, January's interest is recognized in January and paid on February 1. The interest rate is 9%.

13. The investment in Calhoun Company paid dividends of $5,000 in 20x2. All of it had been received by year end. The receipt of dividends from an investment is treated as investment income, a revenue.

14. Dividends of $15,000 were declared on Dec. 15, 20x2, and were scheduled to be paid on Jan. 10, 20x3.

2-31 (Transaction analysis and financial statement presentation)

The Hughes Tool Company started business on October 1, 20x3. Its fiscal year runs through to September 30 of the following year. Following are the transactions that occurred during fiscal 20x4 (the year starting Oct. 1, 20x3, and ending Sept. 30, 20x4).

Required:

a. Use the basic accounting equation to analyze the transactions for 20x4.

b. Prepare an income statement, a balance sheet, and a cash flow statement for fiscal 20x4.

Transactions:

1. On Oct. 1, 20x3, J. Hughes contributed $100,000 to start the business. Hughes is the only owner. She received 10,000 shares.

2. On Oct. 2, 20x3, Hughes borrowed $300,000 from a venture capitalist (a lender who specializes in startup companies). The interest rate on the loan is 11%.

3. On Oct. 3, 20x3, Hughes rented a building. The rental agreement was a two-year contract that called for quarterly rental payments (every three months) of $20,000, payable in advance on Dec. 31, March 31, June 30, and Sept. 30. The first payment was made on Oct. 3, 20x3, and covers the period from Oct. 3 to Dec. 31.

4. On Oct. 3, 20x3, Hughes purchased equipment costing $250,000. The equipment had an estimated useful life of seven years and a residual value of $40,000.

5. On Oct. 3, 20x3, Hughes purchased initial inventory with a cash payment of $100,000.

6. Sales during the year totalled $800,000, of which $720,000 were credit sales.

7. Collections from customers on account totalled $640,000.

8. Additional purchases of inventory during the year totalled $550,000, all on account.

9. Payments to suppliers totalled $495,000.

10. Inventory on hand at year end amounted to $115,000.

11. The company declared and paid a dividend of $40,000 to J. Hughes.

12. Interest on the loan from the venture capitalist was paid at year end, Sept. 30, 20x4, as well as $20,000 of the principal.

13. Other selling and administrative expenses totalled $90,000 for the year. Of this, $20,000 was unpaid as at year end.

14. The income tax rate is 30%. Assume that Hughes made payments during the year equal to three quarters of the ultimate tax bill, and that the rest are accrued at year end. Also, assume that the way net income is calculated for tax purposes does not differ from the method used for reporting purposes.

2-32 (Transaction analysis and financial statement preparation)

The A.J. Smith Company started business on Jan. 1, 20x1. Following are the transactions that occurred during 20x1.

Required:

a. Use the basic accounting equation to analyze the transactions for 20x1.

b. Prepare a balance sheet, an income statement, and a cash flow statement for fiscal 20x1.

Transactions:

1. On Jan. 1, 20x1, the company issued 25,000 common shares at $15 per share.

2. On Jan. 1, 20x1, the company purchased land and buildings from another company in exchange for $50,000 in cash and 25,000 common shares. The land's value is approximately one fifth of the total value of the transaction. Hint: You need to determine a value for the common shares using the information you were given in Transaction 1 and you must record the land and building in separate accounts.

3. Equipment worth $100,000 was purchased on July 1, 20x1, in exchange for $50,000 in cash and a one-year, 10% note, principal amount $50,000. The note pays semi-annual interest, and interest was unpaid on Dec. 31, 20x1.

4. The equipment is amortized using the straight-line method, with an estimated useful life of 10 years and an estimated residual value of $0. Because the equipment was purchased on July 1, only a half year of amortization is recognized in the first year.

5. The buildings purchased in Transaction 2 are amortized using the straight-line method, with an estimated useful life of 30 years and an estimated residual value of $40,000.

6. During the year, inventory costing $200,000 was purchased, all on account.

7. Sales during the year were $215,000, of which credit sales were $175,000.

8. Inventory costing $160,000 was sold during the year.

9. Payments to suppliers totalled $175,000.

10. At the end of the year, accounts receivable had a positive balance of $10,000.

11. On March 31, 20x1, the company rented out a portion of its building to Fantek Company. Fantek was required to make quarterly payments of $5,000 each. The payments were due on March 31, June 30, Sept. 30, and Dec. 31 of each year, with the first payment to be made on March 31, 20x1. All scheduled payments were made during 20x1.

12. Selling and distribution expenses amounted to $30,000, all paid in cash.

13. The company pays taxes at a rate of 30%. During the year, $3,000 was paid to Revenue Canada.

14. Dividends of $4,000 were declared during the year, and $1,000 remained unpaid at year end.

2-33 (Preparation of cash flow statement)
Following are descriptions of line items that should appear on a cash flow statement for the Clarkson Company. Organize these items in a formal cash flow statement, and comment on the health of the company to the extent that you can.

Cash flow line items:

Cash receipts from customers $5,000

Purchase of equipment $12,000

Proceeds from the issuance of shares $20,000

Investment in Canadian Airlines shares $3,000

Cash disbursements to suppliers $3,400

Cash payments to employees (salaries) $1,900

Proceeds from the sale of equipment $6,000

Dividends paid $2,500

Repayment of bank loan $8,000

2-34 (Transaction analysis)

Many transactions take place between two independent entities. How you record a particular transaction depends on whose perspective you take.

Required:

For each of the following transactions, comment on how it would affect the basic accounting equation from each of the perspectives given:

a. Purchase of inventory from a supplier (buyer's and seller's perspectives).

b. Loan from the bank (borrower's and bank's perspectives).

c. Deposit by customer on the purchase of a unit of inventory to be delivered at a later time (company's and customer's perspectives).

d. Company A invests in shares of Company B and obtains the shares directly from Company B (Company A's and Company B's perspectives).

e. Company A invests in shares of Company B and obtains the shares by buying them on the Toronto Stock Exchange; that is, they had previously been issued by Company B and now trade in the stock market (Company A's and Company B's perspectives).

f. Prepayment of insurance premiums (company's and insurance company's perspectives).

Management Perspective Problems

2-35 (Accrual versus cash basis with respect to manipulation of earnings)

Under the accrual basis of accounting, revenues are recognized when the revenue recognition criteria are met and expenses are then matched with the revenues under the matching concept. Discuss management's opportunities to manipulate income reported to shareholders under the accrual basis as compared to the cash basis.

2-36 (Revenue recognition)

Suppose that your company sells appliances to customers under instalment contracts that require them to pay for the appliance over as long a period as two years using monthly payments. Two potential methods of revenue recognition would be to recognize the full purchase price at the time of the sale or to defer recognition of the revenue until you receive the cash from the payments. Discuss the incentives that management might have to choose one method of revenue recognition over the other from both a tax perspective and the perspective of reporting income to shareholders.

2-37 (Cash basis of accounting)
Under the cash basis of accounting, the purchase of a new piece of equipment for cash would be treated as an expense during the accounting period in which it was purchased.

    a. From the perspective of the shareholder of a company, how would this treatment affect your assessment of the income of the company and the value of the remaining assets on the balance sheet?

    b. From the perspective of a buyer of the company (someone who wanted to purchase all of the outstanding shares of the company), how would this treatment affect your assessment of the value of the company as a potential acquisition?

2-38 (Warranty expense and tax implications)
Under accrual basis accounting, warranty expenses are typically estimated at the time of sale and accrued. If you were allowed to determine tax law, would you allow companies to deduct warranty expense at the time of sale, or would you make the company wait until it actually provided the warranty service? Why?

2-39 (Computation of the value of a company)
One of the shareholders of The Really Sinful Cookie Shop is considering selling his ownership and wishes to determine his equity in the cookie shop using good accounting principles. The shareholders know the following transactions have occurred since they started operations at the beginning of the year:

    1. $35,000 was borrowed from the bank to help get the business started and $10,000 was repaid by year end. In addition, the shareholders contributed $15,000 to get the business started.

    2. Ingredients costing $40,000 were purchased during the year, and 80% was used in goods baked during the year. All but $6,000 worth of the ingredients was paid for by the end of the year.

    3. Cookie ovens were rented during the year for $13,000. At year end, an option to purchase the ovens was exercised and $37,000 was paid to acquire ownership.

    4. Salaries of $20,000 were earned by employees during the year; all were paid except income taxes of $3,000, which had been withheld from their paycheques and will be forwarded to Revenue Canada early next year.

    5. After $86,000 had been collected for goods sold, the cash balance at the end of the year was $25,000, and net income of $21,000 was reported.

Required:

    a. List each of the assets and liabilities of the bakery at the end of the year.

    b. Compute the amount of the shareholders' equity at year end.

    c. Prepare a simple balance sheet for the bakery at year end.

    d. For what amount should the shareholder be able to sell his 25% interest?

2-40 (Analysis of a potential investment)
Glancing through the *Globe and Mail* recently, you came across the following business opportunity:

Type of business:	Monthly newsletter
Location:	Isle of Mancala

Market:	Local residents, upscale, approximately 1,200 subscribers
Population:	97,000 residents on the island

Overview: Owned by an individual on the mainland who devotes part of his/her time to the newsletter. The business employs an advertising manager, who sells ads, and it contracts with freelance writers to write stories. The subscribers pay $34.95 annually. The newsletter has a renewal rate of 58% to 70%.

Asking Price:	$150,000		
Financial information:	1997	1998	1999
Gross revenue	$57,800	$86,400	$98,000
After-tax cash inflows	18,200	6,500	7,000

You have $150,000 to invest, and you wonder if this might be a good business opportunity.

Required:
Analyze this potential investment and address the following:

a. Comment on the qualitative characteristics of the information presented in the ad. Is the information

 1. relevant?

 2. reliable?

 3. understandable?

 4. consistent?

b. Can you determine from the information given what revenue recognition principles were applied?

c. Can you determine what expenses were matched with revenues?

d. What other information would you want in order to make an informed decision about this investment opportunity?

Reading and Interpreting Published Financial Statements

2-41 (Determination of items from a Canadian company's financial statements) Base your answers to the following questions on the financial statements of Enerflex Systems Ltd. that you will find in Exhibit 2-11.

a. Determine the amount of cash dividends declared during fiscal 1998.

b. Determine the amount of dividends paid during fiscal 1998.

c. Assuming that all sales were on account, determine the amount of cash collected from customers in 1998.

d. Assuming that the only transactions that flow through the accounts payable and accrued liabilities are purchases of inventory, and assuming that all additions to the inventory account were purchases of inventory, determine the cash payments made to suppliers in 1998.

e. Given the change in income taxes payable, was the tax expense in 1998 greater than or less than the cash paid to Revenue Canada? (Ignore deferred taxes in your answer.)

2-42 (Determination of items from a Canadian company's financial statements) Base your answers to the following questions on the financial statements of Big Rock Brewery Ltd. in Appendix A at the end of the book.

EXHIBIT 2-11

PART A

CONSOLIDATED FINANCIAL STATEMENTS

CONSOLIDATED STATEMENTS OF FINANCIAL POSITION

		December 31	
(Thousands)		**1998**	1997
Assets			
Current assets			
Cash		$ –	$ 19,578
Accounts receivable		54,125	66,096
Inventory	(NOTE 1)	45,094	26,057
Total current assets		99,219	111,731
Rental equipment	(NOTE 2)	22,186	13,403
Property, plant and equipment	(NOTE 3)	36,719	16,170
Goodwill, net of accumulated amortization		1,382	1,423
		$ 159,506	$ 142,727
Liabilities and Shareholders' Equity			
Current liabilities			
Bank loans	(NOTE 4)	$ 3,935	$ –
Accounts payable and accrued liabilities		35,641	46,385
Income taxes payable		514	7,375
Current portion of long-term debt	(NOTE 4)	3,100	–
Total current liabilities		43,190	53,760
Long-term debt	(NOTE 4)	15,200	–
Deferred income taxes		1,060	2,002
		59,450	55,762
Shareholders' equity			
Share capital	(NOTE 5)	34,678	34,630
Retained earnings		65,378	52,335
		100,056	86,965
		$ 159,506	$ 142,727

Commitments and contingencies   (NOTES 6 AND 9)

On behalf of the Board:

P. John Aldred, Director   Patrick D. Daniel, Director

EXHIBIT 2-11

PART B

CONSOLIDATED FINANCIAL STATEMENTS

CONSOLIDATED STATEMENTS OF INCOME

				Years Ended December 31	
(Thousands, except share amounts)				**1998**	1997
Revenue			$	**314,496**	$ 336,220
Cost of goods sold				**244,065**	263,316
Gross margin				**70,431**	72,904
Selling, general and administrative expenses				**32,835**	30,623
(Gain) on sale of equipment				**(200)**	(411)
Income before interest and taxes				**37,796**	42,692
Interest (income), net				**(262)**	(55)
Income before income taxes				**38,058**	42,747
Income taxes	(NOTE 7)			**15,490**	17,526
Net income			$	**22,568**	$ 25,221
Net income per common share – basic			$	**1.50**	$ 1.67
– fully diluted			$	**1.45**	$ 1.61
Weighted average number of common shares				**15,085,177**	15,111,147

CONSOLIDATED STATEMENTS OF RETAINED EARNINGS

				Years Ended December 31	
(Thousands)				**1998**	1997
Retained earnings, beginning of year			$	**52,335**	$ 32,145
Net income				**22,568**	25,221
Common shares purchased for cancellation	(NOTE 5)			**(3,003)**	(496)
Stock options purchased	(NOTE 5)			**(491)**	–
Dividends				**(6,031)**	(4,535)
Retained earnings, end of year			$	**65,378**	$ 52,335

EXHIBIT 2-11
PART C

CONSOLIDATED FINANCIAL STATEMENTS

CONSOLIDATED STATEMENTS OF CHANGES IN FINANCIAL POSITION

	Years Ended December 31	
(Thousands)	**1998**	1997
Operating Activities		
Net income	$ **22,568**	$ 25,221
Depreciation and amortization	**4,616**	4,056
Deferred income taxes	**(942)**	(39)
(Gain) on sale of equipment	**(200)**	(411)
	26,042	28,827
Changes in non-cash working capital	**(24,671)**	1,055
	1,371	29,882
Investing Activities		
Purchase of:		
Rental equipment	**(13,620)**	(5,769)
Property, plant and equipment	**(23,887)**	(3,477)
Proceeds on disposal of:		
Rental equipment	**3,454**	5,211
Property, plant and equipment	**346**	168
	(33,707)	(3,867)
Financing Activities		
Proceeds (repayment) of long-term debt	**18,300**	(4,634)
Common shares purchased for cancellation	**(3,267)**	(532)
Stock options purchased	**(491)**	–
Stock options exercised	**312**	404
Dividends	**(6,031)**	(4,535)
	8,823	(9,297)
Cash (Bank Loans)		
Increase (decrease) in cash	**(23,513)**	16,718
Beginning of year	**19,578**	2,860
End of year	$ **(3,935)**	$ 19,578

a. Determine the amount of dividends declared during fiscal 1999.

b. Assuming that all sales were on account, determine the amount of cash collected from customers in 1999. Should you use Sales less the Government taxes and commissions in your answer, or should you use just the Sales amount?

c. Assuming that the only transactions that flow through the accounts payable and accrued liabilities are purchases of inventory, and assuming that all additions to the inventory account were purchases of inventory, determine the cash payments made to suppliers in 1999.

d. Calculate the following ratios for 1998 and 1999:

   1. profit margin ratio (use sales less government taxes and commissions)
   2. return on assets
   3. return on equity

e. What happened to the profitability in 1999? Search through the annual report and see if you can find an explanation for these results.

2-43 (Determination of items from a Canadian company's financial statements) Base your answers to the following questions on the financial statements of Future Shop Ltd. in Appendix B at the end of the book.

a. Determine the amount of dividends declared during fiscal 1999.

b. Assuming that all sales were on account, determine the amount of cash collected from customers in 1999.

c. Assuming that the only transactions that flow through accounts payable and accrued liabilities are purchases of inventory, and assuming that all additions to the inventory account were purchases of inventory, determine the cash payments made to suppliers in 1999.

d. Calculate the following ratios for 1999:

   1. profit margin ratio
   2. return on assets
   3. return on equity

2-44 (Determination of items from a Canadian company's financial statements) Exhibit 2-12 includes two financial statements from Trimac Company.

Required:

a. Refer to the consolidated cash flow statement (statement of changes in financial position) and compare the net income in each of the last two years to the cash flow from operations in the last two years.

b. In general, why are there differences between cash flows from operations and net income? Refer specifically to the differences due to sales transactions and amortization.

c. Comment on Trimac's ability to pay for its cash needs over the last two years using its cash from operations. Do you think Trimac is in a favourable cash flow position? Support your answer.

2-45 (Determination of items from a Canadian company's financial statements) Base your answers to the following questions on the financial statements of Air Canada that you will find in Exhibit 2-13 and Exhibit 2-5 included earlier in the chapter.

EXHIBIT 2-12

PART A

Consolidated Statement of Earnings

	Year ended December 31 (Note 1)	
(thousands of dollars except per share amounts)	1998	1997
Revenues	$ 607,658	$ 597,669
Operating Costs and Expenses		
Direct	404,780	401,956
Selling and administrative	86,898	82,685
Depreciation and amortization	86,137	79,825
Gain on sale of assets (net)	(8,767)	(5,365)
	569,048	559,101
Operating Earnings	38,610	38,568
Interest – long term debt	22,015	16,465
– other interest (net)	36	1,091
	22,051	17,556
Earnings Before Unusual Items	16,559	21,012
Unusual items – (loss) gain recognized on disposal or write down of investments (Note 6)	(36,067)	77,430
Earnings Before Taxes	(19,508)	98,442
Income tax (recovery) expense (Note 5)	(20,332)	47,688
Earnings Before Equity Accounted Investments	824	50,754
Equity accounted investments (Note 7)	7,655	9,393
Net Earnings	$ 8,479	$ 60,147
Earnings Per Share		
Net earnings - basic	$ 0.22	$ 1.48
- fully diluted	0.22	1.43

Consolidated Statement of Retained Earnings

	Year ended December 31 (Note 1)	
(thousands of dollars)	1998	1997
Retained Earnings, Beginning of Year, As Previously Reported	$ 226,890	$ 166,884
Adjustment – accounting policy change (Note 3)	6,208	—
Retained Earnings, Beginning of Year, as Restated	233,098	166,884
Net earnings	8,479	60,147
Dividend paid on common shares	(7,365)	(7,302)
Repurchase of common shares	(59,948)	(2,322)
Other equity changes	—	9,483
Retained Earnings, End of Year	$ 174,264	$ 226,890

EXHIBIT 2-12
PART B

Consolidated Cash Flow Statement

(thousands of dollars)	Year ended December 31 (Note 1) 1998	1997
Cash Provided (Used)		
Operations		
Net earnings	$ 8,479	$ 60,147
Depreciation and amortization	86,137	79,825
Gain on sale of assets (net)	(8,767)	(5,365)
Future income taxes	(25,346)	42,989
Equity accounted investments (Note 7) – net earnings	(7,655)	(9,393)
Unusual items	36,067	(77,430)
Other	193	1,252
Cash From Operations	89,108	92,025
Cash used by unusual items	(1,050)	—
Net change in non cash working capital balances	(2,091)	(14,055)
Net Cash Flow	85,967	77,970
Investments		
Purchase of fixed assets	(174,699)	(161,884)
Proceeds on sale of fixed assets	78,900	38,137
Net capital expenditures	(95,799)	(123,747)
Acquisition of transportation businesses (Note 8)	—	(12,741)
Increase in investments (Note 7)	(14,677)	(41,867)
Proceeds on disposal of investments (Note 7)	67,053	9,475
Other	(549)	2,600
Cash Used by Investments	(43,972)	(166,280)
Financing		
Increase in long term debt	74,959	80,693
Repayments of long term debt	(30,518)	(5,437)
	44,441	75,256
Net change in bank advances	(3,745)	12,992
Increase in common shares	2,130	3,898
Repurchase of common shares	(75,112)	(2,896)
Dividend paid on common shares	(7,365)	(7,302)
Other interdivisional advances and changes in equity	—	7,104
Cash (Used in) Provided by Financing	(39,651)	89,052
Increase in cash	2,344	742
Cash, beginning of year	4,912	4,170
Cash, End of Year	$ 7,256	$ 4,912

Consolidated Statement of Operations and Retained Earnings
(in millions except per share figures)

Year ended December 31	1998	1997
Operating revenues		
Passenger	$ 4,977	$ 4,533
Cargo	369	387
Other	586	652
	5,932	5,572
Operating expenses		
Salaries and wages	1,363	1,236
Benefits	210	153
Aircraft fuel	657	712
Depreciation, amortization and obsolescence	292	258
Commissions	464	438
Food, beverages and supplies	252	229
Aircraft maintenance, materials and supplies	318	248
Airport and navigation fees	375	228
Aircraft rent	474	383
Customer maintenance materials	76	105
Other (note 1j)	1,307	1,214
	5,788	5,204
Operating income	144	368
Non-operating income (expense)		
Interest income	41	26
Interest expense	(242)	(203)
Interest capitalized	22	43
Amortization of deferred foreign exchange on long-term debt	(32)	(20)
Gain on sale of investments (notes 1a & 4)	57	201
Gain (loss) on sale of other assets	(27)	35
Other	8	16
	(173)	98
Income (loss) before income taxes	(29)	466
Recovery of (provision for) income tax (note 10)	3	(207)
Recovery of prior years income tax benefits previously not recorded (note 10)	10	168
Income (loss) for the year	(16)	427
Retained earnings (deficit), beginning of year	171	(257)
Charge relating to convertible debentures (note 8)	(3)	1
Retained earnings, end of year	$ 152	$ 171
Earnings per share		
– Basic	$ (0.10)	$ 2.74
– Fully diluted	$ (0.10)	$ 2.37

See accompanying notes.

© Air Canada, 1998.

EXHIBIT 2-13

PART B

Consolidated Statement of Financial Position
(in millions)

December 31	1998	1997
Assets		
Current		
Cash and short-term investments (note 1d)	$ 366	$ 650
Accounts receivable	405	467
Spare parts, materials and supplies	258	225
Prepaid expenses	21	17
Deferred income taxes	42	35
	1,092	1,394
Property and equipment (note 2)	3,243	2,817
Deferred charges (note 3)	1,722	1,456
Investments and other assets (note 4)	365	324
	$ 6,422	$ 5,991
Liabilities		
Current		
Accounts payable and accrued liabilities	$ 840	$ 668
Advance ticket sales	360	400
Current portion of long-term debt	79	71
	1,279	1,139
Long-term and subordinated perpetual debt (note 5)	2,917	2,739
Other long-term liabilities	279	218
Deferred credits (note 7)	490	460
	4,965	4,556
Shareholders' Equity		
Convertible debentures (note 8)	–	201
Share capital (note 9)	1,305	1,063
Retained earnings	152	171
	1,457	1,435
	$ 6,422	$ 5,991

See accompanying notes.

On behalf of the Board:

R. Lamar Durrett
President and Chief Executive Officer

John F. Fraser, O.C.
Chairman of the Board

a. Determine the value of share capital issued during 1998.

b. Determine the amount of dividends paid during fiscal 1998.

c. Assuming that all operating revenues were on account, determine the amount of cash collected from customers.

d. A company such as Air Canada has an extensive investment in noncurrent property and equipment. From 1997 to 1998 the property and equipment on the balance sheet (statement of financial position) changed from $2,819 million to $3,243 million, an increase of $426 million. Using the three statements, explain the changes that occurred in this account.

e. Calculate the following ratios for 1998:

1. profit margin ratio (use total operating revenues)

2. return on assets

3. return on equity

2-46 (Determination of items from an international company's financial statements) Base your answers to the following questions on the financial statements of Toys "R" Us, Inc., from the United States that you will find in Exhibit 2-14.

a. Refer to the statement of cash flows and compare the net income in each of the last three years to the cash flow from operations in the last three years.

b. In general, why are there differences between cash flows from operations and net income? Refer specifically to the differences due to sales transactions and amortization (depreciation).

c. Using the income tax expense on the statement of earnings and the income taxes payable on the balance sheets, determine how much cash was sent to the tax authority in fiscal 1998.

d. From the financial statements, discuss the importance of inventory in relationship to other assets on the company's balance sheet.

e. Calculate the following ratios for 1999:

1. profit margin ratio

2. return on assets

3. return on equity

Beyond the Book

2-47 (Find items from a Canadian company's financial statements) Find the annual report of a typical Canadian company in the retail business. Answer the following questions:

a. From the financial statements, discuss how important inventory is in relationship to other assets on the company's balance sheet.

b. How does the company finance its business?

c. Read through the management's discussion of operations and determine if there is any information there that is not included in the financial statements. If you were a shareholder, would you want to know the extra information? Why?

d. How many directors does the company have? What positions do they hold? Are any them directors of other companies?

e. Who are the independent auditors? Was the company given an unqualified opinion by the auditors?

EXHIBIT 2-14

PART A

Consolidated Statements of Earnings

TOYS"R"US, INC. AND SUBSIDIARIES

			Year Ended
(In millions except per share data)	January 30, 1999	January 31, 1998	February 1, 1997
Net Sales	$11,170	$11,038	$ 9,932
Cost of sales	8,191	7,710	6,892
Gross Profit	2,979	3,328	3,040
Selling, advertising, general and administrative expenses	2,443	2,231	2,020
Depreciation, amortization and asset write-offs	255	253	206
Restructuring and other charges	294	–	60
Total Operating Expenses	2,992	2,484	2,286
Operating (Loss)/Income	(13)	844	754
Interest expense	102	85	98
Interest and other income	(9)	(13)	(17)
Interest Expense, Net	93	72	81
(Loss)/Earnings Before Income Taxes	(106)	772	673
Income Taxes	26	282	246
Net (Loss)/Earnings	$ (132)	$ 490	$ 427
Basic (Loss)/Earnings Per Share	$ (0.50)	$ 1.72	$ 1.56
Diluted (Loss)/Earnings Per Share	$ (0.50)	$ 1.70	$ 1.54

See notes to consolidated financial statements.

The "R"Us brand has
successfully captured
young imaginations
and a significant
market share.

EXHIBIT 2-14
PART B

Consolidated Balance Sheets
TOYS"R"US, INC. AND SUBSIDIARIES

Our ever-expanding outdoor and sports headquarters features everything fun under the sun.

(In millions)	January 30, 1999	January 31, 1998
ASSETS		
Current Assets:		
Cash and cash equivalents	$ 410	$ 214
Accounts and other receivables	204	175
Merchandise inventories	1,902	2,464
Prepaid expenses and other current assets	81	51
Total Current Assets	2,597	2,904
Property and Equipment:		
Real estate, net	2,354	2,435
Other, net	1,872	1,777
Total Property and Equipment	4,226	4,212
Goodwill, net	347	356
Other assets	729	491
	$ 7,899	$ 7,963
LIABILITIES AND STOCKHOLDERS' EQUITY		
Current Liabilities:		
Short-term borrowings	$ 156	$ 134
Accounts payable	1,415	1,280
Accrued expenses and other current liabilities	696	680
Income taxes payable	224	231
Total Current Liabilities	2,491	2,325
Long-Term Debt	1,222	851
Deferred Income Taxes	333	219
Other Liabilities	229	140
Stockholders' Equity:		
Common stock	30	30
Additional paid-in capital	459	467
Retained earnings	4,478	4,610
Foreign currency translation adjustments	(100)	(122)
Treasury shares, at cost	(1,243)	(557)
Total Stockholders' Equity	3,624	4,428
	$ 7,899	$ 7,963

See notes to consolidated financial statements.

EXHIBIT 2-14

PART C

Consolidated Statements of Cash Flows

TOYS"R"US, INC. AND SUBSIDIARIES

			Year Ended
	January 30,	January 31,	February 1,
(In millions)	1999	1998	1997
CASH FLOWS FROM OPERATING ACTIVITIES			
Net (loss)/earnings	$ (132)	$ 490	$ 427
Adjustments to reconcile net (loss)/earnings to net cash provided by operating activities:			
Depreciation, amortization and asset write-offs	255	253	206
Deferred income taxes	(90)	18	23
Restructuring and other charges	546	–	–
Changes in operating assets and liabilities:			
Accounts and other receivables	(43)	(40)	(14)
Merchandise inventories	233	(265)	(195)
Prepaid expenses and other operating assets	(27)	(9)	(10)
Accounts payable, accrued expenses and other liabilities	229	22	262
Income taxes payable	(7)	40	44
Net cash provided by operating activities	964	509	743
CASH FLOWS FROM INVESTING ACTIVITIES			
Capital expenditures, net	(373)	(494)	(415)
Other assets	(49)	(22)	(36)
Cash received with the acquisition of Baby Superstore	–	–	67
Net cash used in investing activities	(422)	(516)	(384)
CASH FLOWS FROM FINANCING ACTIVITIES			
Short-term borrowings, net	4	(142)	(10)
Long-term borrowings	771	11	326
Long-term debt repayments	(412)	(176)	(133)
Exercise of stock options	16	62	28
Share repurchase program	(723)	(253)	–
Net cash (used in)/provided by financing activities	(344)	(498)	211
Effect of exchange rate changes on cash and cash equivalents	(2)	(42)	(12)
CASH AND CASH EQUIVALENTS			
Increase/(decrease) during year	196	(547)	558
Beginning of year	214	761	203
End of year	$ 410	$ 214	$ 761
SUPPLEMENTAL DISCLOSURES OF CASH FLOW INFORMATION			
Income Tax Payments	$ 122	$ 192	$ 177
Interest Payments	$ 109	$ 83	$ 109

See notes to consolidated financial statements.

2-48 (Research concerning a Canadian company)
For the company you selected to solve Problem 47, find at least three articles in the financial press that discuss the nature of the markets for this company and the forecast for this sector of the economy. If the company has a website, you may find recent articles about the company posted there. Write a one-page summary of your findings.

Case

2-49 Saskco Chicken Products
Saskco Chicken Products is a new company established by four entrepreneurs from Moose Jaw. They intend to purchase live chickens, process them, and sell them as frozen pieces and whole chickens. They initially anticipate hiring three workers to process the chickens. The four owners will work in the business and have the following titles: President (oversees the whole operation, including finance and accounting), VP Marketing, VP Operations (in charge of the processing operations), and VP Procurement (in charge of purchasing chickens from farmers). The President of Saskco Chicken Products has hired you for three months to help the company set up its accounting system. In anticipation of establishing a computerized accounting package, develop a list of account titles that you think this company will need to start operations. For each account title, write a brief, one-line explanation for its inclusion in the chart of accounts.

Critical Thinking Question

2-50 (Comparison of financing strategies)
Using the statements of changes in financial position (cash flow statements) for Shaw Communications Inc. (Exhibit 2-15) and BCE Inc. (Exhibit 2-16), compare the methods used by the two companies to finance their activities. What are the future implications of the method(s) of financing used? By referring to the statements, explain why they need outside financing.

EXHIBIT 2-15

consolidated statements of cash flows

Years ended August 31	1998	1997
[thousands of dollars except per share amounts]	$	$
OPERATING ACTIVITIES		
Net income from continuing operations	13,525	218
Non-cash items:		
Amortization	147,007	108,842
Amortization of long-term program rights	14,064	9,025
Deferred income taxes	55,140	11,505
Gain on sale of cable systems, net of current taxes	(68,450)	-
Asset writedowns and provisions, net of payments	59,885	23,094
Gain on sale of investments, net of current taxes	(51,174)	-
Equity in Star Choice Communications Inc. loss	21,406	-
Minority interest	(3,413)	-
Other	(4,304)	(937)
Cash flow from continuing operations	183,686	151,747
Net change in non-cash working capital balances		
related to operations *[note 15]*	(54,949)	42,328
	128,737	194,075
INVESTING ACTIVITIES		
Additions to property, plant and equipment	(261,071)	(227,003)
Business acquisitions *[note 4]*	(121,055)	(71,321)
Proceeds on sale of cable systems	185,872	-
Proceeds on sale of investments and other assets	109,653	-
Acquisition of investments, net of share consideration	(332,570)	(72,466)
Additions to deferred charges	(40,188)	(27,498)
	(459,359)	(398,288)
FINANCING ACTIVITIES		
Increase in long-term debt	391,000	497,112
Long-term debt repayments	(540,646)	(319,918)
Proceeds on issue of debenture purchase warrants	-	31,388
Preferred Securities issued net of expenses and related taxes	537,754	-
Issue of Class B Shares	5	
Preferred shares redeemed	-	(2,840)
Dividends	(14,568)	(4,811)
	373,545	200,931
Net increase (decrease) in cash during the year	42,923	(3,282)
Cash position, beginning of the year	(20,876)	(17,594)
Cash position, end of the year	22,047	(20,876)
Cash flow from continuing operations per share *[note 15]*	$ 2.30	$ 2.17

Cash position represents cash and term deposits less bank indebtedness.

see accompanying notes

EXHIBIT 2-16

consolidated financial statements BCE Inc

CONSOLIDATED STATEMENT OF CHANGES IN FINANCIAL POSITION

For the years ended December 31	Notes	1998	($ millions) 1997
Cash provided by (used for) operations			
Net earnings (loss)		4,598	(1,536)
Items not affecting cash			
Extraordinary item	(2)	–	2,950
Depreciation and amortization		3,501	3,897
Purchased in-process research and development expense		688	–
Restructuring and other charges	(5)	518	123
Gain on reduction of ownership in subsidiary and associated companies	(6)	(4,146)	(257)
Net gains on disposal of investments		(1,339)	(227)
Non-controlling interest		(141)	682
Deferred income taxes		90	132
Dividends received in excess of equity in net losses of associated companies		444	208
Other non-cash items		(193)	(317)
Operating cash flow		4,020	5,655
Increase in working capital		(422)	(860)
Other items		174	(405)
Cash flow from operations		3,772	4,390
Cash provided by (used for) investments			
Capital expenditures		(3,774)	(3,413)
Investments		(3,499)	(1,166)
Divestitures		2,750	891
Disposal of capital assets	(12)	768	9
Long-term notes and other receivables		(52)	421
Reduction in cash due to deconsolidation of Northern Telecom Limited	(1)	(3,007)	–
Other items		63	222
		(6,751)	(3,036)
Dividends declared			
By BCE Inc.			
Preferred shares		(93)	(74)
Common shares		(868)	(865)
By subsidiaries to non-controlling interest		(134)	(186)
		(1,095)	(1,125)
Cash provided by (used for) financing			
Notes payable and bank advances		2,227	(218)
Addition to long-term debt		983	1,296
Reduction of long-term debt		(2,174)	(1,314)
Issue of preferred shares		–	245
Issue of common shares		248	124
Purchase of common shares for cancellation		(32)	(134)
Issue of preferred and common shares by subsidiaries to non-controlling interest		950	1,060
Other items		(7)	12
		2,195	1,071
Net (decrease) increase in cash and short-term investments		(1,879)	1,300
Cash and short-term investments at beginning of year		2,249	949
Cash and short-term investments at end of year		370	2,249

From Quill Pens to Computers

In the 1840s, when the maple-sugar operation on this picturesque spot in Lanark County, Ontario (some 60 kilometres west of Ottawa), first went into business, accounting records were kept with quill pens dipped in ink, debits on the left and credits on the right side of the page in a handmade book. Today, bookkeeper Jean LeClaire enters all the accounts for Fulton's Pancake House and Sugar Bush using the Accpac *Simply Accounting* program on a Pentium computer.

But in truth not much has really changed. Four generations later, the sugar bush is still in the same family—and even though they are kept electronically, its accounting records still follow essentially the same principles. In fact, many of the accounts in the general ledger would look very familiar to the farm's first owners: Income from sale of syrup and food; expenses for containers, equipment repairs, payroll, advertising, and so on. And the business still makes most of its over $100,000 of revenue each year from direct sales. "It's unusual today for a producer to sell straight to the buyer, with no middle person," points out owner Shirley Duego.

Of course, those early books probably didn't include among capital assets huge evaporators, which cut down the boiling time of sap into syrup using a reverse osmosis process. Nor did they have to include a system for tracking GST! But they had to be flexible enough to account for the vagaries of Canadian weather—a 19th-century page might well have included, just as Ms. LeClaire's electronic records for 1998 did, a special account for "ice storm expenses."

Essentially, even the simplest and most old-fashioned of accounting systems had the same aim as the most up-to-date electronic ones do today: To provide its users with the information they need to make sound decisions. For Ms. Duego and her co-owner, husband George, these decisions have included diversifying their operation to include a restaurant, craft sales, international group tours, and even an outdoor low-ropes challenge course. These attractions bring some 30,000 visitors to Fulton's each year. With luck, and careful accounting, they will bring in vast numbers of visitors for another four generations.

DOUBLE ENTRY
ACCOUNTING SYSTEMS

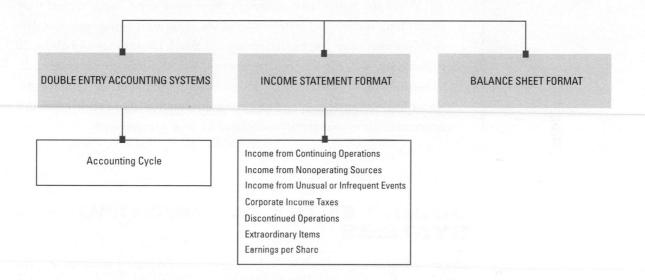

| DOUBLE ENTRY ACCOUNTING SYSTEMS | INCOME STATEMENT FORMAT | BALANCE SHEET FORMAT |

Accounting Cycle

Income from Continuing Operations
Income from Nonoperating Sources
Income from Unusual or Infrequent Events
Corporate Income Taxes
Discontinued Operations
Extraordinary Items
Earnings per Share

Learning Objectives:

After studying this chapter, you should be able to:

1. *Understand the relationship of debits and credits in the recording of transactions.*
2. *Understand the difference between permanent and temporary accounts.*
3. *Identify the steps in the accounting cycle.*
4. *Analyze transactions and record them in journal format.*
5. *Post transactions to T-accounts and prepare a trial balance.*
6. *Understand the necessity of adjusting entries and determine how they should be recorded.*
7. *Describe why closing entries are necessary.*
8. *Understand the difference between a single-step income statement and a multistep one.*
9. *Calculate a profit margin ratio.*
10. *Describe the criteria for unusual items, discontinued operations, and extraordinary items.*
11. *Understand the criteria for listing items on a balance sheet.*

Now that you understand the basic accounting equation and can work through the analysis of some transactions, we are going to take you one step deeper into the practical side of accounting. We are going to show you how to get the amounts into the records in a way that will enable us to pull out information that we need and summarize it into statements. As you read in the opening story, the underlying mechanics of accounting have not changed for years. The double-entry system that we are going to show you can be traced back to the late 15th century. Although the mode of keeping the records—pen and paper to computers—has changed, the system has not.

When you were working through the problems in Chapter 2, you were establishing spreadsheet frameworks of the basic accounting equation. You could see that once you expanded beyond about 10 accounts and about 20 transactions the spreadsheet framework would become unmanageable. Companies have hundreds of accounts and thousands of transactions. Recording, summarizing, and reporting information about their economic activities requires something more elaborate than a spreadsheet.

DOUBLE ENTRY ACCOUNTING SYSTEMS

The recording of transactions in the basic accounting equation is sufficient if the entity has only a few transactions to record. We call this type of system a **synoptic journal**. It is used by clubs that need only to maintain information about dues collected and activities undertaken. However, the plus and minus system used in the spreadsheets becomes confusing and somewhat cumbersome when large numbers of accounts and transactions are considered. To overcome this confusion, accountants have developed an alternative system for recording transactions. This alternative system is known as the **double entry** or **dual entry accounting system**. We will demonstrate the system by using a device known as a **T-account**. To translate from the equation system to the T-account system, imagine replacing the equality sign in the basic accounting equation with a big "T," as follows:

Replace the basic accounting equation:

$$\text{Assets} = \text{Liabilities} + \text{Shareholders' Equity}$$

With a T-account:

Assets	Liabilities + Shareholders' Equity

Note that assets appear on the left side of the T-account and liabilities and shareholders' equity appear on the right side. The equality expressed in the basic accounting equation must still be maintained in the T-account system. Translated, this means that the totals from the left side of the T-accounts must equal the totals from the right side of the T-accounts. The left side of the account is known as the **debit** side, the right side as the **credit** side. The words debit and credit have no meaning in accounting other than "left" and "right." Do not try to attach any other meaning to these terms, as it will likely lead you astray in your thinking about the accounts of the company. The abbreviations for debit and credit are, respectively, Dr. and Cr. The balance in the accounting system can now be expressed in terms of debits and credits rather than in terms of the left and right side of the basic accounting equation. The balance sheet equality requires that debits equal credits.

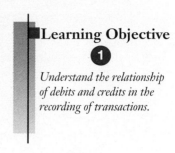

Learning Objective

1

Understand the relationship of debits and credits in the recording of transactions.

The T-account concept also carries over into the accounting for specific asset and liability accounts. Each asset and liability has its own T-account; these accounts, added together, result in the big T-account. See Exhibit 3-1.

INDIVIDUAL T-ACCOUNTS

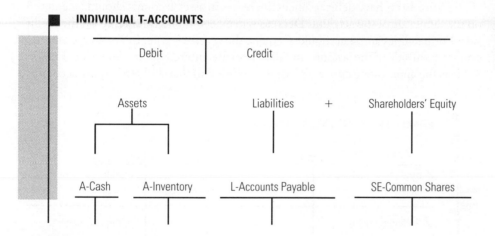

EXHIBIT 3-1

In Exhibit 3-1, note that there are letters preceding the account names. These letters will be used throughout this book to designate the type of account. At this point, there are only three designations to worry about: A represents an asset account, L a liability account, and SE a shareholders' equity account. We will periodically add other designations as we proceed through the book. These letters will be a helpful reminder of the nature of the account with which you are dealing.

Because assets are, by convention, listed on the debit side of the large T-account, they normally have balances on the debit side of the individual T-accounts. Likewise, liabilities and shareholders' equity accounts have credit balances. In Exhibit 3-2, the beginning balances for Demo Retail Company, Ltd., are entered into a set of T-accounts. Beside each balance, you will see a check mark (✓), which is used to designate a balance in the account rather than a new entry. Also, note that the sum of the debit balances ($10,000) equals the sum of the credit balances ($10,000), which means that the system is balanced.

EXHIBIT 3-2

Demo Retail Company, Ltd.

T-Accounts

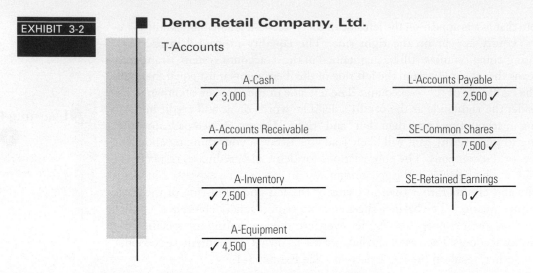

Because assets have debit balances, increases in asset accounts should be entered on the debit side of the account. Decreases in assets should be entered on the credit side. For liabilities and shareholders' equity, the reverse is true. Increases are entered on the credit side of the account and decreases are entered on the debit side. Exhibit 3-3 lists the appropriate entries for asset, liability, and shareholders' equity accounts.

EXHIBIT 3-3

Entries to T-Accounts

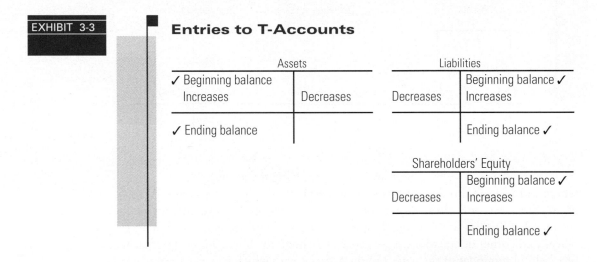

One way to think about the accounts and debits and credits is to imagine that the accounting system is a large warehouse that is balanced on a central point (like the equals sign between the two parts of the basic accounting equation). Inside the warehouse, the company has boxes stacked on either side to maintain the balance. The boxes themselves are weightless, which means that you do not need to have the same number of boxes on each side. The weight is added when something is put in a box. Each box represents an account. When the company needs to keep track of information about a specific financial item, it creates a new box and labels it so that everyone knows what is in that box. For example, there would be a box labelled Cash on one side of the warehouse and box labelled Common Shares on the other side. As financial activities are recorded, things are added to or removed from the appropriate box. Therefore, if you added something to an asset box on one side of the warehouse, you would need to take something out of a different asset box on the same side or go to the other side of the warehouse and add something to one of the boxes there (a liability or a shareholders' equity box). Debiting and crediting accounts is like putting things into boxes and taking things out. If the box is on the left side of the warehouse, it is an asset box. Each time you add something to the box you debit it; each time you take something out of the box you credit it. If the box is on the right side of the warehouse (liabilities and shareholders' equity boxes), it is the opposite. Each time you put something into one of these boxes you credit it; each time you take something out you debit it. If you are careful to ensure that the debits are balanced with credits, your warehouse will not tilt to one side. Periodically you can check all the boxes, record what is in each one, and prepare a balance sheet.

The accounts shown in Exhibits 3-2 and 3-3 are all balance sheet accounts. They have balances that carry over from one period to the next. These accounts are sometimes called **permanent accounts**. One of the permanent accounts is the retained earnings account. You learned in Chapter 1 that the change in the retained earnings account during a given period is the net of the revenues and expenses for the period and the decrease due to dividends declared. In order to keep track of the individual revenue and expense amounts, as well as the dividends declared during the period, you can subdivide the retained earnings account into several separate accounts. These separate accounts are called **temporary accounts**, because they are used temporarily, during the accounting period, to keep track of revenues, expenses, and dividends. The balances in these accounts ultimately have to affect the retained earnings account. Exhibit 3-4 shows the subdivision of the retained earnings account into the temporary revenue, expense, and dividends declared accounts.

Learning Objective
2
Understand the difference between permanent and temporary accounts.

Retained Earnings: Income Statement Accounts

EXHIBIT 3-4

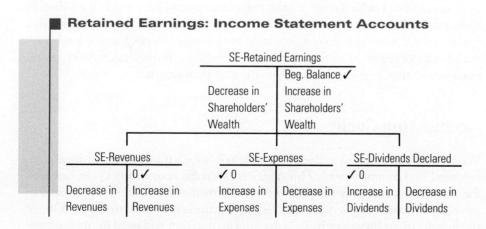

Several things should be noted concerning the revenue, expense, and dividends declared accounts. First, notice that the beginning balance in these accounts is zero.

Because these accounts are used to keep track of revenues, expenses, and dividends declared during the period, their beginning balances must be zero so that the data of the last period are not combined with those of the current period. At the end of the period, the balance in each of the temporary accounts will be used to help prepare the income statement, but then must be transferred into the permanent retained earnings account to produce the final ending balance in the retained earnings account. In this way, the retained earnings account keeps track of the cumulative amounts of revenues and expenses less dividends, and the temporary accounts keep track of only amounts for the current year. In other words, using our warehouse example, the contents of the revenue, expense, and dividends declared boxes are all dumped into the retained earnings box. A revenue box with a credit balance will add to the retained earnings box, which also has a credit balance. An expense or dividends declared box with a debit balance will reduce the contents of the retained earnings box.

Note further that while revenues, expenses, and dividends declared are all shareholders' equity accounts, increases and decreases correspond to different entries. For revenues, credits represent increases and debits represent decreases. For expenses and dividends declared, the opposite is true: debits represent increases and credits represent decreases. Therefore, by the end of a given accounting period (prior to the transfer of the balances to the retained earnings account), revenues have credit balances, expenses have debit balances, and dividends declared has a debit balance. The debit balances in the expense and dividends declared accounts are probably best understood if we remember that they both represent decreases in shareholders' equity. Because shareholders' equity is represented by a credit balance, the decreases in shareholders' equity must be represented by debit balances. Further, because these are temporary accounts and their balances will be transferred to retained earnings, the debit balances will not persist in the permanent accounts. They will be offset by the credit balance revenue accounts. It is possible to have a debit balance in the retained earnings account if expenses have exceeded revenues (i.e., the company has suffered losses). If you look at the balance sheet of Queenstake Resources Ltd. in Exhibit 3-5, you will see that its retained earnings in 1998 and 1997 is a deficit (a debit balance). Most companies do not have a deficit position in their retained earnings. However, it is not unusual for a mining company like Queenstake Resources to have a deficit. Mining companies need to use a substantial amount of resources to find and develop resources. It often takes them several years before they begin to reap the benefit of all their efforts.

Accounting Cycle

Learning Objective

3

Identify the steps in the accounting cycle.

We are now ready to look at the whole system in which transactions are measured, recorded, and communicated. This system is called the **accounting cycle**. Envision for a moment a company that has just been formed and whose managers need to establish an accounting system. What is the first thing they need to decide? One of the first decisions they must make is the information they will need to run the business. What information is important for them in making decisions? What information do outside users need to know about the company? Accounting systems are information systems, so managers should decide at the start what information they

EXHIBIT 3-5

QUEENSTAKE RESOURCES LTD.
CONSOLIDATED BALANCE SHEETS
(in Canadian Dollars)

December 31

	1998	1997
ASSETS		
Current assets		
Cash and cash equivalents	$ 8,152,242	$12,061,060
Accounts receivable	409,388	233,702
Due from joint venture partner	–	348,038
	8,561,630	12,642,800
Mineral properties and equipment (Note 2)	10,234,911	14,442,461
	$18,796,541	$27,085,261
LIABILITIES		
Current liabilities		
Accounts payable and accrued liabilities	$ 466,944	$ 586,823
Non-controlling interest	702,161	467,873
SHAREHOLDERS' EQUITY		
Stated capital (Note 3 (a))		
Authorized: 100,000,000 common shares without par value		
Issued: 39,054,491 shares (1997 – 38,210,879 shares)	46,157,761	45,855,316
Contributed surplus (Note 3 (c))	171,100	–
Share purchase warrants (Note 3 (c))	–	171,100
Deficit	(28,701,425)	(19,995,851)
	17,627,436	26,030,565
	$18,796,541	$27,085,261

Commitments (Note 2)
Contingency (Note 9)

Approved by the Board of Directors

/s/ James Mancuso   /s/ Christopher Serin

J. Mancuso   C. Serin

Director   Director

(See accompanying notes to the Consolidated Financial Statements)

want and need to operate the business. Even for companies in the same industry, each one will develop its own unique information system. As we proceed through a discussion of the accounting cycle, we are going to demonstrate each stage using the transactions from Chapter 2 of Demo Retail Company, Ltd.

Chart of Accounts

The types of accounting information to be recorded in the accounting system are usually summarized in a **chart of accounts**. Exhibit 3-6 lists the chart of accounts for Demo Retail Company, Ltd. The chart of accounts should be viewed as dynamic and not something that can never be changed. As the business changes, there may be a need for a different type of account. For example, suppose that the company originally was unwilling to provide credit to its customers. There would be no need for an accounts receivable account, because the company was strictly a cash business. Later, if the company decided to allow customers to buy on credit, it would need to add an accounts receivable account to the chart of accounts. A key point to note is that the design of the chart of accounts can impart additional information or be a handicap, depending upon how carefully it is conceived.

EXHIBIT 3-6

■ **Demo Retail Company, Ltd.**

Chart of Accounts

Permanent Accounts
    Assets
        Cash
        Accounts Receivable (A/R)
        Inventory (Inv.)
        Prepaid Insurance
        Land
        Equipment
    Liabilities
        Accounts Payable (A/P)
        Interest Payable
        Bank Loan
    Shareholders' Equity
        Common Shares
        Retained Earnings (RE)
Temporary Accounts
    Income Statement Accounts
        Sales Revenues
        Cost of Goods Sold
        Insurance Expense
        Interest Expense
        Amortization Expense
    Dividends Declared

In an actual system, each account in the chart of accounts would be identified by a number to facilitate the ordering of the accounts and the recording of transactions within a computerized system. In this book, accounts will be designated by their names and not by account numbers. An account can be given any name that makes sense and is descriptive of its purpose. Commonly used terms for each type of account will be discussed throughout the book. Several of these names, such as accounts receivable, inventory, accounts payable, and retained earnings, have already been mentioned. Going back to our warehouse example, putting a name on an account is like putting a label on one of the boxes. In order to find a box (or an account) so that you can put something into it or take something out, you need to know what is written on the label.

The chart of accounts is the starting point for the accounting cycle of the company. The complete cycle is illustrated in Exhibit 3-7. Each of the steps in the cycle is discussed in the following subsections.

■ Accounting Cycle

EXHIBIT 3-7

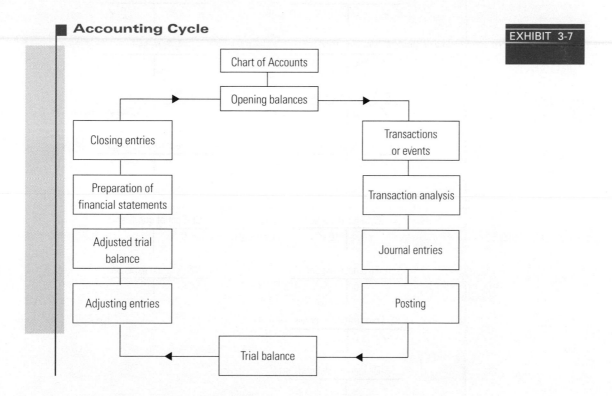

Opening Balances   After the chart of accounts has been established and the company commences business, the accountant needs to record in the accounting system the results of the various transactions that affect the company. The system could be as simple as a notebook with sheets of paper representing the accounts and entries made by hand, or it could be as sophisticated as an on-line computer system in which entries are made via a computer terminal. For the purposes of this book, a manual system will be used, but the same entries apply to any accounting system, no matter how simple or how sophisticated.

In the first year of a company's operations, the first step in the cycle would be to initialize the accounts by entering zero balances in all the accounts. In subsequent accounting periods, the beginning balances will be the balances carried forward from the end of the last accounting cycle. Demo's opening balances at the beginning of 20x1 are shown in Exhibit 3-8.

EXHIBIT 3-8

■ **Demo Retail Company**

T-Accounts: Beginning Balances

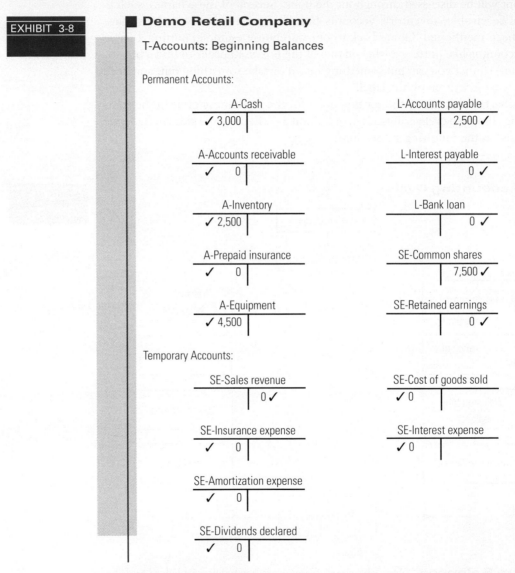

Permanent Accounts:

A-Cash	L-Accounts payable
✓ 3,000	2,500 ✓

A-Accounts receivable	L-Interest payable
✓ 0	0 ✓

A-Inventory	L-Bank loan
✓ 2,500	0 ✓

A-Prepaid insurance	SE-Common shares
✓ 0	7,500 ✓

A-Equipment	SE-Retained earnings
✓ 4,500	0 ✓

Temporary Accounts:

SE-Sales revenue	SE-Cost of goods sold
0 ✓	✓ 0

SE-Insurance expense	SE-Interest expense
✓ 0	✓ 0

SE-Amortization expense
✓ 0

SE-Dividends declared
✓ 0

Note that the temporary accounts for revenues, expenses, and dividends declared have been segregated from the permanent accounts and have zero balances.

TRANSACTIONS OR EVENTS   The next step in the cycle is to recognize that some event or transaction has occurred that affects the assets, liabilities, and/or shareholders' equity of the company. The transaction or event is usually evidenced by some sort of signal such as a source document—a piece of documentation received or created by the company. Examples of source documents would be invoices, cheques, cash register tapes, bank deposit slips, or purchase order forms. For companies, the first transaction to be signalled would be the receipt of cash from the shareholders and the issuance of common shares. This first transaction provides the first inflow of cash, which can then be used to buy the assets necessary to operate the business.

TRANSACTION ANALYSIS   After a signal has been received that a transaction or event has occurred, the accountant must analyze the transaction or event to decide what accounts have been affected and by how much. This phase of the process is called **transaction analysis**. We engaged in this activity in Chapter 2 when we analyzed the effect of various transactions on the basic accounting equation. For routine transactions, such as the purchase and sale of goods, the transaction needs to be analyzed only once. Each subsequent sale or purchase transaction is the same and can be entered into the accounting system without further analysis. Unique and unusual transactions require further transaction analysis, and generally require the services of a professional accountant who understands the use of appropriate (GAAP) accounting methods. For routine transactions, an accountant is probably not needed; an accounting clerk can record the transactions in the accounting system.

JOURNAL ENTRIES   After the accountant has decided how to account for the transaction, an entry must be made to the system. The initial entry is usually made in what is known as the **journal**. The journal is a chronological listing of all the events that are recorded in the accounting system. The entry made to the journal is called a **journal entry**. The journal could be as simple as a piece of paper on which is recorded a chronological list of the transactions that have occurred. The transactions are dated and assigned a transaction number. The journal entry then consists of the date, the transaction number, the accounts affected (and their account numbers), and a listing of the appropriate debits and credits. Exhibit 3-9 demonstrates what a journal entry might look like for the first two transactions for Demo Retail Company, Ltd., in January. For simplicity, assume that all transactions in January took place on January 31. By convention, in a journal entry the debit entries are listed first and credit entries second. Credit entries are also indented from the debit entries. Note that each complete journal entry maintains the balance in the system—that is, debits equal credits. A proper journal entry must always maintain this balance. An explanation of the transaction is included with each transaction so that the circumstances of the transaction are available for future reference.

Learning Objective

Analyze transactions and record them in journal format.

EXHIBIT 3-9

■ Demo Retail Company, Ltd.

Journal Entries

Transaction	Date 20x1	Account name	Debit	Credit
1	Jan. 31	A-Accounts receivable	2,500	
		SE-Sales revenue		2,500
		Sold inventory on account		
2	Jan. 31	SE-Cost of goods sold	1,800	
		A-Inventory		1,800
		Recorded cost of inventory sold		

Note that in Transaction 1 there is a debit to accounts receivable. Accounts receivable is an asset account and a debit to it will increase it. Sales revenue is a shareholders' equity account. Because shareholders' equity accounts normally have a credit balance, a credit to this account will increase it. The increase in these two accounts is appropriate, because Demo has a new asset (customers owe it $2,500) and shareholders' wealth has increased by the sale price of the goods sold. Use the second transaction and see if you can follow the same kind of logic to explain why a debit to cost of goods sold and a credit to inventory are appropriate.

Learning Objective

5

Post transactions to T-accounts and prepare a trial balance.

POSTING TO THE LEDGER Once the journal entries are recorded, the information needed to run the business would be recorded in the accounting system (in the journal) but the information would not be very accessible. If, for example, the manager wanted to know the balance in the cash account, the accountant would have to take the beginning balance in cash and add or subtract all the journal entries that affected cash. If a company has recorded hundreds of journal entries, this could take a long time. To make the individual account information more accessible in a logical and deliberate way, the accountant then proceeds to the next step in the accounting cycle. In this step, the journal entries are **posted to the ledger**.

The **ledger** is a system (in a simple case, a set of notebook pages) in which each account is listed separately (on a separate page). In our warehouse analogy, each account would have its own box. In a computerized system, each account would be represented by a separate computer file accessible by the account number. **Posting** is the process of transferring the information from the journal entry to the ledger account. Each page of the ledger represents a specific T-account. The ledger account would include the name (and number) of the account, its beginning balance, and a listing of all the postings that affected the account during the period. Each listing would include the transaction number, the date, and the appropriate debit or credit. The transaction number would allow a user to go backward in the system to determine the source of an amount in an individual account. Note that if the journal entries are posted properly the balance in the ledger system is preserved. Exhibit 3-10 shows four ledger accounts and the posting of the first two January transactions for Demo Retail Company, Ltd.

■ **Posting to the Ledger**

EXHIBIT 3-10

Demo Retail Company, Ltd.

Ledger

A-Accounts receivable		SE-Sales revenue	
Balance 0			Balance 0
Jan. 31 1 2,500			2,500 1 Jan. 31

A-Inventory		SE-Cost of goods sold	
Balance 2,500		Balance 0	
	1,800 2 Jan. 31	Jan. 31 2 1,800	

The posting to the ledger can take place on a monthly basis, a weekly basis, a daily basis, or with any frequency desired. The timing of the postings is determined to some extent by the management's (or the shareholders') need for up-to-date information. If managers need to know the balance in a particular account—say, inventory—on a daily basis, then the postings should be done at least daily. If management needs to know the amount of inventory on an hourly basis, then the posting has to be done more frequently. Many computer systems account for transactions in what is called "real time," which means that accounts are updated instantaneously. Once the data person has completed the journal entry, the system automatically posts the information to the designated accounts. Other computer systems collect journal entries in "batches" and post them all at one time. In general, managers like to have information sooner rather than later, and, as the cost of computer technology continues to decrease, there has been a proliferation of real-time systems in the corporate world.

At this point it is important to note that a system consisting only of journal entries would make it difficult to determine the balance in any one account. A system of only ledger accounts, without the original journal entries, would make it difficult to understand the sources of amounts in individual accounts. We need both journal entries and ledger accounts in order to collect information in a way that makes it readily accessible and as complete as possible.

TRIAL BALANCE While most errors should be detected at the journal entry and posting phases of the accounting cycle, some errors may persist. Most computerized systems will not post a journal entry unless the debits equal the credits. This type of system catches many errors at the input stage. In a manual system, errors may not be detected at the journal entry stage. If the debits equal the credits at the journal entry stage, it is possible for the amounts to be posted incorrectly to the accounts. One way of detecting errors is to produce a **trial balance**. The trial balance is a listing of all debit and credit balance accounts in the general ledger. To use our warehouse example, we would look into each box and make a list of what we find. A check can then be made to ensure that the total of the debit balances equals the total of the credit balances. If these are not equal, a mistake has been made at some point during the process and must be corrected. The trial balance assists in detecting balance errors, but it does not, in general, allow detection of errors in which the wrong account was debited or credited. Errors such as these can be detected by examining the accounts and their balances for reasonableness. However, if one minor entry was made to a wrong account, it may not be detected in this phase. In a computerized system, a trial balance can be generated by the system at any time. Exhibit 3-11 illustrates the appearance of a trial balance using the data from Demo Retail Company, Ltd.

EXHIBIT 3-11

Account	Debit	Credit
DEMO RETAIL COMPANY		
Trial Balance		
Cash	$ 1,890	
Accounts receivable	300	
Inventory	2,800	
Prepaid insurance	300	
Land	15,000	
Equipment	4,350	
Accounts payable		$ 1,900
Interest payable		50
Bank loan		10,000
Common shares		12,500
Retained earnings		0
Dividends declared	250	
Sales revenues		2,500
Cost of goods sold	1,800	
Amortization expense	150	
Insurance expense	60	
Interest expense	50	
Totals	$26,950	$26,950

Note that this trial balance was prepared before the revenue, expense, and dividends declared accounts were put into retained earnings. Retained earnings still has a zero balance. More importantly, the revenue, expense, and dividends declared accounts still have amounts in them. Note as well the order in which the accounts are listed on the trial balance. They are in the order in which they will appear on the balance sheet and income statement. Accounts will be kept in the ledger in this order to facilitate preparation of the financial statements. If account numbers are assigned to the accounts, as they will be in a computerized system, account numbers will be assigned to a section of the financial statement—say, the current assets section of the balance sheet—and all of the accounts given those numbers will be current assets. When the computerized system prepares a balance sheet it will list the current assets in the current assets section of the balance sheet, in numerical order according to the account numbers they were assigned.

Learning Objective

6

Understand the necessity of adjusting entries and determine how they should be recorded.

ADJUSTING ENTRIES   If an error is detected in the trial balance phase, it must be corrected. A journal entry to correct an error is one type of **adjusting entry** that is made at the end of the accounting period. A second type of adjusting entry is made for transactions or events that were not recognized and recorded during the period. Examples of this type of event are the amortization of the capital assets, the recognition of interest that is owed on loans, and the recognition that wages are owed to some employees. Accountants in most businesses have a set of this second type of adjusting entry that they typically make at the end of every period. Care must be taken to ensure that all events and transactions have been accounted for. The adjusting entry phase of the accounting cycle is used to ensure that the appropriate revenues and expenses have been recorded and reported for the period. Adjusting entries are journalized and posted in the same way that other accounting entries are. In our Demo example, the transactions that would be adjusting entries are the use of insurance in January, the amortization of the equipment, and the recording of the interest owed on the bank loan.

Under GAAP, care is taken by companies to measure their revenues so that all the revenues earned in a period are recorded and reported in that period. The expenses incurred to generate that revenue are recorded and reported (matched) as well. The final adjustments to the revenues and expenses are achieved through the adjusting entries. Although profit-oriented companies adhere to these requirements of GAAP, governments are sometimes not quite as careful, as the following report illustrates:

accounting in the news

ACCRUAL BASED ACCOUNTING

Should the federal government be held to GAAP? In recent years Finance Minister Paul Martin has come under increasing criticism for accounting for major spending programs even before they are approved. This contradicts the principle of accrual based accounting, which calls for recording transactions in the financial periods in which events occur.

One example is the $2.5-billion Millennium Scholarship Fund, which Martin booked for the 1997–98 fiscal year—before legislation for the Fund had been passed. Auditor General Denis Desautels criticized Martin's accounting, saying that when Martin announced the government would have a balanced budget in the fall of 1998, he should have projected a $2.5-billion surplus. Reform Party critics also accused Martin of playing politics: The fund actually starts handing out money to students in the year 2000, just when a federal election is likely to be held.

In his defence, Martin has said this way of accounting for one-time spending programs is more transparent, allowing Canadians to feel the impact of the spending when the programs are created instead of waiting until years later.

What do you think?

Source: "Martin assailed over budget," by Shawn McCarthy, *Globe and Mail*, April 29, 1998, p. B1.

ethics in accounting

■ Many adjusting entries require estimates and judgements by management. These estimates and judgements provide an opportunity to manipulate both balance sheet values and income. Suppose that you, as a staff accountant, are asked to postpone the write-off of some old plant and equipment that is currently idle. It is clear to you that the idled equipment will never be used again. The write-off would need to be recognized as a loss (like an expense on the income statement, it reduces net income) and would, therefore, have a significant negative impact on the income statement. Management has asked you to postpone the write-off because the company has applied for a large loan from the bank and the loss from the write-off could significantly affect the reported performance of the company. What should you do? As you consider your response to this ethical question, it might be helpful to think about who will be affected by your decision (including yourself)—how they will be helped or hurt by it. In particular, think of who might be the users/potential users of the financial statements. This should help you structure your understanding of the situation. Try to justify your decision in the context of these effects.

ADJUSTED TRIAL BALANCE   After all the adjusting entries have been recorded and posted, an **adjusted trial balance** is prepared. This will ensure that debits still equal credits and that any imbalance is corrected before the financial statements are prepared.

FINANCIAL STATEMENT PREPARATION   After the adjusted trial balance has been prepared and any corrections have been made, the financial statements for the period can be prepared. Note that, at this point, the temporary accounts still have balances in them and the retained earnings account has the same balance as it did at the beginning of the period. No entries have been made directly to the retained earnings account. The income statement can, therefore, be prepared from the information in the temporary accounts. Note also that the dividends declared account is not a part of the income statement. Dividends are not an expense of doing business; they are a return to shareholders of part of their accumulated wealth in the company.

The balance sheet can be prepared from the balances in the permanent accounts—with the one exception of retained earnings, which does not, at this point, include the effects of revenues, expenses, and dividends. In a simple case, the cash flow statement could be prepared from the information in the ledger account for cash. For a more complex case, the preparation of the cash flow statement is discussed in greater detail in Chapter 5. Refer back to Chapter 2 to see the income statement and balance sheet for Demo Retail Company, Ltd.

CLOSING ENTRIES   After the income statement is prepared, the balances in the temporary accounts must be transferred to the retained earnings account (a permanent account). This will reset the balance in each temporary account to zero to start the next accounting cycle. The entries that achieve this are called **closing entries**. Closing entries will be distinguished from other entries in the examples in this book by the use of lettering (ABCs) rather than numbering. Sometimes companies use a single temporary account to accumulate all the income statement accounts. This account is usually called an **income summary account**. The balances from all the individual revenue and expense accounts are closed to this summary account. The balance in the income summary account is then closed to retained earnings. This will be demonstrated for Demo Retail Company, Ltd., in the next few pages. Again, because the dividends declared account is not an income statement account, it would be closed directly to retained earnings and would not affect the income summary account. In a computerized system, the accounting program would perform the closing process automatically when instructed to do so. You would make sure that you have finished all of the adjusting entries and have asked the system to prepare the financial statements before instructing the program to close the books for the year, because most computerized systems will not let you go back.

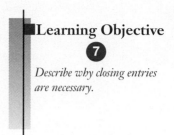

Learning Objective

7

Describe why closing entries are necessary.

ACCOUNTING CYCLE FREQUENCY   One final issue with regard to the accounting cycle is: How often should the cycle be completed? That is, how often should financial statements be prepared? Another way to put it is: How long should an accounting period be? The answer is that financial statements should be prepared as often as necessary to provide timely information to management and shareholders. Since this preparation is not without cost, especially in a manual system, a balance must be struck between the benefits of having up-to-date information and the cost of preparing the statements. In some businesses, the need for up-to-date information is great, in which case daily reports may be necessary. In other businesses, a monthly statement is probably sufficient. Regardless of what time period is selected, the procedures just described are appropriate.

Companies whose shares are traded on a public stock exchange must file financial statements quarterly as well as annually. The frequency with which financial statements are prepared is sometimes expressed in terms of how often a company **closes its books**. If it closes its books monthly, the accounting cycle for the company is one month long, and the temporary accounts are reset on a monthly basis. Adjusting entries, such as those for amortization, interest, and wages, are then made once a month. In a computerized system, the accounts are not reset monthly. Instead, the system produces an income statement just for the month. The system can isolate all of the transactions that were recorded for the month and then prepare an income statement recording only the appropriate transactions. The ease and frequency with which financial statements can be prepared in a computerized system helps to reduce the preparation costs significantly.

Demo Retail Company, Ltd. — The Accounting Cycle

Return now to Demo Retail Company, Ltd. We are going to demonstrate the various stages of the accounting cycle by using the same transactions for January that we used in Chapter 2. The beginning balances in the accounts (the balances that carried over from the end of December 20x0) were displayed in Exhibit 3-8.

We now want to show you the rest of the transactions for Demo. The transactions from January 20x1 are listed here for your convenience. They are described in detail in Chapter 2.

1. Demo sold units of inventory to customers, on account, for $2,500. The units had been in inventory. (Already journalized in Exhibit 3-9.)
2. The cost of the units removed from inventory for the sales in January totalled $1,800. (Already journalized in Exhibit 3-9.)
3. Purchases of new inventory to replace the units sold in January totalled $2,100. All of these purchases were made on account.
4. During the month, Demo received $2,200 from customers as payments on their accounts.
5. Demo made payments of $2,700 on its accounts payable.
6. Demo paid $360 in cash on January 1 for an insurance policy to cover its inventory from January 1, 20x1, through June 30, 20x1.
7. On the first day of January, Demo purchased land for $15,000 as a site for a future retail outlet. In order to pay for the land, Demo raised money by borrowing $10,000 from the bank and issuing new shares for $5,000.
8. Dividends in the amount of $250 were declared and paid in January.
9. Demo's accountant determined that the equipment should be amortized $150 for January.
10. The interest rate charged on the loan from the bank in Transaction 7 is 6%.
11. One month of insurance was used up in January.

Note that the transactions have been organized differently from the way they were described in Chapter 2. Instead of recording the purchase of the insurance and the insurance expense for January as part of the same transaction, we have listed the insurance expense part as a separate transaction—Transaction 11. We have also moved the amortization of the equipment and the interest transaction to Transactions 9 and 10. These three entries are the *adjusting entries* and will be recorded and posted separately in the adjusting entry phase of the accounting cycle.

Exhibit 3-12 shows the first eight transactions for Demo in January in journal entry form.

Demo Retail Company, Ltd.

EXHIBIT 3-12

Journal Entries for Transactions in January 20x1

1.	A-Accounts receivable	2,500	
	SE-Sales revenue		2,500
	Sold inventory on account		
2.	SE-Cost of goods sold	1,800	
	A-Inventory		1,800
	Recorded cost of inventory sold		
3.	A-Inventory	2,100	
	L-Accounts payable		2,100
	Bought inventory on account		
4.	A-Cash	2,200	
	A-Accounts receivable		2,200
	Collected on accounts receivable		
5.	L-Accounts payable	2,700	
	A-Cash		2,700
	Paid amounts owed on accounts payable		
6.	A-Prepaid insurance	360	
	A-Cash		360
	Purchased a six-month insurance policy		
7a.	A-Cash	5,000	
	SE-Common shares		5,000
	Issued common shares		
7b.	A-Cash	10,000	
	L-Bank loan		10,000
	Borrowed from the bank		
7c.	A-Land	15,000	
	A-Cash		15,000
	Purchased land		
8.	SE-Dividends declared	250	
	A-Cash		250
	Declared and paid dividends		

In Exhibit 3-13, all these journal entries have been posted to the ledger T-accounts. Notice how the transactions have been numbered so that it is easy to determine which entries are associated with one another. The title of Exhibit 3-13 indicates that the accounts are in the trial balance phase, which means that the adjusting entries have not been recorded and posted and the temporary accounts have not been closed to retained earnings. The term given to calculating the balance in an account is **footing the account.**

EXHIBIT 3-13

■ **Demo Retail Company, Ltd.**

T-accounts after Posting

A-Cash			
✓	3,000		
(4)	2,200	2,700	(5)
(7a)	5,000	360	(6a)
(7b)	10,000	15,000	(7c)
		250	(8)
✓	1,890		

A-Accounts receivable			
✓	0		
(1)	2,500	2,200	(4)
✓	300		

A-Inventory			
✓	2,500		
(3)	2,100	1,800	(2)
✓	2,800		

A-Prepaid insurance		
✓	0	
(6)	360	
✓	360	

A-Land		
✓	0	
(7c)	15,000	
✓	15,000	

A-Equipment		
✓	4,500	
✓	4,500	

L-Accounts payable			
		2,500	✓
(5)	2,700	2,100	(3)
		1,900	✓

L-Interest payable		
	0	✓

L-Bank loan		
	0	✓
	10,000	(7b)
	10,000	✓

SE-Common shares		
	7,500	✓
	5,000	(7a)
	12,500	✓

SE-Retained earnings		
	0	✓

Temporary Accounts:

EXHIBIT 3-13
CONT.

SE-Sales revenue		
	0	✓
	2,500	(1)
	2,500	✓

	SE-Cost of goods sold	
✓	0	
(2)	1,800	
✓	1,800	

SE-Insurance expense	
✓	0

SE-Interest expense	
✓	0

SE-Amortization expense	
✓	0

SE-Dividends declared	
✓	0
(8)	250
✓	250

After the month's transactions have been posted, a trial balance would be prepared to ensure that debits equal credits. Exhibit 3-14 shows the trial balance before the adjusting entries:

EXHIBIT 3-14

Demo Retail Company, Ltd.

Trial Balance

Account	Debit	Credit
Cash	$ 1,890	
Accounts receivable	300	
Inventory	2,800	
Prepaid insurance	360	
Land	15,000	
Equipment	4,500	
Accounts payable		$ 1,900
Bank loan		10,000
Common shares		12,500
Retained earnings		0
Dividends declared	250	
Sales revenues		2,500
Cost of goods sold	1,800	
Totals	$26,900	$26,900

Note that, except for retained earnings, the accounts that have zero balances have not been listed on the trial balance.

The accountant would then move to the next stage of the accounting cycle and record the adjusting entries. For Demo, those entries are for the amortization of the equipment, the recording of interest for January, and the recording of the use of insurance for one month. Exhibit 3-15 shows the adjusting entries for January.

EXHIBIT 3-15

■ **Demo Retail Company, Ltd.**

Adjusting Entries

9.	SE-Amortization expense	150	
	XA-Accumulated amortization		150
	Recorded the amortization of the equipment for January		
10.	SE-Interest expense	50	
	L-Interest payable		50
	Recorded the interest owed on the bank loan for January		
11.	SE-Insurance expense	60	
	A-Prepaid insurance		60
	Recorded the use of insurance for January		

Note that in Transaction 9 a new account, accumulated amortization, has been introduced. Its account type, XA, is also different. In the detailed explanation of this transaction in Chapter 2, we told you that rather than reduce a capital asset directly as it is used up, we collect the used part in an account called **accumulated amortization**. This is a **contra asset account**, which is why we have labelled it XA. A contra asset account normally has a balance opposite to an asset account. Therefore, it normally has a *credit* balance. Over the life of the equipment, this account will grow by the amortization each year. A contra asset account is shown on the balance sheet contra to the asset account to which it is associated. On the balance sheet you would see:

Equipment	$4,500	
Less: Accumulated amortization	<u>150</u>	$4,350

From now on, we will always use an accumulated amortization account when we are amortizing capital assets.

Exhibit 3-16 shows the accounts after the adjusting entries have been posted. Note that the posted adjusting entries are in bold type.

EXHIBIT 3-16

■ **Demo Retail Company, Ltd.**

T-accounts After Posting of Adjusting Entries

A-Cash			
✓	3,000		
(4)	2,200	2,700	(5)
(7a)	5,000	360	(6a)
(7b)	10,000	15,000	(7c)
		250	(8)
✓	1,890		

L-Accounts payable			
		2,500	✓
(5)	2,700	2,100	(3)
		1,900	✓

A-Accounts receivable			
✓	0		
(1)	2,500	2,200	(4)
✓	300		

L-Interest payable			
		0	✓
		50	**(10)**
		50	✓

A-Inventory			
✓	2,500		
(3)	2,100	1,800	(2)
✓	2,800		

L-Bank loan			
		0	✓
		10,000	(7b)
		10,000	✓

A-Prepaid insurance			
✓	0		
(6)	360	**60**	**(11)**
✓	300		

SE-Common shares			
		7,500	✓
		5,000	(7a)
		12,500	✓

A-Land			
✓	0		
(7c)	15,000		
✓	15,000		

SE-Retained earnings		
	0	✓

A-Equipment		
✓	4,500	
✓	4,500	

XA-Accumulated amortization			
		0	✓
		150	**(9)**
		150	✓

Temporary Accounts:

SE-Sales revenue			
		0	✓
		2,500	(1)
		2,500	✓

SE-Cost of goods sold			
✓	0		
(2)	1,800		
✓	1,800		

SE-Insurance expense		
✓	0	
(11)	**60**	
✓	60	

SE-Interest expense		
✓	0	
(10)	**50**	
✓	50	

EXHIBIT 3-16
CONT.

SE-Amortization expense

✓	0	
(9)	**150**	
✓	150	

SE-Dividends declared

✓	0	
(8)	250	
✓	250	

Exhibit 3-17 shows the Adjusted Trial Balance after the adjusting entries have been posted.

EXHIBIT 3-17

Demo Retail Company

Adjusted Trial Balance

Account	Debit	Credit
Cash	$ 1,890	
Accounts receivable	300	
Inventory	2,800	
Prepaid insurance	300	
Land	15,000	
Equipment	4,500	
Accumulated amortization		$ 150
Accounts payable		1,900
Interest payable		50
Bank loan		10,000
Common shares		12,500
Retained earnings		0
Dividends declared	250	
Sales revenues		2,500
Cost of goods sold	1,800	
Amortization expense	150	
Insurance expense	60	
Interest expense	50	
Totals	$27,100	$27,100

Note that the balance of accumulated amortization, the contra asset account, is listed in the credit column.

At this stage in the accounting cycle, the financial statements would be prepared. The income statement, balance sheet, and cash flow statement for Demo Retail Company, Ltd., for this accounting period were shown in Chapter 2. Because of the introduction of the new account, accumulated amortization, the balance sheet would be slightly different. See the explanation on page 150 about how the change affects the statement. The preparation of the income statement and balance sheet can be made directly from the balances in Exhibit 3-17. The cash flow statement can be prepared using the transactions identified in the cash account in Exhibit 3-16. Exhibit 3-18 shows one additional statement that many companies prepare, a statement of retained earnings. Note that dividends are shown on this statement.

Demo Retail Company, Ltd.

EXHIBIT 3-18

Statement of Retained Earnings
For the month ended January 31, 20x1

Retained earnings, January 1, 20x1		$ 0
Add: Net income		440
		440
Deduct: Dividends declared		250
Retained earnings, January 31, 20x1		$190

The format and order of presentation of the line items on the income statement and balance sheet are addressed in more detail in the remainder of this chapter. The format of the cash flow statement is discussed in more detail in Chapter 5.

The temporary accounts now need to be closed. Exhibit 3-19 shows the closing entries to transfer the balances from the temporary accounts to the permanent account, retained earnings, as well as the temporary accounts and the retained earnings account from Exhibit 3-16. Note that these entries have been lettered (using ABCs) to distinguish them from the regular entries of the period. Also, an income summary account has been used to collect all the revenue and expense balances before closing the net amount ($440) to the retained earnings account. The dividends declared account has been closed directly to retained earnings.

Demo Retail Company, Ltd.

EXHIBIT 3-19

Closing Journal Entries at January 31, 20x1

A.	SE-Sales revenue	2,500	
	SE-Income summary		2,500
B.	SE-Income summary	1,800	
	SE-Cost of goods sold		1,800
C.	SE-Income summary	60	
	SE-Insurance expense		60
D.	SE-Income summary	150	
	SE-Amortization expense		150
E.	SE-Income summary	50	
	SE-Interest expense		50

EXHIBIT 3-19
CONT.

F.	SE-Income summary	440	
	SE-Retained earnings		440
G.	SE-Retained earnings	250	
	SE-Dividends declared		250

Temporary Accounts:

SE-Sales revenue

		0	✓
		2,500	(1)
		2,500	
(A)	2,500		
		0	✓

SE-Cost of goods sold

✓	0		
(2)	1,800		
	1,800		
		1,800	(B)
✓	0		

SE-Insurance expense

✓	0		
(11)	60		
	60		
		60	(C)
✓	0		

SE-Interest expense

✓	0		
(10)	50		
	50		
		50	(E)
✓	0		

SE-Amortization expense

✓	0		
(9)	150		
	150		
		150	(D)
✓	0		

SE-Income summary

		0	✓
		2,500	(A)
(B)	1,800		
(C)	60		
(D)	150		
(E)	50		
(F)	440	440	
		0	✓

SE-Dividends declared

✓	0		
(8)	250		
		250	(G)
✓	0		

SE-Retained earnings

		0	✓
(G)	250	440	(F)
		190	✓

Note that in Exhibit 3-19 each of the revenue and expense accounts has been closed individually. Remember that you must name the account in the journal entry so that you can post the amount to the right account and reduce the account balance to zero. We used four separate journal entries to close all of the expense accounts. We could have used one.

B.	SE-Income summary	2,060	
	SE-Cost of goods sold		1,800
	SE-Insurance expense		60
	SE-Amortization expense		150
	SE-Interest expense		50

This journal entry demonstrates that journal entries can have more than two accounts identified. Even though there are four credits to four different accounts, debits still equal credits.

Note as well that when we closed the revenue account we debited the account. Revenues normally have credit balances, so, to empty the account, we must debit it for the total amount in the account. The expense accounts normally have debit balances, which means that in order to close them we must credit them for their account balances. Once these amounts are posted, each revenue and expense account is back to a zero balance and is ready for the next accounting period.

At this stage, the company would normally prepare a post-closing trial balance. This trial balance would include only the permanent accounts, because all of the temporary accounts now have zero balances. This is the final check on the system to ensure that debits equal credits before transactions for the next period are entered into the system.

Now that you have a better idea of the source of the numbers on the financial statements, we are going to have a more detailed look at the income statement and balance sheet. Up to this point we have kept the preparation of the two statements as simple as possible. Now that you know more about how the numbers are collected, you are ready to expand your knowledge of the statements.

INCOME STATEMENT FORMAT

One of the fundamental objectives of financial reporting is to ensure that the financial statements provide information that is useful to the user. To be useful, information should help current and potential investors, creditors, and other users assess the amount, timing, and certainty of prospective net cash flows to the enterprise.

As you learned in Chapter 1, the purpose of the income statement is to provide information about the performance of the company. The basic format of the income statement summarizes all revenues and expenses to show the net income. The information provided is primarily historical. The revenues are the historical amounts received or receivable from the sale of goods and services, and the expenses are based on the amounts actually paid or payable in the future for the goods and services used to produce the revenues. Some of the expenses may represent very old costs, such as the amortization of very old assets such as buildings.

For the income statement to provide information about future cash flows of the company, the connection between the amounts presented in the income statement and those future cash flows must be understood. Accrual basis accounting requires that revenues and expenses be recorded at amounts that are ultimately expected to be received or paid in cash. For example, to estimate the actual amount of cash that will be collected from sales, the company estimates the amount of sales that will not be collected (bad debts) and deducts that amount from sales. On the expense side, estimates are made for some expenses where amounts are not yet paid, such as interest or tax expenses. In both cases, the figures reflect management's estimates about future cash flows. In this sense, the income statement provides information to the reader about management's assessment of the ultimate cash flows from the business of the period. This means that the income statement, on an accrual basis, provides more information about future cash flows than an income statement prepared on a cash basis, which reflects only cash flows that have already occurred.

A second aspect of providing information about future cash flows is the forecasting ability of the income statement. If the trends in revenues and expenses over several time periods are examined, the revenues and expenses that will occur in the future may be predicted, assuming of course that earning trends in the past continue into the future. An understanding of the relationship of revenues and expenses to future cash flows will allow a reasonable prediction of the amount of cash flows that will result in future periods.

The ability to predict future revenues and expenses depends on the type of item considered, the industry, and the company's history. The sales revenue and cost of goods sold figures are reasonably predictable if the business is in a fairly stable product line. New businesses and new products make this type of forecasting more difficult. Other types of items are not as predictable. Sales of plant and equipment, for example, tend to be more sporadic than the normal sales of goods or services. Some items may occur only once, never to be repeated. The closing of a plant or the sale of a business unit is an event that has income-statement implications in the current period but may not be repeated in the future.

To enable readers of the income statement to make the best estimates of future results, the continuing items should be separated from the noncontinuing items. For this reason, the format of the income statement is designed to highlight these differences.

The result of all this is that the normal income-statement format is designed to provide information about continuing and noncontinuing operations. Exhibit 3-20 provides an overview of the major sections of a typical income statement. Each of these is discussed in the following subsections.

Income Statement Format

Sample Company, Ltd.
Income Statement
For the year ended December 31, 20xx

Income from continuing operations:	
Operating revenues (i.e., sales or service revenue)	$XXX
Operating expenses (i.e., cost of goods sold, selling expenses, and administrative expenses)	(XXX)
Income from continuing operations	XXX
Income from nonoperating sources:	
Financing revenue (i.e., interest revenue)	XXX
Financing expenses (i.e., interest expense)	(XXX)
Gain (loss) on sale of capital assets or investments	XXX
Other	XXX
Income from nonoperating sources	XXX

Income before unusual or infrequent sources	XXX
Income from unusual or infrequent sources	XXX
Income before income tax	XXX
Provision for income tax	(XXX)
Income before discontinued operations and extraordinary items	XXX
Income from discontinued operations (net of tax)	XXX
Income from extraordinary items (net of tax)	XXX
Net income	$XXX

EXHIBIT 3-20
CONT.

Income from Continuing Operations

This section provides information about the revenues and expenses resulting from the sales of goods and services to customers. The operations reported are those that are expected to continue in the future. A separate section later in the income statement contains the results of those operations that management has decided to discontinue.

Income statements can be either single-step or multistep. In Exhibit 3-21, the income statement of Mosaid Technologies Incorporated is an example of a **single-step income statement**. In this type of statement, all the revenues are listed together and all the expenses (except for unusual items and income tax expense) are listed together. Thus Mosaid shows revenues from operations of $40,672,000 plus interest revenue of $707,000, for total revenues of $41,379,000 for the year ended May 1, 1998. The five different expenses total $36,716,000, producing income before the unusual item and taxes of $4,663,000.

On the other hand, in Exhibit 3-22, the income statement of Mitel Company is a **multistep income statement**. In this type of statement, the results of different kinds of operations are segregated. In the top sections of the statement, the results of the main business of the company are reported, resulting in the net line item called "operating income" of $124.4 million. Below that, other continuing operations are reported, such as investment and interest income and interest expense. Note that the figure of $124.4 million is a subtotal of all the amounts above it, which represent the main business activities of Mitel: selling products and providing services. The next items, investment and interest income of $5.7 million and interest expense of $7.7 million, represent financing income, which is considered separate from operating income. Other items that could be included after operating income would be gains (losses) on the sale of capital assets or investments, income from equity investments, and/or unusual items.

Another distinguishing feature of multistep income statements is that the statement often starts with sales less cost of sales, to arrive at a **gross profit** or **gross margin** amount. If a company's major source of revenue is selling goods, it must make enough profit or margin to cover all of the other costs of the business. By examining the gross margin, users can assess the profitability of the company. You can calculate a gross margin percentage, which is the gross margin divided by the sales. You can use this percentage to evaluate a company over time (has this percentage been increasing, decreasing, or remaining stable?) and to compare it to other companies in the same industry. If a company creates a multistep income statement and shows users the gross margin, the statement will be easier to assess.

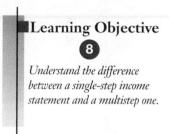

Learning Objective

8

Understand the difference between a single-step income statement and a multistep one.

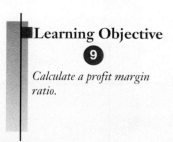

Learning Objective

9

Calculate a profit margin ratio.

EXHIBIT 3-21

MOSAID Technologies Incorporated   financial statements 1998

MOSAID Technologies Incorporated
Consolidated Statement of Earnings and Retained Earnings

(in thousands, except per share amounts)

	Year ended	
	May 1, 1998	May 2, 1997
Revenues		
Operations	$ 40,672	$ 38,853
Interest	707	946
	41,379	39,799
Expenses		
Labour and materials	9,434	9,051
Research and development (Note 8)	13,956	10,009
Selling and marketing	7,157	6,276
General and administration	5,627	5,270
Bad debt	542	–
Unusual item (Note 9)	–	500
	36,716	31,106
Earnings from operations	4,663	8,693
Gain on sale of assets	3,897	670
	8,560	9,363
Income tax (Note 10)	3,012	3,381
Non-controlling interest	337	2,234
Net earnings	5,211	3,748
Retained earnings, beginning of year	20,610	16,862
Retained earnings, end of year	$ 25,821	$ 20,610
Earnings per share (Note 14)		
Basic	$ 0.73	$ 0.53
Fully diluted	$ 0.67	$ 0.49
Weighted average number of shares		
Basic	7,143,500	7,071,576
Fully diluted	8,024,505	7,781,487

See accompanying Notes to the Consolidated Financial Statements.

EXHIBIT 3-22

Pg. 40

Mitel Corporation
Consolidated statements of income and retained earnings

(in millions of Canadian dollars, except per share amounts)	March 27, 1998	March 28, 1997	Years ended March 29, 1996
Revenue:			
Products	$ 806.5	$ 625.0	$ 504.8
Service	82.0	70.5	71.6
	888.5	695.5	576.4
Cost of sales (excluding amortization):			
Products	385.9	297.4	246.7
Service	51.4	47.0	45.6
	437.3	344.4	292.3
Gross margin	451.2	351.1	284.1
Expenses:			
Selling and administrative	231.8	208.4	172.2
Research and development *(Note 14)*	84.5	56.5	42.7
Investment tax credits related to prior years' research and development *(Note 14)*	(40.3)	(11.7)	(7.7)
Restructuring and other charges *(Note 15)*	–	13.0	–
Amortization	50.8	33.5	19.2
	326.8	299.7	226.4
Operating income	124.4	51.4	57.7
Investment and interest income *(Note 16)*	5.7	9.6	10.0
Interest expense *(Note 9)*	(7.7)	(2.4)	(1.7)
Income before income taxes	122.4	58.6	66.0
Income tax expense *(Note 17)*	30.5	20.6	15.0
Net income	91.9	38.0	51.0
Retained earnings, beginning of year	114.2	79.4	31.7
	206.1	117.4	82.7
Dividends on preferred shares	3.2	3.2	3.3
Retained earnings, end of year	$ 202.9	$ 114.2	$ 79.4
Net income attributable to common shareholders after preferred share dividends	$ 88.7	$ 34.8	$ 47.7
Net income per common share *(Note 18)*:			
Basic	$ 0.82	$ 0.32	$ 0.45
Fully diluted	$ 0.80	$ 0.32	$ 0.44

(See accompanying notes to the consolidated financial statements)

Mitel Company (Exhibit 3-22) sells products and provides services. On its income statements it isolates the revenues from the two operations, then discloses the cost of the products and services, and then calculates the gross margin. Because Mitel provides information covering three years, you could determine the stability of its operations by calculating the gross margin percentage for each year for products and services (for products: 1998—52.2%, 1996—52.4%, 1996—51.1%; for services: 1998—37.3%, 1997—33.3%, 1996—36.3%). Both aspects of its operations appear to be relatively stable over time even though the company is growing. Sometimes when a company is growing, it loses some of its control over costs. This does not seem to be the case with Mitel.

Usually when a company discloses the sales minus cost of goods sold section, it will include the other operating expenses that it incurred to generate the revenue. Mitel lists five expenses before it arrives at operating income.

Additional information regarding the performance and profitability of various operating units and operations in different geographical areas can generally be found in the notes to the financial statements under a section called "Segmented Information," if the company has different lines of business that are easily separated or operations in several geographical areas. Additional information may be necessary if the company is very diverse or if it has global operations.

Income from Nonoperating Sources

This section of the income statement reports the results of transactions that do not involve the normal sale of goods and services. Items typically found here are interest income and expense; gain or loss on the sale of capital assets like property, plant, and equipment; restructuring expenses; and other, mainly one-time, events or transactions. Examples can be seen in the Consolidated Statements of Income and Retained Earnings of Mitel Company presented in Exhibit 3-22. The two items in the section following "operating income" are nonoperating items. They include investment and interest income of $5.7 million and interest expense of $7.7 million. Note that although we have indicated that restructuring expenses would normally be included in this section, Mitel has included them as an operating expense. The GAAP guidelines do not strictly specify what should be included in each section of a multistep income statement, which means that Mitel can choose to put the restructuring expenses with the operating expenses.

Income from Unusual or Infrequent Events

Learning Objective

10

Describe the criteria for unusual items, discontinued operations, and extraordinary items.

Sometimes the company chooses to segregate unusual or infrequent events from the rest of the results so the reader of the income statement can understand the nature of the event and make an assessment of its continuing or noncontinuing status. These types of items are reported either with the other nonoperating events or in a section by themselves.

An example of an unusual and infrequent item can be found in Exhibit 3-21, the Consolidated Statement of Earnings and Retained Earnings of Mosaid

Technologies Incorporated. The unusual item is explained in Note 9, which states that "the amount represents redundant lease costs and reparation expenses associated with the Company's planned move to new facilities." These costs are unusual because they are associated with the company's move to new facilities, an event that does not occur very often.

Corporate Income Taxes

At the end of the income statement sections that have been discussed so far, there has been a line item for the corporate income **tax expense** computed on the net of all the items listed above. An example can be seen in the income statement of Mosaid Technologies Incorporated shown in Exhibit 3-21, with the income tax expense of $3,012,000. Sometimes the term *provision for income taxes* is used instead of income tax expense. Taxes are computed on the basis of aggregate net income and are not listed separately for each operating and nonoperating item. The tax expense listed on a company's income statement may not be the actual taxes that are owed to Revenue Canada. The rules used to compute the taxes owed to the government are included in the Canadian *Income Tax Act*. Many of these rules parallel the accounting guidelines, but there are some that are not the same. The income tax disclosure of Tritech Precision Inc. in Exhibit 3-23 shows income tax as "current" and "**deferred**." This means that the total income tax expense calculated on the accounting income is $9,063,000; $5,866,000 of this will be paid to the government this year (based on the rules in the Canadian *Income Tax Act*) and $3,197,000 will likely be paid in taxes in future years, as some of the revenues and expenses that were recognized under accounting become taxable in the future. More will be said about these dual calculations in future chapters.

Two additional items may appear after the computation of tax expenses: *discontinued operations* and *extraordinary items* (although extraordinary items are very rarely found). These items appear below the operating and nonoperating items (they are sometimes called "below-the-line" items) because of their unusual or unique nature. Because they appear after the computation of taxes, the tax effect of these transactions must be reported along with the item itself. The company must pay taxes on these items just as it does on the operating and nonoperating items, so they are reported on what is known as a *net of tax basis*. This means that the tax effects of the item have been netted against the before-tax numbers to produce a net, after-tax number. If, for example, discontinued operations result in a loss of $1,000 before taxes and save $400 in taxes (due to the deductibility of the loss), the net of tax amount would be a $600 loss ($1,000—$400). The tax effects of these below-the-line items are not included in the line item called tax expense.

Discontinued Operations

Discontinued operations are significant segments of the company that management has decided to discontinue. There are criteria for deciding what constitutes a discontinued operation. Once management has decided to discontinue a line of

EXHIBIT 3-23

CONSOLIDATED STATEMENTS OF INCOME
Years ended December 31
000's [except per share amounts]

	1998	1997
Sales	**$ 328,565**	$ 201,312
Cost of goods sold	**254,441**	154,327
Gross profit	**74,124**	46,985
Expenses		
Selling and administration	**26,741**	14,179
Depreciation and amortization	**17,880**	10,831
	44,621	25,010
Income from operations	**29,503**	21,975
Equity in income of Haley Industries Limited	**—**	(1,295)
Interest on long-term debt	**3,652**	1,311
Other interest expense (income)	**393**	(286)
	4,045	(270)
Income before income taxes and minority interest	**25,458**	22,245
Provision for income taxes		
Current	**5,866**	6,048
Deferred	**3,197**	1,364
	9,063	7,412
Income before minority interest	**16,395**	14,833
Minority interest	**1,940**	707
Net income for the year	**$ 14,455**	$ 14,126
Earnings Per Share		
Basic	**$1.71**	$1.77
Fully diluted	**$1.67**	$1.70
Weighted average number of shares outstanding		
Basic	**8,443**	7,971
Fully diluted	**8,717**	8,361

The accompanying notes are an integral component of the consolidated financial statements.

business, there are two types of results that must be reported in the income statement. During the period of time it takes to dispose of the business segment, which may be quite long, the segment may continue to operate. The income from operating these discontinued operations must be reported separately from other income. In prior years, income from these segments was included with regular operations. It is therefore important to show users the income effect of discontinuing this segment. In addition, if the segment is being sold, either in whole or in part, there will be a gain or loss on the disposal of the segment. This gain or loss must also be reported separately from the results of the operations up to the time of disposal. The disclosure of both types of results is illustrated in Exhibit 3-24 for United Dominion Industries Limited. In 1997, the company discontinued a segment of its operations. Note the details of the income from discontinued operations of $3,088,000 in 1997, including the applicable taxes of $2,211,000. The disposal in 1997 resulted in a gain of $50,000,000, which was after a tax deduction of $39,097,000. United Dominion Industries discontinued operations in 1996 as well. You might want to examine the income statement for the details for the prior year.

Extraordinary Items

Although **extraordinary items** are rarely found in income statements, they are interesting. To be classified as extraordinary, items must be unusual, infrequent, and not resulting from management decisions. A recent example was a company that lost money when the armoured car carrying the company's cash was robbed and no insurance could be claimed on the loss because of improper procedures being used. Extraordinary items sometimes arise as a result of natural causes such as earthquakes or floods. Because management may have an incentive to place all of its "bad news" events in this category, the above criteria were developed to restrict what should be included as extraordinary. For example, we noted that losses due to floods might be considered extraordinary. If you had business operations in Saskatoon, Saskatchewan, and the Saskatchewan River overflowed its banks, any losses you incurred would likely be extraordinary because the Saskatchewan River rarely floods in Saskatoon and management could not have prevented or caused the flood. If, however, your business operations were in the Red River Valley south of Winnipeg, Manitoba, damage from a flood might not be considered extraordinary. It is beyond management's control but the Red River often floods, causing extensive damage.

Extraordinary items are shown separately because they are beyond the control of the company and are not expected to recur. It is important to segregate them because they have a material effect on the net income and users need to know that the income will likely not be affected by this item again in the near future. They should, therefore, put more weight on the income before the extraordinary item than they put on the net income after the extraordinary item. The income statement of BCE Inc. in Exhibit 3-25 gives you an example of an extraordinary item in 1997. Note that the extraordinary item resulted in a loss of $2,950 million, which caused a net loss for the year of $1,536 million. The loss was a result of accounting changes associated with BCE's subsidiary and associated companies. Because of the nature of their operations, they were subject to regulatory accounting policies. Changes in

EXHIBIT 3-24

CONSOLIDATED STATEMENTS OF INCOME

UNITED DOMINION INDUSTRIES
Years Ended December 31
(U.S. $ Thousands, Except Per Share Data)

	1998	1997	1996
Sales	$2,020,374	$1,654,679	$1,433,068
Costs and expenses			
Cost of sales	1,401,802	1,168,654	1,009,315
Selling, general and administrative expenses	446,714	341,453	294,564
Restructuring charges (notes 2 and 11)	16,336	–	–
Total costs and expenses	1,864,852	1,510,107	1,303,879
Operating income	155,522	144,572	129,189
Other income (expense)			
Interest – net (note 8)	(35,750)	(18,544)	(19,124)
Gain on sale of business (note 2)	11,285	–	11,792
Other (note 2)	(8,500)	7,700	(3,000)
Income from continuing operations before income taxes	122,557	133,728	118,857
Income tax provision (note 3)	(22,869)	(48,838)	(45,405)
Income from continuing operations	99,688	84,890	73,452
Income from discontinued operations (note 2)			
Earnings, net of applicable income tax expense of $2,211 in 1997 and $7,331 in 1996	–	3,088	21,468
Gain on disposal, net of applicable income tax expense of $39,097	–	50,000	–
	–	53,088	21,468
Net income	$ 99,688	$ 137,978	$ 94,920
Earnings per common share (note 1)			
Continuing operations	$ 2.45	$ 1.91	$ 1.65
Discontinued operations	–	1.19	.48
Net earnings	$ 2.45	$ 3.10	$ 2.13

See accompanying notes to consolidated financial statements.

consolidated financial statements BCE Inc

CONSOLIDATED STATEMENT OF OPERATIONS

For the years ended December 31	Notes	($ millions, except per share amounts) 1998	1997
Revenues	(3)	27,454	34,517
Operating expenses		21,734	26,989
Research and development expense		2,232	2,911
Purchased in-process research and development expense		688	–
Restructuring and other charges	(5)	654	132
Operating profit		2,146	4,485
Gain on reduction of ownership in subsidiary and associated companies	(6)	4,146	257
Other income	(7)	994	108
Operating earnings		7,286	4,850
Interest expense – long-term debt		1,022	1,111
– other debt		259	121
Total interest expense		1,281	1,232
Earnings before income taxes, non-controlling interest and extraordinary item		6,005	3,618
Income taxes	(8)	(1,548)	(1,522)
Non-controlling interest		141	(682)
Net earnings before extraordinary item		4,598	1,414
Extraordinary item	(2)	–	(2,950)
Net earnings (loss)		4,598	(1,536)
Dividends on preferred shares		(93)	(74)
Net earnings (loss) applicable to common shares		4,505	(1,610)
Earnings (loss) per common share			
Net earnings before extraordinary item		7.07	2.11
Extraordinary item		–	(4.64)
Net earnings (loss)		7.07	(2.53)
Dividends per common share		1.36	1.36
Average number of common shares outstanding (millions)		637.6	636.0

CONSOLIDATED STATEMENT OF RETAINED EARNINGS

For the years ended December 31	Notes	($ millions) 1998	1997
Balance at beginning of year		596	3,173
Net earnings (loss)		4,598	(1,536)
		5,194	1,637
Deduct:			
Dividends			
Preferred shares		93	74
Common shares		868	865
		961	939
Purchase of common shares for cancellation	(17)	24	93
Costs related to issuance and redemption of share capital of BCE Inc. and of subsidiaries		2	9
		987	1,041
Balance at end of year		4,207	596

the communication industry in 1997 meant that these companies had to switch from the regulatory accounting practices to GAAP. The switch required that BCE adjust the net carrying values of various assets and liabilities, which resulted in the loss that was classified as extraordinary; because the change in regulatory requirements was beyond the control of management, BCE classified this loss as extraordinary. Users assessing BCE's future profitability should use the net earnings before the extraordinary item of $1,414 million rather than the net loss for the year of $1,536 million. If you compare the $1,414 million to the figure for the following year (1998), you can see that BCE has improved its operations over the year.

Earnings Per Share

In addition to net income, earnings per share is shown, either in the income statement or in a note to the financial statements. **Earnings per share** relates the net income to the common shares outstanding. In many cases, this is a simple calculation that consists of dividing the net income of the company by the average number of common shares outstanding during the year. A weighted average is used if the number of common shares outstanding changed during the year. Note the disclosure of earnings per share in Exhibits 3-21 and 3-22 for Mosaid and Mitel. For Mosaid, the basic earnings per share is $0.73 in 1998. For Mitel, the basic earnings per share figure is $0.82. There are other earnings per share figures that are also disclosed by both these companies—fully diluted earnings per share. Note that the fully diluted earnings per share is lower than the basic earnings per share. The inclusion of a fully diluted earnings per share figure is a signal to users that the company has some financial instruments (i.e., convertible debt or shares) or some obligations like stock options to its employees that could result in more common shares being issued. Remember that earnings per share is calculated by dividing the income by the number of shares outstanding. If more shares are issued, it is possible that the return to current shareholders will decline. The fully diluted earnings per share tells current shareholders the maximum amount the return will decline if all of the new shares are issued. This is discussed in more detail in Chapter 12.

Examples of additional earnings per share figures can be found in Exhibits 3-24 and 3-25. United Dominion Industries discontinued some operations in 1997 and 1996. It disclosed an earnings per share from continuing operations, one from discontinued operations and one for net earnings. The disclosure of the three earnings per share figures enables users to better assess the impact of the decision to discontinue the operations. BCE had the extraordinary item and disclosed an earnings per share amount before the extraordinary item, for the extraordinary item and for the net loss. Again, disclosing all of these figures provides users with more complete information to use in assessing the effect of the extraordinary item on the company. When companies have either discontinued operations or extraordinary items, they must show users the earnings per share before and after the event.

Reports from Other Countries

NAFTA Facts:

The criteria used in other countries to identify extraordinary items are different from those used in Canada. In the United States, for example, transactions or events that are both unusual and infrequent are classified as extraordinary. Note that they do not have the third condition of non-management influence. This means that you are more likely to see an extraordinary item on an income statement from the United States than on one from Canada. Mexico's criteria for classifying an item as extraordinary are the same as those of the United States. The transactions must be both unusual and infrequent. When evaluating an income statement from any of these three countries, you would need to know by which criteria an extraordinary item was classified.

BALANCE SHEET FORMAT

The format of the balance sheet is less varied than that of the income statement. There are separate sections for assets, liabilities, and shareholders' equity. The most commonly used format presents assets on the left-hand side of the page and liabilities and shareholders' equity on the right-hand side. Alternatively, assets may be at the top of the page and liabilities and shareholders' equity at the bottom.

Within both current asset and liability sections, the individual items are generally listed in the order of their **liquidity**. In the case of assets, liquidity refers to the ability to convert the asset into cash. For liabilities, liquidity refers to how quickly the liability will require the use of cash. Current assets and liabilities are generally listed from most liquid to least liquid.

Within the noncurrent asset section, the assets are listed in order of permanency. The asset that will last the longest is listed first. Within the capital asset group, the assets will be listed as land, buildings, and then equipment, because of the time over which they will be useful to the company.

In the noncurrent liability section, accountants do not follow a fixed guideline. The noncurrent liabilities are listed in the order the company thinks is most informative. If you look at Big Rock's balance sheet (BR-13) in the Appendix A at the end of the book, you will see that long-term debt is listed before deferred income taxes.

Some companies choose not to follow the balance sheet format described above. For example, Rogers Communications Inc. in its 1998 balance sheet starts not with current assets but with fixed assets and goodwill, subscribers and licences. Accounts receivable is somewhere in the middle. This format is more commonly seen in Europe. The liabilities also start with noncurrent items and then move to current ones. In Europe, the liability and shareholders' equity sections would be reversed. This part of the balance sheet often starts with shareholders' equity and then moves to liabilities.

Learning Objective

Understand the criteria for listing items on a balance sheet.

Consolidated Balance Sheets

in millions of DM		Consolidated		Financial Services	
Assets	Note	*December 31, 1997*	December 31, 1996	*December 31, 1997*	December 31, 1996
Intangible assets	7	*1,915*	1,951	*100*	80
Property, plant and equipment, net	7	*20,656*	18,225	*76*	57
Investments and long-term financial assets	13	*3,453*	3,536	*205*	60
Equipment on operating leases, net	8	*14,931*	11,941	*15,055*	12,748
Fixed assets		*40,955*	35,653	*15,436*	12,945
Inventories	9	*14,390*	13,602	*988*	645
Trade receivables	10	*12,006*	10,864	*373*	382
Receivables from financial services	11	*25,924*	19,052	*25,953*	19,073
Other receivables	12	*12,251[1]*	8,959	*897*	826
Securities	13	*14,687*	9,783	*91*	92
Cash and cash equivalents	14	*5,833*	4,557	*684*	269
Current assets		*85,091*	66,817	*28,986*	21,287
Deferred taxes	6	*10,462*	9,603	*27*	162
Prepaid expenses		*591*	388	*81*	65
Total assets		*137,099*	112,461	*44,530*	34,459
Liabilities and stockholders' equity					
Capital stock		*2,584*	2,577		
Additional paid-in capital		*5,247*	5,080		
Retained earnings		*26,508[1]*	19,033		
Other equity		*746*	(297)		
Stockholders' equity	16	*35,085*	26,393	*2,642*	2,094
Minority interest		*1,170*	936	*55*	52
Accrued liabilities	17	*36,618*	34,886	*576*	523
Financial liabilities	18	*39,302*	28,850	*38,383*	29,171
Trade liabilities	19	*11,079*	9,027	*176*	132
Other liabilities	20	*10,116*	8,792	*901*	800
Liabilities		*60,497*	46,669	*39,460*	30,103
Deferred taxes	6	*2,003*	2,253	*1,345*	1,244
Deferred income		*1,726*	1,324	*452*	443
Total liabilities and stockholders' equity		*137,099*	112,461	*44,530*	34,459

1) Includes a tax receivable/tax benefit of approximately DM 2.9 billion relating to the special distribution of DM 20 per share.

The accompanying notes are an integral part of these Consolidated Financial Statements.

What we have discussed here are conventions in format. The case of Rogers Communications Inc. shows you that not all companies in Canada follow the conventions. Which format do you think is more understandable? Which format would you find easier to use? Why?

The balance sheet of Daimler-Benz, a German transportation-products manufacturer, shown in Exhibit 3-26, illustrates a European balance sheet. Note that assets start with intangible assets and end with cash and cash equivalents. This is exactly opposite to what you would normally see in Canada. As well, two assets, deferred taxes and prepaid expenses, are separated from the other assets and shown at the end. Liabilities and shareholders' equity starts with common stock and ends with current liabilities like trade liabilities and other liabilities. Again, this is almost exactly opposite to what you would see in Canada. Two items, deferred taxes and deferred income, are segregated at the end of the liabilities.

S U M M A R Y

This chapter added to your understanding of the procedures for collecting, recording and summarizing financial information. You learned about journal entries, debits and credits, ledger accounts, posting, trial balances, adjusting entries, and closing entries. This structure, whether in a manual system or a computerized system, is the same. In a computerized system, the computer takes over more of the mechanical tasks like posting, closing, and preparing trial balances and financial statements. People like you are still required to formulate and input the actual journal entries.

After the in-depth discussion of the accounting cycle, we built on your previous understanding of the income statement and balance sheet. We showed you some of the complexities of the income statement, like operating income, nonoperating income, unusual items, income taxes, discontinued operations, and extraordinary items. As we move through the text, you will have some of these items explained more fully. For now, an awareness of what these items are is sufficient. With the balance sheet, we elaborated on its format, covering the conventional way of preparing the statement and then showing you some other formats used in Canada and elsewhere. By now you should be starting to become familiar with accounting language and procedures. Remember, as you work through the problems at the end of this chapter, that the more effort you put in here, the easier the course will become later.

SUMMARY PROBLEM

1. Use the data from the Sample Retail Company, Ltd., from the summary problem in Chapter 2 and record the effects of the transactions in journal entries, number the entries made, post them to T-accounts, and close the temporary income accounts first to an income summary account and then to retained earnings.

2. The balance sheet of the Template Company Ltd. as at December 31, 20x1, is given in Exhibit 3-27, and the transactions for Template in 20x2 are summarized.

Required:

a. Prepare T-accounts for the Template Company Ltd., and enter the opening balances from the December 31, 20x1, balance sheet. Prepare journal entries for the transactions for 20x2. Open new accounts as you need them. Post the journal entries to the T-accounts. Identify the transactions that represent adjusting entries.

b. Prepare classified balance sheets (beginning and end of the year) and a single-step income statement for the Template Company Ltd. for 20x2.

c. Prepare journal entries for the closing entries and post them to the T-accounts. Use an income summary account.

Transactions for 20x2:

1. Sales for the year totalled $760,000, all of which were on account.

2. A review of accounts receivable at the end of the year showed a balance of $35,000.

3. Amortization of $19,600 was incurred, of which 80% was due to the building and equipment and the remainder to office furniture.

4. Purchases of new equipment totalled $40,700, all paid in cash.

5. Rent is paid for leased equipment. Payments are made quarterly, in advance, on March 31, June 30, September 30, and December 31. Two payments of $15,000 each were made through the end of June. Rent increased to $16,500 per quarter starting with the September 30 payment.

6. Employees earned wages of $150,000 during the year. As at December 31, 20x2, $11,000 was owed to employees.

7. Purchases of inventory, all on account, amounted to $431,000 (assume that this is the only item that affects accounts payable).

8. The company owed inventory suppliers $36,000 as at December 31, 20x2.

9. A count of ending inventories revealed $57,000 in ending inventory.

10. The note payable carries a 9% interest rate, and interest is due annually on December 31. On June 30, 20x2, the company paid off $6,000 of the principal, plus accrued interest. The rest of the principal is not due until June 30, 20x3.

11. Long-term debt at December 31, 20x1, carried an interest rate of 10%, with interest payments due semi-annually on June 30 and December 31. On January 1, 20x2, the company paid off $25,000 of the principal of this long-term debt. On September 30, 20x2, the company issued $27,000 of additional long-term debt at an interest rate of 12% with interest payment terms identical to the existing borrowings.

12. Other selling and administrative expenses of $45,000 were paid in cash.

13. The company's net income is taxed at 30% and, as at December 31, 20x2, $7,442 was owed to Revenue Canada.

14. The company declared $5,000 in dividends each quarter during 20x2; dividends were payable on April 14, 20x2, July 15, 20x2, October 15, 20x2, and January 15, 20x3.

EXHIBIT 3-27

TEMPLATE COMPANY LTD.
Balance Sheet
December 31, 20x1

Assets
Current Assets
Cash		$ 55,000
Accounts receivable		39,500
Inventory		43,000
Prepaid rent		15,000
Total current assets		152,500

Capital Assets
Plant and equipment	$350,000	
Less: Accumulated amortization	100,000	
	250,000	
Office furniture	76,000	
Less: Accumulated amortization	16,000	
	60,000	310,000
Total assets		$462,500

Liabilities
Current Liabilities
Accounts payable		$ 33,000
Wages payable		9,000
Taxes payable		16,000
Total current liabilities		58,000

Noncurrent Liabilities
Notes payable		8,000
Long-term debt		75,000
Total noncurrent liabilities		83,000
Total liabilities		141,000

Shareholders' Equity
Common shares	$185,000	
Retained earnings	136,500	
Total shareholders' equity		321,500
Total liabilities and shareholders' equity		$462,500

SUGGESTED SOLUTION TO SUMMARY PROBLEM

1.   Exhibit 3-28 shows the solution to the Sample Retail Company, Ltd., problem.

2. a. The journal entries are shown in Exhibit 3-29. The T-accounts for Template Company Ltd. are shown in Exhibit 3-30. The December 31, 20x1, balances are shown in bold. The posted transactions from 20x2 are numbered. Additional explanations for various transactions are given below:

Transaction 2. The information given is the ending balance in the account. Cash collections are calculated based on the beginning and ending balances in the account and the debit for sales on account as follows:

■ **Sample Retail Company, Ltd.**
Journal Entries

1.	A-Accounts receivable	80,000	
	SE-Revenue		80,000
	Sold inventory on account		
2.	A-Cash	79,750	
	A-Accounts receivable		79,750
	Collected accounts receivable		
3a.	SE-Salary expense	20,500	
	L-Accrued salaries payable		20,500
	Salaries owed to employees		
3b.	L-Accrued salaries payable	20,375	
	A-Cash		20,375
	Paid salaries		
4.	A-Inventory	39,700	
	L-Accounts payable		39,700
	Purchased inventory on account		
5.	L-Accounts payable	37,300	
	A-Cash		37,300
	Paid accounts payable		
6.	SE-Cost of goods sold	37,500	
	A-Inventory		37,500
	Recorded inventory sold		
7a.	A-Prepaid rent	15,600	
	A-Cash		15,600
	Paid monthly rent		
7b.	SE-Rent expense	15,500	
	A-Prepaid rent		15,500
	Recorded monthly rent used		
8a.	SE-Interest expense	72	
	A-Cash		72
	Paid interest owed on loan		
8b.	L-Bank loan	200	
	A-Cash		200
	Paid part of principal on loan		

9. SE-Amortization expense   2,000
      XA-Accumulated amortization   2,000
    Amortization of equipment

EXHIBIT 3-28
CONT.

10. A-Equipment   4,500
      A-Cash   4,500
    Bought new equipment

11a. SE-Tax expense   1,771
      L-Tax payable   1,771
    Income tax owed

11b. L-Tax payable   1,689
      A-Cash   1,689
    Paid income tax

12. SE-Dividends declared   210
      A-Cash   210
    Declared and paid dividends

T-Accounts

A-Cash

✓	**4,500**		
2	79,750	20,375	3
		37,300	5
		15,600	7a
		72	8a
		200	8b
		4,500	10
		1,689	11b
		210	12
✓	4,304		

A-Accounts Receivable

✓	**500**		
1	80,000	79,750	2
✓	750		

A-Inventory

✓	**7,500**		
4	39,700	37,500	6
✓	9,700		

L-Accounts Payable

		5,400	✓
5	37,300	39,700	4
		7,800	✓

L-Accrued Salaries

		400	✓
3b	20,375	20,500	3a
		525	✓

L-Tax Payable

		360	✓
11b	1,689	1,771	11a
		442	✓

L-Bank Loan

		800	✓
8b	200		
		600	✓

EXHIBIT 3-28
CONT.

A-Prepaid Rent

✓	**1,200**		
7a	15,600	15,500	7b
✓	1,300		

A-Equipment

✓	**9,200**	
10	4,500	
✓	13,700	

SE-Common Shares

		3,600	✓
		3,600	✓

XA-Accumulated Amort. – Equip.

		0	✓
		2,000	9
		2,000	✓

SE-Retained Earnings

		12,340	✓
D	210	2,657	C
		14,787	✓

SE-Dividends Declared

✓	**0**		
12	210	210	D
✓	0		

SE-Revenue

		0	✓
		80,000	1
A	80,000		
		0	✓

SE-Cost of Goods Sold

✓	**0**		
6	37,500		
		37,500	B
✓	0		

SE-Salaries Expense

✓	**0**		
3a	20,500		
		20,500	B
✓	0		

SE-Amortization Expense

✓	**0**		
9	2,000		
		2,000	B
✓	0		

SE-Rent Expense

✓	**0**		
7b	15,500		
		15,500	B
✓	0		

SE-Interest Expense

✓	**0**		
8a	72		
		72	B
✓	0		

EXHIBIT 3-28
CONT.

SE-Income Tax Expense

✓	**0**		
11a	1,771		
		1,771	B
✓	0		

SE-Income Summary

		0	✓
B	77,343	80,000	A
		2,657	
C	2,657		
		0	✓

Closing Entries (already posted)

A.	SE-Revenue		80,000	
	SE-Income summary			80,000
B.	SE-Income summary		77,343	
	SE-Cost of goods sold			37,500
	SE-Salary expense			20,500
	SE-Rent expense			15,500
	SE-Amortization expense			2,000
	SE-Interest expense			72
	SE-Tax expense			1,771
C.	SE-Income summary		2,657	
	SE-Retained earnings			2,657
D.	SE-Retained earnings		210	
	SE-Dividends declared			210

Beginning balance	$ 39,500
Sales	760,000
Total	799,500
Less: Ending balance	35,000
Payments received	$764,500

Transaction 3. The amortization for the period is split between the accounts for plant and equipment and office furniture. Both of these could use the same amortization expense account, but accumulated amortization must be recorded in the appropriate contra asset account.

Transaction 5. The beginning balance in the prepaid rent account on December 31, 20x1, of $15,000 represents the payment made on December 31, 20x1, that covers rent for the first quarter of 20x2. The first two payments in 20x2 of $30,000 (2 × $15,000) cover quarters 2 and 3. The third payment of $16,500 on September 30, 20x2, covers the fourth quarter. Therefore, the rent expense during 20x2 (entry 5b) should be the sum of these amounts, or $61,500 [(3 x $15,000) + $16,500]. The last payment of $16,500 on December 31, 20x2, applies to the first quarter of 20x3 and should be the ending balance in the prepaid rent account (entry 5b). The cash payments during the period total $63,000 [(2 × $15,000) + (2 × $16,500)].

Transaction 6. The amount of wages earned by employees ($150,000) and the ending balance in the wages payable account ($11,000), given in the problem, allow the calculation of the amount paid for wages during 20x2 as follows:

Beginning balance	$ 9,000
Wages earned	150,000
Total	159,000
Less: Ending balance	11,000
Wages payments	$148,000

Transaction 9. The beginning and ending balances in inventory and amount of inventory purchased are used to determine cost of goods sold as follows:

Beginning inventory	$ 43,000
Purchases	431,000
Total	474,000
Less: Ending inventory	57,000
Cost of goods sold	$417,000

Transaction 10. The interest is paid for six months on the initial balance of $8,000. For the last six months of the year the interest is calculated on the new balance in the account, $2,000. It can be calculated according to the following schedule:

$8,000 × 9% × 6/12 =	$360
$2,000 × 9% × 6/12 =	90
Interest expense	$450

Transaction 11. The interest incurred during the year on the initial long-term debt is calculated on the new balance of $50,000 after the principal was reduced by $25,000 on January 1, 20x2. The interest on the new debt that was taken out on September 30, 20x2, is calculated only on the last three months of the year. The interest is calculated as follows:

$$\$50,000 \times 10\% \times 12/12 = \qquad \$5,000$$
$$\$27,000 \times 12\% \times 3/12 = \qquad \underline{810}$$
Interest expense $\qquad \underline{\$5,810}$

Transaction 13. Taxes are computed on the income before taxes, which is $60,640 in 20x2 (see the income statement in Exhibit 3-31). The tax expense is $18,192 (30% × $60,640). The ending balance in the taxes payable account is then used to calculate how much Template paid in taxes in 20x2, as follows:

Beginning balance	$16,000
Tax expense	18,192
Total	34,192
Less: Ending balance	7,442
Tax payments	$26,750

Transaction 14. Because the last dividend declared in 20x2 is still payable as of December 31, 20x2, a new account, dividends payable, must be created. The first three dividends are paid in cash.

b. The income statement and balance sheet for Template Company Ltd. are shown in Exhibit 3-31.

c. The closing entries for the temporary accounts in Exhibit 3-30 are shown in Exhibit 3-32. Only the balances in the temporary accounts are shown in Exhibit 3-32, along with the closing entries. See Exhibit 3-30 for the entries made during the year to arrive at these balances.

■ **Template Company Ltd.**

EXHIBIT 3-29

Journal Entries for 20x2

1.	A-Accounts receivable	760,000	
	SE-Sales revenue		760,000
	Sold inventory on account		
2.	A-Cash	764,500	
	A-Accounts receivable		764,500
	Recorded receipt of accounts receivable		
3.	SE-Amortization expense	19,600	
	XA-Accumulated amortization—plant and equipment		15,680
	XA-Accumulated amortization—office equipment		3,920
	Amortization of capital assets		
4.	A-Plant and equipment	40,700	
	A-Cash		40,700
	Purchased new equipment		

EXHIBIT 3-29

CONT.

5a.	A-Prepaid rent	63,000	
	A-Cash		63,000
	Paid rent in quarterly instalments		
5b.	SE-Rent expense	61,500	
	A-Prepaid rent		61,500
	Recorded rent for the year		
6.	SE-Wages expense	150,000	
	L-Wages payable	9,000	
	A-Cash		148,000
	L-Wages payable		11,000
	Recorded wages owed to employees		
7.	A-Inventory	431,000	
	L-Accounts payable		431,000
	Bought inventory on account		
8.	L-Accounts payable	428,000	
	A-Cash		428,000
	Paid suppliers		
9.	SE-Cost of goods sold	417,000	
	A-Inventory		417,000
	Recorded cost of inventory sold		
10a.	L-Notes payable	6,000	
	SE-Interest expense	360	
	A-Cash		6,360
	Paid on principal of notes payable plus accrued interest		
10b.	SE-Interest expense	90	
	A-Cash		90
	Recorded interest paid on notes payable		
11a.	L-Long-term debt	25,000	
	A-Cash		25,000
	Paid on principal of long-term debt		
11b.	A-Cash	27,000	
	L-Long-term debt		27,000
	Borrowed additional funds		
11c.	SE-Interest expense	5,810	
	A-Cash		5,810
	Recorded interest paid on the long-term debt		

12.	SE-Selling and administrative expenses	45,000	
	A-Cash		45,000
	Paid selling and administrative expenses during the year		

EXHIBIT 3-29
CONT.

13a.	SE-Income tax expense	18,192	
	L-Taxes payable		18,192
	Income taxes owed for the year		

13b.	L-Taxes payable	26,750	
	A-Cash		26,750
	Paid income taxes		

14a.	SE-Dividends declared	20,000	
	L-Dividends payable		20,000
	Dividends declared during the year		

14b.	L-Dividends payable	15,000	
	A-Cash		15,000
	Paid dividends		

Transactions 3, 5b, the part of 6 that records the amount of wages unpaid at the end of the year, and 13a would be adjusting entries.

■ **Template Company Ltd.**

T-Accounts with posted balances

EXHIBIT 3-30

	A-Cash				L-Accounts Payable		
✓	**55,000**					**33,000**	✓
2	764,500	40,700	4	8	428,000	431,000	7
11b	27,000	63,000	5a			36,000	✓
		148,000	6				
		428,000	8				
		6,360	10a		L-Wages Payable		
		90	10b			**9,000**	✓
		25,000	11a	6	9,000	11,000	6
		5,810	11c			11,000	✓
		45,000	12				
		26,750	13b				
		15,000	14b				
✓	42,790						

EXHIBIT 3-30
CONT.

A-Accounts Receivable

✓	**39,500**		
1	760,000	764,500	2
✓	35,000		

L-Taxes Payable

		16,000	✓
13b	26,750	18,192	13a
		7,442	✓

A-Inventory

✓	**43,000**		
7	431,000	417,000	9
✓	57,000		

L-Dividends Payable

		0	✓
14b	15,000	20,000	14a
		5,000	✓

A-Prepaid Rent

✓	**15,000**		
5a	63,000	61,500	5b
✓	16,500		

L-Notes Payable

		8,000	✓
10a	6,000		
		2,000	✓

A-Plant and Equipment

✓	**350,000**		
4	40,700		
✓	390,700		

L-Long-term Debt

		75,000	✓
11a	25,000	27,000	11b
		77,000	✓

XA-Accumulated Amort. – P & E

		100,000	✓
		15,680	3
		115,680	✓

SE-Common Shares

		185,000	✓
		185,000	✓

A-Office Furniture

✓	**76,000**		
✓	76,000		

SE-Retained Earnings

		136,500	✓
D	20,000	42,448	C
		158,948	✓

XA-Accumulated Amort. – Off. Furn.

		16,000	✓
		3,920	3
		19,920	✓

SE-Dividends Declared

✓	**0**		
14a	20,000		
		20,000	D
✓	0		

SE-Sales Revenue

		0	✓
		760,000	1
A	760,000		
		0	✓

SE-Cost of Goods Sold

✓	**0**		
9	417,000		
		417,000	B
✓	0		

SE-Wages Expense

✓	**0**		
6	150,000		
		150,000	B
✓	0		

SE-Amortization Expense

✓	**0**		
3	19,600		
		19,600	B
✓	0		

SE-Rent Expense

✓	**0**		
5b	61,500		
		61,500	B
✓	0		

SE-Interest Expense

✓	**0**		
10a	360		
10b	90		
11c	5,810	6,260	B
✓	0		

SE-Selling & Admin. Expense

✓	**0**		
12	45,000		
		45,000	B
✓	0		

SE-Income Tax Expense

✓	**0**		
13a	18,192		
		18,192	B
✓	0		

SE-Income Summary

		0	✓
B	717,552	760,000	A
		42,448	
C	42,448		
		0	✓

EXHIBIT 3-30
CONT.

2. b. The financial statements for Template Company Ltd. are included in Exhibit 3-31.

Template Company Ltd.

Financial Statements

EXHIBIT 3-31

Template Company Ltd.
Income Statement
For the year ended December 31, 20x1

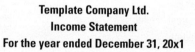

Sales revenue		$760,000
Less operating expenses:		
Cost of goods sold	$417,000	
Wages expense	150,000	
Amortization expense	19,600	
Rent expense	61,500	
Interest expense	6,260	
Selling and administrative expense	45,000	
Total operating expenses		699,360
Income before income tax		60,640
Income tax expense		18,192
Net income		$ 42,448

EXHIBIT 3-31
CONT.

Template Company Ltd.
Balance Sheet
December 31, 20x2 and 20x1

	20x2		20x1	
Assets				
Current Assets				
Cash		$ 42,790		$ 55,000
Accounts receivable		35,000		39,500
Inventory		57,000		43,000
Prepaid rent		16,500		15,000
Total current assets		151,290		152,500
Capital Assets				
Plant and equipment	$390,700		$350,000	
Less: Accumulated amortization	115,680		100,000	
	275,020		250,000	
Office furniture	76,000		76,000	
Less: Accumulated amortization	19,920		16,000	
	56,080	331,100	60,000	310,000
Total Assets		$482,390		$462,500
Liabilities				
Current liabilities				
Accounts payable		$ 36,000		$ 33,000
Wages payable		11,000		9,000
Taxes payable		7,442		16,000
Dividends payable		5,000		
Notes payable		2,000		
Total current liabilities		61,442		58,000
Noncurrent liabilities				
Notes payable				8,000
Long-term debt		77,000		75,000
Total noncurrent liabilities		77,000		83,000
Total Liabilities		138,442		141,000
Shareholders' Equity				
Common shares	$185,000		$185,000	
Retained earnings	158,948		136,500	
Total shareholders' equity		343,948		321,500
Total liabilities and shareholders' equity		$482,390		$462,500

Note that the notes payable is classified as a current liability in 20x2 but was a noncurrent liability in 20x1. The reason for the different treatment is that the last $2,000 of the notes payable is due in 20x3, which means that it is now current. The current portion of any long-term debt is classified as current.

2. c. The closing entries are included in Exhibit 3-32. These transactions are labelled with letters instead of numbers. They have been posted to the T-accounts in Exhibit 3-30. Note that, after posting, all of the revenue and expense accounts and the dividends declared account have zero balances. They are now ready for transactions in 20x3.

■ **Template Company Ltd.**

EXHIBIT 3-32

Closing Entries

A	SE-Sales revenue	760,000	
	SE-Income summary		760,000
B	SE-Income summary	717,552	
	SE-Cost of goods sold		417,000
	SE-Amortization expense		19,600
	SE-Wages expense		150,000
	SE-Rent expense		61,500
	SE-Interest expense		6,260
	SE-Selling and administrative		45,000
	SE-Income tax		18,192
C	SE-Income summary	42,448	
	SE-Retained earnings		42,448
D	SE-Retained earnings	20,000	
	SE-Dividends declared		20,000

ABBREVIATIONS USED

A	Asset	L	Liability
A/P	Accounts payable	PP&E	Property, plant, and equipment
A/R	Accounts receivable	S&A	Selling and administrative
GAAP	Generally Accepted Accounting Principles	SE	Shareholders' equity
		XA	Contra asset account

SYNONYMS

Tax expense/Provision for taxes/Tax provision

GLOSSARY

Accounting cycle The sequence of steps that occurs in the recording of transactions and events in the accounting system.

Accrued expense An expense that has been incurred and recognized in the financial statements but has not yet been paid for.

Accumulated amortization The total amortization that has been taken on an asset up to a particular point in time.

Adjusted trial balance A listing of the account balances after adjusting entries are made but before the closing entries are made.

Adjusting entry An entry made at the end of the period to record an event or transaction that has not been recorded during the current accounting period. Events or transactions that are not signalled in any other way are recorded through adjusting entries.

Chart of accounts A listing of the names of the accounts used in the accounting system.

Close the books The process by which the company makes closing entries to complete one accounting period and sets the balances in the accounts to start the next period. The temporary accounts are closed into the retained earnings account.

Closing entries Entries made at the end of the accounting period to transfer the balances from the temporary income statement and dividend accounts to the retained earnings account.

Contra asset account An account used to record reductions in a related asset account. An example is accumulated amortization.

Credit An entry made to the right side of an account or a reference to the right side of an account.

Debit An entry made to the left side of an account or a reference to the left side of an account.

Deferred taxes A tax entry made to the books of a company for taxes on the difference between the income reported to shareholders during a given period and the income reported to the taxing authority during the same period. These differences arise when the company uses one accounting method for tax purposes and another method for tax reporting purposes.

Discontinued operations Operations of the company that are being phased out and will, therefore, not continue in the future.

Double entry accounting system An accounting system that maintains the equality of the balance sheet equation. Each entry requires that equal amounts of debits and credits be made.

Dual entry accounting system Synonym for double entry accounting system.

Earnings per share A calculation in which the earnings of the company are divided by the average number of common shares outstanding during the period.

Extraordinary item A gain or loss appearing on the income statement that meets three criteria: (1) it is unusual, (2) it is infrequent, and (3) it is not caused primarily by a decision made by someone inside the company.

Footing the account Calculating the balance in a T-account.

Gross margin Sales minus cost of goods sold.

Gross profit Synonym for gross margin.

Income summary account An account used to summarize all the temporary income statement accounts prior to their being closed to retained earnings.

Journal A place where transactions and events are originally recorded in the accounting system.

Journal entry An entry made to the journal to record a transaction or event.

Ledger A place where transactions and events are summarized in account balances. Entries are recorded in the ledger by a process known as posting.

Liquidity A quality of an asset that describes how quickly it can be converted into cash.

Multistep income statement An income statement in which revenues and expenses from different types of operations of the company are shown in separate sections of the statement.

Permanent accounts Accounts whose balance carries over from one period to the next. All balance sheet accounts are considered permanent accounts.

Posting A synonym for posting to the ledger.

Posting to the ledger The process of transferring the information recorded in a journal entry to the ledger system.

Provision for taxes A synonym for tax expense.

Single-step income statement An income statement in which all revenues are listed in one section and all expenses except income taxes are listed in another section.

Synoptic journal   A journal in which transactions are recorded in a spreadsheet format. Each account is assigned its own column and amounts are added or subtracted inside the columns.

T-account   A device used to represent a ledger account.

Tax expense   The expense for income taxes calculated on the accounting income (revenues minus expenses).

Temporary accounts   Accounts used to keep track of information temporarily during an accounting period.

Balances in these accounts are transferred to a permanent account at the end of the period, using a closing entry.

Transaction analysis   The process by which the accountant decides what accounts are affected, and by how much, by an economic transaction or event.

Trial balance   A listing of the account balances.

ASSIGNMENT MATERIAL

Review Questions

3-1 In the adjusted trial balance phase of the accounting cycle, the retained earnings account has its beginning of period balance, whereas the rest of the permanent accounts have their proper end of period balance. Explain why this is the case.

3-2 Respond to each of the following statements with a true or false answer:

   a. Debits increase liability accounts.

   b. Revenues are credit entries to shareholders' equity.

   c. Cash receipts from customers are debited to accounts receivable.

   d. Dividends declared decrease cash at the date of declaration.

   e. The cash basis recognizes expenses when they are incurred.

   f. There is no such thing as a prepaid rent account on the cash basis.

   g. Dividends are an expense of doing business and should appear on the income statement.

3-3 Indicate whether each of the following accounts normally has a debit or a credit balance:

   a. Accounts Receivable

   b. Accounts Payable

   c. Sales Revenue

   d. Dividends Declared

   e. Dividends Payable

   f. Amortization Expense

   g. Common Shares

   h. Prepaid Rent

   i. Retained Earnings

3-4 Draw the accounting cycle, and briefly describe each step.

3-5 "Expense accounts have debit balances, and debit entries increase these accounts." Reconcile this statement with the normal effects of entries on shareholders' equity accounts and the resulting balances.

3-6 Discuss why one company might close its books monthly and another might close them weekly.

3-7 Identify and briefly describe the major sections of the income statement.

3-8 What is the standard format of the balance sheet?

3-9 Explain the meaning of the terms *current* and *noncurrent* as they apply to the balance sheet.

3-10 Explain the meaning of the term *liquidity*.

3-11 What two types of disclosure are made in the income statement with regard to discontinued operations?

3-12 What is an extraordinary item and why is it disclosed separately on the income statement?

Applying Your Knowledge

3-13 (Debit and credit balance identification)
For each of the following accounts indicate whether the account would normally have a debit or a credit balance:

 a. Cash

 b. Accounts Payable

 c. Common Shares

 d. Sales Revenues

 e. Inventory

 f. Cost of Goods Sold

 g. Wages Expense

3-14 (Debit and credit balance identification)
For each of the following accounts indicate whether the account would normally have a debit or a credit balance:

 a. Accounts Receivable

 b. Retained Earnings

 c. Accumulated Amortization

 d. Interest Revenue

 e. Prepaid Insurance

 f. Amortization Expense

 g. Bank Loan

3-15 (Construction of journal entries)

For each of the following transactions construct a journal entry:

a. Inventory costing $1,500 is purchased on account.

b. Inventory costing $1,200 is sold on account for $1,800.

c. Accounts receivable of $800 are collected.

d. The company borrows $10,000 from the bank.

e. The company issues common shares for $2,500.

f. New equipment costing $3,500 is purchased with cash.

3-16 (Journalize, post, and prepare a trial balance)

Treetop Food Distributors Ltd. began operations on January 1, 20x1. During 20x1 the following transactions occurred:

1. Issued common shares for cash, $500,000.

2. Purchased inventory on credit, $760,000.

3. Sold inventory on credit for $920,000. The original cost of the inventory that was sold was $650,000.

4. Collected $600,000 from customers.

5. Paid $720,000 to the suppliers for inventory previously purchased on account.

6. Paid rent for the year, $60,000.

7. Paid other expenses, $54,000.

8. Paid wages of the employees, $102,000.

9. Purchased an investment for $100,000.

10. Declared and paid dividends of $20,000.

Required:

a. Prepare journal entries to record each of the above transactions.

b. Create T-accounts and post the journal entries to the T-accounts.

c. Prepare a December 31, 20x1, trial balance.

3-17 (Journalize, post, and prepare a trial balance)

The Riders Shop Ltd. repaired motorcycles. It had two major sources of revenue, one from the sale of repair parts (parts were sold for twice their cost) and the other from the performance of repair services. The company began operations in March 20x1 with the following chart of accounts:

Cash

Accounts receivable

Parts inventory

Shop supplies on hand

Prepaid insurance

Equipment

Accumulated amortization, equipment

Accounts payable

Advances from customers

Common shares

Retained earnings

Sale of parts

Service revenue

Cost of parts sold

Wages expense

Rent expense

Other expenses

During March the following transactions occurred:

March	1	Issued common shares for $80,000.
	2	Paid the March rent, $1,800.
	5	Purchased spare parts from a supplier on credit for $21,000.
	7	Purchased shop supplies for cash, $9,100.
	9	Billed a customer $310 for parts and $180 for labour in repairing a motorcycle.
	11	Purchased additional motorcycle parts from a supplier, paying $560 cash.
	12	Paid the supplier for the spare parts purchased on March 5.
	15	Charged a customer $218 for parts and $250 for labour for repairing a motorcycle. The customer paid in cash.
	15	Paid the wages for the first two weeks, which totalled $800.
	16	Signed an agreement with Cruising Wheels Ltd., a local used-motorcycle dealer, to perform maintenance repairs on all used motorcycles to make them available for sale. The dealer agreed to pay $600 per quarter for the work. All parts used will be extra. The contract started on March 16 and was concluded with the dealer paying the first quarter's $600.
	20	Purchased a one-year fire insurance policy for cash of $540. The policy comes into effect on April 1.
	22	Repaired several motorcycles, charging $946 for parts and $1,200 for labour. The customers paid in cash.
	25	Billed Cruising Wheels Ltd. $490 for parts used in repairing some motorcycles.
	28	The customer whose work was completed on March 9 paid the amount owed.
	31	Paid wages for the last half of March, $825.

Required:

a. Prepare the journal entries to record the above transactions.

b. Draw a T-account for each account. Organize them in the order in which they will appear on the financial statements. Post the journal entries to the T-accounts.

c. Prepare a trial balance for March 31.

d. From the trial balance, prepare an income statement and balance sheet for the month of March.

3-18 (Journalize, post, and prepare a trial balance and closing entries)
Refer back to Problem 30 in Chapter 2, T. George Company. (1) Prepare journal entries for each of the transactions listed in the problem. (2) Prepare the necessary T-accounts and post the transactions to them. (3) Prepare a trial balance. (4) Prepare the closing entries and post them to the T-accounts.

3-19 (Journalize, post, and prepare a trial balance and closing entries)
Refer back to Problem 31 in Chapter 2, Hughes Tool Company. (1) Prepare journal entries for each of the transactions listed in the problem. (2) Prepare the necessary T-accounts and post the transactions to them. (3) Prepare a trial balance. (4) Prepare the closing entries and post them to the T accounts.

3-20 (Journalize, post, and prepare a trial balance and closing entries)
Refer back to Problem 32 in Chapter 2, A. J. Smith Company. (1) Prepare journal entries for each of the transactions listed in the problem. (2) Prepare the necessary T-accounts and post the transactions to them. (3) Prepare a trial balance. (4) Prepare the closing entries and post them to the T-accounts.

3-21 (Income statement determination)
Jake Redding owns and operates a tire and auto repair shop named Jake's Jack 'em and Fix 'em Shop. During the month the following events occurred:

1. The shop charged $8,300 for repair work completed. All but one of his customers had paid and collected their vehicles. The one customer who had not paid owed Jake $250. Jake still has the car parked in the shop's parking lot and he intends to keep it until the customer pays the bill. The $250 is included in the $8,300.

2. The total cost of parts used in repair work during the month was $2,700. Jake usually pays for the parts with cash. For items like fan belts and oil, which he orders in bulk, he buys from a supplier with 30 days' credit. At the end of the month, he still owes $450 to his supplier.

3. Jake earned $120 in interest on the company's bank account.

4. Jake paid $600 monthly rent on the repair shop. He pays on the first day of each month.

5. Jake paid the previous month's utility bills of $250 on the 10th of the month. At the end of this month, he has this month's utility bills totalling $198, which he intends to pay on the 10th of next month.

6. Jake paid his friend David $350 for helping him in the repair shop.

7. Other expenses related to operating the repair shop for the month totalled $990. All of these have been paid.

Required:
Using the concepts discussed so far in the text, determine the amounts that would properly be reported in the income statement for Jake's shop. If an item is excluded, explain why.

3-22 (Determination of expenses using matching)

For each of the following independent cases, indicate how much of the cost should be recognized as expense in the months of September and October, applying the matching concept:

1. Employees work Monday through Friday and are paid on Monday for the previous week's work. The total payroll is $5,000 per week. September 30 falls on Wednesday.

2. A new lease for the business premises goes into effect on October 1 and increases the rent from $800 to $900. Rent for the next month is always prepaid on the last day of the current month.

3. The company borrowed money on September 1. The loan is to be repaid on the last day of October along with $90 for interest.

4. The company purchased a large barrel of lubricant for $140 on September 1. The lubricant is to be used in the company's operations and is expected to last until the middle of October.

3-23 (Journalize, post, and prepare an income statement and balance sheet; prepare closing entries)

On December 31, 20x1, Sheridan Office Supplies Ltd. had the following account balances:

Cash	$106,000
Accounts receivable	50,000
Inventory	120,000
Investment	100,000
Accounts payable	60,000
Wages payable	7,000
Common shares	300,000
Retained earnings	9,000

During 20x2 the following transactions occurred:

1. On January 1, bought equipment for cash, $60,000. The equipment was expected to last for 10 years and have a residual value of $10,000.

2. On January 1, paid $1,800 for a three-year fire insurance policy.

3. Purchased inventory on credit for $360,000.

4. Sold inventory for $410,000 on account. The inventory that was sold originally cost $270,000.

5. Received $420,000 from customers in settlement of amounts owed to the company.

6. Paid $300,000 to the suppliers to settle some of the accounts payable.

7. Paid $9,000 for advertising.

8. Paid $24,000 for rent for the year.

9. Paid $88,000 for wages over the year. In December, still owed $3,500 to the employees for the last 10 days of work in December.

10. Received a $4,000 dividend from the investment.

11. Paid dividends of $12,000.

Required:

a. Prepare the journal entries to record the above transactions.

b. Create T-accounts, enter the beginning balances from 20x1, and post the 20x2 transactions.

c. Prepare a trial balance.

d. If you haven't already done so, prepare journal entries for the adjusting entries to record the amortization of the equipment, the expiration of the insurance, and the amount owed for wages. Post these journal entries and prepare an adjusted trial balance.

e. Prepare an income statement and a balance sheet for 20x2.

f. Prepare the closing entries and post them to the T-accounts.

3-24 (Journalize, post, and prepare an income statement and balance sheet; prepare closing entries)
On the Go Pizza had the following account balances at December 31, 20x1:

Cash	$140,000
Accounts receivable	20,000
Supplies inventory	5,000
Prepaid rent	48,000
Equipment	40,000
Delivery vehicles	60,000
Wages payable	4,000
Common shares	200,000
Retained earnings	109,000

During 20x2 the following transactions occurred:

1. Sales of pizzas for cash, $450,000. Sales of pizzas on account, $30,000.

2. Purchase of ingredients for the pizzas and other supplies (supplies inventory) amounted to $190,000. All of these items were paid for.

3. During 20x2, supplies inventory valued at $185,000 was used.

4. During 20x2, the company paid $65,000 for wages.

5. During 20x2, $42,000 was used for other expenses.

6. At the end of 20x2, a dividend of $10,000 was declared and paid.

Adjusting entries:

7. Wages owed to employees at the end of the year were $3,000.

8. By the end of 20x2, half of the prepaid rent had been used.

9. The equipment had a useful life of eight years with no residual value at the end of the eight years. Record the amortization.

10. The delivery vehicles had a useful life of five years with a residual value of $5,000 at the end of the five years. Prepare the amortization.

Required:

a. Prepare journal entries for transactions 1 through 6. Create new accounts if necessary.

b. Create T-accounts, enter the beginning balances from 20x1, and post the 20x2 transactions.

c. Prepare a trial balance.

d. Prepare journal entries for adjusting entries 7 through 10. Post these journal entries and prepare an adjusted trial balance.

e. Prepare an income statement and a balance sheet for 20x2.

f. Prepare the closing entries and post them to the T-accounts.

3-25 (Journal entries, trial balances, and closing entries)
Evergreen Retail Company had the following transactions. Assume that the fiscal year end of the company is December 31.

1. Borrowed $4,500 from the bank on January 1, 20x1.

2. Bought equipment on January 1, 20x1 for $8,000.

3. Purchases of inventory on account during 20x1 totalled $17,600.

4. Sales for the period totalled $25,500, of which $14,300 were on account. The cost of the products sold was $16,900.

5. Collections from customers on account totalled $12,700.

6. Payments to suppliers for the inventory totalled $15,800.

7. Employees were paid $2,300 during the year.

8. Dividends were declared and paid in the amount of $1,500.

9. Paid the interest on the bank loan on December 31, 20x1. The interest rate is 10%.

Adjusting entries (you may need to use information recorded in the first nine transactions):

10. The equipment purchased on January 1 has an estimated useful life of five years and an estimated residual value at the end of five years of $900. Record the amortization for the equipment as at December 31, assuming the company uses the straight-line method.

11. Wages in the amount of $200 were owed to employees at the end of the year. They will be paid early in 20x2.

Required:

a. Prepare journal entries for transactions 1 through 9.

b. Create T-accounts and post the 20x1 transactions.

c. Prepare a trial balance.

d. Prepare journal entries for adjusting entries 10 and 11. Post these journal entries and prepare an adjusted trial balance.

e. Prepare the closing entries and post them to the T-accounts.

3-26 (Journal entries, trial balances, and closing entries)

Classic Ltd. had the following transactions. Assume the fiscal year end of the company is December 31.

1. Issued common shares for $30,000.

2. Paid an insurance premium of $600 on July 1 that provides coverage for the 12-month period starting July 1.

3. Purchased $31,350 of inventory on account.

4. Sales recorded for the period totalled $65,000, of which $30,000 were cash sales.

5. Cash collections on customer accounts totalled $32,000.

6. Inventory costing $35,800 was sold.

7. Payments to suppliers for inventory totalled $30,500.

8. Purchased a piece of equipment that cost $11,000. Paid cash.

9. Dividends of $1,300 were declared.

10. Dividends of $1,250 that had previously been declared were paid.

Adjusting entries (you may need to use information recorded in the first 10 transactions):

11. Recognize the amount of insurance expense that was used from July 1 through December 31.

12. Amortization of $3,300 was taken on plant and equipment.

Required:

a. Prepare journal entries to record transactions 1 through 10.

b. Create T-accounts and post the transactions.

c. Prepare a trial balance.

d. Prepare journal entries for adjusting entries 11 and 12. Post these journal entries and prepare an adjusted trial balance.

e. Prepare the closing entries and post them to the T-accounts.

3-27 (Adjusting entries)

The trial balance for Snowcrest Ltd. for December 31, 20x1, is presented below:

	Debit	Credit
Cash	$ 9,000	
Inventory	21,000	
Advances to sales persons	1,000	
Prepaid rent	3,000	
Office supplies	2,000	
Equipment	20,000	
Accumulated amortization, equipment		$ 2,000
Deposits from customers		500

Common shares		40,000
Retained earnings		3,500
Sales		200,000
Cost of goods sold	120,000	
Sales persons' commission	30,000	
Office salaries	25,000	
Miscellaneous expense	10,000	
Dividends	5,000	
Totals	$246,000	$246,000

Adjusting entries:

1. The sales include deposits from customers of $2,000. As at December 31, the total deposits from customers should be $2,500.

2. Half of the advances to sales persons have been earned by the sales people by December 31.

3. Office salaries owed at year end but not paid are $600.

4. One half of the prepaid rent was used in 20x1.

5. A count of the office supplies revealed that $500 was still on hand at year end.

6. Amortization on the equipment for 20x1 was $1,000.

7. Income tax for the year should be calculated using a tax rate of 25%. Hint: You will have to determine income before income tax so that you have a basis on which to calculate the 25%. Remember that you have to calculate this amount after you finish the other adjusting entries.

Required:
Prepare the adjusting entries.

3-28 (Prepare income statement and balance sheet)
You have been retained by the Downunder Company to straighten out the company's accounting records. It seems that the company's trusted accountant for the past 25 years, Icabod Cranium, has just run off to the Bahamas. Unfortunately, in his rush, he seems to have misplaced the company's books. Now the bank is asking for the latest financial statements so it can determine whether or not to renew the company's loan. Luckily, you manage to find a listing of accounts and balances he left on the back of a travel brochure:

Cash on hand (in third desk drawer)	$ 120
Accounts receivable from customers	24,200
Sales to customers	71,500
Loan balance owed to Last National Bank	15,000
Wages owed to employees (not yet paid)	1,215
Cash in bank account	725
Wages expense	3,500

Interest income	515
Equipment	51,500
Cost of inventory sold	40,000
Inventory still on shelves	8,900

Required:

a. Prepare an income statement for the end of the current year, 2001.

b. Prepare a balance sheet as at December 31, 2001.

3-29 (Effect of transactions on balance sheet accounts)
Ann and Greg Fenway run a small art gallery and custom framing business. Using the basic balance sheet accounts of assets, liabilities, and shareholders' equity, explain how each of these would be affected by the following transactions and activities:

a. The Fenways purchased five pictures for cash.

b. Framing materials are purchased on credit.

c. A loan from the bank is repaid (ignore interest).

d. A picture is sold for cash at an 80% profit.

e. A plaster statue falls from a shelf and is broken and discarded.

f. A receivable is collected on a major framing project completed last month for a local law office.

g. Payment is made for the framing materials previously purchased.

Management Perspective Problems

3-30 (The year end closing process)
The accounting system closing process takes some time at the end of the accounting period, in checking for errors, making adjusting entries, and preparing the financial statements. In recent years there has been a real push to speed up this process for most companies. Discuss the incentives that companies might have to make this a faster process.

3-31 (Correction of errors and omissions revealed during the audit)
At year end during the audit process, the auditing firm may find errors and omissions in the recording of transactions and will then ask management to make an adjusting entry to correct these errors. In light of the purpose of the audit opinion (see discussion in Chapter 1), discuss plausible arguments that management might give to convince the auditor to waive making these suggested adjustments.

3-32 (Revision of income statement amounts)
Leadfoot Al decided to retire from stock-car racing and invest all his winnings in a fish farm. He had majored in genetics in college and experimented with many different species of fish before coming up with a catfish that has the texture and taste of ocean trout. Moreover, contacts from his previous profession made it possible for him to acquire feed for his unique form of fish at very low prices. After operating for a little over a year, Al decided to explore expansion possibilities. He talked with his banker about getting a loan and presented an income statement for the past year, based strictly on cash flows as follows:

Cash collected from sale of Al's Gourmet Fish		$420,000
Less: Feed purchases	$390,000	
Purchase of new fish tank	40,000	
Wages paid	70,000	500,000
Operating loss		(80,000)
Plus: Sale of land		120,000
Net income		$ 40,000

From discussions with Al, the banker learned the following:

- $120,000 of the cash collected in the current period was from shipments delivered prior to the start of the year. Payment of all the sales this year was collected prior to year end.

- The feed can be stored indefinitely, and about half of this year's purchases remain on hand at year end.

- Two fish tanks were purchased last year at a total cost of $80,000. These tanks, along with the one purchased at the beginning of this year, were used all year. Each tank is expected to last five years.

- The land sold for $120,000 had been purchased two years earlier for $55,000.

Required:
Provide Al and his banker with responses to the following:

a. Why is the matching concept important in this case?

b. What amount of revenue from the sale of merchandise should be included this period?

c. What amount of expense for fish food should be reported this period? How should the remainder of the food purchased be reported?

d. Should some amount for the fish tanks be included in computing income for the current period? How much?

e. The land was sold for more than its original purchase price. This difference is called a gain and is usually included on the income statement. What is the amount of the gain on the sale of the land that should be included in income this period?

f. Should Al stay in the fish business or go back to auto racing? What factors other than the income computations would be relevant to evaluating the potential future for Al's fish farm?

3-33 (Multistep income statement)
Northland Enterprises sells snowmobiles and recreational equipment and has reported the following revenues and expenses in 2001:

Equipment sales	$6,500,000
Cost of parts and equipment sold	4,200,000
Wages and salaries	1,000,000
Sales of replacement parts	900,000
Revenue from labour charges for repair work	700,000
Income tax expense	730,000

Shipping and delivery costs	690,000
Property taxes	100,000
Interest expense on mortgage payable	90,000
Interest income on investments	70,000

Required:

a. Prepare a 2001 multistep income statement for Northland Enterprises.

b. In 2000, Northland reported net income of $1,050,000 and earned an 18% return on total revenue (net income divided by revenue). The goal for 2001 was to earn income in excess of $1,150,000 and earn a 20% return on total revenue. What amounts were reported? Did Northland attain its goals in 2001?

c. In setting its goals for net income and return on sales for future periods, what types of factors should Northland take into consideration?

Reading and Interpreting Published Financial Statements

3-34 (Income statement and balance sheet items)
Western Star Trucks Holdings Ltd. manufactures trucks and buses. Refer to its 1998 financial statements in Exhibit 3-33 and answer the following questions:

a. Has Western Star Trucks Holdings used a single-step or multistep income statement? What aspects of the statement influenced your decision?

b. Explain why Western Star Trucks Holdings has two earnings per share amounts for each year.

c. Western Star Trucks Holdings has $143,563,000 in capital assets at the end of 1998. However, there is no mention on the income statement of amortization or depreciation expense. In the cash flow statement, there were two line items in the operating section indicating that depreciation and amortization amounted to $16,506,000 and $9,086,000, respectively, in 1998. Explain why you do not see these expenses on the income statement.

d. At the end of 1998 what percentage of Western Star Trucks Holdings' total assets is invested in inventory? What percentage is invested in capital assets?

3-35 (Income statement items)
Use Big Rock's financial statements in Appendix A at the end of the book to answer the following questions:

a. Explain whether it prepares a single-step or multistep income statement.

b. Big Rock lists its earnings per share as "Basic and fully diluted." What do you think this means?

3-36 (Income statement and balance sheet items)
Refer to the 1998 financial statements of Xerox Canada Inc., Exhibit 3-34, and answer the following questions:

a. Has Xerox Canada used a single-step or multistep income statement? What aspects of the statement influenced your decision?

b. You will notice that Xerox has two kinds of operating revenue, sales and service and rental. It also discloses the costs associated with these two revenues, cost of sales and cost of service and rental. For 1998 and 1997, calculate the ratio of gross profit (sales minus cost of sales) to its revenue. Has the gross profit

EXHIBIT 3-33
PART A

Consolidated Balance Sheets

As at June 30	1998	1997
(in thousands of Canadian dollars)		
ASSETS		
Current		
Cash	—	92,027
Accounts receivable *[note 6]*	201,218	203,196
Unbilled revenue *[note 1]*	85,167	21,023
Inventories *[note 3]*	237,312	182,157
Prepaid expenses and other	12,341	11,621
Total current assets	536,038	510,024
Capital assets *[note 4]*	143,563	136,046
Deferred costs *[note 5]*	76,069	61,724
Goodwill [net of accumulated amortization		
of $996; 1997 - $469]	10,986	9,635
Prepaid pension expense *[note 13]*	14,134	11,373
Investments and other assets	2,334	5,278
	783,124	734,080
LIABILITIES AND SHAREHOLDERS' EQUITY		
Current		
Bank indebtedness	1,843	—
Accounts payable and accrued liabilities *[note 6]*	305,393	260,607
Short-term indebtedness *[note 7]*	34,335	—
Current portion of customer deposits and advances	8,122	33,781
Current portion of long-term debt *[note 8]*	33,346	15,383
Total current liabilities	383,039	309,771
Deferred income taxes	553	6,076
Customer deposits and advances	327	1,800
Long-term debt *[note 8]*	171,088	185,502
Total liabilities	555,007	503,149
Commitments and contingencies *[notes 8[ii] and 9]*		
Shareholders' equity		
Share capital *[note 10]*	121,841	119,587
Retained earnings	106,276	111,344
Total shareholders' equity	228,117	230,931
	783,124	734,080

See accompanying notes

On behalf of the Board:

Director   Director

EXHIBIT 3-33
PART B

Consolidated Statements of Operations and Retained Earnings

Years ended June 30	1998	1997	1996
(in thousands of Canadian dollars, except share and per share amounts)			
Revenue	1,552,272	1,236,349	783,319
Cost of sales	1,423,248	1,110,715	683,773
Gross profit	129,024	125,634	99,546
Selling and administrative	109,726	72,170	47,619
Interest expense - net	21,189	8,149	1,477
Net income (loss) before taxes	(1,891)	45,315	50,450
Income tax expense *(recovery) [note 11]*	(2,215)	11,325	13,927
Net income	324	33,990	36,523
Retained earnings, opening balance	111,344	82,962	51,225
Share issue costs *(net of tax)*	296	(90)	40
Dividends paid	(5,688)	(5,518)	(4,826)
Retained earnings, closing balance	106,276	111,344	82,962
Per common share			
Net income	0.02	2.48	3.08
Fully diluted net income	0.02	2.26	2.89
Dividends	0.40	0.40	0.40
Weighted average number of common shares			
outstanding (thousands)	14,214	13,723	11,860

See accompanying notes

EXHIBIT 3-34
PART A

XEROX CANADA INC.
CONSOLIDATED STATEMENTS OF EARNINGS

Year ended December 31
(Dollars in thousands, except per share data)

	1998	1997
REVENUES		
Sales (Note 18)	$ 1,034,473	$ 825,490
Service and rental	420,006	390,746
Finance	95,933	92,434
Total revenues	1,550,412	1,308,670
COSTS AND OTHER DEDUCTIONS		
Cost of sales (Note 18)	764,223	584,590
Cost of service and rental (Note 18)	275,922	260,544
Selling, administrative and general expense	300,110	290,766
Interest expense, net (Note 11, 18)	30,170	28,763
Other, net (Note 12)	14,414	4,043
Restructuring provision (Note 13)	59,500	–
Total costs and other deductions	1,444,339	1,168,706
EARNINGS BEFORE INCOME AND OTHER TAXES AND NON-CONTROLLING INTEREST	106,073	139,964
Income and other taxes (Note 14)	34,486	57,157
Non-controlling interest in earnings (Note 2)	1,761	–
NET EARNINGS	$ 69,826	$ 82,807
NET EARNINGS PER CLASS A AND CLASS B SHARE AFTER PREFERENCE SHARE DIVIDENDS (NOTE 15)	$ 2.17	$ 2.56

CONSOLIDATED STATEMENTS OF RETAINED EARNINGS

Year ended December 31
(Dollars in thousands)

	1998	1997
Retained earnings at beginning of year	$ 380,569	$ 384,133
Net earnings	69,826	82,807
Dividends declared (Note 10)	(4,712)	(73,470)
Premium on Class B Shares and other costs (Note 10)	(19,429)	(12,901)
RETAINED EARNINGS AT END OF YEAR	$ 426,254	$ 380,569

The accompanying notes are an integral part of the consolidated financial statements.

EXHIBIT 3-34
PART B

XEROX CANADA INC.
CONSOLIDATED BALANCE SHEETS

As at December 31
(Dollars in thousands)

	1998	1997
ASSETS		
Cash (Note 8)	$ 6,681	$ 6,021
Trade receivables	70,049	55,115
Accrued revenues	51,342	45,409
Due from related parties (Note 18)	758,241	–
Inventories (Note 4)	169,082	123,909
Net investment in financed receivables (Note 5)	1,119,984	987,734
Land, buildings and equipment (Note 6)	137,983	126,161
Other assets	37,844	14,451
Discontinued operations (Note 3)	224,412	244,321
	$ 2,575,618	$ 1,603,121
LIABILITIES		
Notes payable (due within one year) (Note 8)	$ 1,331,718	$ 442,279
Accounts payable and accrued liabilities (Note 13)	160,825	120,740
Due to related parties (note 18)	–	37,348
Income taxes payable	28,382	33,570
Deferred revenue	17,810	21,178
Debt with original maturity exceeding one year (Note 8)	151,500	177,600
Deferred income taxes	296,701	301,085
Non-controlling interest (Note 2)	75,016	–
	2,061,952	1,133,800
SHAREHOLDERS' EQUITY		
Stated capital (Note 10)	85,328	88,752
Retained earnings	426,254	380,569
Cumulative translation adjustment	2,084	–
	513,666	469,321
	$ 2,575,618	$ 1,603,121

The accompanying notes are an integral part of the consolidated financial statements.

On behalf of the Board of Directors

KEVIN FRANCIS
Chairman of the Board

JOCELYNE CÔTÉ-O'HARA
Chairman of the Audit Committee

increased, decreased, or stayed the same over the two years, for each type of revenue? Is the gross profit ratio the same for the two types of revenue? Would you expect it to be? Explain.

c. Does Xerox Canada prepare a classified balance sheet? What aspects of the statement influenced your decision?

d. Identify the items on the balance sheet that appear to be noncurrent liabilities. What influenced your decision?

3-37 (Income statement items)
Use the income statement of Domtar Inc. in Exhibit 3-35 to answer the following questions:

a. Has Domtar used a single-step or multistep income statement? What aspects of the statement influenced your decision?

b. You will notice that Domtar has an "unusual item" in 1996. The 1997 financial statements described this item as: "The Company provided $35 million of costs related to the restructuring of its specialty fine paper operations, consisting primarily of asset write-downs." Explain why this item could not be disclosed as extraordinary.

c. In 1996 Domtar had earnings from discontinued operations. Why is this item reported at the very end of the income statement? It does not say that the discontinued operations amount is net of tax. Is it? Explain your reasoning.

d. In some years Domtar reports as many as four earnings per share amounts. Explain why each of those earnings per share is important to users.

Beyond the Book

3-38 (Financial statement disclosures)
Find the annual report of a Canadian company that is listed on a Canadian stock exchange. Answer the following questions:

a. From the financial statements, discuss the importance of inventory in relationship to other assets on the company's balance sheet. Address the importance of capital assets to the company.

b. How does the company finance its business (debt or equity)?

c. Does the company prepare a single-step or multistep income statement? How do you know?

d. Does the company have any unusual items, discontinued operations, or extraordinary items? If so, search through the information provided with the financial statements and explain why these items were classified as they were.

e. Has the company prepared a classified balance sheet? Using the items on the balance sheet, explain what liquidity is and how it is used on the balance sheet.

f. How many directors does the company have? How old are they and what percentage of the board is female?

3-39 (Finding additional information about companies)
For the company you selected for problem 38, find at least three articles in the financial press that discuss the nature of the markets for this company and the forecast for this sector of the economy. Write a short, one-page summary of your findings.

EXHIBIT 3-35

DOMTAR INC.

CONSOLIDATED EARNINGS

Year ended December 31
(in millions of Canadian dollars, except per share amounts)

	1998	1997	1996
	$	$	$
Sales	2,348	1,938	1,977
Operating expenses			
Cost of sales	1,815	1,615	1,591
Selling, general and administrative *(Note 12)*	149	123	134
Amortization	184	144	143
	2,148	1,882	1,868
Operating profit before unusual item	200	56	109
Write-down of assets	–	–	35
Operating profit	200	56	74
Financing expenses *(Note 3)*	91	50	72
Premium and write-off on early redemption of long-term debt	–	–	127
Gain on contribution to Norampac, including amortization of deferred gain *(Note 16)*	(5)	(25)	–
Earnings (loss) from continuing operations before income taxes and non-controlling interest	114	31	(125)
Income taxes *(Note 4)*	42	8	(37)
Earnings (loss) from continuing operations before non-controlling interest	72	23	(88)
Non-controlling interest	(2)	(2)	(1)
Earnings (loss) from continuing operations	74	25	(87)
Earnings from discontinued operations, including a net gain on divestitures of $172 *(Note 5)*	–	–	184
Net earnings	74	25	97
Dividend requirements of preferred shares	3	2	3
Interest on equity element of convertible debentures	–	–	3
Net earnings applicable to common shares	71	23	91
	$	$	$
Per common share *(Note 13)*			
Earnings (loss) from continuing operations			
Basic	0.44	0.15	(0.69)
Fully diluted	0.42	*	*
Net earnings			
Basic	0.44	0.15	0.68
Fully diluted	0.42	*	0.63

* No dilution or antidilutive

The accompanying notes are an integral part of the consolidated financial statements.

Part of the
Growing Pains

In a few short years, *Shift Magazine* exploded from a tiny alternative publication to a Canadian success story with a circulation of over 80,000 and poised to expand into the U.S. market. Its young publishers know you have to be more than hip, creative, and tuned in to new technology to put out 10 issues a year of a hit magazine. You need a certain business sense, including the ability to navigate the complex accounting issues that come with the territory.

"When you start up a publication like this," explains Wayne Leek, *Shift*'s Consumer Marketing Director, "everything is on a cash basis. Accounting is kept dead simple: All money that comes in, from subscriptions to donations, to a dollar found on the street, goes into the revenue pot right away—and is spent again instantly, as likely as not, to keep the business alive."

But as the company has grown it has had to make some changes. For example, advertising revenues are now invoiced on a per-issue basis even if the advertiser has a contract for several issues. "We recognize all advertising dollars as soon as the invoice goes out," confirms General Manager Kevin Siu, "even though we usually don't get paid until 30 to 60 days later."

On the subscription revenue side, it doesn't really make accounting sense to recognize revenue from a subscription payment before the subscriber has been sent a single issue. "Eventually you get to a point where you switch to spreading out the revenue over the life of the subscription," says Mr. Leek. "You realize the cash right away, but you defer the revenue for each issue of a subscription until that issue is shipped. Making the switch is just another 'part of the growing pains,'" he explains, "but in the long run the new revenue policies will better reflect the performance of the company."

REVENUE RECOGNITION

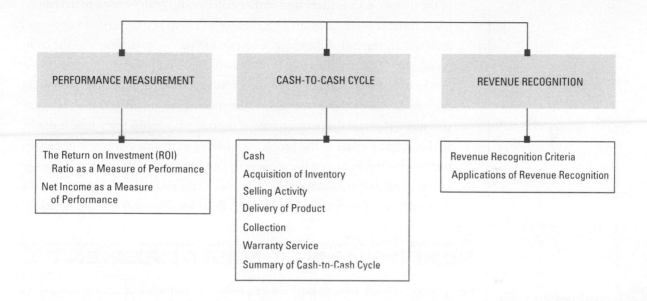

| PERFORMANCE MEASUREMENT | CASH-TO-CASH CYCLE | REVENUE RECOGNITION |

PERFORMANCE MEASUREMENT

- The Return on Investment (ROI) Ratio as a Measure of Performance
- Net Income as a Measure of Performance

CASH-TO-CASH CYCLE

- Cash
- Acquisition of Inventory
- Selling Activity
- Delivery of Product
- Collection
- Warranty Service
- Summary of Cash-to-Cash Cycle

REVENUE RECOGNITION

- Revenue Recognition Criteria
- Applications of Revenue Recognition

Learning Objectives:

After studying this chapter, you should be able to:

1. *Understand how return on investment can give you one measure of performance.*
2. *Calculate the return on investment under some basic scenarios.*
3. *Describe the cash-to-cash cycle of a retail company.*
4. *Describe the relationship between performance and revenue recognition.*
5. *Describe the criteria for revenue recognition.*
6. *Describe various applications of the revenue recognition criteria.*
7. *Calculate amounts to be recognized under the completed contract method and the percentage of completion method.*
8. *Explain the impact various revenue recognition methods have on earnings recognition.*

The opening story describes a new company that changed its revenue recognition policy as it grew. The magazine business is not an over-the-counter retail sales business. Rather, it has two basic sources of revenue: Amounts paid to it for advertisements in one or more issues and amounts paid by subscribers for future issues. For these two sources, the company must decide at what point it has earned revenue. Cash from the subscriptions comes in before the magazines are shipped each month, and cash from the advertisers comes in after the advertisement has been printed in an issue. Should the revenue be tied to the cash flow, or is there some other criterion that can be used to determine when revenue is recognized? This chapter will help you understand the issues involved. By the end of the chapter you should be able to explain why the owners of *Shift Magazine* changed its revenue recognition policy.

In Chapters 1 through 3, the basic financial statements of a company were discussed. Two of those statements, the income statement and the cash flow statement, measure the performance of the company across some time horizon. In this chapter, some of the problems inherent in the measurement of performance are considered, and the accounting concepts and guidelines for the recognition of income are discussed. In Chapter 5, the cash flow statement and the measurement of performance using cash flows are discussed in more detail.

PERFORMANCE MEASUREMENT

Learning Objective

Understand how return on investment can give you one measure of performance.

Let us have a closer look at how we can measure performance. After making an investment, investors generally want to know how well their investment is performing. To put this in a simple context, suppose an investment is made in a savings account at a bank. Periodically, statements are received from the bank that detail any new deposits or withdrawals and any interest earned by the savings. The interest earned can then be compared with the balance on the account to give an indication of the performance of the investment. The comparison of the interest earned to the balance in the account is called a ratio. Ratios can help us assess performance.

The Return on Investment (ROI) Ratio as a Measure of Performance

A common measure of performance used in business is a ratio called the **return on investment**, or ROI, which is generally computed as follows (in Chapter 12 we will discuss several other ratios that also calculate returns):

$$\text{ROI} = \frac{\text{Return}}{\text{Average investment}}$$

In the case of the bank account, the numerator is the interest earned during the period and the denominator is the average amount invested over the period. By averaging the denominator, you take into account additional deposits or with-drawals made during the period. A simple average of the beginning balance and the ending balance in the investment is often used; however, more sophisticated averaging methods may be more appropriate. Suppose the average investment in a bank account was $1,000 and the return was $50. The ROI from the investment would be:

Learning Objective

2

Calculate the return on investment under some basic scenarios.

$$ROI = \frac{\$50}{\$1,000} = 5\%$$

Based on this return, two questions might be asked: (1) Is this a good return on investment? and (2) How confident is the investor that this really is the return?

To answer question (1), the return on this investment should be compared with the returns that could have been earned on other, alternative investments, or with the returns that similar investors are earning. If the next best alternative would have returned only 4%, the bank account was a good investment. If, however, similar investors are earning 6.5% for investments of similar risk, it would seem that the best investment was not made.

To answer question (2), the investors must assure themselves that their $1,000 investment plus their $50 return is really worth $1,050 today. Ultimately, the only way to be sure that the investment is worth $1,050 is to sell the investment; that is, to withdraw the $1,050 from the bank. If the investor does not sell the investment, there is still some chance that the bank will not have the money to repay them; the bank might, for example, file for bankruptcy. In the late 1980s and early 1990s, this was not an inconceivable event as several small Canadian banks went out of business. In banks insured by the Canada Deposit Insurance Company (CDIC), small accounts (those up to $60,000) are insured, so that even in the event of a bank collapse the investor would be repaid by the CDIC. A bank account of this type is about as safe an investment as can be made. An uninsured account would not give the same comfort level with regard to the failure of the banking institution.

Now suppose that an investment is made in a house instead of in a savings account. Assume that the house is bought for investment purposes for $200,000. Assume further that there are no other cash outlays or inflows during the year from this investment. In assessing the return on the investment, the value of the investment at the end of the period must be determined. This value could be estimated by getting an appraisal of the house by a real estate agent, or by comparing the house with other houses in the area that have recently sold. The selling prices of those houses could serve as a basis for estimating the value of the investment. In either case, the value will be an estimate. Confidence in these estimates will surely be lower than the confidence in the estimate of the return earned from the investment in the savings account at the bank. In fact, the only sure way to determine the return on the house would be to sell it; that is, sell the investment. If the investor does not want to sell the investment, however, the only alternative would be to use an estimate of the selling price to measure performance. If the investor estimates the selling price to be $225,000, the ROI will be:

$$ROI = \frac{\$225,000 - \$200,000}{\$200,000} = 12.5\%$$

Measuring the performance of a business is much like estimating the return on the investment in a house. The business makes investments in capital assets (property, plant, and equipment), inventory, accounts receivable, and other assets, and periodically measures the performance of these investments. However, it does not want to sell its investment in these assets at the end of every accounting period simply to determine the proper ROI. It must, therefore, estimate any changes in the value of its assets and liabilities that may have occurred during the accounting period, and report these as net income. We then use that net income amount to calculate a couple of ROIs that you will see later in this book. The first is a return on assets (ROA). This ratio measures the amount of income earned per $1 of assets. It attempts to provide the user with information about how effectively the assets are being used to generate income. A second ratio is the return on equity (ROE). This ratio measures the amount of income earned per $1 invested in shares in the company. It provides users with information about the amount of return being earned by shareholders. They can compare this ROI with investments of other types and risks to determine whether investing in this company is still a good idea.

Some of the changes in value (returns), such as the interest earned on a savings account, are easy to measure. Other changes, such as the change in the value of property, plant, and equipment, are not as easily measured—as the example concerning the investment in a house demonstrates. Because accounting data should be reliable as well as relevant (in Chapter 1 we discussed these terms), accountants have established concepts and guidelines for recognizing the changes in value of assets and liabilities to ensure that the measure of performance most commonly used (net income) provides a reliable measure of the effects of the transactions that took place during the period.

Net Income as a Measure of Performance

The income statement attempts to measure the return to the shareholders on their investment in the company; that is, it measures changes in shareholders' wealth in the company. The accounting value of this shareholders' wealth is measured by the value of shareholders' equity accounts. Remember that these accounts include common shares and retained earnings.

Shareholders' equity accounts are typically affected by three general types of transaction: shareholder investment activities, the declaration of dividends, and transactions that result in profits or losses. Shareholders may invest more money in the company by buying, for example, new shares when they are issued. This does not directly affect their return on the investment, but it does affect the amount of investment they have in the company. Second, shareholders may declare themselves a dividend (via a vote of the Board of Directors), which reduces their wealth in the company by reducing the total assets in the company. This also does not directly affect the return on investment, but again affects the amount of investment. Finally, those transactions that result in profits or losses will affect shareholders' wealth through their effects on retained earnings. It is this last set of transactions, and their impact on value, that is measured by the income statement.

Because the company does not want to sell its investments each period to determine its performance, some concepts and guidelines have been developed to help in estimating changes in value. These concepts and guidelines are sometimes called revenue recognition principles. To understand them, it is useful to understand the corresponding relationship between the cash-to-cash cycle of the company and the estimation of changes in value. The cash-to-cash cycle of a typical retail company is used as an illustration.

CASH-TO-CASH CYCLE

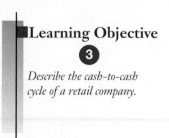

As we have seen, corporate managers engage in three general types of activity: financing, investing, and operating. Let us focus for a moment on operating activities.

Operating activities include all the normal day-to-day activities of every business, which almost always involve cash. Operating activities involve the normal buying and selling of goods and/or services for the purpose of earning profits, for which the business was created. The typical operation of a business involves an outflow of cash followed by an inflow of cash, a process commonly called the **cash-to-cash cycle**. In Exhibit 4-1, the cash-to-cash cycle of a typical retail company is shown. Each phase in the cash-to-cash cycle is discussed in the following subsections.

■ **Cash-to-Cash Cycle of a Retail Company**

EXHIBIT 4-1

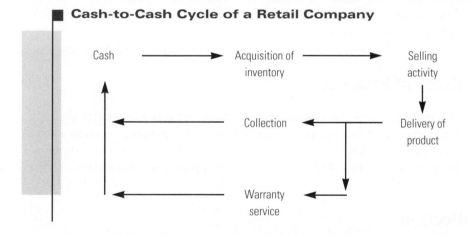

Cash

We have already discussed how the initial amount of cash in a company comes from the initial investment by shareholders, as well as from any loans that the company may have taken out to provide the initial financing. In Chapter 12, the difference between the return on the investment made by the shareholders and the investment made by the lenders is considered; at this point, however, no distinction will be made between them. To simplify matters, you might think of the company as being totally financed by shareholders; that is, there are no loans.

Acquisition of Inventory

Before the company acquires the inventory needed to sell to customers or to provide services, it must undertake the investing activities of acquiring property, plant, and equipment. Next, it hires labour and purchases the first shipments of inventory (or signs contracts to acquire them). Note that, in a retail company, the costs involved in this initial phase may be more substantial that those in a service-oriented company. If you visualize even a small retail store, you will see that the amount of inventory that must be purchased to initially fill the shelves can be substantial.

Selling Activity

The selling phase includes all those activities that are designed to promote and sell the product. These may include pricing the product, advertising the product, hiring and managing a sales force, establishing retail sales outlets, contracting with agencies, signing supply agreements, and attending trade shows. The end result of this phase is sales contracts between the buyer and seller. These may be verbal agreements or formal, written documents. For most retail outlets selling to customers, the agreement occurs when the goods are paid for in the sales outlet (the store). Some retail outlets, however, sell to other businesses or to large enterprises such as hospitals or schools. For these sales, it is more likely that a formal contract is drawn up specifying prices, amounts, and times of delivery.

Delivery of Product

Once a sales contract has been drawn up, the product must be delivered to the customer. Depending on the type of product, this may be instantaneous (as in a grocery store), or it may take months (as in a car dealership). Some sales contracts require periodic deliveries of inventory (as in baked goods to a hospital).

Collection

Upon delivery of the product, collection of the sales price in cash may be immediate, such as in a grocery store, or it could take place at some later date, resulting in an amount owing at the time of delivery, which is called an **account receivable**. Payment at a later date is the same as the seller making a loan to the buyer and accepting the risk that the buyer will not pay (this is called credit risk). The loan to the buyer may carry explicit interest charges, but usually no interest is charged if payment is made within a specified short period of time (typically 30 to 60 days). If the buyer does not pay within the specified period of time, the seller may try to take the product back (repossession) or may try other methods of collecting on the account, such as turning it over to a collection agency.

Other events could also affect the collection of cash. The goods may be returned for various reasons, resulting in no cash collection. The goods may be damaged in shipment, and the buyer may ask for a price adjustment (generally called a **price allowance**). There may also be an incentive built in to encourage prompt payment of cash, such as a **cash discount**, which means that less than the full amount will be accepted as full payment. For example, a seller may offer a 2% price discount if the account is paid within 10 days instead of the usual 30 days. These terms are sometimes stated as "2/10 net 30," which means that a 2% discount is offered if payment is made within 10 days; otherwise, the total amount is due at the end of 30 days.

Warranty Service

Some goods carry a written or implied guarantee of quality. Automobiles, for example, are warranted for a certain number of years or for a certain number of kilometres. During this period, the seller is responsible, to some extent, for replacement or repair of the product. Because the provision of warranty work often involves additional outlays of cash for employees' time and for the purchase of repair parts, warranty service affects the ultimate amount of cash that is available at the end of the cycle.

Summary of Cash-to-Cash Cycle

The net amount left in cash after this cycle is completed is then available to purchase more goods and services in the next cycle. If the cash inflows are less than the cash outflows, the amount of cash available is reduced, and the company may be unable to begin a new cycle without getting additional cash from outside the company in the form of equity or debt. To the extent that cash inflows exceed cash outflows, the company can expand its volume of activity, add another type of productive activity, or return some of the extra cash to shareholders in the form of dividends.

Note that the order of the phases in the cash-to-cash cycle may differ from one company to the next. For example, a transportation contractor such as Bombardier may do most of its selling activity early in the cycle to obtain contracts to deliver products at a future date, with much of the acquisition of raw materials and production taking place after the contract is signed. Also, in some companies the separate phases may take place simultaneously. In Safeway, for example, the delivery of goods to the customer and the collection of cash take place at the same point in time.

REVENUE RECOGNITION

Managers do not want to wait until the end of the cash-to-cash cycle to assess the performance of their company, because they must make day-to-day decisions that will ultimately affect the final cash outcome. If they wait until the end, they may not

Learning Objective
4

Describe the relationship between performance and revenue recognition.

be able to make appropriate adjustments. For example, if the sale of the first few items results in significant uncollected accounts or requires significant warranty service, the managers might want to rethink their policies on granting credit and providing warranties. If the cost of warranty service is too high, they might want to purchase a better quality of inventory so that the products last longer. Furthermore, the cash-to-cash cycle is a continual process that is constantly beginning and ending for different transactions. There is no specific point in time when all of the cash-to-cash transactions reach an end.

To measure operating performance as accurately as possible, accountants divide normal operating activities into two groups, revenues and expenses. **Revenues** are the inflows of cash or other assets from the normal operating activities of the business, which mainly involve the sale of goods or provision of services. **Expenses** are the costs incurred to earn revenues. The difference between revenues and expenses, called **net income**, is one of the key measurements of performance. The expression "in the red" is related to net income. In the past if a company had a negative net income (expenses > revenues), the net loss figure was actually written in red ink. The expression came to mean that a company had experienced a loss. The expression "in the black," although it was less commonly used, meant that you had a positive net income.

The need for timely information to make decisions argues for recognizing revenue as early as possible in the cash-to-cash cycle. The earlier in the cycle revenue is recognized, however, the greater the number of estimates needed to measure the net performance. For example, if the company chooses to recognize revenue at the time of delivery of the product to customers (a common practice for many businesses), it will have to make estimates regarding the collectibility of the receivables and costs of warranty service. To accurately measure the return (profitability) on the sale of a product, these items should be considered; otherwise, the company may be over-estimating the return on the sales of its products. To produce the most accurate measurement of net operating performance, all costs incurred to earn revenues are matched to the revenues they helped earn. In accrual accounting, this is called the **matching principle** (refer again to Chapter 2). The matching principle requires that all costs incurred or to be incurred (in the past, present, or future) to produce the revenue must be recognized at the same time that the revenue is recognized.

The question of when to recognize revenue is quite straightforward for some industries (e.g., clothing retailers). Revenue is recognized when the customer buys the goods in the store. For other industries the decision is not as clearly defined. Note the example on the following page.

The earlier in the cash-to-cash cycle the company chooses to recognize revenues, the less reliable is the company's estimate of the effects of future events. In return, however, the company receives more timely information. To reduce the uncertainty inherent in estimating future events, the company would need to recognize revenues later in the cash-to-cash cycle, when those estimates are more reliable, but the information would be less useful for making management decisions. The decision about when to recognize revenue is a very important one for managers. Knowing about the revenue recognition policy is also important for users, so that they can assess the reliability of the information.

accounting in the news

REVENUE RECOGNITION IN THE COMPUTER INDUSTRY

In the computer industry, some companies view the distributor as a customer while others view the distributor as a middleman. This appears to be at the heart of different revenue recognition styles in Silicon Valley. Accounting guidelines specify that revenue can be counted only after risks involved in the transaction no longer exist and after returns can be "reasonably" estimated. Companies such as Altera, a chipmaker, book sales as soon as the product leaves its factory for distributors; others, such as its competitor Xilinx, wait until distributors actually sell products in the U.S. before booking sales.

If business is good, companies usually don't have problems with booking revenue upon shipment to distributors. But when business isn't good, it can be tempting to convince distributors to take more than they want or need. This is called "stuffing the channel," and it can help smooth over rough spots on earnings reports. It's a gamble, though. If distributors can't return products, they aren't likely to re-order unless they can sell the goods—in this industry products quickly become obsolete—and if distributors have return rights, companies can face large returns that show up in write-offs and restated quarters.

Source: "Shipping Bricks and Other Tricks," by Herb Greenberg, *Fortune*, Sept. 29, 1997, pages 30 and 34.

There is obviously a conflict between the desire to measure performance on a timely basis (early in the cycle) and the ability to measure performance reliably (late in the cycle). **Revenue recognition criteria** have been developed within GAAP to resolve this conflict and to produce a measure of performance that is intended to balance the need for timely information with the need for reliable information. The issue is further complicated when the company is involved in two or more lines of business in which the cash-to-cash cycles may differ. A revenue recognition policy must be developed for each line, and they may not be the same.

AN INTERNATIONAL PERSPECTIVE

Reports from Other Countries

In countries other than Canada, income recognition may be based on different attributes. For instance, in Mexico, Argentina, Brazil, and the Netherlands,
income is determined on a current-cost basis; that is, net income reflects
adjustments of the property, plant, and equipment, and inventory to their
current replacement costs. The following excerpt from the annual report of
Tubos de Acero de México, S.A. (a Mexican company that manufactures and
sells seamless steel pipe, primarily for use in the petroleum industry) illustrates the income recognition principles:

> The Company recognizes the effects of inflation in its financial statements
> in accordance with accounting principles generally accepted in Mexico.
>   Inventories are stated at their estimated net replacement cost, which
> is not in excess of their realizable value. The cost of products sold reflects
> their estimated replacement cost at the time of sale, restated by apply-
> ing factors derived from the NCPI (National Consumer Price Index).
>   Property, plant and equipment (fixed assets) are stated at their esti-
> mated net replacement value determined based on appraisals made by
> independent experts registered with the National Securities Commission.
> Depreciation is calculated by the straight-line method, based on the esti-
> mated useful lives of the assets determined by the appraisers.

There are three specific factors to be considered before a revenue can be recognized. The first factor is whether the revenue has been **earned**. A revenue is considered to have been earned when the company has substantially completed what
it must do to be entitled to the benefits of the revenue. This is sometimes referred
to as "the earnings process being substantially complete." In general, this would
mean that the company has completed most of what it agreed to do and there are
very few costs yet to be incurred in the cash-to-cash cycle, or that the remaining
costs are subject to reasonable estimation, or both. Another way to consider this factor is to determine if all of the risks and rewards of the goods or service have been
transferred to the buyer. If they have, there can be very little left for the seller to do.

The second factor to consider is whether it is possible to measure how much has
been earned. This is often a straightforward answer. When goods or services are
sold for cash or an agreed selling price, the measurement issue is easy to determine.
Sometimes, however, goods or services are sold in exchange for other products,
services, or assets (other than accounts receivable). Then the measurement problem is more difficult. The accountant must examine the value of the goods or services sold and compare them with the value of the products, services, or assets
received. In deciding which of these values to use, the accountant will look for the
most reliable amount, the amount that can be most objectively determined.

The third factor is that there must be reasonable assurance that the amounts
earned can be collected from the buyer. If cash is collected at the time of sale, this third

factor is automatically satisfied. If, however, the goods or services are sold on credit, the seller must be reasonably assured that the amount owed will be collected. Companies will rarely sell goods or services on credit without running a credit check on the buyer, in order to obtain assurance of future collection of the accounts receivable. Even with this assurance, some customers may not pay the amounts owed. Because of this possibility, companies that recognize credit sales as revenue must, in the same period, recognize an expense that measures the probable uncollectibility of the accounts receivable, in order to keep the revenues from being overstated. We call this expense "bad debt expense." More will be said about this expense in Chapter 6.

Revenue Recognition Criteria

1. The revenue has been earned. (The company has completed substantially everything it has to do with respect to the sale.)
2. The amount earned can be measured.
3. There is reasonable assurance of collectibility of the amount earned.

Learning Objective 5

Describe the criteria for revenue recognition.

In conclusion, if revenues have been earned, and the amounts earned can be measured and there is reasonable assurance that they will be collected, they should be recognized in the financial statements. These conditions are usually met at the time of delivery of the product to the customer, so this is the point at which many companies recognize their revenues. The following sections discuss various applications of revenue recognition, including the point of sale to the customer as well as at other points on the cash-to-cash cycle.

Applications of Revenue Recognition

The revenue recognition criteria can be met at different points on the cash-to-cash cycle. Therefore, the point at which different companies recognize revenues can vary, as you observed in the article about Silicon Valley. Several applications that you will see in practice are discussed in the following subsections.

Learning Objective 6

Describe various applications of the revenue recognition criteria.

Revenue Recognition at the Time of Sale

The most common point at which revenues are recognized is the time of sale and/or shipment of goods to the customer. Once the goods have been taken by or shipped to the customer, the company has completed everything it has to do with respect to the transaction. The title to the goods has been transferred and the revenue has been earned. The first criterion has been met. At the time of sale, the amount that is earned is known. Often the customer will pay cash, which is easy to measure. If the company sells the goods on credit, the amount owed is still fairly easy to determine, which means the second criterion has been met. Lastly, the company will have to be reasonably assured of collecting the accounts receivable before revenue can be recognized. Most companies will not sell on credit if they have doubts about the collectibility of the amount.

In annual reports, most companies state their revenue recognition policy as part of the first note, which includes a summary of the significant accounting policies of the company. For example, in its 1998 financial statements, Mosaid Technologies Incorporated states its revenue recognition policy in Note 1 to the financial statements:

> *Revenue from design contracts is recognized on a percentage of completion basis. Revenue from product sales is generally recognized on shipment. A provision for potential warranty claims against shipments is provided for at the time of sale, based on warranty terms and prior claims experience. Service revenue is recognized when the service is performed, or, in the case of maintenance contracts, is recognized on a straight-line basis over the term of the contract.*

The disclosure by Tyco Toys Inc. states that:

> *Sales are recorded as product is shipped, F.O.B. point of shipment. The Company provides for defective returns based upon a percentage of gross sales, based on historical experience.*

The term "F.O.B." means "free on board" and is a legal term used to describe the point at which title to the goods passes. In this case, because the goods are shipped *F.O.B. shipping point*, the title passes after the goods leave the seller's loading dock (the shipping point). If they were shipped *F.O.B. destination*, the goods would remain the property of the seller until they reached their destination, the buyer's receiving dock. The way the goods are shipped will affect the point at which revenue can be recognized. The point at which title to the goods passes is a clear indication that the seller has earned the revenue. Prior to that point, the seller is still responsible for the goods.

Another example of this basis for recording revenues appears in the 1998 financial statements of Haley Industries Limited.

HALEY INDUSTRIES LIMITED

B) Basis of recording revenue
Revenue is recognized when title passes to the purchaser, which is usually when the goods are conveyed to a carrier or when the tooling is accepted by the customer.

To illustrate revenue recognition at the time of sale, assume that Hawke Company sells 1,000 units of its product during the year 20x1 at $30 per unit. Assume further that the costs of these units totalled $22,000 and that, at the time of sale, Hawke estimated they would cost the company an additional $500 in warranty expenses in the future. The income statement for Hawke for 20x1 would appear as in Exhibit 4-2.

■ Revenue Recognition at Time of Sale

EXHIBIT 4-2

HAWKE COMPANY
Income Statement
For the period ended December 31, 20x1

Revenues	$30,000
Cost of goods sold	22,000
Gross profit	8,000
Warranty expense	500
Net income	$ 7,500

Note that although Hawke Company may not have incurred any actual warranty expenses yet, it recognizes an expense equal to its estimate of what the future warranty costs might be. This is what Mosaid Technologies was referring to in its note describing its revenue recognition criteria. Recognizing the warranty expense is appropriate, because the future warranty costs are directly related to the revenue. Therefore, if the company wants to recognize the revenue before it knows the actual warranty cost, it must estimate what those costs might be—so that the revenue is not overstated. At the same time that it recognizes the warranty expense, it recognizes a liability for these future costs. When actual costs are incurred, the liability is reduced and no further expense is recognized.

In some cases, a company might receive a deposit for a product to be delivered in the future. Because it is unlikely that the revenue recognition criteria would be met by this transaction (until the product is delivered, the company has not *earned* the revenue), the revenue from this order is not recorded until the goods are delivered (title passes). The deposit is then recorded as revenue received in advance or unearned revenue (a liability account that represents an obligation to either deliver the goods or return the deposit). For example, if Hawke Company received a $500 deposit on an order, it would make the following entry:

A-Cash   500
    L-Unearned revenue   500

When the goods are delivered, the liability to provide the product is satisfied (the company has done what it had to do with respect to completing the sale), and the deposit can then be recognized as a revenue with the following entry:

L-Unearned revenue   500
    SE-Sales revenue   500

Businesses that require deposits or advance payments on products or services may disclose this in their note on revenue recognition. Typical disclosures for this type of situation are shown here for Canadian Airlines Corporation (1998). Note that liabilities are created for the obligation to provide the service or product in the future.

> **CANADIAN AIRLINES CORPORATION (1998)**
>
> **1. Significant Accounting Policies**
> **g) Revenue recognition:**
> Air transportation revenue is recognized when the transportation is provided. The value of unused tickets or portions thereof is included in the balance sheet as advance ticket sales under current liabilities.
> **h) Frequent flyer program:**
> The incremental costs of providing travel awards under the Corporation's "Canadian Plus" and affiliated carriers' frequent flyer programs are accrued as the entitlements to such awards are earned and are included in accounts payable and accrued liabilities.

Revenue Recognition at the Time of Contract Signing

Even though the point of sale—or, more correctly, the point at which title to the product is transferred to the buyer from the seller—is the most common method used to recognize revenues, there are several situations that require exceptions to this application of revenue recognition. Over the years, certain types of transaction have caused concern, among investors and accountants, about the revenue recognition practices employed. Two of these were in the areas of franchising and retail land sales. Both of these industries initially recognized revenues at the date of contract signing. In the case of franchisers, this contract was the initial franchise agreement. In the case of retail land sale companies, it was the land sale agreement. The problem was that, in both cases, there was a considerable amount of uncertainty with regard to future costs on the seller's part subsequent to contract signing and with regard to the collectibility of the receivables from buyers. Questions were raised as to whether any of the revenue recognition criteria were being met.

The uncertainty stemmed from industry practices. Franchisers (such as McDonald's) typically agree to provide a significant amount of service, such as assistance in locating and designing the franchise facility and in training the staff, subsequent to the signing of a franchise agreement and prior to the opening of the business. Therefore, at the time of contract signing, is the earning process complete? In addition, the initial franchise fee is typically paid in instalments, which raised questions about the reasonableness of future collectibility.

Retail land sale companies often sell land before it is developed and, therefore, have yet to incur the development costs. This means that the seller has not completed everything that must be done; the earning process is not substantially complete. There is also the problem of matching the future development costs to the revenues. Remember that if you want to recognize revenue before all of the costs associated with the sale are incurred (note the warranty example), you must be able to estimate those future costs so that they can be recognized at the same time as the revenue (matching). Sales contracts typically require low downpayments and sometimes below-market interest rates to entice buyers to sign contracts. These conditions make it relatively easy for a buyer to back out of the transaction before all the cash is collected, thereby negating the sale.

Given the fact that in the past the earning process was rarely complete, coupled with the uncertainties with regard to future costs and the collectibility of the receivables, revenue for franchisers and retail land sale companies is now recognized at the time of contract signing only if certain basic criteria are met. These criteria are, first, that only minimal costs are yet to be incurred (this means that the seller has completed substantially everything that has to done to conclude the sale), and, second, that the receivables created in the transaction have a reasonable chance of being collected. These industries have special accounting guidelines because of the special nature of the activities surrounding revenue recognition. The following excerpts from the financial statements of Comac Food Group Inc. and H. Jager Developments Inc. typify the revenue recognition policies of franchisers and land sale companies.

COMAC FOOD GROUP INC. (1998)

Franchise revenue

Income from the sale of franchised stores is recognized when the franchise commences store operations. Revenue received for franchised store locations not open at year end are recorded as deferred revenue.

Franchise royalties are based on retail store sales of the franchises and recorded as earned.

H. JAGER DEVELOPMENTS INC. (1999)

Revenue recognition

Revenue is recognized when a contract for sale is signed, a minimum of 15 percent of the sale proceeds has been received and the collectibility of the remaining proceeds is reasonably assured. Proceeds due from sale of land are presented as agreements receivable.

Revenue Recognition at the Time of Production

Revenue recognition at the time of production is common in two different kinds of industry: mining and long-term construction. If the market value and the sale of the product are both fairly certain at the time of production, as in certain mining operations, the inventories produced can be valued at their net realizable value (selling price) and the resulting revenues can be recognized immediately. The reason for this practice is that the critical event in the revenue-earning process for the mine is not the sale of the ore, but the *production* of the ore. Because the market for the ore is well established, with fairly stable prices, the sale is assured as soon as the ore is produced. By recording the revenues as soon as possible, these companies have more timely information for making decisions.

An example of this revenue recognition method is Bema Gold Company, which operates gold and silver mines.

BEMA GOLD CORPORATION (1998)

Revenue Recognition
Revenue is recorded at the estimated net realizable value when the gold is shipped. Adjustments to these amounts are made after final prices, weights and assays are established. The Company may fix the price it will receive for part or all of its production by entering into forward or option contracts.

Note that for Bema Gold Corporation the earning process is complete when the gold is shipped. At this point the final amount of the sale is fairly certain, but it can still change as a result of final prices, weights, and assays. Although the exact amount earned is not known, Bema Gold is able to make a reasonable estimate of the amount, and it adjusts future revenues for any differences that occur. If it uses forward or option contracts, the amount earned is known for certain. A forward or option contract is a contract that stipulates the amount that will be paid for the gold in the future.

The second type of industry that recognizes revenue at the time of production is one in which the production period is long, such as in the long-term construction industry. Disclosures for Western Star Trucks Holdings Ltd. and Bombardier Inc. illustrate this type of revenue recognition:

WESTERN STAR TRUCKS HOLDINGS LTD. (1998)

Revenue recognition
Revenue from the sale of manufactured buses is recognized on a percentage of completion method, applied on the basis of defined milestones. Provisions are made for anticipated losses, if any, as soon as they become evident. Unbilled revenue represents revenue that has been recorded under the percentage of completion method but has not yet been invoiced to the customer.

BOMBARDIER INC. (1998)

Long-term contracts and programs
Revenues and income from long-term contracts are recognized in accordance with the percentage-of-completion method of accounting. The degree of completion is generally determined by comparing the costs incurred to date to the total costs anticipated for the entire contract, excluding costs that are not representative of the measure of performance. Estimated revenues from long-term contracts include the future revenues from claims when it is reasonably assured that such claims, resulting from work performed for customers in addition to the work contemplated in the original contracts, will result in additional revenues in an amount that can be reliably estimated.

In the long-term construction industry, two methods of recognizing revenue are generally accepted: the **completed contract method** and the **percentage of completion method**. The completed contract method defers the recognition of revenue until the contract is completed and is generally used for projects that are completed in a reasonably short period of time. Longer-term projects are generally accounted for using the percentage of completion method (you will have noticed that both Western Star Trucks and Bombardier use this method), which recognizes a portion of the revenues and expenses of a project during the construction period based on the percentage of completion. The basis for determining the percentage that is complete is usually the costs incurred relative to the estimated total costs.

As an example, suppose that the Solid Construction Company agrees to construct a building for $100 million that will take three years to build, and the company expects to incur costs of $25 million, $35 million, and $10 million in years 1, 2, and 3, respectively. The total expected costs are $70 million, and, therefore, the profit on the project is expected to be $30 million. If all goes according to plan, Solid Construction would recognize the revenues and expenses (and related profits) shown in Exhibit 4-3 during the three years with the percentage of completion method.

Revenue Recognition with the Percentage of Completion Method

EXHIBIT 4-3

(Amounts in thousands)

Year	Degree of Completion		Revenue Recognized		Expenses Recognized	Profit
1	$25,000/$70,000 =	36%	36% x 100,000 =	$ 36,000	$25,000	$11,000
2	$35,000/$70,000 =	50%	50% x 100,000 =	$ 50,000	$35,000	$15,000
3	$10,000/$70,000 =	14%	14% x 100,000 =	$ 14,000	$10,000	$ 4,000
		100%		$100,000	$70,000	$30,000

The formulae to arrive at these amounts are as follows:

$$\frac{\text{Expenses for this period}}{\text{Total cost of project}} = \text{Percentage completed}$$

$$\text{Percentage completed} \times \text{Total revenue} = \text{Revenue to be recognized this period}$$

How well does the percentage of completion method apply the revenue recognition criteria? The first criterion is that the amount has been earned (or the work the company agreed to do has been performed). Instead of waiting until all of the contract work has been completed (which can take several years), the company can, using this method, measure how much work has been completed so far and then recognize as revenue the same percentage of the total contract price. The expenses for the period and the percentage of revenue earned are recognized each period, which provides information to users more often. The second criterion is that you can measure how much you have earned. We do that using the above formulae. The third criterion is that there is a reasonable probability of collection. For many long-term construction contracts, the buyer is billed periodically through the construction process. The periodic billing and collection provide the seller with the ability to estimate collectibility. Because the revenue recognition criteria have been satisfied, it is preferable to use the percentage of completion method rather than wait until the contract work is complete.

If Solid Construction had used the completed contract method, all the revenues and expenses would have been deferred and recognized at the time of completion. That is, the entire $100 million in revenue, $70 million in expenses, and $30 million in profit would have been recognized in year 3. Considering how the percentage of completion method works, and considering that it satisfies the revenue recognition criteria, under what circumstances would it be appropriate to use the completed contract method? Some contracts take less than a year to complete. For such contracts, it might be just as informative to users to wait until the entire contract is finished. If the contract took longer than a year, and if one or more of the revenue recognition criteria were not met, the company would choose to use the completed contract method. It may not be possible to measure how much of the project is completed, which would make the measurement of the revenue earned difficult to determine. There could also be a question about the future collectibility on the contract although it is doubtful if a company would continue to work on a project if it was concerned about future payment for its work.

With either the percentage of completion method or the completed contract method, if an overall loss is projected on the project, Generally Accepted Accounting Principles (GAAP) require that the loss be recognized as soon as it can be estimated. For example, if it turned out that, at the end of year 2, the total estimated costs to complete the contract of Solid Construction were $105 million ($60 million in year 2 and $20 million in year 3, plus the $25 million already incurred in year 1), instead of the original $70 million, an overall loss of $5 million would be indicated for the contract. At the end of year 2, Solid Construction would have to recognize a loss of $16 million. This loss would offset the $11 million profit reported in year 1 and would result in a net loss at this point of $5 million on the contract. If the actual costs equalled the new estimated costs in year 3, no additional profit or loss would be recorded in year 3, as the overall loss on the contract would already have been recognized.

The recognition of the estimated loss in the preceding example is partially a result of the conservative nature of accounting. Conservatism requires that losses generally be recognized as soon as they can be estimated, but profits are seldom recognized until they are realized.

Revenue Recognition at the Time of Collection

Except for cash sales, seldom will the revenue recognition criteria not be met prior to the collection of cash. Therefore, for reporting purposes, the collectibility of cash rarely delays the recognition of revenue. In some circumstances, however, the collection of the receivable is so uncertain that GAAP would require that revenue recognition be postponed until cash is actually collected. In these rare situations, the **instalment method** can be used. This method delays the recognition of revenue until the actual cash is received. The revenue recognition policy of PGI Inc., which follows, refers to the use of the instalment method in certain circumstances. Note that the use of the instalment method postpones the recognition of revenue until cash is collected, which means that the company would not record revenues at the normal point of sale.

PGI INC.

Prior to July 1992, homesites were generally sold under contracts for deed or deed, note and mortgage which provide for a down payment and monthly instalments, including interest, for periods up to ten years. Prior to 1990 income from sales of homesites was recorded when minimum down payment (including interest) and other requirements were met. However, because of collectibility problems with certain off-site broker/foreign sales programs, effective January 1, 1990, the Company adopted the instalment method of profit recognition.

In an instalment type of sale, the buyer agrees to pay for the goods or service over time, sometimes over many months or years. The seller sets the payments that the buyer makes so that all costs incurred can be recovered, a profit is made on the sale, and suitable interest is charged for the loan the seller is making to the buyer. Therefore, the payments received by the seller can be viewed as covering three things: cost recovery, interest, and profits.

The instalment method can be illustrated with a simple example. Assume that the Sunshine Land Company sells for $100,000 a homesite that has a cost of $70,000. Further, assume that the buyer has agreed to make three instalment payments, over the next three years, of $40,000, $40,000, and $40,000, or a set of payments of $120,000. The excess of the payments over the selling price, $20,000, represents interest. Assume that Sunshine decides to recognize interest evenly over the three years, or $6,667 per year. This is not generally done, but it will simplify matters for the purposes of this example. Exhibit 4-4 shows the amount of income that will be recognized with the instalment method.

■ Revenue Recognition with the Instalment Method

EXHIBIT 4-4

Profit %   = ($100,000 − $70,000)/$100,000 = 30%
Gross profit = Payments applied to principal × profit %
              = (Cash received − interest) × profit %

Year	Gross Profits	Interest
1	($40,000 − $6,667) × 30% = $10,000	$ 6,667
2	($40,000 − $6,667) × 30% = $10,000	$ 6,667
3	($40,000 − $6,666) × 30% = $10,000	$ 6,666
Total	$30,000	$20,000

In year 1, an account receivable of $100,000 would be recognized along with a deferred gross profit of $30,000. The deferred gross profit would be included with the liabilities and represents profit that will be recognized in the future. When the first payment of $40,000 is received, the following journal entry would result:

A-Cash	40,000	
L-Deferred gross profit	10,000	
A-Accounts receivable		33,333
SE-Revenue		10,000
SE-Interest revenue		6,667

In subsequent years as payments are received the account receivable and the deferred gross profit will be reduced and revenue will be recognized.

Although we have shown you some of the accounting behind the instalment method, we do not expect that you will be required to learn the details behind the method, for two reasons. First, it is quite complicated and more appropriately handled in an intermediate accounting course. For an introductory course, it is important only that you know a little about the method so that you will understand how revenue is recognized in a company that uses the instalment method. Second, this method is not used very often in Canada. If you think about companies in which the instalment method might be used, such as Sears Canada or The Bay, which allow customers to use their credit cards and pay over time, you will probably be surprised to learn that neither of these companies uses this method. Remember that this method is used only if there is a question about the potential collectibility of the amount owed. Both of these companies have been using credit card sales for a long time and have developed reliable methods for estimating uncollectibility. If they can estimate the potential uncollectibility, they can recognize both the revenue and potential uncollectibility at the point of sale. Therefore, the instalment method becomes unnecessary.

Revenue Recognition with Multiple Lines of Business

For companies that have multiple lines of business or that sell products in standard as well as customized models, the revenue recognition criteria may be met at different points for different products. The disclosures for CHC Helicopter Company illustrate this point.

CHC HELICOPTER COMPANY

Revenue Recognition
Revenues from helicopter operations are recognized based on the terms of customer contracts which generally provide for revenue on the basis of hours flown at contract rates or fixed monthly charges or a combination of both.

    Revenues from engine and component repair and overhaul operations are recognized on the percentage of completion basis, measured on the basis of the sales value of the actual costs incurred and work performed.

Learning Objective

8

Explain the impact various revenue recognition methods have on earnings recognition.

The choice of a revenue recognition policy is one of the critical policy decisions made by a company. The timing of revenue recognition will affect future profitability measures. Even when a company has a policy that meets the revenue recognition criteria, users may have concerns. Note the news item about Yogen Früz presented on the next page.

ethics in accounting

■ Pressures to show profit or growth in revenues, or both, can create ethical dilemmas for managers and accountants. Some of these pressures are self-imposed, particularly if the manager's remuneration is tied to reported profits or revenues. Other pressures may be externally imposed, by someone more senior in the organization or by the shareholders. Suppose, for example, that you are the accountant of a division of a company and that the manager of the division has asked you to make an adjusting entry for the period to recognize a large order. Revenue in your company is usually recorded when the goods are shipped, not when the order is placed. The manager has indicated that this order will bump the division over its sales target for the year and that the bonuses of several managers in the division will be significantly affected. She has also indicated that the company is about to issue more common shares and that her boss would like to show improved results from last year to get the most favourable price for the shares that will be issued. What should you do? Identify the individuals who will be helped and hurt by your decision in order to help you determine what to do.

accounting in the news

DOUBTS ABOUT BOOKING REVENUE EARLY

How a company recognizes revenue can be a subject of debate, even when its methods fall within generally accepted accounting principles (GAAP). In fiscal 1997, frozen yogurt franchiser Yogen Früz recognized some $5.5 million in revenue from the sale of franchise agreements, although it did not receive payment in that accounting period.

Yogen Früz received criticism for booking revenue early. Under GAAP, the revenue recognition principle says that revenue should be recognized in the accounting period in which the revenue is earned. But Yogen Früz defended its accounting practices, saying that the conditions of the sale had been met, the company had fulfilled its obligations, and the revenue had a reasonable chance of being collected. Further, Yogen Früz pointed out that a "significant portion" of the receivable had indeed already been collected.

Was Yogen Früz too aggressive in its accounting? Despite GAAP, revenue recognition retains a large element of subjectivity.

Source: "Yogen Früz defends accounting policy," from Dow Jones News, *Toronto Star*, Sept. 11, 1998, page E4.

The preceding article illustrates that even though a company establishes a policy that is within an accounting guideline, users may have concerns. It is important for companies to respond to concerns, as Yogen Früz did in this instance. Otherwise users will begin to question the validity of the performance results reported by the company, which could, in turn, undermine investor and creditor confidence.

S U M M A R Y

In this chapter, we first discussed some measures of performance—namely, ROI. This discussion led to an explanation of the cash-to-cash cycle and its importance in understanding the performance of a company. Tying in with the cash-to-cash cycle are the concepts underlying the recognition of revenue. We looked at revenue at the time of sale, at the time of contract signing, at the time of production, and at the time of collection. These concepts were explored to improve your understanding of net income as a measure of performance of the business. Companies use different revenue recognition criteria, according to the type of revenue they are generating. When assessing the performance of a company it is important for you to understand the type of revenue it is generating and the revenue recognition policy it has established. If you know these two things you will be better able to understand its cash-to-cash cycle.

While net income is a useful measure of performance, it is not the only measure of performance in which users of financial statements should be interested. In the next chapter, the cash flow statement will be considered. We had a brief look at this statement in Chapter 1. Now we will explore it in more detail. The construction of the statement itself, as well as the interpretation of the information contained in the statement, will be discussed. The implications regarding the health of the company above and beyond those shown on the income statement will also be discussed.

SUMMARY PROBLEMS

1. Suppose that Guenther Construction Ltd. is in the construction business and enters into a contract with a customer to construct a building. The contract price is $10 million and the estimated cost of the building is $6 million. The construction is estimated to take three years to complete.

   Required:
   Prepare a schedule of the revenues and expenses that would be recognized in income in each of the three years with each of the following methods:

   a. Recognition of income at contract signing.

   b. Percentage of completion method, assuming the following schedule of estimated costs:

Year	Amount
1	$3,000,000
2	$1,800,000
3	$1,200,000

   c. Completed contract method.

2. Jonathan, Anthony, and Kendra operated a bicycle shop, The Silver Spoke. They sold assembled bicycles and bicycle accessories. They had a shop in the back where

Kendra repaired bicycles. Occasionally they would be given a contract to assemble 20 to 50 bicycles for one of the major retailers like The Bay. Customers used either cash or credit cards when buying bicycles or bicycle accessories. For minor repairs, the customer paid upon completion of the repairs. For major repairs, The Silver Spoke asked for a downpayment equal to 25% of the estimated cost of the repair. The remaining 75% was paid when the work was complete. When the company assembled bicycles for another retailer, it billed the other retailer upon completion of the work. The company normally received payment within 30 days of submitting the bill.

Required:
Using the revenue recognition criteria, recommend when The Silver Spoke should recognize revenue for each of its various revenue-generating activities.

SUGGESTED SOLUTIONS TO SUMMARY PROBLEMS

1. a. Recognizing revenue at the time of contract signing would probably not be allowed under GAAP because of the extended construction period of the contract. If it were allowed, all the profit, $4 million, would be recognized in the first year and none in later years.

    b. Percentage of completion method (answers in thousands)

Year	Degree of Completion		Revenue Recognized		Expenses Recognized	Profit
1	$3,000/$6,000 =	50%	50% × $10,000 =	$ 5,000	$3,000	$2,000
2	$1,800/$6,000 =	30%	30% × $10,000 =	$ 3,000	$1,800	$1,200
3	$1,200/$6,000 =	20%	20% × $10,000 =	$ 2,000	$1,200	$ 800
		100%		$10,000	$6,000	$4,000

    c. Completed contract method (answers in thousands)

Year	Revenue	Expense	Profit
1	0	0	0
2	0	0	0
3	$10,000	$6,000	$4,000
	$10,000	$6,000	$4,000

2. Sales of bicycles and bicycle accessories: The company should recognize revenue at the time of the sale. At this time, the customer leaves with the merchandise (title transfers); therefore, the company has completed what it has to do, the amount that has been earned is measurable, and the amount has been collected either with cash or through a credit card.

    Minor repairs: The company should recognize revenue when the work is completed. Similar to the situation for the sale of bicycles, the company has completed the work, the amount owed has been measured, and the customer has already paid.

    Major repairs: The company should recognize revenue when the work is completed. When the customer makes the 25% downpayment, the work has not been completed yet. As well, the total amount owed is still unknown. Therefore, two of the criteria have not been met. The company should record the downpayment as unearned revenue. When the repairs are completed, the company will have completed the work (therefore, earned the revenue), the total amount owed is known, and the customer pays for the work with cash or a credit card. At this time, all three of the criteria have been met.

Assembly contract: The company should recognize revenue when the assembly work is completed. At the time of the contract signing, although the company knows how much it will receive and is likely confident that it will receive that amount, the company has not assembled any bicycles. Because a substantial amount of work is yet to be done, the company has not earned the revenue. When the work is complete, the amount it has earned is known and it is reasonable to assume that it will collect the amount owed. At this time, the revenue recognition criteria have been met and revenue should be recognized.

ABBREVIATIONS USED

FOB	Free on board	ROE	Return on equity
GAAP	Generally accepted accounting principles	ROI	Return on investment
ROA	Return on assets		

GLOSSARY

Account receivable   An amount owing as a result of the sale of a product or service.

Cash discount   A reduction in the amount that has to be paid on an account payable or account receivable if payment is made within a specified time limit.

Cash-to-cash cycle   The operating cycle of the company, describing the operating activities of the company from the initial outlays of cash to make a product or to provide a service, to the replacement of cash through collections from customers.

Completed contract method   A method of revenue recognition used in the construction industry in which the revenues from a contract are recognized only when the contract is completed.

Cost   The value of whatever is given up to acquire an item.

Earned   A term used to indicate that the company has completed its earnings process sufficiently to allow the recognition of the revenues from the sale.

Expenses   The costs incurred to earn revenues.

Financing activities   Those activities that involve acquiring cash from long-term loans and investments by owners.

Instalment method   A method of revenue recognition based on cash collections in which each payment received is viewed as part profit and part recovery of costs. A fraction of each payment received is recorded as profit.

Investing activities   Those activities that involve the buying and selling of long-term assets.

Matching principle   A concept that requires all expenses related to the production of revenues to be recorded during the same time period that the revenues are recorded. The expenses are said to be matched with the revenues.

Measurement   The process of determining an appropriate amount or value of some attribute of the item being measured.

Net income   The difference between revenues and expenses.

Operating activities   Those activities involving the cash effects of the normal operations of a business, such as the buying and selling of goods and services.

Percentage of completion method   A method of revenue recognition used in the construction industry in which a percentage of the profits that are expected to be realized from a given project is recognized in a given period, based on the percentage of completion of the project. The percentage complete is typically measured as the fraction of costs incurred to date relative to the total estimated costs to complete the project.

Price allowance   An adjustment made to the selling price of a good or service to satisfy a customer, typically for some defect in the good or service provided.

Recognition   Recognizing an item for inclusion in a financial statement, including both the description and the amount.

Return on investment   A measure of performance of an investment, calculated as the ratio of the return from the investment to the average amount invested.

Revenues The inflows of cash or other assets from the normal operating activities of the business, which mainly involve the sale of goods or provision of services.

Revenue recognition criteria Criteria developed in GAAP that specify the conditions under which revenue should be recognized.

ASSIGNMENT MATERIAL

Assessing Your Recall

4-1 Explain how ROI measures performance.

4-2 Draw a diagram of a typical cash-to-cash cycle of a retail company, and briefly describe the various components of the cycle.

4-3 List the three major revenue recognition criteria that exist under GAAP.

4-4 Describe the concept of a revenue being "earned," and contrast it with the concept of a revenue being "realized."

4-5 Explain the difference between the percentage of completion method and the completed contract method.

4-6 Describe how the instalment method is implemented and explain why it is rarely used in practice.

4-7 Explain the meaning of the matching principle.

4-8 Describe the accounting treatment for a deposit made by a customer for the future delivery of inventory. Using the revenue recognition criteria, explain the rationale for this treatment.

Applying Your Knowledge

4-9 (Revenue recognition criteria)
In the opening story of this chapter, the Consumer Marketing Director of *Shift Magazine* explained how the company recognized revenue. Using the revenue recognition criteria described in this chapter, explain the appropriateness of the revenue policy the company has adopted for revenue from advertisers and revenue from subscribers.

4-10 (Calculate the ROI)
Calculate the ROI for the following investments:

a. Christie Jamison had $430 in her savings account at the beginning of the year. During the year she deposited $60 on her birthday and $100 at Christmas. She earned interest of $18.80.

b. Juan Garcia bought five shares in Nortel for $79.40 each. He kept the shares all year. During the year he received $0.30 per share in dividends. By the end of the year the share price had risen to $84.50.

c. Paul Hancock received a one-year guaranteed investment certificate for $1,200 from his grandmother. At the end of the year when he cashed it in, he received $1,266.

d. The Apple Crisp Cookie Company had $635,900 in assets at the beginning of the year and $670,300 at the end. During the year it earned net income of $22,900.

e. Harjit Sangra has an uncle in the United States. For her birthday, he sent her $50 in U.S. money. On her birthday, if she had sold the $50 U.S. to the bank for Canadian money she would have received $70.42 in Canadian dollars. If she sells the $50 U.S. today she will receive $75.75 in Canadian funds.

4-11 (Calculate the ROI)
Calculate the ROI for the following investments:

a. The Melrose Motor Company bought an investment in a supply company for $90,000. During the year it received dividends equal to $2,000.

b. Jack Valaas bought 5,000 shares in his sister's retail company for $15,000. The company earned a net income of $75,000, which resulted in an earnings per share of $3.75.

c. Margot Chan bought 10 shares in Air Canada for $7.50 per share. One year later she had not received a dividend but the shares were selling at $14.75 per share.

d. The Down Rite Dirty Disposal Company had $1,340,000 in assets at the beginning of the year and $1,150,000 at the end. During the year it earned net income of $112,000.

e. The Bainbridge family bought a home in Calgary for $160,000. Two years later, a real estate agent told them that they could probably sell their home for $210,000.

4-12 (Revenue recognition and the income statement)
Jones Sales Company was incorporated on January 1, 2000. During 2000, it bought products costing $126,500, and at midnight on December 31, 2000, it had $12,200 of the products left in its warehouse. The accounts payable balance at the end of the year was $6,500. It had recorded sales of $221,000 during 2000. The accounts receivable balance at the end of the year was $20,000. The accountant determined that $500 had been earned on one of its investments although the cash amount would not be received by the company until the following year.

> *Required:*
> Prepare as much of the income statement for Jones for 2000 as you can, showing the proper amount of sales, cost of goods sold, gross profit, and any other amounts that can be included. Show all calculations.

4-13 (Revenue recognition and the income statement)
The Tinder Box Furnace Company installed furnaces and air conditioners in homes and businesses. Each of the furnaces carried a five-year warranty and the air conditioners had a four-year warranty. During 2001, the company had sales of $1,230,000. Customers paid half of the sales price when they made arrangements for the installation of a furnace or air conditioner and paid the other half after it was installed. At the end of the year, $65,000 of the sales amount represented amounts paid for furnaces or air conditioners, but they were not yet installed, and the second half of the payment had not been received yet. The cost associated with the sales was $580,000 for the actual furnaces and air conditioners that have been installed this year. An additional cost of $245,000 was incurred for the labour costs associated with the installation. The accountant estimated that future warranty costs associated with the installed items would be $65,000 over the next five years.

> *Required:*
> Prepare as much of the income statement for Tinder Box Furnace Company for 2001 as you can, showing the proper amount of sales, cost of goods sold, gross profit, and any other amounts that can be included. Show all calculations.

4-14 (Revenue recognition on long-term contract)
Brickstone Construction Company signs a contract to construct a building over four years for $20,000,000. The expected costs are:

Year 1:	$ 4,750,000
Year 2:	$ 5,000,000
Year 3:	$ 3,500,000
Year 4:	$ 3,000,000
Total	$16,250,000

The building is completed in year 4.

> *Required:*
> Compute, for each year, the total revenue, expense, and profit using each of the following methods:
>
> a. The percentage of completion method
>
> b. The completed contract method

4-15 (Revenue recognition on instalment sale)
Sandra Carlson sold her house costing $180,000 to Bob Fletcher for $250,000. Bob agreed to pay $60,000 per year for a period of five years.

> *Required:*
> Compute the accounts receivable, interest revenue, and profit at the end of each of the five years, assuming that the interest is earned evenly over the five years.

4-16 (Revenue recognition on instalment sale)
Imperial Company purchases a factory from Superior Manufacturing Company for $1.5 million. The cost of the factory in Superior's records is $975,000. The terms of agreement are that yearly payments of $705,000, $505,000, $455,000, and $255,000 will be made over the next four years. Each of these payments includes an interest payment of $105,000 per year.

> *Required:*
> a. Under what conditions would it be reasonable for Superior to recognize all of the profit on the sale in the first year?
>
> b. Under what conditions would it be important to delay recognition until the actual cash payments are received?
>
> c. Compute the accounts receivable, interest expense, and profit at the end of each of the four years, assuming all of the profit is recognized in the first year.

4-17 (Revenue recognition on long-term contract)
Cruise Shipping Inc. agreed to rebuild the *Santa Marice*, an old cargo ship owned by the Oceanic Shipping Company. Both parties signed the contract on November 28, 2000, for $120 million, which is to be paid as follows:

$10 million at the signing of the contract
$20 million on December 30, 2001
$40 million on June 1, 2002
$50 million at completion, on August 15, 2003

The following costs were incurred by Cruise Shipping Inc. (in millions):

2000:	$21.2
2001:	$36.4
2002:	$26.0
2003:	$12.4
Total	$96.0

Required:

a. Compute the revenue, expense, and profit for each of the four years (ignoring interest) that Cruise Shipping Inc. should report using each of the following methods:

1. Percentage of completion method

2. Completed contract method

b. Which method do you think should be employed by Cruise Shipping Inc. to show the company's performance under the contract? Why?

4-18 (Revenue recognition on long-term contract)
Computronics Company received a contract on March 3, 2000, to set up a central communications centre for a college. The contract price was $1 million, to be paid as follows:

$200,000 at the signing of the contract
$ 60,000 on July 1, 2000
$ 50,000 on December 31, 2000
$ 50,000 on March 25, 2001
$100,000 on August 25, 2001
$150,000 on December 31, 2001
$390,000 on June 30, 2002

The system was completed on June 30, 2002.

Estimated and actual costs were:

$140,000	for the four months ending June 30, 2000
$210,000	for the six months ending December 31, 2000
$240,500	for the six months ending June 30, 2001
$ 90,000	for the six months ending December 31, 2001
$ 69,500	for the six months ending June 30, 2002
Total $ 750,000	

Required:

a. Compute the revenue, expense, and profit that Computronics should report for each of the six-month periods ending June 30 and December 31, using each of the following methods:

1. Percentage of completion method

2. Completed contract method

b. Which method should be used by Computronics Company? Why?

4-19 (Loss on long-term contract)
Free Form Builders Inc., a construction company, recognizes revenue from its long-term contracts using the percentage of completion method. On March 29, 2000, the company signed a contract to construct a building for $500,000. The company estimated

that it would take four years to complete the contract and estimated the cost to the company at $325,000. The expected costs in each of the four years are as follows:

Year	Cost
2000	$110,750
2001	$100,500
2002	$ 84,250
2003	$ 29,500
Total	$325,000

On December 31, 2001, the date Free Form closes its books, the company revised its estimates for the cost in 2002 and 2003. It estimated that it would cost $200,000 in 2002 and $100,000 in 2003 to complete the contract.

Required:
Compute the revenue, expense, and profit/loss for each of the four years.

4-20 (Revenue recognition on instalment sale)
Samson Industries purchased furniture and appliances from the Metal and Wood Company for $75,000 under the following payment plan, which called for semi-annual payments over two years:

Payment	Amount
1	$33,600
2	$22,400
3	$16,800
4	$11,200
Total	$84,000

Each payment includes interest (assume that the proportionate share of interest in each payment is the same as the proportion of that payment to the total payments). Assume that the cost of the furniture and appliances is $60,000 and that Metal and Wood is quite confident Samson will make its payments on time.

Required:
Compute the revenue, expense, accounts receivable, and profit that Metal and Wood Company would report at the end of each of two years.

4-21 (Revenue recognition on long-term contract)
On June 21, 2000, Tristar Electric Company signed a contract with Denton Power Incorporated to construct a small hydroelectric generating plant. The contract price was $10 million, and it was estimated that the project would cost Tristar $7,850,000 to complete over a three-year period. On June 21, 2000, Denton paid Tristar $1 million as a default-deposit. In the event that Denton backed out of the contract, Tristar could keep this deposit. Otherwise, the default-deposit would apply as the final payment on the contract (assume, for accounting purposes, that this is treated as a deposit until the contract is completed). The other contractual payments are as follows:

Date	Amount
October 15, 2000	$3,150,000
April 15, 2001	$1,350,000
December 15, 2001	$1,800,000
March 15, 2002	$1,755,000
August 10, 2002	$ 945,000
Total	$9,000,000

Estimated costs of construction were as follows:

Year	Amount
2000	$3,532,500
2001	$2,747,500
2002	$1,570,000
Total	$7,850,000

The contract was completed on January 10, 2003. Tristar closes its books on December 31 each year.

Required:

Compute the revenue, expense, and profit to be recognized in each year using each of the following methods:

a. The percentage of completion method

b. The completed contract method

4-22 (Revenue recognition decision)

Sonya's Christmas Tree Company began operations on April 1, 1996. She bought a parcel of land on which she intended to grow Christmas trees. The normal growth time for a Christmas tree is six years, so she divided her land into six plots. In 1996 she planted the first plot with trees and watered, cultivated, and fertilized her trees all summer. In 1997 she planted her second plot with trees and watered, cultivated, and fertilized both planted plots. She continued with her plantings and care every year through 2001, when she planted the last plot. On November 1, 2001, she harvested the plot of trees that she had planted in 1996. In 2002 she replanted this first plot.

Required:

a. Describe Sonya's cash-to-cash cycle.

b. What revenue recognition options are open to her? Which one would you recommend, and why?

c. Using your recommended revenue recognition policy, how would Sonya account for all of her costs for growing the trees?

4-23 (Revenue recognition decision)

Terry Park, after graduating with a degree in computer systems and design, set up a business to design and produce computer games for use in arcades. Terry hired two other designers because of the anticipated volume of business. One designer, Kim, is paid an hourly wage. The second, Sandy, is paid 50% of the revenue received by Terry on the games designed or redesigned by Sandy. Terry rents an office where they all work and provides all the necessary equipment, supplies, and other items. Terry is not paid a wage but keeps all of the profits earned.

Terry quickly realized there were two kinds of business: speculative design and custom design. For the speculative designs, Terry or one of the designers would think of a new game, and design, program, and test it. Terry would then try to sell it to a distribution company, either for a fixed price or for a percentage (which ranges from 10% to 25%) of the total revenues earned by the games. To date, Terry has sold three of the four games produced. Terry is currently negotiating the sale of the fourth game.

For the custom design business, Terry would receive an order from a distribution company for either the design of a new game or the redesign of an existing game (which occurs frequently, as games have a useful life of only six months because players quickly get bored with games). Terry negotiates either a fixed fee payable upon completion or an hourly rate based on the estimated length of time it should take to redesign the game. Terry sets the hourly rate based on the perceived difficulty of the project, but the rate is always at least triple the amount paid to Kim. For the hourly-rate contracts, Terry submits monthly invoices showing the number of hours worked on the project.

Required:

a. Describe Terry's cash-to-cash cycle.

b. What revenue recognition options are open to Terry? Which one(s) would you recommend, and why?

c. Using your recommended revenue recognition policy, how would you account for all of the costs incurred by Terry?

d. What recommendations would you make to Terry about the running of this business?

Management Perspective Problems

4-24 (Revenue recognition and earnings)
Financial analysts frequently refer to the "quality" of a company's earnings. Discuss how the quality of two companies' earnings might differ depending on the revenue recognition method that both companies use.

4-25 (Changing revenue policy to affect earnings)
Suppose that a company is currently private (its shares do not trade on a public stock market) but it is thinking of going public (issuing shares in a public stock market). Discuss the incentives that the company might have to misstate its income statement via its revenue recognition policies. If a company decided to change its revenue recognition policy so that its earnings would be enhanced, would the investors realize what it was doing? Where would a new investor look for information about the changes?

4-26 (Revenue policy and management performance measurement)
Suppose that you are the sales manager of a company with an incentive plan that provides a bonus based on meeting a certain sales target. Explain how meeting your sales target is influenced by the revenue recognition principles of the company.

4-27 (Revenue policy and sales targets)
Suppose that you are a sales manager of a Canadian-based company that sells products in Brazil. Brazil has traditionally had a high inflation rate, which means that the exchange rate of the Brazilian *real* per the Canadian dollar typically increases dramatically from year to year. If your compensation is a function of sales as measured in dollars, what risks do you face in meeting your targets and how might you mitigate the risks that you face in meeting those targets?

4-28 (Revenue policy for accounting and tax purposes)
Explain the incentives that a company has in choosing its revenue recognition method for both financial reporting and tax purposes.

4-29 (Revenue policy and return policies)
In the toy industry it is common to allow customers (retail stores) to return unsold toys within a certain specified period of time. Suppose that a toy manufacturer's year end is December 31 and that the majority of its products are shipped to customers during the last quarter of the year in anticipation of the Christmas holidays. Is it appropriate for the company to recognize revenue upon shipment of the product? Support your answer, making reference to revenue recognition criteria.

4-30 (Revenue policy and modes of shipping goods)
Suppose that an exporter in Vancouver sells goods to a customer in Australia. The goods are shipped by cargo vessel. For goods that are in transit at year end what recognition should the Vancouver exporter make of these goods in its financial statements? Support your answer based on revenue recognition criteria.

4-31 (Sale of accounts receivable)

Companies sometimes sell their accounts receivable to raise cash to support their operations. Suppose that a company sells its accounts receivable with recourse. Recourse means that the buyer can return the account receivable to the selling company if it cannot collect on the receivable. How do you think this transaction should be treated in the financial statements of the selling company?

4-32 (Advertising revenue recognition)

Suppose that ESPN (the sports channel) sells $10,000,000 in advertising slots to be aired during the games that it broadcasts during the World Cup soccer tournament. Suppose further that these slots are contracted for during the month of October with a downpayment of $2,000,000. The ads will be aired in June and July of the following year. If the fiscal year end of ESPN is December 31, how should ESPN recognize this revenue in its financial statements?

4-33 (Revenue recognition for gift certificates)

Suppose that The GAP (a clothing retailer) sells gift certificates for merchandise. During the Christmas holiday period suppose that it issues $500,000 in gift certificates. If the company's fiscal year end is December 31, how should it recognize the issuance of these gift certificates in its financial statements at year end?

4-34 (Revenue recognition on software sales)

Suppose that the XYZ Software company produces inventory-tracking software that it sells to retail companies like Future Shop. Further suppose that the software programs sell for $100,000 each and require the company to provide customization to the buyer's operations, which can take several months. If the fiscal year end is September 30 and the company sells 10 units of the product in August, how should it recognize these "sales" in the financial statements at year end?

4-35 (Revenue and expenses associated with obsolete inventory)

Suppose that you are the auditor of ABC Department Store and during your audit of the company's inventory you observe a significant amount of inventory that appears to be extremely old. How would you recommend that the company deal with this inventory, and how will it affect the revenues and expenses recognized during the period? Explain the incentives that the management of the company might have for keeping the inventory in its warehouse.

Reading and Interpreting Published Financial Statements

4-36 (Revenue recognition on layaway sales)

Zale Company sells fine jewellery and giftware in a chain of stores nationwide. Some of its sales are layaway sales; that is, the customer buys an item but takes delivery and makes payment on that sale at a later date. There may be an initial downpayment on the layaway sale. During 1989, Zale changed its method for recognizing the revenues from these sales. The following excerpt is from the first note in their annual report for the year ended March 31, 1991:

> The Company also changed its method of accounting for layaway sales effective April 1, 1989. Prior to that time, sales were not recorded until the final layaway payment is received from the customer. Under the new method, a sale is recorded when the initial layaway payment is received from the customer.

> *Required:*
> As the auditor of the financial statements of Zale, how would you respond to this change? Discuss the circumstances under which each method would be appropriate, based on the revenue recognition criteria under GAAP.

4-37 (Catalogue production, revenue recognition and matching)
Eddie Bauer Outdoor Outfitters sells clothing and other items both from retail stores and through catalogue mailings. The cost of catalogue production and mailing is fairly substantial for a company such as Eddie Bauer. Discuss how the costs associated with catalogue production and mailing should be treated for accounting purposes. Frame your answer in terms of the revenue recognition criteria and the matching principle discussed in the chapter.

4-38 Refer to the balance sheet of Air Canada in Exhibit 2-13. In the notes to the financial statements, Air Canada states its Air Transportation Revenue policy as:

> Airline passenger and cargo sales are recognized as operating revenues when the transportation is provided. The value of unused transportation is included in current liabilities.

Required:

a. By referring to the balance sheet in Exhibit 2-13, calculate the value of the unused transportation in 1998 and 1997.

b. By referring to the revenue recognition criteria, explain why Air Canada's revenue recognition policy is appropriate.

c. Air Canada has a frequent flyer program where customers earn travel miles that can be exchanged at a later date for trips. Suggest how you think Air Canada should account for these free trips.

4-39 (Application of revenue recognition criteria)
The revenue recognition policies used by Mitel Corporation, an international communications products supplier, according to Note 2 to its 1998 financial statements, are as follows:

> 2. (H) Revenue Recognition

> Revenue from the sale of products is recognized at the time goods are shipped to customers. Revenue from the sale of communications systems, including integration and installation services, is recognized on a percentage of completion basis. Revenue from service is recognized at the time services are rendered. Billings in advance of services are included in deferred revenue. Estimated warranty costs associated with these revenues are provided for at the time of sale.

Required:
For each of the parts of Mitel's recognition policy, explain why that application of revenue recognition is suitable for recognizing Mitel's revenues and explain why the application conforms to GAAP.

4-40 (Application of revenue recognition criteria)
The revenue recognition policy of Queenstake Resources Ltd., a mining company, from Note 1 to its 1997 financial statements, is as follows:

> Revenues from the sales of metals are net of royalties and treatment charges, and are recognized when legal title passes to the buyer. Settlement adjustments arising from final determination of metal weights and assays are reflected in sales when received.

Required:

a. Explain why this revenue recognition conforms to GAAP. Include consideration of the treatment of royalties (fees based on actual quantity or value of minerals produced) and settlement adjustments (adjustments caused by selling product based on the actual mineral content when the actual mineral content is not known until a final analysis is undertaken by the purchaser).

b. What alternative revenue recognition policies and recording could Queenstake use that would also conform with GAAP?

4-41 (Application of revenue recognition criteria)

The revenue recognition policies used by Canadian Pacific Limited, a transportation, accommodations, and energy provider, according to Note 1 to its 1997 financial statements, are as follows:

Transportation: Railway freight revenues are recognized on the percentage of completion basis.

Revenues from shipping operations, costs directly attributable to loaded container movements and vessel costs are accounted for on the basis of voyages completed in the period.

Energy: Revenues from crude oil, natural gas and natural gas liquids are recognized at the time of product delivery.

Coal sales revenues are recognized when the coal has been loaded and has departed the shipping locations. Industrial minerals sales revenues are recognized upon shipment from the plant.

Hotels: Revenues from hotel operations are recognized when services are provided and ultimate collection is reasonably assured.

Required:

For each of the five parts of Canadian Pacific's recognition policy, explain why that policy is suitable for recognizing Canadian Pacific's revenues and explain why the policy conforms to GAAP.

4-42 (Revenue recognition decision-making)

There are companies today that are set up to provide additional funds to retired individuals. They offer reverse mortgages. A reverse mortgage is a loan against the person's home that requires no repayment for as long as the person lives there. The person still owns the home and must pay for property taxes, insurance, and upkeep. However, when the person stops living in the home the loan comes due. The person receives the loan either as an immediate cash advance, as a creditline account, as monthly cash payments, or as a combination of the other options. The amount that must be paid back cannot be higher than the equity in the home, which means that the company cannot seek additional funds from the owner or the owner's heirs. The company runs the risk of the person staying in the home a long time and/or of the equity in the home not growing as quickly as anticipated.

Required:

a. If you were a manager in the company offering the reverse mortgage, how would you decide how much money you should loan to the home-owner?

b. Having decided on the amount, how would you recognize revenue over the life of this agreement?

c. Given your revenue recognition method outlined in b, how would you treat the payments made to the home-owners and the various expenses incurred in administering the agreement?

d. Are there any ethical dilemmas that the managers of the company might face in contracting reverse mortgages?

Beyond the Book

4-43 (Change in revenue recognition criteria)
Using an electronic database, search for a company that has changed its revenue recognition methods during the last three years. Using that company, answer the following questions:

a. Describe the method that was used before the change as well as the new method.

b. Does the company give a reason for the change? If so, describe the reason; if not, speculate on why the change occurred.

c. How significant an effect did the change have on the company's financial statements? As in investor, how would you view this change?

d. Did the auditor agree with the change? Do you agree? Why or why not?

Case

4-44 Quebec Supercheese Company (QSC)
Quebec Supercheese Company (QSC) produces many varieties of cheese that are sold in every province in Canada, mainly through large grocery stores and specialty cheese shops. The cheese is produced at its factory in Montreal and shipped across Canada using commercial refrigerated trucks that pick up the cheese at the factory loading dock. All cheese is shipped F.O.B. shipping point, meaning the purchasers pay for the trucking and assume responsibility for the cheese as soon as the trucks pick it up at the factory. In accordance with generally accepted accounting principles, QSC recognizes the sale as soon as the trucks load the cheese, as the purchasers have title and responsibility for the cheese at this point.

QSC is not happy with these arrangements because it has received many complaints from purchasers about spoilage. Even though the purchasers and their truckers have full responsibility for this spoilage, many disputes have occurred because the truckers insist the cheese is spoiled when they pick it up. QSC is considering setting up its own fleet of trucks to deliver its cheese across Canada. It estimates the additional freight costs to QSC can be regained through the higher prices it would charge for including shipping in the price (F.O.B. destination).

If the company makes the deliveries the title to the cheese will not transfer until the cheese is delivered. QSC's president was not happy when she learned that sales would be recognized and recorded only upon delivery to the customer, since she knew that an average of five days' sales are in transit at all times because of the distances involved. One day's sales total approximately $100,000 on average. The effect of this change would be an apparent drop in sales of $500,000 and a decrease of $50,000 in net income in the year of the change.

Required:

a. Advise the president about revenue recognition guidelines.

b. Do you see a solution to the problem of changing the shipping method but avoiding the resulting effect on the income statement?

Critical Thinking Questions

4-45 (Inclusion of items in revenue)
The statement of operations and part of Note 2 from Big Rock Brewery Ltd. for the year ended March 31, 1999, are shown in Exhibit 4-5.

Required:

a. Explain what the "Government taxes and commissions" are.

b. Argue why they should (and should not) be included in the revenues of Big Rock Brewery.

4-46 (Revenue recognition decision-making)
An article by Mahendra Gujarathi ("Bridging the GAP in GAAP: A Case Study of Accounting for Frequent Flyer Plans," *Accounting Horizons*, September 1991) examines accounting for frequent flyer plans offered by airlines.

Required:

a. Briefly summarize the three alternative methods proposed to account for frequent flyer plans. Describe how, and examine why, the revenue recognition alternatives are linked to liability recognition.

b. Do you agree with the recommendations made by the author?

4-47 (Revenue recognition decision-making)
Alliance Atlantis Communications Inc. is a fully integrated supplier of entertainment products whose origins are in the television and motion-picture production industry. It produces, among other products, series for television that it sells to television networks. Some of these series involve the incurring of costs to develop an idea and produce a pilot show, followed by attempts to market the show to television stations. If the series is sold, weekly shows are produced for later airing by participating stations.

Required:

Discuss the revenue production process of this kind of television series, emphasizing the critical points in the revenue recognition process and pointing out the similarities and differences between the revenue process for Alliance Atlantis and for a company manufacturing television sets.

EXHIBIT 4-5

Consolidated Statements of Operations and Retained Earnings

For the years ended March 31, 1999 and 1998 ($ Canadian)

	1999	1998
Revenue		
Sales	$ 26,466,241	$ 25,184,850
Government taxes and commissions	(9,821,360)	(9,531,799)
	16,644,881	15,653,051
Cost of sales	7,691,231	7,676,372
Gross profit	8,953,650	7,976,679
Expenses		
Selling, general and administrative	7,716,517	5,525,157
Interest on long-term debt	647,317	820,974
Interest on short-term debt	14,323	20,591
Amortization	1,132,161	1,103,976
Loss on sale of capital assets (note 4)	228,577	–
	9,738,895	7,470,698
(Loss) income before income taxes	(785,245)	505,981
Income tax (recovery) expense (note 8)	(268,500)	172,000
Large Corporation tax	40,000	45,000
Net (loss) income for year	(556,745)	288,981
Retained earnings, beginning of year	6,903,471	6,614,490
Redemption of common shares (note 7)	(371,278)	–
Retained earnings, end of year	$ 5,975,448	$ 6,903,471
(Loss) earnings per share (note 2)		
Basic & fully diluted	$ (0.11)	$ 0.06

See accompanying notes

Revenue Recognition

Revenue is recognized upon shipment of product at the gross sales price charged to the purchaser. Invoices for sales to Canadian customers are submitted to the respective provincial Liquor Control Boards who pay the Company after deducting Liquor Control Board commissions. Excise taxes, which are assessed on production, and Liquor Control Board Commissions, which are assessed on sales, are recorded as reductions to gross sales prices.

Expect the
Unexpected

Just because an organization isn't out to make a profit doesn't mean it can ignore its accounting. In fact, in today's tough financial climate a charity or any other not-for-profit organization needs to watch its money more carefully than ever.

Just ask Dorothy Hooper, controller for the Manitoba Theatre Centre (MTC). Since 1982, this widely acclaimed theatre has presented top-quality shows to Winnipeg audiences as well as touring productions and co-productions with other theatre companies—though outside Winnipeg the MTC is perhaps best known for its 1995 production of Hamlet, which headlined Hollywood movie star Keanu Reeves.

Not surprisingly, that season sold out completely. But most years, income from ticket sales at the MTC is very hard to predict. "You can never accurately determine how the public will respond to the shows we've selected," explains Ms. Hooper. "Of course the artistic director always tries to make choices that are both artistically interesting and appealing to the public. And he's very, very good. But you just can't tell what people are going to want to see."

This uncertainty makes cash flow a real accounting challenge for a theatre. The costs for the season are pretty much fixed once the plays have been chosen, and most of the expenses of mounting a show must be paid up front: Sets must be built, costumes created, designers paid, and marketing materials prepared long before the curtain rises on the first performance, when box office revenues, which account for about 50% of MTC's income, are still a great unknown. Income from subscriptions, which used to come in at the beginning of the season, is now often paid in instalments throughout the year. Grant money usually comes in instalments as well.

Amazingly, the MTC only very rarely has had to borrow to make ends meet. "We plan very carefully," says Ms. Hooper. "Everyone gets involved." And if there's a cash crunch? "We count on everyone to get us through it. We make an announcement to all the senior staff, and they defer any expenses they can. One department will put off its purchase of a computer so another one that needs the cash can get it sooner. We all pitch in; people will bring in their own pens if that's what it takes."

CASH FLOW STATEMENT

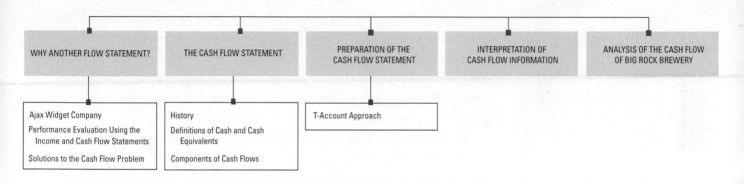

Learning Objectives

After studying this chapter, you should be able to:

1. *Understand the importance of cash to the financial health of a company.*
2. *Describe the relationship between the cash flow statement and the income statement in assessing management performance.*
3. *Describe the cash-to-cash cycle for a retail company through a discussion of the lead/lag relationship.*
4. *Identify some solutions to cash flow problems.*
5. *Identify the three major activities disclosed in the cash flow statement and describe the components of each activity.*
6. *Prepare a cash flow statement from the company's balance sheet and income statement.*
7. *Provide a basic analysis of a company's financial health using a cash flow statement.*

Every organization, whether it is a profit-oriented business or a not-for-profit theatre company as described in the opening story, needs to manage its cash flow. The health of the organization depends on its ability to predict when cash will be coming in and when it will need to be spent. For a not-for-profit organization like the Manitoba Theatre Centre, cash prediction and management is a fine balancing act. Most not-for-profit organizations have a fixed access to funds, from either granting agencies or donations. If they experience a cash shortage, they can't just sell more items or provide more services. When a not-for-profit organization provides a service, it may or may not get paid for it. These organizations cannot issue shares and often cannot borrow money. This greatly limits their choices and makes management of cash essential to their survival.

Profit-oriented companies have similar concerns with respect to cash. They need to know how cash is flowing in and out. If a profit-oriented company has difficulty paying its debts on time, it soon loses its credit rating, and suppliers and lenders will be reluctant to continue to sell it goods on credit or to lend it money. These actions will affect its ability to grow and could contribute to its eventual slide into bankruptcy.

In Chapter 4, the basic concepts underlying the recognition of revenue were discussed from the point of view of the shareholders of the company. Although this is an important perspective, there are other measures of performance affecting the overall health of the company that are not adequately captured by the income statement. Because the income statement is based on accrual accounting, the flows represented on it do not necessarily correspond to the cash flows of the company; and because the company cannot operate without cash, its cash-generating performance during the period must be understood. Considering the importance of cash flow, outside users need some way to assess the future cash position of an organization. This chapter discusses the second major measure of performance, the cash flows that are summarized in the statement called the cash flow statement. The cash flow statement is quite simple in intent, but is rather difficult to prepare and understand properly. Because of this difficulty you may find that your instructor has chosen to leave this chapter until later in the course.

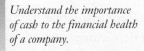

Learning Objective

❶

Understand the importance of cash to the financial health of a company.

WHY ANOTHER FLOW STATEMENT?

The need for another flow statement is probably best conveyed by the use of an example, the Ajax Widget Company (a fictitious company). The assumptions for the example are listed in the boxes below.

Ajax Widget Company

PRODUCT LINE

The Ajax Widget Company sells widgets. A widget* is a hypothetical product for this example.

*Widget is also the trade name for a paint scraper produced by the Gillette Company.

SUPPLIER CREDIT

Widgets cost Ajax $4 apiece. Since Ajax's suppliers do not allow it credit, all inventory must be paid in cash when it is ordered.

SALES/CUSTOMER CREDIT

The widgets currently sell for $5 apiece. Ajax allows its customers up to 30 days to pay for the widgets they buy. For the purpose of this example, it is assumed that all customers pay Ajax on the 30th day after a sale.

   Ajax is a relatively new company and has been experiencing fairly rapid growth in sales. Exhibit 5-1 shows this growth during the first three months of 20x1. Ajax expects that sales will continue to grow at the rate of 600 units per month for at least the next year.

INVENTORY POLICY

Ajax's supply of widgets is such that it cannot get them from the supplier instantaneously. Therefore, it must maintain a certain level of inventory so that units are available when a customer comes in to buy one. Ajax's policy is to maintain inventory at the end of the period equal to 50% of the current month's sales. The relationship can be seen in the data in Exhibit 5-1, which lists the sales in each month and the ending inventory.

■ **AJAX WIDGET COMPANY**

EXHIBIT 5-1

Sales/Inventory Data

(Data in units)

	January	February	March
Beginning inventory	250	500	800
New inventory purchases	1,250	1,900	2,500
Goods available for sale	1,500	2,400	3,300
Sales	1,000	1,600	2,200
Ending inventory	500	800	1,100

Performance Evaluation Using the Income and Cash Flow Statements

As discussed earlier, the performance of Ajax can be measured by constructing an income statement. Assuming that the revenues are recognized at the time of sale and that no other expenses are incurred except inventory costs, Exhibit 5-2 shows the income statement for the first three months of 20x1.

EXHIBIT 5-2

■ AJAX WIDGET COMPANY

Income Statement

	January	February	March
Revenues	$5,000	$8,000	$11,000
Cost of goods sold	(4,000)	(6,400)	(8,800)
Net income	$1,000	$1,600	$ 2,200

As can be seen from Exhibit 5-2, net income is growing at a predictable rate—the shareholders and managers should certainly be happy with this growth. Assuming that sales continue to increase at a rate of 600 units per month, this growth in income should continue. In the long run, the investment in Ajax should be profitable.

Exhibit 5-3 provides some information about the balance sheet of Ajax. The trends in cash, accounts receivable, and inventory shown in Exhibit 5-3 reflect rapid business growth. Accounts receivable reflects an increased level of sales, as does inventory, because ending inventory is a function of sales. The disturbing trend in Exhibit 5-3 is, of course, the decline in the amount of cash on hand for Ajax. To understand the decline in cash, you must consider the cash-to-cash cycle. Exhibit 5-4 shows the cycle for Ajax.

EXHIBIT 5-3

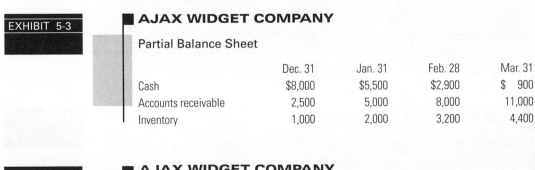

■ AJAX WIDGET COMPANY

Partial Balance Sheet

	Dec. 31	Jan. 31	Feb. 28	Mar. 31
Cash	$8,000	$5,500	$2,900	$ 900
Accounts receivable	2,500	5,000	8,000	11,000
Inventory	1,000	2,000	3,200	4,400

EXHIBIT 5-4

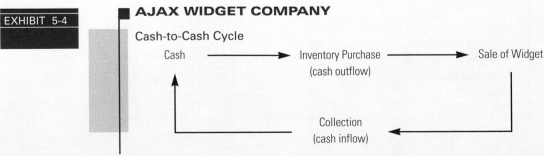

■ AJAX WIDGET COMPANY

Cash-to-Cash Cycle

The cash-to-cash cycle illustrates the **lead/lag relationship** between the cash paid out to buy inventory and the cash coming in from collections of accounts receivable. The lag between inventory purchase and sale varies according to which units are involved. Some units are bought and sold in the same month. Other units are bought in one month, remain in ending inventory, and are sold in the following month. This creates a one-month lag between the outflow of cash for inventory purchases and the sale of those widgets that are carried over in ending inventory. Therefore, considering units purchased and units sold in the same period, as well as units that end up in ending inventory, the average lag between purchase and sale is somewhat less than a month. Once a widget is sold, the lag between sale and collection is one month, because the collection policy is to allow customers 30 days to pay. Consequently, the total lag between cash outflow and cash inflow is somewhere between one and two months.

Because the income statement measures performance at a particular point in the cash-to-cash cycle, it ignores all the timing differences between revenues and expenses recognized and the related cash flows. Therefore, the income statement is not very useful in tracking the cash flows of the company. The income statement will continue to be positive as long as sales are increasing for Ajax. The growth in sales, however, forces Ajax to buy more and more units each month. It is possible that the inventory costs paid in cash in a given month could exceed the cash collections from the previous month's sales. It is evident from the decline in the cash balance in Exhibit 5-4 that this has happened during the first three months of 20x1. Thus, even though net income is increasing each month, the cash position of the company is declining. Because Ajax cannot operate without a sufficient amount of cash, it would make sense to prepare a separate statement, in addition to the income statement, to measure the performance of the company on a cash basis. Hence the need for a cash flow statement.

The cash flow statement cannot replace the income statement; each provides useful information. The income statement summarizes the profitability of the company's operations, while the cash flow statement summarizes the cash flows. To analyze the operations of any company properly, you must consider both profits and cash flows. In the long run, the total profits and net cash flows will be very similar, but they may be quite different for any single year or even over a period of several years.

To understand the usefulness of the information provided by the cash flow statement, think of the management of cash as one of the basic duties of the company's management. Management must ensure that sufficient cash is maintained on hand both to generate profits now and to invest in assets that will generate profits in the future. Simply producing profits now is not sufficient to ensure the company's long-term survival. Without sufficient cash to make investments in revenue-producing assets, the company's long-term viability may be in doubt.

Learning Objective

3

Describe the cash-to-cash cycle for a retail company through a discussion of the lead/lag relationship.

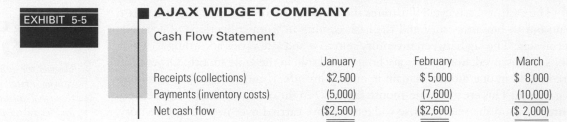

■ AJAX WIDGET COMPANY

Cash Flow Statement

	January	February	March
Receipts (collections)	$2,500	$ 5,000	$ 8,000
Payments (inventory costs)	(5,000)	(7,600)	(10,000)
Net cash flow	($2,500)	($2,600)	($ 2,000)

As can be seen from Exhibit 5-5, the cash flow of the Ajax Widget Company has been negative for the first three months of 20x1. The receipts in the cash flow statement are collections from the previous month's sales, and the payments are the inventory purchase costs for the month. The inventory costs can be calculated by taking the units purchased in Exhibit 5-1 and multiplying them by the unit cost of $4.

The cash flow statement paints a picture of the performance of Ajax during the first quarter of 20x1 that is very different from the picture painted by the income statement. Cash flow is obviously a problem for Ajax. Because Ajax has only $900 left in its cash account, the questions it faces are whether cash will run out in April and, if so, what will it do to continue doing business? In order to decide whether the problem will persist, Ajax should prepare a forecast for the next several months.

Assuming continued growth in sales of 600 units a month and no change in the collection, inventory, and payment policies of the Ajax Widget Company, Exhibit 5-6 illustrates the forecast for the next several months.

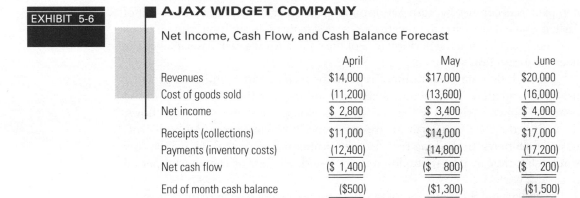

■ AJAX WIDGET COMPANY

Net Income, Cash Flow, and Cash Balance Forecast

	April	May	June
Revenues	$14,000	$17,000	$20,000
Cost of goods sold	(11,200)	(13,600)	(16,000)
Net income	$ 2,800	$ 3,400	$ 4,000
Receipts (collections)	$11,000	$14,000	$17,000
Payments (inventory costs)	(12,400)	(14,800)	(17,200)
Net cash flow	($ 1,400)	($ 800)	($ 200)
End of month cash balance	($500)	($1,300)	($1,500)

As can be seen from Exhibit 5-6, income continues to grow by $600 each month, reflecting the growth in sales of 600 units times the net profit margin of $1 per unit. The cash flow statement indicates that net cash flow will be negative for the next three months, but the trend is that net cash flow is improving and it looks as though it will be positive by July. The ending cash balance is projected to be negative for the next three months and will take longer to return to a positive cash balance. This is a problem, because Ajax cannot operate with a negative cash balance. Operating with a negative cash balance is feasible only if the bank permits a company to overdraw its bank accounts; that is, if it allows more cash to be withdrawn than has been deposited. A negative cash balance is really a loan from the bank. Companies will often make arrangements with the bank for circumstances like this. The loan arrangement is called a **line of credit**. The bank will set a maximum limit on how much can be borrowed in this way and will also establish the repayment schedule if the line of credit is used.

The problem is perhaps best portrayed by Exhibit 5-7 on the next page, which graphs the situation with regard to net income, cash flow, and cash balance for the entire year 20x1. Note the cash balance line, which drops below zero in April and returns to a positive balance in September. In reality, the company cannot have a negative cash balance without making special arrangements with its bank, and something must be done to prevent the problem from continuing for too long. Nevertheless, the graph clearly shows the magnitude and duration of Ajax's cash flow problem.

Cash flow problems such as the one just described may appear to be extreme, and indeed we developed it so that you could easily identify that Ajax had a cash flow problem. The following report concerning Cott Corp., a soft-drink manufacturer, illustrates how cash flow problems can affect a real company.

accounting in the news

LONG-TERM DEBT USED TO OVERCOME CASH FLOW PROBLEM

Looking at the ability to meet internal cash needs is an important measure of a company's financial health. Cott Corp. is one high-profile company that has struggled with cash problems in recent years. In the early 1990s, Cott carved a lucrative niche market out of the soft-drink industry for its private-label soft drinks. Success came quickly, followed by acquisitions of independent bottlers in Canada and abroad and expansion into other product lines such as frozen dinners and pet food.

But heated competition from Coca-Cola and Pepsi, and less than enviable results from new product lines, started taking their toll. By the late 1990s, Cott was struggling under a tremendous debt burden. According to its 1998 annual report, Cott had long-term debt of about $618 million, more than double the figure of a year earlier. This was a symptom of a continuing problem: The company wasn't meeting its cash needs. On average in each of the three previous years, Cott had used up $105 million more in cash than it generated. The shortage of cash would certainly curtail expansion, at least in the near future, and necessitate other cost-cutting measures.

Source: "Is this pop a flop?" by Peter S. Taylor, *Canadian Business*, August 28, 1998, pages 18–20.

Cott is attempting to manage its cash flow problem through borrowing, curtailing expansion, and reducing costs. Would these solutions work for Ajax? There are many ways in which Ajax can address its cash flow problem. Before you read on, you might want to take a few moments to think about how you would solve it.

EXHIBIT 5-7

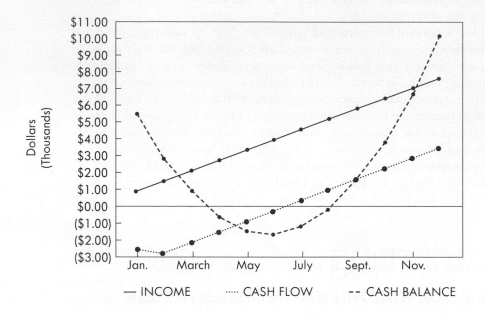

EXHIBIT 5-8

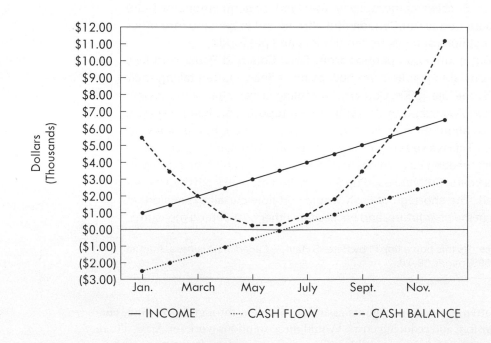

Solutions to the Cash Flow Problem

The cash flow difficulties that Ajax is experiencing are typical of new companies. These problems have three fundamental causes: high growth rates in sales, significant lead/lag relationships in cash inflows and outflows, and under-capitalization. The use of the term **capitalization** in this situation refers to how much cash the company has to start with. Startup companies generally experience a rapid rate of growth in sales. This increase in sales requires them to buy or produce more and more inventory as well as to expand their storage or operating capacity. Buying more inventory and expanding capacity both require cash.

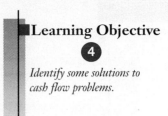

Learning Objective

4

Identify some solutions to cash flow problems.

Compounding the growth problem is the presence of significant lead/lag relationships between the company's cash inflows and outflows. If there were no lead/lag relationship, then, as long as the product could be sold for more than it cost to produce or buy there would be no cash flow problem. Most companies, however, do have some significant lead/lag relationships in their cash flows, which are magnified in periods of high growth.

Finally, startup companies tend to be under-capitalized; that is, they do not have a large pool of cash to start with. When the large cash needs appear, imposed by rapid growth and lead/lag relationships, the company has no cash reserves to get it through prolonged periods of cash outflows. Startup companies (as well as other companies in rapid-growth phases) will experience cash flow problems at some point. In Ajax's case, the problems create a crisis during the month of April. Solutions to the three causes of the cash flow problems of Ajax are discussed in the following subsections.

Growth One way to solve Ajax's problem is to slow down the rate of growth of sales. Exhibit 5-8 shows graphically what happens when the rate of growth in sales is 500 units, rather than 600, per month. All other facts and assumptions are unchanged. You can see from the graph that this solves the cash flow problem of Ajax, because the cash balance line does not dip below zero in any month. Cash flows are still negative in some early months, but the balance in cash is sufficient to absorb these cash outflows. Limiting growth may not be the proper response in this case, because it may be detrimental to the company in the long run. Limiting growth is likely to divert customers to competitors, and those customers may develop loyalties to those competitors and reduce the company's long-run potential in terms of developing a customer base.

Capitalization A second way to solve the cash problem is to address the under-capitalization problem; that is, to start with a larger amount of cash. This larger amount of cash may be obtained in numerous ways. Two typical ways are to issue additional shares in the company and to borrow the cash (debt). If Ajax issues new shares, the cash flow projections will have to be adjusted to incorporate the additional cash inflow from the issuance and any subsequent outflows for dividends. If money is borrowed, the cash flow projections will have to be adjusted for the initial inflow from the borrowing as well as for the payments of principal and interest that will occur in the future. Exhibit 5-9 shows what will happen if an additional $2,000 is obtained at the beginning of January from the issuance of shares. For simplicity, it is assumed that there are no dividends. Note, again, that this solves the cash flow problem.

EXHIBIT 5-9

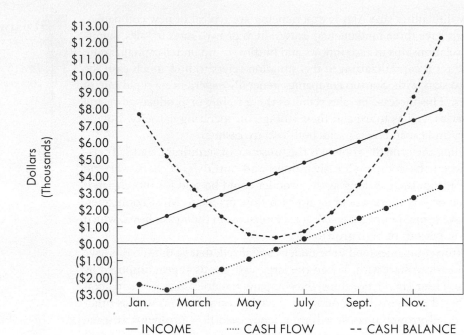

EXHIBIT 5-10

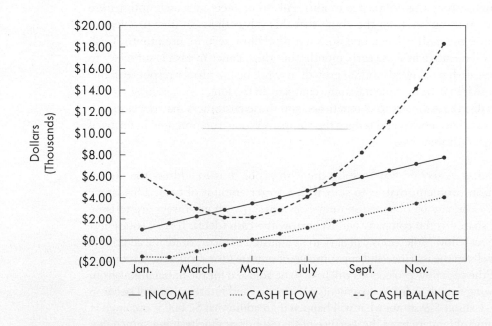

This solution—increased capitalization—is not without its own problems. The first problem is that if shares are issued, the current shareholders of Ajax will be giving up control of some portion of their investment in the company, and they may not want to do that. It may also be difficult to find additional investors willing to take the risk of buying shares in the company. Second, if Ajax decides to attempt to borrow the additional capital, it may not be able to convince a lender that it is worthy of a loan. Lenders are typically very sceptical of new ventures.

Lead/Lag Relationships The third way to solve the cash flow problem of Ajax is to change the lead/lag relationships between the cash inflows and outflows. There are numerous ways to do this. One way to change the relationship is to change Ajax's accounts receivable, accounts payable, or inventory policy. Collecting on accounts receivable sooner or selling for cash or via credit card, paying accounts payable later, or reducing the amount of inventory on hand would all have the effect of reducing the difference between cash outflow and cash inflow in a given month. Exhibit 5-10 shows what will happen if, for example, the accounts receivable policy is changed to require customers to pay within three weeks rather than one month.

This change would be sufficient to solve the cash flow problem, assuming everything else remains the same. Of course, everything else may not stay the same. If Ajax institutes this change, it is likely that some customers will no longer do business with Ajax because they can get better payment terms from a competitor. Thus the rate of growth in sales may be affected. Ajax, therefore, may need to make changes in some other assumptions before it can realistically conclude that this will solve its problem. In this case, however, you know from Exhibit 5-8 that slowing the rate of growth will actually help solve the cash flow problem.

In our example, Ajax must pay cash for the inventory that it buys from its supplier. A supplier may be reluctant initially to sell inventory on credit to a new company. The company has no track record on which the supplier can gauge its credit worthiness. Once Ajax has proved to the supplier that it can pay cash for increasing amounts of inventory, the supplier may be willing to grant 30-day credit terms. Establishing this credit worthiness takes time, however, and does not solve Ajax's initial cash flow problem.

Besides changing the receivables, payables, and inventory policies of Ajax, there are other ways to alter the lead/lag relationship. Changing either the price or the cost of a widget would affect the amounts in the lead/lag relationship and could therefore solve the problem. Remember, however, that changes in these items may also affect other assumptions, such as sales growth.

To summarize, it is clear that a cash flow statement provides information that is not captured by the income statement and balance sheet alone. It is important for a shareholder, manager, or other user of the financial statements to understand the relationship between a company's income, cash-to-cash cycle, and cash flow statement. Also, understanding how receivables, payables, and inventory policies affect the cash flows of the company is extremely important in evaluating the performance of the company. We discuss in greater detail how users interpret cash flow information later in the chapter.

We now turn to the components of cash flow. Then we will explain the preparation of a cash flow statement. Finally, we will explain how the cash flow statement can be used to assess the financial health of the company.

THE CASH FLOW STATEMENT

History

In 1985, the cash flow statement, then called the statement of changes in financial position, became a true cash flow statement. Prior to 1985, companies could prepare a statement of cash flows *or* a statement of **working capital** flows (working capital is current assets minus current liabilities). As of 1985, companies no longer had a choice; they had to show the changes in cash flows, through three functions: operating, financing, and investing. The cash flow statements that you see illustrated in this text will all be statements that follow the 1985 guideline.

In 1998, some changes were introduced to the statement. First, the title "cash flow statement" replaced the "statement of changes in financial position." As well, the articulation of what to include in operating, financing, and investing was more clearly defined. What you see discussed in this chapter will follow the new guidelines. However, because the financial statements that we use as illustrations will not have adopted the new guidelines yet, you will still see the statement referred to as the statement of changes in financial position. You may also see some items that will not be included in future years. We will alert you to these additional items when they appear.

Definition of Cash and Cash Equivalents

As we have seen above, proper management of cash is one of the critical tasks that management of any organization must achieve. Having too little cash on hand results in an inability to cover liabilities and expenses. If such a situation continues, bankruptcy will result. Having too much cash on hand is also a problem in that it is not efficient. Cash held in chequing accounts typically earns little or no interest. It is much better to invest excess cash in some kind of temporary investment that will earn interest. Thus the proper management of cash involves not only cash, but also short-term borrowings and temporary investments.

Therefore, in considering cash flows that are to be summarized in the cash flow statement, rather than restricting our consideration to just cash, we must consider the broader concept of cash and cash equivalents, sometimes called the **cash position**. We use the term **cash equivalents** to include the short-term, highly liquid investments that are readily convertible into known amounts of cash. Also, they must be close enough to maturity that there is little risk of their value changing due to changes in interest rates. The time frame suggested is three months or less. Items that commonly meet these criteria are Government of Canada Treasury Bills and demand loans of other companies. A demand loan is a loan payable on demand, which means that it is very liquid. Cash equivalents also include short-term borrowings that companies use to cover their cash shortages for brief periods, such as lines of credit. However, a normal short-term bank loan would not be called a cash equivalent. Rather, it would be a financing activity.

Components of Cash Flows

In discussing the components of cash flows, we are going back to Chapter 1 where we discussed the three components of the management of any business. First, you must find sufficient long-term financing from investments by shareholders or long-term borrowings to provide for capitalization of the business. Next, you must invest these funds in assets that you will use to produce revenues and profits. Finally, you must operate the business—carry on the revenue-generating activities for which the company was established.

Learning Objective
5

Identify the three major activities disclosed in the cash flow statement and describe the components of each activity.

The basic format of the cash flow statement summarizes all the cash flows into these three groups of activities. Exhibit 5-11 shows the cash flow statement for Big Rock Brewery for the years ended March 31, 1999, and March 31, 1998. We will use its cash flow statement as an example. Note that the cash flow statement is divided into three activities: Operating Activities with a net cash inflow of $2,113,702 for 1999, Financing Activities with a net cash outflow of $2,548,712 for 1999, and Investing Activities with a net cash inflow of $318,616 for 1999. The Net Cash Outflow for 1999 is $116,394. The final section of the cash flow statement shows how this net cash outflow, when added to the cash position of $191,628 at the beginning of the year, results in a cash position of $75,234 at the end of the year. Prior to issuing the 1999 financial statements, Big Rock used the bank indebtedness, which results from short-term borrowings using a line of credit, as a cash equivalent. During the 1999 fiscal year, Big Rock decided that the debt resulting from the line of credit would more appropriately be classified as a financing activity. In summary, the cash flow statement summarizes all the cash flows for 1999 that resulted in the decrease in cash position during the year.

Financing Activities

Financing activities are described as the activities involved in obtaining resources from shareholders and lenders and repaying those shareholders and lenders. Transactions classified as financing typically involve balance sheet accounts associated with equity capital and with short- and long-term borrowing. Typical cash inflows would be those from issuing shares, bonds, mortgages, notes, and other borrowings. Outflows include dividends paid to shareholders, repurchase of shares, and repayment of the principal on any debt obligation.

A special word is needed about interest and dividends. A company pays interest to lenders in exchange for the use of their money. Shareholders are repaid with dividends. Interest expense is associated with a debt, which is a financing activity, but because interest is used in the determination of net income, interest payments are included in the operating section. Dividends, on the other hand, are not used in the determination of net income. They are therefore included in the financing section. Some analysts (particularly bank lenders) would prefer, in their own analyses, to show the interest outflow in the financing section. They might therefore simply move the interest from the operating section to the financing section.

EXHIBIT 5-11

Consolidated Statements of Cash Flows

For the years ended March 31, 1999 and 1998 ($ Canadian)

	1999	1998
Operating Activities		
Net (loss) income for year	$ (556,745)	$ 288,981
Items not affecting cash		
Amortization	1,132,161	1,103,976
Write-off of deferred charges	302,221	18,854
Deferred income taxes	(268,500)	972,000
Loss on sale of capital assets	228,577	—
Cash flow from operations	837,714	2,383,811
Net change in non-cash working capital (note 12)	1,275,988	(717,948)
Cash provided by operating activities	2,113,702	1,665,863
Financing Activities		
(Decrease) increase in bank indebtedness	(297,731)	546,994
Repayment of long-term debt	(1,524,000)	(2,682,692)
Share repurchase (note 7)	(726,981)	—
Cash (used) by financing activities	(2,548,712)	(2,135,698)
Investing Activities		
Additions to capital assets	(294,898)	(517,001)
Additions to deferred charges and other assets	(141,486)	(107,476)
Proceeds on disposal of capital assets	755,000	1,059,755
Cash provided by investing activities	318,616	435,278
Net increase (decrease) in cash	(116,394)	(34,557)
Cash, beginning of year	191,628	226,185
Cash, end of year	$ 75,234	$ 191,628

See accompanying notes

In the cash flow statement of Big Rock shown in Exhibit 5-11, the items included in the financing activities section are fairly typical:

(Decrease) increase in bank indebtedness: outflows of $297,731 and inflows of $546,994
Repayment of long-term debt: outflows of $1,524,000 and $2,682,692
Share repurchase: outflow of $726,981

Not included in Big Rock's cash flow statement are dividends paid to shareholders (an outflow of cash). Dividends do not appear in Big Rock's cash flow statement simply because none were paid in either 1999 or 1998. Note that in both 1999 and 1998 Big Rock was reducing its debt load. In 1997 Big Rock built a new brewery. It financed that construction with debt and share issuances. In the years subsequent to the expansion, it has been paying back the amount borrowed.

An International Perspective

Reports from Other Countries

The categorization of cash flows in Canada, under Canadian GAAP, is somewhat different from that in other countries. In the UK, for instance, cash flows are categorized into five sections as described in footnote K to the 1995 20-F filing of Cadbury Schweppes PLC:

k) Cashflows

Under UK GAAP the Group complies with the Financial Reporting Standard No. 1 "Cashflow Statement" (FRS 1), the objective and principles of which are similar to those set out in SFAS No. 95 "Statement of Cashflows" (SFAS 95). The principal difference between the two standards is in respect of classification. Under FRS 1, the Group presents its cashflows for (a) operating activities; (b) returns on investments and servicing of finance; (c) taxation; (d) investing activities; and (e) financing activities. SFAS 95 requires only three categories of cashflow activity: (a) operating; (b) investing; and (c) financing.

Cash flows arising from taxation and returns on investments and servicing of finance under FRS 1 would, with the exception of dividends paid, be included as operating activities under SFAS 95; dividend payments would be included as a financing activity under SFAS 95. In addition, under FRS 1, cash and cash equivalents include short term borrowings with original maturities of less than 90 days.

Investing Activities

Transactions classified as **investing activities** typically involve balance sheet accounts classified as long-term assets. Typical transactions in this section would be investment in property, plant, and equipment and its subsequent sale or disposal, as well as investments in long-term marketable securities. The purchase or sale of any short-term investments that are not classified as cash equivalents would also be included in the investing section. In Big Rock's cash flow statement, examples of these types of items are:

Additions to capital assets: outflows of $294,898 and $517,001
Additions to deferred charges and other assets: outflows of $141,486 and $107,476
Proceeds on disposal of capital assets: inflows of $755,000 and $1,059,755

Note that Big Rock had an inflow of cash for investing activities in 1999 and 1998. This is not typical of companies. Usually as companies are going through the normal process of replacing long-lived assets, they spend more for the new assets than they get for the old ones they sell. This usually results in a net cash outflow for investing activities. (To see an example of a more typical outflow of cash for investing activities, look at the statement of changes in financial position for Future Shop Ltd. in Appendix B at the end of the book.) Big Rock's cash flow for investing is different because in 1997 they built a new brewery. On the 1997 cash flow statement there was an outflow of $8,599,290 for the new brewery. Since 1997, it has had surplus land, buildings, and production equipment that it has been selling. This has caused the net inflow of cash from investing activities.

Before going on to operating activities, we want to give you some more information about the construction of the new brewery in 1997. The brewery cost Big Rock $8,599,290, and, in order to finance the construction, Big Rock borrowed $7,248,754. We call this a direct-financing type of capital asset acquisition. When the cash flow statement was prepared in 1997, the cost of the brewery was reported under investing activities and the additional borrowings were reported under financing activities. In reality, because additional debt was taken on to build the new brewery, cash and cash equivalents were not used. One of the requirements under the new 1998 cash flow guideline is that when a company acquires assets by assuming directly related liabilities (as was the case with Big Rock) neither the new debt nor the asset acquisition is reported on the statement. Why? Because the cash and cash equivalents were not used. So, if they are not reported on this statement, how do users find out about them? One source is the balance sheet where the increase in both the long-term borrowings and the capital assets would be apparent. Also, it is probable that both items would be discussed fully in notes to the financial statements. Most companies have a note on capital assets and another on long-term debt. Look at the annual report of both Big Rock and Future Shop at the end of the book. Users now need to be aware that they must read these notes more carefully, because they may contain information that was not specifically reported on one of the financial statements.

Operating Activities

Operating activities include all transactions not covered by financing or investing activities. The operating section typically includes the cash flows that result directly from the sale of goods and services to customers. Transactions classified as part of operating activities typically involve balance sheet accounts classified as current assets and current liabilities. The major cash inflow comes from the collection of revenues from customers. The major cash outflow is the payment to suppliers (for inventory, materials, labour, etc.). As mentioned in the Financing Activities section, interest payments are also included in this section of the cash flow statement. One other cash flow worth noting in the operating section is related to taxes. Even though taxes are affected by all three types of activity, the net results of the taxes on the company are reported in the operating section of the cash flow statement.

A complete record of the gross amount of cash coming into the company from operating activities would show the total amount of cash received from revenues and collections from customers as inflows, and the total amount of cash paid out to suppliers for expenses and accounts payable as outflows. This approach, called the **direct approach**, is theoretically very informative but is rarely used in the cash flow statement. When we prepared the cash flow statement for Demo Retail Company, Ltd., in Chapter 2, we used the direct approach. The method normally used in published cash flow statements is the **indirect approach**. Note that these two approaches differ only in the format and content of the Operating Activities section. The Investing Activities and Financing Activities sections are the same for both approaches.

The indirect approach does not report the full gross cash flows from operating activities; it shows only the net cash flows. In the indirect approach, the operating section starts with reported net income and then shows adjustments to net income to arrive at the net cash flows from operations. The adjustments fall into two groups. The first group includes items from the income statement that do not involve cash flows. Note that in the Big Rock cash flow statement the net income is adjusted by the items listed under the heading "Items not affecting cash." The items in this group are amortization, write-off of deferred charges, deferred income taxes and loss on sale of capital assets. If you think about amortization, you will realize that it does not involve a cash payment the way other expenses such as wages do. Amortization expense merely involves recognizing the use of a long-term asset. The cash outflow related to that asset occurred when the asset was purchased— probably several years ago—and initially reported in the investing section of the cash flow statement as an outflow of cash. As a result of the recognition of amortization, the net income figure has been reduced by the amount of the amortization expense that does not represent a current cash outflow. The amortization expenses are thus added back to net income to determine the actual net cash flows from operating activities for the year. The write-off of deferred charges and the deferred income taxes are similar. Deferred charges represents costs that were paid some time ago but not recognized as expenses at that time. When they first occurred, the intent was to recognize them as expenses over time. Thus when they appear on the income statement as a write-off of a deferred charge, no outflow of cash is associated with them; like amortization, these charges must be added to net income to arrive at the cash position. On the income statement, the income tax expense represents the amount of taxes that will likely have to be paid on the revenues less expenses that are recognized in the current period. All of those income taxes may not be owed to Revenue Canada in the current year, because Revenue Canada's rules concerning recognition are not always the same as those used in accounting. Income tax expense that is deducted to arrive at net income is the amount owed for this year (which probably is paid and thus is a cash outflow) plus that amount that will be owed in future years (the deferred taxes). To arrive at the net cash flow from operating activities, it is necessary to add the deferred income taxes to the net income amount, because they do not represent a cash outflow yet. For now we are going to leave aside the explanation of the loss on the sale of capital assets.

The second group of adjustments is needed because all revenues and expenses do not result in immediate cash flows. If accounts receivable increases, not all of the revenues have been collected in cash; some will be collected later. Thus Big Rock's cash flow statement shows an adjustment for net change in noncash working capital of $1,275,988. Remember that working capital is current assets minus current liabilities. If we look at Note 12 referred to on the cash flow statement, we will see that the 1999 changes in the following current assets and liabilities are identified:

Accounts receivable	($ 246,150)
Income taxes receivable	712,403
Inventories	220,206
Prepaid expenses and other	(30,587)
Accounts payable and accrued liabilities	620,116
	$1,275,988

On Big Rock's balance sheet in Appendix A at the end of the book, the accounts receivable has gone from $1,302,336 in 1998 to $1,548,486 in 1999, an increase of $246,150. This means that $246,150 of the Sales amount reported on the income statement has not yet been collected. More accounts receivable is owed at the end of the year than was owed at the beginning of the year. The cash flow is represented by the following formula:

Beginning A/R + Sales − Ending A/R = Cash Flow from Sales

When the amounts from Big Rock's financial statements are put into this formula, the following emerges:

$1,302,336 + $26,666,241 − $1,548,486 = $26,420,091

The cash flow from sales is $246,150 less than the sales amount ($26,420,091 − $26,666,241). To summarize, when there is an increase in accounts receivable over the year, the sales figure that is included in the income statement does not represent the amount of cash flow from sales. It is too large. Thus an increase in accounts receivable is subtracted from the net income amount in order to determine the cash flow from operations.

Changes in other current assets and liabilities included in this second group follow similar reasoning. An increase in current assets reflects a decrease in the amount of cash inflow, or a net cash outflow from operating activities. A decrease in current assets reflects a cash inflow. A decrease in current liabilities such as accounts payable means that cash was used to pay down the liabilities, which is a cash outflow adjustment. An increase in current liabilities indicates that cash was saved by not paying the liabilities this year. This cash saving is the same as an increase in cash from operations. The following chart should help you learn whether to add or subtract the change in the current assets and liabilities:

Change in the Current Account

	Increase	Decrease
Current Asset	Subtract	Add
Current Liability	Add	Subtract

Referring back to Note 12 in Big Rock's financial statements, the accounts receivable and prepaid expenses and other are negative. This means that they increased. The income taxes receivable, inventories, and accounts payable and accrued liabilities are positive. This means that the income tax receivable and inventories decreased and the accounts payable and accrued liabilities increased. You can verify these changes by calculating the changes in these accounts on the balance sheet in Appendix A at the end of the book.

AN INTERNATIONAL PERSPECTIVE

Reports from Other Countries

NAFTA Facts

United States—A cash flow statement is required and can be prepared using either the direct or the indirect approach. As in Canada, in the United States the indirect approach is used most often. Cash flows are segregated into operating, investing, and financing. The disclosure requirements in the United States are very similar to those in Canada under the 1998 changes.

Mexico—The statement of changes in financial position is typically presented as a cash flow statement. Mexican GAAP requires that the financial statements be adjusted for the effect of inflation. A portion of inflation adjustment is typically shown in the operating section, and another portion due to adjustments to the debt balances of the company is adjusted in the financing section.

PREPARATION OF THE CASH FLOW STATEMENT

Learning Objective

6

Prepare a cash flow statement from the company's balance sheet and income statement.

To illustrate the preparation of a cash flow statement, another example will be used. Exhibit 5-12 shows the balance sheet for Huskies Industries Ltd. (a fictitious company) for the year ended December 31, 20x1. Exhibit 5-13 shows the income statement for Huskies Industries for the same period.

EXHIBIT 5-12

■ HUSKIES INDUSTRIES LTD.

Balance Sheet

	Dec. 31, 20x1	Dec. 31, 20x0
Cash	$ 6,050	$ 19,500
Accounts receivable	10,000	20,000
Inventory	40,000	30,000
Prepaid rent	600	500
Total current assets	56,650	70,000
Property, plant, and equipment	159,000	100,000
Accumulated amortization	(69,200)	(50,000)
Net fixed assets	89,800	50,000
Total assets	$146,450	$120,000
Accounts payable	$ 11,000	$ 6,000
Notes payable	200	100
Accrued salaries	400	300
Dividends payable	470	300
Total current liabilities	12,070	6,700
Bonds payable	46,000	40,000
Total liabilities	58,070	46,700
Common shares	29,000	25,000
Retained earnings	59,380	48,300
Total shareholders' equity	88,380	73,300
Total liabilities and shareholders' equity	$146,450	$120,000

EXHIBIT 5-13

■ HUSKIES INDUSTRIES LTD.

Income Statement
For the year ended December 31, 20x1

Sales revenue	$130,000	
Cost of goods sold	80,000	
Gross profit margin	50,000	
Rent expense		$7,100
Miscellaneous cash expenses		600
Amortization		20,000
Salaries expense		9,600
Total expenses	37,300	
Income from operations	12,700	
Gain on sale of property, plant, and equipment	300	
Income before income tax	13,000	
Income tax	520	
Net income	$12,480	

In addition to the balance sheet and income statement, the following information applies to the transactions of Huskies Industries Ltd. for 20x1:

1. Huskies Industries is a retailer; therefore, all amounts added to its inventory reflect purchases at wholesale prices. All inventory is purchased on credit from suppliers.
2. Huskies Industries sells its products to customers on credit. There are no cash sales.
3. During the year, Huskies Industries sold (for $500 in cash) equipment that had an original cost of $1,000 and a book value of $200, thus recording a gain on sale of $300.
4. Huskies Industries borrowed an additional $8,000 by issuing bonds in 20x1.
5. Notes payable were used during 20x1 for short-term financing.

T-Account Approach

Our objective is to construct a cash flow statement from the information given above, which is typical of most companies although simplified for illustrative purposes. We want to determine all of the cash flows that would have occurred to produce the balances shown above. Several methods can be used to determine the underlying cash flows, but all of them require, at a minimum, a balance sheet showing balances at the beginning and end of the year, plus an income statement for the current year. Some additional information may be required as well.

Two of the most common methods for determining the underlying cash flows are to use a set of T-accounts and to use a worksheet. The T-account approach will be used here, but remember that a worksheet could be used for the same task. Also, we will show the preparation of a cash flow statement using only the indirect approach, as virtually all published cash flow statements use this format. For completeness, we include the T-account preparation of the cash flow statement using the direct approach in the Appendix to this chapter.

Exhibit 5-14 shows the set-up for the T-account approach. Note that a large T-account has been included for cash, because the objective of this exercise is to reconstruct all of the transactions that affected cash in this account. All of the accounts from the balance sheet are listed, including their beginning and ending balances. The objective is to reconstruct the transactions that occurred during 20x1 and to include as much detail as possible regarding the nature of the cash transactions. Within the cash account, the transactions are categorized into the three basic activities discussed above: operating, financing, and investing. Note that as we start to reconstruct the transactions we are working outside the formal company records. The transactions that we are reconstructing occurred during the year and were recorded as isolated transactions. We are trying to determine the aggregate of those transactions and how the transactions relate to cash.

EXHIBIT 5-14

■ **Huskies Industries Ltd.**

Cash Flow T-Accounts

A-Cash

✓	19,500	

Operating:

Financing:

Investing:

✓	6,050	

A-Acc. Rec.		A-Inventory		A-Prepaid Rent	
✓ 20,000		✓ 30,000		✓ 500	
✓ 10,000		✓ 40,000		✓ 600	

A-PP&E		XA-Accum. Amort.		L-Acc. Pay.	
✓ 100,000			50,000 ✓		6,000 ✓
✓ 159,000			69,200 ✓		11,000 ✓

L-Note Pay.		L-Accrued Salaries		L-Dividends Payable	
	100 ✓		300 ✓		300 ✓
	200 ✓		400 ✓		470 ✓

L-Bonds Payable		SE-Common Shares		SE-Retained Earnings	
	40,000 ✓		25,000 ✓		48,300 ✓
	46,000 ✓		29,000 ✓		59,380 ✓

In Exhibit 5-15, the analysis for the cash flow statement has been reconstructed for 20x1. The entries in the T-accounts have been given transaction numbers and each is discussed in its section.

Huskies Industries Ltd.

Cash Flow T-Accounts

EXHIBIT 5-15

A-Cash

	✓	19,500				
Operating:						
Net income	(1)	12,480	10,000	(3)	Increase in inventory
Decrease in A/R	(2)	10,000	100	(4)	Increase in ppd. rent
Increase in A/P	(5)	5,000	300	(8)	Gain on sale of equip.
Incr. in acc. sal.	(6)	100			
Amortization	(7)	20,000			
Financing:						
Proceeds from note	(10)	100	2,000	(12)	Prepay. of bond
Proceeds from bond	(11)	8,000	1,230	(15)	Pay. of dividends
Issue of shares	(13)	4,000			
Investing:						
Sale of equip.	(8)	500	60,000	(9)	Purchase of PP&E
	✓	6,050			

A-Acc. Rec.

✓	20,000		
		10,000	(2)
✓	10,000		

A-Inventory

✓	30,000		
(3)	10,000		
✓	40,000		

A-Prepaid Rent

✓	500		
(4)	100		
✓	600		

A-PP&E

✓	100,000		
(9)	60,000	1,000	(8)
✓	159,000		

XA-Accum. Amort.

		50,000	✓
(8)	800	20,000	(7)
		69,200	✓

L-Acc. Pay.

		6,000	✓
		5,000	(5)
		11,000	✓

L-Note Pay.

		100	✓
		100	(10)
		200	✓

L-Accrued Salaries

		300	✓
		100	(6)
		400	✓

L-Dividends Payable

		300	✓
(15)	1,230	1,400	(14)
		470	✓

L-Bonds Payable

		40,000	✓
(12)	2,000	8,000	(11)
		46,000	✓

SE-Common Shares

		25,000	✓
		4,000	(13)
		29,000	✓

SE-Retained Earnings

		48,300	✓
(14)	1,400	12,480	(1)
		59,380	✓

In the indirect approach, the operating activities section is constructed by starting with net income and then reconciling it to its net cash flow equivalent. In this approach, net income is initially assumed to increase cash by the amount of the net income (or decrease cash by the amount of the net loss). This is not strictly true, because many of the items in income do not represent cash flows. For example, as we discussed on page 259, amortization has no effect on cash. The remaining entries in the operating section, except for the gain on sale of equipment, use the current asset and liability accounts to adjust all the items that form the net income to the amount of the cash flows that actually occurred.

In using the T-account method, it is very convenient to reconstruct the summary journal entries that would have been recorded for each of the accounts to determine the net cash flows. These reconstructed journal entries are not essential, but they are a convenient method of determining what happened. Remember that they are intended only for you to understand what occurred; they are not recorded in the accounting system. For example, the cash impact of net income is as follows:

(1) The entry is:
A-Cash (Operating)   12,480
    SE-Retained Earnings   12,480

One adjustment that must be made when all the net income is assumed to increase cash results from the assumption that all the revenues under net income are collected in cash. The change in the balance of accounts receivable shows the net effect of the difference between the sales revenue recorded during the period and the cash collected from customers.

In the case of Huskies Industries, the accounts receivable balance decreased during the year, which means that there were more collections (credit entries to the accounts receivable account) than sales (debit entries to the accounts receivable account). This, in turn, means that Huskies collected more cash than its sales figure shows. The adjustment to the cash account, therefore, shows a cash increase over that represented by the revenues included in net income. In effect, this adjustment adds $10,000 to the revenues shown of $130,000 and is included in net income to produce a net of $140,000 in cash received from customers, as follows:

Sales revenues	$130,000
Decrease in accounts receivable	10,000
Cash collections from sales	$140,000

The net or summary entry to represent this adjustment is as follows:

(2) The entry is:
A-Cash (Operating)   10,000
    A-Accounts receivable   10,000

A second assumption that requires an adjustment is that the cost of goods sold reduced cash during the period by the same amount. There are two reasons why this may be incorrect. The first is that the goods sold, represented by the amounts shown in cost of goods sold, may have come from the beginning inventory (i.e., purchases that were made last year) and may not have required an outflow of cash this year (assuming the accounts payable associated with the inventory purchased were paid last year). The change in the balance of inventory provides information about this potential adjustment.

A second reason would be that purchases of inventory during the period resulted in accounts payable, assuming all purchases are bought on credit. Therefore, if these accounts were not paid as of year end the expenses reported would not yet have resulted in cash outflows. The effects of both these reasons can be corrected by adjusting the net income figure by the net change in the inventory balance and the net change in the accounts payable balance. The effect of these two entries is to adjust the cost of goods sold amount included in the net income ($80,000) to its cash equivalent of cash paid to suppliers ($85,000), as follows:

Cost of goods sold as reported (assumed cash outflow)	($80,000)
Increase in inventory (requiring extra cash outflow)	(10,000)
Increase in accounts payable (meaning less cash paid out)	5,000
Actual cash paid to suppliers	($85,000)

The entries to represent these adjustments are as follows:

(3) and (5) The entries are:

A-Inventory	10,000	
A-Cash (Operations)		10,000
A-Cash (Operations)	5,000	
L-Accounts payable		5,000

Two other expenses on the income statement have corresponding current assets or liabilities: rent expense (prepaid rent) and salaries expense (accrued salaries). Since there is prepaid rent on the balance sheet, Huskies evidently prepays its rent. The increase in the prepaid rent ($100) indicates that more cash was paid out than is reflected in the rent expense. The entry to represent this adjustment is as follows:

(4) The entry is:

A-Prepaid rent	100	
A-Cash (Operating)		100

The salaries expense account has a related liability account, accrued salaries. The increase in accrued salaries ($100) means that Huskies reduced the outflow of cash by owing more to employees at the end of the year than at the beginning of the year. The salaries expense on the income statement is $100 larger than the actual cash outflow for salaries. The entry to represent this adjustment is as follows:

(6) The entry is:

A-Cash (Operations)	100	
L-Accrued salaries		100

A third type of adjustment results from the assumption that all other expenses represent cash outflows. Amortization expense is not a cash expense. Amortization is merely a recognition that part of the long-term assets are used up each year, but no cash flows are associated with amortization expense. The associated cash flow occurred years before, when the assets were purchased. Therefore, because amortization expense is included in calculating net income and results in a decrease in net income, its effect must be removed by adding it back to net income to show the net income figure that would have resulted had we not included amortization expense.

One caveat at this point: Because this adjustment is on the debit side of the cash account, it looks as though amortization is a source of cash. This is not true. Cash collections from customers are the source of cash from operations. It is only because the indirect method is attempting to correct the misstatements made by assuming that all net income increases cash that this item appears as if it were a source of cash. Many analysts approximate the cash from operations of a company by adding amortization to the net income of the company. This is a quick and reasonably close approximation to cash received from operations. However, this method ignores the adjustments due to the other accounts that are shown in Exhibit 5-15.

The entry to adjust for amortization is as follows:

(7) The entry is:
A-Cash (Operations)	20,000	
XA-Accumulated amortization		20,000

The last adjustment in the operating section adjusts the net income for the gain from the sale of the equipment. The $300 gain shown in income assumes that $300 was received in cash. However, point #3 from the additional information provided at the outset of the example indicated that $500 cash was received on the disposal of the equipment. Thus the effect on cash is $500, not $300. Therefore, it is incorrect to assume that the $300 increase in the net income figure represents the cash inflow.

The second problem is that, even if this were the right amount, it would be reported in the wrong section of the cash flow statement. Companies invest in property, plant, and equipment, so cash flows resulting from disposals of property, plant, and equipment are also investing (or, more properly, disinvesting) activities. These are not operating cash flows. The entry to correct for these two misstatements makes two adjustments. It adjusts the amount of cash that actually was received, and it corrects the activity that was affected. The entry to represent these two items is as follows:

(8) The entry is:
A-Cash (Investing)	500	
XA-Accumulated amortization	800	
A-Cash (Operating)		300
A-PP&E		1,000

Remember when we were discussing Big Rock's cash flow statement earlier (Exhibit 5-11)? In the operating activities section, it had added a "loss on sale of capital assets" of $228,577 in 1999. The loss means that less cash was received for the capital assets that were sold than their carrying value (or book value). The actual cash received is shown in the investing section as "proceeds on disposal of capital assets" of $755,000. So just as the gain was deducted from the operating section in the Huskies Industries example, a loss is added back to the operating section. Then the actual cash proceeds from the sale (including the gain or loss) is included in the investing section.

The remaining items adjust for the cash flows that resulted from the financing and investing activities. To determine these cash flows, look for changes in long-term assets, financing liabilities both short- and long-term, and shareholders' equity accounts. The amount of the purchases of new property, plant, and equipment can be determined by considering the beginning and ending balances in the property, plant, and equipment summary account and the credit entry made to this account in entry (8). Note that to reach the ending balance of $159,000 an additional debit of $60,000 is needed. We assume that additional assets were purchased for cash. This cash outflow is shown in the investing section. The entry is represented as follows:

(9) The entry is:

A-PP&E	60,000	
A-Cash (Investing)		60,000

The other accounts that still have changes that remain to be explained at this point are the notes payable, dividends payable, bonds payable, common shares, and retained earnings accounts. Using the extra information provided, an analysis is now made of each of these accounts.

The entry for notes payable is a net entry. It is net because not enough information is given to determine how many new notes were issued for cash or how many were retired (paid off by paying cash). All that is known is the net change in the notes payable account. The net change indicates that more notes were issued during this period than were retired because the balance in the account increased. This net effect is then shown as increasing the notes payable account. The net cash inflow appears in the financing section. The entry is represented as follows:

(10) The entry is:

A-Cash (Financing)	100	
L-Notes payable		100

Entry (11) for the bonds payable is similar to that in (10) except that, in this case, the additional information indicated that there was $8,000 in long-term borrowings this year. Therefore, there would be a new credit of $8,000 to this account. However, the balance in this account increased by only $6,000. It can, therefore, be inferred that $2,000 worth of bonds was paid off during the year. The entries are represented as follows:

(11) The entry is:

A-Cash (Financing)	8,000	
L-Bonds payable		8,000

(12) The entry is:

L-Bonds payable	2,000	
A-Cash (Financing)		2,000

In the common shares account, credits represent new issuances of shares and debits represent repurchases of shares. Again, because there is no explicit information indicating that there were new issuances or repurchases, you can only infer the net effect. The net effect is that the account increased, indicating that more shares were issued than were repurchased. The entry is represented as follows:

(13) The entry is:
A-Cash (Financing)   4,000
    SE-Common shares   4,000

Because all the income statement transactions have now been explained, attention can be turned to the retained earnings account to determine whether the entire change in this account has been explained. The account needs an additional debit of $1,400 to explain the change in the balance. The logical assumption concerning this debit is that it represents the dividends declared during the period. The entry is represented as follows:

(14) The entry is:
SE-Retained earnings   1,400
    L-Dividends payable   1,400

When dividends are declared they become legally payable, but there may be a lag between the time they are declared and the time they are paid. Therefore, the credit side of entry (14) is to a dividends payable account. The cash entry for dividends takes into consideration the change in the balance of the dividends payable account. The balance in the dividends payable account probably reflects the last quarter's dividend, which has yet to be paid. The entry is represented as follows:

(15) The entry is:
L-Dividends payable   1,230
    A-Cash (Financing)   1,230

Entry (15) completes the cash flow analysis. All the net changes in the balance sheet accounts have been explained. The cash account now contains all the information necessary to produce a cash flow statement. The net cash flows from the three types of activity, as taken from the Cash T-account, are as follows:

Huskies Industries Ltd.
Cash Flow Statement
For the Year Ended December 31, 20x1

Operating activities		
Net income	$ 12,480	
Add back items not representing cash flows:		
Amortization	20,000	
Gain on disposal	(300)	
Adjustments for working capital items:		
Decrease in Accounts Receivable	10,000	
Increase in Inventory	(10,000)	
Increase in Prepaid Rent	(100)	
Increase in Accounts Payable	5,000	
Increase in Salaries Payable	100	
Cash from operating activities		$ 37,180
Financing activities		
Issue of Notes Payable	$ 100	
Issue of Common Shares	4,000	
Issue of Bonds Payable	8,000	
Payment of Bonds Payable	(2,000)	
Payment of Dividends	(1,230)	
Cash from financing activities		8,870
Investing activities		
Purchase of Property, Plant, and Equipment	$(60,000)	
Sale of Property, Plant, and Equipment	500	
Cash used for investing activities		(59,500)
Decrease in Cash		(13,450)
Cash − beginning of the year		19,500
Cash − end of the year		$ 6,050

The information from the Cash T-accounts was used to prepare a proper cash flow statement. The totals of the cash flows from the three types of activity, net cash outflow of $13,450 ($37,180 + $8,870 − $59,500 = ($13,450)), must be the same as the net change in cash for the year, a $13,450 reduction ($19,500 − $6,050 = $13,450), which it is. Although the cash flow statement is technically finished with the Decrease in Cash amount, most companies will add the final two lines to the statement so that users can more easily verify the change in cash. In our example, we had cash but no cash equivalents. Many companies have cash equivalents added (or subtracted if they happen to be liabilities) to the cash to arrive at a change in cash and cash equivalents. Such companies must inform users as to which accounts are used for cash equivalents.

Remember that debits in the cash account represent sources or inflows of cash, and credits represent uses or outflows of cash. The formal cash flow statement shows the operating, investing, and financing activities separately.

INTERPRETATION OF CASH FLOW INFORMATION

Learning Objective

7

Provide a basic analysis of a company's financial health using a cash flow statement.

Once the cash flow statement has been prepared, users will want to interpret what the statement tells them about the company. While many users will be interested in what has happened to cash in the current period, they are likely to be more interested in predicting the future cash flows of the company. A bank loan officer, for example, wants to be sure that, if money is lent to the company, the company will be able to pay it back. A stock analyst, on the other hand, will want to know what the cash flows will be over a long period of time, to ensure an adequate return on the investment in shares. Users interested in the future of the company will try to decide which cash flows will continue and which will not continue.

In addition to deciding which cash flows are likely to continue, users will want to make sure that cash from continuing operations is sufficient, over the long run, to pay for the continuing investing and financing activities. There is a limit to the cash inflows that can be achieved from investing and financing activities. Investing inflows are limited by the kinds of return that can be earned from investments in long-term assets and the level of investment by the company. The financing inflows are limited by the willingness of lenders and investors to invest their money in the company. At some level of debt, the company becomes so risky that no lender will agree to lend more. Because the inflows from investing and financing are limited, the company, if it is to remain in business, must generate sufficient cash inflow from operating activities to pay the interest and dividends on the financing activities and to continue investing at appropriate levels in property, plant, and equipment and other long-term assets.

Huskies Industries, as an example, generated $37,180 from operations. Assuming that these are continuing operations (as opposed to discontinued operations), and assuming that Huskies is in a fairly stable industry, you would expect this amount of cash flow to continue into the future. One way to evaluate this is to look at the trend in cash flow from operations over the last five years to see how stable this figure is. The next question to address is whether this flow is sufficient to cover the continuing cash needs of Huskies.

If you look at the uses of cash in the investing and financing sections, you will see that Huskies spent $60,000 to buy new equipment, $1,230 to pay dividends, and $2,000 to pay off debt. It is likely that purchasing new property, plant, and equipment will be a continuing need, because buildings and equipment wear out over time. But does the company buy $60,000 in property, plant, and equipment every year, or is this year's purchase larger (or smaller) than usual? If Huskies pays $60,000 every year, you could quickly conclude that the cash from operations will not be sufficient in the long run to pay for this one need, not to mention other needs. If, however, Huskies has this large need only once every three years and if, in the other two years, the purchases are, say, $15,000, then the average yearly amount of property, plant, and equipment purchases is $30,000 [($60,000 + 15,000 + 15,000)/3 = $30,000]. Cash flow from operations would be sufficient to cover this need, with $10,000 left over for other needs. Again, this can be learned by looking at the trend in property, plant, and equipment spending over the last five years to determine the spending pattern.

Once started, the payment of dividends is generally a continuing need. Companies are reluctant to stop or reduce the payment of dividends, because such action sends a negative signal to the market about the future profitability of the company. The amount of dividends paid, of course, is affected by the number of shares outstanding. If there was an additional issuance of shares in a given year, some growth in the total amount of dividend payments would be expected. Huskies is, in fact, in this position. New shares were issued in 20x1, and this could mean more dividends paid in future years.

The repayment of debt is another generally continuing item, but it is not dependent, for repayment, on cash from operations. Most companies maintain a certain amount of debt. The level of debt is sometimes measured by comparing the dollar amount of debt on the balance sheet to the total amount of debt plus shareholders' equity. This measure is called a **debt/equity ratio**. For Huskies, this ratio, at the end of the year, was $58,070/$146,450 = 39.7%. This measure indicates that 39.7% of Huskies' total financing is in the form of debt. As will be discussed in Chapter 12, there is a theoretical optimal level of debt that will maximize the return to shareholders. Most companies try to maintain this optimal level of debt. Therefore, if some debt must be paid off in a given year (which would lower the debt/equity ratio), it is generally replaced by a new borrowing (which would bring the debt/equity ratio back to its original value). This process of replacing old debt with new debt is sometimes called the rollover of debt. In the cash flow statement, this type of transaction would show up in the financing section as both an inflow of cash and an outflow of cash. If the financing activities involved short-term debt like the note payable used by Huskies, it is acceptable to show the net cash flow rather than the inflows and outflows separately.

With regard to debt, Huskies did pay off some long-term debt, but at the same time it borrowed additional long-term debt, increasing the long-term borrowings by $6,000. It may be that Huskies saw an opportunity to acquire long-term debt at acceptable interest rates. Huskies also took out some additional short-term borrowings to finance the company. Recognize that this short-term debt will probably require a cash payoff in a relatively short period of time, whereas the long-term borrowing will require cash payments over a longer period. If the company has some short-term cash inflow shortages, short-term debt can be a difficult problem. As a reader of the financial statements, you should have some understanding of how soon the debt of a company comes due, because this will affect its need for cash. In the notes to the financial statements, companies usually describe their borrowings quite extensively, including information about interest rates and due dates.

In addition to the borrowing, Huskies generated cash from two other sources: the sale of equipment and the issuance of common shares. Neither of these sources of cash is considered a continuing one. Also, the inflow of cash from the sale of the equipment is very small.

In summary, Huskies required $63,230 in cash to pay for the purchase of property, plant, and equipment, to pay dividends, and to repay debt. It generated a total of $49,780 from operations, issuance of notes and bonds payable, issuance of common shares, and sale of property, plant, and equipment. This produced a shortfall of $13,450 for the period, which was covered by the beginning balance of cash. Cash declined during this period from $19,500 to $6,050. If all the items in the cash flow statement were continuing items, Huskies could continue to operate for only another partial year before it ran out of cash. Nothing definitive can be said about Huskies' cash flow health, because not enough historical data are available. You can say that, if all items are continuing, Huskies will be in trouble next year. If, on the other hand, the purchase of property, plant, and equipment does not continue at its present level, then Huskies may be in reasonable shape.

Cash from operations can also be examined further to determine whether there are any problems in the operations of the company. This analysis is easily carried out using the indirect format of the cash flow statement, where net income is reconciled to cash from operations. For Huskies Industries, the operating section shows that the two reasons for the increase in cash from operations during this period were that accounts receivable decreased and accounts payable increased. This gives some information about the management of the receivables and payables of the company, which is critical in determining the lead/lag relationship in the cash-to-cash cycle. In general, these two accounts would be expected to move in unison. When business is growing, a company generates both more receivables and more payables. When business contracts, both these accounts decrease. In the case of Huskies, they are moving in opposite directions, with accounts receivable decreasing and accounts payable increasing. This should raise a red flag, leading the reader of the statement to question why these amounts are moving in opposite directions. It could mean that there is a problem in the management of receivables or payables, especially the accounts payable.

Another concern regarding cash from operating activities is that Huskies increased inventories during the period, causing cash from operations to decline. If a business were expanding, you would expect a larger inventory. However, increased sales normally mean a larger amount of accounts receivable, which was not the case. Again, this raises a red flag, which should prompt the user to ask why inventory has increased so much. It is possible that Huskies is stockpiling inventory in anticipation of a strike by employees, or it may be that its product is not selling and it has not adjusted inventory purchases sufficiently. This situation may lead to obsolete inventory that cannot be sold.

ANALYSIS OF THE CASH FLOW OF BIG ROCK BREWERY

Refer back to Exhibit 5-11 to find the cash flow statement for Big Rock Brewery Ltd.

First of all, Big Rock uses the indirect approach for the operating section. Note that the two largest adjustments to net income in 1999 are amortization and write-off of deferred charges for the period. Also note that Big Rock produces a substantial amount of cash from operations ($2,113,702 in 1999, even though it had a net loss of $556,745) and that the amount has increased from the previous year. The two biggest uses of cash in 1999 are the repayment of long-term debt ($1,524,000) and the repurchase of shares ($726,981). The trend over the last two years in these items indicates that the repayment of debt is a continuing item but the repurchase of shares is not. To understand more fully the impact of these two items, the user would need to examine the balance sheet to see the level of long-term debt and to review the impact of the repurchase of shares. For example, with the repurchase of shares, the number of shares outstanding will have decreased. Earnings per share should be higher and the amount paid out in dividends may decrease.

In addition to the largest cash flows, let us look more closely at the cash flows associated with borrowings. To gain an understanding of the net effects of borrowing, combine all the debt cash flows into one item, as follows:

	(in thousands)	
	1999	1998
Net change in borrowings (<90 days)	(298)	547
Newly issued (>90 days)	-0-	-0-
Repayments (>90 days)	(1,524)	(2,683)
Totals	(1,822)	(2,136)

The totals show that Big Rock has been repaying its debt over the last two years. This trend in debt repayment can probably be partially explained by other line items in the cash flow statement. Operations has been a good source of cash over the last two years; this has enabled Big Rock to repay the debt and thereby establish a good credit rating, which will enable them to borrow again in the future if the need arises.

Returning to the overall analysis, in 1999 the cash flow from operations ($2,113,702) was almost sufficient to cover the continuing needs for the repayment of debt. The inflow of cash from the disposition of capital assets ($755,000) was more than sufficient to cover the purchases of capital assets ($294,898). This is an unusual situation. It is unlikely that the high amount of the inflow of cash from the sale of capital assets will be a continuing activity. Capital assets are sold, but usually for much less than new acquisitions. It could be concluded that Big Rock performs quite well when it comes to cash generation. It also appears, based on the past trend, that this will continue into the future.

S U M M A R Y

This chapter opened with a discussion about the importance to organizations of effective cash management. We showed you how a company can be earning profits yet at the same time have serious cash flow problems. We outlined the information that users can obtain from the cash flows that are summarized in the cash flow statement. Remember that, for a business to be successful, both cash flows and profits must be generated. We also traced through the cash flow statement, describing the three essential components of the statement and the kinds of activity that are included in each section. We then described the procedure for preparing a cash flow statement. This statement is more complex than the balance sheet and the income statement, in that you need to analyze the income statement and the balance sheet as well as seek out additional information before you can organize all the data that you need in order to prepare the statement. With the income statement and balance sheet, you mostly copy balances from accounts to the right place on the statement. Little analysis is required.

The last part of this chapter is more important than the actual preparation of the statement. It outlined for you how the cash flow statement could be used in assessing the future cash flow of a company. Remember that it is important to see a positive cash flow from operations. The operations are the lifeblood of the company; it is through them that the company will live or die.

The next chapters provide details of the items that appear in the balance sheet to give you a better understanding of the source of the amounts that appear in the financial statements.

SUMMARY PROBLEMS

1. The 2001 balance sheet and income statement of Hayes Industries, Inc., are provided in Exhibit 5-16. Hayes Industries manufactures and distributes a broad range of clothing and related services to retailers. Using these statements, construct the cash flow statement for Hayes for the year ended May 31, 2001. Use T-accounts and the indirect approach. The following additional information and assumptions are also provided (all numbers are in thousands unless otherwise indicated).

   a. The beginning and ending balances in the accumulated amortization account were $69,653 and $71,693, respectively.

   b. Dividends declared in fiscal 2001 totalled $6,654.

   c. Amortization totalled $7,805 in 2001.

   d. Purchases of new property, plant, and equipment totalled $14,790 in 2001.

   e. Property, plant, and equipment sold in 2001 produced a gain of $1,169.

   f. All changes in the shareholders' equity accounts other than earnings and dividends are due to the issuance of new common shares.

   g. Treat the issuance and repayment of long-term debt on a net basis.

   h. Changes in the Other Assets account are considered operating items by Hayes.

HAYES INDUSTRIES, INC.

EXHIBIT 5-16

Balance Sheet

($ in thousands)

	May 31, 2001	May 31, 2000
Assets		
Current Assets:		
Cash and equivalents	$ 2,225	$ 3,227
Accounts receivable	83,962	75,165
Inventories	169,978	114,465
Prepaid expenses	13,023	12,402
Total Current Assets	269,188	205,259
Property, Plant, and Equipment	38,650	33,217
Other Assets	1,190	1,471
Total Assets	$309,028	$239,947
Liabilities and Shareholders' Equity		
Current Liabilities:		
Notes payable	$ 43,500	$ 19,500
Accounts payable	54,331	45,023
Accrued salaries	8,235	11,687
Other accrued expenses	13,039	12,977
Income taxes	4,732	5,352
Dividends payable	1,739	1,555
Total Current Liabilities	125,576	96,094
Long-Term Debt	50,873	16,118
Total Liabilities	176,449	112,212
Shareholders' Equity		
Common shares	15,714	14,791
Retained earnings	116,865	112,944
Total Shareholders' Equity	132,579	127,735
Total Liabilities and Shareholders' Equity	$309,028	$239,947

HAYES INDUSTRIES, INC.

Income Statement
Consolidated Statements of Earnings
($ in thousands except per share amounts)

Year Ended	May 31, 2001	May 31, 2000
Net Sales	$656,987	$624,568
Costs and Expenses:		
Cost of goods sold	543,624	498,790
Selling, general and administrative	91,601	91,209
Interest	4,136	2,297
	639,361	592,296
Earnings Before Income Taxes	17,626	32,272
Income Taxes	7,051	13,071
Net Earnings	$ 10,575	$ 19,201
Net Earnings Per Common Share	$ 1.22	$ 2.23

2. Based on the answer to Question 1 and the previous two years' cash flow statements for Hayes Industries shown in Exhibit 5-17, answer the following questions:

 a. Discuss the company's ability to meet its needs for cash over the last three years. Comment on the continuing nature of the major items that have appeared over the last three years.

 b. Explain why so much cash was generated from operations in 2001.

HAYES INDUSTRIES, INC.

Cash Flow Statements
($ in thousands)

Year Ended	May 31, 2000	May 31, 1999
Operating Activities:		
Net earnings	$19,201	$14,786
Adjustments to reconcile net earnings to net cash provided by operating activities:		
Amortization	7,041	6,457
(Gain) loss on sale of property, plant, and equipment	488	(211)
Changes in working capital:		
(Increase) decrease in:		
Receivables	(7,072)	(935)
Inventories	(11,872)	(19,687)
Prepaid expenses	(704)	(1,851)
(Decrease) increase in:		
Accounts payable	10,121	(3,734)
Accrued salaries and other current expenses	2,428	1,078
Income taxes payable	-0-	(402)
Other noncurrent assets	52	(513)
Net cash provided by operating activities	19,683	(5,012)

EXHIBIT 5-17
CONT.

Investing Activities:		
Purchase of property, plant, and equipment	(9,395)	(8,050)
Proceeds from sale of property, plant, and equipment	414	1,824
Net cash used in investing activities	(8,981)	(6,226)
Financing Activities:		
Short-term borrowings	1,000	18,500
Dividends on common shares	(5,956)	(5,486)
Payments on long-term debt	(4,913)	(14,733)
Addition to long-term debt	-0-	10,000
Purchase and retirement of common shares	(1,885)	(2,449)
Net cash used in financing activities	(11,754)	5,832
Net Change in Cash	(1,052)	(5,406)
Cash at Beginning of Period	4,279	9,685
Cash at End of Period	$ 3,227	$ 4,279

SUGGESTED SOLUTIONS TO SUMMARY PROBLEMS

1. T-Accounts:

The only difficult item to deal with in the set-up of the T-accounts is the balance in the PP&E account and its corresponding accumulated amortization account. The balance sheet presents only one item for the net of the two accounts. To get the beginning and ending balances in the PP&E account, add the net amount reported on the face of the statement to the accumulated amortization balance that is given in the extra information to the problem (this information was provided in a note to the financial statements of Hayes). Therefore, the beginning balance is $102,870 ($33,217 + $69,653) and the ending balance is $110,343 ($38,650 + $71,693).

A-Cash

	✓	3,227			
Operations:					
Net income	(1)	10,575	8,797	(2)	Incr. in A/R
Increase in A/P	(5)	9,308	55,513	(3)	Incr. in inventory
Incr. other acc. exp.	(7)	62	621	(4)	Incr. in ppd. exp.
Decr. in other assets	(9)	281	3,452	(6)	Decr. in accrued sal.
Amortization	(10)	7,805	620	(8)	Decr. in inc. taxes
			1,169	(12)	Gain on sale of PP&E
Investing:					
Proceeds from sale of PP&E	(12)	2,721	14,790	(11)	Purchase of PP&E
Financing:					
Issuance of notes pay.	(13)	24,000	6,470	(15)	Dividends
Iss. of LT debt	(16)	34,755			
Iss. of shares	(17)	923			
	✓	2,225			

A-Accounts Receivable

✓	75,165	
(2)	8,797	
✓	83,962	

A-Inventories

✓	114,465	
(3)	55,513	
✓	169,978	

A-Prepaid Expenses

✓	12,402	
(4)	621	
✓	13,023	–

A-PP&E

✓	102,870		
(11)	14,790	7,317	(12)
✓	110,343		

XA-Accum. Ammort.

		69,653	✓
(12)	5,765	7,805	(10)
		71,693	✓

A-Other Assets

✓	1,471		
		281	(8)
✓	1,190		

L-Notes Payable

		19,500	✓
		24,000	(13)
		43,500	✓

L-Accounts Payable

		45,023	✓
		9,308	(5)
		54,331	✓

L-Accrued Salaries

		11,687	✓
(6)	3,452		
		8,235	✓

L-Other Accrued Expenses

		12,977	✓
		62	(7)
		13,039	✓

L-Taxes Payable

		5,352	✓
(8)	620		
		4,732	✓

L-Dividends Payable

		1,555	✓
(15)	6,470	6,654	(14)
		1,739	✓

L-Long-term Debt

		16,118	✓
		34,755	(16)
		50,873	✓

SE-Common Shares

		14,791	✓
		923	(17)
		15,714	✓

SE-Retained Earnings

		112,944	✓
(14)	6,654	10,575	(1)
		116,865	✓

Explanations of selected transactions.

Transaction 10. The debit entry to the cash account is the amortization of property, plant, and equipment which is a noncash expense and therefore must be put back. The reconstruction entry is:

A-Cash (Operating)	7,805	
XA-Accumulated amortization		7,805

Transaction 12. The sale of property, plant, and equipment resulted in a gain of $1,169. The cost (in the PP&E account) and the accumulated amortization associated with this sale are determined by balancing these two accounts in the T-accounts. The reconstruction entry that results is as follows:

A-Cash (Investing)	2,721	
XA-Accumulated amortization	5,765	
A-Property, plant, and equipment		7,317
A-Cash (Operating)		1,169

Transactions 14 and 15. Determining the amount of dividends that were actually paid for during 2001 involves first determining the amount of dividends declared. If you balance the retained earnings account, it becomes obvious that an additional debit of $6,654 is needed. This debit represents the dividends declared. The reconstruction entry to record this is as follows:

SE-Retained earnings	6,654	
L-Dividends payable		6,654

With the additional entry to the dividends payable account, it is now possible to determine the amount of dividends actually paid for during the year by balancing the account. An additional debit of $6,470 is required to reach the end balance of $1,739. The reconstruction entry to record this is as follows:

L-Dividends payable	6,470	
A-Cash (Financing)		6,470

HAYES INDUSTRIES INC.
Cash Flow Statement
For the year ended May 31, 2001

Operating Activities		
Net earnings	$10,575	
Adjustments to reconcile net earnings to cash provided by operating activities		
Amortization	7,805	
Gain on sale of equipment	(1,169)	
Changes in working capital:		
Increase in accounts receivable	(8,797)	
Increase in inventory	(55,513)	
Increase in prepaid expenses	(621)	
Increase in accounts payable	9,308	
Decrease in accrued salaries	(3,452)	
Increase in other accrued expenses	62	
Decrease in income taxes	(620)	
Decrease in other assets	281	
Cash provided by operating activities		($42,141)
Investing Activities		
Sale of property, plant, and equipment	2,721	
Purchase of property, plant, and equipment	(14,790)	
Cash provided by investing activities		(12,069)
Financing Activities		
Issuance of notes payable	24,000	
Issuance of long-term debt	34,755	
Issuance of shares	923	
Payment of dividends	(6,470)	
Cash provided by financing activities		53,208
Net Change in Cash		(1,002)
Cash at Beginning of Period		3,227
Cash at End of Period		$ 2,225

2. a. The two major continuing needs for cash over the last three years have been the purchase of property, plant, and equipment and the payment of dividends. The combination of these two items has averaged $16,715 over the three years. Only in 2000 did Hayes produce enough cash from operations to cover these needs. In both 1999 and 2001 Hayes used cash in its operations, with a significant amount used in 2001.

In 1999 Hayes also used a significant amount of cash to retire long-term debt and buy back shares. Since operations did not provide cash that year, short-term borrowings were used to meet the company's cash needs. Hayes also drew down its cash balance significantly in 1999 to pay for its cash needs. In 2000 Hayes continued to retire long-term debt and buy back shares. In that year, however, there was some extra cash left over from operations after paying for property, plant, and equipment and dividends. Additional cash was raised from short-term borrowings such that Hayes ended the year in about the same cash position it was in at the beginning of the year.

      In 2001 cash from operations was significantly negative and the expenditures for property, plant, and equipment and dividends were the largest in the three-year period shown on the cash flow statements. Hayes primarily paid for these items by issuing more debt, with more than half of the issuance being long-term (the rest short-term). A look at the balance sheet indicates that long-term debt increased approximately four-fold in 2001. Short-term debt more than doubled. This has significant implications for 2002, as this debt carries with it additional interest expense that will appear in the income statement next year.

b. In analyzing the operating section of the cash flow statements for Hayes, it becomes clear to you that the biggest negative adjustment over the last three years has been the changes in inventories. These changes represent increases in inventories. In 2001, inventories increased $55,513, or almost 49% over year 2000 levels ($114,465). There is clearly a problem here, as sales have not increased this dramatically—only $32,419, or 5.2%, in 2001. Receivables have also increased fairly dramatically—by $8,797, or 11.7%, in 2001. As an offset to the increase in receivables, accounts payable have also increased, by $9,308, or 20.7%, in 2001. While this helps the cash flow of the company, it may also indicate that it is having trouble paying its bills and is slowing down payment on its accounts. The biggest concern is the increase in the level of inventory; you would want to investigate why inventories have grown this much.

GLOSSARY

Capitalization The amount of resources contributed to the company by shareholders and debtholders. The term *capitalization* is used in several ways in accounting. Besides the definition given above, it can also mean the recording of an asset or the deferring of a cost.

Cash equivalents Current assets and liabilities that are very liquid and readily convertible into cash or that can require the short-term use of cash. Examples are short-term investments and bank overdrafts or lines of credit.

Cash flow The net change in cash that occurs from the beginning to the end of an accounting period.

Cash position The amount of cash and cash equivalents.

Debt/equity ratio The ratio calculated by dividing total liabilities by the sum of total liabilities and shareholders' equity. It indicates whether the company relies more heavily on debt or equity to finance the company.

Direct approach A method of calculating the cash from operations of a company in which the direct gross cash receipts and payments are shown.

Financing activities The activities of a company that are directed to obtaining resources for the company from investors or debtholders. The return of resources to shareholders and debtholders is also considered part of these activities.

Indirect approach A method of calculating the cash from operations of a company in which the net income is adjusted for all noncash revenues or expenses to convert it from an accrual basis to its cash basis equivalent.

Investing activities The activities of a company that are directed to investing its resources over extended periods of time in long-term assets.

Lead/lag relationship The relationships between the recognition of revenues and expenses for income statement purposes and the recognition of their cash flow effects.

Line of credit An arrangement with a financing institution that allows a company to overdraw its accounts. The overdrawn amount becomes a loan that must be repaid.

Operating activities The activities of a company that are directed to selling goods and services to customers.

Working capital Current assets minus current liabilities.

ASSIGNMENT MATERIAL

Assessing Your Recall

5-1 Discuss why it is important for companies to prepare a cash flow statement in addition to an income statement.

5-2 Discuss how a company's receivables, inventory, and payables policies affect cash flows relative to the income produced in a given period.

5-3 What is meant by a lead/lag relationship in terms of the cash flow statement?

5-4 For a company with a cash flow problem, list at least three potential reasons for the problem, and suggest a possible solution for each of these reasons.

5-5 Describe the three major categories of activity that are shown on the cash flow statement.

5-6 Discuss the major difference between the direct approach and the indirect approach for constructing the operating section of a cash flow statement.

5-7 "Amortization is a source of cash." Explain your reasons for agreeing or disagreeing with this statement.

5-8 In what section of the cash flow statement (operating, financing, or investing) would each of the following items appear:

    a. Purchase of new property, plant, and equipment

    b. Proceeds from a bank loan

    c. Collections from customers

    d. Dividends to shareholders

    e. Proceeds from the sale of marketable securities

    f. Retirement of debt

    g. Changes in accounts receivable

    h. Net income

    i. Gain or loss on the sale of property, plant, and equipment

5-9 Indicate whether each of the following items should be classified on the cash flow statement as an operating, investing, or financing activity. If an item does not belong on the statement, indicate why.

    a. Payment of cash dividends on common shares

    b. Sale of a warehouse

    c. Interest payments on an outstanding long-term bank loan

    d. Purchase of a company's own common shares on the stock market

    e. Acquisition of land

    f. Borrowing cash by taking out a long-term bank loan

    g. Purchase of an investment in another company by buying its shares

h. Collection of an account receivable

i. Declaration of dividends on common shares

j. Purchase of operating equipment

Applying Your Knowledge

5-10 (Identification of sources and uses of cash)
In the chapter's opening story, Dorothy Hooper, controller of the Manitoba Theatre Centre, described the importance of cash to the viability of the company.

Required:
Identify three possible sources of cash and three possible uses of cash of the Manitoba Theatre Centre.

5-11 (Cash flow and sales growth)
Explain why a high sales growth rate can create significant cash flow problems for a company.

5-12 (Cash flow and capital assets)
Explain the timing of the cash flows related to the purchase, use, and ultimate sale of property, plant, and equipment.

5-13 (Cash flow and interest)
Discuss the classification of interest cash flows in the cash flow statement and discuss whether you believe this is appropriate.

5-14 (Effect of transactions on cash flows)
Classify each of the following transactions as increasing, decreasing, or having no effect on cash flows:

a. Selling inventory to customers on account

b. Amortizing equipment

c. Paying accounts payable (amounts owed to suppliers)

d. Borrowing by establishing a mortgage on a building

e. Prepaying premiums on a two-year insurance policy

f. Collecting accounts receivable

g. Estimating and recording warranty expense for expected future warranty costs on inventory sold to customers

h. Purchasing new equipment using cash

i. Declaring a dividend

j. Paying interest on a bank loan

k. Paying a dividend that was previously declared

5-15 (Effect of transactions on cash flows)
For each of the following items: (1) identify the accounts affected and give the amounts by which they would be increased or decreased; (2) state the amount of any cash flow and whether cash is increased or decreased; and (3) identify how each item would be reported in the cash flow statement.

a. A capital asset is sold for $80,000. The asset originally cost $165,000 and the accumulated amortization is $95,000.

b. A capital asset is purchased for $350,000. A cash payment of $50,000 is made and the remainder is paid with a long-term note of $300,000.

c. Annual interest of 8% is paid on bonds that were issued for $1,000,000.

d. Several years ago a patent was purchased for $80,000. The patent is amortized over five years at a rate of $16,000 per year.

e. Income tax expense for the year is $130,000. The tax payment during the year was $95,000. The remainder will be paid next year.

5-16 (Effect of transactions on cash flows)
For each of the transactions listed in Part b of this question:

a. Indicate the effect on balance sheet categories by using the following format:

Trans. No.	Cash	Current Assets	Noncurrent Assets	Current Liabilities	Noncurrent Liabilities	Other Shareholders' Equity

b. For the transactions affecting cash shown below, state whether they relate to an operating, investing, or financing activity.

Transactions:

1. Purchases on credit, $35,000.

2. Cash paid to suppliers, $32,000.

3. Sales on credit, $60,000.

4. Cost of goods sold, $39,000.

5. Cash payments received on accounts receivable, $58,000.

6. Salaries accrued, $2,500.

7. Salaries paid (previously accrued), $2,000.

8. Machine purchased for $2,800 in cash.

9. Amortization expense, $1,200.

10. Borrowed (long-term) $5,000 to purchase equipment.

11. Interest of $350 paid on the amount borrowed for the purchase of equipment.

12. Borrowed $10,000 using long-term debt.

13. Equipment having a book value (cost minus accumulated amortization) of $700 sold for $700 cash.

14. Dividends declared, $750.

15. Dividends paid, $600.

16. Insurance premium for the next year paid, $575.

17. 1,000 shares issued at $10 per share.

18. Rent received for building, $2,000.

19. Income taxes accrued and paid, $1,325.

5-17 (Effect of transactions on cash flows)

For each of the transactions listed in Part b:

a. Indicate the effect on balance sheet categories by using the following format:

Trans. No.	Cash	Current Assets	Other Noncurrent Assets	Current Liabilities	Noncurrent Liabilities	Shareholders' Equity

b. For the transactions affecting cash, state whether they relate to an operating, investing, or financing activity.

Transactions:

1. 5,000 common shares are issued at $20 per share.

2. Property, plant, and equipment worth $120,000 are purchased for $80,000 in cash and the balance in common shares.

3. Rent payment of $3,000 is received in advance.

4. A sales contract for $100,000 is signed, and a $25,000 deposit is received in cash.

5. Merchandise inventory costing $185,000 is purchased on account.

6. Goods costing $25,000 were found defective and returned to suppliers. These goods had been purchased on account.

7. Sales were $350,000, of which $100,000 were on account.

8. Cash in the amount of $175,000 is paid to suppliers on account.

9. Equipment recorded at $10,000 was destroyed by fire.

10. The company purchased 100 shares of X Company at $15 per share for short-term investment purposes.

11. The company purchased 20,000 shares of Z Company at $18 per share in an effort to buy a controlling interest in the company (a supplier).

12. Interest expense for the year amounted to $2,500 and was paid in cash.

13. The sales contract in transaction 4 was cancelled; $10,000 of the deposit was returned and the rest was forfeited.

14. A bank loan for $100,000 was taken out and is due in five years.

15. Equipment with a cost of $40,000 was sold for $50,000. The buyer agreed to pay $50,000 in the future and signed a note receivable, which required interest payments.

16. During the year, warranty services costing $7,500 were provided to customers. A provision for warranty services was provided earlier in a separate transaction.

17. Amortization for the year totalled $15,000.

18. Dividends of $7,000 were declared, and $5,000 remained unpaid at year end.

19. Patents on a new manufacturing process were purchased for $10,000.

20. Research and development expenses amounted to $25,000 and were charged to expense as incurred.

5-18 (Cash flow from operations)
Compute the cash flow from operations in each of the following cases:

	I	II	III
Sales revenues	$225,000	$335,000	$465,000
Cost of goods sold	150,000	248,000	380,000
Other expenses	45,500	65,700	50,200
Amortization expense	3,000	8,000	20,000
Dividends paid	3,000	-0-	5,000
Increase/(Decrease) in:			
Inventories	5,000	(10,000)	15,000
Accounts receivable	3,500	1,000	(2,000)
Prepaid expenses	(500)	(1,000)	1,800
Salaries payable	(3,000)	2,000	(7,000)
Interest payable	(1,000)	(500)	4,000
Accounts payable	4,000	(9,000)	800

5-19 (Cash flow from operations)
Compute the cash flow from operations in each of the following cases:

	I	II	III
Sales revenues	$175,000	200,000	$225,000
Cost of goods sold	100,000	165,000	175,000
Amortization expense	20,000	15,000	10,000
Interest expense	3,000	5,000	6,000
Gain/(Loss) on sale of equipment	-0-	(2,000)	500
Dividends paid	8,000	-0-	5,000
Increase/(Decrease) in:			
Common shares	10,000	50,000	-0-
Bonds payable	20,000	(30,000)	(15,000)
Interest payable	(500)	(700)	100
Accounts payable	(2,000)	1,000	1,500
Accounts receivable	5,000	(4,000)	3,500
Inventories	(10,000)	(5,000)	15,000
Building and equipment	100,000	(50,000)	(8,000)

5-20 (Preparation of cash flow statement)
Financial statement data for Dennison Company for 2001 are as follows:

Dennison Company
Comparative Balance Sheets

	Dec. 31, 2001	Dec. 31, 2000
Assets		
Cash	$ 4,400	$ 25,500
Accounts receivable	35,000	59,000
Inventories	50,000	30,000
Total current assets	89,400	114,500
Property, plant, and equipment	180,000	165,000
Accumulated amortization	(80,400)	(61,900)
Total noncurrent assets	99,600	103,100
Total assets	$189,000	$217,600
Liabilities and shareholders' equity		
Accounts payable	$ 28,500	$ 38,600
Salaries payable	12,000	24,000
Total current liabilities	40,500	62,600
Bank loan	40,000	50,000
Total liabilities	80,500	112,600
Common shares	100,000	100,000
Retained earnings	8,500	5,000
Total liabilities and shareholders' equity	$189,000	$217,600

Dennison Company
Income Statement
For the year ended December 31, 2001

Sales		$185,500
Expenses		
Cost of goods sold	$87,500	
Salaries expense	48,000	
Amortization expense	23,500	
Interest expense	8,000	
Loss on sale of equipment	5,000	
Total expenses		172,000
Net income		$ 13,500

Additional information:
1. Equipment originally costing $35,000 was sold for $25,000.
2. Dividends declared and paid during the year were $10,000.

Required:
Prepare a cash flow statement for Dennison Company for the year ended December 31, 2001, supported by a set of T-accounts.

5-21 (Preparation of financial statements)

Financial statement data for Matrix Incorporated are as follows:

Matrix Incorporated
Balance Sheet
December 31, 2000

Assets

Cash	$ 15,500
Accounts receivable	10,000
Notes receivable	5,000
Inventories	20,500
Total current assets	51,000
Property, plant, and equipment	160,000
Accumulated amortization	(35,500)
Total noncurrent assets	124,500
Total assets	$175,500

Liabilities and shareholders' equity

Accounts payable	$ 5,000
Salaries payable	18,000
Total current liabilities	23,000
Bonds payable	50,000
Total liabilities	73,000
Common shares	100,000
Retained earnings	2,500
Total liabilities and shareholders' equity	$175,500

Matrix Incorporated
Trial Balance for the Year Ended December 31, 2001

	Debits	Credits
Cash	$ 2,900	
Accounts receivable	12,500	
Prepaid rent	6,000	
Inventories	18,900	
Property, plant, and equipment	160,000	
Accumulated amortization		$ 45,500
Accounts payable		13,800
Interest payable		9,000
Salaries payable		6,000
Bonds payable		10,000
Common shares		100,000
Retained earnings		2,500
Sales		350,000
Cost of goods sold	275,500	
Amortization expense	10,000	
Rent expense	12,000	
Interest expense	15,000	
Salaries expense	24,000	
Totals	$536,800	$536,800

Required:

a. Prepare an income statement and a reconciliation of retained earnings for the year ended December 31, 2001.

b. Prepare a balance sheet as at December 31, 2001.

c. Prepare a cash flow statement for the year ended December 31, 2001.

5-22 (Preparation of cash flow statement)

Athabasca Company reported the following abbreviated balance sheet and income statement for 2001.

Athabasca Company
Income Statement
For the year ended December 31, 2001

Sales		$400,000
Cost of goods sold		180,000
Gross profit		220,000
Other expenses:		
Supplies expense	$25,000	
Amortization expense	40,000	
Wages and salaries	90,000	
Interest expense	18,000	173,000
		47,000
Other income		14,000
Net income		$ 61,000

Athabasca Company
Balance Sheet

	2001	2000
Cash	$ 11,000	$ 60,000
Accounts receivable	100,000	120,000
Inventory	320,000	260,000
Buildings and equipment (net)	400,000	350,000
Total Assets	$831,000	$790,000
Accounts payable	$ 80,000	$ 90,000
Wages and salaries payable	25,000	20,000
Bonds payable	300,000	350,000
Common shares	170,000	100,000
Retained earnings	256,000	230,000
Total Liabilities and Shareholders' Equity	$831,000	$790,000

Required:

a. Prepare a cash flow statement for Athabasca Company for the year ended December 31, 2001.

b. Did the working capital change by the same amount as cash generated by operations? Should these two be the same? Explain.

5-23 (Preparation of cash flow statement)
The financial statement data for Crescent Manufacturing Company are as follows:

Crescent Manufacturing Company
Comparative Balance Sheets

	Dec. 31, 20x1	Dec. 31, 20x0
Assets		
Cash	$ 12,800	$ 17,800
Temporary investments	25,000	125,000
Accounts receivable	69,600	38,600
Prepaid insurance	-0-	6,000
Inventories	93,300	43,300
Total current assets	200,700	230,700
Property, plant, and equipment	300,000	255,000
Accumulated amortization	(86,300)	(66,300)
Total noncurrent assets	213,700	188,700
Total assets	$414,400	$419,400
Liabilities and shareholders' equity		
Accounts payable	$ 15,000	$ 12,600
Interest payable	5,600	8,000
Dividends payable	30,000	20,000
Total current liabilities	50,600	40,600
Mortgage payable	75,000	100,000
Bonds payable	75,000	75,000
Total long-term liabilities	150,000	175,000
Total liabilities	200,600	215,600
Common shares	190,000	200,000
Retained earnings	23,800	3,800
Total shareholders' equity	213,800	203,800
Total liabilities and shareholders' equity	$414,400	$419,400

Income Statement
For the year ended December 31, 20x1

Sales	$508,000	
Interest revenue	10,500	
Gain on sale of temporary investments	25,000	
Total revenues		$543,500
Expenses:		
Cost of goods sold	330,000	
Amortization expense	50,000	
Insurance expense	12,000	
Interest expense	41,500	
Salaries expense	60,000	
Total expenses		493,500
Net income		$ 50,000

Additional information:
1. The temporary investments are not cash equivalents.

2. 10,000 shares of Sigma Company, which were purchased at a cost of $10 per share, were sold at a price of $12.50 per share.

3. Dividends declared during the year amounted to $30,000 and remained unpaid at year end.

Required:
Prepare a cash flow statement for Crescent Manufacturing Company for the year ended December 31, 20x1.

5-24 (Preparation of cash flow statement)
The balance sheets for Simco Company as at the beginning and end of 20x1 are shown below:

Simco Company
Balance Sheets

	Dec. 31, 20x1	Dec. 31, 20x0
Assets		
Current assets		
Cash	$ 28,000	$ 10,000
Accounts receivable	90,000	76,000
Inventories	102,000	112,000
Total current assets	220,000	198,000
Property, plant, and equipment	600,000	485,000
Accumulated amortization	(150,000)	(125,000)
Total noncurrent assets	450,000	360,000
Total assets	$670,000	$558,000
Liabilities and shareholders' equity		
Current liabilities		
Accounts payable	$ 85,000	$ 68,000
Wages payable	50,000	40,000
Total current liabilities	135,000	108,000
Bonds payable	125,000	100,000
Total liabilities	260,000	208,000
Shareholders' equity		
Common shares	175,000	150,000
Retained earnings	235,000	200,000
Total shareholders' equity	410,000	350,000
Total liabilities and shareholders' equity	$670,000	$558,000

Additional information:
1. No dividends were declared or paid.
2. No property, plant, or equipment was sold.
3. No debt was repaid.
4. Net income was $35,000, including $25,000 of amortization expense.

Required:

Prepare a cash flow statement for the year ended December 31, 20x1.

5-25 (Preparation of cash flow statement)

Comparative balance sheets of Janxen Jeans Company for 20x1 and 20x2 are as follows:

Janxen Jeans Company
Comparative Balance Sheets

	Dec. 31, 20x2	Dec. 31, 20x1
Assets		
Current assets		
Cash	$ 200,000	$ 188,000
Accounts receivable	120,000	133,000
Notes receivable	70,000	61,000
Inventories	439,000	326,000
Total current assets	829,000	708,000
Noncurrent assets		
Land	525,000	500,000
Machinery	483,000	238,000
Accumulated amortization	(143,000)	(97,500)
Total noncurrent assets	865,000	640,500
Total assets	$1,694,000	$1,348,500
Liabilities and shareholders' equity		
Current liabilities		
Accounts payable	$ 145,000	$ 158,000
Interest payable	17,500	10,000
Total current liabilities	162,500	168,000
Long-term debt	350,000	200,000
Total liabilities	512,500	368,000
Shareholders' equity		
Common shares	650,000	550,000
Retained earnings	531,500	430,500
Total shareholders' equity	1,181,500	980,500
Total liabilities and shareholders' equity	$1,694,000	$1,348,500

Additional information:
1. Net income is $151,000 and includes amortization expenses of $105,500.
2. Dividends declared and paid during the year were $50,000.
3. A machine costing $80,000 was sold at its book value (cost minus accumulated amortization) of $20,000.
4. No repayment of long-term debt occurred in 20x2.

Required:

Prepare a cash flow statement for the year ended December 31, 20x2.

5-26 (Preparation of income statement and cash flow statement)

The financial statement data for Pharmex Pharmaceutical Company for 20x3 are as follows:

**Pharmex Pharmaceutical Company
Comparative Data**

	Dec. 31, 20x3	Dec. 31, 20x2
Debits		
Cash	$ 50,000	$ 80,000
Accounts receivable	235,000	185,000
Inventories	325,000	296,000
Machinery	555,000	545,000
Total debits	$1,165,000	$1,106,000
Credits		
Accumulated amortization	$ 172,500	$ 122,500
Accounts payable	82,500	97,500
Bonds payable	175,000	150,000
Common shares	400,000	350,000
Retained earnings	335,000	386,000
Total credits	$1,165,000	$1,106,000

Income statement data	
Sales	$1,052,000
Gain on sale of machinery	15,000
Cost of goods sold	878,000
Amortization expense	75,000
Interest expense	60,000
Rent expense	85,000

Additional information:
Acquisition cost of new machinery is $135,000. Old machinery having an original cost of $125,000 was sold at a gain of $15,000. Dividends of $20,000 were declared and paid.

Required:

a. Prepare an income statement including a reconciliation of retained earnings for the year ended December 31, 20x3.

b. Prepare a cash flow statement for Pharmex for the year ended December 31, 20x3.

5-27 (Determine cash collected from customers and paid to suppliers)
Lazard Company had sales of $673,400 for the year. The company reported accounts receivable of $85,500 at the end of last year and $78,600 at the end of this year. Lazard's cost of goods sold this year was $490,000. In last year's balance sheet, Lazard reported inventory of $121,000 and accounts payable of $43,700. In this year's balance sheet, Lazard reported inventory of $132,600 and accounts payable of $54,900.

Required:

a. How much cash did Lazard collect from customers during the year?

b. How much cash did Lazard pay to suppliers for inventory during the year?

5-28 (Preparation of cash flow statement)
Downsview Company had a $261,800 cash balance at the beginning of 2000. The company reported net income of $388,900 for 2000. Included in the company's income statement was amortization expense of $67,000, interest expense of $31,600, and income tax expense of $102,000. The following also occurred during 2000:

1. Accounts receivable increased by $13,000.

2. Inventory decreased by $7,000.

3. Accounts payable increased by $3,500.

4. Wages payable decreased by $1,300.

5. Income taxes payable increased by $3,100.

6. The patent account increased by $27,400. One patent was purchased during the year for $31,200.

7. The plant and equipment account increased by $465,000. One piece of equipment was sold during the year for $22,000. It originally had cost $51,000 and had a $17,000 book value at the time of the sale.

8. Downsview declared and paid cash dividends of $52,000 during 2000.

9. The company repurchased some of its common shares during the year for $44,000.

10. The company issued $100,000 in bonds during the year.

Required:
To help the management of Downsview Company better understand its sources and uses of cash, do the following:

a. Compute the cash generated from operations.

b. Compute the cash flow related to investing activities.

c. Compute the cash flow related to financing activities.

d. Prepare a cash flow statement for Downsview for 2000 in good form.

5-29 (Interpretation of cash flow statement)
The following are the comparative cash flow statements for Sherman Brothers Incorporated:

Sherman Brothers Incorporated
Comparative Cash Flow Statements
($ millions)

	20x3	20x2	20x1
Operating activities			
Net income	486	415	287
Add back:			
Amortization	458	327	138
Changes in working capital items:			
Receivables	(150)	(80)	10
Inventories	(5)	(50)	(30)
Prepaid expenses	(5)	(3)	2
Accounts payable	(25)	15	5
Cash from operations	759	624	412

Investing activities

Acquisition of noncurrent assets	(728)	(464)	(205)
Proceeds from sale of noncurrent assets	37	19	13
Cash used for investing	(691)	(445)	(192)

Financing activities

Issuance of long-term debt	25	450	400
Repayment of long-term debt	(500)	(25)	-0-
Issuance of common shares	1,000	-0-	-0-
Repurchase of common shares	-0-	(400)	(150)
Dividends paid	(510)	(315)	(200)
Cash flow from financing	15	(290)	50

Net increase (decrease) in cash	83	(111)	270
Cash position at beginning of year	174	285	15
Cash position at end of year	257	174	285

Required:

a. Discuss the company's ability to meet its needs for cash over the last three years. Comment on the continuing nature of the major items that have appeared over the last three years.

b. Comment on the accounts receivable, accounts payable, and inventory policies of Sherman Brothers.

c. How did Sherman Brothers finance its repayment of long-term debt and acquisition of noncurrent assets in 20x3?

Management Perspective Problems

5-30 (Cash flow statement and lending decisions)
From the perspective of a bank loan officer, discuss why the cash flow statement may or may not be more important than the income statement in your analysis of a company that is applying for a loan.

5-31 (Cash flow statement and investing decsions)
From the perspective of a stock analyst, discuss why the cash flow statement may or may not be more important than the income statement in the analysis of a company for which you must make a recommendation.

5-32 (Cash flow and compensation plans)
If you were a CEO (Chief Executive Officer) of a company and wanted to use a management compensation plan to motivate your top management, would you want to base your performance targets on cash flows from operations or net income? Discuss the pros and cons of using these two measures of performance.

5-33 (Format of the cash flow statement from a lending perspective)
As a lender, discuss whether you would be satisfied with the current method of classifying cash flows into only three categories. In particular, comment on the classification of interest cash flows and whether you think placing them under operating activities is appropriate.

5-34 (Cash flow analysis)

Chantelle Wong is considering investing in the shares of Titalussa Company. Looking at Titalussa's balance sheet, Chantelle is reassured that the company seems to face little risk of insolvency because it keeps large amounts of cash on hand. Further, the company has no long-term debt and little short-term debt. In fact, management's discussion accompanying the financial statements indicates that management does not believe in incurring debt and, therefore, does not borrow except in unusual cases and normally pays suppliers immediately upon being billed. Because of the large amount of liquid assets held by Titalussa, the company is paying only 6% interest on the small amount of debt it currently owes.

Chantelle also notices that the company's accounts receivable and inventory have been growing at the rate of about 20% per year, so the company has a large amount of current assets, an amount that is several times that of the company's current liabilities. The company's revenues and income both have been growing at about 10% each year, so the company appears not only safe, but very successful as well. Overall, the company seems to be earning annual profits averaging about 18% of shareholders' equity. However, Chantelle notices that the company's cash, while still exceeding the total of all liabilities, has been declining slightly each year.

Chantelle thinks that Titalussa is a safe and potentially profitable investment for her, although she is not sure the company is run as efficiently as it should be. However, she decides that she probably will invest $10,000 in Titalussa's shares if she is satisfied with the answers to a few questions.

Required:

Help Chantelle with her decision by answering the following questions:

a. Does the fact that Titalussa is holding a large amount of cash and other current assets mean that management is doing a good job? Explain in detail.

b. Do you think the company's policy of borrowing very little is a good policy? Explain.

c. If Titalussa Company is so profitable, why is its cash declining slightly, rather than growing? Describe several factors that might account for this phenomenon.

d. If the management of Titalussa Company estimates that the company's shareholders individually can earn 10% returns on their money, what should management do with any excess cash on hand? Why? What should management do with the excess cash if it estimates the shareholders can earn 20% returns on their money elsewhere? Why?

5-35 (Cash flow analysis)

The year 2000 financial statements of Green Company include the cash flow statement reproduced below.

Required:

a. Prepare an analysis of Green Company's year 2000 cash flow statement showing the total sources of cash and the percentage of cash coming from each source.

b. Prepare an analysis of Green's 2000 cash flow statement showing the uses of Green's cash and the percentage going to each use.

c. Did Green Company increase or decrease its current assets other than cash in 2000? Is this change consistent with an increase or decrease in sales during the period? Explain. Has Green Company become more or less risky during 2000 from an investor's viewpoint? Explain why.

d. Does Green appear to be expanding or contracting its operations? How can you tell? What other financial statement information might you examine to determine if Green is expanding? Does Green appear able to maintain its productive capacity without additional financing? Explain.

Green Company
Cash Flow Statement
For the year ended December 31, 2000

Operating:		
Net income		$544,000
Adjustments to convert to cash:		
Amortization		230,000
Gain on sale of operating assets		(14,000)
Change in current assets other than cash		(120,000)
Change in current liabilities		80,000
Cash provided by operations		720,000
Investing:		
Purchase of operating assets	($1,200,000)	
Sale of operating assets	400,000	
Cash used for investing		(800,000)
Financing:		
Issuance of common shares	1,000,000	
Retirement of bonds	(1,300,000)	
Dividends paid	(250,000)	
Cash used by financing		(550,000)
Decrease in cash		($630,000)

5-36 (Operating section analysis)

The operating section of Johann Manufacturing Company's cash flow statement is shown below.

Required:

Using this information, answer the following questions. If a question cannot be answered from the information given, indicate why.

a. Have accounts receivable increased or decreased this year?

b. Does the company appear to be more or less inclined to prepay expenses now than in the past? Does this help or hurt its cash position? Explain.

c. Has inventory increased or decreased this year? Explain how this affects cash.

d. Compared with last year, does the company seem to be relying more or less heavily on trade credit to finance its activities?

e. Has amortization expense increased from last year?

f. If you were a potential creditor of Johann, do you see any warning signs in the cash flow statement that you would want to investigate further before lending the company money? Explain.

g. Johann has $2,000,000 in bonds maturing on January 12, 2002. Johann does not have a bond sinking fund (cash fund used to repay the bond debt) established to pay off the bonds. Do you think Johann will be able to meet its obligation to pay off the bonds without additional long-term financing? Explain.

Johann Manufacturing Company
Cash Flow Statement
For the year ended December 31, 2000

Cash flows from operations:		
Net income		$632,000
Adjustments to convert to cash		
Amortization		220,000
Loss on sale of investments		50,000
Change in current noncash items:		
Accounts receivable	($160,000)	
Inventory	(20,000)	
Prepaid expenses	5,000	
Accounts payable	95,000	
Income tax payable	2,000	(78,000)
Cash provided by operations		824,000
Cash balance, January 1		166,000
Cash balance, December 31		$990,000

Reading and Interpreting Published Financial Statements

5-37 (Analysis of cash flow statement)
Exhibit 5-18 shows the consolidated statement of changes in financial position (cash flow statement) for Purcell Energy Ltd. for the years ended December 31, 1998 and 1997. There has been a dramatic change in Purcell's cash position since the end of 1997.

Required:

a. Prepare a list of all of the sources of cash and the percentage of cash coming from each source. Use "cash from operations" as one source.

b. Prepare a list of all of the uses of cash and the percentage going to each use.

c. Describe the changes in each of the current noncash assets and liabilities.

d. Comment on the change in cash position and sources and uses of cash during the year, including an explanation of the major changes that Purcell made during the year.

5-38 (Analysis of cash flow statement)
Exhibit 5-19 shows the consolidated statement of changes in financial position (cash flow statement) for CCL Industries Inc. for the years ended December 31, 1998 and 1997. CCL Industries uses "cash and short-term investments less bank advances" for its definition of cash and cash equivalents.

Required:

a. Prepare a list of all of the sources of cash and the percentage of cash coming from each source. Use "cash from operations" as one source.

b. Prepare a list of all of the uses of cash and the percentage going to each use.

c. Comment on the change in cash position and sources and uses of cash during the year, including an explanation of the major changes that CCL Industries made during the year.

EXHIBIT 5-18

CONSOLIDATED STATEMENTS OF CHANGES IN FINANCIAL POSITION

For the years ended December 31	1998	1997
Cash provided (used) by:		
Operating activities		
Net income (loss) for the year	$ (2,545,249)	$ 221,147
Item not involving cash		
Depletion, amortization and site restoration	4,431,532	2,474,658
Cash flow from operations	1,886,283	2,695,805
Changes in non-cash working capital balances		
Accounts receivable	1,231,649	(965,738)
Prepaid expenses, deposits and inventories	(44,643)	(59,196)
Accounts payable and accrued liabilities	(5,099,780)	5,538,039
Corporate taxes payable	57,121	9,649
	(1,969,370)	7,218,559
Financing activities		
Payments from (to) Liard Resources Ltd.	(47,455)	165,657
Dividends on preferred shares	–	(5,386)
Issue of common stock, net of related expenses and before effect of deferred taxes	1,111,570	4,240,429
Repurchase of common stock, net (Note 6)	–	(37,818)
Issue of share purchase warrants before effect of deferred taxes	–	9,494,915
Loans receivable	20,000	(57,500)
Net obligation incurred for capital leases	23,907	479,077
Long term debt, net	4,465,107	(731,087)
	5,573,129	13,548,287
Investing activities		
Proceeds on sale of marketable securities	–	761,831
Purchase of Altmark Energy Inc., net of cash acquired	–	(7,705,406)
Purchase of North Rim Oils Limited, net of cash acquired	–	(151,558)
Purchase of marketable securities	–	(164,330)
Purchases of property, plant and equipment, before effect of deferred taxes.	(5,558,331)	(13,262,891)
Proceeds on disposition of property, plant and equipment	54,076	2,313,220
	(5,504,255)	(18,209,134)
Increase (decrease) in cash	(1,900,496)	2,557,712
Cash (bank indebtedness), beginning of year	2,513,602	(44,110)
Cash, end of year	$ 613,106	$ 2,513,602
Cash flow from operations per share	$ 0.096	$ 0.192

The accompanying notes are an integral part of these financial statements.

EXHIBIT 5-19

CONSOLIDATED STATEMENTS OF CHANGES IN FINANCIAL POSITION

Years ended December 31, 1998 and 1997

(in thousands of dollars)	1998	1997
Cash provided by (used for)		
Operations		
Net earnings	$ 44,394	$ 40,710
Items not requiring cash:		
Depreciation and amortization	75,710	56,464
Deferred income taxes	12,314	19,064
Unusual items	—	(4,672)
	132,418	111,566
Net change in non-cash operating working capital	(27,431)	(4,436)
Total cash provided by operations	104,987	107,130
Financing		
Proceeds of long-term debt	162,194	143,334
Retirement of long-term debt	(2,131)	(89,693)
Issue of shares and other paid-in capital	61,076	23,927
Settlement of exercised stock options	—	(1,932)
Repurchase of shares	—	(2,716)
Dividends	(10,259)	(9,797)
Total cash provided by financing	210,880	63,123
Investment		
Additions to capital assets	(85,468)	(65,390)
Business acquisitions (note 2)	(154,005)	(306,252)
Proceeds on disposals	15,436	111,579
Translation adjustment	1,442	(4,147)
Other	(12,906)	(6,021)
	(235,501)	(270,231)
Change in non-cash investment working capital	124,392	(106,694)
Total cash used for investment	(111,109)	(376,925)
Increase (decrease) in cash position	204,758	(206,672)
Cash position at beginning of year	(197,180)	9,492
Cash position at end of year	$ 7,578	$ (197,180)

Cash position is comprised of cash and short-term investments, less bank advances.

5-39 (Analysis of cash flow statement)

Exhibit 5-20 shows the consolidated statements of cash flows for Bema Gold Company (a mining exploration company) for the years ended December 31, 1998, 1997, and 1996.

Required:

a. Considering only the information presented in the cash flow statement, describe the apparent operations and cash management policies of Bema Gold over these three years.

b. Assume you are considering investing in shares of Bema Gold. What additional information would you require before you could make your decision?

5-40 (Analysis of cash flow statement)

Exhibit 5-21 shows the consolidated statements of changes in cash position for Algoma Central Company (a shipping and real estate company) for the years ended December 31, 1998 and 1997.

Required:

a. Discuss the company's ability to meet its need for cash over the last two years. Comment on the continuing nature of the major items that have appeared over the last two years.

b. Which items would require more investigation or further explanation, or both, to help you understand the company's financial health?

c. Discuss why, although there is a large difference in the amount of net income between the two years, the cash from operations is virtually the same.

5-41 (Analysis of cash flow statement)

Exhibit 5-22 shows the consolidated statements of changes in financial position (cash flow statement) for AT Plastics Inc. for the years ended December 31, 1998 and 1997.

Required:

a. Discuss the company's ability to meet its needs for cash over the last two years. Comment on the continuing nature of the major items that have appeared over the last two years.

b. Which items would require more investigation or further explanation, or both, to help you understand the company's financial health?

c. Discuss why there was a significant decrease in cash during 1997 although the company's net income for 1997 was not that different from 1998.

5-42 (Analysis of cash flow statement)

The consolidated statements of changes in financial position (cash flow statement) for Mackenzie Financial Corporation for the years ended March 31, 1998, 1997, and 1996 are presented in Exhibit 5-23. Mackenzie Financial provides investment management and related services to public mutual funds, corporate pension-fund clients, and other institutional investors.

Required:

Explain why the presentation of this cash flow statement differs from the presentations discussed in this chapter under Financing Activities and Investing Activities.

EXHIBIT 5-20

Consolidated Statements of Cash Flows

for the years ended December 31
(in thousands of United States dollars)

	1998	1997	1996
Operating activities			
Loss for the year	$(46,127)	$ (5,871)	$ (2,699)
Non-cash charges (credits)			
Depreciation and depletion	6,711	5,497	2,047
Amortization of deferred financing costs	1,300	1,082	310
Equity in losses of associated companies	1,555	2,213	3,333
Deferred revenue	(1,531)	8,945	–
Investment gains	–	(2,594)	(1,493)
Write-down of mineral properties	32,738	–	49
Write-down of inventory	3,634	–	–
Write-down of notes receivable	2,042	–	–
Other	665	25	(38)
Changes in non-cash working capital			
Accounts receivable	1,685	(1,017)	(1,142)
Inventories	446	(5,506)	(5,514)
Accounts payable	(7,423)	(741)	7,317
Cash from (to) operating activities	(4,305)	2,033	2,170
Financing activities			
Common shares issued *(Note 8)*	39,747	27,894	92,016
Subsidiary's shares issued	–	–	740
Debenture conversions	–	(22,667)	(10,333)
Convertible debentures interest payments	–	(1,692)	(2,078)
Joint venture partner loan (repayment)	–	(10,000)	2,000
Refugio loan proceeds	308	4,000	–
Refugio loan repayments	(6,000)	(4,250)	(4,250)
Gold loan monetization gain *(Note 7)*	–	(8,308)	–
Deferred financing costs	(1,954)	(1,776)	(238)
Other	(123)	1,054	1,088
Cash from (to) financing activities	31,978	(15,745)	78,945
Investing activities			
Acquisition of Arian Resources Corporation *(Note 2)*	(19,398)	–	–
Refugio mine	(4,808)	(6,706)	(14,193)
Julietta development and construction	(6,170)	–	–
Acquisition, exploration and development	(7,220)	(15,706)	(13,483)
Net proceeds from the Aldebaran transaction *(Note 5)*	–	4,698	–
Investment purchases in associated companies	(152)	(6,895)	(20,030)
Promissory notes issued by associated companies, net *(Note 11)*	(590)	(7,693)	(307)
Short-term investments	–	1,459	2,631
Proceeds on sale of investments	–	3,631	4,118
Other	(167)	(1,334)	310
Cash to investing activities	(38,505)	(28,546)	(40,954)
Increase (decrease) in cash	(10,832)	(42,258)	40,161
Cash, beginning of year	24,336	66,594	26,433
Cash, end of year	$13,504	$24,336	$66,594

See accompanying notes to consolidated financial statements.

31

EXHIBIT 5-21

CONSOLIDATED STATEMENTS OF CHANGES IN CASH POSITION

Algoma Central Corporation

Years ended December 31 (In thousands of dollars)	1998	1997
NET INFLOW (OUTFLOW) OF CASH		
RELATED TO THE FOLLOWING ACTIVITIES:		
OPERATING		
Net income	$ 15,963	$ 75,950
Items not affecting cash		
Amortization	21,479	11,797
Deferred income taxes	8,122	7,829
Gain on sale of forest lands	—	(61,299)
Effect of exchange rates	832	—
Other	(141)	(502)
	46,255	33,775
Net change in non-cash operating working capital (Note 9)	(15,100)	(684)
	31,155	33,091
INVESTING		
Additions to capital assets	(90,107)	(32,581)
Investment in joint venture (Note 2)	—	(32,008)
Cash acquired on investment in joint venture (Note 2)	—	17,451
Proceeds from sale of capital assets	47	61,321
Other assets	2,568	(1,511)
	(87,492)	12,672
FINANCING		
Proceeds from long-term debt	16,118	3,614
Dividends paid	(3,793)	(3,793)
	12,325	(179)
TOTAL CASH (DECREASE) INCREASE FOR YEAR	(44,012)	45,584
CASH POSITION, BEGINNING OF YEAR	50,556	4,972
CASH POSITION, END OF YEAR	$ 6,544	$ 50,556

18

24 AT Plastics 1998 Annual Report

consolidated statements of changes in financial position

Years ended December 31, 1998 and 1997

(thousands of dollars)	1998	1997
Cash from (used in)		
Operations		
Net income for the year	$ 10,768	$ 10,341
Add items charged to income not affecting cash		
Depreciation and amortization	9,680	9,741
Deferred income taxes	6,104	5,629
Amortization of exchange on long-term debt	1,432	462
Write-off of discontinued projects	–	877
Cash flow before change in working capital and other liabilities	27,984	27,050
Change in non-cash working capital and other liabilities	11,145	(3,412)
	39,129	23,638
Financing activities		
Long-term debt issued	100,433	70,000
Long-term debt repaid	(8,641)	(6,070)
Common shares issued	24,949	–
	116,741	63,930
Dividends paid	(3,086)	(2,753)
Investing activities		
Purchase of fixed assets	(140,457)	(92,612)
Change in other assets	(8,446)	(7,018)
	(148,903)	(99,630)
Increase (decrease) in cash during the year	3,881	(14,815)
Cash at beginning of year	411	15,226
Cash at end of year	$ 4,292	$ 411

See accompanying notes to consolidated financial statements.

thousands of dollars

CONSOLIDATED STATEMENTS OF CHANGES IN FINANCIAL POSITION

For the years ended March 31	1998	1997	1996
Operating Activities			
Net earnings for the year	$ 80,658	$ 65,514	$ 40,728
Items not affecting cash –			
Depreciation and amortization	124,204	78,604	46,106
Deferred taxes	53,220	35,586	44,380
Adjustment for impaired loans	—	—	(390)
Equity in earnings of affiliated company net of dividends received of $1,260 (1997 – $910; 1996 – $840)	(8,899)	(8,995)	(4,390)
Dilution (gain) loss	638	(3,062)	—
Minority interest share of earnings	1,945	526	—
Currency exchange adjustment *(note 2)*	2,249	—	—
	254,015	168,173	126,434
Net decrease (increase) in non-cash balances related to operations *(note 11)*	35,784	(22,978)	(43,203)
	289,799	145,195	83,231
Financing Activities			
Proceeds from (repayment of) bank loans	2,828	(7,995)	1,788
Repayment of notes payable	(7,082)	(6,632)	(6,211)
Proceeds from issue of senior debentures *(note 8)*	—	99,053	—
Net proceeds from issue of Mackenzie Investment Management Inc. shares	1,610	7,174	—
Increase (decrease) in customer deposits	(24,010)	(5,176)	69,598
Payment of dividends	(9,926)	(9,044)	(8,316)
Issue of common shares	14,768	11,859	2,215
	(21,812)	89,239	59,074
Investing Activities			
Purchase of capital assets	(17,188)	(14,465)	(13,463)
Payment of selling commissions	(253,829)	(210,715)	(138,168)
Decrease (increase) in loans	12,093	6,935	(34,500)
Decrease (increase) in other assets	(7,285)	6,683	2,628
Other	(1,146)	681	(69)
	(267,355)	(210,881)	(183,572)
Increase (decrease) in cash and cash equivalents	632	23,553	(41,267)
Currency exchange adjustment on cash *(note 2)*	503	—	—
Cash and cash equivalents – beginning of year	126,741	103,188	144,455
Cash and cash equivalents – end of year	$ 127,876	$ 126,741	$ 103,188
Cash	$ 17,912	$ 11,145	$ 8,907
Short-term investments	109,964	115,596	94,281
	$ 127,876	$ 126,741	$ 103,188

(The accompanying notes are an integral part of these consolidated financial statements.)

5-43 (Analysis of cash flow statement)
The cash flow analyses of The Volvo Group, Inc., from its 1997 annual report are provided in Exhibit 5-24. Volvo is a Swedish vehicle manufacturing company. Its financial statements are in Swedish krona.

> ### *Required:*
> Based on the above information, respond to the following statements and questions:
>
> a. Discuss the company's ability to meet its needs for cash over the last three years. Comment on the continuing nature of the major items that have appeared over the last three years.
>
> b. Which items would require more investigation or further explanation, or both, to help you understand the company's financial health?
>
> c. Discuss the ability of Volvo to generate cash from operations over the last three years.
>
> d. Identify the major difference between this cash flow statement from Sweden and a typical cash flow statement from Canada.

Beyond the Book

5-44 (Analysis of cash flow statement)
For a company of your own choosing, answer the following questions related to its cash flow statement.

> a. Summarize the results of the cash from operating, investing, and financing activities over the last two years.
>
> b. Explain any significant changes from last year to this year in the items listed in part a.
>
> c. What were the four most significant uses of cash (from the investing and financing sections)?
>
> d. What were the four most significant sources of cash, including operations?
>
> e. How is the company financing its investing activities, through operating activities or financing activities, or both? Support your answer with numbers.

Case

5-45 Atlantic Service Company
Atlantic Service Company was established five years ago to provide services to the home construction industry. It has been very successful, with assets, sales, and profits increasing each year. However, Atlantic is experiencing serious cash shortages and is in danger of going into bankruptcy because it cannot pay its suppliers and already has a very substantial overdraft at its bank. The president has asked you to analyze the cash flow statement for the years ended December 31, 2001 and 2000, in Exhibit 5-25, to explain what appears to be causing the cash shortage problem, and to recommend a plan to save the company from bankruptcy.

EXHIBIT 5-24

Volvo Group

Cash flow analyses

SEK M	1995		1996		1997	
Year's operations						
Net income	9,262		12,477		**10,359**	
Depreciation and amortization	5,656		5,351		**6,796**	
Write-down of shareholdings and fixed assets	1,817		–		**–**	
Income from investments in associated companies after taxes	(730)		(222)		**220**	
Dividends received from associated companies	404		119		**145**	
Gain on sales of securities	(1,180)		(8,169)		**(4,068)**	
Gain on sales of subsidiaries	(3,032)		–		**–**	
Minority interests after taxes	45		(99)		**112**	
Increase in current assets:						
Receivables	(962)		(4,777)		**(7,452)**	
Inventories	(516)		(547)		**(2,575)**	
Increase (decrease) in current operating liabilities and other provisions	570		(618)		**7,280**	
Increase (decrease) in deferred tax liabilities	(267)	(1,175)	23	(5,919)	**711**	(2,036)
Cash flow from year's operations		11,067		3,538		**11,528**
Investments (increase)						
Property, plant and equipment, etc:						
Capital expenditures for property, plant and equipment	(6,491)		(8,200)		**(9,863)**	
Investments in leasing vehicles	(2,585)		(3,851)		**(9,773)**	
Disposals	1,351		1,958		**1,855**	
Investments in shares, net	1,953		14,080		**10,669**	
Long-term receivables, net	(1,953)		(2,804)		**(6,031)**	
Acquisitions and sales of companies	(4,420)	(12,145)	(878)	305	**(1,303)**	(14,446)
Remaining after net investments		(1,078)		3,843		**(2,918)**
Financing, dividends, etc						
Increase (decrease) in short-term bank loans and other loans	(3,993)		5,151		**995**	
Increase (decrease) in long-term loans and provisions for pensions	6,166		(1,844)		**3,404**	
Increase (decrease) in minority interests	(37)		45		**(21)**	
Dividends paid to AB Volvo shareholders	(1,512)		(1,854)		**(1,993)**	
Dividends paid to minority shareholders	(3)		(33)		**(83)**	
Redemption of shares	–		–		**(5,807)**	
New issue of shares	–		–		**116**	
Settlement of loan to Renault	–		(1,536)		**–**	
Other	46	667	(121)	(192)	**(22)**	(3,411)
Increase (decrease) in liquid funds excluding translation differences		(411)		3,651		**(6,329)**
Translation differences on liquid funds		(732)		(296)		**271**
Increase (decrease) in liquid funds		(1,143)		3,355		**(6,058)**
Liquid funds, January 1		24,449		23,306		**26,661**
Liquid funds, December 31		23,306		26,661		**20,603**

In the Cash flow analyses, the effects of major acquistions and divestments of subsidiaries in each year, including the distribution of the shareholding in Swedish Match in 1996, have been excluded from other changes in the balance sheet. The effects of changes in foreign exchange rates at translation of foreign subsidiaries have been excluded, since they do not affect cash flow. Liquid funds include Cash and bank accounts and Marketable securities.

EXHIBIT 5-25

■ **Atlantic Service Company**

Cash Flow Statement
For the years ended December 31, 2001 and 2000

	2001	2000
Operations:		
Net income	$ 150,000	$ 135,000
Adjustments to convert to cash:		
Amortization	25,000	20,000
Changes in noncash working capital:		
Increase in accounts receivable	(35,000)	(30,000)
Increase in inventory	(30,000)	(25,000)
Increase in accounts payable	55,000	45,000
	165,000	145,000
Financing:		
Increase in one-year bank loan	50,000	30,000
Dividends paid	(15,000)	(10,000)
	35,000	20,000
Investing:		
Purchase of equipment	(300,000)	(250,000)
Net cash used in the year	(100,000)	(85,000)
Cash position, beginning of the year	(130,000)	(45,000)
Cash position, end of the year	($230,000)	($130,000)

Critical Thinking Question

5-46 (Universality of the definition of cash and cash equivalents)
As discussed in this chapter, the cash flow statement provides users of financial informa-tion with another "flow" measure of a company's performance. However, several issues have been raised in both academic and practitioner-oriented research relative to the meaning, usefulness, and calculation of cash flows. For example, Wallace and Collier ("The 'Cash' in Cash Flow Statements: A Multi-Country Comparison," *Accounting Horizons*, December 1991) describe how various countries, including Canada, have issued standards regarding the presentation of cash flows but have failed to define the term "cash" both consistently and adequately. The changes made in 1998 in Canada with respect to the cash flow statement define cash as "cash on hand and demand deposits" and cash equivalents as "short-term highly liquid investments that are readily con-vertible to known amounts of cash and which are subject to an insignificant risk of changes in value" (*CICA Handbook*, Sec. 1540.06). It goes on to define short-term as three months or less and to restrict investments to non-equity ones. It also includes bank overdrafts that are payable on demand in the cash equivalents.

Required:
Look up the Wallace and Collier article in your library, briefly summarize the authors' arguments, and discuss the potential problems associated with the lack of a uniform definition of cash for both companies that have only domestic operations and companies that have both domestic and foreign operations. Discuss whether the new Canadian requirements address their arguments.

APPENDIX

Cash Flow Statement Preparation: Direct Approach

Although the indirect approach for preparing and presenting the cash flow statement is standard practice, a few companies use the direct approach. The direct approach differs from the indirect approach in its analysis of the operating activities section. While the indirect approach starts with net income and reconciles net income to the net cash flow from operations, the direct approach summarizes all cash inflows and outflows from operations. The financing and investing sections of the cash flow statement are unaffected and remain the same under both approaches.

In this Appendix, we present the preparation and format of the cash flow statement using the direct approach. We do this by using the same information for Huskies Industries Ltd. that we used earlier in the chapter to present the indirect approach.

Exhibit 5-26 shows the completed T-account approach with all the reconstructed transactions for Huskies Industries for 20x1. The entries in the T accounts have been given transaction numbers, and each is discussed in this section. The cash flow statement will be constructed using the direct approach for the operating section.

■ **Huskies Industries Ltd.**

Cash Flow T-Accounts

	A-Cash				
✓	19,500				
Operating:					
Collections from	(2)	140,000	85,000	(5)	Payments to suppliers
customers			7,200	(7)	Rent payments
			600	(8)	Cash expenses
			9,500	(13)	Payments of salaries
			520	(14)	Payment of taxes
Financing:					
Proceeds from note	(14)	100	2,000	(18)	Prepay. of bond
Proceeds from bond	(17)	8,000	1,230	(16)	Pay. of dividends
Issue of shares	(19)	4,000			
Investing:					
Sale of equip.	(10)	500	60,000	(11)	Purchase of PP&E
✓	6,050				

	A-Acc. Rec.				A-Inventory				A-Prepaid Rent		
✓	20,000			✓	30,000			✓	500		
(1)	130,000	140,000	(2)	(4)	90,000	80,000	(3)	(7)	7,200	7,100	(6)
✓	10,000			✓	40,000			✓	600		

EXHIBIT 5-26 CONT.

A-PP&E

✓ 100,000	
(11) 60,000	1,000 (10)
✓ 159,000	

XA-Accum. Amort.

	50,000 ✓
(10) 800	20,000 (9)
	69,200 ✓

L-Acc. Pay.

	6,000 ✓
(5) 85,000	90,000 (4)
	11,000 ✓

L-Note Pay.

	100 ✓
	100 (14)
	200 ✓

L-Accrued Salaries

	300 ✓
(13) 9,500	9,600 (12)
	400 ✓

L-Dividends Payable

	300 ✓
(16) 1,230	1,400 (15)
	470 ✓

L-Bonds Payable

	40,000 ✓
(18) 2,000	8,000 (17)
	46,000 ✓

SE-Common Shares

	25,000 ✓
	4,000 (19)
	29,000 ✓

SE-Retained Earnings

	48,300 ✓
(3) 80,000	130,000 (1)
(6) 7,100	300 (10)
(8) 600	
(9) 20,000	
(12) 9,600	
(14) 520	
(15) 1,400	
	59,380 ✓

The transactions for 20x1 are reconstructed starting with those that are most easily identifiable because they appear on the income statement. For example, the first transaction that was reconstructed was that for the recognition of sales revenue for the period, as follows:

(1) The entry is:

A-Accounts receivable	130,000	
SE-Retained earnings		130,000

This entry records the sales for the period. The amount is found on the income statement, and an assumption must be made regarding how many of the sales were cash sales and how many were credit sales. A common assumption to make in preparing the cash flow statement is that all sales were on account. The credit entry recognizes that the effect of sales revenue on the balance sheet is to increase retained earnings. Note that there is no need to break out the retained earnings account into temporary accounts, because the individual income statement accounts are not important to the calculation of the cash flow statement. The important thing is to make sure that the change in the retained earnings account is fully explained.

The amount of the cash collection is then determined by considering the accounts receivable account. Because the beginning balance was $20,000, the sales (from transaction 1) were $130,000, and the ending balance was $10,000, the collection had to be $140,000 to make the account balance. The cash collections are shown in the operating section as follows:

(2) The entry is:

A-Cash (Operating)	140,000	
A-Accounts receivable		140,000

To record the cost of goods sold for the period, the following reconstruction entry was made:

(3) The entry is:

SE-Retained earnings	80,000	
A-Inventory		80,000

After making entry (3) and considering the beginning and ending balance in inventory, the purchases for the period can be calculated, because, in this company, purchases are the only type of item that affects the debit side of the inventory account. All these purchases of inventory are credited to accounts payable, because we assumed all purchases were on account. Again, this is a common assumption to make when the percentage of credit purchases is unknown.

(4) The entry is:

A-Inventory	90,000	
L-Accounts payable		90,000

When the credit purchases of $90,000 from entry (4) and the beginning and ending balance in accounts payable ($6,000 and $11,000, respectively) are known, the amount that represents the payments to suppliers on the accounts payable can be calculated ($6,000 + $90,000 − $11,000). Reconstructed entry (5) then records this amount.

(5) The entry is:

L-Accounts payable	85,000	
A-Cash (Operating)		85,000

The next item on the income statement is rent expense. Since there is a prepaid rent account on the balance sheet, Huskies evidently prepays its rent. The reconstruction entry to record rent expense is therefore a debit to the expense and a credit to the prepaid account. This is shown as entry (6).

(6) The entry is:

SE-Retained earnings	7,100	
A-Prepaid rent		7,100

Using the information from entry (6) and the balances from the prepaid rent account, we can determine the amount of cash actually paid for rent during the year. This is shown in entry (7). Recognize that in Huskies' accounting system, entry (7) was made before entry (6). They occur in the order shown here only because we are backing into the transaction.

(7) The entry is:

A-Prepaid rent	7,200	
A-Cash (Operating)		7,200

The amount listed on the income statement as "other cash expenses" directly reduces cash and retained earnings, as follows:

(8) The entry is:

SE-Retained earnings	600	
A-Cash (Operating)		600

The amount of amortization expense is given on the income statement and it reduces retained earnings as well as increasing the accumulated amortization. However, it does not appear on the cash flow statement using the direct approach. *NOTE CAREFULLY: Amortization does not affect the cash flow of the company.* The cash outflow relating to property, plant, and equipment occurred when the asset was originally purchased (an investing activity). A cash inflow could occur when a piece of property, plant, or equipment is sold, as we will see with entry (10) below. The entry for the amortization is:

(9) The entry is:

SE-Retained earnings	20,000	
XA-Accumulated amortization		20,000

At this point, all the information on the income statement, with the exception of the gain from the sale of property, plant, and equipment, has been used. Because some information regarding that transaction was given in the statement of the problem, it can now be reconstructed. In the extra information given, the original cost of the equipment is stated as $1,000 (the amount taken out of property, plant, and equipment), and the book value as $200. A book value of $200 means that the balance in the accumulated amortization account must have been $800 because the asset was originally purchased for $1,000. The $800 of accumulated amortization must be removed from the accumulated amortization account. The cash proceeds from this transaction were $500, and, therefore, a gain of $300 must have been reported. The gain appears on the income statement and, as shown earlier, increases retained earnings. Note, in the cash account, that the cash proceeds are shown in the investing section. This is not an operating item.

(10) The entry is:

A-Cash (Investing)	500	
XA-Accumulated amortization	800	
A-Property, plant, and equipment		1,000
SE-Retained earnings		300

The final entries, (11) to (19), are identical to those described for the indirect approach, entry numbers (9) to (15).

The cash account now contains all the information necessary to produce a cash flow statement. The cash from operations can be taken directly from the figures in the cash T-account, as follows:

Collections from customers	$140,000
Payments to suppliers	(85,000)
Rent payments	(7,200)
Cash expenses	(600)
Payments for salaries	(9,500)
Payment for taxes	(520)
Net cash from operations	$ 37,180

The net cash from operations of $37,180 is the same amount as was determined under the indirect approach.

The remainder of the cash flow statement—that is, the financing and investing activities—will be the same as that produced using the indirect approach, as shown previously. The direct and indirect approaches differ only in the format and details of the operating activities section.

What If They Won't Pay?

Sales are brisk at Stiff Sentences, Inc.: The ten-person Ottawa company recorded receivables of about $750,000 in the year 2000 and expected to reach $1 million in 2001. Their product? Words. Mostly strung together into sentences, as the company name suggests, to form annual reports, letters, speeches, advertising copy, and other communications tools—though Stiff Sentences also sometimes sells words in ones and twos, as it creates names for companies, products, and brands.

Most of the company's clients, which have included Bell Canada, Nortel, Canada Post, the CBC, the United Way, and numerous government departments and agencies, are satisfied customers who bring repeat business and keep the eight seasoned writers busy. But because the company sells a creative process rather than a tangible item, judgements of its products' quality are subjective.

So, despite strict quality-control procedures—the company is only a few steps short of gaining ISO 9000 certification, in fact—"it can happen," says Deborah Johnson, co-owner and business manager, "that a client isn't happy with the result. The biggest problems come when we don't find out about it until we're trying to determine why the bill hasn't been paid two months later."

When this happens, "we try to work something out," she explains. Sometimes the work is redone; often, however, Stiff Sentences ends up writing off all or part of the fee as a bad debt. The writer(s) involved share in the responsibility in such cases. "They're not employees, but associates," says Ms. Johnson, explaining that the company's financial relationship with the writers is much like that of a real-estate company with its agents. "They pay a fee to belong to the group, and they keep a percentage of the revenue from the work that they do."

Most of them make an excellent living (rare in the writing profession). But while they share in the profits at Stiff Sentences, they also share in the risk. Writers are paid twice a month for work completed to date; but if the fee for a job is written off and the writer has already been paid for working on it, he or she refunds the payment.

"It's important, therefore, that we remain very clear about who's responsible for what in each job," stresses Ms. Johnson. Of course, it's also important to keep these uncollectible amounts to a minimum. "The best way to do that is to stay on top of our receivables," she explains, "so if someone isn't paying we find out right away. We're also instituting a clause in our client contracts that says a customer has to let us know within 15 days if they're dissatisfied, or they're liable for the fee anyway."

chapter 6

CASH, TEMPORARY INVESTMENTS, AND ACCOUNTS AND NOTES RECEIVABLE

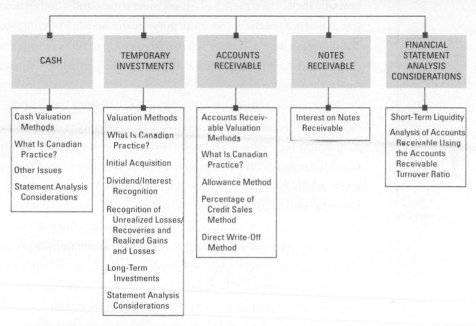

Learning Objectives:

After studying this chapter, you should be able to:

1. *Discuss the control issues related to cash.*
2. *Recognize the importance of cash to the success of a business.*
3. *Prepare a simple bank reconciliation.*
4. *Identify the criteria for the classification of an investment as temporary.*
5. *Explain why temporary investments are recorded using the lower of cost and market.*
6. *Prepare the journal entries associated with the acquisition, holding, and selling of temporary investments.*
7. *Explain why estimating the potential uncollectibility of accounts receivable is required.*
8. *Identify a method for recognizing uncollectibility and describe the circumstances under which its use is appropriate.*
9. *Describe a note receivable and explain the circumstances under which it is used.*
10. *Calculate interest associated with notes receivable and prepare the necessary journal entries.*
11. *Using financial statement information, calculate the current ratio, the quick ratio, and the accounts receivable turnover ratio.*
12. *Explain how the current ratio, the quick ratio, and the accounts receivable turnover ratio help users to understand short-term liquidity issues.*

With this chapter we begin a deeper analysis of some of the more common balance sheet accounts. Starting with the current assets, over the next five chapters we will work our way through noncurrent assets, current liabilities, noncurrent liabilities, and finally shareholders' equity.

In this chapter, the accounting methods and principles that apply to cash, temporary investments, and accounts receivable are considered. In each account category, recognition criteria, valuation methods, income statement implications, financial statement analysis considerations, and other issues that will help you to understand the account category are discussed. The complexities of financial statement analysis associated with this group of accounts are discussed in this chapter and each subsequent chapter in a section entitled "Financial Statement Analysis Considerations."

Our opening story focuses on accounts receivable, one of the topics in this chapter. Stiff Sentences, Inc., describes the difficulty it encounters in collecting its accounts receivable. In Chapter 4 we discussed revenue recognition and the matching principle. If a company like Stiff Sentences wants to recognize revenue when it bills its customers, it will have to somehow measure the potential for noncollectibility to ensure that the revenues are not overstated. This topic will come up again when we discuss accounts receivable later in the chapter.

All the assets discussed in this chapter have the unique property that they either are cash or very soon will become cash. In accounting terms, we often call them *monetary assets* because they are defined in monetary terms. Obviously they are very important to every business, since, as we learned in Chapter 5, sufficient cash must be available at all times to pay for purchases and for debts as they become due for payment.

CASH

Learning Objective

1

Discuss the control issues related to cash.

In the first chapter of this book we discussed the criteria that are used to determine whether, for accounting purposes, something is an asset. Assets were identified as items that: (1) have probable future value that can be measured, (2) the company owns or has the right to use, and (3) arose from a past event. In this chapter we will use these criteria to decide if and how we will categorize cash, temporary investments, and accounts receivable as assets.

Cash meets the criterion of probable future value. Cash does not have any intrinsic value other than the value of the paper or metal from which it is made. It derives its value from its ability to be exchanged for goods and services in the future, which is also called its **purchasing power**. It serves as the medium of exchange in every economy. The ability of cash to serve as a medium of exchange depends on the faith of the individuals in the economy who use it. If there is a loss of confidence in its ability to be exchanged in the future, the currency loses its value. For example, in Russia after the change in government from communism to democracy, Russian currency lost much of its value as a form of exchange because, in an attempt to encourage growth in the economy, the government printed an excessive amount of money, thus lowering its value.

Cash also meets the criterion of ownership/right to use. Ownership of cash is generally evidenced by possession: currency, cheques, money orders, and so on, in safes; monies deposited in banks. One type of cash, currency (bills and coins), cannot be differentiated except by the use of serial numbers on bills. It is therefore a very difficult asset to control. To deal with this problem, companies have learned to make extensive use of banks. As you know, more and more cash transactions are conducted electronically using credit or debit cards, thus eliminating the physical handling of cash. This greatly facilitates the control of cash and the efficiency of transactions. All companies must establish effective internal control procedures for handling and controlling their cash. Auditors review the internal control systems established by a company and design special audit procedures for determining whether the controls adequately safeguard the handling and recording of cash.

Cash also meets the third criterion. A past event transferred the cash to the company. Cash flowing in or out of a company is a signal that a transaction has occurred. If cash is present, an event has taken place.

Cash Valuation Methods

Assuming that cash meets the recognition criteria, the next problem is how to record the cash in the accounting system. For this account and for all other accounts discussed in this text, possible valuation methods will be used. Some of these methods are not allowed under Canadian GAAP but are allowed in other countries. The purpose in discussing the range of possible methods is to lay out conceptually the possibilities that serve as the basis for current practice. A separate section is devoted to the requirements of Canadian GAAP. In some cases, the methods used under Canadian GAAP are a combination of the various possible valuation methods discussed here.

One method of valuing cash is to record it at its face value. This means that as long as cash is held, its value is assumed not to change. If we had $100 in cash, the cash would be valued at $100. If that same $100 was present several weeks later, it would still be valued at $100. Its face value does not change.

However, even though the face value of the $100 does not change, its ability to be converted into goods and services may change. The ability to be exchanged for goods and services, or purchasing power, is affected by the level of inflation or deflation during the period. During periods of inflation, cash is said to have sustained a loss in purchasing power because of its relative loss in terms of exchangeability for goods and services. The $100 can buy fewer goods and services than it could before. In the example we are using here, the attribute of face value does not change but the attribute of purchasing power does. If, however, the attribute of purchasing power is used to value cash, then income would have to be recognized for the change in purchasing power during the accounting period. Consequently, the choice of which attribute of cash to measure is critical to how cash is represented on the balance sheet and how it affects the income statement.

What Is Canadian Practice?

Learning Objective

2

Recognize the importance of cash to the success of a business.

In Canada there is an underlying assumption, referred to as the **unit-of-measure assumption**, which specifies that the results of a company's activities be measured in terms of a **monetary unit** (e.g., the Canadian dollar). This precludes the measurement of activities in terms of purchasing power; cash is, therefore, measured at its face value rather than in any other way.

While the unit-of-measure assumption requires that Canadian currency be measured at face value, this is not the case for foreign currency. Suppose, for example, that a company does business with a Swiss customer and that the agreement with the customer is denominated in euros (the new currency in the European Community). This means that the customer is required to pay in euros rather than Canadian dollars. The company will receive euros and will probably hold a certain amount of euro currency at the beginning and end of the accounting period. Because this asset is measured in a different monetary unit to the rest of the assets of the company, a conversion will have to be made—from euros into Canadian dollars.

In Canada, euros are converted into dollars using the exchange rate that is in effect on the date of the balance sheet. For example, suppose the exchange rate is 1.0 euro = 1.5 Canadian $ at the beginning of the year and 1.0 euro = 1.45 Canadian $ at the end of the year. Suppose further that the company holds 1,000 euros at the beginning and at the end of the year. Exhibit 6-1 shows how the euro would be valued on the balance sheet. You can see that, while there is no gain or loss during the year in terms of euros (the face value does not change), there is a loss in terms of dollars. This loss will appear on the income statement and will be called a *foreign currency transaction loss*.

EXHIBIT 6-1

Foreign Currency Valuation

Date	Amount of Foreign Currency	Amount of Exchange Rate	Cdn. Currency
Jan. 1, 20x1	1,000 euros	1.0 euro = $1.50	$1,500
Dec. 31, 20x1	1,000 euros	1.0 euro = $1.45	$1,450
Loss	0 euros		$50

Exchange rates are determined in the foreign currency markets. Reasons for changes in the exchange rates of currencies are difficult to pinpoint precisely, but, in theory, one of the major reasons is differential inflation rates in the two countries concerned (the economic theory that describes this is called the *purchasing power parity theory*). Individuals who hold currencies in countries with high inflation rates lose more purchasing power than those who hold currencies in countries with low inflation rates. Exchange rates adjust to compensate for these differences in purchasing power. In effect, Canadian GAAP recognizes the changes in purchasing power of foreign currency by allowing the dollar value of foreign currencies to rise and fall with the exchange rate.

One final note with regard to purchasing power. In the mid- to late 1970s and early 1980s, Canada experienced high rates of inflation (by Canadian standards). Accounting regulators became concerned with the problem that income, as measured by GAAP, did not take into consideration the changes in purchasing power of a company's assets and liabilities. In 1982 the CICA adopted guidelines requesting that companies present supplementary information regarding the effects of changing price levels on the financial results. These guidelines were dropped in 1992 when inflation had returned to more normal levels. Therefore, in Canada, there is currently no systematic reporting of the effects of inflation or changing prices on the financial results of companies.

An International Perspective

Reports from Other Countries

NAFTA Facts

United States—In the U.S., inflation levels are very low. American accounting is, like Canadian, based primarily on historical cost. U.S. accounting currently does not require any inflation adjustments.

Mexico—Mexico does have relatively high inflation. In 1999 its inflation was approximately 13%. Inflation adjustments are required for changes in the general price level. Alternatively, inventory, fixed assets, and related expenses may be adjusted to replacement costs.

Other Issues

Despite the complexity of the issues discussed so far, the accounting for cash is relatively straightforward. You simply report how much cash is owned by the company. By cash, we mean currency, cheques, money orders, and amounts in bank accounts that can be used with very short notice.

The main issues in dealing with cash are the control of cash to ensure that it is not lost or stolen and the management of cash balances. Proper control of cash involves policies on such matters as ensuring that all cash is deposited into bank accounts daily or even more frequently, using secure safes and tills to hold cash until it is deposited, using cheques instead of cash to pay expenses, and keeping minimal amounts of cash on hand.

Control of cash is one part of a company's **internal control system**. Management is responsible for safeguarding all of the assets of a company. It establishes policies and procedures to help protect and manage assets like cash, inventory, supplies, equipment, and buildings. Besides the control features discussed above, an effective control system should include the following measures:

1. Physical measures to guard against theft and vandalism. Management protects its assets by securing the premises through the use of locks and alarms, depositing cash in the bank regularly, and keeping cash that is maintained on the premises securely stored in tills and safes.

2. Separation of duties. Employees have the opportunity to defraud a company if one person is responsible for purchasing assets, inspecting them on arrival to ensure that what was ordered has been received, and entering the receipt of the assets in the accounting records. To reduce opportunity for fraud, management attempts to ensure that one person is not responsible for all of these functions. When one employee is responsible for verifying the work of another, dishonest behaviour requires collusion, which is more difficult to plan and execute. With respect to cash, separation of duties means that one person receives cash, another is authorized to write cheques, and a third records the receipt or payment of cash in the accounting records. In a small company, separation of duties may be difficult to implement because of the limited number of employees. Then, management itself must periodically verify the work of employees.

3. An effective record-keeping system. Management establishes an accounting system such that all transactions are recorded on a timely basis, only authorized personnel record transactions, and all personnel authorized to record transactions have the appropriate training, to ensure that errors are minimized.

You may think that all of this concern about internal control is excessive. However, as the summary on the next page indicates, a large number of Canadian companies lose profits due to fraud perpetrated by their employees.

Learning Objective

3

Prepare a simple bank reconciliation.

One control procedure used by virtually every company is the **bank reconciliation**. The bank reconciliation ensures that the accounting records agree with the bank records. Every bank account has a corresponding general ledger account in the company's accounting system. The company's records and the bank ledgers reflect the same transactions, such as cash deposits and cheques written, but the transactions may be recorded at different times. For example, a company may write, record, and mail a cheque on November 1, and the payee may receive it on November 7 and deposit it in its bank account on November 8. The payee's bank will forward the cheque to the company's bank, which will then withdraw the money from the company's account on November 9. The transaction takes a few days to be completed, so the cheque will be outstanding from the time the company records it on November 1 until the bank shows it as a withdrawal from the account on November 9. During the period in which the cheque is outstanding, the two accounts (the general ledger and the bank's records) will be different. The bank reconciliation is the process used to account for all such differences. As an individual, to manage your cash most effectively, you should reconcile your personal bank balance every month.

accounting in the news

COMPANIES AND FRAUD

One 1998 survey found that more than half of major Canadian businesses questioned had been victimized by fraud in the previous year. Further, the majority of cases involved senior employees.

Only half of the companies surveyed by Ernst & Young had a policy in place to deal with fraud, and only half of these companies had communicated the policy to their employees in an effective manner. This despite survey findings that the perpetrators were employees in more than 80% of instances of corporate fraud; of these instances, managers were responsible for more than 60%.

Companies should be explicit with their employees about what constitutes fraud, and should train their employees in methods of identifying suspicious circumstances. Companies should also implement a system for the mandatory reporting of fraud.

The Ernst & Young survey found that 87% of companies do not recover the losses resulting from fraud. The costs are substantial: The survey found that four out of five Canadian companies had been victimized by fraud in the previous five years.

Source: "Corporate Crime and Corruption," by Colin Perkel, *Canadian Press Newswire*, July 8, 1998.

The following information about Gelardi Company illustrates a bank reconciliation:

- The balance in Gelardi's cash account on March 31 was $9,763.42.
- The balance in Gelardi's bank account on March 31 was $9,043.92.
- The accountant reviewed the bank statement and the transactions in the cash account and discovered the following:
  - Cheque #8889 for $462.89 and cheque #8891 for $65.78 were still outstanding (they had been mailed but had not yet been presented to the bank for payment).
  - The last deposit of the month, for $1,035.62, was made as a night deposit and the bank did not record the deposit in Gelardi's bank account until April 2.
  - The bank had included a bank charge of $25.75 for March, but the accountant had not yet recorded it in the company's books.
  - The bank had returned the cheque of one of Gelardi's customers marked NSF (not sufficient funds). This was a cheque for $186.80 that a customer had given the company in exchange for some merchandise. Gelardi had accepted

the cheque, recorded it as an increase to the cash account, and deposited it in its bank account. However, when Gelardi's bank presented the cheque to the customer's bank for payment, it was informed that the customer did not have enough money in his bank account to cover the cheque. Gelardi's bank returned the cheque to Gelardi and removed the amount from the bank account.

Using this information, the accountant would prepare the following bank reconciliation:

Bank Reconciliation		
For the Month of March		
Balance per bank statement		$ 9,043.92
Add: Outstanding deposit		1,035.62
		10,079.54
Deduct: Outstanding cheques		
#8889	$ 462.89	
#8891	65.78	528.67
Adjusted cash balance		$ 9,550.87
Balance per cash account		$ 9,763.42
Deduct: Bank charges	$ 25.75	
NSF cheque	186.80	212.55
Adjusted cash balance		$ 9,550.87

The accountant now knows that the appropriate cash balance is $9,550.87 and also that the company's records and the bank's records are in agreement with respect to cash. After the bank reconciliation is complete, the accountant needs to make a journal entry to adjust the cash account so that it reflects the information that was just received from the bank. The entry would be:

SE-Bank charge expense	25.75	
A-Accounts receivable	186.80	
A-Cash		212.55

After posting, the balance in the cash account would be $9,550.87.

Bank reconciliations are an important control procedure. They ensure that all transactions affecting the bank account have been properly recorded, so the company knows that no transactions have been missed. They are normally made every month, for every bank account, as soon as the bank statement is received. The bank reconciliation procedure consists of reconciling the balance recorded by the company with the balance recorded by the bank. The main reconciling items are outstanding cheques, outstanding deposits, bank service charges that have been deducted from the bank account but not recorded by the company, errors in recording items, and any other item that affects cash and is recorded by either the company or the bank.

Another important control measure is to ensure that the person who reconciles the bank account is not the person who is responsible for the bank account or the accounting records. This will ensure that any error or discrepancy will be found and properly corrected. It also ensures that an individual is not given the opportunity to take cash and then change the books to cover the theft.

The other issue associated with cash is cash management. Proper cash management requires that sufficient cash be maintained in readily accessible bank accounts to pay expenses, while at the same time excess amounts of cash be kept neither on hand nor in bank accounts. Cash is a non-earning asset; that is, it is not earning a return. The company will want to keep as much of its cash invested in income-earning assets as possible. Income-earning assets include savings accounts and short-term investments. A company's cash management policies are critical to the effective management of its cash position and to the maximization of total earnings. Advanced cash management techniques are not discussed in this book but are very important to the shareholders and the management of companies.

ethics in accounting

■ Because of the easy portability of money and the difficulty of identifying one owner's money from another's, handling of cash in any business can be a source of ethical dilemmas for managers and employees. Strict controls must be placed on who within the organization handles cash and how they handle it. The set of controls put in place by a business to manage cash (or any other asset or liability) is sometimes referred to as the internal control system. Internal controls are not based on the assumption that people are dishonest. Rather, their purpose is to ensure that employees do not have the opportunity to become dishonest.

Suppose, for example, that you own a parking lot and have hired an employee to collect fees from individuals who park their vehicles in the lot. What controls do you think would be necessary to ensure that all the cash the employee collects is received by you? What characteristics would you look for in the person you hire to do this job?

There are certain basic control guidelines that companies should consider. Control can provide assurance regarding a broad range of objectives in three general categories: The effectiveness and efficiency of operations, the reliability of financial and management reporting, and compliance with applicable laws and regulations and with company policies.

Ethical questions arise with respect to management's attitudes towards its employees. Should management assume that all employees are dishonest and will steal if they think they can get away with it? Or should management establish controls to ensure that employees are not given any opportunity to steal?

Statement Analysis Considerations

Concern might be expressed regarding restrictions placed on the use of cash. Sometimes a company's cash is restricted with regard to withdrawal from the bank because of a feature known as **compensating balances**. These are minimum balances that must be maintained in the bank account to avoid significant service charges or, in some cases, to satisfy restrictive loan covenants (which are clauses in loan agreements that are designed to reduce the risk to the lender). A company might also restrict cash for a specific use. In such a case, the restricted cash should be segregated from other amounts of cash. Other than these, and those discussed in conjunction with the understanding of the cash flow statement in Chapter 5, there are no special considerations with regard to cash for financial statement analysis.

TEMPORARY INVESTMENTS

Learning Objective

4

Identify the criteria for the classification of an investment as temporary.

As discussed in the last section, the management of cash is an important function in managing a company. One of its aspects is the company's need to minimize its cash balance, given that current or chequing accounts normally earn no returns. One way to convert cash into an earning asset is to invest it in temporary (short-term) marketable securities. **Marketable securities** are securities (i.e., assets that are publicly traded) that represent either a debt interest (Treasury Bills, bonds, or Guaranteed Investment Certificates) or an equity interest (shares) in another entity. The more active the trading in the security, the easier it will be to convert the security back into cash when the cash is needed for other purposes. The ability to turn an investment back into cash quickly is known as *liquidity*, and it is an important aspect of managing the company's cash position.

Securities that are not marketable would likely not qualify as current assets of the company, because they might not be easily converted into cash within one year. They would probably be classified as noncurrent investments. The discussion in this section is restricted to marketable securities.

The probable future value associated with marketable securities comes from two sources. One source is the periodic payments that these securities produce while they are being held. If the security is a debt security, these payments are interest. If the debt security matures in three months or less, the company would likely classify it as a cash equivalent. Payments received from equity securities are dividends. Because equity securities do not have a maturity date, they are not classified as cash equivalents. The second source of probable future value is the value of the securities when sold in the future. If the intention is to hold these securities for the short term (less than one year), the resale price becomes very important. If the intention is to hold them for the long term (more than one year), the resale price is less important. Securities held for the long term are usually called long-term investments and do not appear under the heading of temporary investments in the balance sheet.

The uncertainty, or risk, associated with the future value of temporary investments relates to both the periodic payments and the ultimate sales value. For example, the issuers of debt may default on the interest payments. This not only causes uncertainty with regard to the periodic payments, but it also reduces the value of a security in terms of its final price. If a company cannot make interest payments, it is unlikely that it will be able to pay back the principal when the debt matures. With regard to equity securities, there is no guarantee that dividends will continue at present levels, nor is there any guarantee of the ultimate sales value. The company may grow, increasing its future selling price, or it may fail, rendering the equity shares worthless.

The uncertainty with regard to the future cash flows of a security is sometimes evidenced by the volatility of the price of the security in the securities markets. If you read the business section of the newspaper, you are well aware of the volatility of the markets for equity securities (shares). The market prices of shares fluctuate for many reasons. For example, during the year August 14, 1997, to August 14, 1998, the shares of BCE Inc. (Bell Canada Enterprises) varied from a low of $37.00 to a high of $68.05. The variability in the price is partially a function of the highly competitive telecommunications market in which this company operates.

A similar volatility has existed in recent years in the markets for debt securities (bond markets). The degree of uncertainty depends on the type of security and on the financial health of the issuing entity. Debt securities, for instance, may be viewed as quite safe if they are issued by the government. Canadian government bonds are an example. At the other extreme are corporate bonds issued by very highly leveraged companies (highly leveraged means that total liabilities greatly exceed total equity). These bonds are sometimes called junk bonds. Junk bonds pay very high interest rates to compensate for the high risk of their principal's not being repaid. Equity securities offer a similar spectrum of risk.

The ownership criterion of these assets is relatively straightforward. For some securities, ownership can be represented by pieces of paper (share certificates and bonds). In many cases, however, no certificates are issued and ownership is evidenced by entries in an account maintained by an outside party (such as a broker).

Valuation Methods

One way to value temporary investments is to record them at their original acquisition cost, or **historical cost**. With this method, changes in the market value of the investments have no effect on the balance sheet or income statement until the investment is actually sold. Income is recognized at the time the investment is sold and is termed a **realized gain or loss**. In addition, income is recognized with this method as periodic payments are received in the form of dividends or interest revenue.

A second method would be to value the temporary investments at their market value. In its pure form, this method requires that changes in the market value of the investments cause changes in the carrying value on the balance sheet and a corresponding recognition of income (or loss) on the income statement. The changes in market value are called **unrealized gains or losses**. If you have adjusted the value of the securities to market value, and if the market value remains stable up to the point of sale there will be no further recognition of income upon sale of the investments, because the investment is already valued at its market value at the time of sale. In addition, the periodic receipt of interest and dividends is recognized as income.

What Is Canadian Practice?

The accounting for temporary investments is a combination of the above methods. Temporary investments are held in place of cash, so the intention is to show them at the amount of cash that is expected to be received from them. However, this intention is modified to show a conservative figure. Therefore, temporary investments are shown at their cost—unless their market value has declined to below cost, in which case they are shown at the market value. We call this method the **lower of cost and market (LCM)**. This is a hybrid of the two methods discussed above, historical cost (i.e., the amount paid for the securities when they were purchased) and market value. The lower of cost and market method uses cost—except in situations where the market value of the portfolio is less than the historical cost, when the market value is used. The gain resulting from a market value higher than cost is not recognized until the investment is sold. This one-sided rule with regard to market values is based on the conservative principle in accounting that, in essence, states that losses should be recognized as soon as they can be estimated but gains should be deferred until they are realized.

AN INTERNATIONAL PERSPECTIVE

Reports from Other Countries

In the United States, all short-term marketable securities are carried at their market value. Americans used to use the lower of cost and market method but in 1994 moved to market value. Canada has been discussing moving to market value for temporary investments but so far has stayed with the lower of cost and market method.

The implementation of the lower of cost and market method presents several issues that must be resolved. The first issue is one of classification. When a company invests in a marketable security, it must first decide whether to classify the investment as a current or noncurrent asset. The classification is generally based on the **intent** of management and on the **marketability** of the asset. If management intends to hold the security for less than one year, and if the security is readily marketable, it will be classified as a current asset. Otherwise, it will be classified as noncurrent, in which case the account will be called a long-term investment rather than a temporary or short-term investment.

A second issue that is important in the accounting for investments arises with respect to equity securities. When one company buys shares in another, the buyer will be able to have some voting power based on the number of shares it owns. The larger the proportion of shares the buyer owns, the more control the buyer can exercise over the other company. Most equity securities are shares that carry a vote entitling the owner to vote for the board of directors, which has direct authority over management. For short-term investments, there is usually no intention on the part of the buying company to exercise control. In fact, the relatively small number of shares usually purchased as a short-term investment does not allow a buying company to exercise much control. With long-term investments in shares, there may be some intention to control the company. In some cases, for example, the acquiring company will buy 100% of the outstanding shares of the company. In this case, the acquiring company exercises absolute control over the acquired company. The accounting for investments in which a company exercises significant control is different from that in which the company has little control (i.e., a passive investment). The accounting for investments in which there exists significant control is discussed in Appendix C. In this chapter, only passive investments in securities are considered.

The data in Exhibit 6-2 for the Clifford Company illustrate the application of the lower of cost and market method to short-term investments. Assume that Clifford's year end is December 31 and that the company prepares income statements on a quarterly basis. You will notice that Clifford buys three securities during the first quarter (the first three months in the year). The exhibit then tracks the performance of the portfolio during the year, valuing each security each quarter until it is sold. Dividend and interest payments received over the year are also included.

■ **CLIFFORD COMPANY**

EXHIBIT 6-2

Temporary Investments Data

Security	Type	Quarter Acquired	Acquisition Cost	Quarter Sold	Selling Price
HTMS Corp.	Bonds	1	$10,000	3	$12,000
ATS Inc.	Shares	1	$20,000	4	$18,000
LFS Ltd.	Shares	1	$30,000	-	NA

Values as at the End of

Security	Quarter 1 Cost	Quarter 1 Market	Quarter 2 Cost	Quarter 2 Market	Quarter 3 Cost	Quarter 3 Market	Quarter 4 Cost	Quarter 4 Market
HTMS Corp.	$10,000	$11,000	$10,000	$13,000	NA	NA	NA	NA
ATS Inc.	$20,000	$17,000	$20,000	$21,000	$20,000	$17,000	NA	NA
LFS Ltd.	$30,000	$29,000	$30,000	$28,000	$30,000	$29,000	$30,000	$28,500
Portfolio	$60,000	$57,000	$60,000	$62,000	$50,000	$46,000	$30,000	$28,500

Dividends/Interest Received

Quarter	Amount
1	$1,200
2	$1,200
3	$ 500
4	$ 500

Initial Acquisition

The initial acquisition entry is the same as the entry for the acquisition of any other asset. The only distinction at this point is that each security must be classified as HTMS, ATS, or LFS. To illustrate, the following entry would record the acquisition of the temporary investments during the first quarter of the year:

A-Investment in HTMS	10,000	
A-Investment in ATS	20,000	
A-Investment in LFS	30,000	
A-Cash		60,000

Notice that each investment is recorded in its own account. These accounts would be **subsidiary accounts**. There would also be a control account (probably called short-term investments), which holds the sum of all of the subsidiary accounts (see below).

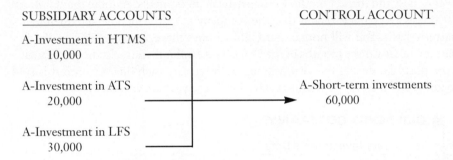

It is the control account that is reported on the financial statements. Transactions are recorded in the subsidiary accounts, which are then used to update the control account.

Dividend/Interest Recognition

Dividend and interest income is recognized each period, as it is earned. In the case of Clifford Company we will assume that all dividend and interest income is received in cash. However, recognize that the interest could be accrued and result in interest receivable rather than cash, and dividends could have been only declared, and not paid, which would result in dividends receivable. In Exhibit 6-2, the dividends and interest from all three investments have been aggregated into one amount. The entry to record these dividends in Quarter 1 would be as follows:

A-Cash	1,200	
SE-Dividend/interest income		1,200
(income statement account)		

Recognition of Unrealized Losses/Recoveries and Realized Gains and Losses

The lower of cost and market rule requires that, at any financial statement date, the company compare the aggregate market value of its portfolio to its original cost, to determine the lower of the two. The company is then required to carry its portfolio at this lower value. Note that for Quarter 1 at March 31 in Exhibit 6-2 the portfolio should be carried at $57,000, because this is the lower of cost and the market value. The writedown from the cost of $60,000 would result in an unrealized loss of $3,000, which would appear in the income statement.

The lower of cost and market rule can be applied in one of two ways: by comparing the totals for the entire portfolio of investments, or by applying the rule to individual securities. For example, if we were to apply the lower of cost and market rule on an individual basis, the investments in ATS and LFS would be written down to their market values, but the investment in HTMS would remain at cost. This would result in an unrealized loss of $4,000, which is larger than the loss that results when the rule is applied on a portfolio basis. This occurs because the portfolio basis allows unrealized gains on some securities (such as HTMS) to offset unrealized losses on other securities (ATS and LFS). Most companies tend to use the portfolio basis. Because they manage their temporary investments on a portfolio basis, this valuation method better reflects the value of the portfolio to the company.

The entry to record the reduction in the carrying value of the temporary investments and the unrealized loss would be:

SE-Unrealized loss on valuation of temporary investments	3,000	
XA-Valuation allowance for temporary investments		3,000

For the current portfolio, the preceding debit entry affects the income statement; that is, unrealized losses are shown on the income statement. The credit entry is to a contra-asset account (see Chapter 3 for a discussion of contra-asset accounts). The account is reported contra to the temporary investments account and reduces the portfolio of securities to its aggregate market value. Notice that the original cost of the securities is unaffected by the above transaction. The **valuation allowance** account is sometimes called *the allowance for the excess of cost of marketable securities over market value* account. It is similar to an accumulated amortization account in that it preserves the historical-cost amounts in the temporary investments accounts that are needed for disclosure and tax purposes. Unlike accumulated amortization, the allowance for the excess of cost of marketable securities over market value is rarely disclosed as a separate item on the balance sheet. Instead, companies will report the temporary investments as a *net* amount (the original cost less the allowance).

In Quarter 2, Clifford again recognizes dividend revenue. At the end of Quarter 2, at June 30, when the company applies the lower of cost and market rule again, you should note that the market value of the portfolio has recovered and, in fact, has gone up above the original cost of the securities purchased. Companies can recover unrealized losses but can never recognize unrealized gains above the original cost of the securities. This means that Clifford can recover the $3,000 unrealized loss it recorded in the first quarter to bring the portfolio back to its original cost of $60,000, but that it cannot recognize the unrealized gain of $2,000 above the original acquisition cost. The entry to record the recovery would be as follows:

XA-Valuation allowance for temporary investments	3,000	
SE-Recovery of unrealized loss on valuation of temporary investments		3,000

The *recovery of unrealized loss on valuation of temporary investments* is an income statement account, and, like a gain, it increases net income, thereby offsetting the loss recorded in Quarter 1.

    The effects on the balance sheet and income statement of the application of the lower of cost and market rule, as well as the other events that affect marketable securities, are summarized in Exhibit 6-3.

EXHIBIT 6-3

■ **CLIFFORD COMPANY**

Financial Statements (Partial)

Income Statement

For the Quarter	Quarter 1	Quarter 2	Quarter 3	Quarter 4
Unrealized holding loss on valuation of temporary investments	($3,000)	–	($4,000)	–
Recovery of unrealized holding loss on valuation of temporary investments	–	$3,000	–	$2,500
Realized gain (loss) on sale of temporary investments	–	–	$2,000	($2,000)
Dividend/interest income	$1,200	$1,200	$ 500	$ 500
Effect on net income of temporary investments	($1,800)	$4,200	($1,500)	$1,000

Balance Sheet

As at the end of	Quarter 1	Quarter 2	Quarter 3	Quarter 4
Temporary Investments (at cost)	$60,000	$60,000	$50,000	$30,000
Less valuation allowance	($ 3,000)	-0-	($ 4,000)	($ 1,500)
Temporary Investments (at LCM)	$57,000	$60,000	$46,000	$28,500

    As shown in Exhibit 6-3, the effect of the preceding entries would be to record a recovery (gain) on the income statement in Quarter 2, and the debit entry brings the balance in the valuation allowance account to zero.

In the third quarter, Clifford recognized dividend/interest revenue and sold investment HTMS for $12,000. Bonds have a face value (in this case $10,000), and the promise of the issuer is that the purchaser will be paid the face value when the bond matures. The fact that Clifford sold the bonds for $12,000 means that they have not reached maturity. If they had, Clifford would have received only $10,000. It is possible that between the date of issue and the date of maturity the value of the bond will change. The difference between the acquisition cost and the selling price ($2,000) represents a gain on the sale. It is appropriate to recognize a gain, because a market transaction has occurred. To record this sale in the third quarter, the following entry would be made:

A-Cash	12,000	
A-Investment in HTMS		10,000
SE-Realized gain on sale of temporary		
investment		2,000

At the end of Quarter 3, at September 30, the company again applies the lower of cost and market rule. Recognize that the portfolio now has one less security, because HTMS was sold during the period. The analysis indicated that the portfolio should be carried at market because it is lower than cost. The adjustment to the allowance account represents the full difference between cost and market, because the balance in the valuation allowance account from the previous quarter is zero. The entry at the end of Quarter 3, at September 30, is:

SE-Unrealized loss on valuation of		
temporary investments	4,000	
XA-Valuation allowance for temporary		
investments		4,000

In the fourth quarter of the year, Clifford sells the investment in ATS for $18,000 and continues to hold the investment in LFS at the end of the quarter, which is also the year-end date of December 31. The sale of ATS results in a realized loss of $2,000, because its acquisition cost was $20,000. The amount of unrealized losses is not considered in calculating the realized loss. The determination of a realized gain or loss is always made by comparing the original acquisition cost with the selling price. The following entry is made for the sale of security B:

A-Cash	18,000	
SE-Realized loss on sale of temporary		
investment	2,000	
A-Investment in ATS		20,000

The evaluation of the lower of cost and market rule at the end of Quarter 4 indicates that the market value of the portfolio (the portfolio now consists of only one security) is lower than the cost by $1,500. As the balance in the allowance account is $4,000, Clifford will have to recognize a recovery of $2,500 to bring the balance back to $1,500. The following entry will accomplish this:

XA-Valuation allowance for temporary investments	2,500	
SE-Recovery of unrealized loss on valuation of temporary investments		2,500

Exhibit 6-3 summarizes the results of the transactions affecting the marketable securities in Quarter 4.

The disclosure of the effects of transactions involving temporary investments in a typical set of financial statements tends to be somewhat limited because of the insignificant nature of these transactions relative to the other transactions of the company. Although Canada does not follow the U.S. lead and maintain its temporary investments at market all of the time, it does require that companies disclose the market value of temporary investments. A company may simply list a line item for temporary investments on the balance sheet and include a note stating that the securities are carried at cost, which approximates market. No details need be provided concerning the amount of dividend or interest revenue or the amount of realized and unrealized gains and losses that are recognized. When the amounts are significant, however, a note to the financial statements generally provides the details.

Examples of disclosures of market values of temporary investments are provided in Exhibit 6-4.

EXAMPLES OF DISCLOSURE OF TEMPORARY INVESTMENTS

Imperial Metals Company (1998)

	December 31 1998	December 31 1997
Marketable securities [Market value $379,542 (1997–$233,794)]	300,593	219,292

MOSAID Technologies Incorporated (1998)

Short-term marketable securities
Short-term marketable securities are recorded at cost plus accrued interest, which approximates fair market value.

The note disclosure used by MOSAID is typical of those used by many companies in Canada. The short-term nature of the investments means that there is often very little difference between original acquisition price and market value. This means that a note like the one used by MOSAID is sufficient.

Long-Term Investments

Accounting rules for noncurrent investments are different from the rules for short-term investments and are discussed in Appendix C at the end of the book.

Statement Analysis Considerations

If temporary investments make up a significant portion of the current assets of the company being analyzed, the potential effects of the unrecognized gains and losses on the financial health of the company should be recognized. If the portfolio is being held at the lower of cost and market, the user has some idea of the loss potential of the securities, as some portion of it has already been recognized. Remember, however, if the lower of cost and market rule is applied on a portfolio basis, gains on some securities can offset losses on others. Also, if the market value of the securities is above the cost, this unrealized gain will not have been recognized. Unrecorded gains or losses could render any ratio using net income misleading. The disclosure requirements for temporary investments are such that you can usually get information about both of these amounts from the notes to the financial statements, since Canadian GAAP requires that the market values be disclosed. Because of this disclosure, it is possible for users to use the market value of the temporary investments in any financial statement analysis.

ACCOUNTS RECEIVABLE

Accounts receivable are amounts owed from customers as a result of the normal business transactions of selling goods and services on credit. The ownership criterion for accounts receivable is evidenced either by a formal contractual agreement or by some other, informal, arrangement such as a sales invoice. The sale itself represents the past event that gave rise to the accounts receivable. The probable future value criterion would be met by the fact that a receivable is the right to receive payment at some future date. The cash that is received at that future date can then be exchanged for other goods and services. The value of the cash that is to be received in the future is affected by the same uncertainties described earlier in the section on cash. In addition to those uncertainties, there is the uncertainty that the customer will not pay the cash as agreed. A complete default by the customer would be called a bad debt. This makes the valuation of accounts receivable less certain than the valuation of cash.

Other uncertainties with accounts receivable are that the customer may return the goods for credit, the customer may request a price adjustment if the goods are damaged in shipment, or the customer may pay less than what is listed on the bill if allowed a discount for prompt payment. All of these factors can not only affect the uncertainty of collecting accounts receivable, but also complicate the determination of the appropriate amount to record.

Accounts Receivable Valuation Methods

An account receivable is an agreement to pay a certain amount at some point in the future. A simple way to value the receivable is to add up the gross payments called for in the agreement. This *gross payments method* ignores the effects of bad debts (customers who do not pay), returns, and so forth, as well as the effects of the *time value of money*.

A second method for valuing an account receivable is to take into consideration the time value of the gross payments to be received. The time value of money refers to the concept that a dollar paid tomorrow is worth less than a dollar paid today, the reasoning being that an investor can invest the dollar received today and have more than a dollar by tomorrow. Therefore, if the company has a receivable for $100 to be received a month from now, that receivable is worth less than $100 received today. Using the terminology of the time value of money, we would want to compute the *present value* of the future cash flows of the receivable. We would discount the future cash flows, using an appropriate interest rate to arrive at this present value. See Appendix D for a full discussion of the computation of present values.

A third method is to take into consideration the possibility that the receivable will not be paid. This could result from either a default by the customer or the return of the goods. Partial payment might also result, if the customer pays early to take advantage of a cash discount, or if the customer demands a price concession. Incorporating these events into the valuation would mean reducing the receivable. This alternative can be used in conjunction with either the first (gross payments) or the second (present value) method of valuing the receivable.

Finally, a valuation method based on the market value of the account receivable might also be considered. Accounts receivable can be sold to other parties, who then collect from the customer. The process of selling accounts receivable is referred to as **factoring**. If a ready market is available in which to sell a receivable, a market price can be used as a value for the receivable.

What Is Canadian Practice?

Most Canadian companies show receivables at the gross payments amount less appropriate allowances for bad debts, returns, and so forth. Ideally the use of present value would be more appropriate, but there is a materiality consideration. If there is little difference between the present value and the gross payments, such as occurs with receivables expected to be paid in a relatively short period of time, the gross payments can be used. The use of present value adds some complications to the accounting for receivables and, unless the accounting for present value makes a significant difference, it is probably not worth the effort. For most companies, the time between sale and collection is relatively short (30 to 60 days). Unless interest rates are extremely high, the difference between the present value and the gross payments for these types of receivable is relatively small. Therefore, most companies account for their accounts receivable at the gross amount less the allowance for bad debts, returns, and so forth. The adjustment for these allowances is necessary because the company does not want to overstate its assets or its income from sales to customers. For example, consider a company that sells $10,000 worth of goods during the accounting period, all on account. The entry to record this transaction is:

A-Accounts receivable	10,000	
SE-Sales revenue		10,000

If the company anticipates that it will collect the entire $10,000, the preceding entry would appropriately state the effects of the transaction on assets and shareholders' wealth. However, if the company anticipates that some customers will not pay, this entry overstates the receivables as well as the shareholders' wealth.

The likelihood that a customer will default on a payment depends on the customer's credit worthiness. A company can improve its chances of receiving payments by performing a credit check on its customers before it grants them credit. The company must balance its desire to sell its product to the customer against the likelihood that the customer will pay. A credit policy that is too strict will result in many customers being denied credit and therefore purchasing their goods from other suppliers. A credit policy that is too loose may cause the company to lose more money from bad debts than it makes from good sales. The company should do a cost/benefit analysis before setting its credit policy. Also, the company must stay abreast of changes in both the industry in which it operates and the economy in general. Changes in interest rates, inflation, or the global economy can alter the credit worthiness of a customer within a short period of time. The following article summary illustrates how a changing economy can affect a company's ability to collect its accounts receivable.

accounting in the news

ACCOUNTS RECEIVABLE AND COLLECTIONS

While the accounts receivable department of any business should expect to experience some doubtful accounts, a sluggish economy will heighten collection problems. In spring 1999, one Vancouver accountant observed that small and mid-sized business clients had accounts receivable outstanding 120 days to six months, in contrast to the two to three months previously observed. He also observed that for some businesses doubtful accounts amounted to a fifth of their revenues.

To protect themselves, some retailers were demanding immediate payment, while major department stores were refusing personal cheques. One law firm even set up a business solely to help companies secure their receivables using techniques as straightforward as customized business documents.

Professionals in the collections business point out that when a company provides a service or product before receiving payment it is giving credit—just as a bank does. Businesses can protect themselves by checking their clients' credit records and using the right language in purchase orders and fee agreements to ensure that their credit is secured.

Source: "Getting paid taking longer than ever for small business," by Jenny Lee, *Vancouver Sun*, April 26, 1999, page F1.

In addition to a policy on bad debts, other policies can affect the amounts collected. One of these is the returns policy of the company. Are customers permitted to return goods, and, if so, under what circumstances? Again, the strictness or looseness of the policy will influence a customer's decision to buy goods from the company. A second policy that should be considered is that concerning cash discounts for early payment. If the company decides to offer a cash discount, the amount of cash that will be collected from the receivable will depend on the number of customers who pay early. The number of customers who pay early will depend on the attractiveness of the discount. Both of these policies require some adjustment to the amounts recorded in the accounts receivable as well as those recorded in the sales revenue account.

The accounting methods for anticipated bad debts or doubtful (sometimes referred to as "uncollectible") accounts are illustrated in the next section. Recognize that similar methods could be used to account for the other adjustments to accounts receivable, such as cash discounts and sales returns. For a more complete description of the accounting for discounts and returns, refer to an intermediate accounting text.

Accounting for doubtful accounts requires adjustments to the accounts receivable account as well as recognition of the related bad debts expense in the income statement. Some smaller businesses use the direct write-off method, but medium-sized and large companies generally use what is called the **allowance method** to recognize doubtful accounts.

Allowance Method

Learning Objective

7

Explain why estimating the potential uncollectibility of accounts receivable is required.

Let us review two key points discussed earlier in the text. First, the matching concept requires that when a company recognizes revenue from a sale it must also recognize all expenses relating to that sale. Second, bad debts are technically not expenses but reductions in revenues. These reductions in revenues should be recognized when the revenues are recognized. Because the company does not know, at the point of sale, which customers will end up as bad debts, it must make some estimates of what dollar amount of sales will ultimately be uncollectible. These estimates are usually based on the company's past experience with its customers. New businesses have little basis for making initial estimates and therefore must use some other method of doing so.

Consider the example accompanying the preceding journal entry. Assume that the company estimates that, of the $10,000 in sales, $325 will ultimately prove to be uncollectible. One method for arriving at this estimate is discussed later in this chapter. As the company is not able to identify the customers who will not pay, the $325 cannot directly reduce specific accounts receivable. Therefore, the following entry records this amount in an account that is contra to the accounts receivable account. This contra account, which is usually called the allowance for doubtful accounts, reduces that aggregate amount of accounts receivable for the anticipated effects of **uncollectible accounts**. The debit is to the bad debt expense account.

SE-Bad debt expense	325	
XA-Allowance for doubtful accounts		325

The allowance for doubtful accounts normally has a credit balance, because its purpose is to show that the full debit balance amount in the accounts receivable will not be collected. In effect, it reduces the accounts receivable total to the net amount of cash that the company actually expects to receive. Remember that the allowance account is contra to the accounts receivable and is grouped with that current asset on the balance sheet.

Note that this entry has the effect of reducing the net carrying value of the accounts receivable (the accounts receivable balance less the balance in the allowance account) from \$10,000 to \$9,675 (\$10,000 − \$325) and reducing the net income by the same amount. Accounts receivable are now stated at the amount the company ultimately expects to collect in cash.

The actual write-off of an account receivable, under the allowance method, occurs when the cutoff date specified in the write-off policy is reached. A company's decision that an account is uncollectible is usually based on a bad debt policy. For example, the policy may state that accounts will be declared uncollectible if they have been outstanding for more than 120 days. This policy is based on the company's experience with collecting from its customers and usually means that the probability of collecting the account after 120 days is so small that payment is not worth pursuing. The company may still try to collect this account, but it will probably turn it over to a collection agency. Assume that we are using this policy for the company in our example; that is, accounts that have not been collected within 120 days are written off. Assume that nonpayments resulted in \$300 in actual write-offs. With the allowance method, this means that we have now specifically identified customer accounts that are bad, which we were unable to identify at the point when we recognized the bad debt expense. Because we recognized the expense when the estimate was made, no further expense should be recognized. We should simply remove the specific account from the accounts receivable and remove an equivalent amount from the allowance account because some portion of the allowance account is no longer necessary. The entry is:

XA-Allowance for doubtful accounts	300	
A-Accounts receivable		300

What happens if one of the accounts we have written off is finally paid by the customer? This is called a **recovery**. Recoveries, under the allowance method, are accounted for by reinstating the account receivable. This is done by reversing the write-off entry and then showing the normal cash collection entry. The following two entries would be made if an account worth \$50 was recovered after having been written off. Note that, whereas one net entry can be made to record this transaction, if no entry is made to the accounts receivable account the customer's account will always be shown in the records as having been a bad debt.

A-Accounts receivable	50	
XA-Allowance for doubtful accounts		50
A-Cash	50	
A-Accounts receivable		50

Assume that this was the first year of the company's operations and that the company had collected $8,500 from its customers by the end of the year. Exhibit 6-5 illustrates the entries and balances in the accounts receivable and the allowance for doubtful accounts.

The ending balance in the accounts receivable account ($1,200) represents those accounts that have not been collected as at the end of the accounting period. In our example, the maximum amount of time any of these accounts can have been outstanding is 120 days; any account beyond that time is written off. The ending balance in the allowance for doubtful accounts should be the remaining allowance that applies to the ending balance in accounts receivable. In other words, the company expects that, of the remaining $1,200 in accounts receivable, $75 will prove to be uncollectible.

EXHIBIT 6-5

■ Allowance Method for Doubtful Accounts

A-Accounts Receivable			
✓	0		
Credit sales	10,000	8,500	Cash collections
Recoveries	50	300	Write-offs
		50	Collections from recoveries
✓	1,200		

XA-Allowance for Doubtful Accounts			
		0	✓
Write-offs	300	325	Bad debt expense
		50	Recoveries
		75	✓

In most financial statements, the allowance account is netted against the accounts receivable account to produce a single line item on the balance sheet. Few companies provide details of the amount of the allowance, neither by showing the balance in the allowance for doubtful accounts nor by including information about it in the notes to the financial statements.

One final point to consider about the accounting for doubtful accounts is the method used to estimate the dollar amounts that are doubtful. One commonly used method is called the *percentage of credit sales method*. This method will be described below. Another method is called the *aging of accounts receivable method*. We will leave the discussion of this method to intermediate accounting texts.

Learning Objective

8

Identify a method for recognizing uncollectibility and describe the circumstances under which its use is appropriate.

Percentage of Credit Sales Method

The **percentage of credit sales method** is based on the assumption that the amount of bad debt expense is a function of the total sales made on credit. It estimates the bad debt expense for the period by multiplying the credit sales during the period by an appropriate percentage. The percentage is determined based on the collection history of the company. In the example above, the $325 of bad debt expense that was used could have been the result of using 3.25% of credit sales as an estimate of the bad debts (3.25% of the $10,000 in credit sales would have resulted in the estimate of bad debt expense of $325). In a new company, the percentage may be determined initially by considering the bad debt experience of other companies in the same industry. In an existing company, historical data is generally used to estimate this percentage as adjusted for present and anticipated future economic conditions. For example, during an economic downturn, bad debt percentages often rise.

The initial estimate of the percentage must be adjusted from time to time to reflect the recent credit experience of the company. If the company is experiencing more write-offs than were estimated, the percentage should be increased. Companies typically do not go back to prior periods to adjust this percentage but adjust it on a prospective basis. Therefore, an over-estimate or an under-estimate in one period will be adjusted in the following period. The percentage can be affected by the types of customers that the company has, a change in credit policy, and general economic conditions such as economic downturns and changes in unemployment levels.

Note that, with the percentage of credit sales method, the ending balance in the allowance for doubtful accounts results from simply totalling the entries to the account. The percentage relationship between the ending balance in the allowance account and the accounts receivable account has nothing to do with the percentage used to estimate bad debt expense. In the example, the ratio of the ending balance in the allowance account to the accounts receivable account is 6.25% ($75/$1,200). This is considerably higher than the 3.25% bad debts the company estimated as its percentage of sales. This is not necessarily inconsistent, however, as a higher percentage of the accounts receivable that are left at the end of the period may not be paid. For example, many of them may be approaching the 120-day limit, which means that the probability of collecting them is becoming extremely small.

AN INTERNATIONAL PERSPECTIVE

Reports from Other Countries

In some countries such as France and Germany, uncollectible accounts are estimated by considering the circumstances of individual accounts rather than by determining an overall percentage rate such as with the percentage of credit sales method. This method is similar to the aging of accounts receivable used in Canada. It is also used by some companies in Japan.

Direct Write-Off Method

The direct write-off method is often used by small companies. It recognizes the loss from the uncollectible account in the period in which the company decides that the account is, in fact, uncollectible. Assume that we are using the policy that applied with the allowance method—that is, accounts are written off after 120 days. In our example, $300 worth of accounts receivable was identified as being more than 120 days overdue. These accounts should be written off. With the direct write-off method, the entry to record this is:

SE-Bad debt expense	300	
A-Accounts receivable (specific accounts)		300

Note that the debit to the bad debt expense account reduces net income in this period. Bad debt expense is somewhat different from other "expenses." It is not accompanied by a related cash outflow. It is more like a reduction in a revenue account in the sense that it represents revenues the company will never receive. In recognition of this, a small number of companies report this as a direct reduction in the sales revenue amount on the income statement. These companies report a line item that they call *net sales—net* meaning that the bad debt expense has been netted out against the sales revenue amount. The majority of companies, however, show bad debts as an expense grouped with other expenses and not as a reduction of the revenues.

The credit entries to the accounts receivable account are to specific customer accounts; the company has identified the exact parties who have not paid. For example, the $300 might be in two specific accounts, a $180 account from Joe Lee and a $120 account from Mary Smith. The accounts receivable balance is generally supported by what is called a subsidiary ledger, similar to the subsidiary ledger used with the temporary investments, in which individual separate receivable accounts are maintained for each customer. This entry would cause reductions in the accounts of both Joe Lee and Mary Smith.

The direct write-off method is a simple way of accounting for bad debts. The company makes every reasonable effort to collect the account, and when it finally decides that an account is uncollectible it records the preceding entry to remove it from the accounting system. The problem with this method is that it violates the matching concept discussed in Chapter 4. As you will recall, the matching concept requires that all expenses related to the production of revenue be matched with the revenue in the period in which the revenue is recognized. The direct write-off method could result in the revenue being recognized in one accounting period and the associated bad debt expense recorded in the next. If bad debts are not material, this mismatching can probably be ignored. If bad debts are significant, however, this mismatching can sufficiently distort the measurement of performance that most accountants would find this method unacceptable. A more appropriate method to use when bad debts are significant is the allowance method discussed earlier.

NOTES RECEIVABLE

Notes receivable are very similar to accounts receivable in their fundamental characteristics. Therefore, we will not discuss the recognition criteria and valuation methods; they are the same as those for accounts receivable. The difference between an account receivable and a note receivable is that the note receivable is evidenced by a more formal agreement, referred to as a **promissory note**. A promissory note is a written contract between two parties, the *maker* and the *payee*. The maker promises to pay a specific amount either upon demand by the payee or at a definite date in the future.

Interest may be shown explicitly as a part of the note, or it may be implicit in the contractual payments. When interest is explicit, it is typically calculated by multiplying the explicit interest rate times the face value of the note times the time factor. The presumption here is that the face value is the amount that has been borrowed via the note. A note in which the interest is implicit specifies the amount to be paid at maturity (the face value), which will be larger than the initial amount borrowed. The interest is the difference between the amount borrowed and the face value. These are sometimes called *discounted notes*.

Notes receivable generally take longer to mature than accounts receivable, but usually less than a year; hence, they are usually considered current assets. Long-term notes receivable are classified in the noncurrent assets section, along with the long-term investments.

Notes are most commonly arranged with banks or other financial institutions. These financial institutions may require that the maker of the note put up some type of **collateral** for the note. Collateral is some asset that the payee has the right to receive if the maker defaults on the note. As an example, think of an individual who purchases a car using a loan from a bank or finance company. The bank uses the new car as collateral for the loan. If the person defaults on the loan, the bank or finance company can reclaim the car and sell it to satisfy the outstanding debt.

A note secured by collateral is called a **secured note**. The collateral may be some type of real property, such as real estate, or personal property, such as equipment or inventory. Depending on the credit worthiness of the maker, a payee may agree to issue an unsecured note, which means that no collateral is specified. Companies will sometimes agree to issue a note to a customer if the customer cannot pay an account receivable within the normal payment period. If the customer requests a longer period of time to pay, the company may agree to this arrangement provided the customer pays interest on the outstanding debt. Extending credit beyond the normal credit terms without demanding interest is not effective cash management.

Interest on Notes Receivable

As stated earlier, interest on notes receivable can be either implied or explicit. A note with implied interest might state: "The maker of the note agrees to pay $1,050 at maturity in exchange for $1,000 today." The maker is borrowing $1,000, and, as the maturity payment is $1,050, the difference ($50) is interest. A note with explicit

Learning Objective

9

Describe a note receivable and explain the circumstances under which it is used.

Learning Objective

10

Calculate interest associated with notes receivable and prepare necessary journal entries.

interest might state: "The maker agrees to pay the principal amount of $1,000 at maturity plus interest at a rate of 12% [always stated as an annual rate unless otherwise indicated] in exchange for $1,000 today." The dollar amount of interest in this case depends on how long it is between the date of the note and maturity.

Short-term notes receivable generally require that interest payments be based on simple-interest calculations. Long-term notes, on the other hand, generally use compound-interest calculations. **Compound-interest** calculations are discussed in Appendix D. **Simple-interest** calculations are demonstrated in the following equation.

Interest charges are calculated based on the amount borrowed, the interest rate, and the amount of time that elapses. The formula is:

SIMPLE-INTEREST FORMULA
Interest = Principal × Interest Rate × Time

The principal is the amount borrowed, the interest rate is specified in the note and is stated as a yearly amount, and the time is the time that has elapsed, stated as a fraction of a year. The calculation of the time that has elapsed is generally measured in days. While the actual number of days can be used, many lenders simplify the calculation by considering each month as comprising 30 days and, therefore, 360 days as equivalent to one year. This convention is used in the calculations that follow.

To illustrate the computation of interest and the accounting for notes, assume the following:

1. On November 30, 20x1, the Bierstaker Company agrees to accept a note of $1,000 from the Wilkicki Company to satisfy an outstanding account receivable from Wilkicki. (This could happen if Wilkicki is having trouble meeting its payment or if it temporarily has more pressing needs for its cash.) The note has a maturity of two months (60 days) and an interest rate of 12%.

2. Bierstaker's fiscal year end is December 31, and Wilkicki does not pay the note until maturity.

On acceptance of the note from Wilkicki, Bierstaker makes the following entry:

A-Notes receivable	1,000	
A-Accounts receivable		1,000

Bierstaker's entry reflects receipt of the note from Wilkicki and the reduction in its accounts receivable.

On December 31, 20x1, one month after receiving the note, Bierstaker must close its books. This means that it must record the accrual of interest on the note from Wilkicki. The interest through December 31, 20x1, is calculated as follows:

Interest = Principal × Interest Rate × Time
= $1,000 × 12% × 30/360
= $10

The entry to record this amount is:

A-Interest receivable	10	
SE-Interest revenue		10

At the end of January, 20x2, Bierstaker will receive payment of $1,020 from Wilkicki. Bierstaker will have to record the accrual of interest for the month of January and the receipt of cash. The calculation of interest is the same as the earlier one because another 30 days has passed. Two entries are shown on January 31, 20x2. The first records the accrual of the interest and the second records the cash payment. Recognize that one combined entry could have been made. The entries are:

A-Interest receivable	10	
SE-Interest revenue		10
A-Cash	1,020	
A-Notes receivable		1,000
A-Interest receivable		20

Other entries are possible if the note has been paid off early or if the note is extended for an additional period of time. Another possibility is that the note may be sold to another party. This is the same as factoring accounts receivable. The note may be sold **with** or **without recourse**, meaning that if the maker does not pay the note at maturity, the purchaser of the note will or will not have the right to collect from the payee the amount owed. Further information about the accounting for the factoring of notes receivable can be found in intermediate accounting courses.

Relatively few short-term notes receivable appear on balance sheets, because they are not common and their amounts are relatively small. Normally, notes receivable are grouped with accounts receivable.

FINANCIAL STATEMENT ANALYSIS CONSIDERATIONS

Short-Term Liquidity

As discussed in Chapter 1, liquidity refers to the ability of a company to convert assets into cash to pay liabilities. An important part of the analysis of short-term liquidity comes from considering the short-term monetary assets on the balance sheet. At least two ratios provide quantitative measures of short-term liquidity: the current ratio and the quick ratio.

Current Ratio

The current ratio is measured by comparing the current assets directly with the current liabilities. It is calculated as:

Learning Objective

Using financial statement information, calculate the current ratio, the quick ratio, and the accounts receivable turnover ratio.

$$\text{Current Ratio} = \frac{\text{Current Assets}}{\text{Current Liabilities}}$$

Learning Objective

Explain how the current ratio, the quick ratio, and the accounts receivable turnover ratio help users to understand short-term liquidity issues.

Remember that current assets are those that are going to be converted into cash in the next year or operating cycle of the company, and that current liabilities are going to require the use of cash in the next year or operating cycle. Therefore, this ratio should normally be greater than 1; otherwise, it is difficult to see how the company will remain solvent in the next year. The rule of thumb for this ratio is that for most businesses it should be approximately 2 or greater, to provide a margin of safety. However, the size of this ratio depends on the type of business and the type of assets and liabilities that are considered current.

Refer to the balance sheet of Big Rock Brewery Ltd. in Appendix A at the end of the book. The current ratio for Big Rock in 1999 is:

CURRENT RATIO—BIG ROCK BREWERY: 1999

$$\text{Current Ratio} = \frac{\$4,115,116}{\$2,294,778} = 1.79$$

One caveat: The current ratio is sometimes subject to manipulation by a company at the end of the year. Therefore, this ratio may not be a very reliable measure of liquidity. For example, consider a company that has $100 in current assets and $50 in current liabilities just before the end of a given year. Its current ratio would be 2 ($100/$50). Suppose that $25 of the $100 is in cash and the rest is in inventory. Suppose further that the company uses up all of its $25 in cash by paying off $25 worth of current liabilities at the end of the year. The current ratio becomes 3 ($75/$25). Now the company looks more liquid. Notice, however, that the company is actually less liquid; in fact it is virtually illiquid in the short term, because it has no cash and must sell its inventory and wait until it collects on those sales before it will have any cash to pay its bills. In this case, the current ratio is deceptive. We have therefore developed a second short-term liquidity ratio, the quick ratio, to help provide more information on the company's liquidity.

Quick Ratio

As illustrated in the above example, one of the problems with the current ratio is that some assets in the current section may be much less liquid than others. For example, inventory is less liquid than accounts receivable, which is less liquid than cash. In some industries, inventory is very illiquid because of the long period of time that it may have to be held before sale. Consider, for example, the holding period in the manufacture of 12-year-old Scotch whisky. The current ratio in such cases will not adequately measure the short-term liquidity of the company. The quick ratio is used in this case to assess the short-term liquidity. It differs from the current ratio in that inventories (and often prepaid expenses) are omitted from the numerator. It is calculated as:

$$\text{Quick Ratio} = \frac{\text{Current Assets} - \text{Inventory} - \text{Prepaid Expenses}}{\text{Current Liabilities}}$$

The rule of thumb for this ratio is that it should be approximately 1 or more. Again, the actual value depends somewhat on the type of industry. For Big Rock, the calculation results in:

QUICK RATIO—BIG ROCK BREWERY: 1999

$$\text{Quick Ratio} = \frac{\$4,115,116 - \$2,050,703 - \$433,785}{\$2,294,778} = .71$$

Analysis of Accounts Receivable Using the Accounts Receivable Turnover Ratio

A company's cash flows are critical to its profitability and even to its survival. Because most companies receive a significant amount of operating cash from the collection of their accounts receivable, the analysis of a company's short-term liquidity should consider its success rate in collecting its accounts receivable.

One of the common ratios used to assess the management of accounts receivable is the accounts receivable turnover ratio. This is calculated by dividing the sales revenue for the period by the average accounts receivable, as follows:

$$\text{Accounts Receivable Turnover Ratio} = \frac{\text{Total Sales Revenue}}{\text{Average Accounts Receivable}}$$

Calculation of this ratio from financial statement data is usually based on the assumption that all sales are on account. If the analyst has more detailed information on the composition of sales, some adjustment can be made in the numerator to include only credit sales. In addition, information in the financial statements may indicate that not all receivables are from customers. Therefore, a more sophisticated calculation might include only customer receivables in the denominator, as only these relate to the sales revenue figure in the numerator.

As an example, consider the information provided in Exhibit 6-6 from the 1999 and 1998 financial statements of Big Rock Brewery Ltd.

EXHIBIT 6-6

■ **BIG ROCK BREWERY LTD.**

1999 and 1998 Financial Statements

BALANCE SHEET (Excerpts)

Current assets	1999	1998	1997
Accounts receivable	$1,548,486	$1,302,336	$1,278,196

INCOME STATEMENT (Excerpts)

Sales	$26,466,241	$25,184,850	$24,163,841

A quick review of this information shows that Big Rock's accounts receivable grew slightly, from $1,302,336 in 1998 to $1,548,486 in 1999. This growth in accounts receivable should not be a surprise in that the sales grew as well, from $25,184,850 in 1998 to $26,466,241 in 1999. A detailed analysis in Exhibit 6-7 shows how this growth affected the collection rate.

EXHIBIT 6-7

■ **BIG ROCK BREWERY LTD.**

Accounts Receivable Turnover

$$1999: = \frac{26,466,241}{\frac{(1,548,486 + 1,302,336)}{2}} = \frac{26,466,241}{1,425,411} = 18.57$$

$$1998: = \frac{25,184,850}{\frac{(1,302,336 + 1,278,196)}{2}} = \frac{25,184,850}{1,290,266} = 19.52$$

In this context, "turnover" means the frequency at which the accounts receivable are "turned over," or the frequency at which they are collected in full and replaced by new accounts. Thus the turnover analysis shows that Big Rock's collection record was better in 1998 than in 1999; the turnover decreased from 19.52 to 18.57.

Another way of analyzing performance of accounts receivable collection is to calculate sales based on number of days in the average balance of the receivables. This analysis assumes that the sales are spread evenly over a 365-day year. Based on this calculation, Big Rock's average daily sales increased from $69,000 ($25,184,850/365) in 1998 to $72,510 ($26,466,241/365) in 1999. Therefore, the 1998 average accounts receivable balance of $1,290,266 represents 18.7 days of average sales ($1,290,266/$69,000), and the 1999 average balance of $1,425,411 represents 19.7 days ($1,425,411/$72,510). Thus Big Rock's 1999 balance of accounts receivable represents 1.0 more day than the 1998 balance, indicating that it is a little slower in collecting its receivables in 1999. A comparison should also be made with the company's normal credit terms. If normal credit terms are 30 days, approximately 30 days of sales would be expected to remain uncollected in accounts receivable.

These analyses indicate that Big Rock is a little slower in collecting cash from its accounts receivable in 1999 than in 1998. Even though it is slower, however, the fact that it is collecting the accounts receivable within 20 days is an indication of good collection management.

In doing these analyses, several complicating factors should be considered. For example, some receivables, such as "financing receivables," do not correspond directly to the revenues produced during the period. These may reflect loans made by the company to its customers. Such loans do not immediately generate an equivalent amount of revenue the way sales of goods or services do. Revenue from the financing receivables is earned over time as the loans accrue interest. Therefore, an accounts receivable turnover based on these receivables would have little meaning.

Finally, trends should be considered. For example, in analyzing the performance of a company you may find that the amounts written off over the last several years have been increasing. Whether this is good or bad depends on how the accounts receivable balance has changed over the same period. To address this question, you could calculate a ratio such as amounts written off to the balance in the receivables. If this ratio has been increasing over the last several years, it may represent some relative degradation in the quality of the receivables. If this were to continue, it would not be good news for the company.

Another way of addressing the same issue would be to compare the ratio of the ending balance in the allowance for doubtful accounts to the ending balance in the accounts receivable (before deducting the allowance). An increase in this ratio over time would indicate that a higher percentage of the ending accounts receivable was considered uncollectible. This, too, would be a negative indication.

SUMMARY

In this chapter we have discussed four major types of current assets that either are cash or are about to become cash. We discussed methods for valuing each and the current Canadian practice with respect to valuation. For cash, we spent some time outlining the importance of internal controls. For the temporary investments, we outlined how the lower of cost and market is applied to their valuation. We discussed the measuring and recording of potential bad debts associated with accounts receivable. The discussion of notes receivable included a section on accounting for the interest that is earned on the notes.

The discussion of these four types of current assets was completed with the introduction of three ratios, the current ratio, the quick ratio, and the accounts receivable turnover ratio, which can be used to assess the short-term liquidity of a company.

The next chapter considers the last major component of current assets: inventory. Because of the complexities associated with inventory accounting, an entire chapter is devoted to this discussion. Other current assets that appear on balance sheets from time to time are considered in other chapters in this book. For the remaining current assets, reference to the notes to the company's financial statements or to an intermediate accounting text should help you understand their nature.

SUMMARY PROBLEMS

1. Exhibit 6-8 provides information on the transactions involving short-term investments for Labbé Ltée. Assuming that Labbé prepares financial statements on a quarterly basis, construct the journal entries that Labbé would make each quarter to record these transactions (do not bother making closing entries for income statement accounts). Assume that all dividends are received in cash during the quarter.

EXHIBIT 6-8

■ LABBÉ LTÉE

Temporary Investments Data

Security	Quarter Acquired	Acquisition Cost	Quarter Sold	Selling Price
Alpha Co.	1	$20,000	–	–
Beta Co.	1	$35,000	4	$29,000
Gamma Co.	1	$15,000	2	$19,000

| | Values as at the End of | | | | | | | |
| | Quarter 1 | | Quarter 2 | | Quarter 3 | | Quarter 4 | |
Security	Cost	Market	Cost	Market	Cost	Market	Cost	Market
Alpha	$20,000	$21,000	$20,000	$22,000	$20,000	$17,000	$20,000	$15,000
Beta	$35,000	$32,000	$35,000	$36,000	$35,000	$37,000	–	–
Gamma	$15,000	$14,000	–	–	–	–	–	–
Portfolio	$70,000	$67,000	$55,000	$58,000	$55,000	$54,000	$20,000	$15,000

| Dividends Received | |
Quarter	Amount
1	$650
2	$525
3	$550
4	$150

2. The Gujarathi Company sells goods on credit to its customers. During 20x4, Gujarathi sold $150,000 worth of goods on credit and collected $125,000 from its customers. The company started the period with a balance of $15,000 in accounts receivable and a balance of $450 in the allowance for doubtful accounts. During 20x4, Gujarathi wrote off $2,925 of accounts receivable. Gujarathi estimates that 2% of the sales amount will ultimately be uncollectible. Calculate the amount of bad debt expense that should be recorded. Also, show all journal entries during the period that would affect accounts receivable and the related allowance account.

3. Using the financial statements of Future Shop Ltd. in Appendix B at the end of the book, calculate the current ratio, the quick ratio, and the accounts receivable turnover ratio for 1999. Write a brief interpretation of the ratios.

SUGGESTED SOLUTIONS TO SUMMARY PROBLEMS

1. The journal entries that Labbé Ltée would make each quarter are as follows:

Quarter 1

Acquisition entry:		
A-Investment in Alpha	20,000	
A-Investment in Beta	35,000	
A-Investment in Gamma	15,000	
A-Cash		70,000
Dividend revenue:		
A-Cash	650	
SE-Dividend revenue		650
Unrealized loss/recovery:		
SE-Unrealized loss on valuation of temporary		
investment	3,000	
XA-Valuation allowance for temporary		
investment		3,000
Realized gain/loss on sale:		
No sales this quarter.		

Quarter 2

Acquisition entry:		
No acquisitions this quarter.		
Dividend revenue:		
A-Cash	525	
SE-Dividend revenue		525
Unrealized loss/recovery:		
XA-Valuation allowance for temporary		
investment	4,000*	
SE-Recovery of unrealized loss on		
valuation of temporary investment		4,000
Realized gain/loss on sale:		
A-Cash	19,000	
A-Investment in Gamma		15,000
SE-Realized gain on sale of temporary		
investment		4,000

*Because the portfolio has recovered from its loss position in Quarter 1, the portfolio should now be carried at cost and the balance in the valuation allowance account ($3,000) should be reduced to zero.

Quarter 3

Acquisition entry:		
No acquisitions this quarter.		
Dividend revenue:		
A-Cash	550	
SE-Dividend revenue		550
Unrealized loss/recovery:		
SE-Unrealized loss on valuation of temporary		
investment	1,000	
XA-Valuation allowance for temporary		
investment		1,000
Realized gain/loss on sale:		
No sales this quarter.		

Quarter 4

Acquisition entry:		
No acquisitions this quarter.		
Dividend revenue:		
A-Cash	150	
SE-Dividend revenue		150
Unrealized loss/recovery:		
SE-Unrealized loss on valuation of temporary		
investment	5,000	
XA-Valuation allowance for temporary		
investment		5,000
Realized gain/loss on sale:		
A-Cash	29,000	
SE-Realized loss on sale of temporary		
investment	6,000	
A-Investment in Beta		35,000

2. The following journal entries would be made by Gujarathi Company during the year:

Credit sales:		
A-Accounts receivable	150,000	
SE-Sales revenue		150,000

Collections from customers:		
A-Cash	125,000	
A-Accounts receivable		125,000
Write-off of bad debts:		
XA-Allowance for doubtful accounts	2,925	
A-Accounts receivable		2,925
Recording of annual bad debt expense:		
SE-Bad debt expense	3,000	
XA-Allowance for doubtful accounts		3,000
($150,000 × .02 = $3,000)		

3. Current ratio

$$\frac{\$221,329}{\$253,878} = .87$$

Quick ratio

$$\frac{\$221,329 - \$160,092 - \$1,544 - \$14,343}{\$253,878} = .18$$

Accounts receivable turnover ratio

$$\frac{\$1,960,274}{(\$25,099 + \$15,121)/2} = 97.5$$

$$365/97.5 \qquad = 3.7 \text{ days}$$

Interpretation:

Both the current ratio and the quick ratio fall below the "rule of thumb" amounts. The quick ratio, in particular, indicates that Future Shop has very few liquid assets available to pay for the $219,550 of accounts payable and accrued liabilities that are probably due within the first couple of months of the new fiscal year. An examination of the balance sheet reveals that during the last fiscal year the company activated a line of credit (see Bank indebtedness). It is probably using the line of credit to cover the cash shortfall. A review of the statement of changes in financial position shows a negative cash flow from operations, which is likely the major contributing factor to the cash shortfall.

The accounts receivable turnover is very favourable. It indicates that the accounts receivable are collected every 3.7 days. This is very fast. The ratio is likely distorted. To calculate the ratio, we used the sales amount. We did not have the "credit" sales amount available. Future Shop Ltd. probably sells the majority of its merchandise for cash or by credit card. This means that the majority of its sales amount is probably cash sales. Because it is not possible to determine the credit sales amount, we cannot calculate a more accurate ratio and we should not put much weight on the accounts receivable turnover ratio.

GLOSSARY

Accounts receivable Assets of a seller that represent the promise by a buyer to pay the seller at some date in the future.

Allowance method A method used to value accounts receivable by estimating the amount of accounts receivable that will not be collected in the future.

Bank reconciliation The procedure used to reconcile a company's record of its bank account balance to the record provided by the bank.

Collateral An asset that is pledged against a debt. If the borrower defaults on the debt, the lender receives title to the asset, which can then be sold to cover the amount owed to the lender.

Compensating balances Minimum balances that must be maintained in the bank account to avoid significant service charges or, in some cases, to satisfy restrictive loan covenants (which are clauses in loan agreements that are designed to reduce the risk to the lender).

Compound interest Interest computed by adding the interest earned in a period to the balance in the account and multiplying the total by the interest rate. The interest earned in one period then earns interest itself in the next period.

Direct write-off method A method of recognizing bad debts. Bad debt expense is recognized under this method at the time the account receivable is written off.

Factoring The process of selling the accounts receivable of a company.

Historical cost A valuation attribute or method that values assets at the price paid to obtain those assets.

Lower of cost and market (LCM) A valuation method that reports the value of an asset at the lower of its historical cost and its current market value.

Marketable equity securities Investment in shares that actively trade in a market.

Marketable securities Shares or debt securities that actively trade in a market.

Monetary An attribute of an asset or liability that indicates that the asset or liability represents a fixed number of monetary units.

Monetary unit The nominal units used to measure assets and liabilities. Usually, the monetary unit used is the local currency unit (such as the Canadian dollar).

Nonmonetary An attribute of an asset or liability that indicates that the asset or liability does not represent a fixed number of monetary units. The value of a nonmonetary item can change over time.

Note receivable An asset that represents the right of the holder of the note to receive a fixed set of cash payments in the future.

Percentage of credit sales method A method of estimating the bad debt expense of a company by estimating the expense as a percentage of the credit sales for the period.

Promissory note A document in which the issuer of the note agrees to pay fixed amounts to the holder of the note at some point in the future.

Purchasing power An attribute of an asset that measures its ability to be exchanged for goods and services.

Realized gain/loss A gain or loss from the sale of an asset or liability that is the result of a completed transaction (in general, it means that cash or an agreement to pay cash has been received in exchange for the asset or liability).

Recourse A provision in agreements to sell receivables in which the buyer of the receivables has the right to return a receivable to the seller if the buyer cannot collect the receivable.

Recovery (accounts receivable) The reinstatement and collection of an account receivable that was previously written off.

Recovery (marketable securities) An unrealized gain from revaluing the portfolio of marketable securities according to the lower of cost and market rule.

Secured note A note receivable secured by collateral.

Security A financial instrument, usually a share or a debt, that may be publicly traded.

Simple interest Interest that is calculated by multiplying the interest rate in the agreement by the principal involved. Interest earned in one period does not earn interest in a subsequent period.

Uncollectible accounts Accounts receivable that are deemed to be uncollectible. The point at which they are uncollectible is generally established by company policy.

Unit-of-measure assumption An assumption made under Canadian GAAP that all transactions are measured using a common unit, the Canadian dollar.

Unrealized gain/loss A gain or loss recognized in the financial statements that has not resulted in the receipt of cash or the right to receive cash, but represents a change in value of an asset.

Valuation allowance An account used to hold the adjustments necessary to lower the carrying value of the temporary investments from historical cost to market value when the market value is lower.

Write-off The process by which an account receivable is removed from the books of a company when it is deemed uncollectible.

ASSIGNMENT MATERIAL

Assessing Your Recall

6-1 Briefly describe how cash, temporary investments, accounts receivable, and notes receivable meet the criteria of probable future value and ownership to qualify as assets.

6-2 Explain what the unit-of-measure assumption means in accounting.

6-3 Discuss why cash is subject to purchasing power risk and why inventory may or may not be subject to this risk.

6-4 Describe the process that accountants use to establish the lower of cost and market value for temporary investments.

6-5 What are the guidelines accountants use to decide if an investment should be classified as a temporary investment?

6-6 Describe and compare the direct write-off method and the allowance method for determining bad debt expense. Is one more consistent with GAAP than the other?

6-7 Describe two ratios that measure current liquidity. Compare the information they provide.

6-8 Describe a ratio that measures the management of accounts receivable and explain what information it provides.

Applying Your Knowledge

6-9 (Preparation of a bank reconciliation)
The Comet Company reconciles its bank account every month. At July 31, 20x2, the bank balance according to its general ledger cash account was $4,643.22 but the bank statement at July 31 showed a balance of $7,582.45. After every item on the bank statement was compared to the detailed transactions recorded in the ledger, the following items were noted. The cheques that were not yet cashed were: cheque number 466 dated July 29 for $1,250.00, cheque number 467 dated July 30 for $520.00, cheque number 468 dated July 31 for $360.50, and cheque number 470 dated July 31 for $1,350.75. The deposit made on July 31 for $1,532.02 was not yet recorded by the bank. The July bank service charges of $25.00 had not been recorded by Comet. On the bank statement, the bank reported that it had collected a note receivable for Comet. The face amount of the note was $1,000 and there was an additional $15 collected for interest owed on the note.

Required:

a. Prepare a bank reconciliation at July 31.

b. How much cash does Comet actually have in its account at July 31?

c. Prepare adjusting journal entries to record all necessary adjustments to bring the cash account to its adjusted balance.

6-10 (Placement of items on a bank reconciliation)

Henrietta Walters is attempting to prepare a bank reconciliation. Indicate whether each of the following items would be added to the bank balance, deducted from the bank balance, added to the cash account balance, or deducted from the cash account balance. If any items do not have to be included, explain why.

a. The bank indicates that two cheques received by Walters and deposited in her account had been returned as uncollectible (NSF).

b. A monthly service charge has been deducted from the account by the bank.

c. Two cheques written by Walters were paid by the bank; however, Walters had forgotten to record them in the cash account.

d. Cash received by Walters during the last day of the month and deposited that evening was not shown as deposits by the bank.

e. An automatic deduction for Walters's electricity bill was made by the bank. She had recorded the amount in the cash account earlier in the month.

f. A loan to Walters from the bank reached maturity during the month and was deducted by the bank from the bank account. Walters had forgotten about the loan coming due.

g. A customer deposited an amount owed to Walters directly into Walters's bank account. Walters had not recorded it yet.

h. An outstanding deposit from the previous month was shown as having been received by the bank at the beginning of the month.

i. Five cheques written by Walters during the month had not yet cleared the bank.

6-11 (Reconciliation of personal bank account)

Peter Hayes notices that the balance recorded in his cheque-book is $840, which is $440 less than the balance shown on his bank statement. Examining the cheques included with the bank statement, he sees that three cheques he wrote, totalling $432, have not yet cleared the bank. Also, he notices that a cheque that did clear was written for $86 but mistakenly recorded in his cheque-book as $68. In addition, a $15 cheque given to him by a co-worker was returned because of insufficient funds, and an automatic deposit for $50 was made to his account but not yet recorded by him. The bank also deducted a service charge, but the bank statement is smeared and he cannot determine the amount of the charge. Calculate the bank service charge.

6-12 (Temporary investments)

Duggan Company purchased 100 preferred shares of Green Company for $25 each on March 1, 2000. It also purchased 200 common shares of White Company for $40 per share on that date. At December 31, 2000, the preferred shares of Green were selling at $26 and the common shares of White were selling at $32. Duggan Company considers the shares to be a temporary investment.

Required:

a. At what amount will the investments be reported in the December 31, 2000, balance sheet?

b. Will any other balance sheet or income statement accounts be affected by the accounting treatment of these securities? If so, which accounts will be affected, and what will the effect be?

6-13 (Dividends earned on temporary investments)

During 2000, Duggan received dividends from the two companies in Problem 6-12. Green Company paid preferred dividends of $2 per share, and White paid a common dividend of $3.50 per share.

Required:

a. If Duggan Company reports income of $45,000 from operations (before any financing income or expenses) during 2000, what amount of net income will it report for the year?

b. Duggan Company has a goal of attaining a 10% annual return on investments. Has Duggan reached its goal for 2000?

6-14 (Temporary investments)

The following transactions relate to the TinCan Company for 20x1 and 20x2. TinCan closes its books on December 31 each year.

Transactions:

20x1

March 25	TinCan purchases 2,500 shares of Meta-Solid Corp. at $20 per share. It also pays fees to its stockbroker of $0.20 per share.
June 30	The market value of each share of Meta-Solid is $23.
August 15	Meta-Solid declares a dividend of $0.50 per share.
October 25	Dividend cheque is received from Meta-Solid Co.
December 31	The market value of each share of Meta-Solid is $25.

20x2

February 18	500 shares of Meta-Solid Corp. are sold at the prevailing market price of $24.50 per share. Brokerage fees are $0.15 per share.

Required:

a. Prepare journal entries for recording all of the preceding transactions in the books of TinCan Company. Assume that the shares purchased are considered to be temporary investments. Note that we have not discussed fees to stockbrokers or brokerage fees in the chapter. In answering this question, use your knowledge of accounting to determine a logical method of recording them.

b. What amount of temporary investments would appear in TinCan's balance sheet at December 31, 20x1?

6-15 (Temporary investments and the lower of cost and market)

The Corona Company holds a portfolio of temporary investments. The aggregate cost and aggregate market value of the entire portfolio in four years is as follows:

Dates	Aggregate Cost	Aggregate Market Value
Dec. 31, 20x1	$250,000	$210,000
Dec. 31, 20x2	300,000	280,000
Dec. 31, 20x3	320,000	325,000
Dec. 31, 20x4	350,000	345,000

Required:

a. Give the necessary journal entries for each year. The accounting period ends on December 31 each year.

b. What amount of temporary investments would appear in Corona's balance sheet for each of these years?

6-16 (Temporary investments and the lower of cost and market)
Upper Company purchased 500 shares each of Jack, Queen, and King Companies on June 30, 2000, at a cost of $45, $30, and $100, respectively, per share. On December 31, 2000, the market values of the shares were $41, $38, and $95, respectively. Upper Company considers the shares to be temporary investments.

   a. At what amount will the investments be reported in the December 31, 2000, balance sheet of Upper Company?

   b. Will any other balance sheet or income statement accounts be affected by the accounting treatment of these securities? If so, which accounts will be affected, and what will the effect be?

6-17 (Dividends earned on temporary investments)
During 2000, Upper received dividends of $5, $7, and $12 per share from the common shares of, respectively, Jack, Queen, and King Companies acquired in Problem 6-16.

   Required:

   a. If Upper Company reports income from operations of $640,000 for 2000, what amount will it report for net income for the year after the dividend revenue is added?

   b. If Upper Company has a goal of earning a 20% annual return on its temporary investments, has it reached its goal for 2000?

6-18 (Temporary investments including lower of cost and market)
The following information relates to the temporary investments held by Trimex Corp. as current assets.

Security	Acquisition Date	Acquisition Cost	Date Sold	Selling Price	Market Value Dec. 31 20x1	20x2	20x3
A	Mar. 13/x1	$ 35,000	NA	NA	$ 38,000	$ 30,000	$ 33,000
B	June 24/x1	65,000	May 27/x2	70,000	60,000	NA	NA
C	Oct. 8/x2	95,000	NA	NA	88,000	100,000	90,000
D	Aug. 3/x3	100,000	June 30/x3	105,000	102,000	98,000	NA

Trimex Corp. closes its books on December 31 each year.

   Required:

   a. Prepare journal entries relating to these temporary investments for each year.

   b. Show how the marketable securities would be presented on the income statement and balance sheet for each year.

6-19 (Temporary investments)

The following information relates to Faun & Faun Inc. for the year ended December 31, 20x2.

Balance sheet at December 31, 20x2

Current assets	
Temporary investments—at cost	$313,000
Less: Valuation allowance for temporary investments	13,000
Net balance (lower of cost and market)	$300,000

The income statement includes the following:

	20x1	20x2
Unrealized loss on valuation of temporary investments		($ 3,850)
Recovery of unrealized loss on valuation of temporary investments	$ 2,000	
Realized gain (loss) on sale of temporary investments	(4,950)	(5,650)
Net income	96,325	103,825

During 20x2, the company sold temporary investments for $50,000 in cash. These investments had a market value of $53,000 on December 31, 20x1. The company also purchased new temporary investments, at a cost of $85,000.

Required:

a. Compute the cost of the temporary investment sold in 20x2, and create the necessary journal entry to show the sale of the investment.

b. Compute the beginning balance (at cost) of the temporary investment for the year 20x2.

c. Compute the beginning balance in the valuation allowance for temporary investments for the year 20x2.

6-20 (Accounts receivable and uncollectible accounts)

The trial balance of P & S Inc. shows a $50,000 outstanding balance in the accounts receivable account at the end of its first year of operations, December 31, 20x1. During this fiscal year, 75% of the total credit sales had been collected and no accounts had been charged off as uncollectible. The company estimated that 1.5% of the credit sales would be uncollectible. During the following fiscal year, the account of James Cordon, who owed $500, was judged uncollectible and was written off. At the end of the year, on December 31, 20x2, the amount previously written off was collected in full from Mr. Cordon.

Required:

a. Prepare the necessary journal entries for recording all of the preceding transactions in the books of P & S.

b. Show the accounts receivable section of the balance sheet at December 31, 20x1.

6-21 (Accounts receivable and uncollectible accounts)

Dundee Company started business on January 1, 2000. The company made credit sales of $750,000 during 2000 and received payments of $680,000 to the end of the year. It also wrote off as uncollectible $12,000 of its receivables when it learned that the customer who owed the $12,000 had filed for bankruptcy. Other than the entry to write off the $12,000, Dundee Company has made no entries related to bad debt expense for the period. The industry average for bad debt expense for companies similar to Dundee is 3% of credit sales. If Dundee uses the allowance method of accounting for bad debts and adopts the industry percentage in estimating bad debt expense for 2000:

  a. What should be the balance reported in the allowance for doubtful accounts at December 31, 2000?

  b. What accounts receivable balance would be reported in the balance sheet at December 31, 2000?

  c. Evaluate the reasonableness of the balance in the allowance for doubtful accounts at December 31, 2000.

6-22 (Accounts receivable and uncollectible accounts)

The Sabre Razor Company's accounts receivable show the following balances at October 31, 20x1, before adjustment: accounts receivable: $1,348,000; allowance for doubtful accounts: $11,000 (credit). Total sales for the year then ended were $21,500,000. Sabre has a policy that 1% of its sales on credit are expected to be uncollectible. Of the total sales, 20% are cash sales and 80% are made on credit.

Required:

  a. Prepare the necessary journal entry to record the bad debt expense for the year.

  b. Show the accounts receivable section of Sabre's balance sheet at October 31, 20x1.

  c. What amount of bad debt expense would appear in the income statement for the year ended October 31, 20x1?

6-23 (Accounts receivable and uncollectible accounts)

The Ace Company's credit sales during the first year of its operations were $925,000. On December 31, 20x1, the accounts receivable had a debit balance of $125,000. Management estimated that 2% of all credit sales would be uncollectible. The company wrote off accounts worth $5,650 at the end of the first year.

On December 31, 20x2, the unadjusted trial balance showed the following:

	Debit	Credit
Accounts receivable	$138,000	
Allowance for doubtful accounts	6,350	
Credit sales		$1,250,000
Bad debt expense	-0-	

After reviewing the write-off of accounts receivable during 20x2, the company decided that the estimate of uncollectibility should be increased from 2% to 2.5%.

Required:

  a. Give the journal entry to record the bad debt expense for 20x2.

  b. Prepare a T-account for the allowance for doubtful accounts and enter into the account all of the transactions that have affected it since the company started operations.

  c. What is the net accounts receivable at the end of 20x2?

6-24 (Note receivable with interest calculations)

On March 1, 2000, Moon Company determined that it would not be able to pay the accounts receivable that it owed to Gamma Company. Moon was confident that it would have the necessary cash near the end of the year. It therefore signed a nine-month, 11% note for the $10,000 that was owed. This note was recorded at its face amount. On August 31, 2000, Gamma Company closed its books for the year.

Required:

a. Prepare all of the necessary journal entries associated with this note up to the end of August 31, 2000, assuming that the interest that is owed on this note will be paid when the note matures (when it is due).

b. Prepare the journal entry to record the payment by Moon of the amount owed to Gamma.

6-25 (Note receivable with interest calculations)

On February 1, 2000, Skeemo Company sold equipment to South Company for $18,040. In payment for the equipment Skeemo accepted a six-month, 14% note. The interest is payable when the note matures. Skeemo's year end is June 30.

Required:

a. Prepare all of the necessary journal entries associated with this note, including the end of year entries and the receipt of payment from South.

b. What items would be included on the balance sheet and income statement of Skeemo on June 30 with respect to this note?

6-26 (Note receivable with interest calculations)

On October 1, 2000, the Sussex Bank lent $2,800 to Cynthia Tsang to buy a laptop computer. She was expecting to have $3,000 at the end of January 2001 when a GIC she owned matured. Cynthia signed a four-month note with interest at 9%. All interest is to be paid at the end of January when the note is due. The year end of Sussex Bank is December 31.

Required:

a. Calculate how much interest has been earned by Sussex Bank by the end of December and by the time the note is due.

b. Prepare the journal entries that Sussex Bank would make at the end of December and when the note is collected in full.

6-27 (Current and quick ratios)

The following amounts were reported by Liquid Company in its most recent balance sheet:

Cash	$ 25,000
Accounts receivable	70,000
Short-term investments	10,000
Inventory	210,000
Prepaid insurance	30,000
Accounts payable	45,000
Wages payable	20,000
Income tax payable	25,000
Sales tax payable	6,000
Short-term notes payable	60,000

Required:

a. Calculate the current ratio and the quick ratio for Liquid Company.

b. Based on a review of other companies in the industry, the management of Liquid Company thinks it should maintain a current ratio of 2 or more and a quick ratio of 1 or more. The ratios at the end of the prior year were 1.8 and 1.2, respectively. How successful has the company been in achieving the desired results this period?

c. How could the company improve its current position?

6-28 (Liquidity decisions)

The following balance sheet accounts and amounts are found at year end on the books of Faraday Products Company:

Building and equipment	$230,000
Tax refund receivable	3,000
Bonds payable (long-term)	125,000
Prepaid insurance	5,000
Accumulated amortization	90,000
Taxes payable	16,000
Inventory	80,000
Wages payable	20,000
Accounts receivable	62,000
Unearned service revenue	26,000
Retained earnings	60,000
Trademarks (capital assets)	35,000
Common shares	120,000
Cash	44,000
Accounts payable	47,000
Land	45,000

Required:

a. Prepare a classified balance sheet in good form.

b. Compute the amount of Faraday's working capital (current assets minus current liabilities).

c. At the beginning of the period, Faraday reported total current assets of $120,000 and current liabilities of $55,000. Compute the current ratios for Faraday at the beginning and end of the period. Has the current ratio improved or declined during the period?

d. At the beginning of the current period, working capital was $65,000. Has Faraday's working capital position and its overall liquidity improved or declined during the year?

e. How might Faraday evaluate the adequacy of its overall liquidity?

6-29 (Cash flow analysis)

The Smythe Company balance sheets for 1999 and 2000 and income statement for the year 2000 are given below. In addition to these statements, the following information is available:

Transactions:

1. There were no sales of property, plant, or equipment during 2000.

2. No dividends were declared or paid during 2000.

3. Temporary investments costing $75 were sold for $100.

Smythe Company
Balance Sheet
At December 31

	2000	1999
Assets		
Cash	$ 540	$ 500
Accounts receivable	900	850
Allowance for doubtful accounts	(15)	(10)
Temporary investments	600	500
Allowance for doubtful accounts	(100)	(50)
Inventory	1,800	1,350
Property, plant, and equipment	8,000	5,800
Accumulated amortization	(2,800)	(1,800)
Total assets	$ 8,925	$7,140
Liabilities and Shareholders' Equity		
Accounts payable	$ 1,700	$1,550
Common shares	3,000	3,000
Retained earnings	4,225	2,590
Total liabilities and shareholders' equity	$ 8,925	$7,140

Smythe Company
Income Statement
For the year ended December 31, 2000

Revenues		$10,000
Cost of goods sold		6,500
Gross profit		3,500
Expenses:		
Bad debt expense	$ 150	
Amortization	1,000	1,150
Operating income		2,350
Unrealized loss on valuation of		
temporary investments		(50)
Realized gain on sale of		
temporary investments		25
Income before taxes		2,325
Income taxes		690
Net income		$1,635

Required:
Prepare a statement to show why cash increased from $500 to $540.

Management Perspective Problems

6-30 (Estimation of uncollectibility of accounts receivable)
Suppose that there is a stock option plan at the SeeSaw Company that rewards managers for achieving a certain level of reported net income. What incentives might management have for influencing the estimation of uncollectibility of accounts receivable?

6-31 (Market value of temporary investments and decision-making)
As a loan officer at a bank, why would you be interested in the market value of temporary investments? Would you want them *recorded* at their market value or would you be satisfied with the lower of cost and market valuation? Explain your reasoning.

6-32 (Bank reconciliation and decision-making)
As a manager of a company, explain why a bank reconciliation is important to your management of cash.

6-33 (Accounts receivable and uncollectibility)
Ontario Company is involved in the manufacture and sale of high-quality racing and mountain bicycles. At the end of 2000, Ontario Company's balance sheet reported total accounts receivable of $250,000 and an allowance for doubtful accounts of $22,000. During 2001, the following events occurred:

1. Credit sales in the amount of $1,250,000 were made.

2. Collections of $1,050,000 were received.

3. Ontario recorded bad debt expense for 2001 as 3% of credit sales.

4. Customers with total debts of $18,000 to Ontario were declared bankrupt and those accounts receivable were written off.

As the Director of Finance for Ontario Company, you have been asked by a member of the executive committee to:

a. Analyze the above activities by giving the journal entries to be recorded by Ontario for each of the transactions.

b. Illustrate Ontario's balance sheet disclosure of accounts receivable at December 31, 2001.

c. Evaluate the adequacy of Ontario's allowance for doubtful accounts at December 31, 2001.

6-34 (Accounts receivable and uncollectible accounts)
Lowrate Communications is involved in the cellular phone market. The following selected information is taken from the financial statements of Lowrate Company (in thousands of dollars):

	2001	2000	1999
Accounts receivable (net)	$ 1,469.8	$ 1,230.6	$ 1,044.8
Allowance for doubtful accounts	128.9	121.9	118.0
Accounts written off	309.9	270.2	296.8
Bad debt expense	312.4	271.5	267.0
Net operating revenues	12,661.8	11,367.8	10,420.0

Required:

Based on the information from Lowrate's financial statements, answer the following questions:

a. What percentage of total accounts receivable is considered uncollectible in each of the three years presented?

b. What percentage of sales is bad debt expense in each of the three years presented?

c. Did Lowrate's collection of accounts receivable improve over the three-year period?

d. The cloning of cellular phones currently is a serious problem. Cloning involves copying access/billing codes from cellular phones belonging to others. Cellular phone companies typically absorb charges for unauthorized calls on cellular phones, amounts in the thousands of dollars. If cloning continues to be a problem as the cellular industry grows, how would this affect the financial statements of a company like Lowrate?

Reading and Interpreting Published Financial Statements

6-35 (Cash and temporary investments)
Information from the balance sheet of Air Canada at December 31, 1998, shows a cash and short-term investments balance of $366 million in 1998 and $650 million in 1997. Note 1d to the financial statements states: "Cash and short-term investments include short-term investments of $295 million (1997 $611 million). All short-term investments may be liquidated promptly and have maturities of less than one year."

Required:

a. Explain why the short-term investments are included with the cash.

b. Describe what you think are the cash management policies of Air Canada.

6-36 (Cash and temporary investments)
In the balance sheet of MOSAID Technologies Incorporated, shown in Exhibit 6-9, cash is described as "Cash and short-term marketable securities." Why are cash and short-term marketable securities shown together?

6-37 (Accounts receivable turnover)
Using data for MOSAID Technologies Incorporated (Balance sheet in Exhibit 6-9 and income statement in Exhibit 3-21), calculate the accounts receivable turnover ratios for 1998 and 1997 using balances of accounts receivable at each year end rather than average balances. Use revenues from operations rather than total revenues. Comment on the ratios and trend.

6-38 (Accounts receivable turnover ratio)
The following appeared in the 1998 balance sheet of Domtar Inc. (in millions of dollars):

	1998	1997
Receivables, net of allowance for doubtful accounts of $12 (1997 – $7)	$ 322	$ 242
The following amounts were reported as Sales on the income statement (millions of dollars)	$2,348	$1,938

EXHIBIT 6-9

MOSAID Technologies Incorporated (INCORPORATED UNDER THE ONTARIO BUSINESS CORPORATIONS ACT)
Consolidated Balance Sheets

(in thousands)

	As at	
	May 1, 1998	May 2, 1997
Current Assets		
Cash and short-term marketable securities	$ 19,625	$ 18,337
Accounts receivable	9,489	11,250
Revenues recognized in excess of amounts billed	4,003	3,656
Inventories (Note 2)	5,512	4,490
Prepaid expenses	476	576
	39,105	38,309
Capital Assets (Note 3)	14,593	7,440
Technology Acquisitions (Note 4)	1,239	995
Long-term Investments (Note 5)	5,814	1,712
	$ 60,751	$ 48,456
Current Liabilities		
Accounts payable and accrued liabilities	$ 5,150	$ 4,988
Mortgage payable (Note 6)	128	–
Income taxes payable	1,069	301
Deferred revenue	630	636
Deferred income taxes	430	383
	7,407	6,308
Mortgage Payable (Note 6)	5,842	–
Deferred Income Taxes	461	713
	13,710	7,021
Shareholders' Equity		
Share capital (Note 7)	21,220	20,825
Retained earnings	25,821	20,610
	47,041	41,435
	$ 60,751	$ 48,456

See accompanying Notes to the Consolidated Financial Statements.

Thomas I. Csathy
Director

Robert F. Harland
Director

Required:

a. What percentage of accounts receivable is considered to be uncollectible in 1998 and 1997?

b. Calculate the accounts receivable turnover for 1998 and 1997 using the balance of the receivables for each year rather than the average receivables. Convert the turnover into the number of days that it takes to collect a receivable.

c. For 1998, reconstruct the journal entries to record transactions relating to sales and collections of accounts receivable assuming that all sales were on account.

6-39 (Accounts receivable, uncollectible accounts, and the turnover ratio)
On the 1998 balance sheet of Suncor Energy Inc. the accounts receivable balance is given as $190 million in 1998, $267 million in 1997, and $292 million in 1996. Note 3 to the financial statements states that the allowance for doubtful accounts for those years was $3 million, $3 million, and $9 million, respectively. Sales on the income statement were reported as $2,068 million (1998), $2,148 million (1997), and $2,097 million (1996).

Required:

a. What percentage of accounts receivable is considered to be uncollectible in 1998, 1997, and 1996?

b. Although sales increased between 1996 and 1997, the allowance for doubtful accounts decreased dramatically. Suggest some reasons why this occurred.

c. Calculate the accounts receivable turnover for 1998 and 1997 using the average of the receivables. Convert the turnover into the number of days that it takes to collect a receivable. What do you observe?

d. For 1998, reconstruct the journal entries to record transactions relating to sales and collections of accounts receivable assuming that all sales were on account.

6-40 (Accounts receivable)
Sears Canada is a major department store chain that sells merchandise on account to customers through its Sears card. In its 1998 financial statements, it includes the following note about its accounts receivable:

2. Charge Account Receivables

Details of charge account receivables are as follows:

(in millions)	1998	1997
Charge account receivables	$1,682.5	$1,655.7
Less: amounts securitized	(1,087.5)	(965.6)
Net charge account receivable	$ 595.0	$ 690.1

Required:

a. What do think Sears Canada means when it says its accounts receivable have been "securitized"?

b. How does a company like Sears Canada protect itself from customers defaulting on amounts charged against credit cards?

Beyond the Book

6-41 (Examination of a company's financial statements)
Acquire the financial statements of a large retail company such as the Hudson's Bay Company, a large resource-industry company such as MacMillan Bloedel Ltd., and a large bank such as the Royal Bank of Canada. Prepare a short report in which you include the following:

a. An in-depth analysis of the cash and other financial asset balances held by each company. Be sure to review the balance sheet accounts and all related notes.

b. An examination of the cash flow statement in search of the major sources of cash inflows and outflows during the past year. Did the companies borrow money during the year? Did they issue shares?

c. A list comparing the operating characteristics of the companies that might affect the amount of financial assets they have on hand. For example, which of the three businesses is likely to have the most dependable and predictable cash inflows and outflows? Which of the three companies realizes the most profits from holding financial assets?

6-42 (Examination of a company's financial statements)
Choose a company as directed by your instructor and answer the following:

a. Prepare a quick analysis of the cash (and equivalents), marketable securities, accounts receivable (gross), and allowance for doubtful accounts by listing the beginning and ending amounts in these accounts and calculating the net change in both dollar and percentage terms for the most recent year.

b. If any of the accounts in part a. has changed more than 10%, give an explanation for this change.

c. If the company has any temporary investments, list the cost and market value of the securities at the beginning and end of the current year and calculate any unrealized gain or loss (if possible) that was recognized during the year. If there was an unrealized gain or loss, describe where it was reported in the financial statements.

d. Compute the following ratios for the most recent two years:

Bad debt expense divided by net sales

Allowance for doubtful accounts divided by gross accounts receivable

Accounts receivable turnover (in times and days)

Comment on both the reasonableness of these ratios and on any significant changes in these ratios.

Case

6-43 Saintjay Supplies Limited
Saintjay Supplies Limited is concerned about its ability to pay its debts. Analyze the information provided below and explain why Saintjay is experiencing problems with its cash balance. What can Saintjay do to reduce these problems?

Saintjay Supplies Limited
Selected Financial Information (in thousands)

Years Ended March 31	1999	2000	2001
Sales on credit	$12,700	$14,100	$17,100
Cash	310	50	10
Temporary investments	25	-0-	-0-
Accounts receivable	1,180	1,510	1,980
Inventories	940	1,250	1,470
Short-term bank loans	-0-	240	760
Accounts payable	610	390	440
Other short-term liabilities	80	80	80

Critical Thinking Questions

6-44 (Temporary investments)
The balance sheet, statement of income, and statement of changes in financial position for Petromet Resources Limited at December 31, 1998, are shown in Exhibit 6-10. Analyze the Investments in the Current Assets and related amounts in the other statements and notes.

Required:

a. Reconstruct the journal entries that would have been made by Petromet in 1996 relating to these temporary investments.

b. Explain what changes occurred in the investments in 1998. Why is it confusing?

6-45 (Accounts receivable)
The balance sheet and Note 3 of Semi-Tech Corporation at March 31, 1998, are shown in Exhibit 6-11.

Required:

a. Describe the policies used by Semi-Tech to record its accounts receivable, paying particular attention to sales that are payable by instalment receivables. Advance reasons why Semi-Tech uses these policies.

b. What alternative policies could Semi-Tech use to record instalment receivables?

EXHIBIT 6-10
PART A

balance sheets

DECEMBER 31 ($ THOUSANDS)		1998		1997
ASSETS				
Current				
Cash	$	147	$	204
Accounts receivable		9,408		8,430
Inventory		2,261		1,912
Investments		125		125
		11,941		10,671
Property, plant and equipment (Note 2)		202,348		152,517
	$	214,289	$	163,188
LIABILITIES				
Current				
Accounts payable and accrued liabilities	$	11,258	$	13,705
Long-term bank debt (Note 3)		60,986		19,814
Convertible debentures (Note 4)		23,530		23,250
Future abandonment and site restoration costs		2,262		1,661
Deferred income taxes		8,623		6,891
SHAREHOLDERS' EQUITY				
Share capital (Note 5)		86,538		78,980
Paid-in capital (Note 4)		2,800		2,800
Retained earnings		18,292		16,087
		107,630		97,867
	$	214,289	$	163,188

See accompanying notes.

On Behalf of the Board:
(Director)   (Director)

EXHIBIT 6-10
PART B

statements of income

YEAR ENDED DECEMBER 31 ($ THOUSANDS, EXCEPT PER SHARE)	1998	1997	1996
REVENUE			
Petroleum and natural gas	$ 39,369	$ 33,927	$ 27,911
Royalties, net of Alberta Royalty Tax Credit	(5,519)	(5,802)	(4,258)
	33,850	28,125	23,653
EXPENSES			
Operating	4,894	3,548	3,191
General and administrative	2,430	1,127	1,373
Depletion and depreciation	17,096	11,924	9,496
Interest on long-term debt	4,911	2,854	3,178
	29,331	19,453	17,238
Income before other item and taxes	4,519	8,672	6,415
Gain on sale of investments	-	-	3,738
Income before taxes	4,519	8,672	10,153
Taxes (Note 7)	2,314	4,275	4,035
Net income	$ 2,205	$ 4,397	$ 6,118
Earnings per share	$ 0.05	$ 0.11	$ 0.18
Weighted average number of common shares outstanding	43,644,058	38,522,103	34,347,166

statements of retained earnings

YEAR ENDED DECEMBER 31 ($ THOUSANDS)	1998	1997	1996
Balance, beginning of year (Note 2)	$ 16,087	$ 11,690	$ 5,572
Net income	2,205	4,397	6,118
Balance, end of year	$ 18,292	$ 16,087	$ 11,690

EXHIBIT 6-10
PART C

statements of changes in financial position

YEAR ENDED DECEMBER 31 ($ THOUSANDS)	1998	1997	1996
Cash provided by (used in)			
Operating activities			
Net income	$ 2,205	$ 4,397	$ 6,118
Items not affecting cash:			
Depletion and depreciation	17,096	11,924	9,496
Deferred income taxes	1,881	3,960	3,774
Amortization of debt discount	280	280	280
Gain on sale of investments	-	-	(3,738)
Cash flow from operations	21,462	20,561	15,930
Change in non-cash working capital related to operations	(979)	570	(472)
	20,483	21,131	15,458
Investing activities			
Property, plant and equipment, net	(66,447)	(49,569)	(23,167)
Site restoration expenditures	(58)	(54)	-
Purchase of investments	-	-	(1,650)
Sale of investments	-	-	5,388
Change in non-cash working capital related to investments	(3,091)	3,583	1,112
	(69,596)	(46,040)	(18,317)
Financing activities			
Common shares, net of issuance costs	7,588	20,797	9,578
Long-term bank debt	41,172	4,290	(7,356)
Change in non-cash working capital related to financing	296	19	72
	49,056	25,106	2,294
Increase (decrease) in cash	(57)	197	(565)
Cash, beginning of year	204	7	572
Cash, end of year	$ 147	$ 204	$ 7

See accompanying notes.

EXHIBIT 6-11
PART A

consolidated financial statements

(Incorporated under the laws of Ontario)

**CONSOLIDATED
BALANCE SHEETS**

(As at March 31, 1998 and 1997)

In millions of U.S. dollars		March 31, 1998		March 31,1997
				Restated – Notes 1(c) and 1(p)
ASSETS				
Current Assets:				
Cash and cash equivalents	$	53.6	$	239.9
Accounts receivable		538.7		591.7
Inventories		395.4		346.5
Prepaid expenses		10.7		13.1
Total current assets		998.4		1,191.2
Investments in Operating Affiliates		372.4		366.8
Property, plant and equipment, net		359.7		349.9
Future income tax assets		84.2		–
Other assets, including goodwill of $421.9 (1997 – $653.0)		531.1		701.4
	$	2,345.8	$	2,609.3
LIABILITIES AND SHAREHOLDERS' EQUITY				
Current Liabilities:				
Notes and loans payable	$	473.7	$	524.7
Accounts payable and accrued liabilities		415.1		343.1
Future income tax liabilities		6.5		2.4
Total current liabilities		895.3		870.2
Long-term debt		781.9		641.5
Pension obligations		159.7		56.3
Other non-current liabilities		51.7		32.7
Total liabilities		1,888.6		1,600.7
Non-controlling interests		266.8		338.2
Contingencies (Notes 9 and 15)				
Shareholders' Equity:				
Capital stock		669.8		669.8
Contributed surplus		0.4		0.4
Cumulative translation adjustment		(7.3)		8.8
Deficit		(472.5)		(8.6)
Net shareholders' equity		190.4		670.4
	$	2,345.8	$	2,609.3

(See accompanying notes to consolidated financial statements)

On behalf of the Board:

(signed) Frank E. Holmes   (signed) Douglas A.C. Davis
        Director   Director

EXHIBIT 6-11
PART B

3. ACCOUNTS RECEIVABLE

	March 31, 1998	March 31, 1997
Trade:		
Installment	$ 168.5	$ 183.3
Other	389.5	335.3
Miscellaneous	78.3	139.1
	636.3	657.7
Less:		
Unearned carrying charges	24.7	35.0
Allowances for doubtful accounts	72.9	31.0
	$ 538.7	$ 591.7

Tracking the Books In Halifax

Until about five years ago, the staff at Dalhousie University's bookstore, as at almost any other retail operation, had to periodically carry out the tedious task of taking manual inventory of the store's thousands of books—not to mention clothing, giftware, stationery supplies, and other items—in order to get a reasonably accurate picture of how many of its items had been sold.

Today, however, thanks to sophisticated inventory and bookkeeping systems that connect to point-of-sale terminals, the store has a perpetual inventory system that is tracked entirely by computer.

"At any time, we can tell how many copies of a title we have in stock," explains Chris MacNeil, Accounting Supervisor at the store, which is located in Halifax. "The system tracks each book from the time it is ordered to the time it is sold—and beyond, if it is returned—by its ISBN." The staff also enter the relevant information when books are returned to the publisher, as they periodically are because too many copies were purchased or a course was cancelled.

State-of-the-art systems like the one at Dalhousie can produce reports on everything from weekly sales by category to the value of current inventory (which the Dalhousie bookstore, like most Canadian businesses, tracks according to first-in, first-out, or FIFO, principles). They cannot do everything, however. If a book purchased in the United States is returned, for example, adjustments have to be made for any changes in the exchange rate. "We'll get back the exact same amount in U.S. dollars that we paid for it," points out Mr. MacNeil, "but if the dollar has gone down in the meantime, then we've taken a loss in Canadian dollars. Of course, it can work out in our favour just as easily."

Another thing the system cannot do is let you know when items have been stolen. Unless an item is recognized through the sales terminal, the system thinks it is still there. "We have had to stick resonant marker strips onto some of our merchandise, like the books, that activate alarms at the doors if someone attempts to take them out of the bookstore," explains Mr. MacNeil. "This stops most of the theft. We still do a count at the end of the year to ensure the accuracy of our records. Over the last five years, the discrepancy between our records and the annual inventory count has been small, so we're definitely doing something right."

chapter 7

INVENTORY

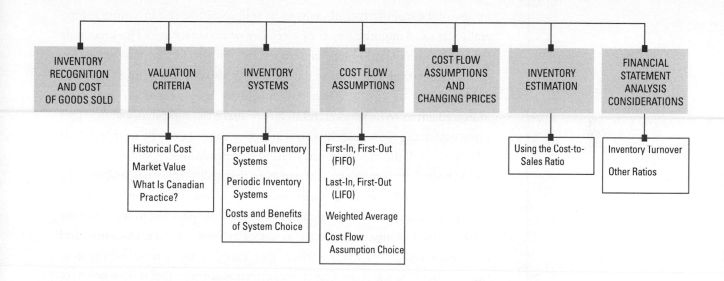

Learning Objectives:

After studying this chapter, you should be able to:

1. *Discuss the importance of inventory to the overall success of a company.*
2. *Describe the evaluation criteria used for inventory in Canada.*
3. *Describe how the lower of cost and market rule is applied to inventory.*
4. *Explain the difference between the perpetual inventory system and the periodic inventory system.*
5. *Discuss some criteria used by companies when choosing an inventory system.*
6. *Describe the three cost flow assumptions and calculate cost of goods sold and ending inventory under each assumption.*
7. *Explain the shortcomings of LIFO and why it is rarely used in Canada.*
8. *Describe the impact of inflation on each of the cost flow assumptions.*
9. *Estimate a value for ending inventory using the cost-to-sales ratio method.*
10. *Calculate the inventory turnover ratio and explain how it can be interpreted by users.*

Purchasing, stocking, and selling inventory is a complicated process. Through the use of a computerized inventory system, the bookstore at Dalhousie University in our opening vignette has attempted to make that process easier. Now it can get information more quickly so that it knows which items are selling and which are not, which items need re-ordering and which need to be returned. The article mentioned terms like FIFO and perpetual inventory system. As you study this chapter these items will be explained to give you a better understanding of how the bookstore is managing its inventory.

Inventory is any item purchased by a company for resale to customers, or for use in the manufacture of items to be sold to customers. Inventory is generally the most important asset of a retailer or manufacturer. The success or failure of the company is dependent upon its ability to buy or make inventory with a unit cost lower than its selling price. It is also dependent upon the company's ability to buy or make the inventory that people want to buy. Management must be very careful to buy or make the right items, at the right price, and in the right quantities so that sufficient profit can be made on their sale to cover all the other necessary business expenditures.

Visualize, for a moment, a music store that sells CDs, tapes, and movies. Imagine the complications that can arise with inventory: The store must select from its suppliers' lists the music and movies that people want to buy, in quantities that will ensure it does not run out of an item (called a **stockout**) and force buyers to go elsewhere—where they may buy more than just the item that was out of stock at the first store. It must make sure that it does not have too many items in inventory, because there are storage and handling costs associated with inventory on hand, as well as the risk of obsolescence. It must also make sure that it sets prices that are competitive yet high enough to provide sufficient profit for the company. The store must also provide safeguards so that people cannot steal the inventory. Complicating this decision even further are the variety and volume of items typically sold by any one company.

The management of inventory can sometimes entail unforeseen problems. Note what happened to the retail business in a small Ohio town discussed in 'Accounting in the News' on the following page.

Learning Objective

Discuss the importance of inventory to the overall success of a company.

When you think about inventory you probably think about items you have purchased recently in stores. Inventory includes those items, but also much more. To a property developer, inventory is land and buildings; to an oil and gas company, it is oil in the ground; to a recycler, it is old newspapers and aluminum cans. Exhibit 7-1 provides two other examples of inventory.

accounting in the news

INVENTORY AND Y2K

While rushing to fill orders is a sign of success for many small-business owners, Galen Lehman and employees at Lehman's Hardware & Appliances have found themselves overwhelmed by a flood of new customers fearful of a Y2K meltdown. For the past 40 years, the Lehman family, who are Mennonites, have run a store and catalogue business selling electricity-free equipment, mainly among the Mennonites and the Amish.

A referral on a Y2K website changed that. By January 1999, fully a third of Lehman's business was coming from people trying to protect themselves from the direly predicted Y2K mayhem. Lehman had to install an answering service, update his web page, and hire more employees. And then there was the problem of inventory: Many of his suppliers were tiny Amish businesses who could not keep up with the orders.

These are the headaches of growth. And Lehman pointed out that this rush of business wouldn't even do him much good financially. How could he react in a meaningful way knowing the added business would last only a few months?

Source: "Y2K orders swamp Mennonite shop owner," by Karen Thomas, *National Post (Financial Post)*, Jan. 29, 1999, page C10.

■ Examples of Inventory

EXHIBIT 7-1

Suncor Energy Inc. is an integrated oil and gas company operating in the tarsands in northern Alberta. The first example below shows Note 6 from its 1998 annual report, which describes its inventory.

Comac Food Group Inc. owns and holds franchise interests in a chain of retail bakery cafés, retail coffee shops, and restaurants in Canada. Note 4 from its 1998 annual report lists its inventory items. Note how the value of the stores held for resale has greatly declined from the previous year.

Suncor Energy Inc.
Excerpt from the Notes to the Statements

6. Inventories
($ millions)

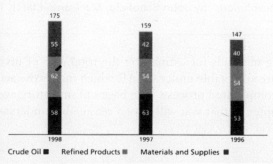

	1998	1997	1996
Crude Oil ■	58	63	53
Refined Products ■	62	54	54
Materials and Supplies ■	55	42	40
	175	159	147

©1997–1998—Suncor Energy Inc. Used with permission

EXHIBIT 7-1
CONT.

■ Comac Food Group Inc.
Excerpt from the Notes to the Statements

4. Inventories
Inventories are comprised of the following:

	1998	1997
Franchise stores under construction	$507,000	$ 98,000
Stores held for sale	294,000	858,000
Ingredients, uniforms and selling supplies	150,000	170,000
	$951,000	$1,126,000

Investment in inventory can be substantial, so companies manage inventory levels carefully to maximize their returns and minimize their costs. The following article about Wal-Mart Canada describes its strategy for inventory management:

accounting in the news

INVENTORY MANAGEMENT IN THE RETAIL BUSINESS

Only five years after stepping into the Canadian market, Wal-Mart has changed the face of this country's retailing industry. With more than 150 outlets nationwide, Wal-Mart Canada Inc. accounts for 30% of department store sales—and it continues to expand. The key to its success lies in great part in its distribution system, viewed as the world's most efficient: In Canada, Wal-Mart has the highest rate of stock turnover of all department stores.

The company invested billions of dollars in the creation of Wal-Mart Retail Link, a computer system that tracks inventory from the point of shipping to the moment it leaves the store. The company has its own satellite to transmit the information. Suppliers are required to make deliveries to distribution centres within a 15–30-minute window; missing shipments can mean fines. Because Wal-Mart has 3,600 stores around the world, it can negotiate cutthroat prices from suppliers that translate into retail prices as low, for high-turnover items, as some retailers pay wholesale.

Source: "The Retail Revolution," by John Schofield, *Maclean's*, March 1, 1999, pages 34–36.

A variety of accounting methods for estimating the total cost of inventory have been developed and are acceptable under GAAP, which makes the accounting for inventory a fairly complicated process. The basics of inventory accounting are covered in this chapter so that you will have a reasonable understanding of how inventory is measured, recorded, and reported. You can then use this information to make informed evaluations of companies.

INVENTORY RECOGNITION AND COST OF GOODS SOLD

Does inventory meet the criteria for being an asset? The probable future value associated with inventory is measured by the company's ability to sell it in the future, and to use the proceeds to buy other goods and services. Since inventory has not yet been sold, the collection of cash from its sale is even more uncertain than the collection of accounts receivable. All the uncertainties associated with the collection of accounts receivable also apply to inventory. Two others are unique to inventory: the availability of buyers, and obsolescence/spoilage. If a sufficient number of buyers cannot be found at the initial price set for the product or service, the price may have to be changed in order to attract buyers. As for obsolescence and spoilage: Computer hardware, for instance, is at considerable risk of technological obsolescence; spoilage, on the other hand, is a major factor for food inventories.

Ownership of inventories is evidenced by possession and, sometimes, by legal title. Ownership of low-priced inventories is usually evidenced by possession, because it is impractical to keep track of legal title to such inventories. They are very much like cash in terms of management. Adequate controls must be maintained so that the inventory is not lost or stolen. Ownership of high-priced inventories may also be evidenced by possession, but in this case there are also legal documents to prove ownership. The ownership of automobiles, for instance, is evidenced by registration.

The fact that the company has possession of inventory indicates that a transaction has occurred. Inventory, therefore, meets the recognition criteria for an asset, and should be recorded as such in the company's accounts. The amount that is placed in the accounts depends on the valuation or measurement criteria that are applied.

Cost of goods sold represents the expense side of an asset. Once inventory is sold, it is no longer an asset. Its cost is reported on the income statement as cost of goods sold and is matched against the revenue that its sale generated. Determining what that cost is can be problematic. Much of the discussion in this chapter will centre around establishing an appropriate cost for the inventory and for the cost of goods sold.

VALUATION CRITERIA

The valuation method allowed under GAAP is a combination of several valuation approaches. GAAP generally specifies cost, but it recognizes that the cost figure used should not differ materially from recent cost. If it does, the company can use one of a number of methods to recognize a decline in inventory value. Before discussing GAAP in detail, however, we need to examine these different approaches to valuation.

Learning Objective

2

Describe the evaluation criteria used for inventory in Canada.

Historical Cost

One possible valuation method is to carry inventory at its historical cost. According to this method, inventory is recorded at its cost on the date it was acquired. In the purest application of the historical cost method, no recognition is made of changes in the market value of the inventory while it is held. Income is recognized only when the inventory is sold. At that time, a profit or loss is recorded.

Market Value

A second possible valuation method is to carry inventory at its market value. When this method is applied, the term **market** must be more clearly defined. Inventory really has two markets. The first is the market in which the company buys its products. In the case of a retailer, this is called the **wholesale market**. For a manufacturing company, there is no one market in which the company buys its inventory, because it incurs numerous costs in constructing its product. If the market price can be found in the market where the inventory is bought, the term **replacement cost** is used. Replacement cost refers to what it would cost the company to replace the product today. The market in which these products are acquired is called the **input market**, or **entry market** (or wholesale market), since this is the market from which the products enter the company.

Another measure of market value might be obtained from the market in which the company *sells* its products. This is called the **retail market**. The company, of course, hopes that prices in the retail market are higher than those in the wholesale market so that it can earn a profit. The markets in which companies sell their products are also sometimes referred to as **output markets**, or **exit markets**. In accounting terminology, the exit price is sometimes referred to as the **net realizable value** (NRV), which is defined as the net amount that can be realized from the sale of the product in question. Net realizable value is not the same as selling price. The "net" part of NRV refers to the company's need to net some costs against the selling price. For example, there are generally some selling costs that must be incurred to sell a product. Net realizable value is, then, the selling price less the costs necessary to sell the item. In a manufacturing company, some inventory is not ready for sale (work in process). Net realizable value, in this case, is the selling price less the selling costs as well as the costs necessary to complete the item.

There is one final issue with regard to the definition of market. The markets referred to in the preceding paragraphs are assumed to be the normal markets in which the company does business. There also are markets for goods that must be sold quickly (such as in a "fire sale") or in abnormally large or small quantities. The prices in these markets do not reflect the value of inventory in its normal use and should not be used in valuing inventory of a **going concern** (a company that will continue to operate in the foreseeable future). These markets may be important in valuing inventory, however, if the company is in bankruptcy or going out of business. Under these distress conditions, normal accounting procedures would not be appropriate, because the conditions violate the **going-concern assumption** that underlies GAAP financial accounting.

Replacement Cost

If a company uses a pure replacement cost valuation system, inventory is carried at its replacement cost. At acquisition, replacement cost is the same as historical cost. As the company holds the inventory, however, unrealized increases and decreases in value are recognized as the replacement cost of the inventory changes. The balance sheet reflects the replacement cost of the inventory at the end of each period, and the income statement shows the unrealized profits and losses. At the time of sale, the only additional profit or loss that is recognized is the difference between the replacement cost at the date of sale and the selling price. This difference is called a *realized profit or loss*.

Net Realizable Value

In a pure net realizable value system, inventory is recorded at its net realizable value. At the date of acquisition, a profit or loss is recorded equal to the difference between the historical cost and the net realizable value. This system requires that, while the inventory is held, changes in net realizable value be recognized as unrealized profits or losses. At the time of ultimate sale no profit is recognized, because the item has already been recorded at its net realizable value.

What Is Canadian Practice?

The application of historical cost is used extensively in Canada. When the use of historical cost results in a figure that is materially different from recent cost figures, companies should apply a lower of cost and market (LCM) rule at the end of the period. This treatment is very similar to the treatment given to temporary investments. Market, as defined here, is most commonly either replacement cost or net realizable value. In Canada, most companies describe their inventories as being valued at the lower of cost and market. In order to help you to understand the implications for inventory, we will first discuss what should be included in the cost of inventory, and then consider how to apply the LCM rule.

Acquisition Costs

The value assigned to inventory should contain all **laid-down costs**. For a retailer, laid-down costs include the invoice price as well as any customs duties, tariffs, or excise duties, in addition to freight and cartage costs. As a practical matter, it is often difficult to assign the exact dollar amount of freight and cartage to a specific item of inventory. Imagine, for example, that a major grocery store receives a new shipment of inventory containing everything from cereal to heads of lettuce. It would be totally impractical to assign freight costs to a single head of lettuce. Therefore, many companies do not assign these costs to inventory, but instead treat them as period costs (for the period in which they are incurred). The shipping costs, often called **transportation in**, or **freight in**, may be assigned to inventory but are more commonly treated as period costs in the cost of goods sold calculation. The calculation of cost of goods sold was first introduced in Chapter 2. With the inclusion of transportation costs, the calculation becomes:

Beginning inventory
+ Purchases
+ Transportation in
= Goods available for sale
− Ending inventory
= Cost of goods sold

For a manufacturing company the inventory costs are more complicated. Typically, a manufacturing company buys materials that it intends to use to make new products. These materials are called **raw materials** and their cost is kept in a raw materials inventory account. The costs assigned to this account include the cost of the materials plus any transportation costs. The company takes the raw materials and begins to make its new products. The process of manufacturing involves additional costs such as the labour costs of the workers, the costs of the machines and buildings, the cost of utilities to run the facilities in which the manufacturing occurs, and so on. The labour costs associated with manufacturing are referred to as **direct labour**, and all of the other, more indirect, costs are referred to as **overhead**. The manufacture of a typical product entails raw materials, direct labour, and overhead.

A company uses three inventory accounts in the manufacturing process: a raw materials inventory account, a work-in-process account, and a finished goods account. The **work-in-process account** collects all of the costs (raw materials, direct labour, and overhead) that are incurred as the product is being made. Once the product is complete, the full cost of making it is transferred from the work-in-process account to the **finished goods account**. Products that are sold are deducted from the finished goods account. Exhibit 7-2 diagrams how the costs flow through the three inventory accounts to cost of goods sold.

■ Manufacturing Cost Flows

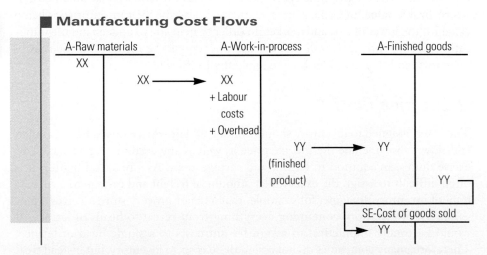

Exhibit 7-3 presents the 1998 inventory disclosure of a manufacturing company, Moore Corporation Limited. Moore Corporation Limited is an international supplier of business forms and a leading provider of information management and business communications services. Moore provides paper and electronic forms and related products such as manual forms, computer forms, labels, commercial printing services, and mailing systems. Moore also offers communications services such as the printing, processing, and distribution of invoices and statements.

EXHIBIT 7-3

■ **Moore Corporation Limited**

Excerpt from the Notes to the Statements

2. INVENTORIES

IN THOUSANDS	1998	1997
Raw materials	$ 42,175	$ 52,584
Work in process	17,620	23,048
Finished goods	112,248	114,584
Other	4,607	5,047
	$176,650	$195,263

AN INTERNATIONAL PERSPECTIVE

Reports from Other Countries

Most countries require that overhead costs be included as a part of the carrying value of inventory. However, some countries, including India, Chile, and Denmark, require that overhead costs be treated as period expenses. The disclosure from Danisco (an international food-industry company in Denmark) illustrates this treatment:

Stock

Raw material, consumables, and goods for resale are entered at the lower of cost or market price. The value of finished goods and goods in course of production is fixed at the value of the material involved and the direct production costs.

Lower of Cost and Market

Because inventory is crucial to the success of companies in the retail and manufacturing industries, users are very interested in its value. When inventory is listed as a current asset on the balance sheet, users assume that it will be sold in the subsequent period for at least its stated value, and, more optimistically, at a profit. During an accounting period, economic circumstances may arise that negatively affect the value of the inventory. At the end of every accounting period, most companies compare the cost of the inventory to its market value and apply the lower of cost and market (LCM) rule. The rule is similar to that applied to temporary investments, discussed in Chapter 6. Companies can use either the **direct method** or the **allowance method**. Under the direct method the ending inventory is reduced to the lower market value. In the subsequent year the lower market value becomes part of cost of goods sold when it becomes the beginning inventory. Under the allowance method the inventory account remains at the original cost and an

Learning Objective
3

Describe how the lower of cost and market rule is applied to inventory.

allowance account is used to hold the decline in value. The allowance account, which is shown contra to the inventory on the balance sheet, is usually adjusted each year to reflect the changing value of the inventory (similar to the treatment of the allowance used with temporary investments). The lower of cost and market rule can be applied to individual items, to pools of similar items, or to the inventory as a whole. Because it is generally impractical to apply it on the basis of an individual item, companies will use either pools of similar items or the total inventory.

AN INTERNATIONAL PERSPECTIVE

Reports from Other Countries

In Canada, the LCM is usually applied on a total inventory basis, because companies are required to use the total inventory basis for tax purposes. It is more efficient to apply this method for both purposes.

In the United States, the LCM is more commonly applied on an individual item basis, because the U.S. tax department requires the application on an individual basis.

Under the direct method, the unrealized losses that result from the application of the LCM rule are often hidden in the cost of goods sold expense. Remember that the cost of goods sold calculation is:

Cost of beginning inventory
+ Purchases
+ Transportation in
= Goods available for sale
− Ending inventory
= Cost of goods sold

If the market value of the inventory is lower than the calculated cost, ending inventory is assigned the lower value. If the ending inventory value goes down, the cost of goods sold expense goes up, thereby incorporating the loss. Under this method, users will not know how large the loss was.

Under the allowance method, a separate loss account is created to hold the amount of the loss. It is usually called Loss Due to Market Decline of Inventory. This loss account could be listed separately on the income statement but is more frequently summarized with other expenses listed after Cost of Goods Sold. Similar to the direct method, under the allowance method the amount of the loss is frequently not known. Companies probably would disclose the inventory loss in value as a separate item on the income statement if it was a material amount. They could also discuss it in a note to the financial statements.

To determine the appropriate market value to use in applying the LCM rule, we need to go back to the discussion about market value. In Canada, companies usually define market as net realizable value, or net realizable value less a normal profit margin, or replacement cost. The most common value is net realizable value (NRV). This makes sense, because if the selling price has dropped below the cost, the company will likely experience a loss in the next period when the inventory is sold. Because the decline in value occurred in the current period, we reduce the value of the inventory in the current period. Then, when it is sold in the next period, it will sell at no profit if the selling price does not change. The option of net realizable value less a normal profit margin reduces the inventory value even more in the current period, so that when it is sold in the next period it will sell at a profit. This option is not used very often, but it is available to companies under GAAP. When replacement cost is used, often it is applied to inventory that is used to manufacture items rather than to inventory that is held for resale.

Exhibit 7-4 presents the inventory disclosure for Western Star Trucks Holdings Ltd., which designs and assembles highly customized automotive vehicles. Note that it uses net realizable value as well as specific identification, standard, and first-in, first-out in its inventory disclosure. More will be said about these other cost bases later in the chapter.

■ Western Star Trucks Holdings Ltd.

Excerpt from the Notes to the Statements

Inventories

Inventories are stated at the lower of cost and net realizable value. Cost is determined for trucks, buses and work in process on a specific identification basis and for parts and components using standard costs which approximate costs determined on a first in first out basis.

AN INTERNATIONAL PERSPECTIVE

Reports from Other Countries

Most countries require the application of the lower of cost and market rule. Some countries, including the United States, refer to it as the lower of cost or market rule. The application of this rule, however, can vary across countries. The *market* value used in the rule is interpreted to mean replacement cost in some countries (Italy and Japan, for example), whereas it is interpreted as net realizable value in many more countries (France, Germany, and the United Kingdom, for example). The **International Accounting Standards Committee (IASC)** defines market value as net realizable value. Very few countries allow the flexibility that exists under Canadian GAAP. The United States uses all three values for market when it requires that, regardless of how high the replacement costs are, the company cannot carry the inventory at a value higher than net realizable value (called a ceiling value). As well, the carrying value cannot be lower than net realizable value less a profit margin (called a floor value). Another difference with the United States is that it views the writedown of inventory as permanent. Almost all other countries (including Canada) either require or permit the recovery of value back to original cost if the market recovers.

INVENTORY SYSTEMS

Now that we have discussed the valuation of inventory in a general way, we need to look at the various systems that companies have developed to manage the volume and variety of inventory that they purchase and subsequently sell. Keeping track of inventory units and their associated costs is essential to the profitable management of a company. Information concerning the units sold and those in inventory is necessary for intelligent decision-making on pricing, production, and re-ordering. An inventory system keeps track of this information. As you saw in our opening story, computerized inventory systems are greatly facilitating the task of inventory management.

At least two types of information about inventory are required. The first relates to the number of units sold during a period and the number that remain. This information is needed to establish a value for cost of goods sold, to trigger the re-ordering of inventory, or to set the level of production for the current period. It may also be necessary to fill sales orders. The second type of information concerns the cost of goods sold during the period and the cost of goods that remain. This information is needed to prepare the financial statements, to evaluate performance, and to make pricing decisions.

Some inventory systems keep track of units of inventory but not their cost; others keep track of both units of inventory and their cost. Systems that keep track of units but not costs are referred to as *physical inventory systems*. In major grocery chains, for example, the cash registers are connected to computers that record the sale of each item of inventory when the item is scanned for its bar code. The computerized inventory system is programmed to trigger new orders when the number of items remaining drops to a predetermined level. Unless the computer program is very sophisticated, it will not identify the purchase cost of the item sold. Systems that keep track of the number of units and the costs associated with units of inventory are referred to as *cost inventory systems*. A cost inventory system can most easily be implemented when the inventory items are uniquely identifiable. For example, a car dealership records the unique characteristics of each vehicle that it buys for resale. When a vehicle is sold, it is relatively easy to record the sale of that specific vehicle and to record its original cost to the dealer. A grocery store, on the other hand, would not be able to determine the original cost of a can of peas because it would have no way of identifying the case from which the can was sold. The bar code on the can tells the computer simply that it is a can of peas of a particular brand. With the increasing sophistication of computer technology, more businesses will be able to convert to cost inventory systems and manage their inventories in a more detailed fashion.

Whatever inventory system is used, it is important for you to understand how inventory flows through it. To illustrate: Consider the inventory T-account in Exhibit 7-5. The company starts the period with a certain amount of beginning inventory, which in a physical inventory system is the number of units and in a cost inventory system is the number of units times the cost of those units. These amounts are known from the end of the last period. The number of units purchased and the cost of those purchases are known from the invoices for the period (in the case of a manufacturer, the debits are for direct materials, labour, and overhead, all of which are known during the period). What is unknown is the cost of goods sold (the number of units sold in a physical system) and the cost (number) of units left in ending inventory. The sum of the cost of the beginning inventory and the cost of purchases is known as the cost of **goods available for sale**. The problem is deciding how to divide the total cost between the cost of goods sold and the cost of those that remain in ending inventory. Whatever inventory system is in place, it must be able to allocate the goods available for sale between the cost of goods sold and ending inventory.

■ Inventory Information

	A-Inventory		
Beginning balance	KNOWN		
Purchases	KNOWN	?????	Cost of goods sold
Ending balance	?????		

EXHIBIT 7-5

The choice of inventory system depends on the type and size of inventory involved and the cost of implementing the system. We will discuss two general types of inventory systems: perpetual and periodic.

Perpetual Inventory Systems

A **perpetual inventory system** keeps track of units or their associated costs, or both, on a continual basis. This means that, as soon as a unit is sold, it (or its cost) is immediately removed from the inventory account. In terms of the T-account in Exhibit 7-5, a credit is made to the account at the time of sale. The ending balance in the account can be computed at any time to provide information about what is left in the account. In this type of system, the ending inventory balance and the cost of goods sold account are always up to date in terms of units or costs. Therefore, the information provided by this type of system is the most timely for decision-making purposes. This is the system used by the Dalhousie University bookstore in the opening story.

Up-to-date information, which is useful in any business, is crucial in some businesses, such as car dealerships. In the automobile business, the sales personnel must know what stock is still available for sale so that a car is not sold twice. Because selling prices are negotiated and the cost of cars may vary dramatically, the cost of a specific car must be known at the time of sale so that an appropriate profit margin will be earned on the sale. The dealer's profitability depends on up-to-date information. Fortunately, the cost of keeping track of this information on a perpetual basis is not very high, because the number of units of inventory is relatively small.

Contrast this situation with that faced by the owner of a hardware store. Here, prices are not negotiated at the time of sale, but rather each item is pre-priced and the stated price is what the customer pays. Therefore, knowing the cost of each unit on a per-sale basis is not necessary. The amount of inventory must be known in order to re-order stock, but re-ordering is probably not done on a daily basis. The cost of keeping track of each inventory item on a perpetual basis would be fairly substantial,

■**Learning Objective**
4

Explain the difference between the perpetual inventory system and the periodic inventory system.

because the hardware store deals with numerous items in relatively large quantities. Consider, for example, using the perpetual system to keep track of all of the nuts and bolts of various types the store sells. The cost to implement a perpetual system in this case would probably outweigh the benefits of having up-to-date information. The hardware store would therefore probably develop a periodic inventory system.

Periodic Inventory Systems

In a **periodic inventory system**, there is no entry to record the reduction in inventory at the time of sale. This may be because a perpetual inventory tracking system is too expensive to maintain, or it may be because the cost of the item sold is not known at the time of sale. In a retail store, for example, clerks know the retail price of an item because it is written on the sales tag, but they probably do not know the cost of the item to the store. To determine the amount sold and the amount left in inventory, the company must periodically stop business and physically count the units that are left, then assign costs to them. The cost of goods sold is then determined by subtracting the ending inventory value, established by the count, from the sum of the beginning inventory value and the purchases made during the period. This process assumes that all items included in the cost of goods sold were indeed sold, which may not always be the case. If items were stolen or misplaced they would not be on the shelves or in the warehouse when the inventory was counted, and we would assume they had been sold. With a periodic inventory system, the company does not have up-to-date information during the period regarding the level of inventory or the cost of goods sold. Therefore, it must develop other methods to determine re-order points.

The counting and costing of ending inventory can be an expensive process, particularly for companies with large amounts of inventory. The company must close during the counting process and perhaps even turn away business. It must also pay individuals to do the counting. Because of the cost, it generally makes sense to count inventory only once a year. For internal control purposes, some companies count key items of inventory more frequently than once a year and prepare financial statements more frequently than once a year. Accountants have developed estimation methods that are used to establish inventory values for these interim reports.

A company may use a perpetual system to keep track of the physical units (remember the use of bar codes in the grocery store) but, because of the difficulty in determining unit costs, use a periodic system to assign costs to units. This type of mixed system provides up-to-date information regarding the number of units available to aid in re-ordering or in making production decisions. It does not provide up-to-date cost information. This may be perfectly acceptable to management if up-to-date unit information is more important than cost information.

Learning Objective

5

Discuss some criteria used by companies when choosing an inventory system.

Costs and Benefits of System Choice

One of the key factors in the choice of inventory system is the cost of maintaining it. The perpetual system provides better information than the periodic system but does so at a higher cost. However, as the cost of computer technology continues to decline, perpetual systems have become a real possibility for companies that formerly would not have considered them. For example, the introduction of the bar code scanner in the grocery business has allowed grocers to keep track of units of inventory on a perpetual basis. Further, with the introduction of **Electronic Data Interchange** (EDI) some retailers use this information to automatically re-order inventory directly from the wholesaler or manufacturer.

One advantage of the perpetual system that we have not discussed is that it can identify **inventory shrinkage**. *Shrinkage* is a general term that refers to losses of inventory due to theft, damage, or spoilage. Periodic systems cannot identify shrinkage because it appears as a part of the cost of goods sold when the ending inventory value is subtracted from the beginning inventory plus purchases. A perpetual system can identify shrinkage because the system tells the company what the ending inventory should be. The company can then do a count to see what is actually left in its physical inventory. The difference is the shrinkage. Physically counting the inventory is necessary under both systems; the fact that shrinkage can be identified under the perpetual system is a bonus. Companies using perpetual systems may, however, stagger the counting of inventories so that not all items are counted at the same time. The closest a periodic system can come to a perpetual system in the identification of shrinkage is through the use of estimation methods. A company may be able to estimate how much inventory should be on hand; when it counts the inventory it can compare it with the estimated amount and get a crude measure of shrinkage.

accounting in the news

INVENTORY SHRINKAGE

Large shrinkage costs are worrisome because they can signal an inability to manage inventory. When T. Eaton Co. Ltd. reported results for its first year as a public company in March 1999, year-end losses included $10 million in higher-than-expected inventory shrinkage costs. The department store chain even closed stores for two hours one day to count inventory.

Analysts expressed worries that Eaton's did not have its inventory under control. In response, Eaton's indicated it would handle the problem by improving anti-theft efforts. The chain, a Canadian institution, has been under the microscope in financial circles since it filed for bankruptcy protection in 1997 and had to be restructured.

Source: "Eaton's posts $72M loss in first year as public company," by Zena Olijnyk, *National Post (Financial Post)*, March 17, 1999, pages C1, 6.

Note: Analysts were right to be concerned about Eaton's management of its inventory. In August 1999 the company declared bankruptcy and turned its assets over to a liquidator.

The cost of an inventory system must be balanced against the benefits of the information it provides. The main benefit of the perpetual system is its timely information. When inventory information is needed on a timely basis for pricing, re-ordering, or other important functions, the benefits of the perpetual system must be carefully considered even though this system is likely to be more expensive.

COST FLOW ASSUMPTIONS

In order to determine the cost of goods sold and the cost of ending inventory, a company must somehow link the cost of specific units to the actual physical units that either were sold (cost of goods sold) or remain in ending inventory. For some businesses, this is not difficult because the physical units are unique and records specifically identify the unit and its cost. Under these circumstances, the company can match the physical units with their costs using the **specific identification** method. Western Star Trucks (Exhibit 7-4) would be able to identify the cost of each unit in its inventory. Each vehicle would have its own invoice price and registration number and therefore would be unique.

In some businesses, the ability to specifically identify costs of individual physical units is not feasible. Consider a shoe retailer that buys shoes in multiple styles, sizes, and colours in a single order. If the retailer never ordered the same shoe again, it would be possible to determine the cost of a specific pair of shoes. However, once a second order is placed and arrives at the store, it is no longer possible to identify whether a specific pair of shoes came from the first order or the second, unless the retailer took the time to mark the second purchase to distinguish it from the first. It is unlikely that retailers would incur the additional cost of specifically identifying each new order. Therefore, in businesses in which specific identification is not feasible, a logical assumption is generally made about how costs flow through the company.

Learning Objective

6

Describe the three cost flow assumptions and calculate cost of goods sold and ending inventory under each assumption.

POSSIBLE COST FLOW ASSUMPTIONS

1. The first item purchased is the first item sold (FIFO).

2. The last item purchased is the first item sold (LIFO).

3. The cost of the items is determined using a weighted average of the cost of the items purchased.

Note as we go through the following assumptions that we are discussing *cost flows*, not *physical flows*. We will be suggesting logical assumptions for cost flows that may be completely opposite to the way inventory physically flows through the company. To illustrate these assumptions, we will use the data in Exhibit 7-6 for Ted's Toasters, Inc.

Three cost flow assumptions—first-in, first-out (FIFO), last-in, first-out (LIFO), and weighted average—form the basis of three logical ways of assigning costs to units sold or remaining in inventory. FIFO assumes that the first unit purchased is also the first unit sold, hence first-in, first-out. LIFO assumes that the last unit purchased is the first unit sold, hence last-in, first-out. Weighted average assigns an average cost to both cost of goods sold and ending inventory. Let us look at each of these approaches in more detail.

ethics in accounting

■ The determination of the ending balance in inventory is crucial not only for determining the balance sheet value for inventory, but also for establishing the cost of goods sold for purposes of the income statement. Any overstatement of ending inventory will result in an understatement of cost of goods sold and, therefore, an overstatement in income. There are many situations that put pressure on managers and employees to show higher net income, such as budget targets and bonus plans. There may also be incentives to overstate ending inventory—for example, if it is to serve as collateral for loans. Also, auditors are interested in establishing ending inventory values and typically are required, under audit guidelines, to be present at the physical count of ending inventory to make sure inventory values are appropriately determined.

Ted's Toasters starts the period with six toasters in inventory. Note that the beginning inventory cost is $84 and that the unit cost is $14. Only in the very first period of operations are the beginning values in inventory the same under all three assumptions. Because different cost flow assumptions assign costs to units in different ways, in subsequent periods each assumption will result in different per-unit amounts being assigned to ending inventory, which in turn becomes beginning inventory for the next period. Each of these cost flow assumptions is discussed in the following subsections. Refer to Exhibit 7-6 as each method is discussed.

■ **Ted's Toasters, Inc.**

EXHIBIT 7-6

Inventory of toasters

Date		Units	Unit cost	Total
January 1	Beginning inventory	6	$14.00	$ 84.00
January 10	Purchase #1	20	14.25	285.00
January 20	Purchase #2	10	14.50	145.00
Goods available for sale		36		$514.00

Sale record

		Units	Unit price	Total
January 15	Sale #1	12	$32.00	$384.00
January 25	Sale #2	15	32.50	487.50
		27		$871.50

First-In, First-Out (FIFO)

The **first-in, first-out,** or **FIFO,** method is still the most commonly used method in Canada, although weighted average is a very close second. FIFO assigns the first costs to the first units sold. This means that ending inventory units will be matched to costs for the most recent purchases. One way to visualize this method is to consider the flow through a pipeline, as shown in Exhibit 7-7. Purchases enter one end of the pipeline. As new purchases are made, they enter the same end of the pipeline, pushing the first purchases further into the pipe. Goods that get sold come out the other end of the pipeline. Therefore, the ones that get sold first are also the ones that entered the pipeline first. The goods still left in the pipeline at the end of the period are the ending inventory. While the acronym FIFO is appropriate for this method, it refers to what happens to the cost of goods sold, not to the ending inventory. A more accurate acronym for ending inventory is **LISH,** for **last-in, still-here.**

EXHIBIT 7-7

■ **FIFO Visualization**

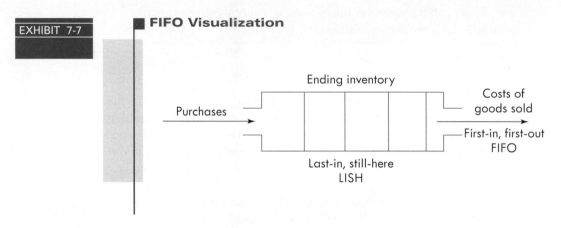

Using the data for Ted's Toasters (Exhibit 7-6) and the FIFO assumption, we can assign a cost to the cost of goods sold and ending inventory as follows:

Cost of goods sold (27 units)

6	units @ $14.00 (beginning inventory)	$ 84.00
+ 20	units @ $14.25 (first purchase)	285.00
+ 1	unit @ $14.50 (second purchase)	14.50
27	units	$383.50

Ending inventory (9 units)

9	units @ $14.50 (second purchase)	$130.50

Note how the sum of units in cost of goods sold and ending inventory (27 + 9) equals the 36 units in goods available for sale. The sum of the dollar amounts ($383.50 + $130.50) equals the dollar amount of the goods available for sale, $514.00. If the dollar amount of ending inventory were to increase, the dollar amount of the cost of goods sold would have to decrease, because the sum of the two must add up to the dollar amount of the goods available for sale. Any errors in counting ending inventory or assigning costs will have an immediate impact on the cost of goods sold and, therefore, net income.

FIFO describes fairly accurately the physical flow of goods in most businesses. For example, in grocery stores new items are put behind old items on the shelf so that old items are sold first. If the grocery store did not rotate inventory in this way, some items would sit on the shelf for months, risking spoilage.

Under GAAP, the matching of costs to physical units does not depend on the physical flow of goods. GAAP attempts to provide the best measure of periodic net income, which is not necessarily achieved by choosing a cost flow assumption that matches the physical flow of the goods. Under FIFO, the costs assigned to the cost of goods sold are the costs from beginning inventory and from earlier purchases.

Last-In, First-Out (LIFO)

The **last-in, first-out,** or **LIFO,** method is used very infrequently in Canada. It assigns the last costs in (i.e., the costs of the most recent purchases) to the first units sold. This means that ending inventory is assigned the costs associated with the first purchases (or beginning inventory). The LIFO method is illustrated in Exhibit 7-8. Imagine inventory as something stored in a bin. New purchases are added to the bin from the top, placing new layers of inventory on top of what is already in the bin (beginning inventory). Goods sold are taken from the top layer. The costs associated with these units are, therefore, the costs associated with the most recent purchases. Ending inventory, on the other hand, is associated with the cost of the layers at the date each was purchased. The bottom layers could have been purchased in a much earlier period. The acronym used to refer to ending inventory is **FISH,** for **first-in, still-here.**

■ **LIFO Visualization**

EXHIBIT 7-8

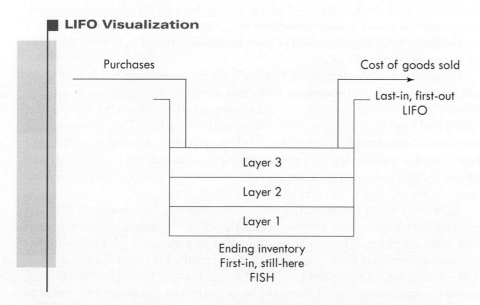

Using Ted's Toasters (Exhibit 7-6) and the LIFO assumption, let us now assign a cost to cost of goods sold and ending inventory.

Cost of goods sold (27 units)

10	units @ $14.50 (second purchase)	$145.00
17	units @ $14.25 (first purchase)	242.25
27	units	$387.25

Ending inventory (9 units)

3	units @ $14.25 (first purchase)	$ 42.75
6	units @ $14.00 (beginning inventory)	84.00
9	units	$126.75

Note again how the sum of the units in cost of goods sold and ending inventory (27 + 9) equals the 36 units in goods available for sale. The sum of the dollar amounts ($387.25 + $126.75) equals the dollar amount of the goods available for sale, $514.00. Note also that the dollar amount of ending inventory is lower than it is under FIFO and, therefore, that the dollar amount of the cost of goods sold is higher. The unit cost of inventory has been rising through January, and because the cost of goods sold is assigned costs from the most recent purchases it receives higher unit costs than under FIFO.

The main problem with LIFO is the cost assigned to ending inventory. In Ted's Toasters, the cost was the $14.00 from beginning inventory and the $14.25 from the first purchase. When purchases are made in February, LIFO will assign those new purchase costs to the cost of goods sold, and again assign the $14.00 and $14.25 to ending inventory. Several years from now, the unit cost assigned to ending inventory could still be the $14.00 and the $14.25. These old costs will not show the inventory on the balance sheet at a very realistic value. In fact, if it was left unadjusted the inventory costs could be substantially below market value. Recognizing this problem with LIFO, accountants have developed several techniques for adjusting the inventory amount to a more realistic value while still assigning the most recent costs to the cost of goods sold. The discussion of these methods is, however, beyond the scope of an introductory textbook.

Learning Objective

7

Explain the shortcomings of LIFO and why it is rarely used in Canada.

Remember that the diagram in Exhibit 7-8 is concerned with the flow of costs, not the physical flow of inventory. Not many inventories actually follow a LIFO physical flow, although there are examples: using steel plates from the top of a pile, taking coal from the top of a pile, or selling nails from a keg. This, however, does not prevent companies from using the LIFO cost assumption to assign costs. LIFO represents a systematic, logical way of assigning costs. In fact, the cost of goods sold on the income statement includes the most recent cost and is, therefore, a good match to the revenue of the period.

LIFO and FIFO represent the two extremes of cost assumption. LIFO will produce the highest cost of goods sold and, therefore, the lowest net income when unit costs are rising. This might be of interest to a manager who wants to discourage shareholders from requesting cash dividends. FIFO, on the other hand, will produce the lowest cost of goods sold and, therefore, the highest net income under the same conditions. This might be of interest to a manager who wants to attract new investors. Because these two assumptions produce dramatically different financial results during times of changing prices, it is important for users of financial statements to know which method is being used and to understand the managerial objectives that might underlie the selection of that method.

Of the three methods we have examined thus far (specific identification, FIFO, and LIFO), LIFO is used the least often in Canada, for several reasons. First, it produces the lowest net income when costs are rising. Second, the value of inventory on the balance sheet quickly becomes an unrealistic value. Third, Revenue Canada does not accept it as a method for determining inventory costs for tax purposes, probably because it produces the lowest net income and would therefore produce the lowest taxable income. We now turn our attention to the fourth and final potential cost flow assumption: the weighted average method.

Weighted Average

The **weighted average** method, the second most commonly used method in Canada, computes an average cost for all the units available for sale in a given period and assigns that average cost to both the units that are sold during the period and the units that remain in ending inventory. Exhibit 7-9 illustrates this method. Imagine inventory as a liquid stored in a tank, such as gasoline at a filling station. Purchases are dumped into the tank and mixed with beginning inventory and previous purchases. Inventory that is sold is therefore a mixture of beginning inventory and recent purchases.

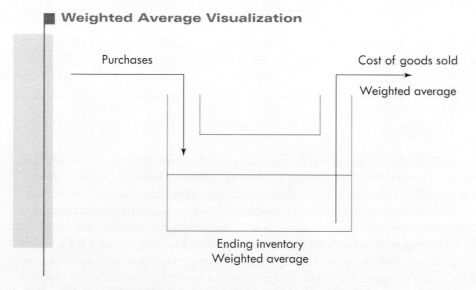

■ **Weighted Average Visualization**

EXHIBIT 7-9

In Ted's Toasters, the average cost is computed by taking the total cost of the goods available for sale ($514.00) and dividing it by the number of toasters available (36) to produce an average cost of $14.278 per unit. This unit cost is then assigned to all the units in ending inventory (9 × $14.278 = $128.50) and to the 27 units sold (27 × $14.278 = $385.51). Note that when the ending inventory of $128.50 is added to the cost of goods sold of $385.51, the total is $514.01—a 1¢ difference from the total value of goods available for sale. This error occurred because we had to round the unit cost. When using the weighted average method, use the calculated unit cost to determine either the ending inventory or the cost of goods sold. Determine the other amount by subtracting your calculated amount from the value of goods available for sale.

Note that the weighted average method produces results on the income state-ment and balance sheet that lie somewhere between those of LIFO and FIFO. Because the weighted average method produces a lower pre-tax income than FIFO, many companies in Canada choose it for tax purposes. They like the higher net income produced by FIFO for reporting purposes and so will maintain two sets of inventory records. This is acceptable practice. The recent increase in the use of the weighted average method for reporting purposes is an indication that companies are choosing to maintain only one set of inventory records.

Cost Flow Assumption Choice

All three of the cost flow assumptions we have discussed are in accordance with GAAP. Given free choice, which method should Ted's Toasters use to represent the operating results for the period? This depends on the fundamental objectives of management. Examine Exhibit 7-10 to see the different financial statement effects of each of the three assumptions.

EXHIBIT 7-10

■ Financial Statement Results

| | | Cost flow assumption | |
	FIFO	Weighted Average	LIFO
Sales revenue	$871.50	$871.50	$871.50
Cost of goods sold	383.50	385.50	387.25
Gross profit	$488.00	$486.00	$484.25
Balance sheet			
Inventory	$130.50	$128.50	$126.75

Ted's Toasters would probably like to use LIFO because it produces the smallest profit and would therefore result in the least tax liability. However, because Revenue Canada will not allow it, Ted's tax adviser would instead recommend weighted average.

Management at Ted's Toasters, however, may be more interested in getting a bonus to increase their own remuneration. If Ted's managers calculate their bonuses based on reported net income, they would be more likely to choose FIFO, which produces the highest amount of net income. Management may be tempted to use FIFO if the company has a loan agreement with a lender that requires the company to maintain a specified current ratio (current assets/current liabilities) and the com-pany is in danger of failing the required ratio test. FIFO produces the highest value of inventory that goes into the numerator of the current ratio.

Political sensitivity may also influence the cost flow decision. Suppose that the company is in the oil and gas industry, and that recent disruptions in world oil mar-kets have caused the price of oil to rise significantly. Consumer advocates have been criticizing the oil and gas industry for profiting from this situation by raising prices beyond what is required by the change in world prices. They advocate an excess-profits tax on the industry. In this situation, the company may want to avoid report-ing income at any higher level than is necessary. Last-in, first-out may be the best choice for minimizing the income effects of these changing prices.

Constraints on Selection

The choice of inventory method is not entirely without constraints. First of all, GAAP requires the company to select the method that represents the fairest matching of costs with revenues regardless of the actual physical flow of inventory. To understand what is meant by fair matching, consider the situation at Ted's Toasters. It has been experiencing a rise in its costs—that is, a period of inflation. Presumably, it has been able to adjust the prices it charges to customers to reflect this rise in costs.

Consider the income reported using the LIFO method. The $484.25 in the gross margin is a result of matching the cost of $387.25 (the most recent purchases) with the current revenue of $871.50. If prices were to stabilize at this point, Ted's could continue to produce a steady profit margin on future sales, because it can continue to buy goods at $14.50. On the other hand, the gross margin of $488.00 produced by using FIFO matches a cost of $383.50 (old costs) against the current revenue. Considering that the current replacement cost of that unit is $14.50, the income produced under FIFO can be split into a **current gross margin** and a **realized holding gain**, as shown in Exhibit 7-11. The sum of the current gross margin and the realized holding gain is the amount of profit reported in Exhibit 7-10 under GAAP. The presentation in Exhibit 7-11 is intended for illustration purposes only and is not used under GAAP. It does show that income produced using FIFO is a combination of a gross margin that can be expected to continue into the future and a realized holding gain that cannot be duplicated in the future. The holding gain is often referred to as a **paper profit**. Users should be aware that because lower older costs form part of the cost of goods sold, some of the resulting gross margin is not a true profit, as some of it must be used to replace the sold inventory with more expensive units.

■ FIFO Income and Holding Gains

EXHIBIT 7-11

Sales revenue	$871.50		
Replacement cost of goods sold	391.50	(27 @ $14.50)	
Current gross margin			$480.00
Replacement cost of goods sold	$391.50		
Historical cost of goods sold	383.50		
Realized holding gain			8.00
Reported gross margin			$488.00

As indicated in Exhibit 7-11, holding gains on inventory are, in fact, recognized at the point when the item is sold. Holding gains on items in ending inventory are not recognized under GAAP. Holding losses on items in ending inventory are recognized to the extent that writedowns occur in the application of the lower of cost and market rule. Therefore, under GAAP, the only changes in the value of inventory that are not recognized are the unrealized holding gains on ending inventory. For companies using FIFO, these holding gains are probably small because ending inventory is stated at the most recent prices. With LIFO, however, these unrealized holding gains can be large.

Given Ted's circumstances, it could be argued that LIFO produces a better measure of periodic net income because the realized holding gains that are contained in net income using FIFO will not persist into the future. It is generally true that during periods of inflation LIFO produces a better measure of net income. Note, however, that under such circumstances LIFO may also produce the least accurate measure of the value of ending inventory, because the prices in inventory may be very old and very low compared to current prices.

Under another set of circumstances, LIFO might not be the best choice. For example, if prices had been stable throughout the period (say, all units had a cost of $14), then all the cost flow assumptions would produce the same income. Under these circumstances the least expensive inventory method should be applied.

AN INTERNATIONAL PERSPECTIVE

Reports from Other Countries

The predominant practice with regard to cost flow assumptions around the world is to assume either FIFO or weighted average. In most countries other than the United States, LIFO is either not permitted (France and the United Kingdom) or used only in limited situations. The significant use of LIFO in the U.S. is partially driven by the LIFO conformity rule (if you use LIFO for tax purposes, you must also use it for reporting purposes) and its allowance for tax purposes. In Germany, the reporting books are essentially the same as the tax books, and prior to 1990 LIFO was not permitted under the tax code. In 1990, however, German law was changed to allow LIFO. Note the following inventory disclosure by Daimler-Benz in its 1997 financial statements:

> Inventories—Inventory is valued at the lower of acquisition or manufacturing cost or market, cost being generally determined on the basis of an average or first-in, first-out method (FIFO). Certain of the Group's U.S. businesses' inventories are valued using the last-in, first-out method (LIFO). Manufacturing costs comprise direct material and labor and applicable manufacturing overheads, including depreciation charges.

COST FLOW ASSUMPTIONS AND CHANGING PRICES

Learning Objective

8

Describe the impact of inflation on each of the cost flow assumptions.

As the Ted's Toasters example illustrates, the use of LIFO during periods of rising prices generally produces the lowest net income, whereas the use of FIFO produces the highest net income. The reverse would be true during periods of deflation, although the use of the lower of cost and market rule would tend to modify this. Canada has had virtually no sustained periods of deflation in recent memory. However, that is not to say that some companies have not faced periods of decreasing unit prices in the goods they use or produce. Take, for example, the microchip industry, which has seen significant drops in the cost per unit of its products. For these types of business, FIFO would make sense for tax purposes; in cases of declining costs, FIFO would produce the highest cost of goods sold and the lowest net income.

In periods of stable prices, all three cost flow assumptions produce the same values for cost of goods sold and ending inventory. The differences among the assumptions are driven by changes in prices across time. The magnitude of the effect depends on the size of the price changes and the size and turnover characteristics of the inventory. Users of financial statements, therefore, need to know more than just the inventory method being used. They must also know the type of inventory being sold and how the economy may be affecting the cost of that inventory.

Consider the use of FIFO and the effects of changing prices. The balance sheet reflects the most recent prices. The cost of goods sold reflects older prices. How old can these prices be? The oldest costs in the cost of goods sold figure are those that existed in beginning inventory. Those costs may have been incurred in the last month of the last year, or even earlier, depending on how often the company turns over its inventory. Inventory turnover measures the number of times the total inventory is sold during the period.

If the inventory turnover ratio is 12, the inventory turns over on average once a month, and the ending inventory costs come from the purchases made in the last month of the year. If inventory turnover is four, the company turns over its inventory on average once a quarter, and the oldest costs in ending inventory could come from the beginning of the last quarter of the year. Therefore, while these costs are viewed as "old," in reality they are not very old. When prices are not rising very rapidly, the differences between prices for the current year and those from the end of the last year will be relatively small.

Now, consider LIFO. Cost of goods sold reflects the most recent prices. Inventory, on the other hand, reflects old prices. How old can these old prices be? The oldest prices in ending inventory are associated with the oldest layer of inventory, which could have been acquired the first year the company was in business. For a 100-year-old company, these unit prices could be from a century ago. Even with small levels of annual inflation, the cumulative difference in prices for these layers and current prices can be substantial. The effects of inflation can cause the LIFO inventory value of a company to be very different from the current replacement cost of the inventory. For this reason, LIFO companies often provide information in the notes to their annual reports to inform the reader of the current cost of their inventories.

The choice of cost flow assumption depends on the nature of the inventory, but the same assumption does not have to apply to all inventories held by a company. For example, note the multiple inventory methods used by Imasco Limited in Exhibit 7-12.

Imasco Limited, 1998

EXHIBIT 7-12

Excerpt from the Notes to the Statements

1. Significant accounting policies
Inventories
Raw materials and supplies are valued at the lower of average cost and replacement cost. Finished goods and development land are valued at the lower of cost and net realizable value. Cost is determined substantially as follows: Tobacco—average cost; Drugstore—first-in, first-out; Land Development—specific item basis (cost of development land includes the original cost of properties and the cost of services such as roads and sewerage and water systems; carrying costs such as interest and property taxes are not capitalized).

AN INTERNATIONAL PERSPECTIVE

Reports from Other Countries

NAFTA Facts

United States—Inventory accounting is very similar to that used in Canada, but LIFO is more commonly used because it is acceptable for tax purposes and if it is used for tax purposes it must also be used for reporting purposes.

Mexico—Inventory is initially recorded at its acquisition or production cost and then restated at the balance sheet date using either price level adjusted or replacement cost amounts subject to the constraint that this amount cannot exceed net realizable value. Cost flow methods are essentially the same as those used in Canada.

INVENTORY ESTIMATION

There are several circumstances in which a company needs to know the cost of goods sold or inventory value but either chooses not to count inventory (it is too costly to close the business to count inventory) or simply cannot count it (it has been stolen or destroyed). In such cases, the company may attempt to estimate the cost of goods sold amount in order to prepare monthly income statements. It may need to estimate the amount and value of inventory for insurance purposes if the inventory is destroyed or stolen. As discussed earlier, it is difficult to determine inventory shrinkage if the periodic system is being used. Companies will often estimate the inventory before they start the annual physical inventory count in order to determine whether shrinkage has occurred.

Using the Cost-to-Sales Ratio

Learning Objective

9

Estimate a value for ending inventory using the cost-to-sales ratio method.

One way to estimate the cost of goods sold is to multiply the sales revenue for the period (a figure that is readily determinable) by the normal **cost-to-sales ratio**. The normal cost-to-sales ratio reflects the normal markup that the company applies to its products. For example, a company that normally marks up its products by 50% prices an item that costs $60 at $90. The cost-to-sales ratio, then, is 67% ($60/$90). If the sales for a given month are $12,000, the estimated cost of goods sold is $8,000 (67% × $12,000).

The cost-to-sales ratio can be used to estimate ending inventory as well. The company would be able to determine the cost of the goods available for sale by referring to the accounting records and finding the beginning inventory and the purchases for the period. For example, if the beginning inventory is $2,000 and the purchases for the period were $9,000, the goods available for sale would be $11,000. If we use the cost-to-sales ratio and the sales amount from the previous paragraph, we can determine that the cost of goods sold is $8,000 for the period. Because we know that goods available for sale must equal cost of goods sold plus ending inventory, all we need to do is subtract the calculated cost of goods sold ($8,000) from the goods available for sale ($11,000) to find the cost of ending inventory ($3,000). This method is often referred to as the **gross margin estimation method**.

FINANCIAL STATEMENT ANALYSIS CONSIDERATIONS

Because of the diversity of cost flow assumptions that are possible, and the significant differences that these assumptions can cause in a company's financial statements, adjustments must be made when inventory ratios are compared across companies. Cross-industry analyses are most affected by cost flow assumptions. Analyses of the same company over time are less affected, providing the inventory method has been consistently applied (e.g., the company always has used FIFO, or has always used weighted average). Changes in the cost flow assumption across time make it difficult to do time-series analyses. When using the inventory or cost of goods sold amounts in ratio analysis, keep these points in mind as you evaluate your results.

Inventory Turnover

The one ratio that looks exclusively at inventory is the **inventory turnover ratio**. This ratio tells the user how fast inventory is sold or how long it is held before it is sold. It is calculated as:

$$\text{Inventory turnover} = \frac{\text{Cost of goods sold}}{\text{Average inventory}}$$

Learning Objective

10

Calculate the inventory turnover ratio and explain how it can be interpreted by users.

The numerator contains the cost of goods sold, which measures the costs assigned to all the items of inventory that were sold. The denominator contains the average inventory. Where possible, average inventory is used rather than ending inventory, because it represents a more appropriate measure if the inventory level has changed over the year. Inventory turnover for Big Rock Brewery Ltd. for 1999 was:

1999
$$\frac{\$7,691,231}{\dfrac{(\$2,050,703 + \$2,270,909)}{2}} = 3.6$$

If the turnover is 3.6, it takes Big Rock about three and a half months to sell an average-sized batch of inventory. In order to determine if a turnover of 3.6 is reasonable for Big Rock, you would need to calculate the ratio for previous years, to see if it was changing. You would also compare Big Rock's ratio with those of other companies in the same industry. A look at the 1998 inventory turnover shows that turnover was slightly faster in 1998 (just over three months):

$$
\text{1998} \qquad \frac{\$7,676,372}{\frac{(\$2,270,909 + \$1,900,215)}{2}} = 3.7
$$

Another way of evaluating this ratio is to calculate the number of days that inventory is held. If you divide the number of days in a year (365) by the inventory turnover, you will know approximately how many days the inventory is held before it is sold. For Big Rock Brewery, the number of days the inventory was held in 1999 and 1998 was:

$$
\text{1999} \qquad 365/3.6 = 101.4 \text{ days}
$$

$$
\text{1998} \qquad 365/3.7 = 98.6 \text{ days}
$$

There is one concern about this ratio when LIFO is used. The ratio attempts to provide information about the speed at which the physical inventory turns over. Ideally, the ratio would put the number of units sold in the numerator and the number of units in ending inventory in the denominator. Because information about the number of units sold or in ending inventory is not provided in the financial statements, we use the cost figures provided in the statements and divide cost of goods sold by the average cost of inventory. With FIFO and weighted average we can use values in the numerator and denominator without risk of distortion, since the two values were determined in similar time frames. Because LIFO assigns the most recent costs to the cost of goods sold, the units in the numerator are stated at current prices. The units in the denominator, however, may be stated at very old unit prices because of the layers that exist with LIFO. Because of this, during periods of rising prices the ratio is likely to overstate the turnover, since higher-priced units are in the numerator and lower-priced units are in the denominator. As very few companies in Canada use LIFO, this will not pose a problem for most of the analyses that you do.

Other Ratios

Other ratios are affected by the use of LIFO versus FIFO if they contain inventory figures or the cost of goods sold. The most dramatic effects are in those ratios that use balance sheet information. The ratio that is probably most affected is the current ratio, which compares current assets to current liabilities (current assets/current liabilities). If costs are rising, the choice of LIFO can cause this ratio to be significantly lower than it would be with FIFO. Also, remember that the current ratio is used in many debt agreements. If a company using LIFO is in danger of violating the requirement for this ratio, a switch to FIFO might solve the problem.

On the income statement, the gross profit percentage (gross profit/sales) is also affected by the choice of FIFO versus LIFO. In Exhibit 7-10, the gross profit for Ted's Toasters varies from $488.00 under FIFO to $484.25 under LIFO. The difference is less than $4.00, but remember that we are dealing with the sale of only 27 units of a single type of inventory. The gross margin percentage is 56% under FIFO and 55% under LIFO. With a greater fluctuation in unit costs and more years of application of the individual methods, the difference between the two would be more dramatic.

SUMMARY

This chapter discussed inventory, the current asset that is vital to the health of a company and its related expense, cost of goods sold. Because of the many kinds of inventory, managing all aspects of inventory is a very complex task. Managers need to order the right kind and the right amount of inventory, price it competitively yet high enough to ensure that the company makes a profit, and safeguard it against theft. Accountants have developed two major systems for accounting for inventory: the perpetual system, which keeps a continuous record of the inventory on hand, and the periodic system, which records the purchase of inventory but does not cost the amount that has been sold until the end of an accounting period. Within these two systems, four methods have developed for assigning costs to inventory: specific identification, FIFO, LIFO, and weighted average. Each of these methods results in a different cost for ending inventory and cost of goods sold. Users need to be aware of how these methods are used so that they can factor their effect into any ratio analysis that they perform. Because counting inventory to determine the amount on hand is a costly endeavour, accountants have developed methods for estimating inventory. Estimates are used for interim reports and for establishing a pre-count value against which management is able to compare the actual physical count of inventory. In this chapter we described the cost-to-sales ratio method for estimating inventory. We finished the chapter by discussing the inventory turnover ratio, a ratio that helps users evaluate the management of inventory.

At this point all the major current asset accounts have been covered. Attention turns next to the noncurrent assets, which have a longer life than current assets; the benefits of these assets are realized over much longer periods of time than the current assets. The next chapter considers all noncurrent asset accounts, with an emphasis on the property, plant, and equipment accounts.

SUMMARY PROBLEM

The income statement, balance sheet, and Note 4 from the 1997 annual report of Meridian Technologies Inc. are shown in Exhibit 7-13. Meridian is a Canadian company that supplies manufactured parts and components to the automotive and service industries. Note 1 of the report states that "inventory is valued at the lower of cost and net realizable value. Cost is determined substantially on a first-in, first-out basis."

1. What are the implications of the word "substantially" in Note 1?

2. In Note 4, you will see that Tooling makes up nearly half the total inventory amount. What kind of inventory is Tooling?

3. In 1996 Meridian had a loss of $5.5 million and in 1997 it had a profit of $6.5 million. Based solely on the sale of inventory, can you suggest reasons why it may have done better in 1997?

4. Calculate the inventory turnover for Meridian for 1997. Briefly discuss what this ratio means.

5. Calculate the current ratio for Meridian for 1996 and 1997. How important is the inventory value in this ratio?

SUGGESTED SOLUTION TO SUMMARY PROBLEM

All figures in the solution are in thousands.

1. The word "substantially" implies that most of the inventory is assigned a cost under the first-in, first-out assumption but that some of the inventory is likely assigned a cost using some other assumption. The note does not state the nature of that other assumption. It is likely that the inventory costed under the other assumption does not materially change the derived inventory value.

2. Meridian manufactures automotive parts, so tooling probably refers to tool and die masters, which are used to cut precision shapes.

3. In 1996 the gross margin on $237,016 of revenues was $24,163, or 10.2%. In 1997 the revenues increased to $365,834, an increase of $128,818, or 54%. The gross margin on the 1997 revenue was $47,289, or 12.9%. In other words, revenues increased but the cost of sales increased proportionately less than the revenue. The increase in the margin from 10.2% to 12.9% makes it easier for Meridian to cover all of its other costs.

4.
$$\frac{\$318,545}{\frac{(\$21,526 + \$16,781)}{2}} = 16.63$$

$$365/16.63 \quad = 21.9 \text{ days}$$

Meridian's inventory turnover is 16.63. It takes about 22 days for it to sell its inventory. Without additional information about Meridian's activities in previous years or about its competitors, it is not possible to comment further on this ratio.

5.
$$\text{Current ratio (1996)} \quad = \frac{\$78,681}{\$62,715} = 1.25$$

$$\text{Current ratio (1997)} \quad = \frac{\$92,780}{\$83,113} = 1.12$$

Inventory represents approximately 21% of the current assets in 1996 and approximately 23% in 1997. This means that it has a significant impact on this ratio. Without the inventory, the ratio in both years would be below one. The company could not meet its current liabilities without selling inventory.

EXHIBIT 7-13
PART A

CONSOLIDATED BALANCE SHEETS
As at December 31

	1997	1996 (note 2)
	($000)	($000)
Assets		
Cash		4,098
Accounts receivable	**60,860**	49,983
Inventory (note 4)	**21,526**	16,781
Prepaid expenses	**10,394**	7,819
Total current assets	**92,780**	78,681
Land, buildings and equipment (note 5)	**178,980**	170,218
Other (note 10)	**667**	3,242
	272,427	252,141
Liabilities and Shareholders' Equity		
Bank indebtedness	**4,537**	
Accounts payable and accrued liabilities	**71,074**	55,102
Current portion of long-term debt (note 6)	**7,502**	7,613
Total current liabilities	**83,113**	62,715
Long-term debt (note 6)	**65,036**	75,187
	148,149	137,902
Capital stock (note 8)	**168,287**	163,629
Deficit	**(45,743)**	(52,197)
Cumulative translation adjustment	**1,734**	2,807
Total shareholders' equity	**124,278**	114,239
	272,427	252,141

See accompanying notes

On behalf of the Board:

Director

Director

16

EXHIBIT 7-13
PART B

CONSOLIDATED STATEMENTS OF OPERATIONS
Year ended December 31, 1997 and nine months ended December 31, 1996 (note 3)

	1997	1996 (note 2)
	($000)	($000)
Revenues	**365,834**	237,016
Expenses:		
Cost of sales	**318,545**	212,853
Selling and general	**16,412**	10,680
Depreciation	**17,596**	12,705
	352,553	236,238
Earnings before interest and taxes	**13,281**	778
Interest expense	**(6,368)**	(6,036)
Earnings (loss) before income taxes	**6,913**	(5,258)
Income tax expense (note 9)	**(459)**	(240)
Net earnings (loss)	**6,454**	(5,498)
Earnings (loss) per share	**$0.20**	$(0.17)
Weighted average number of shares	**32,917,081**	32,431,713

EXHIBIT 7-13
PART C

4. Inventory

	1997	1996
	($000)	($000)
Raw materials	**5,500**	5,263
Work in process	**786**	1,338
Finished goods	**5,279**	4,095
Tooling	**9,961**	6,085
	21,526	16,781

ABBREVIATIONS USED

EDI	Electronic Data Interchange	LCM	Lower of cost and market
FIFO	First-in, first-out	LIFO	Last-in, first-out
FISH	First-in, still-here	LISH	Last-in, still-here
IASC	International Accounting Standards Committee	NRV	Net realizable value

SYNONYMS

Entry market/Input market/Wholesale market

Exit market/Output market/Retail market

Entry price/Input price/Replacement cost

Exit price/Output price/Net realizable value

Freight in/Transportation

GLOSSARY

Cost flow assumption An assumption about how the costs of inventory should be assigned to individual units when it is impossible or impractical to assign costs specifically to units.

Current gross margin The difference between the current selling price of a unit of inventory and its current replacement cost.

Electronic Data Interchange (EDI) The computer linkage of two companies such that inventory is ordered directly over the computer connection.

Entry market The market from which goods or materials enter the company; sometimes referred to as the input market or wholesale market.

Exit market The market in which goods exit the company; sometimes referred to as the output market or retail market.

FIFO An acronym (first-in, first-out) for the cost flow assumption that assigns the cost of the first unit into the company to the first unit sold.

FISH An acronym (first-in, still-here) that describes the ending inventory units with the LIFO cost flow assumption.

Freight in The transportation cost paid when inventory is acquired; also referred to as transportation in.

Going-concern assumption An assumption made in GAAP that the company for which the financial statements are being prepared will continue to exist into the foreseeable future.

Goods available for sale The units of inventory available to be sold during the period. These units consist of those available from the beginning inventory and those produced or purchased during the current period.

Input market The market from which goods or materials enter the company; sometimes referred to as the entry market or wholesale market.

Inventory shrinkage The losses of inventory due to spoilage, damage, or theft.

Laid-down cost Costs such as invoice cost, customs and excise duties, tariffs, and transportation. Although transportation in should be included in the laid-down cost it is often treated as a period cost because it is impractical to allocate it to inventory items. In a manufacturing company, the laid-down cost is direct material, direct labour, and overhead.

LIFO   An acronym (last-in, first-out) for the cost flow assumption that assigns the cost of the last unit purchased by the company to the first unit sold.

LISH   An acronym (last-in, still-here) that describes the ending inventory units under the FIFO cost flow assumption.

Market   Net realizable value (NRV), less a profit margin or replacement cost.

Net realizable value (NRV)   Selling price of a unit of inventory less any costs necessary to complete and sell the unit.

Nonmonetary asset   An asset that is not fixed in terms of the number of monetary units it represents. Examples include inventory and property, plant, and equipment.

Output market   The market in which goods exit the company; sometimes referred to as the exit market or retail market.

Periodic inventory system   An inventory system in which cost of goods sold is determined by counting ending inventory, assigning costs to these units, and subtracting the ending inventory value from the sum of the beginning inventory plus purchases for the period.

Perpetual inventory system   An inventory system in which the cost of goods sold is determined at the time of sale of the unit.

Realized holding gain   A gain that results from the sale of a unit of inventory that had been held over a period during which prices increased. The profits that result from the change in price are the portion referred to as a holding gain.

Replacement cost   The current price at which a unit of inventory can be replaced by the company.

Retail market   The market in which goods exit the company; sometimes referred to as the exit market or output market.

Specific identification   A method of assigning costs to units of inventory in which the cost of a unit can be specifically identified from the records of the company.

Stockout   A situation that arises when a company sells all of a specific item of inventory and has no more in stock.

Transportation in   A synonym for freight in.

Weighted average   A method for assigning costs to units of inventory whereby each unit is assigned the average cost of the units available for sale during the period.

Wholesale market   The market from which goods or materials enter the company; sometimes referred to as the entry market or input market.

ASSIGNMENT MATERIAL

Assessing Your Recall

7-1 Describe the inventory valuation methods allowed under GAAP.

7-2 Describe how the lower of cost and market rule is applied to inventory under GAAP and how this application is similar to that used for temporary investments.

7-3 Define and explain the difference between replacement cost and net realizable value.

7-4 Describe the basic differences between the periodic and the perpetual inventory systems.

7-5 Discuss the advantages and disadvantages of the periodic inventory system compared to the perpetual inventory system.

7-6 Describe the three major cost flow assumptions for inventory that are most commonly used in Canada.

7-7 Discuss a company's incentives for choosing one cost flow assumption over another. Be sure to include a discussion of the choice from both a reporting and a tax perspective.

7-8 Explain the term "holding gain" and discuss how it might arise with various cost flow assumptions.

7-9 Under what circumstances would a company want or need to estimate cost of goods sold or inventory?

7-10 Describe the effects the choice of LIFO or FIFO may have on the ratios related to inventory. Discuss specifically the inventory turnover ratio and the current ratio.

Applying Your Knowledge

7-11 (Calculation of ending inventory and cost of goods sold)
Burke Ltd. held no inventory at the beginning of August. The company's inventory purchases during August were as follows:

August	7	8,000	units	@	$18.00
	14	4,000	units	@	$17.50
	23	12,000	units	@	$15.00
	28	6,000	units	@	$14.50
		30,000	units		

Burke uses a periodic inventory system. At the end of August, the company had 10,000 units of inventory on hand.

Required:

a. Compute the cost of goods sold for August using the weighted average cost flow assumption.

b. Compute the cost of goods sold for August using the first-in, first-out cost flow assumption.

c. Compute the cost of goods sold for August using the last-in, first-out cost flow assumption.

d. Which inventory cost flow assumption results in the greatest net income for August? Which results in the smallest?

e. Which inventory cost flow assumption results in the largest inventory balance at August 31? Which results in the smallest?

7-12 (Calculation of the cost of ending inventory)
The Clean Scent Company, a manufacturer of soaps and cosmetics, had raw materials inventory worth $30,000, at a unit cost of $15, on May 31. The purchases made during the month of June are as follows:

Date	Units Purchased	Total Cost
June 3	3,000	$45,000
June 10	1,000	16,000
June 14	4,000	66,000
June 23	2,500	42,500
June 29	1,000	19,000

A physical count of inventory showed that 2,500 units were still remaining on June 30.

Required:
Compute the cost of ending inventory on June 30 using each of the following cost flow assumptions:

a. FIFO

b. LIFO

c. Weighted average

7-13 (Calculation of cost of goods sold and gross profit)

Yoder Company recorded the following inventory transactions during 2000:

	Number of Units	Unit Purchase Price	Unit Sale Price
Inventory balance, January 1, 2000	60	$4	
Purchase #1	200	$5	
Sale #1	100		$9
Purchase #2	40	$9	
Purchase #3	60	$7	
Sale #2	170		$10

Required:

a. Calculate the cost of goods sold and gross profit for Yoder Company for 2000 assuming Yoder uses a first-in, first-out cost flow assumption.

b. Calculate the cost of goods sold and gross profit for Yoder Company for 2000 assuming Yoder uses a last-in, first-out cost flow assumption.

c. Which of the two methods provides the most conservative estimate of the carrying value of inventory? Which provides the best estimate of the current cost of replacing the inventory? Explain your answers.

d. Which method provides the most conservative estimate of reported income? Under what circumstances would the opposite be true?

7-14 (Calculation of ending inventory and cost of goods sold)

Exquisite Jewellers purchases chiming clocks from around the world for sale in Canada. According to its records, Exquisite Jewellers had the following purchases and sales of clocks in 2001:

Clock No.	Date Purchased	Amount Paid	Date Sold	Sale Price
423	Jan. 22	$1,800	Mar. 8	$3,200
424	Feb. 9	6,000		
425	June 6	2,800	June 16	4,900
426	June 6	3,000	Aug. 9	4,800
427	Sept. 27	2,000		
428	Dec. 8	1,200	Dec. 24	2,000

Exquisite Jewellers has used the average cost in computing its cost of goods sold and inventory balances, but is thinking of changing to specific identification.

Required:

a. Compare the dollar amounts that would be reported as cost of goods sold and ending inventory under average cost and specific identification.

b. What conditions generally must exist for specific identification to be used? Explain why.

c. Which of the two methods best represents the operating results for Exquisite Jewellers? Explain your answer.

7-15 (Calculation of ending inventory and cost of goods sold)

The following information relates to the merchandise inventory of Aspen Company for the month of October:

October	1	Beginning inventory	6,000 units	$60,000
October	3	Purchased	4,000 units	$44,000
October	7	Sold	5,000 units	
October	15	Sold	3,000 units	
October	23	Purchased	5,000 units	$60,000
October	29	Sold	3,500 units	

Required:

Compute the cost of goods sold and ending inventory as of October 31 using the following inventory systems and cost flow assumptions:

a. FIFO

b. LIFO

c. Weighted average

7-16 (Calculation of ending inventory and cost of goods sold)

Dragon Crafts Ltd. had a beginning inventory of 200 units with a cost of $17 each. During January the company engaged in the following transactions:

Jan. 1   Purchased 1,500 units of inventory at a cost of $19 each; because of the frequency of purchases, Dragon Crafts was given a special 10% quantity discount and payment terms of net 30 (30 days). The $19 per unit is prior to the quantity discount.

    5   Paid freight charges of $1,500 on the Jan. 1 purchase. Freight charges are charged to a transportation in account if they are paid separately.

    7   Sold 500 units for $26 each, with terms of net eom (end of month).

    9   Paid for the Jan. 1 purchase.

   10   Purchased 200 units of inventory for $20 each, freight included; terms: net 30.

   11   Sold 300 units for cash for $25 each.

   12   Purchased 800 units of inventory for $22 each, freight included; terms: net 30.

   13   Sold 1,200 units for $30 each; terms 2/10, net 30 (2% discount if paid within 10 days; if not paid, the account is due in 30 days).

   14   Purchased 200 units of inventory for $23 each, with terms of net 30; freight charges of $400 will be due in five days. The freight is not included in the $23.

Dragon Crafts Ltd. uses a periodic system. The company assigns inventory costs on a FIFO basis.

Required:

a. Prepare a schedule showing the computation of Dragon Crafts' cost of goods sold for January.

b. Prepare a schedule showing the composition of Dragon Crafts' inventory at the end of January.

c. If Dragon Crafts assigned inventory costs on a LIFO rather than FIFO basis, compute the company's cost of goods sold and ending inventory for January.

d. If Dragon Crafts assigned inventory on a weighted average basis, compute the company's cost of goods sold and ending inventory for January.

7-17 (Gross margin and the lower of cost and market)
The Corral Saddle Company's information about merchandise inventories is as follows:

			Ending Inventory	
Year	Purchases	Sales	Cost	Market Value
1	$140,000	$145,000	$75,000	$70,000
2	85,000	175,000	80,000	65,000
3	155,000	253,000	72,000	85,000
4	104,000	225,000	21,000	21,000

There was no beginning balance in inventories prior to Year 1.

Required:

a. Compute the gross margin for each year using the acquisition cost basis for valuing inventory.

b. Compute the same gross margin using the lower of cost and market basis for valuing inventory.

c. Compare the gross margin for each year using the two methods, and explain the reason(s) for any differences you observe.

7-18 (Lower of cost and market)
Canadian Lumber Company carries a number of different types of screwdrivers. At the end of 2000, the chief financial officer of Canadian Lumber noted that the international price of screwdrivers had been dropping appreciably. Screwdrivers currently on hand that had been purchased in July 2000 for $9 per unit could be replaced at the end of December for $6 per unit.

Required:

a. If Canadian Lumber Company has 3,000 screwdrivers on hand at December 31, 2000, at what dollar amount should inventory be reported? Is any other information needed to determine the year-end reporting amount? Explain.

b. Why is the decline in the replacement cost of screwdrivers relevant in this situation?

c. Which accounting concepts are relevant in deciding the dollar amount of inventory to be reported? Explain why these concepts are important.

7-19 (LIFO, FIFO, and the lower of cost and market)
The following presentation relates to the inventory valuations of Aurora Inc. using different inventory methods (the company started operations in 20x1):

Period	LIFO	FIFO	Lower of FIFO Cost and Market
December 31, 20x1	$ 65,000	$ 60,000	$ 55,000
December 31, 20x2	135,000	125,000	120,000
December 31, 20x3	150,000	143,000	130,000
December 31, 20x4	100,000	125,000	125,000

There was no beginning balance of inventory in 20x1.

Required:

a. For 20x1, state whether the prices went up or down.

b. For 20x4, state whether the prices went up or down.

c. State which method would show the highest income in each year.

d. Which method would show the lowest income for the four years combined?

7-20 (LIFO and the production of additional inventory)

In mid-September, Waterford Incorporated needed to decide how many units should be produced for the balance of the accounting year, which ends on December 31. The company began its operations in the current year with an inventory of 15,000 units at a unit cost of $15. During the year, it produced 85,000 units at a unit cost of $18. The annual capacity of the plant is 200,000 units. It is estimated that the unit cost of producing additional units (for the remaining part of the year) will be $20. The company, after doing time-series and cross-industry analyses, expects annual sales to be 125,000 units at a selling price of $30 per unit. The company uses a periodic LIFO inventory system.

Required:

a. Assume the company produces just enough units to cover the 125,000 units it sells. Determine the cost of goods sold and the gross profit at this level of production.

b. Assume the company produces the maximum that the plant can produce, but still sells only 125,000 units. Determine the cost of goods sold and the gross profit at this level of production.

c. If the company sold the same number of units under assumptions a. and b., why is there a difference in the value of cost of goods sold and gross profit?

7-21 (Inventory estimation)

Sammellias Ltd., a clothing store, has an inventory count every December 31. It closes its store on that day and hires several university students to help with the counting. Although it has installed an electronic detection device in the doorway of the store to stop people from taking clothing for which they have not paid, the company is still concerned that it is losing some inventory due to theft. Sammellias uses the periodic inventory system. While the inventory is being counted, the accountant decides to estimate the amount of inventory that should be on hand. In the accounting records she finds the following information:

Sales for the year	$490,000
Beginning inventory	30,000
Transportation in	1,200
Purchases	210,000

From previous years, she determines that the normal cost-to-sales ratio is 40%.

Required:

a. Complete the calculation for the accountant and determine how much inventory should be on hand.

b. Assume that when the count is complete, the accountant determines that there is $38,500 in ending inventory. Is there a problem of missing inventory? What criteria would you use to determine whether this is a serious problem? Outline what options may be open to Sammellias if it wishes to do something about the problem.

7-22 (Inventory estimation)

On March 31, 20x2, Cedar Grove Ltd. had a major fire in its main lumber yard. All the inventory was destroyed. In order to complete the insurance claim, the accountant needed an estimate of the inventory that had been in the lumber yard at the time of the fire. A search through the accounting records (which, luckily, had been kept in another building that was not destroyed by the fire) produced the following information:

A cost-to-sales ratio of 64%

Purchases for the year up to March 31	$ 84,000
Sales for the year up to March 31	140,000
Inventory on hand on January 1, 20x2	28,000

Required:

a. Calculate how much inventory should be on hand.

b. Cedar Grove had two other small lumber yards. On April 1, it counted the inventory in the other yards and determined that there was $9,500 in inventory in the other yards. How much should the company claim from the insurance company?

c. What factors could make the estimate of ending inventory inaccurate?

7-23 (FIFO, LIFO, and holding gains)

At the beginning of the year, the Sintex Company had merchandise inventory consisting of 3,500 units at a cost of $250 per unit. During the year, the company produced 5,000 units at an average cost of $400. The company sold 4,000 units for $600 each. The replacement cost on December 31 was $500 per unit.

Required:

a. Compute the cost of goods sold and gross margin using both the FIFO and the LIFO cost flow assumption.

b. Separate the gross margin on sales into operating gross margin and realized holding gains using both FIFO and LIFO.

c. Compute the unrealized holding gains and the total gains (operating margin + realized gain + unrealized gain) using both FIFO and LIFO.

d. Compare the total gains and explain any variance using both cost flow assumptions.

7-24 (Inventory turnover and gross margin calculations)

Stream Ltd. reported total inventory at January 1 and December 31, 2001, of $200,000 and $160,000, respectively. Cost of goods sold for 2001 was $470,000. Stream's nearest competitor reported inventories of $400,000 and $450,000 at January 1 and December 31, 2001, respectively, and reported cost of goods sold of $900,000 for 2001. Total 2001 sales for Stream Ltd. and its competitor were $600,000 and $1,250,000, respectively.

Required:

a. Compute the inventory turnover ratios for the two companies for 2001.

b. Compute the gross margin percentage (gross margin divided by sales) for the two companies for 2001.

c. On the basis of inventory turnover, which company is superior?

d. On the basis of gross margin percentage, which company is superior?

e. Which company would you recommend as best managed? Indicate why.

7-25 (Evaluation of the inventory turnover ratio)

The inventory turnover ratios for Canadian Manufacturing, Honest John's Car Dealership, and Sweet Green Grocery Ltd. are 4.5, 8.7, and 18.2, respectively.

Required:

a. How is the inventory turnover ratio calculated? What information is provided by this ratio?

b. Is the company with the highest turnover ratio run the most efficiently? Explain your answer.

c. Evaluate the turnover ratios for the three companies. Are the differences in ratios consistent with what you would expect? Explain.

d. What other ratios would you examine in assessing the operating efficiency of the companies?

7-26 (Inventory ratio analysis with international competitors)

Describe the concerns that you might have for the ratio analysis of inventories when comparing a Canadian company with a foreign competitor.

Management Perspective Problems

7-27 (Ratio analysis and foreign currencies)

Suppose that you are analyzing two competitors, one a Canadian company and the other a company in Japan whose statements are expressed in yen. Discuss whether it is necessary to convert the statements of the Japanese company into Canadian dollars before computing ratios.

7-28 (Measurement issues related to ending inventory)

As an auditor, what concerns might you have about the measurement of inventories at year end? What effects might misstatements in these amounts have on the financial statements of the company?

7-29 (Effects of changing inventory costing method)

Suppose that a company has used LIFO since it began operations and that prices have generally risen from that point to the present. In one of the company's debt agreements there is a restrictive covenant stating that the company must maintain a current ratio of 2, or it is in violation of the debt agreement and the debt immediately becomes due. If you represent the lender, what reaction would you have if the company wanted to change its inventory method from LIFO to FIFO? How would your answer change if you knew that the company was already financially distressed?

7-30 (Use of ratio analysis during audit procedures)

Auditors typically conduct a preliminary review of a company's financial statements using analytical procedures that include ratio analysis. As an auditor, why would you find ratio analysis useful for auditing the financial statements?

7-31 (Decision-making with respect to inventory valuation)

Your company manufactures a line of processed snack foods using a soybean base with a low fat content. The line was very popular until publicity emphasized that the product is very high in salt and contains numerous chemical preservatives. Now you have inventory on hand that will be hard to sell. The inventory originally cost $3,500,000. Its wholesale selling price prior to the publicity had been $7,000,000. The sales division has presented the following alternative proposals to the executive committee, of which you are a member.

Proposal 1: Offer the product at deep discounts to regular customers. If the discount is large enough, all of the inventory will probably sell. The selling price for the total inventory under these conditions is estimated to be $2,000,000.

Proposal 2: Market the product in third world countries as a nutritious soybean-based food. Marketing costs will probably be $1,000,000, but the entire inventory could be sold at the regular list price of $7,000,000. Nutrition disclosure requirements are virtually non-existent in most of these countries.

Required:

a. Do any accounting entries need to be made to reflect the inventory problem?

b. Which proposal would you favour? Would you suggest any other alternatives?

c. What type of financial disclosure would you expect your company to make if financial statements were prepared prior to the selection of an alternative for disposing of the inventory?

7-32 (Decision-making with respect to inventory estimation)
Black Light Company reported sales of $700,000 in the first quarter of 2001. Because the company does not keep a running tally of the cost of the inventory sold, the controller does not know how much inventory is actually on hand at the end of the quarter. The company, for the first time, is going to prepare quarterly financial reports to issue to its shareholders, but counting the inventory at the end of each quarter is too costly. Therefore, the controller decides to estimate how much inventory is on hand. By looking at the last annual balance sheet, the controller is able to determine that inventory on hand on January 1, 2001, was $250,000, and he knows that an additional $750,000 of inventory was purchased during the first quarter, providing a total $1,000,000 of goods available for sale. The company normally earns a 30% gross profit on sales. Based on this information, and using the cost-to-sales method, the controller arrives at what he thinks is a reasonable estimate of the cost of inventory on hand at the end of the first quarter of 2001.

Required:

a. What would you estimate as the cost of Black Light's inventory on hand at the end of the first quarter of 2001? Explain how you arrived at your estimate. Assume the company earned a consistent 30% gross margin on its sales.

b. If the gross margin estimation method works reasonably well for interim estimates of inventory on hand, why not use it at year end as well and avoid altogether the cost of an annual inventory count?

c. Under what conditions might this method of estimating inventory provide reliable results?

d. Under what conditions might this method of estimating inventory provide unreliable results?

e. Based on your estimate of Black Light's inventory at the end of the first quarter, what is your assessment of the company's inventory position? What factors might have contributed to it?

7-33 (LIFO and ending inventory problems)
Suppose that your company has always used LIFO and that prices have been rising over the years. In order to increase efficiency you have recommended that the company change its manufacturing process and adopt a just-in-time process, in which the raw materials are purchased just in time for production and goods are produced just in time for sale. The new system will either eliminate or significantly reduce inventory levels. What are the financial statement implications of your decision, and what might be the financial tradeoffs that you should consider in implementing your decision?

Reading and Interpreting Published Financial Statements

7-34 (Interpreting the inventory turnover ratio)
Big Rock Brewery Ltd.'s balance sheet, income statement, and notes on inventory are included in Appendix A at the end of the book.

Required:
Using the information in these statements, answer the following questions:

a. In this chapter the inventory turnover ratio for Big Rock was calculated for 1999 and 1998 at 3.6 (101.4 days) and 3.7 (98.6 days), respectively. Knowing that Big Rock is a brewery company, how would you interpret the ratios?

b. Note 3 on inventory shows the components of the inventory amount. Three of those items are part of the manufacturing process; the other one is not. What impact did this other item have on the calculation and interpretation in part a.?

c. One of the items listed as a component of the inventory is returnable glass (bottles). Some of these bottles will be returned and re-used. Suggest some alternative ways that Big Rock could account for these bottles.

d. Big Rock values its raw materials, supplies, promotional goods, and dispensing units at the lower of cost (FIFO) and replacement cost. Assume that for 1999 the replacement cost for the raw materials and returnable glass was $970,000. Recalculate the inventory turnover for 1999 using this new information. What impact does this have on the turnover ratio?

7-35 (Inventory turnover)
The balance sheet, statement of earnings, and note on inventory valuation of Future Shop Ltd. are included in Appendix B at the end of the book.

Required:
Using the information in these statements, answer the following questions:

a. Calculate the inventory turnover ratio for 1999 and 1998 (the inventory amount for 1997 was $244,074,000). Convert it into days.

b. Knowing the type of merchandise that Future Shop sells, does this ratio seem reasonable?

c. Question 7-34 gives the inventory turnover ratios for Big Rock Brewery. How do they compare with the ratios for Future Shop? Why is such a comparison not very useful?

d. What costing method is Future Shop using to value its inventory? Where did you find this information?

7-36 (Inventory turnover)

SoftQuad International Inc. reported the following amounts for inventory and cost of sales in its 1997 financial statements:

Inventory:
1997 $1,628 thousand
1996 $410 thousand

Cost of sales:
1997 $9,794 thousand
1996 $2,585 thousand

Required:

a. Calculate the inventory turnover (by ratio and by days) for SoftQuad International for 1997 and 1996 using the inventory value within the year instead of the average inventory amount.

b. SoftQuad International provides digital authoring and publishing software tools including its flagship HoTMetaL hypertext markup language (HTML) editor that lets non-technical and technical users create content via the Internet and internal corporate networks. It also markets family and children's video games. Using this information about the activities of SoftQuad, evaluate the appropriateness of the inventory turnover that you calculated in part a.

7-37 (Components of inventory)

Comac Food Group Inc. owns the franchises of Domino's Pizza, Grabbajabba Fine Coffee, Pastel's Café, and Company's Coming Bakery Café. It builds the retail outlets and sells the franchise for operation to interested entrepreneurs. A franchisee buys the right to sell the merchandise sold by that outlet (pizza in the case of Domino's Pizza), but the franchisee must run the business under the direction of the franchisor (Comac), which establishes the ingredients, furnishing for the store, and even management style. In its 1998 financial statements Comac has the following note for its inventory:

4. Inventories
    Inventories are comprised of the following:

	1998	1997
Franchise stores under construction	$507,000	$ 98,000
Stores held for resale	294,000	858,000
Ingredients, uniforms and selling supplies	150,000	170,000
	$951,000	$1,126,000

Required:

a. In most of the inventory examples that you have seen in this book, inventory has been retail items that we normally think of as inventory. Explain why it is appropriate for Comac to include the stores in its inventory.

b. Comac Food Group Inc. reports cost of sales at $5,285,000 and $2,472,000 for 1998 and 1997, respectively. Explain why calculating an inventory turnover for Comac would not be meaningful.

7-38 (Inventory turnover)

Mitel Company makes corporate telephone systems and semiconductors used by the computer telephone market. Because it is a manufacturing company, its inventory is composed of raw materials, work-in-process, and finished goods, as follows:

5. Inventories (in millions)

	1998	1997
Raw materials	$ 53.4	$29.4
Work-in-process	60.3	26.9
Finished goods	48.5	26.8
	$162.2	$83.1

The cost of sales for products was $385.9 million and $297.4 million for 1998 and 1997, respectively.

Required:

a. Calculate an inventory turnover for Mitel for 1998 and 1997 using first cost of sales divided by total inventory and then cost of sales divided by finished goods. Use the inventory value in the given year rather than the average inventory.

b. The inventory turnover using total inventory is quite different from the inventory turnover using only finished goods. Which amount do you think is more useful to users? Why?

7-39 (Impact of inventory on current ratio; gross profit impact of changing sales levels) Chai-Na-Ta Corp. is the largest producer of ginseng in the world. It produces, markets, and distributes North American ginseng root and value-added products. Ginseng reaches maturity and can be harvested in three years, but Chai-Na-Ta sometimes allows the crops to mature longer to allow for higher yields and additional seed harvests. The balance sheet and statement of earnings for 1998 and 1997 are presented in Exhibit 7-14.

Required:

a. Calculate the current ratio (CA/CL) for both 1998 and 1997. Comment on the impact that inventory has on this ratio in each year.

b. Included with the current assets and long-term assets is an asset called Ginseng crops. This account collects all of the cost of growing the ginseng. The portion in the current asset section includes the accumulated costs associated with the ginseng that is expected to be sold in the following year. Is this an inventory item? Explain why you think that it is or is not.

c. Calculate the gross profit percentage on the income statement for both 1998 and 1997. Sales declined sharply in 1997 but then improved dramatically in 1998. What effect has this had on the gross profit? What conclusions can you draw from the results that you found?

Beyond the Book

7-40 (Examination of a company's financial statements)
Choose a Canadian company as directed by your instructor and answer the following questions:

a. What kind of inventory does your company carry?

b. Calculate the inventory turnover for each of the last two years using the inventory of the year instead of the average inventory. Report any difficulties that you had in finding the appropriate numbers to make this calculation.

c. Describe any significant changes that occurred in the inventory balance and try to determine what caused the change.

d. Calculate a current ratio for each of the last two years. Describe the significance that inventory has on this ratio in each year.

EXHIBIT 7-14
PART A

Consolidated Balance Sheets

| | | As at November 30 | |
		1998	1997
(Stated in Canadian Dollars)			
ASSETS			
Current assets			
Cash and cash equivalents	$	1,068,993	$ 3,435,077
Accounts receivable		2,952,800	3,642,073
Inventory		16,549,615	16,211,219
Ginseng crops *(Note 5)*		10,318,142	11,277,297
Prepaid and other assets		596,080	615,555
		31,485,630	35,181,221
Investment in Dalian Pegasus Ginseng Pharmaceutical Co., Ltd. *(Note 4)*		3,372,413	6,337,184
Ginseng crops *(Note 5)*		14,961,861	15,867,255
Capital assets *(Note 6)*		12,418,169	14,199,112
Other assets *(Note 7)*		2,372,025	2,649,705
	$	64,610,098	$ 74,234,477
LIABILITIES			
Current liabilities			
Line of credit *(Note 8)*	$	4,600,083	$ 1,007,710
Short-term borrowing *(Note 9)*		300,760	296,595
Accounts payable and accrued liabilities		4,645,778	5,777,179
Current portion of term debt *(Note 10)*		860,596	8,742,562
		10,407,217	15,824,046
Term debt *(Note 10)*		28,241,951	21,642,038
Deferred gain *(Note 11)*		665,000	614,600
Capital due to co-venturer *(Note 11)*		937,500	1,125,000
Deferred income taxes *(Note 15)*		3,126,781	6,596,781
Non-controlling interests		–	74,008
		43,378,449	45,876,473
SHAREHOLDERS' EQUITY			
Share capital *(Notes 12 and 13)*		17,221,262	17,221,262
Equity component of convertible debt and warrants *(Note 10(a) and (b))*		1,062,069	1,416,092
Cumulative translation adjustments		483,074	192,459
Retained earnings		2,465,244	9,528,191
		21,231,649	28,358,004
	$	64,610,098	$ 74,234,477

Going Concern *(Note 2)*
Commitments *(Note 16)*
APPROVED BY THE BOARD

Director *GJ gill*   Director *Michael Harcourt*

18 / *chai-na-ta*

EXHIBIT 7-14
PART B

Consolidated Statements of (Loss) Earnings

		Years ended November 30	
	1998	1997	1996
(Stated in Canadian Dollars)			
Revenue	$ 17,294,375	$ 9,052,647	$ 34,429,647
Costs of goods sold	16,119,501	8,201,600	18,440,782
	1,174,874	851,047	15,988,865
Selling, general and administrative expenses *(Note 1)*	5,862,734	7,867,554	5,787,157
Bad debts	432,112	586,434	212,769
Interest and financing charges	1,650,001	1,237,203	745,501
	7,944,847	9,691,191	6,745,427
	(6,769,973)	(8,840,144)	9,243,438
Loss on sales contracts *(Note 14)*	–	(7,325,925)	–
Operating (loss) income	(6,769,973)	(16,166,069)	9,243,438
Provision on impairment of investment *(Note 4(a))*	(3,372,413)	–	–
Other (expense) income	(818,592)	307,231	109,201
Non-controlling interests	74,008	519,654	(189,312)
(Loss) earnings before income taxes	(10,886,970)	(15,339,184)	9,163,327
Provision for income taxes (recovery) *(Note 15)*	(3,470,000)	(4,703,000)	3,059,748
NET (LOSS) EARNINGS	$ (7,416,970)	$ (10,636,184)	$ 6,103,579
Basic (loss) earnings per share	$ (1.84)	$ (2.64)	$ 1.53
Fully diluted (loss) earnings per share	$ (1.84)	$ (2.64)	$ 1.26
Weighted average number of shares used to calculate basic (loss) earnings per share	4,021,553	4,021,553	3,982,677

Consolidated Statements of Retained Earnings

		Years ended November 30	
	1998	1997	1996
(Stated in Canadian Dollars)			
Balance, beginning of year	$ 9,528,191	$ 20,164,375	$ 14,060,796
Amortization of equity component of convertible debt and warrants *(Note 10(a) and (b))*	354,023	–	–
Net earnings (loss)	(7,416,970)	(10,636,184)	6,103,579
Balance, end of year	$ 2,465,244	$ 9,528,191	$ 20,164,375

Case

7-41 Bema Gold Company
Bema Gold Company is a Canadian company headquartered in Vancouver, British Columbia. It explores and develops gold properties in South America. Raj, a Business Administration student, has recently inherited some money from a grandparent. She intends to create a diversified portfolio of share investments. On the riskier side, she has heard that investing in gold properties can be quite profitable. Raj is contemplating investing in Bema Gold Company. She has the annual report, which includes the financial statements (see Exhibit 7-15). She is concerned because the company has not shown a profit for the last three years, yet issued 8,045,000 new shares for cash in 1998 and 907,807 new shares for cash in 1997. If other investors are willing to buy almost 9,000,000 new shares over the last two years, they obviously have confidence in this company.

> *Required:*
>
> a. Knowing that Bema explores and develops gold properties, explain the significance of gold inventory on its balance sheet by calculating a current ratio for each year and explaining the impact that inventory has on this ratio.
>
> b. Review the three financial statements and draw up a list of questions you would like to ask an investment advisor about this company.

Critical Thinking Question

7-42 (Inventory decision-making with respect to buying and selling)
You and two of your friends have decided to apply some of the knowledge that you are learning in your business classes. You plan to start a wholesale business, buying goods in the Czech Republic and selling them to small specialty stores in the city. One of your friends has an uncle in the Czech Republic who has some contacts that will enable you to buy the merchandise you want. Another friend has an aunt who owns a trucking company that transports merchandise all over Europe. You hope to use the trucking company to transport your merchandise from the Czech Republic to Amsterdam for shipment to Canada.

   You are going to have a meeting to discuss the necessary details surrounding the buying and selling of the inventory. In preparation for the meeting, write a short report outlining the items that you think should be discussed. To make this more realistic and to make your task easier, decide on what types of inventory you are going to buy. The type of inventory you import will affect some of the decisions you make.

EXHIBIT 7-15
PART A

Consolidated Balance Sheets

as at December 31
(in thousands of United States dollars)

	1998	1997
Assets		
Current		
Cash	$ 13,504	$ 24,336
Accounts receivable	2,047	3,130
Notes receivable from associated companies *(Note 11)*	7,303	8,755
Inventories *(Note 3)*	6,858	11,115
Other	454	708
	30,166	48,044
Investments *(Note 4)*	30,561	31,966
Property, plant and equipment *(Note 5)*	131,419	127,533
Other assets *(Note 6)*	8,341	8,451
	$200,487	$215,994
Liabilities		
Current		
Accounts payable	$ 6,737	$ 8,883
Current portion of long-term debt *(Note 7)*	6,000	5,938
	12,737	14,821
Deferred revenue *(Notes 7 and 9)*	7,414	8,945
Long-term debt *(Note 7)*	20,000	25,754
Other liabilities	1,575	1,333
	41,726	50,853
Shareholders' Equity		
Capital stock *(Note 8)*		
Authorized 300,000,000 common shares with no par value		
Issued 122,898,999 common shares (1997 – 104,067,453)	239,690	199,943
Deficit	(80,929)	(34,802)
	158,761	165,141
	$200,487	$215,994

Commitments *(Note 9)*

Approved by the Board

(signature) Director   *(signature)* Director

See accompanying notes to consolidated financial statements.

EXHIBIT 7-15
PART B

Consolidated Statements of Operations and Deficit

for the years ended December 31
(in thousands of United States dollars, except shares and per share amounts)

	1998	1997	1996
Gold revenue	**$ 32,120**	$ 27,991	$ 10,808
Operating costs	**24,912**	22,376	6,603
Gross profit from mine operations	**7,208**	5,615	4,205
Expenses (Income)			
Depreciation and depletion	**6,711**	5,497	2,047
Mine royalty	**469**	642	378
General and administrative	**3,983**	3,516	3,269
Interest on long-term debt	**2,666**	2,188	851
Amortization of deferred financing costs	**1,300**	1,082	310
General exploration	**1,056**	1,120	380
Insurance proceeds	**(2,256)**	(738)	–
Other	**(77)**	217	(1,189)
	13,852	13,524	6,046
Loss before the undernoted items	**(6,644)**	(7,909)	(1,841)
Equity in losses of associated companies	**(1,069)**	(556)	(2,302)
Investment gains	**–**	2,594	1,493
Write-down of mineral properties *(Note 5)*	**(32,738)**	–	(49)
Write-down of inventory *(Note 3)*	**(3,634)**	–	–
Write-down of notes receivable *(Note 11)*	**(2,042)**	–	–
Loss for the year	**(46,127)**	(5,871)	(2,699)
Deficit, beginning of year	**(34,802)**	(27,768)	(23,377)
Imputed interest on equity component of convertible debentures	**–**	(1,163)	(1,692)
Deficit, end of year	**$(80,929)**	$(34,802)	$(27,768)
Loss per common share	**$ (0.40)**	$ (0.07)	$ (0.05)
Weighted average number of common shares outstanding *(in thousands)*	**114,679**	94,698	80,286

See accompanying
notes to consolidated
financial statements.

EXHIBIT 7-15
PART C

Consolidated Statements of Cash Flows

for the years ended December 31
(in thousands of United States dollars)

	1998	1997	1996
Operating activities			
Loss for the year	$(46,127)	$ (5,871)	$ (2,699)
Non-cash charges (credits)			
Depreciation and depletion	6,711	5,497	2,047
Amortization of deferred financing costs	1,300	1,082	310
Equity in losses of associated companies	1,555	2,213	3,333
Deferred revenue	(1,531)	8,945	–
Investment gains	–	(2,594)	(1,493)
Write-down of mineral properties	32,738	–	49
Write-down of inventory	3,634	–	–
Write-down of notes receivable	2,042	–	–
Other	665	25	(38)
Changes in non-cash working capital			
Accounts receivable	1,685	(1,017)	(1,142)
Inventories	446	(5,506)	(5,514)
Accounts payable	(7,423)	(741)	1,317
Cash from (to) operating activities	(4,305)	2,033	2,170
Financing activities			
Common shares issued (Note 8)	39,747	27,894	92,016
Subsidiary's shares issued	–	–	740
Debenture conversions	–	(22,667)	(10,333)
Convertible debentures interest payments	–	(1,692)	(2,078)
Joint venture partner loan (repayment)	–	(10,000)	2,000
Refugio loan proceeds	308	4,000	–
Refugio loan repayments	(6,000)	(4,250)	(4,250)
Gold loan monetization gain (Note 7)	–	(8,308)	–
Deferred financing costs	(1,954)	(1,776)	(238)
Other	(123)	1,054	1,088
Cash from (to) financing activities	31,978	(15,745)	78,945
Investing activities			
Acquisition of Arian Resources Corporation (Note 2)	(19,398)	–	–
Refugio mine	(4,808)	(6,706)	(14,193)
Julietta development and construction	(6,170)	–	–
Acquisition, exploration and development	(7,220)	(15,706)	(13,483)
Net proceeds from the Aldebaran transaction (Note 5)	–	4,698	–
Investment purchases in associated companies	(152)	(6,895)	(20,030)
Promissory notes issued by associated companies, net (Note 11)	(590)	(7,693)	(307)
Short-term investments	–	1,459	2,631
Proceeds on sale of investments	–	3,631	4,118
Other	(167)	(1,334)	310
Cash to investing activities	(38,505)	(28,546)	(40,954)
Increase (decrease) in cash	(10,832)	(42,258)	40,161
Cash, beginning of year	24,336	66,594	26,433
Cash, end of year	$13,504	$24,336	$66,594

See accompanying
notes to consolidated
financial statements.

31

How Much Is That Whooping Crane Worth?

One of the most important concepts in accounting is that of "value," which can have many different meanings, depending on the situation—especially when it comes to capital assets. At the Calgary Zoological Society, the question "What is it worth?" has several answers, explains Ken Huyghe, Supervisor, Financial Services.

"Our office furnishings, vehicles, etc., are all capital assets," he says. "We use a four-year depreciation for them," which means that some assets are completely depreciated and have no value on the books any more.

The computers in the Zoo's offices, however, don't appear on its books at all—nor do the buildings, animal enclosures, or land. "Those belong to the city," says Mr. Huyghe. "It's a bit of an unusual situation: For any big item like that, as soon as it's complete its ownership is transferred to the City of Calgary. So we never depreciate it at all."

An example of such an item is the Zoo's Canadian Wilds exhibit, a large forest with various areas, each representing a different habitat and sheltering a number of species native to Canada: mountain goats, wolves, moose, buffalo, deer, and—rarest of all—whooping cranes. Completed in 1998, Canadian Wilds was built entirely with Zoological Society funds but has now been transferred to the City. "It's still on our books," says Mr. Huyghe, "but only because we still owe money for it—or, rather, our capital fund is repaying our operating fund for some of the expenses the one fund 'borrowed' from the other. But it's not an asset of the Zoo's for accounting purposes."

And what about the most important asset of all—the animals? "Believe it or not, they have no value at all on the books," Mr. Huyghe explains. "They're not even inventoried." If the Zoo buys an animal, it turns up as an expense, and, similarly, a sale creates a revenue; they pretty much cancel each other out. In any case, zoos are more likely, these days, to lend one another or exchange animals than to buy and sell them.

"How would you determine the value of an animal?" muses Mr. Huyghe. "And how would you account for something dying or being born? I guess you could." But for now the Calgary Zoo prefers to keep the animals in their cages but off the books. "Still, they obviously have a super value in reality," Mr. Huyghe points out. "For one thing, if they weren't there, we wouldn't have any admissions, would we?"

CAPITAL ASSETS

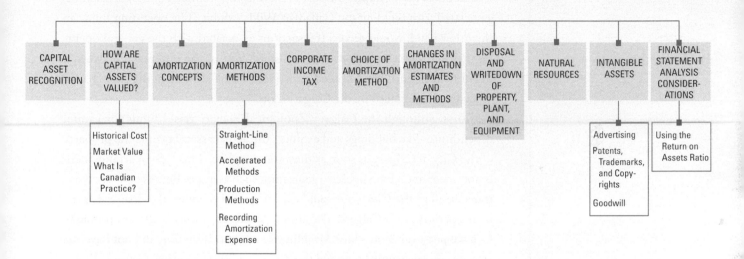

| CAPITAL ASSET RECOGNITION | HOW ARE CAPITAL ASSETS VALUED? | AMORTIZATION CONCEPTS | AMORTIZATION METHODS | CORPORATE INCOME TAX | CHOICE OF AMORTIZATION METHOD | CHANGES IN AMORTIZATION ESTIMATES AND METHODS | DISPOSAL AND WRITEDOWN OF PROPERTY, PLANT, AND EQUIPMENT | NATURAL RESOURCES | INTANGIBLE ASSETS | FINANCIAL STATEMENT ANALYSIS CONSIDER-ATIONS |

HOW ARE CAPITAL ASSETS VALUED?
- Historical Cost
- Market Value
- What Is Canadian Practice?

AMORTIZATION METHODS
- Straight-Line Method
- Accelerated Methods
- Production Methods
- Recording Amortization Expense

INTANGIBLE ASSETS
- Advertising
- Patents, Trademarks, and Copy-rights
- Goodwill

FINANCIAL STATEMENT ANALYSIS CONSIDERATIONS
- Using the Return on Assets Ratio

Learning Objectives:

After studying this chapter, you should be able to:

1. *Describe the valuation methods used for capital assets.*
2. *Identify the acquisition costs that are usually added to the capital asset account at acquisition.*
3. *Describe the purpose of amortization and identify and implement four methods of amortization, including capital cost allowance.*
4. *Identify the factors that influence the choice of amortization method.*
5. *Describe and implement changes in amortization estimates and methods.*
6. *Account for the disposal and writedown of capital assets.*
7. *Describe and implement the amortization method used most frequently for natural resources.*
8. *Explain the accounting difficulties associated with intangible assets.*
9. *Amortize intangible assets.*
10. *Calculate the return on assets ratio and discuss the potential implications of the results.*

Our opening story describes some difficulties associated with recording and reporting capital assets at the Calgary Zoological Society. The Zoo faces some unique problems because of the nature of its assets and because of its relationship with the City of Calgary. The Calgary Zoological Society is a not-for-profit entity similar to the Manitoba Theatre Centre described at the beginning of Chapter 5. Because it is a not-for-profit entity, it has some unique ways of accounting for things—namely, using "funds" to account for specific functions. A "fund" is a complete accounting system that keeps track of specific transactions. For example, the capital fund would record all of the transactions associated with building the Canadian Wilds exhibit. The operating fund, on the other hand, would record transactions associated with the general operations of the Zoo. Now that you have some idea of the difference between a not-for-profit entity and a profit entity, let us look at some of the capital asset recording issues faced by the Calgary Zoo.

First, although the Calgary Zoological Society raises funds for capital expenditures like buildings and exhibits, the actual assets become the property of the City of Calgary as soon as they are complete. This type of arrangement is not uncommon for a public organization such as a zoo. Because the assets are transferred to the City, you would expect to find them on the financial statements of the City of Calgary. The animals represent a whole different problem. Can we put a value on a life? Mr. Huyghe is right: If the Zoo did not have the animals, no one would come and the Zoo would cease to exist. They are, therefore, essential to its continued operation. But can we value them? You know from your accounting studies so far that we do not record people as assets in the accounting system although, like the animals, they may be essential to the organization's operations. There may be some animals that the Zoo actually does buy, which would give you a starting point for valuation. For those animals, you could estimate their expected life and amortize the original cost over that lifetime. But there are probably more animals that the Zoo receives by trading with another zoo or that are born in the Zoo. How would we value those animals? This is a problem that accountants have not yet solved. Until they do, zoos like the Calgary Zoo will continue to expense the cost of animals when they are purchased instead of recording them in the accounting system as capital assets.

This chapter will discuss the measurement, recording, and reporting issues surrounding capital assets. In the previous two chapters, current assets whose value would be realized within one year (or one operating cycle) of the company were discussed. In this chapter, assets with lives longer than a year (or operating cycle) are discussed. We are going to focus on capital assets. Long-term investments that also have lives longer than a year will not be discussed in this text. You will be studying these assets if you take courses in intermediate financial accounting.

Of the capital assets that we are going to study, property, plant, and equipment are the most recognizable. These are a type of noncurrent asset called **tangible assets**, which are usually defined as those assets with some physical form ("tangible" comes from the Latin word for "to touch"). In other words, you can usually see them and touch them. **Intangible assets**, on the other hand, are noncurrent assets that are associated with certain rights or privileges of the company, such as patents, trademarks, leases, and goodwill.

In the sections that follow, the recognition and valuation issues for capital assets are discussed, much as they were for current assets. Because of the long-term nature of these assets, the issue of how to show the income statement effects (expensing of the cost) of the purchase of these assets over time must be addressed. The expense that is recorded is referred to as amortization, or depreciation.

CAPITAL ASSET RECOGNITION

Assets must have a future value to the company. The company must have the right to use them and must have earned that right through a past transaction. When a company buys a capital asset, it has the right to use it—and the transaction has occurred. Therefore, the only asset criterion that merits further discussion is the probable future value, which takes at least two forms. Capital assets are used, first and foremost, to generate revenue, usually by facilitating sales, producing products, or providing services. Therefore, the future value is represented by the cash that will be received from the sales of products and services in the future. Because of the long-term nature of capital assets, these cash flows will be received over several future periods. This type of value is sometimes referred to as **value in use**.

The second source of value for capital assets is their ultimate sales value. Many capital assets are used until the company decides to replace them with a new asset. For example, a business may use a truck for three or four years and then trade it in for a new one. This type of value is called **residual value** (or **resale value**) and can be very important, depending on the type of asset.

Value in use is normally the most appropriate concept for capital assets, because companies usually invest in them to use them, not to sell them. Residual value cannot, however, be totally ignored, because it affects the value of the asset at the end of the period for which the company uses the asset. You saw in Chapter 2 how we use residual value to determine amortization.

The difficulty with the value in use concept for capital assets is the inherent uncertainty with regard to future revenue generated by the sale of inventory or the provision of a service. The company does not know whether the demand for its products or services will continue into the future. Neither does it know what prices the company will be able to command for its products or services. Other uncertainties relate to technology. Equipment can become obsolete as a result of technological change. New technology can give competitors a significant advantage in producing and pricing the product. Technological change can also eliminate the need for the company's product. Consider the manufacturer of 8-track tapes when CDs came on the market. Or consider the typewriter manufacturer with the advent of the personal computer.

The uncertainty of the ultimate residual value is similar to that of the value in use, because the ultimate residual value depends on whether the asset has any value in use to the ultimate buyer. It also is a question of whether a buyer can even be found. Equipment that is made to the original buyer's specifications may not have much of a residual market, because it may not meet the needs of other potential users.

HOW ARE CAPITAL ASSETS VALUED?

Learning Objective

1

Discuss the valuation methods used for capital assets.

In the sections that follow, the discussion is limited to valuation issues regarding property, plant, and equipment, which are similar to those relating to other non-current capital assets. At the end of the chapter, specific concerns and issues with regard to natural resources and intangible assets are discussed.

In Canada, property, plant, and equipment is usually valued at the historical cost with no recognition of market value unless there is a permanent decline in the value of the asset. Some countries do allow for the recognition of changes in market values of property, plant, and equipment, and there have been historical instances of companies disclosing information about the market values of their property, plant, and equipment. Before Canadian practice is discussed in detail, several possible valuation methods will be considered.

Historical Cost

In a historical-cost value system, the original cost of the asset is recorded at the time of acquisition. Changes in the market value of the asset are ignored in this system. During the period in which the asset is used, its cost is expensed (amortized) using an appropriate amortization method (these methods will be discussed later). Market values are recognized only when the asset is sold. The company then recognizes a gain or loss on the sale, where the gain or loss is determined by the difference between the proceeds from the sale and the net book value (carrying value) of the asset at the time of sale. The **net book value**, or **carrying value**, is the original cost less any amortization that had been taken to the point of sale. This net book value is sometimes called the **amortized cost** of the asset.

Market Value

Another possible valuation method records capital assets at their market value. There are at least two types of market values: replacement cost and net realizable value.

Replacement Cost

In a replacement cost valuation system, the asset is carried at its replacement cost. By **replacement cost**, accountants mean the amount that would be needed to acquire an equivalent asset. At acquisition, the historical cost is recorded because this is the replacement cost at the time of purchase. As the asset is used, the carrying value of the asset is adjusted upward or downward to reflect changes in the replacement cost. Unrealized gains and losses are recognized for these changes. The periodic expensing of the asset, in the form of amortization, has to be adjusted to reflect the changes in the replacement cost. For example, if the replacement cost of the asset goes up, the amortization expense will also have to go up, to reflect the higher replacement cost. A gain or loss is also recognized upon disposal of this asset. The amount of the gain or loss is determined by the difference between the proceeds from the sale and the amortized replacement cost at the time of sale. The Accounting Standards Board at one time recommended that companies report supplementary information on the replacement cost of their property, plant, and equipment. At that time, inflation in Canada exceeded 10% and users were expressing concern over the historical cost-carrying values of capital assets. The level of inflation declined and the interest of users in the replacement cost declined along with it. The AcSB removed the recommendation from the *CICA Handbook*. In countries experiencing extreme rates of inflation, capital assets may be recorded at replacement value to provide a better measure of the results for the period. In Mexico, for example, replacement cost of property, plant, and equipment is required for companies whose shares trade on stock exchanges.

Net Realizable Value

With a net realizable value system, assets are recorded at the amount that could be received by converting the asset to cash in the normal course of business—in other words, selling it. During the periods in which assets are being used, gains and losses are recognized as the net realizable value changes over time. Amortization under this type of system is based on the net realizable value and is adjusted every year for the change in this value. At the time of sale, there is no further recognition of gain or loss, as the asset should be carried at net realizable value at the date of sale. This system is not consistent with the notion of value in use of the asset, which assumes that the company has no intention of selling the asset. Therefore, this method is generally not used in Canada even in times of high inflation.

The word *market* must be used with some care. The preceding discussions assume that both the replacement market and the selling market are the markets in which the company normally trades. There are, however, special markets for assets that a company must liquidate quickly. The values in these markets can be significantly different from those in the normal market. As long as the company is a going concern, these specialty markets are not appropriate markets to establish values for the company's assets. On the other hand, if the company is bankrupt or going out of business, these specialty markets may provide the most appropriate estimates of the market value of its assets.

Reports from Other Countries

While most countries value property, plant, and equipment at historical cost, a few (the United Kingdom, France, and Switzerland) allow for revaluation of these assets based on current replacement cost. In France, these revaluations are seldom done, because a conformity requirement between the reporting and tax books would make these revaluations taxable. In the United Kingdom, such revaluations are quite common. The increase in the valuation of the assets that occurs under the replacement cost valuation does not typically pass through income but is recorded directly to the shareholders' equity section, to an account called a *revaluation reserve*.

What Is Canadian Practice?

Capital assets are normally valued at their historical cost (their original acquisition cost). During the period of use, the cost of the asset is expensed using an amortization method that is rational, systematic, and appropriate to the asset. The estimated period of use is generally assumed to be a maximum of 40 years, because estimates longer than 40 years tend to be very uncertain. Changes in market values of the assets are generally not recognized. If it is ever perceived that the net recoverable amount is less than the net carrying value, the difference is recognized as an expense and the carrying value of the asset must be written down. The net recoverable amount is the total of all future cash flows without discounting them to present values. Unlike the case for temporary investments and inventory, once a capital asset is written down it is not written back up if the net recoverable amount subsequently increases.

Capitalizable Costs

Learning Objective

2

Identify the acquisition costs that are usually added to the capital asset account at acquisition.

At the date of acquisition, the company must decide which costs associated with the purchase of the asset should be included or capitalized as a part of the asset's cost. The general guideline is that any cost that is necessary to acquire and prepare the asset for use is a **capitalizable cost**. The following is a partial list of costs that would be considered capitalizable costs:

CAPITALIZABLE COSTS
Purchase price (less any discounts)
Installation costs
Transportation costs
Legal costs
Direct taxes
Interest cost (self-constructed assets)

ethics in accounting

■ The ability to control the timing of a writedown of property, plant, and equipment provides management with an opportunity to manage or manipulate earnings. The issue of earnings management has been studied by many researchers in an attempt to demonstrate its existence and to estimate its effects. In one piece of research along these lines, Bruns and Merchant[1] surveyed 649 managers using a questionnaire describing 13 earnings-management situations and asking respondents to judge the situation as ethical, questionable, or unethical. To quote the authors directly on their results:

"We found striking disagreements among managers in all groups. Furthermore, the liberal definitions revealed in many responses of what is moral or ethical should raise profound questions about the quality of financial information that is used for decision-making purposes by parties both inside and outside a company. It seems many managers are convinced that if a practice is not explicitly prohibited or is only a slight deviation from rules, it is an ethical practice regardless of who might be affected either by the practice or the information that flows from it. This means that anyone who uses information on short-term earnings is vulnerable to misinterpretation, manipulation, or deliberate deception."

The write-off of property, plant, and equipment is but one way that management may attempt to manipulate earnings. The reader of financial statements must be aware of this possibility when analyzing statements, so as not to be misled.

[1] Bruns, W.J., and Merchant, K.A., "The Dangerous Morality of Managing Earnings," *Management Accounting*, August 1990, pp. 22–25.

It is not always easy to determine which costs appropriately belong in an asset account. For example, the cost associated with the salaries of the employees who plan for and order the new asset are normally not included in the acquisition cost itself. This is true even though the time spent by the employees is necessary to acquire the asset. On the other hand, if employee time is required to install a new piece of equipment, the employees' wages usually are included. The costs associated with clearing land in preparation for the construction of a new building are usually included in the land account. The cost of digging the hole to build the foundation of the building, on the other hand, is included in the building account. Land is a unique capital asset. Even though it is used by a company for several years, it is still there. Unlike other capital assets, it does not need to be replaced, and, therefore, its original cost is not amortized. Assigning costs to land means that these costs will not appear in the future on the income statement.

The determination of which costs to capitalize is also influenced by the rules followed for tax purposes. For tax purposes, the company would like to expense as many costs as possible—to reduce taxable income and thus reduce taxes. Capitalizing a cost means that the company will have to wait until the asset is amortized before the cost can be deducted for tax purposes. There is, therefore, an incentive to expense rather than capitalize costs that are only indirectly related to the acquisition of the asset. A company may decide to expense the cost for reporting purposes to bolster their argument that the cost is an expense for tax purposes. The materiality criterion also plays a part in the decision concerning which costs are capitalized. Small expenditures related to the purchase of the asset may be expensed rather than capitalized because it is easier to expense them and the addition of the amount to the asset account would not change it significantly.

Basket Purchases

Sometimes a company acquires several assets in one transaction. This is called a **basket purchase**. For example, when a forest products company acquires timberland, it is buying both land and timber. The price paid for the timberland must then be divided between the land and the timber. In Canada, the price paid for these two assets must be divided between them on the basis of their relative fair values at the time of acquisition. There are two reasons for this. First, full disclosure requires that each important type of asset be shown separately. Second, each type of asset that has a different rate of amortization should be separated in the accounts.

Suppose that the purchase price of the timberland was $1 million and the relative fair values of the land and the timber were assessed at $300,000 and $900,000, respectively. In this case, 25% [$300,000/($300,000 + $900,000)] of the cost, or $250,000, should be assigned to the land and the remaining 75%, or $750,000, to the timber. In the case of timberland, splitting the cost has significant implications for the company, because the cost of land is not amortized and the cost of timber can be expensed as the timber is harvested.

The above example of a basket purchase involved timberland. Another example could be the purchase of a building. Part of the real estate cost must be allocated to the land on which the building is sitting and the remainder must be allocated to the building. If the building includes various pieces of equipment or furniture, part of the purchase cost will have to be allocated to these items as well.

Interest Capitalization

Interest capitalization deserves special consideration. Companies often borrow money to finance a capital asset. The interest paid on the borrowed money is capitalized when it is included in the capital asset account rather than being expensed. This is an issue for companies that construct some of their own capital assets. For example, some utility companies construct their own buildings. In addition to the costs incurred in the actual construction of the asset, such as those for raw materials, labour, and overhead, the company will also incur interest costs if it has to borrow money to pay for the materials, labour, and overhead. In Canada, companies can capitalize interest costs for capital assets that are constructed or acquired over time if the costs are directly attributable to the acquisition. The interest costs can be capitalized only until the capital asset is substantially complete and ready for use. For assets that are purchased rather than constructed, interest costs are usually not capitalized. The time period between acquisition and use is usually too short to make interest capitalization meaningful.

AN INTERNATIONAL PERSPECTIVE

Reports from Other Countries

NAFTA Facts

United States—The accounting for property, plant, and equipment is essentially the same as that used in Canada.

Mexico—Property, plant, and equipment is initially recorded at acquisition cost and then restated to current value at balance sheet dates, using either price indices or replacement cost.

AMORTIZATION CONCEPTS

Amortization, or **depreciation**, is a systematic and rational method for allocating the cost of capital assets to the periods in which the benefits from the assets are received. This matches, in a systematic way, the expense of the asset to the revenues earned from its use. The allocation of any cost across multiple periods will always be somewhat arbitrary. In Canada, the amortization method used must be a rational and systematic method appropriate to the nature of the capital asset with a limited life and to its use by the enterprise. In addition, the method of amortization and estimates of the useful life should be reviewed on a regular basis.

Amortization as used in accounting does not refer to valuation. While it is true that the capital assets of a company generally decrease in value over time, amortization does not attempt to measure this change in value.

Matching some portion of a capital asset's cost to the revenues of the company, along with the other expenses of the company, results in a net profit or loss during the period. The company does not show the entire cost of the capital asset as an expense in the period of acquisition, because the asset is expected to produce revenues over multiple future periods. If these revenues do not materialize, the company will have overstated its profitability in earlier periods and will have to write off the remaining cost of the asset.

To systematically allocate the expense to the appropriate number of periods, the company must estimate the **useful life** of the asset—that is, the periods over which the company intends to use the asset to produce revenues. The company must also estimate the ultimate residual sales value of the asset at the end of its useful life.

Once the useful life and residual value of the asset have been estimated, the **amortizable cost** (cost minus residual value) must be allocated in a systematic and

Learning Objective

Describe the purpose of amortization and identify and implement four methods of amortization, including capital cost allowance.

rational way to the years of useful life. Even though in Canada we do not specify which amortization methods may be used, most Canadian companies use one of three methods. These methods will be discussed in the next section.

AMORTIZATION METHODS

As GAAP developed in the 20th century, "rational and systematic" methods of amortizing capital assets were also developed. The simplest and most commonly used method (used by more than 50% of Canadian companies) is the **straight-line method** (illustrated in Chapter 2), in which the amortizable cost of the asset is allocated evenly over the useful life of the asset. Many accountants have argued in favour of this method for two reasons. First, it is very simple to apply. Second, it properly matches (they argue) expenses to revenues for costs associated with assets that generate revenues evenly throughout their lives. It might also be argued that if an asset physically deteriorates evenly throughout its life, straight-line amortization would capture this physical decline.

For certain assets, decline in revenue-generating capabilities (and physical deterioration) do not occur evenly over time. In fact, many assets are of most benefit to the company during the early years of their useful lives. In later years, when an asset is wearing out and requires more maintenance and perhaps produces inferior products, the value to the company declines significantly. This scenario argues for a more rapid amortization in the early years of the asset's life when a larger amortization expense is matched to the larger revenues produced. Methods that match this pattern are known as **accelerated** or **diminishing balance amortization**.

A third type of amortization recognizes that the usefulness or benefits derived from some capital assets can be measured fairly specifically. These methods are called the **production** or **unit of production methods**. Their use requires that the output or usefulness that will be derived from the asset be measurable as a specific quantity. For example, a new truck might be expected to be used for a specific number of kilometres, such as 250,000. Then the amortization cost per kilometre can be calculated and used to determine amortization expense based on the number of kilometres driven in the accounting period.

A fourth but rarely used amortization method argues that, for some assets, the greatest change in usefulness and/or physical deterioration takes place in the last years of the asset's life rather than in the first few years. A method that captures this pattern is called **decelerated amortization**. Although this type of amortization is not used much in practice, it is conceptually consistent with **present-value amortization**, sometimes called **compound interest amortization**.

Exhibit 8-1 illustrates the pattern of decline in the carrying value of an asset under the three basic methods: straight-line, accelerated, and decelerated. Exhibit 8-2 illustrates the pattern of amortization expense recognition under the same methods. The graphs are based on a 40-year useful life, a zero residual value, and a $10,000 original cost. The methods used are straight-line, accelerated, and decelerated. These methods will be discussed in detail later. Note that Exhibits 8-1 and 8-2 do not show production methods, because there is no consistent pattern with production methods. The amount of amortization expense depends on the actual usage each year.

EXHIBIT 8-1

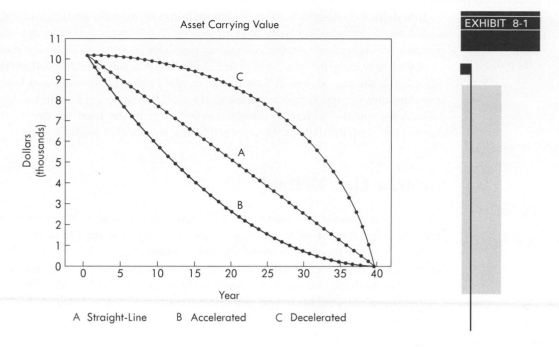

Asset Carrying Value

A Straight-Line   B Accelerated   C Decelerated

In Exhibit 8-1, note that using the straight-line method produces an even (or straight-line) decline in the carrying value of the asset. The accelerated method produces a more rapid decline in the carrying value. The decelerated (present value) method produces a less rapid decline. Note that all methods start and end at the same value.

EXHIBIT 8-2

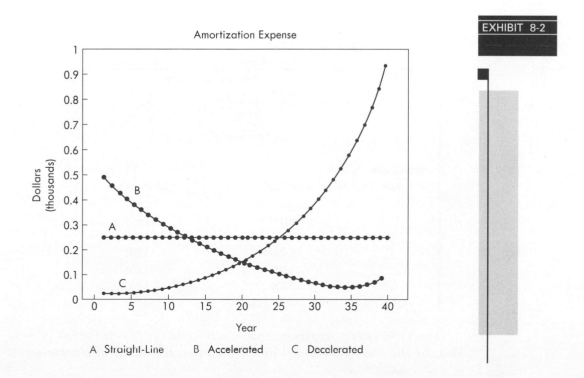

Amortization Expense

A Straight-Line   B Accelerated   C Decelerated

In Exhibit 8-2, you can see that the amortization expense for each period is the same with the straight-line method. With an accelerated method, the amortization expenses are higher in the earlier years of the asset's life, corresponding to the more rapid decline in carrying value, as seen in Exhibit 8-1. A decelerated method, on the other hand, shows a slower decline in the carrying value of the asset and hence small amounts of amortization expense in the earlier years compared to the later years. Although the pattern of recognition is different, the total amount of the expense taken over the life of the asset will be the same for all methods.

Straight-Line Method

The most common method used for financial reporting is the straight-line method. It assumes that the cost of the asset is allocated evenly over the life of the asset. Estimates must be made of the useful life and residual value. A simple example will serve to illustrate the straight-line calculation and the calculation of amortization using other methods. Assume that a company buys an asset for $10,000. The asset has an estimated useful life of five years and an estimated residual value of $1,000. Straight-line amortization would be computed as shown in Exhibit 8-3.

EXHIBIT 8-3

Straight-Line Method

Assumptions:

Original Cost	$10,000
Estimated Residual Value	$ 1,000
Estimated Useful Life	5 years

Calculation:
Straight-Line Amortization

$$\text{Amortization Expense} = \frac{\text{Original Cost} - \text{Estimated Residual Value}}{\text{Estimated Useful Life}}$$

$$= \frac{\$10,000 - \$1,000}{5 \text{ years}}$$

$$= \$1,800 \text{ per year}$$

Amortization Schedule:

Year	Book Value Beginning	Amortization Expense
1	$10,000	$1,800
2	8,200	1,800
3	6,400	1,800
4	4,600	1,800
5	2,800	1,800
		$9,000

The $1,800 of amortization expense is recorded each year for five years so that, by the end of the useful life of the asset, the entire amortizable cost

($9,000 = $10,000 − $1,000) will have been expensed and the residual value of $1,000 will remain on the books of the company.

Whereas the straight-line method can be described by the estimated useful life and estimated residual value, it is sometimes characterized by a rate of amortization. Under the straight-line method, the rate of amortization is determined by taking the inverse of the number of years, 1/N, where N is the number of years of estimated useful life. In the case of the asset in the example, amortizing it over five years means a rate of 0.2 (1/5), or 20% per year. This is referred to as the **straight-line rate**. Note that 20% of the amortizable cost, $9,000, is $1,800.

Accelerated Methods

In most accelerated methods, the amortization is computed by multiplying the carrying value of the asset by a fixed percentage. Because the carrying value (cost less accumulated amortization) decreases each year (since the accumulated amortization increases each year by the amount of the amortization recorded), the computed amount of amortization to be recognized as an expense decreases each year.

The percentage used in these computations is selected by management, based on their judgement of the rapidity of the decline in usefulness of the asset. The faster the decline, the higher the percentage selected. Different types of capital assets have different percentages. A capital asset with a relatively long expected useful life (such as a building) would have a fairly small percentage (such as 5% or 10%). A capital asset with a relatively short expected useful life (such as equipment) would have a larger percentage (such as 20% or 30%).

One method of establishing the percentage rates to be used is called the **double declining balance method**. With this method, the percentage selected is double the straight-line rate. Thus, using the example shown in Exhibit 8-3, the five-year expected useful life of an asset would be amortized over five years on a straight-line basis (that is, 1/20 per year, or 20%), but would be amortized at 40% using the double declining balance method (2 x 20%). However, even though this method appears to be based on fairly concrete numbers, it must be remembered that the 40% rate is still somewhat arbitrary (the 20% is an estimate).

Double declining balance amortization is calculated for our sample asset in Exhibit 8-4. Note that the residual value of the asset does not enter into the computation of the amortization expense. In accelerated methods, the estimated residual value serves as a constraint. This means that, in the example in Exhibit 8-4, the company would not take the full amortization expense determined by the calculation in Year 5, because this would reduce the carrying value of the asset to less than the estimated residual value. In other cases, the residual value may not be reached prior to the end of the useful life so that additional amortization must be taken in the year of disposal of the asset. Alternatively, a loss on disposal could be recognized. In the example given in Exhibit 8-4, suppose that the residual value was $500. The amortization schedule would be the same as that in Exhibit 8-4 except that in Year 5 the company would have to recognize $796 in amortization expense, so the carrying value of the asset would be $500, which is the amount of the residual value.

EXHIBIT 8-4

■ Double Declining Balance Method

Assumptions:

Original Cost	$10,000
Estimated Residual Value	$ 1,000
Estimated Useful Life	5 years
200% Declining Balance Method	

Calculation:

$$\text{DB rate} = \text{DB\%} \times \text{SL rate}$$
$$= 200\% \times 1/n$$
$$= 200\% \times 1/5 = 40\%$$

Amortization Schedule:

At the beginning of the year

Year	Balance in PP&E	Accumulated Amortization	Net Book Value	Calculation of Expense	Amortization Expense
1	$10,000	$ 0	$10,000	40% × 10,000 =	$4,000
2	10,000	4,000	6,000	40% × 6,000 =	2,400
3	10,000	6,400	3,600	40% × 3,600 =	1,440
4	10,000	7,840	2,160	40% × 2,160 =	864
5	10,000	8,704	1,296	40% × 1,296 =	296[a]
					$9,000

[a] The calculation of amortization expense in Year 5 results in a calculated amortization expense of $518, which would reduce the balance to less than the residual value. Therefore, only the amount of expense necessary to bring the balance to the residual value ($1,000) is recorded.

Production Methods

Another method used to calculate amortization is based on the assumption that benefits derived from a capital asset are related to the output or use of that asset. Note that the straight-line and accelerated methods of amortization assume that benefits derived from capital assets are related to time, disregarding how much the assets are actually used during the period. Production methods relate benefits to actual usage.

Use of production methods requires that the useful life of the asset be known or can be estimated and expressed as units of output. For example, trucks can be amortized using a production method if their expected useful life can be expressed in kilometres driven or hours used. Machinery used in producing products may have an expected useful life based on the total number of units of output. Amortization expense is determined by calculating the amortization cost per unit, then multiplying this cost per unit by the actual number of units produced for the period. The formula for calculating amortization expense per unit for production methods is as follows:

$$\text{Amortization expense per unit} = \frac{(\text{cost} - \text{residual value})}{\text{estimated total units of output}}$$

To calculate total amortization expense, simply multiply this per-unit cost by the total number of units produced. Exhibit 8-5 illustrates this method using our previous example.

■ **Production Method**

EXHIBIT 8-5

Assumptions:

Original Cost	$10,000		
Estimated Residual Value	$ 1,000		
Estimated Usage	Year 1	5,000 units	
	Year 2	4,500 units	
	Year 3	5,500 units	
	Year 4	3,000 units	
	Year 5	2,000 units	
		20,000 units	

Calculation:

$$\text{Amortization Expense per Unit} = \frac{(\text{Cost} - \text{Residual Value})}{\text{Estimated Total Units of Output}}$$

$$= \frac{(\$10,000 - \$1,000)}{20,000 \text{ units}}$$

$$= \$0.45 \text{ per unit}$$

Amortization Schedule:

Year	Cost per Year	Units Used	Expense
1	$0.45 x	5,000	$2,250
2	$0.45 x	4,500	2,025
3	$0.45 x	5,500	2,475
4	$0.45 x	3,000	1,350
5	$0.45 x	2,000	900
			$9,000

Recording Amortization Expense

Regardless of the amortization method used, the recording of the expense is the same. Amortization expense is debited and accumulated amortization is credited. The credit side of the entry is made to an accumulated amortization account, *not* to the asset account. The accumulated amortization account is a contra asset account used to accumulate the total amount of amortization expense that has been recorded for the capital asset. It might help you to think of the asset account being used to show the original historical cost of the asset, and the accumulated amortization account being used to show how much of the asset cost has already been expensed.

In financial statements, companies normally show the total original costs of all tangible capital assets separately by category (such as land, buildings, and equipment) with accumulated amortization for each category. Some companies show only one total for accumulated amortization for all the various categories of assets. Some companies show capital assets grouped not by category but by operating division. Many companies show only the total net book value (cost less accumulated amortization) in the balance sheet, with the details provided in a note to the financial statements.

Examples of disclosure of capital assets (sometimes called *fixed assets*) and related accumulated amortization (sometimes called *depreciation*) are shown in Exhibits 8-6 and 8-7. Note that Cara Operations Limited discloses that it is constructing some capital assets and that it is capitalizing the interest costs. The capitalization of interest was discussed earlier in this chapter. In 1997, Algoma Central Corporation disclosed that it was implementing a new capital expenditure program, which would extend the life of its lake vessels significantly. It therefore changed the estimates associated with the capital assets, and the new amortization expense was lower because the original cost was being amortized over a longer period of time. More will be said about this later.

EXHIBIT 8-6

Cara Operations Limited
Excerpt from the Notes to the Statements

3. PROPERTY, PLANT AND EQUIPMENT

In thousands of dollars	Cost	Accumulated Amortization	1999 Net	Cost	Accumulated Amortization	1998 Net
Land	$ 28,839	$ —	$ 28,839	$ 28,927	$ —	$ 28,927
Buildings	80,417	33,557	46,860	81,975	31,884	50,091
Equipment	187,769	75,074	112,695	161,150	64,007	97,143
Leasehold improvements	60,336	20,943	39,393	43,742	17,571	26,171
Equipment under capital leases	33,477	11,456	22,021	37,363	11,040	26,323
	$ 390,838	$ 141,030	$ 249,808	$ 353,157	$ 124,502	$ 228,655

Included in the cost of property, plant and equipment is construction in progress amounting to $16.7 million (1998 – $8.6 million). Interest in the amount of $0.3 million (1998 – $0.3 million) has been capitalized during the year.

CORPORATE INCOME TAXES

The issue of corporate income taxes arises quite naturally at this point and is therefore introduced here. Revenue Canada does not allow companies to deduct amortization expense when calculating **taxable income**. However, it does allow a similar type of deduction, called **capital cost allowance (CCA)**. Capital cost allowance is calculated in a manner similar to accelerated amortization, with several exceptions.

Algoma Central Corporation
Excerpt from the Notes to the Statements

EXHIBIT 8-7

5. Capital Assets

		Land	Amortizable Assets	Accumulated Amortization	Net
		1998			
Marine	$	171	$ 555,514	$ 296,184	$ 259,501
Real Estate		5,029	69,374	19,784	54,619
	$	5,200	$ 624,888	$ 315,968	$ 314,120
		1997			
		Land	Amortizable Assets	Accumulated Amortization	Net
Marine	$	171	$ 480,982	$ 276,783	$ 204,370
Real Estate		1,326	51,894	17,871	35,349
	$	1,497	$ 532,876	$ 294,654	$ 239,719

The calculation of amortization expense for accounting income and CCA for taxable income means that the net capital asset under each calculation is different. This difference is known as a **temporary difference**. Although the amortization expense and the CCA will likely not be the same in a given year, the net capital asset amount under the two calculations will, over time, be the same. When there is a difference in the net capital asset amounts because accounting guidelines and tax rules are different, the result is a **future tax asset or liability**, which accounts for the difference.

In December 1997, Canada introduced a new accounting guideline with respect to corporate income tax. The new guideline measures the future income tax liability or asset using the tax basis of assets and liabilities and the carrying values of those same assets and liabilities on the balance sheet. The guideline came into effect on January 1, 2000, although companies were encouraged to start earlier. The old guideline on corporate income taxes concentrated on the **timing differences** represented by the amortization expense calculated for accounting purposes and the CCA calculated for tax purposes. This difference was referred to as **deferred tax**. Because companies just started to implement this new guideline in 2000, many of the financial statements that you will be examining, including all of the examples used in this book, will refer to deferred taxes.

While it is not the purpose of this text to teach you about income taxes, which are subject to very complex rules, you should understand the basic rules of CCA. Because CCA is required for tax purposes, many smaller companies use it for the accounting amortization calculation as well, so that they have to do only one calculation. For tax purposes, capital assets are grouped into classes as defined by Revenue Canada. For example, most vehicles are grouped into Class 10 and most equipment into Class 8. For each class, a prescribed rate is used to calculate the maximum amount that may be deducted. For example, Class 10 has a maximum rate of 30% and Class 8 has a maximum rate of 20%. Companies may deduct any part of the **undepreciated capital costs (UCC)** in the class up to the stated maximum in a year, except for assets acquired in the current year. In the year of acquisition, the maximum CCA that may be deducted for new assets is restricted to 50% of the normal amount.

For example, assume that Central Corp. purchases new equipment (Class 8) in Year 1 at a total cost of $20,000. For tax purposes, it may deduct a maximum, as follows:

CCA Year 1	50% × $20,000 × 20% = $2,000
CCA Year 2	20% × ($20,000 − $2,000) = $3,600
CCA Year 3	20% × ($20,000 − $2,000 − $3,600) = $2,880

Note that the UCC declines each year by the amount of CCA claimed the previous year.

The cost of new capital assets is added to the class to increase the UCC. When capital assets are sold, the lesser of the original cost or the proceeds from the sale is deducted from the UCC.

The differences between tax and financial statement amounts can produce significant differences between the carrying value of the asset measured in accordance with accounting guidelines and the UCC used as the basis for the CCA reported to Revenue Canada. For example, assume that a company has only one asset. Assume further that there are no other differences in the revenues and expenses for accounting and tax purposes. For tax purposes, assume that the maximum CCA rate is 30%. For financial statement purposes, assume the use of straight-line, and use the deductions shown in Exhibit 8-3. Exhibit 8-8 presents some additional data for this hypothetical company and the computation of income before taxes for the first year of the asset's life.

EXHIBIT 8-8

Future Tax Computations

Income Statement

	Accounting	Tax
Revenues	$90,000	$90,000
Expenses (except amortization or CCA)	50,000	50,000
Income before amortization and taxes	40,000	40,000
Amortization/CCA	1,800	1,500
Income before taxes	$38,200	$38,500
Tax expense (30%)	$11,460	
Taxes payable (30%)		$11,550
Carrying value of the asset	$ 8,200	$ 8,500

Future tax asset = ($8,200 − $8,500) × 30% = $90

If the tax rate is 30%, the company will owe $11,550 ($38,500 × 30%) in taxes based on the income reported to Revenue Canada. What should the company report as tax expense to the shareholders? Some accountants would argue that the tax expense should be calculated based on the accounting income times the tax rate. In this case, the tax expense would be $11,460 ($38,200 × 30%). Others would argue that the company should report the actual taxes payable to Revenue Canada, $11,550, as the expense. In the second case, the tax expense for accounting purposes would not bear any relationship to the income before taxes; that is, $11,550/$38,200 = 30.2% would not reflect the actual tax rate of 30%.

In Canada, the tax expense reported in the income statement must be based on the accounting income before taxes multiplied by the tax rate—that is, the $11,460 just discussed. The entry that would be recorded for our sample company would therefore be:

SE-Tax expense	11,460	
A-Future tax asset	90	
L-Income taxes payable		11,550

As you can see in the preceding entry, the debit to tax expense would then be less than the credit to the taxes payable account, because the latter is based on what is actually owed to Revenue Canada. The difference between these two entries, the **future tax asset**, represents the difference between the carrying values of the asset under accounting and tax multiplied by the tax rate. If the future tax amount has a debit balance, the carrying value of the asset for tax is larger than the carrying value for accounting; therefore, less tax will be paid in the future, because there is still $8,500 of taxable asset remaining—compared to $8,200 for the accounting asset. If the future tax amount has a credit balance (a **future tax liability**), the carrying value of the asset for tax is smaller than the carrying value for accounting; therefore, more tax will be paid in the future, because the smaller tax carrying amount represents a smaller future deduction. These taxes will have to be paid by the company later in the asset's life, when the deduction for tax purposes is significantly less than the amortization for reporting purposes.

Future income tax, therefore, arises from differences in the carrying value of assets for tax purposes and the carrying value for financial statement purposes. The discussion of income taxes goes into more detail in Chapter 9.

CHOICE OF AMORTIZATION METHOD

Companies are free to choose from among the amortization methods that have been discussed. The majority of companies use the straight-line method, probably because of its simplicity and possibly because it usually produces the highest net income in the early years of an asset's life. Some small companies choose to calculate amortization expense using CCA in order to simplify bookkeeping.

Learning Objective

4

Identify the factors that influence the choice of amortization method.

CHANGES IN AMORTIZATION ESTIMATES AND METHODS

Because the amounts used for useful life and residual value are estimates, the assumptions used in their estimation may change over time. Companies must periodically revisit these estimates to ensure that they are still valid. For example, after an asset has been in service for several years, the company may change its estimate concerning the remaining useful life of the asset. The asset may last longer or deteriorate more quickly than originally anticipated. Changes in the estimates used to calculate amortization expense are accounting estimate changes. Accounting estimate changes are handled prospectively.

Learning Objective

5

Describe and implement changes in amortization estimates and methods.

The amortization example in Exhibit 8-3 can be used to illustrate a prospective change in amortization assumptions. Assume that during Year 4 the company decides that the asset has three more years of useful life left (i.e., it should have had an original life of six rather than five years) and that the residual value at the end of the sixth year will be $400. The company recalculates the amortization for Years 4, 5, and 6 based on these new assumptions. The new calculation is based on the remaining book value at the end of Year 3, which is $4,600 [$10,000 − (3 × $1,800)]. The entire schedule of amortization, then, is as shown in Exhibit 8-9. Note that there is no restatement of prior periods with a change of estimate.

EXHIBIT 8-9

■ **Straight-Line Method**
Change in Estimate of Useful Life and Residual Value

Assumptions:

Original Cost	$10,000
Estimated Residual Value	$ 1,000
Estimated Useful Life	5 years

Change during Year 4:

Remaining Estimated Useful Life	3 years
Estimated Residual Value	$ 400

Calculation of Remaining Amortization (years 4–6):
Straight-Line Amortization

$$\text{Amortization Expense} = \frac{\text{Remaining Book Value} - \text{Estimated Residual Value}}{\text{Estimated Useful Life}}$$

$$= \frac{\$4,600 - \$400}{3 \text{ years}}$$

$$= \$1,400 \text{ per year}$$

Amortization Schedule:

Year	Book Value Beginning	Amortization Expense
1	$10,000	$1,800
2	8,200	1,800
3	6,400	1,800
4	4,600	1,400
5	3,200	1,400
6	1,800	1,400
		$9,600

The disclosure of changes in estimates in financial statements usually describes the nature of the change and the effects on the current year. Refer back to Exhibit 8-7. In 1997, Algoma Central Corporation stated that the life of its lake vessels had been extended to 15 years and that, as a result of this change, the amortization expense was lower by $8,694,000. Companies are not required to make this type of disclosure, but voluntary disclosure improves the usefulness of the financial information.

Amortization amounts can also change as new costs are added to the asset account for major repairs and improvements. These generally will require new estimates of useful life and residual value. These are handled as changes in accounting estimates.

A company may also decide that a different amortization method more appropriately aligns the amortization expense with the benefits received from the asset. If the decision to change comes from changed circumstances, experience, or new information, the change is treated in the same way as the changes in estimates were treated. The new amortization method is applied to the carrying value of the asset at the point when the change is made, and the company continues with the new method over the asset's remaining useful life. It is possible that changes in the useful life and residual value might also be applied with the new amortization method.

DISPOSAL AND WRITEDOWN OF PROPERTY, PLANT, AND EQUIPMENT

At the end of an asset's useful life, a company usually sells the asset for another asset of similar productive capacity, especially if the line of business is growing and prospering. In lines of business that are on a decline or are discontinued, old assets are not replaced and assets may be sold or written off before they reach the end of their useful lives.

Normally, at the end of an asset's life, the asset is sold. If the company has accurately projected the residual value, there is no gain or loss on the transaction. If the residual value was not accurately estimated, either a gain or a loss results from this transaction. For example, suppose that the asset in Exhibit 8-3 is sold for $1,200 at the end of its useful life. Recall that its original cost was $10,000 and that its residual value was $1,000. The following entry would be made to record the transaction:

Learning Objective

6

Account for the disposal and writedown of capital assets.

A-Cash	1,200	
XA-Accumulated amortization	9,000	
A-Property, plant, and equipment		10,000
SE-Gain on sale of property, plant,		
and equipment		200

In this entry, the accumulated amortization is removed from the account, as well as the original cost from its account. Note that the net of these two amounts is the carrying value of the asset at the point of sale, $1,000 ($10,000 − $9,000). This amount is also known as the *book value* or *net book value* at the time of sale. Note also that you cannot credit the property, plant, and equipment account for the amount of the book value of $1,000, as that would leave $9,000 in the asset account and $9,000 in the accumulated amortization account, even though the asset is no longer owned by the company.

If the asset had been worthless at the end of its useful life, the disposal of the asset would be recorded as above except that no cash is received. If we assume that no cash is received, then the write-off of the asset in our example results in the following entry:

XA-Accumulated amortization	9,000	
SE-Loss on disposal of property, plant, and equipment	1,000	
A-Property, plant, and equipment		10,000

Note that the remaining book value of $1,000 is recorded as a loss on disposal, not as an adjustment to the amortization that has been recorded.

Sometimes the future recoverable amount of a capital asset (reflecting its ability to generate revenue in the future) declines below its carrying value. Some of the reasons for this decline could be technological change, damage to the asset, or change in the market direction of the company. When the recoverable amount declines, the company must write down the carrying value of the asset to its new lower value. This is done by recognizing a loss on the income statement and increasing the accumulated amortization account by the amount of the loss. Increasing the accumulated amortization decreases the net book value of the asset. For example, suppose that at the end of the third year, when the book value of the asset in Exhibit 8-3 is $4,600, the company determines that as a result of some damage the asset's future recoverable amount has declined to $3,600. The following entry would be made to record this change:

| SE-Loss due to damage to asset | 1,000 | |
| XA-Accumulated amortization | | 1,000 |

In all likelihood, subsequent to this decline in value the company would review the estimated residual value and the useful life so that any necessary changes could be made to the amortization in future periods.

NATURAL RESOURCES

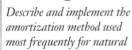

Learning Objective

7

Describe and implement the amortization method used most frequently for natural resources.

Companies that deal with natural resources face some unique problems not associated with investments in property, plant, and equipment. For example, consider the situation of an oil exploration company. The company incurs large costs to find oil. Some explorations are successful in finding oil and others are not. Should the costs of unsuccessful explorations be capitalized on the balance sheet as assets, or should they be written off? Capitalizing these costs as assets implies that they have future value. But do they? If the costs of successful explorations are capitalized, how should they be expensed? That is, what is the useful life of the asset created, and what is a reasonable pattern of expense allocation across the useful life?

In Canada, oil exploration companies have a choice of two methods to account for exploration costs: the **full costing method** and the **successful efforts method**. Under the full costing method, the costs of all explorations, both successful and unsuccessful, are capitalized as long as the expected revenues from all explorations are estimated to exceed the total costs. Under the successful efforts method, on the other hand, only the costs of successful explorations are capitalized, and unsuccessful exploration costs are expensed. Sufficient time is allowed to determine whether an effort is successful. Generally, smaller oil companies use the full costing method, as use of the successful efforts method would make their income appear to be very uneven from year to year, depending on the results of the wells they drilled during the year. Larger oil companies drill more wells every year, so they tend to use the successful efforts method, as it is simpler to apply and its use over a large base does not result in uneven results from year to year.

Exhibit 8-10 includes examples from two companies:

■ Examples of the Full Costing and Successful Efforts Methods

Excerpts from the Notes to Statements

Petromet Resources Limited (1998)

Note 1 (c)(i)

Petroleum and natural gas properties: The Company follows the full cost method of accounting for petroleum and natural gas operations whereby all costs of exploring for and developing petroleum and natural gas reserves are capitalized and accumulated in a single cost centre representing the Company's activity undertaken exclusively in Canada. Such costs include land acquisition costs, geological and geophysical expenses, lease rental costs on non-producing properties, costs of drilling both productive and non-productive wells, related plant and production equipment costs, and overhead charges directly related to these activities.

Suncor Energy Inc. (1998)

Summary of Significant Accounting Policies
(d) Capital assets

The company follows the successful efforts method of accounting for its crude oil and natural gas operations. Under the successful efforts method, acquisition costs of proved and unproved properties are capitalized. Costs of unproved properties are transferred to proved properties when proved reserves are confirmed. Exploration costs, including geological and geophysical costs, are expensed as incurred. Exploration drilling costs are capitalized initially. If it is determined that the well does not contain proved reserves, the capitalized exploratory drilling costs are charged to expense, as dry hole costs, at that time. The related land costs are expensed through the amortization of unproved properties as covered under the Exploration and Production section of the following policy.

Note that Suncor Energy uses the successful efforts method for its acquisition costs and exploration drilling costs. On the other hand, it expenses exploration costs as they are incurred.

Under the full costing method, all capitalized costs are then expensed over the life of the exploration site. Under the successful efforts method, only the capitalized costs associated with the successful site are amortized over the life of the exploration site. The amortization of natural resources is often referred to as **depletion**. The amortization method most commonly used is the production method. With this method, the total number of barrels of oil (in the case of an oil field) that exists in the field is estimated. The amortization expense is then calculated by dividing the number of barrels extracted during the period by the estimated total and multiplying this ratio by the capitalized costs. For example, assume a company estimates a field to have two million barrels of oil. In a given period, 500,000 barrels are extracted. If the capitalized costs are $6 million, the amortization expense during the period would be $1.5 million (500,000/2,000,000 × $6,000,000).

INTANGIBLE ASSETS

Learning Objective

8

Explain the accounting difficulties associated with intangible assets.

As discussed earlier in the chapter, some assets can have probable future value to the company but have no physical form. The knowledge gained from research and development, or the customer loyalty and awareness spawned by a well-run advertising campaign, are examples of intangible assets. The company certainly hopes that it will benefit from having spent money in this way. The difficulty in trying to quantify the benefits and assess the costs of producing intangible assets, such as research and development or advertising, is what makes intangible assets a troublesome area for accountants. Although accountants would generally agree that these might constitute assets, the inability to provide reliable data concerning the costs and future value of the assets prevents accountants from recording these items objectively on the books of the company.

The capitalization guideline for intangible assets is that if an intangible asset is developed internally by the company, the costs associated with its production are generally expensed as incurred. If the intangible asset is purchased from an independent third party, however, the intangible asset can be capitalized at its acquisition cost.

An exception to this guideline occurs with the **development costs** for a product or process. If certain guidelines are met, these development costs may be capitalized and amortized over the useful life of the product. However, the basic **research costs** that were incurred prior to any decision being reached to develop the product or process are still expensed. The guideline is intended to ensure that development costs will be capitalized only if the product or process is actually marketable. The guideline stipulates that the product or process be clearly definable, that technical feasibility be established, that management intend to market the product in a defined market, and that the company have the resources needed to complete the project.

Learning Objective

9

Amortize intangible assets.

The amortization of the cost of an intangible asset is similar to the amortization of other capital assets. The company must estimate the useful life and residual value (if any) of the asset. Because of the estimation problems associated with intangible assets, this is sometimes very difficult to do. Typically, the method used to amortize intangibles is the straight-line method, with an estimated residual value of zero. The useful life depends on the type of intangible. The one aspect of amortization that is different for intangibles is that the accumulated amortization account is rarely used. Most often the company reduces the intangible asset directly. Because of the uncertain valuation of intangibles it is not as important for users to know the original cost. For example, the journal entry to record the amortization of a patent would most likely be:

SE-Amortization expense	xxx	
A-Patents		xxx

One additional point is worth noting. When estimating the useful life of an intangible asset, you should consider both economic life and legal life. Many intangible assets, such as patents, copyrights, and trademarks, have very well-defined legal lives, but may have less well-defined and much shorter economic lives. For intangible assets that have indeterminate lives, a maximum of 40 years can be used for amortization purposes. If at any time it is determined that an intangible no longer has future value, it should be immediately written down. Note the following example:

accounting in the news

INTANGIBLES IN BIOTECH COMPANIES

S mall biotech companies are often founded on the strength of intangible assets in the form of scientific patents that hold potential for drug discovery. The costs associated with developing a drug are high, however, and pharmaceutical companies can spend a lot of money with no guarantee of their drug ever reaching the marketplace.

In 1997, Novopharm Biotech Inc., a drug development company in Toronto, acquired Genesys Pharma of Winnipeg largely on the potential of an anti-cancer drug in development by the smaller company. Two years later, Novopharm stopped development following reports of side effects during Phase 1 clinical trials. Novopharm planned to account for the costs associated with development of the drug by taking a $19.6 million writedown.

Source: "Novopharm Biotech suspends drug," by John Greenwood, *National Post (Financial Post)*, Feb. 11, 1999, page C9.

Several types of intangible assets involve special problems. They are discussed in the following sections.

Advertising

Companies spend enormous amounts of money advertising their products to increase current and future sales. Does the incurrence of advertising costs create an asset for the company? If the advertising is successful, the answer is likely to be yes, but how will the company know whether the advertising is successful, and what time periods will receive the benefits from advertisements that were purchased during the current period? If a customer buys a product, did he/she buy it because of the advertisement, because he/she happened to be in the store and saw it on the shelf, or because the neighbour has one? These questions are very difficult to answer. The intent of advertising is clearly to create an asset, but measuring its value can be extremely difficult. These measurement uncertainties are so severe that accountants generally expense all advertising costs. If a company does capitalize this cost, it has to provide very strong evidence to support the creation of an asset.

Patents, Trademarks, and Copyrights

Patents, trademarks, and copyrights are legal agreements that give the owner rights to use protected information. If the protected information is valuable, the agreements are considered assets. Of course, determining whether they have value is a difficult task, as is estimating the period over which the agreements will continue to have value. Each agreement has a legal life associated with it. For example, a patent has a legal life of 20 years. However, this does not mean that it will have an economic life of 20 years. The patent on a computer chip, for example, may have a useful economic life of only a year or two as a result of technological innovation.

A company records these types of intangible assets only when it buys them from a third party. Development costs of most internally developed patents, trademarks, and copyrights are expensed. Some minor costs, such as registration, and the legal costs of filing a patent, trademark, or copyright can be capitalized. The costs are then usually amortized on a straight-line basis over the estimated useful life of the asset. Legal life serves as a maximum in the determination of the asset's useful economic life.

It is sometimes difficult to establish and defend patents, trademarks, and copyrights. Note the example on the next page.

Goodwill

Goodwill is an asset that represents the above-average profits a company can earn as a result of a number of factors. Above-average management expertise, for example, could give a company an advantage over another company in the same industry. An excellent location could provide a comparative advantage over other companies in the same business. Excellent employee or customer relations can also create an advantage in the marketplace.

Companies incur costs to create these types of goodwill. Advertising campaigns, public service programs, charitable gifts, and employee training programs all require outlays that to some extent develop goodwill. This type of goodwill is sometimes referred to as *internally developed goodwill*.

As with other intangible assets, the costs of developing internally developed goodwill are expensed as they are incurred. In practice, goodwill is recorded as an asset only when it is part of the purchase price paid to acquire another company. Goodwill is not an easily identifiable asset, but is represented by the dollar figure paid by the acquiring company for various valuable—but intangible—characteristics of the acquired company (such as good location or good management). These characteristics, in effect, give the acquired company more value than its identifiable assets

accounting in the news

VALUE OF A RECIPE

How valuable is a recipe for tomato-clam juice? Enough to fuel a decade-long legal battle between two producers, Cadbury Schweppes Inc. and FBI Foods Ltd. In January 1999, the Supreme Court of Canada overturned a lower-court order forbidding FBI Foods from using confidential information to make it.

Clamato, the original tomato-clam juice, was developed by a U.S. company called Duffy-Mott Co. Inc., then licensed to Caesar Canning Inc. of British Columbia. Caesar Canning soon joined with FBI to distribute clamato juice with the consent of Duffy-Mott. In 1982, Cadbury Schweppes took over Duffy-Mott, terminated the licensing agreement with Caesar Canning, and licensed Cadbury Beverages Canada Inc. to produce clamato juice.

In 1988, Cadbury Schweppes took FBI to court for infringement of trademark and breach of confidentiality. The judgement favoured Cadbury Schweppes and the judge set damages to be paid by FBI of $29,900, or the cost saved by Caesar Canning by not developing its own recipe. Following an appeal by Cadbury, FBI was ordered to pay Cadbury a year's worth of profits from Caesar Cocktail and forbidden to produce tomato-clam juice using confidential information.

Overturning the lower-court order against FBI was not the end of this story, however. A referee was to work out a fair compensation package from FBI to Cadbury.

Source: "11-year legal battle over clamato juice ends," by Alan Toulin, *National Post (Financial Post)*, Jan. 24, 1999, pages C1 and C6.

(its buildings, inventory, etc.). Recorded goodwill arises only in situations in which one company buys ownership rights in another company. When the cost of the ownership right exceeds the fair value of the identifiable net assets acquired, then the company has purchased goodwill.

The recording of goodwill and its computation are discussed in more detail in Appendix C at the end of the book. Once recorded, goodwill is amortized over a maximum of 40 years, because of the indeterminate nature of its useful life. Note that if goodwill can be traced to a specific cause and its useful life is known to be shorter than 40 years, it should be amortized over its useful life rather than over 40 years.

Examples of the disclosure of goodwill and other intangible assets are provided in Exhibit 8-11 for Métro-Richelieu Inc. and in Exhibit 8-12 for AT Plastics Inc.

EXHIBIT 8-11

Notes to consolidated financial statements   MétroRichelieu

5. Capital assets

	1998			1997			1996
	Cost	Accumu-lated depre-ciation	Net book value	Cost	Accumu-lated depre-ciation	Net book value	Net book value
Tangible assets							
Land	$ 23.1	$ —	$ 23.1	$ 20.7	$ —	$ 20.7	$ 13.2
Buildings	105.2	36.9	68.3	98.6	34.0	64.6	58.5
Equipment	211.9	110.0	101.9	212.6	121.7	90.9	80.2
Leasehold improvements	73.3	47.1	26.2	63.8	44.4	19.4	14.3
	413.5	194.0	219.5	395.7	200.1	195.6	166.2
Intangible assets							
Goodwill	98.8	29.3	69.5	97.5	26.7	70.8	73.2
Leasehold rights	88.5	23.8	64.7	88.5	21.4	67.1	70.4
Improvements and development of retail network loyalty, software and other	118.2	51.9	66.3	89.1	43.4	45.7	31.1
	305.5	105.0	200.5	275.1	91.5	183.6	174.7
	$719.0	$299.0	$420.0	$670.8	$291.6	$379.2	$340.9

EXHIBIT 8-12

4. Other assets

(thousands of dollars)

		1998	
	Cost	Accumulated Depreciation	Net Book Value
Development costs	$ 10,803	$ 2,471	$ 8,332
Deferred exchange	9,795	2,574	7,221
Deferred financing costs	3,468	610	2,858
Deferred pension costs	6,403	–	6,403
Goodwill	1,109	296	813
Investment tax credits recoverable	1,674	–	1,674
Pre-operating costs	7,739	–	7,739
	$ 40,991	$ 5,951	$ 35,040

(thousands of dollars)

		1997	
	Cost	Accumulated Depreciation	Net Book Value
Development costs	$ 9,111	$ 1,675	$ 7,436
Deferred exchange	5,515	1,320	4,195
Deferred financing costs	2,439	184	2,255
Deferred pension costs	6,165	–	6,165
Goodwill	1,109	222	887
Investment tax credits recoverable	1,287	–	1,287
	$ 25,626	$ 3,401	$ 22,225

FINANCIAL STATEMENT ANALYSIS CONSIDERATIONS

The choice of amortization method for capital assets can produce significantly different results in the financial statements of similar companies. For the first few years, a company using the straight-line method will show higher carrying values for its capital assets than a similar company using the double declining balance method. This affects the balance sheet value as well as the amortization expense that is reported in the income statement. Unfortunately, there is no easy way for the user to convert from one method to another to make the statements more comparable.

Probably the biggest concerns in the analysis of capital assets are understanding which assets have been left out and what market values can be assigned to the assets listed. The historical cost figures for property, plant, and equipment can be very old. Even though the company is not holding these assets for resale, it will have to replace them at some point; therefore, the replacement cost may be relevant. In Canada, companies are not required to disclose replacement cost information. If a company reports property, plant, and equipment as a single amount, the user is not able to determine how much is invested in each of the components. This information could be important to users when attempting to anticipate future outflows of cash for the replacement of some of these assets. Even if a company assigns three separate amounts for property, plant, and equipment, the user is still missing some important pieces of information that could be useful in evaluating the company. For example, if a single amount for buildings is disclosed, the user still does not know: (1) how many buildings are included, (2) where the buildings are located, or (3) when the buildings were acquired. Without this information, the user does not have any way of determining replacement cost or market value.

Another problem is that many intangible assets that have been developed internally do not appear on the books of the company because their costs have been expensed as they were developed. It is possible for a company to have the rights to a patent that it has developed and that will generate revenues for several years. This valuable asset is often not listed as an asset. The large dollar amounts that companies are willing to pay for goodwill when taking control of other companies testifies to the substantial value of these unrecorded assets. A failure to consider these assets can lead different analysts to draw significantly different conclusions about the value of a company.

One final general concern with regard to statement analysis is whether the capital assets listed on the company's balance sheet are really worth the amounts recorded. For example, the conditions that gave rise to goodwill at the date of acquisition may have changed since acquisition. Suppose the goodwill was a result of the technical expertise of a key employee of the business that was acquired. If the employee dies or decides to leave the company after acquisition, the goodwill could be worth less. For this reason, analysts generally have a healthy scepticism about the value of goodwill and other intangibles.

Using the Return on Assets (ROA) Ratio

Despite the unknowns associated with the capital asset values, a ratio using assets has been developed. This ratio, called the return on assets ratio, or ROA, is used to calculate how well management managed the assets used in the company. This ratio simply expresses the total return earned as a percentage of total assets. The return on the investment in assets should be computed prior to any payments or returns to the debtholders or shareholders. Net income has interest expense already deducted, but not dividends. Therefore, the net income, if it is to be used as a measure of return on assets, must be adjusted for the effects of interest expense, so its treatment is similar to that of dividends.

A complicating factor is that interest is a deductible expense in the computation of income tax expense. Therefore, if interest expense is to be removed from the net income figure, the amount of income tax expense that would result must also be adjusted. In other words, the tax savings (i.e., the reduction in income tax expense) associated with this interest deduction must also be removed. The ROA ratio is then calculated as the ratio of the return (income before interest) divided by the investment in total assets, as follows:

$$\text{ROA} = \frac{\text{Income Before Interest}}{\text{Average Total Assets}}$$

$$= \frac{\text{Net Income} + \text{Interest Expense} - \text{Tax Savings of Interest Expense}}{\text{Average Total Assets}}$$

$$= \frac{\text{Net Income} + \text{Interest Expense} - (\text{Tax Rate} \times \text{Interest Expense})}{\text{Average Total Assets}}$$

$$\text{ROA} = \frac{\text{Net Income} + [\text{Interest Expense} \times (1 - \text{Tax Rate})]}{\text{Average Total Assets}}$$

For Big Rock Brewery Ltd. the calculation of ROA for 1998 is as follows:

$$\text{ROA} = \frac{\text{Net Income} + [\text{Interest Expense} \times (1 - \text{Tax Rate})]}{\text{Average Total Assets}}$$

$$= \frac{\$288,981 + [\$841,565 \times (1 - .43)]}{(\$31,919,676 + \$32,866,657)/2}$$

$$= \frac{\$288,981 + \$479,692}{\$32,393,167}$$

$$\text{ROA} = .024$$

Big Rock Brewery's ROA of 2.4% seems low. In 1997, Big Rock built a new brewery facility at a cost of approximately $10,000,000. The new facility is intended to allow growth in sales throughout North America. Growth is taking place, but because it is gradual the ROA is still low at this point. In 1999, Big Rock Brewery had a net loss of $556,745, which means that the ROA in 1999 would be negative. As a user of this information, you would be interested in following this ratio over the next few years to determine whether the company meets its expansion goals and improves its ROA.

As with many ratios, the ROA by itself is not as meaningful as a comparison over time or among companies. However, before using ROA to compare different companies, you should be sure their amortization policies are comparable, as different amortization policies will affect the total assets figure. As the Big Rock Brewery example made clear, you should also determine whether the companies you are comparing have recently invested in new assets. The acquisition of new assets will significantly increase the total asset amount and thus decrease the ROA.

SUMMARY

In this chapter, we described the initial acquisition of capital assets, paying attention to the costs that are included in the asset account. Capital assets include land, buildings, vehicles, equipment, natural resources, intangibles, and many other assets that have a useful life of more than one year. We explored several systematic, rational methods of amortizing capital assets. Amortization of capital assets is an estimate of the expense that relates to the use of the assets each year. Because it is an estimate, it is up to management to determine appropriate amortization rates incorporating useful lives and residual values. We took a brief look at what happens with respect to Revenue Canada and amortization. Because Revenue Canada has restricted the amortization method to CCA, the income tax recorded on the accounting income statement often differs from the income tax that is actually owed to Revenue Canada. This difference is referred to as a future tax asset or liability.

Because amortization methods are estimates, it is important for you to periodically review the useful life and residual value assumptions to determine whether they are still appropriate. If new values are established, the book value of the asset is amortized over its remaining useful life using the new values. As well, if the company decides to change amortization methods, it will amortize the asset over its remaining useful life under the new method.

We completed the chapter with a discussion of the calculation of ROA and its limitations.

SUMMARY PROBLEM

Pete's Trucking Company has a fleet of 10 large trucks that cost a total of $1,410,000. The trucks have an estimated useful life of 10 years and an estimated residual value of 10%. For tax purposes, their Capital Cost Allowance (CCA) rate is 30%. The trucks are each expected to be driven 1,000,000 kilometres. At the end of the 10th year, the trucks were sold for $5,500 each.

Required:

1. Prepare a schedule showing the straight-line amortization that would be recorded over the life of these trucks.

2. Prepare a schedule showing the amortization that would result if Pete's had used the double declining balance method.

3. Prepare a schedule showing amortization on a production basis if the following usage was recorded:

Year 1:	125,000	km
Year 2:	120,000	km
Year 3:	115,000	km
Year 4:	110,000	km
Year 5:	105,000	km
Year 6:	100,000	km
Year 7:	90,000	km
Year 8:	80,000	km
Year 9:	70,000	km
Year 10:	60,000	km

4. Prepare journal entries to record the disposal of the trucks, assuming:

   a. Pete's used straight-line amortization

   b. Pete's used double declining balance amortization

   c. Pete's used a production method of amortization

5. Compare the difference in tax saving in the first two years if Revenue Canada accepted straight-line amortization rather than CCA. Assume a 34% tax rate.

SUGGESTED SOLUTION TO SUMMARY PROBLEM

1. The residual value of the equipment would be $141,000 (10% of $1,410,000 rounded to the nearest thousand). The straight-line amortization would be:

$$\text{Amortization Expense} = \frac{\text{Original Cost} - \text{Estimated Residual Value}}{\text{Estimated Useful life}}$$

$$= (\$1,410,000 - \$141,000)/10 \text{ years}$$

$$= \$126,900/\text{year}$$

2. Double declining balance method:
   Declining balance rate = 200% × straight-line rate
   $$= 200\% \times 1/10 = 20\%$$

   The amortization schedule for double declining balance is (in thousands):

Year	Asset Balance			Calculation		Amortization Expense
1		1,410.0		20% ×	1,410.0	$282.0
2	(1,410.0 − 282.0) =	1,128.0		20% ×	1,128.0	225.6
3	(1,128.0 − 225.6) =	902.4		20% ×	902.4	180.5
4	(902.4 − 180.5) =	721.9		20% ×	721.9	144.4
5	(721.9 − 144.4) =	577.5		20% ×	577.5	115.5
6	(577.5 − 115.5) =	462.0		20% ×	462.0	92.4
7	(462.0 − 92.4) =	369.6		20% ×	369.6	73.9
8	(369.6 − 73.9) =	295.7		20% ×	295.7	59.1
9	(295.7 − 59.1) =	236.6		20% ×	236.6	47.3
10	(236.6 − 47.3) =	189.3		See note		48.3

Note: The calculation in Year 10 would result in amortization of $37,800, which would be insufficient to reduce the carrying value of the asset to its residual value ($141,000). Therefore, additional amortization would be taken in Year 10 to bring the asset to its residual value of $141,000 at the end of Year 10.

3. Cost per km: $(1,410,000 - 141,000)/1,000,000 = \$1.269$

Amortization in Year	1:	$\$1.269 \times 125,000$	$= \$158,625$
Amortization in Year	2:	$\$1.269 \times 120,000$	$= \$152,280$
Amortization in Year	3:	$\$1.269 \times 115,000$	$= \$145,935$
Amortization in Year	4:	$\$1.269 \times 110,000$	$= \$139,590$
Amortization in Year	5:	$\$1.269 \times 105,000$	$= \$133,245$
Amortization in Year	6:	$\$1.269 \times 100,000$	$= \$126,900$
Amortization in Year	7:	$\$1.269 \times 90,000$	$= \$114,210$
Amortization in Year	8:	$\$1.269 \times 80,000$	$= \$101,520$
Amortization in Year	9:	$\$1.269 \times 70,000$	$= \$ 88,830$
Amortization in Year	10:	$\$1.269 \times 60,000$	$= \$ 76,140$

4. a. Straight-line method:

A-Cash	55,000	
XA-Accumulated amortization	1,269,000	
SE-Loss on disposal	86,000	
A-Trucks		1,410,000

b. Double declining balance method:

A-Cash	55,000	
XA-Accumulated amortization	1,269,000	
SE-Loss on disposal	86,000	
A-Trucks		1,410,000

c. Production method:

A-Cash	55,000	
XA-Accumulated amortization	1,237,275	
SE-Loss on disposal	117,725	
A-Trucks		1,410,000

5. Year 1: Straight-line amortization: $126,900
CCA: $50\% \times 30\% \times \$1,410,000 =$ 211,500
                                                $\overline{\$ \ 84,600}$

Difference in tax: $34\% \times \$84,600 = \$28,764$ less tax paid under CCA.

Year 2: Straight-line amortization: $126,900
CCA: $30\% \times (\$1,410,000 - \$211,500) =$ 359,550
                                               $\overline{\$232,650}$

Difference in tax: $34\% \times \$232,650 = \$79,101$ less tax paid under CCA.

ABBREVIATIONS USED

AcSB	Accounting Standards Board	ROA	Return on assets
CCA	Capital cost allowance	UCC	Undepreciated capital cost
DB	Declining balance		

SYNONYMS

Amortization/depreciation

Amortized cost/net book value/carrying value

GLOSSARY

Accelerated amortization   A method of amortization in which, unlike the straight-line method, higher expenses are allocated to the early years of an asset's life.

Amortizable cost   The amount of an asset that can be amortized over its useful life; calculated as the original cost less residual value.

Amortized cost   The amount of an asset's cost that remains after it has been amortized. It is another term for net book value or carrying value.

Amortization   The allocation of the cost of capital assets to expense over their useful lives.

Basket purchase   A purchase of assets in which more than one asset is acquired for a single purchase price.

Book value   The value of an asset or liability carried on the books of a company. For capital assets, this value is the acquisition cost of the asset less the accumulated amortization of the asset.

Capital assets   Assets that have expected useful lives of more than one year (or normal operating cycle, if longer) that are used in the business and are not intended for resale.

Capital cost allowance (CCA)   The deduction permitted by Revenue Canada for tax purposes in place of amortization.

Capitalizable cost   A cost that can be recorded as an asset on the financial statements rather than being expensed immediately.

Carrying value   The acquisition cost of a capital asset minus its accumulated amortization. Synonym for net book value or amortized cost.

Compound interest amortization   An amortization method in which the amortization expense for a period is calculated by the change in the present value of the asset. Synonym for present value amortization.

Decelerated amortization   A method of amortization in which the earlier years of an asset's life are allocated lower expenses than the later years.

Declining balance amortization   Methods in which the amortization for each period is calculated by multiplying the rate of amortization by the carrying value of the asset.

Deferred tax   An asset or liability account that arose under the old method of accounting for timing differences associated with tax expense calculated under accounting guidelines and taxes payable calculated using Revenue Canada's rules.

Depletion   A term sometimes used to describe amortization of the cost of natural resources to expense over the useful life of the resource.

Depreciation   A term sometimes used for amortization, especially for tangible assets that are not natural resources.

Diminishing balance amortization   Synonym for accelerated amortization.

Double declining balance method   A particular type of declining balance amortization method in which the percentage rate is double the rate that would be used for straight-line amortization.

Full costing method   A method of accounting for the drilling and exploration costs of an oil exploration company in which all costs of exploration are capitalized and amortized without regard to the success or failure of individual wells; common in smaller oil and gas companies.

Future tax asset or liability   An asset or liability account that arises when there is a difference in revenues or expenses used for tax purposes and for book purposes. With respect to capital assets, it represents the tax effect of the temporary difference in the net carrying value of the capital assets under accounting versus the carrying value for tax purposes.

Goodwill   An intangible asset that represents the above-average earning capacity of a company as a result of reputation, advantageous location, superior sales staff, expertise of employees, etc. It is recorded only when a company acquires another company and pays more for it than the fair market value of its identifiable net assets.

Intangible asset   A non-physical capital asset that usually involves a legal right.

Interest capitalization   The recording of interest as a part of the construction cost of a capital asset.

Net book value   The carrying value of an asset on the books of a company. Also called amortized cost or carrying value.

Net realizable value The selling price of an asset less any costs to complete and sell the asset.

Net recoverable amount The estimated future net cash flow from use of a capital asset together with its residual value.

Present value amortization An amortization method in which the amortization expense for a period is calculated by the change in the present value of the asset.

Production method A method of amortization in which the amortizable cost of the asset is allocated to the years of its useful life as a function of the volume of production or usage for the period.

Rate of amortization A ratio or percentage that describes the amount of amortization that may be taken during a given period. For straight-line amortization, the rate is the reciprocal of the number of years of useful life (1/N).

Replacement cost A market value of an asset determined from the market in which the asset can be purchased by the company. In a manufacturing company, replacement cost is the cost to reproduce the asset based on current prices of the inputs.

Resale value Synonym for residual value.

Residual value The estimated net realizable value of a capital asset at the end of its useful life to the company.

Straight-line method A method of amortization in which the amortizable cost of the asset is allocated evenly over its useful life.

Straight-line rate The rate of amortization for the straight-line method; calculated as the reciprocal of the number of years of useful life (1/N).

Successful efforts method A method of accounting for the drilling and exploration costs of an oil exploration company in which the costs of exploration are capitalized and amortized only for successful wells.

Tangible asset An asset that has a physical substance.

Undepreciated capital cost (UCC) The carrying value of an asset in a class that has not yet been deducted as capital cost allowance for tax purposes.

Unit of production method Synonym for production method.

Useful life An estimate of the period of time over which an asset will have economic value to the company.

Value in sale The value of an asset if the intent is to sell the asset.

Value in use The value of an asset if the intent is to use the asset rather than sell it.

ASSIGNMENT MATERIAL

Assessing Your Recall

8-1 Describe what is meant by "value in use" versus "value in sale" as applied to capital assets.

8-2 Discuss the types of costs that should be capitalized for a piece of equipment.

8-3 Describe the procedure used in Canada to allocate the cost of a basket purchase of assets to the individual assets.

8-4 Describe why interest can be capitalized as a part of the construction costs of an asset.

8-5 Discuss the purpose of amortization expense and the possible patterns of amortization for a company.

8-6 Discuss the motivations that a company might have for choosing one amortization method over another.

8-7 Describe how residual value and useful life are used in the calculation of amortization under the following methods: straight-line, production, and declining balance.

8-8 Describe the differences between Capital Cost Allowance and accelerated amortization.

8-9 Discuss the nature of future income taxes in the context of differences between amortization and CCA.

8-10 Describe the conditions under which intangible assets can be recorded on the books of a company, and the guidelines under which that value can then be expensed over the life of the asset. Specifically, discuss goodwill, research and development, and patents.

8-11 Discuss the conditions under which a company is required to write down its capital assets.

Applying Your Knowledge

8-12 (Acquisition cost)
Four years ago, Litho Printers Ltd. purchased a large, four-colour printing press for $240,000 with the intent of using it for 10 years. Recently, the production manager learned that replacing the press with a comparable new one would cost $400,000. On the other hand, the production manager estimates that if the company were to sell the current machine it would receive $110,000. The manager also estimates that the company could make $850,000 from selling materials produced on the press over the next six years.

Required:

a. What should be the value assigned to the press in Litho Printers' financial statements?

b. Under what conditions should the press be valued at $850,000?

c. Under what conditions should the press be valued at $400,000?

d. Under what conditions should the press be valued at $110,000?

8-13 (Acquisition cost and interest capitalization)
Cedar Homes Ltd. decided to upgrade some of its log preparation equipment and to expand its facilities. The following events occurred during the year:

Jan.   4   Equipment with an invoice price of $75,000 was received.

         9   Construction on a new addition to the main building was started.

        24   A bill in the amount of $2,400 was received for transporting the equipment (received Jan. 4) to Cedar Homes.

        27   Architect's fees of $7,500 were paid for the preliminary design of the addition to the building.

Feb.   3   Payment was made for the equipment and transportation.

March   9   Payment was made to the construction company in the amount of $250,000 following completion of the addition to the building.

        14   Work crews installed the equipment and were paid $900.

        15   A special ad was run in the local paper at a cost of $250 informing residents that the company would begin interviewing for new employees in two weeks.

        24   A party costing $850 was held to celebrate the completion of the new building.

Apr.   7   Testing of the new equipment was completed and it was placed in service. Total testing costs were $900.

Required:

a. Determine the costs that should be capitalized as assets by Cedar Homes in the buildings and equipment accounts.

b. What should be done with any costs not capitalized?

c. If Cedar Homes had borrowed money to finance the expansion of the facilities, what two options would it have had with respect to the interest expense?

8-14 (Acquisition cost and interest capitalization)
Welborne Company incurred the following costs in opening a new production area in its main factory building:

May 7 Paid $110,000 for the removal of old structures to accommodate the new production area.

10 Paid $180,000 for restructuring and finishing the new production area.

15 Paid $80,000 for the cement foundation for the placement of the new machinery.

20 Received new production equipment with an invoice price of $480,000. A business discount of 10% had been applied to the gross selling price to arrive at the figure of $480,000.

27 Paid freight charges on the equipment of $25,000.

29 Paid the invoice for the equipment.

30 Paid $15,000 for the installation of the new equipment.

June 2 Paid the president's salary of $14,000 for June.

7 Received a refund of $8,000 on the cement work for the equipment foundation.

9 Paid excise taxes of $18,000 on the equipment.

Required:

a. Compute the amount that should be capitalized as equipment cost.

b. What treatment should be accorded those costs not included in the equipment cost?

c. How should amortization on the equipment be reported in Welborne's income statement?

d. If Welborne had borrowed money to pay for the equipment, how should it report the interest on the amount borrowed?

8-15 (Valuation of capital assets)
Lundon Company purchased a tract of land for $150,000 roughly 20 years ago and has now divided the land into two parcels. The company intends to sell one of the parcels and keep the other. Lundon estimates it can sell the one parcel for $240,000. It already has an offer of $190,000 from a local business, and it has a tentative offer from the brother of the president of Lundon Company for $320,000.

Required:

a. What accounting concepts and objectives might be used by the accountant in support of recognizing the value of the parcel at $240,000?

b. What accounting concepts and objectives might be used to argue against recognizing either of the proposed offers?

c. Is it appropriate to revalue one of the parcels and not the other?

d. At what amount should the parcel be valued?

8-16 (Calculation of amortization)
A machine is purchased on January 1, 20x1, for $90,000. It is expected to have a useful life of six years and a residual value of $5,000. The company closes its books on December 31.

Required:
Compute the amount of amortization to be charged each year using each of the following methods:

a. Straight-line method.

b. Double declining balance method.

8-17 (Straight-line amortization with disposal)
On June 1, 20x1, Sherman Bros. Corp. purchased a new machine for $30,000. A useful life of 12 years and a residual value of $1,200 were estimated. On November 30, 20x1, another machine was acquired for $75,000. Its useful life was estimated to be 15 years and its residual value $3,000. On April 30, 20x3, the first machine was sold for $25,000. Sherman Bros. closes its books on December 31 each year and uses the straight-line method of amortization.

Required:
Give the necessary journal entries for the years 20x1 through 20x3 for both machines. Assume that Sherman Bros. calculates amortization on a monthly basis.

8-18 (Disposal of capital assets)
On March 31, 20x4, Hammer & Holding Inc. purchased new machinery. The company acquired the new machinery by trading in its old machine, paying $20,100 in cash and issuing a 12% note payable for $6,000. The old machinery was acquired on June 30, 20x1, for $22,000. At that time, its estimated useful life was 10 years, with a $1,000 residual value. The old asset's market value was approximately the same as its book value at the date of the trade-in. The new machinery's estimated life is six years, with a residual value of $2,500. The company uses a straight-line method of amortization and closes its books on December 31.

Required:

a. Give the necessary journal entry to record the amortization of the old asset up to the date of the trade-in in 20x4. Assume that the amortization was correctly recorded for 20x1, 20x2, and 20x3. Give the necessary journal entry to record the trade-in of the old asset and the acquisition of the new one.

b. Assume that on March 31, 20x9, the machinery acquired in 20x4 could not be sold and the company decided to write it off. Give the necessary journal entries for 20x9.

8-19 (Amortization calculation)
Polar Company purchased a building with an expected useful life of 30 years for $350,000 on January 1, 2001. The building is expected to have a residual value of $50,000.

Required:

   a. Give the journal entries that would be made by Polar to record the purchase of the building in 2001 and then amortize expense for 2001 and 2002 assuming straight-line amortization is used.

   b. Give the journal entries that would be made by Polar to record the amortization expense for 2001 and 2002 assuming the double declining balance method is used.

8-20 (Amortization calculation)

On January 1, 2001, Joy of Life Company paid $220,000 to purchase equipment with an expected useful life of six years. Estimated residual value of the equipment is $16,000. The equipment is expected to be used a total of 22,000 hours, as follows: 2001 – 2,400; 2002 – 3,000; 2003 – 4,400; 2004 – 6,000; 2005 – 4,800; and 2006 – 1,400.

Required:

The controller of Joy of Life Company has requested your assistance in determining the annual amortization expense and the balance in accumulated amortization at the end of each of the years using the following methods:

   a. straight-line method.

   b. double declining balance method.

   c. production method.

8-21 (Amortization [including CCA] and income calculation)

On January 1, 2001, Johnson Company invested $750,000 in equipment with an expected useful life of 20 years and an anticipated residual value of $50,000. For tax purposes, this is a Class 8 asset with a CCA rate of 20%. In 2004, Johnson reported sales of $1,100,000 and operating expenses other than amortization of $800,000. At December 31, 2004, Johnson held $250,000 of assets in addition to its equipment. Johnson's tax rate is 30%.

Required:

   a. Assuming Johnson uses straight-line amortization, what amount of net income will it report for 2004? What will be the return on assets for 2004 using the total assets reported at December 31, 2004, and assuming there is no interest expense on the income statement?

   b. What is the maximum amount of CCA (capital cost allowance) that Johnson would be able to claim for tax purposes in 2004? Assuming the company used straight-line for accounting purposes, what would be the new future tax asset or liability in 2004?

   c. Assuming Johnson uses double declining balance amortization, what amount of net income will it report for 2004? What will be the return on assets for 2004 using total assets reported at December 31, 2004?

   d. For what type of asset would it be appropriate to use double declining balance amortization?

8-22 (Change in estimates)

On October 31, 20x3, Steelman Company acquired a new machine for $105,000. The company estimated the useful life to be 10 years and expected a residual value of $5,000. During 20x6, the company decided that the machine was to be used for another 10 years beyond that date, including all of 20x6, and that the residual value would be $1,500. On June 30, 20x8, the machine was sold for $50,000. The company uses the straight-line method of amortization and closes its books on December 31.

Required:
Give the necessary journal entries for December 31, 20x3, 20x6, and 20x8.

8-23 (Amortization of natural resources)
The Pure Oil Company estimated that the new oil field that it acquired has 8 million barrels of oil. The company extracted 500,000 barrels in Year 1, 700,000 barrels in Year 2, and 1 million barrels in Year 3. The costs capitalized for the oil field total $25 million. The company amortizes oil field capital costs using the production method.

Required:
Compute the amortization expense for each year.

8-24 (Intangibles and amortization)
Pinetree Manufacturing Company reports both equipment and patents in its balance sheet.

Required:

a. Explain how the dollar amount for each type of asset is determined.

b. If both types of assets were purchased three years ago for $10,000 each and had estimated useful lives of 10 years, what amount would be reported in the balance sheet at the end of the current period? Explain.

c. Financial analysts sometimes ignore intangible assets in analyzing financial statements. Do you think this is appropriate? Explain.

8-25 (Intangibles and amortization)
Vinay Company purchases several intangible assets as follows:

Asset	Cost
Patent	$ 60,000
Copyright	200,000
Licence	720,000

In addition to the purchase cost of each asset, legal fees associated with the acquisition of the licence are $34,000. While the patent has a legal life of 20 years, technological changes are expected to render it worthless after about five years. The copyright is good for another 20 years, but nearly all of the related sales are expected to occur during the next eight years. The licence is good in perpetuity, and sales under the licence are expected to continue at the same level for many decades.

Required:

a. Compute the annual amortization, if any, for each of Vinay's intangible assets.

b. Show the balance sheet presentation of the Intangible Asset section of Vinay's balance sheet prepared at the end of the fourth year after acquisition of the intangible assets.

8-26 (Asset valuation and financial statement analysis implications)
Black Daniel Brewing Company is preparing its balance sheet at year end and needs guidelines on how a variety of its assets should be valued. For each of the items listed, indicate the valuation process normally used and the potential impact on financial statement analysis if an alternative measure is used.

		Book Value	Fair Value	Present Value
a.	Cash	$45,000	$45,000	$45,000
b.	Accounts receivable	30,000	28,000	28,000
c.	Inventory A	12,000	32,000	32,000
d.	Inventory B	9,000	8,000	7,500
e.	Land	25,000	24,000	24,000
f.	Machinery	65,000	83,000	94,000
g.	Patents	18,000	24,000	29,000

Management Perspective Problems

8-27 (Valuation of assets in discontinued business)
Suppose that a company decides to discontinue a line of business. Describe what you think would be the most appropriate valuation basis for the property, plant, and equipment for the discontinued operations. As an investor in the shares of the company, discuss what disclosure might be most useful to you in this circumstance.

8-28 (Capital assets as collateral for a loan)
As a lender, discuss how much comfort you might get from the existence of long-term assets, specifically plant and goodwill, in making a long-term loan to a company.

8-29 (Auditor and valuation of capital assets)
As an auditor, discuss how you might evaluate a company's property, plant, and equipment to decide whether it should write down the value of these assets.

8-30 (Goodwill's effect on financial statements)
In some countries (such as the United Kingdom) companies can write off goodwill at the date of acquisition by directly reducing shareholders' equity—that is, the write-off does not pass through net income. Suppose that a Canadian company and a UK company agreed to purchase the same company for the same amount of money. As a stock analyst, describe how the balance sheet and income statement would differ for the two companies after the acquisition. Discuss whether this provides any differential advantage to either of the two companies.

8-31 (Impact of writedowns on remuneration)
Suppose that you are the accounting manager of a division of a large company and your remuneration is partly based on meeting a net-income target. In the current year it seems unlikely that your division will meet its target. You have some property, plant, and equipment that has been idle for a while but has not yet been written off. What incentives do you have to write off its value during the current year? If you do write it off, how will it affect your future ability to meet the income targets for your division?

8-32 (Basket purchase)
Companies that buy real estate often face a basket purchase situation. The purchase of real estate usually involves both the land that is purchased and the building that is on the land. If you are the accounting manager, how would you attempt to allocate the purchase price of the real estate between the land and the building? Why must you allocate between the two assets? What incentives might you have to allocate a disproportionate amount to either the land or the building?

8-33 (Interest capitalization and liquidity analysis)
Suppose that you are evaluating the liquidity of a company. What effect does the capitalization of interest have on your analysis—that is, how does it affect the ratios that you might compute to evaluate liquidity?

8-34 (Analysis of an R & D company)
As a stock analyst, discuss any inadequacies that you might find with the financial statements of a company that is predominately a research and development company.

8-35 (Capital assets and company valuation)
Suppose that you have been asked to provide an analysis of a potential acquisition by your company. Which long-term assets that exist on its financial statements are the most likely to be misstated by their book value, and why? Discuss the long-term assets of the potential acquisition company that might not be represented on the financial statements at all.

8-36 (Accounting for idle assets)
Conservative Company purchased a warehouse on January 1, 2000, for $750,000. At the time of purchase, Conservative anticipated the warehouse would be used to facilitate its expanded product line. The warehouse is being amortized over 20 years and is expected to have a resale value of $120,000. On January 1, 2005, Conservative concluded that the warehouse would no longer be used and should be sold for its book value. At the end of 2005 the warehouse still had not been sold and its net realizable value was estimated to be only $400,000.

> ***Required:***
>
> a. Compute the book value of the warehouse on January 1, 2005.
>
> b. Prepare all journal entries that Conservative would make during 2005 related to the warehouse.
>
> c. If, during 2006, Conservative sells the warehouse for $450,000, what entry would be made for the sale?
>
> d. During 2005, the financial vice-president expressed concern that if Conservative put the building up for sale the company might have to report a loss, and he didn't want to reduce 2005 earnings any further; he wanted to continue treating the warehouse as an operating asset. How would the financial statements be different if the warehouse were still treated as an operating asset during 2005? From a shareholder's perspective, do you think the treatment makes any difference? Explain.

8-37 (Analysis of a company with goodwill)
The 2001 annual report of Fedders Company contained the following financial statement information:

	2001	2000
Inventory	$19,270,000	$ 50,939,000
Net property, plant, and equipment	31,637,000	78,399,000
Other assets	8,125,000	35,236,000
Total assets	81,285,000	179,249,000
Net loss	1,775,000	24,931,000

The notes further indicate that the figures of $8,125,000 and $35,236,000 for other assets reported for 2001 and 2000, respectively, included goodwill of $5,823,000 and $17,670,000.

Fedders' sales are concentrated in room air conditioners. Sales are made directly to dealers and through private-label arrangements with dealers and distributors.

Required:

a. What factor or factors are most likely to have led to the $46,762,000 reduction in net property, plant, and equipment?

b. According to the information in the annual report, a significant portion of the reduction in inventory was not directly related to the reduction in property, plant, and equipment. What factors are most likely to have led to a reduction in inventory?

c. As noted, more than half of other assets was goodwill. Given that the company reported a net loss in both 2000 and 2001, is it appropriate to continue to report goodwill in the balance sheet? Explain.

d. In light of the net loss for the year, ratios such as return on equity may not be meaningful. What ratios might be useful in evaluating Fedders' performance over the 2001 fiscal year?

e. What is your conclusion about Fedders' activities during 2001? What additional information would you like to have for analysis?

Reading and Interpreting Published Financial Statements

8-38 Exhibit 8-6 provided a summary of the capital assets of Cara Operations Limited at March 28, 1999, and March 29, 1998. The 1999 Consolidated Statements of Cash Flows are shown in Exhibit 8-13.

Required:
Using the information provided in Exhibits 8-6 and 8-13, prepare summary journal entries to reconstruct the changes that occurred in the capital asset accounts and related accumulated amortization accounts for the 1999 fiscal year.

8-39 (Research and development)
MOSAID Technologies Incorporated incurs substantial costs in researching and developing computer software. MOSAID's income statements for 1998 and 1997 are shown in Exhibit 3-21.

Required:

a. Rewrite this income statement to show the results if MOSAID were to capitalize these costs. Assume MOSAID amortizes intangible capital assets at 20% using the straight-line method.

b. Explain why MOSAID is not allowed to capitalize these costs.

8-40 (Examination of capital assets)
The note about capital assets from the 1999 financial statements of Mark's Work Wearhouse Ltd. is shown in Exhibit 8-14.

Required:

a. Has Mark's Work Wearhouse bought or sold any land and buildings within the last three years? Explain your answer.

b. Assume Mark's Work Wearhouse bought new furniture, fixtures, and equipment during 1999 but did not sell any. Reconstruct the journal entries for 1999 associated with the furniture, fixtures, and equipment. Include the amortization entries.

c. You will notice that Mark's Work Wearhouse has leased computer equipment and operating software. Although leasing was not discussed in the chapter, suggest some reasons why it would be advantageous for Mark's to lease rather than buy its computers and software.

EXHIBIT 8-13

Consolidated Statements of Cash Flows

For the years ended March 28, 1999 and March 29, 1998

In thousands of dollars	1999	1998
CASH FLOWS PROVIDED BY (USED IN)		
OPERATING ACTIVITIES		
Earnings from continuing operations	$ 18,991	$ 35,437
Adjustments for:		
Amortization of property, plant and equipment	23,803	20,685
Loss on disposal of property, plant and equipment	858	906
Amortization of goodwill and other assets	4,129	3,771
Future income taxes	(4,782)	2,114
Equity earnings	(1,857)	(2,896)
Restructuring costs	12,183	–
Change in franchise notes	(220)	(747)
Change in investments	(236)	128
Change in pension liability	800	1,000
Change in non-cash operating working capital (note 15)	1,868	5,488
Cash flows from continuing operations	$ 55,537	$ 65,886
Discontinued operations	–	(938)
	$ 55,537	$ 64,948
INVESTING ACTIVITIES		
Purchase of property, plant and equipment (note 15)	$ (45,166)	$ (31,681)
Proceeds on disposal of property, plant and equipment	1,657	664
Purchase of goodwill and other assets	(2,792)	(6,309)
Change in mortgages and notes	(582)	(172)
Repayment of Employee Stock Plan Loans	1,047	3,303
Business Acquisition (note 15)	(3,898)	(18,169)
Discontinued operations	–	1,240
	$ (49,734)	$ (51,124)
FINANCING ACTIVITIES		
Share repurchase	$ (1,389)	$ (2)
Share repurchase in excess of book value	(25,578)	(24)
Proceeds from issuance of long-term debt, net of issuance costs	149,377	11,000
Repayment of capital lease obligations	(6,000)	(3,703)
Repayment of long-term debt	(71,106)	(15,685)
Dividends paid	(11,443)	(10,824)
Issuance of capital stock	38	5,308
	$ 33,899	$ (13,930)
NET CHANGE IN CASH	39,702	(106)
CASH – BEGINNING OF YEAR	3,200	3,306
CASH – END OF YEAR	$ 42,902	$ 3,200

7. CAPITAL ASSETS

EXHIBIT 8-14

	1997		1998		1999	
	Cost	Net Book Value	Cost	Net Book Value	Cost	Net Book Value
Land	$ 45	$ 45	$ 45	$ 45	$ 45	$ 45
Building	452	351	452	334	452	312
Leasehold improvements	5,127	2,036	4,654	1,144	4,494	689
Furniture, fixtures and equipment	18,291	8,342	18,873	6,993	21,720	7,453
Fixtures and equipment under capital leases	4,491	3,834	8,645	6,696	13,319	9,520
Computer equipment and operating software under capital leases	—	—	6,346	4,860	9,047	5,512
	$28,406	$14,608	$39,015	$20,072	$49,077	$23,531

8-41 (Accounting for oil and gas properties)
The 1998 balance sheet and income statement of Purcell Energy Ltd. are shown in Exhibit 8-15. Note 1 (D), relating to its accounting policies for capital assets, is also shown in Exhibit 8-15.

Required:

a. Explain in your own words how Purcell records and amortizes capital assets relating to oil and gas properties. Use amounts from the balance sheet and income statement where appropriate.

b. Explain how Purcell's policies would be different if it used the successful efforts method.

8-42 (Labour capitalization)
The 1999 annual report, including the complete financial statements, for Big Rock Brewery Ltd. at March 31, 1999, is shown in Appendix A at the end of the book.

Required:

In Note 4 to the financial statements, Big Rock discloses that it capitalized labour relating to work at its brewery facilities. What changes would result in the balance sheet and income statement if Big Rock did not capitalize labour?

8-43 (Goodwill)
The 1998 balance sheet of Tritech Precision Ltd. is shown in Exhibit 8-16. During 1998 the company acquired two new subsidiaries and increased its ownership interest in another subsidiary.

Required:

a. Using the information on the balance sheet, determine the amount of goodwill that was recorded from the new acquisitions.

b. Over how many years does Tritech appear to be amortizing goodwill?

c. When Tritech reviews its goodwill to see if the carrying amount is still valid, what kinds of issues should it consider?

EXHIBIT 8-15
PART A

CONSOLIDATED BALANCE SHEETS

As at December 31	1998	1997
ASSETS		
Current		
Cash and temporary investments	$ 613,106	$ 2,513,602
Accounts receivable (Note 8)	1,388,254	2,572,448
Loans receivable (Note 2)	92,500	112,500
Prepaid expenses, deposits and inventories	198,443	153,800
	2,292,303	5,352,350
Property, plant and equipment (Note 3)	27,423,253	26,696,508
	$ 29,715,556	$ 32,048,858
LIABILITIES		
Current		
Accounts payable and accrued liabilities	$ 1,786,352	$ 6,886,132
Corporate taxes payable	66,770	9,649
Current portion of obligations under capital leases	194,480	137,490
	2,047,602	7,033,271
Long term debt (Note 5)	5,156,020	690,913
Obligations under capital leases (Note 4)	308,504	341,587
Provision for future site restoration costs	452,000	269,468
	7,964,126	8,335,239
SHAREHOLDERS' EQUITY		
Equity instruments (Note 6)		
Common shares	23,824,354	14,241,871
Share purchase warrants	–	8,999,423
Preferred shares	128,000	128,000
Contributed surplus	529,818	529,818
	24,482,172	23,899,112
Deficit	(2,730,742)	(185,493)
	21,751,430	23,713,619
	$ 29,715,556	$ 32,048,858

Director   Director

The accompanying notes are an integral part of these financial statements.

EXHIBIT 8-15
PART B

CONSOLIDATED STATEMENTS OF OPERATIONS AND DEFICIT

For the years ended December 31	1998	1997
Revenue		
Oil and gas sales, net of royalties	$ 5,538,162	$ 5,623,446
Interest and other	39,722	47,187
	5,577,884	5,670,633
Expenses		
Production	2,493,502	2,154,426
Depletion, amortization and site restoration	4,431,532	2,474,658
General and administrative, net	782,019	543,379
Interest on long term debt	280,967	267,374
	7,988,020	5,439,837
Income (loss) before corporate taxes	(2,410,136)	230,796
Corporate taxes (Note 7)		
Capital	135,113	9,649
Income taxes	–	12,497
Utilization of loss carryforwards	–	(12,497)
	135,113	9,649
Net income (loss) for the year	(2,545,249)	221,147
Dividends	–	(5,386)
Deficit, beginning of year	(185,493)	(401,254)
Deficit, end of year	$ (2,730,742)	$ (185,493)
Earnings (loss) per share	$ (0.130)	$ 0.015

The accompanying notes are an integral part of these financial statements.

EXHIBIT 8-15
PART C

(D) PROPERTY, PLANT AND EQUIPMENT

The Company follows the full cost method of accounting for oil and gas operations whereby all costs of exploring for and developing oil and gas reserves are initially capitalized. Such costs include land acquisition costs, geological and geophysical expenses, carrying charges on non-producing properties, costs of drilling and overhead charges directly related to acquisition and exploration activities.

Costs capitalized, together with the costs of production equipment, are depleted on the unit-of-production method based on the estimated gross proved reserves. Petroleum products and reserves are converted to equivalent units of natural gas using their relative energy content.

Costs of acquiring and evaluating unproved properties are initially excluded from depletion calculations. These unevaluated properties are assessed periodically to ascertain whether impairment has occurred. When proved reserves are assigned or the property is considered to be impaired, the cost of the property or the amount of the impairment is added to costs subject to depletion calculations.

Proceeds from a sale of petroleum and natural gas properties are applied against capitalized costs, with no gain or loss recognized, unless such a sale would significantly alter the rate of depletion. Alberta Royalty Tax Credits are included in oil and gas sales.

In applying the full cost method, the Company performs a ceiling test which restricts the capitalized costs less accumulated depletion and amortization from exceeding an amount equal to the estimated undiscounted value of future net revenues from proved oil and gas reserves, as determined by independent engineers, based on sales prices achievable under existing contracts and posted average reference prices in effect at the end of the year and current costs, and after deducting estimated future general and administrative expenses, production related expenses, financing costs, future site restoration costs and income taxes.

8-44 (Analysis of changes to capital assets)

Notes 1(e) and 5 from the 1998 financial statements of Celanese Canada Ltd. are shown in Exhibit 8-17.

Required:

a. Explain the changes in the property, plant, and equipment during 1998.

b. Does Celanese Canada ever write down its capital assets? If so, how does it write them down?

c. What does Celanese do with additions, improvements, renewals, and expenditures for maintenance and repairs, that are significant? Are all repairs treated in this way?

d. What method of amortization does Celanese Canada use?

Beyond the Book

8-45 (Financial statement disclosures)

Choose a company as directed by your instructor and answer the following questions:

a. Use the balance sheet and the notes to the financial statements to prepare an analysis of the capital assets, by listing the beginning and ending amounts in the various asset and accumulated amortization amounts and calculating the net change in both dollar and percentage terms for the most recent year.

b. If any of the amounts in part (a) have changed more than 10%, provide an explanation for this change.

EXHIBIT 8-16

CONSOLIDATED BALANCE SHEETS
As at December 31
000's

Tritech Precision Inc.
Incorporated under the laws of Ontario

	1998	1997
ASSETS		
Current		
Cash and short-term deposits	$ 8,025	$ 14,980
Accounts receivable	81,394	56,966
Income taxes recoverable	380	—
Inventory	45,376	37,082
Prepaid expenses and other assets	2,739	1,694
Total current assets	137,914	110,722
Fixed assets, net	186,177	100,074
Goodwill, net of accumulated amortization of $1,349 [1997 - $981]	15,093	13,281
Other assets	8,155	3,448
	$ 347,339	$ 227,525
LIABILITIES AND SHAREHOLDERS' EQUITY		
Current		
Bank indebtedness	$ 39,257	$ 2,816
Accounts payable and accrued liabilities	69,217	42,710
Income taxes payable	—	3,047
Current portion of long-term debt	10,924	4,859
Total current liabilities	119,398	53,432
Long-term debt	69,682	40,981
Deferred income taxes	11,138	7,941
Minority interest	20,665	11,098
Total liabilities	220,883	113,452
Shareholders' Equity		
Share capital	75,842	75,656
Retained earnings	50,846	38,417
Cumulative translation adjustment	(232)	—
Total shareholders' equity	126,456	114,073
	$ 347,339	$ 227,525

On behalf of the Board:

W. B. Ferguson
Director

J. D. Mackin
Director

The accompanying notes are an integral component of the consolidated financial statements.

EXHIBIT 8-17

e) Property, plant and equipment

Property, plant and equipment are recorded at cost. Additions, improvements, renewals and expenditures for maintenance that add materially to productive capacity or materially extend the life of an asset are capitalized.

Depreciation is generally provided over the estimated useful lives of the depreciable assets using the straight-line method. Additional depreciation is provided on particular assets if required to recognize the effects of significant technological or market changes. Site improvements are depreciated primarily over 20 years, buildings and their improvements over 10 to 30 years, and machinery and equipment for periods ranging from three to 10 years.

When facilities are retired or otherwise disposed of, the cost and related accumulated depreciation are removed from the asset accounts and gains or losses on disposals are reflected in income in the year of disposal.

5. Property, plant and equipment

	Cost	Accumulated Depreciation	1998 Net Book Value	1997 Net Book Value	1996 Net Book Value
Land	$ 5,394	$ –	$ 5,394	$ 5,394	$ 5,329
Site improvements	9,671	4,933	4,738	4,978	4,944
Buildings and improvements	104,465	64,840	39,625	41,352	36,235
Machinery and equipment	715,904	493,609	222,295	241,756	204,979
Construction in progress	12,103	–	12,103	5,692	56,490
Total	$847,537	$563,382	$284,155	$299,172	$307,977

Expenditures for maintenance and repairs, which were $45,837 for the year ($38,202 in 1997, $42,536 in 1996) are charged to income.

c. What percentage of the company's total assets are invested in property, plant, and equipment? Has this percentage changed significantly over the last year?

d. What amortization method(s) does the company use for its financial statements?

e. Use the following formulae to examine the property, plant, and equipment for the company:

Average age of PP&E = Total Accum. Amort. / Total Amort. Expense

Average Useful Life of PP&E = Total Gross PP&E / Total Amort. Exp.

Note: Remember that amortization (depreciation) expense may not be disclosed in the income statement but will usually appear in the cash flow statement. Compare your results to any information disclosed in the notes. Do these results make sense?

f. Does the company have any significant intangible assets? If so, describe each of them.

Case

8-46 Onta and KewBee Sales Companies
Summary balance sheet and income statement information for Onta Sales Company and KewBee Sales Company for the year ended December 31, 20x1 (the first year of operations for both companies), are shown below. The two businesses are similar.

Upon investigation, you find that Onta is financed mainly by shareholders' equity, KewBee mainly by long-term debt. Onta amortizes all equipment at 10% straight-line and buildings at 5% straight-line, while KewBee amortizes equipment at 20% declining balance and buildings at 10% declining balance. Both have effective corporate income tax rates of 25%.

Required:

a. Which company has the higher return on assets without adjusting for differences in amortization policy?

b. Which company has the higher return on assets after adjusting for differences in amortization policy? (Determine this using two different calculations.)

c. Explain why, using numbers from this example, the ROA adjusts for interest after taxes in the numerator.

d. Explain why, using numbers from this example, you should adjust for differences in amortization policy when comparing different companies.

	Onta	KewBee
Balance Sheet Information		
Total current assets	$ 75,000	$ 80,000
Capital assets		
Land	150,000	125,000
Equipment	200,000	200,000
Accumulated amortization	(20,000)	(40,000)
Buildings	500,000	500,000
Accumulated amortization	(25,000)	(50,000)
Total assets	$ 880,000	$ 815,000
Total liabilities	$ 300,000	$ 700,000
Total shareholders' equity	580,000	115,000
Total liabilities and equity	$ 880,000	$ 815,000
Income Statement Information		
Revenues	$1,000,000	$1,000,000
Expenses:		
Amortization	45,000	90,000
Interest	30,000	70,000
Other	770,000	770,000
Income taxes	38,750	17,500
Net income	$ 116,250	$ 52,500

Critical Thinking Question

8-47 (Capital asset analysis)
The balance sheet, income statement, and selected notes of H. Jager Developments Inc. at February 28, 1999 and 1998, are shown in Exhibit 8-18. H. Jager develops and sells real estate.

Required:

a. Explain why H. Jager does not classify land under development as capital assets.

b. Explain why H. Jager does not split its assets or liabilities into current and non-current sections

EXHIBIT 8-18
PART A

H. Jager Developments Inc.
Consolidated Balance Sheets

February 28	1999	1998
Assets		
Cash	$ 6,014	$ 28,341
Receivables	124,796	17,477
Agreements receivable	799,362	–
Deposits	100,371	249,663
Land under development	6,659,849	7,214,095
Resort facilities (Note 4)	469,919	496,481
Investment (Note 5)	–	236,406
	$ 8,160,311	$ 8,242,463
Liabilities		
Payables and accruals	$ 426,121	$ 866,179
Customer advances	14,370	43,716
Payable to related parties (Note 6)	220,815	167,901
Morgages and loans (Note 7)	3,603,853	6,343,680
	4,265,159	7,421,476
Shareholders' Equity		
Capital stock (Note 8)	10,235,648	9,361,885
Contributed surplus (Note 8)	105,000	–
Deficit	(6,445,496)	(8,540,898)
	3,895,152	820,987
	$ 8,160,311	$ 8,242,463

Contingencies and Uncertainty (Notes 12 and 16)

On behalf of the Board

Signed "Deep Shergill"   Director   Signed "Tim Duffin"   Director

See accompanying notes to the consolidated financial statements.

Grant Thornton

2

EXHIBIT 8-18
PART B

H. Jager Developments Inc.
Consolidated Statements of Operations and Deficit

Years Ended February 28	1999	1998
Revenue		
Lot sales	$ 1,827,383	$ –
Utility fees	41,474	16,870
	1,868,857	16,870
Direct costs	1,413,367	–
Cost of lots sold	85,630	73,276
Utility service costs	1,498,997	73,276
	369,860	(56,406)
Expenses		
General and administrative	398,375	638,012
Depreciation	29,364	29,462
Interest	20,792	70,347
	448,531	737,821
Loss before undernoted	(78,671)	(794,227)
Gain on debt settlements (Note 15)	2,117,541	–
Gain on sale of securities	56,532	66,880
Net earnings (loss) before income taxes	2,095,402	(727,347)
Income taxes	935,000	–
Recovery of income taxes due to utilization of losses carryforward of prior years	(935,000)	–
Net earnings (loss)	2,095,402	(727,347)
Deficit, beginning of year	(8,540,898)	(7,813,551)
Deficit, end of year	$ (6,445,496)	$ (8,540,898)
Earnings (loss) per share (Note 10)	$ 0.06	$ (0.04)

See accompanying notes to the consolidated financial statements.

Grant Thornton

3

EXHIBIT 8-18
PART C

H. Jager Developments Inc.
Notes to the Consolidated Financial Statements
February 28, 1999

3. Summary of significant accounting policies (continued)

Land under development

Land under development is carried at the lower of cost and estimated net realizable value. Cost includes the cost of land, option payments, carrying costs and other direct costs associated with development. Carrying costs include interest on borrowings directly related to land development as well as property taxes and the applicable portion of general and administrative overheads. During the year, overhead costs and interest of $39,998 (1998 – $63,690) and $401,540 (1998 – $382,697) respectively were capitalized.

The cost of land is pro-rated to each phase of a project on an acreage basis up to and including the time that a plan of subdivision is established. Cost of land sold, including devlopment and capitalized costs, are allocated, generally within each subdivision to saleable lots or acreage in proportion to anticipated revenues. Housing units sold are costed on an individual basis whereby specific and identifiable costs are applied to each unit.

Revenue recognition

Revenue is recognized when a contract for sale is signed, a minimum of 15 percent of the sale proceeds has been received and the collectibility of the remaining proceeds is reasonably assured. Proceeds due from sale of land are presented as agreements receivable.

4. Resort facilities	1999	1998
Land	$ 20,000	$ 20,000
Water treatment plant	533,685	533,685
Equipment	65,174	62,372
	618,859	616,057
Accumulated depreciation	(148,940)	(119,576)
	$469,919	$ 496,481

Grant Thornton

Good Accounting Makes for Good Employee Relations

The Mountain Equipment Co-op, which sells outdoor clothing and gear in stores across Canada as well as through its catalogue worldwide, has a reputation among customers for its helpful, knowledgeable staff. Vivian Li, Account Manager for MEC, regards its staff as the company's greatest asset—which is why she considers payroll to be the most important aspect of its accounting for liabilities.

"Payroll accounting may not seem that interesting, but it can actually be quite complex," she explains, "especially for a national organization. It's a crucial service. For a mid-sized business like ours, it's often the highest administrative cost. And there's a very minor margin for error, because you're dealing with people's pay…People are understandably sensitive about their money."

All payroll functions for MEC's stores across Canada are handled at the Vancouver head office by three staff members (two full-time and one part-time), who are "thankfully, very competent," says Ms. Li. Each store has salaried workers, hourly workers, full- and part-time employees. Sales staff, who are all active in outdoor activities themselves, do not receive commissions—because MEC is a cooperative, its primary goal is not to make a profit but to serve its members. All customers must be members; a lifetime membership costs $5.

The actual calculation of pay, and of deductions (for the Canada Pension Plan and Employment Insurance) and benefits (both statutory benefits and supplemental disability and premium health-care plans),

is no problem with today's computerized accounting systems, says Ms. Li. Tracking these changes was actually easier several years ago, when MEC had an external firm take care of all its payroll functions. But they now do them "in-house." "We wanted more flexibility," Ms. Li explains. "External services have standardized reports, and we wanted to keep track of different information." For example, employees at each store report on how much of their time is spent in different functions: working the floor area, the cash area, the stock room, and so forth. The head office tracks and collates this information so store managers can keep informed about how their resources are allocated.

By taking care of payroll and other accounting functions at the central office, MEC can benefit from dealing with a single bank, and from economies of scale. More importantly, it can allow its store managers to focus on selling merchandise and serving members.

LIABILITIES

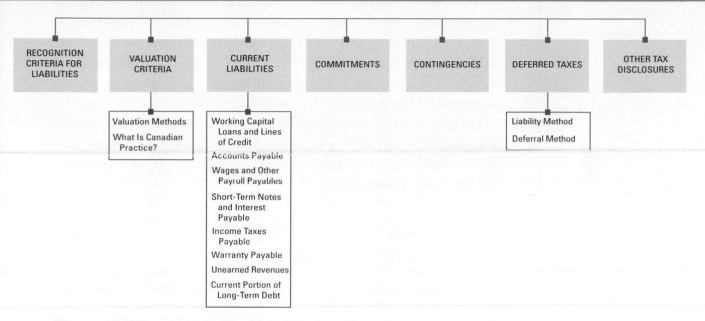

Learning Objectives:

After studying this chapter, you should be able to:

1. *Describe the valuation methods used for liabilities in Canada.*
2. *Explain why companies use working capital loans and lines of credit.*
3. *Explain why accounts payable is sometimes thought of as "free debt."*
4. *Prepare journal entries to record the payroll of a company.*
5. *Calculate the amount of interest that is owed on short-term notes payable.*
6. *Describe how warranties payable is different from current liabilities such as accounts payable.*
7. *Describe situations in which unearned revenue must be recorded.*
8. *Explain why the portion of long-term debt that is due in the next year is recorded as a current liability.*
9. *Explain what a commitment is and how it is recognized by a company.*
10. *Describe the criteria necessary for a contingency and discuss when it is recorded.*
11. *Explain why deferred taxes exist.*
12. *Discuss how the liability method and deferred method for determining deferred taxes are different.*
13. *Calculate future income taxes in amortization and warranty situations.*

People like Vivian Li of Mountain Equipment Co-op would agree that good employee relations are important to a successful business. One of her ways of fostering good relations is by paying strict attention to detail with respect to payroll. Successful businesses also pay attention to obligations to people outside the company. A reputation for paying debts on time enables a company to use credit to operate effectively and to embark on new initiatives. A poor credit rating, on the other hand, results in limited options for outside financing.

In this and the next two chapters, our attention turns to the credit side of the balance sheet and the accounting for liabilities and shareholders' equity. Both liabilities and shareholders' equity can be viewed as sources of assets. Liability holders contribute assets in return for a promise of repayment at some future date, usually with interest. Shareholders contribute assets in return for an ownership interest and the right to share in the future profits of the company.

The general nature of liabilities will be discussed first, followed by current liabilities, contingent liabilities, and deferred taxes. Chapter 10 covers major noncurrent liabilities, such as bonds, leases, and pensions. Chapter 11 covers shareholders' equity transactions.

RECOGNITION CRITERIA FOR LIABILITIES

Liabilities represent obligations agreed to by the company through some past transaction. For an item to be classified as a liability, it must meet three requirements. First, the company must settle the obligation through the transfer of assets, delivery of services, or the conferring of some other benefit specified in the transaction. Usually, the settlement must take place within a specified time. Second, usually the company has little or no discretion with respect to the liability; if it does not meet its obligation, the creditor has the right to pursue legal action. Third, the transaction or event that gave rise to the obligation must have already occurred.

The transfer of assets or services criterion is similar to the probable future value criterion for assets. The uncertainty associated with liabilities concerns the dollar value of assets to be given up, and when that sacrifice will be made.

To avoid uncertainty about the amount and timing of the settlement, some liabilities are divided into fixed payments with fixed due dates. Most loans and accounts payable are of this type. The interest and principal payments are specified in the loan agreement, as are the dates on which those payments will be made. Other liabilities, such as warranty liabilities, may have neither fixed payments nor fixed dates. The settlement of a warranty obligation will depend on when the customer detects a warranty problem, and the cost incurred by the company to fix the problem. Liabilities, therefore, vary in the amount of uncertainty that is associated with them.

If the uncertainty associated with either the amount or the timing of the future transfer is sufficiently great, the liability will probably not be recognized in the financial statements. Suppose, for example, that the company is under investigation by the government for an alleged chemical spill into a river. Does the company have an obligation to transfer assets in the future? If the company is found negligent, there could be a significant liability if a fine is imposed or if the company cleans up the spill, or both. The company may have a difficult time, however, predicting the outcome—whether it will be found negligent and, if found negligent, how much it will cost to satisfy the obligation. In this case, it is likely that no liability will be recorded. However, because of the *possibility* of the future transfer of assets, the company could disclose information about the investigation in a note to the financial statements. Such an item would be referred to as a **contingent liability**, because the future obligation is contingent on certain events occurring.

The ownership criterion that is used for assets does not, strictly, apply to liabilities, but a similar notion does prevail. A company should record only those obligations that it will be required to satisfy. For example, if a customer falls on the company's sidewalk and successfully sues for medical costs, the company may not be obligated to make the payment. If the company is insured against such claims, the insurance company will pay the claim. The company does not record the obligation to pay this liability on its books, because it is the insurance company's obligation. If the insurance does not cover all of the obligation, the company needs to record any excess obligation as a liability.

The third characteristic of a liability, that the transaction that gave rise to the obligation has already occurred, is sometimes difficult to evaluate. For example, in the case of the lawsuit mentioned in the preceding paragraph, what is the event that gave rise to the obligation? Is it the customer falling on the sidewalk, the filing of a lawsuit, or the decision of the court? In this case, the certainty of the obligation increased as each subsequent event occurred. However, the event that ultimately gave rise to the obligation depends on the sequence of events.

Evaluation can also be made difficult when the company signs a binding contract. Suppose, for example, that the company signs a contract to purchase 1,000 units of inventory at $30 per unit, to be delivered 30 days from now. Is the signing of the contract the event that gives rise to the obligation to pay for the inventory, or is it the delivery of the inventory? The obligation of the company is contingent upon the seller fulfilling its part of the contract by delivering the goods on time. If the goods are not delivered, the company is not obligated to pay. The signing of the contract creates what is known as a **mutually unexecuted contract**: At the time of signing, neither the buyer nor the seller has fulfilled its part of the contract; the seller has not delivered any inventory, and the buyer has not paid any cash. Such contracts are normally not recorded in the accounting system.

A **partially executed contract** is one in which one party has fulfilled all or part of its obligation. In the example just given, the contract would be viewed as partially executed if the buyer had made a deposit of $3,000. A partial transaction would then be recorded. In this case, the seller would show an inflow of cash of $3,000 and would create a liability account to represent its obligation to deliver inventory valued at $3,000. The liability account would be called "unearned revenue." Once inventory valued at $3,000 was delivered to the customer, the obligation would be satisfied and the revenue would be earned. Note that only the amount of the deposit is recorded at this time, not the full amount of the contract ($30,000 = 1,000 units × $30 per unit). The buyer would show an outflow of cash of $3,000 and would create an asset account for the right to receive the inventory valued at $3,000. The account would be called "deposits on purchase commitments."

VALUATION CRITERIA

Just as there are different methods for valuing assets, there are several different methods for valuing liabilities. Theoretically, liabilities are valued at their net present value as at the date they are incurred. However, we will consider several valuation methods before discussing Canadian practice in depth.

Valuation Methods

One way to value a liability is to record it at the *gross amount* of the obligation—that is, the total of the payments to be made. For example, if an obligation requires the company to pay $1,000 each month for the next three years, the gross obligation would be $36,000. While this amount accurately measures the total payments to be made, it may not accurately measure the obligation of the company as at the date it is recorded on the balance sheet. For example, suppose that the obligation is a rental agreement for a piece of machinery. If the company can cancel the rental agreement at any time, it is obligated to pay only $1,000 each month. The remaining payments are an obligation only if the company decides to keep using the asset. If the contract was noncancellable, the full $36,000 would make more sense.

Another reason why the gross obligation may not adequately measure the value of the liability is that it ignores the time value of money. Suppose that, in the example, the $1,000 a month is for repayment of a loan. The total payments of $36,000 include both the repayment of principal and the payment of interest. Interest is an obligation only as the company uses the money over time. If the company has the option to pay off the loan early, it merely has to pay off the principal balance and any accumulated interest. It does not have to pay the full amount of the payments. Suppose, for example, that the principal of the loan is $31,000. The difference ($5,000) between this amount and the gross amount is the interest that accrues over time. The company could settle the obligation today with a payment of $31,000. Therefore, recording the liability at $36,000 would overstate the obligation of the company at the present time.

To recognize the time value of money, a company may record its obligations at their **net present value**. Both the future payments on the principal and the interest payments are discounted back to the current period using a discount rate. Chapter 10 will go into more detail about present value calculations. Under this valuation system, the company records the obligation at the net present value. As payments are made, the obligation is reduced and interest expense is recorded to represent the use of the money over time. It is important to remember that interest is recorded only as time passes.

Just as there is concern about the purchasing power of monetary assets, there is concern about liabilities, because most liabilities are also monetary items (i.e., they are fixed in terms of the cash flows that are required to settle them). They are, therefore, subject to changes in purchasing power. As the purchasing power of the dollar changes, the "cost" (in terms of purchasing power) to the company of repaying the obligation changes. For example, suppose that the company takes out a fixed-payment loan to buy a piece of equipment. If inflation occurs during the period when the company is paying off the loan, the purchasing power of the dollar decreases, and the company pays off the obligation with "cheaper" dollars. It experiences a purchasing power gain during this period. Lending institutions attempt to counter future inflationary effects by requiring higher interest rates. Another valuation possibility is to record liabilities using some measure of purchasing power.

What Is Canadian Practice?

In Canada, liabilities should be recorded at the present value of the future payments. The interest rate used depends on the type of liability and the company's credit worthiness. The interest rate should be the appropriate rate for an arm's-length transaction of the type that gave rise to the obligation. However, because the time to maturity is so short, accountants do not use present value calculations for short-term liabilities such as accounts payable. Instead, they record current liabilities such as accounts payable and wages payable at the gross amount that is owed. Short-term notes payable that have an interest component are recorded at the total principal amount. The interest is recorded as it accrues.

Once a liability is recorded, the carrying value is not usually adjusted until the liability is paid. A company in financial trouble, however, may restructure its debt in negotiations with its creditors. Based on concessions that the company may obtain from the lender, it might be able to reduce the amount owed on the obligation, reduce the interest rate used to calculate interest expense on the existing balance, or extend the period over which the debt is to be paid. This is called **troubled debt restructuring**.

CURRENT LIABILITIES

Current liabilities are those obligations that require the transfer of assets or services within one year, or one operating cycle, of the company. As just discussed, most of these are carried on the books at the gross amount. In order for a company to stay solvent (able to pay its debts as they fall due), it must have sufficient current assets and/or assets generated by operations to pay the current liabilities. Creditors such as banks will often use total current liabilities to assess the company's ability to remain viable. The most frequently encountered current liabilities are discussed in the following subsections.

Working Capital Loans and Lines of Credit

As discussed in the preceding paragraph, companies need to have sufficient current assets or inflows of cash from operations to pay debts as they fall due. However,

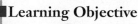
Learning Objective

2

Explain why companies use working capital loans and lines of credit.

they may not be able to convert some of those current assets into cash quickly enough to meet current debt obligation deadlines. To manage this shortfall, companies have a few options. For example, they can arrange for a **working capital loan** from a bank. This short-term loan is often secured by customer balances in accounts receivable, or by inventory. As money is received from accounts receivable, or as the inventory is sold, the amounts received are used to pay off the loan.

Another way for companies to deal with cash shortages is to arrange for a **line of credit** with a bank. In this case, the bank assesses the company's ability to repay short-term debts and establishes a short-term debt balance that it feels is reasonable for the company. This provides the company with more freedom to take advantage of opportunities and/or to settle debts. If cheques written by the company exceed the current cash balance in the bank, the bank covers the excess by immediately activating the line of credit and establishing a short-term loan. Subsequent cash deposits by the company are used by the bank to draw down the loan. A company that is using a working capital loan or has activated a line of credit might have a negative cash balance, which must be shown with the current liabilities. This negative cash balance would be obvious to users on the cash flow statement, because the end cash balance would also be negative. For example, Big Rock Brewery Ltd. has a "demand revolving credit facility with a maximum limit at March 31, 1999 and 1998 of $5,000,000." This line of credit bears interest at Royal Bank prime rate, which at March 31, 1999 and 1998, was 6.5%. (Big Rock's Annual Report, p. BR-18, is included in Appendix A at the end of the book.) Big Rock's line of credit has been expanded over the years. In 1995 the line of credit was for only $750,000 and the rate charged by the bank was prime plus 1/8%. Obviously, Big Rock's need for short-term financing has been growing. The decline in interest charged from prime plus 1/8% to prime indicates that the bank is more confident in Big Rock's ability to pay back the debt even though the potential amount borrowed is much higher. On March 31, 1999, its short-term loan balance was $624,909, whereas its cash balance was $75,234. This resulted in a cash deficiency of $549,675.

Accounts Payable

Learning Objective

3

Explain why accounts payable is sometimes thought of as "free debt."

Accounts payable occur when a company buys goods or services on credit. These are sometimes referred to as *trade accounts payable* (for an example, see the excerpt from the liability section of Domtar Inc., Exhibit 9-1). Payment is generally deferred for a relatively short period of time, such as 30 to 60 days. These accounts generally do not carry explicit interest charges and are sometimes thought of as "free" debt. Under some agreements, there can be either a penalty for late payment or a discount provision for early payment. The penalty and the difference between the discounted payment and the full payment can both be viewed as interest charges for delayed payments on these liabilities.

■ **Domtar Inc. 1998**

Excerpt from the Consolidated Balance Sheets
As at December 31, 1998 and 1997
(in millions of dollars)

Liabilities and Shareholders' Equity

	1998	1997
Current liabilities		
Bank indebtedness	$ 31	$ 35
Trade and other payables	562	333
Income and other taxes payable	52	18
Long-term debt due within one year	49	22
	$ 694	$408
Long-term debt	$1,147	$852

Wages and Other Payroll Payables

Wages owed to employees can be another significant current liability. The magnitude of the liability depends somewhat on how often the company pays its employees, because the balance in the account reflects the accrual of wages since the last pay period. In addition to the wages themselves, the company may provide fringe benefits that must also be quantified. These accruals for health care, pensions, vacation pay, and other benefits also need to be recognized in the periods in which they occur. Because these may be paid in periods other than those in which they are earned, liabilities have to be recorded.

Additionally, the company acts as a government agent (federal and provincial) in the collection of certain taxes. For example, income taxes must be withheld from employees' wages and remitted to the government. While this is not an expense to the company, the company must nevertheless keep track of the amounts deducted from employees' earnings and show the liability to pay these amounts to the government. The liability to pay the employee is reduced by the amount withheld. Other deductions, such as Canada Pension Plan (CPP) or Quebec Pension Plan (QPP) amounts and Employment Insurance (EI), are also deducted from employees' total wages and remitted to the government. This further reduces the amount paid to employees. Beyond the amount deducted from employees' wages, companies must make additional payments to the government for CPP or QPP, EI, and Workers' Compensation. These amounts are shown as an expense to the employer and are recorded as liabilities until they are remitted to the government.

As an example, assume that Angelique's Autobody Shop has a two-week payroll of $7,500 for its seven employees. Income tax of $990 is deducted from the employees' cheques, as well as 3.2% for CPP and 2.7% for EI. The employer has to submit an additional 3.2% for CPP and 3.78% for EI on behalf of its employees. The journal entries to record the payroll would be:

■**Learning Objective**

4

Prepare journal entries to record the payroll of a company.

DEDUCTIONS FROM EMPLOYEES' EARNED INCOME		
SE-Wages expense	7,500.00	
L-Employee income tax payable		990.00
L-CPP contribution payable		240.00
L-EI taxes payable		202.50
A-Cash		6,067.50
Additional Deductions Paid by Employer:		
SE-Wages expense	523.50	
L-CPP contribution payable		240.00
L-EI taxes payable		283.50

The amounts in the three liability accounts are remitted periodically to the government according to its regulations. Note that the total amount recorded by the employers as an expense ($8,023.50) exceeds the amount they have agreed to pay the employees ($7,500.00). Because of these extra amounts that the government requires companies to remit, businesses complain each time the government makes changes to the Canada Pension Plan or Employment Insurance. These rates are set by the government each year, usually in November or December. The additional amounts must always be taken into account by an employer, whether it is considering hiring new staff, or maintaining its current number of employees.

Short-Term Notes and Interest Payable

Learning Objective

5

Calculate the amount of interest that is owed on short-term notes payable.

Short-term notes payable represent borrowings of the company that require repayment in the next year or operating cycle. They either carry explicit interest rates or are structured such that the difference between the original amount borrowed and the amount repaid represents implicit interest. Interest expense and interest payable should be recognized over the life of these loan agreements.

Assume that the Checkerboard Taxi Company borrowed $10,000 at 9% from the local bank. The loan was to be repaid by monthly instalments of $1,710.70 over six months. The monthly instalments included reductions of the principal ($10,000) and interest at 9% per annum. The interest is calculated on the decreasing amount of principal. The following amortization table illustrates the interest component and the reductions of the principal.

Month	Payment	Interest	Principal Reduction	Principal Balance
				$10,000.00
1	$1,710.70	$75.00[a]	$1,635.70	$ 8,364.30
2	$1,710.70	$62.73	$1,647.97	$ 6,716.33
3	$1,710.70	$50.37	$1,660.33	$ 5,056.00
4	$1,710.70	$37.92	$1,672.78	$ 3,383.22
5	$1,710.70	$25.37	$1,685.33	$ 1,697.89
6	$1,710.70	$12.81[b]	$1,697.89	-0-

[a] $10,000 × .09 / 12 = $75.00
[b] rounding error of $.08

The journal entry at the end of the first month to record the first payment would be:

SE-Interest expense	75.00	
L-Short-term note payable	1,635.70	
A-Cash		1,710.70

Try to reconstruct the journal entries for the remaining months. The short-term note payable would initially have been recorded at the principal amount of $10,000, then gradually reduced as monthly payments were made.

Income Taxes Payable

Companies are subject to both federal corporate income taxes, and provincial corporate taxes. As mentioned earlier in the book, the rules governing the calculation of income for tax purposes may differ from the accounting guidelines. The discussion in Chapter 8 concerning future income taxes highlighted this difference (future income taxes will be discussed in greater detail later in this chapter). The taxes that become payable under the rules of Revenue Canada must be recorded as a liability of the company. Multinational companies may also be subject to taxation in the countries in which they operate.

The payment of taxes does not always coincide with the incurrence of the tax. In Canada, companies are required to make monthly tax payments, usually based on taxes paid the previous year, so that the government has a steady flow of cash during the year on which to operate. The deadline for filing the annual tax return is six months after the corporate year end, but the balance of taxes owed for a year must be paid within two months of the year end. Penalties are imposed if the company significantly under-estimates the amount of tax payable.

Warranty Payable

When a company sells a good or service, it makes either explicit or implicit guarantees to the buyer. If the product or service fails to satisfy the customer, the seller may have to provide warranty service. Because the amount of warranty service is unknown at the time of sale, the company should estimate an amount in order to match the expense of the warranty to the revenue from the sale. If the company has been in business for a reasonable length of time, this estimate can be made fairly easily, based on the past history of defects in the product. For new products and new companies, this process may be much more difficult.

As warranty service is provided (paid for by cash or other resources), the estimated liability amount is reduced. For tax purposes, companies claim a deduction when warranty service is actually provided. This creates a difference between the recognition of warranty expense for accounting purposes and for tax purposes. The difference between estimated warranty expense and the actual amounts spent on warranty work gives rise to a future income tax asset in much the way that accounting amortization and CCA give rise to a future income tax asset or liability.

Learning Objective

Describe how warranties payable is different from current liabilities such as accounts payable.

As an example of a warranty situation, let us consider Hubble Appliance Company Ltd. It sells large appliances such as stoves and refrigerators. During the month of January 20x2 it sold eight refrigerators, each of which carried a three-year warranty against mechanical defects. If the refrigerators sold for an average price of $1,150, Hubble would record revenues of $9,200 ($1,150 × 8). Although Hubble buys quality merchandise from its supplier, it is possible that within three years of sale one or more of these refrigerators will break down. In reviewing its past record of mechanical breakdowns, Hubble estimates that, over the long term, it costs approximately 5% of every sticker price to fix all units that ultimately require repair work. Over the next three years, therefore, Hubble expects to spend about $460 ($9,200 × .05) to fix one or more of the eight refrigerators just sold. Depending on the quality of the eight refrigerators, it may spend more than $460 or less than $460. Experience and knowledge of the merchandise make it possible for companies to make reasonably accurate estimates. To record the estimated warranty obligation, Hubble makes the following journal entry:

| SE-Warranty expense | 460 | |
| L-Estimated warranty obligation | | 460 |

If Hubble needed to spend $126 in 20x3 to replace a leaking seal on one of the refrigerators, it would record the repair work by reducing the liability account.

| L-Estimated warranty obligation | 126 | |
| A-Cash | | 126 |

As you can see, an expense is not recorded when actual repair costs are incurred. By estimating its potential future obligation at the time that it records revenue from the sale, Hubble is able to record the warranty expense in the period that it records the revenue. This way, users get a clearer picture of the actual amount of revenue earned on the sale. If Hubble had delayed recognizing an expense until it actually incurred some warranty costs, that expense could easily appear in a period other than the one in which the revenue was recognized. The profit reported for the sale would then have been overstated. For this reason, companies are asked to estimate the potential future warranty obligation and to record it at the time of sale, if the amount of warranty costs is material.

In the airline industry, frequent flyer programs are treated the way warranties are. As customers accrue travel miles, the company records an expense to represent the cost of providing a free flight and a liability to represent the company's future obligation to honour the credits earned by a customer. But some customers never collect enough points to earn a free flight, and others may not redeem their points even though they have enough for a free flight. Should companies accrue a liability for all of the potential free flights, or would it be more appropriate for them to estimate future redemptions of points and accrue a liability to represent that estimate? The following article summary should provide some insight into this dilemma:

accounting in the news

FREQUENT FLYER POINTS

Frequent flyer programs, which allow people to accumulate points they later trade in for air travel, are a good example of a future liability. Airlines need to account for them because people eventually redeem their points. By one estimate, two trillion points were outstanding in 1997—enough to fill 440,000 300-seat planes and send airlines into bankruptcy!

However, major airlines only rate the liability at 25 cents per $1,000 of outstanding cashable miles. Why? They don't expect to pay for every mile outstanding. Many people never claim their miles: Some forget, and some never fly enough to reach minimum award levels.

Source: "Frequent Travellers: How a Frequent Flyer Can Make a Point," Advertising Special Report, *Globe and Mail*, April 25, 1997, page C11.

Unearned Revenues

In many businesses, customers are required to make downpayments prior to the receipt of goods or services. This creates partially executed contracts between buyers and sellers. Because the sellers have not fulfilled their part of the contract, it would be inappropriate for them to recognize revenue from the sale. Therefore, sellers must defer the recognition of revenue from downpayments. These deferrals create liabilities known as **unearned revenues**, or **deferred revenues**.

Businesses that require prepayments generally show unearned revenues as a part of the liability section. Magazine and newspaper publishers and airline companies are among these types of businesses. The current liability section of Air Canada's 1998 annual report includes $360 million ($400 million in 1997) for Advance Ticket Sales. The note on revenue recognition states: "Airline passenger and cargo sales are recognized as operating revenues when the transportation is provided. The value of unused transportation is included in current liabilities."

Learning Objective

7

Describe situations in which unearned revenue must be recorded.

Current Portion of Long-Term Debt

When long-term debt (discussed in Chapter 10) comes within a year of being due, it must be reclassified as a current liability. This reclassification enables users to better estimate the outflow of cash expected during the following year. Therefore, this account category, known as **current portion of long-term debt**, is used for all the debt that was originally long-term but that is now within one year, or one operating cycle, of being paid off or retired. This account is also referred to as the

Learning Objective

8

Explain why the portion of long-term debt that is due in the next year is recorded as a current liability.

current maturity of long-term debt. In the case of long-term mortgages or other debt obligations requiring monthly or annual payments, the current maturity part that is shown with the current liabilities represents the amount of principal that will be paid off in the next year. Remember that the interest paid on this debt is not recorded until it accrues or is paid. In Exhibit 9-1, note that in 1998 about 4.1% of Domtar's long-term debt was due to be paid within the next year.

COMMITMENTS

Learning Objective

9

Explain what a commitment is and how it is recognized by a company.

In the course of business, many companies sign agreements committing them to certain transactions. A common type of commitment transaction is a **purchase commitment**, which is an agreement to purchase items in the future for a negotiated price. As discussed earlier, this is an example of a mutually unexecuted contract and, under Canadian accounting guidelines, therefore, is not recorded on the books of the company. The company would, however, discuss it in a note to the financial statements if it felt that the commitment would have a material effect on future operations. An example of this type of disclosure can be seen in Exhibit 9-2, which is the inventory note for AT Plastics Inc.

EXHIBIT 9-2

AT Plastics Inc. 1998

Excerpt from the Notes to the Statements

Note 10. Commitments and contingencies

Purchases
The Company has entered into a new 15 year cost of manufacture-related ethylene supply contract commencing in 1999 for approximately 125,000 tonnes per year under a limited take or pay arrangement.

AT Plastics likely disclosed this information because of the type of contract that is involved, and because it is committed for the next 15 years. A **take or pay contract** means that the company must pay for the 125,000 tonnes of ethylene whether or not it actually takes that much from the supplier. No monetary amounts are discussed, but the fact that the take or pay contract is *limited* may mean that the amount that must be paid each year has a top limit.

In analyzing the financial statements of a company, undisclosed purchase commitments are a significant risk to be considered. The problem this can pose for the reader of financial statements is illustrated by the case of Westinghouse Company (which became CBS Company in 1997) in the United States in the mid-1970s. Westinghouse was in the business of building nuclear power plants for utility companies. To secure the construction business, Westinghouse offered utility companies fixed-price contracts to supply them with uranium after the plants were completed and running. The average prices stated in these contracts were approximately $8 to $10 US per pound of uranium. By the mid-1970s, Westinghouse was committed to providing a total of approximately 70 million pounds over a 20-year period. Since these were mutually unexecuted contracts, they were not recorded or disclosed in the financial statements.

When the market price of uranium was close to the fixed price in the contracts, these mutually unexecuted contracts were a break-even proposition for Westinghouse (i.e., no gain or loss would occur when the contracts were satisfied), and no disclosure was required. The problem began when a cartel formed in the uranium supply market and drove up the price of uranium. When, in September 1975, the price reached $26 US per pound, Westinghouse informed the utility companies that it had to be excused from fulfilling its contracts because of a legal doctrine called "commercial impracticability." The utility companies then brought lawsuits against Westinghouse, alleging breach of contract. By 1978, the price of uranium had risen to $45 US per pound.

Because the price escalated so significantly above the contract price of $8–$10 US per pound, Westinghouse had to disclose the loss on these commitment contracts. In 1975, the estimated cost to Westinghouse of settling the contracts approached $2 billion, which was about 75% of its total equity at the time. Over the next 15 years, Westinghouse settled most of the suits, the first in 1977 for $20.5 million. The audit opinion of Westinghouse was qualified by the auditors for several years until 1979, when Westinghouse accrued a loss of $405 million (net of taxes) to cover the estimated costs of settling the remaining suits. Remember that auditors qualify their opinion concerning a company's financial statements if the company does not follow GAAP. Failing to accrue the potential liability for the lawsuits would have led to such a qualification. The effects of these suits lingered for 19 years, as indicated by the note in Exhibit 9-3, excerpted from Westinghouse's 1994 annual report.

■ **Westinghouse 1994**

EXHIBIT 9-3

Note 16: Contingent Liabilities and Commitments

Uranium Settlements
The Corporation had previously provided for the estimated future costs for the resolution of all uranium supply contract suits and related litigation. The remaining uranium reserve balance includes assets required for certain settlement obligations and reserves for estimated future costs. The reserve balance at December 31, 1994, is deemed adequate considering all facts and circumstances known to management. The future obligations require providing the remainder of the fuel deliveries running through 2013 and the supply of equipment and services through approximately 1995. Variances from estimates which may occur are considered in determining if an adjustment of the liability is necessary.

CONTINGENCIES

Contingent liabilities (also referred to as **contingent losses**) arise when the incurrence of the liability is contingent upon some future event. The settlement of a lawsuit, for example, is a situation in which the company may or may not incur a liability, depending upon the judgement in the case. The note in Exhibit 9-4, from the 1998 annual report of Canadian National Railway Company, outlines one such contingency.

Learning Objective

Describe the criteria necessary for a contingency and discuss when it is recorded.

■ **Canadian National Railway Company 1998**

Excerpt from the Notes to the Statements

21. Major commitments and contingencies

C. Contingencies

In the normal course of its operations, the Company becomes involved in various legal actions, including claims relating to injuries and damage to property. The Company maintains provisions for such items which it considers to be adequate. While the final outcome with respect to actions outstanding or pending as at December 31, 1998 cannot be predicted with certainty, it is the opinion of management that their resolution will not have a material adverse effect on the Company's financial position.

Another example of a contingency is the guarantee of one company's loan by another company. This happens many times when a subsidiary company takes out a loan and the parent company (the company that owns most of the shares of the subsidiary) guarantees repayment of the loan. The liability to repay the loan is a contingent liability to the parent company, because it is contingent upon the default of the subsidiary. Such a contingency is illustrated in the 1998 annual report of Cominco Ltd., shown in Exhibit 9-5.

■ **Cominco Ltd. 1998**

Excerpt from the Notes to the Statements

Note 13 Commitments and Contingencies

(b) Red Dog Mine

Cominco Alaska Incorporated (CAK), a subsidiary company, has an advanced royalty agreement with NANA Regional Corporation (NANA) on whose land the Red Dog mine is situated. Under the terms of the agreement, NANA receives a royalty equal to the greater of 4.5 percent of Red Dog's net smelter return or US$1 million. After CAK recovers certain capital expenditures, the royalty will be 25 percent of net proceeds of production from the Red Dog mine increasing in 5 percent increments every fifth year to a maximum of 50 percent.

CAK leases road and port facilities from the Alaska Industrial Development and Export Authority (AIDEA) through which it ships substantially all ore concentrate produced at the Red Dog mine. The lease requires CAK to pay a minimum annual user fee to AIDEA of approximately US$18 million, for which CAK is granted priority rights in the use of the facilities. The lease contains a fee escalator based on increases in the five year moving average price per pound of zinc in excess of 50 cents per pound, and on increases in annual tonnages of concentrate shipped in excess of 850,000 tons. Payments related to excess tonnage fees are deposited into an interest-bearing reserve fund held by AIDEA to a maximum of US$23 million, of which 50 percent may be recovered at the end of the initial term of the lease in 2040. Cominco guarantees CAK's obligations pursuant to this agreement and CAK has an option to extend the lease at the end of the initial term for five additional ten year periods.

As a third and final example, the selling of accounts receivable with recourse creates a contingent liability for the selling company because it may be required to buy back the receivables under the recourse provision if the customers default on the payments. A further discussion of the sale of receivables can be found in Chapter 6. Cominco, in its 1998 financial statements, reports the sale of its accounts receivable.

■ **Cominco Ltd. 1998**

EXHIBIT 9-6

Excerpt from the Notes to the Statements

Note 13 Commitments and Contingencies

(e) Sale of accounts receivable
The company has a program to sell, on a revolving basis and with limited recourse, up to US$50 million of its trade metal receivables to a special purpose trust. The program expires in December 2001 and may be terminated at any time by the company or the purchaser. At December 31, 1998, US$33 million of receivables had been sold pursuant to this program.

In Canada, a contingent loss should be recognized as a loss on the income statement and a liability on the balance sheet if it meets the following criteria:

1. It is likely that some future event will result in the company incurring an obligation that will require the use of assets or the performance of a service.

2. The amount of the loss can be reasonably estimated.

If either of these criteria is not met, but the potential for loss is significant, the company should provide users with information about the potential loss in a note disclosure similar to the three examples presented.

DEFERRED TAXES

Deferred taxes arise because, although the company uses accounting revenues and expenses to determine income tax expense on the income statement, it also uses Revenue Canada's calculations of revenues and expenses to determine the income tax payable (that is, the amount that must actually be paid to the government). In Chapter 8, deferred taxes were mentioned because companies must use capital cost allowance (CCA) for tax purposes. Companies can, however, use one of several amortization methods in preparing financial statements.

Other areas that create differences between what is taxed by the government and what is reported on the income statement include the warranty costs discussed earlier in this chapter. The warranty expense on the income statement is an estimate of future warranty costs based on revenue that was recognized in the current period. The deduction for tax purposes is the actual amount that the company paid in the current period to repair items under warranty. Amortization and warranties are examples of how the tax expense reported on the income statement, as calculated based on the accounting revenues and expenses reported on the statement, will be different from the actual taxes payable to the government.

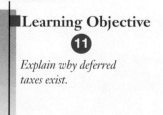

■**Learning Objective**

11

Explain why deferred taxes exist.

Two methods have been used to calculate deferred taxes: the **deferral method** and the **liability method**. The deferral method was used in Canada until the end of 1999, but as of January 1, 2000, companies must use the liability method. Companies were encouraged to implement the change to the liability method prior to 2000, so you may see some financial statements prepared in 1998 and 1999 using the new method. The liability method is used in the United States and is also recommended by the International Accounting Standards Committee. Because Canada now requires the liability method, this section will concentrate on that method. Following this discussion, the deferral method will be briefly described.

Liability Method

Learning Objective

12

Discuss how the liability method and deferred method for determining deferred taxes are different.

The liability method focuses on the balance sheet, not on the income statement. It attempts to measure the liability to pay taxes in the future based on a set of assumptions about future revenues and expenses. Once the liability for these future taxes is calculated and the amounts currently payable to Revenue Canada are established, the tax expense to be reported on the income statement is arrived at as a "plug" figure. With this method, there is no attempt to calculate tax expense using tax rates and income reported to shareholders.

To illustrate the liability method, we will use the data and calculations in Exhibit 9-7. The data represent a company that sells fitness equipment. The motorized equipment like treadmills carries a three-year warranty. The company estimates the probable future costs associated with the sale and records a liability (obligations under warranties) and a warranty expense in the year of the sale. Revenue Canada allows a tax deduction for the actual costs incurred by the company to repair equipment under warranty. Assume that the warranty is the only difference between the accounting and tax methods of the company.

EXHIBIT 9-7

Liability Method Computations

Assumptions:

Income before tax and warranties	$10,000

Warranty expense (accounting purposes):
    Year 1: $200
Actual warranty costs incurred:
    Year 1: $50
    Year 2: $70
    Year 3: $80

Tax rate   40%

Learning Objective

13

Calculate future income taxes in amortization and warranty situations.

The liability method requires the company to do a *pro forma* (as if) calculation of the amounts of income tax that will be payable in the future based on the **temporary differences** that exist in the current period. The pro forma calculations require that the company prepare a schedule of the differences that exist and how they will reverse in future periods. In the case of warranties, in the current period the company accrues a warranty liability that will become a tax deduction in the current and future periods as actual costs are incurred. This creates a **future tax asset**, because fewer taxes will be paid in the future as these deductions are included. Exhibit 9-8 illustrates how this occurs.

■ **Liability Method—Future Tax Asset Computation**

EXHIBIT 9-8

	Year 1	Year 2	Year 3
Beginning warranty obligation	$200	$150	$ 80
Actual warranty costs incurred	50	70	80
Ending warranty obligation	$150	$ 80	$-0-
Tax rate	40%	40%	40%
Future tax asset	$ 60	$ 32	$-0-
Reduction of future tax asset		($28)	($32)
Income tax payable calculation:			
Income before warranty costs and			
income tax	$10,000	$10,000	$10,000
Actual warranty costs	50	70	80
	9,950	9,930	9,920
Taxes payable	3,980	3,972	3,968
	$ 5,970	$ 5,958	$ 5,952
Taxes payable	$ 3,980	$ 3,972	$ 3,968
Future tax asset	(60)	28	32
Accounting tax expense	$ 3,920	$ 4,000	$ 4,000

Note how the original difference of $150 (future tax obligation of $60) reverses in Years 2 and 3 as actual warranty costs are incurred. The amount of actual taxes owed to the government is lower than the accounting tax expense, because the actual warranty costs are deductible for tax purposes in Years 2 and 3. This future reduction in actual taxes owed allows us to create the future tax asset of $60 in Year 1. Note as well that the accounting tax expense is less than taxes payable in Year 1 but higher than taxes payable in Years 2 and 3.

This example assumes that the original estimate in Year 1 was accurate (actual warranty costs over the three years were exactly $200). It also assumes that the tax rate of 40% does not change. Under the liability method, the company must review the estimates to ensure that the future tax asset still exists and that the amount estimated is still valid. In calculating the future tax asset the company must also use the tax rate that will be in effect in Years 2 and 3. If there is a planned change in rates for Years 2 and 3 the new rates must be used. The purpose of these two provisions is to ensure that the amount represented on the balance sheet for the future tax asset or liability is as accurate as possible.

To keep the example simple, we created a warranty obligation in Year 1 and then traced it through Years 2 and 3. In reality, there would be more sales of inventory with warranty provisions in Years 2 and 3. These new sales would create new warranty obligations, and actual warranty costs incurred in Years 2 and 3 would probably be incurred on inventory sold in any or all of the three years. Once we start to deal with multiple years, the calculations become more complex but the concept is the same. Warranty obligations are recognized in Year 1, and over the next two years of the warranty, costs will be incurred as the obligations are met. A future tax asset is created in Year 1 that will be reversed over Years 2 and 3.

Refer back to Chapter 8 for an example of how the liability method is applied when the source of the tax difference is the use of amortization for accounting and the use of CCA for tax.

Deferral Method

The deferral method focuses on the income statement. In this method, the amount of tax expense to be reported to shareholders is calculated based on the recognized revenues and expenses on the income statement using the tax rates in effect in the current year. Since the income reported to shareholders may differ from that reported to Revenue Canada, the amount of tax expense that is reported can differ from the amount that is payable to Revenue Canada. The difference between the expense and the amount payable becomes the amount of deferred tax. We will use the data in Exhibit 9-7 to illustrate the deferral method.

| EXHIBIT 9-9 | | | |

■ Deferral Method—Deferred Tax Calculation

	Year 1	Year 2	Year 3
Tax expense calculation			
Income before warranty and taxes	$10,000	$10,000	$10,000
Warranty expense	200	-0-	-0-
	9,800	10,000	10,000
Income tax expense	3,920	4,000	4,000
Net income	$ 5,880	$ 6,000	$ 6,000
Taxes payable (Exhibit 9-8)	$ 3,980	$ 3,972	$ 3,968
Deferred taxes	$ 60	(28)	(32)

Note that because the tax rate does not change over the three years the net effect is the same as that for the liability method.

The difference between the tax expense reported to shareholders and the taxes payable reported to Revenue Canada is a result of the time lapse between the point when the warranty cost is reported for tax purposes and the point when the warranty expense is reported for accounting purposes. Under the deferral method, the differences are referred to as **timing differences**. Differences in the first year increase the balance in the deferred taxes (an asset in this case). These differences are reversed in the next two years (referred to as **reversing differences**), causing the balance in deferred taxes to decline. The extra taxes that are paid in the first year of the warranty are recovered in Years 2 and 3 as the actual warranty costs reduce taxes payable (the amount actually owed to the government).

Some users misunderstand deferred taxes on the balance sheet, especially if these taxes have a credit balance and are included with the long-term liabilities. The user can incorrectly assume that these deferred taxes represent an amount owed by the company to Revenue Canada, whereas in reality the amount owed is shown as taxes payable. Deferred taxes on the balance sheet represent an amount that will *likely become payable* in the future, if conditions do not change. If we take the example of deferred taxes arising because of amortization (CCA for tax and straight-line for accounting, as illustrated in Chapter 8), in the early period of a capital asset's life, CCA could be larger than accounting amortization. This means that the company will pay less tax today than is measured for accounting purposes. The capital asset for tax purposes (the UCC) will be smaller (representing smaller deductions for tax in the future) than the capital asset for accounting purposes. In the latter part of the asset's life, CCA will be less than the accounting amortization, which means that the company will pay more in tax. Over the life of any asset, the total tax expense will be the same as total taxes payable.

There are three major differences between the liability method and the deferral method. First, the focus is different. The liability method focuses on the balance sheet and the deferral method focuses on the income statement. Second, the tax rate used may be different. The liability method uses the tax rate that will be in effect in future periods. Any time a rate changes, the previously recorded future tax assets and liabilities must be recalculated to reflect the change. Under the deferral method, previously recorded amounts of deferred taxes are not changed when tax rates change. Rather, the amounts are reversed at the previously recorded rates. This means that the amount disclosed on the balance sheet for deferred taxes may not represent the actual future tax impact. Third, under the liability method, the future tax assets and liabilities must be reviewed to ensure that they still accurately reflect the future tax impact. Under the deferral method, the deferred taxes are drawn down as time passes but periodic reviews are not conducted.

Big Rock has a substantial investment in capital assets. In 1997 it increased its investment in capital assets by just over $7 million. In 1998, that balance was reduced by approximately $1.5 million, and in 1999 it was reduced by a further $460,000. Big Rock uses straight-line amortization for reporting purposes but, like every other company in Canada, must use CCA for tax. The deferred tax balance rose by just over $300,000 in 1997 and by a further $1 million in 1998. In 1999 it was reduced by approximately $270,000, indicating that the timing differences are starting to reverse. A note disclosure tells us that "The Company follows the deferral method of accounting for the tax effect of the timing differences between taxable income and accounting income. Timing differences result principally from claiming capital cost allowance for income tax purposes in excess of amortization on capital assets." In its 2000 financial statements, Big Rock will have changed to the liability method.

Although the difference between amortization and CCA is not the only timing difference that results in deferred taxes, it usually has the most impact. The warranty expense discussed earlier also results in deferred taxes. However, the **originating differences** for warranties create debits to deferred taxes and the reversing entries are credits—the opposite of the usual pattern for amortization/CCA.

Deferred taxes can represent a significant amount on the balance sheet (23% of the total liabilities of Big Rock in 1999). It is therefore important that you understand what they are and what they are not. They are the difference between the tax expense as calculated on accounting income and the tax payable as calculated on taxable income. They are not the amount owed to the government for the current period. In fact, whether or not the company ever pays the amount to the government depends on the future activities of the business, and on whether or not the government maintains the same tax rules.

Deferred taxes can appear in various parts of the balance sheet as current assets or liabilities, or as long-term assets or liabilities. Where they appear is a function of the differences that caused them and whether they have a debit or credit balance. Deferred taxes that arise from warranty costs are often classified as current because the actual costs for warranties (those that are tax deductible for tax purposes) are usually incurred in the same year as the expense or in the following year. This is true if the warranty is a one-year warranty. For three-year warranties, the deferred taxes would take longer to reverse and are therefore classified as noncurrent. Deferred taxes that result from the CCA/amortization situation are classified as noncurrent because it takes several years for the deferred taxes to reverse. Because of the difficulty in determining whether deferred taxes are actually a liability, you will often see them classified on their own at the end of the noncurrent liabilities section.

One more issue regarding the deferral method should be considered because it also applies to the liability method. Some differences between the methods used for accounting and for tax purposes are considered **permanent differences**. One example is the recognition of dividend revenue received from an investment in another Canadian company. This is a legitimate revenue for accounting purposes. For tax purposes, however, it is not taxable income because the company that paid the dividends already paid taxes on it. To tax the recipient of the dividend would, in effect, tax the same income twice. If deferred tax were to be computed on this permanent difference, it would never reverse, and the balance in the deferred tax account would never disappear. Refer back to the example in Exhibit 9-7. The company earned $10,000 before tax and warranties. Assume that in Year 1 the source of $500 of that income was dividends from an investment in another company. The computation of taxes payable and accounting tax expense under the liability method would be as presented in Exhibit 9-10.

EXHIBIT 9-10

■ **Liability Method—Future Tax Asset Computation Including a Permanent Difference**

	Year 1	Year 2	Year 3
Beginning warranty obligation	$200	$150	$ 80
Actual warranty costs incurred	50	70	80
Ending warranty obligation	$150	$80	$-0-
Tax rate	40%	40%	40%
Future tax asset	$ 60	$ 32	$-0-
Reduction of future tax asset		($28)	($32)

EXHIBIT 9-10
CONT.

■ Income tax payable calculation:

Income before warranty costs and income tax	$10,000	$10,000	$10,000
Less: permanent difference	500		
	9,500		
Actual warranty costs	50	70	80
	9,450	9,930	9,920
Taxes payable	3,780	3,972	3,968
	$5,670	$5,958	$5,952
Taxes payable	$ 3,780	$ 3,972	$ 3,968
Future tax asset	(60)	28	32
Accounting tax expense	$ 3,720	$ 4,000	$ 4,000

Note that the income before taxes is adjusted for the permanent difference before the taxes payable is determined. The example given above used the liability method but the treatment of permanent differences is the same for the deferral method and the liability method.

AN INTERNATIONAL PERSPECTIVE

Reports from Other Countries

In some countries, such as Italy, Norway, and Chile, accounting practices follow the tax requirements of the country. No deferred tax account is necessary, since there are no differences between accounting and tax. In most countries (Denmark, France, and Japan, to name just a few), the provision for income taxes is based on the taxable income, not on the accounting income reported to shareholders. In these countries, no deferred taxes will be shown either. A relatively small number of countries (including the United States and South Africa) follow the Canadian practice of computing deferred taxes on all timing (temporary) differences (excluding permanent differences). The United Kingdom follows the Canadian practice except that differences that will not reverse in the foreseeable future are not recorded as deferred taxes but are instead treated as permanent differences. Virtually no country allows deferred tax amounts to be present-valued.

NAFTA Facts

United States—The liability method is used.
Mexico—The partial liability method is used, which recognizes deferred taxes only for identifiable non-recurring differences.

OTHER TAX DISCLOSURES

Included in the usual tax disclosure of a company are three basic types of disclosure. The first is a breakdown of the tax expense (sometimes referred to as the tax provision) into the amounts currently payable and the amounts deferred. If the company has significant foreign operations, foreign taxes are sometimes broken out in this disclosure. Trimac Company's financial statements disclose this in Note 5, where the breakdown of the tax expense occurs in the first table (Exhibit 9-11).

EXHIBIT 9-11

Note 5 – Income Taxes

The income tax provision is comprised of the following:

	Year ended December 31	
	1998	1997
Current	$ 5,014	$ 4,699
Future	(25,346)	42,989
	$ (20,332)	$ 47,688

Note 5 – Income Taxes - continued

The provision varies from what would otherwise be expected for the following reasons:

	Year ended December 31			
	1998		1997	
	Amount	Percentage of earnings before tax	Amount	Percentage of earnings before tax
Computed "expected" tax	$ (8,701)	(44.6)	$ 43,905	44.6
Recognition of previously unrecorded loss benefits	(9,553)	(49.0)	(3,278)	(3.3)
Loss for which no tax benefit has been recognized	—	—	426	0.4
Difference between accounting and tax cost base on gains net of non taxable/deductible portion of capital disposals	3,904	20.0	4,200	4.3
Increase in tax base of certain investments	(7,512)	(38.5)	—	—
Capital taxes	1,555	8.0	1,277	1.3
Other	(25)	(0.1)	1,158	1.1
	$ (20,332)	(104.2)	$ 47,688	48.4

During 1989, the Trimac Limited consolidated group acquired two contract drilling businesses. One of the assets acquired related to losses and tax costs in excess of book costs carried forward for income tax purposes. A benefit of $11.6 million which has been recognized as income, is subject to the ultimate acceptance by taxing authorities. In the opinion of management, such claim will be accepted.

The second tax disclosure is a discussion of the items that cause the deferred tax amounts. In Exhibit 9-11, Trimac has not provided this breakdown. Instead, it has moved directly into the third type of disclosure.

The third major disclosure in the notes is a reconciliation of the difference between the tax expense reported and the amount that would have been reported based on statutory rates. This disclosure takes into consideration the tax credits and other items that cause the average (effective) rate to be different from the statutory Revenue Canada rate. The second table in Exhibit 9-11 shows that the differences are significant and are due mainly to the recognition of previously unrecorded loss benefits, the difference between accounting and tax cost based on gains net of non-taxable/deductible portion of capital disposals and the increase in tax base of certain investments.

SUMMARY

This chapter opened with a description of commonly reported current liabilities. It traced through the financial statement impact of lines of credit, accounts payable, wages payable, short-term notes, income tax, warranties, and unearned revenue. It also described some of the anomalies that can affect the decisions made by users but that may or may not be actually reflected on the balance sheet or income statement. These items are commitments (often described in notes to the financial statements) and loss contingencies (reported on the financial statements if likely to occur and to be measurable, but in the notes to the financial statements only if likely to occur but not to be measurable). The chapter concluded with a discussion of deferred income taxes (including coverage of both the liability method and the deferral method), an item that can be confusing to users because it can be either current or noncurrent, depending on its source. Unlike previous chapters, this one did not include a discussion of financial statement analysis concerns regarding liabilities. This topic will be dealt with once the discussion of the remaining liabilities in Chapter 10 is complete. In Chapter 10, attention turns to noncurrent liabilities, of which the primary accounts are bonds payable, pension liabilities, and lease liabilities.

SUMMARY PROBLEM

The Lundkvist Company purchased a piece of equipment on January 1, 20x2, for $21,000. The company will amortize the asset straight-line for book purposes over its useful life, which is estimated to be seven years. The residual value is estimated to be zero. The asset qualifies as a class 10 asset for tax purposes, with a 30% CCA rate. During 20x2, Lundkvist generated $4,500 in income before amortization and taxes. The tax rate in 20x2 is 25%. The amortization of the asset purchased in 20x2 is the only difference between the book methods and the tax methods used by Lundkvist.

Required:

1. Construct the entry for taxes that Lundkvist will make in 20x2 using the liability method of calculating deferred taxes.

2. Prepare a note to accompany the 20x2 financial statements.

SUGGESTED SOLUTION TO SUMMARY PROBLEM

1. The tax expense and taxes payable for 20x2 are calculated as shown in Exhibit 9-12 under the liability method.
   The entry to record taxes in 20x2 therefore is:

SE-Tax expense	375.00	
L-Tax payable		337.50
L-Future tax liability		37.50

Liability Method Computations

Amortization:

   $21,000 / 7 = $3,000
   Book value of asset at the end of 20x2 = $18,000
      ($21,000 − $3,000)

CCA:

   $21,000 × 30% × 50% = $3,150
   UCC at the end of 20x2 = $17,850
      ($21,000 − $3,150)

Computation of future tax liability:

   $18,000 − $17,850 = $150 Difference in ending asset carrying values
   Tax rate = 25%
   Future tax liability = $150 × 25% = $37.50

	Accounting	Tax
Income before amortization/CCA	$4,500	$4,500
Amortization/CCA	3,000	3,150
Income before taxes	1,500	1,350
Taxes	375	338
Net income	$1,125	$1,012

2. The following note could be included with Lundkvist Company's financial statements:

Income Taxes
Income taxes for 20x2 consist of:

Current	$338
Future	37
	$375

Future income taxes arise as a result of temporary differences from claiming capital cost allowance for income tax purposes in excess of amortization on capital assets.

Statutory rate	25.0%
Effect on taxes of capital cost allowance	(2.5)
Effective tax rate	22.5%

ABBREVIATIONS USED

CCA	Capital Cost Allowance	QPP	Quebec Pension Plan
CPP	Canada Pension Plan	UCC	Undepreciated Capital Cost
EI	Employment Insurance		

SYNONYMS

Contingent liability/Contingent loss

Current maturities of long-term debt/Current portion of long-term debt

GLOSSARY

Commitments Obligations to which a company has agreed but which do not yet meet the recognition criteria for liabilities.

Contingencies Events or transactions whose effects on the financial statements depend on the outcome of some future event.

Contingent liability A liability of a company that is contingent on some future event, such as the resolution of a lawsuit.

Contingent loss Synonym for contingent liability.

Current portion of long-term debt That portion of long-term debt that is within one year of coming due.

Deferral method A method of computing deferred taxes in which the tax expense to shareholders is calculated by multiplying the current tax rate by the income before taxes reported to shareholders. The entry to the deferred tax account is the difference between this expense and the taxes owed to Revenue Canada on the company's tax return.

Deferred revenues Synonym for unearned revenues.

Deferred taxes Accounts used to reconcile the differences between the taxes reported to Revenue Canada (taxes payable) and those reported to shareholders (tax expense).

Future tax asset/liability Accounts used to record the future tax effect of the differences between the carrying values of assets/liabilities with respect to accounting records and tax records.

Liability An obligation that will require a probable future sacrifice of resources of the company.

Liability method A method of computing deferred taxes in which the balance in the future tax asset/liability account is calculated based on the tax calculation of future years at future tax rates. The tax expense reported to shareholders is then determined based on the calculated deferred tax amount and the taxes owed to Revenue Canada.

Line of credit A credit limit established by a bank that allows the company to write cheques for amounts greater than the amount of cash in a bank account.

Monetary liability A liability that is fixed in terms of the number of currency units it represents.

Mutually unexecuted contract A contract between two entities in which neither entity has performed its part of the agreement.

Net present value The value today of an amount or series of amounts to be received or paid in the future.

Originating differences The initial differences between book and tax reporting that arise in the accounting for the transactions of the company. When these differences reverse themselves, the reversals are referred to as reversing differences.

Partially executed contract A contract between two entities in which one or both of the parties has performed a portion of its part of the agreement.

Permanent differences Differences between book and tax reporting that never reverse themselves; that is, they are "permanent." An example would be a manufacturing deduction that reduces taxable income but is not an accounting expense.

Purchase commitment   A contract between two entities in which one entity agrees to buy goods or services from another entity but neither party has executed the contract.

Reversing differences   Timing or temporary differences that are reversals of previously recognized originating differences.

Take or pay contract   A contract in which the buyer must pay for a minimum level of merchandise whether or not delivery of those goods is taken.

Temporary difference   Differences that arise because of the different carrying values of assets/liabilities as they are recorded in the accounting records versus as they are recorded in the tax records. The term is used in the liability method of computing deferred taxes.

Timing differences   Differences that arise in the accounting for the transactions of a company between the tax rules and the accounting guidelines. The differences are restricted to those that involve only timing issues—that is, the period in which the items are reported. The term is used in the deferral method of computing deferred taxes.

Troubled debt restructuring   The renegotiation of the terms of a debt agreement when the debtor is financially distressed.

Unearned revenues   Cash receipts from customers that have not yet met the criteria for revenue recognition.

Working capital loan   A short-term loan, often a demand loan, that is arranged with a bank to cover short-term cash shortages experienced by a company.

ASSIGNMENT MATERIAL

Assessing Your Recall

9-1 List three essential characteristics of a liability.

9-2 Describe the term *mutually unexecuted contract* and explain how it is accounted for in Canada.

9-3 Describe the appropriate valuation method for liabilities. Include a discussion of both current and noncurrent liabilities in your response.

9-4 Explain why warranty expense and the actual costs incurred with respect to warranties often do not occur in the same period.

9-5 Describe the nature of an account called *unearned revenues* and provide an example.

9-6 Explain why employers often object when the government changes CPP/QPP and/or EI rates.

9-7 What is the "current portion of long-term debt"? Why is it recorded with the current liabilities?

9-8 Describe the circumstances under which a commitment would be recognized in the financial statements.

9-9 Describe the circumstances under which a loss contingency would be recognized in the financial statements.

9-10 Explain how deferred taxes are calculated in the liability method.

9-11 Explain how the liability method differs from the deferral method.

9-12 Describe or discuss the meaning of the following terms: temporary differences, permanent differences, originating differences, and reversing differences.

Applying Your Knowledge

9-13 (Future tax liabilities)

Some accountants do not believe that future tax liabilities meet the criteria for recognition as a liability. Discuss future tax liabilities in terms of the three criteria for a liability, and provide your own arguments in support of whether or not they meet the criteria.

9-14 (Recording and reporting current liabilities)

Northern Catalogue Sales Ltd. operates a catalogue service out of Saskatoon. The company year end is September 30. At the beginning of September 2001, Northern had the following current liabilities listed on its books:

Bank indebtedness (line of credit)	$12,300
Accounts payable	45,700
Unearned revenue	1,900
Wages payable	3,500
Personal income tax payable	2,100
CPP payable	1,100
EI payable	1,230
Short-term note payable	10,000

During September 2001, the following events occurred:

1. Northern purchased new inventory on account for an invoice cost of $65,300. During the month, $74,600 was paid to suppliers.

2. Merchandise totalling $1,900 was sent to customers, which satisfied the unearned revenue outstanding at the beginning of the month. At the end of the month, merchandise on order by customers totalled $6,500. This merchandise was paid for but was back ordered from the supplier and would be sent in October.

3. Northern paid $5,000 on its line of credit on September 1, 2001. On September 30, interest at 7.5% per annum was paid on the outstanding balance.

4. During September the wages owed to employees at the beginning of the month were paid. Additional wages of $18,000 were incurred. Personal income tax at a rate of 25% was deducted from the employees' cheques. CPP and EI were recorded as well (use the rates given in the chapter to determine the amounts for these items).

5. The personal income tax, CPP, and EI that were outstanding at the beginning of September were paid to Revenue Canada. The new amounts owed for September wages were still outstanding at the end of the month.

6. The short-term note payable was still outstanding at the end of September. It carried an interest rate of 8% per annum.

7. As a result of cash flow needs in September, the line of credit increased by $4,000 on September 30, 2001.

Required:

a. Prepare journal entries to record the September transactions.

b. Prepare the current liability section of Northern's balance sheet at September 30, 2001.

9-15 (Recording and reporting current liabilities)

Shamous Ltd. operates on a calendar-year basis. At the beginning of December 2003, Shamous had the following current liabilities listed on its books:

Accounts payable	$82,300
Rent payable	24,000
Unearned revenue	4,500
Obligations under warranties	33,000

During December 2003, the following events occurred:

1. Shamous purchased a new computer system at a cost of $23,000 on account, payable on January 15, 2004. The company paid an installer $3,500 to set up the new system and train the employees.

2. Shamous purchased inventory for $96,000 on account and made payments of $89,000 to the suppliers.

3. Shamous borrowed $35,000 from the Sussex Bank on December 15 at 8% annual interest. Principal and interest are due three months from the date of the loan.

4. The rent that was owed at the beginning of December represented the rent payments that should have been made in October and November. In December, Shamous paid the past rent owed as well as the rent owed for December. It leases its business space under a lease that requires equal monthly payments, with payments due in advance on the first day of each month.

5. The company earned one half of the income for prepaid services that had been prepaid by a customer on November 30.

6. Shamous's products are sold with a two-year warranty. The company estimates its warranty expense for the year (not previously recorded) as $18,000. During December the company paid $1,100 in warranty claims.

7. Employees of the company are paid a total of $1,400 per day. Three work days elapsed between the last payday and the end of the fiscal year. (Ignore deductions for income tax, CPP, and EI.)

8. At the end of December, Shamous had a five-year bank loan of $20,000 outstanding. The loan required that annual interest payments at 9.5% be paid each December 31. The loan further required that $4,000 of the principal be repaid on January 1 of each year.

> *Required:*
>
> a. Prepare the journal entries to record the December transactions. Ignore the income tax, CPP, and EI on the wages.
>
> b. Prepare the current liability section of Shamous's balance sheet at December 31, 2003.
>
> c. Explain your treatment of the five-year bank loan.

9-16 (Recording and reporting current liabilities)

Joan's Golf Shoppe had the following transactions involving current liabilities:

1. The company ordered golfing supplies from a supplier for $556,400. The parts were ordered on credit. During the year, $521,500 was paid to suppliers.

2. Joan offered her customers a one-year warranty on golf clubs. She estimated that warranty costs would total 2% of sales. Sales for the year were $2,188,200. During the year, she actually spent $39,040 to replace faulty golf clubs under warranty.

3. Joan has four employees involved in sales and one involved in accounting and marketing. During the year, they earned gross wages of $142,000. From this amount, Joan deducted 27% for income tax, 3.2% for Canada Pension deductions, and 2.7% for Employment Insurance contributions before giving the cheques to her staff. As an employer, she was also required to make additional contributions of 3.2% for Canada Pension and 3.78% for Employment Insurance on behalf of her employees.

Required:

a. Journalize the above transactions.

b. Prepare the current liability section of the balance sheet as it would appear at the end of the year after these transactions had been made.

9-17 (Recording and reporting current liabilities)

The University Survival Magazine was a small operation run by two enterprising university students. They published a magazine once a month from September through April. The magazine reported on various university activities, providing tidbits of knowledge on how to get the best tickets, where the best beer was sold for the best price, where the good study spots were located, and how to get library personnel to help with research. They sold their magazine by single copy in the bookstore for $2.75 an issue or by subscription for $18.00 per year for eight issues. In August, they canvassed various local businesses and managed to raise $18,000 in advertising for the magazine. The advertisements were to be included in all eight issues of the magazine. In early September of 20x1, they sold 5,000 subscriptions. Up to the end of December, they sold 7,000 single copies in each of the four months. The cost of printing the first four issues of the magazine was $66,000.

Required:

a. Journalize all of the transactions for August through to the end of December. Where there are alternative ways of recording a transaction, explain why you chose to record it the way you did.

b. Prepare any necessary adjusting entries on December 31.

c. Prepare an income statement for the students for the period up to the end of December.

d. Write a brief memo to the students explaining why the net income amount on the balance sheet will not equal the cash balance in the bank account.

9-18 (Recording and reporting warranties)

Computers Galore Ltd. sold computers, computer accessories, and software. On its computers, the company offered a one-month warranty, which was covered in the cost of the computer, but offered extended warranties of one or two years for an additional charge. The company charged $79 for a one-year warranty and $135 for a two-year warranty. Most customers took advantage of this additional coverage and paid Computers Galore the extra amount. Claims against the warranty varied from replacing parts in computers to providing the customer with a new computer if repairs could not be made. During 2001, Computers Galore sold 1,400 one-year warranties and 850 two-year warranties. Also during 2001, costs associated with the warranties amounted to $64,200 and $79,100, respectively, for the one- and two-year warranties.

Required:

a. Should Computers Galore classify the warranty obligation as current or noncurrent? Explain.

b. Should Computers Galore record a warranty expense associated with its computers? Explain.

c. Prepare journal entries to record the warranty transactions for 2001.

d. If the actual warranty costs incurred by the company are less than the amount collected from customers for the warranty coverage, how should the company account for the difference? How should the company account for the difference if the actual warranty costs are greater?

9-19 (Recording and reporting unearned revenue)
The Cool Air Conditioning Company services air conditioners on a quarterly basis. It offers its customers a service plan that costs $500 per year and includes four service visits during the year. The company collects the entire $500 when the contract is signed and recognizes the revenue on a quarterly basis when each of the four service visits is completed. On January 1, 750 contracts were outstanding. Of these, 200 expired at the end of the first quarter, 250 at the end of the second quarter, 200 at the end of the third quarter, and 100 at the end of the fourth quarter. Sales of new contracts and expenses during the year are as follows:

Quarter	Contracts Sold	Expenses
1	250	$ 80,000
2	400	66,000
3	450	98,000
4	200	115,000

Assume that the sale of new contracts takes place at the beginning of each quarter.

Required:

a. Give the necessary journal entries for each of the four quarters.

b. How many contracts were still outstanding at the end of the fourth quarter, and what is the value of these contracts?

c. Determine the amounts that would appear on the balance sheet and income statement on December 31 with respect to the above activities. Prepare a partial balance sheet and income statement to show how these amounts would be reported.

9-20 (Contingent liability)
On April 10, 20x2, while shopping for new furniture for her home, Mia Thorne, a world-renowned pianist, cut her finger because some of the nails on the table she was looking at were not hammered in properly. On June 10, 20x2, Ms. Thorne sued the furniture store for $5 million. The case came to trial on September 13, 20x2, and the jury reached a decision on December 13, 20x2, finding the store liable and awarding Ms. Thorne a sum of $1.5 million. On February 3, 20x3, the furniture store, dissatisfied with the judgement, appealed to a higher court. The higher court reheard the case beginning on July 18, 20x3. On November 25, 20x3, a jury again found the store liable and awarded $4 million to Ms. Thorne. On January 15, 20x5, the furniture store negotiated a reduced payment to Ms. Thorne and paid her the agreed amount of $2 million.

Required:
Using the stated events in the case, identify the various times at which a loss could be recognized. Using the criteria for a contingent liability, recommend and justify which of those times would be the most appropriate for reporting a note to the financial statements and for making an actual journal entry on the books. Assume the company's year end is December 31.

9-21 (Income taxes and capital assets)

On January 1, 20x1, the Precision Machining Company purchased a new machine costing $38,000. The company uses straight-line amortization for book purposes and CCA for tax purposes. The machine has an estimated useful life of eight years and zero residual value. For tax purposes, the machine is in the 20% asset class, and the company is in the 25% marginal tax bracket and closes its books on December 31.

Required:

a. Calculate the income tax asset/liability for 20x1 and 20x2, and give the necessary journal entries for recording the tax expense for each year. The company uses the liability method. Assume that income before amortization and taxes is constant at $80,000 each year.

b. What amount would appear on the balance sheet for future tax assets/liabilities for 20x1 and 20x2? Where on the balance sheet would these amounts be reported?

c. If you were a banker reviewing this company's financial statements in anticipation of granting it a loan, what importance would you place on the future tax asset/liability balance? Explain.

9-22 (Income taxes and capital assets)

On January 1, 20x1, the Canadian Works Company purchased a new capital asset costing $18,000. The company estimated the useful life of the asset to be five years with a $3,000 residual value. The company uses straight-line amortization for book purposes and the asset qualifies for a 30% CCA rate for tax purposes. The company closes its books on December 31. The income before amortization and taxes in 20x1 is $75,000.

Required:

a. Calculate the future tax asset/liability amount, income tax expense, and taxes payable for 20x1 using the liability method. Assume a tax rate for 20x1 and all future years of 40%. Give the necessary journal entry.

b. Calculate the future tax asset/liability amount to the end of years 20x2 and 20x3.

c. Explain why the future tax account has changed over the three years.

9-23 (Income taxes and warranties)

The Hudson Motor Company manufactures engines for small airplanes and helicopters. The company offers its customers a warranty of five years or 7,500 flying hours. To maintain the warranty, customers must have their engines serviced every 1,000 flying hours. In 20x2, the company sold engines valued at $2,590,000. It estimates that the future warranty costs on these engines will be 4% of sales. During 20x2 it incurred costs of $25,000 associated with warranty work on engines.

Required:

a. Calculate the future tax asset/liability amount associated with the warranties in 20x2 assuming that the company uses the liability method. The tax rate in effect in 20x2 and future years is 32%.

b. Where on the balance sheet would the future taxes balance be reported? Why?

c. If the tax rate in 20x5 changed to 40%, what impact would this have on the calculation of the future tax asset/liability?

Management Perspective Problems

9-24 (Future income taxes and investment decisions)
As a stock analyst, discuss how you might view the nature of future tax liabilities and whether you would treat them in the same way that you might a long-term bank loan.

9-25 (Contingent liabilities and investment decisions)
Suppose that you have been asked by your company to evaluate the potential purchase of another company. The company has been in the chemical business for more than 60 years and has several plants scattered throughout Alberta, Ontario, Texas, and Mexico. Because of the nature of the chemical industry, every company must recognize the possibility of environmental problems associated with the manufacture and transportation of its products. Describe what you might find in terms of disclosure in the company's financial statements relative to environmental liabilities and what additional information you would like to have in assessing its liabilities.

9-26 (Commitments)
Suppose that you are the sales manager for a construction company and you are responsible for securing contracts. As a part of your negotiations with customers you offer a "sweetener" to your contracts, which is an agreement to supply raw materials to the customer at a fixed price over an extended period of time. The price fixed in the contract is currently right at the fair market price for the raw materials.

> *Required:*
>
> a. What does the accounting department need to know about these "sweeteners" to appropriately account for these agreements?
>
> b. How should the accounting department record these transactions?
>
> c. Under what circumstances might your answer to part b. change?
>
> d. What should shareholders know about these agreements?

9-27 (Effect of changes in the CPP and EI rates)
You are the manager of a company with approximately 20 employees. The government has just announced its new rates for CPP and EI. With respect to employee contributions, the CPP is going up from 3.2% to 3.6% and the EI is dropping slightly, from 2.7% to 2.5%. The company's contribution for CPP is rising from 3.2% to 3.6% and the EI is dropping slightly, from 3.78% to 3.7%.

> *Required:*
>
> a. Assume a gross wages amount of $10,000. Calculate the financial impact that this change in rates has on the company.
>
> b. Write a memo to the President of the company explaining the financial impact of this change in rates.
>
> c. Suggest some actions that the company could take to reduce the impact of this rate change.

Reading and Interpreting Published Financial Statements

9-28 (Future costs of reclamation)
Imperial Metals Corporation is a Canadian mining company with operations in Canada and the United States. In the notes to the financial statements of its 1998 annual report, Imperial Metals states:

FUTURE SITE RESTORATION COSTS

The estimated costs for reclamation of producing resource properties are accrued and charged to operations over commercial production based upon total estimated reclamation costs and recoverable reserves. The estimated costs for reclamation of non-producing resource properties are accrued as liabilities when the costs of site clean-up and reclamation are likely to be incurred and can be reasonably estimated. Actual site reclamation costs will be deducted from the accrual.

Required:

a. Explain how and why Imperial Metals treats future reclamation costs for producing properties differently from costs for non-producing properties.

b. Using accounting concepts, explain why it is not appropriate for Imperial Metals to wait until it actually incurs reclamation costs before it recognizes an expense on its income statement for reclamation.

9-29 (Lines of credit)
Note 7B of CAE Inc.'s 1999 financial statements describes the details of its short-term debt.

7. B. SHORT-TERM DEBT

The Corporation has unsecured bank lines of credit available in various currencies totaling $84.0 million (1998 – $91.8 million). The effective interest rate on short-term borrowings was 7.6% (1998 – 5.9%).

Required:

a. CAE has lines of credit available in various currencies. What is a line of credit? Why would CAE want to have lines of credit in various currencies?

b. The lines of credit carry interest at prime or close to prime. What is a prime rate? What does the prime rate tell you about the bank's estimate of riskiness of this debt?

c. The lines of credit are unsecured. What do you think this means? Would CAE be able to get a lower rate of interest if the debt was secured? Explain.

9-30 (Current liabilities in an investment company)
Mackenzie Financial Corporation's balance sheets for March 31, 1998 and 1997, are shown in Exhibit 9-13. Mackenzie provides investment management and related services to public mutual funds, corporate pension fund clients, and other institutional investors.

Required:

a. Mackenzie has a liability called "customer deposits" among its liabilities. What does this liability represent?

b. The company does not distinguish between current and noncurrent liabilities. Are the customer deposits current or noncurrent? Give reasons for your answer.

c. Mackenzie has an asset called "loans." Usually, accounts called loans are liabilities. What is this item and why is it listed with the assets?

EXHIBIT 9-13

Consolidated Financial Statements

thousands of dollars

CONSOLIDATED BALANCE SHEETS

As at March 31		1998		1997
Assets				
Cash and short-term investments *(note 7)*	$	127,876	$	126,741
Accounts and other receivables *(notes 7 and 14)*		93,093		106,296
Income taxes recoverable		22,025		52,844
Loans *(notes 3, 7 and 14)*		205,702		217,795
Deferred selling commissions and investment				
in related partnerships *(note 4)*		515,173		368,285
Investment in affiliated company		77,581		68,682
Management contracts		11,903		12,497
Capital assets *(note 5)*		29,668		26,648
Goodwill		5,153		6,099
Other assets *(notes 6 and 14)*		13,945		6,660
	$	1,102,119	$	992,547
Liabilities				
Bank loans	$	9,633	$	6,805
Accounts payable and accrued liabilities		78,030		86,268
Customer deposits *(notes 7 and 14)*		254,292		278,302
Debentures and notes *(notes 8 and 14)*		124,259		131,341
Deferred taxes		181,609		128,389
Minority interest		9,263		4,661
		657,086		635,766
Shareholders' Equity				
Capital stock *(note 9)*				
Authorized – Unlimited number of common shares				
Issued and outstanding				
– 124,904,630 (1997 – 122,259,630) common shares		67,655		52,887
Retained earnings		374,626		303,894
Currency exchange adjustment *(note 2)*		2,752		—
		445,033		356,781
	$	1,102,119	$	922,547

(The accompanying notes are an integral part of these consolidated financial statements.)

Signed on behalf of the Board

ALEXANDER CHRIST
Director

F. WARREN HURST
Director

9-31 (Short-term borrowings)

The 1998 balance sheet of Xerox Canada Inc. includes the current liability "Notes payable (due within one year)" in the amount of $1,331,718,000 (1997 − $442,279,000). This liability is further described in the following note:

> ### 8. BORROWINGS
>
> The notes payable are promissory notes issued pursuant to the Company's commercial paper program. The notes are of varying maturities not exceeding 365 days and are at interest rates ranging from 5.10% to 5.74%.

The Company has various other long-term debt instruments with varying rates of interest, ranging from 10.1% to 12.15%.

Required:

a. What is a commercial paper program? Does the bank consider this company to be a good credit risk? Explain.

b. Suggest some reasons why the short-term borrowing rate is so much lower than the long-term borrowing rate.

c. It does not say in the notes whether the notes payable are secured. Explain what is meant if a debt is secured. Why would a company choose to issue secured debt?

9-32 (Income tax disclosure)

In Exhibit 9-14, Note 10 to Dofasco Inc.'s 1998 financial statements describes how the income tax on the income statement is determined.

Required:

a. What is Dofasco's statutory rate for income tax in 1998?

b. Dofasco's tax at statutory rates is adjusted by various items to arrive at an actual income taxes expense of $104.7 million. Determine the actual tax rate.

c. In the second table, several items are listed that explain how the income tax expense of $120.4 million (calculated using statutory income tax rates) became $104.7 million. These items represent permanent differences. What are permanent differences? Select two of these items and explain why you think they are permanent differences.

d. In 1998, how much did Dofasco actually pay to Revenue Canada for income taxes? Explain how you determined the amount.

9-33 (Commitments and contingencies disclosure)

Laidlaw Inc. is in the transportation and environmental services industry. In its 1997 financial statements, Laidlaw Inc. had the note found on page 521.

EXHIBIT 9-14

10. Income taxes

The income tax expense is comprised of:

(in millions)	1998	1997
Current	$ 108.2	$ 119.2
Deferred	(3.5)	(18.7)
	$ 104.7	$ 100.5

The income tax expense differs from the amount that would be computed by applying statutory income tax rates, as follows:

(in millions)	1998	1997
Income before income taxes	$ 280.1	$ 293.7
Income tax expense computed using statutory income tax rates	$ 120.4	$ 122.8
Add (deduct):		
Manufacturing and processing credit	(24.1)	(28.0)
Resource allowance	(11.5)	(9.3)
Unrecorded income tax benefit arising from losses of U.S. subsidiaries	14.6	7.4
Mining duties	6.1	5.0
Minimum taxes	3.5	3.4
Other	(4.3)	(.8)
	(15.7)	(22.3)
Income tax expense	$ 104.7	$ 100.5

At December 31, 1998, U.S. subsidiaries have accumulated losses for tax purposes of approximately U.S. $44.6 million (1997 – U.S. $15.3 million) for which no future tax benefit has been recognized in the accounts. These losses can be applied against future taxable income in varying amounts up to 2018.

18. COMMITMENTS AND CONTINGENCIES

Legal Proceedings

In June 1992, the Ministry of the Environment of the Province of Quebec requested a subsidiary of the Company to advise the Ministry of its intentions concerning the carrying out of certain characterization studies of soil and water and restoration work with respect to certain areas of the subsidiary's property in Ville Mercier. In 1968, the Quebec government issued two permits to an unrelated company to dump organic liquids into lagoons on this property. By 1971, groundwater contamination had been identified. In July 1992, the subsidiary responded by first denying any responsibility for the decontamination and restoration of its site and secondly, by proposing that the Ministry and the subsidiary form a working group to find the most appropriate technical solution to the contamination problem. In November 1992, the Ministry served the subsidiary with two Notices alleging the subsidiary was responsible for the presence of contaminants on its property and that of its neighbor and ordering the subsidiary to take all the necessary measures to excavate, eliminate or treat all the contaminated soils and residues located within the areas defined in the Notices and to recover and treat all of the contaminated waters resulting from the aforementioned measures or the Ministry would proceed to do the work and would claim from the subsidiary the direct and indirect costs relating to such work. The subsidiary responded by reiterating its position that it had no responsibility for the contamination and proposing to submit the question of responsibility to the Courts for determination. The subsidiary has filed legal proceedings to obtain a Court determination of its liability, if any, associated with the contamination of the former Mercier lagoons. The Company does not believe that these matters will be material to the Company's operations or financial position.

Required:

a. The above note describes what is called a contingent liability. Although the circumstances that gave rise to the note happened several years ago and the company does not think that the courts will decide against it, the company still decided to include this note in its 1997 financial statements. Provide some plausible reasons why Laidlaw included this note.

b. For how much longer do you anticipate that Laidlaw will continue to provide a note about this issue in its financial statements? Explain.

c. Up to the end of August 1997, Laidlaw still did not have this issue resolved in the courts. Use the SEDAR website to access the 1998 financial statements of Laidlaw. Is this issue described in the notes to the financial statements? Write a short report describing how the issue currently stands. If it has been resolved, describe the impact the resolution has on the company's financial statements.

9-34 (Line of credit disclosure)

Chai-Na-Ta Corporation grows and sells ginseng. The ginseng is grown in Canada and sold in North America and Asia. Ginseng takes three to five years to grow before it is ready for harvesting. In its 1998 annual report Chai-Na-Ta included the following note about its line of credit:

---

8. LINE OF CREDIT

During 1998, the Company had available a $5,000,000 line of credit that bore interest at prime plus 3/4% with a Canadian chartered bank secured by a first charge over certain assets of the Company. Borrowings of $4,600,083 against this line of credit were outstanding at November 30, 1998 (1997 — $1,007,710). On December 15, 1998 the Company renewed this line of credit bearing interest at prime plus 1%, repayable on or before November 15, 1999, subject to quarterly reviews.

Required:

a. What is a line of credit?

b. When Chai-Na-Ta renewed its line of credit in December 1998, the bank raised the interest rate by a quarter of a point. What reasons would the bank have for increasing the interest rate? What actions on the part of Chai-Na-Ta would convince the bank to lower the rate next time it renewed the line of credit?

c. This line of credit is secured against certain assets. What does it mean when a debt is secured? What would be the impact on the interest rate if the debt was not secured?

9-35 (Guarantees and commitments)

In the 1998 annual report of Alcan Aluminium Limited, the following note was included under Commitments and Contingencies (in millions of US$):

The Company has guaranteed the repayment of approximately $7 of indebtedness by third parties. Alcan believes that none of these guarantees is likely to be invoked. Commitments with third parties and certain related companies for supplies of goods and services are estimated at $373 in 1999, $212 in 2000, $35 in 2001, $35 in 2002, $25 in 2003, and $97 thereafter. Most of the commitments in 1999 and 2000 relate to the construction of the new smelter at Alma, Quebec. Total fixed charges from these entities, excluding $175 in relation to the smelter at Alma, were $23 in 1998, $9 in 1997 and $14 in 1996.

Required:

a. What is meant by "guaranteeing the indebtedness of third parties"?

b. With respect to the guarantees, why was it important for Alcan Aluminium to include a note about them with the financial statements.

c. With respect to the commitments for the supplies of goods and services, has Alcan Aluminium recorded these transactions in its accounting records? If not, why not?

Beyond the Book

9-36 (Financial statement disclosures)
Choose a company as directed by your instructor and do the following exercises:

a. Prepare a quick analysis of the current liability accounts by listing the beginning and ending amounts in these accounts and calculating the net change in both dollar and percentage terms for the most recent year. If the company you have selected does not prepare a classified balance sheet, you will need to determine which liabilities are current.

b. If any of the accounts change by more than 10%, give an explanation for this change.

c. What percentage of the company's total assets are funded by current liabilities? Has this percentage changed significantly in the last year?

d. Does the company have any significant commitments or contingencies? Read any related notes and then write a short paragraph summarizing each significant item. For the contingencies, are you aware of anything that has happened since the financial statements were issued related to these contingencies? If so, please describe.

e. Does the company have any significant (greater than 3% of total liabilities) accrued liabilities, such as warranties? If so, please read any notes discussing these items and summarize in a short paragraph the nature of these liabilities.

f. Read the note on income taxes and answer the following questions:

1. What is the company's effective tax rate? What are the major items that cause it to be different from the statutory rate?

2. What are the major items that result in deferred tax assets and liabilities for the company?

3. Can you reconcile the total net deferred tax assets (liabilities) presented in the note with what is reported in the financial statements? Note: To do this, you will need to consolidate all of the deferred tax accounts from the balance sheet.

9-37 (Disclosure of environmental liabilities)
Use an electronic database to search for a company that discloses significant environmental liabilities. Then answer the following questions:

a. What is the nature of the environmental liability?

b. Has the company accrued a liability for its potential environmental costs? If so, attempt to reconstruct the entries made in the most recent year with regard to these environmental costs. If not, discuss the criteria that the company must evaluate to decide whether it should accrue the liability in the future.

c. Evaluate how significant the impact of environmental liabilities might be on the company's financial statements.

Case

9-38 The Bigger Motor Company
The Bigger Motor Company manufactures and sells outboard motors for pleasure boats. Sales are relatively constant from February through November. December and January are very slow months and the company usually has its employees take holidays in these

months. The company has recently signed a contract with Henley Leisure Products Ltd. in North Battleford, a large dealership that sells everything from campers to boats and motors to life jackets. Bigger was given the contract because it was willing to offer extended credit terms to Henley. Because the credit terms were longer than normal, Bigger needs about $60,000 in additional working capital. The senior manager has identified three possible ways of acquiring these funds:

1. Line of credit. The bank would agree to extend a line of credit to Bigger for $75,000. The cost of the line of credit would be 9% per annum, with equal repayments expected in each of the four months after an amount was drawn on the line of credit.

2. Accounts payable. The company purchases about $50,000 per month on credit with terms of 2/30, net 90. Up to this point, the company had always taken advantage of the cash discount of 2% and paid all accounts within 30 days. The company could forfeit the discount and take 90 days to pay.

3. Short-term bank loan. The bank would agree to lend the company $75,000 at 7% interest. Payments could be made over 10 months. As security for the loan, the bank would require that the company maintain a cash balance equal to 15% of the loan amount.

Required:

a. Evaluate each of the three alternatives, doing your best to assess the total cost of the alternative and its riskiness.

b. Recommend one of the alternatives and write a memo to the president of the company explaining why your recommendation would be the best one for the company.

Critical Thinking Question

9-39 (Recognition and disclosure of contingent liabilities)
An issue discussed in Chapter 9 is financial statement recognition and disclosure of contingent liabilities, such as the potential claims associated with litigation. Loss and liability recognition is a function of whether it is likely that an asset has been impaired or a liability has been incurred and the degree to which a loss can reasonably be estimated. Evaluating whether these conditions exist is often a matter of judgement by management and auditors, perhaps more so than with any other issue of recognition or disclosure. Research has shown that reliance on judgement leads to differences among companies in whether and how contingencies associated with lawsuits are disclosed.

Required:

a. In today's environmentally conscious world, regulatory bodies are making more demands on resource companies to be environmentally responsible. For example, companies involved in mineral exploration are often required to plan for the cleanup and restoration of resource sites. A review of the annual reports of several resource companies reveals that some companies create liabilities each year in anticipation of this future event, some companies mention a contingent liability in the notes to the financial statements, and some companies do or say nothing about it. In a brief essay, discuss the criteria that a company should use when deciding on the kind of disclosure necessary to account for future cleanup and restoration costs.

b. As discussed in this chapter, some long-term liabilities are measured using present values. Discuss the appropriateness of using present values for long-term liabilities, and determine whether liabilities that are recorded for lawsuits are, or should be, subject to present value measurement.

Borrowing Money to Pay Money Back: "It Makes Sense."

Borrow money to pay money back? Sometimes this strategy makes sense, especially for a large corporation with long-term goals in mind. Hence when Teleglobe Inc., the Montreal-based international long-distance phone carrier, raised well over $1 billion through bond issues in July of 1999, $750 million of the funds was used to pay off the company's short-term debt. The rest helped Teleglobe kick off a five-year, $5-billion capital spending plan.

"We'll be increasing the capacity of our network to sustain the growth of the industry, which is in the midst of an explosion," explains Pierre VanGheluwe, Assistant Treasurer at Teleglobe. "Our capacity will increase 200-fold over five years. A cable that once carried 80 calls will soon be carrying 300,000."

The bonds were issued in the U.S. market through Merrill Lynch Canada, Inc., in association with its American parent. Large U.S. issues of this kind are unusual for Canadian companies, but are becoming more and more common now that the American bond market is on an upswing. Marc Brunet, a director with Merrill Lynch's investment banking group in Montreal, told the *Globe and Mail* at the time of the issue that "institutions are definitely clamouring for good-quality investment-grade bonds" south of the border. "More specifically, they are interested in the media and telecommunications sector."

Teleglobe's issue, which consisted of $600 million (U.S.) in 10-year debentures at a coupon rate of 7.2%, and another $400 million (U.S.) in 30-year debentures at 7.7%, was quickly snapped up by more than a hundred U.S. investing institutions.

These interest rates are higher than the 5.45% Teleglobe was paying on its short-term debt at the time, but that debt was at a floating rate during a period of potential volatility. Furthermore, explains Mr. VanGheluwe, Teleglobe needs access to the funds for a longer period than the market would have allowed. "You issue long-term debt to fund your long-term assets," he says simply. "It makes sense."

LONG-TERM LIABILITIES

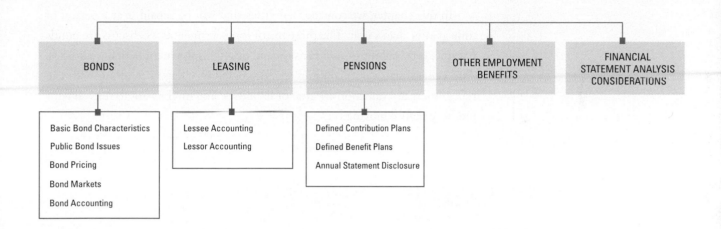

BONDS | LEASING | PENSIONS | OTHER EMPLOYMENT BENEFITS | FINANCIAL STATEMENT ANALYSIS CONSIDERATIONS

Basic Bond Characteristics
Public Bond Issues
Bond Pricing
Bond Markets
Bond Accounting

Lessee Accounting
Lessor Accounting

Defined Contribution Plans
Defined Benefit Plans
Annual Statement Disclosure

Learning Objectives:

After studying this chapter, you should be able to:

1. *Describe the basic characteristics of a bond.*
2. *Explain how bonds are issued and how pricing of bonds is affected by risk.*
3. *Calculate the issue price of a bond and prepare journal entries for the issuance of the bond and interest payments subsequent to the issuance for bonds issued at par, below par, and above par.*
4. *Discuss the advantages and disadvantages of leasing.*
5. *Distinguish between an operating lease and a capital lease and prepare journal entries for a lessee under both conditions.*
6. *Explain the distinguishing features of a defined contribution pension plan and a defined benefit plan.*
7. *Describe other employment benefits and explain how they are treated in Canada.*
8. *Calculate the debt/equity ratio and the times interest earned ratio and write a statement describing the financial health of a company using the information from these ratios.*

Companies like Teleglobe Inc., frequently use long-term debt or the issuance of new shares as a means of raising outside capital, which they then use to finance growth. They use the new cash to buy long-term assets or invest in other companies in order to expand their operations or enter new markets. Long-term debt is often preferable to short-term debt, because the benefits from their expansion efforts will be long-term. They can use the cash generated from the growth to repay the debt. Teleglobe used some of its new long-term debt to repay its short-term debt. The conversion of short-term debt to long-term debt enables a company to spread its debt payments over a greater period of time and puts less pressure on short-term cash needs.

In this chapter, we consider liabilities that will be repaid over a period of time greater than a year. The three major long-term debts we discuss are bonds payable, lease liabilities, and pension and other employment benefit liabilities. The general nature of liabilities was discussed in Chapter 9, along with the recognition and valuation criteria for liabilities. You might want to refresh your memory before moving on.

BONDS

When a public company wants to raise long-term funds to support its operations, it has two basic alternatives: the equity (stock) market, or the debt market. Issuing shares in the equity market is discussed in Chapter 11. Issuing debt in the debt market is the subject of this section. Within the debt market, there are various sources of funds. The company may borrow money from a commercial bank, much the way individuals borrow money from the bank to buy a new home or car. These borrowings are often listed on a company's financial statements as notes payable. The note can be short-term or long-term, and it can carry a fixed or floating interest rate. Another source of funds is what is known as the commercial paper market. A **commercial paper** is an unsecured promissory note that is generally sold to another business by a company that has a fairly high credit rating. In effect, one company borrows from another.

Another market in which the company may borrow money is the **bond market**. Generally, bonds are sold initially to institutional and individual investors through an investment banker (who earns a commission for handling the transaction). The **investment banker**, or a group of investment bankers (sometimes known as a **syndicate**), works with the company to decide which bond terms will be the most attractive to investors. In our opening story, you learned that Teleglobe Inc., used Merrill Lynch as its investment banker when it issued its debentures. Once all the bonds have been sold by the investment bankers, they can be freely traded among investors in a bond market much the way shares are traded on the stock market. The most widely known bond market is the New York Bond Market, which is a **public bond market**. Some bonds are sold to investors through what is referred to as a **private placement**. These types of bonds do not trade in public markets. Private placements are usually made to institutional investors such as trustees in charge of pension funds.

A full explanation of how the various debt markets differ is beyond the scope of this book. Various markets are mentioned so that you can gain some appreciation of the disclosures you will typically find as you read annual reports. Publicly traded bonds in Canada are used to illustrate the accounting issues surrounding long-term debt. There are some complex issues related to **foreign-denominated debt** that we will mention briefly, but in-depth coverage falls outside the parameters of this book.

Basic Bond Characteristics

A bond is a formal agreement between a borrower (the company) and a lender (the investor) that specifies how the borrower is to pay back the lender and any conditions that the borrower must meet during the period of the loan. The conditions of the loan are stated in a document called the **indenture agreement**. The indenture agreement may specify certain restrictions on the company. Known as **bond covenants**, these restrictions may limit the company's ability to borrow additional amounts, to sell or acquire assets, or to pay dividends. Bond covenants are intended to protect the investor against default on the loan by the company.

Learning Objective

1

Describe the basic characteristics of a bond.

Bonds that are traded in public markets are fairly standardized. The indenture agreement will state a **face value** for the bonds, which, in almost all cases, is $1,000 per bond. Unless it is stated otherwise, you should assume that the face value of a bond is $1,000. The face value specifies the cash payment the borrower will make to the lender at the **maturity date** of the bond (which is also specified in the indenture agreement). In addition to the cash payment at maturity, most bonds make semi-annual interest payments to the lender. The amount of these payments is determined by multiplying the bond interest rate times the face value and dividing by two (because they are semi-annual payments). The **bond interest rate** is stated as an annual percentage; it is *not* an effective or true interest rate but simply a means of determining the periodic amount of the interest payments.

One other important item described in the indenture agreement is the collateral the company pledges to the lenders. Some bonds specify particular assets as collateral. A bond known as a **mortgage bond** has some type of real property as collateral. A **collateral trust bond** provides shares and bonds of other companies as collateral. A bond that carries no specific collateral but is backed by the general credit worthiness of the company is known as a **debenture bond**. General debenture bonds can be either **senior debenture bonds** or **subordinated debenture bonds**. The distinction between senior and subordinated is the order in which creditors are paid in the event of bankruptcy: Senior creditors are paid first.

Some indenture agreements specify special provisions of the bond that are designed to make it more attractive to investors. **Convertible bonds**, for example, are convertible to a specified number of common shares in the company issuing the bond. In the 1970s and 1980s investors became concerned about the effects of inflation on the fixed payments, particularly the large final payment, that characterize bond agreements. You will recall from earlier chapters that, in a period of inflation, fixed payments decline in terms of their purchasing power. Therefore, the payment the investor receives at the maturity date may be worth considerably less (in terms of purchasing power) than the dollars lent to the company initially. To protect investors from the effects of inflation, some companies have issued bonds that index the final payment to a commodity. Sunshine Mining Corporation issued one of the first of these bonds, in 1980. It indexed the maturity payment as the greater of $1,000 (the normal maturity payment of a bond) or the market value of 50 ounces of silver. If inflation was significant, the market value of silver would rise and the investor would get the market value at maturity. Since that time, other bonds have indexed maturity values to oil and other commodities.

Public Bond Issues

Learning Objective

2

Explain how bonds are issued and how pricing of bonds is affected by risk.

When a company decides to issue bonds in the public bond market, it contracts the services of an investment banker, who will assist the company in issuing the securities. The investment banker will consult the company about its objectives, and will help design an issue that will both meet the company's objectives and attract investors. All the basic features of the bond that have been discussed above will be considered in structuring the issue.

The investment banker will not only help design the bond issue, but will also be responsible for the initial sale of the issue to its investor clients. Because most issues involve larger amounts than one investment banker can easily sell, the investment banker usually forms a syndicate with other investment bankers, who will be jointly responsible for selling the issue. The members of the syndicate are sometimes known as the **underwriters** of the issue.

The syndicate will agree on a price for the bond issue and will attempt to sell all the bonds to its clients. The price of the bond is fixed at this point and will not change until the syndicate has sold all its bonds. If events occur that make the price unattractive to the clients of the investment bankers, it is likely that the syndicate will not sell the entire issue. In some cases, the syndicate will agree to sell the issue on what is known as a **best efforts basis**. If the syndicate cannot sell all the securities, it simply returns the securities to the company, which means that the company will not be able to raise the amount of money it had hoped to raise. For financially strong companies, however, the syndicate guarantees to sell the entire issue, thereby accepting the risk that it will not be able to sell all the issue to its clients.

Once all the bonds have been sold to the clients of the syndicate, the bonds are "thrown on the open market." This means that holders of the bonds are free to trade them with any other investors. Prices of the bonds might then fluctuate with changes in economic conditions.

Bond Pricing

The prices of bonds are established in the marketplace through negotiations between buyers and sellers. At the initial issuance of the bonds, the buyers are institutional and individual investors, and the seller is the company issuing the bonds. The buyers calculate the present value of the cash flows they will receive from the bond, then decide how much they are willing to pay for the bond. The process of calculating the present value of the bond involves discounting (at the desired earning rate) the future cash flows (repayment of principal and periodic interest) of the bond. The seller does a similar calculation to decide what it is willing to accept for the bond. The buyer weighs the yield (desired) rate against the rate that could be earned from the next-best alternative investment, and also against the risk involved with the particular bond issue. The higher the risk, the higher the yield rate should be. In other words, if buyers are going to accept a greater risk of default, they want to be compensated for that risk with a greater return. In addition to the calculation of the present value, the buyer has to factor in any special features of the bond such as convertibility into shares or any indexing of the maturity value to a commodity. In the rest of this section, these special features are ignored as we move on to a discussion of bond pricing.

The starting point in determining the value of a bond is calculation of the cash flows that will be received by the buyer (and paid by the seller). To illustrate the calculation of interest payments: Assume a company issues bonds on January 1, 20x1, with a total face value of $100,000 and a bond interest rate of 10%. The company issues 100 bonds, each has a face value of $1,000, and each reaches maturity on December 31, 20x7. The company must make a $100,000 payment to the lenders on December 31, 20x7, and must make an interest payment of $5,000 every six months. The $5,000 amount is calculated as follows:

$$\text{Interest Payment} = \text{Face Value} \times \text{Bond Interest Rate} \times 1/2$$
$$= \$100,000 \times 10\% \times 1/2 = \$5,000$$

There will be a total of 14 interest payments, because there are seven years to maturity and two interest payments per year. The interest payments of a bond are typically structured to come at the end of each six-month period. The stream of interest payments is an annuity in arrears, meaning the payments are made at the end of the period.

To illustrate the pricing of a bond, we will use a very simple example. Suppose the Baum Company Ltd. wishes to issue a $1,000 bond (a single bond will be used to make it simple) with two years to maturity. The bond is to have a bond interest rate of 10% and is to pay interest semi-annually. Suppose that Baum expects the investor to demand a return of 8% compounded semi-annually from an investment in its bonds. What price can Baum expect to get from this offering? The cash flows that Baum will pay must be discounted using the yield rate of 8%. The yield rate is sometimes referred to as the **discount rate** or the **market rate**. Exhibit 10-1 shows the time line and the cash flows that would result from this bond.

Learning Objective

Calculate the issue price of a bond and prepare journal entries for the issuance of the bond and interest payments subsequent to the issuance for bonds issued at par, below par, and above par.

Baum Company Ltd.

Assumptions:

Face value	$1,000
Bond interest rate	10%
Time to maturity	2 years
Yield rate	8%

Calculation:

Number of periods
= Time to maturity × 2
= 2 years × 2 = 4

Yield rate per period
= Yield rate / 2
= 8% / 2 = 4%

Interest payments
= Face amount x bond interest rate × 1/2
= $1,000 × 10% × 1/2 = $50

					$1,000
Cash flows		$50	$50	$50	$50
End of period (semi-annual periods)	0	1	2	3	4

Note that the interest payments (the four payments of $50 each) are an annuity in arrears and that the maturity payment ($1,000) is a lump sum cash flow at the end of the fourth period. There are four periods because interest payments are made at the end of each six-month period. The total net present value of the bond, based on a 4% desired or yield rate, is calculated below. To calculate the net present value, we will use the Time Value of Money tables[1] found in Appendix D at the end of the book.

We need to calculate the present value of each of the future cash flows.

					$1,000
		$50	$50	$50	$50
1		4%			
2			4%		
3				4%	
4					4%

For illustrative purposes we will use Table 2, Present value of $1, found in Appendix D.
($50 × 0.96154) + ($50 × 0.92456) + ($50 × 0.88900) + ($50 × 0.85480) + ($1,000 × 0.85480)

48.08	+	46.23	+	44.45	+	42.74	+	854.80	=	$1,036.30

---

[1] There are four time value of money tables in Appendix D. We will be using Table 2, Present value of $1, and Table 4, Present value of an annuity in arrears. These tables contain pre-calculated factors for given interest rates and time periods. When the factors are multiplied times the cash flow amount, the present value of that cash flow is determined.

The result of this calculation is that Baum should expect buyers to pay up to $1,036.30 for the bond. If buyers pay exactly this amount they will earn an 8% return (compounded semi-annually). If they pay more for the bond they will earn less than 8%, and if they pay less than this amount they will earn more than 8%. Note that, because the payments to be paid by Baum are fixed by the terms of the bonds, the only way buyers of the bonds can change the return is to change the amount they invest initially (i.e., the price they pay). If Baum thinks 8% is too high an interest rate, it should not offer these bonds at the price calculated here. It should offer them at a higher price (which will lower the interest rate). Recognize, however, that buyers may not be willing to buy the bonds at that higher price.

An easier way to arrive at the above amount of $1,036.30 is to treat the interest payments of $50 as an annuity (calculate the present value by using Table 3 from Appendix D, Present value of an annuity in arrears) and add to this calculation the present value of the payment at maturity ($1,000). The calculation would be as follows:

$50 × 3.62990 (present value for 4 periods at 4%) + ($1,000 × 0.85480)
$181.50 + $854.80 = $1,036.30

This is the method we will use for subsequent calculations of the present value of a bond issue. These calculations can also be made using a financial calculator that has present value and future value functions.

How does a different desired or yield rate affect the value of the bond? Suppose that, instead of 8%, buyers demand a 12% return from this type of investment. The only thing that would change in the calculation would be the factors that enter the present value calculation. The computation would then be:

Present value of the Baum Company Ltd. bond at 12%:
PV of bond = PV of interest payments + PV of maturity payment
= PV of the annuity of $50 for 4 periods at 6% (Table 4) + PV of the $1,000 for 4 periods at 6% (Table 2)
= ($50 x 3.46511) + ($1,000 × 0.79209)
= $965.35

Consistent with the preceding explanation, if buyers pay less for the bond (in this case $965.35), they earn a higher return (12%). Baum Company Ltd., in this case, receives a lower initial amount from this borrowing and effectively pays a higher interest rate (12%).

According to the terminology used to describe bond pricing, when the bond is issued (or sells) at a price higher than its face value (i.e., greater than $1,000), it is issued (sells) at a **premium**. When the bond is issued for less than its face value, it is issued at a **discount**. If it is issued for exactly its face value, it is said to be issued at **par**. You should avoid placing any connotations on the words premium and discount. They do not mean either that buyers paid too much or that they got a good deal. The price they pay, whether it is par, premium, or discount, is the appropriate value for the bond, given the desired or yield rate used.

A question that might be asked is: What rate would have to be used to present value or discount the cash flows in the example for the bonds to be issued at par? The answer is 10%. Whenever the yield rate of a bond is exactly equal to the bond interest rate, the bond will sell at par. Consequently, if the yield rate is higher than the bond interest rate the bond sells at a discount, and when the yield rate is lower than the bond interest rate it sells at a premium. This relationship is represented in the table in Exhibit 10-2, which shows the price of the bond in the example for various combinations of bond interest rates and yield rates.

EXHIBIT 10-2

■ Relationship of Bond Price to Bond Interest and Yield Rates

		Yield Rates			
		6%	8%	10%	12%
Bond Interest Rates	6%	$1,000.00	$963.70	$929.08	$896.05
	8%	$1,037.17	$1,000.00	$964.54	$930.70
	10%	$1,074.34	$1,036.30	$1,000.00	$965.35
	12%	$1,111.51	$1,072.60	$1,035.46	$1,000.00

Note that, in Exhibit 10-2, all the prices on the diagonal, which represent situations in which the bond interest rate equals the yield rate, are at par. Prices below the diagonal represent premium price situations, where the yield rate is below the bond interest rate; the area above the diagonal represents discount prices.

Another question might be: Why would a company agree to issue (sell) a bond at other than its par value? Remember the earlier discussion about the company seeking advice from investment bankers when it is deciding on the terms of a new bond issue? The investment bankers will provide information to the company about how the market is assessing its risk. The company takes this information into consideration, but it also assesses its ability to pay the interest and the length of time over which the company needs the money. The interest rate set for the bond may or may not be close to the market's interest rate demands. The company takes this into consideration when it is trying to determine how much capital it will be able to raise by issuing the bonds. The other aspect of the issue price that must be considered is the time factor. When a company decides to issue bonds as a way of raising capital, it must get financial advice as to what interest rate it can afford and legal advice as to aspects of the indenture agreement. Once all of those decisions are made, the bond certificates have to be printed and prepared for issue. By the time the bonds are actually issued to investors, the market's risk assessment of the company may have changed, which will cause the issue price to change.

Bond Markets

All financial newspapers and many local newspapers provide information about bond prices for interested investors. Bond prices are quoted in the *Financial Post* in a section entitled "Bonds." An excerpt from this section is shown in Exhibit 10-3. You will notice that it lists Canada, Provincial, Corporate, and International bonds. Look for a moment at the Corporate listing. The first column of the listing shows who is

Bonds

Supplied by RBC Dominion Securities Inc./International from Reuters

RBC DS Index	Index level	Total ret	Price ret	MTD tot.ret
Market	322.67	0.23	0.17	-0.39
Short	277.09	0.10	0.05	-0.23
Intermed	326.95	0.25	0.19	-0.43
Long	391.62	0.41	0.35	-0.62
Govts	320.98	0.22	0.17	-0.39
Canadas	313.22	0.21	0.16	-0.38
Provs	341.19	0.25	0.20	-0.42
Munis	117.93	0.22	0.18	-0.32
Corps	341.71	0.23	0.17	-0.36

	Coupon	Mat. date	Bid $	Yld%
Canada	5.000	Dec 01/00	99.60	5.36
Canada	7.500	Mar 01/01	102.70	5.47
Canada	10.500	Mar 01/01	106.67	5.49
Canada	9.750	Jun 01/01	106.47	5.59
Canada	4.500	Jun 01/01	98.40	5.52
Canada	7.000	Sep 01/01	102.42	5.64
Canada	5.250	Dec 01/01	99.45	5.52
Canada	9.750	Dec 01/01	108.12	5.68
Canada	8.500	Apr 01/02	106.41	5.70
Canada	10.000	May 01/02	110.04	5.74
Canada	5.500	Sep 01/02	99.47	5.70
Canada	11.750	Feb 01/03	117.71	5.80
Canada	7.250	Jun 01/03	104.84	5.76
Canada	5.250	Sep 01/03	98.26	5.75
Canada	7.500	Dec 01/03	106.26	5.78
Canada	10.250	Feb 01/04	116.71	5.81
Canada	6.500	Jun 01/04	102.86	5.79
Canada	5.000	Sep 01/04	96.92	5.73
Canada	9.000	Dec 01/04	114.02	5.81
Canada	12.000	Mar 01/05	128.13	5.85
Canada	8.750	Dec 01/05	114.96	5.82
Canada	14.000	Oct 01/06	146.15	5.85
Canada	7.000	Dec 01/06	106.84	5.82
Canada	7.250	Jun 01/07	108.67	5.83
Canada	10.000	Jun 01/08	127.65	5.88
Canada	6.000	Jun 01/08	101.20	5.82
Canada	5.500	Jun 01/09	97.76	5.81
Canada	5.500	Jun 01/10	97.32	5.84
Canada	9.500	Jun 01/10	128.18	5.90
Canada	9.000	Mar 01/11	125.29	5.92
Canada	10.250	Mar 15/14	141.44	5.94
Canada	9.750	Jun 01/21	144.40	6.04
Canada	8.000	Jun 01/23	125.45	5.98
Canada	9.000	Jun 01/25	138.62	6.02
Canada	8.000	Jun 01/27	127.79	5.94
Canada	5.750	Jun 01/29	98.58	5.85
CMHC	5.000	Jun 01/04	96.12	5.97
EDC	5.500	Jun 18/04	98.10	5.97
EDC	5.000	May 04/06	94.37	6.05
EDC	5.000	Feb 09/09	92.41	6.08

Provincial

	Coupon	Mat. date	Bid $	Yld%
Alberta	6.250	Mar 01/01	100.92	5.55
Alberta	6.375	Jun 01/04	101.65	5.96
B C	9.000	Jan 09/02	106.48	5.88
B C	7.750	Jun 16/03	105.71	6.00
B C	5.250	Dec 01/06	94.99	6.13
B C	6.000	Jun 09/08	98.60	6.21
B C	9.500	Jan 09/12	126.81	6.32
B C	8.500	Aug 23/13	119.86	6.33
B C	6.150	Nov 19/27	95.45	6.50
B C	5.700	Jun 18/29	89.60	6.49
B C MF	7.750	Dec 01/05	107.85	6.19
B C MF	5.500	Mar 24/08	95.06	6.26
HydQue	10.875	Jul 25/01	108.67	5.72
HydQue	5.500	May 15/03	98.25	6.05
HydQue	7.000	Jun 01/04	103.60	6.10
HydQue	10.250	Jul 16/12	132.80	6.44
HydQue	9.625	Jul 15/22	135.35	6.60
HydQue	6.000	Aug 15/31	92.00	6.60
Manit	7.875	Apr 07/03	105.91	5.98
Manit	5.750	Jun 02/08	97.17	6.18
Manit	7.750	Dec 22/25	116.67	6.43
NewBr	8.000	Mar 17/03	106.24	5.97
NewBr	5.700	Jun 02/08	96.84	6.18
NewBr	6.000	Dec 27/17	95.87	6.39
Newfld	6.150	Apr 17/28	93.09	6.70
NovaSc	5.250	Jun 02/03	97.33	6.07
NovaSc	6.600	Jun 01/27	99.92	6.61
Ontario	10.875	Jan 10/01	106.33	5.58
Ontario	8.000	Mar 11/03	106.18	5.98
Ontario	7.750	Dec 08/03	106.30	6.01
Ontario	4.875	Jun 02/04	95.38	6.03
Ontario	9.000	Sep 15/04	112.41	6.05
Ontario	8.250	Dec 01/05	110.91	6.09
Ontario	7.500	Jan 19/06	107.21	6.10
Ontario	7.750	Jul 24/06	109.03	6.10
Ontario	6.125	Sep 12/07	99.91	6.14
Ontario	5.700	Dec 01/08	96.84	6.16
Ontario	7.600	Jun 02/27	115.03	6.43
Ontario	6.500	Mar 08/29	100.97	6.43
OntHyd	10.000	Mar 19/01	106.03	5.61
OntHyd	8.625	Feb 06/02	105.88	5.88
OntHyd	9.000	Jun 24/02	107.67	5.89
OntHyd	5.375	Jun 02/03	98.05	5.97
OntHyd	7.750	Nov 03/05	108.24	6.10
OntHyd	5.600	Jun 02/08	96.31	6.16
OntHyd	8.250	Jun 22/26	122.76	6.45
Quebec	10.250	Oct 15/01	108.40	5.79

	Coupon	Mat. date	Bid $	Yld%
Quebec	5.250	Apr 01/02	98.50	5.91
Quebec	7.500	Dec 01/03	105.15	6.07
Quebec	7.750	Mar 30/06	108.10	6.21
Quebec	6.500	Oct 01/07	101.40	6.27
Quebec	11.000	Apr 01/09	133.00	6.32
Quebec	5.500	Jun 01/09	94.20	6.31
Quebec	8.500	Apr 01/26	123.60	6.60
Quebec	6.000	Oct 01/29	92.15	6.60
Saskat	6.125	Oct 10/01	100.67	5.77
Saskat	5.500	Jun 02/08	95.52	6.18
Saskat	8.750	May 30/25	128.65	6.45
Toronto	6.100	Aug 15/07	98.53	6.34
Toronto	6.100	Dec 12/17	100.46	6.06

Corporate

	Coupon	Mat. date	Bid $	Yld%
407ETR	6.050	Jul 27/09	96.73	6.51
407ETR	6.470	Jul 27/29	94.09	6.94
AGT Lt	8.800	Sep 22/25	119.00	7.18
Air Ca	6.750	Feb 02/04	94.50	8.29
AssCap	5.400	Sep 04/01	98.72	6.12
Avco	5.750	Jun 02/03	98.25	6.29
Bell	6.150	Jun 15/09	97.95	6.44
BMO	5.550	Aug 27/02	98.51	6.12
BMO	5.400	Jun 02/03	97.54	6.16
BMO	5.650	Dec 01/03	97.94	6.22
BMO	5.350	Mar 01/04	96.74	6.21
BNS	5.400	Apr 01/03	97.38	6.25
BNS	6.250	Jul 16/07	98.13	6.56
BNS	5.650	Jul 22/08	93.73	6.60
CardTr	5.510	Jun 21/03	97.58	6.25
Cdn Oc	6.300	Jun 02/08	91.73	7.62
Cdn Pa	5.850	Mar 30/09	94.60	6.63
Clearn	0.000	May 15/08	60.50	12.30
CnCrTr	5.625	Mar 24/05	96.52	6.39
Coke	5.650	Mar 17/04	97.14	6.40
Crestar	6.450	Oct 01/07	93.50	7.55
Domtar	10.000	Apr 15/11	113.68	8.15
Ford C	5.730	Dec 01/03	97.65	6.38
GldCrd	5.894	Jul 15/02	99.47	6.10
GldCrd	6.010	Jul 15/04	99.03	6.25
GrtAA	5.400	Dec 03/02	98.43	5.95
GrtAA	5.950	Dec 03/07	97.11	6.41
GrtAA	6.450	Dec 03/27	94.90	6.86
GrtAA	6.450	Jul 30/29	94.99	6.85
GTC Tr	6.200	Jun 01/07	97.45	6.63
HolRec	6.205	Sep 21/04	99.61	6.30
IBM Ca	5.810	Aug 07/03	98.50	6.25
IntrAm	5.625	Jun 29/09	96.15	6.16
IPL	8.200	Feb 15/24	114.88	6.93
LdnIns	9.375	Jan 08/02	106.71	6.13
Legacy	5.930	Nov 15/02	97.32	6.90
Loblaw	6.650	Nov 08/27	95.71	7.00
MilitA	5.750	Jun 30/19	95.11	6.18
Morgua	6.600	Oct 09/07	93.47	7.71
MstrCr	5.760	Aug 21/02	99.01	6.14
MstrCr	5.700	Nov 21/03	97.92	6.28
MstrCr	6.150	Dec 21/04	99.21	6.33
NavCda	7.560	Mar 01/27	109.57	6.79
Oxford	6.860	Jul 21/04	95.19	8.09
Renais	6.850	Feb 06/07	98.94	7.04
Rogers	10.500	Jun 01/06	113.50	7.85
Rogers	8.750	Jul 15/07	100.63	8.63
RoyBnk	5.400	Sep 03/02	98.10	6.12
RoyBnk	5.400	Apr 07/03	97.64	6.16
RoyBnk	6.750	Jun 04/07	101.91	6.43
SaskWP	6.600	Jul 18/07	91.84	8.03
TD Bnk	5.600	Sep 05/01	99.25	6.02
Trizec	7.950	Jun 01/07	98.43	8.23
Trlium	5.690	Apr 22/03	98.18	6.27
UniGas	8.650	Nov 10/25	120.05	6.97
Weston	7.450	Feb 09/04	104.35	6.29
Wstcoa	6.750	Dec 15/27	97.04	6.99
YrkRec	5.670	Apr 21/02	98.91	6.14

International

	Coupon	Mat. date	Bid $	Yld%
Australia	12.00	15 Ap 00	112.81	5.48
Australia	9.00	15 Au 03	113.07	5.91
Australia	7.50	15 Au 08	108.53	6.33
Britain	7.00	07 De 00	101.48	6.23
Britain	6.75	07 De 03	102.01	6.28
Britain	5.75	13 Oc 08	100.44	5.69
France	3.00	12 Jy 00	98.60	3.83
France	3.50	12 Jy 03	95.09	4.67
France	4.00	25 Oc 08	89.96	5.32
Germany	3.50	16 Jn 00	99.26	3.90
Germany	4.13	15 Jy 03	97.94	4.60
Germany	4.50	04 Jy 08	94.85	5.18
Italy	3.00	01 Jy 01	96.86	4.29
Italy	4.00	15 Jy 03	96.66	4.85
Italy	4.25	01 My 08	91.35	5.45
Japan	6.30	20 Se 00	111.88	0.21
Japan	4.60	22 Se 03	118.34	0.76
Japan	1.70	22 Se 08	100.83	1.61
U.S.	5.63	30 Se 00	99.91	5.68
U.S.	6.00	15 Au 03	100.72	5.83
U.S.	6.63	15 My 07	102.84	6.15
U.S.	6.00	15 My 08	100.50	5.93
U.S.	6.63	15 Fe 27	102.77	6.41
U.S.	6.13	15 No 27	96.70	6.38
U.S.	6.13	15 Au 28	100.50	6.09

issuing each bond. An abbreviation of the company name is given, followed by a set of numbers, a date, and then numbers again in the next two columns. These columns identify the bond interest rate of the issue, the maturity date, and then, in the final two columns, the current selling price and the yield rate at that selling price. For instance, locate the line "RoyBnk 5.400 Sep 03/02 98.10 6.12." This is a bond from the Royal Bank that carries a 5.40% interest rate and that matures on September 3, 2002. Prices in the market are quoted as a percentage of the face value. The bond is currently selling at 98.10, which means that investors are paying $981.00 for a $1,000 bond. In other words, the bond is selling at a discount. When investors buy this bond at a discount they will earn a return of 6.12%. The yield is higher than the actual interest on the bond because the bond sold for less than the face or principal value. This higher yield is likely demanded by investors because they can invest their money elsewhere at the same risk and earn a slightly higher return.

Bond Accounting

The accounting for bonds will be illustrated using the simple examples developed earlier for a bond issued at par, at a discount, and at a premium. For each of the bonds, the entries made at issuance, to recognize the interest accrual and payments, and to record the final payment of the face amount at maturity will be illustrated.

Bonds Issued at Par

Consider the issuance of the Baum Company Ltd. bond (see data in Exhibit 10-1) when bond interest rates were 10%. To record the bond issued at par, you must record the cash proceeds in the cash account and the present value of the bond in the liability account. When bonds are issued at par they are said to be issued at 100. Because the cash proceeds equal the present value at issuance, the following entry is made (any commissions paid to the underwriters are ignored to keep the entries simple):

BAUM COMPANY LTD. BOND ISSUED AT PAR—ISSUANCE ENTRY		
A-Cash	1,000	
L-Bond Payable		1,000

No interest is recognized on the date of issuance, because interest accrues as time passes. The recognition of interest requires two entries. The first is to accrue the interest expense for the period and the amount payable to the bondholders. The second is to record the cash payment made. The recognition of expense should be based on a time value of money computation using the yield rate (10% for the Baum Company Ltd. bond sold at par) and the carrying value of the bond ($1,000 when sold at par). The amount payable to the bondholders is dictated by the bond interest rate. The following calculations and entries would be made at the end of the first interest payment period (six months):

BAUM COMPANY LTD. BOND ISSUED AT PAR—INTEREST ENTRIES
(at the end of first interest period)

SE-Interest Expense[a]	50	
L-Interest Payable[b]		50
L-Interest Payable	50	
A-Cash		50

[a]Interest expense = Carrying Value × Yield Rate × Time
= $1,000 × 10% × 6/12 = $50
[b]Interest payable = Face Amount × Bond Interest Rate × Time
= $1,000 × 10% × 6/12 = $50

The calculation of the interest expense (the interest incurred during the period) and the interest payable (the cash amount owed based on the bond contract) results in the same figure for a bond sold at par. This is not the case for bonds issued at a premium or at a discount.

The calculation of the interest payable amount will be the same in all four interest periods over the life of the bond. The calculation of interest expense in each period will depend on the carrying value of the bond at the beginning of each period. The carrying value will equal the face value of the bond less the discount or the face value of the bond plus the premium. The carrying value (book value) at the end of each period can be calculated using the following formula:

Carrying Value (ending) = Carrying Value (beginning) + Interest Expense − Interest Payments

In the first period:

Carrying value (ending) = $1,000 + 50 − 50 = $1,000

Because the expense and the cash payment are the same in every period, a bond sold at par will have a carrying value of $1,000 at the end of every period. The entries for interest recognition, therefore, would be exactly the same at the end of each of the four interest periods.

At the end of the fourth period, the company will make the final payment of the face value. The entry will be:

BAUM COMPANY LTD. BOND ISSUED AT PAR—MATURITY PAYMENT ENTRY
(at maturity date)

L-Bond Payable	1,000	
A-Cash		1,000

The carrying value of the bond over time is shown graphically in Exhibit 10-4. Note that the carrying value of the bond remains constant over the four six-month periods. The balance in the liability account at the end of the four interest periods is $1,000. This is the balance prior to the maturity payment and, therefore, should be exactly $1,000.

EXHIBIT 10-4

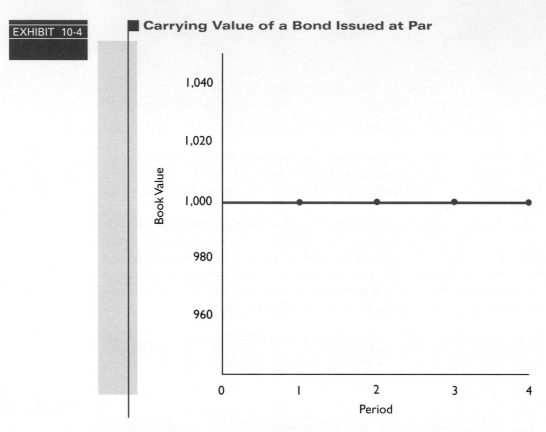

■ **Carrying Value of a Bond Issued at Par**

Sometimes the change in the value of a bond over its life is also summarized in what is known as an amortization table. Exhibit 10-5 shows a typical amortization table for the bond issued at par.

EXHIBIT 10-5

■ **Amortization Table—Bond Issued at Par**

Period	Beginning Carrying Value	Interest	Payment	Ending Carrying Value
1	$1,000.00	$50.00	$50.00	$1,000.00
2	$1,000.00	$50.00	$50.00	$1,000.00
3	$1,000.00	$50.00	$50.00	$1,000.00
4	$1,000.00	$50.00	$1,050.00	$0.00

Bonds Issued at a Discount

Now, assume that investors demanded a 12% return for the bond issued by Baum. As calculated earlier in the chapter, the bond would be issued at a price of $965.35 under these conditions. Another way of expressing the issue price would be to say that the bond sold at 96.535. The following entry would then be made by Baum Company Ltd. at issuance:

BAUM COMPANY LTD. BOND ISSUED AT A DISCOUNT—ISSUANCE ENTRY		
A-Cash	965.35	
XL-Discount on Bond Payable	34.65	
L-Bond Payable		1,000

In this case, the present value of the liability is $965.35, and this is the amount that should be recorded on the books of Baum. This amount could be credited directly to the bond payable account. However, in Canada we normally credit the bond payable account with the face value of the bond and then reduce the amount by creating a contra liability account called *discount on bond payable*. The contra account (note that the XL notation in the journal entry represents a contra liability account) is most commonly reported directly with the bond payable account. The net of these two amounts is the present value—that is, $1,000 − $34.65 = $965.35. Note that this presentation allows for both the disclosure of the face amount of the bonds and the net present value at the date of issuance. Over the life of the bond, we will gradually reduce the discount on the bond payable account such that at maturity the discount will be zero.

The interest entries for the bond issued at a discount are shown in the box below. Notice that the interest expense is now different from the amount payable. The reason for this is that the yield rate and the carrying value are now different from the bond interest rate and the face amount. The difference between the interest expense and the interest payable is credited to the discount account, thus decreasing the balance in the account. This is known as the **amortization of the discount**. This method of calculating interest expense is known as the **effective interest method**. The yield rate times the carrying value of the debt determines the interest expense for the period.

BAUM COMPANY LTD. BOND ISSUED AT A DISCOUNT—INTEREST ENTRIES		
(at the end of first interest period)		
SE-Interest Expense[a]	57.92	
XL-Discount on Bond Payable		7.92
L-Interest Payable[b]		50.00
L-Interest Payable	50.00	
A-Cash		50.00

[a]Interest expense = Carrying Value × Yield Rate × Time
                = $965.35 × 12% × 6/12 = $57.92

[b]Interest payable = Face Amount × Bond Interest Rate × Time
                = $1,000 × 10% × 6/12 = $50

Because the discount is being amortized each period, the net carrying value changes from period to period. The amortization of the discount can be calculated in a straight-line fashion—that is, the same amount is paid each period—as long as the effect on the financial statements is not materially different from the effect of applying the effective interest method, which is illustrated in this section. The carrying value at the end of the period would be calculated as before:

Carrying Value (ending) = Carrying Value (beginning) + Interest Expense − Payments

In the first period:

Carrying Value (ending) = $965.35 + 57.92 − 50.00 = $973.27

Notice that the carrying value has increased a little by the end of the first period. This new carrying value balance is used to calculate the interest expense in the second period. Therefore, the interest expense will increase slightly each period to reflect the increase in the carrying value. The ending carrying value could also be calculated by subtracting the balance in the discount account from the face amount in the bond payable account. The discount account will have a balance of $26.73 ($34.65 − $7.92) at the end of the first period. The face amount minus this discount will give the carrying value of $973.27, the same amount as calculated in the preceding equation.

Exhibit 10-6 shows graphically how the carrying value of the bond changes over time. Notice that because this bond is issued at a discount, the beginning carrying value is below $1,000. As time passes, the discount is amortized (decreases) and the carrying value increases, reaching $1,000 by the maturity date, when the final payment of $1,000 is made.

EXHIBIT 10-6

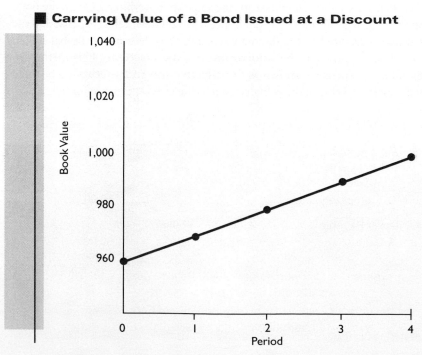

Carrying Value of a Bond Issued at a Discount

At the maturity date, the final maturity payment is made with the same entry made in the par case, because the final carrying value is the same ($1,000). Recognize that what is happening is that the payments made at the interest dates are not sufficient to pay for the interest that has accrued during the period. The excess of the interest expense over the payment decreases the discount, creating the rising carrying value shown in the graph. Exhibit 10-7 shows the amortization table for the bond issued at a discount.

■ **Amortization Table—Bond Issued at a Discount**

Period	Beginning Carrying Value	Interest	Payment	Ending Carrying Value	Beginning Discount
1	$965.35	$57.92	$50.00	$973.27	($34.65)
2	$973.27	$58.40	$50.00	$981.67	($26.73)
3	$981.67	$58.90	$50.00	$990.57	($18.33)
4	$990.57	$59.43	$1,050.00	$0.00	($9.43)

AN INTERNATIONAL PERSPECTIVE

Reports from Other Countries

In Canada and the United States, the amortization of the discount on a bond is calculated using effective interest methods as described earlier. In some countries (Australia and Denmark, for example), the discount is typically amortized in a straight-line fashion, in much the way straight-line amortization is used for a capital asset. Straight-line amortization of the discount (and premium) is acceptable in Canada and the United States as long as the results are not materially different from the results of using the effective interest method.

In some countries, the amount of the discount is written off in the year of the issuance rather than being amortized to income over the life of the bond.

Bonds Issued at a Premium

If the interest rate demanded by investors is 8%, then the Baum Company Ltd. bond would be issued at a premium. The issue price in this scenario was calculated earlier in the chapter as $1,036.30. Another way of expressing the issue price would be to say that the bond sold at 103.63. The following entry would be made at issuance by Baum Company Ltd.:

BAUM COMPANY LTD. BOND ISSUED AT A PREMIUM—ISSUANCE ENTRY		
A-Cash	1,036.30	
L-Premium on Bond Payable		36.30
L-Bond Payable		1,000.00

As in the case of the bond issued at a discount, the $1,000 face value is credited to the bond payable account. The excess of the proceeds over the face amount is credited to an account called *premium on bond payable*. This account is a liability account, but it is also known as an **adjunct account**. The balance in this account is reported directly with the bond liability account; that is, the accounts are linked together. Adjunct accounts are used when they contain balances that *add* to a related account in the way that contra accounts subtract from related accounts. The sum of the two accounts creates a liability that is measured at its net present value.

The interest entries for the bond issued at a premium would be:

BAUM COMPANY LTD. BOND ISSUED AT A PREMIUM—INTEREST ENTRIES		
(at the end of first interest period)		
SE-Interest Expense[a]	41.45	
L-Premium on Bond Payable	8.55	
L-Interest Payable[b]		50.00
L-Interest Payable	50.00	
A-Cash		50.00

[a]Interest expense = Carrying Value × Yield Rate × Time
= $1,036.30 × 8% × 6/12 = $41.45
[b]Interest payable = Face Amount × Bond Interest Rate × Time
= $1,000 × 10% × 6/12 = $50

The premium on the bond payable is amortized in much the way the discount is amortized. As the premium is amortized, the premium account is reduced; consequently, the carrying value of the bond is reduced from period to period. The cash payments made each period are more than enough to pay for the interest expense. The excess of the payments over the expense (i.e., the **amortization of the premium**) reduces the carrying value of the debt. The carrying value at the end of the period would be calculated as before:

Carrying Value (ending) = Carrying Value (beginning) + Interest Expense − Payments

In the first period:

Carrying Value (ending) = $1,036.30 + 41.45 − 50.00 = $1,027.75

Exhibit 10-8 shows graphically how the carrying value of the liability changes over time. Notice that, because this bond is issued at a premium, the beginning carrying value is above $1,000. As time passes, the premium is amortized (decreases), and the carrying value decreases, eventually, by the maturity date, reaching $1,000.

At the maturity date, the final payment is made using the same entry as that used in the par case in that the final carrying value is the same ($1,000). Exhibit 10-9 shows the amortization table for the bond issued at a premium.

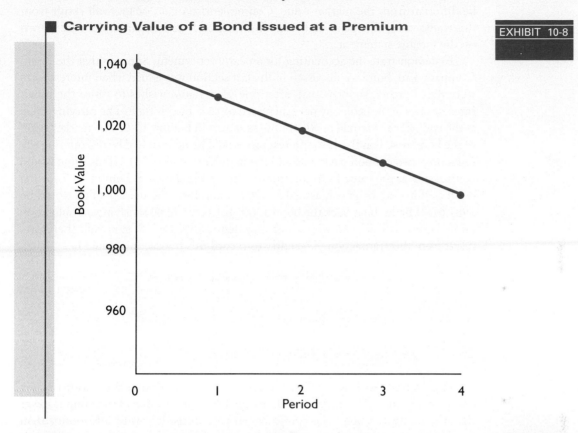

■ **Carrying Value of a Bond Issued at a Premium**

EXHIBIT 10-8

■ **Amortization Table—Bond Issued at a Premium**

EXHIBIT 10-9

Period	Beginning Carrying Value	Interest	Payment	Ending Carrying Value	Beginning Premium
1	$1,036.30	$41.45	$50.00	$1,027.75	$36.30
2	$1,027.75	$41.11	$50.00	$1,018.86	$27.75
3	$1,018.86	$40.75	$50.00	$1,009.62	$18.86
4	$1,009.62	$40.38	$1,050.00	$0.00	$9.62

Early Retirement of Debt

Although a company does not have to pay off its debts until the maturity date, there are times when it makes sense for it to pay the debt earlier than that. Such a transaction is known as **early retirement of debt** or **early extinguishment of debt**. Bonds can be retired by buying the bonds in the bond market or by **calling the bonds**. The bonds may have a call feature that allows the company to buy them back from the investors at a predetermined price. If the intention is to buy them in the bond market, it should be remembered that the interest rates in the economy will likely have changed between the issuance date and the date at which the company wants to buy back the debt. Because the interest rate used to account for the bond is fixed at the issuance date, it is likely that the carrying value of the bond will be different from the market value. Consequently, a gain or loss will result from this transaction. The gains and losses from the early retirement of debt are shown on the income statement.

To demonstrate the accounting for an early retirement: Suppose that the Baum Company Ltd. bond we discussed in the last section was issued when interest rates were 8%. Further, suppose that, after one year, Baum wishes to retire the bond. Interest rates in the economy have increased to 12% by this time. The carrying value at the end of Year 1 would be $1,018.86, as shown in Exhibit 10-9. The market value of the bond based on the 12% interest rate would be determined by discounting the remaining two coupon payments and the maturity value at 12%. This value would be the same as the value from the amortization table shown in Exhibit 10-7 for the bond as if it were originally issued at 12%. Therefore, the market value would be $981.67. If Baum buys back the bond at this price, it will be satisfying an obligation on its books at $1,018.86 with a cash payment of $981.67. A gain will, therefore, result from this transaction. The entry to record this transaction would be:

EARLY RETIREMENT ENTRY		
L-Bond Payable	1,000.00	
L-Premium on Bond Payable	18.86	
A-Cash		981.67
SE-Gain on Early Retirement of Bond		37.19

The example with Baum Company Ltd. illustrates one of the reasons why a company may decide to retire its debt early: The market value of the bond is lower than the maturity value. The company can pay off its debt with less money than would be required at maturity. The downside of this is that if the company needs to raise more capital through the use of debt, it probably will have to pay a higher rate of interest.

LEASING

Learning Objective

4

Discuss the advantages and disadvantages of leasing.

When a company needs to use an asset, such as a piece of machinery, it can obtain the use of the asset in two ways. One is to purchase the asset outright. A second is to enter into a **lease agreement** whereby another company (the **lessor**) buys the asset and the company (the **lessee**) makes periodic payments to the lessor in exchange for the use of the asset over the length of the lease agreement (**lease term**).

There are benefits and costs to both alternatives. One benefit of ownership of the asset is that the company can amortize the asset for tax purposes and, in some cases, obtain an investment tax credit for the purchase. Investment tax credits are incentives provided by Revenue Canada to encourage investment in certain types of assets. These credits usually take the form of a direct reduction in the company's tax bill based on a fixed percentage of the asset's acquisition cost.

Profit from appreciation in the value of the asset is another benefit of ownership. Loss from the amortization of the asset, which could be dramatic if the asset becomes technologically obsolete or loses its market popularity, is the downside. If the company has to borrow to buy the asset, the company's debt/equity and interest coverage ratios will change, which could affect its future borrowing capabilities (these ratios are discussed later in this chapter as well as in Chapter 12). This also ties up capital that might be used for other projects.

To the lessee, the benefits of leasing are several. The lessee does not have to put up its own capital to buy the asset. It also does not have to borrow to buy the asset, which means that its debt/equity and interest coverage ratios will not be affected. If the company is in a tax situation in which little taxable income is generated, the tax advantages of amortizing the asset or claiming an investment tax credit would be of limited value to the lessee. If the lessor can take advantage of the capital cost allowance deduction, the lease payments that the lessee makes will be reduced as a result of the decrease in the lessor's costs. Because the lessee does not own the asset, the risk of loss from obsolescence falls on the lessor. Another advantage, along these same lines, is that the lessee may not want to use the asset for its full useful life. If the company wants to use the asset for only a short time, there is significant risk associated with the resale value if the company decides to buy the asset rather than to lease it.

Lessee Accounting

The accounting issues for a lessee can be illustrated using two extreme situations. At one extreme, suppose that the lease contract is signed for a relatively short period of time—say, two years—whereas the useful life of the asset leased is eight years. In this case, it is clear that the lessee is not buying the asset, but is renting it for only a short period of time. The lease contract may be viewed as a mutually unexecuted contract, and the cash payments required by the lease are recorded by the lessee as rent expense and an outflow of cash. This type of lease is known as an **operating lease**.

Suppose, at the other extreme, that the lease contract was signed for the entire useful life of the asset and that the title to the asset passes to the lessee at the end of the lease term (not an uncommon event). In this case, the substance of the transaction is that the lessee has bought an asset and has agreed to pay for it in instalments. There is essentially no difference between this arrangement and one in which the lessee borrows the money and buys the asset for cash. The lender, in this case, is the lessor. It seems appropriate for the lessee to account for this as a borrowing and as a purchase of an asset. The asset is therefore recorded at its cost (in this case, the present value of the lease payments), and is amortized over time. The asset account name often includes the lease aspect (i.e., Equipment under capital leases). The obligation to the lessor is recorded as a liability, and interest expense is recognized over time. This type of lease is known as a **capital lease**.

Although the appropriate accounting procedures for these extreme situations seem fairly clear, the question arises: What does the company do when the lease is somewhere in between these extremes? Suppose, for example, that the lease term is for 70% of the useful life of the asset and the company has an option to buy the asset at the end of the lease term. Should this qualify as a capital lease? In terms of

Learning Objective
5

Distinguish between an operating lease and a capital lease and prepare journal entries for a lessee under both conditions

the financial statement effects, a company would generally prefer to treat the lease as an operating lease. This would keep the lease obligation off the books, and there would be no effect on the debt/equity and interest coverage ratios. To address this issue, criteria have been developed to distinguish capital leases from operating leases. From the lessee's point of view, the lease qualifies as a capital lease if one of the following criteria is met:[2]

CAPITAL LEASE CRITERIA

1. The title to the asset passes to the lessee at the end of the lease term.
2. The lease term is equal to or greater than 75% of the useful life of the asset.
3. The present value of the minimum lease payments is greater than 90% of the fair value of the leased asset.

If the transaction does not meet any of the three criteria, the lease is an operating lease.

Criterion 1 indicates that the company will own the asset by the end of the lease term and, hence, is buying an asset. Many leases provide an option for the lessee to buy the asset at the end of the lease term. If the price to buy the asset is considered a bargain (i.e., it is likely that the company will exercise its option and buy the asset), then Criterion 1 would be met. Criterion 2 means that the company will have use of the asset during most of its useful life, even though it may not retain title to it at the end of the lease term. Criterion 3 means that if the price the lessee pays to lease the asset is close to the price it would pay to buy the asset, it should account for the transaction as a purchase.

The following simple situation will serve to illustrate the differences in accounting under a capital lease and an operating lease: Suppose that an asset is leased for five years and requires quarterly lease payments of $2,000, payable in advance. The title does not pass at the end of the lease term, and there is no purchase option. The interest rate that is appropriate for this lease is 12%.

If the lease qualifies as an operating lease, the only entry to be made would be the entry to record the payments as rent expense each quarter, as follows.

OPERATING LEASE ENTRY

SE-Rent expense (Lease expense)	2,000	
A-Cash		2,000

If the lease qualifies as a capital lease, the transaction must be recorded as the purchase of an asset and a related obligation. Both the asset and the obligation would be recorded at the present value of the lease payments. This transaction is structured as an annuity in advance (the first payment is made immediately and then there are 19 more payments). Because there are quarterly payments and the lease term is five years, there would be a total of 20 payments. The interest rate per period for use in discounting would be 3% (the quarterly rate based on the 12% annual rate). Based on Table 4 from Appendix D for the present value of an annuity, the following would be the computation of the present value:

---

[2] *CICA Handbook*, Section 3065.06.

PV of lease payments = First payment + PV of 19 payments at 3%
= $2,000 + ($2,000 × 14.32380)
= $2,000 + $28,647.60
= $30,647.60

The entry to record the purchase of the asset and the related obligation at the time of contract signing would be:

CAPITAL LEASE ENTRY
(at date of signing)

A-Asset under capital lease	30,647.60	
L-Obligation under capital lease		30,647.60

The lease obligation would result in a recognition of interest expense similar to that generated by a bond. In the first quarter, two things happen. The first is that a payment is made at the beginning of the quarter (the first payment). This entire payment reduces the principal of the obligation because no time has passed and no interest has accrued. The principal at the beginning of the quarter is, therefore, $28,647.60 ($30,647.60 − $2,000). The second is that interest is calculated on this principal in the amount of $859.43 ($28,647.60 × 12% × 3/12). The entries to record these transactions in the first quarter are:

CAPITAL LEASE PAYMENT ENTRY
(on the first day of each quarter)

L-Obligation under capital lease	2,000	
A-Cash		2,000

CAPITAL LEASE EXPENSE ENTRY
(on the last day of the quarter)

SE-Interest expense	859.43	
L-Obligation under capital lease		859.43

An amortization table of the lease obligation, similar to those constructed earlier for bonds, could be prepared. By the end of the lease term, the lease obligation would be zero. Note that, in the case of a lease, the interest is added directly to the lease obligation account, and the cash payments directly reduce the balance.

In addition, subsequent to acquisition, the asset would be amortized over its useful life (in this case, the lease term, since the title does not pass at the end of the lease term). Assuming the company uses straight-line amortization, the amortization for the first quarter would be $1,532.38 ($30,647.60/20 quarters). Note that the residual value is zero in this calculation because the lessee does not retain title to the asset at the end of the lease term. The entry to record amortization would be:

CAPITAL LEASE EXPENSE ENTRY	
(on the last day of the quarter)	
SE-Amortization expense	1,532.38
XA-Accumulated amortization	1,532.38
(on leased assets)	

These transactions have certain effects on the financial statements. If the asset qualifies as a capital lease, the assets and liabilities of the company would be higher by $30,647.60 than they would be under an operating lease. On the income statement, the company would report both amortization expense and interest expense with the capital lease, whereas with the operating lease, the company would report only rent expense. In the first quarter, the amortization plus interest would be $2,391.81 ($1,532.38 + $859.43). The expense under the operating lease would be $2,000. Therefore, in the first quarter, the capital lease reports higher expenses (they would be even higher if the company used an accelerated method of amortization). The total expenses reported over the life of the lease would be the same, however, regardless of which method is used to record the transaction. With the operating lease, the total expenses would be $40,000: $2,000 × 20 payments. The total capital lease expenses would also be $40,000: $30,647.60 in amortization and $9,352.40 in interest (total payments minus principal = $40,000 − $30,647.60). The difference, then, is in the pattern of expense recognition over the life of the lease, with operating leases showing a level amount of expense but capital leases showing larger expenses in the early years (when amortization and interest are high) and smaller expenses in later years. Exhibit 10-10 graphs the pattern of expense recognition over the life of the lease, treating the lease as an operating lease versus a capital lease.

EXHIBIT 10-10

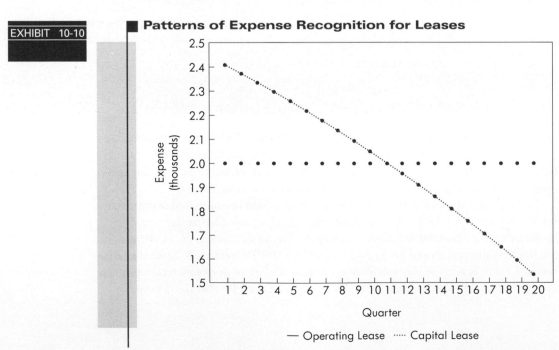

■ Patterns of Expense Recognition for Leases

Because, in Canada, no asset or liability is recorded under operating leases, companies that have significant operating leases have to disclose their commitments to pay for these leases. Companies are required to disclose the future lease payments to be made in total and for each of the next five years. Capital leases require similar disclosure. The obligations associated with leases would typically be shown in a note that relates either to long-term debt or to commitments or contingencies. In the financial statements for CHC Helicopter Corporation, these disclosures can be found in Note 18 (Exhibit 10-11). Assets under capital leases are sometimes also segregated in the plant, property, and equipment section of the balance sheet.

EXHIBIT 10-11

Notes to the Consolidated Financial Statements

April 30, 1998 and 1997 *(Tabular amounts in thousands, except per share amounts)*

---

18. Commitments

The Company has commitments with respect to operating leases. As at April 30, 1998 the minimum lease payments required under such leases were $48,893,000 payable as follows:

1999	$ 6,797,000
2000	5,708,000
2001	4,680,000
2002	4,413,000
2003	3,574,000
and thereafter	23,721,000

AN INTERNATIONAL PERSPECTIVE

Reports from Other Countries

A significant number of countries (such as France, Italy, and Japan) do not require the capitalization of leased assets. In other countries, the capitalization of capital assets is required or is the predominant practice (United States, United Kingdom, and Canada).

Lessor Accounting

Lessor accounting is designed to be a mirror image of the accounting by the lessee. If the lessee qualifies for capital lease treatment, the lessor should be viewed as having provided an asset to the lessee (the lessor will replace the capital asset with a receivable asset). If the lessee must treat the lease as an operating lease, the lessor should retain the asset on its books as the owner and record lease revenue from the lease payments. In both of these situations, the lessor does not have a long-term liability (the subject of this chapter) on its books. Your intermediate financial accounting courses will discuss lease accounting in more detail.

PENSIONS

Pensions are agreements between employers and employees that provide employees with specified benefits (income) upon retirement. To the extent that the company is obligated to make payments under these agreements, some recognition should be given of the cost of these benefits in the years when the company receives the benefits from the work of its employees. Because the payments to retired employees are made many years in the future, pensions represent an estimated future obligation. Two kinds of pension plan are commonly used by employers: **defined contribution plans** and **defined benefit plans**.

Defined Contribution Plans

Learning Objective

Explain the distinguishing features of a defined contribution pension plan and a defined benefit plan.

In a **defined contribution plan**, the employer agrees to make a set (defined) contribution to a retirement fund for the employee. The amount is usually set as a percentage of the employee's salary. Employees sometimes make their own contributions to the same fund to add to the amounts invested. The benefits to the employee at retirement depend on how well the investments in the retirement fund perform. The employer satisfies its obligation to the employee upon payment into the fund. The fund is usually managed by a trustee, and the assets are legally separated from the assets of the company, which means they are not reported with the other assets on the balance sheet of the company.

The accounting for defined contribution funds is relatively straightforward. The company accrues the amount of its obligation to the pension fund, and then records a payment. Because the liability is settled, no other recognition is necessary in the financial statements. The entry to recognize pension expense and the related payment is:

SE-Pension expense	XXX	
L-Pension obligation		XXX
L-Pension obligation	XXX	
A-Cash		XXX

Companies generally make cash payments that coincide with the accruals, because they cannot deduct the cost for tax purposes if no cash payment is made. Therefore, no net obligation usually remains with a defined contribution plan.

Defined Benefit Plans

In a **defined benefit plan**, the employee is guaranteed a certain amount of money during each year of retirement. The formula used to calculate the amount to be paid usually takes into consideration the length of time the employee has worked for the company as well as the highest salary (or an average of the highest salaries) that the employee earned while working for the company. For example, a plan might guarantee that the employee will receive 2% of the average of the highest three years of salaries multiplied by the number of years the employee works for the company. If the employee worked for the company for 30 years and had an average salary of $40,000 for the highest three years, the pension benefit would be $24,000 per year [($40,000 × 2%) × 30 years].

Each year that employees provide a service to the company, they earn pension benefits obliging the company to make cash payments at some point in the future. In estimating the cost of the obligation today (the present value of the liability), several projections must be made. These include: the length of time the employee will work for the company, the age at which the employee will retire, the employee's average salary at retirement, the number of years the employee will live after retiring, and whether the employee will work for the company until retirement. All these factors will affect the amount and timing of the cash flows. In addition, the company must choose an appropriate rate of interest at which to calculate the net present value.

A given employee may leave the company at some point prior to retirement. If the pension benefits belong to employees only so long as they remain in the employ of the company, there may be no obligation on the part of the company to pay out pension benefits. In most plans, however, there is a provision for **vesting** the benefits. Benefits that are vested belong to employees, regardless of whether they leave the company. In addition, while one employee may leave, many others will stay. Thus, even without vesting, it is likely that some fraction of the employees will continue to work for the company until retirement. The total obligation of the pension plan may, therefore, have to be estimated based on the characteristics of the average employee rather than on particular employees.

Calculating the present value of the future pension obligation generally requires the services of an **actuary**. The actuary is trained in the use of statistical procedures to make the types of estimates required for the pension calculation.

The accounting entries for defined benefit pension plans are essentially the same as the preceding entry for defined contribution plans. The company must make an accrual of the expense and the related obligation to provide pension benefits. The amounts are much more difficult to estimate in the case of defined benefit plans, but the concept is the same as that for defined contribution plans. The entry made to recognize the pension expense is called the **accrual entry**. Setting aside cash to pay for these future benefits requires a cash entry. This is sometimes called the **funding entry**. Many employee pension plan agreements have clauses that require the company to fund the pension obligation. Because of the uncertainties associated with the amounts of the liabilities, some companies have been somewhat reluctant to fully fund their pension obligations. There is no requirement that the amount expensed be the same as the amount funded. Therefore, a net pension obligation may result if more is expensed than funded, or a net pension asset may exist if funding is larger than the amount expensed. The actual calculation of the pension expense incorporates many factors and is beyond the scope of this book. To keep the problem simple, we will provide you with information about the pension expense.

Pension funds are described as **overfunded** if the assets in the fund exceed the present value of future pension obligations. In **underfunded** pension plans, the present value of future obligations exceeds fund assets. Pension plans in which the assets actually equal the present value of the future obligations are called **fully funded** plans. The pension fund itself is usually handled by a trustee, and contributions to the fund cannot be returned to the employer except under extraordinary circumstances. To provide sufficient funds to pay benefits, the trustee invests the assets contributed to the fund. Benefits are then paid out of these fund assets.

accounting in the news

AN OVERFUNDED PENSION PLAN

Making decisions about pension funds can be difficult, but some tasks are less onerous than others. Recently, the province of Nova Scotia realized its pension fund for government employees was overfunded—that is, the fund had more money in assets than it needed to pay out to retired employees. Pension funds are not allowed to build up large surpluses. According to provincial figures, the fund had about eight percent more than it required.

The solution: Pay out some of the surplus to government employees and put an equal amount back into government coffers. The government decided to give employees a total of $28 million. Each employee would receive six percent of their gross salary: A person who earned $30,000 would receive $1,800. Hence, a pension cheque before retirement!

Source: "Employees get windfall on pensions," by Brian Flinn, *Halifax Daily News*, March 21, 1998, p. 9.

Annual Statement Disclosures

In Canada, for a defined contribution plan, contribution amounts for the period are disclosed. For a defined benefit plan, the required disclosure is the present value of the future obligations of the company plus the value of the pension fund assets. In light of the fact that the dollar values of future obligations and fund assets are usually substantial, this appears to be barely adequate. Some companies comply strictly with this required disclosure, but others offer additional information about their plans. BCE Inc., for example, provides extensive disclosure about its plan (a defined benefit plan) and the components of its pension expense (see Exhibit 10-12).

OTHER EMPLOYMENT BENEFITS

Employers sometimes offer other types of benefits in addition to pensions. Health care and life insurance are two of the most commonly offered types of additional employee benefits. The obligation to provide these benefits has, for the most part, been ignored in the financial statements of companies in Canada. The benefits have been recorded on a pay-as-you-go basis; that is, the costs are expensed as the cash is paid out to the insurance companies that cover the costs of the benefits. To date, corporate exposure in Canada has been limited because of publicly funded health care. This may not be true in the future.

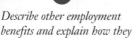

Learning Objective

7

Describe other employment benefits and explain how they are treated in Canada.

Employers also sometimes offer extended health-care benefits to retired employees. In the past, most employers also recorded these on a pay-as-you-go basis. Several years ago in the United States, companies were required to accrue the obligation for future benefits from these post-retirement benefits in much the same way they accrued regular future pension benefits. As a result, several companies reported losses in the first year the accrual was made. As of January 1, 2000, Canada also requires that these benefits be accrued. As the year 2000 annual reports are produced, you should be able to see examples of this accrual of benefits. If companies in Canada follow the same pattern as those in the United States, you will be reading reports of losses in the financial press.

For the many companies that have made no liability provision for these benefits, this new standard could have a significant effect on their financial statements. The standard could cause liabilities to increase and shareholders' equity to decrease. Some of the effects may be deferred and amortized to income over future periods, similar to how other components of the pension expense are amortized.

EXHIBIT 10-12

18. PENSIONS

The Corporation and most of its significant subsidiary companies maintain non-contributory defined benefit plans that provide for pensions for substantially all their employees based on length of service and rate of pay. BCE's funding policy is to make contributions to its pension funds based on various actuarial cost methods as permitted by pension regulatory bodies. The companies are responsible to adequately fund the plans. Contributions reflect actuarial assumptions concerning future investment returns, salary projections and future service benefits. Plan assets are represented primarily by Canadian and foreign equities, government and corporate bonds, debentures, secured mortgages and real estate.

The pension credit and the projected plan benefits are based on management's best estimates including long-term rate of return on the pension asset portfolio and long-term salary escalation rates. Variances between such estimates and actual experience, which may be material, are amortized over the average remaining service lives of the employees. From 1994 to 1997, adjustments to accrued benefits arising from workforce reduction programs were deferred and amortized over five years in conformity with a CRTC ruling. As a result of the discontinued application of regulatory accounting provisions, the unamortized balance of these pension credits was written-off in 1997 and included in the extraordinary item (see Note 2). In addition, included in the restructuring charges (see Note 5) are pension credits associated with employee severance.

The following table sets forth the consolidated financial position of the pension plans and BCE's net pension asset:

At December 31	1998	1997
Plan assets at market value	**10,824**	17,244
Actuarially projected plan benefits		
Accumulated plan benefits	**6,622**	12,299
Effect of salary projections	**721**	1,597
Projected plan benefits	**7,343**	13,896
Plan assets in excess of projected plan benefits	**3,481**	3,348
Unrecognized net experience gains (i)	**(2,282)**	(2,495)
Unrecognized net assets existing at January 1, 1987 (i)	**(42)**	(56)
Unrecognized prior period costs (i)	**108**	141
Net pension asset reflected on the consolidated balance sheet	**1,265**	938
Deferred pension asset, included in deferred charges (see Note 9)	**1,364**	1,363
Deferred pension obligation, included in other long-term liabilities	**(99)**	(425)
Net pension asset	**1,265**	938

(i) Amortized over the employees' expected average remaining service lives (15 years at December 31, 1998).

The components of BCE's pension credit follow:

	1998	1997
Service cost – benefits earned	**288**	343
Interest cost on projected plan benefits	**939**	1,084
Expected return on plan assets	**(1,217)**	(1,307)
Net amortization and other	**(82)**	(167)
Pension credit	**(72)**	(47)

An International Perspective

Reports from Other Countries

While a significant number of countries require accrual of pension cost, many other countries require only that the costs of pension plans be recognized as benefits are paid—the pay-as-you-go method. Countries with this type of accounting include Belgium, India, Norway, and Spain.

NAFTA Facts

The accounting for pension benefits in the United States and Mexico is essentially the same as it is in Canada. However, both Canada and the United States have additional requirements with respect to accrual of post-employment benefits.

FINANCIAL STATEMENT ANALYSIS CONSIDERATIONS

Two ratios that are commonly used to evaluate a company's ability to repay its obligations are the debt/equity ratio and the times interest earned ratio. Using the balance sheet and income statement (Exhibit 10-13) of Métro-Richelieu Inc., a Montreal-based company that is a leader in the food distribution industry in Quebec, we will demonstrate how these two ratios can provide insights into the riskiness of a company.

The formula for the debt/equity ratio is:

$$\frac{\text{Total liabilities}}{\text{Total liabilities} + \text{Shareholders' equity}}$$

Learning Objective

Calculate the debt/equity rates and the times interest earned ratio and write a statement describing the financial health of a company using the information from these ratios.

The 1998 and 1997 debt/equity ratios of Métro-Richelieu Inc. are:

1998	1997
$444.9	$429.3
$444.9 + $342.6	$429.3 + $296.2
56.5%	59.2%

These calculations demonstrate that in 1997 almost 60% of Métro-Richelieu's assets were financed through debt. The ratio dropped a little in 1998, to about 56.5%. From the balance sheet we can see that Métro-Richelieu Inc. increased its short-term liabilities by approximately $43 million, increased its total liabilities by approximately $14 million, and increased its shareholders' equity by approximately

Consolidated statement of earnings

MétroRichelieu

Year ended September 26, 1998 (Millions, except for earnings per share)	1998	1997	1996
Sales	$ 3,653.0	$ 3,432.3	$ 3,266.0
Cost of goods sold and operating expenses	3,483.1	3,277.7	3,124.0
Depreciation and amortization (note 2)	39.7	39.2	37.0
	3,522.8	3,316.9	3,161.0
Operating income	130.2	115.4	105.0
Financing costs			
Short-term	1.1	1.2	1.2
Long-term	3.8	4.1	1.8
	4.9	5.3	3.0
Earnings before income taxes and the following items	125.3	110.1	102.0
Labour relations settlement	24.1	—	—
Gain on disposal of investment	(6.1)	—	—
Earnings before income taxes	107.3	110.1	102.0
Income taxes (note 3)	41.9	43.9	41.0
Net earnings	$ 65.4	$ 66.2	$ 61.0
Earnings per share			
Basic	$ 1.28	$ 1.29	$ 1.00
Fully diluted	$ 1.25	$ 1.26	$ 0.96
Weighted average number of shares outstanding	50.9	51.2	61.1

See accompanying notes

Additional information excluding labour relations settlement and gain on disposal of investment			
Net earnings	$ 75.9	$ 66.2	$ 61.0
Earnings per share			
Basic	$ 1.49	$ 1.29	$ 1.00
Fully diluted	$ 1.45	$ 1.26	$ 0.96

EXHIBIT 10-13
PART A

Consolidated balance sheet

MétroRichelieu

EXHIBIT 10-13
PART B

As at September 26, 1998
(Millions of dollars)

	1998	1997	1996
Assets			
Current			
Cash	$ —	$ —	$ 3.1
Accounts receivable	160.9	147.1	144.2
Income taxes	10.7	3.5	—
Inventories	166.9	164.8	145.0
Prepaid expenses	11.3	10.3	10.0
Current portion of investments *(note 4)*	0.7	2.4	2.5
	350.5	328.1	304.8
Investments *(note 4)*	17.0	18.2	17.4
Capital assets *(note 5)*	420.0	379.2	340.9
	$ 787.5	$ 725.5	$ 663.1
Liabilities and shareholders' equity			
Current			
Bank loans	$ 0.5	$ 7.5	$ —
Outstanding cheques	33.1	11.6	5.9
Accounts payable	329.3	301.7	285.4
Income taxes	—	—	6.0
Current portion of long-term debt *(note 6)*	3.5	2.7	6.5
	366.4	323.5	303.8
Long-term debt *(note 6)*	48.6	94.6	106.2
Deferred income taxes	29.9	11.2	12.6
	444.9	429.3	422.6
Shareholders' equity			
Capital stock *(note 7)*	159.0	157.7	155.3
Retained earnings	183.6	138.5	85.2
	342.6	296.2	240.5
	$ 787.5	$ 725.5	$ 663.1

See accompanying notes

On behalf of the Board:

Jean-Pierre Boyer
Director

Gilles Lamoureux
Director

$46 million, practically all of which came from earnings. The increase in the short-term liabilities in 1998 puts increased demands on the company's cash flows in the short run. It would be important to follow this ratio for more than two years before drawing too many conclusions about any major shifts in financing strategy by the company.

The times interest earned ratio provides a measure of the company's ability to make interest payments out of earnings. It is calculated by the following formula:

$$\frac{\text{Income before interest and taxes}}{\text{Interest}} = \frac{\text{Net income} + \text{Taxes} + \text{Interest}}{\text{Interest}}$$

The calculation of the times interest earned ratio for Métro-Richelieu Inc. for 1998 and 1997 would be:

$$1998 \quad \frac{\$65.4 + \$41.9 + \$4.9}{\$4.9} = 22.9 \text{ times}$$

and

$$1997 \quad \frac{\$66.2 + \$43.9 + \$5.3}{\$5.3} = 21.7 \text{ times}$$

In 1997, Métro-Richelieu Inc. could pay its interest obligation almost 22 times out of earnings. This is a very comfortable position. The risk of nonpayment of interest is very low. By the end of 1998, interest costs had declined such that Métro-Richelieu could now pay its interest obligations 23 times out of earnings. Any creditor would likely be very confident about lending funds to Métro-Richelieu Inc. The increase in the times interest earned ratio, coupled with the small decrease in the debt/equity ratio, demonstrates to creditors that the risk of nonpayment of interest or principal of the debt has declined in the two years.

The biggest concern for analysts regarding liabilities is the possibility of unrecorded liabilities. As seen in the last chapter, commitments and contingent liabilities can have a significant effect on the health of a company. In this chapter, obligations of the company for operating leases and other post-retirement health-care benefits are examples of liabilities not reported on the financial statements. Unrecorded liabilities will cause the debt/equity ratio to be understated and the times interest earned ratio to be overstated. Certain disclosures give the analyst some help in understanding the effects of these unrecorded liabilities. For example, the disclosure of the next five years of lease payments for operating leases allows an analyst to approximate the present value of these lease payments for inclusion in ratio analysis. The effects of commitments and other off-balance-sheet liabilities such as health care are difficult to estimate, but the analyst should have a good understanding of the company and the type of contracts it enters into with suppliers, customers, and employees, so that these liabilities do not come as a surprise.

Another concern is whether the book values of liabilities reflect their current market values. Because liabilities are recorded at the interest rates that were in effect when the debt was issued, changes in market rates can cause changes in the value of these liabilities that are not reflected on the company's books. This does not mean that the company will be paying more or less interest as a result of the market changes, but it does mean that the company may be paying more or less than it would if it had taken out new debt today. Knowledge of this change in interest rate is particularly important when one company is trying to buy another. Book value can be adjusted either by looking at the market value of the debt (for publicly traded debt) or by recalculating the present value of the debt based on current market interest rates. This, of course, requires some detailed information about the terms of the outstanding debt.

Another risk that the analyst should consider is that posed by debt that is denominated in a foreign currency. As you can imagine, if the company is required to repay a debt in a foreign currency, fluctuations in the exchange rate for that currency will cause increases or decreases in the liability as expressed in Canadian dollars. Another risk is that the company may enter into debt agreements in which the interest rate is not fixed but floats with interest rates in the economy (sometimes called variable-rate debt). If interest rates go up, the company can find itself paying significantly higher interest payments. Both of these risks can be managed through the use of sophisticated hedging techniques involving financial instruments such as interest rate and foreign currency options and swaps. To help readers of financial statements understand these complex transactions and the risks posed to the company, companies in Canada are required to disclose these types of transactions and to provide some details concerning the risks the company faces because of them. Many of these risks are associated with amounts that are off-balance-sheet. As an example, consider the disclosure made by Meridian Technologies Inc. in its 1997 annual report (Exhibit 10-14).

■ MERIDIAN TECHNOLOGIES INC. 1997

Excerpt from the Notes to the Statements

7. Financial Instruments

With the exception of the items noted below, the estimated fair values of all financial instruments at December 31, 1997 approximate the carrying values.

At December 31, 1997, the Company had cross-country swaps converting Canadian $42,000,000 of floating rate debt to US $30,205,000 fixed rate debt at an average rate of 7.3% maturing as to one-third in each of 1998, 1999 and 2000. Including the financing spread, this has the effect of fixing the rate at 8.7%. These swaps have a fair value payable of $2,072,000.

At December 31, 1997, the Company also had two forward exchange contracts converting US into Canadian dollars. One converts a total of US $4,500,000 for settlement between January and March 1998, with a fair value payable of $75,000. The other contract converts a total of US $30,900,000 for settlement of certain specified amounts between January 1998 and December 2000. This contract has a fair value payable of $1,690,000.

The fair values of the swaps and forward contracts reflect the estimated amount that the Company would receive/pay to terminate the contracts at December 31, 1997, calculated as the difference between the present value of estimated future receipts and future payments under the terms of each instrument.

SUMMARY

This chapter completes the discussion of liabilities. The risks associated with long-term liabilities are more extensive than those associated with the short-term liabilities discussed in the previous chapter, because of the longer time frame, the larger amounts being borrowed, and the uncertainty of the future. Large companies use bonds as a way of raising additional funds for financing growth in the company. The issuance of bonds is a complex procedure involving the use of financial experts and investment bankers. Depending on the market's perception of the riskiness of the company, the bonds will be issued at par, above par, or below par. This chapter described the accounting for the bonds once they are issued.

The other two items described in this chapter are leases and pensions. Leasing is used extensively across Canada. When a company needs to buy or replace a capital asset, it will determine whether it is more advantageous to buy the asset or to lease it. The details of the leasing contract will determine whether the company must account for the lease as an operating lease or as a capital lease. Many large companies have pension plans for their employees. The two basic types of plan are defined contribution plans and defined benefit plans. We did not go into great detail about the accounting for either leases or pensions, but rather tried to give you a basic understanding of what these items are and how they are reported on the financial statements. Because these two items can have a significant effect on the financial statements, knowledge of them is essential to any evaluation of the future profitability of an organization.

The two ratios that are important in this chapter are the debt/equity ratio and the times interest earned ratio.

The discussion of balance sheet accounts concludes in the next chapter with a discussion of shareholders' equity. Following that chapter, you will find a complete review of the ratio analysis used in this book.

SUMMARY PROBLEMS

1. The Higgins Company Ltd. issued $100,000 face-value bonds with a bond interest rate of 8% on January 1, 20x1. The bonds mature on December 31, 20x10 (i.e., there are 10 years to maturity), and pay interest semi-annually, on June 30 and December 31. The issue price set for these bonds reflected an assumption that investors would need a 10% return (yield rate) in order to be convinced to buy the bonds.

   a. What issue price was set for these bonds under the assumptions set forth above? (In your answer, ignore commissions to the underwriters.)

   b. If the bonds were issued at the price calculated in part (a), what entries would the Higgins Company make during 20x1 to account for these bonds?

   c. If, prior to the issuance of the bonds, interest rates increase in the economy such that investors demand a 12% return from investments such as Higgins's bonds, what price would they be willing to pay on January 1, 20x1, for these bonds?

2. The Acme Company Ltd. enters into a lease for the use of a computer system. The lessor paid $35,000 for the computer system and will lease the system to Acme for five years. At the end of the lease term, the computer will be returned to the lessor, who estimates that the computer will have a zero residual value. The lease

contract will call for monthly payments of $778.56 to be made at the end of each month. These payments provide the lessor with a 12% return on the contract.

  a. Based on the above facts, how should Acme account for this lease?

  b. Construct the entries that Acme should make during the first two months of the lease, assuming that the lease is signed on January 1, 20x1, and that payments are made on the last day of each month.

  c. Give some reasons why Acme would choose to lease the computer system rather than buy it.

3. Exhibit 10-15 shows the pension footnote for Cominco Ltd. (an integrated natural resource corporation involved in mineral exploration, mining, smelting, and refining).

  a. What kind of pension plan does Cominco Ltd. have?

  b. How is Cominco accounting for its post-employment benefits?

  c. On its income statement, Cominco does not disclose the total pension expense for 1998. On its balance sheet, it has a deferred liability for the accrued pension obligation of $23 million. This is down from the 1997 balance of $31 million. By listing this as a deferred liability, what information is Cominco giving users about its pension plan?

■ Cominco Ltd.

Excerpt from the Notes to the 1998 Statements

1 Significant Accounting Policies

Pensions and post-employment costs

    Pension costs and obligations for the company's defined benefit plans are determined using actuarial estimates. Pension expense includes current service costs and the amortization of past service cost, pension surpluses and deficiencies, experience gains or losses, and the effects of changes in plan assumptions on a straight-line basis over the expected average remaining service lives of the relevant employee group. The cumulative difference between amounts expensed or credited to income and the funding contributions is deferred on the balance sheet.

    Pension costs under defined contribution plans are expensed when the contributions are made. The costs of non-pension post-employment benefits are expensed as incurred.

SUGGESTED SOLUTIONS TO SUMMARY PROBLEMS

1. a. Present Value of the Higgins Company Bond at 10%:

> PV of Bond = PV of Interest Payments + PV of Maturity Payment
>   = ($4,000 × 12.46221 (Table 4)) + ($100,000 × 0.37689 (Table 2))
>   = $87,537.84

b.

HIGGINS COMPANY BOND—ISSUANCE ENTRY (at date of issuance)		
A-Cash	87,537.84	
XL-Discount on Bond Payable	12,462.16	
L-Bond Payable		100,000.00

HIGGINS COMPANY BOND—INTEREST ENTRIES (at the end of the first interest period)		
SE-Interest Expense[a]	4,376.89	
XL-Discount on Bond Payable		376.89
L-Interest Payable[b]		4,000.00
L-Interest Payable	4,000.00	
A-Cash		4,000.00

[a]Interest expense = Carrying Value $\times$ Yield Rate $\times$ Time
= \$87,537.84 $\times$ 10% $\times$ 6/12 = \$4,376.89
[b]Interest payable = Face Amount $\times$ Bond Interest Rate $\times$ Time
= \$100,000 $\times$ 8% $\times$ 6/12 = \$4,000.00

HIGGINS COMPANY BOND—INTEREST ENTRIES (at the end of the second interest period)		
SE-Interest Expense[a]	4,395.74	
XL-Discount on Bond Payable		395.74
L-Interest Payable[b]		4,000.00
L-Interest Payable	4,000.00	
A-Cash		4,000.00

[a]Interest expense = Carrying Value $\times$ Yield Rate $\times$ Time
= \$87,914.73 $\times$ 10% $\times$ 6/12 = \$4,395.74
Ending Carrying Value = Beginning Carrying Value + Interest − Payment
= \$87,537.84 + 4,376.89 − 4,000 = \$87,914.73
[b]Interest payable = Face Amount $\times$ Bond Interest Rate $\times$ Time
= \$100,000 $\times$ 8% $\times$ 6/12 = \$4,000.00

c. Present Value of the Higgins Company Bond at 12%:

PV of Bond = PV of Interest Payments + PV of Maturity Payment
= (\$4,000 $\times$ 11.46992 (Table 4)) + (\$100,000 $\times$ 0.31180 (Table 2))
= \$77,059.68

2. a. Because the lease covers more than 75% of the useful life of the asset, Acme should account for it as a capital asset. You can assume that the useful life of the computer system is the full years, because the residual value at the end of that time is zero.

  b. The following entries should be made in the first two months:

  The present value of the lease payments at 12% per year over 60 months is equal to 778.56×44.95504 (Table 4 (60 periods at 1%)) = $35,000

CAPITAL LEASE ENTRY (at January 1, 20x1)		
A-Asset under Lease	35,000	
L-Lease Obligation		35,000

The amortization of the obligation and the first payment must be recorded in the first month. Because this is an annuity in arrears, the first payment reduces the principal of the obligation at the end of the month. The following entries would be made:

CAPITAL LEASE EXPENSE ENTRY (on January 31, 20x1)		
L-Lease Obligation	778.56	
A-Cash		778.56
SE-Interest Expense[a]	350.00	
L-Lease Obligation		350.000

[a]Interest expense = Carrying Value $\times$ Interest Rate $\times$ Time
= $35,000 \times 12\% \times 1/12$
= $350.00

Assuming that the corporation amortizes its leased assets straight-line over the lease term, the following entry would be made at the end of the first month:

CAPITAL LEASE EXPENSE ENTRY (on January 31, 20x1)		
SE-Amortization expense[a]	583.33	
XA-Accumulated amortization (on leased assets)		583.33

[a]Straight-line amortization = $35,000/60 months = $583.33 per month

In the second month, similar entries would be made, as follows:

CAPITAL LEASE EXPENSE ENTRY		
(on February 28, 20x1)		
L-Lease Obligation	778.56	
A-Cash		778.56
SE-Interest Expense[a]	345.71	
L-Lease Obligation		345.71

[a]Interest expense = Carrying Value × Interest Rate × Time

$$= (\$35,000 - \$778.56 + \$350.00) \times 12\% \times 1/12$$

$$= \$34,571.44 \times 12\% \times 1/12$$

$$= \$345.71$$

CAPITAL LEASE EXPENSE ENTRY		
(on February 28, 20x1)		
SE-Amortization expense[a]	583.33	
XA-Accumulated amortization		583.33
(on leased assets)		

[a]Straight-line amortization = $35,000/60 months = $583.33 per month

c. There are several reasons why Acme would choose to lease the computer system:

1. Acme may not have $35,000 available to buy the system. Rather than borrow the $35,000 from the bank, it may choose to lease the asset and make monthly payments. The interest rate charged on the lease may be less than what the bank would charge.

2. Because Acme does not own the computer system, if something goes wrong with the system the lessor is responsible for fixing it. It is likely that the lease agreement contains clauses outlining the types of problems that the lessor agrees to fix and the types of problems that are Acme's responsibility.

3. At the end of the five years Acme is required to return the system to the lessor. This means that it will have to replace it. The end of the lease term forces Acme to stay technologically current (if you assume that five years is not too long to keep a computer system without replacing it). There may be clauses in the lease agreement concerning annual upgrades to the system and specifying who is responsible for these upgrades. If the lessor is responsible, it is to Acme's advantage to lease the system.

3. a. Cominco Ltd. has both defined benefit and defined contribution pension plans.

   b. Cominco Ltd. is accounting for its post-employment benefits by paying for them as they are incurred. This means they are using pay-as-you-go.

   c. Cominco Ltd. is telling users that its pension plan is not fully funded. The amount Cominco has expensed for pension funds is greater than the amount it has deposited in a pension fund to pay for those future benefits. During 1998 the unfunded portion decreased, which means that during 1998 the amount put into the pension fund to cover future benefits exceeded the amount expensed as pension expense.

SYNONYMS

Bond interest rate/coupon rate/stated rate

Early retirement of debt/early extinguishment of debt

Market rate of interest/yield rate/effective rate/discount rate

GLOSSARY

Accrual entry   In the context of pension accounting, this is the entry to accrue pension cost and create the pension obligation.

Actuary   A professional trained in statistical methods who can make reasonable estimates of pension costs.

Adjunct account   An account that adds to a related account; thus, it has the same type of balance as the related account. In this chapter, an example of this type of account is the premium on bond payable account.

Amortization of the discount   The systematic reduction of the discount account balance over the life of a bond. The reduction of the discount account each period adds to the interest expense recorded during the period.

Amortization of the premium   The systematic reduction of the premium account balance over the life of a bond. The reduction of the premium account each period reduces the interest expense recorded during this period.

Best efforts basis   The basis on which underwriters sometimes sell bonds for companies. The underwriters make their "best effort" to sell the bonds, but if they cannot sell them the bonds are returned to the company.

Bond   A long-term borrowing of a company that is evidenced by a bond certificate. The borrowing is characterized by a face value, interest rate, and maturity date.

Bond covenants   Restrictions placed on a company when it issues bonds. The restrictions usually either apply to the company's ability to pay dividends or require that the company maintain certain minimum ratios.

Bond interest rate   An interest rate specified in a bond used to determine the interest payments to be made on the bond.

Bond market   A market in which bonds of companies are actively traded.

Capital lease   A lease that the lessee must record as an asset and a related borrowing, as if the transaction represented the purchase of the asset.

Collateral trust bond   A bond that provides marketable securities as collateral in the event of default by the company.

Commercial paper   A short-term borrowing in which the lender is another company rather than a financial institution.

Convertible bond   A bond that is convertible, under certain conditions, into common shares.

Debenture   A bond that is issued with no specific collateral.

Defined benefit plan   A pension plan that specifies the benefits that employees will receive upon retirement. The benefits are usually determined based on the number of years of service and the highest salary earned by the employee.

Defined contribution plan   A pension plan that specifies how much the company will contribute to the pension fund of its employees. No guarantee is made concerning the amount that will be available upon retirement.

Discount   A term used to indicate that a bond is sold or issued at a value below its face value.

Early extinguishment of debt   Synonym for early retirement of debt.

Early retirement of debt   The settlement of debt (by paying the obligation) prior to its scheduled maturity date.

Effective interest method   A method of calculating interest expense in which the interest is determined by multiplying the carrying value of the debt times the yield rate.

Face value   A value specified in a bond that determines the cash payment that will be made at the maturity date of the bond. The face value is also used to determine the periodic interest payments made on the bond.

Foreign-denominated debt   A borrowing of a company that must be repaid in a foreign currency.

Fully funded   Refers to a pension plan in which the pension plan assets equal the projected benefit obligation.

Funding entry   In the context of pensions, this is the entry made to show the cash payment made to the pension plan to fund the obligation.

Indenture agreement   An agreement that accompanies the issuance of a bond specifying all the terms and restrictions of the borrowing.

Interest payment   The periodic interest payments made on a bond. The payments typically are made semiannually. The amount is calculated by multiplying the face value of the bond by the bond interest rate.

Investment banker   The intermediary who arranges the issuance of a bond in the public debt market on behalf of a company. The investment banker sells the bonds to its clients before the bond is traded in the open market.

Lease agreement   An agreement between a lessee and a lessor for the rental or purchase of an asset, or both.

Lease term   The period or term over which a lessee makes payments to a lessor, as specified in the lease.

Lessee   The party or entity that is renting or purchasing the asset in a lease.

Lessor   The party or entity that is selling or lending the asset in a lease.

Maturity date   A date specified in a bond as the final payment date of the bond.

Mortgage bond   A bond that provides some type of real asset as collateral in the event of a default by the company.

Note   A long-term or short-term borrowing.

Operating lease   A lease in which the lessee does not record an asset and related obligation but treats the lease as a mutually unexecuted contract. Lease expense is then recognized as payments are made per the lease contract.

Other post-employment benefits   Benefits provided to retirees other than pensions. These benefits typically are health-care or life-insurance benefits.

Overfunded   Refers to a pension plan in which the plan assets exceed the projected benefit obligation.

Par   A term used to indicate that a bond is sold or issued at its face value.

Pension   A plan that provides benefits to employees upon retirement.

Premium   A term used to indicate that a bond is sold or issued at a value above its face value.

Private placement   A borrowing arranged privately between two companies or entities.

Public bond market   A market in which bonds are publicly traded.

Senior debenture   A general borrowing of the company that has priority over other types of long-term borrowings in the event of bankruptcy.

Subordinated debenture   A general borrowing of the company that has a lower priority than senior debenture bonds in the event of bankruptcy.

Syndicate   A group of underwriters that collectively helps a company sell its bonds.

Underfunded   Refers to a pension plan in which the plan assets are less than the projected benefit obligation.

Underwriter   An investment bank or group of investment banks that are responsible for selling the original issuance of a company's bonds.

Vesting   A process by which employees are granted pension benefits even if they leave the employ of the company.

ASSIGNMENT MATERIAL

Assessing Your Recall

10-1 Describe the following terms relating to a bond: indenture agreement, bond covenants, face value, maturity date, bond interest rate, interest payments, and collateral.

10-2 Discuss the role of the investment banker in the issuance of bonds by a company.

10-3 Describe what the term "best efforts basis" means in the issuance of bonds and why it is important to a company.

10-4 Discuss how bonds are priced and how the price is affected by changes in market interest rates.

10-5 Describe the following terms as they relate to the issuance and sale of bonds: par, premium, and discount.

10-6 Discuss the meaning of the term "bond discount" and what is meant by the amortization of a bond discount.

10-7 Describe the procedure for the retirement of debt before maturity. Why would a company retire debt early?

10-8 Discuss the benefits of leasing from the point of view of both the lessee and the lessor.

10-9 List and discuss the criteria used to distinguish capital leases from operating leases for lessees.

10-10 Differentiate between defined contribution pension plans and defined benefit plans.

10-11 Define the following terms: overfunded, underfunded, and fully funded.

10-12 What are post-employment benefits? Why are we now required to treat them similarly to pension obligations?

10-13 Explain what the following ratios tell you about a company's financial health: debt/equity ratio and times interest earned ratio.

Applying Your Knowledge

10-14 (Entries for bond transactions)
The Standard Mills Corporation issues 100 bonds, each with a face value of $1,000, that mature in 30 years. The bonds carry a 10% interest rate and are sold to yield 12%. They pay interest semi-annually.

Required:

a. Compute the issuing price of the bonds and show the journal entry to record the issuance of the bonds.

b. Compute interest expense for the first year and show the journal entries to record this expense and the corresponding interest payments.

10-15 (Bond amortization tables)
The Comp Tech Corporation issued 8% bonds with a face value of $200,000, maturing in three years. The bonds pay interest semi-annually.

Required:
Prepare an amortization table for the three years under each of the following conditions:

a. Market yield at issuance is 8%.

b. Market yield at issuance is 10%.

c. Market yield at issuance is 6%.

10-16 (Entries for bond transactions)

Spring Water Company Ltd. needed to raise some additional capital to finance the expansion of its bottled water company. After consulting an investment banker and the VP Finance of the company, it decided to issue bonds. The bonds had a maturity value of $750,000, an annual interest rate of 9%, paid interest semi-annually, on June 30 and December 31, and matured on December 31, 2010. The bonds were issued on January 1, 2001, for $703,267, which represented a yield of 10%.

Required:

a. Show the journal entry to record the issuance of the bonds.

b. Compute the interest expense for the first year and show the journal entries to record the interest expense and the corresponding interest payments.

c. Spring Water Company wanted to raise $750,000 but succeeded in raising only $703,267. Explain why the investors may not have been willing to pay $750,000 for the bonds.

10-17 (Computation of bond issuance amounts)

Fraser Equipment Company Inc. issues 200, $1,000, 10% bonds maturing in eight years. The bonds pay interest semi-annually and are issued to yield 10%.

Required:

a. Compute the issue price of the bonds and give the journal entry to record the issuance.

b. Compute the book value of the bonds five years after issuance—that is, at the beginning of the sixth year.

c. Compute the market value of the bonds five years after issuance, if the market yield has increased to 14%.

d. Compare the book value (calculated in part b.) and the market value (calculated in part c.) at the end of five years. Explain why a difference exists.

10-18 (Issuance of bonds)

The Alphabet Toy Company has plans for a major plant expansion and needs to raise additional capital to pay for the construction. The company is considering issuing six-year, 8% first mortgage bonds with a par value of $500,000. The bonds will pay interest semi-annually.

Required:

a. Compute the amount of cash the company will receive if the bonds are sold at a yield rate of:

   1. 8%

   2. 6%

   3. 10%

b. Prepare the journal entry Alphabet Toy would record at the time of the issuance under each of the three alternative yields.

c. What is a mortgage bond? Explain how the fact that this is a mortgage bond would affect the interest rate dictated by the market (the yield rate).

10-19 (Interest expense)

Pen & Ink Stationery Ltd. sold 10-year, 8% bonds with a $400,000 maturity value on January 1, 2000. Interest is paid semi-annually, on June 30 and December 31.

Required:

a. If the bonds sold at par value, give the journal entries for June 30 and December 31 for 2000 and 2001.

b. If the bonds were sold at 104 for a yield approximating 7.43%, give the journal entries for June 30 and December 31 for 2000 and 2001.

c. If the bonds were sold at 94 for a yield approximating 8.92%, give the journal entries for June 30 and December 31 for 2000 and 2001.

d. Why must amortization of the premium or discount be included in the computation of the annual interest expense?

10-20 (Interest accrual with bond premium)

Crocus Company Ltd. issued 15-year, 12% first mortgage bonds with a par value of $600,000 on January 1, 2001. The bonds pay interest semi-annually and were issued at 134.58 to yield 8%. The company's year end is December 31.

Required:

a. Compute the amount Crocus Company Ltd. received on January 1, 2001, and prepare the journal entry for the bond issuance.

b. What amount of cash does Crocus Company Ltd. pay its bondholders every six months? Prepare the journal entries at June 30, 2001, and December 31, 2001, to record the interest expense and interest payments.

c. How would the journal entries recorded by Crocus Company Ltd. in part b. differ if interest payments were made on July 1, 2001, and January 1, 2002, rather than June 30, 2001, and December 31, 2001?

10-21 (Interest accrual with bond discount)

On January 1, 2001, Rupert Company Ltd. issued $300,000 of 10-year, 8% debentures. The effective yield on the bonds at the time of issue was 12%. Interest is paid semi-annually.

Required:

a. Compute the issue price of the bonds and prepare the journal entry for the issuance.

b. What amount of interest will Rupert pay every six months? Prepare the journal entries for June 30, 2001, and December 31, 2001, to record the accrual of interest expense and the payment of the interest owed.

c. Give the balance sheet presentation of the bond liability at December 31, 2001.

10-22 (Interest computation on a bond)

Birch Company Ltd. issued bonds twice in recent years. The first issue has a $400,000 par value, 10% bond interest rate, and a 10-year maturity; it sold on January 1, 2000, to yield 8%. The second issue has a $200,000 par value, a 6% bond interest rate, and a five-year maturity; it sold on January 1, 2001, to yield 8%. Both issues pay interest on July 1 and January 1.

Required:

a. What amount of interest expense will Birch report for the year 2001?

b. Prepare journal entries to record Birch's interest expense and payments in 2001.

c. Explain why it is reasonable that both bonds sold to yield 8%.

10-23 (Lease)

Boulder Dash Corporation leases automobiles from Speedy Leasing for use by its sales personnel. The leased vehicles are used for two years and then returned to Speedy Leasing. All maintenance and repair is done by Speedy. Boulder Dash makes a deposit of $5,000 at the beginning of the lease on each car and makes monthly payments of $400 per car. The deposit is refunded when the car is returned. Boulder Dash currently has 22 cars under lease from Speedy.

Required:

a. Is the lease an operating lease or a capital lease? Explain.

b. What amount of expense related to the lease will Boulder Dash record for the current year?

c. How should the $5,000 deposit per car be reported by Boulder Dash?

10-24 (Lease)

Transprovincial Buslines Service experienced a major increase in people using the buses in the last three months of 20x0. On January 1, 20x1, Transprovincial entered into an agreement to lease four new buses from NewBus Leasing Ltd. The 10-year lease agreement on each bus requires Transprovincial to pay $1,000 per month at the end of each month starting January 31, 20x1. At the end of the lease term, title to the buses transfers to Transprovincial. The lease is structured with a 10% interest rate. The buses have a useful life of 20 years and are amortized on a straight-line basis with no anticipated residual value.

Required:

a. Is the agreement a capital or an operating lease? Explain.

b. Assuming Transprovincial records the leases on the four buses as capital leases, compute the present value of the lease payments.

c. Present the amounts related to the lease that would appear on the income statements and balance sheets of Transprovincial Buslines at the end of January 20x1 and February 20x1.

10-25 (Capital lease)

On July 1, 20x1, the Turlotec Manufacturing Corporation leased one of its machines costing $800,000 to Start Mechanical Corporation. The 10-year lease was classified as a capital lease for accounting purposes. The lease agreement required equal semi-annual payments of $70,795 payable on December 31 and June 30 each year, and an interest rate of 14%. Both companies close their books annually on December 31.

Required:

Show the necessary journal entries relating to the lease in the books of Start Mechanical Corporation during 20x1. Assume the machine has a useful life of 10 years and zero residual value. Further assume that both companies use straight-line amortization.

10-26 (Operating or capital lease)

The *Provincial Star* newspaper has decided to lease a truck to deliver its newspapers. The company signs an agreement on January 1, 20x1, to lease a truck for $450 per month for the next three years. The title to the truck reverts to the lessor at the end of the lease term. The lease calls for payments on the last day of the month starting on January 31, 20x1. The *Provincial Star* closes its books monthly and believes that 9% is an appropriate yield rate for the lease.

> *Required:*
>
> a. Assuming that the market value of the truck is $20,000 and that the lessor believes its useful life is five years, how should the *Provincial Star* account for this lease?
>
> b. Show the appropriate accounting entries for the first two months of 20x1 for the lease under both the operating lease method and the capital lease method. Assume that the *Provincial Star* amortizes its assets using the straight-line method.

Management Perspective Problems

10-27 (Bond convenants)

As a bond investor, explain the importance of bond convenants in assessing the risk of a particular bond investment.

10-28 (Seniority of bond investments)

In assessing the riskiness of a particular bond, discuss the importance of the seniority of various liabilities of the company and how it affects your assessment.

10-29 (Bond covenants)

Discuss the types of covenants bond investors might like to include in a bond indenture agreement to protect their investment. Explain why these covenants would be effective.

10-30 (Collateral for long-term debt)

As a lender, discuss how much comfort you might get from knowing about the existence of long-term assets, specifically property, plant, and equipment and goodwill, in making a long-term loan to a company.

10-31 (Liabilities not recorded)

In assessing the riskiness of a company, stock analysts are often concerned more with the liabilities that do not appear on the company's financial statements than with those that do appear. Discuss the major types of liabilities that might not appear on the company's financial statements. Describe the information that may be included in the notes to the financial statements concerning these liabilities.

10-32 (Operating leases)

Suppose that you are a stock analyst and you are evaluating a company that has a significant number of operating leases.

> *Required:*
>
> a. Discuss the potential misstatement of the financial statements that may occur because of this treatment. Specifically, address the impact of this type of accounting on the debt/equity ratio and return on assets ratio.
>
> b. Using the disclosures provided in the financial statements, explain how you would adjust the statements to address the issues discussed in part a.

10-33 (Impact of lease treatment on net income)

Suppose that you are a manager whose remuneration is partially tied to meeting a particular net income target for your company. How would the choice of an operating lease over a capital lease affect your ability to meet the target? Given a choice, which accounting treatment would you select? Does your answer depend on whether you are in the early years of the lease versus the later years?

10-34 (Post-employment benefits)

In Canada, accountants are now starting to record the future obligation for post-employment benefits. In the past, the cost of these benefits was recorded as it was incurred (pay-as-you-go). As a manager, explain why you would prefer to continue to use the pay-as-you-go method. What accounting concepts support the change in accounting method from pay-as-you-go to recording of the future obligation before the employees retire?

10-35 (Pension plans)

Describe the two types of pension plans. As a manager, which plan would you recommend to the senior executive of the company? Explain your answer. As an employee, which plan would you prefer? Explain your answer.

10-36 (Lease or buy)

Starburst Brewery Ltd. must replace some of its old equipment with new stainless steel equipment to avoid losing its licence. The controller is unsure as to whether to purchase the equipment with borrowed money or to lease the equipment. If purchased, the equipment will cost $500,000 and have an estimated useful life of 20 years and no residual value. The Sussex Bank is willing to provide the $500,000 to Starburst. The terms of the note are that the 10-year note would carry interest at 12%. Starburst would be required to pay the interest annually at the end of the year. The principal amount would be due at the end of the 10 years. A local rental company is willing to lease the equipment to Starburst for nine years at an interest rate of 12%. At the end of each year, Starburst would be required to pay the leasing company $90,000.

> *Required:*
>
> a. Compute the present value of the future cash flows under both arrangements.
>
> b. State what amounts would appear in Starburst's income statement and balance sheet for the first year under both alternatives.
>
> c. Which of the two financing alternatives would you recommend to the controller? Why? What factors, other than cash payments directly related to financing, might be important to the decision?

Reading and Interpreting Published Financial Statements

10-37 (Long-term notes and debentures)

Notes 7 and 8 to the 1998 financial statements of CHC Helicopter Corp. (Exhibit 10-16) describe the senior subordinated notes and subordinated debentures currently held by the company.

EXHIBIT 10-16

Notes to the Consolidated Financial Statements

April 30, 1998 and 1997 *(Tabular amounts in thousands, except per share amounts)*

7. Senior subordinated notes

The senior subordinated notes bear interest at a fixed rate of $11\frac{1}{2}$% per annum, payable semi-annually on January 15 and July 15. The notes are unsecured, denominated in U.S. dollars, and mature on July 15, 2002 (Note 22(b)).

The outstanding balance at April 30 is as follows:

	1998	1997
Principal amount	$ 121,550	$ 119,000
Repurchased and held by the Company	11,833	11,585
Net amount outstanding U.S.$76,725,000 (1997 - U.S.$76,725,000)	$ 109,717	$ 107,415

8. Subordinated debentures

The subordinated debentures bear interest at 8% per annum, interest only payable semi-annually on April 30 and October 31, and are due August 2007. The debentures are subordinated to all senior indebtedness. The Company may redeem the debentures at a redemption price ranging from 103.6% to 100% of the principal amount of the debentures being redeemed. The trust indenture requires mandatory sinking fund payments of $743,650 on August 31 of each of the next nine years. The Company has pledged its shares of CHC Helicopter Holdings Limited, a wholly-owned subsidiary, as collateral for the debentures.

Required:

a. What are senior subordinated notes and subordinated debentures?

b. The senior subordinated notes pay interest each January 15 and July 15. CHC Helicopter Corp.'s year end is April 30. Assume interest was paid on January 15, 1998, as required. Prepare the journal entry to accrue the interest to April 30, 1998, and then prepare the journal entry on July 15, 1998, to pay the second instalment of interest.

c. Note 8 states that the company "may redeem [buy them back from the investors] the debentures at a redemption price ranging from 103.6% to 100% of the principal amount of the debenture being redeemed." Under what circumstances would the company want to exercise this option?

d. Are the debentures secured or unsecured? Explain.

10-38 (Short- and long-term debt)
On March 29, 1998, Comac Food Group Inc. had 11 outstanding debt instruments (see Exhibit 10-17). The debt instruments are mainly loans and notes payable.

EXHIBIT 10-17

8. LONG TERM DEBT

Long term debt is comprised of the following:

	1998	1997
a) Demand bank loan	$ –	$ 150,000
b) Bank loan	101,000	113,000
c) Demand bank loans	262,000	324,000
d) Term loan	440,000	698,000
e) Loan	20,000	70,000
f) Notes payable	487,000	800,000
g) Note payable	106,000	156,000
h) Note payable	58,000	158,000
i) Note payable	5,000	13,000
j) Due to Manhattan Bagel Company Inc.	284,000	284,000
k) Other	1,000	7,000
	1,764,000	2,773,000
Less current portion	909,000	1,130,000
	$ 855,000	$ 1,643,000

a) The loan is collateralized by a general security agreement and floating charge debenture covering all assets of the Company, bears interest at the bank's prime rate plus 2%. The loan has been repaid in full.

b) The loan was issued under the Small Business Loan program to finance the construction of a corporate store. The loan is collateralized by a chattel mortgage on the store, bears interest at the bank's prime rate plus 3% and has principal repayments of $1,000 per month to August 2006. As the company is in violation of a specific debt covenant, the loan has been classified as current.

c) The loans are collateralized by security agreements covering the assets at specific store locations, bear interest at the bank's prime rate plus 1.5% and have principal repayments of $6,945 per month to June 2000 and $1,200 per month to September 30, 2003.

Providing the Company satisfies the conditions of the loan agreements, the lender has indicated that they do not intend to demand repayment and accordingly the loan is classified as long term.

d) The loan is collateralized by a first floating charge on all Domino's assets except the Domino's Master Franchise Agreement. The loan bears interest at the lender's cost of funds plus 3% and has principal repayments of $21,500 per month to November 1999.

e) The loan is unsecured and bears interest at 9% and is repayable in equal monthly installments of principal and interest of $5,000 to July, 1998.

f) The notes payable are collateralized by a general security agreement covering all the assets of the Company, bear no interest and have monthly principal repayments of $30,000 for the next 11 months, $11,800 for the following 12 months and $4,200 for the next 12 months. The notes are also convertible at the holder's option into Class B common shares of the Company at a rate of $0.70 per share to March 3, 1999 and $1.00 per share to March 3, 2001.

The Company has calculated the debt component as the present value of the required interest and principal repayments discounted at a rate of 6% which approximates the interest rate that would have been applicable to non-convertible debt at the time of its issuance. The difference at acquisition date of $83,000 between the face amount of the loan and the calculated debt component has been presented as contributed surplus.

g) The note payable is collateralized by a general security agreement covering all the assets of the Company, bears no interest and has principal repayments of $58,000 on March 4, 1999 and $58,000 on March 4, 2000. The amount has been discounted to reflect an interest rate of 6% per annum.

h) The note payable is collateralized by a general security agreement covering all the assets of the Company, bears no interest and has a principal repayment of $62,000 on March 4, 1999. The amount has been discounted to reflect an interest rate of 6% per annum.

i) The note payable bears interest of 11% and is repayable in equal monthly installments of principal and interest of $700 to October 1998.

j) A $210,000 (US) loan is payable at the rate of $5,000 (US) for each franchise location sold under the Manhattan Bagel master franchise agreement up to a total of 42 units, with the balance due December 31, 2000. As a result of the closure of the Manhattan Bagel division, the Company terminated the master franchise agreement. Pending final settlement of the loan, it has been classified as long term. The Company disputes any liability to Manhattan Bagel Company Inc. (MBI) with respect to this loan on the basis of default by MBI of its contractual obligations to the Company.

Lenders' prime rates at March 29, 1998 ranged from 5.4% to 6.5% (1997-3.6% to 4.75%).

As at March 29, 1998 principal repayments are as follows.

1999	$ 909,000
2000	460,000
2001	360,000
2002	14,000
2003	14,000
Thereafter	7,000
	$ 1,764,000

Operating Credit Facility

In addition to the long term credit facilities, the Company has a demand operating credit facility of $500,000 which is scheduled to reduce to $350,000 on June 1, 1998 and to $200,000 on September 1, 1998. The line of credit is due on demand and bears interest at the bank's prime rate plus 2%. A general security agreement and floating charge debenture covering all assets of the Company are pledged as collateral. At March 29, 1998, $15,000 (1997 - nil) was drawn on the credit facility.

Required:

a. From the information given, identify which of the debt instruments are short-term and which are long-term.

b. What is collateral? What impact would the type of collateral have on a company's ability to borrow money? Identify the collateral attached to each debt instrument.

c. Some of the debt instruments are identified as bearing "no interest" and yet the company has attached an interest factor to them. Why would an entity lend funds to Comac Food Group and not charge it any interest? Why has Comac assigned an interest factor to these debt instruments?

10-39 (Long-term debt)

In Exhibit 10-18, Note 6 to the 1999 financial statements of Cara Operations Limited describes the long-term debt currently held by the company.

Required:

a. What is the difference between a medium-term note and a mortgage?

b. The average effective rate of interest on the bankers' acceptances rose from 4.2% in 1998 to 5.5% in 1999. Provide some reasons why the interest rate is higher in 1999.

c. Provide some reasons why the interest rate on the capital leases is higher than the interest rate on the medium-term notes and the bankers' acceptances.

d. In Note 6, Cara Operations discloses the principal repayments that will be made in each of the next five years as well as the aggregate amount due after the end of the five years. This is a required disclosure under GAAP. Explain why users need this information.

10-40 (Long-term debt)

Placer Dome Inc. includes information about its long-term debt in Note 6 of its 1998 financial statements. This note is included in Exhibit 10-19. Amounts are stated in millions of U.S. dollars.

Required:

a. Placer Dome Inc. has three bond issues outstanding at the end of 1998. Were these bonds issued at par, below par, or above par? How do you know?

b. Calculate the amount of bond interest that would be paid out by Placer Dome Inc. in 1999 assuming that no new bonds were issued and that none of the bonds were retired early.

c. Although the bonds have maturity dates several years apart, the bond interest being paid on each issue is very similar. Provide some reasons why the interest rates would be similar.

10-41 (Operating and capital leases)

The balance sheet and obligation under capital leases note from the 1999 annual report of Dylex Limited are included in Exhibit 10-20 for this problem.

EXHIBIT 10-18

6. LONG-TERM DEBT

In thousands of dollars		1999		1998
Medium Term Notes (i)	$	149,377	$	—
Bankers' Acceptances (ii)		10,000		81,000
Obligations under Capital Leases (iii)		22,831		27,337
Mortgages		5		111
	$	182,213	$	108,448
Less: Current Portion		4,389		6,322
	$	177,824	$	102,126

(i) Unsecured Medium Term Notes ("Notes") with a face value of $150 million bear interest at 5.95% per annum paid semi-annually in arrears on December 12 and June 12 and unless prepaid fall due in June 2008. The Notes have been issued under a *trust indenture. The Notes are net of a discount on issuance in the amount of $0.6 million.*

(ii) Bankers' Acceptances are unsecured and have been issued under non-revolving arrangements due May 2001. During the year, the average effective rate of interest was 5.5% (1998 – 4.2%). This non-revolving arrangement will be renegotiated and/or repaid as it falls due.

(iii) Obligations under capital leases bear interest at an average rate of 8.1% (1998 – 8.1%) per annum; equipment under capital leases having an aggregate net book value of $22 million (1998 – $29 million) is pledged.

Repayments of principal planned and/or required over the next five years are as follows:

In thousands of dollars

2000	$	4,389
2001		4,125
2002		14,003
2003		4,056
2004		4,159
Thereafter		151,481
	$	182,213

EXHIBIT 10-19

6. Long-term Debt

Consolidated long-term debt comprises the following:

	December 31 1998	1997
Placer Dome Inc.		
Bonds		
May 15, 2003 at 7.125% per annum	$200	$200
June 15, 2007 at 7.125% per annum	100	100
June 15, 2015 at 7.75% per annum	100	100
Medium – term notes (i)	200	200
Placer Pacific bank loans	–	20
	600	620
Current portion	–	(20)
	$600	$600

(i) The interest rates range from 6.1% to 8.0% and the notes mature between 2001 and 2026.

The weighted average interest rate on loans was 7.2% in 1998, 7.2% in 1997 and 7.3% in 1996.

Interest expense and payments on long-term debt included in earnings was $44 million in 1998, $46 million in 1997, and $41 million in 1996. Interest and financing expense excludes capitalized amounts of nil in 1998, $2 million in 1997, and $5 million in 1996.

At December 31, 1998, Placer Dome had unused bank lines of credit of $807 million (including A$5 million and Cdn$25 million). The majority of these facilities are long-term at interest rates determined with reference to LIBOR which at December 31, 1998 was 5.07% (three-month term).

7. Income and Resource Taxes

(a) Details of income and resource tax expense (reduction) related to operations are as follows:

	Years ended December 31 1998	1997	1996
Income taxes			
Current			
Canada	$ 2	$ 6	$ (4)
Foreign	53	11	44
Deferred			
Canada (i)	24	(21)	2
Foreign	5	(3)	–
	84	(7)	42
Mining taxes – Canada			
Current	5	12	1
Deferred	2	(6)	1
	7	6	2
	$91	$ (1)	$44

(i) For 1997, includes a provision of $25 million for taxes payable upon repatriation of funds to Canada.

EXHIBIT 10-20
PART A

Consolidated Statements of Financial Position

Dylex Limited (Incorporated under the laws of Canada)

(thousands of dollars)		January 30 1999		January 31 1998
Current assets				
Cash and short-term investments	$	29,498	$	37,501
Accounts receivable		9,605		8,448
Inventories		166,347		147,971
Prepaid expenses		3,126		4,616
Income taxes recoverable		499		815
Notes and other investments due within one year		411		549
		209,486		199,900
Current liabilities				
Accounts payable		108,062		88,033
Other taxes payable		4,459		4,155
Long-term debt due within one year		116		116
Obligations under capital leases due within one year		803		330
		113,440		92,634
Working capital		96,046		107,266
Other assets				
Notes and other investments		154		1,122
Fixed assets (note 3)		98,366		67,233
Assets under capital leases (note 4)		4,793		1,192
Deferred charges (note 5)		5,463		4,785
		108,776		74,332
Assets employed	$	204,822	$	181,598
Financed by				
Other liabilities				
Long-term debt (note 6)	$	313	$	421
Obligations under capital leases (note 7)		3,888		673
Deferred revenue		15,661		9,454
		19,862		10,548
Shareholders' equity				
Share capital (note 8)		115,730		104,949
Retained earnings		69,230		66,101
		184,960		171,050
Capital employed	$	204,822	$	181,598

Approved on behalf of the Board of Directors

Elliott Wahle
Elliott Wahle
Director

William J. Anderson
William J. Anderson
Director

EXHIBIT 10-20

PART B

7.   Lease Commitments

The future minimum lease payments are as follows:

(thousands of dollars) Fiscal year ending January	Capital leases	Operating leases
2000	$ 1,561	$ 57,147
2001	1,445	51,238
2002	1,067	44,201
2003	547	39,142
2004	717	34,192
Thereafter	–	111,597
Total minimum lease payments	$ 5,337	$337,517
Less amount representing imputed interest at varying rates	646	
Present value of obligations under capital leases	4,691	
Due within one year	803	
Long-term obligations under capital leases	$ 3,888	

Aggregate rentals paid on operating leases for property and equipment for the 52 weeks ended January 30, 1999 amounted to $65,064,000 (for the 52 weeks ended January 31, 1998 – $63,210,000).

Required:

a. Dylex has considerably more operating leases than capital leases. What advantages are there for Dylex in having operating leases rather than capital leases? In your answer, go beyond financial-statement implications.

b. You will notice that the structure of the balance sheet (statement of financial position) is different from the other balance sheets displayed in this book. As a user, do you find Dylex's format more informative or less informative than the other formats? Explain.

c. Calculate the debt/equity ratios for Dylex Limited for 1999 and 1998. Write a short report evaluating your findings. Include comments on the changes in the components of the debt and shareholders' equity.

10-42 (Pension plans)

The note on employee retirement plans from the 1998 financial statements of CCL Industries Inc. is included in Exhibit 10-21.

Required:

a. Describe the pension plan structure of CCL Industries.

b. Is the pension plan overfunded or underfunded? How do you know?

EXHIBIT 10-21

16. EMPLOYEE RETIREMENT PLANS

The Company and its subsidiaries maintain pension plans that include defined benefit and defined contribution segments, which are available to all salaried employees and to hourly employees not covered by union pension plans. Employees hired subsequent to January 1, 1994 enroll in the defined contribution segment.

The defined benefit segment provides a pension based on years of service and earnings. For the defined contribution segment, the Company's contributions are based on a percentage of an employee's earnings with the employee's pension benefits based on these contributions along with investment earnings from those contributions. For the defined contribution segment, the Company's obligations are satisfied upon crediting contributions to the employees' accounts and no further obligation accrues.

Based on the most recent actuarial valuations of these defined benefit plans as of December 31, 1997 there was no unfunded liability for past services. The status of the defined benefit pension plans is as follows as at June 30:

	1998	1997
Pension fund assets	$216.0	$204.2
Present value of accrued pension benefits	$200.1	$197.8

10-43 (Pension plans)

The note on pension costs and obligations from the 1998 financial statements of Bombardier Inc. is included in Exhibit 10-22.

Required:

a. Describe the pension plan structure of Bombardier Inc.

b. Is the pension plan overfunded or underfunded? How do you know?

c. Bombardier goes into considerable detail to describe the underlying assumptions of the pension plan and to discuss the risk associated with the plan. Suggest reasons why all of this detail is included.

EXHIBIT 10-22

Pension costs and obligations

The Corporation maintains pension plans for the benefit of substantially all employees.

The pension obligations of the defined benefit pension plans are valued using an accrued benefit actuarial method and Management's best estimate assumptions. The assets of these pension plans are valued on the basis of market-related values. Current service costs are determined using the projected benefit method pro-rated on services. Adjustments arising from past service benefits and experience gains and losses are amortized on a straight-line basis over the average remaining service lives of the employee groups covered by the plans.

Costs related to post-retirement benefits other than pension costs offered to certain employees are recognized when paid by the Corporation.

10-44 (Debt/equity ratio and times interest earned ratio)
The balance sheet and income statement from the 1998 annual report of Western Star Trucks Holdings Ltd. are included in Exhibit 10-23.

Required:

a. Calculate the debt/equity ratios and the times interest earned ratios for 1997 and 1998.

b. Write a short report evaluating the ratios that you calculated in part a.

c. Western Star Trucks' amount of debt increased between 1997 and 1998, while the amount of shareholders' equity decreased over the same year. Analyze the components that caused this increase (decrease) and comment on how these items might affect your evaluation of the health of this company.

10-45 (Debt/equity and times interest earned ratios)
The balance sheet and income statement from the 1998 annual report of Petromet Resources Limited are included in Exhibit 10-24.

Required:

a. Calculate the debt/equity ratios and the times interest earned ratios for 1997 and 1998.

b. Write a short report evaluating the ratios you calculated in part a.

c. Petromet Resources' amount of debt and shareholders' equity increased between 1997 and 1998. Analyze the components that caused this increase and comment on how these items might affect your evaluation of the health of this company.

Beyond the Book

10-46 (Analysis of a company's liabilities)
Choose a company as directed by your instructor and do the following exercises:

a. Prepare a quick analysis of the noncurrent liability accounts by listing the beginning and ending amounts in these accounts and calculating the net change in both dollar and percentage terms for the most recent year.

b. If any of the accounts change by more than 10%, give an explanation for this change.

c. What percentage of the company's total liabilities comes from long-term bank loans? Long-term bonds? Has this percentage changed significantly over the last year?

EXHIBIT 10-23
PART A

Consolidated Balance Sheets

As at June 30	1998	1997
(in thousands of Canadian dollars)		
ASSETS		
Current		
Cash	—	92,027
Accounts receivable *[note 6]*	201,218	203,196
Unbilled revenue *[note 1]*	85,167	21,023
Inventories *[note 3]*	237,312	182,157
Prepaid expenses and other	12,341	11,621
Total current assets	536,038	510,024
Capital assets *[note 4]*	143,563	136,046
Deferred costs *[note 5]*	76,069	61,724
Goodwill [net of accumulated amortization		
of $996; 1997 - $469]	10,986	9,635
Prepaid pension expense *[note 13]*	14,134	11,373
Investments and other assets	2,334	5,278
	783,124	734,080
LIABILITIES AND SHAREHOLDERS' EQUITY		
Current		
Bank indebtedness	1,843	—
Accounts payable and accrued liabilities *[note 6]*	305,393	260,607
Short-term indebtedness *[note 7]*	34,335	—
Current portion of customer deposits and advances	8,122	33,781
Current portion of long-term debt *[note 8]*	33,346	15,383
Total current liabilities	383,039	309,771
Deferred income taxes	553	6,076
Customer deposits and advances	327	1,800
Long-term debt *[note 8]*	171,088	185,502
Total liabilities	555,007	503,149
Commitments and contingencies *[notes 8[ii] and 9]*		
Shareholders' equity		
Share capital *[note 10]*	121,841	119,587
Retained earnings	106,276	111,344
Total shareholders' equity	228,117	230,931
	783,124	734,080

See accompanying notes

On behalf of the Board:

Director   Director

westernstar

EXHIBIT 10-23
PART B

Consolidated Statements of Operations and Retained Earnings

Years ended June 30	1998	1997	1996
(in thousands of Canadian dollars, except share and per share amounts)			
Revenue	1,552,272	1,236,349	783,319
Cost of sales	1,423,248	1,110,715	683,773
Gross profit	129,024	125,634	99,546
Selling and administrative	109,726	72,170	47,619
Interest expense - net	21,189	8,149	1,477
Net income (loss) before taxes	(1,891)	45,315	50,450
Income tax expense *(recovery) [note 11]*	(2,215)	11,325	13,927
Net income	324	33,990	36,523
Retained earnings, opening balance	111,344	82,962	51,225
Share issue costs *(net of tax)*	296	(90)	40
Dividends paid	(5,688)	(5,518)	(4,826)
Retained earnings, closing balance	106,276	111,344	82,962
Per common share			
Net income	0.02	2.48	3.08
Fully diluted net income	0.02	2.26	2.89
Dividends	0.40	0.40	0.40
Weighted average number of common shares			
outstanding (thousands)	14,214	13,723	11,860

See accompanying notes

western**star**

EXHIBIT 10-24
PART A

balance sheets

DECEMBER 31 ($ THOUSANDS)	1998	1997
ASSETS		
Current		
Cash	$ 147	$ 204
Accounts receivable	9,408	8,430
Inventory	2,261	1,912
Investments	125	125
	11,941	10,671
Property, plant and equipment (Note 2)	202,348	152,517
	$ 214,289	$ 163,188
LIABILITIES		
Current		
Accounts payable and accrued liabilities	$ 11,258	$ 13,705
Long-term bank debt (Note 3)	60,986	19,814
Convertible debentures (Note 4)	23,530	23,250
Future abandonment and site restoration costs	2,262	1,661
Deferred income taxes	8,623	6,891
SHAREHOLDERS' EQUITY		
Share capital (Note 5)	86,538	78,980
Paid-in capital (Note 4)	2,800	2,800
Retained earnings	18,292	16,087
	107,630	97,867
	$ 214,289	$ 163,188

See accompanying notes.

On Behalf of the Board:
(Director)

(Director)

EXHIBIT 10-24
PART B

statements of income

YEAR ENDED DECEMBER 31 ($ THOUSANDS, EXCEPT PER SHARE)	1998	1997	1996
REVENUE			
Petroleum and natural gas	$ 39,369	$ 33,927	$ 27,911
Royalties, net of Alberta Royalty Tax Credit	(5,519)	(5,802)	(4,258)
	33,850	28,125	23,653
EXPENSES			
Operating	4,894	3,548	3,191
General and administrative	2,430	1,127	1,373
Depletion and depreciation	17,096	11,924	9,496
Interest on long-term debt	4,911	2,854	3,178
	29,331	19,453	17,238
Income before other item and taxes	4,519	8,672	6,415
Gain on sale of investments	-	-	3,738
Income before taxes	4,519	8,672	10,153
Taxes (Note 7)	2,314	4,275	4,035
Net income	$ 2,205	$ 4,397	$ 6,118
Earnings per share	$ 0.05	$ 0.11	$ 0.18
Weighted average number of common shares outstanding	43,644,058	38,522,103	34,347,166

statements of retained earnings

YEAR ENDED DECEMBER 31 ($ THOUSANDS)	1998	1997	1996
Balance, beginning of year (Note 2)	$ 16,087	$ 11,690	$ 5,572
Net income	2,205	4,397	6,118
Balance, end of year	$ 18,292	$ 16,087	$ 11,690

d. What interest rates is the company paying on its long-term debt? (You will likely need to look in the notes to the financial statements to find the answer to this question.)

e. Calculate the debt/equity ratio and the times interest earned ratio for the company. Comment on the financial health of the company.

f. Does the company have any other long-term liabilities? Is so, describe each of them.

Case

10-47 Wasselec's Moving and Storage Corporation

Wasselec's Moving and Storage Corporation is a small company based in the Halifax area. It operates in both the residential and business markets. To serve its various clients, Wasselec's Moving and Storage owns two large moving trucks (tractor and trailer units), six medium-sized cartage trucks, two large vans, and two cars. Because its business relies on its vehicles, it has always been the policy of the corporation to purchase new vehicles on a regular rotation basis. Its accountant and vehicle service manager have established guidelines that trigger when a new vehicle should be purchased. For example, the large vans are replaced every 100,000 kilometres, the tractors every nine years, and the trailers every 15 years. The President of the corporation recently read an article about the increasing trend towards leasing. She wonders if Wasselec should start leasing its vehicles instead of buying them, and has asked the accountant for some guidance in this matter. The accountant has asked you, a recent addition to the accounting department, for a summary of the advantages and disadvantages of ownership versus leasing.

Required:

Draft a memo to the accountant summarizing the advantages and disadvantages of ownership versus leasing. Be sure to specifically discuss the assets currently owned by Wasselec. Remember as well that the accountant is very busy. Therefore, your memo should be concise.

Critical Thinking Question

10-48 (Pension plans)

For defined benefit pension plans, a formula has been devised for use in calculating the pension expense for each accounting period. When the calculated pension expense is compared to the amount of cash transferred to a trustee to invest in managing the future obligations of the pension plan, there could be a difference between the two amounts. If the amount of cash transferred is less than the pension expense, a liability for the difference results. If the amount of cash transferred is greater, an asset results. The difference between the two amounts is a reflection of either an overfunded or underfunded pension plan. These amounts are insignificant compared to the total liability of the corporation with respect to the pension plan. Describe the current disclosure requirements for pensions in Canada. Should companies be required to include a liability on the balance sheet which reflects the future obligation of the corporation with respect to its pension plan? What impact would such a requirement have on the debt/equity ratio? Are users being given enough information about pension plans allow them to make informed decisions?

All Your Requests, All the Time

"The radio station you always wanted to listen to, but were never able to find," is how Wolfgang Spegg describes radiomoi.com. This groundbreaking service from musicmusicmusic, of which Mr. Spegg is President, offers subscribers personalized broadcast music through the World Wide Web. Listeners can choose a program from among a variety of formats, or use the Interactive Jukebox either to request individual songs or to create fully personalized shows—all *your* requests, all the time.

A former computer salesman, Spegg knows his way around the high-tech sector—he helped design much of the radiomoi software himself—and is convinced his young company is poised to be one of Canada's "dot com" success stories. Musicmusicmusic also offers Web Bar listening posts, which allow shoppers to preview CDs before making a purchase; an archiving and retrieval service for radio stations; and custom-programmed background music piped into restaurants, malls, and so on. A hardware and software department, The Solutions Group (TSG), makes use of the company's expertise by providing other companies with multimedia applications and large-scale databases for Web delivery.

But when he went looking for bank help to get his ideas off the ground, Spegg came up empty-handed in Canada. "They were all useless, even the bank that publishes a brochure on how people should 'do business on the Internet'."

So Spegg turned to other financing options. He raised $500,000 from friends, relatives, and his own reserves, then, through contacts in his native Germany, another $500,000 from German and Swiss private investors. "Contacts led to contacts," says Spegg, and soon he had another $3 million from European institutional investors.

As with most Internet start-ups, musicmusicmusic's early-year actual revenues have been low; the company grossed US$1.4 million in 1998 and most of that was from TSG. Radiomoi itself generated only US$100,000 in its first 18 months or so of operation. But Spegg predicts the firm will be breaking even by 2002.

In the meantime, in the now-classic fashion of Web-based businesses of the late 1990s, musicmusicmusic went public, issuing 1.5 million shares on October 1, 1999. Given that the initial investors were European—the largest, holding 47.6% of the company, was Germany's Sonstige Aktionäre—and that Spegg has always envisioned a global future for the company, he chose to issue the shares on the German Neuer Markt, a branch of the Frankfurt exchange that specializes in high-tech stocks. All shares in the initial public offering (IPO) were common and the subscription price was Euro 9.00. The IPO was underwritten by the German investment firm Berliner Effektenbank.

Only time will tell how shareholders' equity grows in a newly public corporation. Shares in musicmusicmusic have fluctuated significantly in price since its IPO, and traded actively. And activity, after all, is what the fast-growing Web-based sector is all about. When it comes to online entrepreneurship, comments Spegg, you need to "move fast, or you'll be an also-ran."

Sources: Koch, George, "Canadians.com," *Profit* 18, no. 5 (September 1999, p. 28); musicmusicmusic inc. information materials; Neuer Markt website: www.neuer-markt.de

SHAREHOLDERS' EQUITY

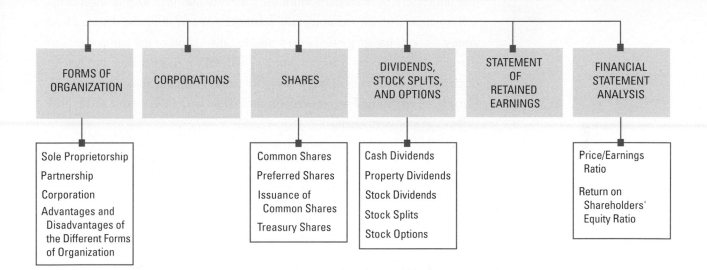

| FORMS OF ORGANIZATION | CORPORATIONS | SHARES | DIVIDENDS, STOCK SPLITS, AND OPTIONS | STATEMENT OF RETAINED EARNINGS | FINANCIAL STATEMENT ANALYSIS |

Sole Proprietorship
Partnership
Corporation
Advantages and Disadvantages of the Different Forms of Organization

Common Shares
Preferred Shares
Issuance of Common Shares
Treasury Shares

Cash Dividends
Property Dividends
Stock Dividends
Stock Splits
Stock Options

Price/Earnings Ratio
Return on Shareholders' Equity Ratio

Learning Objectives:

After studying this chapter, you should be able to:

1. *Distinguish among different types of organizations and explain the advantages and disadvantages of each form.*
2. *Describe the different types of shares and explain why corporations choose to issue a variety of share types.*
3. *Prepare journal entries for share transactions, including the issuance and payment of dividends.*
4. *Describe the different types of dividends and explain why companies might opt to issue one type of dividend rather than another.*
5. *Explain the purpose of the statement of retained earnings.*
6. *Calculate and interpret the price/earnings ratio and the return on shareholders' equity ratio that are often used in decision-making.*

The opening story describes how a new Internet company, musicmusicmusic inc., arranged the financing to start operations. Getting financing is not an easy task, especially for new companies with no proven track record. Musicmusicmusic first got financing from family and friends, then received additional support from private investors in Germany and Switzerland. Finally, it took its company public through an initial public offering (IPO) of shares. This procedure is not uncommon for new companies.

In this chapter, we will provide more information about many of the activities undertaken by musicmusicmusic inc. Our exploration of balance sheet items will conclude with a discussion of the accounts that constitute the shareholders' equity section. Before getting into a detailed discussion of the components of shareholders' equity in a corporation, we will take a short detour and briefly discuss alternative forms of business organization. Although most companies in Canada are established as corporations, they could have been established as proprietorships or partnerships.

FORMS OF ORGANIZATION

Sole Proprietorship

Learning Objective

1

Distinguish among different types of organizations and explain the advantages and disadvantages of each form.

As discussed briefly in Chapter 1, the simplest form of business is the **sole proprietorship**. The sole proprietorship is a single-owner business. All profits and losses belong to the owner, and all decisions are made by the owner. It is probably this aspect of control that keeps the proprietorship form of business alive. Most owners like to be the one making decisions and like to be active in the day-to-day operations.

Proprietors must assume all the risk if the business runs into trouble. They have unlimited liability. **Unlimited liability** means that if the business cannot make its debt payments, creditors can sue the owner and take not just the business assets but also the personal assets of the owner. It is the aspect of unlimited liability that makes many single owners consider establishing the business as a corporation rather than as a proprietorship.

Because the sole proprietor does not have to report to shareholders, there is not a great deal of concern in a sole proprietorship about preparing reports according to Canadian standards. However, the sole proprietor might want to follow Canadian standards if the business requires a bank loan, since loan officers would probably insist on financial statements prepared according to GAAP. GAAP statements might also be required if the sole proprietorship is regulated. If the owner deviated from Canadian standards, it would likely be because preparing the information in another way is more useful for decision-making in terms of running the business.

Revenue Canada also requires information about the financial results of a sole proprietorship. Sole proprietors are required to combine the profits or losses from their business with their personal income for tax purposes. Unlike corporations, sole proprietorships are not taxed separately. The rules for reporting income to Revenue Canada are, therefore, likely to be the single most important motivating factor in producing financial statements. The accounting methods used by the sole proprietor are more likely to follow those used for tax purposes than those set forth under GAAP.

With regard to owner's equity accounts, there is little reason for the owner to distinguish the initial investment from the income retained in the business. For this reason, the owner's equity section of a sole proprietorship typically has only one account, which is sometimes called **owner's capital**. This account is used when the owner puts new capital in the business, when the business earns income (revenues and expenses are closed to this account), and when the owner withdraws cash from the business. Cash withdrawn from the business for personal use is usually referred to as a withdrawal by the owner. These withdrawals are the equivalent of dividends in a corporation. Because the owner is taxed on the combined basis of personal income and business income, these withdrawals are not taxed in the same manner as corporate dividends.

Partnership

A form of business very similar to a sole proprietorship is a **partnership**. In a partnership, two or more individuals agree to conduct business under one name. The involvement of each partner can vary greatly. The rights and responsibilities of the partners are generally specified in a document called a **partnership agreement**. This document is very important because it specifies how the partners will make decisions about the business, including how they will share in the profits and losses of the partnership and how the assets of the partnership will be distributed if the partnership dissolves. In the absence of a partnership agreement, the distribution of assets and profits is assumed to be equal for all partners. If the partners intend to share profits in some other proportion, this must be stated in the partnership agreement. For tax purposes, partnerships are not taxable entities; the income earned by the partners is passed through to them and must be reported on their personal tax returns, similar to the treatment of sole proprietorship income.

Partners can assume different responsibilities and risk in a partnership. **General partners** normally make day-to-day decisions about the business, share in profits and losses, and have unlimited liability. If the partnership defaults on its debts, creditors can sue one, more than one, or all of the general partners for business assets as well as personal ones. **Limited partners**, on the other hand, have limited involvement in the partnership. Normally, they invest in the partnership but do not make day-to-day decisions about its operations. They share in profits and losses but creditors cannot normally sue them if the partnership runs into financial difficulty.

One of the major accounting problems in a partnership is distinguishing among the roles that partners play as owners, creditors, and employees. For example, should the remuneration paid to a partner who works as an employee of the partnership be treated as an expense of the partnership? That is, should all partners share in this expense, or should it be treated as a part of the partner's share of the profits from the business? As another example, suppose a partner lends money to the partnership. Should this be viewed as a liability of the partnership, or as part of the equity contributed by this partner? If the partnership liquidates, should this partner first be paid back as a creditor and then share in whatever is left, or should the loan be considered a part of the partner's equity? There is no single "right" answer to these questions, which is why these issues should all be addressed in the partnership agreement.

The accounting for the owners' equity section of a partnership requires that the partnership keep a separate account for each partner, usually called the **partner's capital account**. Each period, the profits or losses of the partnership must be distributed among the partners' capital accounts. This is usually a relatively complex process that takes into consideration the issues discussed in the preceding paragraph. Sometimes there is also an account for each partner called a **drawings account**. This is an account that keeps track of the amounts withdrawn by the partner during the period. It is similar to a dividends declared account in a corporation in that it collects payments made to owners. In the case of the drawings account, at the end of each accounting period it is closed into the capital account of the specific partner. As with sole proprietorships, such withdrawals are not taxable.

Detailed accounting rules for partnerships are covered in advanced accounting texts and will not be discussed here. The accounting for the transactions of a partnership other than owners' equity is essentially the same as that discussed in this book for corporations.

Corporation

The third major form of business organization is the corporation, which has been the focus of most of this book. It differs from the sole proprietorship and the partnership in at least two significant ways. The first is that the corporation is legally separate from the shareholders. While the owners of sole proprietorships and partnerships can be held liable for the debts of their businesses, corporate shareholders have limited liability for the debts of the companies they own. Corporate shareholders cannot be made to pay for the debts of the company out of their personal assets. Sole proprietors and partners do not enjoy this limited liability.

The second significant way in which corporations differ from proprietorships is the manner in which they are taxed. Because the corporation is viewed as a separate legal entity, Revenue Canada and provincial governments impose a corporate tax on the income it earns. This corporate tax is additional to the personal income tax that shareholders pay when they receive dividends or when they sell their shares and experience a gain or loss.

The basics of accounting for shareholders' equity in a company are covered in preceding chapters of this book. Later in this chapter, details will be provided concerning more complex transactions that involve shareholders' equity.

Advantages and Disadvantages of the Different Forms of Organization

While there are many differences among sole proprietorships, partnerships, and corporations, the two primary differences just discussed, legal liability and taxes, are sufficiently important to warrant more detailed discussion here. With regard to legal liability, the owners of a sole proprietorship or partnership are fully liable for the debts of the business. If the business does not have sufficient assets to pay its debts, creditors have the right to try to collect from the personal assets of the owners. As we have seen, this feature is sometimes referred to as unlimited liability. The shareholders of corporations, on the other hand, enjoy limited liability. The most a shareholder can lose is the amount of the investment in the shares. Creditors cannot seek satisfaction of their claims from the personal assets of corporate shareholders.

Limited liability is obviously an advantage of the corporate form of organization. A form of partnership called **limited partnership** shares partly in this advantage. In limited partnerships, there are general partners and limited partners. General partners have unlimited liability, whereas limited partners have limited liability. The downside for the limited partners is that they also have a limited say in decision-making within the partnership.

Where taxes are concerned, income of partnerships and sole proprietorships is not taxed at the business level, because the income flows through to the individuals. Personal tax is then assessed according to the tax bracket of the individual owner. Corporations, on the other hand, are subject to corporate taxation. An incorporated small business can obtain a tax advantage through tax deferral when profits are retained in the business, because the corporate tax rate is approximately 22% for a small business. The tax to be paid by individual shareholders on dividends or capital gains (if they sell their shares) is deferred until the dividends are received or the shares are sold. They are then taxed at the individual level. Corporate income is, therefore, subject to double taxation, although the income tax rules provide for methods intended to reduce the impact of this double taxation. This double taxation does not necessarily mean that more tax is paid, because the sum of the corporate tax and individual tax for a small business is roughly equal to the individual tax on business income. For larger corporations that cannot take advantage of the small business tax rate, the tax effect could be a disadvantage of the corporate form.

There are other advantages and disadvantages to each form of business. For example, incorporation requires significantly more paperwork and regulation than establishing a sole proprietorship or partnership. Although partnerships can be formed without any written agreement, a written partnership agreement prepared with legal assistance is advisable in order to avoid possible disagreements among the partners. Once established, corporations can raise additional capital much more easily than partnerships; they simply issue more shares or bonds. Partnerships and sole proprietorships are limited to the assets contributed by the owners and those earned by the business and not withdrawn. It is much easier to change your ownership interest if you are a shareholder than if you are a partner or a sole proprietor. You simply sell your shares on the stock market. If you no longer want to own a proprietorship, you must sell the whole business. If you are a partner and want to withdraw from the partnership, you must convince the other partners to buy you out or find another partner to buy your ownership interest. When establishing a new business it is important for you to weigh all of the issues before deciding on the organizational form that will be most beneficial.

In Canada, corporations own the vast majority of business assets and almost all large businesses are organized as corporations. That is why we focus on accounting for corporations in this text.

CORPORATIONS

Let us look at corporations in more detail. Shareholders of corporations require certain types of legal protection, especially because the owners of most corporations are absentee shareholders; that is, they are not intimately involved in the day-to-day business of the company. This protection is provided by the laws of the jurisdiction under which the company is incorporated. In Canada, companies may be incorporated under the federal *Canada Business Corporations Act* or under similar provincial acts that have been established in all 10 provinces. When investors decide to establish a business in the form of a corporation, they first must decide under which act they want to be incorporated. Most companies in Canada are incorporated under the laws of the province in which the business, or at least the head office of the company, is to be located. Companies that intend to do business interprovincially or internationally may decide that incorporation under federal legislation will provide them with more options. After making this decision, the founding investors prepare a document called the **articles of incorporation**. This document includes information on what type of business the company will conduct, how the Board of Directors will be organized, who the management will be, what kinds of shares will be issued, and so on. The exact content of the articles will depend on the decisions of the incorporating shareholders. Once the company has been incorporated, the articles of incorporation can generally be amended only by a vote of the shareholders.

SHARES

Learning Objective

2

Describe the different types of shares and explain why corporations choose to issue a variety of share types.

For accounting purposes, the most important section of the articles of incorporation is the description of the shares that will be issued. The maximum number of shares that the company can issue is specified in the articles. These are referred to as the **authorized shares**. In the past, companies would establish 500,000, 3,000,000, or some other number of shares that they assumed would carry them for many years. When a company is first starting out, it is hard to imagine that you will ever issue 3,000,000 shares. However, companies have found that issuing all of the authorized shares is not very hard to do. To increase the number of authorized shares requires a change in the articles of incorporation, which in turn requires a vote by the shareholders. To give you some perspective on numbers of shares, Big Rock Brewery, a small to medium-sized company, had issued 4,861,200 shares by the end of March 1999. BCE Inc., one of the largest companies in Canada, had issued 68,000,000 preferred and 640,131,136 common shares by the end of December 1998. Microsoft, in the United States, had issued 2,388,000,000 shares by the end of June 1998. The magnitude of these numbers is difficult to conceive when you are starting a company. To overcome the problem of reaching the authorized limit set in the articles of incorporation, many companies today establish an *unlimited* number of authorized shares. This allows them greater freedom to use the issuance of shares as a means for raising capital.

In the past, the articles could also specify a dollar amount that was attached to each share. This dollar amount was known as the **par value**. Under most jurisdictions in Canada, par value shares are no longer permitted. Instead, most companies issue **no-par value shares**. The original purpose of par value was to protect the company's creditors by setting a limit on the dividends the company could pay. In most jurisdictions, a company was able to declare dividends only up to the value of the retained earnings. It could not pay dividends out of par value (i.e., the balance in the common shares account). If a company were allowed to declare a dividend equal to the total of retained earnings and the balance in the other equity accounts, the shareholders might pay themselves a dividend of this amount (sometimes called a **liquidating dividend** because it liquidated the shareholders' investment). This might have left creditors with insufficient assets to satisfy their claims. Companies were able to avoid this constraint by setting very low par values and selling the shares at prices above the par value. Only the total of the par values was credited to the share account; the excess was credited to an account called paid-in capital or premium on shares. Dividends paid out of this second account were permitted in some jurisdictions and were in fact liquidating dividends since they reduced the paid-in equity of the company.

While this is still theoretically true of par values today, the practical value of a par value is almost nonexistent. The par value of most shares is so small compared to the level of other shareholders' equity accounts and the level of liabilities that it provides very little protection to creditors. For this reason, when the *Canada Business Corporations Act* was changed in 1976, par value shares were no longer allowed. Shares had to be no-par value. When no-par value shares are issued, the total amount received for the shares is put into one account, the share account. This larger amount is referred to as the **legal capital** and must be kept intact. It cannot be paid out as dividends. This provides more protection for creditors. Once the *Canada Business Corporations Act* changed, most of the provincial acts were changed as well.

The articles of incorporation also specify the classes or types of shares that can be issued by the company, if indeed more than one class of share is to be issued. In the example concerning BCE Inc., two types of shares, preferred and common, were used. In many companies, more than one class is authorized so that the company will have the flexibility to attract different kinds of investors. For example, some investors want the assurance of regular dividends to provide a steady income; others prefer no regular dividends but hope for increasing share values so that they can earn capital gains when they eventually sell the shares.

The different classes of shares differ in the rights that accrue to their holders. Two major types, **common shares** and **preferred shares**, are discussed in the following subsections. Different classes of shares can be authorized within each of these two major categories. For example, some companies have multiple classes of common shares and multiple classes (sometimes these are called issues) of preferred shares. BCE Inc., for example, by the end of 1998 had one class of common shares and 11 series of preferred shares (Series P, Q, R, S, T, U, V, W, X, Y, and Z), as shown in Exhibit 11-1. Note that BCE's Board of Directors has the power to set specific terms and conditions for each series. This allows for a great deal of flexibility in attracting investment in BCE.

Common Shares

Every corporation must have one class of shares that represents the basic voting ownership rights of the company. These shares are normally referred to as **common shares**. Corporations generally issue common shares through a firm of investment bankers, known as underwriters, similar to the way that bonds are issued (see Chapter 10 for a discussion of this process). When common or preferred shares are issued, their details and features are discussed in a legal document called a **prospectus**, which is given to potential investors when shares (or a bond) are initially issued (sold).

Common shares carry a basic set of rights that allow the owner to share proportionately (based on the number of shares held) in:

1. Profits and losses
2. The selection of management of the corporation
3. Assets upon liquidation
4. Subsequent issues of shares (although not all jurisdictions in Canada provide for this basic right).

Rather than establishing complex income-sharing rules similar to a partnership, a corporation retains all of its profits. However, it is sometimes useful to think of a corporation's profits or losses as being allocated to its shares, even if these earnings or losses are not actually paid out. The resulting per-share figure is useful in determining if the corporation's profits are increasing or decreasing on an individual share basis. This earnings per share figure that corporations calculate provides a measure of performance that all shareholders can use. Recall from Chapter 3 that this calculation consists of dividing the net income of the corporation by the average number of common shares outstanding during the year. A weighted-average is used if the number of common shares outstanding changed during the year. Different classes of shares are entitled to different portions of the earnings. Normally, preferred shares are restricted to the amounts of their dividends, while common shares have no restrictions on their rights to share in earnings once the claims of the creditors and the preferred shares have been satisfied.

If a corporation opts to pay dividends (it is not obligated to do so), shareholders share proportionately in the distribution of earnings in the form of dividends. Corporations, in addition to reporting earnings per share, often report dividends per share. As will be seen below, the right to share in dividend distribution may be amended for different classes of shares, especially preferred shares.

EXHIBIT 11-1

16. PREFERRED SHARES

Authorized

The articles of incorporation of the Corporation provide for an unlimited number of First Preferred Shares and Second Preferred Shares. The articles authorize the Directors to issue such shares in one or more series and to fix the number of shares of each series, and the conditions attaching to them.

Authorized and outstanding

The following provides a summary of the principal terms and conditions relating to the Corporation's authorized and outstanding series of First Preferred Shares. The detailed terms and conditions of such shares are set forth in the Corporation's articles of incorporation.

CUMULATIVE REDEEMABLE FIRST PREFERRED SHARES

Series	Annual Dividend Rate		Convertible Date (on or after)	Convertible into	Redemption Date	Redemption Price		Authorized Number of shares		Outstanding At December 31 Stated capital 1998	1997
P	$1.600		July 15, 2002 (a)	common shares	April 15, 2002	$25		16,000,000	(h)	400	400
Q	$1.725	(b)	December 1, 2000	Series R	December 1, 2000	$25	(c)	8,000,000	(h)	200	200
R		(g)	December 1, 2005	Series Q	December 1, 2005	$25		8,000,000		–	–
S	$1.320	(b)	November 1, 2001	Series T	November 1, 2001	$25	(c)	8,000,000	(h)	200	200
T		(g)	November 1, 2006	Series S	November 1, 2006	$25		8,000,000		–	–
U(d)	$1.385	(e)	March 1, 2007	Series V	March 1, 2007	$25	(f)	22,000,000	(h)	350	350
V		(g)	March 1, 2012	Series U	March 1, 2012	$25		22,000,000		–	–
W(d)	$1.363	(e)	September 1, 2007	Series X	September 1, 2007	$25	(f)	20,000,000	(h)	300	300
X		(g)	September 1, 2012	Series W	September 1, 2012	$25		20,000,000		–	–
Y	$1.150	(b)	December 1, 2002	Series Z	December 1, 2002	$25	(c)	10,000,000	(h)	250	250
Z		(g)	December 1, 2007	Series Y	December 1, 2007	$25		10,000,000		–	–
										1,700	1,700

All series outstanding as at December 31, 1998 are non-voting except under certain circumstances when the holders are entitled to one vote per share and are convertible at the holder's option.

(a) The Corporation may, at any time, elect to create a further series of preferred shares into which the Series P shares will be convertible on a share-for-share basis at the option of the holder. The Series P shares are, subject to the approval of certain stock exchanges, also convertible into common shares at the Corporation's option.

(b) Holders of Series Q, Series S and Series Y shares will be entitled to floating adjustable cumulative dividends commencing with the month of January 2001, December 2001 and January 2003, respectively.

(c) The Corporation may redeem Series Q, Series S and Series Y shares at any time after December 1, 2000, November 1, 2001 and December 1, 2002, respectively, for $25.50 per share.

(d) The Corporation has entered into interest rate swap agreements until 2007 to effectively convert the Series U and W fixed dividends to floating rate dividends equal to the 90-day Bankers' Acceptance Rate less 0.675% and 0.594%, respectively.

(e) Holders of Series U and Series W shares will be entitled to floating cumulative dividends commencing with the month of April 2007 and October 2007, respectively.

(f) The Corporation may redeem the Series U and Series W shares on and after March 1, 2007 and September 1, 2007, respectively. However, if these Series are listed on the Montreal or Toronto stock exchange, the redemption price after these dates shall be $25.50 per share.

(g) Authorized but not issued.

(h) Authorized and outstanding, except that only 14,000,000 Series U shares and 12,000,000 Series W shares are outstanding.

Common shareholders also have a say in the selection of management for the corporation. The standard rule for voting is one share, one vote. The more shares an individual owns, the greater the influence of the individual in the company. One of the shareholders' most important votes is that of electing members of the Board of Directors. The Board of Directors represents the shareholders, and most decisions are made by a vote of the Board of Directors rather than by a vote of all shareholders. The Board of Directors hires (and fires) top-level management of the company. The Board also declares the dividends that are paid to shareholders. Note the following example of how this right of shareholders was exercised in Spar Aerospace Ltd.:

accounting in the news

SHAREHOLDER POWER

Shareholders wield great power. In 1999, Spar Aerospace Ltd. yielded to dissident shareholders demanding a new Board of Directors and a payout of the bulk of Spar's cash assets. The demands fuelled speculation that Spar's days were numbered.

At Spar's annual meeting, the rebel shareholders, representing 58% of outstanding shares, replaced seven members of the nine-member Board with five of their own choosing. The new Board chairman, Eric Rosenfeld, was a principal in Spar's largest shareholder, Crescendo Partners LP, which held 19.9% of the company. Shareholders then voted for the Board to initiate a shareholder payout of as much as $123 million of Spar's stated capital of $128 million, a move that would leave the maker of the famous Canadarm with virtually no growth potential.

Analysts speculated the Board would sell Spar's aviation services company, its sole business asset following a major period of restructuring, and then shut the company down.

Source: "Dissidents control Spar," by Peter Fitzpatrick, *National Post (Financial Post)*, May 14, 1999, p. C1, C6.

The third right of common shareholders is to share in assets upon liquidation. If a company goes bankrupt or otherwise liquidates, there is an established order for creditors and shareholders to be paid. Common shareholders come last on that list; whatever is left after creditors are paid is divided proportionately among the common shareholders based on their relative number of shares. This means that common shareholders bear the highest risk—since there may be nothing left over for them.

The fourth right of common shareholders is to share proportionately in any new issuance of shares. This is called the **preemptive right**. Preemptive rights are not automatic. They must be explicitly stated in the articles of incorporation. This right allows current holders of shares to retain their proportionate interest in the company when new shares are issued. For example, a shareholder owning 20% of a company's shares has the preemptive right to purchase 20% of any new shares of that class that may be issued. Without this right, an investor with a **controlling interest** in a company (i.e., an investor owning more than 50% of the outstanding shares) could lose that controlling interest if the new shares were issued to another investor. Of course this scenario is unlikely, as controlling interest includes the right to vote for the directors of the company, so that directors who support the majority owner will be elected. The greatest protection is reserved for shareholders who own a **minority** or **noncontrolling interest** in a company. Preemptive rights prevent their ownership interests from being diluted.

When more than one class of common shares is issued, each class is distinguished by some amendment to the fundamental rights just described. For example, a second class of nonvoting common shares issued might be entitled to conversion to voting common shares under certain conditions. This obviously affects the control that holders of the voting common shares have over the operations of the company. There might also be differences in the rights to share in the liquidation values of the assets. As shown in Exhibit 11-2, Comac Food Group Inc. has two classes of common shares, Class A performance shares, which are non-voting, and Class B voting common shares. The Class A performance shares are convertible, on a one-to-one basis, to Class B voting common shares when the company reaches certain performance levels; hence their name.

10. SHAREHOLDERS' EQUITY

Class A performance shares

900,000 Class A non voting performance shares, which convert on a one to one basis in increments of 150,000 shares to Class B common shares upon the Company reaching certain performance levels measured by funds from operations. Each performance level increases in increments of $100,000 with the first performance level starting at $300,000 per annum.

Class B Common shares

Unlimited number of Class B voting common shares.

Class B Preferred shares

Unlimited number of Class B non voting preferred shares.

1,115,318 Class B Series III preferred shares convertible on a 1 to 1.803 basis to Class B common shares at any time. The shares are redeemable by the Company for $1 plus unpaid, cumulative dividends. Cumulative dividends of 7% of the redemption amount are compounded annually. Cumulative dividends in arrears as at March 29, 1998 were $162,000 (1997 - $78,000).

Dividends paid to different classes of common shares may also be paid on a different basis, although each outstanding share of any class of shares will be paid the same amount.

Preferred Shares

Preferred shares are shares that have preference over common shares with regard to dividends. This does not mean that preferred shareholders are guaranteed a dividend. However, if dividends are declared, they will receive dividends before common shareholders will. Often, in addition to the preference for dividends, there is some preference with regard to assets in the event of liquidation.

The amount of the preferred dividend is usually stated as a dollar amount per share, such as a $2 preferred share issue. Such an issue would pay a dividend of $2 per share per year. Examples of this type can be found in the note disclosure of BCE Inc. in Exhibit 11-1, where the company lists $1.60 Series P and $1.725 Series Q preferred shares, among others.

Another difference between common and preferred shares, besides that of priority for dividends, is that preferred shares are usually nonvoting. One of the troubling issues in accounting is how to deal with securities, such as preferred shares, whose characteristics make them look more like debt than common shares. Nonvoting preferred shares with a fixed dividend amount are not much different from debt (which is also nonvoting) that has a fixed interest payment. The only real difference is that the company is not obliged to pay the preferred dividend, whereas the interest on the debt is a true obligation and a legal liability.

Preferred shares have other important features. Preferred dividends may be **cumulative**. **Cumulative preferred shares** mean that if a dividend is not declared in one year, the dividends carry over to the next year. In the second year, both the prior year's preferred dividend and the current year's preferred dividend must be declared before any common dividends can be declared. Dividends from prior years that have not been declared are called **dividends in arrears**. Note that for BCE all of the series of preferred shares are cumulative. In fact, most preferred shares are cumulative.

Convertible preferred shares are convertible, at the option of the shareholder, into common shares based on a ratio stated in the articles of incorporation. Note that for BCE the Series P preferred shares are convertible into common shares with certain conditions attached. However, unlike most convertible preferred shares, these shares are also convertible at the *corporation's option*. Most preferred shares are not convertible. **Redeemable preferred shares** can be bought back by the company (retired) at a price and time specified in the articles of incorporation at the option of the issuing company. All of BCE's preferred shares are redeemable. **Retractable preferred shares** can be sold back to the company (retired) at the option of the shareholder. The price that must be paid for them and the periods of time within which they can be sold are specified in the articles of incorporation.

The last feature we are going to discuss is participation. **Participating preferred shares** are preferred shares that not only have a preference with regard to dividends but, if dividends are declared to common shareholders beyond the level declared to the preferred shareholders, the preferred shareholders share in the excess dividends. Most preferred shares are nonparticipating. At one time, BCE had preferred shares that were participating. However, none of its current series of preferred shares has this feature.

While the features of various classes of shares differ, the accounting issues relating to them are essentially the same. Therefore, in the sections that follow we will limit the discussion to common shares.

Issuance of Common Shares

When common shares are issued for cash, the company accounts for the proceeds from the issuance by debiting the cash account. The credit entry is, then, to a common shares account. This common shares account is sometimes referred to as **paid-in capital** or **legal capital**. Remember that to provide protection for creditors the amount credited to the common shares account cannot be paid out as dividends.

To illustrate the issuance entry: Suppose that Rosman Company issues 1,000 common shares for $20 a share. The following entry would be made:

Learning Objective

3

Prepare journal entries for share transactions, including the issuance and payment of dividends.

SHARE ISSUANCE ENTRY		
A-Cash	20,000	
SE-Common shares		20,000

Historically, companies were permitted to issue shares that had a stated or par value. The terms *stated value* and *par value* were originally intended to indicate the underlying value of the shares. With stated or par value shares, only the total of the stated or par value was credited to the common shares account; any remaining amount was credited to another equity account. The use of stated and par values is no longer permitted in most jurisdictions in Canada, although you may find that some companies are incorporated in jurisdictions that permit them, while some companies from other jurisdictions still have some par value shares that were issued in the past and not converted to no-par shares.

To illustrate the issuance entry for par value shares: Suppose that Green Company issued 1,000 common shares for $15 a share that had a par value of $10 per share. The following entry would have been made:

SHARE ISSUANCE ENTRY		
A-Cash	15,000	
SE-Common shares		10,000
SE-Contributed capital		5,000

Note that the additional $5 per share (the amount in excess of par) is recorded in an account called Contributed capital. This account is sometimes called *contributed surplus in excess of par* or *additional paid-in capital*.

Treasury Shares

Subsequent to issuance, the company may decide to buy back some of its own shares. It might do this because it wants to reduce the number of shares outstanding, or because it wants to use the shares to satisfy its stock option plans rather than issue new shares. Shares that have been repurchased by the issuing company are called **treasury shares**. In most jurisdictions in Canada treasury shares are cancelled immediately upon purchase. In some jurisdictions they are not cancelled immediately and are considered to be issued but not outstanding.

Three terms are used to refer to the number of shares of a company: **authorized**, **issued**, and **outstanding**. **Authorized shares** are those that can be issued by the company according to the articles of incorporation. As discussed earlier, many companies avoid having an authorized limit by stating that they have the right to issue an unlimited number of shares. Those that have been sold (issued) by the company are considered **issued shares**. As long as the shares remain in the possession of shareholders outside the company they are considered to be **outstanding shares**. If, however, the company purchases some of its own shares from the market, the shares remain issued but are no longer outstanding. If the company subsequently cancels the shares, they will cease to be issued. If the company does not have to cancel the shares but instead holds them as treasury shares, the issued shares less those held as treasury shares are the outstanding shares. Examples of the use of these terms can be found in Note 10 to the financial statements of Finning International Inc. shown in Exhibit 11-3. Finning has an unlimited number of authorized preferred and common shares. At the end of December 1998 it had 99,600 preferred shares and 79,427,879 common shares issued and outstanding.

EXHIBIT 11-3

[10] SHARE CAPITAL

AUTHORIZED

| Unlimited | Preferred shares without par value of which 4,400,000 are designated as Cumulative Redeemable Convertible Preferred shares |
| Unlimited | Common shares |

ISSUED AND OUTSTANDING		1998	1997
99,600	Preferred shares, Series E (1997: 116,550)	$ 996	$ 1,166
79,427,879	Common shares (1997: 79,090,612)	207,583	204,425
		$ 208,579	$ 205,591

CHANGES DURING 1997 **At the Company's annual meeting in April 1997, the shareholders approved the subdivision of the Company's common shares on a two-for-one basis.**

COMMON SHARES **A shareholders' rights plan is in place which is intended to provide all holders of common shares with the opportunity to receive full and fair value for all of their shares in the event a third party attempts to acquire a significant interest in the Company. The Company's dealership agreements with subsidiaries of Caterpillar Inc. are fundamental to its business and any change in control must be approved by Caterpillar.**

The plan provides that one share purchase right has been issued for each common share and will trade with the common shares until such time as any person or group, other than a permitted bidder, bids to acquire or acquires 20% or more of the Company's common shares. The rights will then separate and will ultimately entitle each holder of common shares (other than the bidder) to purchase common shares of the Company at a 50% discount to the then market price. The rights may also be triggered by a third party proposal for merger, amalgamation or a similar transaction. The rights will expire on September 13, 1999 unless redeemed earlier by the Board of Directors.

FINNING INTERNATIONAL INC.   48

When a company repurchases its own shares and cancels them, a credit is made to cash for the cost of the shares. The debit entry then has to reduce shareholders' equity, since the shares are no longer issued or outstanding. A problem arises if the cost of the shares repurchased is different from the amount received when the shares were originally issued. Shares that were issued in the past were likely issued at different times and for different amounts. If this is the case, the average issue price must be determined by dividing the total amount in the shares account by the total number of shares outstanding before the repurchase.

As an example, suppose that Lee Industries Ltd. had 150,000 common shares outstanding and a balance of $1,500,000 in its Common shares account. The average issue price is $10 ($1,500,000/150,000). If Lee repurchases 1,000 shares for $9 each, it is paying $1 less than the average issue price. This $1 per share is not considered to be a profit or gain, and therefore does not appear in the income statement. The reason for this is that the $1 does not result from the normal operations of the company. The company was not incorporated to earn money by trading in its own shares. As a general rule, companies never earn revenues or incur losses from transactions involving their own equities. Rather, the $1 is still part of shareholders' equity and is credited to a separate account called "Contributed surplus." The entry to record this repurchase would be as follows:

SE-Common shares	10,000	
A-Cash		9,000
SE-Contributed surplus		1,000

If Lee had paid $12 per share, it would have paid $2 more than the average issue price per share of $10. In this case, the $2 extra per share would reduce shareholders' equity. Normally the $2 is debited to Retained earnings, as follows:

SE-Common shares	10,000	
SE-Retained earnings	2,000	
A-Cash		12,000

If there had been a previous repurchase and cancellation of treasury shares, creating a contributed surplus account (similar to the first part of this example), the Contributed surplus account, instead of Retained earnings, could have been debited. Further details on the accounting for treasury share transactions can be found in more advanced accounting texts.

DIVIDENDS, STOCK SPLITS, AND OPTIONS

Cash Dividends

Dividends are payments to shareholders from the total net income retained in a company in the Retained earnings account. Dividends are payment in return for the

Learning Objective

4

Describe the different types of dividends and explain why companies might opt to issue one type of dividend rather than another.

company's use of the shareholders' money. They are paid to shareholders only if the Board of Directors has voted to declare a dividend. The declaration of a cash dividend by the Board of Directors makes the dividend a legal liability of the company. Dividends are not paid on treasury shares because these are held internally by the company, and companies cannot pay dividends to themselves. Dividends are paid only on outstanding shares.

The dividend notice for SNC-Lavalin Group Inc. in Exhibit 11-4 is a typical dividend notice.

EXHIBIT 11-4

SNC·LAVALIN

Notice of dividend

NOTICE is given that the Directors of SNC-Lavalin Group Inc. have declared a quarterly dividend of six cents ($0.06) per share on the Corporation, payable on the 3rd day of June, 1999, to shareholders of record a the close of business on the 20th day of May, 1999.

By order of the Board of Directors
**Y. Laverdière
Corporate Secretary**

Montreal, Quebec
May 6, 1999

SNC·LAVALIN Group Inc.

Three dates are important in the dividend declaration process. The first is the **date of declaration**. This is the date on which the Board of Directors votes to declare a dividend. For SNC-Lavalin that date is May 6, 1999. On the date of declaration, the company records its obligation to pay the dividend by creating a dividends payable account and a dividends declared account. Suppose that SNC-Lavalin had 44,871,500 common shares outstanding on May 6, 1999. The entry to record the declaration would be:

DIVIDEND DECLARATION ENTRY		
SE-Dividends declared	2,692,290	
L-Dividends payable		2,692,290

The debit is usually to a Dividends declared account, which is a temporary account that is closed to Retained earnings at the end of the accounting period. Dividends declared does not appear on the income statement. It is not an expense of doing business; it is a return to shareholders on their investment. Companies typically declare dividends quarterly. Therefore, the Dividends declared account accumulates all four quarterly dividends by the end of the fiscal year. Not all companies use a Dividends declared account. Some companies debit dividends directly to Retained earnings.

In the dividend declaration, the Board of Directors specifies that the dividend is payable to shareholders of record on the **date of record**. This second important date is the date on which a shareholder must own the shares in order to receive the dividend. For SNC-Lavalin that date is the close of business on May 20, 1999. The date of record is typically two weeks after the date of declaration. This delay is needed because the shares of most public companies are traded every day, so the company has no up-to-date record of the owners of its shares. The delay also gives new owners time to inform the company of their ownership of the shares. If the shareholder sells shares before the date of record, the new owner of the shares will be entitled to receive the dividend.

In the shares market, traders speak about the **ex-dividend day**. The ex-dividend day is the day on which shares are sold without the right to receive the dividend. By purchasing the shares on the ex-dividend day, the buyer will not receive the dividend; it belongs to the seller. As you might expect, the price of the shares decreases on the ex-dividend day to reflect the loss of this dividend.

A couple of weeks after the date of record, the company pays the dividend. This third important date is called the **date of payment**. SNC-Lavalin's date of payment is June 3, 1999. Again, a delay is needed so the company can update its list of shareholders and calculate the total amount of dividends owed to each shareholder. This total amount is calculated as dividends per share times number of shares owned.

At the date of record, no entry is made. The company is simply trying to find out who owns the shares on this date to determine who is entitled to receive a dividend cheque. On the payment date, the company sends out the cheques to the shareholders and must make an entry to record the reduction in cash and the payment of the liability. SNC-Lavalin would make the following entry for the payment of the dividend declared:

DIVIDEND PAYMENT ENTRY		
L-Dividends payable	2,692,290	
A-Cash		2,692,290

Property Dividends

It is also possible for a company to declare a dividend that will be settled with some resource other than cash. Dividends of this type are called **property dividends** or **dividends in kind**. These dividends are rare because the assets other than cash that can be paid out are necessarily limited to those that can be divided into small, equal parts. A story is told of a liquor company that was short on cash but long on excess inventory and declared a dividend of one bottle per share. Whether or not this actually happened is not as important as the concept it illustrates. If a company issues a property dividend it must be able to give each shareholder the same amount per share.

The major accounting question for property dividends is how to value the dividend. Should the property be valued at its fair market value, or at its cost? In Canada, property dividends are valued at their fair market value because this represents the value the company is giving up to pay the dividend. This means that if the property is currently being carried at cost, a gain or loss must be recognized to bring the property to its fair market value. Suppose that a company declares a property dividend that it will make by transferring inventory with a fair market value of $12,000 to its shareholders. The inventory is recorded at $9,000, which is the original cost to the company. The following entries would be made:

PROPERTY DIVIDEND ENTRIES		
Declaration of dividend (at fair market value)		
SE-Property dividend declared	12,000	
L-Dividend payable		12,000

Recognition of fair market value on declaration date and payment of dividend on payment date:

L-Dividend payable	12,000	
A-Inventory		9,000
SE-Gain on inventory		3,000

Stock Dividends

Stock dividends are dividends that are satisfied by issuing to shareholders additional shares of the company instead of cash or property. Stock dividends can be used to issue dividends when the company does not want to, or is not in a position to, use any of its assets for dividends. Shareholders who receive stock dividends have the option of either keeping the new shares, or selling them for cash.

Whereas the issuance of a cash or property dividend reduces the overall value of the company (because cash or other assets have been removed), the issuance of a stock dividend does not alter the overall value of the company. For example, assume that a company has 100 shares outstanding and that these shares are held by 10 different people, each with 10 shares. In other words, each person owns 10% of the company. If the company issues a 10% stock dividend, it will issue 10 additional shares (100 shares × 10%), one for every 10 shares held. Each shareholder will now have 11 shares and the company will have 110 shares outstanding. Whereas previously the company's value was divided among 100 shares, now it is divided among 110 shares. The overall value of the company has not changed, nor has the percentage ownership of each of the shareholders—they still own 10% each—but the value attached to each share is a little lower.

If shareholders are no better off after a stock dividend than they were before, why would a company issue a stock dividend? There are a couple of good reasons. First, it is possible that the shareholders are better off. Going back to our example, if the market value of the shares prior to the stock dividend was $10, the market would have valued the company at $1,000 ($10 × 100 shares). After the stock dividend there are 110 shares, so the market value of the shares should drop to $9.09 ($1,000/110 shares). If the market price drops to $9.09, each shareholder is no better off. However, often the market price does not fully compensate for the increase in the number of shares. If the market price only drops to $9.15, the shareholder is better off. The market value of a 10% interest would now be $100.65 ($9.15 × 11 shares), whereas previously it was $100 ($10 × 10).

The second reason is that issuing a stock dividend provides an opportunity for the company to *capitalize* its retained earnings. When cash or property dividends were declared and subsequently issued, a temporary account called *Dividends declared* was used. At the end of the accounting period this account is closed into retained earnings, causing it to decrease. When stock dividends are issued, the same procedure will be followed. Retained earnings will decrease. However, at the same time that retained earnings decreases, the Share capital account will increase because more shares were issued. Because the amount in the Share capital account represents stated or legal capital (meaning that it cannot be reduced to issue dividends), the company has taken an amount from an account from which dividends can be issued and put it in an account from which they cannot, thus *capitalizing* it. Companies that have a substantial accumulation of retained earnings but do not have cash available for a dividend will sometimes issue a stock dividend to reduce the retained earnings amount.

As with property dividends, the question that underlies stock dividends is: What value should be attached to the shares that are issued? Should the fair market value of the shares be used, or should some other value be selected?

To answer this question, consider the following extreme situations. When a stock dividend is declared, it is stated as a percentage of the outstanding shares. Suppose a company declares a 100% stock dividend. This means that each shareholder will receive an additional share for each share currently held. No cash changes hands in this transaction. What would you expect to happen to the market value of the shares? It is likely that the value of a share would be cut in half. There is no change in the value of the assets or liabilities of the company, only a doubling of the number of shares that represent ownership. If there is no change in the value of the company, the price per share should adjust for the number of new shares that have been issued. This suggests that the value of the new shares issued is zero.

At the other extreme, suppose that the company issues one additional share as a stock dividend. The recipient of the share can probably sell the share for the fair market value of the existing shares on that date. It is unlikely, assuming that there are large numbers of shares already on the market, that the price per share would adjust for the issuance of this one additional share. In this case, then, the fair market value of the share issued would seem to measure adequately the value of the dividend. In theory, the market price should adjust for the issuance of new shares in a stock dividend, regardless of the number of shares issued. As a practical matter, however, it is unlikely that the market will fully adjust for very small stock dividends, which makes the fair market value of the shares a reasonable measure of the value given up by the company.

How, then, does the company value the shares that are issued in a stock dividend? Since most stock dividends are for relatively small percentages of the shares issued (similar to the second extreme example), most companies account for them by using the fair market value of the shares as at the date of declaration.

The market price that is used to record the issuance of a small stock dividend should be the market price on the date the dividend is declared. In the case of a stock dividend, unlike that of a cash or property dividend, the Board of Directors has the power to revoke the dividend at any time prior to its actual issuance. This means that the dividend does not represent a legal liability to the company on the date of declaration, unlike a cash dividend. For this reason, some companies do not record an entry on the date of declaration. If an entry is recorded, the credit part of the entry is made to a shareholders' equity account called Stock dividends issuable, not to a Dividends payable account. Upon issuance, the credit is made to the shares account and the Stock dividends issuable account is removed.

To illustrate, let us suppose that a company decides to issue a 15% stock dividend when 100,000 shares are outstanding and the market price is $30 per share. The following entries would be made for the declaration and issuance:

SMALL STOCK DIVIDEND ENTRIES		
Declaration		
SE-Dividends declared	450,000	
SE-Stock dividends issuable		450,000
Issuance		
SE-Stock dividends issuable	450,000	
SE-Common shares		450,000

Stock Splits

A transaction very similar to a stock dividend is a **stock split**. A stock split is usually stated as a ratio. A two-for-one stock split is one in which each share currently held by shareholders is exchanged for two new shares. When this is done, the numbers of shares authorized and outstanding are adjusted to compensate for the increase in the number of shares. The number of shares outstanding is doubled. Splits typically involve large numbers of shares, and the arguments discussed earlier with regard to large stock dividends apply here as well. The additional shares cause no increase or decrease in value to the company, so their market price simply adjusts to compensate for the split. If you look back at Exhibit 11-3, you will see that Finning International Inc. had a two-for-one stock split approved at the annual meeting in April 1997.

In accounting for a stock split, there is no change in the dollar amounts of any of the shareholders' equity accounts. No journal entry is made in the accounting system. The only change is in the number of shares issued and outstanding. This change can be made using an informal or memorandum note in the accounting system.

Why would a company want to double or triple the number of shares outstanding? The main reason is that a stock split improves the marketability of a company's shares. As a company grows, the market value of its shares generally rises. The share price can get quite high. As the price rises, fewer investors have the necessary funds to buy the shares. To lower the price so that it is within reach of more investors, the company may split its shares, which will cut the market price per share. IBM, for example, has split its shares numerous times since its incorporation as its price per share escalated.

Stock Options

An **option** on common shares is an agreement between two parties to either buy or sell a share at a fixed price at some future date. There are two types of option related to common shares of which you should be aware. One type is granted by a company to an employee, allowing the employee to purchase the company's shares at a fixed price. This type of option is generally used as a form of remuneration and as an incentive to employees. If employees are also shareholders, and thus owners, they will likely work harder for the company. If the company grows because of their efforts, they benefit from that growth by owning shares that are increasing in value. For example, it was reported in many newspapers in 1996 that an executive with the Potash Company of Saskatchewan earned almost $3 million by cashing in stock options, buying 12,900 shares at $17.50 and selling them the same day at $102.50, and then buying 22,500 shares at $25.50 and selling them at $104.125. You might wonder why the price the executive paid was so low. The stock option plans were probably created several years before the executive exercised the options. At the time the plans were created those prices of $17.50 and $22.50 may not have been that different from the market price. It is not uncommon for large corporations to offer their senior executives stock option plans. It is also not uncommon for the **exercise price** on those plans to be significantly below the market value. If the executive, through effective management, can increase the value of the company, which will translate into an increase in the market value of the company's shares, both the executive and the company will benefit.

Stock option plans offered to employees other than top executives often have exercise prices closer to the market price at the time the plan was created. The rationale for these plans is similar to that for the executive plans. They provide an incentive for the employees to work hard to improve the performance of the company so that the market price of the shares exceeds the exercise price. When the time comes for employees to exercise their options, they pay the exercise price, obtain the shares, and can either sell them for the current market price and realize a profit, or continue to hold the shares in the hope that the price will rise even further. Obviously, if the share price never exceeds the exercise price, the employees will not exercise their options.

Companies normally disclose details regarding their stock option plans. Exhibit 11-5 shows the stock option plans outstanding for Big Rock Brewery on March 31, 1999.

EXHIBIT 11-5

Options

At March 31, 1999, 694,000 common shares were reserved for the exercise of stock options by employees, directors and a consultant to the Company. These options are exercisable as follows:

Expiry Date	No. of Shares	Exercise Price
December 30, 2002	94,000	$ 5.75
December 15, 1999 to October 6, 2002	375,200	$ 7.15
March 20, 2001	14,150	$ 12.63
August 30, 2000	15,000	$ 13.50
October 16, 2000	86,650	$ 13.88
December 15, 1999	109,000	$ 14.65

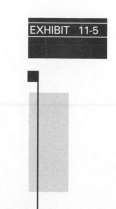

Note that these plans are reserved for employees, directors, and a consultant to the company. It is not specified whether all of these people are part of all of the plans. Note also that the exercise price varies from a low of $5.75 to a high of $14.65 and that the expiry date ranges from December 15, 1999, to December 30, 2002. The market price on November 22, 1999, was $6.00. If the price does not rise, it is unlikely that most of these options will be exercised.

With respect to stock option plans, one of the major questions for accounting purposes is whether to record compensation expense for this type of incentive-based plan. When options are granted, most are not immediately worth anything, since the exercise price may be close to, or even above, the current share price. This situation is sometimes referred to as the option being **out of the money**. In addition, some stock option plans allow employees to exercise them only after a certain period of time, and only if they are still employed by the company. So, even if the option is **in the money**, an employee may not be able to benefit immediately from the granting of the option.

If an option is out of the money, does that mean it is worthless? The answer is a qualified no. Employees may not be able to, nor do they have to, exercise the options immediately. There is generally an extended period of time over which the employees can exercise the option. There may, however, be a specified **expiration date**, after which the option can no longer be exercised. The option will be of some value (in present-value terms) if there is a probability that the share price will exceed the exercise price before the expiration date. The greater the likelihood of this, the higher the value of the option.

Regardless of whether the stock option plans have value, they generally cannot be traded, because they are restricted to the employees to whom they are issued. Therefore, the value of employee stock options is difficult to establish. Under current accounting practice, they are viewed as having no accounting value at the time of granting (when they are out of the money), and no entry is made to record them. Options that are in the money—that is, when the share price is greater than the exercise price as at the date of granting—may be recognized as compensation expense on the date of granting. The expense is measured by the difference between the share price as at the date of granting and the exercise price.

On the date of exercise, the company normally recognizes the receipt of the proceeds from the employee and the issuance of common shares. This entry is no different from any other issuance entry, and the shares are valued at the amount received by the company. No recognition is made of the fair value of the shares at the date of exercise.

A second type of option is a contract between two investors that grants one investor the option to buy (referred to as a **call option**) or to sell (referred to as a **put option**) a company's shares at a fixed price. The shares are bought from, or sold to, the other investor. These options have no effect on the company. They are simply a way for investors to speculate on the share price of a given company. This type of option is traded in open markets, and price quotations for these options appear in newspapers and other financial publications. Because puts and calls have no effect on the company's accounting records, the discussion in this section is restricted to the first type of option, employee stock options.

STATEMENT OF RETAINED EARNINGS

In the preceding discussions of shares and dividends, we made several references to the use of the Retained earnings account. Many companies summarize the changes to their retained earnings in a separate statement, the Statement of Retained Earnings. The format of this statement is very simple. It starts with the opening balance of the retained earnings at the beginning of the year. Then it shows the net income or loss for the year, which comes directly from the income statement. This is followed by the dividends declared in the year. Next appear any other items that affect retained earnings. Finally, the balance of the retained earnings at the end of the year appears. The end balance is the one that appears on the current balance sheet.

An example (for BCE Inc.) is shown in Exhibit 11-6. Note that the balance of the retained earnings at the beginning of the 1998 fiscal year was $596 million, net income (net earnings) for the year was $4,598 million, and dividends of $961 million ($93 million to preferred shareholders and $868 million to common shareholders) were declared. Cancellation of common shares (treasury shares) resulted in a charge of $24 million to retained earnings. This charge to retained earnings means that the price BCE paid for the shares it repurchased exceeded the average issue price of the shares. There was an additional charge of $2 million, which related to legal and financial costs associated with the issuance and repurchase of shares over the year. The balance at the end of the year was $4,207 million. The end balance of $4,207 million is the amount that appears for retained earnings on the December 31, 1998, balance sheet.

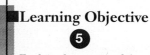

Learning Objective

5

Explain the purpose of the statement of retained earnings.

EXHIBIT 11-6

CONSOLIDATED STATEMENT OF RETAINED EARNINGS

For the years ended December 31	Notes	1998	($ millions) 1997
Balance at beginning of year		596	3,173
Net earnings (loss)		4,598	(1,536)
		5,194	1,637
Deduct:			
Dividends			
Preferred shares		93	74
Common shares		868	865
		961	939
Purchase of common shares for cancellation	(17)	24	93
Costs related to issuance and redemption of share capital of BCE Inc. and of subsidiaries		2	9
		987	1,041
Balance at end of year		4,207	596

BCE Inc. 1998 Annual Report

Reports from Other Countries

The accounting for issuance and retirement of common shares is fairly standard across countries. The greatest difference between Canada and some other countries is the establishment of reserves. Reserves in other countries can be used to set aside retained earnings in separate accounts so that they are unavailable to pay dividends. The part set aside is termed "appropriated retained earnings" and the amount remaining "unappropriated retained earnings." Another way of using reserves is to record changes in the value of assets or liabilities that do not pass through the income statement. In Canada these reserves do not affect earnings for the period. In the United Kingdom property, plant, and equipment can be revalued based on market values. The increase (or decrease) in value does not pass through the income statement but is instead recorded in a separate account in shareholders' equity.

In Japan several types of reserves are permitted in the shareholders' equity section. A portion of the balance sheet and a note of Nippon Steel Corporation are shown in Exhibit 11-7. These disclosures illustrate the use of shareholders' equity reserves. The "legal reserve" is a requirement under the Japanese Commercial Code. The company is required to appropriate a portion of retained earnings as a revenue reserve in amounts equal to at least 10% of cash dividends and exactly 10% of interim cash dividends until the reserve equals 25% of the amount of the capital stock account. Nippon Steel had almost reached the 25% limit by the end of 1998. Note also that the word "reserve" is used in the Nippon Steel report for various liabilities. One of these is also discussed in the note of Nippon Steel. In Canada the use of the word "reserve" is generally discouraged, because users of financial statements may believe it refers to cash that has been set aside, which is erroneous. In Canada its use is limited to references to appropriations of retained earnings.

FINANCIAL STATEMENT ANALYSIS

Price/Earnings Ratio

Learning Objective

6

Calculate and interpret the price/earnings ratio and the return on shareholders' equity ratio that are often used in decision-making.

A key ratio that involves shareholders' equity is **earnings per share**. We introduced this ratio in Chapter 3, and we have discussed it in this chapter as well. Earnings per share provides a measure of the earnings relative to the number of common shares outstanding. It is useful for tracking the return per share earned by the company over time. This ratio can also be related to the current market price per share, by calculating the multiple or **price/earnings ratio**. This is calculated as:

EXHIBIT 11-7

	Millions of yen		Thousands of dollars (Note 3)
	1998	1997	**1998**
LIABILITIES			
Current liabilities:			
Short-term loans and long-term loans due within one year	**¥ 982,162**	¥ 905,999	**$ 7,434,992**
Commercial paper	**10,000**	35,000	**75,700**
Bonds and notes due within one year	**42,372**	80,000	**320,760**
Convertible bonds due within one year	**99,470**	—	**752,990**
Notes and accounts payable (Note 4)	**479,828**	453,959	**3,632,315**
Accrued expenses (Note 4)	**262,493**	278,564	**1,987,078**
Advances received	**72,940**	57,978	**552,162**
Accrued income taxes and enterprise taxes	**38,357**	8,207	**290,367**
Other	**19,677**	25,590	**148,958**
Total current liabilities	**2,007,302**	1,845,298	**15,195,325**
Long-term liabilities:			
Bonds and notes	**532,570**	450,284	**4,031,568**
Convertible bonds	**116,834**	215,573	**884,437**
Long-term loans	**847,643**	788,651	**6,416,681**
Reserve for retirement allowances	**115,538**	128,287	**874,628**
Reserve for repair for blast furnaces	**72,466**	77,307	**548,569**
Other	**45,423**	54,072	**343,858**
Total fixed liabilities	**1,730,476**	1,714,177	**13,099,745**
Minority interests in consolidated subsidiaries	**54,187**	58,925	**410,201**
Total liabilities	**3,791,966**	3,618,401	**28,705,272**
SHAREHOLDERS' EQUITY			
Common stock:			
Authorized — 10,000,000,000 shares			
Issued and outstanding, par value ¥50 per share:			
6,889,903,977 shares of March 31, 1998 and 1997	**419,524**	419,524	**3,175,813**
Statutory reserve:			
Additional paid-in capital	**123,019**	123,019	**931,256**
Legal reserve	**94,513**	92,790	**715,468**
	217,532	215,809	**1,646,725**
Retained earnings	**241,646**	255,802	**1,829,265**
Less: Treasury stock, at cost	**(0)**	(1)	**(3)**
Total shareholders' equity	**878,702**	891,134	**6,651,801**
Total liabilities and shareholders' equity	**¥4,670,669**	¥4,509,536	**$35,357,073**

2. Significant Accounting Policies

(8) Reserve for Repair for Blast Furnaces
The Company's blast furnaces and hot blast stoves including related machines periodically require substantial component replacements, overhauls and repairs. The estimated future costs of such work are provided for and charged to income on a straight-line basis over the periods to the dates of the anticipated replacements and repairs.

In the year ended March 31, 1998, the Company reestimated the provision of reserve for repair based on reflecting a recent technical renovation and its reduced repair costs of blast furnaces and as a result, a reversal of the reserve for repair is shown in the accompanying Consolidated Statements of Income.

$$\frac{\text{Market price per share}}{\text{Earnings per share}}$$

The ratio relates the accounting earnings to the market price at which the shares trade. If two companies in the same industry had the same earnings per share of $5, and Company A's shares were selling for $25 and Company B's shares were selling for $50, the price/earnings ratio would be different. Company A's price/earnings ratio would be 5 ($25/$5) and Company B's would be 10 ($50/$5). The market is placing a higher value on Company B's shares. There are probably many reasons for the higher valuation, such as an assessment of higher earning potential in the future, a lower risk with respect to debt repayment, or an assessment of future market share. When evaluating the price/earnings ratio of a company, it is important for the user to compare the ratio with other companies in the same industry. This comparison will yield information about how the market is valuing the company in relation to others.

Return on Shareholders' Equity Ratio

Another useful indicator of return is **return on shareholders' equity**. This is a more general measure than earnings per share, because it relates the net income available to common shares to the total of the common shareholders' equity. It is calculated as follows:

$$\text{ROE} = \frac{\text{Net income} - \text{Preferred dividends}}{\text{Average common shareholders' equity}}$$

Preferred dividends need to be subtracted from the net income, because preferred shareholders have a senior claim on the income. Preferred dividends must be declared before dividends on common shares. We want this ratio to determine a measure of return to the common shares only. Common shareholders' equity is the shareholders' equity less any amounts that represent owners other than common shareholders. This means that the amount in the preferred shares account would need to be subtracted from the denominator.

This ratio tells you the return the common shareholder is earning on each dollar of income. For Big Rock Brewery in 1999 and 1998 that return is ($0.033) (($556,745)/($16,447,657 + $17,431,383)/2) and $0.017 ($288,981/($17,431,383 + $17,442,402)/2), respectively. Big Rock has no preferred shares issued, so all of the net income (or loss as in 1999) accrues to the common shareholders. The return to common shareholders is negative in 1999 because of the loss of $556,745 incurred that year.

More detailed discussion of other analyses that involve shareholders' equity can be found in Chapter 12.

SUMMARY

This chapter discussed the most common forms of business organization, sole proprietorships, partnerships, and corporations. Advantages and disadvantages for each form were discussed. Because the predominant business structure is the corporation, this form was discussed in more detail. Particular attention was paid to shares. Corporations authorize different types or classes of shares with the intent of attracting capital investment. These shares come with different rights and privileges.

Shareholders are given a return from the company in the form of dividends. Dividends can come in various forms—cash, property, or stock. This section concluded with a brief discussion of stock splits and employee stock option plans.

Because this chapter is devoted to shareholders' equity, we discussed the fourth financial statement, the statement of retained earnings. An example from BCE Inc. was included as an illustration.

The chapter concluded with two ratios, the price/earnings ratio and the return on shareholders' equity ratio (ROE). These two ratios help investors evaluate the current return to common shareholders.

This concludes the discussion of the primary accounts on the balance sheet. In the final chapter of the book, financial statement analysis will be summarized. For those of you who have an interest in understanding some of the complexity behind consolidated financial statements, there is a further discussion of complex companies in Appendix C. This has been included in an appendix because it involves more complex issues that require an understanding of the basic issues we have already discussed, and most introductory courses will not choose to examine this topic.

SUMMARY PROBLEM

The Balukas Company had the following shareholders' equity section balances at December 31, 20x1:

Common shares	$4,700,000
(Unlimited number of common shares authorized, 240,000 shares issued)	
Retained earnings	4,000,000
Total shareholders' equity	$8,700,000

During 20x2, the following transactions occurred:

a. On January 2, 20x2, Balukas repurchased 5,000 of its own common shares at $35 per share and immediately cancelled them.

b. On March 15, 20x2, Balukas issued 10,000 new shares and received proceeds of $40 per share.

c. On June 29, 20x2, Balukas declared and paid a 10% stock dividend. The market price of Balukas' shares on June 29, 20x2, was $45 per share.

d. On June 30, 20x2, Balukas declared a cash dividend of $3.00 per share to shareholders of record on July 15, 20x2, payable on July 31, 20x2.

e. On September 1, 20x2, Balukas issued 100,000 new shares at a price of $50 per share.

f. On December 31, 20x2, Balukas declared a four-for-one stock split.

Required:

1. Construct journal entries for each of the transactions as they occurred during 20x2.

2. Explain why no journal entry was made for transaction f.

SUGGESTED SOLUTION TO SUMMARY PROBLEM

1. a. Repurchase of common shares and cancellation entry:

SE-Common shares	97,917[a]	
SE-Retained earnings	77,083	
A-Cash		175,000

[a]$4,700,000/240,000 \times 5,000 = \$97,917$

b. Common share issuance entry:

A-Cash	400,000	
SE-Common Shares		400,000

c. Small stock dividend entries:

Declaration

SE-Dividends declared	1,102,500[b]	
SE-Stock dividend issuable		1,102,500

Issuance

SE-Stock dividend issuable	1,102,500	
SE-Common Shares		1,102,500

[b]Number of shares $= 240,000 - 5,000 + 10,000 = 245,000$ shares
245,000 shares $\times 10\% \times \$45$ per share $= \$1,102,500$

d. On June 30, 19x2

SE-Dividends declared	808,500[c]	
L-Dividends payable		808,500

On July 31, 19x2

L-Dividends payable	808,500	
A-Cash		808,500

[c]245,000 shares $+$ 24,500 shares $=$ 269,500 shares
269,500 shares $\times \$3.00$ per share $= \$808,500$

e. Issue of new shares

A-Cash	5,000,000	
SE-Common Shares		5,000,000

f. No entry is needed. However, a memorandum entry could be made to indicate that the number of shares outstanding has changed from 369,500 to 1,478,000.

2. During a stock split or a large stock dividend, the number of shares increases but the value of the company does not change. The purpose of the stock split is to lower the current market price of the company's shares. In the four-for-one split that was used in the sample problem, the market price would immediately drop to one quarter of the price before the split. The lower price would make the shares accessible to more investors.

SYNONYMS

Exercise price/Strike price/Option price

Property dividends/Dividends in kind

GLOSSARY

Articles of incorporation A document filed with federal or provincial regulatory authorities when a business incorporates under that jurisdiction. The articles include, among other items, the authorized number of shares and dividend preferences for each class of shares that is to be issued.

Authorized shares The maximum number of shares that a company is authorized to issue under its articles of incorporation.

Call option An option that gives the holder the right to buy shares at a fixed price stated in the contract.

Capital account An account used in a partnership or proprietorship to record the investment and accumulated earnings of each owner.

Common shares Certificates that represent portions of ownership in a corporation. These shares usually carry a right to vote.

Convertible preferred shares Preferred shares that are exchangeable or convertible into a specified number of common shares.

Corporation A form of business in which the shareholders have limited liability and the business entity is taxed directly. Shareholders receive distributions from the entity in the form of dividends.

Cumulative preferred shares Preferred shares that accumulate dividends that are not declared from one period to the next. These accumulated dividends, called dividends in arrears, must be paid before a dividend can be declared for common shareholders.

Date of declaration The date the board of directors votes to declare a dividend. On this date, the dividend becomes legally payable to shareholders.

Date of payment The date on which a dividend is paid to shareholders.

Date of record The date on which a shareholder must own the shares in order to receive the dividend from a share.

Dividend declaration An action by the board of directors of a corporation that makes payment of a dividend a legal obligation of the corporation.

Dividends Payments to shareholders from the total net income retained in a company in the Retained earnings account.

Dividends in arrears Dividends on cumulative preferred shares that have not yet been declared from a prior year.

Dividends in kind Synonym for property dividends.

Drawings account An account used in a partnership or proprietorship to record the cash withdrawals by owners.

Employee stock option An option granted to an employee to buy shares at a fixed price, usually as part of an incentive compensation plan.

Ex-dividend day A date specified in the shares market on which the shares are sold without the most recently declared dividend.

Exercise price The price per share that is required to be paid by the holder of a stock option upon exercise.

Expiration date In the context of stock options, the date on which the option holder must either exercise the option or lose it.

General partners The partners that have unlimited liability in a limited partnership.

In-the-money option An option that would be worth something if exercised immediately.

Issued shares The shares of a corporation that have been issued.

Limited liability A feature of share ownership that restricts the liability of shareholders to the amount they have invested in the corporation.

Limited partners The partners in a limited partnership that have limited liability.

Limited partnership A partnership that allows some partners to have limited liability (limited partners) and others to have unlimited liability (general partners).

Memorandum entry An entry made to record a stock split. No amounts are affected; only the record of the number of shares issued is affected.

No-par value shares Shares that have no par value associated with them.

Option A contract that grants the holder an option to engage in certain types of transactions. In the case of stock options, the contract usually grants the holder the right to buy (call option) or sell (put option) shares at a fixed price (strike price).

Out-of-the-money option   An option that would be worthless if exercised immediately, because the market value is less than the exercise price.

Outstanding shares   The number of shares of a corporation that are held by individuals or entities outside the corporation (i.e., not including treasury shares).

Par value   A value per share of common shares set in the articles of incorporation.

Participating preferred shares   Preferred shares that can participate in dividends declared beyond the level specified by the preferred shares—that is, beyond the fixed dividend payout specified in the preferred shares contract.

Partnership   A form of business in which the owners have unlimited legal liability and the business entity is not taxed directly, but the income from the entity passes through to the partners' individual tax returns.

Partnership agreement   An agreement between the partners in a partnership that specifies how the individual partners will share in the risks and rewards of ownership of the partnership entity.

Preemptive right   The right of shareholders to share proportionately in new issuances of shares.

Preferred shares   An ownership right in which the shareholder has some preference as to dividends; that is, if dividends are declared, the preferred shareholder receives them first. Other rights that normally are held by common shareholders may also be changed in preferred shares; for example, many issues of preferred shares are nonvoting.

Property dividend   A dividend that is satisfied with the transfer of some type of property other than cash.

Prospectus   A document filed with a securities commission by a corporation when it plans to issue public debt or shares.

Put option   An option that provides the holder with the option to sell something at a fixed price (strike price).

Redeemable preferred shares   Preferred shares that can be bought back (redeemed) by the corporation under certain conditions and at a price stated in the articles of incorporation.

Retractable preferred shares   Shares that can be sold back to the company (retired) at the option of the shareholder. The price that must be paid for them and the periods of time within which they can be sold are specified in the articles of incorporation.

Sole proprietorship   A form of business in which there is a single owner (sole proprietor). This form is characterized by unlimited liability to the owner and exemption from corporate taxation.

Stated value   A value per share for common shares established in the articles of incorporation.

Stock dividends   Distribution of additional common shares to shareholders. Existing shareholders receive shares in proportion to the number of shares they already own.

Stock split   Distribution of new shares to shareholders. The new shares take the place of existing shares, and existing shareholders receive new shares in proportion to the number of old shares they already own.

Treasury shares   Shares that are repurchased by a corporation and held internally. Repurchased shares are normally cancelled immediately upon purchase.

Unlimited liability   A characteristic of sole proprietorships and partnerships rendering the owners personally responsible for the liabilities incurred by the business entity.

ASSIGNMENT MATERIAL

Assessing Your Recall

11-1 Characterize the following forms of business in terms of the legal liability of the owners and their tax status: corporations, sole proprietorships, partnerships, and limited partnerships.

11-2 Discuss the purpose of a partnership agreement.

11-3 Describe what is contained in the articles of incorporation and what significance they have for the accounting system.

11-4 List and briefly describe the four rights that common shareholders typically have in a corporation.

11-5 Discuss how preferred shares differ from common shares.

11-6 Briefly describe what each of the following features means in a preferred shares issue:

- a. Participating
- b. Cumulative
- c. Convertible
- d. Redeemable

11-7 Briefly describe each of the following terms: authorized shares, issued shares, and outstanding shares.

11-8 Describe the process of declaring and paying a cash dividend, including information about the declaration date, date of record, and payment date.

11-9 Explain what property dividends are and why they are not used very often by companies.

11-10 Discuss the nature of a stock dividend and why a distinction is made between small and large stock dividends.

11-11 Compare and contrast a 100% stock dividend with a two-for-one stock split.

11-12 Discuss why companies issue employee stock options and what immediate and potential effects these options have on the financial results of the company.

11-13 Explain why companies might declare a stock dividend rather than a cash dividend.

11-14 Describe what the price/earnings ratio is attempting to tell users about a company.

11-15 Explain why the return on shareholders' equity provides information on return to common shareholders only.

Applying Your Knowledge

11-16 (Selecting a business entity)
Indicate whether each of the following business entities is more likely to be established as a sole proprietorship (SP), a partnership (P), or a corporation (C). Provide reasons for your choice.

- a. A dental practice having five dentists.
- b. A clothing store that has six different locations in Ontario.
- c. A paint and body shop owned by Fred Weeks.
- d. A lumber company operating in British Columbia.
- e. A family of three brothers who decided to jointly operate a farm in Saskatchewan.
- f. A lobster fisher from Nova Scotia who owns two boats.

11-17 (Selecting a business entity)
Indicate whether each of the following business entities is more likely to be established as a sole proprietorship (SP), a partnership (P), or a corporation (C). Provide reasons for your choice.

a. Mary's hairstyling salon.

b. A local investment firm consisting of four financial advisors.

c. A potash company.

d. A real estate development company that specializes in shopping malls.

e. One of the big five accounting firms.

f. A car dealership owned by a mother and son.

11-18 (Business formation)

Albert Wong just graduated from university and is planning to start his own software development company. He is trying to decide on the best form of business organization and is debating between setting up practice as a sole proprietor or establishing a corporate entity and serving as its president.

Required:

a. What advantages would there be to operating as a sole proprietorship?

b. What advantages would there be to operating as a corporation?

c. Which form of business organization would his customers likely prefer? Why?

d. Which form of business would be most advantageous to Albert Wong if he anticipated that the business would grow rapidly? Why?

11-19 (Business formation)

Janice Allen just inherited a large amount of money from her grandfather. She intends to start her own architectural company and plans within a few years to expand the operation by bringing in other architects.

Required:

a. What advantages would there be to operating as a sole proprietorship?

b. What advantages would there be to operating as a corporation?

c. What advantages would there be to begin operations as a sole proprietorship and then to switch to a partnership when she expands?

d. Which form of business organization would her customers likely prefer? Why?

e. Which form of business would be most advantageous to Janice Allen if she wanted to maintain control as the business expanded? Why?

11-20 (Equity transactions)

Explain how and by what amount each of the following transactions affects individual shareholders' equity accounts and total shareholders' equity of Northern Lights Ltd.

a. Northern Lights authorizes the issuance of 1,000,000 common shares and 200,000 preferred shares which pay a dividend of $5 each.

b. 100,000 common shares are issued for $15 a share.

c. 20,000 preferred shares are issued for $45 per share.

d. The full annual dividend on the preferred shares is declared.

e. A dividend of $0.20 is declared on the common shares.

f. Both dividends are paid.

g. Northern Lights earns income for the year of $290,000.

11-21 (Equity transactions)
Southern Exposure Ltd. began operations on January 2, 20x1. During the year the following transactions occurred that affected shareholders' equity:

a. Southern Exposure authorized the issuance of 300,000 common shares and 80,000 preferred shares which pay a dividend of $1.50 per share.

b. 90,000 common shares are issued for $12 a share.

c. 25,000 preferred shares are issued for $18 per share.

d. The full annual dividend on the preferred shares was declared and paid.

e. A dividend of $0.75 per share is declared on the common shares but is not yet paid.

f. The company earns income of $240,000 for the year.

g. The dividends on the common shares are paid.

h. A 2% stock dividend is declared on the common shares and distributed. On the date of declaration the market price of the shares was $15.

Required:
Prepare journal entries to record the above transactions.

11-22 (Equity transactions)
Marshall Investigations was owned by four retired police officers. They set up their business as a corporation and during the first year the following transactions occurred:

a. 10,000 common shares were issued to the four owners (2,500 shares each) at $25 per share.

b. 10,000 preferred shares were issued to people other than the owners at $35 per share. The company was authorized to issue 25,000 preferred shares.

c. A dividend of $2 per share was declared for the preferred shareholders.

d. The dividend declared in part c. was paid.

e. The company purchased 500 of its own common shares from one of its owners at an agreed price of $50 per share and immediately cancelled them.

f. During the first year of operations the company earned income of $120,000.

Required:
Prepare journal entries to record the above transactions.

11-23 (Equity transactions)
Green Grocers Ltd. had been operating for several years. It had an unlimited number of common shares authorized and 750,000 shares issued. As well, there were 200,000 preferred shares authorized and 50,000 issued. The preferred shares paid a dividend of $1.00 per share. During 20x1, the following transactions affecting shareholders' equity occurred:

a. 50,000 common shares were issued at $15 per share.

b. The preferred dividend for the year was declared and paid.

c. A 10% comon stock dividend was declared when the market price of the shares was $18. The shares were distributed one month after the declaration.

d. At the very end of the year, a common dividend of $1.50 per share was declared on the common shares. It would be paid in the following year.

e. The company earned income of $2,350,000.

Required:
Prepare journal entries to record the above transactions.

11-24 (Equity transactions)
Give journal entries for the following transactions. If no journal entry is required, explain why.

   a. A two-for-one stock split has been declared by a company that has 80,000 common shares authorized and 40,000 shares outstanding. The shares were originally issued for $5 each and have a market value of $50 each prior to the split.

   b. A 10% stock dividend is declared on the outstanding shares when the market value of each share is $30.

   c. Stock dividends declared in part b. are satisfied with the issuance of shares.

   d. The company purchases 10,000 of its own shares at a market price of $28 per share and cancels them. (Hint: Calculate the average carrying value per share.)

11-25 (Share issuance, repurchase, and cancellation)
On December 31, 20x1, the shareholders' equity section of Ortegren Ltd.'s balance sheet appears as follows:

Preferred shares, no par, $8, redeemable, 50,000 shares authorized, 10,000 shares issued	$ 3,000,000
Common shares, no par, unlimited number authorized, 500,000 shares issued	5,820,000
Retained earnings	5,438,000
Total shareholders' equity	$14,258,000

During 20x2 the following events occurred:

   a. Ortegren issued 40,000 additional common shares for $35 per share.

   b. The company declared and paid the dividend on the preferred shares for the first half of the year.

   c. Immediately after paying the preferred dividend for the first half of the year, the company repurchased the shares on the market for $103 per share.

   d. The company earned income of $966,000 for 20x2.

Required:

   a. Prepare journal entries to record the above transactions.

   b. Prepare the shareholders' equity section of the balance sheet as at December 31, 20x2.

   c. Give possible reasons why Ortegren might change its equity financing by eliminating the preferred shares and issuing more common shares.

11-26 (Stock dividends)
Timmerman Company has 45,000 common shares outstanding. Because it wants to use its cash flow for other purposes, the company has decided to issue stock dividends to its shareholders. The market price of each of Timmerman Company's shares is $60. Give the journal entries for recording the issuance of the stock dividend if:

   a. The company decides to issue a 5% stock dividend.

   b. The company decides to issue a 100% stock dividend.

11-27 (Issuance of shares)

Jimenez Company Ltd. incorporated on June 5 with an unlimited number of authorized common shares. Shortly thereafter, the company issued 50,000 common shares for $30 per share and a month later issued another 10,000 shares for $32 per share. During the remainder of the year, the company incurred a net loss of $47,000 from its operations.

Required:

Prepare the shareholders' equity section of Jimenez Company's balance sheet as at the end of the year.

11-28 (Change in shareholders' equity)

The shareholders' equity of Bamber Ltd. at the end of 2002 and 2001 appears as follows:

	2002	2001
Preferred shares, no par, $1, 50,000 shares authorized, 10,000 shares issued	$100,000	$100,000
Common shares, no par, 1,000,000 shares authorized, 200,000 shares issued (2001 − 180,000 shares)	446,000	305,000
Retained earnings	510,000	430,000
Total shareholders' equity	$1,056,000	$835,000

During 2002, Bamber paid a total of $30,000 in cash dividends.

Required:

a. Assuming the preferred shares were not in arrears, how was the $30,000 in cash dividends distributed between the two classes of shares?

b. Both the common shares and the retained earnings changed during the year. Suggest explanations that would account for the changes.

c. Compute the amount of each of the items that caused the changes.

11-29 (Equity transactions)

The following information relates to the shareholders' equity section of Johnson Ltd. (in thousands):

	December 31, 20x2	December 31, 20x1
Preferred shares (10,000 shares outstanding)	$5,000	$ 5,000
Common shares (375,000 shares outstanding)	?	7,500
Retained earnings	4,400	3,750
Total shareholders' equity	?	$16,250

During 20x2, 10,000 common shares were issued at a price of $32 per share. Cash dividends of $750,000 and $100,000 were paid to common shareholders and preferred shareholders, respectively. The company acquired 15,000 treasury shares during the year at $28 per share and held them. The company issued 5,000 common shares under employee stock option plans at $25 per share.

Required:

a. Calculate the ending balance in common shares at the end of 20x2.

b. Calculate the amount of net income reported in 20x2.

11-30 (Equity transactions)

Give the journal entries for the following shareholders' equity transactions of the Green Sleeves Apparel Company:

a. On January 10, 20x1, the articles of incorporation are filed with the provincial secretary. The company is authorized to issue 1,000,000 common shares and 100,000 cumulative preferred shares which carry a dividend of $10.00 per share.

b. On January 12, 20x1, the company issues 75,000 common shares at $25 each.

c. On January 15, 20x1, the assets of Tritex Knits Ltd. are acquired in exchange for 20,000 common shares and 10,000 preferred shares. The market value of the common shares was $25 and the preferred shares $100 on this date. The assets acquired and their relative fair market values are: land, $500,000; equipment, $250,000; inventory, $200,000; building, $500,000; and accounts receivable, $50,000.

d. On January 20, 20x1, 25,000 of the preferred shares are issued at $100 per share.

e. No dividends are declared in 20x1.

f. On December 2, 20x2, cash dividends are declared on the preferred shares. Once the dividends are paid on the date of payment, January 10, 20x3, no preferred dividends will be in arrears.

g. On December 2, 20x2, a 10% stock dividend is declared for the common shares. The market price of the common shares on this date is $72 per share. The shares are issued on December 15, 20x2, when the market price per share is $75.

11-31 (Issuance of shares)

The Mattle Company was formed on January 1, 20x1, and the shareholders' equity section of the balance sheet on December 31, 20x1, appeared as follows:

Shareholders' Equity as at December 31, 20x1:

$4 Preferred Shares	$250,000
Common Shares	380,000
Retained Earnings	130,000
Total Shareholders' Equity	$760,000

During 20x1, the following transactions took place:

a. Common shares were issued at a price of $50 a share.

b. Preferred shares were issued at $50 per share.

c. 1,000 common shares were acquired at $50 per share and immediately cancelled.

d. A preferred dividend was declared and paid for the year.

e. A cash dividend of $5 per share was declared and paid to common shareholders at year end.

The transactions just listed were the only share capital transactions that occurred during the entire year.

Required:

Given this information, answer the following questions:

a. How many common shares were issued?

b. How many preferred shares were issued?

c. How much net income was reported during the year?

11-32 (Income statement and statement of retained earnings)
The following are selected account balances from Darby Ltd.'s trial balance on December 31, 20x1:

Revenues	$2,240,000
Cost of goods sold	925,700
Wage expense	340,800
Amortization expense	145,000
Miscellaneous expense	220,900
Interest expense	42,000
Preferred dividends declared	167,000
Common dividends declared	252,600
Retained earnings, Jan. 1, 20x1	4,239,500

Required:
Prepare the 20x1 income statement and retained earnings statement in good form for Darby Ltd. Based on this information, how likely does the continuation of Darby's common dividend appear to be? Explain.

Management Perspective Problems

11-33 (New share issuance)
You are a loan officer at a bank. You helped Cedar Ltd. arrange a $1.5-million, 20-year mortgage with your bank just six months ago. Cedar Ltd. has just announced an issuance of new shares from which it intends to raise $5 million. How do you think this new issuance will affect the bank's outstanding loan? Identify some positive outcomes and some negative ones.

11-34 (Price/earnings ratio)
As a stock analyst, explain the importance of the price/earnings ratio.

11-35 (Investment banker)
As an investment banker, describe some of the services that you would perform for a company.

11-36 (Stock dividends and splits)
The shareholders' equity section of Bonanza Ltd.'s balance sheet appears as follows on December 31, 2001:

Common shares, 1,000,000 authorized,	
100,000 issued and outstanding	$2,500,000
Retained earnings	2,345,000
Total shareholders' equity	$4,845,000

Near the beginning of 2002, Bonanza declared and distributed a 10% stock dividend. At the date of declaration, the common shares were selling for $89 per share. By the end of October, the price of the shares had risen to $104 per share. Bonanza's Board of Directors decided to split the shares four-for-one. Late in December, the Board declared a cash dividend on the common shares of $1 per share, payable in early January 2003. In past years, the dividend generally had been about $3 per share. During 2002, Bonanza Ltd. earned net income of $2,355,000.

Required:

a. Prepare the shareholders' equity section of Bonanza's balance sheet at December 31, 2002.

b. What effect has each dividend had on the individual shareholders' equity accounts of Bonanza and on Bonanza's total shareholders' equity?

c. What reasons might the company have for declaring a stock dividend? What is your assessment of these reasons?

d. What reasons might the company have for splitting its shares? What is your assessment of these reasons?

e. If you were one of Bonanza's common shareholders, would you be happy or unhappy with the stock dividend and split? Why? What do you think about the reduction in the cash dividend from $3 to $1? Explain.

11-37 (Retained earnings and dividends)

You have recently been considering investing in some of Cascade Ltd.'s common shares. The company has been relatively profitable over the years and prospects for the future look good. However, it recently has had to make heavy expenditures for new capital assets. The company's summarized balance sheet at the end of 2001 is as follows:

Cash	$ 50,000
Other current assets	943,000
Capital assets (net)	8,279,000
Total	$9,272,000
Current liabilities	$ 588,000
Long-term debt	2,500,000
Common shares	4,000,000
Retained earnings	2,184,000
Total	$9,272,000

The company has 200,000 common shares outstanding and its earnings per share has increased by at least 10% in each of the last 10 years. In several recent years, earnings per share increased by more than 15%. Given the company's earnings and the amount of its retained earnings, you judge that it could easily pay cash dividends of $2 or $3 per share resulting in hardly a dent in retained earnings.

Required:

a. Evaluate the prospects of your receiving a cash dividend from Cascade during the next year if you were to purchase its shares.

b. Evaluate the prospects of your receiving a cash dividend from Cascade during the next five years if you were to purchase its shares.

c. Suppose Cascade borrowed cash of $2 million on a five-year bank loan to provide working capital and additional operating flexibility. While no collateral would be required, the loan would stipulate that no dividends be paid in any year in which the ratio of long-term debt to equity was greater than 2 to 3. Evaluate your prospects for receiving cash dividends from Cascade in the short term and during the next five years if Cascade were to enter into the loan agreement.

11-38 (Cash dividends)

You have been considering buying some common shares of Basker Ltd. Basker has 1,000,000 common shares outstanding. The company has been through difficult times but now is doing better. Your main concern is whether you will receive cash dividends. In addition to the common shares, the company has 20,000 shares of $1, no par, Class A preferred outstanding which are noncumulative and nonparticipating. The company also has 50,000 shares of $6, no par, Class B preferred outstanding. These shares are nonparticipating but are cumulative. The normal dividend was paid on both classes of preferred shares until last year, when no dividends were paid. This year, however, Basker is doing exceptionally well and is expecting net income of $3,600,000. The company has not yet declared its annual dividends but has indicated that it plans to pay total dividends equal to 40% of net income. If you immediately buy 2,000 shares of Basker Ltd. on the stock market:

a. What amount of common dividend would you expect to receive?

b. What amount of common dividend would you expect to receive if the Class B preferred shares were noncumulative?

11-39 (Return on investment)

Stanley Corporation Ltd.'s balance sheet appears as follows:

Cash	$ 160,000
Other current assets	1,842,000
Capital assets (net)	7,841,000
Total	$9,843,000
Current liabilities	$ 512,000
Long-term debt	2,500,000
Preferred shares	1,000,000
Common shares	2,500,000
Retained earnings	3,331,000
Total	$9,843,000

For the year just ended, Stanley reported net income of $928,000. During the year, the company declared preferred dividends of $80,000 and common dividends of $300,000.

Required:

a. Compute the following ratios for Stanley:

   1. Return on assets

   2. Return on long-term capital (long-term debt + shareholders' equity)

   3. Return on common shareholders' equity (do not include the preferred shares)

b. If the company's interest expense related to its long-term debt was $135,000 for the year, after taxes, and the long-term debt could have been replaced with $2,500,000 worth of common shares, what would the return on common shareholders' equity have been for the year without debt financing? What does this imply about the desirability of this company using long-term debt? Will this always be true? Explain.

c. Suppose the company had issued the long-term debt shown on the balance sheet, but had issued an additional $1,000,000 worth of common shares rather than the preferred shares. What would the return on common shareholders' equity have been? What does this imply about the desirability of this company using preferred shares?

Reading and Interpreting Published Financial Statements

11-40 (Share transactions)

The balance sheets of Sears Canada Inc. and Note 10 at January 2, 1999, and January 3, 1998, are shown in Exhibit 11-8.

| EXHIBIT 11-8 PART A | *Consolidated Statements of Financial Position* | SEARS CANADA |

As at January 2, 1999 and January 3, 1998 (in millions)	1998	1997
Assets		
Current Assets		
Cash and short-term investments	$ 190.4	$ 68.3
Charge account receivables (Note 2)	595.0	690.1
Other receivables (Note 3)	505.4	534.5
Inventories	738.7	640.3
Prepaid expenses and other assets	57.4	48.9
Future income tax assets (Note 4)	61.6	41.9
	2,148.5	2,024.0
Investments and Other Assets (Note 5)	50.9	22.8
Net Capital Assets (Note 6)	867.6	825.1
Deferred Charges (Note 7)	131.0	135.4
	$ 3,198.0	$ 3,007.3
Liabilities		
Current Liabilities		
Accounts payable	$ 683.4	$ 560.2
Accrued liabilities	312.4	318.4
Income and other taxes payable	90.8	162.7
Principal payments on long-term obligations due within one year (Note 9)	163.4	11.6
	1,250.0	1,052.9
Long-term Obligations (Note 9)	680.5	836.1
Future Income Tax Liabilities (Note 4)	103.2	75.9
	2,033.7	1,964.9
Shareholders' Equity		
Capital Stock (Note 10)	451.8	450.9
Retained Earnings	712.5	591.5
	1,164.3	1,042.4
	$ 3,198.0	$ 3,007.3

Approved by the Board:

P.S. Walters
P.S. Walters
Director

J.M. Tory
J.M. Tory
Director

10. CAPITAL STOCK

An unlimited number of common shares are authorized. Changes in the number of outstanding common shares and their stated values since December 29, 1996 are as follows:

	1998		1997	
	Number of shares	**Stated value (millions)**	Number of shares	Stated value (millions)
Beginning Balance	**105,959,504**	**$ 450.9**	105,610,910	$ 448.3
Issued pursuant to stock options	**124,460**	**0.9**	348,594	2.6
Ending Balance	**106,083,964**	**$ 451.8**	105,959,504	$ 450.9

Details of stock option transactions under the Employees Stock Plan, including Special Incentive Awards, as at January 2, 1999, are set out below. Special Incentive Awards of options and shares are awarded to Senior Officers of the Company on a conditional basis, subject to achievement of specified performance criteria, within specified vesting periods. In 1998, 140,000 shares were awarded as Special Incentive Awards, 40,000 of which are subject to Plan amendment and obtaining requisite approvals. No shares were issued during the year under Special Incentive Awards.

Options granted and accepted	Option price	Expiry date	Options exercised	Options outstanding
175,975	$ 5.69	Feb. 1998	170,325	-
142,150	$ 7.53	Feb. 1999	110,575	31,575
195,200	$ 7.49	Feb. 2000	144,542	50,658
232,301	$ 5.58	Feb. 2001	182,483	49,818
275,730	$ 5.58	Feb. 2006	70,605	205,125
60,000	$ 9.72	Nov. 2006	-	60,000
286,750	$ 10.65	Jan. 2007	23,006	263,744
30,000	$ 10.82	Feb. 2007	10,000	20,000
306,870	$ 19.63	Jan. 2008	-	306,870
26,000	$ 24.73	Apr. 2008	-	26,000

Special Incentive Award Options

170,000	$ 22.75	Feb. 2008	-	170,000
825,000	$ 28.75	Jul. 2008	-	825,000

Options to purchase up to 342,870 common shares have been authorized to be granted under the Employees Stock Plan in 1999.

In April, 1998, the Company established the Directors' Stock Option Plan to grant stock options to Directors who are not Executive Officers of the Company or Sears, Roebuck and Co. In 1998, 9,000 stock options were granted to six Directors at an option price of $25.98. The options expire in April, 2008. No options were exercised during the year.

The Company is authorized to issue an unlimited number of non-voting, redeemable and retractable Class 1 Preferred Shares in one or more series. As at January 2, 1999, the only shares outstanding were the common shares of the Company.

Required:

a. Reconstruct all journal entries that affected shares for the year ended January 2, 1999.

b. Reconstruct all journal entries that affected shares for the year ended January 3, 1998.

c. Calculate the balance in the common shares account as at December 29, 1996.

d. Reconcile the number of shares outstanding from January 3, 1998, to January 2, 1999.

e. Calculate how many common shares were outstanding on December 29, 1996.

f. Calculate the return on shareholders' equity for the year ended January 2, 1999. Net income for the year ended January 2, 1999, was $146,400,000.

11-41 (Stock options and warrants)
The balance sheets, income statements (called Statement of Operations), and Note 8 of H. Jager Developments Inc. as at February 28, 1999 and 1998, are shown in Exhibit 11-9.

Required:

a. Note that H. Jager had a number of stock options and share purchase warrants outstanding at February 28, 1999. Explain what stock options and warrants are.

b. Who holds the options and warrants?

c. Why would H. Jager have issued these options and warrants?

d. Assume that all of the options and warrants were exercised on March 1, 1998, for the prices specified (for the purposes of this question, ignore when the options and warrants were actually issued). How much additional cash would H. Jager have had to invest during the 1999 fiscal year?

e. Assume that H. Jager could earn 10% after taxes on additional investments. Calculate the net income H. Jager would have earned for 1999 after the activities described in part d.

f. Calculate the revised basic earnings per share that H. Jager would have reported for 1999 if d. and e. had occurred. (Hint: Remember that both net income and the number of shares outstanding change.)

g. Calculate the return on shareholders' equity for the year ended February 28, 1999.

11-42 (Effect of share issuances)
The 1998 and 1997 balance sheets for Mackenzie Financial Corporation and Note 9 as at March 31, 1998, are shown in Exhibit 11-10.

Required:

a. Reconstruct all journal entries that affected common shares for the year ended March 31, 1998. Under what circumstances and at what price were the additional shares issued?

b. Assuming that all holders of stock options exercise all warrants outstanding on March 31, 1998, what is the minimum amount of cash that Mackenzie will receive? What is the maximum amount of cash that Mackenzie could receive?

EXHIBIT 11-9
PART A

H. Jager Developments Inc.
Consolidated Balance Sheets

February 28	1999	1998
Assets		
Cash	$ 6,014	$ 28,341
Receivables	124,796	17,477
Agreements receivable	799,362	–
Deposits	100,371	249,663
Land under development	6,659,849	7,214,095
Resort facilities (Note 4)	469,919	496,481
Investment (Note 5)	–	236,406
	$ 8,160,311	$ 8,242,463
Liabilities		
Payables and accruals	$ 426,121	$ 866,179
Customer advances	14,370	43,716
Payable to related parties (Note 6)	220,815	167,901
Morgages and loans (Note 7)	3,603,853	6,343,680
	4,265,159	7,421,476
Shareholders' Equity		
Capital stock (Note 8)	10,235,648	9,361,885
Contributed surplus (Note 8)	105,000	–
Deficit	(6,445,496)	(8,540,898)
	3,895,152	820,987
	$ 8,160,311	$ 8,242,463

Contingencies and Uncertainty (Notes 12 and 16)

On behalf of the Board

Signed "Deep Shergill"   Director   **Signed "Tim Duffin"**   Director

See accompanying notes to the consolidated financial statements.

Grant Thornton

2

EXHIBIT 11-9
PART B

H. Jager Developments Inc.
Consolidated Statements of Operations and Deficit

Years Ended February 28	1999	1998
Revenue		
Lot sales	$ 1,827,383	$ –
Utility fees	41,474	16,870
	1,868,857	16,870
Direct costs	1,413,367	–
Cost of lots sold	85,630	73,276
Utility service costs	1,498,997	73,276
	369,860	(56,406)
Expenses		
General and administrative	398,375	638,012
Depreciation	29,364	29,462
Interest	20,792	70,347
	448,531	737,821
Loss before undernoted	(78,671)	(794,227)
Gain on debt settlements (Note 15)	2,117,541	–
Gain on sale of securities	56,532	66,880
Net earnings (loss) before income taxes	2,095,402	(727,347)
Income taxes	935,000	–
Recovery of income taxes due to utilization of losses carryforward of prior years	(935,000)	–
Net earnings (loss)	2,095,402	(727,347)
Deficit, beginning of year	(8,540,898)	(7,813,551)
Deficit, end of year	$ (6,445,496)	$ (8,540,898)
Earnings (loss) per share (Note 10)	$ 0.06	$ (0.04)

See accompanying notes to the consolidated financial statements.

Grant Thornton

3

H. Jager Developments Inc.
Notes to the Consolidated Financial Statements
February 28, 1999

---

8. Capital stock

a) Authorized:
   Unlimited common voting shares
   Unlimited preferred shares

b) Common shares issued:

	1999		1998	
	Number	**Amount**	Number	Amount
Balance, beginning of year	**29,156,315**	**$9,361,885**	13,951,315	$7,841,385
Shares issued:				
Pursuant to private placements	**–**	**–**	3,555,000	355,500
Share subscription agreements	**5,371,000**	**537,100**	250,000	25,000
Debt settlement agreements	**1,559,800**	**155,980**	11,400,000	1,140,000
Cancelled	**(420,000)**	**(105,000)**	–	–
Balance, end of year	**35,667,115**	**9,949,965**	29,156,315	9,361,885

Grant Thornton   9

EXHIBIT 11-9
PART D

H. Jager Developments Inc.
Notes to the Consolidated Financial Statements
February 28, 1999

---

8. Capital stock (continued)

c) Preferred shares issued:

	1999		1998	
	Number	Amount	Number	Amount
Balance, beginning of year	–	–	–	–
Shares issued:				
Debt settlement agreements	28,580	285,683	–	–
Balance, end of year	28,580	285,683	–	–
Capital stock, end of year		$10,235,648		$9,361,885

During the year, the Company had 420,000 previously issued common shares returned, for no consideration, to treasury for cancellation. This amount has been reflected as contributed surplus.

d) Stock options:

The following options, granted to directors and employees, to acquire common shares of the Company, are outstanding:

1999 Number of Shares	1998 Number of Shares	Exercise Price Per Share	Expiry Date
–	237,500	$ 1.00	March 31, 1998
1,250,000	1,250,000	$ 0.10	May 30, 2002
1,250,000	1,250,000	$ 0.10	February 3, 2003
250,000	–	$ 0.10	April 7, 2003

e) Warrants

On December 15, 1997, 1,100,000 warrants were issued. Each warrant entitled the holder to acquire one common share for $0.10 per share for each warrant outstanding. These warrants were not exercised and expired on June 30,1998.

Grant Thornton   **10**

Consolidated Financial Statements

EXHIBIT 11-10

PART A

thousands of dollars

CONSOLIDATED BALANCE SHEETS

As at March 31	1998	1997
Assets		
Cash and short-term investments *(note 7)*	$ 127,876	$ 126,741
Accounts and other receivables *(notes 7 and 14)*	93,093	106,296
Income taxes recoverable	22,025	52,844
Loans *(notes 3, 7 and 14)*	205,702	217,795
Deferred selling commissions and investment		
in related partnerships *(note 4)*	515,173	368,285
Investment in affiliated company	77,581	68,682
Management contracts	11,903	12,497
Capital assets *(note 5)*	29,668	26,648
Goodwill	5,153	6,099
Other assets *(notes 6 and 14)*	13,945	6,660
	$ 1,102,119	$ 992,547
Liabilities		
Bank loans	$ 9,633	$ 6,805
Accounts payable and accrued liabilities	78,030	86,268
Customer deposits *(notes 7 and 14)*	254,292	278,302
Debentures and notes *(notes 8 and 14)*	124,259	131,341
Deferred taxes	181,609	128,389
Minority interest	9,263	4,661
	657,086	635,766
Shareholders' Equity		
Capital stock *(note 9)*		
Authorized – Unlimited number of common shares		
Issued and outstanding		
– 124,904,630 (1997 – 122,259,630) common shares	67,655	52,887
Retained earnings	374,626	303,894
Currency exchange adjustment *(note 2)*	2,752	—
	445,033	356,781
	$ 1,102,119	$ 922,547

(The accompanying notes are an integral part of these consolidated financial statements.)

Signed on behalf of the Board

ALEXANDER CHRIST
Director

F. WARREN HURST
Director

EXHIBIT 11-10
PART B

 **9** **C**apital Stock

(a) Stock Split

On October 24, 1997, the Board of Directors of the Corporation approved a 2-for-1 stock split of the common shares of the Corporation. This stock split was effected by declaration of a stock dividend of one additional common share for each common share of the Corporation issued and outstanding on the dividend record date of November 10, 1997. All references to shares and per share amounts in the financial statements have been adjusted retroactively to reflect the 2-for-1 stock split.

(b) Stock Options

The Corporation has granted options to purchase common shares to employees and others, at a minimum of the market price on the date the options were granted. These options have five year terms and are exercisable one year from date of grant.

A maximum number of 4,425,664 common shares has been reserved for future option grants under the share option plan. The maximum number of shares to be allocated to each employee is 1% of the issued and outstanding common shares of the Corporation.

Year Granted	Expiry Date	Option Exercise Price $	Stock Options				
			Outstanding March 31, 1997	Issued in Fiscal 1998	Exercised in Fiscal 1998	Cancelled in Fiscal 1998	Outstanding March 31, 1998
1992	1997	2.48 – 2.75	94,000	—	94,000	—	—
1993	1998	3.81 – 6.00	2,595,800	—	1,436,600	—	1,159,200
1994	1999	3.75 – 4.75	782,000	—	229,000	—	553,000
1995	2000	4.00 – 5.63	1,400,000	—	385,100	—	1,014,900
1996	2001	6.63 – 8.85	1,611,400	—	500,300	10,000	1,101,100
1997	2002	14.13 – 20.48	—	3,264,000	—	191,000	3,073,000
1998	2003	17.65	—	35,000	—	—	35,000
			6,483,200	3,299,000	2,645,000	201,000	6,936,200

During the year ended March 31, 1998, options for 2,645,000 shares (1997 – 3,002,400; 1996 – 729,000) were exercised for cash proceeds of $14,768 (1997 – $11,859; 1996 – $2,215). The average weighted price for options issued during the year ended March 31, 1998 was $13.16 (1997 – $6.85; 1996 – $4.80).

(c) Earnings per Share

Fully diluted earnings per share have been calculated on the basis that all of the options to purchase common shares existing at the end of the year had been exercised at the beginning of the year or date of issuance, if later.

c. Assume that all of the warrants outstanding as at March 31, 1998, were actually exercised on March 31, 1998, for the minimum exercise prices. Redraft the March 31, 1998, balance sheet to include this transaction (this is called a "pro forma" balance sheet). Comment on the changes in the pro forma balance sheet compared to the actual March 31, 1998, balance sheet.

d. Calculate the return on shareholders' equity for the year ended March 31, 1998. Net income for the year was $80,658,000.

11-43 (Effect of share issuances)

The balance sheets for 1998 and 1997 for Petromet Resources Limited and Notes 4 and 5 as at December 31, 1998, are shown in Exhibit 11-11.

Required:

a. Reconstruct all journal entries that affected common shares for the year ended December 31, 1998.

b. What is the maximum number of common shares that could be outstanding on December 31, 1998, if all possible conversions and options were exercised on December 31, 1998? (Ignore the actual dates on which these conversions and options are actually exercisable.)

c. If all possible conversions and options were exercised on December 31, 1998, as assumed in part b., what assets, liabilities, equities, revenues, and expenses would be affected?

d. Calculate the return on shareholders' equity for the year ended December 31, 1998. Net income for the year was $2,205,000.

11-44 (Effects of share issuances)

The balance sheets for 1998 and 1997 for Queenstake Resources Ltd. and Note 3 as at December 31, 1998, are shown in Exhibit 11-12.

Required:

a. Reconstruct all journal entries that affected common shares for the year ended December 31, 1998.

b. Reconstruct all journal entries that affected common shares for the year ended December 31, 1997.

c. Calculate the average issue price per share for each type of common share issued during 1997 and 1998. Comment on the average prices received for each type of placement. Why are they different?

d. Comment on the trends in share prices found in part c. Which type of average issue price best reflects Queenstake's operating success and prospects? Justify your answer.

EXHIBIT 11-11
PART A

balance sheets

DECEMBER 31 ($ THOUSANDS)	1998	1997
ASSETS		
Current		
Cash	$ 147	$ 204
Accounts receivable	9,408	8,430
Inventory	2,261	1,912
Investments	125	125
	11,941	10,671
Property, plant and equipment (Note 2)	202,348	152,517
	$ 214,289	$ 163,188
LIABILITIES		
Current		
Accounts payable and accrued liabilities	$ 11,258	$ 13,705
Long-term bank debt (Note 3)	60,986	19,814
Convertible debentures (Note 4)	23,530	23,250
Future abandonment and site restoration costs	2,262	1,661
Deferred income taxes	8,623	6,891
SHAREHOLDERS' EQUITY		
Share capital (Note 5)	86,538	78,980
Paid-in capital (Note 4)	2,800	2,800
Retained earnings	18,292	16,087
	107,630	97,867
	$ 214,289	$ 163,188

See accompanying notes.

On Behalf of the Board:
(Director)   (Director)

4. CONVERTIBLE DEBENTURES

The 6.5 percent convertible subordinated debentures were issued in 1994 in the principal amount of $25,000, are due March 31, 2004, with interest paid semi-annually. The debentures are convertible into common shares at $9.50 per share and are non-redeemable until March 31, 1999, unless the closing price of the common shares for 30 consecutive trading days is $15.25 per share or more. After March 31, 1999, the debentures are redeemable in the event that the weighted average price at which the common shares are traded during a 30 consecutive trading day period is not less than 130 percent of the conversion price.

5.   SHARE CAPITAL

EXHIBIT 11-11

PART B

(a)   The authorized share capital consists of an unlimited number of common shares and an unlimited number of preference shares, issuable in series. No preferred shares have been issued.

(b)   Issued

	SHARES	AMOUNT
Balance, December 31, 1995	33,932,139	$ 57,226
Issued for flow-through public offering	3,100,000	10,230
Less: issue costs, net of deferred income tax of $291	-	(361)
Less: effect of tax deductions renounced	-	(1,472)
Balance, December 31, 1996	37,032,139	$ 65,623
Issued for cash on exercise of stock options	40,000	50
Issued through public offering	2,933,333	11,000
Issued for flow-through public offering	2,716,049	11,000
Less: issue costs, net of deferred income tax of $557	-	(696)
Less: effect of tax deductions renounced	-	(7,997)
Balance, December 31, 1997	42,721,521	$ 78,980
Issued for cash on exercise of stock options	1,025,522	2,422
Issued for flow-through private placement	1,567,113	5,500
Less: issue costs, net of deferred income tax of $149	-	(185)
Less: effect of tax deductions renounced	-	(179)
Balance, December 31, 1998	**45,314,156**	**$ 86,538**

(c)   Stock option plan

Stock options to acquire common shares are granted to directors, officers and key employees from time to time at exercise prices equal to the market value of the shares at the date of the grant. At December 31, 1998, options to purchase 2,885,000 common shares were outstanding. Options are granted for a five year term. Options granted prior to July 1, 1997 vested immediately. Options granted thereafter vest over a two year period.

OPTIONS OUTSTANDING

	OPTIONS	PRICE PER SHARE	PROCEEDS IF EXERCISED
Balance, December 31, 1995	3,345,000	$ 0.31-8.875	$ 18,402
Granted	415,000	2.80	1,162
Cancelled	(525,000)	4.50-8.875	(4,364)
Balance, December 31, 1996	3,235,000	0.31-8.875	15,200
Granted	815,000	3.00-3.10	2,497
Cancelled	(710,000)	4.50-8.875	(5,733)
Exercised	(40,000)	0.31-2.80	(50)
Balance, December 31, 1997	3,300,000	2.25-8.375	11,914
Granted	1,365,000	3.00-3.95	4,469
Cancelled	(754,478)	2.80-8.375	(4,147)
Exercised	(1,025,522)	2.25-3.15	(2,421)
Balance, December 31, 1998	**2,885,000**	**$ 2.80-4.50**	**$ 9,815**
Exercisable, December 31, 1998	**2,133,750**	**$ 2.80-4.50**	**$ 7,393**

(d)   Flow-through shares

During the year, the Company entered into flow-through share agreements whereby proceeds of $5,500 were received and the Company committed to expend and renounce $5,500 in qualified expenditures. Directors and officers of the Company subscribed for 169,913 flow-through shares for consideration of $610.

EXHIBIT 11-12
PART A

QUEENSTAKE RESOURCES LTD.
CONSOLIDATED BALANCE SHEETS

(in Canadian Dollars)

December 31

	1998	1997
ASSETS		
Current assets		
Cash and cash equivalents	$ 8,152,242	$12,061,060
Accounts receivable	409,388	233,702
Due from joint venture partner	–	348,038
	8,561,630	12,642,800
Mineral properties and equipment (Note 2)	10,234,911	14,442,461
	$18,796,541	$27,085,261
LIABILITIES		
Current liabilities		
Accounts payable and accrued liabilities	$ 466,944	$ 586,823
Non-controlling interest	702,161	467,873
SHAREHOLDERS' EQUITY		
Stated capital (Note 3 (a))		
Authorized: 100,000,000 common shares		
without par value		
Issued: 39,054,491 shares		
(1997 – 38,210,879 shares)	46,157,761	45,855,316
Contributed surplus (Note 3 (c))	171,100	–
Share purchase warrants (Note 3 (c))	–	171,100
Deficit	(28,701,425)	(19,995,851)
	17,627,436	26,030,565
	$18,796,541	$27,085,261

Commitments (Note 2)
Contingency (Note 9)

Approved by the Board of Directors

/s/ James Mancuso   /s/ Christopher Serin

J. Mancuso   C. Serin

Director   Director

(See accompanying notes to the Consolidated Financial Statements)

EXHIBIT 11-12

PART B

3. SHARE CAPITAL

(a)   During the years ended December 31, 1998, 1997 and 1996, changes in share capital were as follows:

December 31	1998		1997		1996	
	Shares	Amount	Shares	Amount	Shares	Amount
Balance begining of year	38,210,879	$45,855,316	28,897,591	$27,367,328	23,979,866	$21,496,561
Issued during the year (net of issue costs)						
For cash:						
Private placements	–	–	7,000,000	15,157,645	3,846,154	4,491,007
Exercise of options	150,000	22,500	275,000	67,500	473,667	306,517
Exercise of warrants	643,612	257,445	1,940,288	3,008,043	445,288	690,918
For bonuses	50,000	22,500	98,000	254,800	30,000	39,000
For mineral properties	–	–	–	–	122,616	343,325
Balance end of year	39,054,491	$46,157,761	38,210,879	$45,855,316	28,897,591	$27,367,328

(b)   The Company has had an established incentive stock option plan since 1986 (the "1986 Plan"). Ten year options were granted to employees and directors at market value at the date of grant. These options are exercisable at any time before expiry from 1998 to 2005. The 1986 Plan includes share appreciation rights, whereby an optionee may, if permitted by the Board of Directors, have the right, when entitled to exercise an option, to terminate such option in whole or in part by notice in writing to the Company, and in lieu of receiving that number of shares permitted to exercised under the option, to instead receive shares equal in value to the "profit" portion of the option only (the difference between the exercise price and the market price of the option shares). The 1986 Plan will remain in place until all existing options are exercised, expire or are cancelled. The Company established another incentive stock option plan on May 17, 1995, amended on May 14, 1997, in accordance with current Toronto Stock Exchange rule changes (the "1995 Plan"). A maximum of 2,800,000 five year options may be granted under the 1995 Plan at market value on the day before granting. One half of the options granted are exercisable immediately and the remainder one year later. At December 31, 1998, there were 115,000 options available for granting under the 1995 Plan.

The Company also established a Share Bonus Plan on May 17, 1995 (the "Bonus Plan") pursuant to which the Board may from time to time grant up to 200,000 bonus common shares of the Company to qualifying individuals within certain parameters. The Company granted 50,000 bonus common shares to one senior officer in 1998 leaving 22,000 available for granting under the Bonus Plan.

Options outstanding at December 31, 1998 under these plans are all exercisable in 1999 in the following amounts and exercise prices:

Number of Shares	Exercise Price	Expiry Dates
40,000	$0.30	June 26, 2003
190,000	$0.50	October 26, 2000
890,000	$0.62	January 30, 2003
77,000	$0.70	October 24, 2004
180,000	$0.76	March 15, 2005
38,000	$1.30	January 6, 2003
235,000	$1.30	November 22, 2001
805,000	$2.60	May 27, 2002
135,000	$3.50	March 17, 2004
2,590,000		

Option activity for the three proceding years is as follows:

Year ended December 31	1998	1997	1996
1986 Plan balance beginning of year	580,000	800,000	1,215,334
Granted	–	–	–
Exercised	(150,000)	(200,000)	(298,667)
Cancelled	–	(20,000)	(116,667)
Balance end of year	430,000	580,000	800,000
1995 Plan balance beginning of year	1,340,000	540,000	440,000
Granted	1,050,000	920,000	275,000
Exercised	–	(75,000)	(175,000)
Cancelled	(230,000)	(45,000)	–
Balance end of year	2,160,000	1,340,000	540,000
Total	2,590,000	1,920,000	1,340,000

EXHIBIT 11-12
PART C

(c)   The Company has outstanding at December 31, 1998 999,950 Group B warrants, each exercisable at $1.00 until they expire on the earlier of 30 days following the triggering event and September 11, 1999; 1,500,100 Group C warrants, each exercisable at $2.10 until they expire or the earlier of 30 days following the triggering event and September 11, 2000, (the "triggering event" will occur if the 10-day weighted average trading price for the Company's common shares exceeds $1.25 for the Group B warrants and $2.47 for the Group C warrants); and, 277,500 warrants, each exercisable at $0.60 until they expire on November 1, 2000, all of which entitle the holder to purchase one common share.

The Company had 1,711,000 warrants outstanding at December 31, 1997 with an aggregate assigned value of $171,000. The warrants expired on April 2, 1998 and the value has been reclassified to contributed surplus.

Warrant activity for the three preceding years is as follows:

Year ended December 31	1998	1997	1996
Balance beginning of year	5,488,500	4,998,789	3,521,000
Issued	–	3,500,000	1,923,077
Exercised	(643,612)	(1,940,288)	(445,288)
Expired	(2,067,338)	(1,070,001)	–
Balance end of year	2,777,550	5,488,500	4,998,789

Beyond the Book

11-45 (Examination of shareholders' equity for a real company)
Choose a company as directed by your instructor and answer the following questions:

a. Prepare a quick analysis of the shareholders' equity accounts by listing the beginning and ending amounts in these accounts and calculating the net change in both dollar and percentage terms for the most recent year.

b. If any of the accounts changes by more than 10%, give an explanation for this change.

c. For each type of share authorized by the company, list the nature of the issue, the number of shares (authorized, issued, and outstanding), par value or no-par value, market price at the end of the year, and any other special features of the issue.

d. What was the market value of the company at the end of the most recent year? (Multiply the number of shares outstanding by the market price.) Compare this with the book value of the company and discuss the reasons why these amounts are different. Be as specific as possible.

e. Did the company pay dividends in the most recent year? If so, what was the dividend per share and has this amount changed over the past three years?

f. Did the company declare any stock dividends or have a stock split during the most recent year? If so, describe the nature of the event and the effects on the shareholders' equity section.

Case

11-46 (Manonta Sales Company)
Manonta Sales Company's summary balance sheet and income statement as at December 31, 20x1, are shown below.

Balance Sheet (in thousands)

Current assets	$178,000
Investments	1,000
Net property, plant, and equipment	56,000
Total assets	$235,000
Current liabilities	$115,000
Long-term debt	93,000
Shareholders' equity	27,000
Total liabilities and shareholders' equity	$235,000

Income Statement (in thousands)

Sales	$550,000
Cost of goods sold, operating and other expenses	525,000
Earnings before income taxes	25,000
Income taxes	10,000
Net income	$ 15,000
Earnings per share	$1.00

The long-term debt has an interest rate of 8% and is convertible into 9,300,000 common shares. You own 100 common shares of Manonta and are trying to decide whether you should keep or sell them. After carefully analyzing all available information about Manonta, you decide the following events are likely to happen. First, Manonta will increase its earnings before income taxes by 10% next year because of increased sales. Second, the effective tax rate will stay the same. Third, the holders of long-term debt will convert it into shares on January 1, 20x2. Fourth, the current multiple of earnings per share to market price of 20 will increase to 22 if the debt is converted because of the reduced risk.

You decide you will sell the shares if you think their market price will not increase by 10% next year. Should you keep the shares or sell them? Support your answer with a detailed analysis.

Critical Thinking Question

11-47 (Stock options)
Corporate executives are normally remunerated with a package that consists of a combination of one or more of the following:

a. Salary

b. "Perks" (a commonly used abbreviation for "perquisites") such as cars, expense accounts, nice offices, and club memberships

c. Bonuses based on reported net income

d. Bonuses based on gross sales

e. Stock option plans

Argue the impact of each of the above items on the actions of executives. What would each item encourage the executive to achieve? Which of these actions might be beneficial to the company? Which might be harmful? If you were designing a remuneration package for executives running a company you owned, what would you include? Explain why you included the items that you did.

Doing Your "Homework" on Investment Opportunities

Early every morning, at a time when many people can face little more than pop-music radio stations or the Weather Channel, Michael Decter sits down for half an hour with a cup of coffee, the business section of the morning newspaper, and a stack of quarterly and annual corporate reports. This habit has made him a millionaire.

Mr. Decter has no professional training or experience in investing or even accounting—his field is consultancy in the health-care sector. By simply researching businesses and analyzing financial statements, however, he has invested his way to an RRSP fund with a value of well over $1 million, ensuring that a comfortable retirement lies ahead.

Mr. Decter literally stumbled across his first big investment. Every day on his way to work, he would walk through Winnipeg's old Grain Exchange Building, because it is connected to the city's underground tunnel system. "One day," he writes, "I noticed an annual report for a company called the Traders Building Association. I picked it up and discovered that this company owned the Grain Exchange Building, as well as a portfolio of stocks and bonds."

"Apparently, the Traders Building Association was set up as a corporation so that the tenants of the Grain Exchange Building, who were largely from the grain transport and related industries, could each own a piece of the action. Its shares were publicly traded on the tiny Winnipeg Stock Exchange. Over the years, income from the building had been used to assemble a portfolio of stocks and bonds.

"As I began to analyze the report, I realized that the stocks and bonds had a combined value greater than the price of the shares…. After I worked over my logic a number of times, it seemed clear to me that if I could obtain shares in Traders Building Association, eventually I would benefit from the unlocking of the company's hidden value."

Mr. Decter bought 300 shares in TBA. His stockbroker thought he was crazy, and assigned them a value on his monthly statement of U.S. $1 each. After about a year and a half of almost no movement in the stock price, Mr. Decter began to think that perhaps the stockbroker was right, and unloaded 50 shares. Six months later he regretted it; sure enough, a local entrepreneur made a takeover bid for TBA, and Mr. Decter sold his remaining shares for over twice their original price.

"My experience with TBA helped me formulate what I now think of as the two founding principles in my investment strategy," he says. "The first principle is to look under your nose…. I knew the territory. And each and every one of us knows some territory…. The second principle is to do your homework." The value of TBA's assets, and of its shares, was clearly outlined in the corporation's financial statements for anyone to see. The key is to look—and to have the confidence and initiative to follow through on your analysis.

chapter 12

FINANCIAL STATEMENT ANALYSIS

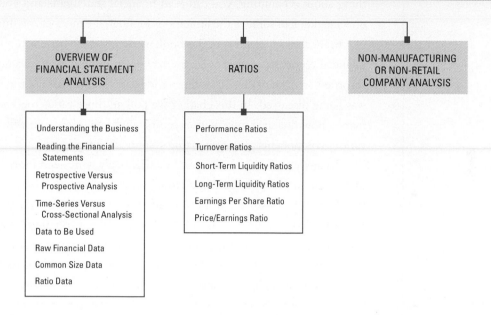

OVERVIEW OF
FINANCIAL STATEMENT
ANALYSIS

RATIOS

NON-MANUFACTURING
OR NON-RETAIL
COMPANY ANALYSIS

Understanding the Business

Reading the Financial
Statements

Retrospective Versus
Prospective Analysis

Time-Series Versus
Cross-Sectional Analysis

Data to Be Used

Raw Financial Data

Common Size Data

Ratio Data

Performance Ratios

Turnover Ratios

Short-Term Liquidity Ratios

Long-Term Liquidity Ratios

Earnings Per Share Ratio

Price/Earnings Ratio

Learning Objectives:

After studying this chapter, you should be able to:

1. *Explain why knowledge of the business is important when attempting to draw conclusions about the future health of a company.*

2. *Describe the various ways that an analysis of a company's financial statements can be made.*

3. *Describe the types of ratios that are best suited to providing insight into specific decisions.*

4. *Calculate specific ratios and explain how the ratios can be interpreted.*

5. *Assess the financial health of a company through the use of ratios.*

Michael Decter picked up an annual report that someone had discarded, learned something about the company described in it, reviewed and analyzed its financial statements and discovered that the shares were trading at a value lower than the value of its assets. Logic told him that if he invested at the current share price, he would be able to sell them later at a higher price. And he did. He employed strategies that you have been learning throughout this book. You have an advantage over Mr. Decter. After studying this text, you know something about accounting, you can read financial statements and you have some understanding of some of the limitations found in the numbers on the statements.

In the first 11 chapters of this book we describe the basic components of the financial reporting system and how accounting numbers are accumulated and recorded. In most of these chapters we identified ratios that use the material that was being discussed. In this chapter we pull all those ratios together and summarize how financial information can be analyzed. Here you will see how the various components of the reporting system work together.

To analyze financial information effectively, you need more than a basic understanding of what each individual statement means. You need to understand the relationships among the three major financial statements and the methods that produce the numbers. You also need to compare and contrast these relationships over time and among different companies. We left this discussion until near the end of the book, because proper analysis requires a good understanding of all components of all the financial statements.

This chapter provides an overview of financial statement analysis and a discussion of the basic ratios used. However, because financial statement analysis is very complex, it can serve only as an introduction. Remember two basic facts as you work through this chapter. First, there is no definitive set of rules or procedures that dictate how to analyze financial statements. Second, every analysis should be tailored to the underlying reason for making the analysis. These two features make comprehensive analysis quite complex. A more detailed discussion of financial statement analysis is left to advanced texts.

OVERVIEW OF FINANCIAL STATEMENT ANALYSIS

Financial statements are typically analyzed for a specific purpose. An investment analyst or a stockbroker, for example, may undertake an analysis in order to recommend that a client buy or sell a stock. A bank lending officer may perform an analysis of a client's financial statements to decide whether the client will be capable of paying back a loan if the bank decides to lend the money. A student looking for a job may perform an analysis of a company to decide whether it will be a suitable company for which to work.

Depending on the type of decision to be made, the analyst will tailor the analysis to the demands of the decision. For example, a banker trying to decide whether to make a short-term loan may restrict the analysis to the short-term cash-producing capabilities of the company. The investment analyst, on the other hand, may focus on the long-term financial health of the company.

In this chapter, we take a very general approach to financial statement analysis. No particular decision is considered as the various ratios are discussed. However, we do attempt to discuss decision contexts in which a particular ratio may be more helpful than others in assessing the health of the company. Whatever the decision, one of the first things you have to do is come to some understanding of the business.

Understanding the Business

Understanding the business means more than understanding a company's financial statements. It means that you must have a grasp of the underlying economics of the business, the risks involved, and the economic factors that are crucial to the long- and short-run health of the company. It means that you must understand the various types of businesses in which the company is engaged. For example, a large company such as BCE Inc. (Bell Canada) is involved in more than just telephones. It has businesses in many communications areas such as production (Northern Telecom), research (Nortel Networks), mobile satellite service (TMI Communications), satellite television signals (Expressvu Inc.), cable television (Jones Intercable), and many other areas. An analyst who thinks that BCE is only in the telephone business has a very inaccurate view of the risks involved in lending BCE money, or in buying its shares.

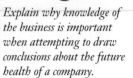

Learning Objective

1

Explain why knowledge of the business is important when attempting to draw conclusions about the future health of a company.

A basic understanding of the range of businesses in which a company is engaged can be obtained by reading the first section of the annual report. In most annual reports, the first sections are devoted to describing the various businesses in which the company is involved and their associated achievements and expectations. Usually the financial statements are found in the second half of the annual report. Although this descriptive section does not usually explain everything you need to know about the company, it does provide some insight into what the company does and the types of risks it faces.

Once you have an overall view of the kinds of businesses operated by the company, you should next read the financial statements, including the auditor's report and the notes to the financial statements.

Reading the Financial Statements

The first step in reading the financial statements is to study the auditor's report attached to them. The auditor's report confirms that appropriate accounting policies were followed and that the statements "present fairly" the financial position of the company. This report is important because the auditor is an independent third party who is stating a professional opinion on the fairness of the numbers and disclosures reported in the financial statements. Remember that the auditor's

EXHIBIT 12-1

Auditors' Report

To the Shareholders of Cara Operations Limited

We have audited the consolidated balance sheets of Cara Operations Limited as at March 28, 1999 and March 29, 1998 and the consolidated statements of earnings and retained earnings and cash flows for the years then ended. These financial statements are the responsibility of the Corporation's management. Our responsibility is to express an opinion on these financial statements based on our audits.

We conducted our audits in accordance with generally accepted auditing standards. Those standards require that we plan and perform an audit to obtain reasonable assurance whether the financial statements are free of material misstatement. An audit includes examining, on a test basis, evidence supporting the amounts and disclosures in the financial statements. An audit also includes assessing the accounting principles used and significant estimates made by management, as well as evaluating the overall financial statement presentation.

In our opinion, these consolidated financial statements present fairly, in all material respects, the financial position of the Corporation as at March 28, 1999 and March 29, 1998 and the results of its operations and its cash flows for the years then ended in accordance with generally accepted accounting principles.

PricewaterhouseCoopers LLP

PRICEWATERHOUSECOOPERS LLP

Chartered Accountants

Toronto, Canada

May 19, 1999

report is not a guarantee of the accuracy of the information contained in the financial statements. Financial statements are prepared by management, and management has primary responsibility for them. Auditors express their opinion on whether the financial statements present the information fairly according to generally accepted accounting principles. The auditor's report does not indicate if the information contained in the financial statements is good or bad. It is the reader's responsibility to interpret the information provided. A typical unqualified auditor's opinion, provided by PricewaterhouseCoopers LLP for the 1999 financial statements of Cara Operations Limited, is shown in Exhibit 12-1.

The second step is to read each of the major financial statements to make sure that the results make sense for the types of activities in which the company is engaged. Use your knowledge from this course to look for unusual account titles and unusually large dollar items. If there is a large loss item on the income statement, for example, the nature of the loss is important. Is it an item that can be expected to continue into the future, or is it a non-continuing item? Unusual account titles may indicate that the company is involved in a line of business that is new, which could have serious implications for future operations. For example, if a manufacturer suddenly shows lease receivables on its balance sheet, this probably indicates that it has started to lease assets as well as sell them. The leasing business is very different from the manufacturing business and exposes the company to different types of risks. You must take this new information into consideration in evaluating the company.

A reading of the financial statements is not complete unless it includes a careful reading of the notes to the financial statements. Because the major financial statements provide summary information only, there is not much room on the statements for all the details necessary for the reader to gain a full understanding of the company's transactions. Therefore, the notes provide a place for more details and discussion about many items on the financial statements. Also, pay attention in the notes to the summary of the significant accounting policies used by the company. Remember that GAAP allows a great amount of flexibility in choosing accounting principles, so you should be aware of the choices that were made by management. These will generally be listed in the first note to the financial statements.

Once you have an overall understanding of the business and the financial statements, you can begin a detailed analysis of the financial results.

Retrospective Versus Prospective Analysis

As discussed earlier, most analyses are made with a particular objective in mind. Almost every analysis of a set of financial statements is, in one way or another, concerned with the future. Because of this, you should make a prospective (forward-looking) analysis of the company to try to determine what the future will bring. For example, loan officers in banks try to forecast future cash flows of companies to ensure that loans will be repaid.

The problem with prospective analysis is that the world is an uncertain place; no one can predict the future with complete accuracy. Analysts, however, are expected to make recommendations based on their predictions of what the future outcomes will be for specified companies. In trying to predict the future, one of the most reliable sources of data you have is the results of past operations of a company as summarized in the financial statements. To the extent that the future follows the trends of the past, you can use these retrospective data to help you predict the future. You must also understand the economics of a company well enough to know when something fundamental has changed in the economic environment to make it unlikely that the past results of the company will predict the future. In such a situation, you cannot rely on the retrospective data.

If you believe that retrospective data may be useful in predicting the future, a complete analysis of that retrospective data is in order. Two major types of analysis of retrospective data are times-series and cross-sectional analyses.

Learning Objective

2

Describe the various ways that an analysis of a company's financial statements can be made.

Time-Series Versus Cross-Sectional Analysis

In a **time-series analysis**, the analyst examines information from different time periods in the life of the company to look for any pattern in the data over time. For example, you may look at the sales data over a five-year period to determine whether sales are increasing, decreasing, or remaining stable. This will have important implications for future sales of the company. The assumption underlying a time-series

EXHIBIT 12-2

Financial Highlights

In thousands of dollars, except for share data	1999	1998	1997
System Sales	1,246,050	1,194,216*	1,097,184*
Gross Revenue	864,890	806,927*	719,125*
Net Earnings Before Restructuring	28,229	35,027	30,369
Net Earnings After Restructuring	18,991	35,027	30,369
Net Earnings per Share Before Restructuring (¢)	29.5	35.7	30.1
Net Earnings per Share After Restructuring (¢)	19.9	35.7	30.1
Dividends per Share (¢)	12.0	11.0	10.0
Shareholders' Equity	248,279	267,660	238,175
Long-term Debt and Notes	182,213	108,448	115,492
Shares Outstanding (000's)	94,638	98,859	97,811

*Includes discontinued operations – 1998 and 1997 (Days Inn).

analysis is that there is some predictability in the time series; that is, past data can be used to predict the future. Without this assumption, there is no reason to do a time-series analysis.

Many companies recognize the importance of time-series information and provide five- or 10-year summaries to facilitate analysis. Exhibit 12-2, from the Cara Operations Limited 1999 annual report, shows selected pieces of financial data across three years. In Cara's information it is interesting to note that sales in 1997 and 1998 included the operations from Days Inn which was discontinued and is not inlcuded in the 1999 amounts. Even without this part of their operations, gross revenues rose in 1999. You will note that the company has provided information before and after restructuring. Restructuring means that the company was restructured its weighting of debt and equity. After the restructuring the number of shares outstanding is down and the amount of long-term debt is up.

A **cross-sectional analysis** compares the data from the company with the data from another company for the same time period. Usually, the comparison is made with another company in the same industry (a competitor perhaps), or with an average of the other companies in the industry. For example, you might look at the growth in sales for General Motors Canada compared to the growth in sales for Ford Canada or Chrysler Canada. Other cross-sectional analyses might compare companies across different industries (General Motors Canada compared to BCE), countries (General Motors Canada compared to Nissan), and so forth. However, any such cross-sectional comparisons must consider that different industries may have slightly different accounting principles (for example, accounting principles for banks and insurance companies are slightly different from those for other industries). Comparing across countries is much more difficult because of different accounting methods and sets of standards used. However, investment analysts use as wide a range of investments as possible in order to recommend the best investment strategy to their clients. To do so, they must consider the return versus risk trade-off across many companies. They must, therefore, directly compare companies in different industries and different countries.

The choice of which type of analysis to conduct is based, in part, on the type of decision that motivated the analysis. In a lending situation, for example, the lending officer is less concerned about other companies than about the time-series of the data for the particular company under consideration. Actually, the lending officer uses both types of analysis. The lender must be aware of industry trends in the analysis of a particular company to get an overall assessment of how well this company performs relative to its competitors to ensure its future viability. The lender must couple the cross-company comparison with a time-series analysis of the financial health of the company to determine its ability to repay any money loaned.

Data to Be Used

The type of data used in a time-series or cross-sectional analysis will vary depending on the purpose of the analysis. Three general types of data that are frequently used are raw financial data, common size data, and ratio data.

Raw Financial Data

Raw financial data are the data that appear directly in the financial statements. An example of a time-series analysis of this type of data might be that of data from income statements, as shown for Cara Operations Limited in Exhibit 12-2, or that of total long-term debt and notes for the past six years. Cross-sectional analysis can also be used with this type of data. For example, you might compare total revenues across companies in the same industry for the past three years.

Time-series data is almost always available directly from financial statements, since they usually show data for a two-year period. In addition to the main financial statements, some annual reports contain time-series data in the form of a five- or 10-year summary such as that shown in Exhibit 12-2. Note that this summary does not include all items that appear on the income statement. Annual reports may also contain data other than strictly financial data, such as numbers of employees or sales volumes expressed in physical units rather than dollars.

In the remainder of the chapter, data from a set of financial statements will be used to illustrate various types of analyses. For purposes of illustration, we are going to continue to use the financial statement data of Cara Operations Limited for the year ended March 29, 1999. Cara Operations, with headquarters in Mississauga, Ontario, is the leading Canadian-owned and the second-largest food service company in Canada. The raw financial statement data for Cara Operations, which include the balance sheets, statements of earnings, and statements of cash flows, appear in Exhibit 12-3.

EXHIBIT 12-3
PART A

Consolidated Balance Sheets

As at March 28, 1999 and March 29, 1998

In thousands of dollars	1999	1998
ASSETS		
Current Assets		
Cash	$ 42,902	$ 3,200
Accounts receivable (net of reserve for bad debts)	65,682	69,732
Inventories	21,629	20,775
Prepaid expenses and other assets	3,171	3,546
Future income taxes (note 8)	3,938	2,277
Current portion of Long-Term Receivables (note 2)	1,830	2,040
	$ 139,152	$ 101,570
Long-Term Receivables (note 2)	16,073	16,989
Property, Plant and Equipment (note 3)	249,808	228,655
Goodwill and Other Assets (note 4)	67,432	66,007
Future Income Taxes (note 8)	6,339	2,613
Equity Investments (note 5)	82,307	80,214
	$ 561,111	$ 496,048
LIABILITIES		
Current Liabilities		
Accounts payable and accrued charges	$ 91,319	$ 88,679
Provision for restructuring costs (note 14)	9,100	–
Income taxes	638	5,306
Current portion of long-term debt (note 6)	4,389	6,322
	$ 105,446	$ 100,307
Unearned Income on Sale of Franchises	702	1,583
Long-Term Liabilities (notes 12 and14)	11,083	7,200
Long-Term Debt (note 6)	177,824	102,126
Future Income Taxes (note 8)	17,777	17,172
	$ 312,832	$ 228,388
SHAREHOLDERS' EQUITY		
Capital Stock (note 7)	$ 30,913	$ 32,264
Retained Earnings	217,366	235,396
	$ 248,279	$ 267,660
	$ 561,111	$ 496,048

Approved on behalf of the Board

M. BERNARD SYRON
Chairman of the Board

GABRIEL TSAMPALIEROS
President and Chief Executive Officer

EXHIBIT 12-3
PART B

Consolidated Statements of Earnings and Retained Earnings

For the years ended March 28, 1999 and March 29, 1998

In thousands of dollars	1999	1998
GROSS REVENUE	$ 864,890	$ 801,202
Earnings before the following:	$ 81,462	$ 84,743
Amortization of property, plant and equipment	23,803	20,685
Amortization of goodwill and other assets	4,129	3,771
Long-term interest expense, net of interest income of $1,673 (1998 – $733)	8,600	5,821
Restructuring costs (note 14)	15,500	–
Earnings before income taxes, equity earnings and discontinued operations	29,430	54,466
Provision for income taxes (note 8)	(12,296)	(21,925)
Earnings before equity earnings and discontinued operations	17,134	32,541
Equity earnings (net of amortization of $706 (1998 – $671)) (note 5)	1,857	2,896
Earnings from continuing operations	18,991	35,437
Discontinued operations – net of tax (note 11)	–	(410)
Net earnings for the year	$ 18,991	$ 35,027
Retained Earnings – Beginning of Year	235,396	211,217
Share repurchase in excess of book value (note 7)	(25,578)	(24)
Dividends	(11,443)	(10,824)
Retained Earnings – End of Year	$ 217,366	$ 235,396
Earnings per share from continuing operations		
Basic	19.9¢	36.1¢
Fully diluted	19.7¢	35.4¢
Net earnings per share		
Basic	19.9¢	35.7¢
Fully diluted	19.7¢	35.0¢

EXHIBIT 12-3
PART C

Consolidated Statements of Cash Flows

For the years ended March 28, 1999 and March 29, 1998

In thousands of dollars	1999	1998
CASH FLOWS PROVIDED BY (USED IN)		
OPERATING ACTIVITIES		
Earnings from continuing operations	$ 18,991	$ 35,437
Adjustments for:		
Amortization of property, plant and equipment	23,803	20,685
Loss on disposal of property, plant and equipment	858	906
Amortization of goodwill and other assets	4,129	3,771
Future income taxes	(4,782)	2,114
Equity earnings	(1,857)	(2,896)
Restructuring costs	12,183	–
Change in franchise notes	(220)	(747)
Change in investments	(236)	128
Change in pension liability	800	1,000
Change in non-cash operating working capital (note 15)	1,868	5,488
Cash flows from continuing operations	$ 55,537	$ 65,886
Discontinued operations	–	(938)
	$ 55,537	$ 64,948
INVESTING ACTIVITIES		
Purchase of property, plant and equipment (note 15)	$ (45,166)	$ (31,681)
Proceeds on disposal of property, plant and equipment	1,657	664
Purchase of goodwill and other assets	(2,792)	(6,309)
Change in mortgages and notes	(582)	(172)
Repayment of Employee Stock Plan Loans	1,047	3,303
Business Acquisition (note 15)	(3,898)	(18,169)
Discontinued operations	–	1,240
	$ (49,734)	$ (51,124)
FINANCING ACTIVITIES		
Share repurchase	$ (1,389)	$ (2)
Share repurchase in excess of book value	(25,578)	(24)
Proceeds from issuance of long-term debt, net of issuance costs	149,377	11,000
Repayment of capital lease obligations	(6,000)	(3,703)
Repayment of long-term debt	(71,106)	(15,685)
Dividends paid	(11,443)	(10,824)
Issuance of capital stock	38	5,308
	$ 33,899	$ (13,930)
NET CHANGE IN CASH	39,702	(106)
CASH – BEGINNING OF YEAR	3,200	3,306
CASH – END OF YEAR	$ 42,902	$ 3,200

Common Size Data

Although the raw data of a company can reveal much about its performance, some relationships are more easily understood when some elements of the raw data are compared with other elements. For example, in the statement of earnings for Cara Operations in exhibit 12-3, you can see that the sales revenue for Cara Operations increased from $801,202,000 in 1998 to $864,890,000 in 1999. Cost of goods sold has also increased over this same period from $716,459,000 to $783,428,000. (The cost of goods sold is not disclosed on the statement of earnings as a separate amount. Rather, Cara Operations discloses the "gross revenue" and then the "earnings before the following." The difference between these two amounts represents the cost of goods sold.) The question is, what happened to profit margins on a relative basis? This is a question of the relationship of the costs to the revenues. One way to address this question is to compare the cost of goods sold expressed as a proportion of the sales revenue. Often, this is done by preparing a set of financial statements called common size statements.

In a common size statement of earnings, all line items are expressed as percentages of net revenues. In the case of Cara Operations, a common size income statement is shown in Exhibit 12-4 with every item calculated as a percentage of net sales.

■ **Cara Operations Limited**

EXHIBIT 12-4

Common Size Statements of Earnings

	1999	1998
Gross revenue	100%	100%
(Cost of goods sold (not included)	90.6%	89.1%
Earnings before the following	9.4%	10.6%
Amortization of property, plant and equipment	2.8%	2.6%
Amortization of goodwill and other assets	0.5%	0.5%
Long-term interest expense, net of interest income	1.0%	0.7%
Restructuring costs	1.8%	–
Earnings before income taxes, equity earnings,		
and discontinued operations	3.3%	6.8%
Provision for income taxes	1.4%	2.7%
Earnings before equity earnings and		
discontinued operations	1.9%	4.1%
Equity earnings	0.2%	0.4%
Earnings from continuing operations	2.1%	4.5%
Discontinued operations	–	0.1%
Net earnings for the year	2.1%	4.4%

This common size statement of earnings shows that Cara's operations have been very stable. Sales have risen and the cost of those sales has risen proportionately slightly more than sales. An analyst will examine a company's financial statements carefully when sales are rising. If the cost of those sales rises proportionately more than the sales, the new sales are costing the company more and management should be looking for ways to control the costs. The rise in cost of sales is slightly more than 1% and it is something analysts will watch. Most of the items on the statement of earnings are proportionately very consistent with the previous year although the amortization of property, plant and equipment and the long-term interest expense are slightly higher. A review of the balance sheet shows that the property, plant and equipment increased just over $20 million and the long-term debt increased over $75 million. Also, on the earnings statement, there is a new expense, "restructuring costs". These costs are associated with the closure of 71 Harvey's restaurants during the 1999 fiscal year. The notes to the financial statements indicate that the company will continue to close more restaurants in 2000 and 2001. This means that you should see this expense again over the next two years. Thus, we can determine the reasons for the decrease in net earnings in absolute numbers.

Common size statements could also be prepared for the balance sheet and the cash flow statement. The common size data can then be used in a time-series analysis, as they were earlier, or they could be used in a cross-sectional analysis of different companies. In fact, in cross-sectional analysis, common size statements allow for a comparison of companies of different sizes.

Ratio Data

Common size data are useful for making comparisons of data items within a given financial statement. They are not useful for making comparisons across the various financial statements. Ratios compare a data element in one statement with an element in another statement, or with an element within the same statement. These ratios can then be used in a time-series or cross-sectional analysis. Ratio data are potentially the most useful data because they reveal information about relationships between the financial statements. To further illustrate this, the remainder of this chapter will be devoted to discussing various ratios, their computation, and their interpretation. Most of these have been introduced in previous chapters, but a discussion of the ratios as they relate to one another should help you understand the usefulness of ratio analysis.

RATIOS

Learning Objective

3

Describe the types of ratios that are best suited to providing insight into specific decisions.

Ratios explain relationships among data in the financial statements. The relationships differ across companies, if for no other reason than that the underlying transactions are different across companies. For example, a manufacturing company is very concerned about the management of inventory, and it focuses on various ratios related to inventory. A bank, on the other hand, has no inventory and would not be able to compute a ratio involving inventory. It might, however, be very concerned about the loans that it makes, whereas the manufacturer would not have any items comparable to loans.

Because of the differences across companies, it is impossible for us to address all the ratio issues related to all types of industries. The focus of our discussion will therefore be restricted to Cara Operations. Most of our discussion will also be applicable to companies in other industries, such as retailing. At the end of the chapter there will be a brief discussion of ratio analysis of non-retailing/manufacturing companies in areas where there may be differences in interpretation.

The ratios that will be discussed are divided into three general categories, but you will see that they are all related. The three categories are performance, short-term liquidity, and long-term liquidity. Most of these ratios apply to any company regardless of the nature of its business, but some (such as inventory ratios) apply only to certain types of businesses.

Before the calculations of the various ratios are presented, one general caveat should be made about the calculation of ratios. Often, one of several ways can be used to compute a given ratio. Therefore, it makes sense to understand the basis of a calculation before you attempt to interpret it. The use of ratios in this book will be consistent with the definitions given. If you use similar ratios from other sources, you should check the definition used in that source to make sure that it is consistent with your understanding of the ratio.

Performance Ratios

Net income and cash flow as measures of performance were discussed in Chapters 4 and 5. Much can be learned from studying the income and cash flow statements, in both their raw data and common size forms; the ratios discussed in this section complement that understanding and also draw out some of the relationships between these statements and the balance sheet.

For example, in Chapter 4 a performance ratio called the **return on investment (ROI)** was briefly discussed. In that chapter, ROI was discussed in generic terms as a measure of performance of an investment. The generic form of the ROI calculation can be used to formulate several different ratios, depending on the perspective taken in measuring performance. One perspective is that of the shareholders, who make an investment in the company and want to measure the performance of their investment. A form of the ROI measure that captures the return to shareholders is referred to as the **return on equity (ROE).**

A second perspective is that of the debtholders, who make an investment in the company by lending money to it. The return they receive is the interest paid by the company. The interest rate paid to them is a measure of their ROI. This type of ROI calculation is not explicitly discussed in this chapter.

The third perspective is that of management. Management obtains resources from both shareholders and debtholders. Those resources are then invested in assets. The return generated by the investment in assets is then used to repay the debtholders and the shareholders. The performance of the investment in assets is therefore very important. This type of ROI is captured in a ratio referred to as the **return on assets (ROA).**

In this chapter, both ROE and ROA are considered. In addition to these two overall measures of performance, three more ratios, referred to as turnover ratios, are discussed. These turnover ratios provide further insights into three major policy decisions that management makes; these decisions concern accounts receivable, inventory, and accounts payable.

Learning Objective

4

Calculate specific ratios and explain how the ratios can be interpreted.

Return on Assets (ROA)

Management must make two fundamental decisions regarding the company. The first is the type of assets the company should invest in (sometimes referred to as the investment decision), and the second is whether to seek more financing to increase the amount the company can invest in assets (referred to as the financing decision). The ROA ratio, in this book, separates the investment decision from the financing decision. Regardless of the mix of debt and shareholder financing, this ratio asks: What type of return is earned on the investment in assets? From this perspective, the return on the investment in assets should be computed prior to any payments or returns to the debtholders or shareholders. Net income is a measure of return on assets that is computed prior to any returns to shareholders, but after the deduction of interest to the debtholders. Therefore, the net income, if it is to be used as a measure of return on assets, must be adjusted for the effects of interest expense so it is treated on a basis that is similar to the treatment of dividends.

However, there is a complicating factor. Interest is a deductible expense in the computation of income tax expense. Therefore, if interest expense is to be removed from the net income figure, we must also adjust the amount of income tax expense that would result. In other words, the tax savings (i.e., the reduction in income tax expense) associated with this interest deduction must also be removed. The ROA ratio is then calculated as the ratio of the return (income before interest) divided by the investment in total assets, as follows:

$$\text{ROA} = \frac{\text{Income before interest}}{\text{Average total assets}}$$

$$= \frac{\text{Net income} + \text{Interest expense} - \text{Tax saving of interest expense}}{\text{Average total assets}}$$

$$= \frac{\text{Net income} + \text{Interest expense} - (\text{Tax rate} \times \text{Interest expense})}{\text{Average total assets}}$$

$$\text{ROA} = \frac{\text{Net income} + [\text{Interest expense} \times (1 - \text{Tax rate})]}{\text{Average total assets}}$$

Based on the data for Cara Operations in 1999, the computation of the ROA is as follows. The income tax rate of 41.8% is found in a note to the financial statements.

ROA–CARA OPERATIONS LIMITED, 1999

$$\text{ROA} = \frac{\text{Net income} + [\text{Interest expense} \times (1 - \text{Tax rate})]}{\text{Average total assets}}$$

$$= \frac{\$18,991 + [\$8,600 \times (1 - 41.8\%)]}{\dfrac{\$561,111 + \$496,048}{2}}$$

$$= 4.54\%$$

This 4.54% ROA indicates that Cara Operations earned 4.54% on the average total assets before making any payments to the suppliers of capital. This 4.54% should be compared to the ROA earned by other, similar, companies and to Cara Operations' ROA in previous years, to determine the trend.

The computation of the appropriate tax rate to use in the ROA formula is somewhat problematic. The rate that should be used is the marginal tax rate of the company. The marginal rate is the rate of tax the company would pay on an additional dollar of income before taxes. This marginal rate would be a combination of the federal and provincial corporate income tax rates. Many analysts use the average tax rate, which is computed by dividing the tax expense by the income before taxes. Many companies, including Cara Operations, show the average tax rates in a note to the financial statements.

The ROA is useful as an overall measure of the performance of the investment in the assets of the company. However, cross-sectional comparisons of ROAs across industries must be made with care. The level of ROA reflects, to some extent, the risk inherent in the type of assets the company invests in. Investors trade off the risk of an investment for the return on the investment. The more risk the investor takes, the higher the return demanded by the investor. If the company invested its assets in a bank account (a very low-risk investment), it would expect a lower return than if it invested in oil exploration equipment (a high-risk business). Although this factor cannot explain all the variations in ROA between companies, it must be kept in mind. It may be more appropriate either to do a time-series analysis of this ratio or to compare it cross-sectionally with a direct competitor in the same business. Data obtained from a source of industry ratios such as Dun and Bradstreet can provide you with median measures of ROA that can be used for comparison purposes to determine whether the calculated ROA is reasonable.

Another breakdown of the ROA ratio can be used to gain insight into the cause of a change in this ratio, as follows:

$$\text{ROA} = \frac{\text{Net income} + [\text{Interest expense} \times (1 - \text{Tax rate})]}{\text{Average total assets}}$$

$$= \frac{\text{Net income} + [\text{Interest expense} \times (1 - \text{Tax rate})]}{\text{Sales revenue}} \times \frac{\text{Sales revenue}}{\text{Average total assets}}$$

$$= \text{Profit margin ratio} \times \text{Total asset turnover}$$

This breakdown of the ratio into a **profit margin ratio** and a **total asset turnover** allows the analyst to assess some of the reasons why the ROA of a company has gone up or down. The profit margin ratio is, of course, affected by the level of the company's costs relative to its revenues. Changes in this ratio would indicate a change in the profitability of the product and may indicate changes in the cost structure or pricing policy. The total asset turnover ratio is the ratio of sales to total assets, or the dollars of sales generated per dollar of investment in assets. Changes in this ratio could reflect an increase or decrease in sales volume, or it could reflect major changes in the level of investment in assets of the company.

The breakdown for Cara Operations in 1999 would be as follows:

ROA (BREAKDOWN)—CARA OPERATIONS LIMITED, 1999

$$\text{ROA} = \frac{\text{Net income} + [\text{Interest expense} \times (1 - \text{Tax rate})]}{\text{Sales revenue}}$$

$$\times \frac{\text{Sales revenue}}{\text{Average total assets}}$$

$$\text{ROA} = \frac{\$18,991 + [\$8,600 \times (1 - 41.8\%)]}{\$864,890} \times \frac{\$864,890}{\dfrac{\$561,111 + \$496,048}{2}}$$

$$= 2.77\% \times 1.64 = 4.54\%$$

These calculations indicate that Cara Operations earned the 4.54% ROA by achieving a profit margin ratio of 2.77% and a total asset turnover of 1.64. Note that the 4.54% could be increased by increasing either the profit margin ratio or the total asset turnover, or both.

Note that the same ROA could be achieved by companies in the same industry with different strategies. For example, a discount retailer operates on smaller profit margins and hopes to make that up by a larger volume in sales relative to investment in assets. Discounters generally have less invested in their retail stores. Full-price retailers have a much larger investment in assets relative to their sales volume and therefore must charge higher prices to achieve a comparable ROA. The two types of business face the same general sets of risks and should earn comparable ROAs.

Return on Equity (ROE)

Return on equity (ROE), discussed earlier in this section, is the return the shareholders are earning on their investment in the company. There is one additional quirk that must be understood in computing this ratio. If there is more than one class of shares (generally the second class of shares would be preferred shares), the ROE calculation should be done from the point of view of the common shareholders. This means that any payments to the other classes of shares (preferred dividends, for example) should be deducted from net income in the numerator of this ratio, because these amounts are not available to common shareholders. The denominator in such cases should include only the shareholders' equity accounts that belong to common shareholders. This usually means that the preferred shares equity account is subtracted from the total shareholders' equity to arrive at the common shareholders' equity.

The computation of the ROE for a company is as follows:

$$\text{ROE} = \frac{\text{Net income} - \text{Preferred dividends}}{\text{Average common shareholders' equity}}$$

Cara Operations Limited has Class A non-voting shares as well as common shares. However, in the information accompanying the financial statements, management indicates that it paid dividends of $11,443,000 thousand. It does not distinguish between the dividends paid on the common shares and those paid on the non-voting shares. We can only conclude that the non-voting shares do not have a preference to dividends. Because we are unable to determine the exact status of the non-voting shares or the amount of dividends paid to this class of share, we are going to calculate the ROE without deducting the non-voting share dividends and we will use all of shareholders' equity, not just the common shareholders' equity. For Cara operations the calculation is the following:

ROE—CARA OPERATIONS LIMITED, 1999

$$ROE = \frac{\text{Net income} - \text{Preferred dividends}}{\text{Average common shareholders' equity}}$$

$$= \frac{\$18,991 - 0}{\dfrac{\$248,279 + \$267,660}{2}}$$

$$= \frac{18,991}{257,970} = 7.36\%$$

This calculation shows that Cara Operations earned 7.36% ROE, indicating that it earned an average of 7.36% on the average shareholders' equity balances. This is down from the previous year's ROE of 13.8%. Just as with the ROA, this 7.36% could be compared with other, similar, companies, or with Cara Operations' results generally over time. Cross-sectional comparisons (between different companies) are also difficult with regard to ROE, for the same reason that ROA is difficult. Differences in the risks involved should result in differences in returns. Differences in the risks cannot, however, always explain large differences in return, as there are many factors that affect ROE.

Leverage

Comparing the ROE computed for Cara Operations with the associated ROA shows that the company, while earning only an 4.54% return on assets, showed a return of 7.36% on the shareholders' equity. This increase in return to equity is a result of the company successfully applying financial leverage. Financial **leverage** means simply that some of the funds obtained to invest in assets came from debtholders rather than from shareholders. A company that has a larger proportion of debt to shareholders' equity is said to be highly leveraged.

In the case of a totally shareholder-financed company—that is, a company with no debt—the ROE (assuming only one class of shares) would equal the ROA. There would be no interest expense; therefore, the numerators of the two ratios would be the same. The denominators would be the same because of the accounting equation (Assets = Liabilities − Shareholders' Equity) as adjusted given the assumed absence of any liabilities (Assets = Shareholders' Equity).

To understand the effects of leverage, consider first the data in Exhibit 12-5 for a 100% equity-financed company, Baker Company (a fictitious company). To keep the illustration simple, all liabilities are considered to be interest-bearing for Baker Company. Note that, in this example, Baker generates a 16.67% return on its assets before taxes (income before interest and taxes/assets = $166.67/$1,000). After the 40% corporate income taxes, this translates into a 10% after-tax return (ROA). Note also that the ROE is the same as the after-tax ROA because there is no debt.

EXHIBIT 12-5

■ Baker Company (100% equity-financed)

Balance Sheet

Assets	Liabilities
$1,000	$ 0
	Shareholders' equity
	$1,000

Income Statement

Income before interest and taxes	$ 166.67
Interest	0.00
Income before taxes	166.67
Income taxes (40%)	66.67
Net income	$ 100.00

ROA = $100/$1,000 = 10%
ROE = $100/$1,000 = 10%

Now consider the data in Exhibit 12-6 for Baker Company, which now assume that the company is only 90% shareholder-financed.

EXHIBIT 12-6

■ Baker Company (90% equity-financed) (16.67% interest rate)

Balance Sheet

Assets	Liabilities
$1,000	$ 100
	Shareholders' equity
	$ 900

Income Statement (assuming an interest rate of 16.67%)

Income before interest and taxes	$ 166.67
Interest	16.67
Income before taxes	150.00
Income taxes (40%)	60.00
Net income	$ 90.00

ROA = [$90 + {16.67 × (1 − .4)}]/$1,000 = $100/$1,000 = 10%
ROE = $90/$900 = 10%

In Exhibit 12-6, note several things. First note that the ROA is the same as that in Exhibit 12-5, because the mix of assets has not changed; only the amount of debt in the balance sheet has changed. The assets should be earning exactly what they would earn in a 100% shareholder-financed company. Second, note that the ROE is the same as the ROA. This will be the case *only* if the after-tax borrowing rate is the same as the after-tax ROA. Note that the before-tax borrowing rate is 16.67%. To adjust the rate to an after-tax rate, multiply it by 1 minus the tax rate, or 16.67% × (1 − 40%) = 10%. This means that the company borrowed $100 at a net cost of 10% (the after-tax borrowing rate) and invested the $100 in assets that return 10% after taxes (ROA). Therefore, the company breaks even on the money it borrowed. The shareholders' return of 10% is the income after taxes ($90) divided by their investment ($900).

Next, consider Exhibit 12-7, in which a lower interest rate is assumed (12%). In Exhibit 12-7, note that the ROE is greater than the ROA. This occurs because the company was able to borrow at a rate that was less than the rate it could earn by investing in assets. The after-tax cost of borrowing is 7.2% [12% × (1 − 40%)], whereas the after-tax return on the assets is 10% (ROA). Therefore, when the company borrowed $100 it cost $7.20 in interest, but the company was able to generate $10 in income. The difference is $2.80, which goes to the shareholders as an incremental return. Therefore, the shareholders earn a 10% (or $90) return on their investment of $900, plus they get the excess return of $2.80 that is earned on the money that was borrowed, for a total ROE of 10.3%. This improves their percentage return (ROE) over what they could have earned as a 100% equity-financed company, without any further investment on their part.

■ **Baker Company (90% equity-financed) (12% interest rate)**

EXHIBIT 12-7

Balance Sheet

Assets	Liabilities
$1,000	$ 100
	Shareholders' equity
	$ 900

Income Statement (assuming an interest rate of 12%)

Income before interest and taxes	$ 166.67
Interest	12.00
Income before taxes	154.67
Income taxes (40%)	61.87
Net income	$ 92.80

ROA = [$92.80 + {12.00 × (1 − .4)}]/$1,000 = $100/$1,000 = 10%
ROE = $92.80/$900 = 10.3%

This, then, is the advantage of leverage. The shareholders can improve their return (ROE) if the company can borrow funds at an after-tax borrowing rate that is less than the after-tax ROA. This is a big "if." The company that leverages itself is committed to making fixed interest payments to debtholders prior to earning a return on its assets. It is betting that the return on assets will be higher than the after-tax cost of its borrowing. If it is wrong, the return to the shareholders (ROE) could fall below what they could have earned with no debt at all. Consider, for example, the results of Baker Company in Exhibit 12-8, where the company commits to paying lenders 20% (before taxes). Return on equity in this case falls below the ROA to 9.8%. This is the risk of leveraging a company.

■ **Baker Company (90% equity-financed) (20% interest rate)**

Balance Sheet

Assets	Liabilities
$1,000	$ 100
	Shareholders' equity
	$ 900

Income Statement (assuming an interest rate of 20%)

Income before interest and taxes	$ 166.67
Interest	20.00
Income before taxes	146.67
Income taxes (40%)	58.67
Net income	$ 88.00

ROA = [$88 + {20 × (1 − .4)}]/$1,000 = $100/$1,000 = 10%
ROE = $88/$900 = 9.8%

If leveraging the company a little is potentially a good thing, as illustrated in Exhibit 12-7, why not leverage it a lot? In other words, why not borrow funds to buy most of the company's assets? In Exhibit 12-7, why not have 90% debt and 10% equity in the company? Exhibit 12-9 illustrates the kind of return the company could expect given 90% debt and the same interest rate as shown in Exhibit 12-7. A return of 35.2% is certainly a very attractive return compared to the ROA of 10% that could be achieved with a 100% equity-financed company. The problem with this financing strategy is that lenders will find the riskiness of their investment much higher in Exhibit 12-9 than they would in Exhibit 12-7. As the company adds more and more debt to its capital structure, it is committing itself to higher and higher fixed interest payments, and lenders will start demanding higher and higher returns from their investments as the risk increases. The interest rates will rise, and Baker Company will no longer be able to borrow at the 12% that was assumed in Exhibit 12-7. When its average borrowing costs start to equal or exceed the ROA of the company, it will become unattractive to borrow any further funds.

In theory, the increase in the borrowing rate would increasingly become a function of the amount of leverage employed by the company. Return on equity would improve over that of a 100% equity-financed company, up to a point. Exhibit 12-10 graphs the change (at least in theory) in ROE for various levels of leverage. Based on this graph, you can see that there is a point (at the top of the curve) at which ROE would be maximized. The amount of leverage that corresponds to this point is sometimes called the **optimal capital structure** of the company. For the hypothetical company illustrated in the graph, the optimal capital structure would be

Baker Company (10% equity-financed) (12% interest rate)

EXHIBIT 12-9

Balance Sheet

Assets	Liabilities
$1,000	$ 900
	Shareholders' equity
	$ 100

Income Statement (assuming an interest rate of 12%)

Income before interest and taxes	$ 166.67
Interest	108.00
Income before taxes	58.67
Income taxes (40%)	23.47
Net income	$ 35.20

ROA = [$35.20 + {108.00 × (1 − .4)}]/$1,000 = $100/$1,000 = 10%
ROE = $35.20/$100 = 35.2%

approximately 40% debt and the rest equity. This point exists in theory but is difficult to determine in the real world. It is true, however, that as you look across industries, different industries have different average levels of leverage. This would indicate that, based on the risk characteristics of those industries, the companies in those industries borrow to the point they think is profitable, and no further.

Leverage and Optimal Capital Structure

EXHIBIT 12-10

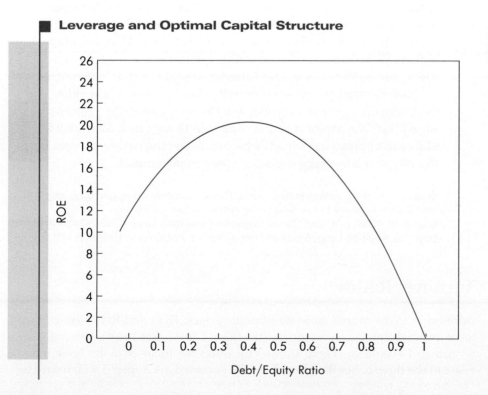

Cara Operations' interest rate on its debt varied from 5.5% to 8.1% before taxes. Its tax rate was approximately 40% which means the after-tax interest rate ranged from 3.3% to 4.9%. If its ROA was 4.54%, it was earning a slightly higher return on its assets than it paid to borrow money. Its ROE of 7.36% illustrates how that slight increase in ROA translated into an increase in its return to shareholders.

The use of leverage by a company can be judged, to some extent, by the difference in its ROE and its ROA, as illustrated in the hypothetical example and by Cara Operations. In addition, several other ratios are used to measure the amount of leverage the company employs, as well as how well it uses that leverage. These include the debt/equity ratio and the times interest earned ratio, which are discussed in a later section on liquidity.

accounting in the news

USE OF LEVERAGE TO BUY OTHER COMPANIES

Some companies make leveraging their business. Toronto-based Onex Corp. has made a name for itself as a leveraged buyout specialist—borrowing money to buy companies by using the assets in the acquired company as collateral.

Onex has invested in a variety of industries, ranging from automotive parts to food distribution to high-tech contract manufacturing. Recently, Onex made its first acquisition in the building industry with American Buildings Corp., an industrial and commercial structure specialist. Onex paid the $405 million price tag with $145 million in cash and the rest with debt, outside investment, and contributions from American Buildings management.

Onex's strategy involves choosing good performers in industries with high growth potential and then improving their returns on equity. One senior manager has said Onex's best asset is its ability to improve a company's performance; the bigger the deal, the bigger the leverage impact of Onex management.

Sources: "Making money in the middle: Onex engineers leveraged buyouts, and then engineers better firms," by Amanda Lang, *Financial Post Daily*, March 18, 1998, p. 8; and "Onex forges into building industry with $405M buy," by Amanda Lang, *National Post (Financial Post)*, April 9, 1999, p. C3.

Turnover Ratios

In addition to the overall measures of performance, ROA and ROE, some other measures are helpful in understanding the specific items that affect the overall performance of a company. Three turnover measures are discussed in this book. They relate to the three policy decisions that were discussed in Chapter 5 with regard to the cash flow performance of a company. They are accounts receivable, inventory, and accounts payable turnovers. These ratios provide some quantitative measures of the lead/lag relationships that exist between the revenue and expense recognition and the cash flows related to these three items.

Accounts Receivable Turnover

The **accounts receivable turnover** ratio attempts to provide information about the accounts receivable policy of the company. This ratio measures how many times during a year the accounts receivable balance "turns over"—that is, how many times old receivables are collected and replaced by new receivables. It is calculated as follows:

$$\text{Accounts receivable turnover} = \frac{\text{Sales on account}}{\text{Average accounts receivable}}$$

When data from financial statements are used, the assumption is usually made that all sales were on account, because there is usually no information in the financial statements about the percentage of sales on account versus percentage of cash sales. If the turnover ratio was being prepared for internal use by management, this type of information would be available and would be used in the computation of this ratio.

When the data from Cara Operations are used, the ratio for 1999 is:

ACCOUNTS RECEIVABLE TURNOVER—CARA OPERATIONS LIMITED, 1999

$$\text{Accounts receivable turnover} = \frac{\text{Sales on account}}{\text{Average accounts receivable}}$$

$$= \frac{\$864,890}{\dfrac{\$65,682 + \$69,732}{2}}$$

$$= 12.8 \text{ times}$$

The level of turnover of accounts receivable depends on several factors, especially the normal credit terms granted by the company. If the company normally gives customers 30 days to pay, and if customers pay in 30 days, the resulting accounts receivable turnover would be 12, because there would be 30 days of sales always outstanding in accounts receivable. If the normal credit term is 60 days, the resulting accounts receivable turnover would be 6. With an accounts receivable turnover of 12.8, it appears that many of Cara Operations' receivables have 30-day credit terms.

The turnover number can also be converted into a measure of the days necessary to collect the average receivable by dividing the number of days in one year by the turnover ratio. To simplify calculations, the number of days in a year is often assumed to be 360 rather than 365. The average days to collect for Cara Operations are:

DAYS TO COLLECT ACCOUNTS RECEIVABLE—CARA OPERATIONS LIMITED, 1999

$$\text{Days to collect} = \frac{365}{\text{Accounts receivable turnover}}$$

$$= \frac{365}{12.8}$$

$$= 28.5 \text{ days}$$

You cannot simply look at the 28.5 days and decide whether it is bad or good. You need to know what the normal credit terms are (if the average monthly sales are fairly equal, large sales in the last month of the fiscal year would result in an apparently lower turnover and higher number of days' sales in the year-end balance) and what proportion of total sales is made on credit. To analyze this 28.5 days, we should also consider a time-series analysis (the trend compared to previous years) and a cross-sectional analysis (a comparison with the performance of competitors of Cara Operations).

Inventory Turnover

The **inventory turnover** ratio gives the analyst some idea of how fast inventory is sold or, alternatively, how long inventory is held prior to sale. The calculation of the turnover is similar to that of the accounts receivable turnover, with a measure of the flow of inventory in the numerator and a measure of the balance in inventory in the denominator. It is calculated as follows:

$$\text{Inventory turnover} = \frac{\text{Cost of goods sold}}{\text{Average inventory}}$$

Note that the numerator contains the cost of goods sold, not the sales value of the goods sold (revenues). Total sales revenue, while it does measure the flow of goods sold to customers, would be inappropriate in the numerator, because it is based on the selling price of the inventory while the denominator is measured at cost. Cost of goods sold measures at cost and so is more appropriate.

The number of days for which inventory is held can be calculated from the turnover ratio in the same way that the accounts receivable turnover ratio is calculated.

INVENTORY TURNOVER—CARA OPERATIONS LIMITED, 1999

$$\text{Inventory turnover} = \frac{\$7,83,428}{\dfrac{\$21,629 + \$20,775}{2}}$$

$$= 36.95 \text{ times}$$

$$\text{Days inventory held} = \frac{365}{\text{Inventory turnover}}$$

$$= \frac{365}{36.95}$$

$$= 9.9 \text{ days}$$

The average number of days that inventory is held depends on the type of inventory produced, used, or sold. In the ratio just calculated, the inventories of Cara Operations were used. Remember that Cara's major operations involve the sale of food products in restaurants, hospitals, schools, and airports. The 9.9 days, therefore, refers to the average length of time that costs remain in inventory from original purchase or for use in food preparation. For Cara, the short period of time reflects the fact that its inventory is food. For a manufacturing company such as Big Rock Brewery you would need to decide whether to use all of the inventories (raw materials, work in process, and finished goods) or only the finished goods in the denominator of the turnover ratio, to determine how long it takes from completion of production to sale. From a note to Big Rock's financial statements, we know that the value of the finished goods inventories in 1999 and 1998 is $549,278 and $418,015, respectively. From this information we can calculate the finished goods inventory turnover as follows:

FINISHED GOODS INVENTORY TURNOVER—BIG ROCK BREWERY LTD., 1999

$$\text{Inventory turnover} = \frac{\$7,691,231}{\frac{\$549,278 + \$418,015}{2}}$$

$$= 15.9 \text{ times}$$

$$\text{Days inventory held} = \frac{365}{\text{Inventory turnover}}$$

$$= \frac{365}{15.9}$$

$$= 23 \text{ days}$$

Based on these numbers, it seems obvious that the finished goods are not held for very long (23 days) before they are sold. Because Big Rock manufactures and sells beer, the holding of the finished product for approximately 23 days seems reasonable. However, as with the accounts receivable turnover figures, deciding whether this is good or bad would require either a time-series or a cross-sectional analysis, as well as some detailed knowledge of the industry.

Accounts Payable Turnover

The **accounts payable turnover** ratio is similar to the accounts receivable ratio, but provides information about the accounts payable policy of the company. In its ideal form, it would be calculated as follows:

$$\text{Accounts payable turnover} = \frac{\text{Credit purchases}}{\text{Average accounts payable}}$$

The problem with the preceding formulation is that the credit purchases of a company do not appear directly in the financial statements. It may be possible to approximate the credit purchases by finding the cash payments made to suppliers in the cash flow statement, assuming that the balance in accounts payable did not change drastically during the period. However, this requires that the company prepare its cash flow statement using the direct approach. As mentioned in Chapter 5, almost all companies use the indirect approach to the cash flow statement, and cash payments to suppliers do not appear directly in that statement.

Another alternative is to use the cost of goods sold figure in place of purchases on credit, because cost of goods sold appears in the income statement. To the extent that the purchase of goods is the main item affecting cost of goods sold, this would be appropriate. In a retailing company, this would probably be a good approximation, again assuming that the level of inventories did not change dramatically during the period. For a manufacturing company, however, many items other than credit purchases affect the cost of goods sold. For example, a manufacturing company like Big Rock will likely include the amortization of its production equipment in the cost assigned to the inventory it produces. When this ratio is calculated, most analysts would use the cost of goods sold in the numerator. It would therefore be calculated as:

$$\text{Accounts payable turnover} = \frac{\text{Cost of goods sold}}{\text{Average accounts payable}}$$

For Cara Operations in 1999, this ratio is:

ACCOUNTS PAYABLE TURNOVER—CARA OPERATIONS LIMITED, 1999

$$\text{Accounts payable turnover} = \frac{\$783,428}{\dfrac{\$91,319 + \$88,679}{2}}$$

$$= 8.7 \text{ times}$$

$$\text{Days to pay} = \frac{365}{\text{Accounts payable turnover}}$$

$$= \frac{365}{8}$$

$$= 42 \text{ days}$$

For Cara Operations, the calculation of this ratio and the average days to pay appear to be high if the normal credit terms received by Cara Operations are 30 days. In this case, it may not be appropriate to use the cost of goods sold as an approximation of purchases on credit if the cost of goods sold includes significant amounts that are not purchased on credit from suppliers. As well, you will notice that we used the "accounts payable and accrued charges" amount from the balance sheet, because accounts payable was not listed separately. It is probable that the accrued charges include amounts like interest payable, which are not included in the cost of goods sold. However, we cannot really understand these numbers without having more details of the operations and the amounts that are included in the cost of goods sold and accrued charges. Again, cross-sectional and time-series analyses should be undertaken.

Short-Term Liquidity Ratios

As discussed in Chapter 1, liquidity refers to the ability of the company to convert assets into cash to pay liabilities. A basic understanding of the short-term liquidity position of the company should result from a consideration of the financial statements, particularly the cash flow statement, as well as the turnover ratios discussed in the performance section. Understanding the liquidity position requires a knowledge of the leads and lags in the company's cash-to-cash cycle. Additionally, at least two other ratios provide quantitative measures of short-term liquidity: the current and quick ratios.

Current Ratio

The **current ratio** is calculated by comparing the total current assets to the total current liabilities. It is calculated as follows:

$$\text{Current ratio} = \frac{\text{Current assets}}{\text{Current liabilities}}$$

Remember that current assets are those assets that are going to be converted into cash in the next year (or operating cycle of the company if it is longer than one year) and that current liabilities are going to require the use of cash in the next year. As such, this ratio should be greater than 1; otherwise, it is difficult to see how the company will remain solvent in the next year. The rule of thumb for this ratio, for most industries, is that it should be 1 or more, but, to be conservative, approximately 2 or more. However, the size of this ratio depends on the type of business and the type of assets and liabilities that are considered current.

One caveat: The current ratio is subject to manipulation by a company at the end of the year. This ratio may not, therefore, be a very reliable measure of liquidity. For example, consider a company that has $100 in current assets and $50 in current liabilities at the end of a given year. Its current ratio would be 2 ($100/$50). Suppose that $25 of the $100 is in cash and the rest is in inventory. Suppose further that the company uses up all of its $25 in cash to pay $25 of current liabilities at the end of the year. The current ratio becomes 3 ($75/$25); now the company looks more liquid. Notice, however, that the company is actually less liquid; in fact, it is virtually illiquid in the short term, because it has no cash and must sell its inventory and wait until it collects on the sale of that inventory before it will have any cash to pay its bills. In this case, the current ratio is deceptive.

The current ratios for Cara Operations in 1999 and 1998 are:

CURRENT RATIO—CARA OPERATIONS LIMITED, 1999 AND 1998

1999

$$\text{Current ratio} = \frac{\$139,152}{\$105,446} = 1.32$$

1998

$$\text{Current ratio} = \frac{\$101,570}{\$100,307} = 1.01$$

The current ratio of 1.32 in 1999 is an improvement over the 1.101 of the previous year. Although this ratio appears to be low, it may be quite acceptable in this industry. Also, remember from the inventory turnover ratio that the inventory sells within 10 days, which means the company's ability to convert the inventory to cash is accelerated.

Quick Ratio

One of the problems with the current ratio is that some assets in the current section are less liquid than others. For example, inventory is usually less liquid than accounts receivable, which in turn is less liquid than cash. In some industries, inventory is very illiquid because of the long period of time that it may have to be held before sale. Consider, for example, the holding period in the manufacture of 12-year-old scotch whisky. The current ratio in such cases will not adequately measure the short-term liquidity of the company, because the inventory will not be converted into cash for a long period of time. In this case, the **quick ratio** is a better measure of short-term liquidity. It differs from the current ratio only in that inventories and, often, prepaid expenses are omitted from the numerator. Prepaid expenses do not convert into cash. Instead, they used cash in the past, and the company will be saving cash because amounts have been paid in advance. The ratio is calculated as:

$$\text{Quick ratio} = \frac{\text{Current assets} - \text{Inventories} - \text{Prepaid expenses}}{\text{Current liabilities}}$$

The rule of thumb for this ratio is that it should be approximately 1 or more. A quick ratio of 1 means that the very short-term current assets are equal to the total of the current liabilities. Again, the actual value depends on the type of industry. For Cara Operations, the calculation results in:

QUICK RATIO—CARA OPERATIONS LIMITED, 1999 AND 1998

1999

$$\text{Quick ratio} = \frac{\$139,152 - \$21,629 - \$3,171}{\$105,446} = 1.08$$

1998

$$\text{Quick ratio} = \frac{\$101,570 - \$20,775 - \$3,546}{\$100,307} = .77$$

Just as with the current ratio, the quick ratio in 1999 of 1.08 is an improvement over the quick ratio in 1998 of .77. The quick ratio in 1999 is very close to the 1.0 rule of thumb amount. Taken together, the current ratio and quick ratio indicate that Cara Operations has significantly improved its liquidity position in the last year. Just reviewing these two years, illustrates the importance of time-series analyses in understanding a ratio. Cross-sectional analyses should also be undertaken.

Long-Term Liquidity Ratios

Long-term liquidity refers to the ability of the company to pay its obligations in the long term (meaning more than one year in the future), or its ability to pay its long-term debt. A time-series analysis of the cash flow statement and the patterns of cash flow over time should provide the insight one needs in order to assess a company's abilities in this regard. There are at least two ratios generally used in assessing long-term liquidity: the debt/equity ratio and the times interest earned ratio.

Debt/Equity Ratio

The **debt/equity ratio** is really a set of ratios that are used to assess the extent to which the company is leveraged. From our earlier discussion about leverage, you know that the more leverage a company has, the riskier is its situation and the more fixed are its commitments to pay interest. Comparing the amount of debt to the amount of equity in a company is important in assessing its ability to pay off these debts in the long term.

Of the many different definitions of the debt/equity ratios that could be used here, we will provide three. They will be referred to as D/E(I), D/E(II), and D/E(III). D/E(I) expresses the total debt of the company as a percentage of total liabilities plus shareholders' equity (the same as total assets). The total liabilities are assumed to include all liabilities of the company, the shareholders' equity to include all shareholders' equity accounts. This ratio is calculated as:

$$D/E(I) = \frac{\text{Total liabilities}}{\text{Total liabilities} + \text{Shareholders' equity}}$$

$$\text{Or} \quad \frac{\text{Total liabilities}}{\text{Total assets}}$$

For Cara Operations in 1999, this ratio is:

D/E(I)—CARA OPERATIONS LIMITED, 1999

$$D/E(I) = \frac{\$312,832}{\$561,111}$$

$$= .56$$

The first debt/equity ratio tells you that Cara's debt makes up just over half of total liabilities and shareholders' equity. In other words, Cara Operations uses equity and debt almost equally to finance its investment in assets.

The second debt-to-equity ratio provides the same information but in a slightly different form. It is calculated as the ratio of the total liabilities to the total shareholders' equity, as follows:

$$D/E(II) = \frac{\text{Total liabilities}}{\text{Total shareholders' equity}}$$

For Cara Operations in 1999, this ratio is:

D/E(II)—CARA OPERATIONS LIMITED, 1999

$$D/E(II) = \frac{\$312,832}{\$248,279}$$

$$= 1.26$$

This ratio tells you, in a different way, that the debt and equity are almost equal. When the debt is compared to the equity, it represents just over 100% of the equity amount. In other words, Cara Operations uses debt slightly more often to finance its assets.

The third debt-to-equity ratio focuses on the long-term debt of the company relative to its equity. It is calculated as the ratio of the total long-term liabilities to the sum of the total long-term liabilities plus the shareholders' equity of the company, as follows:

$$D/E(III) = \frac{\text{Total long-term liabilities}}{\text{Total long-term liabilities + Shareholders' equity}}$$

For Cara Operations in 1999, this ratio is:

D/E(III)—CARA OPERATIONS LIMITED, 1999

$$D/E(III) = \frac{\$207,386}{\$207,386 + \$248,279}$$

$$= .46$$

This ratio tells you that 46% of the financing of the investment in assets is achieved using long-term debt.

Is the level of debt represented in these ratios appropriate for Cara Operations? Again, a cross-sectional analysis of these ratios could reveal whether Cara Operations has excessive debt compared to other companies. A time-series analysis could reveal the trend over time. As a general guide, however, the average of corporate debt on the books of nonfinancial companies is somewhere between 45% and 50%. Cara Operations, with a ratio of 56%, appears to be very close to that average. An inspection of the long-term debt of Cara Operations shows that 5.7% of the total liabilities ($17,777/$312,832) is future income taxes which, if you recall, are not contractual obligations with a fixed payment date. Therefore, the long-term liquidity position of Cara Operations appears to be quite good.

Times Interest Earned Ratio

The final ratio in the long-term liquidity section is the **times interest earned (TIE) ratio**. It compares the amount of earnings available to pay interest to the level of interest expense. Because interest is tax-deductible, the earnings available to pay interest would be the earnings prior to the payment of interest or taxes. One complication in the computation of this ratio is that some companies capitalize interest when they construct long-term assets. This means that, instead of expensing interest, a company can record the interest in an asset account. This generally happens only when a company is constructing an asset and incurs interest on money borrowed to finance the construction. The adjustment to the ratio is that the amount of interest capitalized should be added to the denominator. The numerator does not require adjustment if the amount of interest expensed is added back to net income. The ratio is therefore calculated as:

$$\text{Times interest earned} = \frac{\text{Income before interest and taxes}}{\text{Interest}}$$

Cara Operations indicates in a note to the financial statements that its policy is to capitalize interest on "assets constructed over time." The notes to the financial statements indicate that, in 1999, Cara Operations capitalized $300,000 of interest. Thus to calculate this ratio for 1999, we have included this amount in addition to the interest expense reported on the income statement. The ratio is therefore calculated as:

TIMES INTEREST EARNED—CARA OPERATIONS LIMITED, 1999

$$\text{TIE} = \frac{\$29,430 + (\$8,600 + \$1,673)}{(\$8,600 + \$1,673) + \$300}$$

$$= 3.8$$

Note that in the calculation there appear to be three interest amounts added to the income before taxes. The sum of $8,600 and $1,673 represents the interest expense from the income statement. Cara Operations nets the interest expense and interest income together and reports the net amount, the $8,600. It then discloses the interest income amount, the $1,673. To arrive at the interest expense amount for this ratio it is necessary to add back the interest income amount.

The resulting ratio of 3.8 indicates that Cara Operations earned 3.8 times the amount it needed to pay its interest expense in 1999. This is a comfortable cushion. Income would have to drop to one-quater of its current level before Cara Operations would have trouble paying the interest. When a company indicates that it has capitalized interest but does not disclose the amount of that capitalization, you need to remember that the times interest earned ratio will be overstated. Your problem as a user attempting to evaluate the company's ability to pay the interest owed is that you cannot determine the amount by which it is overstated. When any company shows a times interest earned ratio of close to 1, it indicates that the payment of the interest may be at risk. As a lender, you should be concerned by a low times interest earned ratio.

Earnings Per Share Ratio

The **earnings per share ratio** is one that is quoted quite often in the financial press and one in which shareholders are very interested. In its simplest form, it is the earnings of the company divided by the weighted-average number of common shares outstanding. Although this ratio may be of some help in analyzing a company's results, its usefulness is limited. The major problem with using it as a measure of performance is that it ignores the level of investment. Companies with the same earnings per share might have very different profitabilities, depending on their investment in net assets. The other limitation is that the shares of different companies are not equivalent, and companies with the same overall profitability may have different earnings per share figures because they have a different number of shares outstanding that represent ownership. The best use of the earnings per share figure is in a time-series analysis, rather than in a cross-sectional analysis.

The earnings per share calculation represents the earnings per common share. Therefore, if the company also issues preferred shares, the effects of the preferred shares must be removed in calculating the ratio. With preferred shares outstanding, this means that any dividends that are paid to preferred shareholders should be deducted from net income, because that amount of income is not available to common shareholders. The number of preferred shares outstanding should also be left out of the denominator. The calculation of basic earnings per share then becomes:

$$\text{Basic earnings per share} = \frac{\text{Net income} - \text{Preferred dividends}}{\text{Weighted average number of common shares outstanding}}$$

The preferred dividends that should be deducted are the cumulative preferred dividends, whether or not they are declared in the year, and any non-cumulative preferred dividends that have been declared in the year. Recall from Chapter 11 that cumulative means that if a dividend is not declared on the preferred shares in one year, the dividends then carry over into the next year. In the second year, both the prior year's preferred dividends and the current year's preferred dividends must be declared before any common dividends can be declared.

In addition to preferred shares, another complicating factor in the calculation of earnings per share arises when the company issues securities that are convertible into common shares. Examples of these types of securities are convertible debt, convertible preferred shares, and share option plans. The key feature of these securities is that they are all convertible into common shares under certain conditions. If additional common shares are issued upon their conversion, the earnings per share number could decrease because of the larger number of shares that would be outstanding. This is called the potential dilution of earnings per share.

At the end of a given accounting period, the presence of convertible securities creates some uncertainty about how to report the earnings per share number. Should the company report earnings per share without considering the potentially dilutive effects of the convertible securities, or should it disclose some information that would allow readers of the financial statements to understand these effects? To provide the best information to users of financial statements, we should disclose information about the dilutive effects of convertible securities. Thus financial statements may include several earnings per share figures, the main ones being the basic earnings per share and the fully diluted earnings per share.

Basic Earnings Per Share

Basic earnings per share is usually a very simple number that considers only the net income, preferred dividends, and weighted-average number of common shares outstanding. Every published financial statement shows this figure. Note in Exhibit 12-3 on the statement of earnings for Cara Operations that two basic earnings per share figures are given, a basic earnings per share from continuing operations (19.9 cents) and a basic earnings per share on net earnings (19.9 cents). The reason for the two amounts is that in 1998 Cara Operations discontinued some of its operations. Because these operations were being discontinued, Cara backed these amounts out of the normal continuing operations and showed them separately. In order to create parallel treatment in 1999, the company disclosed two basic earnings per share amounts. When users review the financial statements it is usually with two objectives in mind: to see how the company did during the last year and to assess how it might do in the future. Because of this focus on the future, it is important for companies to separate discontinued operations that will not affect the future and continuing operations that may be a good measure of future operations. To help users in their evaluation, whenever there are non-future items like discontinued items or extraordinary items, the company discloses two basic earnings per share figures: one for continuing operations and one for net income. The basic earnings per share from continuing operations is probably more useful.

Fully Diluted Earnings Per Share

Fully diluted earnings per share is calculated under the worst-case scenario set of assumptions. The company identifies all of the dilutive securities that will have a negative effect on the earnings per share amount if they are converted. For example, if convertible preferred shares are converted to common shares, the number of common shares outstanding will increase. At the same time the numerator will increase, because if the preferred shares are now common shares, there will no longer be any preferred dividends and all of the net income will be available to the common shareholders. Because both the numerator and the denominator increase, the effect of a conversion on earnings per share is not always negative. Under the worst-case scenario for determining fully diluted earnings per share, the calculation includes only those conversions that will have a negative effect on earnings per share. The calculation of fully diluted earnings per share is a "heads-up" calculation for users. It attempts to tell users how much the earnings per share could decline in the future if all of the dilutive convertible securities were converted to common shares.

Cara Operations has stock option plans and share warrants. A **warrant** is a right given to a shareholder to purchase common shares at an assigned price. The shareholder can choose to exercise the warrant (buy the shares) or sell the warrant to someone else, who can then buy the shares or let it expire. As a result of these dilutive securities, in 1999, Cara Operations has reported two fully diluted earnings per share amounts, 19.7 cents for fully diluted earnings per share from continuing operations and 19.7 cents for fully diluted earnings per share from net earnings. As with the disclosure for basic earnings per share, it is important to distinguish between the amounts that reflect possible future earnings and the amounts that represent net earnings. These fully diluted earnings per share amounts are not much lower than the basic earnings per share amounts. In other words, although there will be a negative effect on earnings per share if the stock options or share warrants are exercised, current shareholders can be assured that any negative effect will not be very large.

Price/Earnings Ratio

The **price/earnings ratio**, or **multiple**, is a comparison of the price per share on the stock market with the earnings per share of the company. Many analysts think of this ratio as the price investors are willing to pay for a dollar's worth of earnings. The interpretation of this ratio is somewhat difficult, because stock market price levels are not well understood. It might help to think of the multiple in terms of its inverse. If a company is earning $1.00 per common share and the shares are selling for $20 on the stock market, this indicates that the current multiple is 20. The inverse of this multiple is 1/20, or 5%; this indicates that the shares are returning 5% in the form of earnings per share compared to the market price.

Many factors affect the level of stock market prices, including the interest rates prevailing in the economy and the future prospects of the company. It is sometimes useful to think that the market price reflects the present value of all future expected earnings of the company. The earnings per share figure serves as an important link between the accounting numbers produced in the financial statements and the stock market price of the company's shares.

NON-MANUFACTURING OR NON-RETAIL COMPANY ANALYSIS

Although the above discussion is applicable to most companies in most industries, some differences for non-manufacturing or non-retail companies should be noted. As an example of a non-manufacturing or non-retail company, consider a financial services company such as a bank, an insurance company, or a finance company. Compared to manufacturers and retailers, these types of companies invest in very different kinds of assets, and obtain their financing from different sources.

The assets of financial services companies consist of almost no inventories and relatively little property, plant, and equipment. The majority of their assets are loans made to their customers or other investments. The assets of most nonfinancial companies are mainly property, plant, and equipment; inventories; and receivables.

The liability sections of financial services companies are also very different from those of manufacturers and retailers. The first major difference is the debt/equity ratio. Financial services companies tend to have considerably higher debt/equity ratios than manufacturers or retailers because of the large amounts of cash received from depositors. In the insurance industry, the high ratio results from amounts owed to policyholders. The second major difference is that liabilities of financial services companies such as banks tend to be predominantly short-term in nature because of the deposits received from customers, which are normally payable upon demand. Many customers, however, leave amounts with these companies for long periods of time. This means that although they are technically short-term because the customer can withdraw the funds at any time, in reality they are often long-term in nature.

The higher leverage employed by financial services companies reflects, in part, the lower risk of the types of assets in which these companies invest. Manufacturers, in addition to employing financial leverage, employ something called **operating leverage**. Operating leverage involves investing in large amounts of property, plant, and equipment (capital assets with fixed amortization costs). The property, plant, and equipment allows manufacturers to make their own inventory instead of buying it from an outside supplier (variable costs). The risk is that the manufacturers must operate at sufficient volume for their profit from the sale of goods to cover their fixed costs. At large volumes, this makes manufacturing companies very profitable but, at low volumes, the companies generate large losses because the fixed costs must be paid from the lower sales volumes. Partially because of the amount of operating leverage, lenders generally do not lend to manufacturers as much as they lend to financial services companies.

A complete analysis of financial services companies is beyond the scope of this book. It is hoped that this brief discussion of some of the differences between financial services companies and manufacturers and retailers has provided you with some insights into how analyses may differ according to the type of company being assessed.

SUMMARY

At this point in the book, we have discussed all the major financial statements and specific accounting methods and principles that apply to each category within the asset, liability, and shareholders' equity sections of the balance sheet. We have devoted this final chapter to methods you can use to gain some insights into how to interpret the information that you find reported on the financial statements. By comparing amounts on one financial statement with related amounts on another financial statement, we are able to make some assessments about the impact of various items on the health and future prospects of a company. We have restricted the discussions to fairly simple companies to make it easier for you to learn the basics.

In Appendix C at the back of the book you will find additional information about complex organizations. These are companies (usually called parent companies) that buy an interest in other companies (called subsidiaries) to obtain control of the resources of those companies. The majority of the real companies reported in this book are parent companies that have one or more subsidiaries. You can tell that a company is a parent company if it prepares "consolidated" financial statements. If you flip back to the examples of financial statements throughout the book you will see that most of them are consolidated. The accountant is faced with complex issues, such as how to represent the resources controlled by the shareholders of the parent company.

RATIO SUMMARY

Exhibit 12-11 summarizes the ratios that were developed in the chapter.

■ **Ratio Summary**

$$ROA = \text{Profit Margin Ratio} \times \text{Total Asset Turnover}$$

$$= \frac{\text{Net income} + [\text{Interest expense} \times (1 - \text{Tax rate})]}{\text{Sales revenue}} \times \frac{\text{Sales revenue}}{\text{Average total assets}}$$

$$ROE = \frac{\text{Net income} - \text{Preferred dividends}}{\text{Average shareholders' equity}}$$

$$\text{Inventory Turnover} = \frac{\text{Cost of goods sold}}{\text{Average inventory}}$$

$$\text{Accounts Receivable Turnover} = \frac{\text{Sales on account}}{\text{Average accounts receivable}}$$

$$\text{Accounts Payable Turnover} = \frac{\text{Cost of goods sold}}{\text{Average accounts payable}}$$

$$\text{Current Ratio} = \frac{\text{Current assets}}{\text{Current liabilities}}$$

$$\text{Quick Ratio} = \frac{\text{Current assets} - \text{Inventory} - \text{Prepaid expenses}}{\text{Current liabilities}}$$

$$\text{D/E(I)} = \frac{\text{Total liabilities}}{\text{Total liabilities} + \text{Shareholders' equity}}$$

$$\text{D/E(II)} = \frac{\text{Total liabilities}}{\text{Shareholders' equity}}$$

$$\text{D/E(III)} = \frac{\text{Total long-term liabilities}}{\text{Total long-term liabilities} + \text{Shareholders' equity}}$$

$$\text{Times Interest Earned (TIE)} = \frac{\text{Net income} + \text{Taxes} + \text{Interest}}{\text{Interest}}$$

$$\text{Price/Earnings Ratio} = \frac{\text{Stock market price}}{\text{Earnings per share}}$$

SUMMARY PROBLEM

The income statement, balance sheet, and cash flow statement of Mark's Work Wearhouse Limited are shown in Exhibit 12-12. Calculate the following ratios for 1999 based on the data in the financial statements. Comment on what the ratios tell us about the financial position of Mark's Work Wearhouse and what further analyses you should undertake.

Performance Ratios:

1. ROA (Break down into profit margin ratio and total asset turnover.)
2. ROE
3. Accounts receivable turnover
4. Inventory turnover
5. Accounts payable turnover

Short-Term Liquidity Ratios:

6. Current ratio
7. Quick ratio

Long-Term Liquidity Ratios:

8. Debt/equity ratios
9. Times interest earned

SUGGESTED SOLUTION TO SUMMARY PROBLEM

ROA:

ROA (BREAKDOWN)—MARK'S WORK WEARHOUSE LIMITED, 1999

ROA = Profit Margin Ratio $\times$ Total Asset Turnover

$$= \frac{\text{Net income} + [\text{Interest expense} \times (1 - \text{Tax rate})]}{\text{Sales revenue}} \times \frac{\text{Sales revenue}}{\text{Average total assets}}$$

$$= \frac{\$5,752 + [\$3,365^* \times (1 - 5,244/10,996)]}{\$283,401} \times \frac{\$283,401}{\dfrac{\$132,992 + \$105,617}{2}}$$

$$= 2.65\% \times 2.38 = 6.31\%$$

*The interest expense is the sum of the short-term and long-term interest.

ROE:

ROE—MARK'S WORK WEARHOUSE LIMITED, 1999

$$\text{ROE} = \frac{\text{Net income} - \text{Preferred dividends}}{\text{Average shareholders' equity}}$$

$$= \frac{\$3,923 - 0^*}{\dfrac{\$53,306 + \$46,746}{2}}$$

$$= 7.8\%$$

*Although the company had preferred shares, it always treated them as common shares because they could be converted to common shares whenever the company wanted. The shares were exchanged for common shares during the year ended January 30, 1999.

EXHIBIT 12-12
PART A

Consolidated Balance Sheets

(thousands)	As at January 25, 1997	As at January 31, 1998	As at January 30, 1999
Assets			
Current assets			
Cash and cash equivalents	$ 11,749	$ 349	$ 2,710
Accounts receivable (Note 4)	12,284	12,644	13,364
Merchandise inventories	44,040	60,108	76,982
Other current assets (Note 5)	2,304	2,709	3,304
	70,377	75,810	96,360
Other assets (Note 6)	793	449	975
Capital assets (Note 7)	14,608	20,072	23,531
Future income taxes (Notes 1M & 18)	1,676	2,091	3,413
Goodwill (Note 8)	7,368	7,195	8,713
	$ 94,822	$ 105,617	$ 132,992
Liabilities			
Current liabilities			
Accounts payable and accrued liabilities	$ 36,540	$ 33,280	$ 43,557
Income taxes payable	6,478	6,683	4,976
Current portion of long-term debt (Note 10)	2,286	4,434	7,992
	45,304	44,397	56,525
Long-term debt (Note 10)	11,952	13,414	22,052
Deferred gains (Note 7)	682	1,060	1,109
	57,938	58,871	79,686
Shareholders' Equity			
Capital stock (Notes 12 and 20C)	28,577	31,888	32,696
Retained earnings (Note 1M)	8,307	14,858	20,610
	36,884	46,746	53,306
	$ 94,822	$ 105,617	$ 132,992

Approved by the Board

Michael Fox, Director

Garth Mitchell, Director

EXHIBIT 12-12
PART B

Consolidated Statements of Earnings and Retained Earnings

(thousands except per Common Share amounts)	52 weeks ended January 25, 1997	53 weeks ended January 31, 1998	52 weeks ended January 30, 1999
Corporate and franchise sales (Note 14)	$ 303,756	$ 402,207	$417,468
Corporate operations			
Front-line operations (Note 1B)			
Sales	$ 220,902	$ 252,016	$ 283,401
Cost of sales	136,933	149,923	169,163
Gross margin	83,969	102,093	114,238
Front-line expenses			
Personnel, advertising and other	39,642	47,074	51,869
Occupancy	19,570	21,862	25,868
Depreciation and amortization	3,811	4,724	5,350
Interest – short term	1,176	656	2,015
	64,199	74,316	85,102
Front-line contribution	19,770	27,777	29,136
Franchise royalties and other (Note 15)	4,981	7,604	7,016
Net front-line contribution before back-line expenses	24,751	35,381	36,152
Back-line operations (Note 1B)			
Back-line expenses			
Personnel, administration and other	10,028	14,880	15,124
Occupancy	835	978	998
Depreciation and amortization	612	2,371	3,027
Software development and maintenance costs	727	815	906
Computer services	3,406	946	571
Interest – long term	673	1,676	1,350
Franchise bad debt provisions	160	460	219
Other costs (Note 17)	—	851	—
	16,441	22,977	22,195
Earnings before provision for closure of U.S. pilot stores and income taxes	8,310	12,404	13,957
Provision for closure of U.S. pilot stores (Notes 16 and 20A)	—	—	2,961
Earnings before income taxes	8,310	12,404	10,996
Income taxes (Notes 1M and 18)			
Current expense	4,937	6,268	6,566
Future expense (benefit)	(550)	(415)	(1,322)
	4,387	5,853	5,244
Net earnings	3,923	6,551	5,752
Retained earnings at beginning of year	4,384	8,307	14,858
Retained earnings at end of year	$ 8,307	$ 14,858	$ 20,610
Earnings per Common Share			
Basic	16¢	24¢	21¢
Fully diluted	15¢	23¢	20¢

EXHIBIT 12-12
PART C

Consolidated Statements of Cash Flows

(thousands)	52 weeks ended January 25, 1997	53 weeks ended January 31, 1998	52 weeks ended January 30, 1999
Cash and cash equivalents generated (deployed)			
Operations			
Net earnings	$ 3,923	$ 6,551	$ 5,752
Non-cash items			
Provision for closure of U.S. pilot stores (Note 16)	—	—	2,961
Depreciation and amortization	4,423	7,095	8,377
Loss (gain) on disposition of capital assets	(481)	378	47
Future income taxes (benefits) (Note 1M)	(550)	(415)	(1,322)
Funds provided by operations	7,315	13,609	15,815
Changes in non-cash working capital			
(net of effect of acquisition of subsidiaries and franchise stores)			
Accounts receivable	135	(356)	(605)
Merchandise inventories	1,415	(15,654)	(6,755)
Other current assets	(646)	(404)	(614)
Accounts payable and accrued liabilities	4,510	(3,401)	771
Income taxes payable (Note 1M)	2,002	205	(1,707)
	7,416	(19,610)	(8,910)
	14,731	(6,001)	6,905
Investing			
Acquisitions of subsidiaries net of cash acquired (Note 2)	(7,263)	—	(2,196)
Purchases of franchise stores (Note 3)	(1,312)	(507)	(4,320)
Purchases of capital assets (Note 7)	(2,323)	(874)	(3,183)
Other assets	852	(287)	(720)
Goodwill	(4)	—	—
Disposition of capital assets	(75)	(217)	(160)
	(10,125)	(1,885)	(10,579)
Financing			
Proceeds of long-term debt (Notes 7 and 10)	7,000	—	10,259
Retirement of long-term debt	(216)	(1,413)	(1,417)
Repayment of capital lease liabilities	(533)	(2,412)	(3,615)
Issuance of share capital for cash (Note 12)	807	311	808
	7,058	(3,514)	6,035
Net cash and cash equivalents generated (deployed)	11,664	(11,400)	2,361
Cash and cash equivalents at beginning of year	85	11,749	349
Cash and cash equivalents at end of year	$11,749	$ 349	$ 2,710

Supplementary Schedules to Consolidated Statements of Cash Flows

(thousands)	52 weeks ended January 25, 1997	53 weeks ended January 31, 1998	52 weeks ended January 30, 1999
Schedule of non-cash investing and financing activities:			
Capital assets acquired by means of capital leases	$ (3,509)	$(10,435)	$ (6,969)
Capital lease funding to acquire capital assets	$ 3,509	$ 10,435	$ 6,969
Retirement of long-term debt on conversion to equity	$ —	$ (3,000)	$ —
Issuance of share capital on conversion of long-term debt	$ —	$ 3,000	$ —
Supplement disclosures of cash flow information:			
Cash paid for:			
Short-term interest	$ 1,176	$ 656	$ 1,956
Long-term interest	$ 475	$ 1,874	$ 1,323
Income taxes	$ 2,842	$ 6,063	$ 8,273

Accounts Receivable Turnover:

A/R TURNOVER—MARK'S WORK WEARHOUSE LIMITED, 1999

$$\text{Accounts Receivable Turnover} = \frac{\text{Credit sales}}{\text{Average accounts receivable}}$$

$$= \frac{\$283,401^*}{\dfrac{\$13,364 + \$12,644}{2}}$$

$$= 21.8 \text{ times}$$

$$\text{Days to Collect} = \frac{365 \text{ days}}{\text{Receivable turnover}}$$

$$= \frac{365 \text{ days}}{21.8}$$

$$= 17 \text{ days}$$

*Total sales was used because no amount for credit sales was given. Because the total amount could include some cash sales, the accounts receivable turnover may be inflated. It may actually take longer to collect the accounts receivable than is indicated by this ratio.

Inventory Turnover:

INVENTORY TURNOVER—MARK'S WORK WEARHOUSE LIMITED, 1999

$$\text{Inventory Turnover} = \frac{\text{Cost of goods sold}}{\text{Average inventory}}$$

$$= \frac{\$169,163}{\dfrac{\$76,982 + \$60,108}{2}}$$

$$= 2.47 \text{ times}$$

$$\text{Days Inventory Held} = \frac{365 \text{ days}}{\text{Inventory turnover}}$$

$$= \frac{365 \text{ days}}{2.47}$$

$$= 148 \text{ days}$$

Accounts Payable Turnover:

A/P TURNOVER—MARK'S WORK WEARHOUSE LIMITED, 1999

$$\text{Accounts Payable Turnover} = \frac{\text{Cost of goods sold}}{\text{Average accounts payable*}}$$

$$= \frac{\$169{,}163}{\dfrac{\$43{,}557 + \$33{,}280}{2}}$$

$$= 4.4$$

$$\text{Days to Pay} = \frac{365 \text{ days}}{4.4} = 83 \text{ days}$$

*The company does not disclose accounts payable as a separate item. It provides instead the sum of accounts payable and accrued liabilities. This means that the average accounts payable amount used in the ratio is larger than accounts payable and the number of days to pay is therefore indicating a much longer period than would be the reality for the company.

Current Ratio:

CURRENT RATIO—MARK'S WORK WEARHOUSE LIMITED, 1999

$$\text{Current Ratio} = \frac{\text{Current assets}}{\text{Current liabilities}}$$

$$= \frac{\$96{,}360}{\$56{,}525}$$

$$= 1.70$$

Quick Ratio:

QUICK RATIO—MARK'S WORK WEARHOUSE LIMITED, 1999

$$\text{Quick Ratio} = \frac{\text{Current assets} - \text{inventory} - \text{prepaid expenses}}{\text{Current liabilities}}$$

$$= \frac{\$96{,}360 - \$76{,}982 - \$2{,}396^*}{\$56{,}525}$$

$$= .30$$

*The $2,396 represents the prepaid expenses. This amount was found in Note 5 to the financial statements.

D/E(I):

D/E(I)—MARK'S WORK WEARHOUSE LIMITED, 1999

$$D/E(I) = \frac{\text{Total liabilities}}{\text{Total liabilities} + \text{Shareholders' equity}}$$

$$= \frac{\$79,686}{\$79,686 + \$53,306}$$

$$= 59.9\%$$

D/E(II):

D/E(II)—MARK'S WORK WEARHOUSE LIMITED, 1999

$$D/E(II) = \frac{\text{Total liabilities}}{\text{Shareholders' equity}}$$

$$= \frac{\$79,686}{\$53,306}$$

$$= 1.49$$

D/E(III):

D/E(III)—MARK'S WORK WEARHOUSE LIMITED, 1999

$$D/E(III) = \frac{\text{Total long-term liabilities}}{\text{Total long-term liabilities} + \text{Shareholders' equity}}$$

$$= \frac{\$23,161}{\$23,161 + \$53,306}$$

$$= .30$$

Times Interest Earned:

TIE—MARK'S WORK WEARHOUSE LIMITED, 1999

$$TIE = \frac{\text{Net income} + \text{Taxes} + \text{Interest}}{\text{Interest}}$$

$$= \frac{\$5,752 + \$5,244 + \$1,350 + \$2,015}{\$1,350 + \$2,015}$$

$$= 4.27 \text{ times}$$

Performance Ratios

In analyzing the performance of any company, first consider the net income and its trend. For Mark's Work Wearhouse, the net income is positive. It is down about 12% from 1998 but up 46% from 1997. This indicates that Mark's Work Wearhouse is in a fluctuating environment. Any business that sells clothing is subject to fluctuations in trends and the economy. The earnings per share has been relatively stable. Next, consider the ROA and ROE ratios. The ROA is 6.31% and the ROE is 7.8%. The ROA of 6.31% indicates that Mark's Work Wearhouse is earning a relatively low return on assets, although somewhat greater than could be earned if the assets were invested in bank deposits. From the breakdown in the ROA calculation, the performance by Mark's Work Wearhouse can be seen to be in its total asset turnover (2.38) and not the profit margin ratio (2.65%). Mark's Work Wearhouse sells work and sports clothing at lower mark-ups than department stores. Because of its lower mark-up, it sells more volume, which improves its asset turnover. The ROE of 7.8% is slightly greater than the ROA and that indicates the company is making some use of leverage.

The turnover figures are interesting, and some are likely distorted. The calculation of the accounts receivable turnover of 21.8 times indicates only 17 days' sales in accounts receivable. This compares very favourably to the normal credit terms of 30 days, and implies that there should be no significant collection problems. However, in calculating the ratio we were not able to use "credit" sales, because that amount was not disclosed. Mark's Work Wearhouse sells clothing, and most of its sales are likely for cash. Using the total sales amount to calculate this ratio has obviously inflated the turnover rate; by how much, we cannot determine. The inventory turnover of 2.47 times indicates that there are 148 days' sales of inventory on hand. This indicates that the company is carrying five months of inventory. The clothing industry is seasonal, which means that spring/summer merchandise is replaced by fall/winter merchandise. Five months worth of inventory may be the norm, but it is a ratio that users should monitor over time. The accounts payable turnover of 4.4 times indicates that the company pays its suppliers an average of 83 days after incurring the obligation. This ratio is obviously distorted by the inclusion of accrued liabilities in the denominator. When there are more items included besides the amounts owed to suppliers of inventory, this ratio is rendered meaningless.

Further analyses would include common size financial statements to determine the trends in the cost of goods sold and other expenses (shown in Exhibit 12-13), and trend analyses of the ROA and ROE.

Mark's Work Wearhouse Limited

Common Size Income Statement

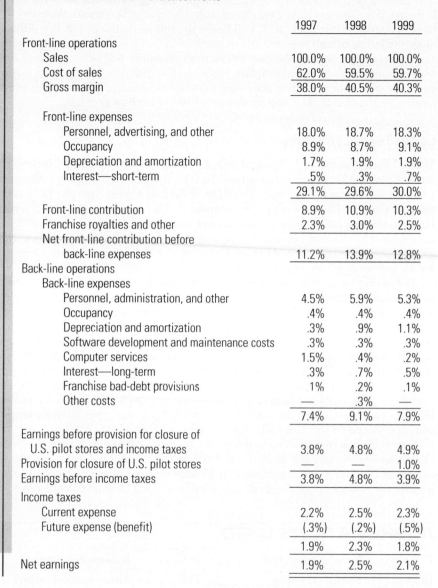

	1997	1998	1999
Front-line operations			
Sales	100.0%	100.0%	100.0%
Cost of sales	62.0%	59.5%	59.7%
Gross margin	38.0%	40.5%	40.3%
Front-line expenses			
Personnel, advertising, and other	18.0%	18.7%	18.3%
Occupancy	8.9%	8.7%	9.1%
Depreciation and amortization	1.7%	1.9%	1.9%
Interest—short-term	.5%	.3%	.7%
	29.1%	29.6%	30.0%
Front-line contribution	8.9%	10.9%	10.3%
Franchise royalties and other	2.3%	3.0%	2.5%
Net front-line contribution before			
back-line expenses	11.2%	13.9%	12.8%
Back-line operations			
Back-line expenses			
Personnel, administration, and other	4.5%	5.9%	5.3%
Occupancy	.4%	.4%	.4%
Depreciation and amortization	.3%	.9%	1.1%
Software development and maintenance costs	.3%	.3%	.3%
Computer services	1.5%	.4%	.2%
Interest—long-term	.3%	.7%	.5%
Franchise bad-debt provisions	.1%	.2%	.1%
Other costs	—	.3%	—
	7.4%	9.1%	7.9%
Earnings before provision for closure of			
U.S. pilot stores and income taxes	3.8%	4.8%	4.9%
Provision for closure of U.S. pilot stores	—	—	1.0%
Earnings before income taxes	3.8%	4.8%	3.9%
Income taxes			
Current expense	2.2%	2.5%	2.3%
Future expense (benefit)	(.3%)	(.2%)	(.5%)
	1.9%	2.3%	1.8%
Net earnings	1.9%	2.5%	2.1%

EXHIBIT 12-13

These common size statements show that net income remained relatively constant in the three years. Although sales have increased, supporting expenses, including cost of goods sold, have remained proportionately the same. There are a few fluctuations in the back-line expenses, but where one has risen another has fallen such that overall the total expense is relatively constant.

Short-Term Liquidity

The current ratio is reasonable at 1.7, although just slightly on the low side. It would be better if the current ratio were closer to 2. The quick ratio shows the effect of the large inventory balance. It is at .3, well below the rule of thumb of 1.0. It is difficult to judge the inflow of cash from the sale of inventory. It is likely that, because of the large cash sales of this company, the cash inflow from inventory will be sufficient to handle what appears to be a potential cash flow problem. The cash flow from operations on the cash flow statement is positive and larger than the net income amount. This provides more reassurance that the company does not have a cash flow problem.

Long-Term Liquidity

Mark's Work Wearhouse is financed 60% by debt and 40% by equity. Just over one third of the total liabilities is long-term debt. The fairly low debt/equity ratio result in a modest increment for leverage. The ROE of 7.8% is higher than the ROA at 6.3% but not by much. This means that the company is able to make modest use of leverage. High debt/equity ratio require a stable market for the products sold. The clothing market is subject to seasonal trends and can change rapidly as fashions and incomes change. Mark's Work Wearhouse's modest use of leverage is probably a prudent use of resources for the market in which it operates.

Interesting information can be found on the cash flow statement. In 1999, the cash inflow from operating activities is positive, as it should be, even though the net income is lower than it was the previous year. The previous year it was negative, mostly as a result of an increase in investment in inventory. This fact makes the positive cash flow from operations even more important. Cash is being used for investing activities in new long-term assets, investments in subsidiaries, franchise stores, and capital assets, which is also a good sign. This new investment is being financed mainly with long-term debt. Some debt was paid off and some new shares were issued, but the predominant inflow of cash was from new long-term debt. Because the company's times interest earned ratio indicates that it can cover the interest payment at least four times from earnings, the company should be able to handle this new debt quite readily.

One thing you may have noticed from the financial statements is that Mark's Work Wearhouse did not pay any dividends in 1999. In fact, neither did it pay any dividends in 1998 or 1997. As an investor, if you were looking for an investment that would pay you periodically in the form of dividends, this would likely not be what you are looking for.

ABBREVIATIONS USED

P/E Ratio	Price/earnings ratio	ROE	Return on equity
ROA	Return on assets	TIE	Times interest earned

GLOSSARY

Accounts payable turnover The number of times that accounts payable are replaced during the accounting period. It is usually calculated as the cost of goods sold divided by the average accounts payable.

Accounts receivable turnover The number of times that accounts receivable are replaced during the accounting period. It is calculated as the sales divided by the average accounts receivable.

Common size data Data that are prepared from the financial statements (usually the income statement and balance sheet) in which each element of the financial statement is expressed as a percentage of some denominator value. On the income statement, the denominator value is usually the net sales revenues for the period. On the balance sheet, the denominator is the total assets for the period.

Cross-sectional analysis A type of financial statement analysis in which one company is compared with other companies, either within the same industry or across industries, for the same time period.

Current ratio A measure of the short-term liquidity of the company. It is measured as the ratio of the current assets of the company divided by the current liabilities.

Debt/equity ratio Measures of the leverage of the company. There are numerous definitions of these ratios, but all of them attempt to provide a comparison of the amount of debt in the company compared to the amount of equity.

Earnings per share ratio A measure of the performance of the company, calculated by dividing the earnings for the period available to common shares by the weighted-average number of common shares that were outstanding during the period.

Fully diluted earnings per share A type of earnings per share calculation that provides the lowest possible earnings per share figure under the assumption that all convertible securities and options of the company are converted into common shares. It measures the maximum potential dilution in earnings per share that would occur under these assumed conversions.

Inventory turnover The number of times that inventory is replaced during the accounting period. It is calculated as the cost of goods sold divided by the average inventory.

Leverage The use of debt in a company to improve the return to the shareholders.

Multiple A synonym for price/earnings ratio.

Operating leverage The replacement of variable costs with fixed costs in the operation of the company. If a sufficient volume of sales is achieved, the investment in fixed costs can be very profitable.

Optimal capital structure The theoretical point at which the leverage of the company maximizes the return to the shareholders (ROE).

Price/earnings ratio A performance ratio that compares the market price per share with the earnings per share.

Profit margin ratio A performance measure that compares the after-tax but before-interest income of a company with the revenues of the company.

Prospective analysis A financial statement analysis of a company that attempts to look forward in time to predict future results.

Quick ratio A measure of the short-term liquidity of a company calculated by dividing the current assets less inventories and, in most cases, prepaid items by the current liabilities.

Raw financial data The data that appear directly in the financial statements.

Retrospective analysis A financial statement analysis of a company that looks only at historical data.

Return on assets (ROA) A measure of performance that measures a company's return on investment in assets. It is calculated by dividing the income after tax, but before interest, by the average total assets of the corporation during the accounting period. The ratio can be split into the profit margin ratio and the total asset turnover ratio.

Return on equity (ROE) An assessment of performance that measures the return on the investment made by common shareholders. It is calculated by dividing the net income less dividends for preferred shares by the average common shareholders' equity during the accounting period.

Time-series analysis A financial statement analysis in which data are analyzed over time.

Times interest earned (TIE) ratio A measure of long-term liquidity of a company. It measures the ability of the company to make its interest payments. It is calculated by dividing the income before interest and taxes by the interest expense.

Total asset turnover A measure of performance of a company that shows the number of dollars of sales generated per dollar of investment in total assets. It is calculated by dividing the sales revenue by the average total assets for the accounting period.

Warrant A certificate that entitles the holder to purchase specific shares at a specified price within a stated period.

ASSIGNMENT MATERIAL

Assessing Your Recall

12-1 Explain the difference between a retrospective analysis and a prospective analysis of a company.

12-2 Compare and contrast time-series analysis and cross-sectional analysis.

12-3 Describe the three major types of data that could be used in a time-series or cross-sectional analysis.

12-4 For each of the following ratios, reproduce the formula for their calculation:

    a. ROA (Break down into profit margin ratio and total asset turnover ratio.)

    b. ROE

    c. Accounts receivable turnover

    d. Inventory turnover

    e. Accounts payable turnover

    f. Current ratio

    g. Quick ratio

    h. D/E(I)

    i. D/E(II)

    j. D/E(III)

    k. Times interest earned

12-5 Explain how the turnover ratios relate to the cash produced from the operations of a company.

12-6 Describe leverage, and explain how it is evidenced in the ROA and ROE ratios.

12-7 Explain, using the profit margin and total asset turnover ratios, how two companies in the same business (use retail clothing stores as an example) can earn the same ROA, yet have very different operating strategies.

12-8 What is the advantage of preparing common size statements in financial statement analysis?

12-9 Explain why the current ratio is subject to manipulation as a measure of liquidity.

12-10 Discuss the problems associated with calculating an accounts payable turnover ratio that make it difficult to interpret.

12-11 Describe how earnings per share is calculated, and discuss the purpose of producing basic and fully diluted earnings per share for a company.

12-12 Explain how the credit risk of a company can be assessed using the times interest earned ratio.

Applying Your Knowledge

12-13 (Liquidity ratios)

The financial data for Spectrum Associates are as follows (amounts in thousands):

	Year 1	Year 2	Year 3	Year 4
Current assets				
Cash	$ 200	$ 100	$ 200	$ 150
Accounts receivable	700	800	600	650
Inventories	500	1,000	1,450	2,100
Other current assets	100	100	250	100
	$1,500	$2,000	$2,500	$3,000
Current liabilities				
Accounts payable	$ 600	$ 700	$ 825	$ 800
Accrued salaries	300	400	495	400
Other current				
liabilities	100	150	165	300
	$1,000	$1,250	$1,485	$1,500

Required:

a. Compute the current and quick ratios for Years 1 through 4.

b. Comment on the short-term liquidity position of Spectrum Associates.

12-14 (Liquidity ratios)

Sundry Ltd. is a thriving company. The Board of Directors wants to declare a cash dividend. The balance sheet of Sundry Ltd. is as follows (in thousands of dollars):

	20x2	20x1
Assets		
Current		
Cash and short-term investments	$ 67,834	$ 62,595
Accounts receivable	98,666	96,242
Inventories	135,836	135,519
Prepaid expenses	8,403	6,635
	310,739	300,991
Capital assets	545,574	540,203
Long-term investments	28,881	24,842
	$885,194	$866,036
Liabilities and Shareholders' Equity		
Current		
Bank indebtedness	$ 74,015	$107,018
Accounts payable	84,637	100,289
Current portion of long-term debt	1,693	32,482
	160,345	239,789
Long-term debt	288,801	143,795
Deferred income taxes	60,528	84,563
Bonds payable	25,311	50,657
Minority interest	14,145	13,960
	549,130	532,764
Shareholders' equity		
Common shares	214,962	210,709
Retained earnings	121,102	122,563
	336,064	333,272
	$885,194	$866,036

Required:

a. Calculate the current ratio for 20x1 and 20x2.

b. Calculate the quick ratio for 20x1 and 20x2.

c. As of the date of preparation of the balance sheet, no dividends had been declared. Did Sundry Ltd. earn income in 20x2? Explain.

d. Calculate a debt/equity ratio for Sundry Ltd. in 20x1 and 20x2.

e. Taking into consideration the information learned in a through d, would you recommend that a dividend be declared for 20x2? Explain.

12-15 (Accounts receivable turnover)
The financial data for Campton Electric Company Inc. and Johnson Electrical Ltd. for the current year are as follows:

	Annual sales	Accounts receivable, Jan. 1	Accounts receivable, Dec. 31
Campton Electric	$3,893,567	$542,380	$628,132
Johnson Electrical	1,382,683	168,553	143,212

Required:

a. Compute the accounts receivable turnover for each company.

b. Compute the average number of days required by each company to collect the receivables.

c. Which company appears to be more efficient in terms of handling its accounts receivable policy?

d. What additional information would be helpful in evaluating management's handling of the collection of accounts receivable?

12-16 (Accounts receivable turnover)
The Super Gym Company Limited sells fitness equipment to retail outlets and fitness centres. The majority of these sales are on credit. The financial data related to accounts receivable over the last three years are as follows:

	20x0	20x1	20x2
Accounts receivable	$ 350,672	$ 362,488	$ 358,562
Sales	3,218,449	3,585,391	3,988,432

Required:

a. Compute the accounts receivable turnover for each year. In year 20x0, use the accounts receivable in 20x0. For the other two years, use the average accounts receivable.

b. Compute the average number of days required to collect the receivables in each year.

c. As a user of this information, describe what trends you see. What additional information would you like to know to help you understand the trends?

12-17 (Inventory turnover)

Information regarding the activities of Polymer Plastics Company is as follows:

	Year 1	Year 2	Year 3	Year 4	Year 5
Cost of goods sold	$463,827	$511,125	$593,350	$679,686	$708,670
Average inventory	65,537	81,560	110,338	166,672	225,895

Required:

a. Do a time-series analysis for the inventory turnover for each year. Also, compute the average number of days that inventories are held for the respective years.

b. Is Polymer Plastics Company managing its inventories efficiently? What information do you need to know before you can answer this question?

12-18 (Inventory turnover)

The financial data for Green Grocers Limited and Fast Lane Foods Inc. for the current year are as follows:

	Annual cost of goods sold	Inventory Jan. 1	Inventory Dec. 31
Green Grocers Limited	$8,554,921	$582,633	$547,925
Fast Lane Foods Inc.	2,769,335	174,725	195,446

Required:

a. Compute the inventory turnover for each company.

b. Compute the average number of days the inventory is held by each company.

c. Knowing the type of inventory these companies sell, comment on the reasonableness of the inventory turnover. Which company manages its inventory more efficiently?

d. Are there any potential problems associated with fast inventory turnovers?

12-19 (Analysis using selected ratios)

The following ratios and other information are based on a company's comparative financial statements for a two-year period:

	Year 1	Year 2
Current ratio	1.84	2.20
Quick ratio	1.01	.89
D/E(I) ratio	.43	.58
D/E(II) ratio	.75	1.38
Earnings per share	.24	.15
Gross profit percentage	42.3%	43.6%
Total assets	$2,143,702	$3,574,825
Current assets	$ 965,118	$1,462,763

Required:

a. What is the amount of current liabilities at the end of Year 2?

b. What is the amount of total debt at the end of Year 2?

c. What is the total shareholders' equity at the end of Year 2?

d. Do you think this company is a retail company, a financial institution, or a service organization? Explain.

e. If the company has 1,650,200 common shares outstanding for most of Year 2 and has issued no other shares, what is its net income for Year 2?

f. Based on the information available, what is your assessment of the company's liquidity? Explain. Given the limited information, what is your assessment of the company's overall financial position? Explain.

g. What changes do you see between Year 1 and Year 2 that appear particularly significant? What explanations might there be for these changes?

12-20 (ROE and ROA)

The following financial information relates to Stanton Publishing Inc. (amounts in thousands):

	Year 1	Year 2	Year 3	Year 4
Sales	$15,472	$19,558	$21,729	$28,493
Average total assets	19,745	25,227	33,146	67,185
Average shareholders' equity	6,278	9,614	13,619	24,729
Net income	200	503	1,105	2,913
Interest expense	50	55	96	89
Tax rate	40%	40%	40%	30%

Required:

For each year, calculate:

a. Return on shareholders' equity (ROE)

b. ROA

   (1) Profit margin ratio

   (2) Total asset turnover

c. Comment on the profitability of Stanton Publishing Inc.

12-21 (ROE and ROA)

The following financial information relates to Cool Cool Brewery Ltd. (amounts in thousands):

	Year 1	Year 2	Year 3
Sales	$42,798	$54,061	$76,023
Average total assets	48,774	65,258	98,654
Average shareholders' equity	24,664	32,415	51,415
Net income	1,533	3,830	6,755
Interest expense	896	1,441	2,112
Tax rate	25%	30%	30%

Required:
For each year, calculate:

a. Return on shareholders' equity (ROE)

b. ROA

   (1) Profit margin ratio

   (2) Total asset turnover

c. Comment on the profitability of Cool Cool Brewery Ltd.

12-22 (ROE and ROA)
Canadian Import Company's summarized balance sheet is as follows:

Total assets	$600,000	Liabilities	$200,000
		Shareholders' equity	400,000
	$600,000		$600,000

The interest rate on the liabilities is 8% and the income tax rate is 30%.

Required:

a. If the ROE is equal to the ROA, compute the net income.

b. Compute the ROE, using the net income determined in part a.

c. Compute the income before interest and taxes for the net income derived in part a.

d. Assume that total assets remain the same (i.e., at $600,000) and that loans increase to $300,000, while shareholders' equity decreases to $300,000. Assume that the interest rate is now 6% and that the income tax rate remains at 30%. What is the net income if the ROA is the same as that calculated in part b.? What is the ROE?

e. Compare the ROE in both situations, and explain why there is a difference.

12-23 (D/E(I), D/E(II), D/E(III), and times interest earned)
Artscan Enterprises' financial data are as follows:

	Year 1	Year 2	Year 3
Income before interest and taxes	$ 500	$ 800	$1,000
Interest	80	100	135
Current liabilities	425	525	750
Noncurrent liabilities	600	1,000	1,400
Shareholders' equity	1,200	1,800	2,200

Required:

a. Compute the debt/equity ratios (I, II, and III) and times interest earned ratio.

b. Comment on the long-term liquidity position of Artscan Enterprises.

12-24 (D/E(I), D/E(II), D/E(III), and times interest earned)
Waverly Company's financial data are as follows:

	Year 1	Year 2	Year 3
Income before interest and taxes	$1,000	$1,300	$1,600
Interest	120	150	165
Current liabilities	390	430	520
Noncurrent liabilities	700	1,100	1,200
Shareholders' equity	1,500	1,500	1,800

Required:

a. Compute the debt/equity ratios (I, II, and III) and times interest earned ratio.

b. Comment on the long-term liquidity position of Waverly Company.

12-25 (Transaction effects on ratios)

Required:
State the immediate effect (increase, decrease, no effect) of the following transactions on:

a. Current ratio

b. Quick ratio

c. Inventory turnover

d. ROE

e. Debt/equity ratio (D/E(I))

Transactions:

1. Inventory costing $25,000 is purchased on credit.

2. Inventory costing $125,000 is sold on account for $158,000.

3. Payments of $65,000 are made to suppliers.

4. A machine costing $120,000 is purchased; $30,000 is paid in cash and the balance will be paid in equal instalments for the next three years.

5. Common shares worth $100,000 are issued.

6. Equipment costing $80,000 with accumulated amortization of $50,000 is sold for $40,000 in cash.

7. Goods that cost $35,000 were destroyed by fire. The residual value of some of the partly burned goods was $3,000, which is received in cash when these goods are sold. The destroyed goods were not insured.

12-26 (Transaction effects on ratios)

Required:
State the immediate effect (increase, decrease, no effect) of the following transactions on:

a. Current ratio

b. ROA

c. Accounts receivable turnover

d. ROE

e. Debt/equity ratio (D/E(I))

Transactions:

1. Goods costing $300,000 are sold to customers on credit for $450,000.

2. Accounts receivable of $350,000 is collected.

3. Inventory costing $550,000 is purchased from suppliers.

4. A long-term bank loan for $750,000 is arranged with the bank, and the cash was received by the company.

5. The bank loan carries an interest rate of 10% and the interest payment is made at the end of the year.

6. The company used $100,000 to buy temporary investments.

7. New common shares are issued for $250,000.

12-27 (Earnings per share)

Transland Equipment Ltd. has 900,000 common shares and 100,000 preferred shares outstanding. The preferred shares pay a dividend of $1.00 per share and are convertible into 200,000 common shares. During the year, Transland earned net income of $720,000.

Required:

a. Calculate the basic earnings per share that should be reported in the financial statements.

b. What relevance does the convertibility of the preferred shares have for reporting earnings per share?

12-24 (Earnings per share)

In 2000, Signal Communications Ltd. reported an earnings per share of $0.46. Signal had 28,500 common shares outstanding during 2000 and 2001. In 2001, Signal reported net income of $14,800.

Required:

a. What was the net income for 2000?

b. Calculate the earnings per share for 2001.

c. Where in the financial statements do you usually find the earnings per share amount?

d. Assume that in December 2001 Signal decided to split its common shares 2 for 1. What effect will this have on the earnings per share amount calculated in b.? Will the year 2000 earnings per share amount be affected as well? Explain.

12-29 (Analysis of assets)

You have inherited money from your grandparents and a friend suggests that you consider buying shares in Galena Ski Products. Because you may need to sell the shares within the next two years to finance your university education, you start your analysis of the company data by computing (1) working capital, (2) the current ratio, and (3) the quick ratio. Galena's balance sheet is as follows:

Current assets	
Cash	$218,000
Inventory	320,000
Other current assets	32,000
Noncurrent assets	
Land	50,000
Building and equipment	266,000
Other	25,000
Total	$911,000
Current liabilities	$165,000
Long-term debt	400,000
Common shares	150,000
Retained earnings	196,000
Total	$911,000

Required:

a. What amount of working capital is currently maintained? Comment on the adequacy of the working capital.

b. Your preference is to have a quick ratio of at least .80 and a current ratio of at least 2.00. How do the existing ratios compare with your criteria? Using these two ratios, how would you evaluate the company's current asset position?

c. The company sells only on a cash basis currently and has sales of $700,000 this past year. How would you expect a change from cash to credit sales to affect the balance sheet ratios?

d. Galena's balance sheet is presented just before the start of shipments for its fall and winter season. How would your evaluation change if these balances existed in late February following completion of its primary business for the skiing season?

12-30 (Ratio analysis of two companies)
You have obtained the financial statements of A-Tec and Bi-Sci, new companies in the high-tech industry. Both companies have just completed their second year of operations. You have acquired the following information for an analysis of the companies. All dollar amounts are stated in thousands.

	A-Tec		Bi-Sci	
	2001	2000	2001	2000
Cash	$ 3	$ 2	$ 1	$ 1
Accounts receivable	30	15	20	20
Inventory	40	20	30	30
Other current assets	5	1	3	1
Capital assets (net)	310	170	115	104
Current liabilities	67	40	24	24
Long-term debt	270	130	0	0
Common shares	18	18	72	72
Retained earnings	33	20	73	60
Sales (all credit sales)	950	675	600	600
Cost of goods sold	665	450	450	450
Net income	95	80	60	60

Required:

a. Calculate the following ratios for the two companies for the two years.

    1. Current ratio

    2. Working capital (dollar amount)

    3. Accounts receivable turnover

    4. Inventory turnover

    5. Asset turnover

    6. D/E(I)

    7. Shareholders' equity to total assets

    8. Gross margin ratio

    9. Return on sales

   10. ROA

   11. ROE

b. Write a brief analysis of the two companies based on the information given and the ratios computed. Be sure to discuss issues of liquidity, leverage, and profitability. Which company appears to be the better investment for the shareholder? Explain. Which company appears to be the better credit risk for the lender? Explain.

Management Perspective Problems

12-31 (Use of ratios in debt restrictions)
Contracts with lenders, such as bond holders, typically place restrictions on a company's activities in an attempt to ensure that the company will be able to repay both the interest and the principal on a debt. These restrictions are frequently stated as functions of ratios. For instance, a restriction could be that the debt/equity ratio (D/E(II)) cannot exceed 2.0. If it does exceed 2.0, the total debt falls due immediately. Two commonly used ratios are the current ratio and the debt/equity ratio. Explain why these might appear as restrictions. How do they protect the lender?

12-32 (Use of ROA in performance measurement)
Management compensation plans typically specify performance criteria in terms of financial statement ratios. For instance, a plan might specify that management must achieve a certain level of return on investment, for example, ROA. If management were trying to maximize their compensation, how could they manipulate the ROA ratio to achieve this maximization?

12-33 (Use of ratios for investing decisions)
You are considering investing in the stock market. As a potential investor, choose four ratios that you think would be most helpful to you in making your investment decision. Explain your choice.

12-34 (Ratio analysis and auditors)
Auditors review the financial statements to determine whether the information reported has been collected, summarized, and reported according to accepted accounting principles. Although auditors are not expected to identify fraud, they do perform tests to see if there are any apparent abnormalities. What ratios or forms of ratio analysis do you think would be helpful to the auditor in identifying abnormalities?

12-35 (Using ratios to evaluate credit worthiness)

You are the sales manager in a company that sells automotive supplies to service stations and car dealerships. You have been contacted by a car dealership that wants you to supply its service department with automotive parts. The dealership would like to purchase on credit with 30 days to pay from the date of invoice. You have access to the dealership's financial statements for last year. Which ratios could be useful to you in making the decision about whether to sell on credit? Explain your choices.

12-36 (Use of ratios in decision-making)

Managers, investors, and creditors usually have a specific focus when making decisions about a business.

Required:

For each of the following cases, identify the ratio or ratios that would help the user in making a decision or in identifying areas for further analysis:

a. A company's net income has declined. Is the decrease in net income from:

(1) a decrease in sales or an increase in cost of goods sold?

(2) an increase in total operating expenses?

(3) an increase in a specific expense such as tax expense?

b. Does a company generate sufficient cash to pay the debts that come due and pay dividends without having to borrow additional money?

c. Does a company rely more heavily on long-term debt financing than other companies in the same industry?

d. In a comparison of two companies, how would you decide which company has been more profitable in relation to invested capital?

e. Has the decline in the economy affected a company's ability to collect its accounts receivable?

f. Has a company been successful in reducing its investment in inventories as a result of installing a new ordering system that was intended to result in better production scheduling?

g. From a group of companies, which company provides the greatest earnings per share? Remember that a share in one company likely does not represent the same proportion of ownership interest as a share in another company.

h. From a group of companies, which company manages its inventory most efficiently?

Reading and Interpreting Published Financial Statements

12-37 (Ratio analysis of CHC Helicopter Corporation)

The 1998 financial statements of CHC Helicopter Corporation (with headquarters in St. John's, Newfoundland) are shown in Exhibit 12-14.

EXHIBIT 12-14
PART A

Consolidated Balance Sheet

April 30 *(in thousands of Canadian dollars)*
Incorporated under the laws of Canada

	1998	1997
Assets (Note 5)		
Current		
Cash	$ 684	$ 883
Receivables	74,812	56,292
Work in progress	33,090	19,363
Inventory	116,770	87,477
Prepaid expenses	8,437	5,092
	233,793	169,107
Property and equipment, net (Notes 3 and 6)	344,661	298,754
Other assets (Note 4)	37,573	32,887
	$ 616,027	$ 500,748
Liabilities		
Current		
Bank indebtedness (Note 5)	$ 53,100	$ 27,120
Payables and accruals	67,281	67,190
Current portion of long-term obligations (Notes 6 and 8)	21,233	16,400
	141,614	110,710
Long-term debt (Note 6)	119,502	97,250
Senior subordinated notes (Note 7)	109,717	107,415
Subordinated debentures (Note 8)	14,129	15,000
Other credits (Note 9)	72,892	65,709
Shareholders' equity	158,173	104,664
	$ 616,027	$ 500,748

Commitments and contingent liabilities (Notes 18 and 19)

On Behalf of the Board

_____ Director   _____ Director

See accompanying notes

EXHIBIT 12-14
PART B

Consolidated Statement of Earnings

Year Ended April 30 *(in thousands of Canadian dollars, except per share amounts)*

	1998	1997
Revenue	$ 354,125	$ 351,749
Operating expenses	300,935	297,498
Earnings before undernoted items	53,190	54,251
Depreciation and amortization	(9,844)	(9,217)
Gain on disposal of assets	2,816	357
Earnings from operations	46,162	45,391
Interest (Note 13)	27,559	26,114
Earnings before income taxes	18,603	19,277
Income taxes (Note 14)	8,498	9,202
Net earnings	$ 10,105	$ 10,075
Net earnings per share (Note 15)	$ 0.75	$ 0.86

See accompanying notes

EXHIBIT 12-14
PART C

Consolidated Statement of Cash Flow

Year Ended April 30 *(in thousands of Canadian dollars, except per share amounts)*

	1998	1997
Operating activities		
Earnings from operations	$ 46,162	$ 45,391
Items not involving cash		
Depreciation and amortization	9,844	9,217
Gain on disposal of assets	(2,816)	(357)
Other	623	251
Funds flow from operations before interest and income taxes	53,813	54,502
Interest, net of amortization (Note 13)	(25,185)	(24,169)
Current income taxes (Note 14)	(2,807)	(3,039)
Cash flow from operations	25,821	27,294
Change in non-cash working capital (Note 16)	(22,488)	(5,040)
	3,333	22,254
Financing activities		
Long-term debt - increase	39,796	16,615
- reduction	(16,604)	(24,737)
Short-term bank indebtedness	25,080	6,458
Government grant	856	—
Capital stock	42,428	407
Dividends	(1,383)	(1,171)
Preferred share redemption	—	(3,002)
	90,173	(5,430)
Cash available for investing activities	93,506	16,824
Investing activities		
Long-term investments (Note 2)	(62,289)	(2,079)
Property and equipment - additions	(37,635)	(21,106)
- proceeds from sale	12,607	12,643
Helicopter overhaul provision, net	(3,423)	(5,827)
Other	(2,965)	(472)
	(93,705)	(16,841)
Change in cash during the year	(199)	(17)
Cash, beginning of year	883	900
Cash, end of year	$ 684	$ 883
Cash flow from operations per share (Note 15)	$ 1.93	$ 2.33

See accompanying notes

Required:

Based on these financial statements, answer each of the following questions:

a. Compute the following ratios for 1998:

(1) ROA (split into profit margin ratio and total asset turnover). Assume that the corporate income tax rate is 43%.

(2) ROE (CHC does have preferred shares outstanding but has not disclosed the dividends that were paid to the preferred shareholders. Because the amount of preferred shares issued is small, in computing this ratio assume that the preferred dividends are zero).

(3) Inventory turnover (assume that 50% of Operating expenses relates to inventory).

(4) Accounts receivable turnover.

b. Compute the following ratios for both 1998 and 1997:

(1) Current ratio.

(2) Quick ratio.

(3) D/E(I).

(4) Times interest earned.

c. Comment on the use of leverage by CHC.

d. Assume you are considering investing in CHC. Comment on the pros and cons of doing so. Use not only the ratios, but also the information from the three financial statements in your analysis.

e. A significant proportion of CHC Helicopter's operations is conducted in other countries. The Canadian dollar has decreased in value relative to the currencies used in most of the countries in which CHC operates. Assume that the Canadian dollar will continue to decrease in value, and that CHC has the ability to choose the currency in which it can receive revenues, pay expenses, and borrow money. How should CHC use this ability to maximize its profits?

12-38 (Ratio analysis for Western Star Trucks Holdings Ltd.)
The 1998 financial statements of Western Star Trucks Holdings Ltd. (based in Kelowna, British Columbia) are shown in Exhibit 12-15.

Required:

Based on these financial statements, answer each of the following questions:

a. Compute the following ratios for 1998:

(1) ROA (split into profit margin ratio and total asset turnover).

(2) ROE (there are no preferred shares outstanding).

(3) Inventory turnover.

(4) Accounts receivable turnover.

b. Compute the following ratios for both 1998 and 1997:

(1) Current ratio.

(2) Quick ratio.

(3) D/E(I).

(4) Times interest earned.

EXHIBIT 12-15
PART A

Consolidated Balance Sheets

As at June 30	1998	1997
(in thousands of Canadian dollars)		
ASSETS		
Current		
Cash	—	92,027
Accounts receivable *[note 6]*	201,218	203,196
Unbilled revenue *[note 1]*	85,167	21,023
Inventories *[note 3]*	237,312	182,157
Prepaid expenses and other	12,341	11,621
Total current assets	536,038	510,024
Capital assets *[note 4]*	143,563	136,046
Deferred costs *[note 5]*	76,069	61,724
Goodwill [net of accumulated amortization of $996; 1997 - $469]	10,986	9,635
Prepaid pension expense *[note 13]*	14,134	11,373
Investments and other assets	2,334	5,278
	783,124	734,080
LIABILITIES AND SHAREHOLDERS' EQUITY		
Current		
Bank indebtedness	1,843	—
Accounts payable and accrued liabilities *[note 6]*	305,393	260,607
Short-term indebtedness *[note 7]*	34,335	—
Current portion of customer deposits and advances	8,122	33,781
Current portion of long-term debt *[note 8]*	33,346	15,383
Total current liabilities	383,039	309,771
Deferred income taxes	553	6,076
Customer deposits and advances	327	1,800
Long-term debt *[note 8]*	171,088	185,502
Total liabilities	555,007	503,149
Commitments and contingencies *[notes 8[ii] and 9]*		
Shareholders' equity		
Share capital *[note 10]*	121,841	119,587
Retained earnings	106,276	111,344
Total shareholders' equity	228,117	230,931
	783,124	734,080

See accompanying notes

On behalf of the Board:

Director   Director

westernstar

EXHIBIT 12-15
PART B

Consolidated Statements of Operations and Retained Earnings

Years ended June 30	1998	1997	1996
(in thousands of Canadian dollars, except share and per share amounts)			
Revenue	1,552,272	1,236,349	783,319
Cost of sales	1,423,248	1,110,715	683,773
Gross profit	129,024	125,634	99,546
Selling and administrative	109,726	72,170	47,619
Interest expense - net	21,189	8,149	1,477
Net income (loss) before taxes	(1,891)	45,315	50,450
Income tax expense *(recovery) [note 11]*	(2,215)	11,325	13,927
Net income	324	33,990	36,523
Retained earnings, opening balance	111,344	82,962	51,225
Share issue costs *(net of tax)*	296	(90)	40
Dividends paid	(5,688)	(5,518)	(4,826)
Retained earnings, closing balance	106,276	111,344	82,962
Per common share			
Net income	0.02	2.48	3.08
Fully diluted net income	0.02	2.26	2.89
Dividends	0.40	0.40	0.40
Weighted average number of common shares			
outstanding (thousands)	14,214	13,723	11,860

See accompanying notes

EXHIBIT 12-15
PART C

Consolidated Statement of Cash Flows

Years ended June 30	1998	1997	1996
(in thousands of Canadian dollars, except per share amounts)			
OPERATING ACTIVITIES			
Net income	324	33,990	36,523
Adjustment for items not involving cash			
Depreciation	16,506	12,375	4,850
Amortization	9,086	3,160	362
Deferred income taxes	(8,178)	5,981	6,902
Cash flow from operations	17,738	55,506	48,637
Changes in non-cash working capital balances			
relating to operations *[note 14]*	(98,576)	(22,343)	(79,152)
Cash provided by (used in) operating activities	(80,838)	33,163	(30,515)
FINANCING ACTIVITIES			
Bank indebtedness	1,843	(32,497)	32,497
Short-term indebtedness	34,335	—	—
Dividends paid	(5,688)	(5,518)	(4,826)
Long-term debt borrowings	16,232	220,806	56,806
Repayment of long-term debt	(7,259)	(128,306)	(8,024)
Decrease in cash collateral deposits	—	—	2,480
Common shares issued (net of issue costs)	2,550	43,474	17,773
Purchase of non-controlling interest in Orion *[note 8]*	(17,237)	—	—
Cash provided by financing activities	24,776	97,959	96,706
INVESTING ACTIVITIES			
Decrease (increase) in investments and other assets	2,944	(885)	(583)
Capital asset additions	(23,979)	(45,655)	(22,609)
Increase in deferred costs	(13,328)	(27,673)	(20,684)
Acquisitions *[note 2]*	(1,602)	(22,190)	(23,841)
Cash used in investing activities	(35,965)	(96,403)	(67,717)
Increase (decrease) in cash	(92,027)	34,719	(1,526)
Cash, beginning of year	92,027	57,308	58,834
Cash, end of year	—	92,027	57,308
Per common share			
Cash flow from operations	1.25	4.04	4.10
Fully diluted cash flow from operations	1.24	3.79	3.88
Supplemental cash flow information			
Income taxes paid	9,442	9,260	10,170
Interest paid	18,807	6,276	2,340

See accompanying notes

c. Assume you are thinking of investing in Western Star Trucks. Comment on the financial health of the company, highlighting any areas that might be of concern. Use not only the ratios, but also the information from all three financial statements in your analysis.

d. Comment on the use of leverage by Western Star Trucks.

e. Western Star Trucks builds its heavy-duty highway transport trucks in Canada and exports many of them to the U.S. and other countries. It buys parts in both Canada and other countries. Assume first that the Canadian dollar strengthens against the U.S. dollar, and second that it weakens. Comment on the effect these changes would have on Western Star Trucks' revenues and expenses.

12-39 (Ratio analysis for Sleeman Breweries Ltd.)
The 1998 financial statements of Sleeman Breweries Ltd. (with headquarters in Guelph, Ontario) are shown in Exhibit 12-16.

Required:
Based on these financial statements, answer each of the following questions:

a. Compute the following ratios for 1998:

(1) ROA (split into profit margin ratio and total asset turnover).

(2) ROE (there are no preferred shares outstanding).

(3) Inventory turnover.

(4) Accounts receivable turnover.

b. Compute the following ratios for both 1998 and 1997:

(1) Current ratio.

(2) Quick ratio.

(3) D/E(I).

(4) Times interest earned.

c. Assume you are thinking of investing in Sleeman Breweries. Comment on the financial health of Sleeman Breweries, highlighting any areas that might be of concern. Use not only the ratios, but also the information from all three financial statements in your analysis.

d. Comment on the use of leverage by Sleeman Breweries. Include comments on the average interest rates paid by Sleeman Breweries on both long-term and short-term debt (include "Bank indebtedness" and the "Current portion of long-term obligations" in your calculations).

e. Sleeman Breweries, like Big Rock Brewery, brews beer. Calculate the same ratios in a. and b. for Big Rock Brewery that you did for Sleeman Breweries. Compare the two companies. Which do you think is the better investment? Why?

12-40 (Ratio analysis for Tritech Precision Inc.)
The 1998 financial statements of Tritech Precision Inc. (with headquarters in Toronto, Ontario) are shown in Exhibit 12-17.

CONSOLIDATED BALANCE SHEETS

EXHIBIT 12-16

PART A

December 26, 1998 and December 27, 1997

	1998	1997
ASSETS		
CURRENT		
Accounts receivable	$ 10,298,798	$ 10,341,943
Inventories *(Note 4)*	11,972,472	8,466,950
Prepaid expenses	1,302,311	473,105
	23,573,581	19,281,998
Property, plant and equipment *(Note 5)*	41,864,535	33,364,805
Long-term investments	3,308,486	4,631,437
Deferred income taxes	566,000	—
Intangibles *(Note 6)*	36,342,108	13,979,640
	$ 105,654,710	$ 71,257,880
LIABILITIES		
CURRENT		
Bank indebtedness *(Note 7)*	$ 2,546,774	$ 280,606
Accounts payable and accrued liabilities	17,483,060	14,028,903
Current portion of long-term obligations *(Note 8)*	4,744,880	3,821,768
	24,774,714	18,131,277
Long-term obligations *(Note 8)*	29,465,021	19,155,713
Deferred income taxes	—	1,510,000
	54,239,735	38,796,990
Shareholders' equity		
Share capital *(Note 10)*	38,309,948	26,110,403
Retained earnings	13,105,027	6,350,487
	51,414,975	32,460,890
	$ 105,654,710	$ 71,257,880

Approved by the board

Ken Hallat, Director

John Withers, Director

18

Sleeman Breweries Ltd. Annual Report 1998

EXHIBIT 12-16
PART B

CONSOLIDATED STATEMENTS OF EARNINGS AND RETAINED EARNINGS

Years Ended December 26, 1998 and December 27, 1997

	1998	1997
Net revenue	$ 76,022,656	$ 54,060,720
Cost of goods sold	34,574,580	26,079,988
Gross margin	41,448,076	27,980,732
Selling, general and administration	26,302,452	18,663,164
Earnings before interest, income taxes, depreciation and amortization	15,145,624	9,317,568
Depreciation and amortization	3,696,743	3,134,909
Interest expense	2,112,129	1,441,847
Earnings before income taxes	9,336,752	4,740,812
Income taxes *(note 9)*	2,582,212	910,560
Net earnings	6,754,540	3,830,252
Retained earnings, beginning of year	6,350,487	2,520,235
Retained earnings, end of year	$ 13,105,027	$ 6,350,487
Earnings per share – basic *(note 12)*	$ 0.44	$ 0.29
Earnings per share – Fully diluted *(note 12)*	$ 0.43	$ 0.28

EXHIBIT 12-16
PART C

CONSOLIDATED STATEMENTS OF CASH FLOWS

Years Ended December 26, 1998 and December 27, 1997

	1998	1997
NET INFLOW (OUTFLOW) OF CASH RELATED TO THE FOLLOWING ACTIVITIES		
OPERATING		
Net earnings	$ 6,754,540	$ 3,830,252
Items not affecting cash		
Depreciation and amortization	3,696,743	3,134,909
Deferred income taxes	924,000	541,000
Gain on disposal of equipment	(92,634)	(190,861)
	11,282,649	7,315,300
Changes in non-cash operating working capital items *(Note 13)*	(4,380,800)	689,025
	6,901,849	8,004,325
INVESTING		
Acquisitions, net of bank indebtedness assumed of $928,773	(15,969,451)	—
Additions to property, plant and equipment	(8,539,442)	(7,354,913)
Additions to intangible assets	(48,124)	(160,961)
Additions to long-term investments	—	(625,000)
Proceeds from property, plant & equipment disposal	3,677,644	214,266
	(20,879,373)	(7,926,608)
FINANCING		
Stock options exercised	779,144	441,062
Long-term obligations – proceeds	20,374,571	6,037,630
Long-term obligations – principal repayments	(9,442,359)	(3,104,032)
	11,711,356	3,374,660
NET CASH FLOW	(2,266,168)	3,452,377
Bank indebtedness, beginning of year	(280,606)	(3,732,983)
Bank indebtedness, end of year	$ (2,546,774)	$ (280,606)

EXHIBIT 12-17
PART A

CONSOLIDATED BALANCE SHEETS
As at December 31
000's

Tritech Precision Inc.
Incorporated under the laws of Ontario

	1998	1997
ASSETS		
Current		
Cash and short-term deposits	$ 8,025	$ 14,980
Accounts receivable	81,394	56,966
Income taxes recoverable	380	—
Inventory	45,376	37,082
Prepaid expenses and other assets	2,739	1,694
Total current assets	137,914	110,722
Fixed assets, net	186,177	100,074
Goodwill, net of accumulated amortization of $1,349 [1997 - $981]	15,093	13,281
Other assets	8,155	3,448
	$ 347,339	$ 227,525
LIABILITIES AND SHAREHOLDERS' EQUITY		
Current		
Bank indebtedness	$ 39,257	$ 2,816
Accounts payable and accrued liabilities	69,217	42,710
Income taxes payable	—	3,047
Current portion of long-term debt	10,924	4,859
Total current liabilities	119,398	53,432
Long-term debt	69,682	40,981
Deferred income taxes	11,138	7,941
Minority interest	20,665	11,098
Total liabilities	220,883	113,452
Shareholders' Equity		
Share capital	75,842	75,656
Retained earnings	50,846	38,417
Cumulative translation adjustment	(232)	—
Total shareholders' equity	126,456	114,073
	$ 347,339	$ 227,525

On behalf of the Board:

W. C. Ferguson
Director

J. D. Mackin
Director

The accompanying notes are an integral component of the consolidated financial statements.

EXHIBIT 12-17
PART B

CONSOLIDATED STATEMENTS OF INCOME
Years ended December 31
000's [except per share amounts]

	1998	1997
Sales	**$ 328,565**	$ 201,312
Cost of goods sold	**254,441**	154,327
Gross profit	**74,124**	46,985
Expenses		
Selling and administration	**26,741**	14,179
Depreciation and amortization	**17,880**	10,831
	44,621	25,010
Income from operations	**29,503**	21,975
Equity in income of Haley Industries Limited	**—**	(1,295)
Interest on long-term debt	**3,652**	1,311
Other interest expense (income)	**393**	(286)
	4,045	(270)
Income before income taxes and minority interest	**25,458**	22,245
Provision for income taxes		
Current	**5,866**	6,048
Deferred	**3,197**	1,364
	9,063	7,412
Income before minority interest	**16,395**	14,833
Minority Interest	**1,940**	707
Net income for the year	**$ 14,455**	$ 14,126
Earnings Per Share		
Basic	**$1.71**	$1.77
Fully diluted	**$1.67**	$1.70
Weighted average number of shares outstanding		
Basic	**8,443**	7,971
Fully diluted	**8,717**	8,361

The accompanying notes are an integral component of the consolidated financial statements.

EXHIBIT 12-17
PART C

CONSOLIDATED STATEMENTS OF CHANGES IN FINANCIAL POSITION
Years ended December 31
000's

	1998	1997
Operating Activities		
Net income for the year	$ **14,455**	$ 14,126
Add (deduct) items not involving a current outflow of cash		
Depreciation and amortization	**17,880**	10,831
Deferred income taxes	**3,197**	1,364
Minority interest	**1,940**	707
Equity in income of Haley Industries Limited	**—**	(1,295)
	37,472	25,733
Net change in non-cash working capital balances		
related to operations	**(22,007)**	(10,244)
Cash provided by operating activities	**15,465**	15,489
Investing Activities		
Net purchase of fixed assets	**(79,687)**	(29,692)
Bank indebtedness assumed on acquisition of subsidiaries	**(3,250)**	(1,504)
Acquisition of subsidiaries	**(2,648)**	—
Additional investments in subsidiaries	**(706)**	(9,875)
Redemption of subsidiary's preferred shares	**(125)**	(125)
Cash used in investing activities	**(86,416)**	(41,196)
Financing Activities		
Increase in long-term debt	**33,389**	1,660
Minority interest investment in subsidiary	**7,786**	—
Repayment of long-term debt	**(10,131)**	(4,421)
Other assets	**(1,691)**	—
Dividends paid	**(2,026)**	—
Issuance of common shares	**186**	27,234
Issuance of subsidiary's common shares	**42**	—
Cash provided by financing activities	**27,555**	24,473
Net decrease in cash during the year	**(43,396)**	(1,234)
Cash position, beginning of year	**12,164**	13,398
Cash position, end of year	$ **(31,232)**	$ 12,164
Cash position represented by		
Cash and short-term deposits	$ **8,025**	$ 14,980
Bank indebtedness	**(39,257)**	(2,816)
	$ **(31,232)**	$ 12,164

The accompanying notes are an integral component of the consolidated financial statements.

Required:

Based on these financial statements, answer each of the following questions:

a. Compute the following ratios for 1998:

(1) ROA (split into profit margin ratio and total asset turnover). The tax rate is 44.6%. Net the two interest expense amounts together.

(2) ROE (there are no preferred shares outstanding).

(3) Inventory turnover.

(4) Accounts receivable turnover.

b. Compute the following ratios for both 1998 and 1997:

(1) Current ratio.

(2) Quick ratio.

(3) D/E(I).

(4) Times interest earned (net the two interest expense amounts together).

c. Assume you are thinking of investing in Tritech. Comment on the financial health of Tritech, highlighting any areas that might be of concern. Use not only the ratios, but also the information from all three financial statements in your analysis.

d. Comment on the use of leverage by Tritech. Be sure to include "Bank indebtedness" and the "Current portion of long-term debt" in your calculations.

e. Tritech produces specialized parts for several industries, including the automotive and defence industries. Approximately 75% of sales are made in the U.S. Most of the costs and liabilities are in Canadian dollars. Calculate the effects on "Income before income taxes and minority interest" under the following assumptions: (i) the Canadian dollar strengthens against the U.S. dollar by 5%; and (ii) the Canadian dollar decreases in value by 5% against the U.S. dollar. Comment on the effect of these changes.

12-41 (Ratio analysis for Enerflex Systems Ltd.)

The 1998 financial statements of Enerflex Systems Ltd. (with headquarters in Calgary, Alberta), which produces compressor equipment used in the natural gas industry, are shown in Exhibit 12-18.

Required:

Based on these financial statements, answer each of the following questions:

a. Compute the following ratios for 1998:

(1) ROA (split into profit margin ratio and total asset turnover).

(2) ROE (there are no preferred shares outstanding).

(3) Inventory turnover.

(4) Accounts receivable turnover.

b. Compute the following ratios for both 1998 and 1997:

(1) Current ratio.

(2) Quick ratio.

EXHIBIT 12-18
PART A

CONSOLIDATED FINANCIAL STATEMENTS

CONSOLIDATED STATEMENTS OF FINANCIAL POSITION

		December 31	
(Thousands)		**1998**	1997
Assets			
Current assets			
Cash		$ –	$ 19,578
Accounts receivable		54,125	66,096
Inventory	(NOTE 1)	45,094	26,057
Total current assets		99,219	111,731
Rental equipment	(NOTE 2)	22,186	13,403
Property, plant and equipment	(NOTE 3)	36,719	16,170
Goodwill, net of accumulated amortization		1,382	1,423
		$ 159,506	$ 142,727
Liabilities and Shareholders' Equity			
Current liabilities			
Bank loans	(NOTE 4)	$ 3,935	$ –
Accounts payable and accrued liabilities		35,641	46,385
Income taxes payable		514	7,375
Current portion of long-term debt	(NOTE 4)	3,100	–
Total current liabilities		43,190	53,760
Long-term debt	(NOTE 4)	15,200	–
Deferred income taxes		1,060	2,002
		59,450	55,762
Shareholders' equity			
Share capital	(NOTE 5)	34,678	34,630
Retained earnings		65,378	52,335
		100,056	86,965
		$ 159,506	$ 142,727

Commitments and contingencies   (NOTES 6 AND 9)

On behalf of the Board:

P. John Aldred, Director   Patrick D. Daniel, Director

EXHIBIT 12-18
PART B

CONSOLIDATED FINANCIAL STATEMENTS

CONSOLIDATED STATEMENTS OF INCOME

		Years Ended December 31	
(Thousands, except share amounts)		**1998**	1997
Revenue		$ **314,496**	$ 336,220
Cost of goods sold		**244,065**	263,316
Gross margin		**70,431**	72,904
Selling, general and administrative expenses		**32,835**	30,623
(Gain) on sale of equipment		**(200)**	(411)
Income before interest and taxes		**37,796**	42,692
Interest (income), net		**(262)**	(55)
Income before income taxes		**38,058**	42,747
Income taxes	(NOTE 7)	**15,490**	17,526
Net income		$ **22,568**	$ 25,221
Net income per common share − basic		$ **1.50**	$ 1.67
− fully diluted		$ **1.45**	$ 1.61
Weighted average number of common shares		**15,085,177**	15,111,147

CONSOLIDATED STATEMENTS OF RETAINED EARNINGS

		Years Ended December 31	
(Thousands)		**1998**	1997
Retained earnings, beginning of year		$ **52,335**	$ 32,145
Net income		**22,568**	25,221
Common shares purchased for cancellation	(NOTE 5)	**(3,003)**	(496)
Stock options purchased	(NOTE 5)	**(491)**	–
Dividends		**(6,031)**	(4,535)
Retained earnings, end of year		$ **65,378**	$ 52,335

EXHIBIT 12-18
PART C

CONSOLIDATED FINANCIAL STATEMENTS

CONSOLIDATED STATEMENTS OF CHANGES IN FINANCIAL POSITION

(Thousands)	Years Ended December 31 1998	Years Ended December 31 1997
Operating Activities		
Net income	$ 22,568	$ 25,221
Depreciation and amortization	4,616	4,056
Deferred income taxes	(942)	(39)
(Gain) on sale of equipment	(200)	(411)
	26,042	28,827
Changes in non-cash working capital	(24,671)	1,055
	1,371	29,882
Investing Activities		
Purchase of:		
Rental equipment	(13,620)	(5,769)
Property, plant and equipment	(23,887)	(3,477)
Proceeds on disposal of:		
Rental equipment	3,454	5,211
Property, plant and equipment	346	168
	(33,707)	(3,867)
Financing Activities		
Proceeds (repayment) of long-term debt	18,300	(4,634)
Common shares purchased for cancellation	(3,267)	(532)
Stock options purchased	(491)	–
Stock options exercised	312	404
Dividends	(6,031)	(4,535)
	8,823	(9,297)
Cash (Bank Loans)		
Increase (decrease) in cash	(23,513)	16,718
Beginning of year	19,578	2,860
End of year	$ (3,935)	$ 19,578

(3) D/E(I).

c. Assume you are thinking of investing in Enerflex. Comment on the financial health of Enerflex, highlighting any areas that might be of concern. Use not only the ratios, but also the information from all three financial statements in your analysis.

d. Calculate the net income and earnings per share figures in 1998 assuming that Enerflex had issued common shares as assumed in part d. and had issued them at the same average price per common share as for the existing common shares. Enerflex had 15,019,000 common shares outstanding at December 31, 1998. Assuming a multiple (price/earnings ratio) of 20, what difference in share price would this change cause? Comment on the use of long-term debt by Enerflex.

12-42 (Ratio analysis for MOSAID Technologies Incorporated)
The 1998 financial statements of MOSAID Technologies Incorporated (with headquarters in Kanata, Ontario) are shown in Exhibit 12-19.

Required:
Based on these financial statements, answer each of the following questions:

a. Compute the following ratios for 1998:

(1) ROA (split into profit margin ratio and total asset turnover).

(2) ROE (there are no preferred shares outstanding).

(3) Accounts receivable turnover.

b. MOSAID is involved in custom computer memory chip design and chip testing. The 1998 inventory of $5,512,000 consists of Raw materials of $3,199,000 and Work in process of $2,313,000. Provide an explanation as to why there is no Finished goods inventory and why inventory turnover would not be meaningful.

c. Compute the following ratios for both 1998 and 1997:

(1) Current ratio.

(2) Quick ratio.

(3) D/E(I).

d. Comment on the use of leverage by MOSAID. Compare the ratios calculated for MOSAID with the ratios calculated in Problem 12-41 for Enerflex Systems Ltd. Compare the use of leverage by the two companies. Explain why a comparison of the leverage of these two companies may not be appropriate.

e. Assume it is May 1, 1998, and MOSAID is considering a major expansion that would cost $30,000,000 and wants to raise $10,000,000 of this from outside sources, either by issuing more shares or by incurring long-term debt. Assume MOSAID would maintain its current ROA and income tax rates.

(1) If it borrowed this $10,000,000 as long-term debt, what is the maximum interest rate it should pay?

(2) Assume it could sell additional common shares at the current market price (assume its multiple is 20 and there would be no issuing costs). How many new shares would MOSAID have to issue?

(3) Assume MOSAID could borrow the $10,000,000 at 10% before taxes. Should MOSAID use debt or shares to finance this expansion?

EXHIBIT 12-19

PART A

MOSAID Technologies Incorporated   financial statements 1998

MOSAID Technologies Incorporated
Consolidated Statement of Earnings and Retained Earnings

(in thousands, except per share amounts)

	Year ended	
	May 1, 1998	May 2, 1997
Revenues		
Operations	$ **40,672**	$ 38,853
Interest	**707**	946
	41,379	39,799
Expenses		
Labour and materials	**9,434**	9,051
Research and development (Note 8)	**13,956**	10,009
Selling and marketing	**7,157**	6,276
General and administration	**5,627**	5,270
Bad debt	**542**	–
Unusual item (Note 9)	**–**	500
	36,716	31,106
Earnings from operations	**4,663**	8,693
Gain on sale of assets	**3,897**	670
	8,560	9,363
Income tax (Note 10)	**3,012**	3,381
Non-controlling interest	**337**	2,234
Net earnings	**5,211**	3,748
Retained earnings, beginning of year	**20,610**	16,862
Retained earnings, end of year	$ **25,821**	$ 20,610
Earnings per share (Note 14)		
Basic	$ **0.73**	$ 0.53
Fully diluted	$ **0.67**	$ 0.49
Weighted average number of shares		
Basic	**7,143,500**	7,071,576
Fully diluted	**8,024,505**	7,781,487

See accompanying Notes to the Consolidated Financial Statements.

EXHIBIT 12-19
PART B

MOSAID Technologies Incorporated (INCORPORATED UNDER THE ONTARIO BUSINESS CORPORATIONS ACT)
Consolidated Balance Sheets
(in thousands)

	As at	
	May 1, 1998	May 2, 1997
Current Assets		
Cash and short-term marketable securities	$ 19,625	$ 18,337
Accounts receivable	9,489	11,250
Revenues recognized in excess of amounts billed	4,003	3,656
Inventories (Note 2)	5,512	4,490
Prepaid expenses	476	576
	39,105	38,309
Capital Assets (Note 3)	14,593	7,440
Technology Acquisitions (Note 4)	1,239	995
Long-term Investments (Note 5)	5,814	1,712
	$ 60,751	$ 48,456
Current Liabilities		
Accounts payable and accrued liabilities	$ 5,150	$ 4,988
Mortgage payable (Note 6)	128	–
Income taxes payable	1,069	301
Deferred revenue	630	636
Deferred income taxes	430	383
	7,407	6,308
Mortgage Payable (Note 6)	5,842	–
Deferred Income Taxes	461	713
	13,710	7,021
Shareholders' Equity		
Share capital (Note 7)	21,220	20,825
Retained earnings	25,821	20,610
	47,041	41,435
	$ 60,751	$ 48,456

See accompanying Notes to the Consolidated Financial Statements.

Thomas I. Csathy
Director

Robert F. Harland
Director

EXHIBIT 12-19
PART C

MOSAID Technologies Incorporated financial statements 1998

MOSAID Technologies Incorporated
Consolidated Statement of Changes in Financial Position
(in thousands)

	Year ended	
	May 1, 1998	May 2, 1997
Operating		
Net earnings	$ 5,211	$ 3,748
Items not affecting cash		
Amortization	3,301	2,405
Gain on long-term investment	(4,103)	–
Loss on disposal of capital assets	206	22
Non-controlling interest	337	2,234
Deferred income taxes	(205)	49
	4,747	8,458
Change in non-cash working capital items	1,301	(3,710)
	6,048	4,748
Investing		
Acquisition of capital assets – net	(10,357)	(5,366)
Acquisition of technology	(547)	(1,169)
Long-term investments	(4,002)	(2,570)
Proceeds of disposition of long-term investment	3,781	–
	(11,125)	(9,105)
Financing		
Issue of mortgage	6,000	–
Repayment of mortgage	(30)	–
Issue of common shares	395	876
	6,365	876
Net cash inflow (outflow)	1,288	(3,481)
Cash position, beginning of year	18,337	21,818
Cash position, end of year	$ 19,625	$ 18,337
Cash comprises the following:		
Cash	$ 1,367	$ 3,028
Marketable securities	18,258	15,309
	$ 19,625	$ 18,337

See accompanying Notes to the Consolidated Financial Statements.

12-43 (Ratio analysis for Shaw Communication Inc.)
The 1998 financial statements of Shaw Communication Inc. (with headquarters in Calgary, Alberta) are shown in Exhibit 12-20.

> *Required:*
> Based on these financial statements, answer each of the following questions:

a. Compute the following ratios for 1998:

(1) ROA (split into profit margin ratio and total asset turnover).

(2) Accounts receivable turnover.

b. Shaw Communication's businesses include cable television, television programming development, radio broadcasting, and expanding telecommunication services. Explain why inventory turnover would not be meaningful.

c. Compute the following ratios for both 1998 and 1997:

(1) Current ratio.

(2) Quick ratio.

(3) D/E(I).

d. Assume you are thinking of investing in Shaw Communications. Comment on the financial health of Shaw Communications, highlighting any areas that might be of concern. Use not only the ratios, but also the information from all three financial statements in your analysis.

Beyond the Book

12-44 (Ratio analysis of a company)
Choose a company as directed by your instructor and answer the following questions:

a. Using the ratios given in the text, prepare an analysis of the company with respect to performance, short-term liquidity, long-term liquidity, and earnings per share ratios.

b. Even though the ratios do not span a long period of time, discuss the financial health of the company. Would you invest in it? Why or why not?

Critical Thinking Questions

12-45 (Discussion of the value of comparability)
One of the qualitative characteristics underlying financial accounting is comparability. As you will recall, comparability refers to similarities of financial information between different companies, and consistency of the financial information produced by a company over time. Two of the many ways of achieving comparability are by limiting the number of different ways transactions may be recorded, or by specifying how assets, liabilities, equities, revenues, and expenses will be disclosed in the financial statements.

One of the arguments against comparability is that it limits the ability of companies to choose among accounting methods, which may result in disclosures that may not be preferred by management.

EXHIBIT 12-20

PART A

consolidated balance sheets

As at August 31	1998	1997
[thousands of dollars]	$	$
ASSETS [note 8]		
Current		
Cash and term deposits	22,047	-
Accounts receivable [note 8]	59,632	45,550
Income taxes recoverable	4,007	-
Prepaids and other	31,152	17,032
	116,838	62,582
Investments and other assets [note 5]	712,689	156,246
Property, plant and equipment [note 6]	997,274	879,391
Deferred charges	69,519	57,334
Subscriber base and broadcast licenses [note 7]	1,304,904	1,294,648
	3,201,224	2,450,201
LIABILITIES AND SHAREHOLDERS' EQUITY		
Current		
Bank indebtedness [note 8]	-	20,876
Accounts payable and accrued liabilities	146,501	116,740
Income taxes payable	-	17,536
Unearned subscriber revenue	37,666	35,779
Current portion of long-term debt	121,976	70,192
	306,143	261,123
Long-term debt [note 8]	1,225,273	1,408,059
Deferred credits	33,304	39,933
Deferred income taxes	220,092	161,012
Minority interest	815	698
	1,785,627	1,870,825
Commitments [note 12]		
Shareholders' equity [note 9]		
Share capital	548,077	5,521
Contributed surplus	657,118	362,410
Retained earnings	210,402	211,445
	1,415,597	579,376
	3,201,224	2,450,201

On behalf of the Board:

Director   Director

60 s h a w

see accompanying notes

consolidated statements of income and retained earnings

EXHIBIT 12-20
PART B

Years ended August 31	1998	1997
[thousands of dollars except per share amounts]	$	$
Revenue [note 3]	783,800	688,363
Operating, general and administrative expenses	467,953	395,201
Operating income before amortization [note 3]	315,847	293,162
Amortization [notes 1, 6 and 7]	147,007	108,842
Operating income before interest	168,840	184,320
Interest [note 8]	135,191	135,403
Operating income before the following	33,649	48,917
Gain on sale of cable systems [note 4]	69,750	-
Gain on sale of investments [note 5]	55,874	-
Asset writedowns and provisions [note 10]	(62,751)	(23,094)
Other revenue including dividends from investees	6,416	1,210
Income from continuing operations before income taxes	102,938	27,033
Income taxes [note 11]	71,420	26,815
Equity in Star Choice Communications Inc. loss	(21,406)	-
Minority interest	3,413	-
Net income from continuing operations	13,525	218
Discontinued operations [note 2]	-	16,374
Net income	13,525	16,592
Retained earnings, beginning of year	211,445	199,664
Dividends	(14,568)	(4,811)
Retained earnings, end of year	210,402	211,445
Earnings (loss) per share		
Net income from continuing operations	(0.01)	0.01
Discontinued operations		0.23
	(0.01)	0.24

see accompanying notes

EXHIBIT 12-20
PART C

consolidated statements of cash flows

Years ended August 31	1998	1997
[thousands of dollars except per share amounts]	$	$
OPERATING ACTIVITIES		
Net income from continuing operations	13,525	218
.Non-cash items:		
Amortization	147,007	108,842
Amortization of long-term program rights	14,064	9,025
Deferred income taxes	55,140	11,505
Gain on sale of cable systems, net of current taxes	(68,450)	-
Asset writedowns and provisions, net of payments	59,885	23,094
Gain on sale of investments, net of current taxes	(51,174)	-
Equity in Star Choice Communications Inc. loss	21,406	-
Minority interest	(3,413)	-
Other	(4,304)	(937)
Cash flow from continuing operations	183,686	151,747
Net change in non-cash working capital balances		
related to operations [note 15]	(54,949)	42,328
	128,737	194,075
INVESTING ACTIVITIES		
Additions to property, plant and equipment	(261,071)	(227,003)
Business acquisitions [note 4]	(121,055)	(71,321)
Proceeds on sale of cable systems	185,872	-
Proceeds on sale of investments and other assets	109,653	-
Acquisition of investments, net of share consideration	(332,570)	(72,466)
Additions to deferred charges	(40,188)	(27,498)
	(459,359)	(398,288)
FINANCING ACTIVITIES		
Increase in long-term debt	391,000	497,112
Long-term debt repayments	(540,646)	(319,918)
Proceeds on issue of debenture purchase warrants	-	31,388
Preferred Securities issued net of expenses and related taxes	537,754	-
Issue of Class B Shares	5	-
Preferred shares redeemed	-	(2,840)
Dividends	(14,568)	(4,811)
	373,545	200,931
Net increase (decrease) in cash during the year	42,923	(3,282)
Cash position, beginning of the year	(20,876)	(17,594)
Cash position, end of the year	22,047	(20,876)
Cash flow from continuing operations per share [note 15]	$ 2.30	$ 2.17

Cash position represents cash and term deposits less bank indebtedness.

see accompanying notes

Required:
Discuss the pros and cons of comparability, with reference to the analysis of financial statements.

12-46 (Use of subsidiaries to manage debt financing)
A major reason that companies such as General Motors form finance subsidiaries (separate companies that they control) is the potential to increase leverage as they seek ways to finance the manufacture and sale of their products. Such subsidiaries are referred to as "captive" finance subsidiaries.

Required:
Explain why a company that finances its operations through a subsidiary has greater debt capacity than a similar company that finances its operations internally.

APPENDIX A
BIG ROCK BREWERY LTD. FINANCIAL STATEMENTS

*Bernd Pieper, Brewmaster; Bob King, President;
Ed McNally, Chairman & Chief Executive Officer*

Last year was very important in the history of Big Rock Brewery. After commencing operations in 1985, Big Rock had enjoyed substantial success growing sales to over $14 million by March 1995. In 1996 a new brewing facility was completed, doubling capacity. Unfortunately, sales increases have slowed since the move was made. In fact, in the first seven months of the past fiscal year, sales were declining.

After 13 years of growth, it was obvious that the success of word-of-mouth promotion and sponsorship had reached its effective limits. Privatization of Alberta liquor stores had created an explosion in beer selection from 212 products in 1994 to 592 in 1998. The Company needed to make an investment in advertising while building internal marketing resources in order to compete with more and more beers from all over the world. This investment increased expenses substantially during the past fiscal year, and had a major impact on sales which increased steadily in the last quarter of this fiscal – a trend that has continued to accelerate into fiscal 2000.

Despite the obvious payoff from this new approach, it has not come without up-front costs. Net income for the year ended March 31, 1999 was down to a $556,745 loss, from a profit of $288,981 a year earlier. Similarly, cash flow from operations declined to $837,714 versus $2,383,811 in 1998. The loss and decline in cash flow primarily reflect an increase of $2,191,360 in selling, general and administrative costs to $7,716,517.

In fiscal 1999, revenues increased to $26.5 million from $25.2 million the previous year, despite declines in the first two quarters. This trend continued and accelerated early in the new fiscal year.

In developing the new successful approach to marketing in both our traditionally strong Alberta market and elsewhere, Big Rock has been assisted by Calgary-based Parallel. In addition, the Company has made a substantial recruiting effort to develop a much deeper marketing team. We are confident both our relationship with Parallel and our investment in internal resources will pay off substantially for our shareholders in the medium and long term.

Our New Marketing Initiatives

In the short six months since adopting a more aggressive marketing approach, Big Rock has initiated a number of programs aimed at increasing short- and long-term sales growth. A new advertising program was developed and launched in late October, with billboard and radio announcements in both Calgary and Edmonton. Sales began a slow increase in January. This was followed by a retail glass giveaway program starting in March. By the fiscal year end March 31, 1999, the sales for the last quarter had risen by 16 percent.

Another major move to create better brand recognition was the implementation of new packaging featuring a clear message about Big Rock and more information about the nine different brands. The packaging, which kept 80 percent of the old look but provided for more consistent branding across the entire product line, was recently awarded gold in the prestigious national Marketing Magazine awards.

The most exciting program undertaken in the last few years began with a secret plan developed by the brewing staff to brew an outstanding lager.

To accommodate the new yeast, the brewmasters required a reliable source of soft spring water. They found exactly the right source, a flowing spring fed by the Thompson Glacier near the southern border of Jasper National Park, Alberta.

The next search was for a name that would clearly describe a lager brewed with cold glacier water, cold fermented, cold filtered, and cold packaged. The word we wanted was obviously "cold", thus the trademark we sought and obtained was Köld, which has a hint of both its German pedigree and the Big Rock personality.

The brewmasters have produced a truly outstanding, distinguished and quaffable lager. It is so good, consumers will immediately recognize its premium quality when compared to other products presently available. Also, they will know exactly what they are drinking, as all the ingredients are listed on the label – hops, malt, yeast and glacier-fed spring water. Early sales of this product are very encouraging.

Thompson Glacier, the source of the glacier-fed spring water used in Big Rock's new lager – Köld.

Finally, Big Rock is delighted to announce the appointment of Bob King, former Chairman and Chief Executive Officer of the Alberta Gaming and Liquor Commission, as President. Bob is one of Canada's leading authorities on liquor distribution and regulations. He will apply his wide experience and recognized administrative skills to build on the growth and success of Big Rock.

The Big Rock staff have dealt with the many challenges and changes with skill and creativity. With their ongoing teamwork they continue to be Big Rock's greatest asset. Big Rock employees remain committed to producing Canada's highest quality beer and solidifying a reputation as an outstanding regional brewer.

Sincerely,

Edward E. McNally
Chairman and Chief Executive Officer

June 10, 1999

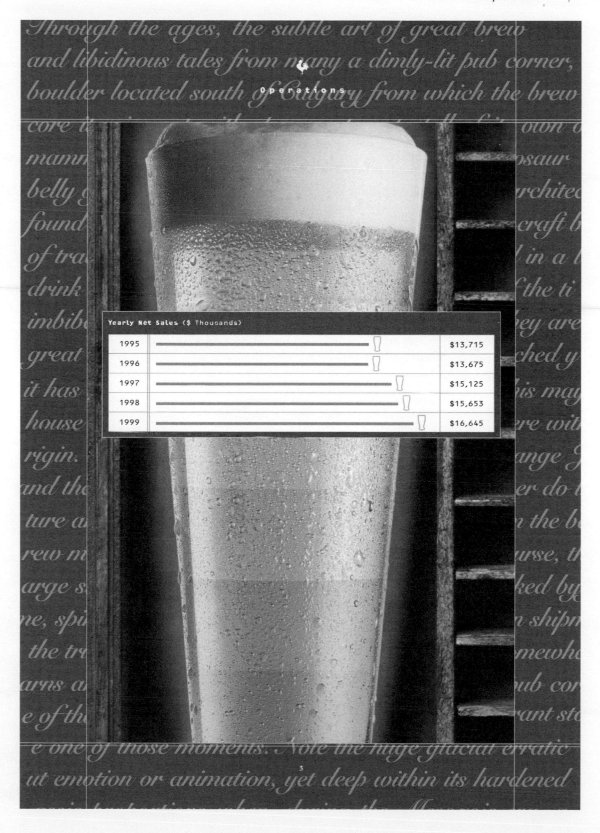

Operations

Yearly Net Sales ($ Thousands)

1995		$13,715
1996		$13,675
1997		$15,125
1998		$15,653
1999		$16,645

3

🐓

A M a r k e t i n g G l a n c e

Brian Rowland, Manager, Sales; Bert Boulet, Chief Financial Officer;
Janine Calb, Manager, Marketing and Communications

Strategic planning, focus and investment were the key words for Big Rock marketing in the last fiscal year. The positive results of these marketing efforts are proven by recent sales increases and positive consumer feedback.

After the very busy summer of 1998, Big Rock's first national marketing plan was developed. This plan outlined efforts to reposition and strengthen branding. It also determined geographic and product priorities within particular target markets. This comprehensive plan outlined strategies for promotions in retail liquor stores as well as bars and restaurants, sponsorship criteria, point-of-sale support, competitive information, market research and budgets.

The first national strategy implemented was the redesign of our packaging. Consumer feedback revealed that our current packaging did not provide enough information to base a purchasing decision on. Also, the Big Rock identity was not prominent. This was, in essence, a lost brand-building opportunity. The packaging was redesigned to create a family look for the brand, while providing more information on product type for the consumer. However, the majority of the original artwork was retained in order to retain existing brand loyalty.

The new packaging was introduced with Big Rock's first advertising campaign in Alberta. A consumer contest to win a trip to any one of nine big rocks around the world was supported by radio, billboard, print, in-store point-of-sale material and viral media. This contest was launched at the Company's special event, Big Rocktoberfest in late October, and ran through the end of November. The contest was successful in increasing brand awareness and educating consumers about the range of beers that Big Rock offers. Sales increases were immediately apparent.

In December the popular variety pack was brought back, this time under the name "Winter Six". Promotion for this variety pack supported trial on a number of our brands while continuing to build the Big Rock brand name. The radio and in-store support drove sales of Winter Six to a 40 percent increase over that of the previous Big Rock variety pack.

Big Rock's new Chinook Pale Ale supports salmon habitat conservation by donating a portion of sales to the Pacific Salmon Foundation.

The new calendar year brought even stronger promotions and sales growth for Big Rock. Based on consumer demand, 12-packs of Grasshopper and Traditional were developed. These new packs were launched with an extremely successful glass promotion. Any consumer who purchased a 12-pack received a Big Rock branded pint glass. This promotion was supported by radio, billboard, print and in-store point-of-sale material. Consumer feedback was extremely positive. The billboards screamed "FREE BEER – glass" and the radio commercials featured Ed McNally offering to give away "free beer (glasses)". Ed's character proved to be so memorable and humorous that he just may make a return to the radio in the new fiscal year.

The glass promotion continues with free Chinook glasses in April and May, free Light glasses in June and free Grasshopper glasses in July. From a marketing perspective this promotion has proved successful for a number of reasons: the Big Rock brand name is strengthened when consumers use this glass at home, trial has increased on the smaller brands and sales have continued to increase with each new product focus.

Big Rock's growth strategy for the fiscal year included portfolio expansion and focus in regions outside of Alberta. Rock Creek Cider was added to offer consumers a light tasting, less sweet alternative to current ciders. This cider is currently available in draught only and has had great success with distribution to date. A sales team was hired in Ontario and an office opened to allow Big Rock to be closer to our customers and potential consumers in the largest beer market in Canada.

Rock Creek Cider, brewed in the Okanagan Valley of British Columbia, was added to the Big Rock portfolio.

KÖLD

The launch of Big Rock's new lager, Köld, has been extremely exciting and opens up tremendous marketing potential for the new fiscal year. Early sales are encouraging and it appears that this product is targeted and positioned exactly where it was intended. The Company is excited to have developed a strong brand for introduction into the lager market – Canada's strongest market for beer sales.

All new marketing initiatives have been supported by our continued community involvement through sponsorships and special events. Following a successful Big Rocktoberfest in October, the sixth annual Eddies Commercial Contest was held in Calgary at the Jubilee Auditorium in May. Once again, this event was a huge success as it continues to build year after year. Big Rock's approach to events has changed slightly as it has developed a partnership with professional event planners, the Event Group, to manage its events. This partnership ensures that Big Rock events will continue to grow and offer more support to the community. This approach has resulted in the addition of two new events for the next fiscal year while allowing Big Rock staff to continue to focus on sales volume growth and developing brand awareness.

While there have been significant personnel changes within the marketing department this year, the result is a team that has synergy and continues to be able to stretch resources beyond expectations. Everyone who has been involved in the development and implementation of the marketing plan had significant influence over the exciting recent sales trends and should be commended. The team is poised for continued growth and exploration of new markets in the next fiscal year.

Now that's Kold.
Photo: John Dunn/Arctic Light

Köld's advertising has successfully reached the 18- to 24-year-old demographic.

Big Rock employees are committed to producing quality beer.

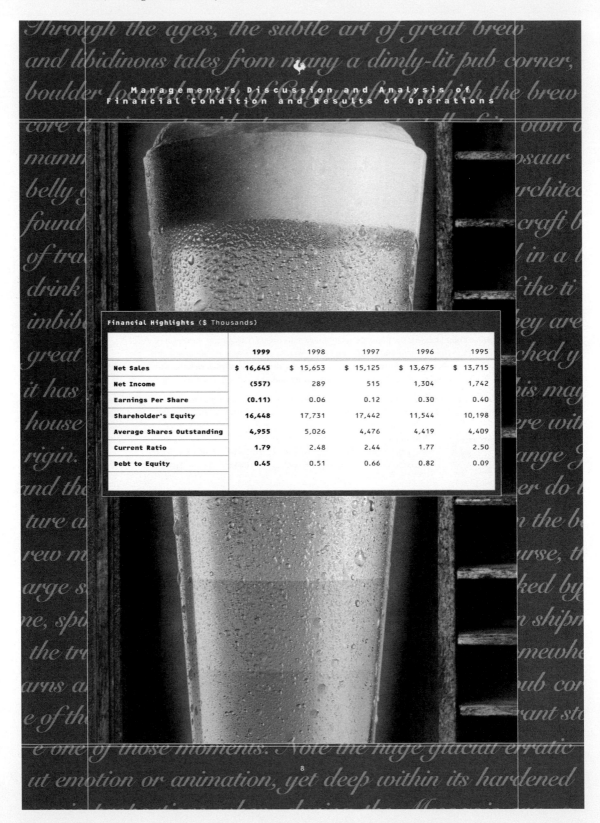

Management's Discussion and Analysis of
Financial Condition and Results of Operations

Financial Highlights ($ Thousands)

	1999	1998	1997	1996	1995
Net Sales	$ 16,645	$ 15,653	$ 15,125	$ 13,675	$ 13,715
Net Income	(557)	289	515	1,304	1,742
Earnings Per Share	(0.11)	0.06	0.12	0.30	0.40
Shareholder's Equity	16,448	17,731	17,442	11,544	10,198
Average Shares Outstanding	4,955	5,026	4,476	4,419	4,409
Current Ratio	1.79	2.48	2.44	1.77	2.50
Debt to Equity	0.45	0.51	0.66	0.82	0.09

The following discussion and analysis should be read in conjunction with the Company's Consolidated Financial Statements and Notes included therein.

Overview

A regional producer and distributor of premium quality speciality beers (also known as "craft" beers), Big Rock is committed to developing its business by following three sound business fundamentals:

- Consistently brewing distinctive, premium quality craft beers;
- Constantly providing superior, personalized customer service; and
- Creating and sustaining strong community relationships.

The Company currently produces nine different brands of bottled and draught beer with six of these distributed in cans. The Company launched a new lager brand in May of 1999. Big Rock currently sells its products in Western Canada, two territories and selected U.S. states. Approximately 80 percent of total sales are in Alberta where Big Rock has a four percent share of the total beer market. In the past, Big Rock used agents in Ontario to market its products. As of March 1999, the Company has opened an office in Ontario, Canada's largest beer market, and hired several key staff to oversee sales and marketing. The Company is confident this added focus in Ontario will increase Big Rock's profile and sales.

With a state-of-the-art, 250,000-hectolitre brewery and a proven reputation for producing world-class, natural beers for any market, the Company is well positioned to continue growth in existing markets and to successfully respond to opportunities in new markets.

Year-end Comparisons

Net sales increased to $16,644,881 in fiscal 1999, up from $15,653,051 in 1998. While Canadian market sales increased by $1,272,368 to $16,136,597, U.S. sales decreased to 3.3 percent of total sales in 1999 from 5.3 percent in 1998.

For the fiscal year ended March 31, 1999, overall sales volumes of 99,623 hectolitres were up from fiscal 1998 volumes of 98,514 hectolitres. The increase in sales can be attributed to a new advertising and marketing campaign launched in late October 1998. This campaign focused on the Alberta market and early indications prove it to be successful. The Company plans to focus future marketing efforts on increasing market share in Alberta and responding to new marketing opportunities in other Canadian markets. It will transfer proven marketing initiatives to these opportunities.

The cost of sales increased slightly from $7,676,372 in 1998 to $7,691,231 in 1999. The increase is a result of increased sales and a one-time writedown of packaging materials. Due to purchasing and production efficiencies encountered through state-of-the-art equipment and the implementation of new cost control measures, cost of sales as a percentage of net sales has decreased to 46.0 percent, as compared to 49.0 percent in fiscal 1998.

Gross profit increased to $8,953,650 or $89.88 per hectolitre in 1999 as compared to $7,976,679 or $80.97 per hectolitre in 1998. The Company was able to increase the gross profit to 54.0 percent of net sales as compared to 51.0 percent in fiscal 1998.

Selling, general and administrative expenses increased to $7,716,517 as compared to $5,525,157 reported in 1998. The increase is directly attributed to the increased advertising and marketing in Alberta as well as the establishment of new and expanded sales teams in British Columbia and Ontario. Historically, Company advertising has been limited, however, current market conditions plus the increased industry competition have warranted increased spending in this area. Growth in these markets has been the result of these initiatives. Included in selling, general and administrative is a $302,211 write-off of deferred charges from prior years.

Amortization expense increased slightly to $1,132,161 in fiscal 1999 from $1,103,976 in 1998.

Interest expense decreased by 21.0 percent to $661,640 in 1999 as compared to $841,565 in 1998. The Company adhered to an aggressive repayment plan and reduced debt by 16.9 percent in the last fiscal year. This aggressive approach to debt reduction will favourably impact subsequent years' interest expense.

The Company reported a net loss of $556,745 and a loss per share of $0.11 for the current year. This loss is attributable to the writedowns and increased marketing and advertising expenditures that occurred this year. By the end of the fiscal year these marketing efforts had increased sales and brand awareness in our main markets.

Liquidity and Capital Resources

As at March 31, 1999, the Company had a positive working capital (current assets minus current liabilities) of $1,820,338. Cash flow from operations decreased to $837,714 from $2,383,811 as reported in 1998. The decrease relates primarily to the increased advertising and marketing initiatives. The Company also reported a write-off of deferred charges and loss on sale of capital assets. The deferred charges were expenditures capitalized in prior years and included professional fees, refinancing and packaging design. The Company also sold the last building at the previous brewery site and recorded a loss of $228,577.

The Company currently has a revolving credit line of $5,000,000 (1998 – $5,000,000) which bears interest at a floating rate of prime. A general security agreement and a general assignment of book debt have been provided as collateral. As at March 31, 1999, $624,909 was drawn against the line of credit.

Long-term debt was reduced by $1,524,000 to $7,476,000 in 1999 from $9,000,000 in 1998. The debt is broken down into two loan commitments, one of which has principal repayment terms of $28,000 per month and the other $437,500 repayable in quarterly instalments. The Company has made sufficient payments of principal on both loans so that no principal repayments are required until April 30, 2000. Collateral for the credit facility consists of a fixed and floating charge debenture on the lands, buildings and equipment, and a fixed mortgage and charge against the brewery.

Financing activities during 1999 consumed $2,548,712. This was a result of long-term debt repayment and a share repurchase plan. Share capital decreased by $355,703 as the Company repurchased 165,000 common shares at a cost of $726,981. The difference between the decrease in share capital and the cost to repurchase common shares was recorded against retained earnings.

Investing activities decreased slightly as the Company does not require major capital expenditures as the current facility was built in 1996 with the latest technologies. The Company received proceeds of $755,000 from the sale of the last building located at the previous brewery site. The proceeds were used to reduce long-term debt.

The Company expects to meet its future financing needs from a number of sources:

- Working capital through operating cash flow;
- Cash on hand; and
- Revolving lines of credit, to the extent required.

Risks and Uncertainties

The Company considers other brewers in the premium-priced category to be its main competitors. This includes import beer and specialty beer brewed by both the craft industry and national brewers.

In this difficult and highly competitive market, the Company must remain focused on the business principles it has implemented so successfully in its home market. The Company is confident it can compete successfully and continue its steady growth.

The Company requires various permits, licenses and approvals from various government agencies to operate in its market areas. In Alberta, where the Company sells the majority of its products, the Alberta Gaming and Liquor Commission provides the necessary documents. Other agencies include the Saskatchewan Liquor and Gaming Authority, Manitoba Liquor Control Commission, Liquor Control Board of Ontario, British Columbia Liquor Distribution Board, Revenue Canada – Excise, and the U.S. Bureau of Alcohol, Tobacco and Firearms. Management believes the Company is currently in compliance with all licences, permits and necessary approvals.

The Company has completed an assessment of its computer systems to identify the possible impact of the Year 2000 Issue. The Year 2000 Issue is the result of computer programs being written using two digits rather than four to define the applicable year. Computer programs with time-sensitive software may recognize a date using "00" as the year 1900 rather than the year 2000. Management believes the Company's major software packages are year 2000 compliant. Upgrades will be required for some secondary systems and these will be completed as soon as they become available.

The Company is working directly with key vendors, suppliers and service providers in order to avoid any business interruptions in the year 2000 and thereafter. However, the Company has no means of ensuring that external agents will be year 2000 ready. In addition, the Company is in the process of completing its contingency planning for all risk areas. The contingency plans include, among other things, manual "work-arounds" for potential software and hardware failures and an increase in year-end inventory to allow for production disruptions that could occur in January 2000. The Company does not anticipate a material effect on its financial position or results of operations from the Year 2000 Issue.

Management's Report

The accompanying consolidated financial statements in the annual report are the responsibility of management. The consolidated financial statements of the Company have been prepared in accordance with Canadian generally accepted accounting principles ("GAAP"). The Company's accounting policies are, in all material respects, in accordance with United States ("U.S.") GAAP. In the opinion of management, the financial statements have been prepared within acceptable limits of materiality and, when necessary, management has made informed judgements and estimates in accounting for transactions which were not complete at the balance sheet date. Where alternative accounting methods exist, management has chosen those it deems most appropriate in the circumstances as indicated in the notes to the consolidated financial statements.

Management maintains appropriate systems of internal control. Policies and procedures are designed to give reasonable assurance that transactions are appropriately authorized, assets are protected and financial records are properly maintained to provide reasonable assurance that financial information is relevant and reliable.

The Audit Committee is appointed by the Board of Directors, and is comprised of directors, the majority of which are not officers or employees of the Company. The Committee meets regularly with management to discuss internal controls over the financial reporting process, auditing matters and financial reporting issues, to satisfy itself that each party is discharging its responsibilities and to review the financial statements and the external auditors' report. The Audit Committee has approved the financial statements.

Edward E. McNally
Chairman and Chief Executive Officer

Bert Boulet
Chief Financial Officer

Auditors' Report

To the Shareholders of Big Rock Brewery Ltd.

We have audited the consolidated balance sheets of Big Rock Brewery Ltd. as at March 31, 1999 and 1998 and the consolidated statements of operations and retained earnings and cash flows for the years then ended. These financial statements are the responsibility of the Company's management. Our responsibility is to express an opinion on these financial statements based on our audits.

We conducted our audits in accordance with generally accepted auditing standards. Those standards require that we plan and perform an audit to obtain reasonable assurance whether the financial statements are free of material misstatement. An audit includes examining, on a test basis, evidence supporting the amounts and disclosures in the financial statements. An audit also includes assessing the accounting principles used and significant estimates made by management, as well as evaluating the overall financial statement presentation.

In our opinion, these consolidated financial statements present fairly, in all material respects, the financial position of the Company as at March 31, 1999 and 1998 and the results of its operations and its cash flows for the years then ended in accordance with accounting principles generally accepted in Canada.

Calgary, Canada
May 4, 1999

Ernst + Young LLP
Chartered Accountants

Consolidated Balance Sheets
As at March 31 ($ Canadian)

As at March 31	1999	1998
Assets (note 6)		
Current		
Cash	$ 75,234	$ 191,628
Accounts receivable	1,548,486	1,302,336
Income taxes receivable	6,908	719,311
Inventories (note 3)	2,050,703	2,270,909
Prepaid expenses and other	433,785	403,198
	4,115,116	4,887,382
Capital assets (note 4)	24,978,339	26,799,179
Deferred charges and other	72,380	233,115
	$ 29,165,835	$ 31,919,676
Liabilities and Shareholders' Equity		
Current		
Bank indebtedness (note 5)	$ 624,909	$ 922,640
Accounts payable and accrued liabilities	1,669,869	1,049,753
	2,294,778	1,972,393
Long-term debt (note 6)	7,476,000	9,000,000
Deferred income taxes	2,947,400	3,215,900
Total liabilities	12,718,178	14,188,293
Commitments (note 9)		
Shareholders' equity		
Share capital (note 7)	10,472,209	10,827,912
Retained earnings	5,975,448	6,903,471
	16,447,657	17,731,383
	$ 29,165,835	$ 31,919,676

See accompanying notes

On behalf of the Board:

Edward E. McNally
Director

J. Angus McKee
Director

Consolidated Statements of Operations
and Retained Earnings
For the years ended March 31, 1999 and 1998 ($ Canadian)

	1999	1998
Revenue		
Sales	$ 26,466,241	$ 25,184,850
Government taxes and commissions	(9,821,360)	(9,531,799)
	16,644,881	15,653,051
Cost of sales	7,691,231	7,676,372
Gross profit	8,953,650	7,976,679
Expenses		
Selling, general and administrative	7,716,517	5,525,157
Interest on long-term debt	647,317	820,974
Interest on short-term debt	14,323	20,591
Amortization	1,132,161	1,103,976
Loss on sale of capital assets (note 4)	228,577	–
	9,738,895	7,470,698
(Loss) income before income taxes	(785,245)	505,981
Income tax (recovery) expense (note 8)	(268,500)	172,000
Large Corporation tax	40,000	45,000
Net (loss) income for year	(556,745)	288,981
Retained earnings, beginning of year	6,903,471	6,614,490
Redemption of common shares (note 7)	(371,278)	–
Retained earnings, end of year	$ 5,975,448	$ 6,903,471
(Loss) earnings per share (note 2)		
Basic & fully diluted	$ (0.11)	$ 0.06

See accompanying notes

Consolidated Statements of Cash Flows
For the years ended March 31, 1999 and 1998 ($ Canadian)

	1999	1998
Operating Activities		
Net (loss) income for year	$ (556,745)	$ 288,981
Items not affecting cash		
Amortization	1,132,161	1,103,976
Write-off of deferred charges	302,221	18,854
Deferred income taxes	(268,500)	972,000
Loss on sale of capital assets	228,577	–
Cash flow from operations	837,714	2,383,811
Net change in non-cash working capital (note 12)	1,275,988	(717,948)
Cash provided by operating activities	2,113,702	1,665,863
Financing Activities		
(Decrease) increase in bank indebtedness	(297,731)	546,994
Repayment of long-term debt	(1,524,000)	(2,682,692)
Share repurchase (note 7)	(726,981)	–
Cash (used) by financing activities	(2,548,712)	(2,135,698)
Investing Activities		
Additions to capital assets	(294,898)	(517,001)
Additions to deferred charges and other assets	(141,486)	(107,476)
Proceeds on disposal of capital assets	755,000	1,059,755
Cash provided by investing activities	318,616	435,278
Net increase (decrease) in cash	(116,394)	(34,557)
Cash, beginning of year	191,628	226,185
Cash, end of year	$ 75,234	$ 191,628

See accompanying notes

15

Notes to Consolidated Financial Statements
For the years ended March 31, 1999 and 1998 ($ Canadian)

1. Description of Business

Big Rock Brewery Ltd. (the "Company") produces and markets its own brands of specialty draught and bottled beer for sale across Canada and the United States. The consolidated financial statements include the accounts of the Company and its wholly-owned subsidiary, Big Rock Brewery (Sask.) Ltd.

2. Significant Accounting Policies

The consolidated financial statements of the Company have been prepared in accordance with Canadian generally accepted accounting principles ("GAAP"). The Company's accounting policies are, in all material respects, in accordance with United States ("U.S.") GAAP. The consolidated financial statements, in management's opinion, have been properly prepared within reasonable limits of materiality and within the framework of the accounting policies summarized below.

All figures are reported in Canadian dollars. Exchange rates between the U.S. and Canadian dollars for each of the years reported in these consolidated financial statements were as follows:

	Canadian Equivalent of $1 US	
	End of year	Average for year
March 31, 1999	1.5087	1.5037
March 31, 1998	1.4166	1.4026

Inventories

Inventories of raw materials, supplies, promotional goods and dispensing units are valued at the lower of cost (first-in first-out method) and replacement cost. Inventories of brews in process and finished product are valued at the lower of cost (including direct materials, labour and overhead costs) and net realizable value.

Returnable glass containers are initially recorded at cost. In order to charge operations for wear and disappearance, the costs of bottles are charged to operations over their estimated useful life.

Capital Assets

Capital assets are stated at cost less accumulated amortization. Amortization is recorded on the straight-line basis over the estimated useful lives of the assets. Amortization rates are as follows:

Buildings	2.5%
Production equipment	3.3% to 15%
Vehicles	25%
Furniture and fixtures	15%

The Company completes a yearly assessment of its capital assets for impairment by assessing the estimated future net cash flows from the assets, less directly attributable general and administrative costs, carrying costs, future removal costs and income taxes of the assets. Any shortfall of this amount from the net carrying amount of the asset less deferred income taxes, is charged to expense in the period.

Revenue Recognition

Revenue is recognized upon shipment of product at the gross sales price charged to the purchaser. Invoices for sales to Canadian customers are submitted to the respective provincial Liquor Control Boards who pay the Company after deducting Liquor Control Board commissions. Excise taxes, which are assessed on production, and Liquor Control Board Commissions, which are assessed on sales, are recorded as reductions to gross sales prices.

Deferred Income Taxes

The Company follows the deferral method of accounting for the tax effect of the timing differences between taxable income and accounting income. Timing differences result principally from claiming capital cost allowance for income tax purposes in excess of amortization on capital assets.

Foreign Exchange

Transactions in foreign currencies are recorded in Canadian dollars at the exchange rates in effect at the date of the transaction. Monetary assets and liabilities in foreign currencies have been converted to Canadian dollars at exchange rates in effect at the balance sheet date. Foreign exchange gains and losses included in earnings are not material for the years presented.

Earnings per Share

Earnings per share are calculated using the weighted average number of shares outstanding during each year which was 4,955,322 for the year ended March 31, 1999 (1998 – 5,026,200). Fully diluted earnings per share is calculated on the assumption that outstanding common share options which are dilutive were exercised at the beginning of the period and the funds derived therefrom were invested at the Company's annual after tax cost of financing.

All potential option issuances for both 1999 and 1998 were anti-dilutive under both Canadian and U.S. GAAP.

Stock options

All stock options are granted at or above the market price of the stock on the date of grant. No compensation expense is recorded for the fair value of options granted.

3. Inventories

	1999	1998
Raw materials and returnable glass	$ 1,026,843	$ 1,416,377
Brews in progress	235,471	234,319
Finished product	549,278	418,015
Promotional goods and dispensing units	239,111	202,198
	$ 2,050,703	$ 2,270,909

4. Capital Assets ($ Thousands)

	1999			1998		
	Cost	Accumulated Amortization	Net Book Value	Cost	Accumulated Amortization	Net Book Value
Land	1,844	–	1,844	2,172	–	2,172
Buildings	7,337	464	6,873	8,728	1,158	7,570
Production equipment	19,624	3,835	15,789	19,541	2,977	16,564
Vehicles	79	67	12	75	58	17
Furniture and fixtures	725	265	460	680	204	476
	29,609	4,631	24,978	31,196	4,397	26,799

During the year ended March 31, 1999, the Company capitalized labour of $19,192 (1998 – $59,680) relating to the enhancement at its brewing facilities.

During the year ended March 31, 1999, the Company sold capital assets which included surplus land, buildings and production equipment with a net book value of $983,577 for aggregate proceeds of $755,000, resulting in a loss on sale of $228,577.

5. Bank Indebtedness

The Company has a demand revolving credit facility with a maximum limit at March 31, 1999 and 1998 of $5,000,000. Advances under the line bear interest at the Royal Bank prime rate (effective rate at March 31, 1999 and 1998 – 6.5%). Collateral provided for this loan is the same as described in note 6.

6. Long-term Debt

	1999	1998
Brewery Facility		
Term loan payable in monthly principal payments of $28,000. The facility has a five-year term and is amortized over 15 years.	$ 3,976,000	$ 4,384,000
Equipment Facility		
Term loan payable over four years in quarterly principal payments of $437,500.	3,500,000	4,616,000
	7,476,000	9,000,000
Less current portion	–	–
	$ 7,476,000	$ 9,000,000

During the year ended March 31, 1999, the Company made sufficient payments of principal on both loans so no principal repayments are required on the brewery commitment and equipment commitment until April 30, 2000. Accordingly, there is no current portion of long-term debt for the fiscal year ended March 31, 2000.

A fixed and floating charge debenture and supplemental debenture for $20,000,000 covering all assets, a general security agreement and an assignment of fire insurance have been provided as collateral for credit facilities.

The facilities impose a number of positive and negative covenants on the Company including the maintenance of certain financial ratios.

These facilities bear variable rates of interest ranging from Royal Bank prime to prime plus 3/4% depending on the Company's average quarterly interest coverage ratios.

At March 31, 1999 the Company had a swap agreement to exchange floating interest rates for fixed interest on $ 7,500,000 (March 31, 1998 – $10,200,000) of the loan at 7.24% interest (1998 – 6.44% to 7.24%) with maturity at April 30, 2001.

Any payments or receipts incurred under the swaps are recorded as part of the interest expense over the terms of the swaps.

The average interest rate on the facilities (including the effect of the swaps) for the year ended March 31, 1999 was 7.91% (March 31, 1998 – 7.77%).

Cash interest payments made during 1999 amounted to $654,536 (1998 – $891,397).

Estimated principal payments required for subsequent fiscal years are as follows:

	Total
March 31, 2000	$ –
March 31, 2001	1,786,000
March 31, 2002	2,086,000
March 31, 2003	636,000
March 31, 2004	336,000
Thereafter	2,632,000
	$ 7,476,000

7. Share Capital

Authorized

Unlimited number of voting common shares.

Unlimited number of preferred shares which may be issued in one or more series with rights, privileges, restrictions and conditions as fixed by the directors prior to the issue of each series.

Issued and outstanding

Common Shares	No. of Shares	Amount
Balance as at March 31, 1997 and 1998	5,026,200	$ 10,827,912
Shares redeemed in normal course issuer bid	(165,000)	(355,703)
Balance as at March 31, 1999	**4,861,200**	**$ 10,472,209**

The $371,278 excess of the redemption price for the shares over the average issue price of the shares has been charged to retained earnings.

Options

At March 31, 1999, 694,000 common shares were reserved for the exercise of stock options by employees, directors and a consultant to the Company. These options are exercisable as follows:

Expiry Date	No. of Shares	Exercise Price
December 30, 2002	94,000	$ 5.75
December 15, 1999 to October 6, 2002	375,200	$ 7.15
March 20, 2001	14,150	$ 12.63
August 30, 2000	15,000	$ 13.50
October 16, 2000	86,650	$ 13.88
December 15, 1999	109,000	$ 14.65

8. Income Taxes

The Company is a public company engaged in manufacturing and processing activities for Canadian income tax purposes. The Company's effective tax expense is summarized as follows:

	1999	1998
Income before income tax expense	$ (785,245)	$ 505,981
Income tax expense at statutory rate of 44.6%	(350,000)	226,000
Effect on taxes of		
Manufacturing and processing profits deduction	59,000	(34,000)
Non-deductible expenses	22,500	18,000
Other	40,000	(38,000)
	(228,500)	172,000
Current income tax expense (recovery)	40,000	(800,000)
Deferred income tax (recovery) expense	(268,500)	972,000
	$ (228,500)	$ 172,000

At March 31, 1999 the Company has non-capital losses of $2,100,000 deductible against future income for tax purposes. The losses expire as follows: 2005 – $100,000; 2006 – $2,000,000.

Cash income taxes paid during the year were $93,808 (1998 – $15,802).

9. Commitments

The Company leases warehouse premises on which the lease expires in October 2001. The Company also leases office equipment and vehicles under operating leases. Annual lease payments including estimated utilities and property taxes are as follows:

	Payment
2000	$ 176,337
2001	142,216
2002	53,037
2003	—
	$ **371,590**

10. Information about Geographic Segments

Substantially all of the Company's assets and revenues are in Canada. Net sales in 1999 in the United States, on a percentage basis, were 3.3% (1998 – 5.3%).

11. Financial Instruments

Financial instruments of the Company consist of cash, accounts receivable, income taxes receivable, bank indebtedness, accounts payable and accrued liabilities, long-term debt and interest rate swaps. As at March 31, 1999 and 1998, there were no significant differences between the carrying amounts reported on the balance sheet (excluding the interest rate swaps), and their estimated market values. At March 31, 1999, a cash payment of approximately $108,095 (1998 – $277,852) would have been required to settle the interest rate swap agreements.

The Company is exposed to currency risk on cash, trade receivables and accounts payable denominated in U.S. dollars, totalling U.S. $20,723 at March 31, 1999 (March 31, 1998 – U.S. $170,396).

The Company has a concentration of credit risk because substantially all of its accounts receivable are from a small number of government-owned Provincial Liquor Boards. However, no individual customer accounts for greater than 10% of sales in any period.

12. Net Change in Non-cash Working Capital

The net change in non-cash working capital relating to operating activities consists of:

	1999	1998
Accounts receivable	$ (246,150)	$ (24,140)
Income taxes receivable	712,403	(118,360)
Inventories	220,206	(370,694)
Prepaid expenses and other	(30,587)	(132,490)
Accounts payable and accrued liabilities	620,116	(72,264)
	$ **1,275,988**	$ (717,948)

13. Year 2000 Issue

The Year 2000 Issue arises because many computerized systems use two digits rather than four to identify a year. Date-sensitive systems may recognize the year 2000 as 1900 or some other date, resulting in errors when information using year 2000 dates is processed. In addition, similar problems may arise in some systems which use certain dates in 1999 to represent something other than a date. The effects of the Year 2000 Issue may be experienced before, on, or after January 1, 2000, and, if not addressed, the impact on operations and financial reporting may range from minor errors to significant systems failure which could affect an entity's ability to conduct normal business operations. Management has developed and is implementing a plan designed to identify and address the expected effects of the Year 2000 Issue on the Company. As at March 31, 1999, the Company had commenced the assessment of the readiness of third parties such as customers, suppliers and others and this is ongoing. However, it is not possible to be certain that all aspects of the Year 2000 Issue affecting the Company, including those related to the efforts of customers, suppliers, or other third parties, will be fully resolved.

14. Comparative Figures

Certain comparative figures have been reclassified to conform with the current year's presentation.

Corporate Information

Directors

Dr. Edward E. McNally
Chairman &
Chief Executive Officer
Big Rock Brewery Ltd.
Calgary, Alberta

Mr. Robert H. Hartley
Rancher
High River, Alberta

Mr. James M. Jackson
Developer
Jackson & Jackson
Durango, Colorado

Mr. Richard W. Jones
Business Consultant
Paine Webber Inc.
Los Angeles, California

Mr. J. Angus McKee
Chairman &
Chief Executive Officer
Gulfstream Resources Limited
Calgary, Alberta

Mr. William G. Turnbull
Chairman of the Board
Ducks Unlimited Canada
Independent
Real Estate Consultant
Calgary, Alberta

Ms. Kathleen M. McNally
Partner
McNally and Cerveny
Associates Limited
Calgary, Alberta

Mr. J. Cameron Millikin
Chairman
Bay Mount Capital
Resources, Inc.
Calgary, Alberta

Mr. John A. Fisher
President
Fisher & Company LLC
San Francisco, California

Officers and Senior Personnel

Edward E. McNally
Chairman &
Chief Executive Officer

Bob J. King
President

Bernd Pieper
Brewmaster

Bert A. Boulet, CA
Chief Financial Officer

Janine E. Calb, MBA
Manager, Marketing and
Communications

Brian T. Rowland
Manager, Sales

Shane C.P. Gerdis
Corporate Secretary

Head Office

5555 – 76th Avenue SE
Calgary, Alberta T2C 4L8
Telephone (403) 720-3239
1-800-242-3107
Fax (403) 236-7523
www.bigrockbeer.com

Auditors

Ernst & Young LLP
Chartered Accountants
1300, 707 – 7th Avenue SW
Calgary, Alberta T2P 3H6

Transfer Agents

CIBC Mellon Trust
Company
600, 333 – 7th Avenue SW
Calgary, Alberta T2P 2Z3

Notice of Annual Meeting of Shareholders

Friday, August 6, 1999. 3:00pm MST to be held at The Big Rock Grill, Big Rock
Brewery Ltd., 5555 – 76th Avenue SE, Calgary, Alberta (52nd Street at Glenmore Trail)

Corporate Profile

Big Rock Brewery Ltd. is a regional producer and marketer of premium quality craft beers in Calgary, Alberta, Canada. The Company's products are available in draught, bottles and cans. Big Rock is committed to three business fundamentals:
• Consistently brewing distinctive, premium quality craft beers;
• Constantly providing superior, personalized customer service; and
• Creating and sustaining strong community relationships.
Big Rock products are marketed in five provinces and two territories in Canada, and in the United States.

5555 – 76th Avenue SE, Calgary, Alberta T2C 4L8
www.bigrockbeer.com

printed in canada

ANNUAL REPORT
1999

FINANCIAL &
OPERATING HIGHLIGHTS

	Fiscal Year ended April 3/99 (in thousands of dollars except per share data)		Fiscal Year ended March 31/98 (in thousands of dollars except per share data)	
	Consolidated	Canada	Consolidated	Canada
Sales	$1,960,274	$1,451,071	$1,760,160	$1,251,197
Earnings before interest, unusual items, taxes, depreciation & amortization	14,696	41,742	31,989	50,541
Earnings (loss) before tax	(102,723)	12,020	3,307	30,548
Net earnings (loss)	(82,245)	38,511	3,961	31,202
Net earnings (loss) per share	($6.48)	$3.03	$0.31	$2.46
Total assets	$338,516	N/A	$441,307	N/A
Shareholders' equity	56,329	N/A	89,866	N/A
Number of stores at end of fiscal year				
Supercentres	80	80	104	76
Electronics Express stores	0	0	6	6
Computer City stores	7	7	-	-
Growth in total sales	11%	16%	16%	14%
Growth in same store sales	7%	6%	6%	9%

CONSOLIDATED SALES

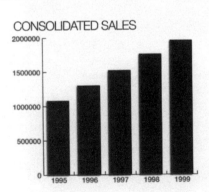

CANADIAN SALES

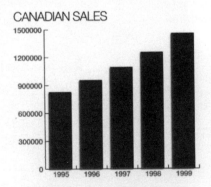

CONSOLIDATED NET EARNINGS

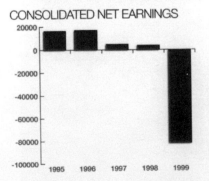

CANADIAN NET EARNINGS

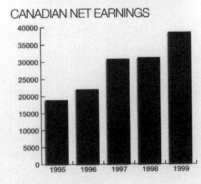

A MESSAGE

TO OUR SHAREHOLDERS

Fiscal 1999 was a very difficult year for Future Shop. For most of the year we concentrated our energies on turning around our U.S. operations. We made significant progress in this respect. Our operations improved and our sales increased. However, we still had a long way to go before we could stem the losses in the U.S. We came to the conclusion that the level of losses being incurred in the U.S. were not sustainable and, regrettably, on March 9th we decided to terminate the operation in the U.S. and exit that market.

Exiting the U.S. market will allow us to concentrate on our Canadian operations. We continued with the expansion of our Canadian stores and opened 5 new stores and relocated another 2 stores during the course of fiscal 1999. We will continue with this program in fiscal 2000 and will be opening 3 new stores and relocating 7 others.

During fiscal 1999 we acquired the Computer City stores in Canada from a U.S. retailer which was exiting the Canadian market. We believe that this was an important strategic acquisition which will enable us to maintain and strengthen our leadership position in the sales of computer products in Canada.

We continued to invest heavily in information technology in order to reduce costs, provide better customer service, produce superior management information reporting and improve distribution channel management. The investment in information systems amounted to approximately $44 million in fiscal 1999 and we plan to invest an additional $20 million in fiscal 2000. We anticipate significant cost savings and efficiencies from this investment.

The systems which are expected to provide the greatest benefits are scheduled to be put into operation later this year. In addition to developing and installing new systems, we have made our legacy system year 2000 compatible and do not foresee any problems in this respect. We continue to believe that our new systems will enable us to run a far more efficient and cost effective operation and thus will give us a significant competitive advantage.

We have had our setbacks during fiscal 1999, however we are looking forward to the future with confidence and optimism. We have a strong brand name. We have a large number of loyal customers. We have loyal, hard working and competent associates and we have a very strong management team. We have built the infrastructure which will enable us to deliver our products and services at the lowest total cost to our customers.

The combination of the above gives us a very strong competitive position in the market and we intend to use this position in order to achieve profitable growth.

We will not have a business without our loyal customers. I would like to thank all our customers for shopping at Future Shop. We shall be making every effort to provide them with better service in the years to come. I would also like to thank our associates for their dedication and hard work. We can only succeed if we have loyal, knowledgeable and hard working associates. Last but not least, I would like to thank our shareholders, suppliers, bankers and professional advisers for their support during the past year.

Hassan Khosrowshahi
Chairman of the Board,
President and C.E.O.

INVESTING In Our PEOPLE

INNOVATION

At Future Shop our people make the difference. We believe in our people and we believe in providing them with the means to grow and realize their potential. Our people foster a culture of dignity, teamwork, openness, innovation, hard work and most of all are proud to be a part of Future Shop. Everyday our associates focus on adding value to each customer's experience, whether in store, over the telephone or on the Internet. Over the past years, the hard work of our associates has built Future Shop into one of the leading retailers in Canada and the largest company in the country in our business sector, with stores operating in communities from British Columbia to Newfoundland. Today, in our Renaissance Program, our associates are developing the business systems that will allow us to accommodate considerable future growth, provide better customer service, offer improved business reporting and furnish us with more sophisticated business management tools. This fiscal year we recognized an opportunity to apply our knowledge of the Canadian computer business by acquiring the operations of Computer City Canada. This move brought us the valuable expertise and knowledge of the associates of Computer City. The acquisition was more than just buying retail stores; it was about adding to our organization a team of associates who are experts in serving the Canadian computer consumer.

Dignity

TEAMWORK

Openness   HARD WORK

②

skills   CUSTOMER SERVICE

Training

Product Knowledge

The G.U.E.S.T. program, a comprehensive training initiative to build
and improve customer service, was launched early this past fiscal year and has prompted
many positive comments. Investing in our people rewards both our associates and our customers
and has always driven the growth of our Company. Today, extensive training programs on product
knowledge and customer service are offered to our retail associates providing them with the skills and expertise
which enables them to offer professional service to our customers. These training programs are part of a larger
effort designed to enhance our associates' ability to meet and exceed our customers' expectations.

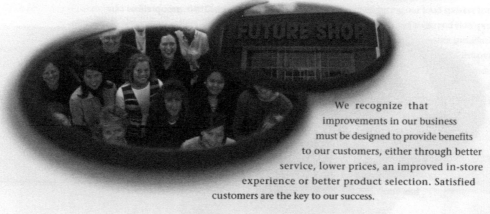

We recognize that
improvements in our business
must be designed to provide benefits
to our customers, either through better
service, lower prices, an improved in-store
experience or better product selection. Satisfied
customers are the key to our success.

we sell STATE of the art technology

Future Shop offers consumers some of the most exciting and sophisticated products available today. Future Shop associates provide our customers with products to enrich their lives, from a digital home theatre with direct to home satellite television to a wireless telephone to respond to e-mail. Our customers find products at Future Shop that give them the opportunity to realize their potential. Products that incorporate breakthrough technology and breathtaking performance enable our customers to improve their lives. This past year we saw particular growth in the popularity of new technologies such as direct to home satellite television systems, digital cameras, DVD video and wireless communications. Future Shop also offers a wide range of services, including product delivery, installation, upgrade, warranty and repair programs.

&COMPUTERS information products

Products in our Home Office group allow our customers to realize their potential in educational, business and creative endeavours. The Home Office category includes computers, printers, scanners, software, fax machines and personal organizers. Future Shop is the Canadian industry leader in the sale of computers to the home PC consumer, and carries information products from quality brand name manufacturers including Apple, Brother, Compaq, Epson, Hewlett Packard, IBM, Panasonic, Sharp, Sony and Toshiba.

④

audio&VIDEO

Future Shop had significant growth in the Audio
Video product categories this past year. These categories
include products such as televisions, videocassette recorders, digital
camcorders, DVD, direct to home satellite systems and home and mobile
stereo components and systems. We experienced dramatic increases in
market share in every department. We are currently the leader in market share
and sales in Canada in these categories and we expect to continue to grow our business
this coming year. Our planned launch of StarChoice and Look Communications digital
television products early this coming fiscal year reflects our commitment to being a
leading retailer of content services in addition to consumer electronics hardware.

NEW TECHNOLOGY

As part of
our commitment
to offering leading
edge products and tech-
nology, we plan to pursue
the retailing of digital cable,
expand our selection of audio products, and are eagerly anticipating the
introduction of high definition television
(HDTV), plasma screen TV and LCD TV. We are
currently introducing HDTV transition products and plan to be
the first to market HDTV in Canada. This past fiscal year we experienced
substantial gains in our sales of projection TVs and surround sound audio systems,
reflecting a shift in consumer tastes to buying home theatre packages rather than purchasing
audio and video products separately. In order to serve this consumer trend we are currently reconfiguring our loud speaker listening
rooms and enhancing our merchandising of audio and video products.
We are also upgrading our facilities for the custom installation of
car audio products and pursuing the offering of innovative
automobile electronics technology such as navigation products.
This past year also saw an expanded program of associate training
on product knowledge and service, encouraging an even
higher level of support of the products we sell and ensuring that customers receive greater value when shopping
in our stores. Future Shop carries all major brands including Bose, Canon, harman kardon, Hitachi, Infinity,
JVC, Kenwood, MTX, Panasonic, Pioneer, Polk,
Proscan, RCA, Samsung, Sharp, Sony and
Toshiba.

Wireless communication products are one of
the fastest growing categories for Future Shop. This category includes
products such as landline and wireless telephones, answering machines, voice and
data messaging systems, personal
digital assistants,
Internet services,
business machines
and digital imaging
products. Future
Shop's
selection of
sophisticated
communication
products
includes quality
brands like @Home,
Cantel AT&T, Bell Mobility,
Clearnet, Fido, Motorola, Nokia, PageMart, Panasonic, Sony,
Sympatico and 3Com.

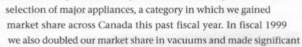

communications

APPLIANCES

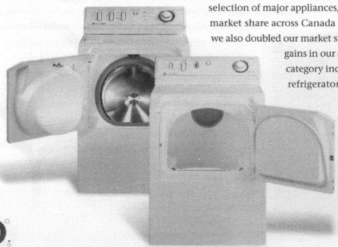

This past year we expanded our appliance
offerings to include small electrical appliances such as breadmak-
ers, fans, and toaster ovens. These products complement our existing wide
selection of major appliances, a category in which we gained
market share across Canada this past fiscal year. In fiscal 1999
we also doubled our market share in vacuums and made significant
gains in our air conditioning business. The appliance
category includes microwave ovens, ranges, laundry,
refrigerators, freezers, dishwashers, vacuum cleaners
and small electrical appliances. In this
category we offer respected brands including Eureka, Frigidaire, General Electric,
Hamilton Beach, Hoover, Jenn-Air,
Magic Chef, Maytag, Moulinex,
Panasonic, Whirlpool and
Whirlpool Gold.

⑥

entertainment

Future Shop experienced significant growth in our share of the entertainment product market this past year; a year that saw relatively flat sales growth in the industry as a whole. Our growth in the DVD category led us to become the number one retailer of DVD software and hardware in Canada and brought Future Shop closer to our goal of becoming the country's premier total entertainment destination retailer of choice for music, movies and DVD. This coming year we plan to expand our commitment to support the development of new artists through our 'Future Stars' program, which encourages the ongoing growth of the industry. Future Shop has been proud to be involved in special events such as Edgefest, MusicWest, North by Northeast, and the Montreal, Toronto and Vancouver Jazz Festivals. Future Shop offers entertainment products by major labels and studios including BMG Music Canada, EMI Music Canada, Sony Music Canada, Universal Music, Warner Music Canada, Twentieth Century Fox Home Entertainment Canada, Universal Studios Canada, Warner Home Video, Paramount Home Video, Columbia Tristar and Buena Vista Home Entertainment Canada, Warner Home Video and Paramount.

QUALITY innovation EXPERIENCE

Future Shop today is Canada's largest retailer of consumer electronics and computers and a major retailer of appliances and entertainment products. We are committed to bringing new technology products to the market first under the banner of Get It First at Future Shop. Our latest prototype stores present innovative displays and an exciting, lively in-store experience for our customers. Spectacular entertainment products including home theatre systems, DVD video and digital satellite systems are displayed for our customers in friendly, interactive settings. The consumer electronics industry expects that the imminent introduction of high definition television and related digital products will create consumer demand and strong sales, and Future Shop is well positioned to lead in this growing market.

guaranteed LOWEST PRICES

Our strategy is to offer the customer a broad selection of merchandise with expert assistance in finding the right products for their needs. Future Shop's Guaranteed Lowest Price program ensures that our customers receive the best prices.

We opened five new Future Shop stores and relocated two others in fiscal 1999 and we plan to open another three new stores and relocate seven in fiscal 2000. Our goal is to increase both the number of our stores in Canada and our market share. We expect the introduction of new products such as HDTV will contribute to the growth of our existing business. We also intend to open Future Shop stores in smaller metropolitan areas within Canada and believe that there are many markets where the chain can be expanded profitably. A variety of standard store sizes have been developed to match the store size to the trade area in which it will be located. We have been successful in making Future Shop a leader in the retailing of consumer electronics, computers, appliances and entertainment products. We expect that a concerted focus on operating an efficient and profitable business and on adding value to improve our customers' experience and enhance the value of our brand will lead to positive growth this coming year. In addition to expanding the Future Shop chain, our immediate plans include creating similarly successful businesses with E-Commerce and Computer City.

E-COMMERCE

With the growing importance of E-Commerce in Future Shop's product categories we have decided to establish a significant presence for Future Shop in this area. During last year, we established a site to sell a limited selection of our products on the internet. We have gradually improved the selection of products and the functionality of the site.

During the past nine months, with the help of outside consultants, we have defined our goals and the route we will be taking in developing our E-Commerce capability. We plan to integrate our Internet business with our existing storefronts, to bring the best of Future Shop to the Internet and provide our retail store customers and sales associates with the best features of our Internet operations in store.

The Company has recently named an experienced VP of E-Commerce and will be making a significant investment in the development of E-Commerce Capabilities. We believe the attributes that have made us successful in the retail market will contribute to our success in the online market: namely hard work, wide selection, low prices and a commitment to providing tremendous service and value to our customers.

Future Shop's strong presence in the Canadian marketplace and high brand awareness provides the Company with a marked advantage in establishing an Internet sales presence. The Future Shop retail store locations will provide customers with a tangible point of reference and build a level of trust, a key element in on line brand and business development.

By this fall we will launch the new release of our site which will have significantly greater functionality, many new features and an extended range of products. After sales service will be available to our customers through our Future Shop locations and our call centre. We plan to improve the site and increase the range of the products on an ongoing basis and are committed to becoming a leader in the field of E-Commerce.

8

ComputerCity

Future Shop Ltd. acquired the operations of Computer City Canada in October 1998. Computer City sells computer hardware, peripherals, software and accessories to retail customers, corporate businesses and government agencies. Significant sales are generated to small, medium and large businesses. Stores average around 20,000 square feet and are located in retail areas adjacent to business districts. The addition of the Computer City banner allows us to build our leadership position in the sale of computer products in Canada, including expanding our current sales to corporations and government offices. The computer training and technical servicing infrastructure offered by Computer City provides customers with a full service environment to take care of all of their computing needs. Located in all Computer City locations, our Service Centres are staffed by up to twenty technicians who are A+ certified by the Computing Technology Industry Association, and who have completed training providing them with the highest manufacturer certified qualifications available.

Our technicians offer our customers computer upgrades, repair and diagnosis services. Our Software Training Centres offer specialized training covering a wide range of business and home office applications for all skill levels. The Training Centres offer our customers the opportunity to receive training in the latest software programs at convenient times and affordable rates. In addition to professional assistance from our associates in store, customers can also take advantage of delivery and expert set up services in their home or office for their computer system purchases. Computer City stores are located in Coquitlam and Richmond, British Columbia; Calgary, Alberta; and Mississauga, North York, Markham and Ottawa, Ontario.

MANAGEMENT'S
DISCUSSION AND ANALYSIS

Results of Operations

The following table presents the results of operations as a percentage of sales for the last two fiscal years:

	Year ended April 3, 1999	Year ended March 31, 1998
Sales	100.0 %	100.0%
Cost of sales	78.9 %	77.9%
Gross profit	21.1 %	22.1%
Selling, general and administrative expenses	22.1 %	21.9%
Earnings (loss) before income taxes & unusual items	(1.0)%	0.2%
Unusual items	(4.3)%	0.0%
Income tax recovery	1.1 %	0.0%
Net earnings (loss)	(4.2)%	0.2%

Sales

Sales for the fiscal year ended April 3, 1999 increased 11% to $1.96 billion compared to $1.76 billion for the previous fiscal year. On a consolidated basis, same store sales increased 7%. All of the sales increase occurred in Canada. Sales in the United States as measured in Canadian dollars showed virtually no change from the prior year. As measured in U.S. dollars, sales in the United States actually declined from the previous year due to the closure of the Utah stores in September 1998 and the closure of the remaining U.S. stores in March 1999. (See "U.S. Operations" on next page). Sales in Canada increased due to the opening of five new stores, the acquisition of the seven Computer City stores and an increase in same store sales of 6%.

	Canada	USA	Total 1999	Total 1998
Sales ($'000)	$1,451,071	$509,203	$1,960,274	$1,760,160
Sales per retail square foot per annum	$1,065	$958	$1,032	$859
Growth in total sales	16%	0%	11%	16%
Growth in same store sales	6%	11%	7%	6%

The product mix changed slightly as the acquisition of Computer City increased the portion of sales derived from home office products to 51% from 49% of sales. The communications category decreased to 4% of sales from 7%.

	1999	1998
Home Office	51%	49%
Audio and Video	29%	29%
Appliances	7%	7%
Communications	4%	7%
Music Software	4%	4%
Other	5%	4%
	100%	100%

Gross Profit

The Company's gross profit margins declined to 21.1% from 22.1% in the prior fiscal year. Gross margins declined in both Canada and the United States across most product categories and was most prevalent in the home office category. Also, the acquisition of Computer City skewed the Company's Canadian sales mix toward lower margin product categories.

Selling, General & Administrative Expenses ("SG&A")

Future Shop's SG&A expenses, as a percentage of sales, increased from 21.9% in the previous fiscal year to 22.1%. The increase is primarily attributable to higher depreciation charges and a significant increase in spending on new information systems.

Unusual Items

During fiscal 1999, management decided to discontinue the U.S. operations. All stores have been closed, substantially all the inventory has been sold and the majority of employees engaged in operations related to those operations have been terminated or reassigned to the Canadian operations.

Included in unusual items, therefore, are costs related to the closure including liquidation of inventories, severance of employees, termination of real estate obligations and other closure expenses of approximately $47.9 million. The loss on disposal and write-down of U.S. capital and other assets was $32.5 million. In addition, the Company incurred other unusual items including approximately $1.6 million in costs related to the closure of the Future Shop Express stores and a $1.9 million write-down of other assets due to a permanent impairment in the value of a long-term investment.

MANAGEMENT'S
DISCUSSION AND ANALYSIS CONTINUED

Income Taxes

The Company recorded an income tax recovery of $20,478,000 versus a recovery of $654,000 for the previous fiscal year.

Canadian Operations

Net earnings from Canadian operations were $38,511,000 compared to $31,202,000 in the previous fiscal year. Net earnings from Canadian operations before income taxes and unusual items decreased to $16,582,000 from $30,548,000 in the previous fiscal year. This decrease was due to lower gross margins and increased SG&A as a percentage of sales.

U.S. Operations

Sales in the United States as measured in Canadian dollars showed no change from the prior year. However, as measured in U.S. dollars, sales in the United States actually declined from the previous year due to the closure of the Utah stores in September 1998 and the closure of the remaining U.S. stores in March 1999. The decline in sales was marginally offset by a 3% growth in same store sales in the United States as measured in U.S. dollars (11% in Canadian dollars). Losses continued as gross margins declined in all product categories from the prior year. The continuing losses led to the decision in March 1999 to close the U.S. operations. Losses before unusual items were $35,475,000 as compared to $27,241,000 in the prior fiscal year.

Consolidated Net Loss

The consolidated net loss for the year was $82,245,000 as compared to consolidated net earnings of $3,961,000 in the prior fiscal year.

Liquidity and Capital Resources

Cash flow used in operations during the year ended April 3, 1999 amounted to $38,732,000 as compared to cash provided by operations of $29,340,000 in the prior year.

At April 3, 1999, working capital had decreased to a negative $32,549.000 compared to a positive $18,720,000 at March 31, 1998. The decline is due to costs associated with the closure of the U.S. operations and the closure of the Future Shop Express stores in Canada, as well as capital expenditures and investing activities.

Net capital expenditures for the year ended April 3, 1999 were $68,905,000 as compared to $32,694,000 in the prior year. The increase is due to expenditures to open five new stores in Canada, upgrades to management information systems and continued renovations of existing stores. In addition, $12,894,000 was used to acquire the Computer City assets.

For the upcoming fiscal year Future Shop plans to incur capital expenditures of approximately $45,000,000. The capital expenditure program will involve $20,000,000 for the opening of new stores and the renovation or relocation of existing stores, $20,000,000 for investment in new technology and information systems and $5,000,000 for an enhanced e-commerce strategy.

Future Shop has a $55,000,000 revolving credit facility, which increases to $85,000,000 between April and December. At April 3, 1999, $23,828,000 had been drawn down against this facility.

Management believes that cash flow from operations, the proceeds of the Offering and existing credit facilities will be sufficient to fund operations and capital expenditures for the coming fiscal year.

Dividend Policy

The Company intends to continue its policy of retaining its earnings for use in its business and does not expect to pay dividends on its Common Shares in the foreseeable future.

Outlook

Future Shop is planning to open three new stores in the coming year, one in Alberta, one in Québec and one in Nova Scotia. Seven existing stores will be relocated and selected departments within existing stores will be renovated and updated to increase sales.

MANAGEMENT'S
DISCUSSION AND ANALYSIS CONTINUED

Management believes that the investments in management information systems and technology will enhance the productivity and efficiency of Future Shop's operations and reduce the costs of doing business. In addition, the development of an enhanced e-commerce program should contribute to the growth of sales and extend Future Shop's market reach.

The closure of the U.S. operations will allow for reductions in corporate overhead as the need to perform administrative functions specific to the U.S. operations will disappear. Management intends to focus on realizing the economic advantages arising from Future Shop's dominant position in the Canadian marketplace. The development and growth of the Computer City chain should also provide a source of growth in sales and earnings in the coming years.

Year 2000

Future Shop uses computer technology throughout its business operations to carry on its day-to-day operations. Thee computer technology used includes not only the hardware and software used in Future Shop's management information systems, point-of sale systems, inventory and distribution management systems, but also embedded technology in a variety of ancillary systems ranging from heating and air-conditioning systems to security systems. Some of these ancillary systems are not under the direct control of Future Shop but instead are the responsibility of third parties. Future Shop also relies on its suppliers and business partners to achieve Year 2000 compliance and to continue to provide the goods and services they currently supply without disruption.

Future Shop cannot test the Year 2000 readiness of suppliers, especially suppliers providing critical services such as public utilities. Future Shop must therefore rely on and has endeavoured to obtain, assurances from these third parties as to the state of their readiness. Nevertheless, there can be no guarantees that problems will not occur and the nature and magnitude of these problems, if they occur, cannot not be foreseen.

Future Shop retails computers and related equipment, software and product that have embedded in them computer hardware and software. While Future shop is not the manufacturer of these products, there is a risk that purchasers of these products may attempt to hold Future Shop liable for damages or losses arising from the failure of these products to perform properly as a result of the Year 2000 issue. Moreover, the nature and magnitude of such claims cannot be foreseen. Future Shop's ability to successfully defend these claims, should they arise, to obtain indemnities from the manufacturers or to obtain coverage for such claims under insurance policies, can only be determined when and if such claims arise.

Internally, Future shop has been addressing the Year 2000 issue as part of a comprehensive project to upgrade most of its information systems. Certain of the new systems include new hardware and packaged software purchased from vendors who have represented that the systems are Year 2000 compliant. The Company also sought assurances from vendors that timely updates will be made available to make the remaining purchased software Year 2000 compliant. Internal and external resources were used to make the required modifications to all "legacy" systems and to test their Year 2000 compliance. These system upgrades are now nearly complete and final testing is expected to be completed by the summer of 1999.

Computer hardware and packaged software generally are capitalized when acquired. Internal and external costs incurred to develop internal-use software are capitalized during the application development stage. Amortization of computer hardware and software is recorded on the straight line method over their expected useful lives, commencing when ready for use following appropriate testing. Costs of computer hardware and software capitalized during the year ended April 3, 1999 totalled $44,432,000. The Company intends to spend a further $20,000,000 in the fiscal year ended April 1, 2000. These costs are part of a comprehensive plan for systems upgrades. Cost otherwise specifically related to the Year 2000 issue are not by themselves material.

SUMMARY OF CONSOLIDATED QUARTERLY RESULTS
OF OPERATIONS (UNAUDITED)

Similar to most retailers, Future Shop's business is seasonal by nature. Sales in the fourth quarter of the calendar year are traditionally significantly higher than sales in any of the first three quarters due to holiday buying in November and December.

SUMMARY OF EARNINGS
(in thousands of dollars, except per share data)

FISCAL 1999	June 30 1998	October 3 1998	January 2 1999	April 3 1999	Total
Sales	$388,700	$487,618	$659,109	$424,847	$1,960,274
Gross profit	$83,717	$106,678	$135,308	$87,848	$413,551
Earnings before taxes & unusual items	($13,530)	$2,304	$9,629	($17,296)	($18,893)
Net earnings	($9,471)	($18,713)	$4,686	($58,747)	($82,245)
Earnings per share	($0.75)	($1.48)	$0.37	($4.63)	($6.48)

SUMMARY OF EARNINGS
(in thousands of dollars, except per share data)

FISCAL 1998	June 30 1997	September 30 1997	December 31 1997	March 31 1998	Total
Sales	$354,310	$414,603	$585,600	$405,647	$1,760,160
Gross profit	$79,215	$89,566	$129,178	$91,428	$389,387
Earnings before taxes	($6,653)	$952	$14,566	$(5,558)	$3,307
Net earnings	($5,027)	$720	$8,908	($640)	$3,961
Earnings per share	($0.40)	$0.06	$0.70	($0.05)	$0.31

FIVE YEAR REVIEW
-CONSOLIDATED

Years ending
(in thousands of dollars, except per share data and sales per retail square foot)

	April 3/99	March 31/98	March 31/97	March 31/96	March 31/95
CONSOLIDATED SUMMARY OF EARNINGS					
Sales	$1,960,274	$1,760,160	$1,523,016	$1,303,828	$1,082,594
Gross profit	413,551	389,387	352,215	282,376	225,191
Selling, general and administrative expenses	432,444	386,080	348,583	261,467	194,800
Earnings before interest, unusual items, taxes, depreciation and amortization	14,696	31,989	27,777	35,824	38,315
Earnings before tax	(102,723)	3,307	3,632	20,909	30,391
Net earnings	(82,245)	3,961	5,015	17,235	16,544
Weighted average shares	12,692	12,670	12,670	12,670	12,670
Earnings per share	($6.48)	$0.31	$0.40	$1.36	$1.31
CONSOLIDATED SUMMARY OF EARNINGS PERCENTAGES					
Gross profit	21.1 %	22.1 %	23.1 %	21.7 %	20.8 %
Selling, general and administrative expenses	22.1 %	21.9 %	22.9 %	20.1 %	18.0 %
Earnings before tax	(5.2 %)	0.2 %	0.2 %	1.6 %	2.8 %
Effective tax rate	19.9 %	(19.8 %)	(38.1 %)	17.6 %	45.5 %
Net earnings	(4.2 %)	0.2 %	0.3 %	1.3 %	1.5 %
CONSOLIDATED SALES STATISTICS					
Total increase over prior year	11.4 %	15.6 %	16.8 %	20.4 %	82.2 %
Same store sales growth	7.4 %	6.4 %	(6.4 %)	(9.7 %)	32.4 %
Sales per retail square foot	$1,032	$859	$822	$1,093	$1,502
CONSOLIDATED SUMMARY BALANCE SHEETS					
Total current assets	$221,329	$333,038	$302,868	$271,789	$209,864
Total assets	338,516	441,307	406,778	354,716	257,019
Total current liabilities	253,878	314,318	280,221	236,604	162,329
Non-current extended warranty plan	26,945	28,283	29,114	27,682	23,340
Total liabilities	282,187	351,441	302,873	273,826	193,364
Total shareholders' equity	56,329	89,866	85,905	80,890	63,655
Total equity and liabilities	338,516	441,307	406,778	354,716	257,019

SUMMARY OF CANADIAN QUARTERLY RESULTS
OF OPERATIONS (UNAUDITED)

Similar to most retailers, Future Shop's business is seasonal in nature. Sales in the fourth quarter of the calendar year are traditionally significantly higher than sales in any of the first three quarters due to holiday buying in November and December.

SUMMARY OF EARNINGS
(in thousands of dollars, except per share data)

FISCAL 1999	June 30 1998	October 3 1998	January 2 1999	April 3 1999	Total
Sales	$272,028	$355,161	$487,707	$336,175	$1,451,071
Gross profit	$63,221	$80,495	$106,135	$71,279	$321,130
Earnings before taxes & unusual items	$56	$7,849	$18,337	($9,660)	$16,582
Net earnings	$4,115	($307)	$14,847	$19,856	$38,511
Earnings per share	$0.32	($0.02)	$1.17	$1.56	$3.03

SUMMARY OF EARNINGS
(in thousands of dollars, except per share data)

FISCAL 1998	June 30 1997	September 30 1997	December 31 1997	March 31 1998	Total
Sales	$252,681	$305,513	$416,855	$276,148	$1,251,197
Gross profit	$57,750	$70,854	$95,067	$63,988	$287,659
Earnings before taxes	($1,310)	$8,223	$21,419	$2,216	$30,548
Net earnings	$316	$7,991	$15,761	$7,134	$31,202
Earnings per share	$0.02	$0.63	$1.25	$0.56	$2.46

FIVE YEAR REVIEW
(UNAUDITED)

Years ending
(in thousands of dollars, except per share data and sales per retail square foot)

	April 3/99	March 31/98	March 31/97	March 31/96	March 31/95
CANADA SUMMARY OF EARNINGS					
Sales	$1,451,071	$1,251,197	$1,093,532	$954,672	$829,290
Gross profit	321,130	287,659	261,103	214,250	176,946
Selling, general and administrative expenses	304,548	257,111	231,685	186,679	142,457
Earnings before interest,unusual items, taxes, depreciation and amortization	41,742	50,541	46,685	38,592	40,525
Earnings before tax	12,020	30,548	29,418	27,571	34,489
Net earnings	38,511	31,202	30,801	22,022	18,906
Weighted average shares	12,692	12,670	12,670	12,670	12,670
Earnings per share	$3.03	$2.46	$2.43	$1.74	$1.49
CANADA SUMMARY OF EARNINGS PERCENTAGES					
Gross profit	22.1 %	23.0%	23.9%	22.4%	21.3%
Selling, general and administrative expenses	21.0%	20.5%	21.2%	19.6%	17.2%
Earnings before tax	0.8%	2.4%	2.7%	2.9%	4.2%
Effective tax rate	(220.4%)	(2.1%)	(4.7%)	20.1%	45.2%
Net earnings	2.7%	2.5%	2.8%	2.3%	2.3%
CANADA SALES STATISTICS					
Total increase over prior year	16.0 %	14.4%	14.5%	15.1%	53.5%
Same store sales growth	6.2 %	9.2%	(3.0%)	(8.6%)	33.2%
Sales per retail square foot	$1,065	$915	$805	$1,048	$1,471

FINANCIAL REVIEW

Management's Responsibility for Financial Statements

The management of Future Shop Ltd. is responsible for the integrity of the accompanying consolidated financial statements and all other information in the annual report. The financial statements have been prepared by management in accordance with generally accepted accounting principles, which recognize the necessity of relying on some best estimates and informed judgements. All financial information in the annual report is consistent with the consolidated financial statements.

To discharge its responsibilities for financial reporting and safeguarding of assets, management depends on the Company's systems of internal accounting control. These systems are designed to provide reasonable assurance that the financial records are reliable and form a proper basis for the timely and accurate preparation of financial statements. Management meets the objectives of internal accounting control on a cost-effective basis through the prudent selection and training of personnel and the adoption and communication of appropriate policies.

The Board of Directors oversees management's responsibilities for financial statements primarily through the activities of its Audit Committee. This committee meets with management and the Company's independent auditors, Deloitte & Touche LLP, to review the financial statements and recommend approval by the Board of Directors. The financial statements have been audited by Deloitte & Touche LLP. Their report is presented below.

Hassan Khosrowshahi
President, CEO and
Chairman of the Board

Gary Patterson, CA
Chief Financial Officer

AUDITORS' REPORT

To the Shareholders of Future Shop Ltd.

We have audited the consolidated balance sheets of Future Shop Ltd. as at April 3, 1999 and March 31, 1998 and the consolidated statements of earnings (loss), retained earnings (deficit) and changes in financial position for the period from April 1, 1998 to April 3, 1999 and the year ended March 31, 1998. These financial statements are the responsibility of the Company's management. Our responsibility is to express an opinion on these financial statements based on our audits.

We conducted our audits in accordance with generally accepted auditing standards. Those standards require that we plan and perform an audit to obtain reasonable assurance whether the financial statements are free of material misstatement. An audit includes examining, on a test basis, evidence supporting the amounts and disclosures in the financial statements. An audit also includes assessing the accounting principles used and significant estimates made by management, as well as evaluating the overall financial statement presentation.

In our opinion, these consolidated financial statements present fairly, in all material respects, the financial position of the Company as at April 3, 1999 and March 31, 1998 and the results of its operations and the changes in its financial position for the period from April 1, 1998 to April 3, 1999 and the year ended March 31, 1998 in accordance with generally accepted accounting principles.

Deloitte & Touche LLP
Chartered Accountants
Vancouver, British Columbia
May 14, 1999

CONSOLIDATED
BALANCE SHEETS

		As at April 3, 1999		As at March 31, 1998
		(in thousands of dollars)		
ASSETS				
CURRENT				
Cash and short-term deposits	$	-	$	58,945
Cash held in escrow (Note 5)		20,251		-
Accounts receivable		25,099		15,121
Inventory		160,092		254,690
Prepaid expenses		1,544		1,634
Future income taxes (Note 7)		14,343		2,648
		221,329		333,038
CAPITAL AND OTHER ASSETS (Note 3)		114,217		108,269
FUTURE INCOME TAXES (Note 7)		2,970		-
	$	338,516	$	441,307
LIABILITIES				
CURRENT				
Bank indebtedness, secured by a general security agreement covering all assets	$	23,828	$	-
Accounts payable and accrued liabilities		219,550		309,838
Current portion of extended warranty plan		10,500		4,480
		253,878		314,318
EXTENDED WARRANTY PLAN		26,945		28,283
DUE TO AFFILIATED COMPANY (Note 4)		1,364		1,364
FUTURE INCOME TAXES (Note 7)		-		7,476
		282,187		351,441
SHAREHOLDERS' EQUITY				
Capital stock (Note 5)		58,051		29,851
Special warrants (Note 5)		20,508		-
Retained earnings (deficit)		(22,230)		60,015
		56,329		89,866
	$	338,516	$	441,307

Commitments (Note 8)

APPROVED BY THE BOARD

Hassan Khosrowshahi _____ (signed) Director

Gary Patterson, CA _____ (signed) Director

CONSOLIDATED
STATEMENTS OF EARNINGS (LOSS)

	Period from April 1, 1998 to April 3, 1999	Year ended March 31, 1998
	(in thousands of dollars except per share amounts)	
Sales	$ 1,960,274	$ 1,760,160
Cost of sales	(1,546,723)	(1,370,773)
Gross profit	413,551	389,387
Selling, general and administrative expenses	(432,444)	(386,080)
Unusual items (Note 6)	(83,830)	–
Earnings (loss) before income taxes	(102,723)	3,307
Income tax recovery (Note 7)	20,478	654
Net earnings (loss)	$ (82,245)	$ 3,961
Earnings (loss) per share	$ (6.48)	$ 0.31
Weighted average number of common shares outstanding ('000)	12,692	12,670

CONSOLIDATED
STATEMENTS OF RETAINED EARNINGS (DEFICIT)

	Period from April 1, 1998 to April 3, 1999	Year ended March 31, 1998
	(in thousands of dollars)	
RETAINED EARNINGS, BEGINNING OF YEAR	$ 60,015	$ 56,054
Net earnings (loss)	(82,245)	(3,961)
RETAINED EARNINGS (DEFICIT), END OF YEAR	$ (22,230)	$ 60,015

CONSOLIDATED STATEMENTS
OF CHANGES IN FINANCIAL POSITION

	Period from April 1, 1998 to April 3, 1999	Year ended March 31, 1998
	(in thousands of dollars)	
OPERATING ACTIVITIES		
Net earnings (loss)	$ (82,245)	$ 3,961
Items not involving cash		
Depreciation and amortization	31,496	28,294
Loss on disposal and write-down of capital and other assets	34,989	41
Future income taxes	(21,634)	(2,125)
Extended warranty plan	(1,338)	(831)
Cash provided by (used in) operations	(38,732)	29,340
Change in non-cash operating working capital	(10,443)	20,736
Net cash provided by (used in) operations	(49,175)	50,076
FINANCING ACTIVITY		
Issue of special warrants	48,201	-
INVESTING ACTIVITIES		
Business acquisition	(12,894)	-
Proceeds on disposal of capital assets	1,056	1,607
Purchase of capital and other assets	(69,961)	(34,301)
	(81,799)	(32,694)
NET CASH (INFLOW) (OUTFLOW)	(82,773)	17,382
CASH POSITION, BEGINNING OF YEAR	58,945	41,563
CASH POSITION (INDEBTEDNESS), END OF YEAR	$ (23,828)	$ 58,945

NOTES
TO THE CONSOLIDATED FINANCIAL STATEMENTS

1. SIGNIFICANT ACCOUNTING POLICIES

These consolidated financial statements have been prepared in accordance with accounting principles generally accepted in Canada. The following includes significant policies that have been adopted by the Company where alternatives are available:

(a) Change in year-end

Commencing in fiscal 1999, the fiscal year of the Company consists of a 52 or 53 week period ending on the first Saturday in April.

(b) Principles of consolidation

The consolidated financial statements include the accounts of the Company and its wholly-owned subsidiaries, Future Shop Protection Corp., Future Shop, Inc. and pursuant to a reorganization in the United States during fiscal 1999, Vycom Partners LLP. All significant intercompany transactions are eliminated upon consolidation.

(c) Inventory

Inventory is valued at the lower of average cost and net realizable value. Cost consists of invoiced cost plus freight and duty, net of discounts.

(d) Capital assets, depreciation and amortization

Capital assets are recorded at cost. Internal and external costs incurred to develop internal-use software are capitalized. Amortization of computer hardware and software commences when ready for use following appropriate testing. Depreciation and amortization are provided using the following methods and rates:

Furniture, fixtures and equipment	20% declining balance
Computer hardware and software	Straight-line over three to ten years
Rental assets	Straight-line over four years
Leasehold improvements	Straight-line over five years

(e) Goodwill and intangible assets

Amortized on a straight line basis over five years.

(f) Extended warranty plan

Estimated costs related to product warranty are recorded at the time of the sale of the extended warranty contract. Management reviews these anticipated costs annually to assess the need for any adjustments which may be required thereto.

(g) Foreign exchange translation

The Company's foreign operation is an integrated subsidiary and its financial statements are translated using the temporal method.

(h) Foreign exchange contracts

The Company is exposed to the risk of exchange fluctuations for goods purchased in the U.S. for sale in Canada. The Company manages this risk with the use of forward exchange contracts which fix the exchange rate on these purchases. All other inventory is purchased in the same currency as it will later be sold. The Company is exposed to foreign exchange fluctuations to the extent of its net investments in the U.S.

NOTES

The liabilities of the Company which are covered by forward exchange contracts (notional amount) equal $4,283,707. The market value at April 3, 1999, translated at the spot rate, is $4,304,321. All of these contracts mature within 2 months.

(i) Earnings (loss) per share

Fully diluted loss per share is equal to basic loss per share as the effects of common shares issuable upon the exercise of options and special warrants would be anti-dilutive.

(j) Adoption of new accounting standards for income taxes

During fiscal 1999, the Company retroactively adopted the new recommendations of the Canadian Institute of Chartered Accountants relating to the accounting for income taxes. Under this new accounting policy, future income taxes reflect the tax effect of differences between the book and tax bases of assets and liabilities. In addition, the future income tax assets including unused tax losses are recognized, subject to a valuation allowance, to the extent that it is more likely than not that a future income tax asset will be realized. Previously, deferred income taxes were based on items of income and expense that were recorded in different years in the financial statements and tax returns, and were measured at the tax rate in effect in the year the difference originated. It is not necessary to restate prior year's financial statements as the adoption of this standard does not have a material impact on the Company's financial position or results of operations in the current or preceding year.

(k) Management's estimates

The preparation of the consolidated financial statements in conformity with generally accepted accounting principles requires management to make estimates and assumptions that affect the reported amounts of assets, liabilities, revenue and expenses, and the disclosure of contingent assets and liabilities at the reporting date and during the reporting period. In particular, the use of estimates is an important factor in determining the anticipated future costs of the extended warranty plan and in the provision for unexpended costs of closing the U.S. operations. The recorded amounts are based on the Company's best information and judgement, however, actual results could differ from the estimates.

2. BUSINESS ACQUISITION

During November 1998, the Company acquired the Canadian business operations of Computer City Inc. ("Computer City") for cash consideration of $12,894,000. Computer City sells computer hardware, peripherals, software and accessories to retail customers, corporate businesses and government agencies and provides its customers with technical support and training. The purchase price was allocated as follows based on the fair value of net assets acquired:

	($'000)
Net working capital	$ 9,366
Capital assets	3,310
Intangible assets	218
	$12,894

The acquisition has been accounted for by the purchase method and accordingly the operating results have been included from the date of purchase.

NOTES
TO THE CONSOLIDATED FINANCIAL STATEMENTS

3. CAPITAL AND OTHER ASSETS

		1999		1998
	Cost	Accumulated Depreciation & Amortization	Net Book Value	Net Book Value
		($'000)		
Computer hardware/ software	$ 37,222	$ 17,386	$ 19,836	$ 4,724
Furniture, fixtures and equipment	66,286	31,397	34,889	45,456
Leasehold improvements	58,451	36,933	21,518	40,860
Rental assets	1,778	1,278	500	1,903
Software under development	37,198	-	37,198	12,627
Goodwill and other	276	-	276	2,699
	$ 201,211	$ 86,994	$ 114,217	$ 108,269

4. DUE TO AFFILIATED COMPANY

The amounts are owing to a company under common control and are unsecured, non-interest bearing and are repayable during the period expiring in 2009 only from taxable income of Future Shop, Inc.

5. CAPITAL STOCK AND SPECIAL WARRANTS

(a) Capital stock

The Company is authorized to issue an unlimited number of common, preferred and employee participation shares, with no par value. The changes in capital stock issued and outstanding during the two fiscal years ended April 3, 1999 are as follows:

	Number of common shares	Amount ($'000)
Issued & outstanding at March 31, 1997 & 1998	12,670,000	$ 29,851
Exercise of special warrants (Note 5(b))	2,000,000	28,200
Issued & outstanding at April 3,1999	14,670,000	$ 58,051

(b) Special warrants

The changes in special warrants issued and outstanding during the two fiscal years ended April 3, 1999 are as follows:

	Number of special warrants	Amount ($'000)
Issued & outstanding at March 31, 1997 & 1998	-	$ -
Issue of special warrants	3,500,000	48,708
Exercise of special warrants	(2,000,000)	(28,200)
Issued & outstanding at April 3,1999	1,500,000	$ 20,508

On March 30, 1999, the company completed special warrant offerings for aggregate net proceeds of $48,708,000.

The first special warrant offering was issued to a company under common control, and consisted of 2,000,000 special warrants for aggregate proceeds of $28,200,000, which were exercised on March 30, 1999 for 2,000,000 common shares.

The second special warrant offering, issued pursuant to an Underwriting Agreement, consisted of 1,500,000 special warrants for proceeds of $20,508,000, net of share issue costs of $1,149,000 less future income tax recoveries of $507,000.

Each special warrant issued under the second offering entitles the holder to acquire one common share of the Company, without further payment, during the period ending on the earlier of March 30, 2000 and the sixth business day after the day on which a receipt for a prospectus qualifying for distribution the common shares underlying the special warrants ("Prospectus") is issued by the last of the Securities Commission of British Columbia and Ontario. Any special warrants not exercised prior to such time will be deemed to be exercised immediately prior to such time.

If a receipt for the Prospectus is not issued by the Securities Commission of each of British Columbia and Ontario on or prior to June 28, 1999, each holder of special warrants may elect within a period of ten business days thereafter, to reconvey all or a portion of its special warrants to the Company and receive repayment of the purchase price plus interest.

The Company is in the process of filing the Prospectus in connection with the above distribution of 1,500,000 common shares. The net proceeds from these special warrants are being held in escrow pending the earlier of the exercise of any special warrants or the clearance of the Prospectus.

(c) Stock options

As at April 3, 1999, the Company had director and employee options outstanding for the purchase of 885,835 common shares. These options, which expire between May 14, 2003 and December 13, 2008, may be exercised as to 25% per year from the date of issue of employee options, at an exercise price equal to the market price of the shares on the date of grant which range from $8.95 to $25.50 per share. If the optionee and the Company jointly so elect, the optionee will be compensated for the cash equivalent of the value of the stock options, rather than the issuance of shares.

6. UNUSUAL ITEMS

During fiscal 1999, the Company decided to discontinue operations in the United States. As at April 3, 1999, all stores have been closed, substantially all of the inventory has been sold and the majority of employees engaged in activities related to those operations have been terminated.

In addition, during fiscal 1999 the Future Shop Express stores in Canada were closed. Unusual items consist of the following:

	($'000)
Closure of U.S. operations	
Cost related to the closure of the U.S. operations, including the liquidation of inventories, termination of real estate obligations, severance of employees & other closure expenses	$ 47,894
Loss on disposal & write-down of capital & other assets used in the U.S. operation	32,465
Cost related to the closure of the Future Shop Express stores	1,583
Write-down of other assets due to a permanent impairment in the value of a long-term investment	1,888
	$ 83,830

Accounts payable and accrued liabilities as at April 3, 1999 include approximately $15 million related to unexpended costs of the closure of U.S. operations.

7. INCOME TAXES

The provision of income taxes is at an effective tax rate which differs from the basic corporate tax rate for the following reasons:

	1999	1998
Combined basic Canadian federal and provincial tax rates	44.05 %	44.05 %
	($'000)	
Recovery of (provision for) income taxes based on above rates	$ 45,249	$ (1,457)
Increase (decrease) resulting from:		
Lower rate on losses of foreign subsidiary	(3,528)	(2,208)
Benefit of losses of foreign subsidiary not recorded	(22,516)	(9,792)
Utilization of income tax benefits not previously recorded	-	15,970
Other	1,273	(1,859)
Income tax recovery	$ 20,478	$ 654

NOTES
TO THE CONSOLIDATED FINANCIAL STATEMENTS CONTINUED

As at April 3, 1999, the Company and its subsidiaries have accumulated non-capital income tax losses and capital losses which they can apply against future earnings. The portion of the non-capital and capital loss carryforwards for tax purposes which has not been recognized in the financial statements amounts to $122 million and $2 million, respectively. The non-capital loss carryforwards expire in varying amounts to 2019 and the capital loss carryforwards are available indefinitely.

Significant components of future income tax assets and liabilities are as follows:

	1999	1998
	($'000)	
Assets		
Depreciable capital assets	$ 31,060	$ 16,478
Tax loss carryforwards	27,059	8,697
Non-deductible accruals & provisions	6,699	2,534
Other	2,293	454
	67,111	28,163
Liabilities		
Extended warranty plan	49,798	32,991
Total future income tax asset (liability)	17,313	(4,828)
Less: current portion	14,343	2,648
Total long-term portion of net future income tax asset (liability)	$ 2,970	$ (7,476)

8. COMMITMENTS

At April 3, 1999, the minimum future annual payments under operating leases for the Company and its subsidiaries were as follows:

Fiscal years ending:	($'000)
2000	$ 62,916
2001	49,965
2002	51,334
2003	51,573
2004	51,291
Thereafter	157,154
Total	$ 424,233

9. RELATED PARTY TRANSACTIONS

Related party transactions and balances not disclosed elsewhere in these financial statements include:

(a) charges by affiliated companies consisting of rental costs paid to a company under common control of $1,091,685 (1998 - $1,368,777) and administration fees paid to the parent company of $238,000 (1998 - $500,000);

(b) accounts payable includes $1,584,397 (1998 - nil) due to the parent company and companies under common control; and

(c) four U.S. real estate leases were assigned to a company under common control for nominal consideration.

10. SEGMENTED INFORMATION

The Company is engaged in one line of business selling computers, consumer electronic products, appliances, communications equipment and music software through its retail stores, and prior to the closure of its United States stores (see Note 6) operated in two geographic segments.

1999	Canada	United States	Total
	($'000)		
Sales	$1,451,071	$ 509,203	$ 1,960,274
Cost of sales	(1,129,941)	(416,782)	(1,546,723)
Gross profit	321,130	92,421	413,551
Selling, general & administrative expenses	(281,455)	(119,493)	(400,948)
Depreciation & amortization	(23,093)	(8,403)	(31,496)
Unusual items	(4,562)	(79,268)	(83,830)
Earnings (loss) before income taxes	$ 12,020	$ (114,743)	$ (102,723)
Capital assets & goodwill	$ 113,265	$ 952	$ 114,217
Total assets	$ 331,366	$ 7,150	$ 338,516

1998	Canada	United States	Total
		($'000)	
Sales	$1,251,197	$ 508,963	$1,760,160
Cost of sales	(963,538)	(407,235)	(1,370,773)
Gross profit	287,659	101,728	389,387
Selling, general &			
administrative expenses	(237,360)	(120,426)	(357,786)
Depreciation & amortization	(19,751)	(8,543)	(28,294)
Earnings (loss)			
before income taxes	$ 30,548	$ (27,241)	$ 3,307
Capital assets & goodwill	$ 73,742	$ 34,527	$ 108,269
Total assets	$ 293,260	$ 148,047	$ 441,307

11. FINANCIAL INSTRUMENTS

(a) Financial risk

The Company is exposed to financial risk arising from fluctuations in foreign exchange rates, and the degree of volatility of these rates. The Company uses forward exchange contracts as described in Note 1 (h) to hedge its exposure to certain foreign currency risk.

(b) Credit risk

The Company's exposure to credit risk is limited. Accounts receivable are primarily from customers which are a large and diverse group.

(c) Fair value

Fair values of cash and short-term deposits, accounts receivable, accounts payable and accrued liabilities approximate their carrying values.

12. UNCERTAINTY DUE TO THE YEAR 2000 ISSUE

The Year 2000 Issue arises because many computerized systems use two digits rather than four to identify a year. Date-sensitive systems may recognize the year 2000 as 1900 or some other date, resulting in errors when information using year 2000 dates is processed. In addition, similar problems may arise in some systems which use certain dates in 1999 to represent something other than a date. The effects of the Year 2000 Issue may be experienced before, on or after January 1, 2000, and, if not addressed, the impact on operations and financial reporting may range from minor errors to significant systems failure which could affect an entity's ability to conduct normal business operations. While the Company is addressing the Year 2000 Issue, it is not possible to be certain that all aspects of the Year 2000 Issue affecting the Company, including those related to the efforts of customers, suppliers or other third parties, will be fully resolved.

13. COMPARATIVE FIGURES

Certain of the prior year figures have been reclassified to conform with the current year's presentation.

BOARD

OF DIRECTORS

Hassan Khosrowshahi (2)
President, Chief Executive Officer &
Chairman of the Board
President, Inwest Investments Ltd.

Behzad Khosrowshahi
Vice President, Mechandising

Edward A. Kotite (2)
Partner, Kotite & Kotite LLP

Gary Patterson (1)
Executive Vice President
and Chief Financial Officer

Edwin Charles Phillips (1,2)
Corporate Director

Ian Thomas (1)
President, Thomas Consultants Inc.

(1) member of the audit committee
(2) member of the compensation committee

CORPORATE
OFFICERS

Alex Brown
Vice President, Western Operations

Michael DeSandoli
Vice President, e-Commerce

Alan Evanston
Director, Service

Robert Golden
Director, Store Design & Merchandise
Presentation

Behzad Khosrowshahi
Vice President, Merchandising

Hassan Khosrowshahi
Chairman, President & C.E.O.

Rozanne Kipnes
Director, Real Estate Development &
Construction

Kevin Layden
Chief Operating Officer

Rick Lotman
Director, Merchandising, Music & Video

Michael McEvoy
Director, Resource Protection

Larry Needham
Chief Information Officer

Gary A. Patterson
Executive Vice President & Chief
Financial Officer

Kevin Primeau
Director, Merchandising Information
Products

Glenn Quarrington
Vice President, Human Resources

Wesley Skitch
Vice President, Eastern Operations

Jeanette Stuart
Director, Human Resources

Don Whilsmith
Director, Distribution

Randolph Zien
Vice President and Corporate Secretary

FUTURE SHOP
STORE LOCATIONS

BRITISH COLUMBIA
Kamloops
Kelowna
Nanaimo
Greater Vancouver (12)
Victoria

ALBERTA
Calgary (3)
Edmonton (5)
Lethbridge
Medicine Hat

Red Deer
Grande Prairie

SASKATCHEWAN
Regina
Saskatoon

MANITOBA
Winnipeg (4)

NEW BRUNSWICK
Moncton

NEWFOUNDLAND
St. John's

NOVA SCOTIA
Halifax

ONTARIO
Ancaster
Barrie
Brampton
Burlington
Hamilton
Kingston
Kitchener
London (2)

Newmarket
Oakville
Ottawa (3)
Stoney Creek
Sudbury
Thunder Bay
Greater Toronto Region (14)
Windsor

QUEBEC
Gatineau
Montreal (7)
Quebec City (2)
Chicoutimi

COMPUTER CITY
STORE LOCATIONS

BRITISH COLUMBIA
Greater Vancouver (2)

ALBERTA
Calgary

ONTARIO
Greater Toronto Region (3)
Ottawa

REGIONAL OFFICES
AND DISTRIBUTION CENTRES

Montreal, Quebec
(Regional Office)

Toronto, Ontario
(Regional Office and Distribution Centre)

Vancouver, British Columbia
(Regional Office and Distribution Centre)

GENERAL
INFORMATION

HEAD OFFICE

8800 Glenlyon Parkway
Burnaby, British Columbia
V5J 5K3

AUDITORS

Deloitte & Touche LLP
Chartered Accountants
Vancouver, British Columbia

COMMON SHARE TRANSFER AGENT & REGISTRAR

Montreal Trust Company
Vancouver, British Columbia

ANNUAL GENERAL MEETING

August 19, 1999
1:30 p.m.
Holiday Inn, Metrotown
4405 Central Boulevard
Burnaby, B.C.

PRICE RANGE
OF COMMON SHARES

Future Shop Ltd. Common shares are traded on The Toronto Stock Exchange (TSE) under the symbol FSS. The following table sets forth quarterly trading information on The TSE:

Fiscal Quarters	Fiscal 1999	
	High	Low
First	$14.15	$12.00
Second	15.50	9.00
Third	11.00	8.50
Fourth	14.50	8.70

FUTURE SHOP

Head Office
8800 Glenlyon Parkway
Burnaby, British Columbia
V5J 5K3

APPENDIX C
COMPLEX ORGANIZATIONS

Throughout this text we have shown you excerpts from the financial statements of various Canadian and international companies. Without exception, all of these financial statements were *consolidated* financial statements. Consolidated financial statements become necessary when one company buys a controlling ownership interest in another, thus creating a complex organization. Before we end this text, we want to provide you with a broad understanding of how financial statements become consolidated and the implications of using consolidated statements for decision-making purposes. Because an investment in the common shares of a company carries with it a right to vote, one company can influence and, under the right circumstances, control the activities of another company. In this chapter, we also consider accounting issues related to organizations that are considered complex because of intercompany investments. We start with a brief discussion of the purpose of such intercompany investments, and then turn to aspects of their accounting and analysis.

PURPOSE OF INTERCOMPANY INVESTMENTS

A company may have many reasons for acquiring an ownership interest in another company. Buying the shares of another company may be viewed as a good short-term or long-term investment. The equity securities that a company carries in its current asset account, called temporary investments, are an example of this type of investment. If the shares are bought for this reason, usually the number of shares purchased is small compared to the number of outstanding shares. Consequently, the acquiring company has little influence or control over the affairs of the acquired company. Such investments are sometimes called **passive investments** or **portfolio investments**, because the acquiring company cannot exercise any control over the decisions of the acquired company. Certain passive investments can also be long-term if the intention of management is to hold the security for long-term returns.

A second major reason for obtaining ownership of the shares of another company is to influence or control the decisions made by that company. Common targets for this kind of purchase are competitors, suppliers, and customers. Acquiring a block of shares in a supplier or customer allows the acquiring company to exercise some influence over the production, buying, and selling decisions of the acquired company to the benefit of the acquiring company. If the block of shares purchased is large enough, the acquiring company could gain a controlling interest in a competitor, which would allow it to increase its market share by increasing its productive capacity or its geographic market, or both. Combining with a competitor is sometimes referred to as **horizontal integration**. Horizontal integration may also offer other benefits resulting from economies of scale. The company may be able to reduce its work force or use the same distribution system to avoid duplication of effort. Buying a controlling interest in a supplier or customer allows the company to secure a market in which to buy its raw materials (in the case of a supplier) or to sell and distribute its product (in the case of a customer). Buying a supplier or customer is sometimes referred to as **vertical integration**. Fletcher Challenge Canada Limited is an example of a company that is vertically integrated. Fletcher Challenge, together with the various companies that it controls, is involved in all aspects of the forest products industry, from the cutting of trees, through the manufacture of lumber and paper products, to the sale of these products to customers.

Another reason for buying and controlling another company is **diversification**. If a company is in a cyclical business, it can protect itself from cyclical declines in one business by investing in another business that is counter-cyclical. **Cyclical businesses** are those that have significant peaks and valleys of activity. A greeting card company is an example of a cyclical business. Some of the cards, like birthday cards, are purchased relatively evenly throughout the year. Others, like Christmas cards and Valentine cards, result in peaks in the generation of revenue. Such a company may wish to diversify by buying into an automobile dealership business. The peak times for the dealership are likely to be the late summer when the new cars are introduced and early spring when people are anticipating travelling over the summer. The greeting card business and the automobile dealership would be experiencing peak activity at different times, which would help to even out the revenue flows for the whole business.

Algoma Central Corporation is an example of a diversified Canadian business. Its main focus of operation is marine transportation. It operates several ships, and it transports goods, provides for the repair and maintenance of ships, and offers marine-engineering services. This business is dependent upon not only the type of goods shipped, but also the economic environment of the countries to and from which goods are transported. Algoma has offset the cyclical nature of the shipping industry by investing in the commercial real estate business. It owns and manages various shopping centres, office buildings, and apartment buildings in Ontario. This business is also subject to the economic environment, but it is much more localized and would be unlikely to experience the same peaks and valleys as marine transportation.

METHODS OF OBTAINING INFLUENCE AND CONTROL

Perhaps the simplest way to gain control of the assets of another company is to purchase the assets directly from that company. This is called an **asset purchase**. The accounting for asset purchases is discussed in Chapter 8. If several assets are acquired at one time, such as in the acquisition of an entire division or plant, a single price may be negotiated. As discussed in Chapter 8, this type of purchase is called a *basket purchase*. The total cost of the assets purchased must be allocated to the individual assets acquired on the basis of their relative fair market values. If one company buys all of the assets of another company, it is not able to either influence or control the second company. Because it has purchased the assets, it controls only the assets it has purchased. The company from which it has purchased the assets can continue to operate, but now it has different assets that it must use to generate revenue. An asset purchase does not require consolidated financial statements. Once the new assets are recorded in the accounting system of the purchasing company, there are no further accounting complications.

The only way to gain influence or control over another company is to buy common shares in a **share acquisition**. For the sake of this discussion, we will refer to the acquiring company as the **investor** and the company whose shares are acquired as the **investee**.

One way the shares can be acquired is payment of cash from the investor to the shareholders of the investee (i.e., the shares are bought in the stock market). Another way is an exchange of the shares of the investor for the shares of the investee. This form of investment is called a **stock swap**. A variation of this is an exchange of the investor's debt (bonds) for shares of the investee in a transaction that may be called a **debt for equity swap**. In fact, some investments involve the exchange of all three (cash, shares, and debt) for the shares of the investee.

In a share acquisition, the investor can gain a large degree of influence or control over the investee by buying (or swapping) more shares. Such influence or control is gained by exercising the voting rights that the investor obtains when buying the shares. Ultimate control over the assets and liabilities of the investee will occur when the percentage ownership of the voting rights is greater than 50%. This is called a **controlling interest**.

An investor can sometimes effectively control an investee even though it owns less than 50% of the shares. This can occur in situations in which the remainder of the shares are owned by a large number of investors, none of whom has a very large percentage ownership in the investee (in such situations, the shares are said to be **widely held shares**); if the investor owns 30% to 50% of the investee and the rest of the shares are widely held, the investor may be able to effectively control the assets and liabilities of the investee. Because it is possible to control with less than 50%, GAAP defines control as occurring when one company can make "strategic operating, investing and financing policies without the cooperation of others."[1] If a company owns 40% of the shares of another company, it may be able to elect the

---

[1] *CICA Handbook*, para. 1590.03(b)

majority of the Board of Directors. It has, however, elected them with the cooperation of the other shareholders. If those other shareholders become dissatisfied with the way in which the Board of Directors manages the company, they could get together and out-vote the 40% shareholder. For this reason, a company with a 40% interest in another company would likely not prepare consolidated financial statements, but a company that owned 51% probably would.

In a share acquisition the investee remains a legal entity separate from the investor. The investor company is like any other owner in that it has limited liability with regard to the debts of the investee. The investor's liability is limited to the amount invested in the shares. The separation of the legal status of the two companies is one reason this form of acquisition is appealing. The tax status of each company is also separate. Each company must file its own return. For accounting purposes, the separate legal status also means that the investor and the investee each keeps its own set of accounting records, even if the investor has acquired 100% of the investee's shares. This presents an accounting problem if the investor controls the investee, because they are, in substance, one accounting entity.

VALUATION ISSUES AT DATE OF ACQUISITION

In any type of acquisition, whether of a single asset or an entire company, the fundamental accounting valuation method is historical cost. The new asset or the investment in the investee is recorded at its cost. If the asset is acquired with a payment of cash, the amount of cash serves as the proper measure of the cost. If debt is exchanged for the asset or company, the value of the debt should be used as the measure of cost. Under GAAP, debt is usually measured at its net present value. The net present value of the debt at the date of issuance is used to measure the cost of an acquisition in which debt is exchanged.

When shares are issued in the acquisition, their fair market value should be used as the measure of cost at the date of acquisition. A problem exists in valuing shares when the issue is large, because the number of shares outstanding increases significantly and the value of the investment acquired is not exact. How the market will adjust the existing share price to reflect this acquisition is not known at the date of acquisition. In these situations, instead of using the value of the shares to measure the acquisition, accountants sometimes turn to the fair market value of the assets acquired to measure the value of the shares given up. If the shares are swapped for the shares of another company, the value of the shares of the other company may not be easily estimated. Stock swaps involving 100% of the shares of another company present the most difficulty in measuring the value of the transaction.

Share Acquisition

In a share acquisition, the investor records the cost of the acquisition in an investment account. There is no breakdown of this cost into individual assets and liabilities, because the assets and liabilities do not technically belong to the investor; they remain the legal property or legal obligation of the investee. An investor that owns a large enough percentage of the investee's shares may control the assets economically through its voting rights, but it does not hold the title to the assets nor is it legally obligated to settle the liabilities. Under GAAP, two methods are currently used to account for an acquisition of a controlling interest: the **purchase method**, and the **pooling of interests method**.

Purchase Method

The **purchase method** assumes that after the shares are purchased or exchanged, one company can be identified as an **acquirer**. This method is always used when the investor pays cash or issues debt in exchange for the shares of the investee. When shares are swapped for the shares of the investee, this method is used when the original shareholders of the investor company control more shares than the new shareholders from the investee company. For example, assume that Company A has 500,000 common shares currently issued. It is interested in purchasing all the shares of Company B, which has 100,000 common shares currently issued.

COMPANY A	COMPANY B
500,000 shares issued	100,000 shares issued
Company A issues 100,000 new shares and exchanges them with the shareholders of Company B on a 1 for 1 basis	
After the exchange	
600,000 shares issued	100,000 shares issued, now owned
(500,000 shares held by the original	by Company A
shareholders of Company A;	
100,000 held by the old	
shareholders of Company B)	
Result: The original shareholders of Company A still hold most of the shares of Company A and therefore still control Company A, which now controls Company B.	

The purpose of most share exchanges in Canada is to gain control of another company. When this is achieved, the acquiring company is called the **parent company** and the acquired company is called the **subsidiary**. Because the subsidiary is an integral part of the total operations of the parent company, users need to know how it is performing. The parent and the subsidiary are separate legal entities, keeping separate books, preparing separate financial statements, and paying separate taxes. To provide users with information about the whole entity (parent and subsidiaries), accountants prepare consolidated financial statements, which add together the components of the various financial statements of the parent and the subsidiaries. Users see the total cash controlled by the entity, the total inventory owned by the entity, the total revenues earned by the entity, and so forth. Complications in this addition arise if there have been transactions between the parent and the subsidiaries. Because such transactions occur within the total accounting entity (parent and subsidiaries), they are deemed not to have occurred. They must be eliminated. More will be said about this later.

As well as providing information about the total entity, consolidated financial statements hide information about the individual companies in the group. When users are not given information about individual companies in the group, they have difficulty determining the risks and rewards contributed by the separate companies. If a company, through its activities, is involved in various industries or geographic locations, it is required to disclose segmented information in the notes to its financial statements. The segmented information provides some breakdown of accounts in the different segments so that users can evaluate the potential future impact of the segments on the total entity.

As we have seen, when the parent company purchases a controlling number of shares in the subsidiary, it has an investment on its books that it has recorded at the cost of the purchase. Because another company is being controlled and consolidated financial statements are going to be prepared, the transaction is viewed as a basket purchase. The cost to acquire the subsidiary needs to be allocated to the individual assets and liabilities of the subsidiary based on their relative fair market values at the date of acquisition, just as with any other basket purchase. This allocation is not recorded on the actual books of the parent or the subsidiary, but rather is determined during the worksheet preparation of the financial statements. When the assets and liabilities of the subsidiary are added to the assets and liabilities of the parent for the purpose of preparing consolidated financial statements, it is the *fair market values* of the subsidiary's assets and liabilities that are added to the *historical cost* assets and liabilities of the parent.

In the allocation of the purchase price, all the assets and liabilities in the subsidiary are first measured at their fair market values. Some assets that did not exist on the books of the subsidiary may be found and included in this measurement process. For example, if the subsidiary developed a patent or a trademark internally, the costs of such an item would have been expensed (see Chapter 8 for a discussion of whether to capitalize or expense the costs of these types of assets). The parent would need to identify all assets that the subsidiary owned or had the right to use, and would have to establish values for those items using similar items currently in the market as a guide, estimations of future benefits, or appraisals. By buying the shares, the parent is controlling these assets as well, and part of the acquisition cost should be allocated to them if they have a measurable market value. All of these assets and liabilities, those on the books and those that have value but are not on the books, are known as the **identifiable net assets** of the subsidiary. In the year that a parent buys a subsidiary, the components of the assets and liabilities that were purchased will be disclosed in the notes to the consolidated financial statements. Exhibit C-1 provides an example of this type of disclosure from the financial statements of Domtar Inc.

2. ACQUISITION OF E.B. EDDY

EXHIBIT C-1

Effective July 31, 1998, Domtar acquired from George Weston Limited all of the issued and outstanding shares of its wholly-owned subsidiaries E.B. Eddy Limited and E.B. Eddy Paper, Inc. ("E.B. Eddy"), an integrated producer of specialty paper and wood products. The acquisition has been accounted for using the purchase method and, accordingly, the purchase price was allocated to the assets and liabilities based on their estimated fair value as of the acquisition date. The results of operations related to the acquisition have been included in these consolidated financial statements from the effective date of acquisition. Details of the acquisition at the effective date are as follows:

	$
Net assets acquired at assigned values:	
Assets acquired	
Operating working capital, including bank indebtedness of $16	58
Fair value adjustments to working capital	(108)
Property, plant and equipment	1,027
Other assets	33
Liabilities assumed	
Long-term debt	(75)
Other long-term liabilities	(127)
	808
Consideration:	
Cash, including transaction fees	440
Common shares issued	368
	808

	$
Net assets acquired at assigned values:	
Assets acquired	
Operating working capital, including bank indebtedness of $16	58
Fair value adjustments to working capital	(108)
Property, plant and equipment	1,027
Other assets	33
Liabilities assumed	
Long-term debt	(75)
Other long-term liabilities	(127)
	808
Consideration:	
Cash, including transaction fees	440
Common shares issued	368
	808

You will note from Domtar's description that values have been assigned to four asset groups and two liability groups. By far the most valuable asset acquired was property, plant, and equipment. The fair market value of the identifiable net assets was $808 million. Domtar's acquisition did not result in goodwill since the purchase price was negotiated at the fair market value of E.B. Eddy's net assets.

However, if the purchase price is more than the fair market value of the identifiable net assets, another asset, called **goodwill**, must be reported (refer to Chapter 8). It represents all the intangible reasons that motivated the investor to pay more for the investee than the sum of the fair market values of its individual assets and liabilities. Perhaps the acquirer expects to earn extra future cash flows, or perhaps the business is located in a high-traffic area and so has a greater chance to earn high revenues than businesses located elsewhere. Perhaps the sales personnel in the business have created a loyal customer following that leads to consistently high revenues, or perhaps advertising campaigns have made this a well-known business. If, on the other hand, the purchase price is less than the fair market value of the identifiable net assets, some amount of the fair market value of the identifiable assets must be reduced. At the time of the writing of this book, GAAP has offered no guidelines regarding which assets should be reduced, other than to specify that they should be nonmonetary in nature. The Accounting Standards Board has been considering some changes specifying that the reduction should be achieved through first reducing intangibles that had no observable market value, and then reducing amortizable capital assets.

Pooling of Interests Method

When one company exchanges its shares for all the shares of another company, the parent company may not be identifiable. Referring to our previous example of Company A and Company B, let us assume that Company A issues 500,000 shares and exchanges them with the shareholders of Company B for all of their 100,000 shares on a five-for-one basis.

COMPANY A	COMPANY B
500,000 shares issued Company A issues 500,000 new shares and exchanges them with the shareholders of Company B on a 5 for 1 basis	100,000 shares issued
After the exchange 1,000,000 shares issued (500,000 shares held by the original shareholders of Company A; 500,000 held by the old shareholders of Company B)	100,000 shares issued, now owned by Company A

Result: The original shareholders of Company A hold half of the 1,000,000 shares of Company A and the old shareholders of Company B hold the other half. Neither group of shareholders can exercise control; they must share it. As in the previous example, Company B is controlled by Company A, but this time there is joint control of Company A.

When no acquirer can be identified, we think of these two companies as having pooled their resources to create a larger organization. Only very rarely are share exchanges arranged for the purpose of pooling. Therefore, we will discuss them only briefly here, and will concentrate for the rest of the chapter on acquisitions made under the purchase method. The guidelines with respect to pooling are quite different in the United States. There, it is acceptable to use the pooling method whenever shares are exchanged in an acquisition; it is not necessary to use the identification of an acquirer as the deciding factor between the two methods. As a result of this difference, pooling is common in the United States.

In a share exchange in which an acquirer cannot be identified, no new shareholders are created; the previous owner groups are simply merged, as are the assets and liabilities. Because one company has not been purchased by the other, there is no reason to change the cost basis of the assets and liabilities. In the pooling of the two companies, therefore, the assets and liabilities are reported at their previous book values rather than at their fair market values. The concept here is that the ownership interests in the net assets of the two companies have been pooled; hence, the term **pooling of interests** is used for this type of transaction.

Implications of Purchase Versus Pooling

At the date of acquisition, the investor company will report a set of values for the assets and liabilities using the purchase method, which will be different from the set of values reported using the pooling method. If the fair market value of the net assets acquired is higher (as it is in many cases) than the historical cost book value, the net assets using the purchase method will be higher, sometimes significantly so, than with pooling. Often, the new asset, goodwill, will be one of the assets forming a purchase acquisition, but will not be part of a pooling.

There is another difference between purchasing and pooling. In pooling, the combined companies are assumed to have been combined (pooled) forever. This means that any income generated by the investee during the accounting period leading up to the merger should be shown on the income statement of the combined company, even if the investee was acquired (pooled) on the last day of the year. If the purchase method is used, no income can be recognized prior to the date of purchase, because the transaction is viewed as a new purchase of assets. Therefore, if the merger was completed on the last day of the year, no income from the investee could be recorded by the combined company in the year of merger using the purchase method. The concept of being together forever (in the pooling method) also means that the retained earnings balances of the two companies are pooled at the date of merger. Under the purchase method, only the retained earnings of the investor company survive in the combined entity. The earnings history of the investee is not preserved under the purchase method, because the assets and liabilities are viewed as having been acquired at the date of merger.

INCOME RECOGNITION ISSUES SUBSEQUENT TO ACQUISITION

Income recognition issues subsequent to acquisition are a consequence of the valuation decisions made at the date of acquisition. In the following subsections, these issues are discussed for asset acquisitions and share acquisitions.

Asset Purchases

Subsequent to purchase, asset acquisitions are accounted for similarly to any other acquisition of assets. If the asset acquired is property, plant, or equipment, it is amortized like any other such asset. If the asset purchased is inventory, it ultimately affects cost of goods sold when it is sold.

Share Acquisitions

The accounting treatment of income subsequent to a share acquisition depends on the level of control the investor exerts over the investee. As examples of the conceptual differences, consider two extreme cases. In the first case, the investor owns only a few shares in the investee; in the second case, the investor buys 100% of the shares of the investee.

Case 1

If the investor buys only a few shares of the investee, it has virtually no control or influence over the investee. The investor may not dictate the dividend policy or any other strategic policy to the investee. As indicated earlier, this is a passive investment. The shareholders of the investor company in such a situation are unlikely to be interested in the full details of the operating performance of the investee. They are probably more interested in the cash flows that have come in from their investment (dividends) and in the current market value of their investment. Therefore, income recognition should probably show dividend revenue.

Case 2

In this case, where the investor owns 100% of the shares of the investee, the shareholders of the investor are likely to want to know the operating details of the performance of the investee, because they economically control all the assets and liabilities. For example, if the investee purchased was a competitor, the results of sales of the company's product are the combined results of the investor and the investee. To show only the details of the investor would be misleading in terms of the resources controlled by the shareholders. The investor's shareholders would probably find information about the combined assets and liabilities of the two companies more useful than simply a listing of the investor's assets and liabilities. A set of statements that conveys this information is the **consolidated financial statements**. Consolidated financial statements are prepared as if the investor and investee were one legal company. Under GAAP the two companies represent one economic accounting entity. In this situation, the investor is typically referred to as the **parent company** and the investee as the **subsidiary**.

What Is Canadian Practice?

This section will describe the guidelines that have been established under Canadian GAAP for the acquisition of various blocks of shares. It is important for you to understand these guidelines, because companies will describe their various acquisitions and tell you how they are accounting for them. You will need to know the various methods used so that you can understand the effects of a given method on the financial statements.

Under Canadian GAAP, control is determined by the investor's ability to determine the strategic operating, investing, and financing activities of the investee without seeking the permission of others. It usually means that the investor owns more than 50% of the voting shares of the investee, but in some circumstances the investor could own less than 50% and still be able to exercise control.

Because control is evidenced by the ability to determine certain activities in another company, GAAP provides guidelines for recommended cutoffs for the percentage ownership (in voting shares) that require different accounting treatment. Exhibit C-2 outlines these cutoffs. For small investments (less than 20%), GAAP specifies the **cost method**. Small investments are subdivided into those that are current, which we usually label temporary investments, and those that are noncurrent, which are generally labelled investments. Larger investments (greater than 50%) require **consolidation**; that is, consolidated financial statements must be prepared. For investments that fall between these two extremes, the acquirer is considered to have **significant influence** over activities in the investee. Significant influence is evidenced by the ability to elect a person to the Board of Directors, significant transactions between the two companies, or an exchange of technology or managerial personnel. When a situation of significant influence exists, another method, called the **equity method**, is required. Each of these methods is discussed in detail in the following pages.

■ **Accounting Methods for Investments**

EXHIBIT C-2

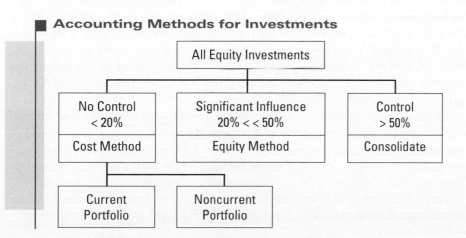

The percentage cutoffs identified in Exhibit C-2 are only a guide. If a company can demonstrate that it possesses either more or less control than the percentage ownership indicates, the company can apply a different method. For example, if a wholly owned subsidiary (100% ownership) goes into receivership, control often passes from the parent company to a trustee. The investment in the subsidiary should then be carried using the cost method. Also, an investor that owns less than 50% of an investee's voting shares but also owns convertible rights on other securities that, if converted, would increase its ownership beyond 50%, would be required to prepare consolidated financial statements. Each method carries its own set of implications for the company, as discussed in the following subsections.

Cost Method   The cost method is discussed in Chapter 6. To refresh your memory, the investment is carried in the investment account at its cost. During the period in which the investment is held, dividend revenue is recognized. If the investment is in marketable securities (short-term), at the end of each period the portfolio of securities is valued at the lower of its cost and market value. The unrealized losses (or recoveries) are shown in the income statement. If the investment is long-term, the portfolio is compared to market, but written down only if the decline is a permanent one. Once a long-term investment is written down, it is not written back up. To review the details of these accounting procedures, see Chapter 6. Note that no recognition is made of the net income results of the investee during the period except to the extent that these results are captured by its willingness to pay dividends.

Consolidation Method   Consolidation is required when an investor (parent company) controls the activities of an investee (subsidiary). For instructional purposes here, we will assume that the investor owns more than 50% of the outstanding shares of an investee. Because the subsidiary is still a legally separate company, the parent company records its investment in the subsidiary company in an investment account on its books. However, because the parent company economically controls the assets and liabilities of the subsidiary, it is probably more useful to the shareholders of the parent company to report the full details of the assets, liabilities, and income statement items rather than a single amount in the investment account and a single amount of income from the subsidiary on the income statement. The purpose of consolidating, therefore, is to replace the investment account with the individual assets and liabilities of the subsidiary. On the consolidated financial statements, then, it looks as if the two companies are legally one—that is, as if they had merged. You must recognize, however, that this is simply an "as if" representation of the combined company. The accounting systems are not merged. In fact, the consolidated statements are prepared "on paper"; no actual entries are made to either company's accounting system.

Because a consolidation tries to make it look as if the two companies were merged, the issues of purchase versus pooling also apply in a consolidation. If the acquisition transaction qualifies as a pooling, the consolidated statements are prepared by combining the book values of the assets and liabilities of the two companies. If the purchase method is indicated, the consolidated statements are prepared using the fair market value of the assets and liabilities acquired, as well as any goodwill. These amounts are combined with the book values of the parent's assets and liabilities.

Equity Method   Between the two extremes of no control and complete control lies the situation in which the investor can significantly influence the investee but not completely control its decisions. The accounting method used, the **equity method**, tries to strike some middle ground between showing the results of all the assets, liabilities, and income items in the financial statements (consolidation) and showing only the dividend revenue from the investment (cost method). The equity method requires that the investor show the effects of its share of the financial results of the investee—that is, as if it consolidated its share of the assets, liabilities, and income statement items. The difference is that its share of the net assets (assets minus liabilities) is reported as a single line item, "Investment in shares," on the balance sheet of the investor. Its share of the net income is also reported as a single revenue item, "Equity in earnings of investment" or simply "Income from investment," on the income statement. Because of the netting of assets and liabilities as well as revenues and expenses, this method is sometimes referred to as **one-line consolidation**.

To illustrate the entries made in a simple case using the cost method and the equity method, let us assume the following facts. Assume that the investor bought 30% of the outstanding shares of an investee for $10,000. During the first year of the investment, the earnings of the investee were $3,000 and dividends of $1,500 were declared. We will assume that in Case A the 30% does not give the investor significant influence (cost method required) and in Case B significant influence is present (equity method required). The entries the investor makes to account for the investment in the first year are as follows:

CASE A (COST METHOD)		CASE B (EQUITY METHOD)	
Investor's entry for acquisition:			
A-Investment in shares 10,000		A-Investment in shares 10,000	
A-Cash	10,000	A-Cash	10,000
Investor's entry to record earnings			
from investee:			
No entry		A-Investment in shares 900	
		SE-Equity in earnings of	
		investment	900[a]
Investor's entry to record dividends			
from investee:			
A-Cash	450[b]	A-Cash	450
SE-Dividend revenue	450	A-Investment in shares	450

[a]Investor's percentage ownership × Earnings of investee = 30% × $3,000
[b]Investor's percentage ownership × Dividends of investee = 30% × $1,500

The entry to record the earnings shows that the investment account increases by the investor's share of the earnings of the investee. Under the equity method, the investment account represents the investor's investment in the investee and, as the investee earns income and increases its shareholders' equity, the investor's investment increases in value as well. The credit part of this entry is to the income statement in a revenue line item called **Equity in earnings of investment**. We will subsequently abbreviate this as **EEI**.

The entry to record the dividends of the investee causes a decrease in the investor's investment account. This should make sense because, on the investee's books, the declaration of dividends causes a decrease in the shareholders' equity of the company. Because the investor's investment account measures its share of that equity, the investment account should decrease with the declaration of dividends. One way to understand this is to imagine that the investment represents a deposit in a savings account. The interest on the savings account would be equivalent to the earnings of the subsidiary. Withdrawals from the savings account would be the equivalent of the dividends declared. Withdrawals decrease the balance in the savings account in the same way that dividends reduce the investment account.

CONSOLIDATION PROCEDURES AND ISSUES

Numerous procedures and issues are important to understanding consolidated statements, but they are so complex that usually they can be understood only at the advanced accounting level. To give you a general idea of the procedures necessary for consolidation, we will show you the consolidation of a 100%-owned subsidiary. This will be followed by a discussion of the issues surrounding the handling of intercompany transactions.

Consolidation Procedures—100% Acquisition

To illustrate the concepts behind the preparation of a consolidated set of financial statements: Let us consider a share acquisition in which the parent acquires a 100% interest in the subsidiary. To make the example as concrete as possible: Exhibit C-3 shows the balance sheets of the parent (referred to as Parent Company) and the subsidiary (referred to as Sub Company) just prior to the acquisition.

EXHIBIT C-3

■ **Parent and Subsidiary Balance Sheets**

Prior to Acquisition

Balance Sheets

	Parent Company	Sub Company
Assets other than PP&E	$2,200	$2,500
Property, plant, and equipment	1,800	1,500
Total assets	$4,000	$4,000
Total liabilities	$2,000	$3,000
Shareholders' equity	2,000	1,000
Total liabilities and shareholders' equity	$4,000	$4,000

Assume that, at acquisition, Parent Company pays $1,400, in cash, for all the outstanding shares of Sub Company. In a cash transaction, the acquisition would be considered a purchase and not a pooling, because the shareholders of Parent Company have not changed. Because the book value of Sub Company's equity (net assets) is $1,000 at the date of acquisition, Parent Company has paid $400 more than the book value for the assets and liabilities of Sub Company. Assume further that $250 of this $400 relates to the additional fair market values of the property, plant, and equipment of Sub. It will be assumed that the fair market values of the other assets and liabilities of Sub are equal to their book values. This means that the remainder of the $400, or $150, is due to goodwill. Exhibit C-4 represents these assumptions.

■ **Representation of the Purchase Price Composition**

EXHIBIT C-4

Parent Company's 100% Acquisition of Sub Company

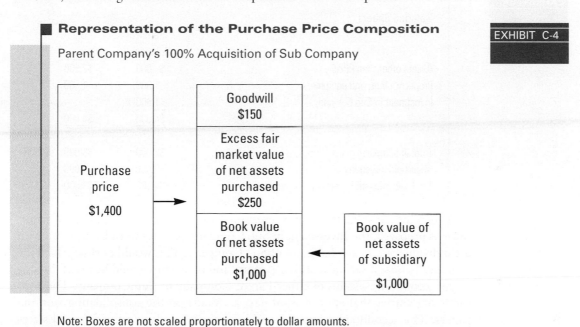

Note: Boxes are not scaled proportionately to dollar amounts.

Parent Company records its investment in an account called Investment in Sub Company. Because Parent Company owns more than 50% of the shares of Sub Company, it controls Sub Company and will have to prepare consolidated financial statements. Because Sub Company remains a separate legal entity, it will continue to record its transactions in its accounting system. Parent Company will also continue to keep track of its own transactions, on what are known as the **parent-only books**. At the end of each accounting period, the separate financial statements of the two entities will be combined on a worksheet to produce the consolidated financial statements, as if the two companies were one legal entity. One question that arises is how Parent Company should account for its investment in Sub Company on its parent-only books. Because the investment in the Sub Company account will be replaced in the consolidation process by the individual assets and liabilities of Sub Company, it does not really matter, from a consolidated point of view, how Parent Company accounts for its investment on the parent-only statements. However, it will make a difference in the parent-only financial statements. GAAP is somewhat silent on this issue, and there is some diversity in practice. Some companies use the equity method to account for the investment; some use the cost method. It will be assumed that Parent Company uses the equity method. The investment entry would be:

INVESTMENT ENTRY		
A-Investment in Sub Company	1,400	
A-Cash		1,400

The above entry would be the same if the company was intending to use the cost method. After recording the investment, the balance sheets of Parent Company and Sub Company will appear as shown in Exhibit C-5.

EXHIBIT C-5

■ **Parent and Subsidiary Balance Sheets at Date of Acquisition**

Balance Sheets

	Parent Company	Sub Company
Assets other than PP&E	$ 800	$2,500
Property, plant, and equipment	1,800	1,500
Investment in Sub Company	1,400	–
	$4,000	$4,000
Total liabilities	$2,000	$3,000
Shareholders' equity	2,000	1,000
Total liabilities and shareholders' equity	$4,000	$4,000

When the consolidated balance sheet for Parent Company at the date of acquisition is prepared, the Investment in Sub Company account must be replaced with the individual assets and liabilities of Sub Company. This would normally be done on a set of **consolidating working papers**, and no entries would be made directly in the accounting systems of either Parent Company or Sub Company. The consolidating entries that are discussed next are made on the consolidating working papers. The accountant starts the working papers by placing the financial statements as prepared by Parent Company and Sub Company side by side, as shown in Exhibit C-6. The working papers will then have columns for the consolidating entries and for the consolidated totals. Note that the exhibit shows debit and credit columns for all four items.

EXHIBIT C-6

■ **Consolidating Working Papers**

Account	Parent Company Debit	Parent Company Credit	Sub Company Debit	Sub Company Credit	Consolidating Entries Debit	Consolidating Entries Credit	Consolidated Totals Debit	Consolidated Totals Credit
Assets other than PP&E	800		2,500					
Property, plant, and equipment	1,800		1,500					
Investment in Sub Company	1,400							
Liabilities		2,000		3,000				
Shareholders' equity		2,000		1,000				
Totals	4,000	4,000	4,000	4,000				

On the consolidating working papers, each row across will be added to obtain the consolidated totals. If no adjustments are made to the balances as stated in Exhibit C-6, several items will be double-counted. In the first place, the net assets of the subsidiary will be counted twice, once in the individual accounts of Sub and again as the net amount in Parent's investment account. One or the other of the two must be eliminated. Because the idea of consolidated statements is to show the individual assets and liabilities of the subsidiary in the consolidated totals, the best option is to eliminate the parent's investment account. The second item that will be counted twice is the shareholders' equity section. The only outside shareholders of the consolidated company are the shareholders of Parent Company. The shareholders' equity represented by Sub's balances is held by Parent Company. The shareholders' equity section of Sub Company must, therefore, be eliminated. Both of these are eliminated in a working paper entry called the **elimination entry**. The elimination entry in the example would be:

WORKING PAPER ELIMINATION ENTRY		
SE-Shareholders' equity (Sub Company)	1,000	
???	400	
A-Investment in Sub Company		1,400

In the preceding entry you can see that, in order to balance the entry, a debit of $400 has been made. What does this represent? It represents the excess amount that Parent Company paid for its interest in Sub Company over the book value of the net assets. Remember the assumption that this excess is broken down into $250 for **excess fair market value** of property, plant, and equipment over its book value and $150 for goodwill. Therefore, the complete entry would be:

WORKING PAPER ELIMINATION ENTRY (ENTRY 1)		
SE-Shareholders' equity (Sub Company)	1,000	
A-Property, plant, and equipment	250	
A-Goodwill	150	
A-Investment in Sub Company		1,400

As a result of the elimination entry, the consolidating working papers would appear as shown in Exhibit C-7. The working paper entries are numbered so that you can follow them from the journal entry form to the working paper form.

▮ Consolidating Working Papers (Balance Sheet Only)

EXHIBIT C-7

Account	Parent Company Debit	Parent Company Credit	Sub Company Debit	Sub Company Credit	Consolidating Entries Debit	Consolidating Entries Credit	Consolidated Totals Debit	Consolidated Totals Credit
Assets other than PP&E	800		2,500				3,300	
Property, plant, and equipment	1,800		1,500		(1) 250		3,550	
Goodwill	–		–		(1) 150		150	
Investment in Sub Company	1,400					1,400 (1)	–	
Liabilities		2,000		3,000				5,000
Shareholders' equity		2,000		1,000	(1) 1,000			2,000
Totals	4,000	4,000	4,000	4,000	1,400	1,400	7,000	7,000

Note that shareholders' equity on a consolidated basis is the same as shown on Parent Company's books. This is true because all that consolidation has really done is replace the net assets represented in the investment account with the individual assets and liabilities that make up the net assets of the subsidiary. In this sense, the statements of Parent Company (which are referred to as the **parent-only statements**) portray the same net results to the shareholders as consolidation. However, the consolidated statements present information to the shareholders that is somewhat different in that ratios, such as the debt/equity ratio, can be quite different from those found in parent-only statements. For example, from Exhibit C-7 you can calculate the debt/equity ratio for the parent-only statements as 1.0 ($2,000/$2,000), whereas in the consolidated statements it is 2.5 ($5,000/$2,000). This occurs because Parent Company has acquired a subsidiary that is more highly leveraged than it is (note that the debt/equity ratio for Sub Company is 3.0 ($3,000/$1,000). The consolidation of the two companies produces a leverage ratio that is a weighted average of the two ratios. Although the debt/equity ratio appears to be less favourable on the consolidated statements, users must remember that Sub Company is a separate legal entity and is responsible for its own debts. Parent Company has limited liability. For this reason, creditors such as banks prefer to see parent-only financial statements when they assess a company's ability to repay debt.

Now, consider what the financial statements of Parent Company and Sub Company might look like one year after acquisition. The accounts of the two companies are shown in Exhibit C-8 (remember that EEI stands for equity in earnings of investment).

EXHIBIT C-8

■ Parent and Subsidiary Balance Sheets & Income Statements

One Year Subsequent to Acquisition

Balance Sheet

	Parent Company	Sub Company
Assets other than PP&E	$1,440	$3,000
Property, plant, and equipment	1,850	1,600
Investment in Sub Company	1,490	–
Total assets	$4,780	$4,600
Total liabilities	$2,420	$3,450
Shareholders' equity	2,360	1,150
Total liabilities and shareholders' equity	$4,780	$4,600

Income Statement

	Parent Company	Sub Company
Revenues	$1,500	$2,000
Expenses	(1,010)	(1,475)
Amortization	(250)	(225)
EEI	240	–
Net income	$480	$300
Dividends declared	$120	$150

Using the equity method, Parent Company would make the following entries during the year to account for its investment using the equity method:

ENTRIES USING THE EQUITY METHOD (ON PARENT COMPANY'S BOOKS)		
Parent's share of Sub's income:		
A-Investment in Sub Company	300	
SE-EEI		300
Parent's share of Sub's dividends:		
A-Cash	150	
A-Investment in Sub Company		150

After these entries have been made, the ending balance in the investment account would be $1,550 ($1,400 + $300 − $150). You will note in the statements in Exhibit C-8 that the investment account has a balance of $1,490. The difference in these amounts is a result of the fact that Parent Company paid more than the book value for the net assets of Sub Company. As we assumed earlier, Parent Company paid $400 more than the book value ($1,000). The $400 is due to the extra fair market value of property, plant, and equipment ($250) and goodwill ($150). Subsequent to acquisition, these amounts must be amortized, and the amortization is shown as part of the EEI. Companies will establish amortization periods based on the expected useful life of the assets acquired. Assume that property, plant, and equipment has a remaining useful life of five years, has a residual value of zero, and is amortized straight-line. Therefore, Parent Company must take an additional $50 ($250/5 years) in amortization expense over that shown on the books of Sub Company. The $150 of goodwill also has to be amortized. If it is assumed that the goodwill is amortized over 15 years (the maximum allowed is 40 years), the goodwill expense will be $10 per year ($150/15 years). Adding these two new expenses together means that Parent Company has to report an additional $60 in expenses during the year subsequent to acquisition. Using the equity method, Parent Company shows these additional expenses as a part of the EEI. The following entry is made (in addition to those shown earlier in the section):

AMORTIZATION ENTRY UNDER EQUITY METHOD (ON PARENT COMPANY'S BOOKS)		
SE-EEI	60	
A-Investment in Sub Company		60

With this additional entry, the balance in the investment in Sub Company account is $1,490, exactly the balance shown in Exhibit C-8.

The consolidated working papers at the end of the first year are presented in Exhibit C-9. You should note that they are shown in the **trial balance phase**. In the trial balance phase, the temporary income statement and dividends declared accounts still have balances that have not been closed to retained earnings (refer to Chapter 3 if you need to refresh your memory concerning the meaning of the trial balance phase). Note that shareholders' equity has the same balance it did at the beginning of the year. This is how the accounts must be listed if the consolidated financial statements are to be properly prepared.

EXHIBIT C-9

■ Consolidating Working Papers (Year Subsequent to Acquisition)

Account	Parent Company Debit	Parent Company Credit	Sub Company Debit	Sub Company Credit	Consolidating Entries Debit	Consolidating Entries Credit	Consolidated Totals Debit	Consolidated Totals Credit
Assets other than PP&E	1,440		3,000					
Property, plant, and equipment	1,850		1,600					
Goodwill								
Investment in Sub Company	1,490							
Liabilities		2,420		3,450				
Shareholders' equity		2,000[a]		1,000[a]				
Revenues		1,500		2,000				
Expenses	1,010		1,475					
Amortization expense	250		225					
Amortization expense—goodwill								
EEI		240						
Dividends declared	120		150					
Totals	6,160	6,160	6,450	6,450				

[a]Beginning of period balances (trial balance phase).

In the year subsequent to acquisition, three basic consolidating working paper entries are made if Parent Company is using the equity method to account for the investment on the parent-only financial statements. In addition to the investment account and the shareholders' equity accounts discussed earlier, the EEI must be eliminated, as well as the dividends declared account of the subsidiary. Otherwise, the income of Sub Company would be counted twice, once as EEI and a second time as the individual revenue and expense items. Dividends declared by the subsidiary are really just intercompany transfers of cash from a consolidated point of view. They are not dividends to outside shareholders and, as such, should be eliminated in the consolidation process. The entry to eliminate EEI and dividends will be called the *reversal of current year entries*, because the entry is, in effect, removing income and dividends recognized during the period. Once these two entries have been made, the third set of entries recognizes the extra amortization expense and goodwill expense discussed earlier. The consolidating working paper entries are as follows:

CONSOLIDATING WORKING PAPER ENTRIES:		
Reversal of current year entries (Entry 1):		
SE-EEI	240	
SE-Dividends declared		150
A-Investment in Sub Company		90
Investment elimination entry (Entry 2):		
SE-Shareholders' equity	1000	
A-Property, plant, and equipment	250	
A-Goodwill	150	
A-Investment in Sub Company		1,400
Amortization of assets and goodwill (Entry 3):		
SE-Amortization expense	50	
A-Property, plant, and equipment or		50
(XA-Accumulated amortization)		
SE-Amortization expense—goodwill	10	
A-Goodwill		10

The preceding entries are added to the consolidating working papers as shown in Exhibit C-10. Note that a separate accumulated amortization account has not been provided and that the amount of extra amortization has simply been credited to the property, plant, and equipment account for the amortization for the period. You can think of property, plant, and equipment as a net account—that is, net of accumulated amortization.

Income, on a consolidated basis, is as follows:

PARENT COMPANY—CONSOLIDATED NET INCOME	
Revenues	$3,500
Expenses	(2,485)
Amortization expense	(525)
Amortization expense—goodwill	(10)
Net Income	$480

Note that this is exactly the same as the net income that was reported by Parent Company using the equity method as shown in Exhibit C-8. This will always be the case. As we have seen, the equity method is sometimes referred to as *one-line consolidation*. It is a one-line consolidation because the balance sheet effects of consolidation are captured in the one-line item called the investment account. The income statement effects of consolidation are captured in the one-line item called EEI. The only difference, then, between the equity method and full consolidation is that the one-line items are replaced with the full detail of the assets and liabilities of the subsidiary on the balance sheet and the full detail of the revenues and expenses of the subsidiary on the income statement.

EXHIBIT C-10

■ **Consolidating Working Papers (Year Subsequent to Acquisition)**

Account	Parent Company Debit	Parent Company Credit	Sub Company Debit	Sub Company Credit	Consolidating Entries Debit	Consolidating Entries Credit	Consolidated Totals Debit	Consolidated Totals Credit
Assets other than PP&E	1,440		3,000				4,440	
Property, plant, and equipment	1,850		1,600		(2) 250	50 (3)	3,650	
Goodwill					(2) 150	10 (3)	140	
Investment in Sub Company	1,490					90 (1)	–	
						1,400 (2)		
Liabilities		2,420		3,450				5,870
Shareholders' equity		2,000[a]		1,000[a]	(2) 1,000			2,000
Revenues		1,500		2,000				3,500
Expenses	1,010		1,475				2,485	
Amortization expense	250		225		(3) 50		525	
Amortization expense - goodwill					(3) 10		10	
EEI		240			(1) 240			–
Dividends declared	120		150			150 (1)	120	
Totals	6,160	6,160	6,450	6,450	1,700	1,700	11,370	11,370

[a]Beginning of period balances (trial balance phase).

Consolidation Procedures—Less than 100% Acquisition

One complication that arises in acquisitions is that the parent company does not always acquire 100% of the shares of the subsidiary. Suppose, for example, that Parent Company buys 80% of the shares of Sub Company for $1,120. The balance sheets of Parent Company and Sub Company immediately after acquisition are shown in Exhibit C-11. A column that represents 80% of the balance sheet of Sub Company is also presented for future reference.

Assume that the same fair market values of the assets and liabilities apply to Sub Company, as before. The only asset that had extra fair market value is property, plant, and equipment, with excess value of $250. Since Parent Company purchased only 80% of Sub Company, it acquired only 80% of this extra fair market value, or $200. The calculation of goodwill would be made as follows:

PARENT COMPANY—CONSOLIDATED NET INCOME	
Purchase price	$1,120
Less 80% of book value acquired (80% of $1,000)	(800)
Less 80% of extra fair market value (80% of $250)	(200)
Goodwill	$ 120

Parent and Subsidiary Balance Sheets at Date of Acquisition (80% Acquisition)

EXHIBIT C 11

Balance Sheet

	Parent Company	Sub Company	80% of Sub Company
Assets other than PP&E	$1,080	$2,500	$2,000
Property, plant, and equipment	1,800	1,500	1,200
Investment in Sub Company	1,120	–	–
Total assets	$4,000	$4,000	$3,200
Total liabilities	$2,000	$3,000	$2,400
Shareholders' equity	2,000	1,000	800
Total liabilities and shareholders' equity	$4,000	$4,000	$3,200

If Parent Company owns 80% of Sub Company, who owns the other 20%? The answer is: other shareholders. Because Parent Company controls Sub Company, it must prepare consolidated financial statements. When consolidated financial statements are prepared, Parent Company adds 100% of Sub Company's assets, liabilities, revenues, and expenses to its own accounts. But Parent Company does not own 100% of Sub Company. It must, therefore, show the 20% as being owned by the other shareholders. It does this by creating an account called **noncontrolling interest (NCI)**, sometimes called **minority interest**. The NCI account on the balance sheet is located at the end of the long-term liabilities. It contains 20% of the book value of Sub Company, or $200 (20% of $1,000). Another NCI account on the income statement holds 20% of Sub Company's net income. It appears as an expense and reduces the income by 20% so that consolidated net income represents only the 80% that belongs to Parent Company. These two NCI accounts allow the parent to consolidate 100% of its subsidiaries and then to back out the part that does not belong to it.

To illustrate the NCI (minority interest) disclosure, we have included the 1998 balance sheet and income statement of Semi-Tech Corporation in Exhibit C-12. The NCI on the income statement in fiscal 1998 is a loss of $119.1 million. This amount of the combined incomes and losses from Semi-Tech's subsidiaries represents the amount that Semi-Tech does not own. The NCI on the balance sheet is $266.8 million. Semi-Tech Corporation has several subsidiaries. Its 1998 annual report lists its subsidiaries and tells the user how much of each subsidiary it owns (see Exhibit C-13). The NCI likely came from the consolidation of Singer (50%). It would consolidate all of the 100%-owned companies, but not Semi-Tech (Global), because it owned only 43% of this company. It likely used the equity method for this investment.

EXHIBIT C-12
PART A

consolidated financial statements

(Incorporated under the laws of Ontario)

**CONSOLIDATED
BALANCE SHEETS**

(As at March 31, 1998 and 1997)

In millions of U.S. dollars		March 31, 1998		March 31,1997
				Restated – Notes 1(c) and 1(p)
ASSETS				
Current Assets:				
Cash and cash equivalents	$	53.6	$	239.9
Accounts receivable		538.7		591.7
Inventories		395.4		346.5
Prepaid expenses		10.7		13.1
Total current assets		998.4		1,191.2
Investments in Operating Affiliates		372.4		366.8
Property, plant and equipment, net		359.7		349.9
Future income tax assets		84.2		–
Other assets, including goodwill of $421.9 (1997 – $653.0)		531.1		701.4
	$	2,345.8	$	2,609.3
LIABILITIES AND SHAREHOLDERS' EQUITY				
Current Liabilities:				
Notes and loans payable	$	473.7	$	524.7
Accounts payable and accrued liabilities		415.1		343.1
Future income tax liabilities		6.5		2.4
Total current liabilities		895.3		870.2
Long-term debt		781.9		641.5
Pension obligations		159.7		56.3
Other non-current liabilities		51.7		32.7
Total liabilities		1,888.6		1,600.7
Non-controlling interests		266.8		338.2
Contingencies (Notes 9 and 15)				
Shareholders' Equity:				
Capital stock		669.8		669.8
Contributed surplus		0.4		0.4
Cumulative translation adjustment		(7.3)		8.8
Deficit		(472.5)		(8.6)
Net shareholders' equity		190.4		670.4
	$	2,345.8	$	2,609.3

(See accompanying notes to consolidated financial statements)

On behalf of the Board:

(signed) Frank E. Holmes   (signed) Douglas A.C. Davis
          Director   Director

EXHIBIT C-12
PART B

CONSOLIDATED STATEMENTS OF LOSS AND DEFICIT

(For the years ended March 31, 1998 and 1997)

In millions of U.S. dollars, except per share data	Year Ended March 31, 1998	Year Ended March 31, 1997
		Restated – Notes 1(c) and 1(p)
Revenues	$ 1,060.4	$ 1,300.0
Costs and expenses:		
Cost of sales	780.3	898.0
Selling and administrative expenses	345.2	314.5
Restructuring and related charges	103.9	–
Goodwill amortization and write-off	309.4	44.1
Operating (loss) income	(478.4)	43.4
Other income (expenses):		
Interest, net of related foreign exchange adjustments	(80.4)	(79.2)
Royalties and license income	10.9	14.3
Miscellaneous, net	12.4	13.7
Loss related to Singer operations including goodwill amortization and write-off	(535.5)	(7.8)
Equity earnings from Semi-Tech (Global) Company Limited	15.3	3.2
Loss related to Singer operations and Semi-Tech (Global) Company Limited equity interest	(520.2)	(4.6)
Corporate items:		
Non-cash interest on Senior Secured Discount Notes	(53.3)	(46.9)
Corporate income (expenses), net	2.6	(5.4)
Loss before income taxes and non-controlling interests	(570.9)	(56.9)
Provision for income taxes	12.1	8.2
Loss before non-controlling interests	(583.0)	(65.1)
Non-controlling interests	(119.1)	14.4
Net loss	(463.9)	(79.5)
(Deficit) retained earnings, beginning of year	(8.6)	71.8
Dividends paid	–	(0.9)
Deficit, end of year	$ (472.5)	$ (8.6)
Loss per share:		
Basic	$ (6.94)	$ (1.19)
Fully diluted	$ (6.94)	$ (1.19)

(See accompanying notes to consolidated financial statements)

EXHIBIT C-13

semi-tech
organization chart

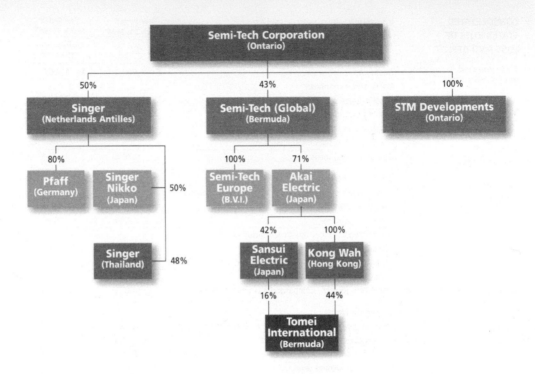

Semi-Tech Corporation (Ontario)

- 50% → **Singer** (Netherlands Antilles)
- 43% → **Semi-Tech (Global)** (Bermuda)
- 100% → **STM Developments** (Ontario)

Singer (Netherlands Antilles)
- 80% → **Pfaff** (Germany)
- **Singer Nikko** (Japan) → 50% **Singer** (Thailand) 48%

Semi-Tech (Global) (Bermuda)
- 100% → **Semi-Tech Europe** (B.V.I.)
- 71% → **Akai Electric** (Japan)

Akai Electric (Japan)
- 42% → **Sansui Electric** (Japan)
- 100% → **Kong Wah** (Hong Kong)

Sansui Electric 16% → **Tomei International** (Bermuda) ← 44% **Kong Wah**

building the organization

SANSUI		PFAFF	1989/1990	• STG acquires Singer (SSMC)

SANSUI

PFAFF

SINGER

KONG WAH   AKAI

1989/1990	• STG acquires Singer (SSMC)
1991	• Singer goes public
1992	• STG acquires Sansui
1993	• Singer transferred from STG to STC • STG acquires Pfaff
1995	• STG acquires 55% of Akai Electric • Akai acquires 77% of Kong Wah
1996	• STG increases Akai stake to 66% • Akai increases Kong Wah stake to 100% • STG acquires Nokia's TV operation
1997	• Pfaff transferred from STG to Singer • Sansui transferred from STG to Akai
1998	• STG increases Akai stake to 71%

When a parent company owns less than 100% of a subsidiary, the accounting can become quite complex. The discussion of these aspects will be left to more advanced texts. It is enough that you understand what the NCI account represents.

Consolidations—Intercompany Transactions

One final complication that deserves mention is the impact that intercompany transactions have on the consolidated financial statements. When a parent company buys a controlling interest in a supplier or a customer, it is likely that there are many transactions between the two companies. Prior to the acquisition these transactions are viewed as taking place between two independent parties, but after the acquisition they are viewed as intercompany transactions. Sales of goods and services between a parent and a subsidiary cannot be viewed as completed transactions unless there has been a sale of the goods or services outside the consolidated entity. Therefore, any profits (revenues and expenses) from those transactions that are not completed by a sale outside the consolidated entity must be eliminated. If there are remaining balances in accounts receivable and accounts payable that relate to intercompany transactions, these too must be removed.

To briefly show you this elimination process, we present the following example. Company A owns 100% of Company B. During 20x1, Company A sells a parcel of land to Company B for $60,000. This land had originally cost Company A $45,000. Company A records the transaction on its books in the following manner:

A-Cash	60,000	
A-Land		45,000
SE-Gain on sale of land		15,000

Company B records the acquisition of the land as follows:

A-Land	60,000	
A-Cash		60,000

Note that Cash went out of one entity into the other. The consolidated entity has the same amount of Cash. Land went from $45,000 on one entity's books to $60,000 on the other entity's books. To the consolidated entity, this is the same parcel of land that was on last year's consolidated balance sheet at its historical cost of $45,000. If it is not reduced back to $45,000 on the consolidated balance sheet, it will be overstated. If we allowed the sale price of items sold intercompany to appear on the consolidated financial statements, the two entities could sell items back and forth merely to increase asset value and to record revenue when, in reality, no external transactions with independent third parties took place. The last item, Gain on the sale of land, must also be removed from the consolidated income statement. No gain can be recognized by the consolidated entity, because the land has not been sold to an outside party. The journal entry to eliminate this unrealized gain on the consolidating working papers would be:

SE-Gain on sale of land	15,000	
A-Land		15,000

An entry similar to this would have to be repeated each year on the consolidating working papers when the consolidated financial statements are prepared. The entry in subsequent years would have a debit to *Retained earnings* rather than *Gain on sale of land*, because in future years the income statement does not have the gain reported. The gain caused the retained earnings of Company A to increase in the year that the land was sold to Company B. Entries similar to these are prepared for all the intercompany transactions that occur between the two entities.

FINANCIAL STATEMENT ANALYSIS CONSIDERATIONS

The consolidation of a subsidiary considerably changes the appearance of both the income statement and the balance sheet from the parent-only financial statements under equity. The income statement is different only in its detail; the net income for the period is the same regardless of whether or not the subsidiary is consolidated. Also, because the balances in the shareholders' equity accounts are the same whichever method is used, ratios such as return on equity are unaffected by the consolidation policy.

Ratios that involve other balance sheet figures can be dramatically affected. Earlier in the chapter, the effect of consolidation on the debt/equity ratio was described using the information provided in Exhibit C-7. The debt/equity for Parent Company was 1.0, whereas the debt/equity for the consolidated entity was 2.5. Users who need information about an entity's ability to repay debt should not rely on consolidated financial statements. These statements contain the liabilities of all the companies in the consolidated entity, but each of those companies is responsible only for its own debt. A parent and its subsidiaries may guarantee each other's debt. This would reduce the risk of nonpayment and could result in lending institutions charging lower rates or lending larger amounts. When the debt is guaranteed, the debt/equity ratio of the consolidated entity is useful. All of the assets are available to service the debt.

Other ratios will also be affected. The ROA ratio, for example, divides the net income before interest by the average total assets. The numerator changes to the extent that the interest expense of the subsidiary is included on the consolidated income statement and is, therefore, added back to the net income. The denominator (average total assets) also changes, because the investment account is replaced with the individual assets and liabilities of the subsidiary. In the example in Exhibit C-8, the total assets of the parent prior to consolidation were $4,780. After consolidation the total assets were $8,230 (Exhibit C-10). This dramatic increase would certainly affect the ROA. Prior to consolidation the ROA would have been 10% ($480 / $4,780). After consolidation the ROA was 5.8% ($480 / $8,230).

The current ratio will also be affected. The current assets and liabilities that are embedded in the investment account are shown in full detail when they are consolidated. The current assets and liabilities of the subsidiary would be added to those of the parent when they are consolidated. Because our example in Exhibit C-7 does not distinguish current from long-term liabilities, it is not possible to demonstrate the change that would occur. Obviously, the quick ratio will also be affected by consolidation, for the same reason that the current ratio is affected.

Shareholders, potential investors, and most other outside users may not be able to determine the impact that various subsidiaries have on the consolidated financial statements. If a parent owns 100% of a subsidiary, the subsidiary will often not publish financial statements for external users other than Revenue Canada. A lender would be able to request individual financial statements for any company that wanted to borrow funds, but most other external users would not have this luxury. This means that users should have some understanding of which ratios are affected by the consolidation process. If the parent owns less than 100% of the shares, the subsidiary, if it is traded on the stock market, must publish publicly available financial statements. Users then have the opportunity to get more information about the components of the consolidated entity. A 100%-owned subsidiary does not trade on the stock exchange and does not need to make its financial statements public. Parent companies often have many subsidiaries. Evaluating each subsidiary individually is usually not necessary. Rather, users determine the ratios but keep in mind that each company is responsible for its own debt and taxes.

SUMMARY

In this Appendix we provided more background to improve your understanding of consolidated financial statements. You learned about the different levels of investments in other companies, from portfolio investments to significant influence investments to controlled subsidiaries. Using simple examples, we demonstrated the acquisition of a 100%-owned subsidiary. We helped you increase your knowledge through a discussion of non-wholly owned subsidiaries and of intercompany transactions. We concluded the Appendix with a brief discussion of the impact of the consolidation process on ratio analysis.

The environment of corporate financial reporting is one of constant change and growing complexity. This book has introduced you to most of the fundamental concepts and principles that guide standard-setting bodies, such as the Accounting Standards Board, as they consider new business situations and issues. You should think of the completion of this Appendix as the end of the beginning of your understanding of corporate financial reporting. As accounting standard-setting bodies and regulators adjust and change the methods and guidelines used to prepare financial statements, you must constantly educate yourself so that you understand the impacts of these changes on the financial statements of your company and of other companies.

AN INTERNATIONAL PERSPECTIVE

Reports from Other Countries

In 1991, the FASB in the United States issued a discussion memorandum entitled "International Accounting Research Project: Consolidations/Equity Accounting." A study conducted by Price Waterhouse surveyed practices in Australia, Canada, France, Germany, Italy, Japan, the Netherlands, the United Kingdom, and the United States as of November 1990.

Price Waterhouse concluded that, in virtually all the countries surveyed, consolidated financial statements were required for companies that were publicly traded on securities exchanges. In some countries, however, the consolidated statements are not considered the primary financial statements. In Japan, for instance, consolidated statements are provided as supplementary information. In many of the countries surveyed, non-publicly traded companies did not prepare consolidated financial statements.

The survey also found widespread use of a criterion of control rather than ownership in deciding whether to consolidate an entity. France, for instance, explicitly allows subsidiaries in which the parent owns more than 40% to be consolidated if no other group of shareholders has a greater share. Finance subsidiaries were generally not consolidated in countries other than the United States, but within seven months of the survey's completion, Canada, New Zealand, and the United Kingdom had revised their standards to require consolidation of these subsidiaries. The revised international standard, IAS 22, on business combinations requires the use of the purchase method with the criterion of control and the consolidation of all subsidiaries.

As this book is being written, standard-setters in Canada and the United States are discussing new consolidation standards that would result in greater similarities between the two countries in the guidelines for consolidation.

SUMMARY PROBLEM

The Peck Company (parent) bought 100% of the shares of the Spruce Company (subsidiary) on January 1, 20x1, for $600,000. On January 1, 20x1, the shareholders' equity section of the Spruce Company was as follows:

Common shares	$125,000
Retained earnings	75,000
Total shareholders' equity	$200,000

The amount paid by Peck for Spruce was larger than the book value of the assets acquired. This excess amount was attributed partially to land ($50,000) and equipment ($250,000). The equipment had a remaining useful life of 10 years and an assumed residual value of zero. Peck amortizes its assets straight-line and amortizes any goodwill over five years.

The following represents the trial balance of Peck and Spruce as at December 31, 20x1 (the end of the fiscal year).

Trial Balance, December 31, 20x1

Account	Peck Company Debit	Peck Company Credit	Spruce Company Debit	Spruce Company Credit
Cash	$ 780,000		$ 240,000	
Accounts receivable	400,000		200,000	
Inventory	525,000		350,000	
Investment in Spruce	675,000		–	
PP&E	800,000		600,000	
Accumulated amortization		$ 300,000		$ 200,000
Accounts payable		425,000		290,000
Long-term debt		900,000		580,000
Common shares		700,000		125,000
Retained earnings (1/1)		400,000		75,000
Revenues		5,000,000		2,000,000
Expenses (other than amort'n)	4,200,000		1,700,000	
Amortization	100,000		100,000	
Equity in Spruce earnings		155,000		–
Dividends declared	400,000		80,000	
Totals	$7,880,000	$7,880,000	$3,270,000	$3,270,000

Required:

a. Reconstruct the entries that Peck made during 20x1 to account for its investment in Spruce using the equity method.

b. Prepare a set of consolidating working papers for Peck and Spruce for 20x1. Separately, show the consolidating entries in journal entry form.

c. Calculate the following ratios for Peck Company using its parent-only financial statement information and the consolidated entity information:

1. Debt/equity
2. Return on equity
3. Return on assets
4. Current ratio

SUGGESTED SOLUTION TO SUMMARY PROBLEM

a. Using the equity method, the following entries would be made:

At acquisition:

A-Investment in Spruce	600,000	
A-Cash		600,000

At year end:

To recognize income: The net income of Spruce is calculated as follows:

Revenues	$2,000,000
Expenses	1,700,000
Amortization	100,000
Net income	$ 200,000

Since Peck's share of Spruce's income is 100%, the following entry would be made:

A-Investment in Spruce	200,000	
SE-Equity in Spruce earnings		200,000

To recognize dividends: Spruce declared $80,000 in dividends and Peck's share is 100%; therefore, the following entry would be made:

A-Cash	80,000	
A-Investment in Spruce		80,000

To recognize amortization of goodwill and excess fair market value: At the date of acquisition, Peck paid $400,000 more for the shares of Spruce than the book value ($200,000) of the net assets. This excess amount would be attributable to the following balance sheet items:

Land	$ 50,000
Equipment	250,000
Goodwill	100,000
Total	$400,000

The land is not amortized, but the excess amount due to the equipment must be amortized. Since Peck uses straight-line amortization, the extra amortization expense would be $25,000 per year ($250,000/10 years). The goodwill would also have to be amortized and, since it is Peck's policy to amortize goodwill over five years, extra amortization expense of $20,000 per year would have to be recognized ($100,000/5 years). Using the equity method, the sum of these two extra expenses would be recognized with the following entry:

SE-Equity in Spruce earnings	45,000	
A-Investment in Spruce		45,000

Based on these entries, the investment account balance would be $675,000 and the equity in Spruce earnings would be $155,000, as shown in the trial balance.

b. The consolidating working papers are shown in Exhibit C-14.

The consolidating working paper entries are as follows:

1. To reverse current income and dividends:

SE-Equity in Spruce earnings	155,000	
SE-Dividends declared		80,000
A-Investment in Spruce		75,000

Consolidating Working Papers, Peck Company and Spruce Company, 20x1—100% Acquisition

EXHIBIT C-14

Account	Peck Company Debit	Peck Company Credit	SpruceCompany Debit	SpruceCompany Credit	Consolidating Entries Debit	Consolidating Entries Credit	Consolidated Totals Debit	Consolidated Totals Credit
Cash	780,000		240,000				1,020,000	
Accounts receivable	400,000		200,000				600,000	
Inventory	525,000		350,000				875,000	
Property, plant, & equipment	800,000		600,000		(2) 300,000		1,700,000	
Accumulated amortization		300,000		200,000		25,000 (3)		525,000
Goodwill					(2) 100,000	20,000 (3)	80,000	
Investment in Spruce	675,000					75,000 (1)	—	
						600,000 (2)		
Accounts payable		425,000		290,000				715,000
Long-term debt		900,000		580,000				1,480,000
Common shares		700,000		125,000	(2) 125,000			700,000
Retained earnings		400,000[a]		75,000[a]	(2) 75,000			400,000
Revenues		5,000,000		2,000,000				7,000,000
Expenses	4,200,000		1,700,000				5,900,000	
Amortization expense	100,000		100,000		(3) 25,000		225,000	
Goodwill expense					(3) 20,000		20,000	
EEI		155,000			(1) 155,000		—	
Dividends declared	400,000		80,000			80,000 (1)	400,000	
Totals	7,880,000	7,880,000	3,270,000	3,270,000	800,000	800,000	10,820,000	10,820,000

[a]Beginning of period balances (trial balance phase).

2. To eliminate the investment account and shareholders' equity and to create extra fair market value and goodwill:

SE-Common shares	125,000	
SE-Retained earnings	75,000	
A-Land (PP&E)	50,000	
A-Equipment (PP&E)	250,000	
A-Goodwill	100,000	
A-Investment in Spruce		600,000

3. To amortize the extra fair market value and to amortize goodwill:

SE-Amortization expense	25,000	
XA-Accumulated amortization		25,000
SE-Goodwill expense	20,000	
A-Goodwill		20,000

c. Parent-only   Consolidated entity

1. Debt/equity

$\$1,325,000/\$1,555,000^a = 0.85$ $\$2,195,000/\$1,555,000^b = 1.41$

[a] $\$700,000 + 400,000 + 5,000,000 - 4,200,000 - 100,000 + 155,000 - 400,000 = \$1,555,000$
[b] $\$700,000 + 400,000 + 7,000,000 - 5,900,000 - 225,000 - 20,000 - 400,000 = \$1,555,000$

2. Return on equity

$\$855,000^a/\$1,555,000 = 0.55$ $\$855,000^b/\$1,555,000 = 0.55$

[a] $\$5,000,000 - 4,200,000 - 100,000 + 155,000 = \$855,000$
[b] $\$7,000,000 - 5,900,000 - 225,000 - 20,000 = \$855,000$

3. Return on assets

$\$855,000/\$2,880,000^a = 0.30$ $\$855,000/\$3,750,000^b = 0.23$

[a] $\$780,000 + 400,000 + 525,000 + 800,000 - 300,000 + 675,000 = \$2,880,000$
[b] $\$1,020,000 + 600,000 + 875,000 + 1,700,000 - 525,000 + 80,000 = \$3,750,000$

4. Current ratio

$\$1,705,000^a/\$425,000 = 4.0$ $\$2,495,000^b/\$715,000 = 3.5$

[a] $\$780,000 + 400,000 + 525,000 = \$1,705,000$
[b] $\$1,020,000 + 600,000 + 875,000 = \$2,495,000$

ABBREVIATIONS USED

EEI   Equity in earnings of investment   PP&E   Property, plant, and equipment
NCI   Noncontrolling interest

GLOSSARY

Asset purchase   An acquisition of assets from another company in which the acquiring company purchases the assets directly rather than buying a controlling interest in the shares of the other company. Title to the assets passes to the acquiring company.

Consolidated financial statements   Financial statements that represent the total financial results of a parent company and its various subsidiaries as if they were one company, even though they are separate legal entities.

Consolidating working papers   A worksheet that adjusts the financial statements of a parent and its subsidiaries so that the statements can be combined to show the consolidated financial statements.

Consolidation   An accounting method that companies are required to use to represent their ownership in other companies when they have control over the activities in other companies. The method requires the preparation of consolidated financial statements.

Controlling interest The amount of ownership of a subsidiary that a parent company must have in order to control the strategic operating, financing, and investing activities of the subsidiary. An ownership interest of greater than 50% usually meets this criterion.

Cyclical business A business that is subject to significant swings in the level of its activity, such as the greeting card business.

Debt for equity swap A transaction in which debt securities are exchanged for equity securities.

Diversification A reason for acquiring ownership in another company. Diversification typically implies that the new company acquired is in a business very different from the current business of the company. The idea is to find a business that is counter-cyclical to the company's current business.

Elimination entry A working paper consolidating entry that eliminates the balance in the investment in subsidiary account against the shareholders' equity accounts of the subsidiary. At the same time, if the price paid by the parent company exceeds the book value of the subsidiary's shareholders' equity section, excess fair market value of the net assets acquired and goodwill are recognized as part of the entry.

Equity in earnings of investment (EEI) An account used in a parent company's books to record its share of the subsidiary's net income for the period using the equity method.

Equity method An accounting method that companies use to represent their ownership in companies in which they have significant influence. This is usually true when the percentage of ownership is between 20% and 50%. In addition, this method is often used in parent-only statements to account for the investment in a subsidiary. In the latter case, the account will be eliminated on the consolidating working papers at the end of the year when consolidated financial statements are prepared.

Excess fair market value The difference between the fair market value and book value of the assets of a subsidiary company whose shares are acquired by a parent company. The difference is measured at the date of acquisition.

Goodwill An intangible asset that arises when a parent company acquires ownership in a subsidiary company and pays more for the shares than the fair market value of the underlying net identifiable assets at the date of acquisition. The difference between the price paid and the fair market value of the identifiable net assets at the date of acquisition is the value of the goodwill. It can represent expected excess earnings that result from the accumulated reputation of the subsidiary, its exceptional sales staff, or an advantageous location.

Horizontal integration A type of acquisition in which a parent company buys a competitor company in order to gain a larger market share or to expand the parent company's markets geographically.

Identifiable net assets The assets and liabilities that can be specifically identified at the date of a merger or acquisition. Some of the identifiable assets, such as patents and trademarks, may not have been recorded on the subsidiary's books.

Investee A company whose shares are being acquired by another company (the investor).

Investor A company that acquires shares of another company as an investment.

Minority interest A synonym for noncontrolling interest.

Noncontrolling interest (NCI) The portion of a less-than-100%-owned subsidiary that is owned by other shareholders.

One-line consolidation The equity method is referred to as a one-line consolidation method because it produces the same net results as the full consolidation method except that the results are shown in a single line on the balance sheet (the investment account) and a single line on the income statement (the equity in earnings of investment).

Parent company A company that acquires control (usually meaning that it can elect a majority of the Board of Directors) of another company. The acquired company is referred to as a subsidiary.

Parent-only books The accounting records of a parent company that have not been combined with its subsidiary's records in consolidated financial statements. The parent typically records the investment in its subsidiary using the equity method on the parent-only books.

Passive investment An investment by one company in another company in which the acquiring company has no capability of controlling or influencing the decisions of the acquired company.

Pooling of interests method An accounting method used in acquisitions involving an exchange of shares that results in neither company being recognized as an acquirer of the other. The underlying concept of the method is that the ownership groups of the two companies are pooled together and, therefore, there is no basis on which to revalue the assets and liabilities of the two companies. In consolidation, the assets and liabilities are combined at their book values at the date of acquisition.

Portfolio investment Synonym for passive investment.

Purchase method   An accounting method used to record the acquisition of another company. The acquisition is treated as a purchase, and the assets and liabilities acquired are measured at their cost. Because this is typically a basket purchase, the cost is allocated to the individual assets and liabilities on the basis of their relative fair market values.

Share acquisition   An acquisition of another company that is achieved through the acquisition of shares of that company. The acquired company continues as a separate legal entity.

Stock swap   An acquisition in which an acquiring company exchanges its shares for the shares of the acquired company.

Subsidiary   A company controlled by another company (the parent), usually by the parent owning more than 50% of its outstanding shares and controlling its strategic operating, financing, and investing decisions.

Trial balance phase   A phase in the preparation of financial statements in which the temporary accounts still contain income statement and dividend information from the period and have not been closed out to retained earnings.

Vertical integration   A type of merger or acquisition in which a parent company buys a supplier or a customer company in order to ensure a supply of raw materials or a market for its end product.

Widely held shares   Shares of a company that are held by a large number of individuals or institutions such that no one shareholder has significant influence on the decisions of the company.

ASSIGNMENT MATERIAL

Assessing Your Recall

C-1   Identify and briefly explain the major reasons why a company might want to buy shares in another company.

C-2   Compare and contrast a share acquisition and an asset acquisition in terms of their effects on the financial statements.

C-3   Explain the financial statement implications of accounting for an acquisition using the purchase method versus the pooling method:

    a. At the date of acquisition

    b. Subsequent to the date of acquisition

C-4   Explain the conceptual differences between an acquisition treated as a purchase and an acquisition treated as a pooling.

C-5   Briefly describe the GAAP guidelines for the accounting of long-term acquisitions in the shares of other companies. In your description, identify the criteria used to distinguish the various accounting methods.

C-6   Describe the nature of goodwill and how it arises in the context of an acquisition.

C-7   The equity method is sometimes referred to as a one-line consolidation. Explain.

C-8   Discuss what a consolidation is trying to achieve.

C-9   Consolidating working paper entries are needed to eliminate double accounting for certain items on the books of the parent and the subsidiary. Explain which items would be accounted for twice if the subsidiary's books were added directly to the parent company's books.

C-10 The consolidated balances in the asset and liability accounts do not exist on the books of either the parent company or the subsidiary. Explain why you agree or disagree with this statement.

Applying Your Knowledge

C-11 (Acquisition of 100%-owned subsidiaries)
Down Company purchased 100% ownership of Topp Company for $80,000 and 100% ownership of Steady Company for $240,000 on January 1, 2001. Immediately after the purchases, the companies reported the following amounts:

Company	Total Assets	Total Liabilities	Total Shareholders' Equity
Down Company	$950,000	$250,000	$700,000
Topp Company	120,000	40,000	80,000
Steady Company	370,000	130,000	40,000

Required:
If a consolidated balance sheet is prepared immediately after the purchase of the two companies:

a. What amount of total assets will be reported?

b. What amount of total liabilities will be reported?

c. What amount of total shareholders' equity will be reported?

d. Why is it necessary to eliminate the balance in Down's investment account in each of the two companies when a consolidated balance sheet is prepared?

C-12 (Investments ranging from 10% to 100%)
On April 1 the Red Tin Company acquired some common shares of the Timber Steel Company. On April 1 the book value of the Timber Steel Company's net assets was $10 million and the market value of the net assets was $12.5 million. During the year, the Timber Steel Company had net earnings of $1,000,000 and declared dividends of $600,000.

Required:
For each of the following assumptions, give the amount of income recognized by the Red Tin Company from its investment in Timber Steel Company, and show the beginning and ending balances for the investment account on Red Tin's books. Both companies close their books annually on December 31. Goodwill is to be amortized over a period of 20 years. Assume that any excess fair market value is to be amortized straight-line over five years. Assume in each case that the market value of the shares on December 31 is the same as the acquisition price.

a. The acquisition price is $1,250,000 for 10% of the common shares of Timber Steel.

b. The acquisition price is $1,500,000 for 15% of the common shares of Timber Steel.

c. The acquisition price is $3,125,000 for 25% of the common shares of Timber Steel.

d. The acquisition price is $6,000,000 for 45% of the common shares of Timber Steel.

e. The acquisition price is $13,000,000 for 100% of the common shares of Timber Steel.

C-13 (Acquisition alternatives of a 100% purchase)

Popular Limited decided to acquire 100% of the Wallflower Company for $250,000. To pay for the acquisition, Popular's management concluded it could (1) sell temporary investments it holds and pay cash, (2) issue new bonds and use the cash receipts, or (3) issue common shares with a market value of $250,000 in exchange for the shares of Wallflower.

Required:

Answer each of the following questions and explain why your answer is appropriate:

a. Under which of the alternatives will total liabilities in the consolidated balance sheet be greater than the amount reported by Popular prior to the purchase of Wallflower's shares?

b. Under which of the alternatives will total assets in the consolidated balance sheet be greater than the amount reported by Popular prior to the purchase of Wallflower's shares?

c. Under which of the alternatives will total shareholders' equity in the consolidated balance sheet be greater than the amount reported by Popular prior to the purchase of Wallflower's shares?

d. Which of the alternatives would appear to increase the riskiness of investing in Popular Limited?

e. Which of the alternatives would appear to reduce the riskiness of investing in Popular Limited?

C-14 (Portfolio investment and significant influence investment)

On January 1, Nix Company acquired portions of the common shares of two companies, Cal Company and Lake Company. The data relating to the acquisition and the first year of operations are as follows:

Company	Common Shares Acquired	Book Value of Net Assets as at 1/1	Market Value of Net Assets as at 1/1	Acquisition Price	Net Income for the year	Dividends Declared for the year
Cal Company	18%	$3,500,000	$5,000,000	$ 900,000	$1,250,000	$ 800,000
Lake Company	40%	8,000,000	9,500,000	4,800,000	3,000,000	2,000,000

All the companies close their books annually on December 31. Goodwill, if any, is to be amortized over a period of 40 years. Property, plant, and equipment acquired has a remaining useful life of six years, has a residual value of zero, and is amortized using the straight-line method. Any excess fair market value in the transaction relates to property, plant, and equipment. The market value of Cal Company and Lake Company shares held on December 31 was $850,000 and $4,500,000, respectively.

Required:

Show the journal entries (including the acquisition) to account for these two investments during the year.

C-15 (Consolidation of a 100%-owned subsidiary)

Large Company owns all of the common shares of Small Company. Income statements for the companies for 2001 contained the following amounts:

	Large Co.	Small Co.
Sales revenue	$600,000	$300,000
Cost of goods sold	400,000	160,000
Gross profit	200,000	140,000
Dividend income from subsidiary	90,000	
Operating expenses	(130,000)	(50,000)
Net income	$160,000	$ 90,000

During 2001, Small Company purchased inventory for $10,000 and immediately sold it to Large at cost. Large has not sold this inventory yet.

Required:

In the consolidated income statement for 2001:

a. What amount will be reported as sales revenue?

b. What amount will be reported as cost of goods sold?

c. What amount will be reported as dividend income from subsidiary?

d. What amount will be reported as operating expenses?

e. Why are some amounts reported in the consolidated income statement not equal to the sum of the amounts from the statements of the parent and the subsidiary?

C-16 (Consolidation of a 100%-owned subsidiary)

On January 1, Lid Company acquired 100% of the common shares of Ant Company at a price of $1,500,000. The book value of the net assets of Ant Company on January 1 was $1,250,000. The book value of the net assets approximates the fair value at the date of acquisition. During the year Ant earned $340,000 and declared dividends of $290,000. At the end of the year the dividends receivable of Lid Company included an amount of $290,000 that was due from Ant Company. (Hint: Lid's balance sheet would have a dividend receivable and Ant's would have a dividend payable. The consolidated entity cannot owe money to itself. Therefore, both of these accounts must be removed on the working papers before consolidated financial statements are prepared.) Goodwill, if any, is to be amortized over a period of 20 years.

Required:

a. Show the journal entries for the acquisition of the common shares and other entries during the year, assuming that Lid uses the equity method on its own books.

b. Prepare the consolidating working paper entries.

C-17 (Consolidation of a 100%-owned subsidiary)

Jennie's Plumbing and Heating recently purchased 100% of the shares of Ron's Repair Service. The balance sheets for the two companies immediately after the purchase of Ron's shares were:

	Jennie's Plumbing	Ron's Repair
Cash	$ 20,000	$ 8,000
Accounts receivable	50,000	30,000
Inventory	80,000	72,000
Investment in Ron's Repair	150,000	
Buildings and equipment	300,000	240,000
Less: accumulated amortization	(110,000)	(80,000)
Total assets	$490,000	$270,000
Accounts payable	$ 60,000	$ 75,000
Taxes payable	70,000	45,000
Common shares	200,000	100,000
Retained earnings	160,000	50,000
Total liabilities and equity	$490,000	$270,000

At the balance sheet date, Ron's Repair owes Jennie's Plumbing $15,000 on accounts payable.

Required:

a. Prepare a consolidated balance sheet for Jennie's Plumbing and its subsidiary.

b. Why are the shareholders' equity balances of Ron's Repair not included in the consolidated balance sheet?

c. Monona Wholesale Supply has extended credit of $10,000 to Jennie's Plumbing, and Winona Supply Company has extended credit of $10,000 to Ron's Repair. Which supplier has the stronger claim on the consolidated cash balance? Explain.

d. Jennie's Plumbing has applied to the Sussex Bank for a $75,000 short-term loan to open a showroom for bathroom and kitchen fixtures. Accounts receivable will be used as collateral, and Jennie's Plumbing has provided the bank with its consolidated balance sheet prepared immediately after the acquisition of Ron's Repair. From the bank's perspective, how would you rate the sufficiency of the collateral? Explain.

e. If Jennie's Plumbing had purchased only 80% of the shares of Ron's Repair, an item labelled "Noncontrolling Interest" would have been reported on the balance sheet. What does the amount assigned to the noncontrolling interest represent?

C-18 (Consolidation of a 100%-owned subsidiary)
The following are the balance sheets and income statements for Jungle Company and Forest Company as at December 31, 20x1:

Balance Sheet as at December 31, 20x1

	Jungle Company	Forest Company
Assets		
Cash	$ 29,000	$ 15,000
Accounts Receivable	35,000	45,500
Investment in Forest Company	128,750	–
Other Assets	61,000	74,500
Total Assets	$253,750	$135,000
Liabilities & Shareholders' Equity		
Accounts Payable	$ 39,500	$ 20,000
Other Current Liabilities	10,500	10,000
Common Shares	150,000	80,000
Retained Earnings	53,750	25,000
Total Liabilities & Shareholders' Equity	$253,750	$135,000

Income Statement for the year ended December 31, 20x1

	Jungle Company	Forest Company
Sales Revenue	$100,000	$ 60,000
Cost of Goods Sold	(55,000)	(35,000)
Amortization	(25,000)	(5,000)
EEI	18,750	–
Net Income	$ 38,750	$ 20,000
Dividends Declared	$ 25,000	$ 15,000

On January 1, 20x1, Jungle had acquired 100% of the common shares of Forest Company. The acquisition price was $125,000. The shareholders' equity section of Forest Company on January 1 was as follows:

Forest Company

Common Shares	$ 80,000
Retained Earnings	20,000
Total	$100,000

The fair market value of Forest's net assets equalled their book values at the date of acquisition. Goodwill, if any, is to be amortized over a period of 20 years.

Required:

a. Prepare the consolidating working papers, supported with the necessary working paper journal entries.

b. Prepare the consolidated balance sheet and income statement.

C-19 (Accounting for a subsidiary)

Varwood Company Ltd. is a subsidiary of Tabor Company Ltd. The balance sheets for Varwood Company and for the consolidated entity at December 31, 2001, contained the following balances:

	Varwood Company	Consolidated Amounts for Tabor Co. and Subsidiary
Cash and receivables	$ 80,000	$120,000
Inventory	150,000	260,000
Land	70,000	200,000
Building and equipment	150,000	450,000
Less: accumulated amortization	(70,000)	(210,000)
Total assets	$380,000	$820,000
Accounts payable	$ 40,000	$ 70,000
Notes payable	90,000	290,000
Noncontrolling interest		100,000
Common shares	80,000	180,000
Retained earnings	170,000	180,000
Total liabilities and equity	$380,000	$820,000

Required:

a. Does Tabor own 100% or less than 100% of Varwood's common shares? How do you know?

b. What percentage of Varwood's assets and liabilities is included in the consolidated balance sheet? Explain.

c. What is the amount of cash and accounts receivable reported by Tabor at December 31, 2001, if (1) there are no intercompany receivables and payables, and (2) Tabor's accounts receivable contain a $20,000 receivable from Varwood?

d. Must Tabor share a portion of Varwood's net income with others? Explain. What portion of the income from Tabor's separate operations must be shared with the other shareholders of Varwood?

e. Which of the questions a. through d. could be answered if only the consolidated financial statements were available?

C-20 (Consolidation of a 100%-owned subsidiary)

On January 1, 20x1, Neptune Company Ltd. acquired 100% of the outstanding shares of Baker Company Ltd. The acquisition price was $250,000, which included $20,000 related to the excess fair market value of the capital assets acquired. The shareholders' equity as at January 1, 20x1, was as follows:

	Neptune Co.	Baker Co.
Common shares	$500,000	$150,000
Retained earnings	10,000	50,000
Total	$510,000	$200,000

During the year, Neptune Company lent $50,000 to Baker Company, which was to be repaid by December 31, 20x1; however, $20,000 was still due from Baker at the end of the year. The trial balances of Neptune and Baker on December 31, 20x1, were as follows:

Trial Balance, December 31, 20x1

Account	Neptune Co. Debit	Neptune Co. Credit	Baker Co. Debit	Baker Co. Credit
Current assets	$ 150,000		$ 90,000	
Capital assets	350,000		200,000	
Investment in Baker	249,800		–	
Cost of goods sold	200,000		75,000	
Other expenses	25,000		10,000	
Dividends declared	50,000		30,000	
Current liabilities		$ 85,000		$ 35,000
Noncurrent liabilities		100,000		50,000
Common shares		500,000		150,000
Retained earnings		10,000		50,000
Sales revenue		300,000		120,000
EEI		29,800		
Totals	$1,024,800	$1,024,800	$405,000	$405,000

The entire fair market value of the capital assets is to be amortized using the straight-line method. The remaining useful life is five years and the residual value is zero. Goodwill, if any, is to be amortized over a period of 25 years.

> *Required:*
>
> a. Prepare the consolidating working papers, supported by the necessary working paper journal entries.
>
> b. Prepare the consolidated balance sheet.

C-21 (Equity method and consolidation of a 100%-owned subsidiary)

On January 1, 20x1, Casey Incorporated acquired 100% of the outstanding common shares of Smith Company Ltd. and List Company Ltd. The details of the acquisitions and the earnings of both companies are as follows:

	Smith Co.	List Co.
Book value of net assets as of 1/1/x1	$140,000	$175,000
Acquisition price	150,000	200,000
Earnings (loss) for 20x1	(20,000)	15,000
Dividends declared for 20x1	–	10,000

Goodwill, if any, is to be amortized over a period of 40 years. Assume that the fair market value of the net assets on 1/1/x1 is adequately measured by the book values.

Required:

a. Construct the journal entries that Casey will make on its own books in 20x1 to account for these investments, assuming it uses the equity method.

b. Prepare the consolidating working paper entries for the consolidation of these investments as of 12/31/x1, assuming the entries in part a. have been recorded.

C-22 (Acquisition of a subsidiary)

The following are the balance sheets for Trident Inc. and Gum Company Ltd. as at December 31, 20x1 (prior to any acquisition):

Balance Sheet as at December 31, 20x1

	Trident Inc.	Gum Co.
Assets		
Current Assets	$175,000	$ 65,000
Noncurrent Assets	500,000	130,000
Total Assets	$675,000	$195,000
Liabilities & Shareholders' Equity		
Current Liabilities	$ 85,000	$ 28,000
Noncurrent Liabilities	190,000	57,000
Common Shares	350,000	100,000
Retained Earnings	50,000	10,000
Total Liabilities & Shareholders' Equity	$675,000	$195,000

On December 31, 20x1, Trident Inc. issued 5,000 shares having a market value of $300,000 in exchange for all 7,500 shares of Gum. Just prior to the new issuance of shares, Trident Inc. had 25,000 shares outstanding. The value of the shares exchanged over the book value of Gum includes $100,000 of excess fair market value of the non-current assets. All other assets and liabilities of Gum were properly valued on its books.

Required:

a. Explain whether this acquisition should be accounted for as a purchase or as a pooling.

b. Construct the entry that Trident would make on its books to account for its investment in Gum.

c. Prepare a consolidated balance sheet as at December 31, 20x1.

C-23 (Calculation of consolidated net income)

Refer to the data in Problem C-22. For 20x1, the details of the net income and dividends reported by the two companies were as follows:

	Trident Inc.	Gum Co.
Net income for 20x1	$250,000	$75,000
Dividends declared for 20x1	$225,000	$65,000

Required:

What is the net income of Trident Inc. on a consolidated basis?

C-24 (Preparation of a consolidated income statement)

Refer to the data in Problem C-22 and assume that the net income and dividends declared for 20x2 are as follows:

	Trident Inc.	Gum Co.
Revenues	$700,000	$280,000
Cost of goods sold	400,000	160,000
Other expenses	95,000	30,000
Net income	$205,000	$ 90,000
Dividends declared	$150,000	$ 75,000

Trident's net income excludes the income from its investment in Gum. Goodwill is to be amortized over a period of 30 years, and any excess fair market value of noncurrent assets is to be amortized using the straight-line method over a 10-year useful life with a zero residual value.

Required:

Prepare a consolidated income statement for 20x2.

Reading and Interpreting Published Financial Statements

C-25 (Business acquisitions)

In its 1998 annual report, Bombardier Inc. listed three business acquisitions. The details are described in Exhibit C-15.

EXHIBIT C-15

Notes to Consolidated Financial Statements

For the years ended January 31, 1998 and 1997 (tabular figures in millions of Canadian dollars, except share capital and share option plan)

1. ACQUISITIONS OF BUSINESSES

a) Deutsche Waggonbau AG

At year-end, the Corporation acquired for a cash consideration of $517.8 million, including acquisition costs, substantially all of the share capital of Deutsche Waggonbau AG, a German manufacturer of transportation equipment. This acquisition has been accounted for by the purchase method and the accounts have been consolidated from January 31, 1998.

Net assets acquired at fair value

Cash and term deposits		$ 662.1
Accounts receivable		184.6
Inventories	$ 136.5	
Less: Advances and progress billings	(110.6)	25.9
Fixed assets		328.5
		1 201.1
Accounts payable and accrued liabilities		(440.4)
Advances and progress billings in excess of related costs		(211.5)
Provision for pension costs		(31.4)
		(683.3)
Net assets acquired		$ 517.8

b) de Havilland Inc.

On January 28, 1997, the Corporation purchased the 49% interest in de Havilland Inc. owned by the Province of Ontario at its carrying amount of $49.0 million. As consideration, the Corporation issued a 15-year promissory note to the Province of Ontario.

c) Business jet completion assets

On December 9, 1996, the Corporation acquired for a cash consideration of $33.8 million the net assets of the business jet completion division of Innotech Aviation Ltd. located in Dorval (Québec). The allocation of the purchase price to the fair value of the net assets acquired resulted in $30.4 million attributed to goodwill.

Required:

a. What accounting method is Bombardier most likely to use to account for its investment in Deutsche Waggonbau AG and de Havilland Inc.? What items in the note led you to that conclusion?

b. From the information provided in part (c) of the note, determine the fair value of the net assets for Innotech's business jet completion division. On the basis of that information, do you think Bombardier paid too much to acquire this division?

c. Bombardier designs and manufactures products for the recreational, aerospace, and transportation markets. Deutsche Waggonbau AG is a German manufacturer of transportation equipment. Knowing these facts about the two companies, explain whether this is horizontal integration, vertical integration, or diversification.

C-26 (Business acquisitions)

Cara Operations made two acquisitions between fiscal 1998 and fiscal 1999. These acquisitions are described in Note 5 of its 1999 annual report. Note 5 is reproduced in Exhibit C-16.

EXHIBIT C-16

5. EQUITY INVESTMENTS

The Corporation has equity interests of approximately 39% and 56% in The Second Cup Ltd. and The Spectra Group of Great Restaurants Inc., respectively. The excess of the original cost over the net book value of the assets of these companies amounted to $28.1 million. This difference comprises principally goodwill which is being amortized over 40 years.

Accumulated amortization as at March 28, 1999 amounted to $1.9 million (1998–$1.2 million).

Required:

a. In fiscal 1999, Cara Operations acquired equity interests in The Second Cup Ltd. and The Spectra Group of Great Restaurants Inc. What accounting method should Cara Operations use to account for these investments? Explain.

b. Assuming that the acquisition of the two investments occurred at the beginning of Cara Operations' fiscal year, calculate the amount of goodwill amortization that would be reported on its income statement for the year ended March 28, 1999.

c. Cara Operations describes itself as being in the Food Services business. Do these two investments represent horizontal integration, vertical integration, or diversification?

d. In 1993, Cara Operations described itself as having two core businesses, Food Services and Office Products. Why do you think Cara Operations exited the office products business?

C-27 (Acquisition of a subsidiary)

In 1996, Western Star Trucks Holdings Ltd. purchased all of the ordinary and preference shares of ERF (Holdings) plc, a manufacturer of heavy-duty commercial vehicles in the United Kingdom. Western Star Trucks Holdings Ltd. manufactures heavy-duty trucks for world markets and supplies transit buses for the North American market. Note 2 from the 1998 annual report of Western Star Trucks describes the transaction (Exhibit C-17):

EXHIBIT C-17

Notes to Consolidated Financial Statements

June 30, 1998
(in thousands of Canadian dollars, except where otherwise indicated)

2. *ERF Holdings Acquisition*

In fiscal 1996, the Company announced a take-over bid to purchase all of the ordinary and preference shares of ERF (Holdings) plc ("ERF Holdings"), a manufacturer of heavy duty commercial vehicles in the United Kingdom. The acquisition was completed in the first quarter of fiscal 1997. The results of ERF Holdings are included with the Company's results commencing July 1, 1996.

The acquisition was accounted for using the purchase method. The acquisition equation is as follows:

Assets acquired	
Current assets (excluding cash of $1,325)	111,793
Capital assets	41,556
Investments	3,809
Prepaid pension expense	10,900
Goodwill	10,019
	178,077
Less liabilities assumed	
Current liabilities (excluding bank indebtedness of $11,923)	94,034
Long-term debt assumed	11,753
	105,787
Net consideration payable	
(includes net bank indebtedness from ERF Holdings of $10,598)	72,290
Net consideration payable comprises	
Common shares issued (represents 730,595 common shares)	26,123
Cash paid (including acquisition costs)	33,708
Loan notes issued	1,861
Consideration payable by the Company	61,692
Net bank indebtedness from ERF Holdings	10,598
Total	72,290

Set out below is certain unaudited pro forma financial information for the Company for the year ended June 30, 1996, which gives effect to the acquisition of ERF Holdings assuming it had occurred on July 1, 1995:

	Pro forma (unaudited)
Revenue	1,247,681
Net income	38,119
Net income per share	3.03

Required:

a. From the information given in Exhibit C-17, how would Western Star Trucks account for its investment in ERF (Holdings)?

b. ERF (Holdings) is based in the United Kingdom. Identify some difficulties that Western Star Trucks will have to resolve when it prepares its consolidated financial statements.

c. Explain whether the purchase of ERF (Holdings) by Western Star Trucks is an example of horizontal integration, vertical integration, or diversification.

C-28 (Business acquisitions and divestitures)

In its 1998 annual report, Shaw Communications Inc. summarizes the net assets acquired through business acquisitions for fiscal 1998 and fiscal 1997 (Exhibit C-18). Shaw Communications Inc. is a diversified Canadian communications company whose core business is providing cable television services.

EXHIBIT C-18

4. BUSINESS ACQUISITIONS AND DIVESTITURES

A summary of net assets acquired through business acquisitions, accounted for as purchases, is as follows:

[thousands of dollars]	1998 $	1997 $
Identifiable net assets acquired at assigned fair values		
Working capital (deficiency)	(1,538)	2,702
Property, plant and equipment	20,596	2,766
Subscriber base	101,997	-
Broadcast licences		47,361
	121,055	52,829
Deferred income taxes	-	1,394
Minority interest	-	631
	-	2,025
Purchase price	121,055	50,804

Effective June 30, 1998 the Company purchased cable television systems in Courtney/Comox, Powell River and Kamloops, British Columbia and Lethbridge, Alberta for $121,055,000 and sold its cable television systems in Windsor, Chatham, Leamington and Smith Falls, Ontario for $185,872,000, resulting in a pre-tax gain of $69,750,000.

In 1997, the Company purchased radio station CKRY-FM ("Country 105") in Calgary, Alberta for $17,764,000; 80% of CMT Canada, the Canadian country music video specialty network for $27,485,000; radio station CING-FM in Burlington, Ontario for $5,555,000; and paid the balance due on acquisitions made in 1996.

Required:

a. In 1998, Shaw Communications Inc. realized a pre-tax gain of $69,750,000. Explain how this gain was realized.

b. The most valuable asset that Shaw Communications Inc. acquired in 1998 was something called "Subscriber base." What do you think this represents? How would you go about estimating a fair value for this asset?

c. In 1998 no minority interest was incurred. What does this tell you about the types of acquisitions Shaw Communications Inc. undertook in fiscal 1998 versus fiscal 1997?

C-29 (Acquisition of assets of another company)

Imperial Metals Corporation is a base and precious metals exploration, development, and production company, concentrating its activities in British Columbia. In 1998 the company acquired, through a subsidiary, all the mining assets of Princeton Mining Corporation. The acquisition is described in Exhibit C-19.

EXHIBIT C-19

3.   ACQUISITION OF SUBSIDIARY

Effective March 1, 1998 the Company acquired, through a wholly owned subsidiary, all the mining assets of Princeton Mining Corporation and assumed certain liabilities, including the outstanding debentures and interest accrued and unpaid thereon. The principle asset acquired in this transaction was a 60% interest in the Huckleberry which owns 100% of the Huckleberry Mine (Note 2). The consideration totaled $12,840,967, paid by issuance of 12,498,763 common shares of the Company at an ascribed value of $12,498,763 and expenses related to the acquisition of $342,204. This acquisition has been recorded using the purchase method of accounting.

Details of the net assets of Princeton Mining Corporation acquired are as follows:

Working capital, including cash of $1,557,133	$2,745,082
Mineral properties	79,116,411
Future site reclamation deposits	5,016,784
Other assets	1,472,922
Short term debt	(2,700,000)
Long term debt	(68,789,011)
Future site reclamation costs	(4,021,221)
Net assets acquired effective March 1, 1998	$12,840,967

Required:

a. Is this transaction an example of a share acquisition or an asset purchase?

b. Explain why it is reasonable that there is no goodwill in this acquisition.

c. Will minority interest arise from Imperial Metals Corporation's acquisition of Princeton Mining Corporation?

C-30 (Acquisition of 100%-owned subsidiaries)

Mark's Work Wearhouse Ltd. completed two acquisitions between 1996 and 1998. These acquisitions are described in Note 2 of its 1999 annual report (see Exhibit C-20).

Required:

a. Read through Mark's Work Wearhouse's 1998 acquisition of Paul John Enterprises Ltd. Explain the difference between assumed goodwill and acquisition goodwill.

b. In the 1996 acquisition of Work World Enterprises, 98% of the purchase price went to acquire goodwill. What impact will the amortization of the goodwill have on Mark's Work Wearhouse's income statement and balance sheet? Why do you think management was willing to pay such a hefty premium above the net assets for Work World Enterprises?

c. For both acquisitions, Mark's Work Wearhouse Ltd. paid cash. Compare the profitability and riskiness of the investments if Mark's Work Wearhouse had issued additional common shares instead of paying cash. What other information would you need to have in order to adequately answer this question?

2. ACQUISITIONS

EXHIBIT C-20

A. Effective November 1, 1998, the Company's wholly owned subsidiary Work World Enterprises Inc. acquired all of the outstanding shares of Paul John Enterprises Ltd. (Paul John) for a cash down payment of $2,253,000. In addition, there may be a further future earnout amount based on sales of the operation over the next five years, payable no later than April 15, 2004. This amount is not determinable at this time, but the amount, if any, will be added to the purchase price as additional goodwill when it can be estimated. Paul John owned and operated 19 Work World franchise stores in British Columbia and the Yukon, which are now being operated as corporate stores in the Company's Work World Division.

The acquisition was accounted for by the purchase method, with the results of operations from the acquired business included from the November 1, 1998 acquisition date. Earnings before income taxes for the period November 1, 1998 to January 30, 1999 were $559,000.

The acquisition resulted in goodwill of $328,000 which is being amortized on a straight-line basis over 27.7 years which represents the average remaining life of the original franchise agreements plus one extension period. The net assets acquired were as follows:

	1999
Cash	$ 57
Other current assets	7,572
Capital assets	781
Assumed goodwill	557
Acquisition goodwill (See Notes 1F and 8)	328
	9,295
Liabilities assumed	(7,042)
Acquisition cost	$ 2,253

B. Effective December 1, 1996, the Company acquired all of the outstanding shares of Work World Enterprises Inc. for cash totalling $7,263,000. Work World was directing the operation of Work World and Workwear World franchises operating retail stores in Canada using a variety of proprietary trademarks and trade names.

The acquisition was accounted for by the purchase method, with the results of the acquired business included from the December 1, 1996 acquisition date.

The acquisition resulted in goodwill of $7,146,000 which is being amortized on a straight-line basis over 33.9 years which represents the average life of the franchise agreements plus one extension period.

The net assets acquired were as follows:

	1997
Other current assets	$ 1,596
Franchise contracts receivable	52
Capital assets	587
Acquisition goodwill (See Notes 1F and 8)	7,146
	9,381
Liabilities assumed	(2,118)
Acquisition cost	$ 7,263

C-31 (Acquisition of a 100%-owned subsidiary)

Bema Gold Corporation acquired Arian Resources Corporation in 1998. The acquisition is described in Exhibit C-21.

2 *Business combination*

Effective June 29, 1998, the Company acquired all of the issued and outstanding shares of Arian Resources Corporation ("Arian") in a business combination accounted for by the purchase method. As consideration for this acquisition, Bema issued 10,010,530 common shares having a fair value of $18,508,000. In addition, Bema has agreed to issue up to 339,204 of its common shares upon the exercise of outstanding Arian common share purchase warrants at a price of $3.63 per share until May 28, 1999. On July 2, 1998, as part of the business combination, Bema settled $1,667,000 of debts owed by Arian by issuing 776,016 common shares.

Arian's principal asset is its 79% interest in Omsukchansk Mining and Geological Company ("OMGC"), a Russian joint stock company which holds the licence ("Julietta licence") for the rights to explore, develop and mine the Julietta gold-silver deposit located in the Magadan region of the Russian Far East (Note 5).

The net assets acquired and consideration given were as follows:

Assets acquired	
Current assets	$ 575
Mineral property and deferred development	25,215
	25,790
Liabilities assumed	(6,392)
	$19,398
Consideration given	
Common shares	$18,508
Acquisition costs	890
	$19,398

Required:

a. Describe the process by which Bema Gold Corp. acquired 100% of Arian Resources Corp.

b. What difficulties will Bema Gold Corp. encounter when it attempts to consolidate Arian Resources Corp. at year end? What business risks does Bema Gold Corp. face with Arian Resources Corp.?

c. Did any goodwill arise from this acquisition? If so, how much? If not, what reasons could you suggest for there not being any?

Critical Thinking Question

C-32 (Strategic planning of future growth)

As explained at the beginning of this chapter, companies buy all or parts of other companies for many reasons. You might assume that this type of activity is undertaken only by large corporations, but that is not the case. Many owners of small businesses will establish or buy subsidiaries as they start to expand. Often these small subsidiaries will represent a specific niche in the business plan of the owner, enabling the owner to undertake various activities without exposing the whole organization to the risk of failure.

Assume that you are the owner of a small business. Your initial business is installing carpets. You have a crew of three people who do the installation for you. Your ultimate goal is to do finishing contract work on residential and commercial construction. You hope eventually to control a multimillion-dollar operation. Think about the path you could take to expand your business from carpet installation to your eventual goal. Draft a plan of expansion that would take you gradually from one to the other. Include in your plan the purchase or establishment of subsidiaries.

APPENDIX D
TIME VALUE OF MONEY

Earlier in the book we discussed the concept of the time value of money with regard to the valuation of assets and long-term liabilities. In particular, the present value of the future cash flows of an asset was suggested as a possible valuation method for almost all asset categories. Except for long-term receivables, present-value methods are not typically used when accounting for assets under GAAP because of the difficulty in estimating the future cash flows that result from the use of those assets. The accounting for liabilities, on the other hand, relies primarily on present-value methods. The basic concepts of the time value of money are discussed in this appendix.

BASIC CONCEPTS

To gain an appreciation for the time value of money, consider the following situation. Lee, a college student on a reasonably tight budget, would like to raise some cash. Lee has a compact disc player that could be sold. Carlos and Darcy have made Lee separate offers to buy the CD player. Carlos has offered to pay $300 today. Darcy has made a higher offer, $330, but will not have the cash for another two months. Regardless of which offer Lee accepts, Lee has agreed to hand over the CD player today. Which offer should Lee accept? Before you read on, come to some decision about what you think Lee should do, and why.

There are numerous reasons why Lee might accept one offer over the other. Carlos's offer is attractive because Lee would get the cash immediately. This may be important because Lee will need to eat; if Lee has run out of money, it may not be feasible to wait two months to collect from Darcy, even though his offer is higher. Another reason why Carlos's offer is attractive is that collecting the cash now presents no **risk**. Carlos will hand over the cash as Lee hands over the CD player. With Darcy's offer, there is some possibility that Lee will never be paid the $330.

A third reason for accepting Carlos's offer is that if Lee does not need the money to live, Lee can invest the $300 today and have more than $300 two months from now. For this reason, it is inappropriate to compare the $330 offer directly with the $300 offer. It is more appropriate to compare the $330 offer with what the $300 would be worth two months from now. In the terminology of the time value of money, the $300 is a **present value** and the $330 is a **future value**. To compare the offers on a dollar-for-dollar basis, Lee would have to calculate either what the $300 will be worth in two months (its future value) or what the $330 is worth today (its present value).

Assume that Lee takes the approach of calculating what the $300 offer will be worth two months from now. How much the $300 will generate depends on what investment opportunities are available to Lee. For example, suppose that the best Lee can do is invest the money at 10% annual interest. The $300 could earn $5 in two months ($300 × 10% × 2/12). Therefore, Lee would have $305 at the end of two months. This is clearly less than the $330 that Darcy is offering, which makes his offer more attractive. But Lee might also want to consider the riskiness of the investment compared to the risk that Darcy will fail to pay. For example, if Lee invests in wildcat oil wells (a risky investment) and no oil is found, the $300 investment will be lost. In this case, it may be more risky to invest than to accept the risk that Darcy will not pay.

The advantage of Darcy's offer is clearly that it is for more money. Considering the next best investment Lee can make with Carlos's offer (invest it at 10%), Darcy's offer is superior (assuming that accepting Darcy's offer and investing pose similar risks). To consider the offers equivalent on a dollar-for-dollar basis, Lee would have to be able to earn a 60% return on the $300 investment ($300 × 60% × 2/12 = $30).

A corporation faces many decisions similar to this one with cash flows occurring at different times, resulting in various alternatives and risks. The only way to properly compare the dollar amounts is to use time value of money concepts and computations. One standard approach is to calculate the present value of all alternatives and then compare them. All other things being equal, the corporation would choose the option that produced the highest present value. Unfortunately, all other things are not usually equal. As our example points out, there may be differences in the risk associated with the alternatives. It may also be that the corporation has objectives other than maximizing the present value; that is, it may need to spend its money in other ways in order to survive, just as Lee may need to get the cash immediately in order to survive. A corporation, for example, may have a loan coming due and so may need cash immediately; it cannot wait to receive cash in the future.

Decisions based on comparison of the present value of alternatives are not the subject of this book. The accountant generally is faced with recording the results of the decisions already made by management, or providing data for management to make those decisions. Time value of money considerations enter into the accountant's work when a present-value method is used to record the results of a particular transaction. Under GAAP, there are at least two situations in which present-value methods are used. The first situation is accounting for liabilities. Under GAAP, most liabilities are carried on the corporation's books at their net present value. Interest on these liabilities is then recorded over time, based on time value of money calculations. The second situation in which present values are used is accounting for long-term receivables. On the books of a lender, long-term receivables are the mirror image of the long-term liabilities that appear on the books of a borrower.

FUTURE VALUE

In the example of Lee and the CD player, the future value of an amount was calculated by using the present value, an assumed interest rate, and the time period between the present and future dates. There are many contexts in which a corporation or an individual must make a future-value calculation of this type. For example, if you are saving money for a future purchase, such as a car or a house, you need to know how long it will take you to accumulate the appropriate amount (the future value), based on the amount deposited in your savings account and the rate of interest offered. In a corporate context, a corporation would need to know whether it will have sufficient funds available from its investments to pay a liability that comes due at some future date.

To illustrate the calculation of a future value, we offer a simple example. Suppose that $100 is invested in a bank savings account that pays interest at a 10% annual rate. (Interest rates are always stated as an annual rate unless otherwise indicated.) How much will be in the savings account at the end of the year? The answer is $110. The calculation of the interest is as follows:

$$\text{Interest} = \text{Principal} \times \text{Interest Rate} \times \text{Time} = P \times I \times T$$
$$= \$100 \times 10\%/\text{year} \times 1 \text{ year} = \$10$$

In addition to calculating the interest, we could also represent the ending balance in the account using an equation. The amount at the end of the period could be calculated using the following formula:

$$\text{Ending Balance} = \text{Beginning Balance} + \text{Interest}$$
$$= \text{Beginning Balance} + (\text{Principal} \times \text{Interest Rate} \times \text{Time})$$
$$= \$100 + (\$100 \times .10/\text{year} \times 1 \text{ year}) = \$110$$

Another way to express the relationship is to use the terminology of the time value of money. The **principal** is the **present value**, and the **interest rate** is sometimes referred to as the **discount rate**. The **beginning balance** is the same as the **present value**, and the **ending balance** is the **future value**. The formula to calculate the ending balance (future value) is:

Calculation of Ending Balance — First Year:
$\quad$ Ending Balance = Beginning Balance + (Principal $\times$ Interest Rate $\times$ Time)

If we let:
$\quad$ PV = Present Value
$\quad$ FV = Future Value
$\quad\quad$ r = Discount rate per period

then:
$\quad$ FV = PV + (PV $\times$ r $\times$ 1)

Simplifying this yields:
$\quad$ FV = PV $\times$ (1 + r)
$\quad\quad$ = \$100 $\times$ (1 + .1) = \$110

How much will be in the account at the end of the second year? The answer depends on whether the interest that was earned in the first year is left in the account or withdrawn, and whether the bank then pays interest on the interest that is left in the account. If the bank does not add the interest to the principal before it calculates the interest in the following period, then the interest calculation is said to be one of **simple interest**. In the case of simple interest, the interest earned in the second period will be the same as the interest earned in the first period, as long as the principal has not changed. In most situations involving more than one year, simple interest is not used. Most banks would calculate **compound interest**, which means that the interest earned in one period is added to the principal and then this amount earns interest in the next period. The standard assumptions used in the discussion that follows are that interest is not withdrawn at the end of the period and that it is compounded. This means that in our example the \$110 that existed at the end of the first year earns interest in the second year, producing \$11 in interest (\$110 $\times$ 10%), for an ending balance of \$121. The formulation for the situation in the second year would be (the time variable is dropped at this point and is assumed to be one year):

Calculation of Ending Balance — Second Year:
$\quad$ Ending Balance = Beginning Balance + (Principal $\times$ Interest Rate)

If we let:
$\quad$ PV = Present Value
$\quad$ FV_i = Future Value

where $_i$ represents the year
$\quad$ r = Discount rate per year

then:
$\quad$ $FV_2 = FV_1 \times (1 + r)$

where FV_1 is the value at the end of the year 1. Substituting for FV_1 from the equation shown earlier, we get:
$\quad$ $FV_2 = [PV \times (1 + r)] \times (1 + r)$
$\quad\quad$ $= PV \times (1 + r)^2$
$\quad\quad$ $= \$100 \times (1 + .1)^2 = \$121$

This result can be generalized to N years into the future so that the relationship between present and future values is as follows:

Future-Value Formula:
$$FV_N = PV \times (1 + r)^N$$

This formula applies to what is known as **lump sum amounts**—that is, single cash flows (or single payments). The future value of a single amount, at the present value (PV), N years into the future, at an interest rate of r per year, can then be calculated by applying this formula.

Note that, in the future-value formula, the last term on the right is a function only of r and N. This last term is called a **future-value factor** and can be summarized in a two-way table with values of r on one dimension and values of N on the other. These factors, which are sometimes called **future value of $1 factors**, are provided in Table 1 at the end of appendix D. The term $FVF_{r,N}$ will be used to represent future value of $1 factors. The formula can, then, be expressed in terms of the factors as:

Future-Value Formula:
$$FV_N = PV \times FVF_{r,N}$$

Suppose that $1,000 is deposited in a savings account today at 12%. What amount will be available in the account at the end of five years, assuming that interest is compounded at the end of each year? Using the preceding formula, the factor from the table for N = 5 and r = 12% is used and plugged into it:

Future-Value Formula:
$$FV_5 = \$1,000 \times FVF_{12\%,5}$$
$$= \$1,000 \times 1.76234 = \$1,762.34$$

COMPOUNDING PERIODS

In the preceding examples, a period of one year was used in computing the compound interest. Interest can be compounded more often than annually. In fact, most banks do compound it more often. Some banks compound it quarterly, some monthly, some daily, and some even compound it on what is known as a continuous basis. How does changing the compounding period affect the calculation?

To incorporate a different compounding period into the future-value formulas (and the present-value formulas that will be discussed later), adjust the number of periods N and the interest rate per period r to reflect the appropriate compounding period. For instance, in the example of the future-value calculation in which $1,000 was deposited at 12% and compounded annually for five years, suppose that the problem is changed so that interest is compounded semi-annually (twice a year). There would now be two compounding periods per year and, therefore, a total of 10 periods (of six months each) over the five years. The interest rate per period would then be adjusted to 6% (12%/2 periods per year). The calculation would be:

Future-Value Formula:
$$FV_{10} = \$1,000 \times FVF_{6\%,10}$$
$$= \$1,000 \times 1.79085 = \$1,790.85$$

Note that the future value is larger when interest is compounded more often (it was $1,762.34, compounded annually). This makes sense, because the interest has a greater chance to earn interest itself.

To compare the effects of different compounding periods, consider the data in Exhibit D-1, which show the effects of changing the compounding period on a $1 investment for one year.

You can see from Exhibit D-1 that the future value increases as the compounding period increases in frequency. The continuous compounding formula will not be discussed, because it is not used often for accounting purposes. It provides the maximum improvement in return that can be obtained based on changes in the compounding period. It is clear that on a yearly basis the compounding period affects the return on the investment: Yearly compounding yields a 12% return; monthly compounding yields a 12.683% return. The two types of investment are based on a 12% interest rate, but they are based on different compounding periods. The 12% is generally referred to as the **nominal rate**, and the 12.683% as the **effective rate**. Because of differences in the compounding periods, banks in Canada are required to disclose effective interest rates (known as the annual percentage rate, or APR), as well as nominal interest rates, on the products they offer.

EXHIBIT D-1

Effects of Compounding Periods

Assumptions:
      Investment (PV) = $1
    Yearly interest rate = 12%
    Investment period = 1 year

Compounding Period	r(%)	N	Factor	Future Value
Yearly	12	1	1.12000	$1.12
Semi-annually	6	2	1.12360	$1.1236
Quarterly	3	4	1.12551	$1.12551
Monthly	1	12	1.12683	$1.12683
Continuously	a	a	1.12750	$1.12750

[a] The continuous method calculates the ending value of e^r, where e is the base of the natural logarithms.

PRESENT VALUE

The calculation of a present value from a future value is simple once the future-value formula is known. Simply rearrange the future-value formula so that the present value appears on one side and the rest of the formula appears on the other. The present-value formula would then be:

> Present-value formula:
> $$PV = FV_N \times \frac{1}{(1 + r)^N}$$

Note again that the second term on the right side of the equation depends only on r and N. Table 2 at the end of Appendix D provides a listing of these present value of $1 factors. The term $PVF_{r,N}$ is used to represent present value of $1 factors. The formula can be written as:

> Present-value formula:
> $$PV = FV_N \times PVF_{r,N}$$

This formula can be used in situations in which the future value is known and the present-value information is needed. For example, if you will need $1,000 five years from now and want to know how much you must deposit in the bank today at 8%, compounded annually, to have the $1,000 by then, the calculation would be:

> Present-value formula:
> $$PV = \$1,000 \times PVF_{8\%,5}$$
> $$= \$1,000 \times 0.68058 = \$680.58$$

Note that the present-value factors are simply the reciprocals of the future-value factors. Two tables of these factors are not really required, as one can be easily derived from the other by taking the reciprocal.

MULTIPLE CASH FLOWS

The foregoing discussion dealt only with single present values and single future values. In many contexts, however, more than one cash amount is involved. For example, an accountant recording the present value of a loan that is to be repaid monthly for five years will record a total of 60 payments. Multiple cash flows can be handled using the formulas that have been derived here. In a present-value problem, the present-value formula derived could simply be applied to each of the cash flows separately, and then the amounts added together to get the total present value. Future values could be handled in a similar fashion.

ANNUITIES

A special and simplifying situation occurs if the multiple cash flows are all equal. This is a fairly common occurrence in business. For example, most loans are structured so that all the payments are the same. Many lease agreements also call for equal payments over an extended period.

A stream of cash flows in which the amounts are the same is called an **annuity**. Annuities are characterized in two ways. The first is by the number of payments required. The second is by the timing of those payments, especially the timing of the first in a series of payments. An annuity in which the first cash flow (payment) comes at the end of the first time period is known as an **annuity in arrears**. It is also sometimes referred to as an **ordinary annuity**. Most equal-payment loans are structured as annuities in arrears. The first payment comes a month after the loan is made.

An annuity in which the first payment comes at the beginning of the first time period is called an **annuity in advance** or, sometimes, an **annuity due**. Most rental agreements and leases are structured as annuities in advance.

An annuity in which the first payment is delayed beyond the end of the first period is referred to as a **deferred annuity**. Some annuities are structured so that there is no terminal date; that is, the payments are theoretically paid forever. Such an annuity is called a **perpetuity**, and it can either be **in advance** or **in arrears**.

Annuities in Arrears (Ordinary Annuities)

The present or future value of an annuity in arrears can be calculated by applying the formulas developed earlier to each of the payments separately, and then adding the amounts together. A more efficient way is to take into consideration the simplifications that result when the payments are equal.

Consider the situation of an annuity in arrears for N periods. The following time line represents the pattern of payments (referred to as PMT):

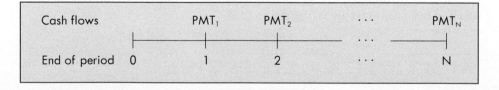

To develop an equation to calculate the present value of the annuity, first create a formula for the sum of the individual cash payments using the formula developed earlier. The equation would be as follows:

> Total present value $= PV_1 + PV_2 + \ldots + PV_N$
>
> where PV_i is the present value of payment i.

Substitute the formula for each PV_i:

> Total present value $= (PMT_1 \times PVF_{r,1}) + (PMT_2 \times PVF_{r,2}) + \ldots + (PMT_N \times PVF_{r,N})$

Now, recognize that $PMT_1 = PMT_2 = \ldots = PMT_N = PMT$, and simplify the preceding equation:

> Total present value $= PMT \times (PVF_{r,1} + PVF_{r,2} + \ldots + PVF_{r,N})$

Note that the last term (i.e., the sum of the present-value factors) is a function of only the interest rate and the number of periods. It is, therefore, a **present-value factor for an annuity in arrears**. It can be expressed in a simplified formula (which will not be derived) as:

> Present value of an annuity in arrears factor:
> $$PV_AF_{r,N} = (PVF_{r,1} + PVF_{r,2} + \ldots + PVF_{r,N})$$
> $$= \frac{[1 - (1 + r)^{-N}]}{r}$$
> where $PV_AF_{r,N}$ is the annuity in arrears factor for N periods at r% interest.

The formula for the present value of an annuity in arrears can then be expressed as:

> Present value of an annuity in arrears formula:
> $$PV = PMT \times PV_AF_{r,N}$$

The present value of an annuity in arrears factors appear in Table 4 at the end of Appendix D. To illustrate the usage of this formula: Assume that the payments on a loan are $300 a month for three years at an interest rate of 12%. Calculate the present value of these payments (i.e., the principal of the loan). Note that because the loan requires monthly payments, the compounding period is, implicitly, monthly. In determining the present value, the following calculation would be made:

> Present value of an annuity in arrears formula:
> $$PV = \$300 \times PV_AF_{1\%,36}$$
> $$= \$300 \times 30.10751 = \$9,032.25$$

The present value of an annuity in arrears formula can also be rearranged to calculate the payments required to pay off a loan, given the principal of the loan, the interest rate, and the number of payment periods. Suppose that you want to borrow $15,000 to buy a car. The bank will lend you money for three years at 12%, with payments to be made monthly. The calculation to determine the monthly payments is:

Annuity in arrears payment formula:
$$PMT = PV/PV_AF_{1\%,36}$$
$$= \$15,000/30.10751 = \$498.21/month$$

The future value of an annuity can also be calculated using the formula derived for the lump sum amounts. Again, because of the unique nature of annuities, a simplified formula has been devised for calculating the future value of an annuity in arrears. The formula is as follows:

Future value of an annuity in arrears factor:
$$FV_AF_{r,N} = (FVF_{r,1} + FVF_{r,2} + \ldots + FVF_{r,N})$$
$$= \frac{[(1 + r)^{N-1}]}{r}$$

where $FV_AF_{r,N}$ is the future value of an annuity in arrears factor for N periods at r% interest.

The future value of an annuity in arrears formula then becomes:

Future value of an annuity in arrears formula:
$$FV_N = PMT \times FV_AF_{r,N}$$

The future value of an annuity in arrears factors appear in Table 3 at the end of Appendix D.

To use this formula, suppose that you were able to save $100 each month out of your pay. At the end of each month you deposit this amount in a savings account that pays interest at 12%, compounded monthly. You want to know how much you will have accumulated in the savings account at the end of two years. This is a future-value calculation that can be made as follows:

$$FV_N = PMT \times FV_AF_{r,N}$$
$$FV_{24} = \$100 \times FV_AF_{1\%,24}$$
$$FV_{24} = \$100 \times 26.97346 = \$2,697.35$$

In another situation, you might want to know how much you must save every month to accumulate a certain amount in the future. Suppose that you want to save

$10,000 for a downpayment on a house. You want to accumulate it over a five-year period, and you can invest your money at 8%, compounded quarterly. How much must you deposit at the end of each quarter to accumulate the $10,000? The solution can be found by rearranging the future value of an annuity in arrears formula to allow you to calculate the payment:

$$PMT = \frac{FV_N}{FV_AF_{r,N}}$$

$$PMT = \frac{FV_{20}}{FV_AF_{2\%,20}}$$

$$= \$10,000/24.29737 = \$411.57 \text{ per quarter}$$

Annuities in Advance (Annuities Due)

An annuity in advance differs from an annuity in arrears only in that the first payment is made at the beginning of the first period rather than at the end. The same total number of payments is made. The following time line shows the pattern of payments for an N-period annuity in advance.

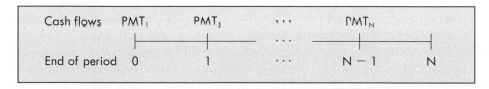

Note that the first payment comes at the beginning of period 1 and the last payment comes at the beginning of period N.

A present-value factor for an annuity in advance can be derived in the same way that it was derived for the annuity in arrears. However, knowledge of the annuity in arrears factors will be used to calculate the present value of the annuity in advance problem.

The trick to using annuity in arrears factors in an annuity in advance problem is to make the annuity in advance problem look like an annuity in arrears problem. To do this, look at the N-period annuity in advance time line and cover up the first cash flow. This leaves N – 1 remaining cash flows, the first of which comes at the end of the first period. This is an annuity in arrears problem for N – 1 periods. You already know how to find this present value. The present value of the cash flow that was covered up is equal to the payment itself, since it comes at time zero. Therefore, if you add this payment to the present value of the annuity in arrears for N – 1 periods, you get the present value of the annuity in advance. In a formula, this relationship can be shown as follows:

PV annuity = PV of first cash flow + PV of remaining N − 1 cash flows in advance
$$= PMT + (PMT \times PV_AF_{r,N-1})$$

This can then be simplified as follows:

$$\text{PV annuity in advance} = \text{PMT} \times (\text{PV}_A\text{F}_{r,N-1} + 1)$$

The last term in this expression (in parentheses) is the factor for an annuity in advance problem. Note that you multiply this factor by the payment to get the present value. Therefore, the conversion of present value of annuity in arrears factors to present value of annuity in advance factors is to take the present value of annuity in arrears factor for one less period ($N-1$) and add 1. In many annuity in arrears factor tables (including Table 4), this conversion is stated in a footnote to the table.

A similar conversion can be made for the future-value factors. The trick, in this case, for making the problem look like an annuity in arrears problem is to add one cash flow. This extra cash flow appears in the diagram below as PMT.*

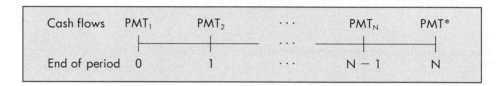

The diagram now shows $N + 1$ payments, which could be viewed as an annuity in arrears if you start at time period $N - 1$. You could then use the future value of an annuity in arrears factor to calculate the future value of this annuity at time N. Then, recognizing that the future value of PMT* is equal to PMT, you could subtract PMT from the future value of the annuity, which would leave the future value of the annuity in advance. In a formula, this is expressed as follows:

$$\text{FV annuity} = \text{FV of } N + 1 \text{ cash flows} - \text{FV of cash flow at time N in advance}$$
$$= (\text{PMT} \times \text{FV}_A\text{F}_{r,N+1}) - \text{PMT}$$

This can then be simplified to:

$$\text{FV annuity in advance} = \text{PMT} \times (\text{FV}_A\text{F}_{r,N+1} - 1)$$

The conversion is, therefore, to take the annuity in arrears factor for one more period ($N + 1$) and subtract 1. Again, this conversion appears in the footnote to Table 3.

Consider a problem in which a company decides to rent a piece of equipment for five years. It will make yearly payments of $1,000 each, in advance. If the corporation can invest its money at 10%, how much would it have to put in the bank today to allow it to make the payments from the bank account? In other words, what is the present value of the payments the corporation has to make? This is an annuity in advance problem. It can be solved as follows:

$$\begin{aligned} \text{PV annuity in advance} &= \text{PMT} \times (\text{PV}_A F_{r,N-1} + 1) \\ &= \$1,000 \times (\text{PV}_A F_{10\%,4} + 1) \\ &= \$1,000 \times (3.16987 + 1) = \$4,169.87 \end{aligned}$$

Perpetuities

A perpetuity is a special form of annuity since it has no ending date (the cash flows continue forever). In this case, the formula for the present value simplifies even more and becomes:

$$\begin{aligned} \text{PV perpetuity in arrears} &= \text{PMT}/r \\ \text{PV perpetuity in advance} &= \text{PMT} + (\text{PMT}/r) = \text{PMT} (1 + 1/r) \end{aligned}$$

As an example of the use of a perpetuity calculation, consider the problem of trying to establish the appropriate price for one corporation to acquire another. While there are several ways for an analyst to estimate the value of a corporation, one approach is to estimate the cash flows that would occur in the future and discount them using an appropriate discount rate. A rough calculation can be made if the analyst estimates the average amount of cash the corporation generates each year. Using this estimate, and assuming that the corporation can continue to generate this level of cash flows forever, the analyst can calculate the present value using the perpetuity formula. For example, if you estimate that the corporation can generate $100,000 a year in cash for the foreseeable future, and that 10% is an appropriate discount rate for the riskiness of the corporation, then the market value of the corporation should be the present value of the perpetuity of cash flows. This would be $1 million ($100,000/10%).

INTERNAL RATES OF RETURN

In the formulas and problems discussed earlier, we were interested in calculating the present value, the future value, or the payments, given the information concerning the number of periods and the interest rate. In these problems we treated the interest rate as having been given. In some situations, the interest rate is not explicitly given but is implicit in the structure of the cash flows. For example, a non-interest-bearing note would state the proceeds from the note (the original principal) and the amount due at maturity. No interest rate would be stated in the contract. The interest, of course, is the difference between the proceeds at issuance and the amount repaid at maturity. To calculate the implicit interest rate, consider the following example.

Suppose that a corporation issues a note (i.e., borrowed money) for $1,000 that requires repayment in two years at $1,210. The $1,000 is the present value of the loan, and the $1,210 is the future value. The interest paid over the life of the note is $210, but no explicit interest rate is stated. The interest rate could be calculated by making some assumptions about how interest is compounded and making use of the formulas derived earlier. Suppose it is assumed that interest is compounded annually. This means that there are two periods between the present value and the future value. The interest rate can then be found using the present-value formula for a lump sum:

Present-value formula:

$$PV = FV_N \times \frac{1}{(1 + r)^N}$$

$$\$1{,}000 = \$1{,}210 \times \frac{1}{(1 + r)^2}$$

To solve for r in the preceding equation, two strategies may be employed. The first is to solve the quadratic equation for r. This requires that you know how to solve a quadratic equation. While many readers may know how to solve this equation, imagine a situation of $N = 15$ instead of $N = 2$. The equation then becomes much more difficult. The second strategy for solving this equation is to make a guess at the appropriate value for r and then compare the right and left sides of the equation. If the right side is higher, you know that the r you picked was too low. Next, try a higher value of r and recalculate the right side. Continue to iterate this process until the right side equals the left side. When they are equal, you have found the interest rate that equates the future value with the present value. This rate is known as the **internal rate of return**.

If you have only the formula or the tables to work with, the calculation of the internal rate of return is probably best done using the iteration procedure. If, on the other hand, you have access to a sophisticated calculator or a computer with a spreadsheet package, you will see that the calculation of the internal rate of return is a built-in function. You simply have to plug in the cash flows and invoke the built-in function. This is a much more efficient way to determine the internal rate of return than using the iterative procedure.

To illustrate the iterative procedure, Exhibit D-2 presents the calculation of the internal rate of return for the problem just posed. The initial guess is 8%.

EXHIBIT D-2

Iterative Procedure of Calculation of Internal Rate of Return

$$PV = FV_N \times PVF_{r,N}$$
$$\$1{,}000 = \$1{,}210 \times PVF_{r,2}$$

Interest Rate, %	Value of Right-Hand Side	Decision
8	$\$1{,}210 \times 0.85734 = \$1{,}037$	Rate too low
12	$\$1{,}210 \times 0.79718 = \$965$	Rate too high
10	$\$1{,}210 \times 0.82645 = \$1{,}000$	Correct rate

Summary Problem

As a final example, consider a situation with multiple sets of cash flows. Suppose that a corporation wants to borrow money from a lender. The corporation wants to borrow the money for seven years. The corporation has determined that it can afford to make periodic payments of $75 at the end of each six-month period (a small dollar amount is used in the example, but you can add more zeros to make the amounts larger and more realistic). The corporation also agrees to make a large payment (sometimes called a **balloon payment**) of $1,000 (in addition to the final $75 payment) at the end of the seven years.

Under the conditions outlined earlier, what would the lender be willing to lend to the company? The lender would have to determine what the payments would be worth based on an appropriate interest rate. Suppose that the lender wants to earn 12%. The lender would present-value the cash flows to be received from the corporation at the 12% discount rate. The present value will then tell the lender what amount it can lend in order to receive a 12% return on its investment.

The loan is structured such that there are to be 14 payments (7 years X 2 payments per year) of $75 and a final payment of $1,000 at the end of the 14 six-month periods. This is an annuity in arrears and a lump sum. The interest rate per period is 6%. The present value of the cash flows is calculated as follows:

$$
\begin{aligned}
PV &= PV \text{ (annuity in arrears)} + PV \text{ (lump sum)} \\
&= PMT \times PV_A F_{r,N} + FV_N \times PVF_{r,N} \\
&= \$75 \times PV_A F_{6\%,14} + \$1,000 \times PVF_{6\%,14} \\
&= \$75 \times 9.29498 + \$1,000 \times 0.44230 \\
&= \$697.12 + \$442.30 = \$1,139.42
\end{aligned}
$$

The $1,139.42 is the amount the lender should be willing to lend the corporation. If the lender lends this amount to the corporation and receives the $75 periodic payments and the $1,000 at the end, the lender will have earned 12% (compounded semi-annually).

The preceding calculation is exactly the same as that used to calculate the price of a bond. Bonds are long-term borrowings of a corporation and are discussed in detail in Chapter 10.

TABLE 1

Future Value of $1

Periods	0.50%	0.75%	1.00%	1.50%	2.00%	3.00%	4.00%	5.00%	6.00%	7.00%	8.00%
1	1.00500	1.00750	1.01000	1.01500	1.02000	1.03000	1.04000	1.05000	1.06000	1.07000	1.08000
2	1.01003	1.01506	1.02010	1.03023	1.04040	1.06090	1.08160	1.10250	1.12360	1.14490	1.16640
3	1.01508	1.02267	1.03030	1.04568	1.06121	1.09273	1.12486	1.15763	1.19102	1.22504	1.25971
4	1.02015	1.03034	1.04060	1.06136	1.08243	1.12551	1.16986	1.21551	1.26248	1.31080	1.36049
5	1.02525	1.03807	1.05101	1.07728	1.10408	1.15927	1.21665	1.27628	1.33823	1.40255	1.46933
6	1.03038	1.04585	1.06152	1.09344	1.12616	1.19405	1.26532	1.34010	1.41852	1.50073	1.58687
7	1.03553	1.05370	1.07214	1.10984	1.14869	1.22987	1.31593	1.40710	1.50363	1.60578	1.71382
8	1.04071	1.06160	1.08286	1.12649	1.17166	1.26677	1.36857	1.47746	1.59385	1.71819	1.85093
9	1.04591	1.06956	1.09369	1.14339	1.19509	1.30477	1.42331	1.55133	1.68948	1.83846	1.99900
10	1.05114	1.07758	1.10462	1.16054	1.21899	1.34392	1.48024	1.62889	1.79085	1.96715	2.15892
11	1.05640	1.08566	1.11567	1.17795	1.24337	1.38423	1.53945	1.71034	1.89830	2.10485	2.33164
12	1.06168	1.09381	1.12683	1.19562	1.26824	1.42576	1.60103	1.79586	2.01220	2.25219	2.51817
13	1.06699	1.10201	1.13809	1.21355	1.29361	1.46853	1.66507	1.88565	2.13293	2.40985	2.71962
14	1.07232	1.11028	1.14947	1.23176	1.31948	1.51259	1.73168	1.97993	2.26090	2.57853	2.93719
15	1.07768	1.11860	1.16097	1.25023	1.34587	1.55797	1.80094	2.07893	2.39656	2.75903	3.17217
16	1.08307	1.12699	1.17258	1.26899	1.37279	1.60471	1.87298	2.18287	2.54035	2.95216	3.42594
17	1.08849	1.13544	1.18430	1.28802	1.40024	1.65285	1.94790	2.29202	2.69277	3.15882	3.70002
18	1.09393	1.14396	1.19615	1.30734	1.42825	1.70243	2.02582	2.40662	2.85434	3.37993	3.99602
19	1.09940	1.15254	1.20811	1.32695	1.45681	1.75351	2.10685	2.52695	3.02560	3.61653	4.31570
20	1.10490	1.16118	1.22019	1.34686	1.48595	1.80611	2.19112	2.65330	3.20714	3.86968	4.66096
24	1.12716	1.19641	1.26973	1.42950	1.60844	2.03279	2.56330	3.22510	4.04893	5.07237	6.34118
36	1.19668	1.30865	1.43077	1.70914	2.03989	2.89828	4.10393	5.79182	8.14725	11.42394	15.96817
48	1.27049	1.43141	1.61223	2.04348	2.58707	4.13225	6.57053	10.40127	16.39387	25.72891	40.21057
60	1.34885	1.56568	1.81670	2.44322	3.28103	5.89160	10.51963	18.67919	32.98769	57.94643	101.2571
120	1.81940	2.45136	3.30039	5.96932	10.76516	34.71099	110.6626	348.9120	1088.188	3357.788	10252.99
240	3.31020	6.00915	10.89255	35.63282	115.8887	1204.853	12246.20	1.22E+05	1.18E+06	1.13E+07	1.05E+08
360	6.02258	14.73058	35.94964	212.7038	1247.561	41821.62	1.36E+06	4.25E+07	1.29E+09	3.79+10	1.08E+12

(continued)

TABLE 1 (continued)

Future Value of $1

Periods	9.00%	10.00%	11.00%	12.00%	13.00%	14.00%	15.00%	16.00%	18.00%	20.00%	25.00%
1	1.09000	1.10000	1.11000	1.12000	1.13000	1.14000	1.15000	1.16000	1.18000	1.20000	1.25000
2	1.18810	1.21000	1.23210	1.25440	1.27690	1.29960	1.32250	1.34560	1.39240	1.44000	1.56250
3	1.29503	1.33100	1.36763	1.40493	1.44290	1.48154	1.52088	1.56090	1.64303	1.72800	1.95313
4	1.41158	1.46410	1.51807	1.57352	1.63047	1.68896	1.74901	1.81064	1.93878	2.07360	2.44141
5	1.53862	1.61051	1.68506	1.76234	1.84244	1.92541	2.01136	2.10034	2.28776	2.48832	3.05176
6	1.67710	1.77156	1.87041	1.97382	2.08195	2.19497	2.31306	2.43640	2.69955	2.98598	3.81470
7	1.82804	1.94872	2.07616	2.21068	2.35261	2.50227	2.66002	2.82622	3.18547	3.58318	4.76837
8	1.99256	2.14359	2.30454	2.47596	2.65844	2.85259	3.05902	3.27841	3.75886	4.29982	5.96046
9	2.17189	2.35795	2.55804	2.77308	3.00404	3.25195	3.51788	3.80296	4.43545	5.15978	7.45058
10	2.36736	2.59374	2.83942	3.10585	3.39457	3.70722	4.04556	4.41144	5.23384	6.19174	9.31323
11	2.58043	2.85312	3.15176	3.47855	3.83586	4.22623	4.65239	5.11726	6.17593	7.43008	11.64153
12	2.81266	3.13843	3.49845	3.89598	4.33452	4.81790	5.35025	5.93603	7.28759	8.91610	14.55192
13	3.06580	3.45227	3.88328	4.36349	4.89801	5.49241	6.15279	6.88579	8.59936	10.69932	18.18989
14	3.34173	3.79750	4.31044	4.88711	5.53475	6.26135	7.07571	7.98752	10.14724	12.83918	22.73737
15	3.64248	4.17725	4.78459	5.47357	6.25427	7.13794	8.13706	9.26552	11.97375	15.40702	28.42171
16	3.97031	4.59497	5.31089	6.13039	7.06733	8.13725	9.35762	10.74800	14.12902	18.48843	35.52714
17	4.32763	5.05447	5.89509	6.86604	7.98608	9.27646	10.76126	12.46768	16.67225	22.18611	44.40892
18	4.71712	5.55992	6.54355	7.68997	9.02427	10.57517	12.37545	14.46251	19.67325	26.62333	55.51115
19	5.14166	6.11591	7.26334	8.61276	10.19742	12.05569	14.23177	16.77652	23.21444	31.94800	69.38894
20	5.60441	6.72750	8.06231	9.64629	11.52309	13.74349	16.36654	19.46076	27.39303	38.33760	86.73617
24	7.91108	9.84973	12.23916	15.17863	18.78809	23.21221	28.62518	35.23642	53.10901	79.49685	211.7582
36	22.25123	30.91268	42.81808	59.13557	81.43741	111.8342	153.1519	209.1643	387.0368	708.8019	3081.488
48	62.58524	97.10723	149.7970	230.3908	352.9923	538.8065	819.4007	1241.605	2820.567	6319.749	44841.55
60	176.0313	304.4816	524.0572	897.5969	1530.053	2595.919	4383.999	7370.201	20555.14	56347.51	652530.4
120	30987.02	92709.07	274636.0	805680.3	2.34E+06	6.74E+06	1.92E+07	5.43E+07	4.23E+08	3.18E+09	4.26E+11
240	9.60E+08	8.59E+09	7.54E+10	6.49E+11	5.48E+12	4.54E+13	3.69E+14	2.95E+15	1.79E+17	1.01E+19	1.81E+23
360	2.98E+13	7.97E+14	2.07E+16	5.23E+17	1.28E+19	3.06E+20	7.10E+21	1.60E+23	7.54E+25	3.20E+28	7.72E+34

TABLE 2

Present Value of $1

Periods	0.50%	0.75%	1.00%	1.50%	2.00%	3.00%	4.00%	5.00%	6.00%	7.00%	8.00%
1	0.99502	0.99256	0.99010	0.98522	0.98039	0.97087	0.96154	0.95238	0.94340	0.93458	0.92593
2	0.99007	0.98517	0.98030	0.97066	0.96117	0.94260	0.92456	0.90703	0.89000	0.87344	0.85734
3	0.98515	0.97783	0.97059	0.95632	0.94232	0.91514	0.88900	0.86384	0.83962	0.81630	0.79383
4	0.98025	0.97055	0.96098	0.94218	0.92385	0.88849	0.85480	0.82270	0.79209	0.76290	0.73503
5	0.97537	0.96333	0.95147	0.92826	0.90573	0.86261	0.82193	0.78353	0.74726	0.71299	0.68058
6	0.97052	0.95616	0.94205	0.91454	0.88797	0.83748	0.79031	0.74622	0.70496	0.66634	0.63107
7	0.96569	0.94904	0.93272	0.90103	0.87056	0.81309	0.75992	0.71068	0.66506	0.62275	0.58349
8	0.96089	0.94198	0.92348	0.88771	0.85349	0.78941	0.73069	0.67684	0.62741	0.58201	0.54027
9	0.95610	0.93496	0.91434	0.87459	0.83676	0.76642	0.70259	0.64461	0.59190	0.54393	0.50025
10	0.95135	0.92800	0.90529	0.86167	0.82035	0.74409	0.67556	0.61391	0.55839	0.50835	0.46319
11	0.94661	0.92109	0.89632	0.84893	0.80426	0.72242	0.64958	0.58468	0.52679	0.47509	0.42888
12	0.94191	0.91424	0.88745	0.83639	0.78849	0.70138	0.62460	0.55684	0.49697	0.44401	0.39711
13	0.93722	0.90743	0.87866	0.82403	0.77303	0.68095	0.60057	0.53032	0.46884	0.41496	0.36770
14	0.93256	0.90068	0.86996	0.81185	0.75788	0.66112	0.57748	0.50507	0.44230	0.38782	0.34046
15	0.92792	0.89397	0.86135	0.79985	0.74301	0.64186	0.55526	0.48102	0.41727	0.36245	0.31524
16	0.92330	0.88732	0.85282	0.78803	0.72845	0.62317	0.53391	0.45811	0.39365	0.33873	0.29189
17	0.91871	0.88071	0.84438	0.77639	0.71416	0.60502	0.51337	0.43630	0.37136	0.31657	0.27027
18	0.91414	0.87416	0.83602	0.76491	0.70016	0.58739	0.49363	0.41552	0.35034	0.29586	0.25025
19	0.90959	0.86765	0.82774	0.75361	0.68643	0.57029	0.47464	0.39573	0.33051	0.27651	0.23171
20	0.90506	0.86119	0.81954	0.74247	0.67297	0.55368	0.45639	0.37689	0.31180	0.25842	0.21455
24	0.88719	0.83583	0.78757	0.69954	0.62172	0.49193	0.39012	0.31007	0.24698	0.19715	0.15770
36	0.83564	0.76415	0.69892	0.58509	0.49022	0.34503	0.24367	0.17266	0.12274	0.08754	0.06262
48	0.78710	0.69861	0.62026	0.48936	0.38654	0.24200	0.15219	0.09614	0.06100	0.03887	0.02487
60	0.74137	0.63870	0.55045	0.40930	0.30478	0.16973	0.09506	0.05354	0.03031	0.01726	0.00988
120	0.54963	0.40794	0.30299	0.16752	0.09289	0.02881	0.00904	0.00287	0.00092	0.00030	0.00010
240	0.30210	0.16641	0.09181	0.02806	0.00863	0.00083	0.00008	0.00001	8.4E-07	8.9E-08	9.5E-09
360	0.16604	0.06789	0.02782	0.00470	0.00080	0.00002	7.4E-07	2.4E-08	7.8E-10	2.6E-11	9.3E-13

(continued)

TABLE 2 (continued)

Present Value of $1

Periods	9.00%	10.00%	11.00%	12.00%	13.00%	14.00%	15.00%	16.00%	18.00%	20.00%	25.00%
1	0.91743	0.90909	0.90090	0.89286	0.88496	0.87719	0.86957	0.86207	0.84746	0.83333	0.80000
2	0.84168	0.82645	0.81162	0.79719	0.78315	0.76947	0.75614	0.74316	0.71818	0.69444	0.64000
3	0.77218	0.75131	0.73119	0.71178	0.69305	0.67497	0.65752	0.64066	0.60863	0.57870	0.51200
4	0.70843	0.68301	0.65873	0.63552	0.61332	0.59208	0.57175	0.55229	0.51579	0.48225	0.40960
5	0.64993	0.62092	0.59345	0.56743	0.54276	0.51937	0.49718	0.47611	0.43711	0.40188	0.32768
6	0.59627	0.56447	0.53464	0.50663	0.48032	0.45559	0.43233	0.41044	0.37043	0.33490	0.26214
7	0.54703	0.51316	0.48166	0.45235	0.42506	0.39964	0.37594	0.35383	0.31393	0.27908	0.20972
8	0.50187	0.46651	0.43393	0.40388	0.37616	0.35056	0.32690	0.30503	0.26604	0.23257	0.16777
9	0.46043	0.42410	0.39092	0.36061	0.33288	0.30751	0.28426	0.26295	0.22546	0.19381	0.13422
10	0.42241	0.38554	0.35218	0.32197	0.29459	0.26974	0.24718	0.22668	0.19106	0.16151	0.10737
11	0.38753	0.35049	0.31728	0.28748	0.26070	0.23662	0.21494	0.19542	0.16192	0.13459	0.08590
12	0.35553	0.31863	0.28584	0.25668	0.23071	0.20756	0.18691	0.16846	0.13722	0.11216	0.06872
13	0.32618	0.28966	0.25751	0.22917	0.20416	0.18207	0.16253	0.14523	0.11629	0.09346	0.05498
14	0.29925	0.26333	0.23199	0.20462	0.18068	0.15971	0.14133	0.12520	0.09855	0.07789	0.04398
15	0.27454	0.23939	0.20900	0.18270	0.15989	0.14010	0.12289	0.10793	0.08352	0.06491	0.03518
16	0.25187	0.21763	0.18829	0.16312	0.14150	0.12289	0.10686	0.09304	0.07078	0.05409	0.02815
17	0.23107	0.19784	0.16963	0.14564	0.12522	0.10780	0.09293	0.08021	0.05998	0.04507	0.02252
18	0.21199	0.17986	0.15282	0.13004	0.11081	0.09456	0.08081	0.06914	0.05083	0.03756	0.01801
19	0.19449	0.16351	0.13768	0.11611	0.09806	0.08295	0.07027	0.05961	0.04308	0.03130	0.01441
20	0.17843	0.14864	0.12403	0.10367	0.08678	0.07276	0.06110	0.05139	0.03651	0.02608	0.01153
24	0.12640	0.10153	0.08170	0.06588	0.05323	0.04000	0.03493	0.02838	0.01883	0.01258	0.00472
36	0.04494	0.03235	0.02335	0.01691	0.01228	0.00894	0.00653	0.00478	0.00258	0.00141	0.00032
48	0.01598	0.01031	0.00668	0.00434	0.00283	0.00186	0.00122	0.00081	0.00035	0.00016	0.00002
60	0.00568	0.00328	0.00191	0.00111	0.00065	0.00039	0.00023	0.00014	0.00005	0.00002	1.5E-06
120	0.00003	0.00001	3.6E-06	1.2E-06	4.3E-07	1.5E-07	5.2E-08	1.8E-08	2.4E-09	3.1E-10	2.3E-12
240	1.0E-09	1.2E-10	1.3E-11	1.5E-12	1.8E-13	2.2E-14	2.7E-15	3.4E-16	5.6E-18	9.9E-20	5.5E-24
360	3.4E-14	1.3E-15	4.8E-17	1.9E-18	7.8E-13	3.3E-21	1.4E-22	6.2E-24	1.3E-26	3.1E-29	1.3E-35

TABLE 3

Future Value of an Annuity in Arrears

Periods	0.50%	0.75%	1.00%	1.50%	2.00%	3.00%	4.00%	5.00%	6.00%	7.00%	8.00%
1	1.00000	1.00000	1.00000	1.00000	1.00000	1.00000	1.00000	1.00000	1.00000	1.00000	1.00000
2	2.00500	2.00750	2.01000	2.01500	2.02000	2.03000	2.04000	2.05000	2.06000	2.07000	2.08000
3	3.01502	3.02256	3.03010	3.04522	3.06040	3.09090	3.12160	3.15250	3.18360	3.21490	3.24640
4	4.03010	4.04523	4.06040	4.09090	4.12161	4.18363	4.24646	4.31013	4.37462	4.43994	4.50611
5	5.05025	5.07556	5.10101	5.15227	5.20404	5.30914	5.41632	5.52563	5.63709	5.75074	5.86660
6	6.07550	6.11363	6.15202	6.22955	6.30812	6.46841	6.63298	6.80191	6.97532	7.15329	7.33593
7	7.10588	7.15948	7.21354	7.32299	7.43428	7.66246	7.89829	8.14201	8.39384	8.65402	8.92280
8	8.14141	8.21318	8.28567	8.43284	8.58297	8.89234	9.21423	9.54911	9.89747	10.25980	10.63663
9	9.18212	9.27478	9.36853	9.55933	9.75463	10.15911	10.58280	11.02656	11.49132	11.97799	12.48756
10	10.22803	10.34434	10.46221	10.70272	10.94972	11.46388	12.00611	12.57789	13.18079	13.81645	14.48656
11	11.27917	11.42192	11.56683	11.86326	12.16872	12.80780	13.48635	14.20679	14.97164	15.78360	16.64549
12	12.33556	12.50759	12.68250	13.04121	13.41209	14.19203	15.02581	15.91713	16.86994	17.88845	18.97713
13	13.39724	13.60139	13.80933	14.23683	14.68033	15.61779	16.62684	17.71298	18.88214	20.14064	21.49530
14	14.46423	14.70340	14.94742	15.45038	15.97394	17.08632	18.29191	19.59863	21.01507	22.55049	24.21492
15	15.53655	15.81368	16.09690	16.68214	17.29342	18.59891	20.02359	21.57856	23.27597	25.12902	27.15211
16	16.61423	16.93228	17.25786	17.93237	18.63929	20.15688	21.82453	23.65749	25.67253	27.88805	30.32428
17	17.69730	18.05927	18.43044	19.20136	20.01207	21.76159	23.69751	25.84037	28.21288	30.84022	33.75023
18	18.78579	19.19472	19.61475	20.48938	21.41231	23.41444	25.64541	28.13238	30.90565	33.99903	37.45024
19	19.87972	20.33868	20.81090	21.79672	22.84056	25.11687	27.67123	30.53900	33.75999	37.37896	41.44626
20	20.97912	21.49122	22.01900	23.12367	24.29737	26.87037	29.77808	33.06595	36.78559	40.99549	45.76196
24	25.43196	26.18847	26.97346	28.63352	30.42186	34.42647	39.08260	44.50200	50.81558	58.17667	66.76476
36	39.33610	41.15272	43.07688	47.27597	51.99437	63.27594	77.59831	95.83632	119.1209	148.9135	187.1021
48	54.09783	57.52071	61.22261	69.56522	79.35352	104.4084	139.2632	188.0254	256.5645	353.2701	490.1322
60	69.77003	75.42414	81.66967	96.21465	114.0515	163.0534	237.9907	353.5837	533.1282	813.5204	1253.213
120	163.8793	193.5143	230.0387	331.2882	488.2582	1123.700	2741.564	6958.240	18119.80	47954.12	128149.9
240	462.0409	667.8869	989.2554	2308.854	5744.437	40128.42	306130.1	2.43E+06	1.97E+07	1.61E+08	1.31E+09
360	1004.515	1830.743	3494.964	14113.59	62328.06	1.39E+06	3.39E+07	8.50E+08	2.15E+10	5.41E+11	1.35E+13

(continued)

TABLE 3 (continued)

Future Value of an Annuity in Arrears

Periods	9.00%	10.00%	11.00%	12.00%	13.00%	14.00%	15.00%	16.00%	18.00%	20.00%	25.00%
1	1.00000	1.00000	1.00000	1.00000	1.00000	1.00000	1.00000	1.00000	1.00000	1.00000	1.00000
2	2.09000	2.10000	2.11000	2.12000	2.13000	2.14000	2.15000	2.16000	2.18000	2.20000	2.25000
3	3.27810	3.31000	3.34210	3.37440	3.40690	3.43960	3.47250	3.50560	3.57240	3.64000	3.81250
4	4.57313	4.64100	4.70973	4.77933	4.84980	4.92114	4.99338	5.06650	5.21543	5.36800	5.76563
5	5.98471	6.10510	6.22780	6.35285	6.48027	6.61010	6.74238	6.87714	7.15421	7.44160	8.20703
6	7.52333	7.71561	7.91286	8.11519	8.32271	8.53552	8.75374	8.97748	9.44197	9.92992	11.25879
7	9.20043	9.48717	9.78327	10.08901	10.40466	10.73049	11.06680	11.41387	12.14152	12.91590	15.07349
8	11.02847	11.43589	11.85943	12.29969	12.75726	13.23276	13.72682	14.24009	15.32700	16.49908	19.84186
9	13.02104	13.57948	14.16397	14.77566	15.41571	16.08535	16.78584	17.51851	19.08585	20.79890	25.80232
10	15.19293	15.93742	16.72201	17.54874	18.41975	19.33730	20.30372	21.32147	23.52131	25.95868	33.25290
11	17.56029	18.53117	19.56143	20.65458	21.81432	23.04452	24.34928	25.73290	28.75514	32.15042	42.56613
12	20.14072	21.38428	22.71319	24.13313	25.65018	27.27075	29.00167	30.85017	34.93107	39.58050	54.20766
13	22.95338	24.52271	26.21164	28.02911	29.98470	32.08865	34.35192	36.78620	43.67199	48.49660	68.75958
14	26.01919	27.97498	30.09492	32.39260	34.88271	37.58107	40.50471	43.67199	50.81802	59.19592	86.94947
15	29.36092	31.77248	34.40536	37.27971	40.41746	43.84241	47.58041	51.65951	60.96527	72.03511	109.6868
16	33.00340	35.94973	39.18995	42.75328	46.67173	50.98035	55.71747	60.92503	72.93901	87.44213	138.1085
17	36.97370	40.54470	44.50084	48.88367	53.73906	59.11760	65.07509	71.67303	87.06804	105.9306	173.6357
18	41.30134	45.59917	50.39594	55.74971	61.72514	68.39407	75.83636	84.14072	103.7403	128.1167	218.0446
19	46.01846	51.15909	56.93949	63.43968	70.74941	78.96923	88.21181	98.60323	123.4135	154.7400	273.5558
20	51.16012	57.27500	64.20283	72.05244	80.94683	91.02493	102.4436	115.3797	146.6280	186.6880	342.9447
24	76.78981	88.49733	102.1742	118.1552	136.8315	158.6586	184.1678	213.9776	289.4945	392.4842	843.0329
36	236.1247	299.1268	380.1644	484.4631	618.7493	791.6729	1014.346	1301.027	2144.649	3539.009	12321.95
48	684.2804	960.1723	1352.700	1911.590	2707.000	3841.475	5456.005	7753.782	15664.26	31593.74	179362.2
60	1944.792	3034.816	4755.066	7471.641	11761.95	18535.13	29219.99	46057.51	114189.7	281732.6	2.61E+06
120	344289.1	927080.7	2.50E+06	6.71E+06	1.80E+07	4.81E+07	1.28E+08	3.39E+08	2.35E+09	1.59E+10	1.70E+12
240	1.07E+10	8.59E+10	6.86E+11	5.41E+12	4.22E+13	3.24E+14	2.46E+15	1.84E+16	9.92E+17	5.04E+19	7.25E+23
360	3.31E+14	7.97E+15	1.88E+17	4.36E+18	9.87E+19	2.19E+21	4.73E+22	1.00E+24	4.19E+26	1.60E+29	3.09E+35

*To compute the annuity in advance factor use the arrears factor for one more period and subtract 1.

TABLE 4

Present Value of an Annuity in Arrears

Periods	0.50%	0.75%	1.00%	1.50%	2.00%	3.00%	4.00%	5.00%	6.00%	7.00%	8.00%
1	0.99502	0.99256	0.99010	0.98522	0.98039	0.97087	0.96154	0.95238	0.94340	0.93458	0.92593
2	1.98510	1.97772	1.97040	1.95588	1.94156	1.91347	1.88609	1.85941	1.83339	1.80802	1.78326
3	2.97025	2.95556	2.94099	2.91220	2.88388	2.82861	2.77509	2.72325	2.67301	2.62432	2.57710
4	3.95050	3.92611	3.90197	3.85438	3.80773	3.71710	3.62990	3.54595	3.46511	3.38721	3.31213
5	4.92587	4.88944	4.85343	4.78264	4.71346	4.57971	4.45182	4.32948	4.21236	4.10020	3.99271
6	5.89638	5.84560	5.79548	5.69719	5.60143	5.41719	5.24214	5.07569	4.91732	4.76654	4.62288
7	6.86207	6.79464	6.72819	6.59821	6.47199	6.23028	6.00205	5.78637	5.58238	5.38929	5.20637
8	7.82296	7.73661	7.65168	7.48593	7.32548	7.01969	6.73274	6.46321	6.20979	5.97130	5.74664
9	8.77906	8.67158	8.56602	8.36052	8.16224	7.78611	7.43533	7.10782	6.80169	6.51523	6.24689
10	9.73041	9.59958	9.47130	9.22218	8.98259	8.53020	8.11090	7.72173	7.36009	7.02358	6.71008
11	10.67703	10.52067	10.36763	10.07112	9.78685	9.25262	8.76048	8.30641	7.88687	7.49867	7.13896
12	11.61893	11.43491	11.25508	10.90751	10.57534	9.95400	9.38507	8.86325	8.38384	7.94269	7.53608
13	12.55615	12.34235	12.13374	11.73153	11.34837	10.63496	9.98565	9.39357	8.85268	8.35765	7.90378
14	13.48871	13.24302	13.00370	12.54338	12.10625	11.29607	10.56312	9.89864	9.29498	8.74547	8.24424
15	14.41662	14.13699	13.86505	13.34323	12.84926	11.93794	11.11839	10.37966	9.71225	9.10791	8.55948
16	15.33993	15.02431	14.71787	14.13126	13.57771	12.56110	11.65230	10.83777	10.10590	9.44665	8.85137
17	16.25863	15.90502	15.56225	14.90765	14.29187	13.16612	12.16567	11.27407	10.47726	9.76322	9.12164
18	17.17277	16.77918	16.39827	15.67256	14.99203	13.75351	12.65930	11.68959	10.82760	10.05909	9.37189
19	18.08236	17.64683	17.22601	16.42617	15.67846	14.32380	13.13394	12.08532	11.15812	10.33560	9.60360
20	18.98742	18.50802	18.04555	17.16864	16.35143	14.87747	13.59033	12.46221	11.46992	10.59401	9.81815
24	22.56287	21.88915	21.24339	20.03041	18.91393	16.93554	15.24696	13.79864	12.55036	11.46933	10.52876
36	32.87102	31.44681	30.10751	27.66068	25.48884	21.83225	18.90828	16.54685	14.62099	13.03521	11.71719
48	42.58032	40.18478	37.97396	34.04255	30.67312	25.26671	21.19513	18.07716	15.65003	13.73047	12.18914
60	51.72556	48.17337	44.95504	39.38027	34.76089	27.67556	22.62349	18.92929	16.16143	14.03918	12.37655
120	90.07345	78.94169	69.70052	55.49845	45.35539	32.37302	24.77409	19.94268	16.65135	14.28146	12.49878
240	139.58077	111.14495	90.81942	64.79573	49.56855	33.30567	24.99796	19.99984	16.66665	14.28571	12.50000
360	166.79161	124.28187	97.21833	66.35324	49.95992	33.33254	24.99998	20.00000	16.66667	14.28571	12.50000

(continued)

TABLE 4 (continued)

Present Value of an Annuity in Arrears

Periods	9.00%	10.00%	11.00%	12.00%	13.00%	14.00%	15.00%	16.00%	18.00%	20.00%	25.00%
1	0.91743	0.90909	0.90090	0.89286	0.88496	0.87719	0.86957	0.86207	0.84746	0.83333	0.80000
2	1.75911	1.73554	1.71252	1.69005	1.66810	1.64666	1.62571	1.60523	1.56564	1.52778	1.44000
3	2.53129	2.48685	2.44371	2.40183	2.36115	2.32163	2.28323	2.24589	2.17427	2.10648	1.95200
4	3.23972	3.16987	3.10245	3.03735	2.97447	2.91371	2.85498	2.79818	2.69006	2.58873	2.36160
5	3.88965	3.79079	3.69590	3.60478	3.51723	3.43308	3.35216	3.27429	3.12717	2.99061	2.68928
6	4.48592	4.35526	4.23054	4.11141	3.99755	3.88867	3.78448	3.68474	3.49760	3.32551	2.95142
7	5.03295	4.86842	4.71220	4.56376	4.42261	4.28830	4.16042	4.03857	3.81153	3.60459	3.16114
8	5.53482	5.33493	5.14612	4.96764	4.79877	4.63886	4.48732	4.34359	4.07757	3.83716	3.32891
9	5.99525	5.75902	5.53705	5.32825	5.13166	4.94637	4.77158	4.60654	4.30302	4.03097	3.46313
10	6.41766	6.14457	5.88923	5.65022	5.42624	5.21612	5.01877	4.83323	4.49409	4.19247	3.57050
11	6.80519	6.49506	6.20652	5.93770	5.68694	5.45273	5.23371	5.02864	4.65601	4.32706	3.65640
12	7.16073	6.81369	6.49236	6.19437	5.91765	5.66029	5.42062	5.19711	4.79322	4.43922	3.72512
13	7.48690	7.10336	6.74987	6.42355	6.12181	5.84236	5.58315	5.34233	4.90951	4.53268	3.78010
14	7.78615	7.36669	6.98187	6.62817	6.30249	6.00207	5.72448	5.46753	5.00806	4.61057	3.82408
15	8.06069	7.60608	7.19087	6.81086	6.46238	6.14217	5.84737	5.57546	5.09158	4.67547	3.85926
16	8.31256	7.82371	7.37916	6.97399	6.60388	6.26506	5.95423	5.66850	5.16235	4.72956	3.88741
17	8.54363	8.02155	7.54879	7.11963	6.72909	6.37286	6.04716	5.74870	5.22233	4.77463	3.90993
18	8.75563	8.20141	7.70162	7.24967	6.83991	6.46742	6.12797	5.81785	5.27316	4.81219	3.92794
19	8.95011	8.36492	7.83929	7.36578	6.93797	6.55037	6.19823	5.87746	5.31624	4.84350	3.94235
20	9.12855	8.51356	7.96333	7.46944	7.02475	6.62313	6.25933	5.92884	5.35275	4.86958	3.95388
24	9.70661	8.98474	8.34814	7.78432	7.28288	6.83514	6.43377	6.07203	5.45095	4.93710	3.98111
36	10.61176	9.67651	8.87859	8.19241	7.59785	7.07899	6.62314	6.22012	5.54120	4.99295	3.99870
48	10.93358	9.89693	9.03022	8.29716	7.67052	7.12960	6.65853	6.24497	5.55359	4.99921	3.99991
60	11.04799	9.96716	9.07356	8.32405	7.68728	7.14011	6.66515	6.24915	5.55529	4.99991	3.99999
120	11.11075	9.99989	9.09088	8.33332	7.69230	7.14286	6.66667	6.25000	5.55556	5.00000	4.00000
240	11.11111	10.00000	9.09091	8.33333	7.69231	7.14286	6.66667	6.25000	5.55556	5.00000	4.00000
360	11.11111	10.00000	909091	8.33333	7.69231	7.14286	6.66667	6.25000	5.55556	5.00000	4.00000

*To compute the present value factor for an annuity in advance use the arrears factor for one less period and add 1.

ABBREVIATIONS USED

FV	Future value	PV	Present value
$FVAF_{r,N}$	Future value of an annuity in arrears factor	$PVAF_{r,N}$	Present value of an annuity in arrears factor
$FVF_{r,N}$	Future value of $1 factor	$PVF_{r,N}$	Present value of $1 factor
N	Number of periods	r	Interest rate per period (discount rate)
PMT	Payment (in an annuity)		

SYNONYMS

Annuity in advance/Annuity due

Annuity in arrears/Ordinary annuity

Discount rate/Effective rate/Market rate

GLOSSARY

Annuity due   Synonym for annuity in advance.

Annuity in advance   A series of equal cash flows in which the amounts are received or paid at the beginning of each period.

Annuity in arrears   A series of equal cash flows in which the amounts are received or paid at the end of each period.

Compound interest   Interest calculated by multiplying the interest by the principal. Interest earned in one period is added to the principal to calculate the interest in the next period.

Compounding period   The shortest period over which interest is earned and added to the balance of the principal.

Deferred annuity   An annuity in which the first cash flow is deferred until a subsequent time period.

Discount rate   The interest rate per period used to discount or present-value a set of cash flows.

Effective rate   The interest rate per period (sometimes annualized) used to discount or present-value a set of cash flows.

Future value   The value at some date in the future of a single amount of cash or a series of cash amounts.

Future-value factor   A factor used to convert a present-value amount into a future-value amount.

Internal rate of return   The interest rate that equates a current outflow of cash with a single future cash flow or a series of cash flows.

Nominal rate   The annual interest rate used to present-value a set of cash flows. The nominal rate does not take into consideration the compounding of interest during the year.

Ordinary annuity   Synonym for annuity in arrears.

Perpetuity   An annuity in which there is no maturity date; that is, the cash flows are assumed to continue forever.

Present value   The value today of cash to be received at some date or multiple dates in the future.

Present-value factor   A factor used to convert a future-value amount into a present-value amount.

Simple interest   Interest calculated by multiplying the interest rate by the principal. Interest earned in one period is not added to the principal to calculate the interest in the next period; that is, it is not compounded.

ASSIGNMENT MATERIAL

Applying Your Knowledge

D-1 Fred and Cathy plan to buy a house in three years. They will need $15,000 for the downpayment. How much must they deposit today in order to earn 8% interest, compounded in each of the following ways?

    a. Annually

    b. Semi-annually

    c. Quarterly

D-2 Pimlico Inc. has excess cash that it wants to invest for five years. It can deposit $25,000 either in a money-market account and earn 9%, compounded annually, or in a bank account that pays 8%, compounded quarterly. What should it do?

D-3 The law firm of Taylor & Smith decided to lease (rent) a computer system for its offices. The firm signed an 18-month contract, and the first payment was due upon signing. The lease (rental) payments of $2,000 are due on the first of each month. If the firm is able to invest at 9% annually, how much does it need today in order to ensure that it will be able to meet all of the lease payments?

D-4 a. Olivia is saving to buy a car. She plans to deposit $50 at the end of each month into an account that pays 6%, compounded monthly. How much will she have for a downpayment in two years?

      b. If Olivia uses the amount arrived at in part a. to put a downpayment on a $15,000 car, how much will her monthly payments be? The loan is set at 12% for four years, and the payments will come due at the end of the month.

D-5 Joe Inc. has issued bonds that pay $100 at the end of each year indefinitely. If you require a 15% rate of return (i.e., the discount rate is 15%), what is the value of such a bond?

D-6 Today is your niece's 14th birthday. You anticipate that she will enter university on her 18th birthday. She will need $10,000 at the end of each of the four years of university. You plan to make a deposit one year from today into an account that pays 12% annually, and to make three more identical deposits, one each year until she starts university. To reach your goal, how much do you have to deposit annually?

D-7 Mr. Lee wants to buy a house that costs $200,000. He is evaluating the possible ways of paying for the house and has come up with the following alternatives. Calculate the monthly payments that Mr. Lee will have to make under each alternative.

    a. 20% down, monthly payments, maturity 30 years, rate 12%

    b. 10% down, monthly payments, maturity 20 years, rate 9%

    c. 0% down, monthly payments, maturity 10 years, rate 9%

D-8 Suzy is the lucky winner of $2 million in a special lottery. She will receive 20 annual payments of $100,000, starting today. She can earn 8% on this money. Are her winnings actually worth $2 million?

D-9 Mr. Street takes out a three-year graduated-payment loan. The monthly payments on this loan are as follows:

Year 1: $100/month

Year 2: $125/month
Year 3: $150/month

If interest rates are currently 12%, how much did Mr. Street borrow, given the payments that are to be made?

D-10 Ms. Black wants to establish a scholarship that will pay out $6,000 a year indefinitely in monthly instalments. The first monthly instalment of the scholarship is to be paid immediately. How much will Ms. Black have to donate if the university can invest at 9% compounded monthly?

D-11 How does the answer to Question 10 change if the first monthly instalment is to be paid one month after the initial donation was made instead of immediately?

D-12 A finance company advertises that it will pay a lump sum of $8,115 at the end of six years to any investor who deposits $1,000 annually (at the end of the year) for six years. Calculate the interest rate that is implicit in this offer.

D-13 You want to obtain a university education, for which you will need $11,000 per year for four years, starting next year. Your parents agree to support you in this endeavour and decide to deposit an amount of money today sufficient to cover the four years. They can deposit the amount in an account that pays 8%, compounded annually.

    a. Calculate the amount that your parents should deposit.

    b. Calculate the amount that will be left in the account after the first withdrawal.

D-14 On your retirement, you deposit $2,000,000 in a bank that pays 10% annual interest. Calculate how much you will be able to withdraw at the end of each year to deplete the fund in exactly 10 years.

D-15 A manufacturing corporation is considering an option to sell a machine via a lease. The machine cost the manufacturer $500,000. The lease agreement requires that lease payments be made at the end of each month for three years, with the title to the machine passing to the buyer at the end of the lease term. If the manufacturer wants to earn a return of 9%, what monthly payments must be set for the lease?

D-16 Mr. Grump is considering two investment alternatives:

    a. a bond that costs $1,000 today and makes interest payments of $75 at the end of each year for the next three years and a final payment of $1,075 at the end of year 4

    b. a zero coupon bond that costs $735.03 today and pays back $1,000 at the end of year 4

Which alternative should Mr. Grump choose, and why?

D-17 XYZ Corporation wants to establish a fund that will be used to meet a $900,000 commitment at the end of 10 years. The corporation plans to deposit a fixed amount in the fund each year for 10 years, beginning today. The corporation estimates that the assets in the fund will earn a return of 9%. Calculate the annual contribution that XYZ should make to the fund.

D-18 Suppose that an investment corporation offers you a contract that will pay you and your heirs $950 a year for your lifetime and for that of your heirs. If your next best alternative is to invest at 9%, how much should you be willing to invest in this contract?

D-19 You have just won $1 million in a special lottery. This amount will be paid to you in yearly instalments of $50,000 for 20 years. You are expecting to receive the first cheque today. If you can invest this money at 10%, how much are your winnings worth today?

APPENDIX: TIME VALUE OF MONEY PROBLEM SOLUTIONS

Applying Your Knowledge

D-1 $PV_N = FV_N * PVF_{r,N}$

 a. Annual Compounding
$$PV = \$15,000*(PVF_{8\%,3})$$
$$= \$15,000*(.79383)$$
$$= \$11,907.45$$

 b. Semi-annual Compounding
$$PV = \$15,000*(PVF_{4\%,6})$$
$$= \$15,000*(.79031)$$
$$= \$11,854.65$$

 c. Quarterly Compounding
$$PV = \$15,000*(PVF_{2\%,12})$$
$$= \$15,000*(.78849)$$
$$= \$11,827.35$$

D-2 $FV_N = PV * FVF_{r,N}$

Money-market account:
$$FV_5 = \$25,000* FVF_{9\%,5}$$
$$= \$25,000*(1.53862)$$
$$= \$38,465.50$$

Bank deposit:
$$FV_{20} = \$25,000* FVF_{2\%,20}$$
$$= \$25,000*(1.48595)$$
$$= \$37,148.75$$

Pimlico Inc. should deposit the money in the money-market account.

D-3 PV annuity in advance $= PMT*(1 + PV_AF_{r,N-1})$
$$= \$2,000*(1 + PV_AF_{0.75\%,17})$$
$$= \$2,000*(1 + 15.90502)$$
$$= \$2,000*(16.90502)$$
$$= \$33,810.04$$

D-4 a. $FV_N = PMT*FV_AF_{r,N}$
$$= \$50*(FV_AF_{0.5\%,24})$$
$$= \$50*(25.43196)$$
$$= \$1,271.60$$

 b. Financing amount $= \$15,000 - 1,271.60 = \$13,728.40$
Since the payments are monthly, the compounding period is also monthly.

$$PMT = PV / PV_AF_{r,N}$$
$$= \$13,728.40 / PV_AF_{1\%,48}$$
$$= \$13,728.40 / 37.97396$$
$$= \$361.52/month$$

D-5 $PV = PMT / r$ (perpetuity)
$= \$100 / 15\%$
$= \$666.67$

D-6 Amount needed by 18th birthday (4 years from now):

$PVN = PMT^* PV_AF_{r,N}$
$= \$10,000^*(PV_AF_{12\%,4})$
$= \$10,000^*(3.03735)$
$= \$30,373.50$

Deposits to be made in order to have $30,373.50 in four years:

$FV = \$30,373.50$

$PMT = FV / FV_AF_{r,N}$
$= \$30,373.50 / FV_AF_{12\%,4}$
$= \$30,373.50 / 4.77933$
$= \$6,355.18$

You must deposit $6,355.18 each year for the next four years in order to reach your goal.

D-7 Assume that monthly payments are made at the end of the month. Since the payments are monthly, the compounding is also monthly.

a. 20% downpayment = $40,000
Balance of $160,000 to be paid in monthly instalments for 30 years:

$PMT = PV / PV_AF_{r,N}$
$= \$160,000 / PV_AF_{1\%,360}$
$= \$160,000 / 97.21833$
$= \$1,645.78 / month$

b. 10% downpayment = $20,000
Balance of $180,000 to be paid in monthly instalments for 20 years:

$PMT = PV / PV_AF_{r,N}$
$= \$180,000 / PV_AF_{0.75\%,240}$
$= \$180,000 / 111.14495$
$= \$1,619.51 / month$

c. $200,000 to be paid in monthly instalments for 10 years:

$PMT = PV / PV_AF_{r,N}$
$= \$200,000 / PV_AF_{0.75\%,120}$
$= \$200,000 / 78.94169$
$= \$2,533.52 / month$

D-8 PV annuity in advance $= PMT^*(1 + PV_AF_{r,N-1})$
$= \$100,000^*(1 + PV_AF_{8\%,19})$
$= \$100,000^*(1 + 9.6036)$
$= \$100,000^*(10.6036)$
$= \$1,060,360$

D-9 Mr. Street has to have borrowed the present value of all the monthly payments. The present value could be calculated as follows:

$$PV = \$100^*PV_AF_{1\%,12} + \$125^*[PV_AF_{1\%,24} - PV_AF_{1\%,12}] + \$150^*[PV_AF_{1\%,36} - PV_AF_{1\%,24}]$$
$$= \$100^*11.25508 + \$125^*[21.24339 - 11.25508] + \$150^*[30.10751 - 21.24339]$$
$$= \$3,703.67$$

Mr. Street borrowed $3,703.67.

D-10 Since the payments are for an indefinite period and the first payment is to be made immediately, this is a perpetuity in advance.

$$PV \text{ perpetuity in advance} = PMT^*(1 + 1/r)$$
$$= \$500^*(1 + 1/0.0075)$$
$$= \$67,166.67$$

Ms. Black will have to donate $67,166.67.

D-11 PV perpetuity in arrears $= PMT^*1/r$
$$= \$500^*1/0.0075$$
$$= \$66,666.67$$

D-12
$$FV_N = PMT^*FV_AF_{r,N}$$
$$\$8,115 = \$1,000^*(FV_AF_{r,6})$$
$$FV_AF_{r,6} = 8.115$$
$$r = 12\%$$

D-13 a. $PV_N = PMT^*PV_AF_{r,N}$
$$= \$11,000^*(PV_AF_{8\%,4})$$
$$= \$11,000^*(3.31213)$$
$$= \$36,433.43$$

b. Balance after first withdrawal
$$PV_N = PMT^*PV_AF_{r,N}$$
$$= \$11,000^*(PVAF8\%,3)$$
$$= \$11,000^*(2.57710)$$
$$= \$28,348.10$$

D-14
$$PV_N = PMT^*PV_AF_{r,N}$$
$$\$2,000,000 = PMT^*(PV_AF_{10\%,10})$$
$$\$2,000,000 = PMT^*(6.14457)$$
$$PMT = \$325,490.64 \text{ / year}$$

D-15 This is an annuity in arrears, with a present value of $500,000.

$$PV = PMT^*PV_AF_{r,N}$$
$$\$500,000 = PMT^*(PV_AF_{0.75\%,36})$$
$$\$500,000 = PMT^*(31.44681)$$
$$PMT = \$15,899.86$$

D-16 Mr. Grump should choose the option that offers the highest rate of return. The calculation of the rate of return could be computed using the formula below. Note that the bond offers an annuity of $75 at the end of each year and a lump sum of $1,000 at the end of the four years.

$$PV = FV_N * PVF_{r,N} + PMT * PVAF_{r,N}$$
$$\$1,000 = \$1,000 * PVF_{r,4} + \$75 * PVAF_{r,4}$$

The problem in solving this equation is that there appear to be two unknown factors. There is really only one unknown factor, the interest rate, but there is no easy way to determine the value for the two factors. A trial-and-error method could be employed, whereby you select a trial interest rate, compare the left-hand side of the equation with the right-hand side, and then incrementally change the interest rate until both sides are equal.

In this particular case, an easier solution is possible. Note that the original principal of the loan to the company is the $1,000 initial proceeds from the bond. That principal is not paid off until the end of the bond's life. Since the principal is the same each year and the interest payments are the same every period, the rate of interest is the same every year and is calculated by dividing the interest amount by the principal, as follows:

Return = 75/1,000 = 7.5%

The rate of return for a zero coupon bond is calculated as follows:

$$PV_N = FV_N * PVF_{r,N}$$
$$\$735.03 = \$1,000 * PVF_{r,4}$$
$$PVF_{r,4} = 0.73503$$
$$r = 8\%$$

Thus the zero coupon bond has the higher return and Mr. Grump should make that investment.

D-17 This is an annuity in advance, with a future value of $900,000.

$$FV = PMT * FVAF_{r,N+1} - 1$$
$$\$900,000 = PMT * FVAF_{9\%,11} - 1$$
$$\$900,000 = PMT * (17.56029 - 1)$$
$$PMT = \$54,346.88$$

D-18 Treat this as a perpetuity, as you are not sure how long your longest-living heir will live.

$$PV = PMT / r \quad \text{(perpetuity)}$$
$$= \$950 / 9\%$$
$$= \$10,555.56$$

D-19 PV annuity in advance $= PMT * (1 + PVAF_{r,N-1})$
$$= \$50,000 * (1 + PVAF_{10\%,19})$$
$$= \$50,000 * (1 + 8.36492)$$
$$= \$50,000 * (9.36492)$$
$$= \$468,246$$

COMPANY
INDEX

SUBJECT INDEX

By sharing your opinions about Financial Accounting, you will help us ensure that you are getting the most value for your textbook dollars. After you have used the book for a while, please fill out this form. Fold, tape, and mail it, or fax us toll free @ 1(800)565-6802!

Course name: _____   School name: _____

Your name: _____   Instructor's Name: _____

1) Did you purchase this book (check all that apply):

  ❏ From your campus bookstore

  ❏ From a bookstore off-campus

  ❏ New   ❏ Used   ❏ For yourself

  ❏ For yourself and at least one other student

2) Was this text available at the bookstore when you needed it:

  ❏ Yes   ❏ No

3) How far along are you in this course (put an X where you are now)?

  ❏ _____ ❏ _____ ❏
  Beginning   Midway   Completed

4) How much of this text have you used (put an X where appropriate)?

  ❏ _____ ❏ _____ ❏
  Skimmed   Read half   Read entire book

5) Have you read the introductory material (i.e., the preface)?

  ❏ Yes   ❏ No   ❏ Parts of it

6) Even if you have only skimmed this text, please rate the following features:

Features:	Very valuable/effective	Somewhat valuable/effective	Not valuable/effective
Value as a reference			
Readability			
Design			
Study & review material			
Problems & cases			
Relevant examples			
Overall perception			

7) What do you like most about this book?

  _____

  _____

  What do you like least?

  _____

  _____

8) May we quote you?   Yes _____ No _____

If you would like to receive information on other Wiley business books, please fill in the following information:

Mailing address: _____

                (Street)   (Apt. #)

_____

(City)   (Province)   (Postal Code)

9) At the end of the semester, what do you intend to do with this text?

❑ Keep it   ❑ Sell it   ❑ Unsure

Thank you for your time and feedback!

WILEY

---------------------------------- (fold here) ----------------------------------

MAIL POSTE

Canada Post Corporation / Société canadienne des postes

Postage paid
if mailed in Canada

Port payé
si posté au Canada

Business Reply

Réponse d'affaires

0108529899   01

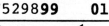

0108529899-M9W1L1-BR01

COLLEGE DIVISION
JOHN WILEY & SONS CANADA LTD
22 WORCESTER RD
PO BOX 56213 STN BRM B
TORONTO ON   M7Y 9C1